# Inside AutoCAD® Release 12 for Windows™

By
*Rusty Gesner*
*Tom Boersma*
*Kevin Coleman*
*Dennis Hill*
*Peter Tobey*

*Original Authors:*
*D. Raker*

*H. Rice*

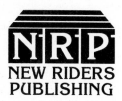

## NRP
### NEW RIDERS
### PUBLISHING

New Riders Publishing
Indianapolis, Indiana

# Inside AutoCAD® Release 12 for Windows™

By Rusty Gesner, Tom Boersma, Kevin Coleman, Dennis Hill, and Peter Tobey

Published by:
New Riders Publishing
201 W. 103rd Street
Indianapolis, IN 46290-1097 USA

Printed in the United States of America          7 8 9 0

**Library of Congress Cataloging-in-Publication Data**

Inside AutoCAD release 12 for Windows / by Rusty Gesner ...[et al.].
    p. cm.
"Original authors: D. Raker, H. Rice."
Includes index.
ISBN 1-56205-146-6 : $37.95
1. Computer graphics.  2. AutoCAD for Windows.  I. Gesner, Rusty.  II.
Raker, Daniel.  III. Rice, Harbert.  IV. Title: Inside AutoCAD release
twelve for Windows.
T385.I4765  1993
620'.0042'02855369—dc20          93-16079
                    CIP

*Composed in MCPdigital, Palatino, and Stone Sans Serif.*

**Publisher**
David P. Ewing

**Associate Publisher**
Tim Huddleston

**Managing Editor**
Cheri Robinson

**Acquisitions Editor**
John Pont

**Product Director**
Rusty Gesner

**Production Editor**
Margaret Berson

**Editor**
Faye Kagele

**Editorial Assistance**
Karla J. Barnhart

**Technical Editor**
Janis Brown

**Editorial Secretary**
Karen Opal

**Book Design and Production**
Amy Peppler-Adams, Katy Bodenmiller, Christine Cook, Lisa Daugherty,
Dennis Clay Hager, Jay Lesandrini, Tom Loveman, Roger Morgan, Juli Pavey,
Angela M. Pozdol, Michelle Self, Susan Shepard, Greg Simsic, Alyssa Yesh

**Proofreaders**
Julie Brown, Terri Edwards, Carla Hall-Batton, Howard Jones, John Kane,
Tim Montgomery, Linda Seifert, Marcella Thompson

**Indexed by**
Johnna Van Hoose

# About the Authors

**B. Rustin Gesner** is publishing director of New Riders Publishing in Gresham, Oregon. Prior to joining New Riders, he was founder and president of CAD Northwest, Inc., in Portland, Oregon. He is a registered architect and formerly practiced the profession in Oregon and Washington after attending Antioch College and the College of Design, Art, and Architecture at the University of Cincinnati. Mr. Gesner is coauthor of the New Riders books *Maximizing AutoCAD Release 12* (formerly titled *Maximizing AutoCAD Volume I*), *Maximizing AutoLISP* (formerly titled *Maximizing AutoCAD Volume II*), *AutoCAD for Beginners*, *Inside AutoCAD*, *Inside AutoCAD Release 12*, and *Inside AutoCAD for Windows*.

**Tom Boersma** is a certified manufacturing engineer, an ATC trainer, and a CAD/CAM training specialist at Grand Rapids Community College in Michigan. He is coauthor of *Inside AutoCAD for Windows* and *Inside AutoCAD Release 12*.

**Kevin J. Coleman** has been working with AutoCAD since 1985. He joined New Riders Publishing in 1989 and has produced illustrations and done technical editing for many of the New Riders AutoCAD books. Mr. Coleman attended the University of Oregon. He is a special contributor to *Maximizing AutoCAD Release 12* and *Maximizing AutoLISP*.

**Dennis Hill** is a computer consultant who provides services in AutoCAD and general computer systems to clients of his company, Bandit E.D.S. He has been using AutoCAD since 1985 and studied engineering at San Jose State University. He is a special contributor to *Maximizing AutoCAD Release 12* and *Maximizing AutoLISP*.

**Peter Tobey** has pursued a lifelong interest in drafting and design, including the creation of kinetic sculptures, toys, medical equipment prototypes, and the design of large-scale industrial waste-treatment facilities. His continuing self-education in the use of AutoCAD began with version 1.4 in 1984. He is currently employed as Senior Designer and CAD Manager at a consulting engineering firm outside Portland, Oregon. He is a special contributor to *Maximizing AutoCAD Release 12* and *Maximizing AutoLISP*.

# Acknowledgments

New Riders Publishing thanks Jim Boyce for his many contributions to *Inside AutoCAD for Windows* (Release 11 version) and *Inside AutoCAD Release 12*, upon which some of the material in this book was based.

The authors express their thanks to Margaret Berson and Faye Kagele for editing this book. Special thanks to Cheri Robinson and Tim Huddleston for their assistance.

Special thanks to Janis Brown for speedy and accurate technical editing.

Rusty Gesner offers profuse thanks for helping facilitate this project to Chris Bradshaw, Cary Fulbright, John Lynch, and Neele Johnston, and to numerous other friends and colleagues at Autodesk for their encouragement and support over the past nine years. Rusty also thanks Patrick Haessly and Harbert Rice for their contributions to earlier editions of this book, upon which this book is based.

# Trademark Acknowledgments

New Riders Publishing has made every attempt to supply trademark information about company names, products, and services mentioned in this book. Trademarks indicated below were derived from various sources. New Riders Publishing cannot attest to the accuracy of this information.

1-2-3 and Lotus are registered trademarks of Lotus Development Corporation.

AutoCAD, AutoCAD Training Center, Autodesk, Autodesk Animator, AutoLISP, AutoShade, AutoSketch, ADI, and ATC are registered trademarks of Autodesk, Inc. The following are trademarks of Autodesk, Inc.: ACAD, Advanced Modeling Extension, Advanced User Interface, AME, ATLAST, AUI, AutoCAD Development Systems, AutoCAD SQL Extension, AutoCAD SQL Interface, Autodesk Training Center, AutoFlix, DXF, and 3D Studio.

Borland Resource Workshop is a trademark of Borland International, Inc.

CompuServe is a registered trademark of CompuServe Information Serve, Inc., and H&R Block, Inc.

IBM/PC/XT/AT, IBM PS/2, OS/2, and PC DOS are registered trademarks of the International Business Machines Corporation.

Microsoft is a registered trademark of Microsoft Corporation. Word, MS-DOS, and Excel are registered trademarks, and Microsoft Windows is a trademark of Microsoft Corporation.

Norton Utilities is a trademark of Symantec Corporation.

PostScript is a trademark of Adobe Systems Incorporated, registered in the U.S.A. and other countries.

Quarterdeck Expanded Memory Manager, DESQview, and DESQview 386 are trademarks of Quarterdeck Office Systems.

RenderMan is a registered trademark of Pixar used by Autodesk under license from Pixar.

UNIX is a registered trademark of UNIX System Laboratories, Inc.

Trademarks of other products mentioned in this book are held by the companies producing them.

# Warning and Disclaimer

This book is designed to provide information about the AutoCAD program. Every effort has been made to make this book as complete and as accurate as possible, but no warranty or fitness is implied.

The information is provided on an "as is" basis. The author and New Riders Publishing shall have neither liability nor responsibility to any person or entity with respect to any loss or damages arising from the information contained in this book or from the use of the disks or programs that may accompany it.

# Contents at a Glance

# Contents

# INTRODUCTION

AutoCAD is a software phenomenon; its users far outnumber the users of any other CAD system. Since its introduction, AutoCAD has grown from a microcuriosity to a full-fledged CAD system by any set of standards. AutoCAD has also grown from a relatively simple program to a large and complex one. Even if you are new to AutoCAD, however, you do not need to be intimidated by its size and complexity. More than a million designers and drafters have learned to use AutoCAD; hundreds of thousands of them have mastered the program with the help of previous editions of *Inside AutoCAD*.

*Inside AutoCAD Release 12 for Windows* is your guide to a significant step in the evolution of AutoCAD: AutoCAD Release 12 for Windows. Like AutoCAD, Windows has become a phenomenal success story in the microcomputer industry. Like AutoCAD, Windows has evolved from a seemingly basic system to an obviously powerful and complex one. The current version of Windows—version 3.1—is an accessory to PC DOS/MS-DOS, but one that transforms it into a much more flexible and powerful computing environment. Because AutoCAD for Windows utilizes the flexibility of Windows, it offers you a far more productive design environment than AutoCAD under DOS.

*Inside AutoCAD Release 12 for Windows* helps you take advantage of the many features that AutoCAD for Windows offers over previous versions of AutoCAD. In this book, you learn how to perform the following tasks in AutoCAD for Windows:

- Access files and directories through the program's easy-to-use graphical interface

- Start up and operate different application software packages in a similar manner

- Run several application programs simultaneously, and easily switch between them

- Transfer data from AutoCAD to an external program, process or analyze the data, and then move it back to AutoCAD to update your drawing

- Copy or link data from AutoCAD into other Windows programs to create spreadsheets, reports, or manuals that contain AutoCAD-created data or graphics

- Add frequently used commands and macros to the AutoCAD toolbar

- Customize the AutoCAD for Windows interface by changing the fonts and colors used for the AutoCAD interface

Release 12 has been dubbed "the user's release." Like most previous releases of AutoCAD, Release 12 adds many new features. The most noticeable new feature of Release 12 is the more productive design environment that results from enhancements to the user interface. Release 12 provides a more comprehensive set of pull-down menus and dialog boxes, an integrated screen menu, and several improvements in input and editing that make AutoCAD easier and more intuitive to use.

*Inside AutoCAD Release 12 for Windows* helps you take advantage of the many features that AutoCAD Release 12 offers over previous versions of AutoCAD. In this book, you learn how to use the following features, which are new to, or improved in, AutoCAD Release 12:

- **More dialog boxes.** Release 12 includes easy-to-use dialog boxes for many kinds of operations and for virtually all settings. The enhanced dialog boxes make AutoCAD easier to learn and use than ever before.

- **Better menus.** The main menu is gone, replaced by the File pull-down menu. The pull-down menu is better organized and more complete than the old main menu, and it features nested child submenus for related sets of commands and options. The screen menu automatically displays pages of options for most commands, whether you enter the command by menu or from the keyboard.

- **Enhanced object selection.** You can use several new methods to select objects to edit more quickly and precisely. These methods include automatic windowing and selecting objects that cross irregular lines, or selecting windows with irregular boundaries.

- **Noun/verb editing.** You can now select entities, then specify the command to edit them with.

- **Grips editing.** You can select entities and then pick geometric points (like object snap points) on them to drag them around and modify them by using several of the most common editing operations.

- **Locked layers.** You can lock layers to leave them visible, while preventing object selection or editing on them.

- **Plotting.** The task of plotting is greatly improved in Release 12, with dialog-box control, your choice of any number of alternative plotters or plot configurations, and optional plot preview.

- **PostScript.** You can use, plot, and export PostScript fonts and fills for presentation-quality graphics.

- **Graphics file formats.** AutoCAD Release 12 can import PostScript, TIFF, GIF, and PCX graphics files and can export these and other common graphics-file formats.

- **Dimensioning.** AutoCAD Release 12 makes dimensioning fast and easy through a new set of submenus (which give you fast access to dimensioning commands), and a dialog box (for setting variables and managing styles). You no longer need to remember all those cryptic variable names.

- **Linetypes.** Broken linetypes now display with polylines of all types.

- **Automated boundary and hatch generations.** You can automatically generate complex boundary polylines defined by multiple entities, and you can then hatch those boundaries.

- **Regions.** You can create editable single-entity flat objects from polylines and circles, and then extract properties such as area, perimeter, centroid, bounding box, moment of inertia, products of inertia, principal moments, and radius of gyration.

# Who Should Read this Book—and How

The AutoCAD for Windows program does not include a Windows-specific version of the *AutoCAD Reference Manual*. Although the complete *AutoCAD Reference Manual* is provided as an enhanced help file, it documents and illustrates only the DOS-to-AutoCAD interface. Whether you are a new AutoCAD user, a new Windows user, new to both programs, or experienced in both, *Inside AutoCAD Release 12 for Windows* is your only complete and integrated Windows-specific introduction, tutorial, and reference manual for AutoCAD for Windows.

# The Benefits of this Book to AutoCAD Users Who Are New to Windows

If you are an experienced AutoCAD user who is new to Windows and AutoCAD for Windows, you should read Part One. Then you can skim through Part Two for an overview of AutoCAD for Windows, pausing to learn about the new menus, the toolbar, and the dialog boxes before you delve into Part Three. In Part Three, you learn how to customize AutoCAD for Windows to enhance your productivity. This book does not require any previous Windows experience, but you will want to read Appendix B to familiarize yourself with the basics of Windows.

As you will see throughout this book's exercises, you can more easily access programs, files, and directories through AutoCAD for Windows' graphical interface. You also gain productivity by switching from one application program to another without exiting from them, as you must do in DOS. You can now easily transfer data from AutoCAD to an external program, process or analyze it, and then use it to update your AutoCAD drawing.

In the more advanced sections of the book, you learn to apply new sophistication and power to your AutoCAD work. You can extend your system's power and flexibility almost endlessly by programming AutoCAD with Visual Basic, copying and linking AutoCAD data to other programs, and customizing the AutoCAD for Windows interface.

# The Benefits of this Book to Windows Users Who Are New to AutoCAD

If you are an experienced Windows user who is new to AutoCAD, you can skim through the sections on the Windows interface. You should carefully read most chapters and work through the exercises, however, to become familiar with the program's commands, menus, and dialog boxes. This book requires no previous AutoCAD experience; it takes you from the beginning level and makes you an expert.

You can now apply your Windows skills to easily learn to use the world's best-selling CAD program. You can transfer data from AutoCAD to other Windows applications, process or analyze the data, and then use the results to update your drawing.

See Appendix B for tips to help you optimize the performance of Windows for AutoCAD, as well as other applications programs.

# The Benefits of this Book to New AutoCAD and Windows Users

If you are new to both Windows and AutoCAD, you can skim through the book for an overview. After that, you should read all chapters and work through the exercises.

They will teach you how to use the Windows interface and the program's commands, menus, and dialog boxes. Remember that this book requires no previous AutoCAD or Windows experience. The book takes you from the beginning level and makes you an AutoCAD expert. If you need more information on the basics of Windows before you start working with AutoCAD, start by reading Appendix B.

This book covers AutoCAD for Windows more completely than any other available source of information. Study the book well and you will become an expert in the program's use. After you have completed Parts One and Two, you will be able to take advantage of the book's benefits to experienced users.

## The Benefits of this Book to Experienced AutoCAD and Windows Users

If you are experienced with both Windows and AutoCAD, you can skim through the book for a overview of how they work together, then delve into Parts 3 and 4 to add customization and 3D to your repertoire.

Now you can merge the productivity of AutoCAD with the productivity of Windows' graphical interface. You can switch from Windows application programs to AutoCAD without exiting from any program. You can also easily transfer data from AutoCAD to an external program, process or analyze it, and then use it to update your AutoCAD drawing. You will find discussion and tips in Appendixes A and B to help you optimize the performance of both AutoCAD and Windows.

Even if you are experienced with previous releases of AutoCAD, Release 12 has enough new features to make this book valuable to you. Although you can skim through parts of the book, you should explore the new dialog boxes and menus in Chapter 2 and the new editing techniques in Chapter 6, then delve into Parts 3 and 4 to add advanced 2D drawing and editing techniques to your repertoire.

If you have been using only AutoCAD's 2D features, you also may want to use Part Five of this book to expand into 3D surface and solid modeling. You will find discussion and tips in Appendixes A and B that will help you optimize the performance of both AutoCAD and Windows.

## If You are Upgrading from AutoCAD Release 11

This book is written specifically for the Release 12 version of AutoCAD. If you are upgrading from AutoCAD Release 11, AutoCAD Release 12 offers you many new features, including those described earlier. This book provides comprehensive coverage of these new features.

# If You are Upgrading from AutoCAD Release 10

You will also find a great deal of useful information in this book if you are upgrading from AutoCAD Release 10. If you are making this upgrade, you will find an enormous number of added features and enhancements in Release 12, and these features are comprehensively covered in this book. They include paper space, dimension styles, new text alignments, external references, new 3D-input methods, and a new 3D polyface surface entity.

You can use paper space to easily compose multiple-view 2D or 3D drawing sheets, so that when you plot, what you see on the screen is what you get on paper. You can use external references (xrefs) to insert one drawing into another, which protects the inserted drawing from being edited and ensures that the other drawing updates automatically when the inserted drawing is edited. You can use dimension styles to create and control dimensioning standards and to protect associative dimensions from accidental changes during editing.

# The Benefits of this Book to All Readers

No matter how proficient you are with AutoCAD, Windows, or your computer, and no matter how you read this book, you will revisit it again and again as a reference manual. You will find *Inside AutoCAD Release 12 for Windows* indispensable as you use it to find explanations and examples of specific commands and techniques. You can also refer to the table of AutoCAD system variables in Appendix C for more information.

# How this Book Is Organized

*Inside AutoCAD Release 12 for Windows* is organized for both the beginner and the experienced AutoCAD user. The book is designed both as a tutorial to help new users learn to master AutoCAD for Windows, and as a reference guide you can use long after you have mastered the basics of the program. To accomplish these goals, the book is organized into parts, each of which covers a specific group of concepts and operations.

*Inside AutoCAD Release 12 for Windows* starts with the basics of 2D CAD drafting and ends with the construction and presentation of 3D models. The exercises and discussions do not assume that you have any prior knowledge of CAD in general or of AutoCAD in particular. If you study the entire volume, you will be able to use AutoCAD for Windows for 2D drafting, 3D modeling, and presentation. Further, you will be able to customize AutoCAD for Windows so that it works in a way that best suits your unique needs, even if you have no programming knowledge.

# Part One: Getting Started

The three chapters in Part One teach you some Windows basics and prepare you to begin drawing in AutoCAD for Windows. You learn how to start the AutoCAD for Windows program, set up AutoCAD to follow the exercises, and set up specific drawing parameters in the drawing editor. The chapters familiarize you with the AutoCAD drawing editor and interface. At the end of Part One, you will be ready to begin creating and editing drawings in AutoCAD.

Chapter 1 teaches the bare essentials of Windows—just the basics you need to run AutoCAD. (You can get more detailed information about Windows from Appendix B or a Windows reference guide.) The chapter then shows you how to set up AutoCAD for Windows for the exercises in this book. You also learn how to install the *Inside AutoCAD Release 12 for Windows* disk (referred to as the IAW DISK). Even if you are an experienced AutoCAD or Windows user, you need to create a special command line and specify directories so that AutoCAD can work in sync with this book's exercises.

Although Chapter 2 teaches a few basic AutoCAD drawing and editing commands, the chapter's real purpose is to teach you about the AutoCAD for Windows interface. Chapter 2 identifies and discusses the parts of the drawing screen, and covers the various menus and methods of command entry. It emphasizes the use of the toolbar, pull-down menus, and dialog boxes, because they help you take full advantage of the Windows interface. Chapter 2 also shows you how to use AutoCAD Release 12 for Windows' on-line help system.

Chapter 3 covers drawing setup. CAD, like manual drafting, requires some planning and setup before you actually start drawing. Although several basic drawing commands are used in the exercises, Chapter 3 emphasizes setting up layers, linetypes, colors, and drawing units.

When you complete Part One, you will be familiar with your AutoCAD drafting system so that you can begin learning how to draw productively in Part Two.

# Part Two: Basic 2D AutoCAD Drafting

Part Two covers basic 2D drafting. To produce good 2D drawings, you must know how to control the accuracy of AutoCAD's drawing tools. Part Two teaches you how to control the drawing display and how to create and edit 2D drawings.

Chapter 4 shows you how to use AutoCAD's snap, grid, object snaps, and other accuracy aids. These tools help you create extremely precise drawings. You also learn how to control the standard AutoCAD coordinate system and to create your own coordinate system.

In Chapter 5, you learn how to control the drawing window so that you can draw and arrange images of any size on the screen. You develop a mastery of single and multiple views in the drawing area, and learn to control the amount of the drawing displayed, including the use of the new Aerial View bird's-eye feature. The chapter also demystifies the concept of paper space, which is the bridge between your computer and the paper.

Chapter 6 covers several basic drawing commands and introduces several of the editing features new to Release 12. New users will find these editing methods intuitive and easy to use; experienced AutoCAD users may need to study this chapter more carefully and practice to break old habits and take advantage of more efficient ways to create and edit drawings.

Chapter 7 shows you how to use every remaining 2D drawing command, so that you can draw virtually anything you want.

Chapter 8 comprehensively covers all the features of the basic editing commands introduced in Chapter 6 for moving, copying, rotating, arraying, and mirroring existing entities in your drawings. The job of editing goes beyond fixing mistakes and making changes. In fact, you can often draw more efficiently by editing existing entities than you can by creating new ones.

When you finish Part Two, you will be able to complete nearly any 2D drawing; however, the features covered in Part Three will make your drafting much more efficient.

# Part Three: Advanced 2D AutoCAD Drafting

Part Three of *Inside AutoCAD Release 12 for Windows* introduces many new and advanced features of AutoCAD. The previous chapters cover several basic commands and features; this section teaches you how to use those commands more efficiently and to improve your drawing versatility. Additional advanced commands are covered, and Part Three offers in-depth coverage of dimensioning and plotting. You learn drawing-construction techniques, how to create and insert drawing symbols, dimensioning techniques, and how to prepare drawings for plotting and presentation. By the time you complete Part Three, you will know all of AutoCAD's 2D commands and many drawing and editing techniques, tips, and tricks for producing accurate, professional-looking 2D drawings.

Chapter 9 covers advanced editing commands that enable you to use many methods to extend, stretch, trim, scale, and offset existing objects. In this chapter, you also learn several additional methods for creating new objects.

Chapter 10 describes a wide range of drawing tips and techniques. This chapter combines commands from the previous chapters and shows you how to use construction lines and point filters to build accurate drawings quickly. You also learn how to use all the AutoCAD UNDO features so that you can easily try different edits without wasting time.

Chapters 11 and 12 show you how to use AutoCAD blocks (symbols) and xrefs (externally referenced files). In Chapter 11, you learn how to save drawing time and file space by using blocks to insert repetitive objects in your drawings. You also learn how to update your drawings quickly by redefining blocks. Chapter 11 teaches the use of external references—xrefs—which are insertions into a drawing that reference the contents of other drawing files. Xrefs coordinate the cooperative editing of a master drawing by enabling several people to work on parts of it simultaneously. Xrefs also make drawings smaller by storing parts in their own separate drawing files; the master file updates automatically if the referenced file is edited.

Chapter 12 is another techniques chapter, which teaches the application of blocks, xrefs, and other drafting techniques when creating a drawing. In this chapter, you draw a complete site plan.

Chapter 13 shows how to compose and plot your drawings the way you want them using Windows' concurrent capabilities to plot while you continue to draw. You learn how to use paper space to compose drawings, making multiple-view plotting a cinch. Chapter 13 also includes dozens of plotting tips.

Chapter 14 contains techniques for dressing up your drawings with hatching, linetypes, and freehand sketching using Windows' concurrent capabilities to plot while you continue to draw. This chapter closes by examining AutoCAD's inquiry commands, which tell you what, where, and when you are drawing.

Chapter 15 covers the basic use of AutoCAD's dimensioning settings and commands to dimension your drawings. (Advanced dimensioning is discussed in Chapter 17.)

When you complete Part Three, you will have learned how to create complex 2D drawings, from initial setup to final plot.

# Part Four: Advanced AutoCAD Features

Part Four introduces you to new and more advanced features of AutoCAD Release 12. Part Four shows you how to customize and tailor AutoCAD to your specific needs—from storing nongraphic information in your drawings, to customizing and using advanced dimensioning, to using AutoCAD data and images in conjunction with other applications.

Chapter 16 teaches you how to use AutoCAD's attribute entities as tags you attach to blocks in your drawing to maintain information about various items. If you are creating a drawing that details the equipment in a factory, for example, you can use attributes to keep track of cost, function, manufacturer, purchase date, maintenance data, and other types of information about the equipment. Chapter 16 also shows you how to extract data from the attributes in a drawing. You can use the extracted data to create reports or bills of materials, or to otherwise collect and analyze data.

Chapter 17 shows you how to set variables and create and use dimension styles to customize and control dimensions so they meet your standards. Chapter 17 also covers several of AutoCAD's advanced dimensioning capabilities, such as ordinate, chain, and datum dimensioning.

Chapter 18 describes techniques and commands for customizing AutoCAD's interface. Chapter 18 shows you how to customize AutoCAD to define command abbreviations, use prototype drawings, and add commands and macros to the AutoCAD toolbar, so that you can save time and avoid entering repetitive steps manually. Chapter 18 also examines other interface customization topics, such as changing the fonts and colors used for the AutoCAD interface.

Chapter 19 describes techniques and commands for importing and exporting AutoCAD data and images to and from other programs. This chapter shows how to copy and link data from AutoCAD to other applications using the Window Clipboard and OLE to create reports or manuals that contain AutoCAD graphics. Chapter 19 also covers the use of Dynamic Data Exchange (DDE) to move data from AutoCAD to an external program, process or analyze it, and then move it back to AutoCAD to update your drawings.

The capability to copy a drawing or part of a drawing to another document can save considerable time in developing training materials, manuals, reports, and other documents. Chapter 19 also covers two file standards for CAD data exchanges: Autodesk's DXF format and the international IGES file formats. AutoCAD Release 12 can also import and export PostScript, PCX, TIFF, and GIF files, as well as export several other industry-standard graphics-file formats. This capability opens up some new ways to use AutoCAD, such as for desktop publishing and presentation work.

When you finish Part Four, you will have a complete mastery of AutoCAD for 2D design and drafting. You will be able to extract data from your drawings, customize your dimensioning methods, and exchange graphic and nongraphic data with other users and programs.

# Part Five: AutoCAD and 3D Drawing

Part Five covers 3D modeling, from planar 2D entities to extruded 2D entities, to true 3D surface entities. You learn how to create, edit, and display models. You can use 3D models to create complex shapes or find intersections and other design relationships that are difficult or impossible to draw manually.

Chapter 20 teaches you how to use the user coordinate system (UCS) to position construction planes anywhere in 3D space. You can draw on these construction planes by using standard 2D AutoCAD drawing commands, creating a 3D model from extruded 2D entities. Chapter 20 also teaches you to control your viewpoint and viewports to visualize your model in 3D, and to view your model more realistically with hidden lines removed.

Chapter 21 introduces 3D entities, such as 3D polylines, 3D faces, and 3D surface meshes. You learn to use the basic 3D surface commands as well as AutoLISP-defined commands that create 3D objects, such as boxes, wedges, cones, and spheres. You also use surface shading to view your 3D model quickly and clearly.

Chapter 22 shows you how to move around in and present your 3D drawings. You learn to dynamically adjust your 3D viewpoint and create perspective views to help you plan and preview 3D presentations. You learn to put dynamic views, slides, and scripts together to create a walk-through presentation.

By the time you finish Part Five, you will be an expert in AutoCAD Release 12 for Windows, from 2D to 3D.

## The Appendixes

*Inside AutoCAD Release 12 for Windows* also has three useful appendixes.

Appendix A covers installation, configuration, and troubleshooting.

Appendix B teaches you the basics of using Windows, and how to improve the performance of both AutoCAD and Windows.

Appendix C is a useful table of AutoCAD's system variables.

# How To Use the Tutorials

Each chapter is divided into a series of exercises, each of which teaches one or more AutoCAD commands. Explanatory text accompanies each exercise, puts commands and techniques into context, explains how commands behave, and shows you how to use different options. If you just read the text and exercises and look at the illustrations, you will learn a great deal about the program. But if you want to gain a greater mastery of AutoCAD Release 12, you need to sit down at a computer equipped with AutoCAD Release 12 and work through the exercises.

# Where To Find Specific Topics

You should work through each part of the book in order, but you can choose specific topics, if you want. The IAW DISK enables you to enter the exercise sequence at several different points in most chapters. If you want to begin immediately, examine the following Quick Start Guide to locate key topics and techniques.

*Wherever you start, you should first do the setup (and IAW DISK installation) exercises in Chapter 1 so that your system setup corresponds with the directions and illustrations in the exercises.*

**Table 1.1**

**Quick Start Guide to *Inside AutoCAD Release 12 for Windows***

| If you want to: | Turn to: |
| --- | --- |
| Set up to use the book and IAW DISK | Chapter 1 |
| Set up AutoCAD Release 12 | Chapter 1 |
| Install or configure AutoCAD Release 12 | Appendix A |
| Learn to use Windows | Appendix B |
| Use menus and dialog boxes | Chapter 2 |
| Use various forms of input | Chapter 2 |
| Set up drawings | Chapter 3 |
| Use the user coordinate system (UCS) in 2D | Chapter 4 |
| Use the user coordinate system (UCS) in 3D | Chapter 20 |
| Use multiple views (viewports) in 2D | Chapter 5 |
| Use multiple views (viewports) in 3D | Chapter 20 |
| Use MVIEW (paper space) viewports in 2D | Chapters 5 and 13 |

| If you want to: | Turn to: |
| --- | --- |
| Use MVIEW (paper space) viewports in 3D | Chapter 20 |
| Learn 2D drawing commands | Chapters 2, 6, and 7 |
| Use 2D drawing commands to draw 3D objects | Chapters 10 and 20 |
| Learn 3D drawing commands | Chapters 20, 21, and 22 |
| Edit 2D drawings | Chapters 8, 9, and 10 |
| Edit 3D drawings | Chapters 20, 21, and 22 |
| Create 2D regions and extract information from drawings | Chapter 14 |
| Create 2D drawings from 3D entities | Chapter 20 |
| Plot 2D and 3D drawings | Chapter 13 |
| Compose paper space drawing sheets to plot | Chapters 13 and 20 |
| Use blocks (symbols and parts) in drawings | Chapters 11 and 12 |
| Use external references (xrefs) | Chapters 11 and 12 |
| Add attribute information to drawings | Chapter 16 |
| Dimension drawings | Chapters 15 and 17 |
| Customize dimensioning | Chapter 17 |
| Use associative dimensions and styles | Chapter 17 |
| Control 3D views and perspectives | Chapters 19 and 21 |
| Customize menus, toolbar, and toolbox | Chapter 18 |
| Customize the AutoCAD for Windows interface | Chapter 18 |
| Use DDE | Chapter 19 |
| Copy images to the Windows Clipboard | Chapter 19 |
| Copy and link AutoCAD data to other applications | Chapter 19 |

# Using the IAW DISK

The best way to use *Inside AutoCAD Release 12 for Windows* is to work through every exercise in sequence. You can work selected exercises to cover topics of particular interest, but many exercises require drawings created in earlier exercises or chapters. In most cases, you can create the drawing you need without investing too much time and effort. But you often can easily choose exercises to perform without backtracking by using files from the IAW DISK. This disk contains exercise drawings saved at various stages of completion. Whenever an exercise gives you the option of using a file from the IAW DISK, doing so will ensure that your drawing matches the book's for the exercise.

Chapter 1 explains how to set up directories on your hard disk for use with *Inside AutoCAD Release 12 for Windows*. The setup is designed so that the IAW directory structure and exercises will not interfere with your normal AutoCAD settings or any other work you are doing. Chapter 1 also explains how to install the drawing and support files included in the IAW DISK.

# A Special Note to AutoCAD Instructors

Several editions of *Inside AutoCAD Release 12* have been used for classroom instruction, and *Inside AutoCAD Release 12 for Windows* is equally suitable for classroom use. Each chapter begins with a brief description of its contents and tells the student what he or she should be able to learn from it. Each chapter ends with a summary.

# Following the Book's Conventions and Exercises

The conventions used for showing various types of text throughout this book are, insofar as possible, the same as those used in the *Microsoft Windows Users Guide* and the *AutoCAD Reference Manual*. These conventions are shown in this section. Some conventions, such as the use of italics to introduce a new term, are pretty simple. Others, such as those used in the exercises, are worth a closer look.

A sample exercise follows. You do not need to work through it, but you should study the format so that you will know what to expect from the exercises throughout the book. Most exercises are accompanied by one or more illustrations, most of which were captured from the screen during an actual exercise. Exercises are arranged in two columns, with direct instructions on the left and explanatory notes on the right. Lengthy explanations sometimes extend across both columns. The numbers shown in circles refer to points in the illustrations (see fig. I.1).

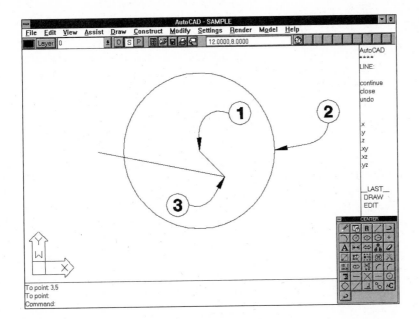

## A Sample Exercise

Continue in the SAMPLE drawing from the previous exercise.

| | |
|---|---|
| `Command:` *Turn on the S toolbar button* | Sets snap mode on |
| `Command:` *Choose* **D**raw, *then* **C**ircle, *then* Center, **R**adius | Issues the CIRCLE command from the **C**ircle child menu |
| `_circle 3P/2P/TTR/<Center point>:` *Pick point at* ① *(see fig. I.1)* | Specifies the circle's center point |
| `Diameter/<Radius>:` **3** ↵ | Draws a 6" circle |
| `Command:` *From the screen menu, choose* DRAW, *then* LINE: | Issues the LINE command |
| `From point:` *From the toolbox, choose* CENTER | Specifies the CENter object snap |
| `_center of` *Pick the circle at* ② | Starts the line at the circle's center |
| `To point:` *Pick at* ③ | Draws the line |
| `To point:` **3,5** ↵ | Specifies the coordinates you typed |
| `To point:` *Press Enter* | Ends the LINE command |

Because AutoCAD for Windows is a Windows application, its interface uses many of the elements used by other Windows applications. Some of AutoCAD's traditional AUI pull-down menus have been replaced by icon menus. The status line is now a toolbar, which incorporates buttons for a few commonly used commands. The toolbar also contains two of the status line's traditional elements: the current layer name and the coordinates display. The menu bar no longer pops up when you move the pointer to the status line—instead, it always appears above the toolbar. Another new feature is the toolbox, which also contains buttons for commonly used commands and all of the object snap modes.

When you see an instruction such as *Choose* Item in an exercise, it means to move the pointer to Item on the menu bar and click the left mouse button. Or, you can use a hot key—a key combination consisting of the Alt key and the letter underlined in the menu bar item—to display the menu. You can choose any menu item by moving the pointer to the item and clicking the left mouse button. You can choose pull-down menu items by clicking on them, or by pressing the hot key indicated with an underlined letter or number in the menu. If you are not familiar with the Windows interface, you will be introduced to it in Part One; Appendix B covers it in more detail.

If a pull-down menu or dialog box is currently displayed, *Choose* refers to an item on it. The *screen menu* is the menu that appears at the right side of the drawing area. All instructions to choose from the screen menu are prefaced with *"From the screen menu, choose...."* Instructions to use the toolbar or toolbox are prefaced with *"From the toolbar (or toolbox), choose...."* Otherwise, the exercises assume that you will use the pull-down menu. See Chapter 2 for more information on using menus, dialog boxes, and the toolbar and toolbox.

In some cases, you will see the instruction *Press Enter*. Your computer may have a key labeled Enter, or one labeled Return, or one with an arrow symbol. In any case, *Press Enter* means to press the key that enters a carriage return.

In some cases, you will see the symbol ↵ in the exercises. Your computer may have a key labeled Enter, or one labeled Return, or one with an arrow symbol. In any case, ↵ means that you need to press the key that enters a return.

You often enter commands from the keyboard. Similarly, point coordinates, distances, and option keywords often must be typed. The exercise text generally indicates when typed input is required by showing it in bold text following a prompt, such as `Command:` **UNITS** ↵ or `To point:` **3,5** ↵. You should type the input as it appears, and then press Enter.

Early in the book, you will notice that exercises contain numerous prompts and explanations of what is (or should be) happening as you enter commands. Later exercises often omit prompts that have become routine, and explanations of familiar effects.

Many exercises end with an instruction to end or save the drawing. You may not want to end a drawing, because some chapters can be completed in one or two sittings. You should save your drawings when instructed, however, to help you build a habit of saving drawings at regular intervals. If you want to proceed at a leisurely pace, you can end your drawing whenever you see the save instruction, and reload it later. If you want to take a break where a save or end instruction is not shown, just close and save or end your drawing and reload it later.

In addition to the conventions shown here, you may find it easier to follow the material in this book if you look over the Windows material in Appendix B.

# Notes, Tips, and Warnings

*Inside AutoCAD Release 12 for Windows* features many special "sidebars," which are set apart from the normal text by icons. The book includes three distinct types of sidebars: "Notes," "Tips," and "Warnings." These passages have been given special treatment so that you can instantly recognize their significance and easily find them for future reference.

A note *includes "extra" information you should find useful, but which complements the discussion at hand instead of being a direct part of it. A note may describe special situations that can arise when you use AutoCAD for Windows under certain circumstances, and* may tell you what steps to take when such situations arise. Notes may also tell you how to avoid problems with your software and hardware.

A tip *provides you with quick instructions for getting the most from your AutoCAD system as you follow the steps outlined in the general discussion. A tip might show you how to conserve memory in some setups, how to speed up a procedure, or how to perform one* of many time-saving and system-enhancing techniques.

A warning *tells you when a procedure may be dangerous—that is, when you run the risk of losing data, locking your system, or even damaging your hardware. Warnings generally tell you how to avoid such losses, or describe the steps you can take to remedy them.*

# Exercises and Your Graphics Display

The authors created this book's illustrations by capturing screen displays during the process of performing the exercises. All screen displays were captured from systems using SuperVGA display controllers set for the 800×600-pixel resolution, 16-color mode under Windows. If your system has a standard VGA, or EGA card, or a high-resolution display controller, your screen displays may not agree exactly with the illustrations. Menus and screen elements may appear larger or smaller than they do in the illustrations, and you may want to zoom in or out further than the instructions indicate. You should learn from the outset, in fact, that you must adjust to the task at hand and the resources available. You may find that if you use colors different than instructed in the exercises, the entities are easier to see, especially if you are working with a white background rather than a black background.

*The drawing image will probably be clearer if you set AutoCAD for Windows to use a black drawing background. See the AutoCAD Environment Settings dialog box instructions in Chapter 18 for details.*

# What You Need To Use this Book

To use *Inside AutoCAD Release 12 for Windows*, you need the following software and hardware, at the least. This book assumes the following:

- You have a computer with both AutoCAD for Windows and Windows 3.1 or later installed and configured. Appendixes A and B provide more specific information and recommendations on system requirements, and on installing, configuring, and maximizing the performance of AutoCAD for Windows.

- You have at least 3M of free hard disk space left after you have installed and configured Windows and AutoCAD for Windows.

- You have a graphics display and pointing device configured to work with Windows (if the system works with Windows, it should work with AutoCAD for Windows).

- You are familiar with PC DOS/MS-DOS and can use the basic DOS commands and utilities.

- You are familiar with Windows and can use it to run applications (if not, see Appendix B).

# Handling Problems

As you work through the exercises in *Inside AutoCAD Release 12 for Windows*, you may experience some problems. These problems can occur for any number of reasons, from input errors to hardware failures. If you have trouble performing any step described in this book, take the following actions:

- Check the update text file on the IAW DISK.

- Try again. Double-check the steps you performed in the previous exercise(s), as well as earlier steps in the current exercise.

- Check the settings of any AutoCAD system variables modified in any previous exercise sequences. (See the system variables table in Appendix C for a listing of all system variables.)

- See the troubleshooting section of Appendix A.

- Check the *AutoCAD Reference Manual* or the AutoCAD Release 12 on-line help.

If none of the above suggestions help, call New Riders Publishing (503-661-5745) *only* if the problem relates to a specific exercise, instruction, or error in the book. Otherwise, try the following for further help:

- Call your AutoCAD dealer.

- Log in to the Autodesk forum on CompuServe, and ask or search for help.

# Other AutoCAD Titles from New Riders Publishing

New Riders Publishing offers the widest selection of books on AutoCAD available anywhere. Although the following titles are oriented to the command-line interface rather than the Windows interface, their contents still apply to AutoCAD Release 12, and what you learn from this book will make it easy for you to follow them.

*Inside AutoCAD Release 12 for Windows* is written for the beginning to intermediate AutoCAD user. If you prefer a beginning tutorial, see *AutoCAD Release 12 for Beginners*. It covers the 80 percent of AutoCAD that most users use in everyday work, packaged in an easy-to-use text.

For comprehensive coverage of several Autodesk products that can be used to create 3D designs and presentations, see *AutoCAD 3D Design and Presentation*. The book includes coverage of AutoCAD 3D, AME solid modeling, AutoShade, RenderMan, Autodesk Animator Pro, 3D Studio, and AutoFlix.

If you want to turn your AutoCAD drawings into animated presentations—or if you just want to draw cartoons—see *Inside Autodesk Animator*.

If you want to customize AutoCAD to work your way, see *Maximizing AutoCAD*. *Maximizing AutoLISP* covers all aspects of customization, short of writing programs in AutoLISP or the C language. *Maximizing AutoLISP* covers applications development using AutoLISP programs, menus, dBASE, Lotus 1-2-3, and BASIC.

If you want a quick, yet comprehensive reference, see the *New Riders' Reference Guide to AutoCAD Release 12*.

If you want a tutorial workbook or need to pass the Certified AutoCAD Operator's Exam, see the *AutoCAD Tutor*. The workbook is designed specifically to help new AutoCAD users prepare for this exam.

If you manage other AutoCAD users, with or without a network, see *Managing and Networking AutoCAD*. This book provides a comprehensive discussion of the issues facing an AutoCAD manager or network administrator.

If you do technical drafting in 2D or 3D, see *AutoCAD Drafting and 3D Design*. The book is written around ANSI Y14.5M standards.

If you want a comprehensive reference volume on AutoCAD, see *AutoCAD: The Professional Reference, Second Edition*. This generous volume covers everything from basic commands to customization.

# Other Windows Titles from New Riders Publishing

If you are new to Windows and want to learn more about this powerful operating environment, see *Inside Windows 3.1*. This book is a fast-paced tutorial designed for experienced DOS users who want to become productive quickly in the Windows environment. *Inside Windows 3.1* is filled with practical examples to help you quickly master Windows commands. The book also features in-depth discussions of basic Windows concepts, and provides comprehensive instructions that help you benefit from Windows' powerful features, such as Dynamic Data Exchange and Object Linking and Embedding.

If you are already proficient with Windows and you want to start customizing or optimizing your Windows system, see *Maximizing Windows 3.1*. This book shows you how to use Windows to program Windows applications, modify existing Windows applications, and optimize memory management.

Windows users at all levels can use *Windows 3.1 on Command*. This handy reference is task-oriented; you can use it to learn specific operations without knowing the name of the commands you need. The book covers all the basic Windows file-management operations, and shows you how to customize the Windows interface and perform other higher-level functions. This step-by-step guide leads you quickly through even the most complicated Windows-specific tasks.

If you must use Windows on a network, look into *Windows 3.1 Networking*. This advanced reference shows you how to integrate Windows and Windows applications into a network environment. You learn how to set up the Windows environment so that it does not conflict with your network operating system. The book also contains optimization and customization strategies to help you get the most from Windows in a networked system. If you are working with peer-to-peer networking, you may be interested in *Inside Windows for Workgroups*.

For a more advanced book on programming for Windows, see *Windows 3.1 End-User Programming*. This book was written for advanced Windows users who want to write their own Windows applications. This book teaches you how to create your own Windows-based applications by using the new generation of end-user programming tools. The book includes three disks containing sample applications and valuable programming tools.

You can order any New Riders title by calling 1-800-428-5331 for customer service.

*New Riders also carries a line of books on a variety of network products. These include* Inside Novell Netware; Maximizing Novell NetWare; NetWare, the Professional Reference; Novell NetWare on Command; Inside NetWare Lite; Inside LANtastic; *and* Token Ring Troubleshooting.

# Contacting New Riders Publishing

The staff of New Riders Publishing is committed to bringing you the best in computer reference material. Each New Riders book is the result of months of work by authors and staff, who research and refine the information contained within its covers.

As part of this commitment to you, the NRP reader, New Riders invites your input. Please let us know if you enjoy this book, if you have trouble with the information and examples presented, or if you have a suggestion for future editions.

Please note, however, that the New Riders staff cannot serve as a technical resource for AutoCAD Release 12 or any other applications or hardware. Refer to the documentation that accompanies your programs and hardware for help with specific problems. Your AutoCAD dealer can provide general AutoCAD support.

If you have a question or comment about any New Riders book, please write to NRP at the following address:

New Riders Publishing
Attn: Associate Publisher
201 W. 103rd Street
Indianapolis, IN 46290

We will respond to as many readers as we can. Your name, address, or phone number will never become part of a mailing list or be used for any other purpose than to help us continue to bring you the best books possible.

If you prefer, you can FAX New Riders Publishing at the following number:

(317) 581-4670

Thank you for selecting *Inside AutoCAD Release 12 for Windows*!

# Getting Started

# PART 1

# Introduction

The process of getting started is often one of the most challenging aspects of learning to use new software. Perhaps you are new to the computer-aided drafting (CAD) environment or to AutoCAD, or perhaps you do not have much experience with computers. Part One of *Inside AutoCAD Release 12 for Windows* shows you how to set up your system for use with this book's exercises and how to begin working in the AutoCAD drawing editor.

## How Part One is Organized

Part One includes three chapters, which take you through the basics of setting up, starting, and drawing in AutoCAD. In these chapters, you learn how to set up AutoCAD so that you can follow the book's exercises, begin and save drawing files, and set up specific drawing parameters in the drawing editor. These chapters cover six basic topics:

- Using the Windows interface
- Starting up AutoCAD
- Setting up AutoCAD for the exercises in this book
- Learning the parts of the AutoCAD drawing editor
- Using the AutoCAD menus
- Beginning to draw in AutoCAD

# Understanding the Need for Proper Setup

Chapter 1 shows you how to set up AutoCAD so that you can easily duplicate this book's exercises. You can draw these exercises from scratch every time, or you can use the drawing files included on this book's optional disk. This disk (called the IAW DISK throughout this book) contains AutoCAD drawing files that have been specially prepared for use with the book's exercises. By using these disk files, you can better concentrate on the material in the chapter because the drawing being discussed generally continues at the point of creation shown in the file. The disk is also helpful if you do not follow the chapters in order, or if you want to go at any time to some particular topic of interest. Chapter 1 gives you instructions on installing the disk.

# Setting Up for the Drawing Exercises

This book instructs you to run AutoCAD from a special directory, which you will create in Chapter 1. That directory will contain a special AutoCAD configuration file, as well as your exercise drawings. You should set up and use the special directory for the following reasons:

- The tutorials are easier to follow if you are working with the same path names shown in the exercises.

- If you run the exercises from their own directory, they do not interfere with any existing drawings or settings that you already are using on your system.

- By learning how to set up a special directory, you can set up AutoCAD for other special situations in the future, such as varying hardware or multiple projects.

Chapter 1 teaches you how to create a batch file to start AutoCAD from the special directory you set up. By the end of Chapter 1, you should have a basic understanding of the Windows interface and have your system all ready to begin drawing with AutoCAD.

# Moving around in the Drawing Editor

Chapter 2 explains the basics of interacting with the AutoCAD program. It shows you how to begin drawing, how to enter points and coordinates, and how to save your drawing.

Chapter 2 describes the important parts of the drawing screen and explains their functions. AutoCAD sometimes seems more complex than it is because it offers several ways to access the same command. AutoCAD Release 12 for Windows provides a more user-friendly interface than earlier releases of the program because of the increased use of pull-down menus and dialog boxes, which enable you to select items graphically, as well as the immediately accessible toolbar and toolbox. Chapter 2 is designed to help you navigate through the various menu systems, dialog boxes, toolbar, and toolbox, and to introduce you to the different methods of command entry.

Throughout this book, the exercises show you various methods of command entry. Remember, however, that you do not need to master all the methods at once. Determine the method that makes the most sense to you and concentrate on that until you feel ready to try some of the others.

# Learning AutoCAD's Editing and Help Facilities

Among the first AutoCAD commands this book introduces are basic editing tools, such as ERASE and UNDO. If you are new to AutoCAD, you probably will make mistakes often and want to correct them quickly. Even users who have mastered the AutoCAD software still use the editing tools often. The on-line help function enables you to access information that explains the use of commands and the function of available command options. The help system is another good feature to learn early. AutoCAD Release 12 for Windows' help system offers even more help than was previously practical.

# Creating Your First Drawings

Chapter 3 introduces several basic drawing commands in a tutorial fashion to help you with the beginning drawings. Because AutoCAD can work in so many different applications and disciplines, drawing parameters are very important. Chapter 3 explains standard CAD terms as it introduces you to using the basic commands. Drawing layers, linetypes, colors, and drawing units are covered, and the chapter provides practice for you in setting up related drawings. Chapter 3 also makes several comparisons between "manual drafting" and CAD drafting to help you visualize the similarities and differences between the two types of drafting.

The goal of Part One is to familiarize you with the AutoCAD drafting system. When you are done with Part One, you should be comfortable enough with AutoCAD to start learning to draw productively.

CHAPTER 1

# Setting Up

*Inside AutoCAD Release 12 for Windows* is a reference and tutorial about AutoCAD and how it runs in the Windows environment. Chapter 1 helps you to set up and to explore the working relationship between AutoCAD and the Windows operating environment. Whereas Appendix A explains in detail how to load and configure the software, the following pages help you start up AutoCAD with the right parameters and control its operating characteristics.

*Even if you are an experienced Windows user and have already set up AutoCAD for Windows in Windows, you need to set up for this book by performing several exercises in this chapter, starting with the "Making the IAW Directory" exercise.*

## Introducing AutoCAD Release 12 for Windows

In the past decade, during the rapid development of the personal computer, many standards were developed for hardware features and operating characteristics. For this reason, it is not difficult to work with many different brands of personal computers. Fortunately, this same trend has started to develop with the appearance and operating characteristics of software. Windows operating software provides a much friendlier operating environment than does DOS, and all software developed for Windows has a familiar "look and feel" that makes using many different software applications much simpler. Also, Windows provides many tools to share information easily between software packages. Your computer screen may not look quite as busy as the one shown in figure 1.1, but you can do many exciting things through the multitasking capability of Windows.

**Figure 1.1:**

Running AutoCAD
in Windows.

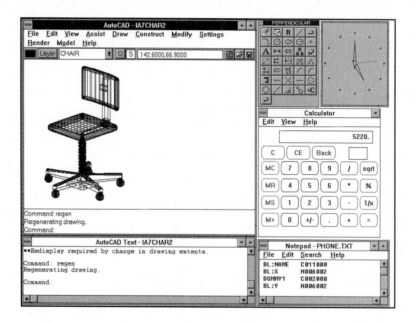

# AutoCAD for Windows Requirements

Before AutoCAD for Windows can run, you must have Windows 3.1 running in 386-enhanced mode. You also must have a version of DOS (PC DOS or MS-DOS) that is 3.3 or later. (DOS version 5.0 or later is recommended strongly for its compatibility and memory management capability.)

Enhancements and improvements to software are often accompanied by increased demands on hardware. At least 8 megabytes of RAM are needed to run AutoCAD for Windows. The software takes about 32 megabytes of space on the hard drive.

# AutoCAD for Windows Features

This version of AutoCAD has many new features available. Some of the most visible changes include the following:

- Icons instead of words in some pull-down menus

- An improved status line, now called the toolbar, which provides convenient command and settings icon buttons

- A floating, customizable toolbox

- Enhanced help with much more information and many more available options

The feature that really makes this package attractive is its Windows compatibility, which includes the following:

- Dialog boxes that conform to Windows standards

- Text and graphic windows that can be resized and moved around on the screen

- The capability of editing multiple files (drawings) at the same time

- Capability of running other application packages simultaneously with AutoCAD for Windows

- Dynamic Data Exchange links for exchanging information with other application packages

- Object linking and embedding for sharing and automatic updating of document files between applications

- Graphics exchange with other Windows application packages through Windows metafiles and vector or bit-mapped images, using Clipboard cut-and-paste commands

In terms of raw processing speed, the DOS 386 version of AutoCAD is faster and may still be preferred for complex drawings. Nevertheless, the Windows interface and its features offer productivity enhancements that may outweigh raw processing speed.

# Using Windows

Now that Windows is loaded and operational on your computer, several key areas should be mentioned that control how AutoCAD functions. Your Windows reference manual is the best source of information about how your specific version of Windows operates. (Two good references are *Inside Windows 3.1* and *Maximizing Windows 3.1*, available from New Riders Publishing.) Like DOS, Windows has many updates and different versions available. Windows itself can be customized extensively, so do not be surprised if your screen looks slightly different than the examples shown in this book.

Start up Windows on your computer.

## Starting Windows

*Enter* **WIN** *at the DOS command prompt*      Starts Windows (see fig. 1.2)

# The Windows Program Manager

The first window you see as the Windows software starts up is the Program Manager. This window, as shown in figure 1.2, shows pull-down menu items and graphical icons that open up other windows, called *applications groups*. (Applications groups are windows containing other icons that activate programs.) As a general rule, one click of the mouse button on a word or icon selects that option. A *double-click* activates an icon to run an application program or open a window.

You can move a window around by holding the mouse button down on the window title bar and dragging the window; you can resize it by holding the mouse button down on the edge or corner of the window border and dragging it. You may have to do some practicing with your own input device before this becomes easy for you.

**Figure 1.2:**

The Windows
Program Manager.

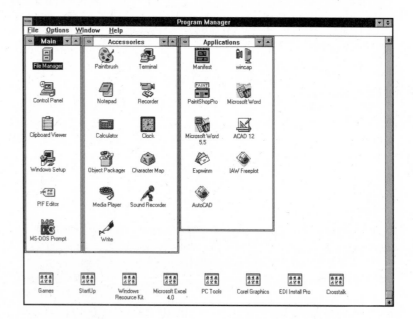

# The Accessories Window

One of the icons in the Windows Program Manager opens the Accessories group window. Open this group by double-clicking on the Accessories icon. The Accessories window is not needed for running AutoCAD, but it is a place in which you find programs that can interface with AutoCAD and be active at the same time. Paintbrush, Write, Calendar, Clock, and many other Windows applications are shown here. Close this window by double-clicking on the control menu box icon (the box with a long dash [-] in it at the left side of the title bar).

*If all of these icons are not showing, select <u>W</u>indow from the Program Manager pull-down menu, then <u>A</u>rrange icons. To retain the icon arrangement when exiting windows, select <u>O</u>ptions, then verify that there is a check next to the <u>S</u>ave settings on Exit option.*

## The Main Window

Several items in the Main group help you set up the Windows environment for AutoCAD. Open the Main group by double-clicking on the Main icon. The Control Panel enables you to select fonts, colors, printers, and other settings for Windows. The File Manager is used for disk- and file-management tasks that are otherwise performed in DOS or with a third-party file-management software package. Windows Setup enables the graphics resolution (800×600 for the screen shots in this book) to be selected. Again, you can close these windows by double-clicking on the control menu box icon at the upper left corner of the window.

*Clicking on the down-arrow button at the upper right corner of the window reduces a window to its icon size and places it near the bottom of the screen. The window is still active; it is pushed out of the way until it is needed again.*

## The WIN.INI File

Many of the Windows operating parameters can be graphically set from the various dialog boxes shown in the windows mentioned here. These settings are really saved in a file called WIN.INI, however. You can use Edit, Notepad, or any ASCII editor to modify this text file directly to change Windows' operating parameters.

*Keep both a printed copy and backup copy of your WIN.INI file in a safe place so that these settings can be restored if the WIN.INI file becomes contaminated with unusable settings.*

Remember, some of the settings created in the Windows environment also control the AutoCAD operating characteristics.

# Setting Up AutoCAD for Exercises in this Book

To run AutoCAD from Windows, you must first understand how both Windows and AutoCAD function. The remainder of this chapter explains specifically how to set up your system to work with the exercises in this book. After successfully completing this chapter, you will probably want to modify your own system to fit your particular needs. Although many of the file commands can be executed at the DOS prompt, this book uses the options found in Windows whenever possible.

## Introducing the IAW DISK

A disk, called the IAW DISK, is included with *Inside AutoCAD Release 12 for Windows*. The book and disk are designed for use on your AutoCAD workstation. The setup for *Inside AutoCAD Release 12 for Windows* exercises requires you to set aside space on your hard disk for a directory called IAW. This setup ensures that any AutoCAD settings and drawings used for the exercises in the book do not interfere with any other AutoCAD settings or projects that you or your co-workers may be working on. As mentioned earlier, learning these setup steps helps you learn how to utilize your system efficiently.

The book assumes that you are using the DOS operating system with Windows, that you are running AutoCAD on a hard disk—designated as the C: drive, and that you have a directory structure similar to the one shown in the following exercise.

*Your drive letter or directory names may differ from those shown in this book. If they do, substitute your drive letter and directory names wherever you encounter drive letters (such as C) or the directory names (such as \ACADWIN) in the book. If you are using an operating system other than DOS, your directory creation and setup will differ from those shown in the following pages. Even so, you should set up a directory structure that is similar to the one shown in this chapter.*

## Making the IAW Directory

Make a special directory called IAW and use it for the exercises in this book, to minimize the chance that you may disturb the existing AutoCAD files. Also, you can easily remove all practice files from the book's exercises after you are through with them. You need to make this directory, and then copy the necessary files into it. By copying the files into the IAW directory, you set up a self-contained AutoCAD environment.

## Making the IAW Directory

Click on or open the Program Manager window. To open it, click on the Program Manager icon.

| | |
|---|---|
| *Double-click on the Main group icon, and then on the File Manager icon* | Opens Main Window, then File Manager |
| *Choose **F**ile from the menu bar, and then* Cr**e**ate Directory | |
| *Enter* **C:\IAW** *in the **N**ame: box and press Enter or choose* OK | Creates the new directory |

Activate the IAW directory by clicking on IAW.

| | |
|---|---|
| *Choose **V**iew, then* **T**ree and Directory | Displays a listing like that shown in figure 1.3 |

Look at the listing to verify that the directory was created. If necessary, click on the scroll bar (at the right side of the Directory Tree window) to display the new name.

| | |
|---|---|
| *Double-click on the control menu box (the box at the top left corner of File Manager)* | Closes File Manager |

# Setting Up the AutoCAD for Windows Command Line

Instead of using batch files to start up application packages such as AutoCAD, Windows enables you to specify the start-up command parameters in a special command line. An appropriate icon is then assigned, so that when you double-click on the icon, the command line executes the commands and parameters to start the software. Software that is specifically designed to run in Windows usually has a special icon available. AutoCAD for Windows includes five icon choices.

## The AutoCAD Startup Command

Unless you specify otherwise, AutoCAD for Windows is loaded into a directory called C:\ACADWIN. The command to start AutoCAD for Windows, therefore, is C:\ACADWIN\ACAD.EXE, which starts up the AutoCAD executable file.

**Figure 1.3:**

The Directory Tree window.

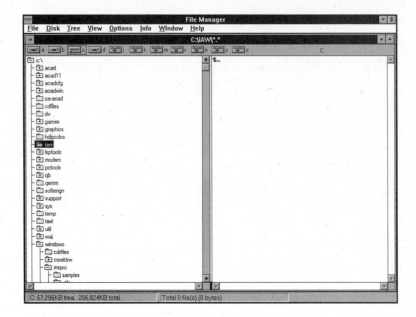

# The /C Command-Line Switch

The directory containing the configuration information is specified with the /C command-line switch. This switch and the path to the configuration directory is placed after the command to start AutoCAD. The command to start AutoCAD for Windows for this book is C:\ACADWIN\ACAD.EXE /C C:\IAW. This tells AutoCAD to look in the C:\IAW directory for the configuration files.

You can place the AutoCAD command line and icon into any of Program Manager's existing groups (Windows Applications, for example) or into its own group. If you want the AutoCAD icon to appear in an existing group window, open the group window by double-clicking on its icon before creating the AutoCAD for Windows command line and icon.

If you want to place the AutoCAD command line and icon into its own group, first create the new program group. To do so, choose **N**ew from the Program Manager **F**ile menu and click on the Program **G**roup radio button instead of the Program **I**tem (as shown in fig. 1.4), and, click on OK. In the Program Group Properties dialog box, enter the name of the new group window in the **D**escription text box and click on OK. The **G**roup File name is created automatically for you. Then you can proceed to add AutoCAD to your new group window using the following instructions.

*You can move an existing program icon from one group to another
by having both windows open and dragging the icon from the old
program group to the new one.*

**Figure 1.4:**

New Program
Object dialog box.

The following exercise installs the Inside AutoCAD Release 12 for Windows command
line and IAW icon in an existing group. If your drive is not C: or your version of
AutoCAD for Windows is not in the \ACADWIN directory, or you have created the
IAW subdirectory with a different path, substitute your drive or directory for that
shown.

## Setting Up the IAW Command Line and Icon

Double-click on the Program Manager icon, or switch to the Program Manager window,
and then create or open the group window in which you want to set up the *Inside AutoCAD
Release 12 for Windows* startup icon.

| | |
|---|---|
| *Choose* **F**ile, *then* **N**ew | Opens New Program Object dialog box |
| *Click on the* **P**rogram **I**tem *radio button (if needed to turn it on as in figure 1.4), then choose OK* | Opens Program Item Properties dialog box |
| *Enter* **IAW** *in the* **D**escription *box (see fig. 1.5), click in the* **C**ommand Line *box and enter* **C:\ACADWIN\ACAD.EXE /c C:\IAW**, *then choose the* **W**orking Directory *box and enter* **C:\IAW** | |
| *Choose* Change **I**con, *click on an icon that you prefer, and then choose* OK | Specifies the AutoCAD icon to display |
| *Choose* OK *again* | Creates the new program item |

→

*The beginning of the command line is cut off in figure 1.5; be sure
you enter the complete command line as shown in the exercise.*

**Figure 1.5:**

The Program Item
Properties
window.

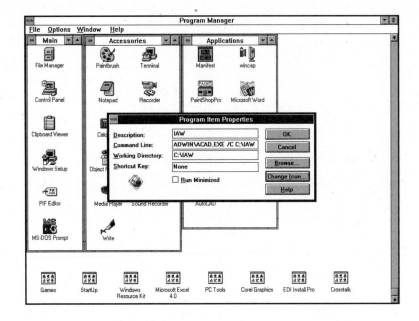

# Configuring AutoCAD To Run from the IAW Directory

Because AutoCAD now looks to the IAW directory for its configuration information (digitizer, plotter, operating parameters, and so on), it asks to be configured when the AutoCAD icon is selected unless the ACAD.CFG file is copied to this directory. (Installing AutoCAD for Windows puts a default ACAD.CFG file in the ACADWIN directory.)

 You should also copy a file named ACAD.INI to the IAW directory. The ACAD.INI file is a text file that controls the appearance of the AutoCAD drawing and text windows. Some of the features it controls are the following:

- Background colors

- Graphic and text window sizes

- Fonts used in the menus

- Floating toolbox buttons and icons

- Toolbar buttons and icons

Some of these features also are controlled from the drawing editor by choosing <u>F</u>ile, and then En<u>v</u>ironment. See Chapter 16 for details.

## Copying the ACAD.INI and ACAD.CFG Files

The following exercise shows how to use File Manager to copy the ACAD.INI and ACAD.CFG files (see fig. 1.6). (If the ACAD.CFG file is not found, instructions later in this chapter help you create it.)

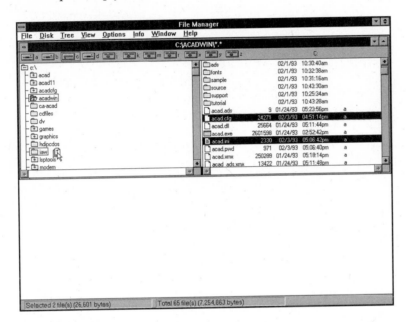

**Figure 1.6:**

Copying ACAD.INI and ACAD.CFG in File Manager.

---

### → Copying ACAD.INI and ACAD.CFG to the IAW Directory

| | |
|---|---|
| *Double-click on Main icon* | Opens Main group |
| *Double-click on File Manager icon* | Opens File Manager |
| *Click on ACADWIN in the C: Directory Tree window* | Displays the ACADWIN directory list |
| *Choose* <u>V</u>iew, *then* <u>N</u>ame, *and then* <u>V</u>iew, *then* <u>S</u>ort by Name | Formats and sorts listing like that shown in figure 1.6 |
| *Click on ACAD.INI, and then hold down the Ctrl key and click on ACAD.CFG (see fig. 1.6)* | Highlights the files to copy |

*continues*

| | |
|---|---|
| *Hold down the Ctrl key and press and hold the mouse button on one of the selected file names while dragging the copy files icon to the IAW directory, then release the key and button, and choose **Y**es to confirm the copy* | Copies the selected files to the IAW directory |
| *Close File Manager and Main groups by double-clicking on their respective control menu boxes* | Closes File Manager and Main groups |

*If you start up a drawing in AutoCAD for Windows and you do not see any icons on the toolbar buttons, ACAD.INI may not have been copied to the subdirectory that has been designated with the /C switch on the command line.*

See Appendix A for more help in setting up AutoCAD's system environment and configuring AutoCAD.

# Installing the IAW DISK

Now you are ready to install the IAW DISK files. In addition to saving time by bypassing initial drawing setup requirements, the disk provides starting drawings for many of the exercises, enabling you to skip material you already know. For example, if you want to learn about dimensioning, but you do not want to first create a drawing to dimension, you can move right to the dimensioning section by using a preset drawing from the disk.

## Installing the IAW DISK

Continue in File Manager, from the previous exercise. Put the IAW DISK in disk drive A:.

| | |
|---|---|
| *Click on the A: drive icon* | Reads the disk and displays its files |
| *Double-click on INSTALL.EXE* | Executes the installation program |

The installation program will prompt you and offer defaults for all necessary information. If you have created your IAW subdirectory on another drive or in a different path, be sure to change the defaults.

| | |
|---|---|
| *When installation is complete, choose* **F**ile, *then* **E**xit | Leaves File Manager |

# Starting AutoCAD

Now that the command line has been defined and the proper files copied to the IAW directory, start AutoCAD by double-clicking on the AutoCAD icon you just made.

## Starting AutoCAD for Windows

*Double-click on the IAW icon you installed*                    Begins AutoCAD

If the dialog box with an ACAD.MSG file displayed in it appears, read it, then click on OK to close it.

*You can delete the ACAD.MSG file to prevent its display after you have once read it. Message files may exist in both the IAW and ACADWIN directories.*

If no configuration file is found, AutoCAD asks you to answer some configuration questions. The video display is automatically selected from Windows. An input device (digitizer) is only configured if it is different from the one that was running under Windows. The plotter may be configured by selecting the correct one from the list or by using the appropriate ADI driver. Leave the default login name and do not use file locking unless you are running from a network.

# Setting the Defaults for the Exercises

To make absolutely sure that you are using the same default settings in AutoCAD as this book uses, take the steps shown in the following exercise to set up AutoCAD and to tell it to not use a prototype drawing. A *prototype drawing* is a drawing that AutoCAD uses as a template for creating a new drawing. All the AutoCAD settings that are stored in a drawing file, other drawing information, and any entities are transferred to the new drawing from the prototype. Without a prototype drawing, AutoCAD begins all new drawings with the same settings as the initial default ACAD.DWG. See Chapter 18 for more information on prototype drawings. The other settings made in the exercise are necessary to ensure that your setup matches this book's. They will be covered in more detail in later chapters.

The **F**ile pull-down menu gives you the choice of creating or editing drawings, plotting drawings, configuring AutoCAD, and using special utilities.

## Starting a New Drawing

| | |
|---|---|
| *Choose* **F**ile | Displays the **F**ile pull-down menu |
| *Choose* **N**ew | Displays the Create New Drawing dialog box (see fig. 1.7) |
| *Unless it already is checked, click on the box to the left of* **N**o Prototype, *then on* **R**etain as Default | Places Xs in the boxes, turning on their settings |
| *Choose* OK | Closes the dialog box and saves your settings |

**Figure 1.7:**

The AutoCAD Create New Drawing dialog box.

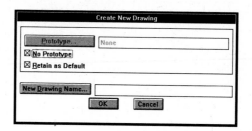

| | |
|---|---|
| *Choose* **S**ettings | Displays the Settings menu |
| *Choose* **S**election Settings | Displays the Entity Selection Settings dialog box |
| *If any of the boxes below* Selection Modes *contains Xs, click on the boxes to clear them* | Clears selection modes |
| *Choose* OK | Closes the dialog box and saves the settings |
| *Choose* **S**ettings, *then* **G**rips | |
| *If checked, click on* Enable Grips *to clear the X from the box* | Turns off grips |
| *Choose* OK | |
| *Choose* **F**ile, *then* **P**references | Opens the Preferences dialog box |
| *Click on* Screen **M**enu *to place a check mark in the check box* | Activates the screen menu |
| *Click on* **S**ave *to* ACAD.INI | Saves the changes for next time |
| *Choose* OK | Accepts the changes |
| *Choose* **F**ile, *and then* E**x**it AutoCAD | Ends this AutoCAD session |

*If you jump from chapter to chapter, choose Settings, then Selection Settings, and then put X marks in the Use Shift to Add and Press and Drag check boxes.*

Instead of using the File Menu, you can also enter the NEW command at the AutoCAD `Command:` prompt. You can access many of AutoCAD's commands from the pull-down and screen menus, as well as from the command line. The commands sometimes act differently, however, depending on the way you access them. The differences between command-access methods are discussed as you learn about AutoCAD's commands and menus in the next chapter.

*If you want to open another software application without ending your AutoCAD for Windows session, click on the down-arrow button in the upper right corner of the AutoCAD window. This step reduces the AutoCAD window to an icon until you double-click on it to open the window again.*

# Summary

Because AutoCAD now has the look and feel of Windows, as do many other software packages conforming to these standards, you should find it easier to become proficient in many different applications. In setting up AutoCAD specifically for this book, you have learned how to start up AutoCAD from Windows and how to specify configuration and support directories.

If you are a new Windows user, this chapter introduced you to the Windows operating environment, which will become familiar as you work through the exercises in this book.

Chapter 2 begins by placing you back into the AutoCAD Drawing Editor and shows you how to begin drawing. The various parts of the graphics screen are explained, and you are introduced to the menus that contain many AutoCAD commands.

# CHAPTER 2

# Getting To Know How AutoCAD Works

You probably are already familiar with manual drafting and design techniques or with CAD techniques used in programs other than AutoCAD. The drawing techniques and design methods you use in AutoCAD, however, are much the same as those used in manual drafting (and with other CAD programs); only the tools are different. The task of learning to use those tools is as simple as learning to use AutoCAD's user interface. In this chapter, you learn about the components that make up the AutoCAD for Windows drawing editor, and put them to use to create a few simple drawings.

## Using the Drawing Editor

One of the best ways to learn AutoCAD is to begin a drawing and start using some of the commands. In this chapter, you open a new CAD drawing file, draw some lines and text, and save the file. By taking these steps, you learn how to access commands from AutoCAD's menus, and you become familiar with AutoCAD's use of the keyboard and pointing device.

When introducing new commands, this book emphasizes the use of pull-down menus, which seem to be the easiest interface for a new user. AutoCAD's pull-down menus are similar to those in other software packages. Figure 2.1 shows an example of an

AutoCAD pull-down menu. Unless otherwise specified in the exercises, the instructions refer to the pull-down menus. The complete AutoCAD for Windows Release 12 pull-down menu system is shown in the menu map at the back of this book. Most of the commands used in the following exercises are covered more completely in later chapters. This chapter focuses more on methods of choosing commands and learning the drawing editor layout than on the specific commands themselves.

**Figure 2.1:**

AutoCAD pull-down and child menus.

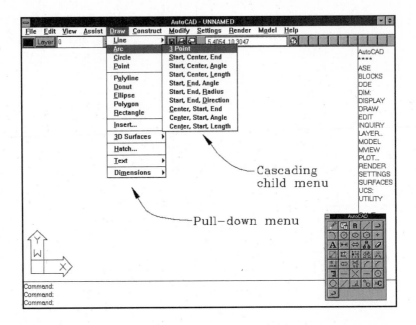

This chapter also examines AutoCAD's other forms of command input, including command-line entry, shortcut-key definitions, the use of the toolbar, the floating toolbox, and the screen menu. You learn about these types of command entry to gain a balanced overview of the many ways in which you can issue commands and choose options.

*Do not be concerned if your AutoCAD does not display the toolbox in the lower right corner of the AutoCAD window. You will set it up to match the toolbox in this book's illustrations near the end of this chapter.*

*Exercise instructions to choose an item refer to pull-down menu items unless a dialog box is open or the toolbar, toolbox, or screen menus are specified.*

For additional information on using dialog boxes and other aspects of the windows interface, see Appendix B.

The exercises in this book often instruct you to use your pointing device to perform certain functions on the graphics window. This pointing device could be a mouse, digitizer tablet, or the keyboard's cursor keys. The button most often used is the *pick* button. The pick button usually is the mouse's left button or the lowest-numbered button (1 or 0) on the digitizer puck or stylus. You use this button to pick a menu selection, click on a dialog box selection, or select an entity on the graphics screen. Sometimes you must *double-click* the input device if you want to choose a selection in a dialog box. This requires pressing the pick button twice in rapid succession. When the term *drag* is used, you must hold down the pick button while you move the cursor to another location.

## Using Hot Keys To Access Commands

While some users prefer to operate AutoCAD by choosing items from the pull-down menu with a mouse, others use the keyboard as much as possible. For fast keyboard access to menu and dialog items, *hot keys* are featured on the pull-down menu title bar, within the pull-down menus, and in dialog boxes. On your graphics screen, the hot key for each item is shown underlined. In this book, the hot keys are shown in a bold and underlined format. By holding down your *Alt* key while pressing the hot key, the dialog or menu item is selected. When a pull-down menu is open, you can select one of its menu items by pressing the hot key character alone, without the Alt key. Similarly, depending on the current focus (what the currently selected or active item is) in a dialog box, you can sometimes use the hot key alone; however, it is easier and more predictable to always use the Alt key along with the hot key.

The next exercise shows the use of hot keys to begin a new drawing. During the exercise in the rest of the book, when the instructions say "choose" an item, you may either choose items by picking them, or use hot keys, if available.

## Beginning a New Drawing

If you followed the exercises in Chapter 1, you can start AutoCAD by double-clicking on the AutoCAD icon in Windows. This runs the Windows command line that you created in Chapter 1. After the AutoCAD logo and software identification information appear, the drawing editor is displayed, as shown in figure 2.2.

**Figure 2.2:**

The AutoCAD
drawing editor.

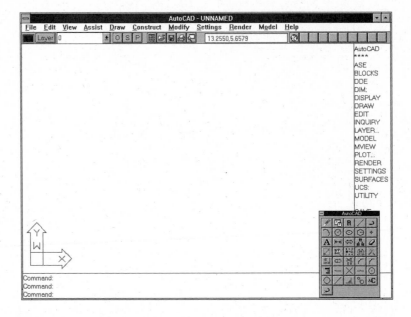

If you choose **F**ile from the pull-down menu, and then **N**ew, AutoCAD displays the
Create New Drawing dialog box shown in figure 2.3. You can type your new drawing's
name in the blank input box, which contains the blinking cursor. If you click on the
New **D**rawing Name button, another dialog box appears, enabling you to choose an
existing file name. This dialog box enables you to replace an existing drawing with the
new one, or to edit the selected name and create a similarly named drawing. You also
can create a drawing with no name, and then name it later by using the SAVE command or the Save **A**s pull-down menu option under **F**ile.

**Figure 2.3:**

The Create New
Drawing dialog
box.

When a dialog box appears on-screen, you can remove it by accepting it or canceling
it. Click on OK to accept the current entries in the box, or click on the Cancel button to
ignore any changes to the current settings. You can press Enter to accept the dialog box
if the OK button is highlighted or shadowed. You can press either Esc or Ctrl-C to
cancel the dialog box.

When a dialog box is on the screen, you can click on an appropriate text box to enable keyboard entry or corrections to the current settings. You can click on an on/off setting to modify the existing setting. You can find more detailed information on the use of dialog boxes near the end of this chapter.

*For your drawing names, you can use alphabetical characters, numbers, and most symbols, but no spaces. AutoCAD adds a file-name extension of DWG when it stores the drawing on disk, creating drawing file names such as CHAPTER2.DWG. Remember: because AutoCAD takes care of the extension (DWG), you should not enter it.*

In the following exercises, you begin a new drawing file named CHAPTER2. AutoCAD sets up a new drawing file called CHAPTER2.DWG in the IAW directory of your current drive (all exercises in this book assume that you are using drive C).

## Starting a New Drawing Using Hot Keys

Command: *Press Alt-F, then Alt-N,*    Begins a new drawing named
*type* **CHAPTER2** *in the* New **D**rawing    CHAPTER2 in the \IAW directory
Name *edit box, and then press Enter*

The new drawing is created in \IAW because the working directory was set from Windows in Chapter 1. This makes \IAW the default directory when you start AutoCAD.

You also can execute the NEW command by typing **NEW** and pressing Enter at the Command: prompt. When you use the NEW command, you can press Enter in response to the drawing-name prompt to clear the existing drawing database from memory and start a new, unnamed drawing. The following exercise starts a new drawing without assigning a name.

## Clearing the Drawing Database

Command: **NEW** ↵                Displays the Create New Drawing dialog box

*Press Enter*                Clears the drawing database without assigning a
                name to the drawing

As you just saw, in AutoCAD you can start a new drawing without naming it right away. When you issue the SAVE command, AutoCAD prompts for a drawing name if there is no current name. The SAVEAS command enables you to save the existing file under a different name.

Now that you have used the pull-down menu and have seen a dialog box, along with typing a command at the keyboard, you are ready to begin drawing with AutoCAD.

## Starting To Draw

Try moving the pointer around in the graphics window. The AutoCAD drawing editor, as shown in figure 2.4, has several different parts. At the top of the graphics window is the *title bar*. The title bar, which is common to many Windows applications, shows the name of the drawing and contains the Windows maximize, minimize, and control-menu buttons. Below the title bar is the *menu bar*, better known as the pull-down menu in AutoCAD. This feature is also common to many Windows applications. The *toolbar* is located just below the menu bar. This is similar to, but much more powerful than, the status line found in non-Windows versions of AutoCAD. Its features are explained later in this chapter. The largest part of the screen is the center area, called the *drawing area*. The *screen menu*, located to the right of the drawing area, has been a part of AutoCAD from the beginning, and users of earlier versions may find the screen menu method of command selection more familiar. The *toolbox*, an icon menu shown in the lower right corner of the graphics window, is a new and exciting part of AutoCAD Release 12 for Windows. Several lines of text appear at the bottom of the screen. This text is referred to as the Command: prompt.

**Figure 2.4:**

The AutoCAD drawing editor.

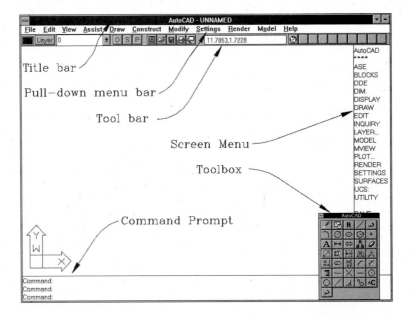

*The toolbox shown in most of this book's illustrations has been resized to be five icons wide and dragged to the lower left corner of the screen, where it does not obstruct the command prompt lines. See Chapter 18 for instructions on resizing and customizing the toolbox.*

You can access the pull-down menu by moving the pointer to the appropriate menu heading and then clicking on it. When the pull-down menu appears, you click on one of the menu's items to execute the command. When you click on some items in a pull-down menu, a *cascading menu* (also called a *child menu*) or dialog box appears to help you execute the command.

In the following exercise, you use a pull-down menu to issue AutoCAD's LINE command, and then experiment with drawing lines.

## Drawing Your First Line

`Command:` *Choose* **D**raw, *then* **L**ine, *then* **1** Segment

Starts the LINE command for a single segment

`Command: line From point:` *Move the cursor and click near* ① *in figure 2.5*

Picks the line's starting point

Move the crosshairs and see a line trailing behind them.

`To point:` *Pick a point near* ②

Specifies the line's endpoint, then ends the LINE command

The **1** Segment menu item terminates the LINE command after a single segment is drawn. Normally, the LINE command continues until you end it, as the following exercise shows. In the next exercise, you continue drawing lines by repeating the LINE command. If you press Enter at the `Command:` prompt, the last command is repeated; in this case, you can press Enter to reissue the normal LINE command.

**Figure 2.5:**

Drawing a line.

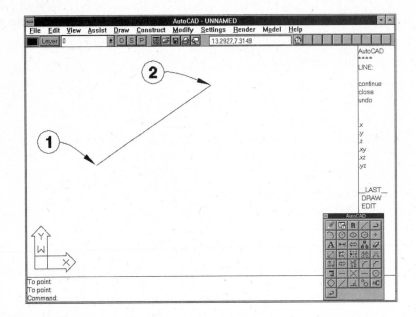

## Continuing the LINE Command

| | |
|---|---|
| `Command:` *Press Enter* | Repeats the previous command |
| `LINE From point:` *Press Enter* | Starts a new line at the first line's endpoint |
| `To point:` *Pick a point near ①* *in figure 2.6* | Specifies the endpoint of the new line segment |
| `To point:` *Pick a point near ②* | Specifies the next line segment's endpoint |
| `To point:` *Press Enter* | Ends the LINE command |

*On most systems, you also can press a mouse or digitizer cursor button to simulate the pressing of the Enter key. This is called AutoCAD's button number 1 and is generally the right button on a mouse or the lowest-numbered button (after the pick button) on a digitizer. On many digitizers, the pick button is marked with a 1 and AutoCAD button 1 is marked with a 2. On a typical digitizer stylus, the pick button is built into the stylus's point and is clicked by pressing the point against the tablet surface. AutoCAD button 1 is often a small button on the barrel of the stylus. AutoCAD button 1 is referred to as the Enter button throughout this book.*

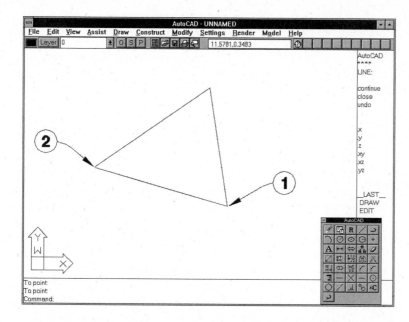

**Figure 2.6:**

Continuing the line.

You can see that AutoCAD's LINE command is simple and straightforward. When you issue the LINE command, AutoCAD begins the process of recording the two endpoints of a line segment. If you press Enter at the `From point:` prompt, AutoCAD continues drawing lines, starting the next line at the last endpoint of the previous line.

You can issue the normal LINE command by clicking on the line icon in the toolbox, by entering **LINE** at the `Command:` prompt, by using the Segments pull-down menu option, or by choosing the LINE: screen-menu option. You can draw another line segment every time you see a `To point:` prompt. AutoCAD helps you visualize the next segment's location by *rubber-banding*, or trailing a segment between your last point and the cursor.

*If you press Ctrl-C, Enter, or the spacebar, AutoCAD ends the LINE command and returns to the `Command:` prompt.*

# Entering Points and Coordinates in AutoCAD

Why is it so easy to draw in AutoCAD? You start the program, which takes you immediately into the drawing editor, then you begin entering points. It does not matter whether you enter points by picking them with your pointer or by entering them at the keyboard. The reason for this ease of use is that AutoCAD uses a standard Cartesian coordinate system and recognizes various types of drawing geometry.

## Using the World Coordinate System (WCS)

When you enter the drawing editor, you enter a coordinate system called the *World Coordinate System* (referred to throughout this book as the *WCS*). When AutoCAD asks you to enter a point, you either locate the point with your pointing device or enter the point's coordinates from the keyboard. The system's coordinates consist of a horizontal X displacement and a vertical Y displacement (and a Z displacement for 3D). These coordinates are called *absolute coordinates*. Although absolute coordinate points are specified with parentheses (3,4) in textbook geometry by convention, coordinates typed at the keyboard in AutoCAD are separated only by a comma, such as 3,4. Both the X and Y are measured from a zero base point that is initially set at the lower left corner of your screen. This base point's coordinates are 0,0.

## Using the User Coordinate System (UCS)

If you look at the lower left corner of your screen, you see an icon near point 0,0. This icon, shown in figure 2.7, is the *UCS icon*. "UCS" stands for *User Coordinate System*. The UCS enables you to establish your own coordinate system and shift your base point in your drawing by changing the position of the coordinate system. You make extensive use of the UCS when you work in 3D, but for now, leave it at the default position.

 *The default UCS is called the World Coordinate System (WCS).*

The WCS X axis is horizontal, left to right, and the Y axis is vertical, down to up. If you look closely at the UCS icon, you see that the X arrow points to the right on the X axis, and the Y arrow points up the Y axis. The "W" on the Y arrow means that you are currently in the default World Coordinate System. The UCS icon displays other information about your location in 3D. The UCS icon, for example, displays a "+" when the icon is shown at the UCS origin (0,0). The box in the icon's corner indicates the Z-axis direction, which is covered later, in the chapters on 3D.

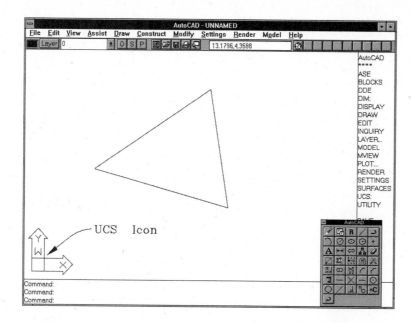

**Figure 2.7:**

The drawing editor with the UCS icon.

If you find the UCS icon distracting when you are working in 2D, you can always turn it off. The following exercise shows you how to turn it off and on. The UCSICON **O**n and Origin selections on the **S**ettings menu control the UCS icon. It can be turned on or off, and placed at the UCS origin or at the lower left corner of the drawing area.

## Turning the UCS Icon Off and On

| | |
|---|---|
| Command: *Choose* **S**ettings, *then* U**C**S, *then* **I**con, *then* **O**n | Turns off the icon, if it was on |
| `'setvar Variable name or ?: ucsicon` | AutoCAD displays the command sequence as the commands are executed |
| `New value for UCSICON <1>: 0` | |
| Command: *Choose* **S**ettings, *then* U**C**S, *then* **I**con, *then* **O**n | Turns the icon back on, if it was off |
| `'setvar Variable name or`<br>`? <UCSICON>: ucsicon` | |
| `New value for UCSICON <0>: 1` | |

You can enter the UCSICON command at the Command: prompt, if you like. In addition to the On/Off/Origin options, the All option enables the setting to affect the UCSICON in all the views in a multiple-view drawing screen setup.

# Finishing the Practice Exercise

In the next exercise, you continue using the pull-down menus to add some text to the drawing, and then zoom in closer to see it. Enter the text and coordinate values shown in the exercise, and complete the entry by pressing Enter.

## Adding Text and Using ZOOM

| | |
|---|---|
| Command: *Choose* **D**raw, *then* **T**ext, | Begins the DTEXT command *then* **D**ynamic |
| _dtext Justify/Style/<Start point>: **c** ↵ | Specifies the Center justification option |
| Center Point: **5.5,4** ↵ | Specifies absolute coordinates |
| Height <0.2000>: **.05** ↵ | Sets the text height |
| Rotation angle <0>: *Press Enter* | Accepts the 0 rotation angle |
| Text: **Welcome To INSIDE AutoCAD** ↵ | Enters the text string |
| Text: *Press Enter* | Ends the DTEXT command |

Where is the welcome? You must zoom in closer to see it.

| | |
|---|---|
| Command: *Choose* **V**iew, *then* **Z**oom, *then* **W**indow | Issues the ZOOM command with the Window option |
| Command: _'zoom All/Center/Dynamic/Extents/Left/ Previous/Vmax/Window/<Scale(X/XP)>: window | |
| First corner: *Pick at* ① *(see fig. 2.8)* | Specifies the zoom window's first corner |
| Other corner: *Pick a point at* ② | Zooms the display (see fig. 2.9) |
| Command: *Press Enter* | Repeats the ZOOM command |
| 'ZOOM | Specifies the All option All/Center/Dynamic/Extents/Left/ Previous/Vmax/Window/<Scale(X/XP)>: **ALL** ↵ |
| Regenerating drawing. | Returns to the full magnification |

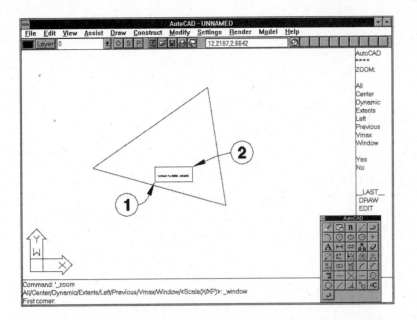

**Figure 2.8:**

Small text prior to ZOOM Window.

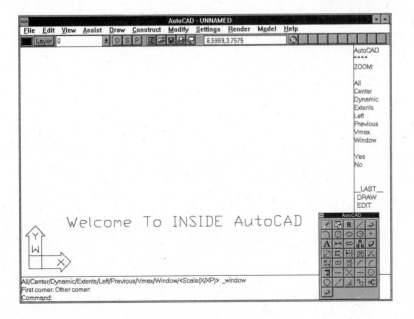

**Figure 2.9:**

The magnified text after ZOOM Window.

*You may have noticed a leading underscore (_) in front of commands issued from the menu. This underscore character is part of AutoCAD's method of making foreign-language translations of menus easier, but you can simply ignore it.*

You have started a new drawing file and created some lines and text by using AutoCAD's pull-down menus. Now you can complete your first pass through the drawing editor by saving your first effort.

## Saving a Drawing File

AutoCAD provides several commands and selections on the **F**ile pull-down menu that write the drawing as a file on a permanent storage device, such as a hard drive. Your work is saved with a DWG file-name extension. AutoCAD further secures your work by renaming the previous version of the drawing file (if one exists) with a BAK extension.

The **F**ile menu's **S**ave and Save **A**s selections and the SAVE command write a DWG file and then return to the drawing editor so that you can continue working on the current file. The **S**ave selection executes the QSAVE command, which automatically saves the drawing under the existing name, as shown at the Command: prompt in figure 2.10.

**Figure 2.10:**

The QSAVE command, issued by the Save menu item.

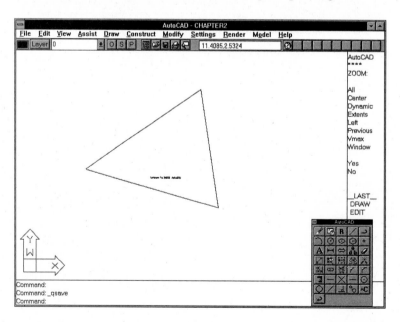

The Save **A**s item gives you the option of saving your current drawing session under the current name or under a file name of your choice. Press Enter to accept the default name shown at the Command: prompt or type in a new name to save the drawing to a different file name. The Save **A**s menu selection displays the File dialog box to enable graphic selection of file names, drives, and directories.

---

### Saving Your File

| | |
|---|---|
| Command: *Choose* **F**ile, *then* Save **A**s | Issues the SAVEAS command and opens the Save Drawing As dialog box |
| *Click in the* File **N**ame *edit box, type* **CHAPTER2**, *then choose* OK | Saves the drawing as CHAPTER2.DWG |

---

The **F**ile menu features several other options, two of which you can use when opening and closing a drawing file. The E**x**it AutoCAD item enables you to exit from AutoCAD. If there are unsaved changes, the Drawing Modification dialog box appears. This dialog box enables you to save the current changes, discard the changes, or cancel out of the dialog box and return to the drawing editor.

The **F**ile menu's Reco**v**er option attempts to restore a damaged drawing file. AutoCAD also attempts to restore a damaged drawing file if you try to open a drawing that is damaged.

You have just navigated the most basic route through AutoCAD. You have started a new drawing file, used a few drawing commands, and saved your work. Now it is time to take a more detailed look at AutoCAD's user interface.

# Communicating with AutoCAD

When you choose menu items, you can glance at the Command: prompt at the bottom of your screen to see what information AutoCAD needs (such as a start point), or what action to take (such as selecting objects). Then watch the center of the graphics window for the action. You also can use the toolbar to keep track of AutoCAD.

## Using the Toolbar

If you look near the top of the graphics window, below the area used by the pull-down menu, you see the toolbar. This line contains a combination of text, icons, and numbers. Here you find status information on current settings, and you can issue certain commands. Think of the toolbar as a medical monitor that gives you AutoCAD's vital signs. Figure 2.11 labels the items on the toolbar. By glancing at the toolbar, you can observe the active layer and color settings. The Ortho, Snap, and Paperspace buttons control whether those settings are on or off. Clicking on the layer and color buttons gives easy access to those dialog boxes. Several icons enable frequently used commands such as toolbox location, OPEN, SAVE, PLOT, and ZOOM Window to be easily accessed. Using the toolbar to issue commands and make settings is covered later in this and other chapters.

**Figure 2.11:**

The toolbar and some of its components.

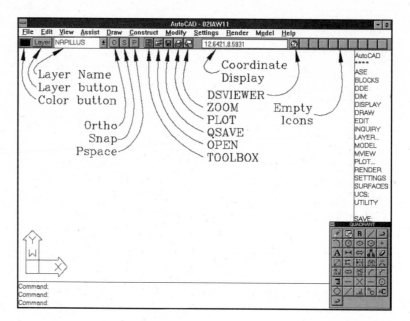

## Using the Coordinate Display

The toolbar's *coordinate display* is helpful when you need to determine drawing positions. These numbers represent the current or last coordinate position defined. When you move the pointer around with the coordinate setting turned off, these numbers do not change; rather, they continue to identify the last point you entered as part of a command or picked with the cursor. Clicking on the display box acts as a switch to activate the coordinate display, so that the coordinates continually update as the crosshairs move around the screen.

Move the cursor to the lower left corner, and the coordinates approach 0,0. When a command that accepts coordinates is active and at least one point has been entered, clicking on the coordinate display really enables three different choices. The display mode switches from off to polar coordinates to absolute coordinates. The polar coordinates are displayed only when you are using a drawing command.

# Keeping Track of AutoCAD at the Command Line

As you work with the AutoCAD program, you come to know what it expects from you and how it reacts when you do something. Many AutoCAD commands set up new drawing environments to receive additional commands. AutoCAD uses the bottom part of the screen to tell you what it is doing. This communication channel is called the Command: prompt. The Command: prompt is usually three lines, depending on your configuration. The Command: prompt shows AutoCAD's prompts and your responses or input. It keeps track of your latest communication with AutoCAD.

AutoCAD has a flexible command and menu structure. You can issue any AutoCAD command by typing the command name at the keyboard in response to the Command: prompt.

As you type, the letters appear after the Command: prompt. In order to execute any typed command, you must press Enter to let AutoCAD know that you are finished typing. (This key might be called the Return key on some systems.) If AutoCAD cannot interpret what you have typed, it lets you know after you press Enter.

---

### Entering Commands at the Command: Prompt

| | |
|---|---|
| Command: **LI** ↵ | Issues an invalid command name |
| Unknown command.   Type ? for list of commands | AutoCAD does not recognize the command as you have typed it |
| Command: **LINE** ↵ | Issues the LINE command with the correct spelling |
| From point: *Pick any point* | |
| To point: *Pick any point* | |
| To point: *Press Enter* | Ends the LINE command |

---

*Remember that you must press Enter to enter input you have typed, such as **LINE** for the LINE command. You also can use the spacebar or the Tab key rather than Enter, unless AutoCAD is expecting a text string (such as when you are using the TEXT command).*

## Using the Text Window

In addition to the Command: prompt, AutoCAD can display a full window of Command: prompt text, as shown in figure 2.12. You can press the F2 key to switch AutoCAD between the text window (this is called running in text mode) and graphics window (graphics mode). Press F2 again to switch back to the graphics window.

**Figure 2.12:**

The AutoCAD text window.

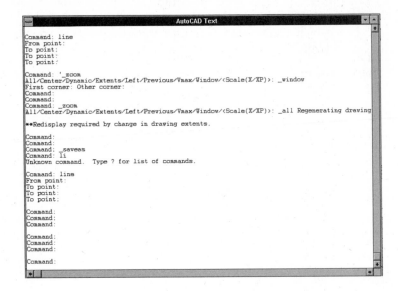

## Switching between Text and Graphics Windows

| Command: *Press F2* | Displays the text window |
| --- | --- |
| Command: *Press F2* | Displays the graphics window |

If you look closely at the text window, you see the last sequence of commands that you have typed (or picked from the menu). You can use this text window to look back through a set of Command: prompts to see what you have done. If you are interrupted by a phone call, for example, you can view the text window to easily find your place and get started again.

# Correcting Errors

AutoCAD is forgiving. The worst thing that can happen when you mistype a command name is that AutoCAD warns you that it does not recognize the command as you typed it. Then AutoCAD gives you another chance or prompts you to get help.

If you notice a typing error before you press Enter, press the Backspace key on the keyboard to erase the characters. Then you can retype the entry. If you just want to start over, you can press Ctrl-X to display *Delete*, ignore all previous characters on the line, and get a blank new line to enter what you intended.

If you start the wrong command, and it is already showing on the Command: prompt, you can press Ctrl-C one or more times to cancel any command and return to the Command: prompt. The toolbox also contains an icon for Ctrl-C.

## Using the ERASE Command

AutoCAD also forgives you if you draw something that you do not want or if you put an object in the wrong place.

You can remove an entity by using the ERASE command, and then you can redraw the entity. When you use ERASE, the crosshairs change to a *pick box*. You move the pick box until it touches the entity that you want to remove. Select the entity by clicking on it with your pointing device's pick button.

*AutoCAD offers you other ways to select entities and other ways to salvage errors without erasing. For now, however, ERASE is enough to get you out of a jam if you get stuck with a screen filled with lines that you do not want.*

In the following exercise, you erase the Welcome... text from your drawing. You find the ERASE command in the **M**odify menu.

---

### Using ERASE To Remove an Entity

| | |
|---|---|
| Command: *Choose* **V**iew, *then* **Z**oom, *then* **W**indow | Begins the ZOOM command with the Window option |
| `_'zoom All/Center/Dynamic/Extents/`<br>`Left/Previous/Vmax/Window/`<br>`<Scale(X/XP)>: window` | |

*continues*

| | |
|---|---|
| First corner: *Pick a point at the lower left corner of the text* | Locates the zoom window's first corner |
| Other corner: *Pick a point at the upper right corner of the text* | Locates the window's second corner |
| Command: *Choose **M**odify, then **E**rase, then **S**ingle* | Issues the ERASE command with the Single option |
| _erase<br>Select objects: single | |
| Select objects: *Place the pick box on the "W" of Welcome, as shown in figure 2.13, and click the pick button* | Selects the object to be erased and erases the text |
| Select objects: 1 found | |

**Figure 2.13:**

Selecting text for erasing.

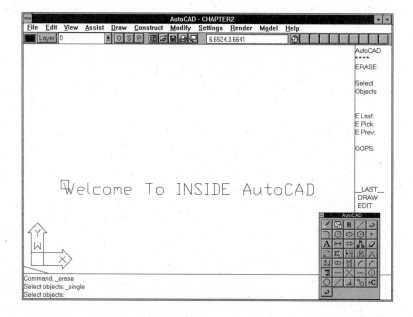

The S**i**ngle menu choice issues ERASE with the Single option, prompts you to select an object, and immediately erases it. You then can select the S**i**ngle menu choice again to erase another entity. If you enter **ERASE** at the Command: prompt or use the toolbox icon, ERASE enables you to select many entities and then erases them at the same time.

You can choose **O**ops to bring back the last entity group erased. You also can enter **E** at the Command: prompt to issue the ERASE command. If you want to try the screen menu, you can find the ERASE command under the EDIT group.

# Using the UNDO Command

Sometimes, you may discover you that have executed many commands, and yet your drawing is not turning out quite right. You may have made a crucial mistake, and you may need to back up in your drawing session to the point where the error was made. You can use AutoCAD's UNDO command to step back, one command at a time. This method can be more helpful than just erasing, because the UNDO command undoes not only entities, but also the zooms and screen settings that you may have changed along the way.

The following exercise introduces you to the UNDO command.

## Using UNDO To Reverse an Erasure

Command: *Choose* **E**dit, *then* **U**ndo        Makes the text reappear

Command: _U GROUP

Command: *Choose* **E**dit, *then* **R**edo        Makes the text disappear again

Command: _redo

The **E**dit pull-down menu has two selections that control undoing: **U**ndo and **R**edo. The **U**ndo selection issues the U command, which cancels the last command or *group*. Any menu choice, even if it issues several commands, is considered one group and is undone in one step. In most cases, this means only the last command. If you repeat a command (such as CIRCLE) several times in succession, however, you can use U to undo several items at the same time. AutoCAD also features the UNDO command, which offers additional controls (these are covered in later chapters).

The **R**edo selection issues the REDO command, which undoes U and UNDO. Although you can select **U**ndo repeatedly to back up step-by-step, you can use **R**edo only once, immediately after U or UNDO.

 *Often, it is just as convenient to enter a **U** from the keyboard as it is to select the U or UNDO commands from a menu.*

# Getting Help from AutoCAD

Help information is always available in AutoCAD for Windows. To get help when you need it, however, you need to know how to use the AutoCAD help feature effectively. Fortunately, the help system even includes help on how to use the help system. The following section briefly gets you started and shows you the main features of the help system. Then you can continue to explore the help system on your own.

## Exploring the Help Dialog Boxes

You can access help in several ways. You can issue the HELP command by entering **HELP** (or its abbreviated alternative, **?** - a question mark) from the keyboard. When you issue the HELP command, or press the F1 key, or choose the **C**ontents item from the **H**elp pull-down menu, AutoCAD displays the main AutoCAD Help dialog box, the Contents for AutoCAD Help (see fig. 2.14).

**Figure 2.14:**

The Contents for AutoCAD Help dialog box.

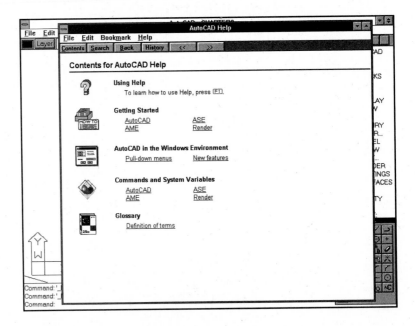

The Contents for AutoCAD Help consist of five main parts, each with one or more subtopics, as shown in figure 2.14. To access any of the subtopics, move the cursor to it (the cursor changes to a hand) and click when the hand's index finger points to the desired item.

- **Using Help** gives instructions on how to use the help system. To access it from AutoCAD, press F1, and then, in the Contents for AutoCAD Help window, press F1 again. Alternatively, you can choose **H**elp, then **H**ow to use Help from the AutoCAD pull-down menu.

- **Getting Started** is a brief guide to procedures for various tasks in AutoCAD, ASE, AME, and Render.

- **AutoCAD in the Windows Environment** describes each item in each pull-down menu and submenu (child menu), as well as providing an introduction to features that are new to AutoCAD for Windows or different from other versions of AutoCAD.

- **Commands and System Variables** contains basically the same information as the help system in non-Windows versions of AutoCAD: help for each command and system variable in for AutoCAD, ASE, AME (and Region Modeling), and Render.

- **Glossary** is a glossary of terms.

## Getting Help

| | |
|---|---|
| Command: *Choose **H**elp, then **C**ontents, or enter* **HELP** *or* **?**, *or press F1* | Displays Contents for AutoCAD Help dialog box (see fig. 2.14) |
| *Move the cursor to* AutoCAD *in the* Commands and System Variables *section and click* | Displays the AutoCAD Commands and System Variables dialog box index for A-C |

You can click on any command to view its help information, or click on D, E-I, L-O, P-R, S, T, or U-Z to view other sections of the index.

| | |
|---|---|
| *Click on* CIRCLE | Displays help for CIRCLE |
| *Click on the* ≤≤ *button* | Displays help for CHPROP (see fig. 2.15) |

*If any help dialog box contains more information than fits in it, it displays scroll bars at the right (and sometimes the bottom) that you can use to see all the information. You can also resize, move, and manipulate the help windows, like any other window.*

**Figure 2.15:**

The AutoCAD
Commands and
System Variables
dialog box for
CHPROP.

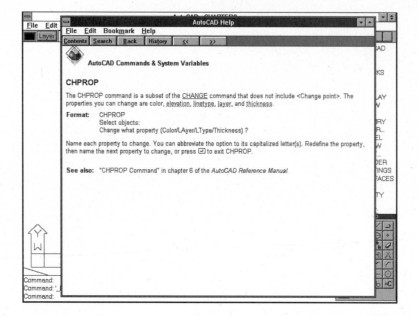

Near the top of the help dialog box in figure 2.15 are the <u>C</u>ontents, <u>S</u>earch, <u>B</u>ack, His<u>t</u>ory, <u><<</u>, and <u>>></u> buttons.

- **<u>C</u>ontents.** This button displays the Contents for AutoCAD Help dialog box.

- **<u>S</u>earch.** This button opens a Search dialog box, in which you can select or enter key words and phrases to search a predefined index for topics. Search does not do a general search of the help data files. In AutoCAD, you can choose <u>H</u>elp, then <u>S</u>earch for Help On to display this dialog box.

- **<u>B</u>ack.** This button returns to the previously displayed help dialog box window.

- **His<u>t</u>ory.** This button displays a list of the previously displayed help dialog box windows from the current help session. You can select one to reopen it.

- **<u><<</u> and <u>>></u>.** These buttons page to the previous and next topics in the alphabetic topic list for the current dialog box, as you saw in the previous exercise.

In the dialog box for CHPROP, you see that CHANGE is underlined with a solid line and that elevation, linetype, layer, and thickness are underlined with broken lines. This formatting indicates that you can obtain further information by clicking on the underlined words. Click on a broken underline to display the glossary definition for that item; click again or press Esc to return to the current dialog box. Click on a solid underline to jump to the help dialog for that topic. Try it in the following exercise.

## Jumping around in Help

Continue from the previous exercise.

| | |
|---|---|
| *Click on* l̲ayer | Pops up the layer glossary definition (see fig. 2.16) |
| *Press Esc or click anywhere* | Closes layer definition |
| *Click on* CHANGE | Displays help for CHANGE |
| *Choose* His̲tory | Pops up Windows Help History dialog box (see fig. 2.17) |
| *Double-click on* Main Table of Contents | Displays Contents for AutoCAD Help dialog box |
| *Double-click on the control icon (the box at the upper left of the help window)* | Closes help and returns to AutoCAD |

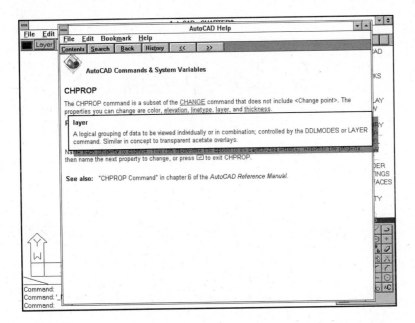

**Figure 2.16:**

The Layer glossary definition.

**Figure 2.17:**

The Windows Help History dialog box.

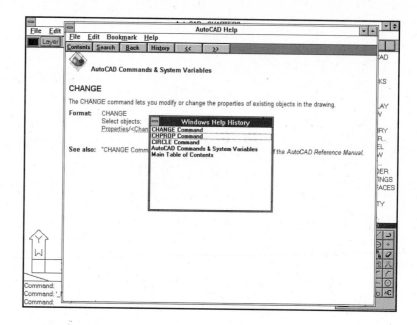

# Getting Context-Sensitive Help in Commands

Another way to use the HELP command is to issue it while using the command about which you want to learn more. This method is called *context-sensitive* help. In the following exercise, you request help while using the COPY command. To do so, you can enter HELP or a question mark prefaced with an apostrophe ('**HELP** or '**?**), or you can press F1. This issues the HELP command as a *transparent* command; that is, you are issuing the HELP command while another command is active. When a command runs transparently, it runs while another command is active.

## More Jumping around in Help

You should be back in AutoCAD.

| | |
|---|---|
| Command: *Choose* **C**onstruct, *then* **C**opy | Issues COPY command |
| _copy | |
| Select objects: *Press F1, or enter* '**?** *or* '**HELP** | Displays help for the COPY command |
| *Choose* **F**ile, *then* E**x**it | Closes help and returns to AutoCAD |
| Resuming COPY command. Select objects: *Press Ctrl-C* | Cancels the COPY command |

*Most dialog boxes contain a Help button, which you can choose to display the Help dialog box for their commands.*

## Other Help Features

The menu bar at the top of the help dialog boxes contains pull-down menus labeled File, Edit, Bookmark, and Help. You can use the Help menu to learn how to use these menus, which offer features that include marking your place in the help files and copying text from help windows.

# Using the File Menu

You learned in earlier exercises how to use several of the command options under the File pull-down menu. The New selection enables you to name a new file when you create it. The Save option enables you to save the file again under that name. By choosing Save As, you can rename the file as it is being saved. Unless you are interested in the prototype drawing file options in the Create New Drawing dialog box, it is really not necessary to name a drawing initially because AutoCAD prompts for a file name as soon as you try to save the drawing.

## Opening an Existing File

If you want to load an existing drawing into the drawing editor, choose Open from the File pull-down menu; the Open dialog box appears. Use the up and down arrows or drag the slider box to find the appropriate drawing file's name, and then double-click on that name. Of course, you can always enter the name in the File Name edit box, or click on the Type It button to type the file name on AutoCAD's command line if you already know it.

You learned in earlier exercises how to begin a new drawing and assign it a name, and how to save a drawing after you have made changes to it. The next exercise shows you how to open an existing drawing file and save it with a new name—two functions you may frequently perform.

### Opening an Existing Drawing

| | |
|---|---|
| Command: *Choose* File, *then* Open | Displays the Drawing Modification dialog box (see fig. 2.18) |
| *Choose* Discard Changes | Discards changes you made to the drawing and opens the Open Drawing dialog box |
| *Double-click on* CHAPTER2 *in the* File Name *list box (see fig. 2.19)* | Loads the drawing CHAPTER2 into the graphics editor |

**Figure 2.18:**

The Drawing
Modification
dialog box.

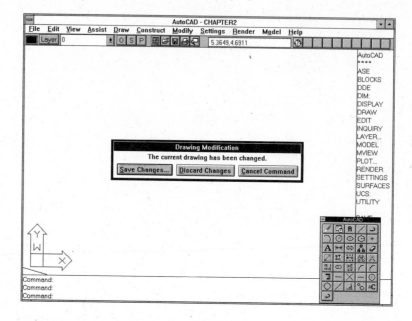

**Figure 2.19:**

The Open dialog
box.

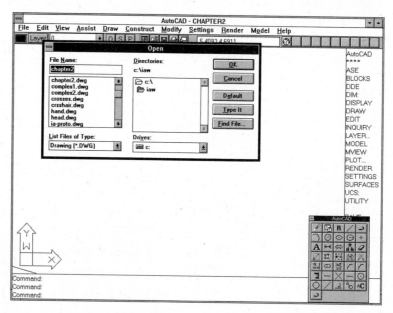

Also found at the bottom of the **F**ile pull-down menu is a feature called Fin**d** File. This feature shows the last four drawings accessed in AutoCAD. You can open any one of these four drawings by clicking on it.

In the next exercise, you save the drawing with a new name.

---

### Saving a File to a New Name

| | |
|---|---|
| `Command:` *Choose* <u>F</u>ile, *then* Save <u>A</u>s | Displays the Save Drawing As dialog box |
| *Type* **CHAP2-B**, *then choose* OK | Saves the drawing to a new file and closes the dialog box |

```
_saveas
Current drawing name set to
C:\IAW\CHAP2-B
```

| | |
|---|---|
| `Command:` *Choose* <u>F</u>ile, *then* <u>N</u>ew, *then* OK | Clears the drawing database without assigning a drawing name |
| `Command:` *Choose* <u>F</u>ile, *then* <u>O</u>pen | Displays the Open dialog box |

The drawing you saved earlier with the SAVEAS command, CHAP2-B, appears in the Open dialog box.

| | |
|---|---|
| *Choose* <u>C</u>ancel | Closes the dialog box |

---

# Specifying File Patterns

After you have used AutoCAD for some time, you will probably have many drawings in your drawing directories. It can be time-consuming to hunt through all the file names in the Open dialog box, so AutoCAD provides a means of displaying only the file names you want to view. The default pattern displayed in the box is *.dwg. If you only want four-character file names to appear, you can enter a pattern of ????.DWG. A pattern of PROJ5*.DWG shows only those files that begin with the characters PROJ5. The following exercise illustrates the use of patterns.

---

### Using File-Name Pattern Filters

| | |
|---|---|
| `Command:` *Choose* <u>F</u>ile, *then* <u>O</u>pen | Displays the Open dialog box and highlights the File <u>N</u>ame edit box |
| *Enter* **C*.DWG** | Lists only drawing names that begin with the letter C |

The <u>L</u>ist Files of type edit box enables many of the popular file extensions such as DXF, IGS, and MNU to be selected as a file type to be listed in the files box.

| | |
|---|---|
| *Choose* Cancel | Aborts the command |

# Changing Directories

You can see from the previous exercise that the File **N**ame edit box is useful for viewing only specific drawings in the selected directory. But what do you do when the drawing you want to load is not in the current directory? Use the **D**irectories list box. The directory window enables you to choose the appropriate directory. Click on the up or down arrows on the scroll bar, or drag the slider box to view the entire list. The arrow buttons in the scroll bar at the right edge of the list box act much like the up- and down-arrow keys on your keyboard. Each click of a scroll arrow button moves the entries in the list box by one item at a time. The slider box, which is located on the scroll bar between the two arrow buttons, enables you to dynamically drag the contents of the list past the viewing window. Double-click on the two dots (..) at the top of the list to move one level closer to the root directory.

Try loading a drawing from the AutoCAD SAMPLE directory in the next exercise.

## Loading Drawings from Other Directories

| | |
|---|---|
| Command: *Choose* **F**ile, *then* **O**pen | Displays the Open dialog box |
| *Double-click on* C:\ *in the* **D**irectories *list box* | Changes to the parent directory |

If AutoCAD is installed in a directory other than \ACADWIN on your system, substitute the appropriate directory in the following step.

| | |
|---|---|
| *Double-click on* ACADWIN *in the* **D**irectories *box* | Selects the AutoCAD directory |
| *Double-click on* SAMPLE | Selects the \ACADWIN\SAMPLE directory |
| *Use the down button in the* File **N**ame *list box to locate the entry* SHUTTLE | |
| *Double-click on* SHUTTLE *in the* File **N**ame *list box* | Loads the drawing SHUTTLE.DWG from the \ACADWIN\SAMPLE directory (see fig. 2.20) |

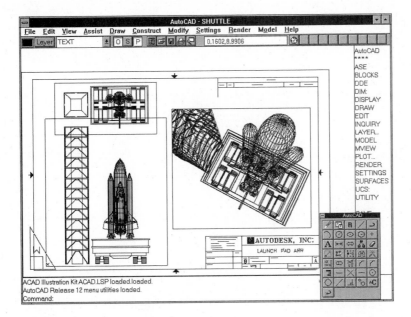

**Figure 2.20:**
The SHUTTLE drawing.

In the next exercise, you close out the SHUTTLE drawing and load another file from the \IAW directory.

## Reloading CHAPTER2 from the \IAW Directory

| | |
|---|---|
| Command: *Choose* File, *then* Open | Displays the Open dialog box |
| *Double-click on* C:\ *in the* Directories *list box* | Selects the root directory |
| *Double-click on* IAW *in the* Directories *list box* | Selects the \IAW directory |
| *Double-click on* CHAPTER2 | Loads the drawing CHAPTER2.DWG |

# Opening a Drawing from File Manager

You can use the Windows File Manager to simultaneously open a drawing file and start AutoCAD. If you already have AutoCAD running, File Manager starts another session of AutoCAD for the selected file. Most of the exercise is setting up File Manager to find the file; if you are familiar with File Manager or have previously set it up so you can find the drawings in the IAW directory (as in Chapter 1), you can skip those steps. If necessary, click on the scroll bar (at the right side of the Directory Tree and File windows) to display the directory and file names.

## Using File Manager To Open a Drawing and Start AutoCAD

Continue from the previous exercise, with a drawing open in AutoCAD.

Open File Manager (in Program Manager, double-click on the Main icon, and then on the File Manager icon).

Choose the drive C icon on the menu bar. If both the Tree and Directory windows are not displayed, choose <u>V</u>iew, then T<u>r</u>ee and Directory. If the File window does not list files in order of name, choose <u>V</u>iew, then <u>N</u>ame, and <u>V</u>iew, then <u>S</u>ort by Name.

| | |
|---|---|
| *Find and click on* IAW *in the C: Directory Tree window* | Displays the ACADWIN directory list |
| *Find and double click on* IAWOFFIC *in the File window* | Starts AutoCAD with a simple office plan in an AutoCAD (2) - IAWOFFIC window |
| Command: *Press and hold the Alt key while pressing the Tab key several times (until the AutoCAD - CHAPTER2 label appears), then release both keys* | Returns to previous AutoCAD session and drawing |
| Command: *Use Alt-Tab again to return to the AutoCAD (2) - IAWOFFIC window* | |
| *Double-click on the control menu box (the box at the top left corner of the AutoCAD (2) window)* | Closes AutoCAD (2) - IAWOFFIC window and returns to AutoCAD - CHAPTER2 window |

The File Manager window is still open in the background. You can use Alt-Tab to display it, then double-click on the control menu box to close it.

# Accessing Files Using Drag-and-Drop Features

Another method of accessing files while running AutoCAD is by using the capability of Windows to "drag and drop" file icons from the Windows File Manager. This feature is quite easy to use if you are familiar with Windows and can open and run several applications at once. To bring files into a drawing, you must open File Manager so that you can drag file icons into the AutoCAD graphics window. When the file is brought in, AutoCAD can determine, by its file type, whether to insert it as a block, load it as an AutoLISP routine, or whatever else the file is intended for in AutoCAD. At that point, the regular AutoCAD command, such as INSERT, takes over. Many of these operations, along with their file extension and AutoCAD command, are shown in table 2.1. Some of the more common uses are:

- Inserting drawing files as blocks

- Inserting text files as dynamic text

- Loading menus, AutoLISP routines, or fonts

- Printing a drawing

The actual operation of these AutoCAD commands is covered in later chapters.

 *Getting a "file icon" refers to clicking on a file name from a list of files in the Windows File Manager. An icon of that file is automatically created and can be dragged to another window.*

## Table 2.1
## Some Common Drag-and-Drop Procedures

| Operation | File Extension | AutoCAD Command |
| --- | --- | --- |
| Insert drawing file | .dwg | INSERT |
| Insert text file | .txt | DTEXT |
| Import DXF file | .dxf | DXFIN |
| Import IGES file | .igs | IGESIN |
| Load linetype | .lin | LINETYPE |
| Load menu | .mnu,.mnx | MENU |
| Import PostScript Images | .eps | PSIN |
| Run script | .scr | SCRIPT |
| Load shape font | .shp,.shx | STYLE |
| Load AutoLISP routine | .lsp | LOAD |
| Load ADS application | .exe | XLOAD |
| Print a drawing | .dwg | PLOT |

Printing a file is a little different than the other functions because the icon must be dragged to the Windows Print Manager application instead of AutoCAD.

# Using Other File Menu Options

In addition to commands that enable you to open and save drawing files, the File menu includes commands that perform many other actions. Several of these commands are examined in more detail in other chapters; however, you may be curious as to what these commands do and when you might need them.

## Print/Plot

The Print/Plot option (see Chapter 13) enables you to create a hard copy or plot file of the current drawing. When you choose Print/Plot, AutoCAD displays the Plot Configuration dialog box, in which you can select the plotting device and examine or change the many parameters and settings associated with plotting.

## Exit AutoCAD

The Exit AutoCAD option does just what its name implies; it closes the AutoCAD window. If you prefer a quicker way to exit AutoCAD, enter the QUIT command at the AutoCAD Command: prompt. The QUIT command performs the same function as the Exit AutoCAD option in the File menu. If unsaved data exists, the Drawing Modification dialog box enables you to save or discard the changes.

## Configure

The Configure option steps you through AutoCAD's interactive configuration, which tells AutoCAD which hardware you are using. The menu header, shown in figure 2.21, gives information ranging from your AutoCAD version and serial number to your current hardware selections. If someone else installed your software, you may want to copy this hardware information, in case you have to reconfigure the software in the future. This configuration also tells who owns your program's license and from which dealer it was obtained; this dealer is required to provide you with support. See Appendix A for more details about the Configure option.

## Utilities

The Utilities option enables you to perform disk-file maintenance operations. The File Utilities dialog box enables you to perform many common file maintenance chores from the drawing editor. This capability is especially helpful if you have not learned how to maneuver about in your computer's operating system. Four of the dialog box's options—List files, Delete file, Copy file, and Rename file—are commands every CAD operator needs to use. The Unlock file option unlocks a file that was accidentally left locked by the file-locking function, which enables only one session to edit the drawing at a time. Choosing any of these options opens the appropriate dialog box, enabling the selections of directories, files, and pattern names.

**Figure 2.21:**

Configuration settings.

You also can perform general maintenance on your files and directories—such as copying, renaming, and deleting files—by using the corresponding commands directly from the operating system. There is no harm in doing so; they perform the same tasks. Table 2.2 lists AutoCAD's file-maintenance commands and their DOS-command equivalents.

*If you get a* `Waiting for file: ... Locked by ... Press Ctrl-C to cancel.` *message, make absolutely sure that no one else is using the file. If you are positively sure that no one else is using it, the file may have been left locked accidentally. If so, you can use the* **U**nlock *option to unlock it. File locking enhances security on networks.*

## Table 2.2
## AutoCAD File Utility Commands

| Command | Equivalent DOS Command |
| --- | --- |
| List files | DIR |
| Copy file | COPY |
| Rename file | REN |
| Delete file | DEL |
| Unlock file | none |
| Exit | none (returns to the Command: prompt) |

You also can access the AutoCAD file utilities from the drawing editor by entering **FILES** at the Command: prompt.

The Compile option is not covered in this book. This option is used for creating custom text fonts. See *Maximizing AutoCAD Release 12* (New Riders Publishing) or the *AutoCAD Reference Manual* for details.

The Recover option is for salvaging a drawing file that AutoCAD does not load because it has detected an error in the file.

## Import/Export, Xref, and Applications Menu Options

The Import/Export functions, which are covered extensively in Chapter 19, enable AutoCAD to exchange data with other software. This import/export feature supports common translation file formats, such as DXF, IGES, and PostScript.

Xref is a function that enables the external reference of other drawings and links to be created between drawing databases. This is an extension of blocking techniques and is explained in Chapter 12.

You can choose the Applications option to bring up a dialog box that enables you to load AutoLISP and AutoCAD Development System (ADS) files.

Now that you have used some of AutoCAD's pull-down menus and entered commands at the Command: prompt, you are ready to examine the other ways in which you can issue commands and control AutoCAD.

# Comparing AutoCAD's Menus and Tools

Menus are the interface by which you communicate with AutoCAD. You do not need to remember all the commands and their options and modifiers. Instead, you use the menu system to choose commands with a pointing device. The AutoCAD menus are organized to make navigation through the software as simple as possible, although the commands themselves require a certain amount of study and practice before you feel comfortable using them.

AutoCAD has more than 150 commands, many of which feature numerous options. Most of these commands relate to specific functions such as drawing, editing, or dimensioning. Because many users are not proficient in typing, AutoCAD provides an ACAD.MNU file that offers the following six alternative ways to enter commands from menus. In addition, you can use the toolbox or toolbar, which are defined in the ACAD.INI file, to issue commands.

- Pull-down menu
- Screen menu
- Tablet menu
- Button menu
- Icon menu
- Pop-up (cursor) menu
- Toolbox
- Toolbar

In addition to these menus and tools, AutoCAD provides many dialog boxes through which you can make and control input. Menus provide a convenient way to organize and group commands so that they can easily be chosen and executed. You have already used the pull-down menu; the rest of this chapter examines all the menus, as well as dialog boxes.

 *Most menu items are programmed first to cancel any existing commands before executing the new one. This means that you can execute a command while another one is still active, and the first one is canceled.*

AutoCAD's standard menus give you many different ways to execute some of the same commands. You should try all the types of menus available to see which menu method you prefer. Feel free to experiment with the menus as you proceed with this chapter. Note that, in addition to the five methods of command entry listed earlier, you also can enter complete commands directly at the Command: prompt, and you can use the command shortcut keys that are defined in the file ACAD.PGP.

## Pull-Down Menus

The pull-down menu was introduced in AutoCAD Release 9. This feature was added to make AutoCAD work more like many of the other software packages that had adopted pull-down menus. The menu bar presents a list of titles that indicate the types of selections available in each pull-down menu. The names of the 11 pull-down menus appear at the top of the graphics window.

Many pull-down menu selections open a child menu to help with subcommand selection, as shown in figure 2.22. Some AutoCAD pull-down menus present dialog boxes for commands with multiple settings and groups of related commands. Many people find pull-down menus easier to use than screen menus because each submenu occupies a different spot on the screen.

*Inside the back cover of this book is a complete map of AutoCAD's pull-down menus.*

**Figure 2.22:**

The Draw pull-down menu and the Circle child menu.

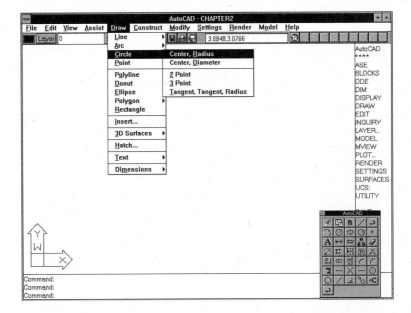

Another special pull-down menu feature of AutoCAD for Windows is the ability to show the Draw, Construct, and Modify menus as icons instead of text items, as shown in figure 23. A choice under Settings called Menu Bitmaps turns on this feature. Selecting that same item again turns the feature off.

---

## Turning the Menu Bitmaps On and Off

Continue from the previous exercise, or in any drawing with the standard ACAD.MNU loaded.

Command: *Choose* **S**ettings, *then* Menu **B**itmaps      Turns on Menu Bitmaps

Command: *Choose* **D**raw, *then* **C**onstruct, *then* **M**odify *(see fig. 2.23)*      Bitmaps (icons) appear in menu

Command: *Choose* **S**ettings, *then* Menu Bitmaps      Turns off Menu Bitmaps

---

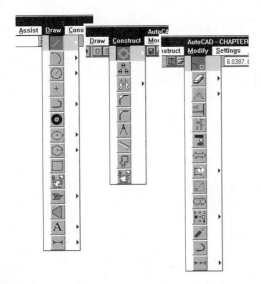

**Figure 2.23:**

Menu Bitmaps turned on.

*Unless otherwise specified, the instructions in this book's exercises refer to the pull-down menus by their text labels.*

The following list presents some minor points you should remember about the pull-down menus.

- If a pull-down selection is followed by three dots (such as <u>H</u>atch...), that selection calls up a dialog box or an AutoLISP program.

- Selections followed by an arrow, such as Di<u>m</u>ensions, call up *child*, or cascading, menus. You can either click on the menu option to open the child menu, or use a hot key to open the child menu.

*Some commands act a little differently, depending on whether you enter them at the Command: prompt, use screen menus, or use pull-down menus. The pull-down menu <u>P</u>oint and <u>D</u>onut items, for example, automatically repeat until canceled. If you enter them from the Command: prompt, they execute only once. Several selections, such as <u>I</u>nsert and <u>S</u>election Settings, automatically load and execute externally defined commands that display dialog boxes for option selection. Dialog boxes are discussed next.*

## Dialog Boxes

AutoCAD's dialog boxes offer a unique and convenient way to view and adjust certain AutoCAD settings, to enter and edit text strings, and to enter file names. Although dialog boxes are usually brought up through menu selections that contain their commands, you also can access them by entering their command names at the Command: prompt. Most names begin with DD, such as DDEMODES. Table 2.3 lists the commands that use dialog boxes.

*Many of these dialog commands are defined through AutoLISP or ADS and must be loaded before you can use them. The ACAD.MNL file (which accompanies the standard ACAD.MNX menu) causes these commands to automatically load when you (or a menu item) enter their command names. If the ACAD menu is not loaded in the current drawing, however, or if the ACAD.MNL file is not on the AutoCAD search path, these commands are not auto-loaded when you try to use them. If you use a different menu file, it needs an MNL file that contains the contents of ACAD.MNL. For example, if your menu is MYOWN.MNU (or MNX), you need a corresponding MYOWN.MNL file that includes the contents of ACAD.MNL.*

## Table 2.3
## Commands that Issue Dialog Boxes

| Command | Pull-Down Menu Selection | Purpose |
|---|---|---|
| DDEMODES | Entity Modes | Sets layer, color, linetype, and other default properties for new entities |
| DDLMODES | Layer Control | Creates layers, sets their default properties, and controls visibility |
| DDRMODES | Drawing Aids | Controls snap, grid, modes, and isometric settings |
| DDATTE | | Edits attributes in blocks |
| DDUCS | Named UCS | Controls the User Coordinate Systems |
| DDEDIT | | Edits text entities or attribute definitions |
| DDIM | Dimension Style | Sets dimensioning styles and variables |
| DDGRIPS | Grips | Controls Autoedit grips |
| DDSELECT | Selection Settings | Enables entity-selection settings to be changed |
| DDOSNAP | Object Snap | Controls running object snaps |
| DDINSERT | Insert | Assists in block insertion |
| DDRENAME | | Enables blocks, layers, views, and so on, to be renamed |
| DDATTEXT | | Controls attribute extraction |
| DDATTDEF | | Helps in defining attributes |
| DDUNITS | Units Control | Controls all the units options |
| DDCHPROP | Properties | Helps to change entity properties |
| All File Commands | Various | Displays and scrolls through lists of file names |

When a dialog box appears on the screen, it shows a list of settings and their current values. Some settings are on/off boxes with a check to indicate when they are on. You click on the box with the pointer's pick button to turn a setting on or off. Other boxes display values such as names, colors, or distances. You change these edit boxes by highlighting and editing them or by entering a new value. Some values, such as file or layer names, are presented in list boxes, which may only show a portion of a long list. These list boxes have scroll bars at the right side to scroll up and down the lists. A typical dialog box, such as the one that defines drawing tools, is shown in figure 2.24.

**Figure 2.24:**

The Drawing Aids dialog box.

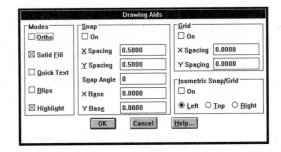

Although dialog boxes duplicate the functions of other commands, they provide clearer and more convenient control over complex commands or groups of commands. You can find additional explanations and practice exercises for dialog boxes later in this chapter.

## Icon Menus and Image Buttons

AutoCAD also can display menu selections as graphic images in a special type of dialog box, called an *icon menu*. AutoCAD uses slide files to construct these special menus. When AutoCAD displays an icon menu, you choose a menu item by clicking on a graphical representation of the selection (an *icon*). AutoCAD executes the corresponding selection the same way as any other menu selection. The Previous and Next buttons flip through other pages of icons. AutoCAD has a number of preset icon menus, such as those used for hatch patterns, as shown in figure 2.25.

Icon menus sometimes show only a selection of icons in addition to the Previous, Next, and Cancel buttons, with no additional controls on the dialog box associated with the icons. Other icon menus include a text list box at the left of the dialog box, which describes each icon's function. In addition to selecting an icon, you also can select a description from the list, and the associated icon is automatically selected, as well.

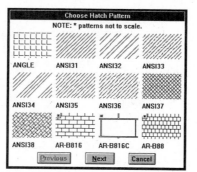

**Figure 2.25:**

The Choose Hatch Pattern dialog box.

AutoCAD also uses other dialog boxes that can display images. These dialog boxes use image buttons to graphically illustrate command options. *Image buttons* are much like standard control buttons, except that they display pictures rather than words. Dialog boxes containing image buttons function much like icon menus; that is, you click on an image button to issue a command function associated with the button, just as clicking on an icon issues a command or selects an option.

## Screen Menu

The *screen menu* appears on the right side of the screen in the drawing editor. Recall that you make your screen menu selections by highlighting the item with your pointing device and pressing the pick button. A *branch* is an item that activates another AutoCAD submenu. The groupings of menu pages are for convenience only and have no effect on AutoCAD's command structure. If you get lost, just choose AutoCAD at the top of any screen menu. This choice returns you to the initial screen menu, called the *root menu*, and restores the initial pull-down menu bar.

*Exercise instructions referring to screen menus assume that their menu selections are currently visible on the screen menu. If they are not visible, choose the AutoCAD selection at the top of the screen menu.*

When you choose a menu item, it changes menu pages or sends a command, option, or a series of commands to AutoCAD for execution. This command execution is the same as if you had entered the input. You may remember from using the pull-down menu that screen menus are often activated from the pull-down selections to help you with command options. In this way, AutoCAD's screen menus are context-sensitive, changing appropriately as you select pull-down menu items.

## Keyboard Access to the Screen Menu

You also can access the screen menu from the keyboard. The keyboard offers two methods of screen menu selection. The first method is to press the menu cursor key (usually Ins) to highlight a menu selection. Use the up- and down-arrow keys to move the highlighted bar to the menu item you want and press Ins again (or press Enter) to choose the item.

The second method of accessing the screen menu from the keyboard is to start typing characters of the menu selection at the Command: prompt. As you type, the menu label beginning with the characters you type becomes highlighted. Most selections are highlighted by typing one or two characters, and then you press Enter or Ins to execute the selection.

## Screen Menu Conventions

As you move through the screen menus, notice that the DIM:, UCS:, and SAVE: selections are followed by colons. These selections often branch to a new menu page and always start the command. Any selection that automatically starts a command has a colon after the menu label. Many commands require subcommands in order to complete their chores. These subcommands usually are listed in lowercase letters. As you flip through menu pages, remember that you can always return to the root menu by choosing AutoCAD at the top of the menu page.

Screen menu items ending in three periods (...), such as LAYER or PLOT, activate a dialog box.

At the bottom of most menu pages are shortcut branches that enable you to return to your LAST menu page or to the DRAW and EDIT menu pages. Some menu pages offer more selections than can fit on one page. In such cases, the next and previous selections flip forward and back through pages to access all the selections available.

Finally, every menu page has * * * * below the AutoCAD selection. This selection presents you with a menu page containing choices for HELP, U (Undo), REDO, RE-DRAW, SAVE, and object snaps. *Object snaps* are aids for drawing objects. Chapter 4 covers the object snap options.

Menus are a powerful tool in AutoCAD, giving you flexibility in command entry. With a little practice, you should soon find your preferences. Many users, however, prefer to use a tablet menu, as described in the next section.

## Tablet Menu

AutoCAD comes with a standard tablet menu that performs many of the same functions as the screen and pull-down menus. Figure 2.26 shows the complete tablet menu. The tablet menu offers a few advantages over the other menu options. You can easily remember where to find tablet menu selections, and you always can find them without flipping through menu pages. The tablet menu also includes graphic images to help you identify your selection. Many selections from the tablet menu call the appropriate screen menu pages to help you in your subcommand option selections.

*To bring up AutoCAD's standard tablet menu, you need to run through a small set of configuration steps. See Appendix A for help in configuring the AutoCAD standard tablet menu.*

## Button Functions

Nearly everyone uses some type of pointing device with AutoCAD—usually a mouse or tablet puck (see fig. 2.27). AutoCAD reserves one button on the puck or mouse for picking points and choosing screen and tablet menu items. This button tells AutoCAD to pick a point or select an object where the cursor or crosshairs are positioned on the screen.

A mouse usually has 2 or 3 buttons, and a puck can have up to 16 buttons. The position of the pick button varies with the device. The second button acts as an Enter key. Most of the other buttons are assigned to do the same duties as the function keys and control settings explored in the next chapter. A digitizer or special mouse driver may be necessary to access these functions.

## Buttons Menu

Some digitizing pucks and other input devices have 16 or more buttons. AutoCAD's standard menu file, ACAD.MNU, also includes a buttons menu that assigns additional functions to the buttons on pointing devices that have more than four buttons. AutoCAD assigns these auxiliary button as follows:

| Button Function | Effect |
|---|---|
| ^B | Snap |
| ^O | Ortho |
| ^G | Grid |
| ^D | Coordinate Display |
| ^E | Isoplane |
| ^T | Tablet On/Off |

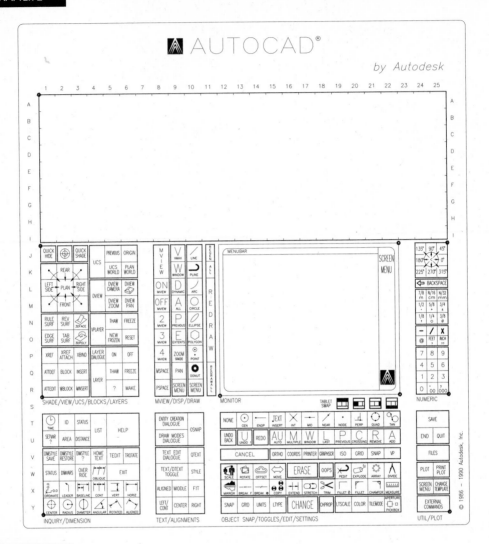

**Figure 2.26:**

The AutoCAD
tablet menu.

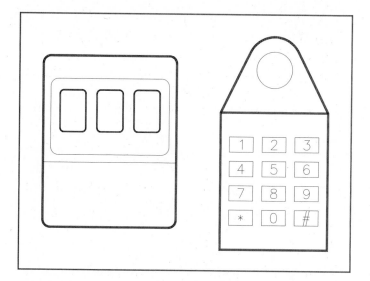

**Figure 2.27:**
A typical mouse and puck.

You can assign the buttons to execute other menu selections by creating a custom button menu. For details on creating button menus, see *Maximizing AutoCAD Release 12* (New Riders Publishing) or Chapter 18 of this book.

# The Toolbar, Toolbox, and Pop-up Menus

In addition to the pull-down, screen, and tablet menus, AutoCAD Release 12 for Windows offers several shortcuts for commands that are used frequently. Depending on your preferences, you may find a few of these methods useful.

 *You will find an annotated illustration of the toolbar and toolbox in the front cover of this book. The position of toolbar icons varies, depending on your window size, but their order remains as illustrated.*

## Toolbar

You can change several of the settings directly from the toolbar. A button is provided for Ortho, Snap, and Paper space to turn those functions on or off. When you click on the layer name, a drop-down list shows the defined layers to enable selection of a different active layer. The Layer button brings up the Layer Control dialog box. The Entity Creation Modes dialog box is accessed by clicking on the color box on the left side of the toolbar. Many other buttons on the toolbar are programmable and defined in the ACAD.INI file. This procedure is explained in Chapter 18. The first five buttons, those already containing icons, are already programmed. These buttons provide easy access to the following commands: toolbox location, OPEN, QSAVE, Print/PLOT, and ZOOM.

## Toolbox

The floating toolbox is a group of 35 icons representing the most often used commands in AutoCAD. Some of these include the basic drawing and editing commands, and the object snap modes. In case you cannot recognize all the icons, the text box at the top displays the name of the commands when you cover them with the pointer. The toolbox is also defined in the ACAD.INI file. The toolbox is referred to as the floating toolbox because you can place it anywhere in the graphics window, or even outside of it. The ACAD.INI file, as well as the toolbox icon in the toolbar, controls the toolbox location and layout.

## Pop-up Menu

AutoCAD button 2 displays the pop-up (cursor) menu on the screen at the pointer position. This enables easy access to the object snap modes. If you use a two-button mouse, you can hold down Shift while you press the right button to display the pop-up menu. On a digitizer puck, AutoCAD button 2 is the next-lowest numbered button after the pick button and the Enter button.

Try the toolbar, toolbox, and pop-up menu in the following exercise. The TOOLBOX icon on the toolbar is a 2×6 grid of tiny icons. The REDRAW icon in the toolbox is on R. The ZOOM icon on the toolbar is a magnifying glass at the corner of a white window. You can choose any of these icons by clicking on them with your pick button. The toolbox title displays the name of the icon under the current cursor location. Your toolbox may currently appear as a 2×18 column at the left or right side of your screen, or it may look similar to the one in this book, or it may not be currently displayed. If your toolbox is not displayed, you can click on the TOOLBOX icon on the toolbar to display it.

---

### Using the Toolbar, the Toolbox, and the Pop-Up Menu

Continue from the previous exercise. If your toolbox is missing, then from the toolbar, choose the TOOLBOX icon to display it.

Command: *From the toolbox, choose*    Issues the REDRAW command
REDRAW

Command: REDRAW

Command: *From the toolbar, choose the*    Issues the Zoom command and Window option
ZOOM Window icon

Command: ZOOM

```
All/Center/Dynamic/Extents/Left/
Previous/Vmax/Window/<Scale(X/XP)>:
Window
```

First Corner: *Pick a point*

Other Corner: *Pick another point*      Zooms

Command: *Click* Button 2 *or hold down*      Displays pop-up (cursor) menu at the pointer
Shift *and click* Button 1      position (see fig. 2.28)

*Press Ctrl-C*      Cancels menu

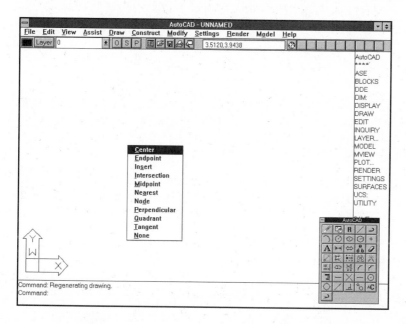

**Figure 2.28:**

The pop-up
(cursor) menu.

 *The child menu displayed by choosing *A*ssist, then Object *S*nap, is
identical to the pop-up cursor menu.*

# Configuring the Toolbox

So that your toolbox configuration matches the 5×8 icon toolbox shown throughout this
book, perform the steps in the following exercise.

## Configuring a 5×8 Toolbox

From the toolbar, click one or more times on the TOOLBOX icon (until it appears similar to that shown in fig. 2.28). Your toolbox probably now appears as 6×6 icons.

| | |
|---|---|
| Command: *Anywhere in the toolbox, right-click (click the right mouse button)* | Displays the Toolbox Customization dialog box |
| *In the* Toolbox Width *area, double-click in the* **F**loating *buttons box and enter* **5** | Sets toolbox to five icons wide |
| *If it does not contain a check mark, choose the* **S**ave to ACAD.INI *check box* | Preserves setting |
| *Choose* OK | Makes and saves change to match figure 2.28 |

*See the inside front cover of this book for a diagram identifying each of the toolbox icons. For details on modifying or adding icons and commands to the toolbox, see Chapter 18.*

# Using Keyboard Commands versus Menus

Many experienced users think that keyboard command entry can be just as fast, if not faster, than menus. AutoCAD's *command alias* feature also makes command entry faster. A command alias is an abbreviation that you can use instead of typing the entire command name. When you use an alias, AutoCAD replaces it with the full command name and executes the command normally. To execute the CIRCLE command from a menu, for example, you pull down the **D**raw menu or choose the DRAW screen menu, then choose the **C**ircle or CIRCLE items, and then choose a circle option. Or, you can merely type a **C**, press Enter, and be done with it. Some of AutoCAD's standard command abbreviations are shown in table 2.4.

### Table 2.4
### Keyboard Command Abbreviations

| Alias | Command | Alias | Command |
|-------|---------|-------|---------|
| A | ARC | LA | LAYER |
| C | CIRCLE | M | MOVE |
| CP | COPY | P | PAN |

| Alias | Command | Alias | Command |
|-------|---------|-------|---------|
| DV | DVIEW | PL | POLYLINE |
| E | ERASE | R | REDRAW |
| L | LINE | Z | ZOOM |

These abbreviations cover only a few of AutoCAD's many commands, but you can easily create your own abbreviations by modifying the ACAD.PGP file. This procedure is explained in Chapter 18, and a more comprehensive IAW-ACAD.PGP file is included on the IAW DISK. You can use that file or create your own custom ACAD.PGP file for your most frequently used commands.

AutoCAD offers a similar keyboard shortcut for command options. Instead of flipping through menus for command options, you can abbreviate virtually any command option to the one or two letters that are unique for that option at the current prompt. For example, recall the ZOOM prompt:

```
All/Center/Dynamic/Extents/Left/Previous/Vmax/Window/<Scale(X/XP)>:
```

The ZOOM Window menu item responds to this prompt with only a W, not with the entire word WINDOW. You need only type the characters that are shown as uppercase in AutoCAD prompts to execute an option.

The purpose of this book is to teach you AutoCAD for Windows thoroughly, so you want to become intimately familiar with the AutoCAD commands. Pull-down menu selection is emphasized because that is probably the easiest interface for a new user. After you learn the commands, you can decide if keyboard entry, abbreviations, or other menus are better for you.

AutoCAD's standard menus are general purpose, but you may do specific types of drawings for which custom menus are much more efficient. You can purchase custom menus for many different applications (see your AutoCAD dealer). Or you can create your own custom menus, as comprehensively covered in *Maximizing AutoCAD Release 12* (New Riders Publishing).

Most users find that a combination of keyboard commands or abbreviations and menu selections works out well.

The following section thoroughly covers the use of dialog boxes. As more software packages are starting to use Windows-style dialog boxes, it becomes easier for a user to learn several software packages. If you are new to the type of dialog boxes that AutoCAD uses, this next section should be of special interest.

# Using Dialog Boxes

Dialog boxes are more convenient than AutoCAD's other data-entry methods because they enable you to view or change several items at a time. In addition, dialog boxes are the only way to view a list of files when you need to specify a file name.

## Entering Text in Dialog Boxes

The Open dialog box and other file dialog boxes in AutoCAD are almost identical to the Save Drawing As dialog box, which is shown in figure 2.29. This dialog box, which contains most of the dialog box features, appears when you enter the SAVE command if you have not yet named the current drawing. Dialog box features that are not part of the Save Drawing As dialog box are explained after the following exercise.

**Figure 2.29:**

The Save Drawing As dialog box.

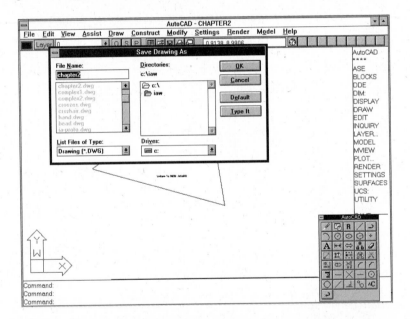

You use *edit boxes* in dialog boxes to enter text and values such as file, color, layer names, distances, or scale factors. In the Save Drawing As dialog box, the long rectangular box under File Name is an edit box. This edit box is highlighted when the Save Drawing As dialog box appears. To highlight an edit box that is not currently highlighted, click on it. Your keyboard's Tab key also moves between the edit boxes and buttons, highlighting each one as you move to it. If the edit box or button name has a single underlined letter, that letter can be typed from the keyboard to highlight that location. The underlined T in the Type It button is a shortcut key. If an edit box is in the text-entry mode, you must hold down Alt while pressing the shortcut key.

When an edit box is highlighted, the characters you type replace the current value. If you want to edit the current value instead of replacing it, click on the edit box or press one of the cursor-control keys. A vertical-bar text cursor appears to mark the current character-entry position. The cursor-control keys are the four arrow keys and the Home and End keys. The left- and up-arrow keys move the text cursor one character to the left; the right- and down-arrow keys move it to the right. The Home and End keys move the text cursor to the beginning and end of the line. The Backspace and Del keys delete the character before and after the current text cursor position. Any characters you type are inserted at the current text cursor position. If the value is too long to fit into the edit box, it scrolls to the left or right. You can use the cursor keys to scroll the text in the box.

When you have the desired text in the edit box, you can accept it by pressing Enter or by clicking on the <u>O</u>K button. <u>O</u>K, <u>C</u>ancel, <u>T</u>ype It, and <u>D</u>efault are examples of dialog box buttons. A *button* is an object that immediately executes an action when you click on it. Some buttons, such as the <u>S</u>et Color button in the Layer Control dialog box, open child dialog boxes, which you use to enter new values. You can select a button by clicking on it or by using its shortcut key (if it has one). In the file dialog boxes, the <u>O</u>K button accepts the current settings, exits, and performs the file action, and the <u>C</u>ancel button exits without making changes. The Enter and Esc keys also are shortcut alternatives to <u>O</u>K and <u>C</u>ancel buttons. If AutoCAD does not accept your new value, it is invalid and you must edit it or cancel the change. The <u>T</u>ype It button closes the dialog box and returns you to the Command: prompt, and the <u>D</u>efault button restores all settings in the file dialog box to what they were when the dialog box appeared.

## Using Dialog Box Lists

You also can enter a file name and make selections in dialog boxes by selecting from lists. To select an item in the list, click on it or use the cursor keys to move up and down the list. If you double-click on an item, the same action occurs as when you select the item and press Enter. When you double-click on a file name in the file list box, the file name is selected and a file action occurs on the chosen item. In the file dialog boxes, the file name you choose from the list appears in the file name edit box. Edit and list boxes that are linked this way are called *combo boxes*.

*If an item is gray in a dialog box, it usually means the item currently is not relevant or cannot be selected.*

The list of directory names below the <u>D</u>irectories label also is a list box. When you select a directory from it, its name appears on the line above the list box. You can, however, use the File <u>N</u>ame edit box to change directories. If you preface the text you enter in the File <u>N</u>ame edit box with a backslash, AutoCAD interprets it as a directory name rather than a file name, changing the current directory and the contents of the file name and directory lists.

The other type of list box found in some dialog boxes is the *drop-down list*. Normally, only a text box is visible, with a drop-down arrow icon at the right of it. When you click on the arrow icon, the list box opens below the text box. Whether the list box is open or not, you can use the cursor keys to scroll up and down the items in the list. When the list is open, you can select an item by pressing the key of that item's first character.

## Filtering File Names in a File Dialog Box

The List Files of Type pop-up list enables common file extensions such as dwg, igs, dxf, or others to be filtered from the entire directory listing. This method is not quite as flexible as entering DOS wild-card combinations in the File Name edit box, but it is much easier to perform.

## Using File Dialog Boxes

When you save your drawing, use the Save Drawing As dialog box to try out various dialog box features. The following exercise tests the features found in this dialog box. If your AutoCAD program directory is not named ACADWIN, substitute your directory's name for \ACADWIN in the next exercise.

### Saving a Drawing with the Save Drawing As Dialog Box

Continue from the previous drawing, with CHAPTER2.DWG loaded.

Command: **SAVE** ↵                          Displays the Save Drawing As dialog box

The File Name edit box is highlighted and displays CHAPTER2, the File Name list shows CHAP2-B.DWG, and the current directory is C:\IAW. Other files from the IAW DISK also appear in the list.

*Double-click on* C:\ *in the* Directories *list box, then double-click on* ACADWIN          Changes to the \ACADWIN directory and redisplays the file and directory lists

*Double-click in the* File Name *edit box, then enter* *.*          Filters the file-name list to display all the files in the \ACADWIN directory

*Click twice on the scroll bar under the slider box to page down the list*

*Click on the scroll bar above the slider box button to page up the list*

*Click on the down arrow to scroll down one line*

*Click on any file name*          Displays the name in the File Name edit box

| | |
|---|---|
| *Click on the right end of the* File **N**ame *edit box and press Backspace four times* | Positions the text cursor and deletes the file extension |
| *Click on the* D**e**fault *button or press Alt-E* ⏎ | Restores CHAPTER2 and \IAW defaults |

You could click on CHAPTER2.DWG and the OK button or press Enter at this point to save to the default, but instead, try the **T**ype It button.

| | |
|---|---|
| *Click on the* **T**ype It *button or press Alt-T* ⏎ | The dialog box disappears and a file-name prompt appears |
| `Save current changes as <C:\IAW\CHAPTER2>:` *Press Enter* | Saves the drawing |

As you invest time in your drawings, they become more valuable and you need to save them frequently. Your work is not secure until it is saved to a file on the hard disk, with periodic backups copied to another disk or tape.

*MS-DOS file names are limited to eight characters. As you work in AutoCAD, it helps to think ahead about naming and organizing your drawing files. Create file and directory names that help identify the contents of the files. Try to anticipate how you are going to sort your files in the DOS environment. For example, in file lists, PROJ01 and PROJ02 sort in order with PROJ??, but PROJ1 sorts after PROJ02. When you use SAVE to record your work-in-progress, you can adopt a temporary naming convention for saving several levels of backup files: PTEMP01, PTEMP02, and so on.*

Choose **F**ile, then Save **A**s to display the Save File As dialog box. Some commands, such as INSERT, do not display a file dialog box unless you request it by entering a tilde (~) at the prompt for a file name.

*You can turn the file dialog box feature off by setting the FILEDIA AutoCAD system variable to 0. With the file dialog box turned off, all file menu selections and commands prompt for the file name on the* `Command:` *prompt. If you have the file dialog box feature turned off, you can still pop up file dialog boxes when you want to use them by entering a tilde (~) when prompted for a file name.*

CHAPTER 2

# Using Other Dialog Box Features

The file dialog boxes contain all dialog features except check boxes, radio buttons, and horizontal slider bars. Figure 2.30 illustrates check boxes and radio buttons in the Drawing Aids dialog box (choose **S**ettings, then **D**rawing Aids).

**Figure 2.30:**

Check boxes and radio buttons in the Drawing Aids dialog box.

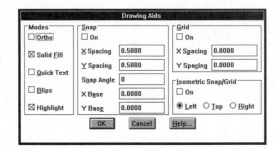

*Check boxes* are on/off switches that appear near key words labeling items that can only be on or off, such as the **G**rid On or **S**nap On items in the Drawing Aids dialog box. If an X mark appears in the box, it is on; if the box is blank, it is off. You click on the box to turn it on or off. *Radio buttons* are groups of settings—only one radio button can be on at any one time. Radio buttons appear as a group of circles or squares enclosed in a box, with a black dot indicating which button is on, such as the **I**sometric Snap/Grid group in the Drawing Aids dialog box.

*Slider bars* are horizontal sliders that control values. They function the same as list box scroll bars. Figure 2.31 shows a slider in the Grips dialog box (choose **S**ettings, then **G**rips). The slider controls the size of AutoCAD grip boxes. The slider bar can be dragged by your input device, or you can click on the arrows to adjust the grip size. A sample of the size is shown beside the slider.

# Ending Your Work

Save your work now by using the END command. The END command makes a backup file from your previously saved file, stores the up-to-date copy, and exits the drawing editor. The END command saves the drawing to the current drawing file name. You can type in the END command at the Command: prompt or access it from the **F**ile menu by choosing the E**x**it AutoCAD option. In previous releases of AutoCAD, the QUIT command left the drawing editor and discarded any unsaved changes. In Release 12 for Windows, the QUIT command still warns you that you have unsaved changes and enables you to save them before exiting.

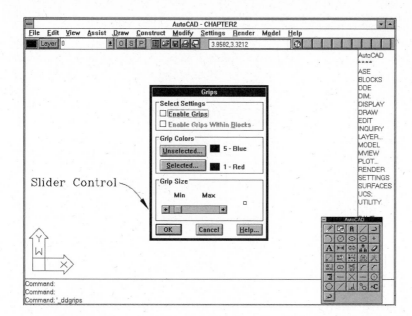

Slider Control

**Figure 2.31:**

Sliders in the AutoCAD Grips dialog box.

*At times, you may need your drawing files to be as small as possible for archiving or exchanging with others. You can sometimes reduce the size of an AutoCAD drawing file by ending twice. That is, end your drawing once, reload it, and end it a second time. When you erase objects in a drawing, they are not actually removed from the drawing database until the drawing is loaded the next time. The process of double-ending a drawing completely purges the drawing of deleted entities. This can save disk space, especially after an extensive editing session.*

# Summary

You have had a chance to set up AutoCAD and experiment with the drawing editor by entering a few commands. AutoCAD is cooperative. It only takes action when you tell it to do something. AutoCAD lets you know that it is waiting for your input with the Command: prompt or other prompts on the prompt line.

Help is always available to you from the pull-down menu, if you type **Help** or **?** at the Command: prompt, or if you type **'Help** or **'?** when you are in commands. If you get stuck in a drawing, you can always undo a command, erase your drawing, or leave the drawing unsaved and start over.

Now that you know your way in and out of AutoCAD, you can move on to organizing AutoCAD's drawing environment and experimenting with using menus. This chapter introduced many exciting features of AutoCAD Release 12 for Windows. If you are not yet comfortable with Windows, or are more familiar with older versions of AutoCAD, you may be anxious to move on to the more traditional AutoCAD commands. Chapter 3 introduces you to more of the drawing and editing commands.

# Setting Up an Electronic Drawing

The preparation required for drawing in AutoCAD is much like preparation for drawing on a drafting board. In manual drafting, you select drawing tools to fit your particular drawing; for instance, you might select a 1/16" scale. Similarly, you set up parameters in AutoCAD to fit your particular drawing. That is, you create custom tools to use with AutoCAD. After you set up the proper units, scale, linetype, sheet size, and text, you can begin drawing.

If you take time to set up AutoCAD before you start your drawing, you can save your settings and use them in future drawings, which saves preparation time.

This chapter continues to discuss the AutoCAD menus that were introduced in Chapter 2 and shows you how to set up AutoCAD for drawing. You also learn how to save settings in a prototype drawing.

## Organizing Your Drawing Setups

A few differences exist between the process of organizing an electronic drawing and the preparation of a manual drawing. Before you prepare an electronic drawing sheet, you need to understand how an electronic drawing's scale, layers, and drawing entities are different from their manual-drawing counterparts. For this reason, take a moment to become familiar with scale, layers, and entities.

# Understanding Full-Scale Electronic Drawings

In AutoCAD, drawing elements are stored in real-world units. AutoCAD can track your drawing data in fractions or decimals, in meters, millimeters, feet, inches, or just about any unit of measurement that you want to use.

When you draw on a drafting board, you usually create the drawing to fit a specific sheet size or scale. The text, symbols, and line widths are generally about the same size from one drawing to another.

In AutoCAD, however, this process is reversed. You always draw the image at actual size (full scale) in real-world units. The only time you need to worry about scale is during plotting. At plot time, AutoCAD enables you to scale your full-size electronic drawings up or down to fit the plot sheet. You must, therefore, plan ahead for scaling a full-size AutoCAD drawing and make settings that adjust the scale of the text, symbols, and line widths so that they plot at an appropriate size.

A bolt that is two inches long may look ten inches long when it is blown up on the screen, but AutoCAD regards the bolt as being two inches long, no matter how you show it or plot it. To help you get comfortable with electronic scaling, this chapter illustrates setups with different units and sheet sizes.

# Working with Electronic Layers

Even in manual drafting, almost everything you design and draw can be thought of as being separated into layers. Printed circuit boards have layers. Buildings are layered by floors. Even schematic diagrams have information layers for annotations. A virtually unlimited number of electronic layers are available in AutoCAD to give you more flexibility and control in organizing your drawing than you would have in manual drafting.

If you have ever done manual drafting, you may have used transparent overlays to separate your drawings into physical layers. Think of AutoCAD's electronic layers in 2D as transparent sheets that are laid one over the other. When you are working in 2D, you are looking down through a stack of sheets (see fig. 3.1). You can see your entire drawing as it is being built from the superimposed sheets. You can pull out a single sheet to examine or modify, or you can work with all the layers at once.

In 3D, layers become more of an organizational concept and have less physical resemblance to overlays. Any layer can contain any group of objects, which may be superimposed in space to coexist with other objects on other layers. In 3D, you should think of each layer as containing a unique class of objects. You can look at all layer groups together, or you can look at any combination by specifying the layers you want to see.

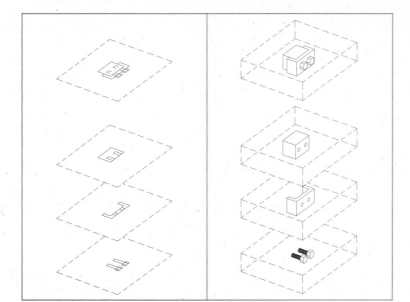

**Figure 3.1:**
2D and 3D layers.

Each layer can have any color and linetype associated with it. When you set up your AutoCAD layers, you need to determine which parts of the drawing you are going to place on each layer and what color and linetype you are going to use with each layer. You can make as many or as few layers as you need.

## Understanding Entities and Properties

When you use AutoCAD's drawing tools to draw on one of these electronic layers, you create a *drawing entity*. Lines, circles, and text are examples of entities. In addition to its geometric location, each entity has an associated color, layer, and linetype. 3D entities also have thickness and elevation. AutoCAD calls these associations *properties*. Color is commonly used in AutoCAD to control the line weight of entities when they are plotted. You can preset each layer's color and linetype.

One part of preparing for an AutoCAD drawing is determining how you group entities on layers and what colors and linetypes to use when you construct drawing entities. The simplest (and in many cases, the best) way to organize a drawing is to use layers to control the properties of entities. If you are going to draw a gizmo by using red dashed lines, you can draw it on the red dashed-line layer. Many of these decisions are determined by drawing standards that you may have established previously. If you need to make exceptions, AutoCAD enables you to change the properties of any entity, regardless of its layer.

*If you are not using color in your plotted and printed output, you may want to use color to control line weight in your plots. Plotter pens are assigned by entity color. Plotting and color-control for plotting are discussed in Chapter 13.*

# Setting Up a Drawing

You can find most of the setup tools you need on the **S**ettings pull-down menu (see fig. 3.2) and on the two pages of the SETTINGS screen menu.

**Figure 3.2:**

The Settings pull-down menu and the first page of the SETTINGS screen menu.

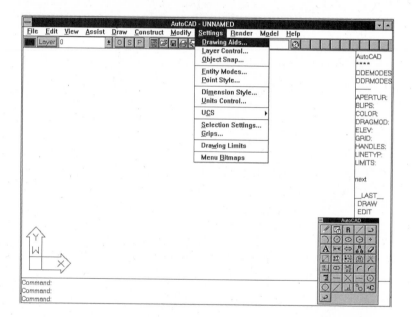

When you begin a new drawing, AutoCAD makes several assumptions about drawing setup, including display and input units, scale, and linetype. These pre-established settings are called *defaults*.

AutoCAD sets up many default settings by reading a prototype drawing, which is stored on your hard disk. The AutoCAD prototype drawing, which comes with your AutoCAD software, is called ACAD.DWG. By telling AutoCAD to use no prototype drawing (as you did in Chapter 1), you begin new drawings with all the defaults found in the original ACAD.DWG.

The standard ACAD.DWG prototype assumes that you want to draw entities on layer 0. By default, layer 0 has white, continuous lines. (These white lines may appear inverted as black lines on a white background on some systems, but AutoCAD still treats them as white lines.) The ACAD.DWG also assumes a default system of measurement display (called *units*) that uses decimal units and initial drawing limits of 12 units in the X direction and 9 units in the Y direction. The drawing *limits* define your intended drawing area.

When you set up your drawing, you actually are modifying settings that were passed by AutoCAD from the prototype drawing into your new drawing. As you set up your drawing, AutoCAD shows you the default values in brackets at the Command: prompt. You can accept the default values by pressing Enter. You also can create one or more custom prototype drawings and tell AutoCAD which prototype drawing you want to use for these defaults. This technique is demonstrated later in this book.

# Determining a Scale Factor and Drawing Limits

How do you calculate the scale you need? First, establish your system of units. Second, determine a scale factor. A *scale factor* is a setting that enables you to produce a plot at the size you want from a drawing that you have created at actual size ( *full scale*). You set your electronic sheet so that you can draw at full scale.

The following sections show you how to tailor AutoCAD settings by examining an architectural drawing and an engineering drawing. After you become familiar with these sample drawings, you learn how to set up layers by creating a simple one-to-one scale drawing.

First, you must determine a drawing scale factor, and then you use it to calculate the following AutoCAD settings:

- Sheet size (limits)
- Line width
- Text height
- Symbol size
- Linetype scale

The limits setting is the most important setting affected by a scale factor because it is the AutoCAD equivalent of sheet size. You set the drawing's limits during the initial drawing setup; other drawing effects are set later.

# Determining Scale Factor and Sheet Size

Sheet size is calculated in much the same way as in manual drafting, except that you use the resulting scale ratio to scale up the sheet size to fit around the full-scale size of your drawing. Then, when you plot the drawing, you scale everything back down by the same factor. In traditional drafting, the drawing is scaled down to fit in the sheet.

If you are working with an architectural calculation for a floor plan that is 75 feet by 40 feet, you may want the drawing to be scaled at 1/4" = 1' (12"). What is your scale factor, and what size electronic sheet are you going to use? The size of your electronic sheet is set by the limits that you choose. The limits are determined by the X,Y values of the lower left and upper right corners of your electronic sheet.

If you convert your drawing scale to a ratio of 1:*n*, then *n* is your scale factor. If you already have selected a drawing scale, you can easily determine the scale factor. Thus, in this example, because you are working at 1/4" = 1'-0", your scale factor is 48. The mathematics look something like this:

> *1/4:12/1 converts to 1:48/1 or 1:48 for a scale factor of 48.*

If, on the other hand, you select a drawing scale of 3/8" = 1'-0", your drawing scale factor is 32. The math looks like this:

> *3/8:12/1 converts to 1:96/3 or 1:32 for a scale factor of 32.*

# Calculating a Sheet Size for a Known Scale and Object Size

Use your scale factor to determine your electronic drawing limits by running some test calculations on possible plotting sheet sizes. You set the limits by multiplying the sheet size by your scale factor. Follow this sample set of calculations:

| | |
|---|---|
| Size of floor plan | 75" × 40' |
| Scale | 1/4" = 12" |
| Determine scale factor | 48 |

Now, test a 17×11-inch sheet:

> 17" × 48 = 816" or 68'
>
> 11" × 48 = 528" or 44'
>
> A 17" × 11" sheet equals 68' × 44' at 1/4" = 12" scale.

This sheet size is too small because the 75' by 40' drawing does not fit on the sheet. Now test a 36×24-inch sheet:

> 36" × 48 = 1728" or 144'

24" × 48 = 1152" or 96'

A 36" × 24" sheet equals 144' × 96' at 1/4" = 12" scale.

This size should work with plenty of room for dimensions, notes, and a border.

In this example, you determined your limits by the number of units that fit across a standard sheet (D size, 36" by 24", because 144' across 36" at 1/4" = 12"). If you have to fit the drawing to a predetermined sheet size, start with that size and the size of what you are drawing, and then calculate the scale factor from them:

36" × 24" sheet and 75' × 40' object:

75' equals 900" (75' × 12" per foot)

36":900" (ratio of sheet size to object size)

36":900" equals a ratio of 1:25

Next typical architectural scale is 1:48, or 1/4:12, which is 1/4" = 1' scale

Your limits do not actually limit the size of your drawing. Think of AutoCAD's limits as an electronic fence, which AutoCAD uses to warn you if you draw outside your boundary. This boundary is an ideal way to represent a sheet size. It gives you a frame of reference for zooming or plotting. If you need to draw outside the electronic sheet, you can expand the sheet by resetting the limits.

# Setting the Drawing's Limits

How do you get these settings into AutoCAD? You can set limits manually or you can use an AutoCAD setup routine that sets limits automatically. The setup routine uses the limits you choose as it steps you through the calculations for sheet size and scale. In the exercises that follow, you use an automatic limits setup on an architectural sheet, and then you try the UNITS and LIMITS commands to set up an engineering drawing. Later in this chapter you learn how to set limits manually.

## Setting Limits Automatically

When you choose **L**ayout from the **V**iew pull-down menu, the **M**V Setup item loads and executes an AutoLISP program that sets up your limits. This program also draws a border around the drawing or inserts a complex title block. The border is drawn around the perimeter of the sheet as a reference line that matches your limits. This border is not intended to be plotted but shows your sheet edges. MVSETUP also includes another option that sets up the drawing in paper space with optional viewports and inserts a complex title block. Paper space and optional viewports are covered in Chapter 5. Figure 3.3 shows the menu selection sequence used for MVSETUP.

**Figure 3.3:**

The MVSETUP
menus.

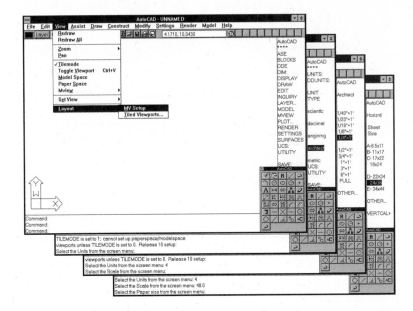

To get started, follow the steps in this exercise to begin AutoCAD, create a new drawing, and step through setting up AutoCAD:

---

## Using MVSETUP To Prepare an Architectural 1/4"-Scale Drawing

Start AutoCAD by double-clicking on the AutoCAD icon in Windows.

| | |
|---|---|
| Command: *Choose* **F**ile, *then* **N**ew | Opens the Create New Drawing dialog box |
| *Type* **ARCH**, *then press Enter or click on* OK | Creates a new drawing named ARCH in the current directory |
| Command: *Choose* **V**iew, *then* **L**ayout, *then* **M**V Setup | Loads and initiates MVSETUP command |

```
Command: _mvsetup

Initializing....MVSETUP loaded
Paperspace/Modelspace is disabled.
The pre-R11 setup will be invoked unless
it is enabled.  Enable Paper/Modelspace?
<Y>: N ↵

TILEMODE is set to 1;  cannot set up
paperspace/modelspace viewports unless
TILEMODE is set to 0.  Release 10 setup:
```

```
Select the Units from the screen
menu: Choose archtect

Select the Scale from the screen
menu: Choose 1/4"=1'

Select the Paper size from the       Completes the setup
screen menu: Choose 24×36
```

A border is drawn around the drawing.

# Setting Units

AutoCAD offers units that are suitable for nearly any normal drawing practice. If you normally use architectural units, use AutoCAD's architectural units. Choose your system of units by using the **U**nits Control option from the **S**ettings pull-down menu. The process of setting units does two things for your drawing. First, it sets up the input format for entering distances and angles from the keyboard. Second, it sets up the output format that AutoCAD uses when displaying and dimensioning distances and angles.

The AutoCAD Units Control dialog box gives you control over the unit options. The next exercise shows you how to complete a detailed description of the units you want to use. Some of the settings called for in the exercise may already be selected in your drawing.

*Even though you may not need finer fractions than 1/2" at this scale, you can ensure precision by setting the smallest fraction displayed to 1/64" (the default is 1/16"). If you set this **P**recision option in the Units area to 1/2", everything you draw is rounded to 1/2" when displayed, even if the dimension is not accurate. Individual errors in drawing are less likely but may cause cumulative errors. Set the option to 1/64" to make drawing errors more likely to show up. Then, if a coordinate displays as 49/64" when it should be 1", you know that it is not drawn correctly.*

Figure 3.4 shows the Units Control dialog box with the default settings. The default setting for zero angle is usually to the right or east. The default setting for angle measurement is counterclockwise. Use these default settings in your setup.

**Figure 3.4:**

The AutoCAD Units Control dialog box, showing the various unit settings.

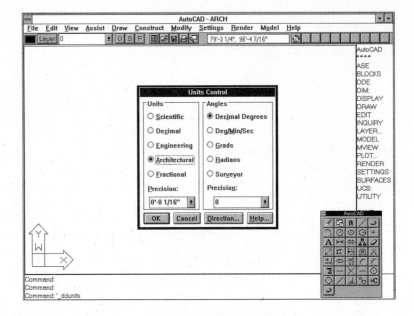

## Using Units To Set Up an Architectural Drawing

| | |
|---|---|
| Command: *Choose* **S**ettings, *then* **U**nits Control | Displays the Units Control dialog box |
| *Choose the* **A**rchitectural *radio button* | Selects units |
| *Choose the* **P**recision *pop-up list box in the* Units *area, then select* 0'-0 1/64" | Changes precision from 1/16" to 1/64" |
| *Choose the* Dec**i**mal Degrees *radio button* | Selects Decimal Degrees angles |
| *Choose the* Precisio**n** *pop-up list box in the* Angles *area, then select* 0.00 | Changes the angular measurement precision from 0 to 2 decimal places |
| *Choose* **D**irection | Opens the Direction Control dialog box |
| *Choose the* **E**ast *radio button in the* Angle 0 Direction *area* | Specifies East (right of screen) as the direction of angle 0 |
| *Choose the* **C**ounter-Clockwise *radio button* | Measures angles counterclockwise from 0 |

| | |
|---|---|
| *Choose* OK, *then* OK *again* | Closes both dialog boxes |
| Command: *Move the cursor and pick a few points, noting the coordinate display in the status bar* | |
| Command: *Choose* **F**ile, *then* **S**ave | Saves your changes to ARCH.DWG |

After you set the units, the coordinates display shows feet, inches, and fractions. If the format of the current coordinate is too long to fit in the coordinates display area, it displays in scientific units, such as 1.704450E+03,95'–9 51/64".

*If the active coordinate display is off, you can press F6 to turn it on. Clicking on the coordinate display box in the toolbar also turns it on or off.*

Usually, you set units only once for a drawing, but you can change units in the middle of a drawing.

*Fractional units represent inches by default, but the inch marks (") are not shown. You can use fractional units for units other than inches by adjusting dimensioning and plot setups.*

# Entering and Displaying Values in Various Units

No matter what units you use, you can enter values in integer, decimal, scientific, or fractional formats. When you are using architectural or engineering units, you can input values as feet, inches, or both. AutoCAD assumes that the value is in inches unless you use a foot mark (') to indicate feet. You can omit the inches mark ("), and if the inches value is zero, you do not need to type anything. The values 2'0" or 2'0 or 2' or 24" are all equivalent in engineering units. Notice that no space is allowed between the foot and inch value. Because the inch mark is optional, you need to specify only the foot mark. Thus, to signify one foot, three inches, you can enter 1'3" or 1'3.

Use a hyphen to separate fractions, as in 1'3-1/2. You must enter fractions without spaces (1-3/4 rather than 1 3/4) because AutoCAD reads a press of the spacebar as a press of the Enter key. The input format and display format differ. You input 1'3-1/2" but AutoCAD displays this value as 1'-3 1/2". You can force feet and inches, angles, and fractions to display in the same form as their entries by setting the UNITMODE system variable to 1. To do so, just enter **UNITMODE** at the Command: prompt and then enter the value **1**.

# Using the Limits Command

In the previous exercises, you used AutoCAD's automatic limits setup to configure an AutoCAD drawing. Next, you are going to follow the steps in a setup sequence for the engineering sheet by using AutoCAD's individual settings commands for units and limits.

## Determining a Scale for a Known Object and Sheet Size

Consider an engineering example as a second case for setting limits. If a 24-inch manhole cover needs to be drawn on an 8 1/2" by 11" sheet, how do you compute your scale factor and determine your electronic limits? Try the following "trial-and-error" method:

| | |
|---|---|
| Size of manhole cover | 24" diameter |
| Sheet size | 11" × 8 1/2" |

Test a scale of 1/2" = 1" scale, which is a scale factor of 2 (1 unit = 2 units):

11" × 2 = 22"

8-1/2" × 2 = 17"

A scale factor of 2 gives 22" × 17" limits; this scale factor is too small. The 24-inch manhole cover drawing is too large for the sheet of paper.

Test a scale of 1/4" = 1" scale, which is a scale factor of 4 (1 unit = 4 units):

11" × 4 = 44"

8-1/2" × 4 = 34"

These limits of 44" × 34" should work.

For this example, select engineering units: feet and inches, with the inch as the smallest whole unit. Engineering fractions are decimals of an inch. This time, use the SETTINGS item from the screen menu to issue the UNITS command.

# Using UNITS To Set Engineering Units for a Drawing

*Choose* <u>F</u>*ile, then* <u>N</u>*ew, and enter* **ENGR**

Begins a new drawing named ENGR

**Command:** *From the screen menu, choose*
SETTINGS, *then* next, *then* UNITS:

Starts the UNITS command

*Press F2*

Displays the text window

```
_UNITS
Report formats:        (Examples)

  1.  Scientific      1.55E+01
  2.  Decimal         15.50
  3.  Engineering     1'-3.50"
  4.  Architectural   1'-3 1/2"
  5.  Fractional      15 1/2
```

With the exception of Engineering and Architectural formats, these formats can
be used with any basic unit of measurement. For example, Decimal mode is perfect
for metric units as well as decimal English units.

Enter choice, 1 to 5 <2>: **3** ↵

Number of digits to right of
decimal point (0 to 8) <4>: **2** ↵

```
Systems of angle measure:       (Examples)
  1.  Decimal degrees            45.0000
  2.  Degrees/minutes/seconds    45d0'0"
  3.  Grads                      50.0000g
  4.  Radians                    0.7854r
  5.  Surveyor's units           N 45d0'0" E
```

Enter choice, 1 to 5 <1>: *Press Enter*

Number of fractional places for display
of angles (0 to 8) <0>: **2** ↵

Direction for angle 0.00:

```
  East    3 o'clock  =  0.00
  North  12 o'clock  =  90.00
  West    9 o'clock  =  180.00
  South   6 o'clock  =  270.00
```

Enter direction for angle 0.00 <0.00>:
*Press Enter*

Do you want angles measured clockwise? <N>
*Press Enter*

By entering **UNITS** at the Command: prompt, you issue the same command you would by selecting UNITS: from the screen menu. If you enter **DDUNITS** at the Command: prompt or choose **U**nits Control from the **S**ettings pull-down menu, AutoCAD displays the AutoCAD Units Control dialog box. The Units Control dialog box appears in an exercise later in this chapter.

# Setting Limits

After you establish your drawing's units, use the Dra**w**ing Limits option from the **S**ettings pull-down menu to set sheet boundaries for your drawing. AutoCAD displays the following prompt to indicate the default location for the lower left corner of the screen:

```
<0'-0.00",0'-0.00">
```

By default, AutoCAD specifies that the lower left boundary of your intended drawing area is X = 0 and Y = 0. You can enter a new lower left corner by assigning new X,Y coordinates. In the following exercise, you accept the default lower left corner by pressing Enter and then enter your estimated limits of 44",34" for the upper right corner.

---

### Setting Limits for an Engineering Drawing Sheet

| | |
|---|---|
| Command: *Choose* **S**ettings, *then* Dra**w**ing Limits | Starts the LIMITS command |
| `'_limits`<br>`Reset Model space limits:`<br>`ON/OFF/<Lower left corner>`<br>`<0'-0.00", 0'-0.00">:` *Press Enter* | Accepts the default location for the lower left corner |
| `Upper right corner <1'-0.00",`<br>`0'-9.00">:` **44",34"** ⏎ | Sets the limits for the upper right corner |

---

You also can issue the LIMITS command by entering **LIMITS** at the Command: prompt or by choosing SETTINGS and then LIMITS: from the screen menu.

Unfortunately, AutoCAD does not insert a border around the drawing area when you set limits manually. You need the border to see the drawing's limits. The following steps solve this problem by setting a drawing grid. A grid is also useful for estimating coordinate values and distances.

## Setting a Grid To Display the Drawing's Limits

| | |
|---|---|
| Command: *Choose* **S**ettings, *then* **D**rawing Aids | Displays the Drawing Aids dialog box |
| *Click the* On *check box in the* **G**rid *area* | Turns on the grid |
| *Double-click in the* X S**p**acing *edit box, then enter* **1**" ↵ | Sets the grid spacing to 1" |
| *Choose* OK | Closes the dialog box and displays the grid |
| Command: *Choose* **V**iew, *then* **Z**oom, *then* **A**ll | Zooms so that limits and the grid cover the drawing area |
| Command: *Press Enter* | Repeats the ZOOM command |
| ZOOM | |
| All/Center/Dynamic/Extents/Left/ Previous/Vmax/Window/ <Scale(X/VP)>: **.75** ↵ | Zooms so that the limits and the grid cover 75 percent of the drawing window |
| Command: *Choose* **F**ile, *then* **S**ave | Saves the drawing as ENGR.DWG |

The grid that appears provides a boundary for your scaled drawing, as shown in figure 3.5.

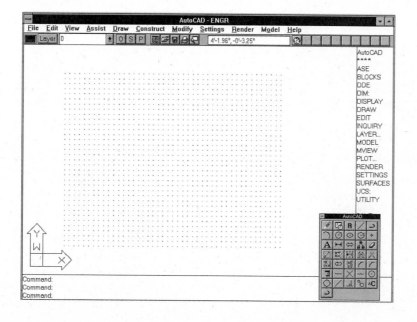

**Figure 3.5:**

The limits shown by a grid.

The area covered by the grid is the defined limits, representing an 8 1/2" × 11" plotting sheet at 1/4" = 1" scale. If you draw outside the grid, you are drawing outside the area that represents the intended plot area. Later in this chapter you learn how to use the Drawing Aids dialog box to set the grid and other drawing settings.

In the preceding exercise, you issued the ZOOM command by selecting the **Z**oom item from the **V**iew pull-down menu. You also can issue the ZOOM command by entering **ZOOM** at the `Command:` prompt or by choosing ZOOM: from the DISPLAY screen menu.

*When you set drawing limits to match your plotting sheet's size, remember that plotters grip a portion of the sheet's edge during plotting. Make sure that your drawing allows enough room at the borders for your plotter. A safe margin is from 1/4" to 1 1/4", depending on the plotter brand and the amount of the paper's edge it grips.*

## Turning On the Limits Warning

You may have noticed the ON/OFF prompt for the LIMITS command. When you turn on limits checking, AutoCAD does not allow you to draw outside the limits. When limits checking is on, AutoCAD checks each point you specify to determine whether the point is within the drawing's established limits. If the point is outside the limits, AutoCAD prevents you from drawing to the point (as in creating a line that passes beyond the limits). The following exercise shows you how to test this capability.

Although your limits represent a plot area of 8 1/2" × 11", they cover 44" × 34" in real-world units. Try drawing a 24-inch diameter circle to represent the manhole cover and see if it fits within your limits.

### Testing Your Drawing Scale Factor and Limits

`Command:` *Choose* **S**ettings, *then*
Dra**w**ing Limits

`_limits`
`Reset Model space limits:`

`ON/OFF/<Lower left corner>`             Turns on limits checking
`<0'-0.00",0'-0.00">:` *From the*
*screen menu, choose* ON

The following steps draw a circle for the outside of the manhole cover:

`Command:` *Choose* **D**raw, *then* **C**ircle,
*then* Center, **R**adius

```
_circle 3P/2P/TTR/<Center point>:
```
*Try to pick a point outside the grid*

```
**Outside limits
```
AutoCAD rejects the point because it is outside the limits

```
3P/2P/TTR/<Center point>: 22,17 ⏎
```
Specifies a center point inside the limits

```
Diameter/<Radius>: 12 ⏎
```
Specifies the circle's radius so that the circle remains within the limits

The manhole should fit neatly on the drawing, as shown in figure 3.6.

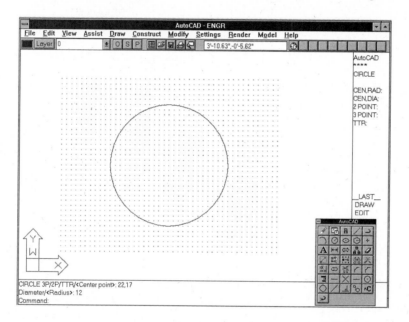

**Figure 3.6:**

A manhole, drawn with a circle.

The **C**ircle selection on the **D**raw pull-down menu displays a cascading menu with several choices, each of which issues the CIRCLE command and the appropriate option for its method of specifying a circle. For example, the Center, **D**iameter menu item issues a CIRCLE command and the Diameter option. You also can issue the CIRCLE command and options from the screen menu by choosing DRAW, then CIRCLE, and then one of the circle options. Enter **CIRCLE** at the Command: prompt to issue the CIRCLE command alone, without options.

# Setting Other Drawing Effects

Other settings, such as text height and symbol scale, are based on your drawing standards. If you have a drawing standard, you should adjust AutoCAD's settings to match your specifications. Just as you set your electronic sheet size to accommodate the manhole cover, you can adjust text, symbols, and line width so that they are in proportion to sheet size. You can easily configure these settings if you have a drawing scale factor. Simply determine the size you want your text, symbols, and other elements to be when the drawing is plotted, then multiply that size by the scale factor.

The following examples are for the manhole cover:

| *Plotted Size* | × | *Scale Factor* | = | *Electronic Size* |
|---|---|---|---|---|
| 0.2" Text height | × | 4 | = | 0.8" |
| 1/2" Bubble | × | 4 | = | 2" diameter (or 1" radius) |
| 1/16" Line width | × | 4 | = | 1/4" |

AutoCAD also provides a variety of linetypes, such as hidden and dashed. You adjust linetypes by using the LTSCALE command to set the correct scale factor for the desired linetype. Like text and symbols, LTSCALE should be set for the plotted appearance, not how it looks on the screen. Linetype scale is largely a matter of personal preference, but setting it to your scale factor is a good starting point. Linetype selection is discussed in detail later in this chapter.

The following exercise shows you how to add scaled text, a bubble callout (the number 1 in a circle), and a circle (the inner lip of the manhole) to your manhole cover. In the exercise, you use a hidden linetype to add the circle to your drawing.

## Setting Text Height, Symbol Size, and Linetype Scale

| | |
|---|---|
| Command: *Choose* **V**iew, *then* **Z**oom, *then* **A**ll | Zooms to the grid and limits |
| Command: *From the toolbar, click on the* S *button* | Turns on snap |
| Command: *Choose* **D**raw, *then* **T**ext, *then* **D**ynamic | |
| _dtext Justify/Style/<Start point>: **M** ↵ | Specifies Middle text justification |
| Middle point: **23,3** ↵ | |
| Height <0'-0.20">: **.8** ↵ | |
| Rotation angle <0.00>: *Press Enter* | |

Text: **MANHOLE COVER** ↵

Move the text cursor by using the coordinate display to pick the point 1'-3.00",0'-3.00".

Text: **1** ↵

Text: *Press Enter*                          Ends the DTEXT command

Command: *Choose* **D**raw, *then* **C**ircle,
*then* Center, **R**adius

_circle 3P/2P/TTR/<Center point>:
**15,3** ↵

Diameter/<Radius>: **1** ↵

Before drawing the inner lip, set the current linetype to HIDDEN.

Command: *From the screen menu, choose*        Starts the LINETYPE command
AutoCAD, *then* SETTINGS,
*then* LINETYP:

'_LINETYPE

?/Create/Load/Set: **L** ↵                  Specifies the Load option

Linetype(s) to load: **HIDDEN** ↵          Displays the Select Linetype File dialog box

*Press Enter*                            Loads the HIDDEN linetype from ACAD.LIN

Linetype HIDDEN loaded

?/Create/Load/Set: **S** ↵

New entity linetype (or ?)                 Sets to HIDDEN linetype
<BYLAYER>: **HIDDEN** ↵

?/Create/Load/Set: *Press Enter*

Command: *Choose* **D**raw, *then* **C**ircle,
*then* Center, **R**adius *and draw a circle*
*at 22,17 with an 11" radius*

The circle has a hidden linetype, but you need to adjust the linetype scale to see it.

Command: **LTSCALE** ↵                     Issues the LTSCALE command

New scale factor <1.0000>: **4** ↵         Sets the linetype scale to the drawing's scale
factor

Regenerating drawing.

The partially completed manhole with text, a bubble, and an inner lip should look like
the drawing in figure 3.7.

**Figure 3.7:**

The manhole
with text, symbol,
and a linetype.

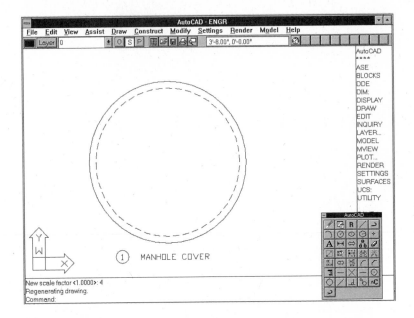

Like the LINETYPE command, the LTSCALE command also appears on the screen menu (choose SETTINGS, then next, then LTSCALE:), or you can enter **LINETYPE** or **LTSCALE** at the Command: prompt to access these commands. You can make a linetype active by using the Set option under the LINETYPE command or as part of the LAYER command. The Entity Creation Modes dialog box also enables selection of linetypes. It can be accessed by clicking on the color box in the toolbar.

As you can see from the exercise, after you calculate a drawing scale factor for your drawing's plot scale and sheet size and you calculate the drawing's limits, it is relatively simple to adjust text height and linetype scale proportionally to that drawing scale factor. The important thing to remember is that this drawing scale factor does not scale the drawing in AutoCAD; you still draw things full-size. The scale is only a factor that you apply to individual commands to size symbols, linetypes, and text appropriately for their eventual plotted output.

*A linetype scale of 0.3 to 0.5 times your drawing scale factor usually yields the best plotted output, but it may not be visually distinguishable on screen. You may need to set a linetype scale for drawing and later reset it for plotting.*

If you have a printer (or plotter) installed on your system and you have AutoCAD configured for that printer (see your *Installation and Performance Guide* or Appendix A), take a moment to make a quick plot before continuing. If you do not have a printer available, skip to the section on layers.

# Making a Quick Plot

If you have a printer configured in AutoCAD, the following exercise enables you to print a hard copy of the manhole drawing. Do not be too concerned about the plotting sequence; it is explained in detail in the plotting chapter. The plot shows how all the calculations that you made provide a plotted drawing at 1/4-inch scale. The following exercise reflects settings for an HP LaserJet printer, but works for any 8 1/2" × 11" or larger printer or plotter. Figure 3.8 shows the Plot Configuration dialog box, which you use in the following exercise to specify plot options.

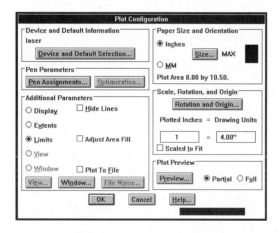

**Figure 3.8:**

The Plot Configuration dialog box.

---

## Making a Quick Plot

Command: *Choose* **F**ile, *then* **P**rint/Plot

Displays the Plot Configuration dialog box (see fig. 3.8)

*Click on the* **L**imits *radio button in the* Additional Parameters *area*

*Double-click on the number in the* Plotted Inches *edit box in the* Scale, Rotation, and Origin *area, and then enter* **1**

*continues*

*Double-click on the number in the Drawing*    Specifies a plot scale of 1:4
*Units edit box, then enter* **4**

*Choose* OK

```
Command: _plot
```

```
Effective plotting area:  10.50 wide x 8.00 high. Position paper in plotter.
Press RETURN to continue or S to Stop for hardware setup
```

*Press Enter*                                Starts the plot

```
Regeneration done 100%
```                              Displays progress

```
Plot complete
```

After you issue the preceding commands, your plotted output should resemble the manhole in figure 3.9.

**Figure 3.9:**

A 1/4-scale plot of the manhole.

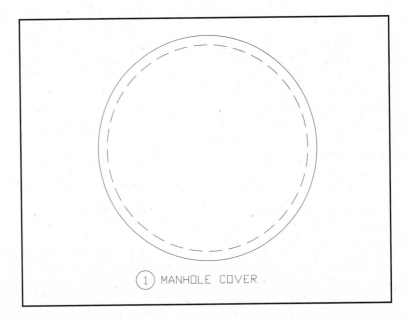

The right side of the plot may be cropped and your plotting area may differ from that shown in the exercise, depending on the size of your printer or plotter. Nevertheless, you should be able to apply a drafting scale to your printout and measure a 24" circle at 1/4 scale and 0.2"-high text with a 0.25" bubble.

When beginning a new drawing, AutoCAD has defaults that enable you to start drawing immediately. A wise practice, however, is to start by first setting up drawing parameters, such as units and limits. Layering of entities also is important when creating a drawing with a well-organized database. The next section shows you how to set up layers, as well as other important drawing elements.

# Setting Up Layers, Colors, and Linetypes

In the following exercise, you begin a new drawing by using engineering units and limits for an 8 1/2" × 11" sheet with a drawing scale factor of 1 (full scale). In this exercise, you use the Units Control dialog box (DDUNITS command) rather than the UNITS command. In this drawing, you create a new list of layers, and you set colors and linetypes by using the Layer Control dialog box.

## Setting Up Units and Limits

| | |
|---|---|
| Command: **NEW** ↵ | Opens the Create New Drawing dialog box |
| *Enter* **CHAPTER3** ↵ | Begins a new drawing |
| Command: *Choose* **S**ettings, *then* **U**nits Control | Displays the Units Control dialog box |
| *Choose the* **E**ngineering *radio button, then the* **P**recision *pop-up list box in the* Units *area, then* 0.00 | Specifies Engineering units, 2 places accuracy |
| *Choose the* Deci**m**al Degrees *radio button, then the* Precisio**n** *pop-up list box in the* Angles *area, then* 0.00 | Specifies Decimal angular measurement |
| *Choose* OK | Closes the dialog box |
| Command: *Choose* **S**ettings, *then* Dra**w**ing Limits | |
| `'_limits`<br>`Reset Model Space limits` | |
| `ON/OFF/<Lower left corner`<br>`<0'-0.00",0'-0.00">`: *Press Enter* | Defaults to 0,0 |
| `Upper right corner <1'-0.00",`<br>`0'-9.00">`:**11,8.5** ↵ | |
| Command: **Z** ↵ | Issues the ZOOM command |

*continues*

```
ZOOM All/Center/Dynamic/Extents/        Performs a ZOOM All
Left/Previous/Vmax/Window/
<Scale(X/XP)>: A ↵

Regenerating drawing.
```

Command: *Choose* **F***ile, then* **S***ave*        Saves the drawing as CHAPTER3.DWG

The drawing is ready for the next exercise, in which you learn how to set up layers.

## Understanding Layers

Layers help you control and organize your drawing. If your drawing becomes too dense or complicated, you can turn off selected layers so that they do not interfere with your work. If you later need to draw certain parts that you did not anticipate, you can create new layers for those parts.

As described earlier in this chapter, layers are comparable to overlay drafting on transparent sheets. You create your drawing by building it on a family of sheets (layers). Each layer has a name, a default color, and a linetype. You can work on any layer. Although editing commands such as ERASE work on any number of layers at once, you can draw on only one layer at a time. The layer you currently are using is called the *current* layer. When you draw an entity, it is attached to the current layer. The current layer name is displayed near the left of the toolbar, as shown in figure 3.10. The new drawing you started in the preceding exercise uses layer 0—the default layer from the ACAD.DWG prototype drawing—as the current layer.

**Figure 3.10:**

The current layer's name, displayed in the toolbar.

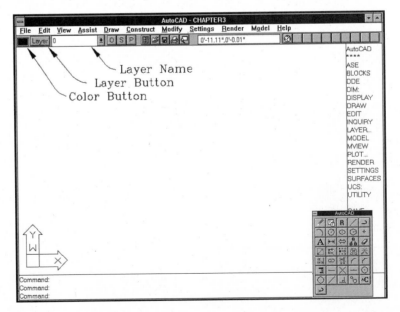

The Layer Control dialog box, which appears in figure 3.11, contains every available tool for defining and setting up new layers. You can modify the properties of existing layers separately or in groups. This dialog box is important if you need to create drawings to specific layering standards or if you want to control the drawing display and plotted output. You can access the Layer Control dialog box in one of four ways:

- Choose the **S**ettings pull-down menu, then choose the **L**ayer Control option.

- Enter the DDLMODES command at the `Command:` prompt.

- Choose LAYER from the screen menu.

- Click on the Layer button in the toolbar.

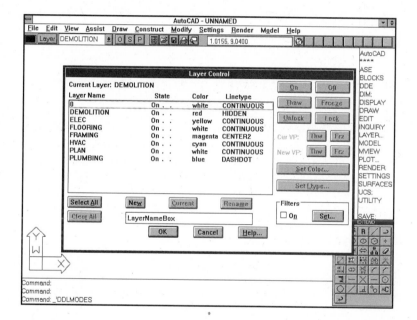

**Figure 3.11:**

The Layer Control dialog box.

To use the dialog box transparently, use the menus or enter '**DDLMODES** in the middle of another command. If you change settings transparently, however, the changes may not affect all current commands. You also can change layer settings by using the LAYER command, which is discussed later in this chapter.

In the Layer Control dialog box, layer 0 is shown with AutoCAD's default drawing properties: white, continuous lines. Layer 0 is fine for experimenting, and it has some special properties that are explained later, but for most drawing work you should set up your own layers.

# Understanding Layering Conventions

Like other drawing parameters, layer setup is a matter of standard practice and style. Layers are most often used to separate different types of objects in your drawing. You may place drawing components on one layer, for example, and their dimensions on another layer. Try to anticipate the types of layers that you want to separate. The following list shows a sample set of layers:

| Objects on Layer | Layer Name |
| --- | --- |
| Components | OBJ01 |
| Dimensions | DIM01 |
| Symbols/Annotations | ANN01 |
| Text | TXT01 |
| Title Sheets | REF01 |

You can create an unlimited number of layers, but for most applications, 10 to 20 layers is more than enough. When you name your layers, it helps to apply DOS-style naming conventions and use wild cards to organize them. Layer names can be up to 31 characters long, but the toolbar shows only the first 8 characters. You can use letters, digits, dollar signs ($), hyphens (-), and underscore (_) characters in your layer names. AutoCAD converts all layer names to uppercase.

Many different layer-naming schemes are currently in use. Some code the color, linetype, and line weight. Others specify the trade and work location, such as ARCH-FLR01 or ELEC-CLG03. One popular convention codes layers with the Construction Specifications Institute (CSI) material code. Whatever scheme you use, remember three things:

1. Coordinate with anyone with whom you may be trading drawings, such as consultants and subcontractors.

2. Whatever types of information you code in your names, always put the same type of information in the same column (character position) so that you can select groups of layers by using wild cards. If you use a layer-naming scheme of ARCH-FLR01 and ARCH-FLR03, for example, you can select all floor plan layers by using the wild cards ????-FLR?? or all architectural layers by using ARCH*. If you name the second floor A-2NDFLR, however, you cannot select it with the same wild cards.

3. Make the scheme expandable, so that it accommodates growth. When you draw a three-story building, for example, use two characters for floor numbers so that the naming scheme is compatible with the 33-story building you design a year later.

Autodesk has even attempted to coordinate all the registered third-party software developers with layer-naming guidelines that prohibit different packages from interfering with each other when used on the same project.

For more information and recommendations on layer-naming schemes, see *Managing and Networking AutoCAD*, by New Riders Publishing.

# Using the Layer Control Dialog Box

You must instruct AutoCAD to draw on the proper layer. You can use the Layer Control dialog box to create layers, to control which layers of the drawing are displayed, and to determine which layer becomes the current drawing layer. The LAYER command and the Layer Control (DDLMODES) dialog box set the following properties for the specified layer or layers:

- **Current.** This property makes the specified layer the current layer; new entities are then placed on this layer.

- **On.** This property makes the layer visible.

- **Off.** This property makes the layer invisible.

- **Color.** This property defines a single default color so that anything drawn on the specified layer is the specified color, unless an entity color overrides it.

- **Ltype.** This property defines a single default linetype for the specified layer. Lines (and other drawing elements) drawn on the specified layer take on the default linetype unless you override it.

- **Freeze.** This property makes the layer invisible so that AutoCAD ignores all the layer's entities during regeneration. This setting increases the performance of AutoCAD searches and displays.

- **Thaw.** This property unfreezes layers.

- **Lock.** This property changes the layer property so that it is visible, but the entities cannot be altered or deleted.

- **Unlock.** This property restores a locked layer back to its original state.

The ability to freeze and thaw layers by viewports also is available and is covered in Chapter 5's discussion of paper space.

# Creating New Layers

The drawing file you created earlier has only one layer. In the following exercise, you define several more layers, change the default parameters, and then save them for future use. The target layers are shown in table 3.1.

## Table 3.1
## Layer Configuration Table

| Layer Name | State | Color | Linetype |
| --- | --- | --- | --- |
| 0 | On | 7 (White) | CONTINUOUS |
| CIRCLE | On | 3 (Green) | CONTINUOUS |
| PARAGRAM | On | 6 (Magenta) | CONTINUOUS |
| SQUARE | On | 2 (Yellow) | CONTINUOUS |
| TEXT | On | 4 (Cyan) | CONTINUOUS |
| TRIANGLE | On | 1 (Red) | CONTINUOUS |

When you create new layers in the Layer Control dialog box, you can enter several names if they are separated by commas without spaces.

## Creating New Layers

Command: *From the toolbar, click on the* Layer *button*    Displays the Layer Control dialog box

*Type* **CIRCLE,PARAGRAM,SQUARE, TEXT,TRIANGLE**

*Choose the* Ne**w** *button*    Creates the new layers, named CIRCLE, PARAGRAM, SQUARE, TEXT, and TRIANGLE

The layer information should now appear in the dialog box, as shown in figure 3.12. Because you did not set any properties for the new layers, AutoCAD automatically set them with the same defaults as layer 0. Each layer is color 7 (white) with a continuous linetype.

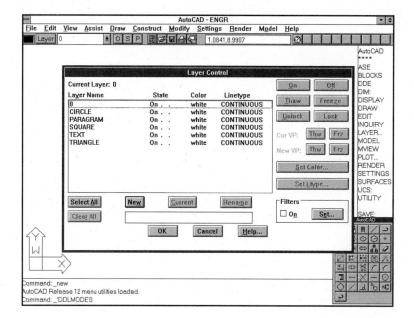

**Figure 3.12:**
The newly
defined layers, as
shown in the
Layer Control
dialog box.

## Understanding Layer Color

A layer has only one color, but several layers can have the same color. Color is assigned to layers by names or numbers (up to 255 different colors). Colors commonly are used to assign plotting line weights to objects in the drawing. AutoCAD uses the following naming and numbering conventions for seven standard colors:

| Color Number | Color |
| --- | --- |
| 1 | Red |
| 2 | Yellow |
| 3 | Green |
| 4 | Cyan |
| 5 | Blue |
| 6 | Magenta |
| 7 | White |

*Colors with numbers higher than 7 do not have names, and their availability depends on your video card and display. You can see colors with numbers higher than 7 by loading the CHROMA or COLORWH drawings from the AutoCAD SAMPLE disk (and probably from the SUPPORT directory). You also can see CHROMA by viewing the slide named ACAD(CHROMA). The VSLIDE command is explained in Chapter 22.*

## Modifying Layer Properties

You can easily change layer properties by using the Layer Control dialog box. The **O**n and O**ff** buttons and the **T**haw and Free**z**e buttons control the visibility of the currently selected layer(s). The **S**et Color and Set **L**type buttons display child dialog boxes (see fig. 3.13), which assign color and linetype to the selected layers. The **C**urrent button makes a single selected layer current. (Chapter 5 discusses the use of the Cur VP Thw and Frz and New VP Thw and Frz buttons.) You must select a layer before you can modify its properties. To select or deselect a layer, click on the layer's name in the list box. You can select or deselect all the drawing's layers at the same time by clicking on the Select **A**ll and Clea**r** All buttons.

The Select Color dialog box enables you to graphically select colors for layers. You can click on a color box to select a color, or enter its name in the Color edit box. The Select Linetype dialog box enables you to graphically select a linetype to assign to a layer. As with the Select Color dialog box, you also can enter the linetype by name in the **L**inetype edit box.

**Figure 3.13:**

The Select Color and Select Linetype dialog boxes.

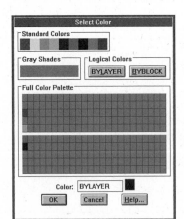

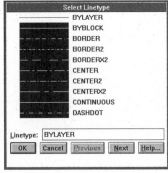

## Setting Layer Color

In the following exercise, you set the layer colors in your drawing.

---

### Setting Layer Colors

Continue from the preceding exercise with the Layer Control dialog box open.

| | |
|---|---|
| *Click on* CIRCLE *in the* La**y**er *name list box, then choose* **S**et Color | Selects the CIRCLE layer and displays the Select Color dialog box |
| *Click on the green box in the* Standard *area, then choose* OK | Changes CIRCLE's color to green in the Layer Control dialog box list |
| *Click on* CIRCLE | Deselects the layer |

Repeat this process by selecting each layer and then setting its color to match the colors listed in figure 3.14.

| | |
|---|---|
| *Click on the* OK *button* | Saves the new layer and color settings and exits from the Layer Control dialog box |

---

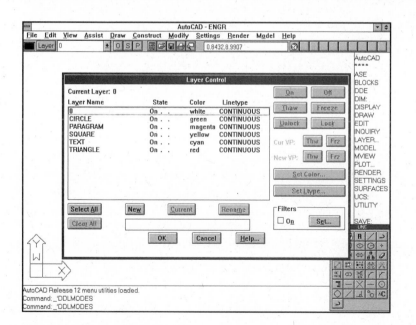

**Figure 3.14:**

The Layer Control dialog box with new color settings.

You also can specify a color in the Select Color dialog box by entering its name or number in the Color edit box.

## Setting Layer Linetype

If you use the LAYER command to set linetypes, they are automatically loaded from the ACAD.LIN file, which contains AutoCAD's linetype definitions. Before the linetypes can be displayed and selected in the Layer Control dialog box, however, they must be loaded. You can use the Load option from the LINETYP: command on the SETTINGS screen menu to load ACAD.LIN, which usually resides in the SUPPORT subdirectory. Until you learn the individual names, it is easiest to specify files by using the asterisk wild-card character (*), which loads all linetypes. Figure 3.15 shows the standard linetypes.

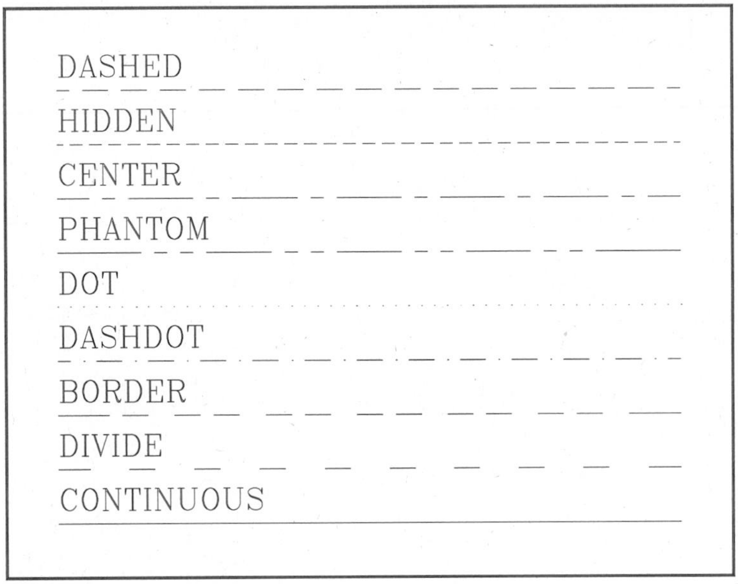

**Figure 3.15:**

AutoCAD's
standard linetypes.

DASHED

HIDDEN

CENTER

PHANTOM

DOT

DASHDOT

BORDER

DIVIDE

CONTINUOUS

Each of the linetypes has corresponding double-scale and half-scale linetypes, such as DASHED2 for a half-scale dashed line and DASHEDX2 for a double-scale dashed line. The half-scale linetypes all end in 2 and the double-scale linetypes end in X2.

In the following exercise, you load and set new layer linetypes.

### Setting Layer Linetypes

Command: *From the screen menu, choose*
SETTINGS, *then* LINETYP:, *then* Load

_LINETYPE ?/Create/Load/Set: _LOAD

| | |
|---|---|
| `Linetype(s) to load: * ↵` | Specifies all linetypes and displays the Select Linetype File dialog box |
| *Choose* OK | Specifies the file \ACADWIN\SUPPORT\ ACAD.LIN |
| `Linetype BORDER loaded.`<br>`Linetype BORDER2 loaded.`<br>`Linetype BORDERX2 loaded.`<br>`Linetype CENTER loaded.`<br>`Linetype CENTER2 loaded.`<br>`Linetype CENTERX2 loaded.`<br>`Linetype DASHDOT loaded.`<br>`Linetype DASHDOT2 loaded.`<br>`Linetype DASHDOTX2 loaded.`<br>`Linetype DASHED loaded.`<br>`Linetype DASHED2 loaded.`<br>`Linetype DASHEDX2 loaded.`<br>`Linetype DIVIDE loaded.`<br>`Linetype DIVIDE2 loaded.`<br>`Linetype DIVIDEX2 loaded.`<br>`Linetype DOT loaded.`<br>`Linetype DOT2 loaded.`<br>`Linetype DOTX2 loaded.`<br>`Linetype HIDDEN loaded.`<br>`Linetype HIDDEN2 loaded.`<br>`Linetype HIDDENX2 loaded.`<br>`Linetype PHANTOM loaded.`<br>`Linetype PHANTOM2 loaded.`<br>`Linetype PHANTOMX2 loaded.` | AutoCAD reports its progress as it loads the new linetypes |
| `?/Create/Load/Set:` *Press Enter* | Ends the LINETYPE command |
| `Command:` *From the toolbar, click on the* Layer *button* | Displays the Modify Layer dialog box |
| *Click on* CIRCLE, *then choose* Set **L**type | Displays the Select Linetype box |
| *Choose* **N**ext, *click on the* DASHED *linetype example, then choose* OK | Assigns the dashed linetype to the CIRCLE layer |

Choose Clea**r** All, then repeat this process to assign a HIDDEN linetype to the PARAGRAM layer. The layer settings will match those in figure 3.16.

| | |
|---|---|
| *Choose* OK | Saves new layer and linetype settings |
| `Command:` *From the toolbar, choose* QSAVE | Saves the drawing |

**Figure 3.16:**

The Layer Control
dialog box with
new linetype
settings.

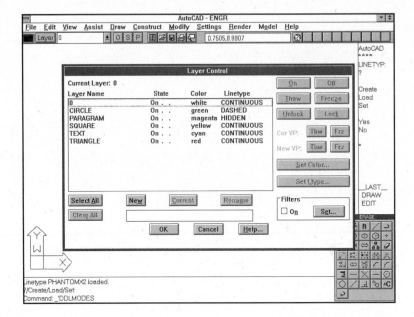

*You can create your own custom linetypes by using the LINETYPE
command. See Chapter 14 or* Maximizing AutoCAD Release 12
*for details.*

You now have a complete set of layers. You can modify their other properties by
choosing the layers and selecting the appropriate buttons in the Layer Control dialog
box.

## Choosing the Current Layer

As you learned earlier, the current drawing layer name always appears near the left
end of the toolbar. To make a different drawing layer active, click on the layer name in
the toolbar and a pop-up list enables you to select another layer name. Or, open the
Layer Control dialog box and select only that layer, then click on the **C**urrent button to
make that layer current. After you click on the OK button to exit from the dialog box,
that new current layer's name appears in the status line.

You can change layer settings at any time while you work in the drawing. If you alter
the properties of layers (such as linetype or color), AutoCAD regenerates the drawing
window to reflect these changes when you exit from the LAYER command.

# Making Layers Invisible

In the exercise that follows, you learn how to turn a layer off and then on again. If you turn off the current layer, AutoCAD prompts you to reconfirm the action. Remember that you have to see what you are drawing!

Follow the steps to draw a square with lines, and then turn the SQUARE layer off and on.

---

## Setting a Current Layer and Layer Visibility

| | |
|---|---|
| **Command:** *From the toolbar, click on the layer name* | Shows the pop-up list of layer names |
| *Select* SQUARE | Displays current layer SQUARE in the layer name box |
| **Command:** *Choose* **D**raw, *then* **L**ine, *then* **S**egments, *and draw a square in the upper left corner of the drawing area (see fig. 3.17)* | |
| **Command:** *Click on the* Layer *button, select* SQUARE, *click on* O**ff**, *then* OK | Warns that the current layer is turned off |
| *Click on* OK | Accepts the warning and the square disappears |
| **Command:** *Press Enter* | Redisplays the dialog box |
| *Select* SQUARE, *choose* **O**n, *then* OK | Turns the SQUARE layer back on |

---

*If you are drawing but you cannot see anything happening, make sure that you have not turned off the current layer.*

You also can make a layer invisible by freezing it. When a layer is frozen, the entities on it do not display, regenerate, or print. This arrangement means that your drawing refreshes more quickly after you invoke a command (such as ZOOM) that requires a regeneration. The disadvantage of freezing layers is that layers have to regenerate when you thaw them. The thawing process takes a little longer to perform. For this reason, freeze layers only when you know you do not need to display, regenerate, or print the frozen layer for a while.

**Figure 3.17:**

A drawn square and the current layer's name in the toolbar.

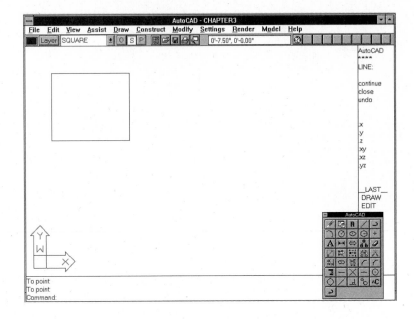

## Locking Layers

Another nice feature to use with layered entities is the Lock option. The Lock option enables you to view the locked layer's entities but not select them for editing. In a complex drawing, you can lock the layers that are not being used, making entity selection much easier. Also, when you give a drawing file to another person for reference or review, you can lock some layers to avoid unwanted changes. The Unlock option unlocks selected layers that have been locked.

## Using the LAYER Command

Although the dialog box usually is easier to use, you can use the LAYER command to create layer names, set color and linetype, control layer visibility, and display layer status. The LAYER command displays the following prompt:

```
?/Make/Set/New/ON/OFF/Color/Ltype/Freeze/Thaw/LOck/Unlock:
```

The ON, OFF, Color, Ltype, Freeze, Thaw, LOck, and Unlock options offer the same settings as their Layer Control dialog box counterparts. The Make option creates a new layer and makes it the current layer. The New option creates new layers. With the New, ON, OFF, Color, Ltype, Freeze, Thaw, LOck, and Unlock options, you can enter multiple layer names separated by commas. The Set option sets the layer you specify as the new current layer. Try using the LAYER command to experiment with setting layers. You can access the LAYER command by entering **LAYER** at the `Command:` prompt.

# Testing Drawing Layer Properties

In the last few exercises, you created a working drawing file that uses real units, limits, and a foundation of layers. How do you know that all these layers work? You just saw the yellow square on the SQUARE layer. In the following exercise, you make the CIRCLE layer current and draw a circle to see how entities adopt other layer settings. After drawing the circle, you save the drawing by naming it to a new file called WORK. This drawing is used as the prototype drawing in the next chapter on drawing accuracy. After saving the drawing near the end of the exercise, you use the LAYER command to change the color of the CIRCLE layer to blue, then enter **U** to undo the change.

## Testing Layers and Saving the WORK Drawing

Continue from the preceding exercise, in the CHAPTER3 drawing.

| | |
|---|---|
| Command: **LAYER** ↵ | Starts the LAYER command |
| Command: LAYER ?/Make/Set/New/ON/ OFF/Color/Ltype/Freeze/Thaw/ LOck/Unlock: | Tells AutoCAD that you want to set a new current layer |
| *From the screen menu, choose* Set | |
| SET New current layer <SQUARE>: **CIRCLE** ↵ | |
| ?/Make/Set/New/ON/OFF/Color/Ltype/ Freeze/Thaw/LOck/Unlock: *Press Enter* | Makes CIRCLE the current layer |
| Command: *Choose* **D**raw, *then* **C**ircle, *then* Center, **R**adius, *and pick two points, placing the circle in upper right corner of the drawing* | |
| Command: *Choose* **F**ile, *then* Save **A**s, *and enter* **WORK** ↵ | Saves the file with the name WORK.DWG |
| Command: **LAYER** ↵ | |
| Command: ?/Make/Set/New/ON/OFF/ Color/Ltype/Freeze/Thaw/LOck/Unlock: *From the screen menu, choose* Color | Specifies the Color option |
| Color: **BLUE** ↵ | Specifies blue |
| Layer name(s) for color 5 (blue) <CIRCLE>: *Press Enter* | Makes the circle blue |
| ?/Make/Set/New/ON/OFF/Color/Ltype/ Freeze/Thaw/LOck/Unlock: *Press Enter* | Ends the command |
| Command: **U** ↵ | Undoes the color change |
| LAYER | |

After you draw the circle, your drawing should look like figure 3.18. You should have a yellow square and a green dashed circle.

**Figure 3.18:**

The square and circle on their respective layers.

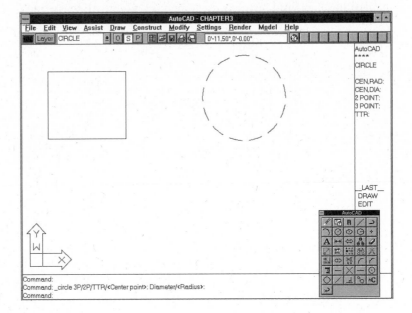

You also can make all layer settings and create new layers by using the LAYER command.

As the next section explains, you do not have to use layers to control all the properties of all your entities. You can just as easily modify the color and linetype properties associated with individual drawing entities.

# Setting Color and Linetype by Entity

You have seen how to control an entity's color or linetype by drawing it on an appropriate layer. You also can set color and linetype explicitly by overriding the layer's defaults and setting an individual entity's color and linetype. You must use separate commands to make these individual changes.

You can use the Entity Creation Modes dialog box (the DDEMODES command) to control the current entity color, linetype, and layer settings. The dialog box appears in figure 3.19. The **C**olor and **L**inetype buttons display the same Select Color and Select Linetype child dialog boxes as the Layer Control dialog box. The **L**ayer button displays a Layer Control dialog box, in which you can review layer settings or double-click on a layer to make it current.

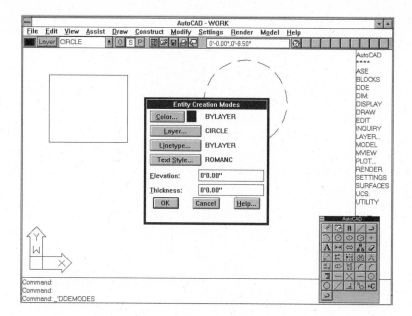

**Figure 3.19:**

The Entity Creation Modes dialog box.

To display the Entity Creation Modes dialog box, you can enter **DDEMODES** at the Command: prompt, click on the color box in the toolbar, or you can choose **E**ntity Modes from the **S**ettings pull-down menu. You also can choose SETTINGS and then DDEMODES from the screen menu. To use the dialog box transparently, you can use the menus or enter '**DDEMODES** while another command is active. You may use the COLOR and LINETYPE commands to ensure that an entity receives the color and linetype you want.

*Before you use linetypes from the Select Linetype dialog box, they must be loaded into the drawing. You can do this with the Load option of the LINETYPE command, or by using the drag-and-drop method. Follow this procedure to load linetypes using the drag-and-drop method:*

*1. Open a window containing the Windows File Manager.*

*2. Click on the ACAD.LIN file in the SUPPORT directory.*

*3. Drag the icon into the AutoCAD window (or icon), and release.*

*Any transparent changes you make to settings may not affect all current commands.*

# Understanding Entity Colors

You can use the Entity Creation Modes dialog box to control the current entity color, linetype, and layer settings. You also can use the COLOR command to ensure that an entity receives the color you want. If you use the COLOR command to set the default entity color to a specific color (rather than by layer), the subsequently created entities take on *explicit* colors. Explicit colors are not affected by the entity's layer or by changes to the layer. When you create a new entity, AutoCAD assigns the current entity color setting to the new entity. When you change the current entity color, it does not affect entities that already exist—only entities that are created after you set the color.

You can set an individual entity's color to any valid color name or number. (Remember, you can have 1 to 255 colors, but only the first 7 have names.) By default, AutoCAD sets colors by layer. When color is set to BYLAYER, AutoCAD does not store new entities with a specific color. Instead, it gives new entities the color property according to layer, which causes any new entity to adopt the color that is assigned to its layer.

*Another color setting is the BYBLOCK color. Chapter 11 covers BYBLOCK assignments.*

Take a look at the color settings in your new drawing. Then, take the following steps to change the color to red by using the Entity Creation Modes dialog box, as shown in figure 3.19. You can see in the exercise that the default color is set to BYLAYER. After you change the color, you draw another circle to see how the explicit color settings override the layer setting.

---

## Using the Entity Creation Modes Dialog Box

Continue with the WORK drawing from the preceding exercise.

| | |
|---|---|
| Command: *Choose* **S**ettings, *then* **E**ntity Modes | Displays the Entity Creation Modes dialog box |
| *Choose the* **C**olor *button* | Brings up the Select Color dialog box |
| *Click on box 1* (RED) *then* OK | Sets the current color to red and exits from the Select Color dialog box |
| *Click on* OK | Exits from the Entity Creation Modes dialog box |

Command: *Choose* **D**raw, *then* **C**ircle, *then*      Draws a circle
Center, **R**adius, *and pick two points below*
*the first circle*

Your drawing should show a red dashed circle, in addition to the green dashed circle and yellow square, as shown in figure 3.20.

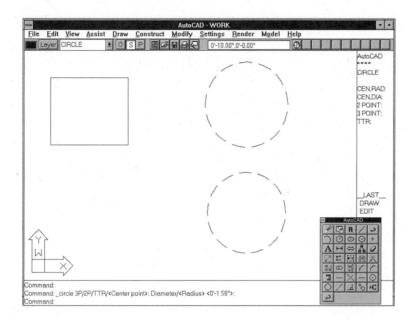

**Figure 3.20:**

A second circle added to the drawing.

In the preceding exercise, you used the pull-down menus to set the current color. The quickest method of accessing the Entity Creation Modes dialog box is by clicking on the color button located at the left side of the toolbar. If you prefer, you can enter **COLOR** at the Command: prompt or choose SETTINGS, then COLOR: from the screen menu. You simply enter a new entity color at the COLOR command's New entity color <BYLAYER>: prompt.

# Understanding Entity Linetypes

After reading about entity colors, you might guess that linetype settings have a similar control. Take a look at the L**i**netype option in the Entity Creation Modes dialog box. This option enables you to set an explicit linetype that overrides the layer's default for all entities that you create after you change the setting. You also can set the linetype to BYLAYER, so that new entities use the layer's default linetype.

The linetype choices are displayed in the Select Linetype dialog box, as shown in figure 3.21. A sample of the highlighted linetype appears in the box. The next exercise shows you how to change the linetype setting independently of the layer setting.

**Figure 3.21:**

The Select Linetype dialog box.

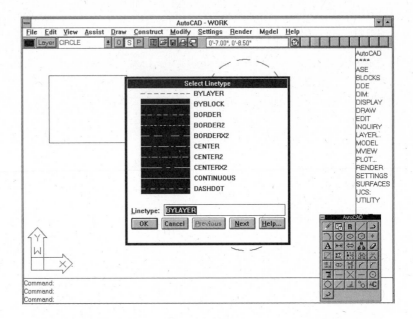

## Setting Entity Linetypes

Continue with the WORK drawing from the preceding exercise.

| | |
|---|---|
| Command: *Choose* Settings, *then* Entity Modes, *then* Linetype | Displays the Entity Creation Modes and Select Linetype dialog boxes |
| *Click on* CONTINUOUS, *then* OK, *then click on* OK *again* | Sets the current linetype to continuous and exits from both dialog boxes |
| Command: *Choose* Draw, *then* Circle, *then* Center, Radius, *and pick two points beneath the square* | Draws another circle |

You should have three circles. The last one is drawn with a red continuous line, even though it is on the CIRCLE layer, which is set to green with dashed lines. (Remember that you changed the individual entity color to red in the previous exercise.) The drawing should now look like the sample in figure 3.22.

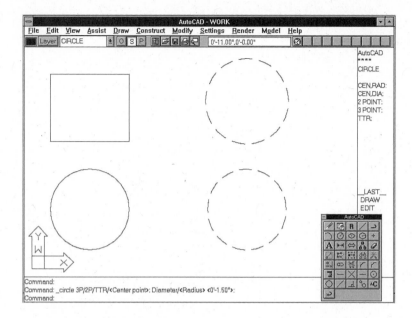

**Figure 3.22:**
The third circle with the continuous linetype.

You also can use the LINETYPE command to set the current linetype; enter **LINETYPE** at the Command: prompt or choose SETTINGS, then LINETYP: from the screen menu. The LINETYPE command displays the following prompt:

    ?/Create/Load/Set:

You can load linetypes, as you did earlier. To load the linetypes, you can enter a **?** to list linetypes, create new linetypes, or enter an **S** to set a new current linetype. To set a new current linetype, enter its name at the New entity linetype <current linetype>: prompt, which appears when you select the Set option.

*Explicit color and linetype settings stay in effect, even when you change current layers. You should not mix explicit color and linetype settings with layer settings, or the drawing may become too confusing. Try to stick with one system of control, with few exceptions.*

# Changing Entity Properties

The COLOR and LINETYPE commands change the properties only for new entities that are drawn after you change the color and linetype settings. But you also can change the properties of existing entities. To do so, you can use the CHPROP (CHange

PROPerties) command. After you select the objects whose properties you want to change, AutoCAD asks which properties you want to modify. You can use CHPROP to change the following properties:

- Color
- Layer
- Linetype
- Thickness

Thickness is a property associated with 3D entities. You can read more about thickness in Chapter 20.

In the following exercise, you use CHPROP to change a circle's layer and color.

## Using CHPROP To Change Layer and Color

`Command:` *From the screen menu,*
*choose* AutoCAD, *then* EDIT, *then* CHPROP:

`CHPROP Select objects:` *Select the green circle (the first circle)*

`1 found.`

| | |
|---|---|
| `Select objects:` *Press Enter* | Ends object selection |
| `Change what property (Color/LAyer/LType/Thickness) ?` *From the screen menu, choose* LAyer | |
| `New layer <CIRCLE>:` **SQUARE** ⏎ | Gives the circle the properties of the SQUARE layer |
| `Change what property (Color/LAyer/LType/Thickness) ?` *From the screen menu, choose* Color | |
| `COLOR New color <BYLAYER>:` *From the screen menu, choose* red | Specifies the color red |
| `Change what property (Color/LAyer/LType/Thickness) ?` *Press Enter* | Turns the circle red |

Like many other commands in AutoCAD, you can issue the CHPROP command by typing it or by choosing it from the screen or pull-down menu. You also can use a dialog box to change properties.

## Using a Dialog Box To Change Properties

When you choose the **M**odify pull-down menu, then **C**hange, then **P**roperties, the Change Properties dialog box appears if entities have previously been selected. (You also can enter **DDCHPROP** at the Command: prompt to display the dialog box.) If you have not yet created a selection set, DDCHPROP prompts you to select objects, then displays the dialog box after the objects are selected. The next exercise demonstrates the use of the DDCHPROP command. Figure 3.23 shows the Change Properties dialog box.

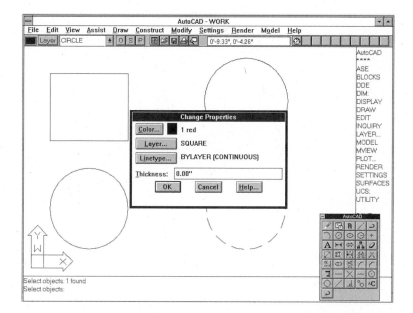

**Figure 3.23:**

The Change Properties dialog box.

## Using DDCHPROP To Change Entity Properties

Command: *Choose* **M**odify, *then* **C**hange, *then* **P**roperties

Starts the DDCHPROP command

Select objects: *Pick the red, hidden circle*

1 found

Select objects: *Press Enter*

Opens the Change Properties dialog box

*Choose* **C**olor, *then click on the magenta color box, then on* OK

Selects magenta

*Click on* OK

Makes the circle magenta

Command: **U** ↵

Undoes the change

The DDCHPROP command may be a little easier to use than CHPROP because of the way options are graphically displayed in the dialog box. The Color and Linetype dialog boxes are helpful, and the layer list is extremely useful because it is often difficult to remember the layer names (and to spell them correctly) when typing them. You also can click on the dialog box's **H**elp button if you forget how to use the command.

*You also can use the Modify <entity> dialog box, which is opened by the En̲tity item on the M̲odify pull-down menu, to change properties and other aspects of existing entities. See Chapter 6 for details.*

# Using the RENAME Command

The RENAME command changes the names of existing drawing objects, such as blocks or layers. The Rename dialog box provides a convenient tool for renaming such items. You can activate the dialog box by entering **DDRENAME** at the Command: prompt or by choosing RENAME:, then Dialogue from the UTILITY screen menu. The dialog box enables you to select the item's category, such as Block. A list box displays the existing name. You then can enter a new name in the edit box.

In the following exercise, you practice using the RENAME command.

---

### Using DDRENAME To Rename Drawing Objects

Continue with the WORK drawing from the preceding exercises.

Command: *From the screen menu, choose* UTILITY, *then* RENAME:          Starts the RENAME command

RENAME Block/Dimstyle/LAyer/LType/ Style/UCS/VIew/VPort: *From the screen menu, choose* Dialogue          Cancels RENAME and starts the DDRENAME command and opens the Rename dialog box

Select the Layer option from the left list box.

*Click on* TRIANGLE *in the right list box*          Selects the TRIANGLE layer for renaming

*Click in the* **R**ename To: *edit box and type* **TRI**, *then click on* **R**ename To:          Renames the TRIANGLE layer to TRI

*Choose* OK          Closes the dialog box

1 Layer(s) renamed.

---

When the RENAME command is issued, the prompt offers a selection of items that you can rename. These items include blocks, dimension styles, layers, linetypes, styles, user coordinate systems, views, and viewports. Many of these items have not yet been discussed in this book, but are covered in later chapters. After you specify a category, such as Block, you first specify the item's old name. Then you specify the new name to replace it.

# Using the STATUS Command

In the following exercise, you use the STATUS command to check your current entity property defaults. You cannot use STATUS to change those default settings. The STATUS command displays its information in a text screen.

## Using Status To Get a Drawing Status Report

Command: *Choose* <u>A</u>ssist, *then* <u>I</u>nquiry, *then* <u>S</u>tatus, *and press F2*    Displays a text screen with status information

Notice the following three lines in the status display (see fig. 3.24):

```
Current layer:      CIRCLE
Current color:      1 (red)
Current linetype:   CONTINUOUS
```

Command: *Press F2 to switch back to graphics window*

The top of the status report shows your drawing limits. The status report lists the current layer, current color, and current linetype, followed by additional information about your settings. These settings become more important as you read through the book. For now, remember that you can access this information and that AutoCAD keeps track of all the data.

**Figure 3.24:**

The status
display.

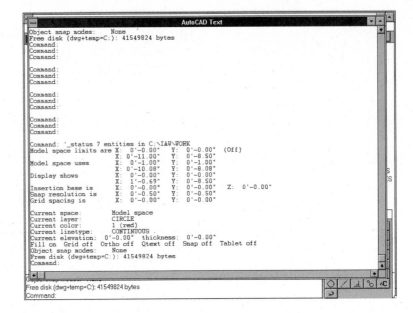

# Modifying and Viewing System Variables

AutoCAD has about 175 variables that are saved with a drawing. These variables cover everything from the units settings to dimensioning options. Fortunately, the default settings in the ACAD.DWG drawing file are established to enable you to start drawing without many adjustments. You will probably never need to use many of the variables in the drawings you create.

You can type all the system variables at the Command: prompt, just as you can enter any AutoCAD command. You already have changed several of the variables, however, by making changes to dialog boxes or screen-menu selections.

You can use the SETVAR command to set and view the values of AutoCAD's system variables. You also can enter the names of system variables directly at the Command: prompt to set their values. The following exercise demonstrates the use of the SETVAR command.

## Using SETVAR To Change System Variables

Continue with the WORK drawing from the preceding exercises.

Command: **SETVAR** ↵            Issues the SETVAR command

Variable name or ?: **BLIPMODE** ↵

```
New value for BLIPMODE <1>: 0 ↵
```
Turns off BLIPMODE, so that blip marks do not appear when you pick points

```
Command: Choose Draw, then Line, then Segments
```

*Draw a few lines, noting that blips do not appear when you pick points*

```
To point: Press Ctrl-C
```
Cancels the LINE command

```
Command: U ↵
```
Undoes the LINE command

```
Command: U ↵
```
Undoes the BLIPMODE change

---

This chapter does not explain all the AutoCAD system variables. Instead, they are covered throughout the book as they apply to different commands. You cannot directly change the value of some system variables because they are *read-only variables*; you can see their value, but AutoCAD does not allow you to change it. You can update such variables by making changes in other areas of your drawing or configuration.

# Keeping Your Work Safe

You have been working on the CHAPTER3 drawing for some time, but you may not have saved it yet. If your system's power failed suddenly or some other event caused you to lose the changes you have made, you would not lose much; CHAPTER3 is not an important or complex drawing. If you were working on a real drawing with a real deadline, however, you could not take lost work so lightly. This section shows you how to ensure that you do not lose changes to your drawing during an editing session.

In the following exercise, you specify an interval (in minutes) for AutoCAD's automatic file-saving feature. You specify the interval through the SAVETIME system variable. The variable's initial default setting is 120 minutes.

## Using SAVETIME To Set Autosave Frequency

Continue with the WORK drawing from the preceding exercises.

```
Command: SAVETIME ↵
```
Accesses the SAVETIME system variable

```
New value for SAVETIME <120>: 15 ↵
```
Sets autosave to 15-minute intervals

```
Command: Choose File, then Exit
AutoCAD, and discard your changes
```
Exits from AutoCAD

The SAVETIME setting is saved in the ACAD.CFG file, in spite of your discarding the current drawing.

Automatic saves are made to the file name AUTO.SV$ in the current directory. If you need to recover a drawing from the saved file, rename AUTO.SV$ with a DWG extension, such as WHEW.DWG, and open it as a drawing.

You have finished setting up drawing parameters in AutoCAD. This task becomes much easier after you have had a little more practice and a better understanding of how AutoCAD works.

# Summary

The exercises in this chapter illustrate the manner in which AutoCAD uses setup commands. AutoCAD begins new drawings by reading many default settings from a prototype drawing named ACAD.DWG. The proper setup of a drawing file requires you to set up units, limits, and a working set of layers. AutoCAD saves you time by offering dialog boxes, defaults, and wild-card options in place of elaborate keyboard entry during your setup.

Several key concepts can help you establish a good drawing setup. Use an appropriate drawing scale factor to set your drawing limits for your electronic sheet size. You also can use AutoCAD's automatic setup routines to select your final sheet size and to set your drawing's limits. You can scale text, linetype, and symbols using your drawing scale factor.

You should organize your layers to hold different types of objects. Adopt a layer-naming convention that enables you to organize your drawing's names with wild cards. The current layer is the active drawing layer. The toolbar always shows the current layer. Default drawing properties for color and linetype are set using the BYLAYER variable. You can explicitly override BYLAYER color and linetype using the COLOR and LINETYPE commands. You also can change properties associated with existing entities by using the CHPROP command. If you are uncertain as to which properties are current in your drawing, use the Entity Creation Modes dialog box or the STATUS command to help you keep track.

The drawing tasks you performed in this chapter were not accurate—you simply picked points on the screen rather than entering exact measurements and coordinates. In the next chapter, you learn to use many of AutoCAD's commands and tools to prepare accurate drawings. Because accuracy is extremely important in CAD drawings to ensure proper dimensioning, Chapter 4 is of special interest to you.

# Basic 2D AutoCAD Drafting

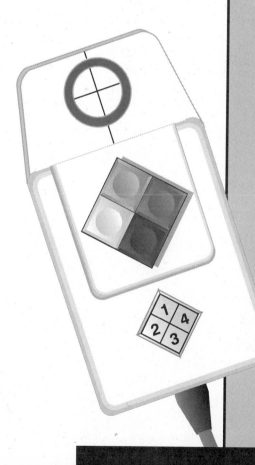

**PART 2**

# Introduction

Two-dimensional (2D) drawings are the workhorses of drafting and design. To obtain good 2D drawings by using AutoCAD, you need to know the basics of object creation and editing. You also need to know how to control the graphics display screen. Part Two of *Inside AutoCAD Release 12 for Windows* teaches you the basic techniques for producing accurate, professional-looking 2D drawings. In the following five chapters, you learn basic drawing and editing techniques, as well as tips and tricks that help you efficiently produce the kind of high-quality drawings you want and expect from AutoCAD.

## How Part Two Is Organized

Part Two includes five chapters that take you from the coordinate system and object snap techniques, through controlling your AutoCAD graphics environment, to basic 2D drawing and editing commands. In addition to giving you more practice in using AutoCAD's various menus, toolbar, and toolbox, these chapters cover the following five subjects:

- Understanding AutoCAD's coordinate systems
- Using object snap features and electronic drawing aids
- Controlling the graphics display
- Using the basic drawing and editing commands
- Creating graphic entities

# Understanding the Coordinate System

One important feature of an electronic CAD drawing is its capability to maintain an accurate database of graphic entities. Chapter 4 explains the importance of accuracy in CAD drawings and the importance of avoiding bad drawing habits. As your first step in learning to create accurate entities, you must develop an understanding of how to use the coordinate system.

Chapter 4 shows you how to create precise drawings by using AutoCAD's object snaps and other electronic drawing aids. You learn how to control your location in the drawing file and how to create your own coordinate system.

# Using the Display Commands

If you know how to control the AutoCAD display, you can save time and frustration when you work with complex drawings. Chapter 5 shows you how to work with a single-viewport and a multiple-viewport drawing area. You also learn how to use zooms and pans to control the displays in the drawing area, including the use of the new AutoCAD Release 12 for Windows *Aerial View* feature. Chapter 5 demystifies paper space, which is the bridge between your computer and the paper. When you are done with Chapter 5, you should be able to set up views and display your work in multiple viewports. You also learn how to zoom in to the view to see fine details, to zoom out to see the big picture, and to save your drawing views and viewports for future use.

# Understanding Basic Drawing and Editing

The 80/20 rule can easily be applied to using AutoCAD; that is, you probably can achieve 80 percent of your initial drawing requirements by using only 20 percent of the available commands. Chapter 6 introduces the drawing and editing commands that enable you to quickly start creating a drawing. The drawing and editing exercises in Chapter 6 are easy to follow, and they should give you the confidence you need to continue learning more AutoCAD commands.

# Creating AutoCAD Graphic Entities

Graphic entities are the building blocks of CAD drawings. Chapter 7 includes complete coverage of all the graphic entities you can create in AutoCAD. Although you may not immediately see a need for all these types of entities, the chapter's drawing exercises show you how entities can be used to reduce the number of steps necessary to complete a drawing. The more time you spend with AutoCAD, the more similarity you can see in the way all entity creation commands operate. Before long, the command prompts should be all you need to remind you of the information necessary to create an entity.

# Editing Graphic Entities

Many entities need to be edited after they are created. AutoCAD's real power and flexibility lie in the program's editing capabilities. In fact, many experienced AutoCAD drafters spend more time using editing commands than drawing commands. Chapter 8 explains many common editing commands and provides some examples that show you when and how to use them. Chapter 8 also explains more about the object-selection process and shows you how to control selection sets so that you can edit exactly the objects you want. The chapter's exercises also teach you how to create multiple copies of objects arranged in a grid or circle, to rotate and trim objects in a variety of ways, and to change an entity's properties.

# Drawing Accurately

Given a straight edge and a ruler, a drafter can locate a point on a drawing sheet with some degree of accuracy; the drafter then can use that point as a location for drawing more objects. In this chapter, you learn how AutoCAD's electronic tools replace manual-drafting tools for locating points and maintaining drawing accuracy.

Some of the benefits of AutoCAD's tools stand out immediately. You never need to clean up eraser shavings, you work at the proper scale, and you never need to lend your 30/60 triangle. Other benefits are not as apparent, such as the 100 percent accuracy of straightedges and triangles, the precise mathematically defined curves, and electronically flexible graph paper to trace over as a guide.

## Examining Electronic Drawing Aids

The first step in creating accurate drawings is to locate your drawing points. One way to locate them accurately is to enter coordinates from the keyboard. Although you may know some of the coordinate values to start a drawing, you rarely have complete information for entering all your drawing points. Besides, this method of coordinate entry is grueling, tedious work and leaves you open to making typing errors.

Most of the time, you can pick drawing points without any help from AutoCAD. As you saw in the last chapter, however, it is hard to pick points accurately. AutoCAD provides two methods for controlling the movement of your cursor so that you can accurately select pick points. The first method is to use the grid and snap functions; the second is to use the object snap functions (see fig. 4.1).

**Figure 4.1:**

Object snap targets and the points they pick.

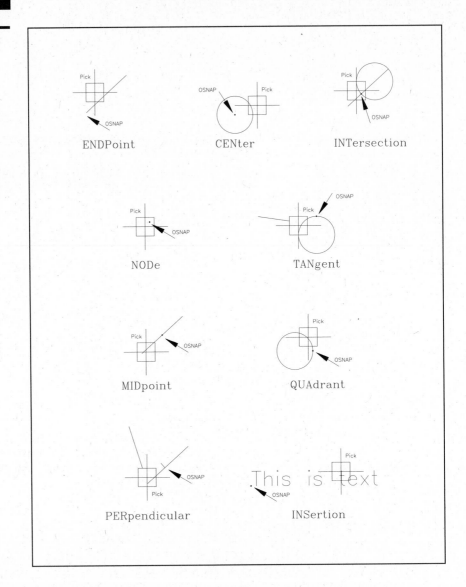

AutoCAD has two other drawing-accuracy aids: ortho mode and XYZ point filters. When AutoCAD is in ortho mode, you can draw or input points only orthogonally—in other words, at right angles to previous points or lines. Ortho mode is discussed in detail in this chapter. For information on XYZ point filters, see Chapter 10.

# Understanding Grid and Snap

AutoCAD is accurate to at least 14 significant digits. If you pick your drawing points without some form of control, however, AutoCAD must translate the cursor's pixel position into the current drawing units. That is, AutoCAD must approximate the coordinates you actually want. If you try to pick the point 2.375,4.625, for example, you may get such numbers as 2.3754132183649,4.6248359103856. If you set the coordinate display to show only three decimal places, these numbers falsely appear to be rounded accurately, but AutoCAD stores them internally with their true precision—with several more decimal places of "inaccuracy." Even if you visually align the crosshairs with the grid or other objects, you seldom locate the desired point with complete accuracy.

You can control your pick points by using grid and snap. AutoCAD's grid serves as a visible template that shows the location of a set of points, but it does not round the input points to accurate locations. *Snap* is an invisible grid template that controls the points that you select with your cursor. If you set snap to 0.5, then you can select only points that fall on 0.5-unit increments.

You can most easily control pick points by coordinating AutoCAD's grid and snap capabilities. If you set them equally, you can select only grid points. If you set the snap increments to half the grid increments, you can select only the grid points themselves or points that lie halfway between the grid points. You control the accuracy of your point selection by using snap; grid enables you to keep track visually of the points to which you are snapping.

# Understanding Object Snap

As your drawing becomes more complex, points on circles, arcs, and intersections of angled lines no longer fall directly on grid and snap points. AutoCAD offers a set of tools called *object snaps* (also called *geometric snaps*) to help you accurately pick such points. To understand object snaps, remember that objects such as lines have middle points and endpoints, and circles have center, quadrant, and tangent points. When you draw, you often attach lines to these points.

AutoCAD's *object snaps* are geometric filters that enable you to select your drawing-attachment points. If, for example, you want to draw to an intersection of two lines, you can set the object snap to filter for intersections, and then pick a point close to the intersection. The point snaps to the precise intersection of the lines. Although it takes a little time to get used to setting object snaps, they are the best way to maintain geometrically accurate drawings.

# Examining the Drawing Accuracy Tools

Drawing accuracy is controlled by the GRID, SNAP, ORTHO, and OSNAP commands and by the Drawing Aids dialog box. This dialog box is accessed from the **D**rawing Aids item in the **S**ettings pull-down menu (see fig. 4.2); when you select **D**rawing Aids, the Drawing Aids dialog box appears, as shown in figure 4.3. The commands also are found on the SETTINGS screen menu. You also can turn Grid, Snap, and Ortho on and off by using function keys and Ctrl-*key* combinations. The O and S buttons in the toolbar switch the Ortho and Snap modes on and off. When the button is highlighted, the mode is on.

**Figure 4.2:**

The Settings pull-down menu and first page of the SETTINGS screen menu.

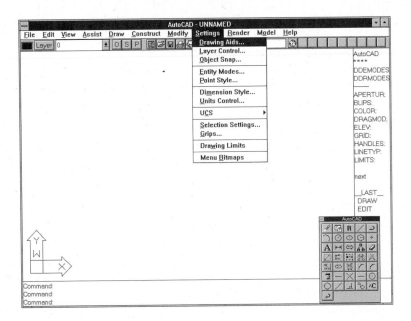

# Using Drawing Aids

In the following exercise, you use a technique of starting a new drawing that makes its settings equal to one of the drawings from the IAW DISK. This new drawing uses the defaults of the IAWWORK drawing from the IAW DISK as a prototype instead of using the ACAD.DWG settings as shown in Chapter 3. IAWWORK is the same as the WORK drawing saved at the end of Chapter 3. AutoCAD begins with a copy of the specified prototype drawing, giving it the new name you specify. Name it WORK, replacing the previously saved WORK drawing.

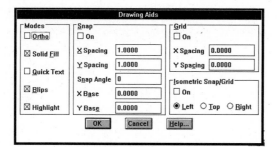

**Figure 4.3:**

The Drawing Aids dialog box.

---

## Editing a New Copy of the WORK Drawing File

*Begin AutoCAD, then choose* **F**ile, *then* **N**ew

Opens the Create New Drawing dialog box

*Choose the* **P**rototype *button, then find and double-click on* IAWWORK *in the list box*

Chooses a prototype drawing

*Click in the text box for a new drawing and type* **WORK**, *then choose* OK

Names the drawing

*Choose* **Y**es *to replace the existing* WORK *drawing, if prompted*

Command: *Choose* **S**ettings, *then* **L**ayer Control, *then verify that your settings match those shown in table 4.1, and choose* OK

Your drawing should look like figure 4.4, which shows a single circle located in the upper right corner of your graphics drawing area.

---

**Figure 4.4:**

The WORK
drawing.

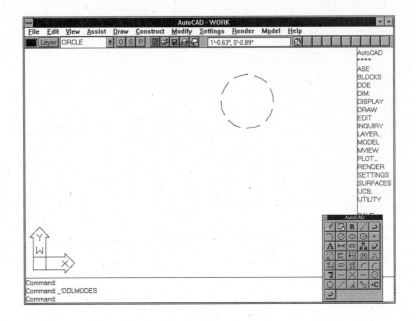

## Table 4.1
## WORK Drawing Settings

**UNITS**   Engineering, 2 decimal places, 2 fractional places for angles,
            defaults for all other settings.

**LIMITS**  0,0 to 11,8.5

| Layer Name | State | Color | Linetype |
| --- | --- | --- | --- |
| 0 | On | 7 (White) | CONTINUOUS |
| CIRCLE | On/Current | 3 (Green) | DASHED |
| PARAGRAM | On | 5 (Blue) | HIDDEN |
| SQUARE | On | 2 (Yellow) | CONTINUOUS |
| TEXT | On | 4 (Cyan) | CONTINUOUS |
| TRIANGLE | On | 1 (Red) | CONTINUOUS |

The drawing's current layer is CIRCLE. In the following exercise, you draw a few
points on the CIRCLE layer.

# Controlling Drawing Points

The POINT command is the simplest of AutoCAD's drawing commands. This command inputs a single drawing point. Try it with the coordinate values shown in the following exercise. To see the actual point entity, you must perform a display redraw after you create the point.

---

## Using the POINT Command

| | |
|---|---|
| Command: *From the toolbox, choose* POINT | Starts the POINT command |
| Command: POINT Point: **3,6.25** ↵ | Displays a small blip mark at the specified coordinate |
| Command: *Choose* **V**iew, *then* **R**edraw | Leaves only a dot |

---

First, a mark appears at the specified coordinates. This mark is actually larger than the point itself, which you drew with the POINT command. This mark is a construction marker (or *blip*) for the point. The REDRAW command clears the construction marker and leaves a small green dot, or *point entity*. (You may not easily see the point, but it is there.) You can be certain of its location because you typed the absolute X,Y coordinate values. (REDRAW is discussed further at the end of this chapter.)

# How Accurate Are Pick Points?

Picking a point accurately with your cursor is difficult. As you move the cursor, the digital readout of your coordinates should display the crosshair cursor's current X,Y location. If the coordinates are not active, you can turn on your coordinate display by clicking on the display in the toolbar, pressing Ctrl-D, or pressing F6. Figure 4.5 shows the coordinate display in the toolbar.

Try the following exercise to see how accurately you can pick your drawing points. To test your pick point, use the coordinate display and the **I**D Point selection from **I**nquiry on the **A**ssist pull-down menu. Try to pick at coordinates 3.25,5. **I**D Point simply displays the picked point's coordinates.

---

## Using ID To Test Pick Points

Make sure that your coordinate display is turned on.

| | |
|---|---|
| Command: *Choose* **A**ssist, *then* **I**nquiry, *then* **I**D Point | Issues ID command transparently |
| '_id Select point: *Try picking a point at exactly 0'-3.25",0'-5.00" on the coordinate display* | |
| X = 3.24"  Y = 5.03"  Z = 0.00" | Your point may differ |

---

**Figure 4.5:**

The coordinate
display.

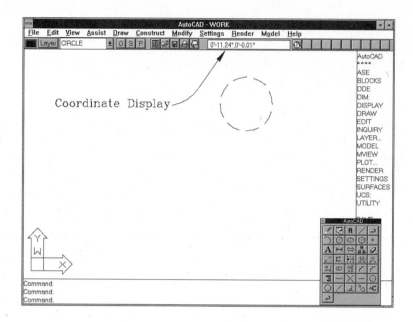

ID Point shows the X, Y, and Z position of your pick point. Try a few more points. As you can see, it is nearly impossible to accurately pick the point you want. Without some form of control over the points you pick, a drawing can contain many inaccurate points.

*The ID command and the coordinates display may claim that the point is exactly at 3.25,5.00. When you change your units to six or eight decimal places, however, you see that AutoCAD really is rounding off an inaccurate point.*

Although the coordinate display shows coordinates with the full precision set by the UNITS command, instructions to pick points at specific coordinates are generally abbreviated in this book's exercises. Leading and trailing zeros, and feet and inch marks that are not required for point entry, may be omitted. For example, rather than "pick at 0'-3.25",0'-5.00"," you may be instructed to "pick at 3.25",5.00"" or to "pick or enter **3.25,5**."

# Using the Grid Display

To get accurate points, first set up a grid template that helps you see points on the screen. A *grid* consists of a series of construction points that appear on the screen, but which are not part of the drawing file. Grids serve as a frame of reference while you draw.

You set up a grid by using the GRID command or the Drawing Aids dialog box. In the next exercise, you set up a one-inch grid. If you move the crosshairs and try to pick a grid point with the ID command, you can see that grid points do not actually control input points.

## Using GRID To Set Up a Grid

| | |
|---|---|
| `Command:` *Choose* **S**ettings, *then* **D**rawing Aids | Displays the Drawing Aids dialog box |
| *In the* **G**rid *area, click on the* On *check box* | Turns on the grid |
| *Double-click in the* X S**p**acing *box and enter* **1**, *then choose* OK | Sets X to 1" and defaults Y to X, then displays the grid |

The one-inch grid appears, as shown in figure 4.6.

Now use the ID command to try to pick a point that lies exactly on one of the grid marks.

`Command:` **ID** ↵

`Point:` *Try picking on the grid at exactly 7.00",5.00"*

AutoCAD displays the following message, which shows the exact location of the point you just picked:

`X = 0'--6.99" Y = 0'--4.99"  Z = 0'--0.00"`

The message confirms that you did pick a point, and it shows that the point is not precisely located on the grid. The message you see on your screen may be different from this one.

*The grid helps you visualize distances and see drawing limits. The grid, however, is only a visual aid, and does not affect point entry or cursor movement. When you set the grid spacing, avoid setting a grid that is too dense (that is, one whose markers are too close together). A too-dense grid obscures the drawing and causes screen redrawing to operate slowly.*

Because you have several options in setting up a grid, you are not limited to creating square grids. You can, for example, change the grid spacing to give different X,Y aspect ratios. Figure 4.7 shows a grid with a 2X:1Y aspect ratio.

**Figure 4.6:**

A grid, added to the WORK drawing.

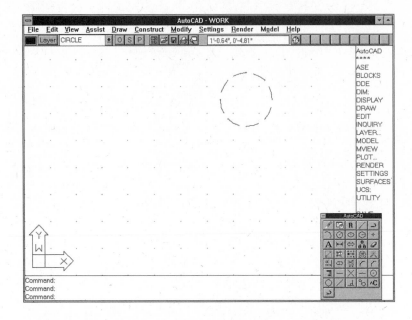

**Figure 4.7:**

A grid with a 2X:1Y aspect ratio.

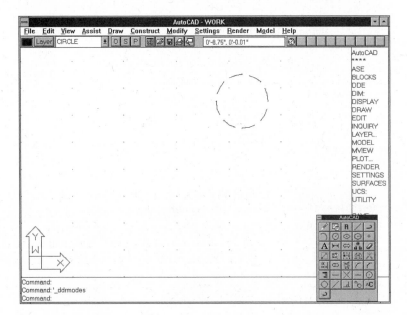

## Setting Up a Grid

You can set the grid by using the Drawing Aids dialog box or the GRID command. The GRID command prompt appears with the following options:

```
Grid spacing(X) or ON/OFF/Snap/Aspect <0'--0.00">:
```

These options perform the following functions:

- **Grid spacing (X).** This option sets the X,Y grid increment and activates it. If you enter **0**, AutoCAD makes the grid equal to the snap spacing, changing automatically when snap changes. If you enter a number followed by an X, AutoCAD sets the grid to the current snap increment times the specified number.

- **ON.** This option makes the grid visible.

- **OFF.** This option makes the grid invisible.

- **Snap.** This option sets the grid increment so that it is equal to the current snap increment (when you enter **0** or **1X** for the grid spacing, for example), except that the Snap option does not automatically change the grid as snap changes.

- **Aspect.** This option enables you to set different increments for the grid's horizontal and vertical markers.

*You can press Ctrl-G or F7 to turn the grid on and off.*

## Setting Snap Points

The SNAP command sets the smallest increment that AutoCAD can recognize when you move the cursor. If you turn snap on and set a spacing value, you notice that your cursor moves with a jerking motion; it jumps from snap point to snap point instead of tracking smoothly. Think of setting snap as setting your smallest drawing increment. When you set snap-spacing values, all drawing pick points are forced to multiples of your snap values.

A good practice is to set your snap to some fraction of your grid spacing. AutoCAD normally aligns snap points with the grid. As you draw, you can easily "eyeball" points that are 1/4 to 1/5 the distance between grid points. In the following exercise, you set the snap increment to 0.25", or 1/4 of your grid spacing.

## Using SNAP To Set Snap Points

| | |
|---|---|
| Command: *Choose* **S***ettings, then* **D***rawing Aids* | Displays the Drawing Aids dialog box |
| *In the* **S***nap area, click on the* On *check box* | Turns on snap |
| *Double-click in the* **X** Spacing *box, enter* **.25***, and click on* OK | Defaults the Y spacing so that it equals the X spacing |

The S button in the toolbar is highlighted, indicating that snap is on, and the coordinates display accurately in 1/4-inch increments (see fig. 4.8). Try moving the cursor around. The crosshairs now jump to the snap increments.

**Figure 4.8:**

The toolbar shows that snap is on.

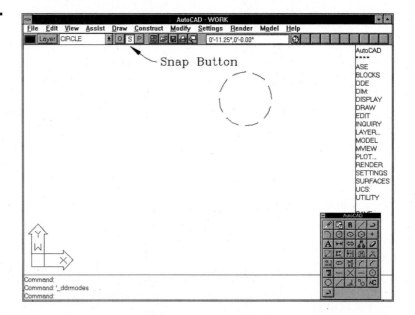

*You can turn snap on and off by clicking on the S button, pressing Ctrl-B, or pressing F9. Turning snap off is helpful if you want to select an object at a point to which you cannot snap.*

## Using Snap Points To Draw Objects

After you set a snap value, you can draw accurately, as long as the object you want to draw is on a snap point. The toolbar shows the correct crosshair position as it rounds the X,Y values to 0.25".

In the following exercise, draw a 2"×2" square with the lower left corner at 0'-7.50", 0'-1.00". Use the coordinate display to help you pick the points used in the following exercise. As you pick points, notice that the cursor snaps to the snap increments.

### Using SNAP To Draw a Square

| | |
|---|---|
| **Command:** *From the toolbar, click on the layer name, then choose* SQUARE | Shows layer list |
| **Command:** *Choose* **D**raw, *then* **L**ine, *then* **S**egments | Issues the LINE command |
| **Command:** _line From point: *Use the coordinates display to pick the point 0'-7.50", 0'-1.00"* | Starts the line and updates the coordinates display to show a distance and an angle, as in 0'–1.500"<0.00 |
| **To point:** *Press F6, then pick point 0'-9.50",0'-1.00"* | Changes coordinates back to X,Y display, then draws the line |
| **To point:** *Pick point 0'-9.50", 0'-3.00"* | Draws a line |
| **To point:** *Pick point 0'-7.50", 0'-3.00"* | Draws a line |
| **To point:** *Pick point 0'-7.50", 0'-1.00"* | Finishes the square |
| **To point:** *Press Enter* | Ends the LINE command |

After you finish, your drawing should look like the one shown in figure 4.9.

**NOTE**

*The* X,Y to distance<angle *coordinate display options seen in this exercise are discussed later in this chapter.*

As you work with the GRID and SNAP commands, you probably need to adjust the grid and snap settings as you zoom, so that you can work in greater detail. If you start with a snap at 1 unit and a grid at 5 units on a whole drawing, you may need to reset your snap to 1/4 unit and your grid to 1 unit when you zoom to work on a portion of the drawing.

You can coordinate your snap and grid spacing to suit your needs. Make it a practice to set your grid and snap, and then leave them on most of the time. If you do not pick your drawing points with snap (or object snap) on, your drawings will not be accurate.

**Figure 4.9:**

A square drawn
with the SNAP
command.

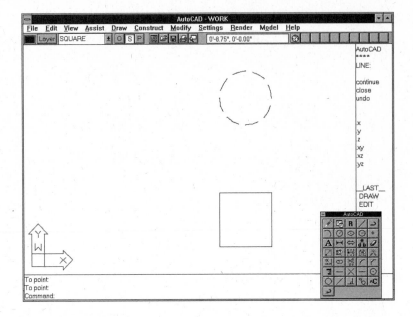

You can use the Drawing Aids dialog box or the SNAP command to set snap. The
SNAP command provides the following options:

```
Snap spacing or ON/OFF/Aspect/Rotate/Style <0'--0.00">:
```

You can use the following options to set snap spacing:

- **Snap spacing.** This option prompts you for a value to set the snap increment and
  to turn on snap.

- **ON.** This option turns on snap.

- **OFF.** This option turns off snap. This is the initial default setting.

- **Aspect.** This option prompts for different horizontal (X) and vertical (Y) snap
  increments (except in isometric mode; see the description of the Style option).

- **Rotate.** This option prompts you to specify an angle and a basepoint, around
  which you can rotate the snap grid (and crosshairs). See the discussion of Ortho
  (later in this chapter) for an example.

- **Style.** This option prompts for Standard or Isometric style. Standard sets the
  normal (default) snap style; Isometric sets an isometric snap grid style by aligning
  the snap points to a 30-, 90-, or 150-degree grid. You use isometric snaps to draw
  in the standard isometric planes. Press Ctrl-E one or more times to rotate the
  current isometric drawing plane from top to right, then to left, and then back to
  top.

# Using Ortho Mode as a Special Snap

If you are drawing horizontal and vertical lines, you can place an additional constraint on your cursor movements by turning on ortho mode. "Ortho" stands for *orthogonal* and limits cursor movement to right angles from the last point. When ortho is on, any lines you enter with the cursor are aligned with the snap axes. In effect, you can draw only at right angles. To turn on ortho mode, click on the O button in the toolbar. You can also use the Drawing Aids dialog box, the ORTHO command, F8, or Ctrl-O.

Ortho is easy to use and helpful any time you draw sets of horizontal and vertical lines. In the following exercise, you access the ORTHO command, and then draw another square around the square you just drew. When you turn on ortho mode , <Ortho on> appears at the Command: prompt and the O button is highlighted. As you draw the square, the cursor is limited to vertical and horizontal movement, which makes it easy to get true 90-degree corners. The rubber-band cursor that normally trails from the last point to the intersection of the crosshairs now goes from the last point to the nearest perpendicular point on the X or Y crosshairs.

As you pick points, notice that you do not actually need to place the cursor on the correct X and Y coordinates. The cursor need only be aligned along one axis, either X or Y, depending on the desired location of the next point.

After you draw the square, undo it and turn off ortho; you use this drawing again later to practice using AutoCAD's object snaps.

## Using ORTHO To Draw a Square

Command: *Choose* **D**raw, *then* **L**ine, *then* **S**egments

| | |
|---|---|
| Command: _line From point: *Pick* ① *at 7.00",0.50" (see fig. 4.10), then move the cursor around* | Starts the line and rubber-bands freely |
| To point: *Click on the* O *button* | Turns on ortho |
| To point: <Ortho on> *Move cursor around, then pick* ② *at 10.00",0.50"* | Rubber-bands orthogonally and draws the line |
| To point: *Pick* ③ *at 10.00",3.50"* | |
| To point: *Pick* ④ *at 7.00",3.50"* | |
| To point: *From the screen menu, choose* close | Closes the series of lines and ends the LINE command |
| Command: *Choose* **E**dit, *then* **U**ndo | Removes the four lines and turns off ortho mode |

**Figure 4.10:**

Using Ortho to
draw a square.

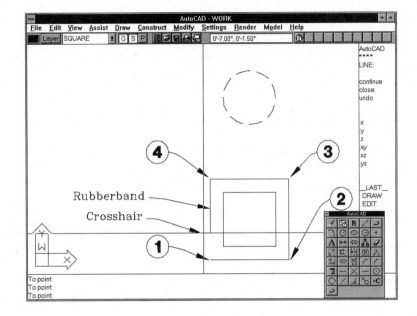

*If you turn on or off a mode such as Ortho, Snap, or Grid in the middle of a command, and later undo the command, the active setting also is undone.*

## Examining Coordinate Entry

If you enter coordinates from the keyboard, they override the Snap and Ortho drawing controls (but not object snap). You may often enter coordinates from the keyboard as you set up drawings or as you draw at specific points or known distances that are relative to known points.

*The Z distance or Z angle is assumed to be zero, unless otherwise specified.*

## Using Absolute Coordinates

If you know the exact coordinates of your point or its distance and angle from the 0,0 drawing origin, you can use the keyboard to enter coordinates in several formats. All of these formats are known as *absolute coordinates* or *explicit coordinates*.

*Absolute Cartesian coordinates* treat coordinate entry as X and Y displacements from 0,0 (or X,Y,Z from 0,0,0 in 3D). For example, the absolute Cartesian coordinates 6,5,4 place a point that is 6 units along the positive X axis, 5 units along the positive Y axis, and 4 units along the positive Z axis from the 0,0,0 base point. The default position for 0,0 is at the lower left of your limits and drawing area, but you can locate it anywhere by using the UCS command. If your displacement is positive, you do not need to use a plus (+) sign. Negative displacement is left and down on the screen. You must use a minus (-) sign for negative displacements. In figure 4.11, the points are located by the Cartesian distances X, Y, and Z.

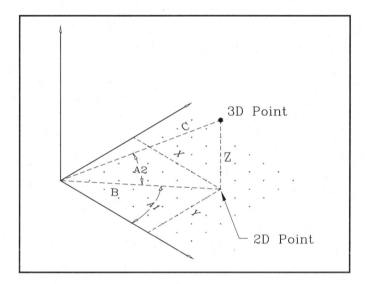

**Figure 4.11:**

Various forms of coordinate entry.

*Absolute Polar coordinates* also treat 2D coordinate entry as a displacement from 0,0, but you specify the displacement as a distance and angle. The distance and angle values are separated by a left-angle bracket (<). Positive angles are counterclockwise, relative to 0 degrees as an imaginary horizontal line extending to the right of 0,0. In figure 4.11, the 2D point is located using B and A1, as in B<A1. In this system of coordinate entry, 90 degrees is vertically above, and 180 degrees is horizontally left (see fig. 4.12). The value 2<60, for example, is two units from 0,0 along a line at 60 degrees from the X axis in the X,Y plane.

*Absolute Spherical coordinates* are 3D polar coordinates and are specified as a distance and two angles. The first angle is from 0,0 in the X,Y plane, and the second angle is the angle toward the Z axis up or down from the X,Y plane. In figure 4.11, the 3D point is located using spherical coordinates by distance C and angles A1 and A2, as in C<A1<A2. For example, 2<60<45 specifies a point 2 units from the 0,0,0 origin along a line at 60 degrees from the X axis in the X,Y plane and at 45 degrees up toward the Z axis from the X,Y plane.

**Figure 4.12:**

Default units angle direction.

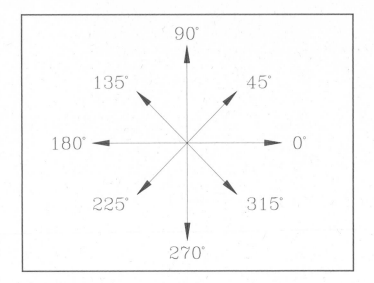

*Absolute Cylindrical coordinates* also are for 3D use. They are like polar coordinates, but they also use a height in the Z axis above or below the X,Y plane. In figure 4.11, the 3D point is located using cylindrical coordinates by distance B, angle A1, and distance Z, as in B<A1,Z. For example, 2<60,3 specifies a point 3 units vertically above the 2D (polar) point that is 2 units from the 0,0,0 origin, along a line at 60 degrees from the X axis in the X,Y plane.

In the following exercise, you review the use of absolute Cartesian coordinates, which you already have used several times, and try absolute polar coordinates as you draw a triangle at the upper left corner of the drawing.

## Specifying Points with Absolute Coordinates

Continue working in the WORK drawing.

| | |
|---|---|
| Command: *From the toolbar, click on the layer name box, then select* TRIANGLE | Sets the current layer |
| Command: *Choose* **D**raw, *then* **L**ine, *then* **S**egments | |
| Command: _line From point: **1.25,5.25** ↵ | Specifies an absolute Cartesian point |
| To point: **3,7.5** ↵ | Specifies an absolute Cartesian point |
| To point: **7.08<47.86** ↵ | Specifies an absolute polar point |
| To point: *From the screen menu, choose* close | Closes the triangle |

The triangle appears in the upper left part of the drawing area, as shown in figure 4.13.

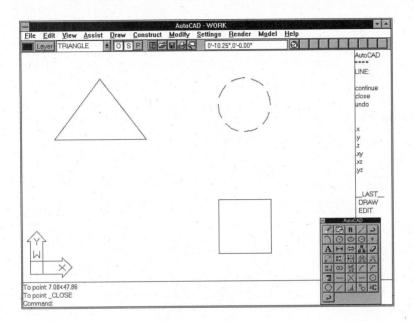

**Figure 4.13:**

A triangle, drawn with absolute coordinates.

The preceding exercise uses simple points, but in a real drawing, points are often harder to calculate. If you examine the drawing database closely, you find that the third point (5 times the square root of 2 at 45 degrees) does not align exactly with the first point because it is entered with two decimal places of precision.

Absolute coordinates can locate the first point of an object in the drawing, but relative coordinates are usually better for locating subsequent points. Relative polar coordinates can be picked easily by using the cursor with the coordinate display.

## Tracking and Picking Polar Coordinates

The precision capability of the SNAP, GRID, and ORTHO commands often is sufficient for accuracy, but drawing is easier if you know how far the cursor is from the last point. You can use the cursor to pick polar coordinates; you can track your cursor movements for polar input by switching the coordinate display to polar mode. To change modes on the coordinate display, you can click on the display, press F6, or press Ctrl-D. Figure 4.14 shows the polar coordinates display.

The coordinate display has three modes:

- On, with polar coordinate display during commands which allow polar coordinate input. This mode has a "split personality" in most commands. When the crosshairs pull a rubber-band line, such as in a LINE command, the second mode automatically switches into a *polar distance<angle* display relative to the last point. This mode is the most frequently used because it enables you to pick the initial point for a command with absolute X,Y coordinates and to pick subsequent points with relative polar points.

- On, with absolute coordinate display. In this position, the X,Y display is constantly updated as you move the cursor.

- Off, sometimes called *static coordinates*. These coordinates are updated each time a point is specified.

The default mode is on, with polar display. Clicking on the coordinate display or pressing F6 switches to the absolute position, then to the off position. If this sounds confusing, it is! Switch the display mode until you get the coordinate display you want.

**Figure 4.14:**

Displaying polar coordinates.

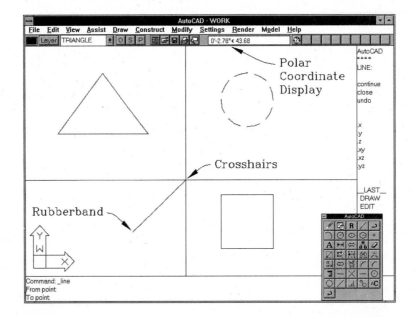

## Using Relative Coordinates

Often you may know the X,Y or X,Y,Z distance, or the distance and angle from a previous point to a point you want to enter, but you may not know the point's displacement from 0,0. Any method of entering coordinates also can be used relative to the last point entered in your drawing, instead of relative to 0,0. To enter a relative point, enter an *at* symbol (@) to precede the first number.

Relative coordinates treat the last point of coordinate entry as a temporary 0,0,0 (stored in the LASTPOINT system variable). If you want to add a horizontal line segment to be two units in the X direction and one in the Y direction from the previous point, enter

@**2,0**. Relative polar, spherical, and cylindrical coordinates specify displacement with distance(s) and angle(s). For example, the relative polar @2<60 is 2 units at 60 degrees.

If you want to enter a new point at the last point, you can use a zero distance, such as @0,0 or @0<*nn* (*nn* can be any angle). This is the same as the last point. A simpler way to enter a new point at the last point is to enter an @ without any number or angle. AutoCAD interprets this symbol as specifying the last point.

*Issue the ID command at the* Command: *prompt to draw relative to a point that is not the last point used in the drawing. The ID command enables you to pick the point you want to work relative to, and it becomes the new last point. You also can check and change the last point with the LASTPOINT system variable.*

In the following exercise, try relative, Cartesian, and polar coordinate entry by drawing a parallelogram. You use the keyboard and the cursor to specify relative polar coordinates. Use the following exercise sequence for your input values.

## Drawing with Relative Coordinates

Continue from the previous triangle exercise.

Command: *From the toolbar, click on the layer name box, then select* PARAGRAM

Command: *Choose* **D**raw, *then* **L**ine, *then* **S**egments

| | |
|---|---|
| Command: _line From point: *Use the coordinate display to pick absolute Cartesian coordinates 0'-4.25", 0',1.00"* | Starts LINE and changes the coordinate display to polar display |
| To point: **@2.25<60** ↵ | Specifies relative polar coordinates |
| To point: **@-3,0** ↵ | Specifies relative Cartesian coordinates |
| To point: *Using the coordinate display, pick relative polar coordinates @ 0'-2.25"<240.00* | |
| To point: *Use the coordinate display to pick absolute Cartesian coordinates 0'-4.25",0',1.00"* | |
| To point: *Press Enter* | Ends the LINE command |
| Command: *Choose* **F**ile, *then* **S**ave | Saves the drawing |

After you finish, your drawing should look like figure 4.15.

**Figure 4.15:**

A parallelogram, drawn with relative coordinates.

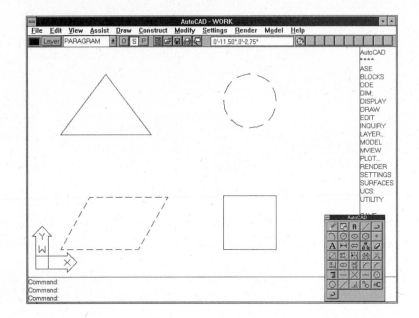

*Do not let the coordinate display fool you; it displays with as much or as little precision as you set when you issue the UNITS or DDUNITS commands. A polar display is rarely precise at angles other than 90-degree increments. For example, 2.10<60 is more likely 2.0976325 at 60.351724 degrees, or some such.*

*Unless relative coordinates are specified or the @ sign is used in exercise instructions, coordinates in exercises refer to absolute coordinates.*

# Creating Your Own Coordinate System

So far you have been using AutoCAD's default coordinate system, the *World Coordinate System* (WCS). You can create your own coordinate system by using the UCS command. The UCS command enables you to position the 0,0 origin anywhere, so that you can work relative to any point you want. You also can rotate the X,Y (and even Z) axes to any angle in 2D or 3D space (see fig. 4.16). Although the *User Coordinate System* (*UCS*) was developed for use in 3D drawing, it also can be useful for 2D-drawing applications.

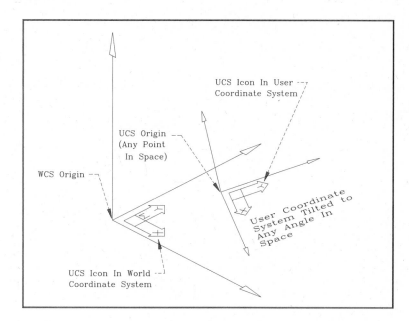

**Figure 4.16:**

A User Coordinate System and the World Coordinate System.

The following two examples and their exercises show you a few of the UCS command's capabilities. The first uses the UCS command to change the location of the 0,0 origin point and the direction of the X and Y axes in your drawing. The second changes the location of 0,0 and keeps the X and Y directions in the default directions. When you draft in 2D, you frequently encounter cases in which you have drawing data relative to known positions. Large sets of offset data or datum-dimensioned work are common examples. To handle this type of drawing, you can set your UCS origin to the known position, input the drawing data relative to the UCS's 0,0 origin, and then return your UCS to its original (default) world setting.

You can modify or change the current UCS by using either the UCS command or the UCS Control dialog box (the DDUCS command—see fig. 4.17). The Settings pull-down menu contains a single UCS menu item, which offers a number of child menus from which you can set or select UCS options. The Named UCS and Presets menu items on the first UCS child menu offer two UCS dialog box options: UCS Control (the UCS Control dialog box) and UCS Presets (an icon menu of preset UCS orientations for 3D work). These options are available through typed commands and on the UCS: screen menu.

**Figure 4.17:**

The UCS Control
dialog box.

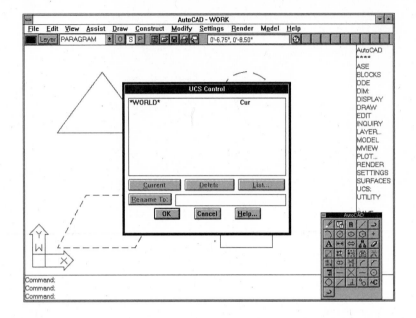

The UCS icon (the X,Y arrows at the lower left corner of the drawing editor) helps you keep track of the UCS by showing the orientation of the X and Y axes. You can set the icon so that it appears aligned on the 0,0,0 origin of the UCS, if there is room in the drawing window. When the UCS icon is set to the origin, and it can fit there, a plus mark appears. If the icon cannot fit at the origin, it appears at the lower left without a plus mark. The UCS icon's appearance is controlled by the UCSICON command or the Icon selection on the UCS child pull-down menu. AutoCAD also offers a UCSICON: selection and a UCS: selection on the SETTINGS screen menu, as well as a UCS: selection on the root screen menu.

Now, make sure that your UCS icon is on. In the following exercise, you use the UCS command to rotate your drawing's coordinate system 90 degrees and set the 0,0 origin near the lower right corner. When you specify the new UCS's coordinates, you specify them in terms of the current coordinate system. Use the coordinates display to pick the new origin.

## Using UCS To Create a User Coordinate System

Command: *Choose* Settings, *then* UCS, *then*      Sets the UCS icon to origin
Icon, *then* Origin

'setvar Variable name or ? <>:
ucsicon New value for UCSICON <1>: 3

Command: **Z** ↵                                     Issues the ZOOM command

| | |
|---|---|
| `ZOOM All/Center/Dynamic/Extents /Left/Previous/Vmax/Window/<Scale (X/XP)>:` **.8** ↵ | Zooms out so that you can watch the UCS icon jump to the origin |
| `Command:` **U** ↵ | Undo zooms back |
| `Command:` *Choose* **S**ettings, *then* U**C**S, *then* **O**rigin | Issues the UCS command with the origin prompt |
| `Origin point <0,0,0>:` *Pick point* 10.25,.5 | Relocates UCS and icon to lower right |
| `Command:` *Choose* **S**ettings, *then* U**C**S, *then* **A**xis, *then* **Z** | Issues the UCS command with the Z rotation angle prompt |
| `Rotation angle about Z axis <0.00>:` **90** ↵ | Reorients the UCS so that the X axis points up |

As shown in figure 4.18, the new coordinate system and icon appear in the lower right corner of the drawing editor.

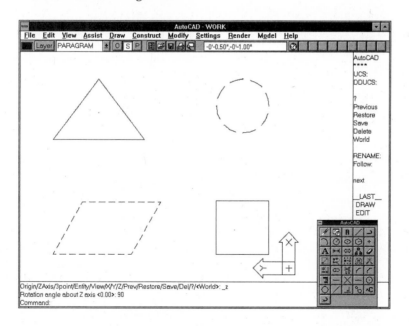

**Figure 4.18:**

The new User Coordinate System.

To see the effect of the changed origin, move the crosshairs and watch the coordinates display. They should show 0,0 at the lower right corner, a vertical X direction, and a horizontal Y direction.

The process of offsetting the origin is straightforward, but you may ask what effect rotating the UCS around the Z axis has on your 2D drawing. Imagine that you are standing on the X axis, looking down at your drawing with your left arm extended to the left to grip a pole rising up from 0,0. Walk forward through 90 degrees and kick the X axis as you walk. You just rotated around the Z axis by 90 degrees. To AutoCAD, the Y axis is North. If you draw a building that fits on the drawing best with North pointing to the left, you find it easier to work if you rotate the UCS. Similarly, if you are datum-dimensioning a part from its lower right corner, you can relocate and rotate its UCS.

Try out the new UCS by making a border around your drawing. Use the following exercise as a guide.

## Drawing a Border in a UCS

`Command:` *Set current layer to* TEXT

`Command:` *Choose* **D**raw, *then* **L**ine, *then* **S**egments

`_line From point:` **0,0** ↵                      Starts the line at the lower right corner

`To point:` *Turn on Ortho, then pick*          Draws the right border
*or enter relative polar coordinates*
*@7.75<0.00*

`To point:` *Pick or enter the relative polar*
*coordinates @9.75<90.00*

Notice that "up" is now to the left (see fig. 4.19).

`To point:` *Pick or enter the relative polar*
*coordinates @7.75<180.00*

`To point:` *Pick or enter the relative polar*
*coordinates @9.75<270.00*

`To point:` *Turn off Ortho and press Enter*     Ends the LINE command

`Command:` **UCS** ↵

`Origin/ZAxis/3point/Entity/View`              Restores the World Coordinate System
`/X/Y/Z/Prev/Restore/Save/Del/?/`
`<World>:` *Press Enter*

If you use the UCS command, rather than the UCS Control dialog box, you see the following prompt:

    Origin/ZAxis/3point/Entity/View/X/Y/Z/Prev/Restore/Save/Del/?/<World>:

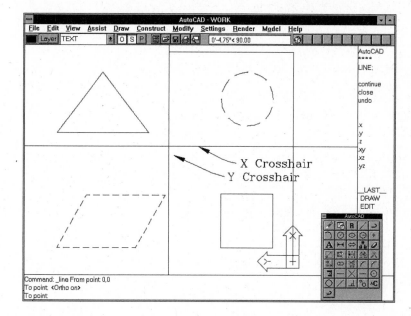

**Figure 4.19:**
The border in progress.

The UCS Control dialog box, the menu items in the **A**xis child menu, and the UCS Orientation dialog box in effect issue the UCS command with the appropriate options preset. You learn how to use all these options in Part Five, which covers 3D. You can use the following subset of options with most two-dimensional applications:

- **Origin.** This option specifies a new X,Y,Z origin point relative to the current origin.

- **Z.** This option rotates the X,Y axes around the Z axis.

- **Prev.** This option steps back to the previous UCS. You can back up through as many as ten previously used UCSs.

- **Restore.** This option sets the UCS to a previously saved UCS.

- **Save.** This option enables you to store the current UCS under a name, which you specify.

- **Del.** This option removes a saved UCS.

- **?.** This option lists previously saved UCSs by name to display point of origin and orientation.

- **<World>.** This option indicates that, by default, the UCS is set to the WCS. Press Enter to accept this option.

The following UCSICON command options control the display of the UCS icon:

- **ON.** This option turns on the UCS icon.

- **OFF.** This option turns off the UCS icon.

- **All.** This option displays the UCS icon in all multiple viewports.

- **Noorigin.** This option displays the UCS icon at the lower left corner of the viewports.

- **ORigin.** This option displays the UCS icon at the 0,0 origin of the current UCS, unless the origin is out of the drawing area or is too close to the edge for the icon to fit. The icon then appears at the lower left corner.

In the following exercise, you change the location of your UCS origin to midway up the drawing. Then you add some text to the drawing.

## Using UCS To Change the Origin Point

Command: *Choose* **S**ettings, *then* U**CS**, *then* **O**rigin

Origin point <0,0,0>: **5.5,4.25** ↵          Sets a new origin

Command: *Choose* **D**raw, *then* **T**ext,          Issues the DTEXT command (see Chapter
*then* **D**ynamic                              7 for more details)

_dtext Justify/Style          Specifies the Center justification option
/<Start point>: **C** ↵

Center point: **0,0** ↵

Height <0'--0.20">: **.25** ↵

Rotation angle <0.00>: *Press Enter*

Text: **Welcome To INSIDE AutoCAD** ↵          Displays the text

Text: *Press Enter*          Accepts the text

Your drawing should look like figure 4.20.

Command: **UCS** ↵          Begins the UCS command

Origin/ZAxis/3point/Entity/View          Restores the World Coordinate System
/X/Y/Z/Prev/Restore/Save/Del/?
/<World>: *Press Enter*

Command: *Set the current layer to* 0

Command: *Choose* **F**ile, *then* Save **A**s,          Saves the drawing under the name
*then type* **BASIC** *and choose* OK          BASIC, for use in the next chapter

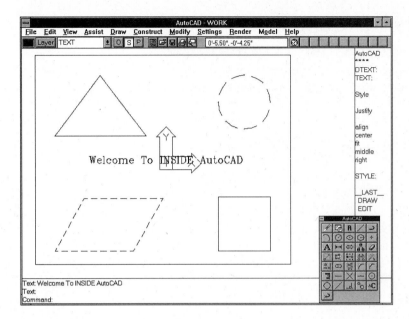

**Figure 4.20:**

Text centered at current UCS origin.

The UCS icon now should be located at the lower left of the display. Each shape should have the color and linetype of its appropriately named layer. Your grid should be 1 unit, and snap should be .25 units. Make corrections if needed and save your drawing again as BASIC. You use this drawing again in the following exercises and in the next chapter on display controls.

If you want to take a break, this is a good stopping point. In fact, whenever you save or quit a drawing, you can safely take a break. For the rest of the chapter, you use the BASIC drawing as a scratch drawing to see how object snaps work.

# Object Snaps: Snapping to Entities

Snap is useful if you want to draw an element that fits the snap increments. You can draw almost anything because of the many absolute or relative coordinate-entry options. If you need to align new points, lines, and other objects with geometric points on entities that you already have drawn, however, you need an easier method.

Suppose, for example, that you want to start a new line at the exact endpoint of an existing line, and it does not fall at a snap point. Or suppose that you want to pick a tangent point to a curve or pick the intersection of two lines that do not fall on a snap point. For both of these examples, you need to use object snaps. The OSNAP command enables you to edit existing entities and to add new entities with precision. OSNAP provides a choice of geometric points that you can snap to by using object snap.

# Using the OSNAP Command
# To Pinpoint a Crosshairs Location

AutoCAD's OSNAP command and filter modes calculate the attachment points you need to make accurate drawings. You tell AutoCAD which object snap attachment mode(s) to use—such as INT for INTersection. After you pick a point or enter coordinates near the geometric point you want, AutoCAD snaps to the precise attachment point.

At the beginning of the chapter, figure 4.1 shows all the filter modes you can use for picking different attachment points on objects. The geometric shapes that make up your BASIC drawing give you the opportunity to exercise all these object snap options.

## Using Overrides versus Running Modes

You can use object snaps as single-pick *override* filters, or you can set a *running* object snap mode that is active until you are prompted for object selection or until you turn it off. You select object snaps as *overrides* (which interrupt the current running mode) by using the floating toolbox icon selections.

> *The floating toolbox can be moved around the graphics window by dragging it or by clicking on the toolbox location icon in the toolbar. Its initial location and size is defined in the ACAD.INI file. If you do not remember what the icons represent, watch the text box at the top of the toolbox as the cursor moves over the icons.*

You may also select object snaps from the pop-up menu or the screen menu that appears when you select the * * * * item at the top of the screen menu (see fig. 4.21). You can make the pop-up menu appear at the cursor's location by pressing the third button on your input device. This is the middle button on a three-button mouse (the lowest-numbered button after the pick and Enter buttons on a digitizer cursor). On many pointing devices, this button is marked with a 3; this book refers to it as the *pop-up button*. Some mouse drivers may not support the middle button, and some mice have only two buttons. You also can access the pop-up menu by pressing button 2 (the Enter button) while holding down the Shift key.

You can find the OSNAP command on the SETTINGS screen menu or on the Running Object Snap dialog box under the **S**ettings pull-down menu. The object snap options are the same for both overrides and running modes. You also can specify object snaps from the keyboard.

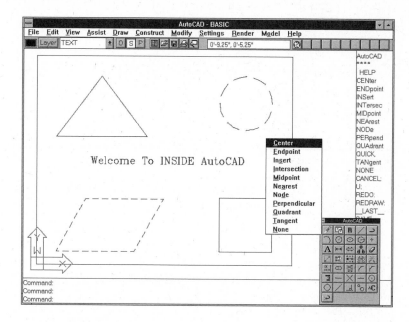

**Figure 4.21:**

The pop-up, screen, and toolbox menus for object snaps.

**TIP**

*If you type the object snap modifiers, just enter the first word or the first three or four characters, such as MID or PER. If you are using ENDPoint, get in the habit of entering* **ENDP** *rather than* **END***, to avoid accidentally ending your drawing.*

## Using Object Snaps as Single-Pick Filters

To learn how overrides work, you use the NODe and ENDPoint object snaps in the following exercise to draw a line from the point entity (the first point you drew in the drawing) in the triangle to the corner of the triangle. NODe snaps to a point entity, not to the triangle's geometric node.

### Using the NODe and ENDPoint Object Snaps

Command: *From the toolbar, click on the*
S *button to turn off Snap*

Command: *From the toolbox, choose* LINE

`_line From point:` **NODE**                              Specifies the NODe object snap

`NODe of` *Pick point* ① *near the point*     Snaps to the point entity
*entity in the triangle (see fig. 4.22)*

*continues*

| | |
|---|---|
| To point: *From the toolbox, choose* **ENDPOINT** | Issues the ENDPoint object snap override |
| endp of *Pick point ② near the triangle's corner (see fig. 4.22)* | Snaps to the end point (see fig. 4.23) |
| To point: *Press Enter* | Ends the LINE command |

**Figure 4.22:**

Using the NODe and ENDPoint object snaps.

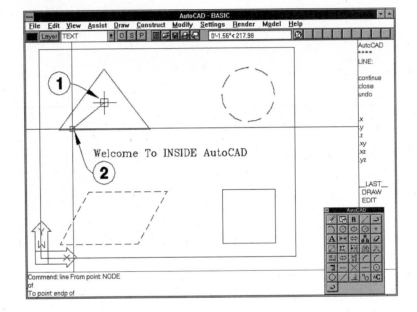

Figure 4.23 shows the result.

You have used object snap successfully. If a pick fails to find an object to snap to when an override mode is set, AutoCAD warns you and reprompts for the point, discarding the object snap setting.

A dense drawing can have several attachment points close to your pick point. If you want to snap to an intersection, AutoCAD may find one, but it may not be the intersection you want. Object snap uses a tolerance or *target* box to identify the points it considers as candidates for the snap attachment (see fig. 4.24). This tolerance is controlled by an *aperture* box, which is an electronic bull's-eye that homes in on object snap points. AutoCAD uses the object snap only for objects that fall in the aperture. You should size your aperture according to the entities you are selecting, the drawing's zoom settings, the display resolution, and the drawing density.

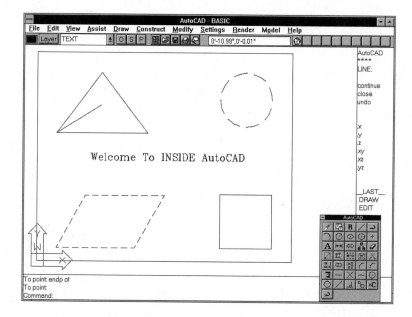

**Figure 4.23:**

The line drawn with object snaps.

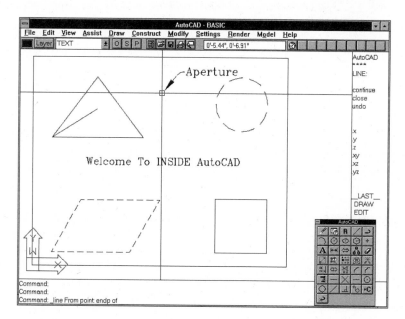

**Figure 4.24:**

The object snap aperture.

## Setting the Aperture and Picking a Point

In the following exercise you set the aperture to control the size of the crosshairs' bull's-eye. You can use the APERTURE command or the APERTUR: selection from the SETTINGS screen menu. You also can adjust the aperture by using a slider bar in the Running Object Snap dialog box. To access this dialog box, choose **O**bject Snap from the **S**ettings pull-down menu.

---

### Using Aperture To Set the Object Snap Target

Continue in the BASIC drawing from the previous exercise.

| | |
|---|---|
| Command: *From the screen menu,* *choose* SETTINGS, *then* APERTUR: | Issues the APERTURE command |
| Command: _APERTURE | |
| Object snap target height (1-50 pixels) <10>: *From the screen menu,* *choose* 5 | Sets the aperture's size to five pixels from the center point |

---

A *pixel* is the smallest dot that your screen can display. Four to six pixels (the default value is ten) give a good target size, depending on the resolution of your display. The size is measured from the aperture's center, so five pixels make a ten-pixel-high aperture box. Try a few different values to see how comfortable you feel with larger and smaller apertures.

*A small aperture size finds points faster and more accurately in crowded drawings, but it is harder to line up. A large aperture is easy to line up, but it is slower and less accurate. If you have 1024×768 or greater screen resolution, you may want to set the aperture size to eight or ten rather than the setting specified in the preceding exercise.*

*Display drivers that use display list (virtual-screen) technology to provide faster pans and zooms can take over control of the aperture setting. See your display driver's manual for information.*

The following exercises demonstrate the operation of the remaining object snaps. These object snaps include INTersection, MIDpoint, PERpendicular, INSert, TANgent, CENter, QUAdrant, and NEAr. The point that INSert finds on a text entity depends on the type of justification that was used to create the text.

## Completing the Object Snap Options

| | |
|---|---|
| Command: **L** ↵ | Issues the LINE command |
| Command: LINE From point: **@** ↵ | Starts the line from the last point that was specified |
| To point: *From the toolbox, choose* INTERSECTION | Issues the INTersect object snap |
| int of *Pick* ① *near the intersection of the parallelogram (see fig 4.25)* | Finds the intersection of the two selected lines |
| To point: *From the toolbox, choose* MIDPOINT | Issues the MIDpoint object snap |
| mid of *Pick* ② *or anywhere on the triangle's base line* | Finds the midpoint |
| To point: *From the toolbox, choose* PERPENDICULAR | Issues the PERpendicular object snap |
| per to *Pick* ③ *or anywhere on the triangle's right side* | Finds perpendicular from base to side |
| To point: *From the screen menu, choose* * * * * , *then* INSert | Displays the screen menu of object snaps and issues the INS override |
| _INSERT of *Pick* ④ *or anywhere on the text* | Finds the center text insertion point |
| To point: *From the toolbox, choose* TANGENT | Issues the TANgent object snap |
| tan to *Pick* ⑤ *on the circle's upper left side (see fig. 4.26)* | Finds the tangent point |
| To point: *From the toolbox, choose* CENTER | Issues the CENter object snap |
| cen of *Pick* ⑥ *or anywhere on the circle* | Finds the circle's center point |
| To point: **QUA** ↵ | Issues the QUAdrant object snap |
| of *Pick* ⑦ *near the circle's bottom* | Finds the 270-degree quadrant point |
| To point: *From the toolbox, choose* NEAREST | Issues the NEArest object snap |
| nea to *Pick* ⑧ *or anywhere on the line from the text to the circle* | Finds the closest point to the point you picked |
| To point: *Press Enter* | Ends the LINE command |

**Figure 4.25:**

Using the
INTersection,
MIDpoint,
PERpendicular,
and INSert object
snaps.

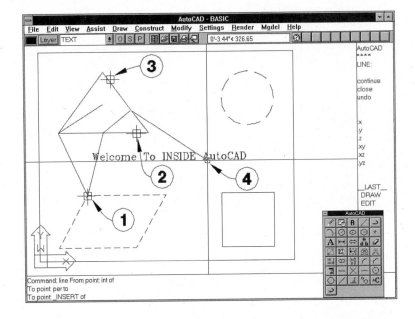

**Figure 4.26:**

Using the
TANgent, CENter,
QUAdrant, and
NEAr object
snaps.

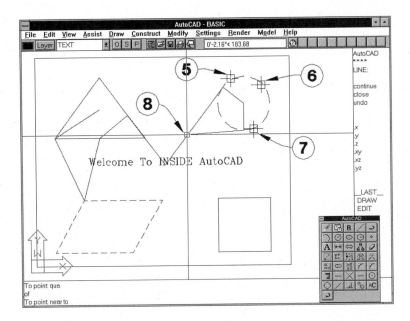

Your drawing should now look like figure 4.27.

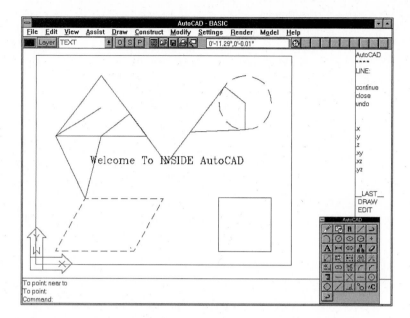

**Figure 4.27:**

The completed line, drawn with object snaps.

# Using QUIck To Optimize OSNAP

When you use an object snap, AutoCAD must search every object in the drawing window to find all the objects that cross the aperture box. The program then calculates potential points for all qualified objects to find the best (closest) fit for the object snap you issue. This process can take some time if the drawing contains many objects.

You can shorten the object snap search process by reducing the size of the aperture to keep extraneous objects out of the target. You also can use the QUIck object snap option, which enables AutoCAD to take the most recently created object that meets your object snap criteria, instead of doing an exhaustive search and comparison to find the closest object. You invoke QUIck by using it as a prefix for other object snap option(s), such as QUI,INT for a quick intersection.

When you invoke QUIck, AutoCAD occasionally finds a different fit from the one you want. If this happens, simply cancel the current command and start the object snap process again without the QUIck modifier. The following list explains all the OSNAP options, including the QUIck modifier:

- **CENter.** This option snaps to the center of an arc or circle.

- **ENDPoint.** This option snaps to the nearest endpoint of a line or arc.

- **INSert.** This option snaps to the origin of text, attributes, and symbols (block or shape) that have been inserted into the drawing file. (You learn more about blocks, shapes, and attributes in Chapter 11.)

- **INTersection.** This option snaps to the nearest intersection of any combination of two lines, arcs, or circles.

- **MIDpoint.** When you choose the MIDpoint option, AutoCAD snaps to the midpoint of a line or arc.

- **NEArest.** This option snaps to the nearest point on an entity. This is generally an endpoint, a tangent, or a perpendicular point.

- **NODe.** This option snaps to a point entity.

- **PERpendicular.** This option snaps to a point on a line, arc, or circle that, for the picked entity, would form a perpendicular (normal) line from the last point to the picked entity. The resulting point need not even be on the entity.

- **TANgent.** This option snaps to a point on an arc or circle that forms a tangent to the picked arc or circle from the last point.

- **QUAdrant.** This option snaps to the closest 0-, 90-, 180-, or 270-degree point on an arc or circle.

- **QUIck.** This option forces all other object snap options to find the first potential target quickly. The point QUIck chooses is not necessarily the closest target. QUIck finds the potential point that is on the most recently qualified object in the target box.

- **NONe.** This option removes or overrides any running object snap.

*In the preceding list,* line *and* arc *refer to line and arc entities and each edge or segment of solid, trace, 3Dface, viewport, polygon mesh, or polyline entities. Polylines are treated as if they have zero width. Although some of these entities may not be familiar to you, the book covers them in later chapters.*

*Generally, references to object snap modes are abbreviated to their first three letters throughout the rest of the book.*

In previous exercises, you used object snaps as overrides in the middle of the LINE command to fine-tune line endpoints. This override mode temporarily sets up an object snap aperture condition to complete the task at hand. Frequently, however, you may need to use the same mode or combination of modes repeatedly. For this reason, AutoCAD enables you to set running modes.

# Using a Running Mode Object Snap

An object snap condition that is set to be in effect until you change it is called a *running mode*. You use the OSNAP command to set running object snap modes. Running mode object snaps remain in effect until you replace them with another running mode setting or until you temporarily override them. If a pick fails to find an object to snap to when a running mode is set, AutoCAD finds the point it would have found if no object snap mode were set. Unlike SNAP, GRID, and ORTHO, the OSNAP command is not transparent; fortunately, overrides are transparent. Use the NONe override to temporarily suppress a running mode.

 *If a running object snap is on, the crosshairs have a bull's-eye aperture during point entry and object selection.*

In the following exercise, you draw a diamond in the square by using a running MID object snap mode.

## Using a Running Object Snap To Put a Diamond in a Square

| | |
|---|---|
| Command: *Choose* **S**ettings, *then* **O**bject Snap | Issues the DDOSNAP command and displays the Running Object Snap dialog box |
| Command: *Put a check in the* **M**idpoint *check box, then choose* OK | Sets MID as the running object snap mode |
| Command: *From the toolbox, choose* LINE | Displays the Aperture box |
| From point: *Pick point* ① *on the top line (see fig. 4.28)* | Snaps to the midpoint of the line |
| To point: *Pick point* ② *on the right line* | Snaps to the midpoint |
| To point: *Pick point* ③ *on the bottom line* | Snaps to the midpoint |
| To point: *Pick point* ④ *on the left line* | Snaps to the midpoint |
| To point: *Pick point* ⑤ *on the top line* | Snaps to the midpoint |
| To point: *Press Enter* | Ends the LINE command |
| Command: **OSNAP** ↵ | Issues the OSNAP command |
| Object snap modes: **NONe** ↵ | Resets the running object snap mode to NONe |

**Figure 4.28:**

Drawing with a running MIDpoint object snap.

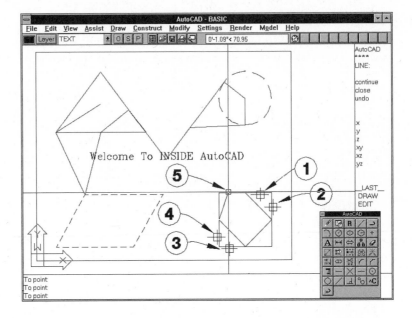

You can specify two or more running or override modes at once; AutoCAD finds the calculated point of whichever mode is closest to the crosshairs. Specify multiple modes by checking multiple check boxes in the Running Object Snap dialog box. If you use the OSNAP command at the Command: prompt, include multiple object snap modes on the Command: prompt and separate them with commas, as in END,MID,CEN.

*The INT,ENDP,MID running object snap mode should cover most of your object selection requirements.*

Use the override modes whenever the need arises; they override running modes. Set up a running object snap whenever you repeatedly use the same object snap mode(s).

# Using REDRAW and BLIPMODE for a Clean Drawing Window

As you worked through the object snap exercises, you probably noticed that when you enter a point (either with a cursor or from the keyboard), AutoCAD places a small cross (blip) on the screen. As you draw, you fill up the drawing area with real drawing entities (such as lines and circles) and construction markers. A few blips are useful for keeping an eye on where you have been (or might want to go again), but they become distracting if they accumulate on the screen.

As you draw, erase, and move entities, pieces of lines and entities seem to disappear. Although they usually are still there, a gap is left in the underlying entity's representation in the drawing window after you erase or move an entity that overlaps another.

You can use the REDRAW command to clean up the drawing, redraw underlying entities, and get rid of blips. Erase a line and try it.

---

### Using REDRAW To Clear Up the Drawing Window

`Command:` *Choose* **M**odify, *then* **E**rase,
*then* **Si**ngle

`_erase Select objects: single`

`Select objects:` *Pick a point on the*          Erases the line
*line from the triangle to the center*
*of the text*

The line is gone (see fig. 4.29). Part of the triangle also seems to be gone.

`Command:` *From the toolbox,*          Redraws the drawing window: the blips are
*choose* REDRAW          gone and the triangle is okay (see fig. 4.30)

`Command:` *Choose* **F**ile, *then* E**x**it          Discards changes to the drawing
AutoCAD, *then* **D**iscard Changes

---

The display appears as before in figure 4.30, but without the blip marks.

If you do not need blips, you can use the BLIPMODE command to suppress construction markers. You can prevent AutoCAD from drawing these temporary markers by turning off BLIPMODE. To suppress blips, set BLIPMODE's value to 0.

**Figure 4.29:**

The display after ERASE and before REDRAW.

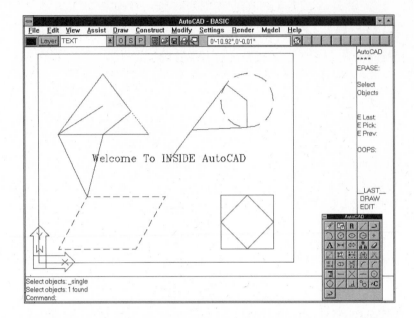

**Figure 4.30:**

The display after REDRAW.

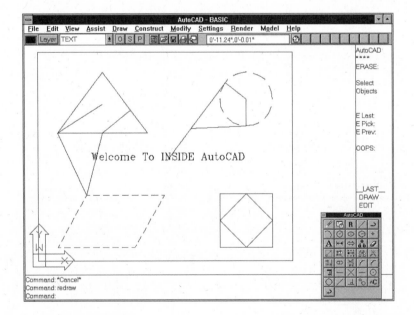

# Summary

A trick for ensuring accurate drawing is to use relative and polar points, with the coordinate display used for reference. Use the GRID command to give you a frame of reference; use the SNAP command to limit your crosshairs and picks to preset increments. If you need to draw at 90-degree increments, activate the ORTHO command. If you need to align your coordinate system with your drawing, you can change the UCS. Many users find it helpful to jot down notes or make up a checklist to keep track of these display settings.

To construct geometrically accurate objects, use coordinate entry and object snap for snapping to objects. You can invoke the Osnap options temporarily as an override to any point-picking command. A running object snap mode sets up a full-time mode and aperture that you can still override. Try to find a good aperture setting to control the reliability and speed of your object snap searches. The toolbox provides easy access to commands you use often. Try to use it instead of searching through other menus for these commands.

Throughout the rest of this book, you often see coordinates given in response to prompts with the exercises. You can type them and press Enter, or you can pick the coordinates with the pointing device if you are sure the pick is accurate. Remember that the crosshairs position is only accurate with snap on or with object snap. Use object snap at every opportunity you can. Your drawing productivity will improve, and you can be confident that your work is accurate. Now that you have had a chance to experiment with object snaps, move on to learning how to get around in AutoCAD.

# Controlling the Graphics Display

Whether you set your drawing limits to represent a drawing that is 2' × 3' or 2,000' × 3,000', your computer's screen is not large enough to give you a one-to-one view of the drawing file. In this chapter, you learn how to use AutoCAD's tools to control your location in the display, your future location, and your movement from one location to another.

In AutoCAD, your graphics window becomes a *viewport* into your drawing, enabling you to zoom in and out, and to move around the drawing. You actually have been working in a viewport all along—a single viewport that uses the entire drawing area. In this chapter, you learn to use multiple viewports, as shown in figure 5.1, to see several parts of your drawing simultaneously, and to scale the viewports to different sizes for eventual plotting.

AutoCAD's display controls make drawing easier. Basic display-control commands, such as ZOOM and PAN, function in AutoCAD just like their photographic counterparts. The ZOOM command enables you to magnify your drawing to do detailed work. PAN enables you to slide your drawing from side-to-side so that you can work on large objects without having to return to a full-drawing view to determine your location in the drawing. Simple controls, such as REDRAW and REGEN, enable you to clean up your drawing or display its most current view.

**Figure 5.1:**

The drawing area, divided into three viewports.

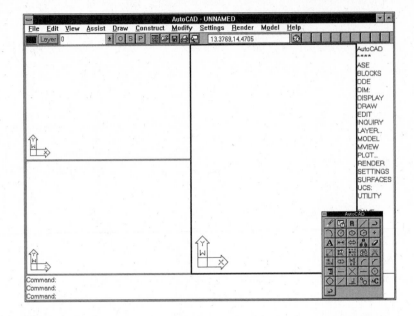

To make drawing easier, you can open multiple viewports in the drawing area to display your model at different scales and from different viewpoints. You also can use these viewports to display areas of your model that normally are not visible at the same time, such as both ends of a long part. You can see your entire object in a single viewport, for example, while you zoom in to work on a drawing detail in a second viewport. You can view a parts schedule in one viewport while you check your drawing annotations in another. You can even set many of AutoCAD's controls—such as snap, grid, and the UCS icon—differently in each viewport. When you save your drawing, the viewport setup is saved with it so that you do not need to re-create the viewports every time you load the drawing.

The display-control tools are located on the **V**iew pull-down menu and the DISPLAY screen menu, as shown in figure 5.2.

# Maximizing the Graphics Display

Before you learn to manipulate the entities in the graphics window, you must understand that the graphics window itself can be controlled, much like any Windows application package. The AutoCAD window can be reduced to an icon by clicking on the *minimize* button, which is a down arrow in the upper right corner of the graphics window. Double-clicking on the icon restores the window.

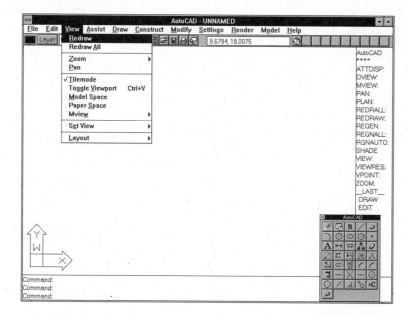

**Figure 5.2:**

The View pull-down menu and DISPLAY screen menus.

*After you have minimized the window to an icon, be sure to return to that same icon to open the window. If you try to return to AutoCAD by clicking on the icon you normally use to start up AutoCAD, you will have two sessions running concurrently.*

When open but not maximized, the AutoCAD window size can be adjusted by moving the cursor to the edge or corner of the window, where the cursor should change to a double arrow. Then hold the button down and drag the edge or corner to a new position. You can move the entire window by dragging the titlebar. The up-arrow button next to the minimize button causes the AutoCAD window to fill the screen. This button is called the *maximize* button. See Appendix B for more information on the Windows interface.

*If you have several Windows applications open with AutoCAD, you may want the AutoCAD window reduced in size to view your other applications concurrently. This arrangement is especially helpful when using "drag-and-drop" features, or "pasting" data between applications.*

# Setting Up the Display Controls

You do not need an elaborate drawing to get a feel for display controls; the simple geometric shapes in the BASIC drawing (which you saved in Chapter 4) work well enough for you to practice getting around the drawing area. You can use the drawing named IAWBASIC.DWG, found on the IAW DISK. It is identical to the BASIC drawing. In Chapter 4, you used the Create New Drawing dialog's <u>P</u>rototype option to specify the IAW DISK prototype drawing. When you know the name of the prototype, you can enter it directly by using an equal sign, as shown in the following exercise. Table 5.1 shows the settings that should be in the BASIC drawing.

**Table 5.1**
**BASIC Drawing Settings**

| GRID | SNAP | ORTHO | UCS | UCSICON |
|---|---|---|---|---|
| On | Off | Off | World | On |

| | |
|---|---|
| **UNITS** | Engineering, 2 decimal places, 2 fractional places for angles, defaults all other settings. |
| **LIMITS** | 0,0 to 11,8.5 |

| Layer Name | State | Color | Linetype |
|---|---|---|---|
| 0 | On/Current | White | CONTINUOUS |
| CIRCLE | On | Green | DASHED |
| PARAGRAM | On | Blue | HIDDEN |
| SQUARE | On | Yellow | CONTINUOUS |
| TEXT | On | Cyan | CONTINUOUS |
| TRIANGLE | On | Red | CONTINUOUS |

## Loading the BASIC=IAWBASIC Drawing

Choose <u>F</u>ile, then <u>N</u>ew, type **BASIC=IAWBASIC** in the drawing name text box and press Enter or choose OK, then choose OK to replace the existing BASIC drawing, if prompted.

Your drawing should look like figure 5.3 and match the settings in table 5.1.

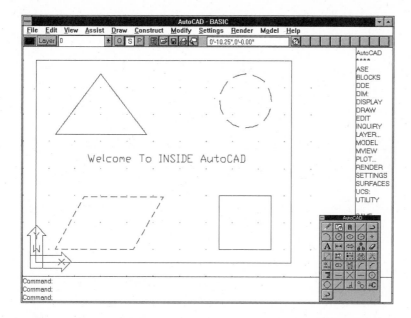

**Figure 5.3:**

The BASIC drawing.

# Controlling the Drawing Display

Now that the drawing is loaded and visible in the drawing editor, suppose that you want to look more closely at the triangle. To do this, you need to zoom in on the drawing. The most common way to tell AutoCAD what part of the current drawing you want to enlarge is to pick diagonal corners of a box, or *window,* around the area of interest. Use the ZOOM command with the Window option to zoom in on your drawing.

## Using Zoom Window

Do the following exercise to become more familiar with the ZOOM command's Window option. You do not need to pick exact coordinates; just indicate roughly the area you want to see in more detail.

### Using ZOOM Window

Use the S toolbar button to turn on Snap.

Command: *Choose* **V**iew, *then* **Z**oom, *then* **W**indow

Issues the ZOOM command with the Window option

Command:_'zoom

*continues*

```
All/Center/Dynamic/Extents/Left/
Previous/Vmax/Window/<Scale(X/XP)>:
_window
```

First corner: *Pick ① (see fig. 5.4)*          Sets the window's lower left window

Other corner: *Pick ②*                          Sets the window's upper right corner

**Figure 5.4:**

Creating a Zoom
Window.

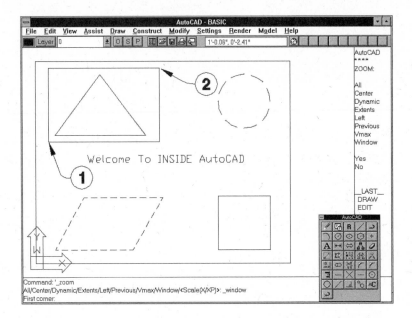

Notice that after you pick the first corner, instead of the normal crosshairs, your cursor
changes to a *rubber-band* box. As soon as you pick the second corner, AutoCAD displays the area of the drawing that you enclosed in the window, as shown in figure 5.5.
The corners that you pick guide AutoCAD in determining the new area to display.
This area usually is not exactly the same shape as originally displayed because
AutoCAD maintains its 1:1 X and Y display aspect ratio, regardless of the aspect
ratio (proportions) of the window you specify.

The following exercise shows you how to zoom closer to the upper point of the triangle by creating another zoom window. After you pick the new corners, AutoCAD
redraws the drawing area. You do not need to specify the Window option. When the
ZOOM command is issued, you can automatically start a window simply by picking a
point on the screen. The toolbar also has an icon that executes the ZOOM command
with the Window option.

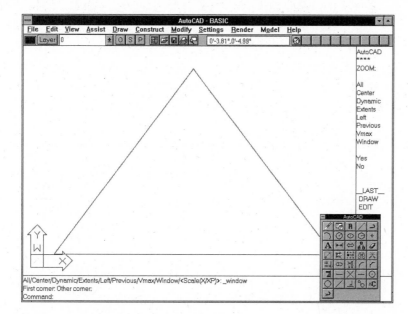

**Figure 5.5:**

The view of the drawing after ZOOM Window.

## Using ZOOM Window To Zoom Closer

Command: **ZOOM** ⏎

All/Center/Dynamic/Extents/Left/Previous/
Vmax/Window/<Scale(X/XP)>: *Pick the window's lower left corner (see fig. 5.6)*

Other corner: *Pick the upper right corner (see fig. 5.6)*

After you pick the upper right corner, AutoCAD redraws the screen and magnifies the top of the triangle, as shown in figure 5.7.

How far can you zoom in? Suppose, for example, that you draw the entire solar system at full scale, which is about 7 million miles across. If you draw the solar system with enough detail, you can position your view at the outskirts of the galaxy and zoom in close enough to read a book on a desk. AutoCAD is capable of such drawings because it is precise within at least 14 significant digits.

**Figure 5.6:**

The second Zoom
Window.

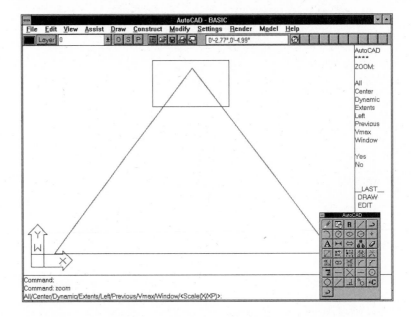

**Figure 5.7:**

The triangle's
magnified top,
after the second
zoom.

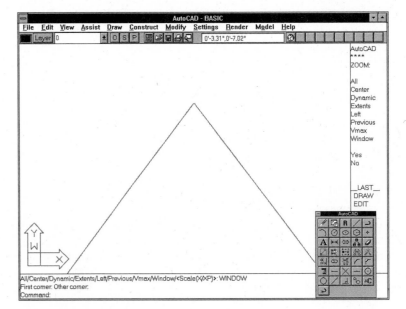

*You do not have to issue the Window option to perform a ZOOM Window. The default ZOOM command accepts two corner points and zooms to the window that they define. Just enter **ZOOM**, and then pick two points to perform a ZOOM Window.*

Try zooming in on your drawing once more, before you zoom back to a full view.

## Zooming Out with Zoom All

If you want to zoom back out to view the entire drawing after you have zoomed in on it, you can use the ZOOM command's All option. The All option is the easiest way to return to the full display of your drawing file. The following exercise shows you how to zoom back out to the drawing's extents after having zoomed in on a detail.

---

### Using Zoom All

Command: *Choose **V**iew, then **Z**oom, then **A**ll*

Issues the ZOOM command with the All option

```
Command: _zoom
All/Center/Dynamic/Extents/
Left/Previous/Vmax/Window/
<Scale(X/XP)>: all
Regenerating drawing.
```

---

Your on-screen view of the drawing should appear as it did when you started. When AutoCAD executes the ZOOM command with the All option, it regenerates the current viewport with everything in the drawing file. If you draw within the drawing limits, ZOOM All returns the display screen to its limits. If your drawing exceeds the limits you set for it, ZOOM All zooms beyond the limits to display everything in the drawing file.

## Examining ZOOM's Other Options

As you have seen, the Window and All options enable you simply to move in closer to your drawing and move back from it. The ZOOM command, however, is one of AutoCAD's most powerful and versatile display-control commands, and it features several useful options, including the following:

- **All.** In 2D (plan view), this option displays the drawing's limits or extents, whichever is larger. In a 3D view, All displays the drawing's extents.

- **Center.** This option zooms to the center point and displays the height (in drawing units) or the magnification that you specify. Pick a new center and press Enter to pan (move the display at the current zoom magnification). The center point you pick becomes the viewport's center. To keep the center point unchanged and to change the display height or magnification, press Enter at the new center point prompt instead of specifying a new point.

- **Dynamic.** This option graphically combines the PAN command with the ZOOM command's All and Window options. Dynamic displays an image of the entire generated portion of your drawing, and you use the cursor to tell AutoCAD where to zoom. Dynamic can zoom in or out, or it can pan the current viewport. Dynamic is explained in more detail later in this chapter.

- **Extents.** This option displays all the drawing entities as large as possible in the current viewport.

- **Left.** This option zooms to the lower left corner and displays the height (in drawing units) or the magnification that you specify. The point you specify becomes the new lower left corner of the current viewport. In all other ways, Left works in the same way as Center.

- **Previous.** This option restores a previous display for the current viewport, whether it was generated by the ZOOM, PAN, VIEW, or DVIEW commands. AutoCAD stores up to ten previous views for each viewport; you can step back through them by using the Previous option repeatedly.

- **Vmax.** This option zooms to the currently generated virtual screen, to display the maximum possible drawing area without a regeneration.

- **Window.** This option zooms to the rectangular area you specify by picking two diagonally opposite corner points. When you issue the ZOOM command, you can automatically begin a zoom window by picking a point on the screen. Unless the X,Y proportions of the window you specify exactly match the proportions of the viewport, a little extra width or height of the image shows.

- **Scale(X/XP).** This option requires you to enter a magnification factor for AutoCAD to use in zooming. The Scale option is the default. In other words, you can type a scale factor without specifying the Scale option. If you enter a number, such as **2**, you create a zoom scale that is twice what is shown by the limits. If you specify a scale factor followed by an X—such as .8X—you create a view with a scale of .8 of the existing view. The XP option is for a scale relative to paper space.

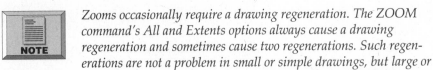

*Zooms occasionally require a drawing regeneration. The ZOOM command's All and Extents options always cause a drawing regeneration and sometimes cause two regenerations. Such regenerations are not a problem in small or simple drawings, but large or complex drawings can take a long time to regenerate. If you use the ZOOM command's Previous or Vmax options, you can often avoid forcing AutoCAD to regenerate your drawing.*

# Keeping Track of Zoom Displays

Every time you zoom in or out, AutoCAD keeps track of the previous display, up to ten zooms. In the following exercise, you learn how to use the Left, Center, and Previous options.

## Using ZOOM Left, Center, and Previous

Command: *From the screen menu, choose* DISPLAY, *then* ZOOM:    Starts the ZOOM command

Command: _'ZOOM

All/Center/Dynamic/Extents/Left/
Previous/Vmax/Window/<Scale(X/XP)>:
L ↵    Specifies the Left option

Lower left corner point: *Pick near the*    Sets the lower left corner
*point 2.50,2.00 or enter the coordinates*

Magnification or Height <0'-8.50">:    Specifies the window's height and zooms
4.5 ↵    (see fig. 5.8)

Use the S button on the toolbar to turn snap off.

Command: *Press Enter*    Repeats the ZOOM command

_'ZOOM

All/Center/Dynamic/Extents/
Left/Previous/Vmax/Window/
<Scale(X/XP)>: C ↵    Specifies the Center option

Center point: *Pick a point on the letter W*    Sets the window's center point

Magnification or Height    Specifies the window's height and zooms in on
<0'-4.50">:.5 ↵    the drawing  (see fig. 5.9)

Command: *Press Enter*    Repeats the ZOOM command

_'ZOOM

All/Center/Dynamic/Extents/Left/
Previous/Vmax/Window/<Scale(X/XP)>:
P ↵    Zooms back to the previous view

Command: *Press Enter*    Repeats the ZOOM command

_'ZOOM

All/Center/Dynamic/Extents/Left/
Previous/Vmax/Window/<Scale(X/XP)>:
P ↵    Zooms to the previous view

If all goes well, you should end up where you started, with a full view of your drawing.

**Figure 5.8:**

The result of the ZOOM command's Left option.

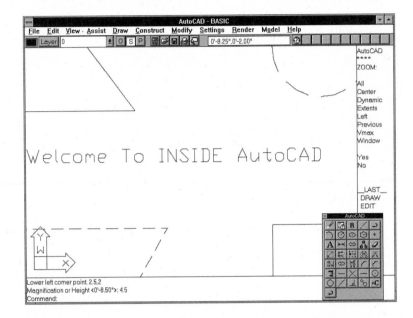

**Figure 5.9:**

The result of the ZOOM command's Center option.

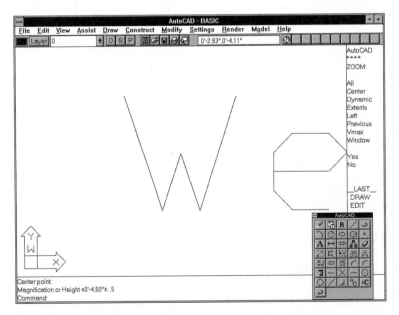

*The Previous option does not necessarily zoom out. It simply returns to a previous view, whether larger or smaller than the current view, including views created by the PAN and VPOINT commands.*

You may have noticed a speed difference between zooms that regenerate the drawing and those that do not. In a complex drawing, this time difference can be considerable. To control drawing regenerations, you need to understand how ZOOM works. The following section explains AutoCAD's virtual screen.

# Understanding AutoCAD's Virtual Screen

To understand the ZOOM command, you need to understand the relationship of REDRAW, REGEN, and the virtual screen. When you load a new drawing or use the REGEN command, AutoCAD recalculates the current view to its full 14 places of precision. The program calculates this as if the display were a 32,000×32,000-pixel display screen, or the *virtual screen*. The virtual screen contains the last regeneration, or recalculation, of the graphic database. AutoCAD translates this calculated image to your actual display area and redraws the current viewport. AutoCAD can perform a redraw quickly, several times as quickly as a regeneration. This translation is what occurs when you use the REDRAW command, turn on the grid, turn on layers, or change other settings that cause a redraw.

Many kinds of zooms require only a redraw, not a regeneration. The drawing does not regenerate as long as you do not zoom outside of the current virtual screen or zoom so far into tiny detail that AutoCAD cannot translate accurately from the virtual screen. When a zoom occurs without a regeneration, it occurs at redraw speed.

*Resizing the AutoCAD graphics window also causes a regeneration and sometimes zooms out as well. If the window is not maximized, you can resize it by moving the cursor to any edge or corner where the cursor changes to a double arrow. Then, press the pointer button, drag the corner or edge, and release the button. (If the window is maximized, first click on the maximize button at the upper right corner of the window.) If the resized window differs in aspect ratio (X:Y size) from the original, AutoCAD will zoom out to avoid clipping off any of the original window's contents.*

If you want your zooms to be fast, you need to avoid regenerations. Zooming in to a larger magnification usually is no problem. The easiest way to control regenerations when zooming out is to use the ZOOM Dynamic option.

# Using ZOOM's Dynamic Option

You have used the basic two-step process of zooming in on your drawing with a window and zooming back out by using the ZOOM command's All option. What if you want to magnify a small portion of the drawing while you already are zoomed in to a different section? The ZOOM command's Dynamic option enables you to control and display your zoom window in a single step without having to use the ZOOM command's All option.

AutoCAD actually has three display subsets. When you work with a dynamic zoom, these subsets are shown in the current viewport. AutoCAD uses the following display sets:

- **Drawing extents.** This set displays everything in the drawing file.

- **Generated area.** This choice displays a portion (up to all) of the drawing file that AutoCAD has regenerated. This is the virtual screen.

- **Current view.** The current view displays a portion (up to all) of the generated data that appears in the current viewport.

When you select a dynamic zoom, you can see these areas graphically in the current viewport before you make a decision on the next view.

Figure 5.10 shows three rectangular areas outlined on the diagram. The large solid rectangle shows the entire drawing extents, and the current view is represented by a dashed rectangle.

**Figure 5.10:**

The ZOOM command's Dynamic option controls.

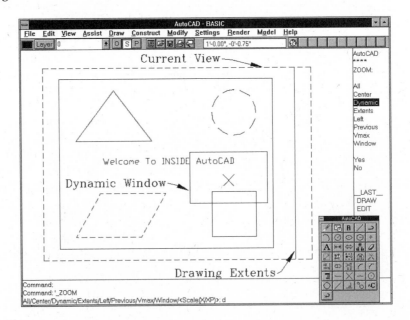

The third rectangular area is a dynamic window, which you can move with your pointer. Use this dynamic window to select the next view you want to see.

In the following exercise, you learn how to use the ZOOM command's Dynamic option. You first must use the ZOOM command's All option and then zoom in to magnify your drawing by a factor of three. Then call up the ZOOM command's Dynamic display.

## Using ZOOM Dynamic

| | |
|---|---|
| Command: *Choose* **V**iew, *then* **Z**oom, *then* **A**ll | Zooms to the drawing limits |
| Command: *Press Enter* | Repeats the ZOOM command |
| _ZOOM<br>All/Center/Dynamic/Extents/<br>Left/Previous/Vmax/Window/<<br>Scale(X/XP)>: **3** ↵ | Magnifies the display by a factor of three (see fig. 5.11) |
| Command: *Press Enter* | Repeats the ZOOM command |
| _ZOOM<br>All/Center/Dynamic/Extents/<br>Left/Previous/Vmax/Window/<br><Scale(X/XP)>: **D** ↵ | Displays the ZOOM command's Dynamic controls (see fig. 5.12) |

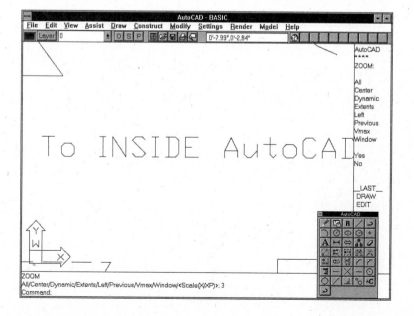

**Figure 5.11:**

The BASIC drawing magnified three times.

**Figure 5.12:**

The beginning of the ZOOM command's Dynamic option.

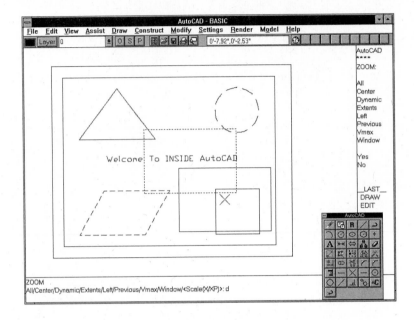

Your display should look like figure 5.12. By moving your pointer around, you can drag the dynamic viewing window around as if it were held by the X handle in the middle of the window. Your pointer also controls the window's size. When you click your pointing device's button, an arrow appears within the dynamic viewing window, enabling you to control the window's size. When you move the arrow to the right, you make the window larger; move the arrow to the left to make the window smaller.

When the window is the size you want, click again to lock in the size. You click the pointer button to move between the dynamic window size and its location.

After you capture the desired viewing area in the window, press Enter while holding the dynamic viewing window in place to select it. AutoCAD zooms to that new window.

## Continuing with the ZOOM Dynamic Command

Continue from the previous exercise, with the ZOOM command active. The following should still show on the prompt lines.

```
All/Center/Dynamic/Extents/Left/
Previous/Vmax/Window/<Scale(X/XP)>: D
```

*Drag the dynamic window around with the X handle shown at ① in figure 5.13*

*Click the pointer button*                    Switches to dynamic window sizing

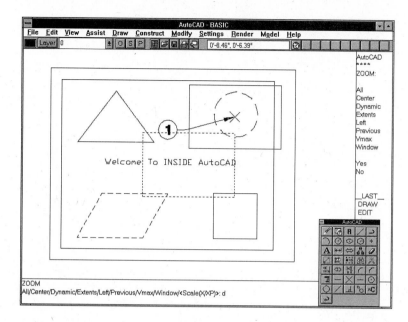

**Figure 5.13:**

Moving the
current view.

| | |
|---|---|
| Move the window horizontally by dragging it to ② in figure 5.14 | Stretches and shrinks the dynamic window |
| Click the pointer button | Switches to dynamic location control |
| Line up the dynamic viewing window (see ③ in fig. 5.15) | Encloses the circle |
| Hold the pointer in place, and press Enter or right-click | Displays the view shown in figure 5.16 |

*You might shrink the dynamic window so far that you see only the arrow or X. If this happens, you need to enlarge the window with the pointer to regain a visible window.*

*See the Aerial View section later in this chapter for a quicker alternative to ZOOM D. You can also do your own style of the Dynamic option of ZOOM by using the other ZOOM options and cutting them short. You can, for example, start the Previous option and cut it short by pressing Ctrl-C as soon as you see enough to decide where to go next. Then follow with your intended zoom.*

**Figure 5.14:**

Resizing the
current view.

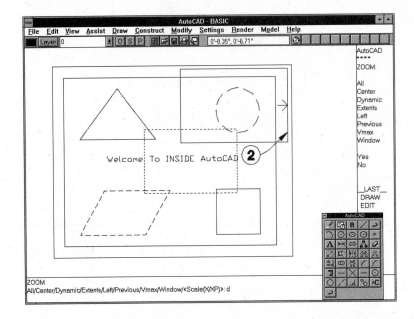

**Figure 5.15:**

The viewing
window that
encloses the circle.

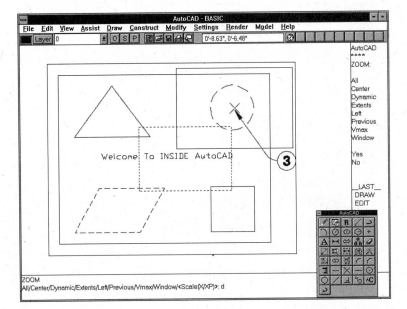

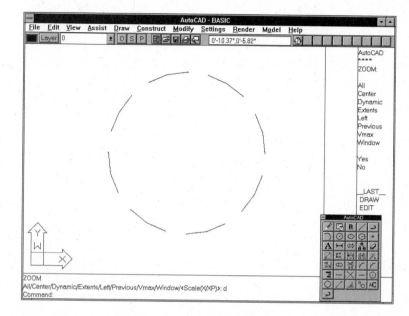

**Figure 5.16:**

The display after the ZOOM command's Dynamic option.

# Using Zoom's Extents Option

Now try zooming back out by using the ZOOM command's Extents option in the following exercise. The Extents and All options zoom out as far as needed, even beyond the limits, to display everything in the drawing file. Unlike All (which never zooms to a smaller area than the limits), the Extents option zooms to the smallest area possible that displays all the entities in the drawing.

## Using ZOOM Extents

| | |
|---|---|
| Command: **z** ↵ | Issues the ZOOM command |
| All/Center/Dynamic/Extents/<br>Left/Previous/Vmax/Window/<br><Scale(X/XP)>: **E** ↵ | Magnifies the drawing to the edge of the drawing border |

Your screen should look like the one shown in figure 5.17.

**Figure 5.17:**

The drawing after using ZOOM Extents.

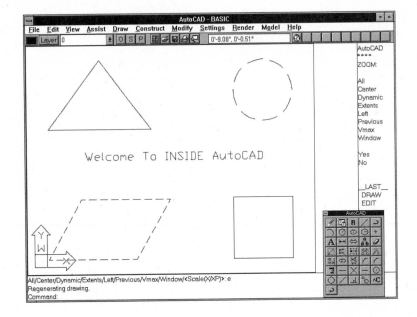

*Always use the ZOOM command's Extents option just before you end your drawing session. Extents acts as a check to let you know if you have drawn anything outside your limits. You can cut the zoom short by pressing Ctrl-C.*

You might notice that you can use the ZOOM command's Dynamic option to move your current view from side to side without changing the magnification. This movement is called *panning*. AutoCAD also has a PAN command, which you can use just for panning.

# Using PAN To Slide a View

The PAN command enables you to view other areas of the drawing by moving the drawing across the current viewport. If you are zoomed in to a given area of the drawing and you need to draw outside the current viewport, the PAN command enables you to shift the drawing to display the area you need to see. The PAN command behaves just like a camera pan. It enables you to move around the drawing at your current magnification.

To use the PAN command, you must supply AutoCAD with a *displacement*. A displacement is defined by two points, which determine the distance and direction of the pan. When you specify two points to identify a displacement, you specify a point at which

AutoCAD picks up the drawing (the *first* displacement point), and then specify another point at which the drawing can be placed (the *second* displacement point). Your display crosshairs trail a line from the first to the second displacement point, showing you the pan's path.

In the following exercise, use the PAN command to isolate the square in the upper left corner of your drawing area.

## Using PAN for Display

| | |
|---|---|
| Command: *Choose* **V**iew, *then* **P**an | Issues the PAN command |
| Command: _'pan displacement: *Pick a point at* ① *(see fig 5.18)* | Specifies the first displacement point |
| Second point: *Pick a point at* ② | Specifies the second point and pans the view |
| Command: *From the toolbar, choose* QSAVE | Saves BASIC drawing for later exercise |

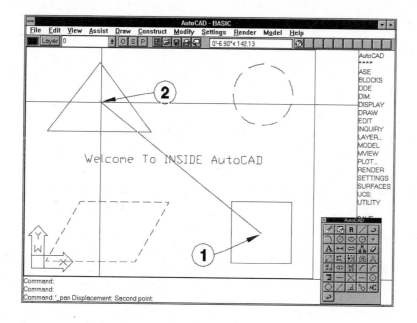

**Figure 5.18:**

Using the PAN command to show displacement.

Your screen should look like the one shown in figure 5.19.

**Figure 5.19:**

The view after the PAN command.

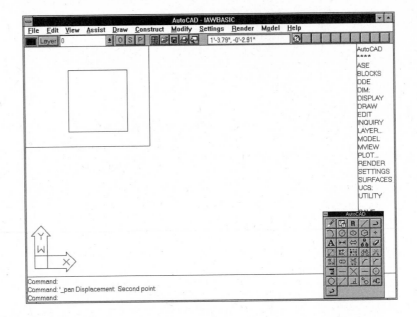

*When you use the ZOOM command's Dynamic option with a constant window size, it functions in much the same manner as the PAN command. You also can do limited panning by using the Center and Left ZOOM options and by keeping the same height.*

# Using the Aerial View and Scroll Bars To Zoom and Pan

AutoCAD Release 12 for Windows includes two viewing features not available in the DOS version (and most other versions) of AutoCAD: Aerial View and graphics window scroll bars. Depending on your configured display driver, you can use one or the other of these features, but not both. If you have configured AutoCAD with the Windows Accelerated Display Driver ADI 4.2 by Autodesk (with the Display-list option on), you can use the Aerial View, a separate little window in which you can specify zooms and pans. If you have configured AutoCAD with the nondisplay-list Windows driver by Autodesk, you can use the graphics window scroll bars to pan the drawing.

## Using Aerial View

The Aerial View feature is most useful in a large drawing, where it is all too easy to lose track of where you are. You could use ZOOM Dynamic, but it must regenerate the screen to display the drawing. This method is often unacceptably slow, particularly if the area of interest is late in the regeneration. Aerial View can display the entire drawing in a separate window that can be kept visible and immediately accessible, and this window requires no regeneration to use. You can quickly indicate and pan or zoom to any area you want. You can open the Aerial View window by either choosing the Aerial View (DSVIEWER) icon from the toolbar or entering DSVIEWER at the command prompt. Either method displays the current extents or the current virtual screen (whichever is less—usually the entire drawing) in the Aerial View window. Depending on the Aerial View option settings, you may need to redisplay Aerial View and/or click on its title bar to use it. When instructed to "Activate Aerial View" in the following exercises, click on the DSVIEWER icon on the toolbar and/or click on the Aerial View title bar as needed to display the Aerial View window and highlight its title bar. Aerial View will then be ready to pan or zoom your drawing. To return to the AutoCAD window when the Aerial View title bar is highlighted, simply click in the AutoCAD window.

The Aerial View menu bar (see fig. 5.20) contains an Options pull-down menu and the + (plus), - (minus), Pan, and Zoom commands.

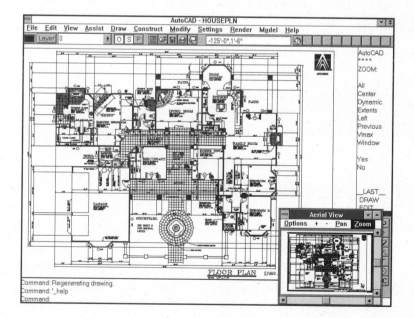

**Figure 5.20:**

The Aerial View window activated.

The **Z**oom command is selected and active by default. You simply pick two points in the Aerial View window to zoom the AutoCAD graphics window, as shown in the following exercise. To better appreciate the savings in time compared to using ZOOM D or multiple zooms, use a moderately complex drawing for this exercise. If you did not install the AutoCAD sample drawings, you can use any other moderately complex drawing.

## Activating Aerial View and Zooming with It

If not already configured for the Accelerated Display-list Driver, choose **F**ile, then **C**onfigure, press Enter, enter **3**, then **Y**, then **1**, make sure there is a check in the Display-list box and choose OK, and then press Enter three times to reconfigure the display driver.

| | |
|---|---|
| Command: *Choose **F**ile, then **O**pen and open the* HOUSEPLN *drawing in the* \ACADWIN\SAMPLE *directory (or use another drawing)* | Opens a sample drawing |
| Command: From the toolbar, choose the Aerial View (DSVIEWER) icon | Issues the DSVIEWER command |
| _DSVIEWER | Displays the Aerial View window |
| *Click on the Aerial View title bar* | Highlights title bar and activates window |
| *Resize the Aerial View window (press and drag on the lower right corner), then press and drag on the title bar to position it as shown in figure 5.20, leaving a bit of the toolbox exposed* | |

The Aerial View window is now active, with the default Zoom command highlighted and active.

| | |
|---|---|
| *Pick a point in the middle of the window, then a second point near the upper right corner* | Zooms to upper right corner in AutoCAD graphics window (see fig. 5.21) and returns to AutoCAD |

*You can choose **F**ile, then **P**references, then **S**ave to ACAD.INI, and then OK to save this Aerial View configuration.*

Notice that the zoomed area of the drawing is now indicated in the Aerial View window by a heavy rectangular line.

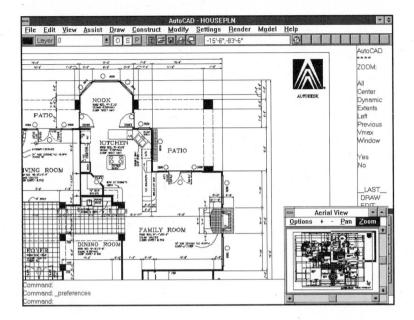

**Figure 5.21:**

AutoCAD window zoomed by Aerial View.

*Like most forms of ZOOM, Aerial View can be used transparently in the middle of most AutoCAD commands in model space; however, it is disabled in paper space mode or perspective views.*

Aerial View accomplishes its action in the AutoCAD window by issuing the AutoCAD ZOOM command, so you can use ZOOM Previous to return the AutoCAD window to previous views. It zooms, however, on the current view or settings within the Aerial View window itself.

*The U and UNDO commands may also return the AutoCAD window to previous views. In some cases, however, AutoCAD may also undo previous commands.*

## The Aerial View Commands and Menu

Although **Z**oom is the Aerial View default, the Aerial View menu bar offers several options and commands. The aerial view menu bar commands are described in the following list.

- **+** Magnifies the image in the Aerial View window 2x to display less of the drawing (does not affect the AutoCAD window).

- **-** Shrinks the image in the Aerial View window .5x to display more of the drawing (does not affect the AutoCAD window).

- **Pan.** Pans the drawing in the AutoCAD window to the view you pick in the Aerial View window (does not change the zoom magnification). The Aerial View window displays a dashed box sized to the current view to aid your view selection.

- **Zoom.** Zooms the drawing in the AutoCAD window to the area defined by the two corner points you pick in the Aerial View window. If you double-click on **Z**oom, it zooms the drawing in the AutoCAD window to the area currently visible in the Aerial View window.

The Aerial View options menu commands are as follows:

- **Global View.** Displays the current extents or the virtual screen (whichever is less) in the Aerial View window (does not affect the AutoCAD window). This option usually displays the entire drawing.

- **Locate.** Displays, in Aerial View, an 8x bird's-eye view of the cursor location as you move it around in the AutoCAD window. You can then right-click to use the Magnification dialog box to adjust the view magnification with a slider bar or by choosing + or **-**. When you pick a point in the AutoCAD window, the AutoCAD window zooms to the view in the Aerial View, but the Aerial View itself reverts to its previous view.

- **Statistics.** Displays memory and entity count statistics for the current viewport.

- **Auto Viewport.** When this option is checked, AutoCAD constantly updates the Aerial View window to the current viewport. Generally, the only change you see is in the heavy rectangular line in the Aerial View window indicating the zoomed area of the drawing. When this option is cleared, AutoCAD does not update the Aerial View window when you switch AutoCAD viewports until you reactivate the Aerial View window.

- **Window on Top.** When this option is checked, the Aerial View window remains on top of the AutoCAD window.

- **Dynamic Update.** When this option is checked, the Aerial View window updates as you edit the drawing in the AutoCAD window. When this option is cleared, the Aerial View window updates only when you reactivate it. You may want to set it off when you edit complex drawings.

In addition to these commands and menu items, you can also use the Aerial View window's scroll bars to pan the view in the Aerial View window. The scroll bars are at the right side and bottom of the Aerial View window. You can click on the arrow buttons at the top/bottom or left/right of the scroll bars, or drag the slider box (the box in the center of the scroll bar) up/down or left/right to pan the view in the Aerial View window. The scroll bars do not affect the AutoCAD window.

*To cancel an Aerial View command or menu item, click on the Aerial View title bar.*

Try the Aerial View +, -, and **P**an commands; the **G**lobal View, **L**ocate and Dynamic **U**pdate menu options; and the Aerial View scroll bars in the following exercise.

## Using Aerial View Commands and Options

Continue from the previous exercise.

| | |
|---|---|
| *Activate the Aerial View window and choose* **P**an | Displays a dashed box |
| *Drag the box to the lower left corner and click* | Zooms AutoCAD window to match area in box |
| *Activate the Aerial View window and choose* - | Displays more of the drawing in the Aerial View window (see fig. 5.22) |

Notice that the **P**an command is now the default.

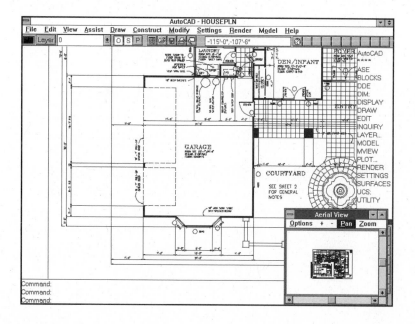

**Figure 5.22:**

Aerial View window zoomed out, with Pan active.

*continues*

| | |
|---|---|
| *Double-click on* **Z**oom | Zooms the AutoCAD window to match the Aerial View |
| *Activate the Aerial View window and choose* **O**ptions, *then* **G**lobal View | Displays original view (entire drawing) in the Aerial View |
| *Choose + three times* | Magnifies the center of the drawing in the Aerial View |

Notice that these last two steps left the AutoCAD window unchanged.

| | |
|---|---|
| *Choose* **O**ptions, *then* **L**ocate, *and drag the small crosshairs that appear in the center of the AutoCAD window* | Enters bird's-eye mode—Aerial View displays 8x view of the AutoCAD window cursor location |
| *Right-click* | Displays Magnification dialog box |
| *Choose* **-** *four times, then choose* OK | Displays 4x view in Aerial View |
| *Move crosshairs to the NOOK (at the upper right of the drawing, near the center—see AutoCAD window in figure 5.23), and click* | Zooms AutoCAD window to area shown in Aerial View |

**Figure 5.23:**

AutoCAD window after Aerial View **L**ocate.

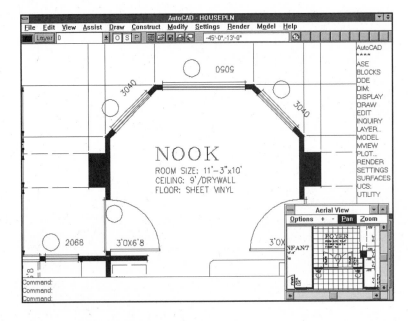

Aerial View now returns to its previous view (see fig. 5.23). You can use the scroll bars to position the Aerial View in the area of the Nook.

| | |
|---|---|
| *Activate the Aerial View window, then press and drag the right-side slider box up to the top three times, and the bottom-side slider box to the right side once* | Pans the Aerial View to approximately match the AutoCAD window's view |
| *Click three times on the the the right-side scroll bar's down-arrow button, then twice on the bottom-side scroll bar's left-arrow button* | Fine-adjusts the Aerial View to match the AutoCAD window's view |
| *Activate (click in) the AutoCAD window, pick the word NOOK, and enter* **E** | Erases the block of attribute text and updates Aerial View |
| Command: **U** ↵ | Unerases the text in AutoCAD and updates Aerial View |
| *Activate the Aerial View window, then Choose* **O**ptions, *then* **D**ynamic Update | Turns off updating during editing |
| *Activate the AutoCAD window, pick the word NOOK, and enter* **E** | Erases the text but does not update Aerial View |
| *Activate the Aerial View window* | Updates Aerial View |
| *Choose* **O**ptions, *then* **G**lobal View, *then Double-click on* **Z**oom *and continue to the next exercise, or exit AutoCAD without saving changes* | Restores original views |

If you have configured AutoCAD with the Windows driver by Autodesk instead of the Display-list driver, you cannot use the Aerial View. You can, however, use optional scroll bars in the AutoCAD graphics window to pan the drawing.

*In addition to Aerial View, the Autodesk display list driver offers performance improvements in redraws and object selection that make the use of the nondisplay-list driver rather inefficient by comparison. A lack of sufficient RAM memory for the display list driver is the only reason you should use the nondisplay-list driver.*

# Using the AutoCAD Graphics Window Scroll Bars

The nondisplay-list Windows driver by Autodesk offers you the use of optional graphics window scroll bars to pan the drawing. You turn on the scroll bars with the Preferences dialog box. Try it in the following exercise. The graphics window scroll bars work similarly to the Aerial View scroll bars described before the previous exercise, except that these scroll bars do affect the graphics window.

## Using Scroll Bars To Pan

If not already configured for the nondisplay-list Windows driver by Autodesk, choose File, then Configure, press Enter, enter 3, then Y, then 2, and then press Enter three times to reconfigure the display driver. The Aerial View disappears if it was present. Exit back to AutoCAD.

Command: *Choose File, then Preferences*     Turns on scroll bars
*and, in the* AutoCAD Graphics Window
*section, choose* Scroll Bars *unless there*
*is already a check in its check box,*
*then choose* OK, *then* Continue

The AutoCAD graphics window now displays scroll bars at the right and bottom. Press and drag the toolbox title bar, if necessary, to move the toolbox clear of the scroll bars.

Choose File, then Open, and open the HOUSEPLAN drawing in the \ACADWIN\SAMPLE directory (or use any moderately large drawing).

Command: *From the toolbar, choose* ZOOM
*and zoom in to the center of the drawing*
*(see fig. 5.24)*

Command: *Press and drag the bottom scroll*     Pans view to the right and redraws graphics
*bar's slider box to the right (see fig 5.25),*     graphics window
*then release*

To return to using the Accelerated Display-list Driver and Aerial View, reconfigure AutoCAD as instructed at the beginning of the earlier "Activating Aerial View and Zooming with It" exercise.

Continue to the next exercise and discard changes to this drawing, or exit AutoCAD without saving changes.

*To save the configuration with scroll bars on, you can choose File, then Preferences, then Save to ACAD.INI, then OK. However, returning to the Accelerated Display-list Driver configuration instead is probably a better choice.*

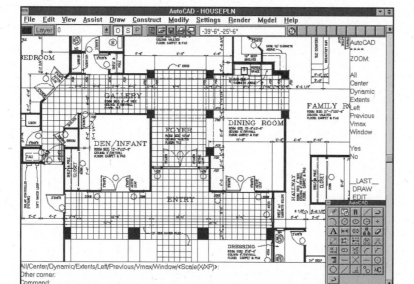

**Figure 5.24:**

Zoomed-in HOUSEPLN, with scroll bars.

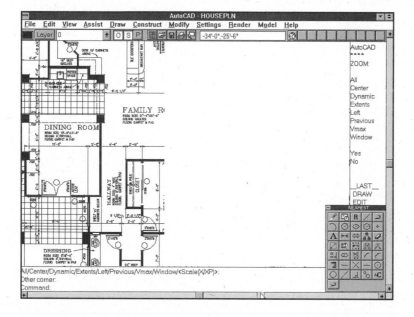

**Figure 5.25:**

HOUSEPLN being panned by scroll bar slider box.

In addition to using the slider box to pan with the scroll bars, you can click on or press and hold on the arrow buttons at the left/right and top/bottom of the scroll bars.

# Using VIEW To Name and Save Working Views

As you work on a drawing, you may find that your zooms and pans frequently return to the same drawing views. You can save time by saving and recalling your zooms and pans.

Suppose, for example, that you are going to concentrate your work on the sample drawing's square for the next few hours. Periodically, you want to zoom out to work in other areas, but most of the time you are zoomed in to the square. Instead of picking a window around the square every time you want to zoom to this area, you can store this view with a name, and then use the name to restore that view whenever you need it.

A stored window is called a *named view*. To save a view, use the VIEW command to name and store it. You can select VIEW from the DISPLAY screen menu, or you can enter **VIEW** at the Command: prompt. You can display the View Control dialog box by entering **DDVIEW** or choosing **N**amed view from the S**e**t View child menu on the **V**iew pull-down menu. The following exercise shows you how to use AutoCAD's VIEW command and save a view named SQUARE. After saving the view, you zoom out and then restore the view.

Before you begin the following exercise, zoom to the area of the drawing shown in figure 5.26.

**Figure 5.26:**

The saved and restored view named SQUARE.

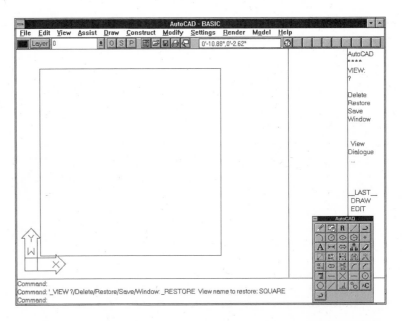

# Using VIEW To Save and Restore a View

| | |
|---|---|
| *Choose* **F**ile, *then* **O**pen, *and enter* **C:\IAW\BASIC** | Reopens BASIC drawing from earlier exercise |
| Command: *From the screen menu, choose* DISPLAY, *then* VIEW:, *then* Save | Starts the VIEW command with Save option |
| Command:_'VIEW ?/Delete/Restore/ Save/Window:_S View name to save: **SQUARE** ↵ | Saves the current view under the name SQUARE |
| Command: *Choose* **V**iew, *then* **Z**oom, *then* **A**ll | Returns to full view (see fig. 5.27) |
| Command: *From the screen menu, choose* DISPLAY, *then* VIEW:, *then* Restore | Starts the VIEW command with the Restore option |
| Command:_'VIEW ?/Delete/Restore/ Save/Window: _RESTORE View name to restore: **SQUARE** ↵ | Restores the saved view named SQUARE as shown in figure 5.26 |

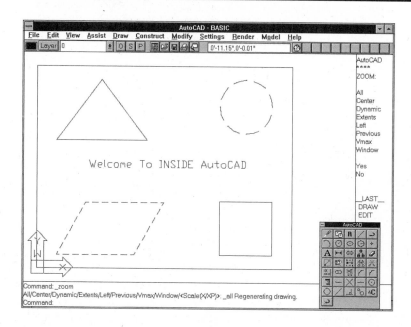

**Figure 5.27:**

The view after ZOOM All.

*Useful named views are L for Limits or A for All. Both are easy to type and can be used instead of issuing the ZOOM command's All option to avoid regenerations. Use a standard named view called PLOT for consistency in plotting.*

The VIEW command has the following five options:

- **?.** This option displays a list of all saved viewport configurations when you enter an asterisk (*). The ? option lists a specific set of views when you enter names with wild cards. The list includes an M or P with the view's name to indicate whether the view is defined in model space (M) or paper space (P).

- **Delete.** This option prompts you to enter the name of a view to delete. You can use wild cards to delete a group of views.

- **Restore.** This option enables you to enter the name of a saved view to display it in the current viewport.

- **Save.** This option saves the current viewport's view.

- **Window.** This option enables you to define a window to save as a view by specifying its corners. You also can enter a name for the view.

*You can rename an existing view by using the RENAME command or the Rename dialog box (DDRENAME command). The RE-NAME command is described in Chapter 3.*

*If you use the ZOOM command's Center option, press Enter to default the center point, enter .8X, and then save the view as A or ALL. This configuration provides a margin of safety in avoiding zoom and pan regenerations. Then use the VIEW command's Restore option to restore the All view, rather than the ZOOM command's All or Dynamic options.*

When many view names are being saved and restored, the View Control dialog box is a useful tool (see fig. 5.28). Enter **DDVIEW** or choose **N**amed View from the S**e**t View child menu on the **V**iew pull-down menu to display this dialog box. The list box shows all the existing named views. You use the radio buttons to restore a named view, create a new view, delete an existing view, or see a description of a view's general parameters. The edit box enables you to type in or change view names. As is the case with most dialog boxes, you can choose OK to accept the most recent changes in the dialog box; select Cancel to disregard the changes.

In the following exercise, you use the View Control dialog box to restore and save named views of the drawing.

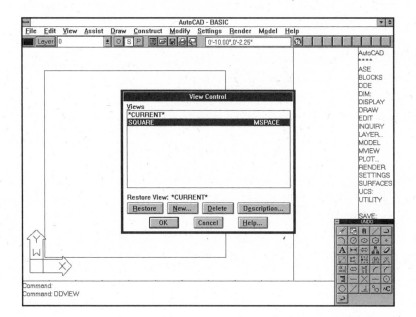

**Figure 5.28:**

The View Control dialog box.

---

## Using DDVIEW To Work with Views

| | |
|---|---|
| Command: *Choose **V**iew, then **Z**oom, then **A**ll* | Returns to full view |
| Command: *Choose **V**iew, then **S**et View, then **N**amed View* | Starts the DDVIEW command and displays the View Control dialog box |
| *Click on* SQUARE *in the view list box, then choose **R**estore, then* OK | Restores the view named SQUARE and closes the dialog box |
| Command: **U** ↵ | Undoes the VIEW command and returns to previous view |
| Command: *Zoom in on the parallelogram* | |

*continues*

| | |
|---|---|
| Command: *Choose* **V**iew, *then* S**e**t View, *then* **N**amed View | Starts the DDVIEW command and displays the View Control dialog box |
| DDVIEW | |
| *Click on the* **N**ew *button, then type* **PARA**, *and choose* **S**ave View | Saves the view with the name PARA |
| *Choose* OK | Closes the dialog box |
| Command: *Press Enter* | Repeats the DDVIEW command |
| The two view names, PARA and SQUARE, appear in the View Control dialog box. | |
| *Choose* Cancel | Closes the View Control dialog box |

The View Control dialog box also can list information such as clipping data, twist angle, and view size. This information may be especially helpful for shading or rendering; you can access it by choosing the Description button. View names also can be deleted if they are no longer needed. (Remember to click on the **H**elp button if you forget how some of these options work.)

# Controlling Display Size and Resolution

As your drawing files become larger, you need to control the display size and resolution of your drawing. You have to be conscious of the amount of your drawing you want AutoCAD to keep active at any one time. In using dynamic zooms, you have seen that AutoCAD keeps three different sets of drawing data active: the drawing extents, generated data, and the current view.

When your drawing file is small and uncomplicated, all these subsets usually are one and the same. As your drawing file gets larger, only portions of the file are generated, and it becomes more efficient to display only portions of your drawing. You usually use redraw (fast) speed to move from one view to another in the generated portion of the drawing file by using a PAN or ZOOM command. To call up a view that contains nongenerated data, however, requires a regeneration of a different set of data and takes more time.

## Using VIEWRES To Control Smooth Curves and Regeneration

The AutoCAD VIEWRES (VIEW RESolution) command controls the speed of your zooms and regenerations in two ways. First, it turns fast zoom on and off. *Fast zoom* means that AutoCAD maintains a large virtual screen so that it can do most pans and zooms at redraw speed. If fast zoom is off, all pans and zooms cause a regeneration. Second, VIEWRES determines how fine the curves should be. When circles or arcs are tiny, AutoCAD needs to display only a few straight lines to fool your eye into seeing smooth curves. When arcs are larger, AutoCAD needs more segments (or vectors) to make a smooth arc. The VIEWRES circle zoom percent tells AutoCAD how smooth you want your curves, and AutoCAD determines how many segments are needed to represent what is to be displayed.

In the following exercise, you learn how to alter the displayed smoothness of the circle by generating fewer segments. To see the effect, you need to change the circle's layer to a continuous linetype.

## Using VIEWRES To Control Resolutions

| | |
|---|---|
| Command: *Choose* **V**iew, *then* **Z**oom, *then* **A**ll | Displays the entire drawing |
| Command: *Choose* **M**odify, *then* **C**hange, *then* **P**roperties | Issues the DDCHPROP command |
| Select objects: *Select the circle and ess Enter, choose* **L**inetype, *select* CONTINUOUS, *and choose* OK, *then* OK *again* | Changes circle's linetype |
| Command: **VIEWRES** ↵ | |
| Do you want fast zooms? <Y>: *Press Enter* | Accepts the fast zoom default |
| Enter circle zoom percent (1-20000)<100>: **5** ↵ | |
| Regenerating drawing. | Displays the circle as an octagon |
| Command: *Press Enter* | Repeats the VIEWRES command |
| VIEWRES Do you want fast zooms? <Y>: *Press Enter* | |
| Enter circle zoom percent (1-20000)<100>: **100** ↵ | |
| Regenerating drawing. | Redisplays the round circle |

Figures 5.29 and 5.30 demonstrate the effect of VIEWRES on circles.

**Figure 5.29:**

The circle before
the VIEWRES
command.

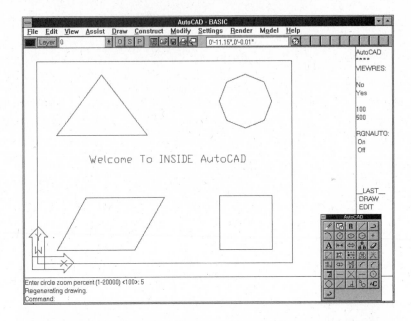

**Figure 5.30:**

The circle after
the VIEWRES
command.

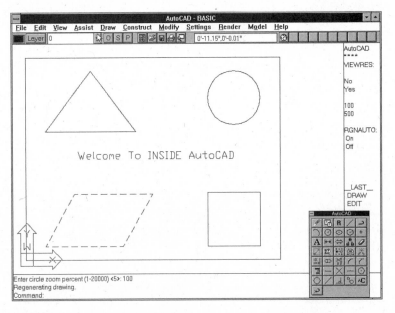

The trade-off for fast zoom is that when a regeneration is required, AutoCAD takes
longer to regenerate the drawing than if fast zoom is off. AutoCAD takes longer
because it must regenerate a larger area.

*If you turn fast zoom off, the ZOOM command's Dynamic option and all other pans and zooms always cause a drawing regeneration. Although you probably never should turn off fast zoom, you might find that AutoCAD is more efficient when zooming large text-filled drawings or doing work that often causes regenerations even if fast zoom is on. In addition, if VIEWRES is set to too high a number, it may cause slow regenerations.*

## Using REGEN To Control Data Generation

You have seen that the VIEWRES command and some zooms cause AutoCAD to regenerate the drawing. When the drawing file is full of many entities, particularly text, arcs, and circles, regeneration takes a long time.

You can force a regeneration of the display and drawing file by using the REGEN command. You can use REGEN to make AutoCAD recalculate the virtual screen at a particular current view so that your dynamic zoom display shows only the desired part of the drawing. To use REGEN, enter **REGEN** at the Command: prompt. AutoCAD displays the message Regenerating drawing. while the drawing regenerates.

*To keep AutoCAD from regenerating extraneous data, freeze layers that you are not using. Thaw the layers when you need them.*

## Using REGENAUTO To Control AutoCAD's Regeneration

When you zoom, pan, or view, you usually want AutoCAD to make sure that everything in the drawing file is displayed accurately. Because large drawings can take a long time to regenerate, however, you may not want AutoCAD to regenerate when you are busy drawing or editing.

You can use the REGENAUTO command to determine when AutoCAD regenerates the drawing. When REGENAUTO is off, AutoCAD avoids regeneration unless absolutely necessary. When necessary, AutoCAD first stops and asks if you want to regenerate. The REGEN command, however, always overrides REGENAUTO and forces AutoCAD to regenerate the drawing.

The disadvantage of turning off REGENAUTO is that reset linetype scales, redefined symbols, and changed text styles do not automatically display with their new settings until you regenerate the drawing. After you are comfortable with these items in AutoCAD, not seeing every change as it occurs is a small penalty to pay for the time savings of keeping REGENAUTO turned off in complex drawings.

*The QTEXT command displays text as only a box outline so that drawings regenerate quickly. Chapter 7 discusses the use of QTEXT.*

# Using Transparent Commands

You can use the PAN, ZOOM, and VIEW commands (as well as REDRAW) while most other AutoCAD commands are active. When you issue a command while a previously issued command is active, the second command is said to be operating *transparently*. You can issue a *transparent* command by placing a leading apostrophe (') before the command's name. Recall that you can get transparent 'HELP the same way. Often the pull-down menu selections issue commands with the apostrophe included.

In the following exercise, draw a line and issue a transparent 'VIEW and 'ZOOM. Then look for the double angle bracket (>>) at the Command: prompt. The double bracket shows that the current command is suspended.

## Using Transparent VIEW and ZOOM

Command: *Issue the ZOOM command with the All option*

Command: *Choose* **D**raw, *then* **L**ine, *then* **S**egments

_line From point: *Pick any point in the triangle*

To point: **'VIEW** ↵　　　　　　　　　　　Issues transparent VIEW command

>>?/Delete/Restore/Save/Window: **S** ↵　　The >> prompt indicates that another command is suspended

>>View name to save: **A** ↵　　　　　　　Saves the current view and completes the VIEW command

Resuming _LINE command.

To point: *Choose* **V**iew, *then* **Z**oom, *then* **W**indow

_'zoom　　　　　　　　　　　　　　　　Begins a transparent ZOOM with the Window option

>>Center/Dynamic/Left/Previous/
Vmax/Window/<Scale(X/XP)>: w

>>First corner: *Pick* ① *(see fig. 5.31)*

| | |
|---|---|
| >>Other corner: *Pick* ② | Completes the ZOOM command |
| Resuming _LINE command. | |
| To point: *Pick any point inside the circle* | |
| To point: '**VIEW** ↵ | Starts the VIEW command transparently |
| >>?/Delete/Restore/Save/Window: **R** ↵ | |
| >>View name to restore: **A** ↵ | Restores view A without regenerating |
| Resuming _LINE command. | |
| To point: *Press Enter* | Ends LINE command |

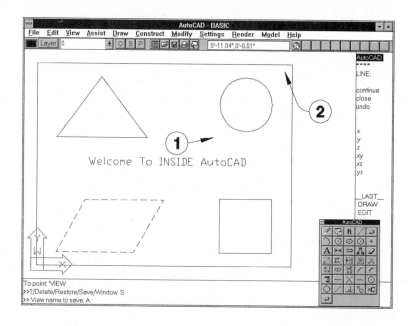

**Figure 5.31:**

A LINE command suspended by issuing a transparent VIEW command.

You may have noticed that the transparent ZOOM prompt omits the All and Extents options. The options are left out because they cause regenerations.

# Displaying Multiple Viewports

So far, all the display controls used in these exercises have looked in on your drawing with a single drawing view in a single viewport. AutoCAD, however, also can display multiple views of your drawing simultaneously in the graphics window. In effect, you divide your drawing area into windows called *viewports* and display different views of your drawing in each of them.

You have been working in a viewport all along—a single viewport that covers the entire drawing area. Multiple viewports work just as if you divide your drawing area into rectangles, making several different drawing areas instead of one. You can have up to 16 viewports visible at one time while still retaining your screen and pull-down menus and Command: prompt area.

You can work in only one viewport at a time. The viewport you are using is called the *current viewport*. You make a viewport current simply by clicking in it. When a viewport is current, its border is thicker than the others and the cursor appears as it normally does in a single viewport display. When you work in any viewport, use your normal display controls just as if you are working with a single viewport. You can retain zoom, pan, grid, and snap settings for that viewport. The key point, however, is that the images shown in multiple viewports are multiple images of the same data. You are not duplicating your drawing; rather, you are just putting its image in different viewports.

Because the viewports look onto the same *model* or drawing, you can draw from viewport to viewport. You can start a line in one viewport, click on another viewport to make it current, and then complete the line. AutoCAD rubber-bands your line segment across the viewports.

Multiple viewports are essential in 3D modeling to give you concurrent views of your model from different viewpoints. You can, for example, display plan, elevation, and isometric views of your model. Viewports also offer advantages over a single-view display in some common 2D drafting situations, such as multiview drawings or drawings with multiple plotted scales. When you are faced with the problem of detailing different areas of a large drawing or you need to keep one area of your drawing (such as a title block or bill of materials) in constant view, use viewports to divide your drawing area.

Two types of viewports are available in AutoCAD—*tiled* viewports (see fig. 5.32) and *untiled* viewports (see fig. 5.33). Untiled viewports (referred to as *mview viewports* because they are defined by the MVIEW command) are much more flexible and must be created in an environment called *paper space*. Tiled viewports were the first type of viewports available in AutoCAD; mview viewports were added in Release 11. Because mview viewports are more natural and similar to manual drafting, this book emphasizes their use.

# Understanding Paper Space and Model Space

*Model space* is the drawing environment that exists in any viewport, whether it is a single full-size viewport, one of several tiled viewports, or an mview viewport entity in paper space. Think of *paper space* as an infinitely large sheet of paper on which you can arrange viewports that show your model. Although model space is a three-dimensional environment, paper space is a two-dimensional environment for arranging views of your model for display or plotting.

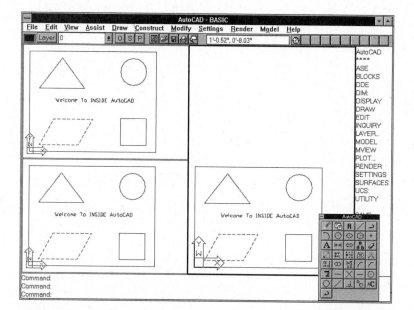

**Figure 5.32:**
Tiled viewports.

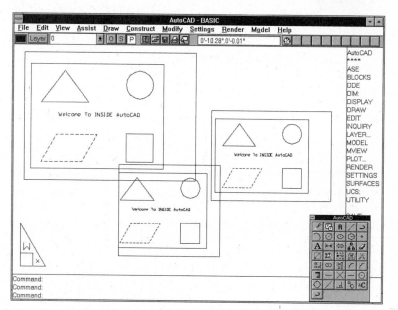

**Figure 5.33:**
Untiled (MVIEW)
viewports.

Whether you are creating two-dimensional or three-dimensional models, you do most of your drawing in model space. You draw in paper space when you add standard items, such as title blocks and sheet borders, and some types of dimensioning or annotation. Paper space dimensioning and annotation are essential in 3D work.

You view paper space only in plan view, which reinforces the two-dimensional nature of paper space. You can draw 3D objects in paper space, but with no way to view them because it makes little sense to do so.

# Working in Paper Space

Along with paper space comes a new type of viewport—mview viewports. *Mview viewports* can be any size; they do not have to touch (as tiled viewports do), and they even can overlap one another. You can think of viewports as glass windows into your drawing that can be either open or closed. If you are in paper space, the window is closed and, although you can still see through it, you cannot reach through it to make changes to the entities behind it. You can move and edit the window frame itself, however. When you are in model space, the current viewport window is open and you can work with the entities shown inside to edit them or draw more entities. You cannot modify the window frame in model space, however, only the entities inside the frame. You also cannot have more than one of those windows open (current) at a time.

You can draw anything in paper space that you can draw in model space, except that 3D objects look flat. Paper space is similar to another semi-independent drawing that overlays your entire group of viewports. What you draw in paper space appears over, but not in, your viewports. You can snap by using object snap commands from paper space to the model-space contents of the underlying viewports. You cannot, however, snap by using object snap commands from model space to paper space. Zooms cause more regenerations in paper space because paper space uses no virtual screen.

When you are working in paper space, viewports are like any other entity. You can, for example, edit the boundary of the viewport itself. Indirectly, that can affect the view of the model shown in the viewport. If you make the paper space viewport larger by stretching it, you might see more of the model. If you make the paper space viewport smaller, some of the model might disappear behind the boundary of the viewport. You can use the MOVE command to move a viewport around without affecting other viewports. You can change the color of a viewport's boundary box by using the CHPROP command, and you can erase a viewport just like any other AutoCAD entity. All these changes can be made in paper space.

When you return to model space, you can select individual viewports and edit individual entities that show up in those viewports. You cannot, however, edit the viewport frame's size, color, or other attributes.

# Examining the Command Set for Mview Viewports

Three primary commands and one system variable enable you to enter and use viewports in paper space. The TILEMODE system variable must be set to 0 (off) before you can enter paper space. Then you use the MVIEW command to create viewports. To enter model space so that you can work in these viewports, use the MSPACE command. Use the PSPACE command to return to paper space to edit viewports, to add title blocks or annotation, or to set up for plotting. All these commands and several preset options are on a child menu displayed by choosing <u>V</u>iew and then Mvie<u>w</u> from the pull-down menu.

# Entering Paper Space and Creating Viewports

When you begin a drawing in AutoCAD, the display shows a single viewport by default, unless you are using a prototype drawing that has been set up for multiple viewports. The system variable TILEMODE is set to 1 (on) by default, which gives you only tiled viewports. As you just saw, to enter paper space, you must set TILEMODE to 0. When you are in paper space and you set TILEMODE back to 1, AutoCAD returns to model space with one or more tiled viewports.

To activate or deactivate paper space, choose <u>V</u>iew, then <u>T</u>ilemode. When <u>T</u>ilemode is checked, paper space is not active. By clicking on <u>T</u>ilemode, you remove the check mark, set TILEMODE to 0, and enter paper space. Clicking again on <u>T</u>ilemode sets TILEMODE back to 1, shown by the check mark reappearing.

You can access the MVIEW command from the DISPLAY screen menu or enter it at the Command: prompt. When Tilemode is off, the P button in the toolbar enables you to switch between MSPACE and PSPACE, and is highlighted when PSPACE is on.

The following example uses the drawing named IAWBASIC.DWG from the IAW DISK as a prototype. It is identical to the BASIC drawing from Chapter 4. This exercise shows you how to enter paper space, create a few mview viewports, then draw some lines and experiment with object selection in paper space.

---

## Creating Viewports in Paper Space

Choose <u>F</u>ile, then <u>N</u>ew, then <u>D</u>iscard Changes, and enter **BASIC=IAWBASIC**, then choose OK to replace the existing BASIC drawing, if prompted.

Command: *Choose* <u>V</u>iew, *then* <u>T</u>ilemode        Sets TILEMODE to 0 and enters paper space

The drawing image disappears until you create viewports.

Command: *Choose* <u>V</u>iew, *then* Mvie<u>w</u>, *then*        Starts the MVIEW command
<u>C</u>reate Viewport

*continues*

| | |
|---|---|
| `Command: _mview`<br>`ON/OFF/Hideplot/Fit/2/3/4/Restore/`<br>`<First Point>:` *From the screen menu,*<br>*choose* Fit | Fits a viewport to fill the display<br>area and redisplays the drawing image |
| `Command:` *Perform a ZOOM with the Center*<br>*option, center point 12,0 and height 19* | Displays the viewport shown in figure 5.34 |
| `Command:` *Choose* **V**iew, *then* Mvie**w**, *then*<br>**2** Viewports | Issues the MVIEW command with the 2 option |
| `Command: _mview`<br>`ON/OFF/Hideplot/Fit/2/3/4/Restore/`<br>`<First Point>: _2` | |
| `Horizontal/<Vertical>:` **H** ↵ | Specifies a Horizontal divider between<br>viewports |
| `Fit/<First Point>:` *From the toolbox,*<br>*choose* INTERSECTION | Specifies the INTersect object snap mode |
| `int of` *Pick the viewport's upper right*<br>*corner at* ① *in figure 5.34* | Sets the first corner of the new viewport pair |
| `Second point:` **26,-9** ↵ | Sets the viewport's other corner |
| `Regenerating drawing.` | Displays the drawing image in two new<br>viewports (see fig. 5.35) |
| `Command:` *Choose* **F**ile, *then* **S**ave | Saves the current drawing |
| `Command:` *Choose* **D**raw, *then* **L**ine, *then*<br>**S**egments, *and draw a few lines across*<br>*two or three viewports* | |
| `Command:` **E** ↵ | Issues shortcut key for the ERASE command |
| `Select objects:` *Select the lines you*<br>*just drew* | Selects the lines |
| `Select objects:` *Select the circle or text* | Ignores entities in the viewports |
| `Select objects:` *Press Enter* | Erases only the selected lines |

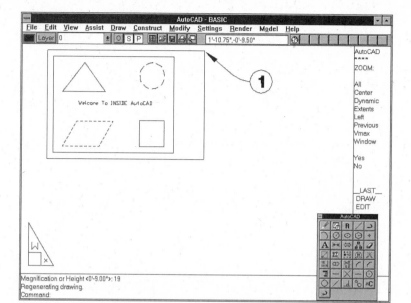

**Figure 5.34:**

The first paper space viewport.

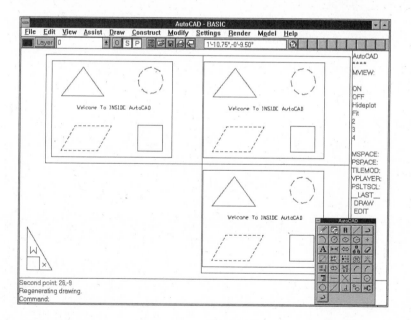

**Figure 5.35:**

Three mview viewports.

You cannot select the entities in the viewports unless you are in model space. The viewports themselves, however, are erased if you select their borders while in paper space.

*If you set TILEMODE to 1 to exit from paper space after you already have created viewports, the viewports remain defined. You can redisplay them later by setting TILEMODE to 0, or by choosing View, then Tilemode, which switches the tilemode from its existing setting.*

The MVIEW command gives you the following options for creating and controlling viewports in paper space:

- **First point.** This option enables you to specify two diagonally opposite corner points to define a new viewport, which becomes the current viewport.

- **ON.** This option makes all model space entities in the selected viewports visible.

- **OFF.** This option makes all model space entities in the selected viewports invisible.

- **Hideplot.** This option enables you to select the viewports from which 3D hidden lines are to be removed during plotting.

- **Fit.** This option creates a single viewport the size of the current paper space view.

- **2/3/4.** This option creates two, three, or four viewports.

- **Restore.** This option creates an arrangement of mview viewports that matches the appearance of a tiled viewport configuration that has been saved by using the VPORTS command. (MVIEW cannot save and restore mview viewport configurations.)

*When you create viewports by using the Fit, 2, 3, or 4 options, the viewports appear tiled, but you can move them apart and resize them by using commands such as STRETCH and MOVE.*

*The MVSETUP program, which is included with AutoCAD, can set up multiple viewports, adjust limits, and insert a title block. You can load this AutoLISP program by entering **MVS** at the* Command: *prompt, or from the pull-down menu by selecting View, then Layout, then **M**V Setup.*

# Drawing in Multiple Viewports

The following exercise begins by entering model space and setting the upper left viewport as current. By zooming in on the triangle and drawing lines to points that are no longer visible in that viewport, you can see some of the benefits of drawing with multiple viewports.

---

## Drawing with Multiple Viewports

Continue in the BASIC drawing from the previous exercise.

Command: *Click on the* P *button*

Switches from paper space to model space and displays the UCS icon in each viewport

Command: *Click in the upper left viewport*

Makes the upper left viewport the current viewport

Command: *Zoom in on the triangle (see fig 5.36)*

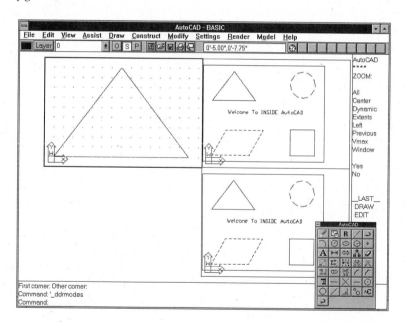

**Figure 5.36:**

The left viewport zoomed, displaying a small grid.

Command: *Choose* **S**ettings, *then* **D**rawing Aids, *and set the grid to .25*

Command: **L** ↵

Issues the LINE command

*continues*

| | |
|---|---|
| `LINE From point:` *Pick a point that is approximately in the center of the triangle (notice the rubber-band cursor)* | Starts the line |
| *Click in the upper right viewport (notice the rubber-band cursor)* | Changes the current viewport |
| `To point:` *Choose* **V**iew, *then* **Z**oom, *then* **W**indow, *and transparently zoom in on the circle (see fig 5.37)* | |
| `Resuming _LINE command.` | |

**Figure 5.37:**

The upper right viewport with the first line.

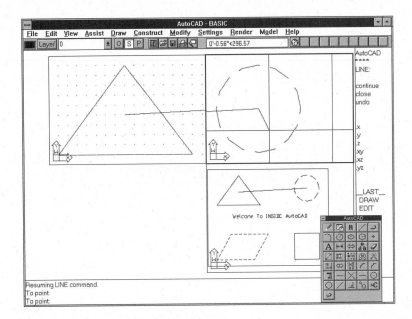

| | |
|---|---|
| `To point:` *Pick a point that is approximately in the center of the circle, as shown in figure 5.37* | Continues the line |
| `To point:` *Click in the bottom right viewport, then pick the approximate center of the square, as shown in figure 5.38* | Makes the viewpoint current and continues the line |
| `To point:` *Pick the approximate center of the parallelogram shown in figure 5.39* | Continues the line |
| `To point: C ↵` | Closes the line in the triangle |

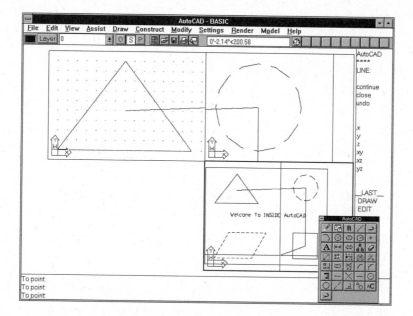

**Figure 5.38:**

The bottom right view with the continuing line.

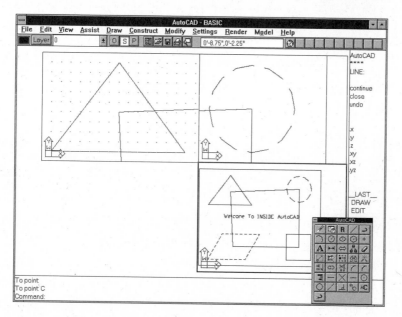

**Figure 5.39:**

The complete line shown in all the viewports.

When you are done, the upper viewports should show portions of the completed lines, and the bottom viewport should show the whole drawing.

# Editing Mview Viewports

In model space, any actions you make, such as erasing or copying, affect the model in the current viewport rather than the viewport itself. When you are working in paper space, the only entities you can access are the boundary boxes around each viewport and any entities you created or inserted in paper space. The key to understanding viewports in paper space is that when you are working in paper space you cannot make any changes to the model—just to the viewport. To make changes to the model, you have to enter model space. Occasionally, you may want your edit commands to change the viewport itself, rather than the model that is displayed inside it. You might, for example, create a viewport that is not quite large enough to display all of the view that is supposed to appear in it at a certain scale for plotting. Use AutoCAD's STRETCH command to resize the viewport while in paper space.

AutoCAD recognizes the boundary box around the viewport as a single entity. If you select one line of the boundary box, the entire viewport is selected. Because the viewports are recognized as single entities, you can move, copy, erase, and scale them. (These editing commands are covered in detail in the chapter on editing. For now, just follow the exercise steps.)

You also can place the viewports on different layers. If the color for a viewport is set to BYLAYER, the boundary box displays at whatever color has been assigned to the layer. You also can change the color of the boundary box lines by using the CHPROP command and by providing an explicit color for the viewport. A change to the layer or color of the boundary does not affect the image inside the viewport, just the boundary box. If you want to plot a drawing without plotting the viewport boundary boxes, place the boundaries on a layer that can be turned off for plotting.

The next exercise continues with the BASIC drawing that was modified in the last exercise and uses AutoCAD's editing commands to change the viewports (see chapters 6–9 for details on the editing commands).

---

## Editing Mview Viewports

Continue in the BASIC drawing.

| | |
|---|---|
| Command: *Click on the P button* | Redisplays the triangle paper space UCS icon |
| Command: *Choose* **M**odify, *then* Stret**c**h | Issues the STRETCH command with the Crossing option |

```
Select objects to stretch by window...
Select objects: c
```

First point: *Pick at ① near the left viewport (see fig. 5.40)*

| | |
|---|---|
| `Second point:` *Pick at ②, across the viewport's bottom left corner* | Selects a corner of the viewport |
| `Select objects:` *Press Enter* | Ends object selection |
| `Base point:` *Pick point ③ on bottom edge of viewport (see fig. 5.40)* | Sets the base point of the stretch |
| `New point:` *Pick point near ④* | Specifies the displacement and stretches the viewport to about twice its original height |
| `Command:` *Choose **M**odify, then **M**ove* | Issues the MOVE command |
| `Select objects:` *Pick each viewport on its boundary, and then press Enter* | Selects all three viewports |
| `Base point or displacement:` *Pick at ⑤ outside bottom left of left viewport* | Sets the move's "from point" |
| `Second point of displacement:` **0,0** ↵ | Moves the viewports into positive X,Y coordinate space |
| `Command:` *Choose **V**iew, then **Z**oom, then **A**ll* | Shows the entire drawing |
| `Command:` **CHPROP** ↵ | |
| `Select objects:` *Pick the upper right viewport's boundary and press Enter* | Selects the viewport to change |
| `Change what property (Color/LAyer/ LType/Thickness) ?` **C** ↵ | Specifies the Color option |
| `New color <BYLAYER>:` **RED** ↵ | Specifies the new color |
| `Change what property (Color/LAyer/ LType/Thickness) ?` *Press Enter* | Ends the command and changes the viewport's color |
| `Command:` *Choose **M**odify, then **E**rase, then **S**ingle* | |
| `Select objects: single` | |
| `Select objects:` *Pick the lower right viewport* | Erases the viewport |
| `Command:` *From the screen menu, choose* OOPS: | Restores the erased viewport |
| *Save the drawing* | |

The results are shown in figure 5.41.

**Figure 5.40:**

The unedited
mview viewports.

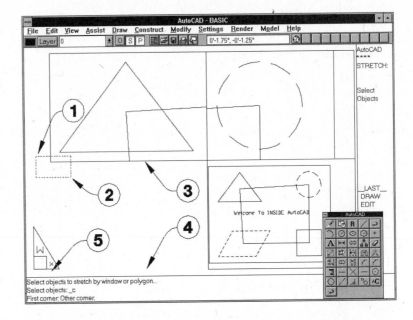

**Figure 5.41:**

The edited
viewports.

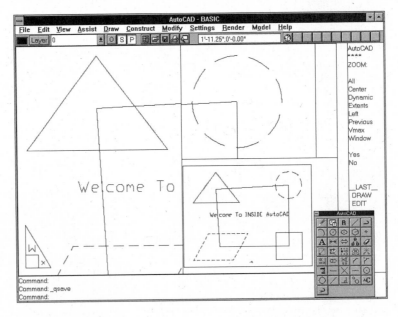

You can see how easy it is to change mview viewports. Just remember that if you want
to change the viewport, you have to be in paper space. If you want to change the
model, you have to be in model space.

# Using VPLAYER To Control Layer Visibility

Normally, when you freeze a layer, that layer disappears from every viewport because the LAYER command affects layers globally. With mview viewports (not tiled viewports), you can control the layer visibility in individual viewports by using the VPLAYER (ViewPort LAYER) command.

Unlike the LAYER command, VPLAYER only affects the way layers appear in a single viewport. This enables you to select a viewport and freeze a layer in it while still enabling the contents of that layer to appear in another viewport. VPLAYER settings affect only the visibility of layers in viewports when TILEMODE is set to 0 (paper space). If you switch back to a single or tiled model view by setting TILEMODE to 1 (tiled viewports), the global layer settings take precedence over any VPLAYER settings.

The VPLAYER command can be executed from either paper space or model space. If you are in model space and use the Select option, the graphics window temporarily switches to paper space so that you can select a viewport. The following exercise uses the VPLAYER command from model space.

The BASIC drawing is a good starting point for this exercise because it is relatively simple and contains entities drawn on different layers.

---

## Controlling Layer Visibility Using VPLAYER

Continue in the BASIC drawing, or open it again.

| | |
|---|---|
| Command: *Click on the P button* | Enters model space |
| Command: *Choose* **V**iew, *then* Mvie**w**, *then* V**p**layer | Begins the VPLAYER command |
| Command: _vplayer ?/Freeze/Thaw/ Reset/Newfrz/Vpvisdflt: *From the screen menu, choose* Freeze | Specifies the Freeze option |
| Layer(s) to Freeze: **CIRCLE** ↵ | |
| All/Select/<Current>: **S** ↵ | AutoCAD prompts for viewports to select |
| Switching to Paper space. | |
| Select objects: *Pick the upper right viewport and press Enter* | Selects the viewport |
| Switching to Model space. | |
| ?/Freeze/Thaw/Reset/Newfrz/Vpvisdflt: *From the screen menu, choose* Freeze | |
| Layer(s) to Freeze: **PARAGRAM** ↵ | |

*continues*

```
All/Select/<Current>: S ↵
```

```
Switching to Paper space.   ·
```

```
Select objects: Pick the lower right
viewport and press Enter
```

```
Switching to Model space.
```

```
?/Freeze/Thaw/Reset/Newfrz/          Specifies the Freeze option
Vpvisdflt: F ↵
```

```
Layer(s) to Freeze: TEXT ↵
```

```
All/Select/<Current>: S ↵
```

```
Switching to Paper space.
```

```
Select objects: Select the left viewport
and press Enter
```

```
Switching to Model space.
```

```
?/Freeze/Thaw/Reset/Newfrz/          Ends the VPLAYER command
Vpvisdflt: ↵
```

```
Regenerating drawing.                Redisplays the viewports with selected layers
                                     frozen in each (see fig. 5.42)
```

**Figure 5.42:**

Using VPLAYER to
freeze layers.

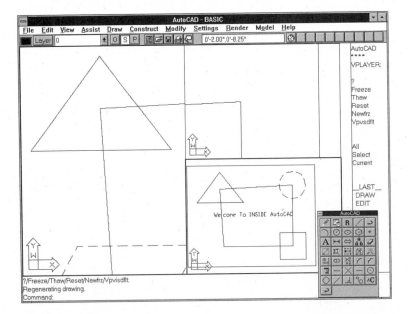

After you use VPLAYER, although a layer is frozen in each of the viewports, the data on it still appears in the other viewports.

# Understanding VPLAYER Options

The VPLAYER command gives you a number of options for selectively controlling layer visibility, as well as creating new layers. The options are available in VPLAYER:

- **?.** This option lists the current viewport's frozen layers. In model space, this option prompts for a viewport selection, temporarily switching to paper space.

- **Freeze.** This option enables you to specify layer name(s) to freeze and the viewport(s) in which to freeze them.

- **Thaw.** This option enables you to specify layer name(s) to thaw and the viewport(s) in which to thaw them.

- **Reset.** This option enables you to specify layer name(s) to restore the current default visibility setting for the specified layer(s), and to specify the viewports in which to reset them. The default is set by the Vpvisdflt option.

- **Newfrz.** This option enables you to specify name(s) to create new layer(s) that are frozen in all viewports. You can enter more than one name, separated by commas.

- **Vpvisdflt.** This option enables you to specify layer name(s) and Frozen or Thawed (the default) to set the current visibility defaults for the specified layer(s) in subsequently created viewports.

- **All.** This option specifies all mview viewports, whether visible or not.

- **Select.** This option enables you to select one or more mview viewports. If model space is current, the graphics window switches to paper space for the selection.

- **Current.** This option specifies the current viewport.

# Controlling Dialog Box Viewport Layers

You also can use the Layer Control dialog box (choose <u>S</u>ettings and then <u>L</u>ayer Control, click on the Layer button, or enter the DDLMODES command) to control layers in mview viewports.

---

## Controlling Layer Visibility Using the Layer Control Dialog Box

Continue in the BASIC drawing from the preceding exercise.

Command: *Click in the left viewport
to make it active*

*continues*

Command: *Click on the* Layer *button and choose the* TRIANGLE *layer,* Cur VP Frz, *then* OK

Displays the Layer Control dialog box (see fig. 5.43) and freezes TRIANGLE

Notice that the TRIANGLE layer is frozen in the left viewport.

Command: *From the Layer Control dialog box, choose* TRIANGLE *layer, then* Cur VP Thw, *then* OK

Thaws the layer in the current viewport

**Figure 5.43:**

The Layer Control dialog box.

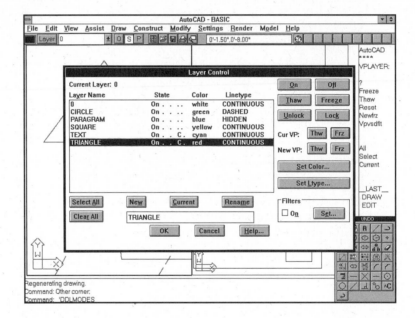

Whereas the VPLAYER command is a more powerful and versatile method of turning layers off and on in different mview viewports, the Layer Control dialog box is a little easier because it enables graphic selection of the layers. The dialog box method can be cumbersome for making many changes at once because the viewport must first be selected before opening the dialog box.

In paper space, the Layer Control dialog box displays the settings of the current viewport, which, in this case, is the current left viewport.

The Cur VP: Thw and Frz (CURrent ViewPort THaW and FReeZe) buttons control the freeze and thaw status of selected layers in the current viewport. The New VP: Thw and Frz buttons control the freeze and thaw status of selected layers for new viewports. These buttons set the layer(s) so that it is automatically frozen in subsequently created viewports. You might choose to do this when setting up several new viewports in a complex drawing. By clicking on the buttons after selecting layers, you can change the states of the current or new viewports. If you are in paper space, the change applies to the paper space view itself, not to any of the viewports.

Notice the five columns in the State column (the On column and four columns of dots). The first column shows the global on and off settings for each layer as On or a dot for off. The second column shows the global freeze and thaw settings as F for frozen or a dot for thawed. The third column shows the layer lock status as L for locked or a dot for unlocked. The fourth colum shows the current viewport mview settings. The fifth column shows the new mview viewport settings as F for frozen or a dot for thawed. A dot in columns for a layer indicates that the layer is set to the default for that setting.

The following exercise shows you tiled viewports and how to convert them to mview viewports. If you set TILEMODE back to 1 (on), the drawing area changes back to a single tiled viewport.

---

### Using TILEMODE To Exit from Paper Space

| | |
|---|---|
| `Command:` *Choose* **V**iew, *then* **T**ilemode | Turns on TILEMODE |
| `New value for TILEMODE <0>: 1` | Displays all the layers in a single tiled viewport |
| *Save the drawing* | |

---

When you exit from paper space, all the layers display in the default single-tiled viewport, regardless of their VPLAYER settings.

# Choosing between Mview Viewports and Tiled Viewports

What is so special about mview viewports? You can work on simultaneous multiple views of your drawing in tiled viewports, but AutoCAD restricts the way you can size tiled viewports. You can resize and place mview viewports, however, any way that you want. Mview viewports also enable you to control layers selectively by viewport, rather than globally in all tiled viewports. If you use mview viewports, you can freeze a layer in one viewport and leave it thawed in another viewport. You can plot several mview viewports simultaneously in paper space to create a multiview drawing, but only one tiled viewport can be plotted at a time.

*To fill the screen with a view when working in a mview viewport for an extended period of time, turn TILEMODE on with a single tiled viewport.*

# Using Tiled Viewports

You can do most, if not all, of your modeling and drawing by using mview viewports. Sometimes, however, you might want to use AutoCAD's tiled viewports for model space work. As you work through the following exercises, keep in mind that all of the drawing features found in tiled viewports, such as the capability to draw from one viewport to another, also are inherent in mview viewports.

The VPORTS command controls tiled viewports. It divides the AutoCAD graphics area into windows. Like mview viewports, each tiled viewport contains a unique view of the drawing. Unlike mview viewports, however, tiled viewports must touch at the edges and they cannot overlap one another. You cannot edit, rearrange, or turn individual tiled viewports on or off. The other limitation of tiled viewports is in layer visibility—VPLAYER and the VP Frz settings of the Layer Control dialog box do not work in tiled viewports. You must use the LAYER command or global settings in the Layer Control dialog box to freeze layers in tiled viewports, and then the corresponding layers in all viewports are affected. In plotting, only the current viewport is plotted.

Tiled viewports are created by using the VPORTS command. Make sure the TILEMODE system variable is set to 1 (on), then enter **VPORTS** or select VPORTS: from the SETTINGS screen menu. VPORTS offers several command options that you can use to build your display by adding, deleting, and joining viewports. After you have the viewports you want, you can save and name the group. A group of viewports is called a *configuration*. Use the same naming conventions to name your configuration that you use for layer names. You can have up to 31 characters, and you can use three special characters ($, -, and _) in your names. Most of the options in VPORTS are similar to the MVIEW command. The capability to save and restore named tiled viewports are the only advantages tiled viewports have over mview viewports.

The VPORTS command offers the following options:

- **Save.** This option saves and names the current viewport configuration (up to 31 characters).

- **Restore.** This option restores any saved viewport configuration. Enter a specific name to restore, enter an asterisk to display a list of all saved viewport configurations, or use any wild cards to list a specific set of names.

- **Delete.** This option deletes a saved viewport configuration.

- **Join.** This option combines the current viewport with a selected viewport. The two viewports must be adjacent and form a rectangle.

- **SIngle.** This option changes the screen to a single viewport and displays the view of the current viewport.

- **?.** This option enables you to enter an asterisk to list all named viewport configurations, or use wild cards to list a specific set of viewports.

- **2.** This option divides the current viewport into a horizontal or vertical pair of viewports.

- **3.** This option divides the current viewport into three viewports. This is the default option.

- **4.** This option divides the current viewport into four viewports.

Creative use of the 2, 3, 4, and Join options often is needed to get the arrangement you want. In the following exercise, use VPORTS to divide your drawing area into three viewports by using IAWBASIC.DWG from the IAW DISK, identical to the BASIC drawing from Chapter 4.

Begin the exercise by making sure TILEMODE is set to 1 (see fig. 5.44). Then divide your drawing area in half. Next, divide the top half into three viewports. Finally, join the top three viewports into two viewports so that you end up with a configuration of two up and one below.

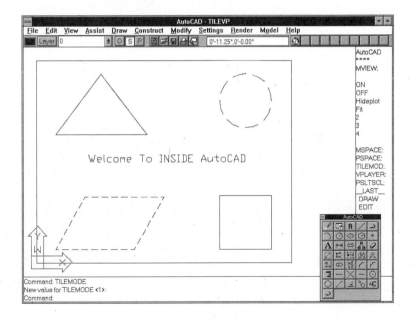

**Figure 5.44:**

The TILEVP drawing before viewports.

# Using VPORTS To Get Multiple Views

Continue from the preceding exercise, or begin a new drawing named TILEVP=IAWBASIC.

Make sure the drawing has the settings shown in table 5.1.

Command: **TILEMODE** ↵

New value for TILEMODE <1>:      Confirms that TILEMODE is set to 1
*Press Enter*

Command: *From the screen menu, choose*     Starts the VPORTS command
SETTINGS, *then* next, *then* VPORTS:

Command: _VPORTS

Save/Restore/Delete/Join/SIngle/?/    Specifies the 2 viewport option
2/<3>/4: **2** ↵

Horizontal/<Vertical>: **H** ↵       Specifies Horizontal

Regenerating drawing.          Divides the drawing area, as shown in figure
                                    5.45

**Figure 5.45:**

The drawing with
two viewports.

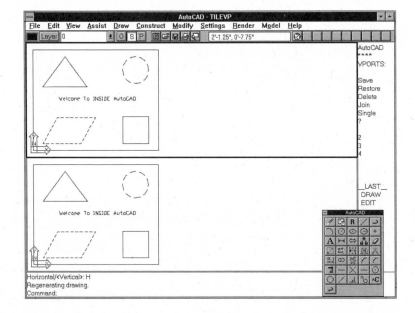

Command: *Press Enter*         Repeats the VPORTS command

_VPORTS

Save/Restore/Delete/Join/SIngle/?/
2/<3>/4: **3** ↵

| | |
|---|---|
| `Horizontal/Vertical/Above/Below/`<br>`Left/<Right>:` **V** ↵ | Divides the current (upper) viewport<br>into 3 vertical viewports (see fig. 5.46) |

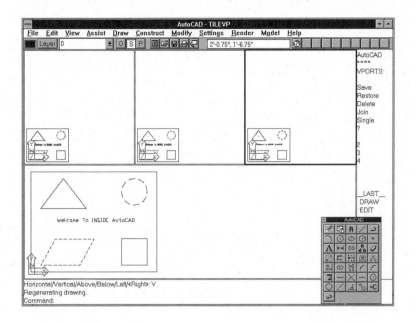

**Figure 5.46:**

The top viewport divided three times.

| | |
|---|---|
| `Command:` *Press Enter* | |
| `_VPORTS` | |
| `Save/Restore/Delete/Join/SIngle/`<br>`?/2/<3>/4:` **J** ↵ | Specifies the Join option |
| `Select dominant viewport <current>:`<br>*Press Enter* | Accepts the top right viewport as dominant |
| `Select viewport to join:` *Pick the top*<br>*center viewport* | Merges the two viewports (see fig. 5.47) |

All viewports that are being joined inherit the current settings of the dominant viewport.

In the following exercise, you save your viewport configuration, return your drawing to a standard single-viewport display, and restore the named viewport configuration.

**Figure 5.47:**

Joining top right
and top center
viewports.

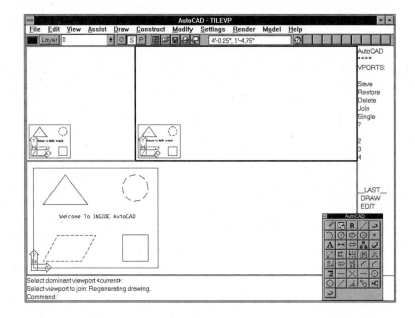

## Saving a VPORT Configuration

Command: **VPORTS** ↵

Save/Restore/Delete/Join/SIngle/          Specifies the Save option
?/2/<3>/4: **S** ↵

?/Name for new viewport                    Saves the viewport configuration as BASIC
configuration: **BASIC** ↵

Command: *Press Enter*

VPORTS

Save/Restore/Delete/Join/SIngle/          Regenerates the drawing with a
?/2/<3>/4: **SI** ↵                        single viewport

Command: *Press Enter*

Save/Restore/Delete/Join/SIngle/?/2/
<3>/4: **R** ↵

?/Name of viewport configuration to
restore: **BASIC** ↵

Regenerating drawing.                      Regenerates the drawing with the BASIC
                                           viewport configuration

Command: *Quit AutoCAD*

When you use the SIngle option, the resulting viewport inherits the settings of the current viewport.

*You can translate previously saved tiled viewports into mview viewports. To do so, use the Restore option of the MVIEW command while you are in paper space.*

## Saving and Restoring Mview Viewports

The VPORTS and VIEW commands cannot save and restore mview viewports. When you save and restore named views in paper space, any viewports currently in the views are visible, just like any other entity. If the arrangement of viewports is changed since the view was saved, the former arrangement is not restored. You can, however, save and restore mview viewports by using the BLOCK, INSERT, and MVIEW commands. (The BLOCK and INSERT commands are covered in detail in Chapter 11.)

To save an arrangement of viewports while in paper space, make a block of the viewport entities you want to save by using an insert base point of 0,0 and any name you want.

To restore a previously saved (blocked) arrangement of viewports while in paper space, insert the saved block of the viewport entities by using an insert point of 0,0 and prefacing the name with an asterisk. Then use the MVIEW command to turn them on (they insert turned off) and select all the viewports. Before you insert the saved viewports, you probably want to erase any current viewports.

*The next chapter includes an exercise with an example of this technique.*

To save an arrangement of viewports to use in other drawings, use the WBLOCK command, rather than the BLOCK command. To import viewports into other drawings, use the INSERT and MVIEW commands as previously described. You also can create several groups of viewports in paper space and pan around to the set in which you want to work.

## Using REDRAWALL and REGENALL

When you use multiple viewports and you want to redraw or regenerate all the ports, use the REDRAWALL or REGENALL commands. The standard REDRAW and REGEN commands affect only the current viewport. REDRAWALL also can be performed transparently.

*You can delete the BASIC and TILEVP drawings because they are not used again in this book.*

# Summary

AutoCAD offers many ways to get around the AutoCAD display. Display commands frame different aspects of your drawing, and viewports give you multiple views. The following tips may help you get around on your display.

ZOOM gives you more (or less) detail. The most common zoom-in method is Window. Window is the most intuitive and convenient way to specify what the next view contains, and the command is conveniently placed as an icon in the toolbar. The most common zoom-out methods are All and Previous, or named views. When zooming out, use ZOOM Dynamic or a view named ALL to get you there in a single step. ZOOM Dynamic enables you to choose your next zoom display view. ZOOM Extents gives you the biggest view possible of your drawing file. Use ZOOM Extents at the end of a drawing session to make sure that you have not drawn outside your limits.

A PAN displacement gives a nearby view while you are still at the same magnification. When moving from one side of the drawing file to another, use ZOOM Dynamic to see the whole view and to help you locate your next view. ZOOM Dynamic is more intuitive than PAN and gives you feedback on how long it takes to generate your requested image. The VIEW command saves and restores zoomed-in windows. Take the time to use names and store views for drawing efficiency.

Watch how often you regenerate your drawing file. The REDRAW command cleans up construction and refreshes the image without regenerating the drawing. Remember, VIEWRES optimizes display generation by trading looks for speed. The REGEN command gets you the latest look at what is in the drawing file. Automatic drawing regeneration is controlled by using REGENAUTO.

The time it takes to name and save standard working views and viewport configurations is worthwhile if you are using multiple views. As your drawings become more complex, named views save you time in editing and plotting. Your hardware performance and drawing sizes help determine how you use these features.

Use mview viewports to see multiple views of your drawing. Use multiple viewports when you need to do detailed (zoomed-in) work while still looking at your whole drawing or when you need to see a schedule or reference part of your drawing.

The next chapter introduces you to editing, which is a new topic. In Chapter 6, you learn how to select entities for editing, learn to use basic editing techniques to modify the drawing, and learn to use a feature that is new in Release 12—grips.

# Basic Drawing and Editing

This chapter is designed to teach you how to create a drawing in AutoCAD. If you have worked through the previous chapters, you should be comfortable with the following procedures:

- Opening existing drawing files, as well as naming and saving new files
- Entering commands from the keyboard or choosing them from the pull-down or screen menus
- Using object snaps and coordinate input
- Manipulating the graphics window
- Setting up a drawing file with the proper units, limits, and other common settings

These steps may seem more involved than you expected in preparation for CAD drafting. A solid foundation of good AutoCAD habits prevents you from having to "unlearn" bad habits that come from trying to draw without understanding how AutoCAD was meant to be used. Now comes the part you have been waiting for: creating a real drawing. This chapter focuses on the basic drawing and editing commands that you first use in creating and modifying graphic entities.

A fundamental difference between manual drafting and CAD drafting is that, in manual drafting, the end product is the sheet of paper with the design shown on it. With CAD, the end product is the graphic database, with hard-copy plots used as one means of sharing that data with others. The task of creating a CAD drawing involves the use of graphic entities, such as lines, arcs, and circles. These entities can be edited and changed as needed to contain the exact geometric shape and properties required of them.

The drawing commands and editing-command options used in this chapter introduce you to drawing and editing and illustrate how powerful, yet easy to use, AutoCAD is. A single view in model space is all that is needed to view the example part, but you can use the ZOOM and PAN commands to show the part at a scale that is easiest for you to work with.

Figure 6.1 shows a drawing of the tool plate you work on in this chapter.

**Figure 6.1:**

The tool plate.

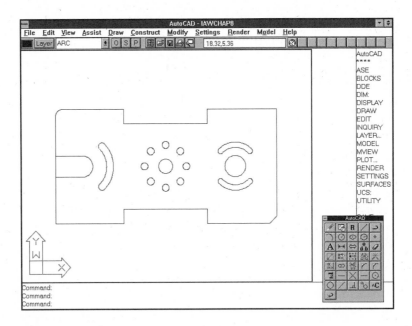

Table 6.1 shows the settings for the TOOLPLAT drawing.

The following exercise begins a new drawing called TOOLPLAT using IAWCHAP6.DWG from the IAW DISK; the drawing settings should be the same as those in table 6.1.

### Table 6.1
### TOOLPLAT Drawing Settings

| COORDS | GRID | SNAP | UCSICON |
|--------|------|------|---------|
| On | .5 in | .25 | ORigin |

| | |
|---|---|
| **UNITS** | Decimal units, 2 decimal places, 0 fractional places for angles, default all other settings. |
| **LIMITS** | –1,–1 to 20,12 in model space; 0,0 to 12,9 in paper space |
| **Viewports** | One mview viewport, from 0,0 to 8.5,11 |
| **Current Space** | Paper space |

| Layer Name | State | Color | Linetype |
|------------|-------|-------|----------|
| 0 | On/ | 7 (White) | CONTINUOUS |
| ARC | On | 4 (Cyan) | CONTINUOUS |
| CIRCLE | On | 1 (Red) | CONTINUOUS |
| LINE | On/Current | 2 (Yellow) | CONTINUOUS |

## Setting Up the TOOLPLAT Drawing

Use the NEW command to begin a new drawing named TOOLPLAT=IAWCHAP6.

Issue a ZOOM with the Extents option.

Command: **MS** ↵                          Switches to model space

Issue a ZOOM with the All option, then verify the settings shown in table 6.1.

The LINE command is one of the most often-used entity-creation commands in AutoCAD. You can issue the LINE command by entering **LINE** (or **L**), by choosing **L**ine and an option from the **D**raw pull-down menu, or by choosing LINE: from the DRAW screen menu.

# Using the LINE Command

You already used the LINE command several times in previous chapters, but you have not used all of its options and techniques for drawing lines. As you use the LINE command, AutoCAD records the two endpoints of each line segment. Remember that you can enter points by using the following methods:

- Use the pointer and crosshairs to pick points

- Use snap, ortho, and object snaps to control your point picking

- Enter coordinates at the keyboard: absolute or relative, Cartesian, polar, spherical, or cylindrical

In the following exercises, you practice using object snap and the various forms of typed and picked coordinate entry you learned in Chapter 4.

After a line is created from two endpoints (regardless of how they were entered), AutoCAD assumes that you want to continue drawing lines until you end the LINE command and return to the Command: prompt.

The LINE command has three useful options: continue, Undo, and Close. The continue option enables you to pick up the last point of the most recent line to start a new line segment. Press Enter in response to the From point: prompt to continue. You specify Undo and Close by entering a **U** or a **C** at the To point: prompt. Undo eliminates the last line segment of the current command and backs up one point so you can try the line segment again. Close makes a polygon by drawing a segment from your last endpoint, closing it to the first point of the line series drawn by the current LINE command.

When you choose **L**ine from the **D**raw pull-down menu, you have several choices. The **S**egments item (which issues the default LINE command) continues to prompt for additional endpoints, while the **1** Segment option exits after a single line is drawn. The **D**ouble Lines option uses an AutoLISP routine to create double lines at a specified width (see Chapter 12 for this technique).

In the next exercise, use the options in the **L**ine child menu of the **D**raw pull-down menu to draw part of the perimeter of the tool plate. Use a mixture of absolute coordinate entry, relative point selection, and polar selection. Your drawing should look like figure 6.2 when you finish the exercise.

---

## Using the LINE Command

Command: *Choose* **D**raw, *then* **L**ine, *then*     Issues the default Line command
**S**egments     (multiple segments)

| | |
|---|---|
| `_line From point:` **0,0** ↵ | Starts the line with an absolute coordinate |
| `To point:` **5,0** ↵ | Specifies an absolute coordinate and draws a line |
| `To point:` **@0,1** ↵ | Draws relative to the last point |
| `To point:` **@6<0** ↵ | Specifies a relative polar point |
| `To point:` *Pick the relative polar point 2.00<270* | Draws a 2" line at 270 degrees |
| `To point:` *From the screen menu, choose* undo | Removes the last line segment |
| `To point:` *Pick the relative polar point 1.00<270* | Draws a 1" line at 270 degrees |
| `To point:` *Pick the relative polar point 4.50<0* | Draws a 4.5" line at 0 degrees |
| `To point:` **@.5,.5** ↵ | Draws a .5" chamfer |
| `To point:` *Press Enter* | Ends the LINE command |

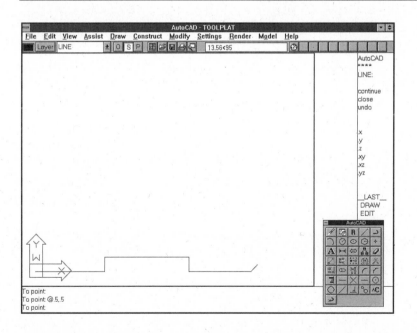

**Figure 6.2:**

The tool plate perimeter started with LINE.

The Undo option is a convenient method of stepping back, one line segment at a time, during the LINE command. Each time you enter **U** or choose undo, AutoCAD backs up one segment. You can do this several times in a row. After the LINE command ends, a U or UNDO command undoes all the segments created during the previous command.

Before continuing with the tool plate perimeter, take a moment to examine the options for the LINE command.

# LINE Options

The following list summarizes the LINE command options:

- **continue.** Choose the continue option from the screen menu or press Enter at the From point: prompt to continue a line from the endpoint of the most recent previously drawn line or arc.

- **Close.** Enter **C** (Close) or choose Close from the screen menu at the To point: prompt to close a series of line segments. This option creates a line from the last segment's endpoint to the first point of the series.

- **Undo.** Press **U** at the To point: prompt to undo the last line segment, back to the previous point.

*You can keep undoing as long as you are in the LINE command and have not exited the command by pressing Enter, the spacebar, or Ctrl-C.*

Next, complete the perimeter of the tool plate using the LINE command. Instead of the pull-down menu, however, use a combination of the screen menu and command line to is-sue and control the LINE command. Your completed perimeter should look like figure 6.3.

## Using a Variety of Line Methods

| Command: *From the screen menu, choose* DRAW, *then* LINE: | Starts the LINE command |
| --- | --- |
| _LINE From point: *Press Enter* | Starts at the last endpoint |
| To point: **16,8** ↵ | |
| To point: **11,8** ↵ | |
| To point: *Pick the relative polar point 1.00<270* | |
| To point: *Pick the relative polar point 6.00<180* | |
| To point: **@1<90** ↵ | |
| To point: *Pick the relative polar point 5.00<180* | |
| To point: *Enter* **C** *or, from the screen menu, choose* Close | Closes to the first point in the series |

The line closes to the first point in this LINE command series, not to the beginning of your perimeter as you may have expected.

Command: **U** ↵                                          Undoes all lines from this LINE command

Command: **REDO** ↵                                    Brings back the lines

Command: *From the toolbox, choose* ERASE          Starts the ERASE command

erase

Select objects: *Pick the last*                 Erases the line and ends the
*diagonal line and press Enter*                  ERASE command

Command: **LINE** ↵                                      Starts the LINE command

From point: *From the toolbox, choose*            Selects the ENDP object snap
ENDPOINT

endp of *Pick at* ① *(see fig. 6.3)*

To point: *From the toolbox, choose*              Draws the last line
ENDPOINT, *then pick at* ②

To point: *Press Enter*                             Ends the LINE command

Use PAN or ZOOM Center to position the tool plate at the center of the viewport.

Command: *From the toolbar, choose* QSAVE    Saves the drawing

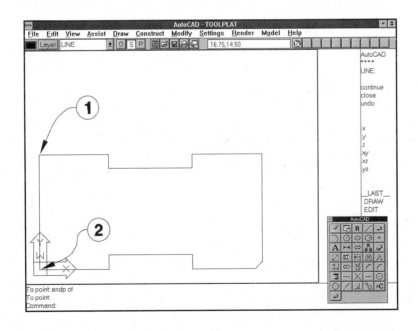

**Figure 6.3:**

The completed tool path perimeter.

*Any time you draw a few line segments and want to close them into an irregular polygon, use Close. (Close creates a closed series of line entities; to make a regular polygon as a single polyline entity, use the POLYGON command. See Chapter 7 for more details.) Just press Enter or Ctrl-C at the* To point: *prompt if you want to terminate the command without closing to the first point.*

In later exercises, you draw the slot at the left of the tool plate, add fillets to the upper corners, and chamfer the lower left corner. For now, you need to learn the ARC and CIRCLE commands.

# Creating Circles and Arcs

Unlike lines, circle and arc entities require more than two simple endpoints. You can create arcs and circles in at least a dozen different ways. Regardless of the parameters (like endpoints, angles, directions, or chords) that you enter to create the entity, arcs and circles are stored as the simplest possible geometry. A circle is stored as a center point and a radius. An arc is a center point, a radius, a start angle, and an end angle. Using this geometric information, AutoCAD can regenerate accurate curves at the best possible resolution and smoothness that your system can display or plot.

## Getting To Know Circles

If you choose **C**ircle from the **D**raw pull-down menu, AutoCAD displays a child menu that lists five circle creation methods. Why so many? For different drafting tasks, you may have different information about where circles should go. Most often, you know the center point and the radius or diameter. In these cases, you use this information to create the circle. The following list describes the circle options:

- **Center point.** Type or pick the center point, and CIRCLE prompts for a diameter or radius. This option is the default.

- **Diameter.** Use this option to enter a distance or pick two points to show a distance for the diameter.

- **Radius.** Use this option to enter a distance or pick two points to show a distance for the radius.

- **3P.** Use this option to specify the circumference with three points.

- **2P.** Use this option to specify two diameter points on the circumference.

- **TTR.** Use this option to select two lines, circles, or arcs that form tangents to the circle, and then specify the circle's radius.

As illustrated in figure 6.4, you can create a circle in at least five ways. Which method do you choose? If you know whether you have a radius, diameter, or points, you can pick the correct option from the menu. If you do not have this information, entering the CIRCLE command (or C) from the keyboard enables you to pick your options in midstream.

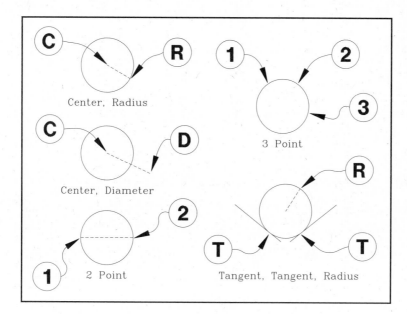

**Figure 6.4:**

Five ways to draw circles.

 *Notice the difference between Center point/Diameter and 2P. Both options enable you to specify a diameter, but if you pick the second point with Center point/Diameter, it merely indicates the diameter's distance, and the circle does not draw through the point. If you pick two points with 2P, you see a circle appear between those two points with the distance as the diameter. The 2P option enables you to draw a diameter circle the way most people intuitively think about diameter.*

In the next exercise, you draw a few circles using **C**ircle on the **D**raw pull-down. Use Center, **R**adius option for the first circle and Center, **D**iameter for the second circle. Figure 6.5 shows what your drawing should look like after this exercise.

## Using the CIRCLE Command

Continue with the TOOLPLAT drawing from the previous exercise.

*continues*

| | |
|---|---|
| `Command:` *Click on* LINE *in the toolbar layer name box, then choose* CIRCLE | Makes the CIRCLE layer current |
| `Command:` *Choose* **D**raw, *then* **C**ircle, *then* Center, **R**adius | Starts the CIRCLE command |
| `_circle 3P/2P/TTR/<Center point>:` *point 8.00,4.00* | Specifies the circle's center |
| `Diameter/<Radius>:` **.5** ↵ | Draws a circle with a .5" radius |
| `Command:` *Choose* **D**raw, *then* **C**ircle, *then* Center, **D**iameter | Issues the CIRCLE command with the Diameter option |
| `_circle 3P/2P/TTR/<Center point>:` *Pick or enter point 13.00,4.00* | Specifies the circle's center |
| `Diameter/<Radius>: <0.50> _diameter Diameter <1.00>:` **2** ↵ | Draws a circle with a 2" diameter |

**Figure 6.5:**

Holes added to the tool plate.

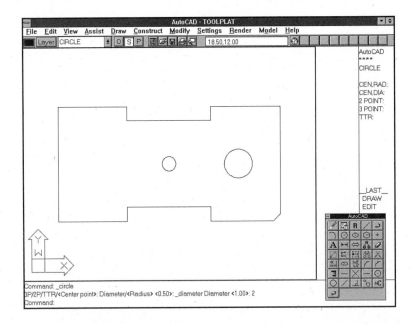

If you pick a center point with the default Center, **R**adius option, AutoCAD prompts you to specify a radius or to use the diameter option. If you specify a point, as you did for the first circle, you get a circle through that radius point. If you enter **D** instead, you get the diameter prompt. After you specify a point at the diameter prompt, AutoCAD draws a circle by the center point/diameter method. If you choose Center, **D**iameter, AutoCAD automatically enters the diameter option for you.

If you enter **2P**, **3P**, or **TTR** at the center point prompt, you get one of those options, and AutoCAD prompts you for the necessary points to complete the circle.

You also can access the CIRCLE command from AutoCAD's DRAW screen menu, from the toolbox, or from the command line. Use the toolbox and the screen menu with the 2P and 3P options to draw a few more circles.

## Drawing 2-Point and 3-Point Circles

| | |
|---|---|
| Command: *From the screen menu, choose* AutoCAD, *then* DRAW, *then* CIRCLE, *then* 2 POINT: | Starts the CIRCLE command with the 2P option |
| _CIRCLE 3P/2P/TTR/<Center point>: 2P First point on diameter: *Pick or enter point 9.25,4.00* | Specifies ① on the diameter (see fig. 6.7) |
| Second point on diameter: DRAG | The menu issues the DRAG option |
| *Pick or enter point 9.75,4.00* | Draws a .5" circle through ② |
| Command: *From the toolbar, choose* ZOOM, *then pick window points* ③ *and* ④ *(see fig. 6.6)* | Zooms in on the hole pattern |
| Command: *From the toolbox, choose* CIRCLE | Starts the CIRCLE command |
| circle 3P/2P/TTR/<Center point>: **3P** ↵ | Specifies the 3-point option |
| First point: *Pick or enter point 7.75,2.50* | Specifies first point on the circumference |
| Second point: *Pick or enter point 8.00,2.25* | Specifies ⑥ on the circumference |
| Third point: *Drag the cursor to dynamically resize the circle, then pick or enter point 8.25,2.5* | Completes the circle through ⑦ on the circumference (see fig. 6.7) |
| Command: **U** ↵ | Undoes the last circle |
| Command: **U** ↵ | Undoes the ZOOM |

**Figure 6.6:**

Zoom points for drawing circles.

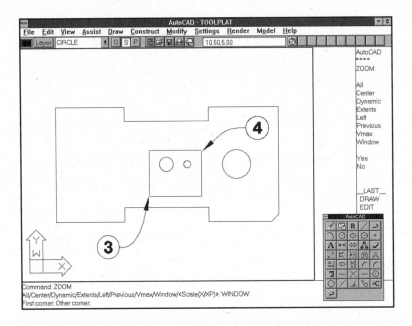

**Figure 6.7:**

Circles drawn with 2P and 3P options.

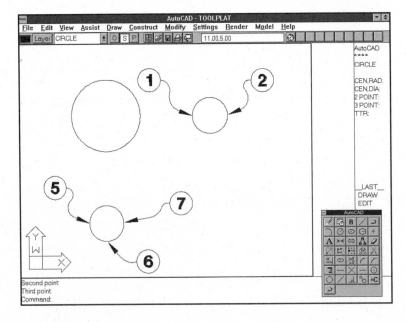

Although the screen menu automatically issued the DRAG option, it is not necessary because drag is on by default. You also can issue the CIRCLE command and options from the AutoCAD `Command:` prompt or use the **C** shortcut command. Use this method, along with the TTR option, to draw a few more circles.

---

## Using the TTR Circle Option

| | |
|---|---|
| `Command:` **CIRCLE** ↵ | Starts the CIRCLE command |
| `3P/2P/TTR/<Center point>:` **T** ↵ | Specifies the TTR option |
| `Enter Tangent spec:` *Pick the line at point ① in figure 6.8* | Selects the first tangent line |
| `Enter second Tangent spec:` *Pick the line at point ②* | Selects the second tangent line |
| `Radius <0.25>:` **.5** ↵ | Draws a 1" circle tangent to the two lines |
| `Command:` **C** ↵ | Issues the CIRCLE command |
| `CIRCLE 3P/2P/TTR/<Center point>:` **T** ↵ | Specifies the TTR option |
| `Enter Tangent spec:` *Pick the line at point ③ (see fig. 6.8)* | Selects the first tangent line |
| `Enter second Tangent spec:` *Pick the line at point ④* | Selects the second tangent line |
| `Radius <0.50>:` *Press Enter* | Uses the default to draw a tangent circle |

*Save the drawing*

---

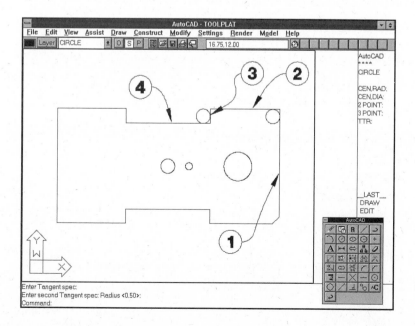

**Figure 6.8:**

Circles drawn with TTR option.

The CIRCLE command has many options, depending on what information you have about the circle. When you use AutoCAD properly, you never need to calculate (or worse yet, guess) the information for correctly drawing a circle. Using the proper option and the right object snaps should give you an accurate circle.

As you learn in chapters 8 and 9, you can break or trim the circles and their adjacent lines to form fillets, or you can use the FILLET command to both draw the fillet and trim or extend lines. This exercise was good practice using the CIRCLE command (and the last two practice circles are edited in Chapter 8), but there are often several ways to accomplish a task in AutoCAD. For example, another way to draw fillets is just to draw an arc. Arcs are explained in the following section.

# Using Three-Point Arcs

If you thought there are many ways to create circles, there are even more ways to create arcs; and AutoCAD offers nearly every possible geometric method for creating them.

The most straightforward way to create arcs is with the three-point default of the ARC command. It works about the same way as a three-point circle. The first point is the arc's beginning; the second and third points define the arc's curve. The last point and first point define the chord of the arc. AutoCAD automatically drags the arc, unless you have turned drag off with the DRAGMODE system variable.

The ARC command can be issued from the DRAW screen menu, from the toolbox, from the **A**rc child menu on the **D**raw pull-down menu, or entered with ARC or A at the Command: prompt. The pull-down **A**rc child menu lists all of the options.

Draw the arc for the guide slot at the left of the tool plate using a three-point arc (see fig. 6.9).

---

## Drawing 3-Point Arcs

| | |
|---|---|
| Command: *Click on* CIRCLE *in the toolbar layer name box, then choose* ARC | Makes the ARC layer current |
| Command: *Choose* **D**raw, *then* **A**rc, *then* **3**-point | Issues the ARC command |
| _arc Center/<Start point>: *Pick or enter point 2.00,3.25* | Starts the arc at ① |
| Center/End/<Second point>: *Pick or enter point 2.75,4.00* | Picks second point at ② |

Move the cursor, noting how the arc drags from the first point through the second point.

| | |
|---|---|
| End point: *Pick or enter point 2.00,4.75* | Draws the arc to ③ |

---

After you enter the first two points, AutoCAD uses drag to show you where the three-point arc is going to be drawn. Although drag is automatically turned on by the **3** point menu item, whenever the DRAGMODE command is set to Auto (the default) AutoCAD drags the results of the command before it is finished. Experiment by dragging during drawing and editing commands.

Next, draw the fillet for the upper left corner of the tool plate using the start point with the Center and End options. Instead of using the pull-down menu option, however, use the AutoCAD command line to experiment with the ARC prompts.

## Drawing Arcs with Start, Center, End

Command: **ARC** ↵

| | |
|---|---|
| _ARC Center/<Start point>: *Pick or enter point 0.50,8.00* | Begins the arc |
| Center/End/<Second point>: **C** ↵ | Specifies the Center option |
| Center: *Pick point 0.50,7.50* | Specifies the center point |

Move the cursor, noting how the arc dynamically follows the third point.

| | |
|---|---|
| Angle/Length of chord/<End point>: *Pick relative polar point at 0.50<180* | Draws the arc |

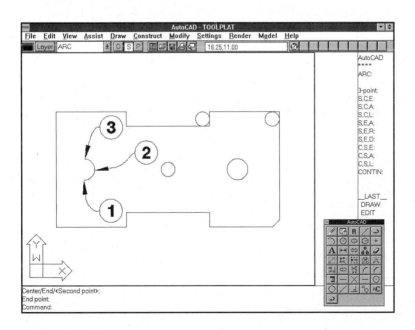

**Figure 6.9:**

A 3-point arc for the guide slot.

As shown in the previous exercise, you can enter points by typing coordinates or by picking from the drawing area with the help of the coordinate display. Remember the first rule of using AutoCAD: read the `Command:` prompt. When you use commands with as many options as ARC offers, reading the default prompt and the available options tells you what type of data AutoCAD is looking for. In many cases, a coordinate can be entered for the default response or another option can be chosen. These options for ARC are explained more fully in the following section.

The ARC command has eight options: the default start point, continue, Center, End point, Angle, Radius, Direction, and Length of chord. These options can be grouped by common functions (see fig. 6.10) to provide ten ways to draw arcs. Try some of these arc options on your SCRATCH layer.

**Figure 6.10:**

Ten different ways to draw arcs.

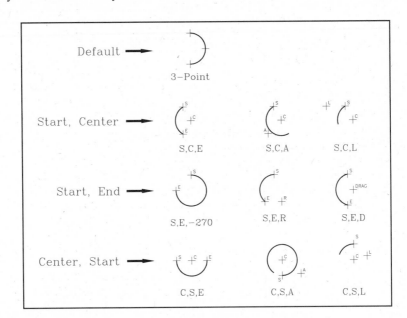

## Using the Arc Options

AutoCAD offers several different methods for drawing arcs, and varying the order of the options enables you to choose the easiest order of input. An example of input order is center-start-end versus start-center-end. The following list explains some combinations of the arc options.

- **3-Point.** This method creates an arc that passes through three specified points. The first point is the start point, the third point is the endpoint, and the second point is any other point lying on the arc.

- **Start,Center.** This method requires an arc starting point and the center point of the arc. This option group has a third parameter, which completes the arc by specifying an endpoint, an angle, or a length of chord.

- **Start,End.** This method enables you to define the starting and ending points of the arc first, and then to define how the arc is to be drawn. You define the arc with an angle, radius, direction, or center point.

- **Center,Start**. This method enables you to first identify the center of the arc, and then the start point. The arc is completed by supplying an angle, length of chord, or endpoint.

- **Continue.** This method is a further default—invoked by pressing Enter at the first arc prompt or by choosing CONTIN from the arc screen menu—that starts a new arc tangent to the last line or arc drawn. Similarly, pressing Enter at the first prompt of the LINE command starts a new line at the end of the last arc.

You can select any of ten predefined combinations of arc options from the pull-down, screen, or tablet menus. The options are abbreviated by mnemonic letters on the screen and tablet menus, or from the keyboard.

You can choose your options midstream by entering **ARC** and the options from the keyboard. If you begin an arc with a picked point, your construction methods narrow to those that begin with Start; if you begin with C, AutoCAD restricts you to options that accept the center point first, and so on.

To finish your examination of the ARC command, use the Angle option, polar point specification, and the CONTINUE: screen menu item to draw one of the radial slots on the tool plate. When you have completed the slot, add a line to the guide slot at the left of the tool plate.

---

## Drawing Arcs with Angles, Polar, and Continue

| | |
|---|---|
| Command: *From the screen menu,* *choose* C,S,A: | Issues ARC with the Center, Start, and Angle options |
| `_ARC Center/<Start point>: _` `C Center:` *Pick or enter point 13.00,4.00* | Locates the arc's center |
| `Start point: @2.25<225` ↵ | Locates the arc's start point |
| `Angle/Length of chord/<End point>:` `_A Included angle: DRAG` | Menu issues Angle and DRAG options |

Move the cursor, noting that graphical included angle input is measured from zero degrees, not from the start of the arc.

| | |
|---|---|
| `Included angle: 90` ↵ | Draws the arc |

*continues*

| | |
|---|---|
| `Command:` *From the screen menu, choose* CONTIN: | Issues ARC with the Continue option |
| `_ARC Center/<Start point>:`<br>`End point: DRAG` | Continues the arc from the end of the last arc drawn |

Move the cursor, noting that the dynamic arc is always tangent to the previous arc.

| | |
|---|---|
| `End point: @.5<135` ↵ | Draws the arc |
| `Command:` *Press Enter* | Repeats the ARC command |
| `ARC Center/<Start point>: C` ↵ | Specifies the Center option |
| `Center:` *Pick or enter point 13.00,4.00* | Locates the center |
| `Start point:` *From the toolbox, choose* ENDPOINT, *and pick at* ① *(see fig. 6.11)* | Locates the start point |
| `Angle/Length of chord/<End point>:`<br>`A` ↵ | Specifies the Angle option |
| `Included angle: -90` ↵ | Draws the arc clockwise |

Next, continue with another tangent arc.

| | |
|---|---|
| `Command:` *From the screen menu,*<br>*choose* CONTIN: | |
| `Endpoint:DRAG` *From the toolbox,*<br>*choose* ENDPOINT, *then pick* ② | Closes the slot with another arc |
| `Command: L` ↵ | Issues LINE command |
| `From point:` *Pick or enter point 2.00,4.75* | Starts the line |
| `To point:` *From the toolbox, choose* PERPENDICULAR, *then pick* ③ | Draws a line |
| `To point:` *Press Enter* | Ends the LINE command |

Instead of trying to memorize every option of the ARC command, try to understand what combinations of data—point, center point, radius, and so on—are needed to define an arc. Usually three pieces of data must be given for AutoCAD to accurately draw an arc. The reason so many options are given is to make sure that you can describe the arc based on the information you have, without having to calculate or guess at unknown information.

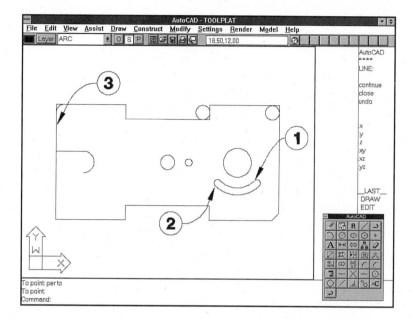

**Figure 6.11:**

The slots added to the tool plate.

Your TOOLPLAT drawing is far from complete, but you are now familiar with all of the options for the LINE, ARC, and CIRCLE commands and have used many of these options in the TOOLPLAT drawing. You may feel, however, that the order and manner in which you created the drawing was a bit haphazard. Actually, it was by design. Now you can experiment with some of the powerful features that are new to AutoCAD in Release 12—autoediting and grips—to complete the TOOLPLAT drawing.

# Using Grips and Autoediting Modes

The remainder of this chapter explains and demonstrates some of the editing techniques you need to finish the drawing. In CAD drafting, editing means much more than erasing entities or correcting mistakes. Editing commands are often used in conjunction with entity-creation commands to make your drawings easy to create, yet extremely accurate. AutoCAD's editing commands have many options suitable for different situations. The following exercises introduce the basic options of each editing command, using the autoediting method with grip controls.

Think of *grips* in AutoCAD as being convenient locations on each entity to help control and manipulate that entity. Each entity has several grip points, which can be chosen accurately (without specifying object snap modes) by picking in the grip box. For instance, the grip points on a line are the endpoints and the midpoint (see fig. 6.12). When the GRIPS system variable is set to 1 (on, the default), the grips appear on an entity when that entity is selected at the Command: prompt.

**Figure 6.12:**

Common entity
grip locations.

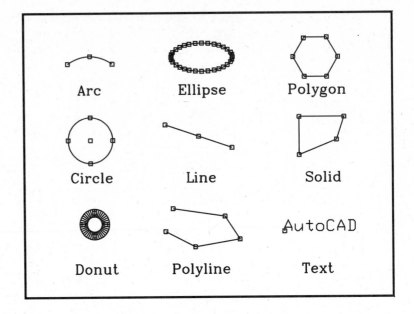

When you click on a visible grip, it becomes "hot" (selected) and displays highlighted. A hot grip becomes a base point for one of the autoediting modes to manipulate the entity. *Autoediting modes* are a special group of common editing commands that are available when a base grip is chosen. These modes are briefly explained in the following list.

- **Stretch.** The stretch mode enables entities to be modified by moving one or more grips to another location while leaving the other part of the entity in its original location. This can easily change the size or shape of an entity or a group of entities. In some cases, the stretch mode moves an entity.

- **Move.** The move mode relocates entities from a base point to another specified location. The size and orientation does not change.

- **Rotate.** This mode enables objects to be rotated around a specified base point. The angle can be entered or specified by dragging.

- **Scale.** The scale mode enables entities to be scaled up or down by a given scale factor about a specified base point. Scale factors can be directly entered, dragged to size, or given, using the Reference option.

- **Mirror.** Selected entities can be mirrored about a line formed by the base point grip and another selected point.

All these autoediting modes have several things in common. First of all, when entities are selected and a base grip is chosen to issue the command, you can choose the proper mode by entering the first two letters of the mode (**SC** for scale, for example) or by pressing Enter, the spacebar, or button 1 to switch between the modes. If you want to make a copy while executing an autoediting mode, use the Copy option or hold down the Shift key while making multiple second point picks. The Undo option undoes the last edit, and the eXit option exits the autoediting modes. These modes are similar to the commands, such as STRETCH and MOVE, which are discussed in the next chapter.

The following exercises introduce you to selecting and editing entities using grips. Zoom in on the upper left corner of the tool plate and stretch the top and side lines to the ends of the arc to form a proper fillet for the corner.

## Stretching Lines with Grips

Continue with the TOOLPLAT drawing from the previous exercises and use ZOOM with the Window option to show the drawing area (see fig 6.13).

| | |
|---|---|
| Command: **GRIPS** ↵ | Accesses GRIPS system variable |
| New value for GRIPS <0>: **1** ↵ | Turns on grips |
| Command: *Turn off Snap, if on, by pressing F9* | |
| Command: *Pick a point on the upper left arc* | Selects and highlights the arc and displays its grips points |
| Command: *Pick line at* ① *(see fig. 6.13)* | Selects and highlights the top line, and displays grips |
| Command: *Pick grip at* ② | Enters stretching autoediting mode |
| \*\* STRETCH \*\* | Stretches the line to the arc endpoint |
| <Stretch to point>/Base point/Copy/ Undo/eXit: *Pick arc's grip at* ③ | |

*Choose* **V**iew, **Z**oom, *then* **P**revious

*If you miss the entity when picking, a rubber-band box (a window) appears from the pick point. Pick again at the same point, and then try again. Window selection is covered later in this chapter.*

**Figure 6.13:**

Grip points and
pick points.

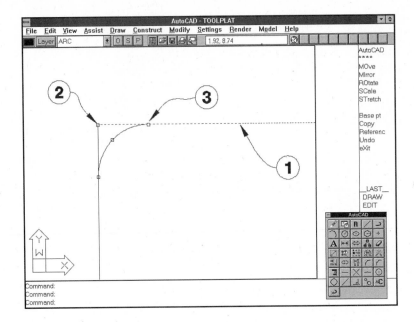

The previous exercise could have used the End point object snap to lock the line onto
the endpoint of the arc. Because the cursor automatically snaps to grips, however, you
generally do not need to use object snaps when editing with grips. (Some entities do
not provide grips for certain object snaps, so you need to use object snaps occasionally.)
The trick to eliminating object snaps for editing, and even for drawing, is to first select
the entities to snap to as well as the entities to edit, which displays all their grips. Then,
click on the grips of the entities to edit, which makes their autoedit grips hot. You then
can snap to any of the displayed grips without using object snap modes. The hot grips
remain hot until the autoedit operation is completed or canceled by pressing Ctrl-C. All
the grips remain displayed until you enter a command or press Ctrl-C at the Command:
prompt.

Depending on the autoediting mode being used, either hot entities only or all highlighted entities are affected. To better control editing with grips, you must understand
AutoCAD's selection settings and methods. The next section explains them.

# Controlling GRIPS and Selection Parameters

Remember that the GRIPS system variable must be on (1) for autoediting modes to
function. You can display the Grips dialog box (see fig. 6.14) by using the DDGRIPS
command or by choosing **G**rips from the **S**ettings pull-down menu. Putting a check
mark in the **E**nable Grips check box turns on the GRIPS system variable; clearing the

box turns it off. You can easily adjust the grip size, which works similarly to object snap aperture size, with the slider bar. You can also specify the color of both displayed and selected grips in this dialog box.

# Controlling Selection with DDSELECT

Two other settings, Use **S**hift to Add and **P**ress and Drag, improve the versatility and interaction of editing with grips. They are found in another dialog box called Entity Selection Settings (see fig. 6.14). The DDSELECT command brings up this dialog box, or you can choose **S**election Settings from the **S**ettings menu. The other settings in this dialog box are covered in Chapter 8.

AutoCAD editing modes and commands operate on a *selection set* of entities that you select. The current selection is generally indicated by highlighting the entities. The **U**se Shift to Add setting controls how entities are added to the selection set (the same as the PICKADD system variable). When this setting is on, (1=the default), entities are added to the selection set as they are selected. When this setting is off (0), newly selected entities replace the existing selection set, unless you hold down Shift as you select them. Whether PICKADD is on or off, holding down Shift and selecting currently highlighted entities removes those entities from the selection set. To add entities when PICKADD is off, hold down Shift while selecting entities. Experiment with PICKADD off in the following exercise.

**Figure 6.14:**

The Grips and Entity Selection Settings dialog boxes.

---

## Controlling Selection

Continue with the TOOLPLAT drawing from the previous exercise.

Command: *Pick any entity*                    Highlights the entity and starts a selection set

Command: *Pick two other entities*            Highlights the entities and adds them to the set

Command: *Shift-pick one of the*              Removes the entity from the set
*highlighted entities*

*continues*

| | |
|---|---|
| Command: *Choose **S**ettings, then **S**election Settings* | Displays the Entity Selection Settings dialog box |
| *Put a check mark in the **U**se Shift to Add check box, then choose OK* | Turns PICKADD off (0) and exits |
| Command: *Pick any entity* | Clears the selection set (leaving grips on) and starts a new set |
| Command: *Pick any other entity* | Clears the selection set again and starts another new set |
| Command: *Shift-pick two other entities* | Adds the entities to the existing set |
| Command: *Shift-pick a highlighted entity* | Removes the entity from the set |

When you are selecting entities, it is obvious whether PICKADD is off or on. How you have it set really depends on your personal preference, but once you are used to it, you will probably find it more versatile to have it off. Remember to use Shift to unselect entities or, when PICKADD is off, to select additional entities.

 *The exercises throughout the rest of this book assume that **U**se Shift to Add is checked (PICKADD is 0, off).*

As an alternative to pressing Ctrl-C to clear a selection set or to clear grips (press twice to clear both), you can pick in a clear area of the drawing to clear the selection set or remove grips from the entities. When you do so, you are actually selecting a window or crossing-window of empty space in the drawing to clear the selection set. You must pick twice. If your first pick finds an entity, it selects the entity. If, however, the first pick misses, it sets the base corner of a rubber-banded window or crossing box. A second pick completes the window or crossing selection. A window selects all entities totally enclosed in its box; a crossing selects all entities in the box or that cross its box. You pick window points left-to-right, and the rubber-band box is shown solid; you pick crossing points right-to-left, and the rubber-band box is dashed. If the selection set is already empty, or if you just emptied it with a window or crossing selection of empty space, making another window or crossing selection removes all grips from the drawing window. The following exercise demonstrates this technique.

## Clearing the Selection Set and Grips

Continue with the TOOLPLAT drawing from the previous exercise. You should have a few entities selected.

Command: *Pick points* ① *and* ②       Clears the selection set
*(see fig. 6.15)*

Command: *Pick points* ① *and* ②       Clears the grip markers
*again*

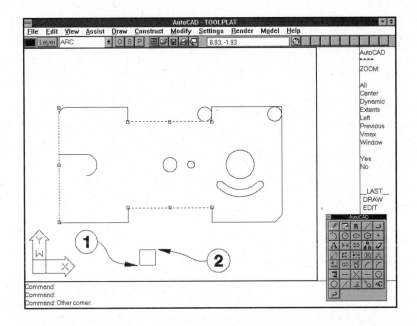

**Figure 6.15:**

Selecting in empty space to clear grips.

The previous exercise cleared the grip boxes and selection set from the drawing. You often need to clear grips to keep the drawing area from becoming to cluttered. Alternatively, you could have used two Ctrl-C's to clear the grips and selection set.

Window and crossing selections, including clearing a selection set and grips using the preceding method, are easier if you change the way AutoCAD makes window and crossing selections. The next section explains why.

# Controlling Press and Drag

Prior to Release 12, AutoCAD always required two picks to show a window. In most software with a graphical interface, you can make a window selection by pressing and holding the button at the first point, dragging to the second point, and then releasing the button. The Entity Selection Settings dialog box now offers a choice in the way a window or crossing is specified. When the <u>P</u>ress and Drag box is checked (the PICKDRAG system variable is on, set to 1), a window is created by pressing the pick button, moving to the other corner of the window, and releasing. Even if you are used to the old two-pick method, once you get used to <u>P</u>ress and Drag you will find it faster and more efficient. It also behaves the same as other software you may use and enables you to clear selection sets or grips with a single pick. Try this technique in the next exercise.

## Controlling Press and Drag

| | |
|---|---|
| Command: **DDSELECT** ↵ | Displays the Entity Selection Settings dialog box |
| *Put a check mark in the* <u>P</u>ress *and* <u>D</u>rag *checkbox, then choose OK* | Turns on PICKDRAG and exits |
| Command: *Press and hold button 1 at* ① *(see fig. 6.16), drag to* ②, *and release button 1* | Creates a Crossing window selection |
| Command: *Press and hold button 1 at* ③, *drag to* ④, *and release* | Creates a Window selection, clears the previous selection set, and starts a new set |
| Command: *Click once in empty space* | Clears the selection set |
| Command: *Click again in empty space* | Removes grip markers |

*Throughout the rest of the book,* <u>P</u>ress *and Drag (PICKDRAG on, 1) is the default window/crossing selection mode. When exercises direct you to use a crossing or window selection, remember to use the* <u>P</u>ress *and Drag technique to select as directed.*

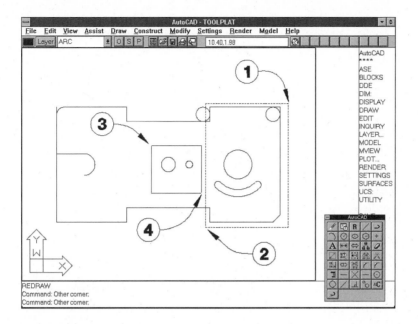

**Figure 6.16:**

Selection points for press and drag windows.

## Controlling Aperture Size

You can easily adjust the pickbox size that appears on the crosshairs by clicking on and dragging the box on the horizontal slider in the Entity Selection Settings dialog box. It also can be set using the PICKBOX system variable or chosen from the APERTUR: item of the SETTINGS screen menu. The size is called out in pixels and usually ranges between 5 and 15, depending on your graphics resolution. Use whatever is comfortable for your display and pointing device.

# Editing with the Autoediting Modes

Now that you have an understanding of <u>U</u>se Shift to Add and <u>P</u>ress and Drag, you can use them constantly to simplify editing tasks. The following exercises continue the use of stretch autoediting mode and show you how to snap to specific points by using only grips. This method can be a great time saver over using the regular object snaps and usually involves fewer steps.

## Object Snapping with Autoediting Grips

Continue with the TOOLPLAT drawing from the previous exercise and zoom to the view shown in figure 6.17.

| | |
|---|---|
| `Command:` *Pick the arc at* ① *(see fig. 6.17)* | Selects the arc and displays its grips |
| `Command:` *Pick line at* ② | Clears the previous set, selects the vertical line, and shows grips |
| `Command:` *Pick grip at* ③ | Grips the line and enters stretch mode |
| `** STRETCH **` | Snaps the line to the arc endpoint |
| `<Stretch to point>/Base point/Copy/`<br>`Undo/eXit:` *Pick the lower left grip on the arc at* ④ *in fig. 6.18* | |

**Figure 6.17:**

Grip and entity selection points before stretching lines.

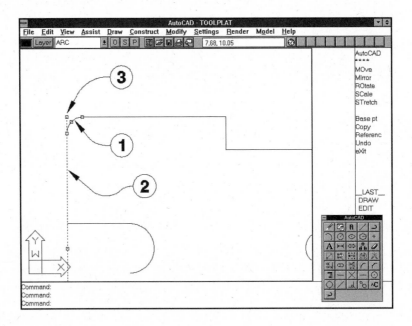

The stretch autoediting mode affects other entities as well. With a few exceptions, depending on which grip you pick, the Stretch autoediting mode changes the shape of entities. In the next exercise, you change one of the arcs in the radial slot.

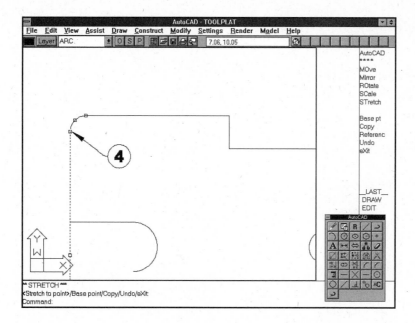

## Stretching Arcs with Autoedit

Zoom to the previous view with ZOOM P.

| | |
|---|---|
| `Command:` *Pick any arc* | Selects arc and displays grips |
| `Command:` *Pick the arc's midpoint grip* | Grips the midpoint and enters stretch mode |
| `** STRETCH **`<br>`<Stretch to point>/Base point/Copy/`<br>`Undo/eXit:` *Move and pick any other point* | Changes the arc's shape |
| `Command:` *Pick an endpoint grip on the arc* | Grips the endpoint and enters stretch mode |
| `** STRETCH **`<br>`<Stretch to point>/Base point`<br>`/Copy/Undo/eXit:` *Pick any other point* | Changes the arc's shape |
| `Command:` **U** ↵ | Undoes the last change |
| `Command:` **U** ↵ | Returns the arc to its original shape |

# Copying and Moving with Stretch Autoediting Mode

The stretch autoediting mode can be used to move an entity, change an endpoint, or resize an entity, depending on what type the entity is and which grip is selected. Picking one grip point on an entity may not have the same effect as picking one of the other grip points. Selecting the end of a line stretches the line, for example, whereas picking the middle grip moves it. You also can use the Copy option or hold Shift down while choosing the second point to create copies while stretching.

Experiment with these methods and options, and use the Copy option of the stretch autoediting mode to complete the guide slot at the left of the tool plate.

## Copying with Autoediting modes

| | |
|---|---|
| Command: *Pick line at* ① *(see fig. 6.19)* | Selects the line and displays grips |
| Command: *Pick the mid grip on the line* | Grips line and enters stretch mode, moving line |
| \*\* STRETCH \*\* <br> &lt;Stretch to point&gt;/Base point/Copy/ <br> Undo/eXit: *Pick a point above the tool plate* | Moves the line |
| Command: **U** ↵ | Undoes the stretch move |
| Command: *Select the guide slot arc* | Selects and displays grips |
| Command: *Pick at* ① | Clears the arc from the set, selects the line, and displays its grips |
| Command: *Pick the line's midpoint grip* | Grips the line and enters stretch autoediting mode, moving the line |
| \*\* STRETCH \*\* <br> &lt;Stretch to point&gt;/Base point/Copy/ <br> Undo/eXit: **B** ↵ | Specifies the Base point option |
| Base point: *Pick the right end grip of the line* | Changes the base (from) point for moving the line |
| \*\* STRETCH \*\* <br> &lt;Stretch to point&gt;/Base point/Copy/ <br> Undo/eXit: **C** ↵ | Specifies the Copy (multiple stretch) option |
| \*\*STRETCH (multiple) \*\* <br> &lt;Stretch to point&gt;/Base point/Copy/ <br> Undo/eXit: *Pick the bottom grip on the arc at* ② | Copies the line |

| | |
|---|---|
| `<Stretch to point>/Base point/Copy/`<br>`Undo/eXit:` *Pick another point below*<br>*the base plate* | Copies the line again |
| `<Stretch to point>/Base point/Copy/`<br>`Undo/eXit:` **U** ↵ | Undoes the last copy |
| `<Stretch to point>/Base point/Copy/`<br>`Undo/eXit:` *Press Enter* | Exits from autoediting mode |
| `Command:` *From the toolbar, choose* QSAVE | Clears the selection sets and grips, and saves the drawing |

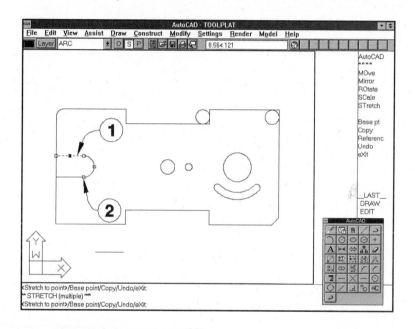

**Figure 6.19:**

Copying with stretch autoediting mode.

NOTE

*You can exit from the multiple autoediting modes by pressing Enter, the spacebar, Ctrl-C, or by entering an* **X.** *If you are not in multiple mode, you can exit from autoediting by pressing Ctrl-C or by entering an* **X.**

Because it is so versatile—capable of stretching, moving, and copying objects—the stretch mode is the first of the autoediting modes to appear when you choose a grip to enter autoediting mode. The move autoediting mode works similarly to stretch and is explained in the next section.

# Using the Move Autoediting Mode

Instead of using the stretch autoediting mode to move something, try using the move mode. To do so, enter **MO** (for MOve) at the autoedit prompt or press the spacebar once, and the move mode prompt appears. Specifying a point moves the selected entity or entities the distance between the base point (the grip you selected) and the specified point. If you want a base point other than the selected grip, the Base point option enables you to specify a new base point, as in the preceding exercise. You can specify points by any combination of grips, object snaps, or by entering the coordinates.

*If you are trying to move or stretch a grip point a small distance, the desired point may fall in the grip box of the gripped point, preventing you from picking the desired point. In such cases, just move or stretch the grip to an out-of-the-way point, pick the grip again, and then pick the desired point, which is now clear of the grip.*

Try using the move autoediting mode in the next exercise.

---

## Using Move Autoediting mode

| | |
|---|---|
| `Command:` *Pick, drag, and release to select from ① to ② (see fig. 6.20)* | Selects the radial slot and displays grips |
| `Command:` *Pick either large arc's mid grip* | Enters stretch mode |
| `** STRETCH **`<br>`<Stretch to point>/Base point/Copy/`<br>`Undo/eXit:` *Press Enter* | Switches to move mode |
| `** MOVE **`<br>`<Move to point>/Base point/Copy/`<br>`Undo/eXit:` | |

Move the cursor and note that the entire radial slot (the entire selection set) now moves with the cursor.

| | |
|---|---|
| *Pick any point below the tool plate* | Relocates the slot |
| `Command:` **U** ↵ | Undoes the move |

---

As with stretch mode, you can make one or more copies from the original by using move mode. Use the Copy option or hold down the shift key while picking the point to copy to. The next exercise uses the Copy option with move mode.

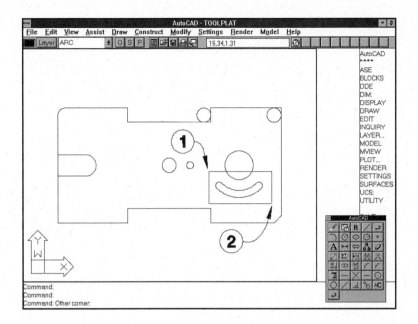

**Figure 6.20:**
Window selection points for moving the slot.

---

## Copying with Move Autoediting Mode

Command: *Select a window from ①*
*to ② (see fig. 6.20)*

Selects the radial slot and
displays grips

Command: *Pick any of the large*
*arc's grips*

Enters stretch mode

** STRETCH **
<Stretch to point>/Base point/Copy/
Undo/eXit: *Press spacebar*

Switches to move mode

** MOVE **
<Move to point>/Base point/Copy/
Undo/eXit: **C** ↵

Specifies the Copy (multiple)
option

** MOVE (multiple) **
<Move to point>/Base point/Copy/
Undo/eXit: *Pick two points below the*
*tool plate (see fig. 6.21)*

Copies two new slots to below
the tool plate

<Move to point>/Base point/Copy/
Undo/eXit: *Press Enter*

Exits from autoediting mode

*Save the drawing*

**Figure 6.21:**

Two copies of the
radial slot.

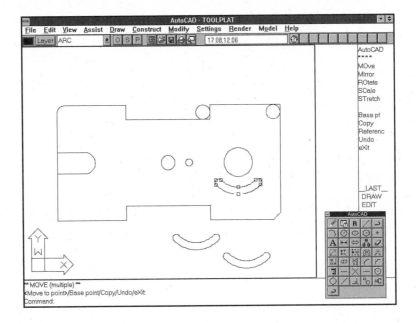

The previous exercise showed how the Move mode of autoedit is used and how you can make multiple copies if necessary. It is important to select all of the entities to be included in the command, as well as to have any additional grips displayed that may be needed for point selection. Rotate mode is shown next.

## Rotating with Autoediting Mode

Often, it is more convenient to draw a shape in a normal orientation and then rotate it or rotate and copy it into a different orientation than it is to draw it at an odd angle. The rotate mode enables selected entities to be rotated about a base point. The default base point is the selected grip. You can use the Base point option to specify a different one. You enter rotate mode by pressing Enter or the spacebar twice or by entering **RO** (ROtate). You are then prompted for a rotation angle. A positive angle produces a counterclockwise rotation by that amount; a negative angle produces a clockwise rotation.

*The autoediting modes, in order, are stretch, move, rotate, scale, and mirror. Autoedit rotates through the modes, in this order, when you press Enter, the spacebar, or the Enter button on your pointing device. If you press Enter when in mirror mode, it rotates back to stretch mode again. You also can pick the modes and options from the screen menu.*

Try using rotate mode in the following exercise.

## Rotating and Moving Entities with Autoedit

Continue with the TOOLPLAT drawing from the previous exercise.

| | |
|---|---|
| Command: *Select a window from* ① *to* ② *(see fig. 6.22)* | Selects the radial slot and displays its grips |
| Command: *Pick either large arc's midpoint grip* | Highlights grip and enters stretch mode |
| `** STRETCH **`<br>`<Stretch to point>/Base point/Copy/`<br>`Undo/eXit:` *Press the spacebar twice* | Switches to rotate mode |
| `** ROTATE **`<br>`<Rotation Angle>/Base point/Copy/`<br>`Undo/Reference/eXit:` | |

Move the cursor, and note that the slot rotates dynamically as you do so.

| | |
|---|---|
| `<Rotation angle>/Base point/Copy/`<br>`Undo/Reference/eXit:` **90** ↵ | Rotates the entities 90 degrees counterclockwise |

Now, using figure 6.23 as a guide, move the slot into position near the guide slot at the left of the tool plate.

| | |
|---|---|
| Command: *Pick either of the mid grips* | Enters stretch mode |
| `** STRETCH **`<br>`<Stretch to point>/Base point/Copy/`<br>`Undo/eXit:` *Press the spacebar once* | Switches to move mode |
| `** MOVE **`<br>`<Move to point>/Base point/Copy/`<br>`Undo/eXit:` *From the screen menu, choose* Base pt | Prompts for a base point |
| `Base point:` *From the toolbox, choose* CENTER, *then pick either of the large arcs* | Sets the base point at the arc's center |
| `<Move to point>/Base point/Copy/`<br>`Undo/eXit:` *From the toolbox, choose* CENTER, *and pick center of guide slot arc* | Moves the slot to a new location |

**Figure 6.22:**

Slot selection window and grips.

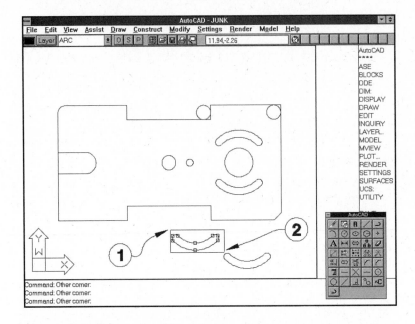

**Figure 6.23:**

The rotated and relocated slot.

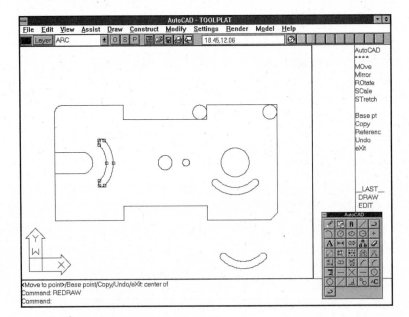

The rotate and move modes of autoedit were used to orient the slot and move it to the proper location. Object snaps were used, instead of grips, because arc centers do not have grips. Remember that picking an empty window once clears the selection set and doing it a second time removes the visible grips. You use that technique again in the following exercise.

Next, use the Copy option of the rotate autoediting mode to complete the hole pattern at the center of the tool plate.

## Rotating and Copying with Autoedit

| | |
|---|---|
| Command: *Double-click at* ① *(see fig. 6.24)* | Clears the selection set and grips |
| Command: *Pick the circle at* ② | Creates the set and displays grips |
| Command: *Pick the circle at* ③ | Clears the previous set, selects the circle, and displays grips |
| Command: *Pick the circle's center grip* ③ | Enters stretch mode |
| `** STRETCH **` `<Stretch to point>/Base point/Copy/` `Undo/eXit:` *Press Enter twice* | Switches to rotate mode |
| `** ROTATE **` `<Rotation angle>/Base point/Copy/` `Undo/Reference/eXit:` **B** ↵ | Prompts for a base point |
| `Base point:` *Pick center grip of circle* ② | Sets the rotation base point |
| `<Rotation angle>/Base point/Copy/` `Undo/Reference/eXit:` **C** ↵ | Specifies the Copy option |
| `** ROTATE (multiple) **` `<Rotation angle>/Base point/Copy/` `Undo/Reference/eXit:` **45** ↵ | Makes the first copy at 45 degrees |
| `<Rotation angle>/Base point/Copy/` `Undo/Reference/eXit:` **90** ↵ | Makes the next copy at 90 degrees |
| `<Rotation angle>/Base point/Copy/` `Undo/Reference/eXit:` **135** ↵ | Makes the next copy at 135 degrees |
| `<Rotation angle>/Base point/Copy/` `Undo/Reference/eXit:` **180** ↵ | Makes the next copy at 180 degrees |

*continues*

`<Rotation angle>/Base point/Copy/`
`Undo/Reference/eXit:` *Press Enter*  Exits from autoediting mode

`Command:` *From the toolbar, choose* QSAVE  Clears grips and the selection set, and saves the drawing

**Figure 6.24:**

Circles copied
with rotate
autoediting mode.

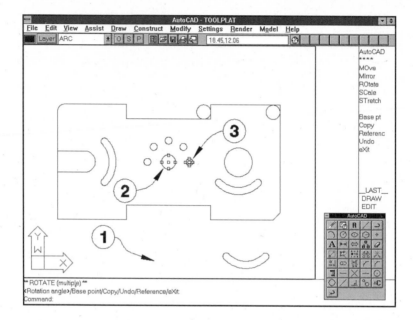

The rotate mode of autoedit is convenient for changing the orientation of entities or creating circular patterns. Most of its options—Base point, Copy, Undo, and eXit—work the same as with the other autoediting modes. The Reference option enables you to specify the current rotation and then the new rotation desired. This method works well when you do not know the incremental distance between the old and new rotation. See Chapter 8 for details.

In this drawing, some of the work that can be accomplished by rotating also can be done with mirroring.

## Mirroring Entities with Autoedit

The mirror mode creates a mirror image of the selected entities over a chosen mirror line. The mirror line is defined with endpoints of the base point and a selected second point. The base point is assumed to be the selected grip, unless a different grip is specified with the Base point option. If Ortho is on, you can easily pick a second point for a horizontal or vertical mirror line. The Copy option creates a mirrored copy of the original entities; otherwise the original entities are transformed. Enter **MI** (MIrror) at the autoedit prompt or cycle through the options by pressing Enter, the Enter button of the pointing device, or the spacebar to access the mirror mode.

Try the mirror autoediting mode on the tool plate. Mirror the right-hand radial slot to make a copy above the hole.

---

## Mirroring Entities with Autoediting mode

| | |
|---|---|
| Command: *Select the circle at ③* | Creates the set and shows grips |
| Command: *Select a window from ①*<br>*to ② (see fig. 6.25)* | Selects the radial slot and displays grips |
| Command: *Pick one of the grips on the slot* | Enters stretch mode |
| `** STRETCH **`<br>`<Stretch to point>/Base point/Copy/`<br>`Undo/eXit:` *Press Enter four times* | Switches to mirror mode |
| `** MIRROR **`<br>`<Second point>/Base point/Copy/Undo/`<br>`eXit:` **B** ↵ | Prompts for a base point |
| `Base point:` *Pick center grip of the*<br>*circle* | Specifies the new base point |
| `<Second point>/Base point/Copy/Undo/`<br>`eXit:` *Pick the circle's right grip*<br>*at ③* | Locates the second point directly to the right of the base point and mirrors the slot |

Because you did not use the Copy option, the original slot was deleted.

| | |
|---|---|
| Command: **U** ↵ | Undoes the edit |
| Command: *Select the circle at ③* | Creates the set and shows grips |
| Command: *Select a window from ①*<br>*to ② (see fig. 6.25)* | Selects the radial slot and displays grips |
| Command: *Pick one of the grips on*<br>*the slot* | Enters stretch mode |
| `** STRETCH **`<br>`<Stretch to point>/Base point/Copy/`<br>`Undo/eXit:` *Press the spacebar four times* | Switches to mirror mode |
| `** MIRROR **`<br>`<Second point>/Base point/Copy/Undo/`<br>`eXit:` **B** ↵ | |

*continues*

```
Base point: Pick the center grip of circle

<Second point>/Base point/Copy/Undo/      Specifies the Copy option
eXit: C ↵

** MIRROR (multiple) **                    Copies and mirrors in one operation
<Second point>/Base point/Copy/Undo/
eXit: Pick the circle's right grip
at ③

** MIRROR **                               Exits from autoedit
<Second point>/Base point/Copy/Undo
/eXit: Press Enter
```

*Save the drawing*

**Figure 6.25:**

Upper slot created
with mirror
autoediting mode.

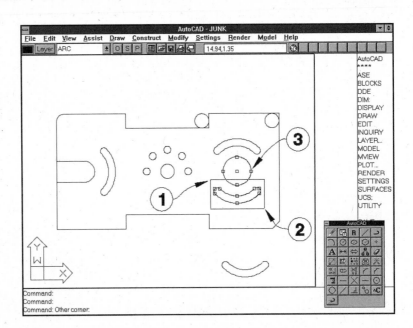

## Using the Shift Key To Copy

Next, use the mirror mode to complete the hole pattern at the center of the tool plate. This time, instead of using the Copy option, press Shift as you pick the second point. Using Shift is an alternate way to copy with autoedit.

## Finishing the Hole Pattern by Mirroring

| | |
|---|---|
| `Command:` *Pick the circle in the center of the hole pattern* | Creates the set and displays grips |
| `Command:` *Select a crossing window from points ① to ② (see fig. 6.26)* | Selects three circles and displays grips |
| `Command:` *Pick any one of the grip points on the small holes* | Enters stretch mode |
| `** STRETCH **`<br>`<Stretch to point>/Base point/Copy/`<br>`Undo/eXit:` **MI** ↵ | Enters mirror mode |
| `** MIRROR **`<br>`<Second point>/Base point/Copy/Undo/`<br>`eXit:` **B** ↵ | |
| `Base point:` *Pick the center hole's center grip* | Sets a new base point |
| `** MIRROR **`<br>`<Second point>/Base point/Copy/Undo/`<br>`eXit:` *Shift-pick (hold down the Shift key and pick) the right grip of the center hole* | Enters multiple mode, to make copies while picking second point(s) |
| `** MIRROR (multiple) **`<br>`<Second point>/Base point/Copy/`<br>`Undo/eXit:` *Press Enter* | Exits autoedit mode |

Your drawing should look like figure 6.27.

Look for opportunities to use mirror mode in your drawings to save time when creating entities. Remember to properly specify the two points that form the mirror line. Also, determine whether the Copy option is needed.

# Scaling with Autoedit

Scaling is another editing feature that is a great time saver. You may need to use the scale mode of autoedit to create blown-up views, scale standard shapes up or down, or change from an inch base to a metric base entity. Like the rotate mode, scaling is done from a base point, which, unless otherwise specified, is the selected grip point.

Next, assume that an engineering change requires that you scale down the size of the hole and radial slots at the right side of the tool plate. The pattern is proportional to its original size—just smaller. Use the scale autoediting mode in the following exercise to scale the slots to 3/4 of their original size.

**Figure 6.26:**

Crossing selection of holes to mirror.

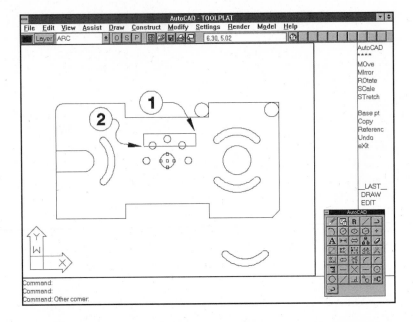

**Figure 6.27:**

Completed hole pattern, with grips.

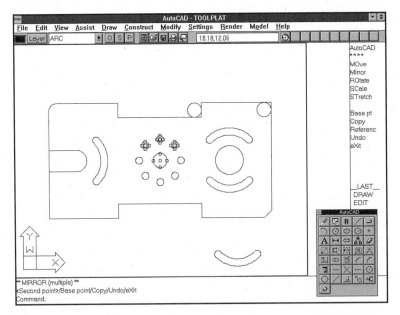

## Using Scale Autoediting mode

`Command:` *Double-click in empty space*          Clears the selection set and grips

`Command:` *Pick a crossing window from*          Selects slots and circle
① *to* ② *(see fig. 6.28)*

`Command:` *Pick center grip of center circle*     Enters stretch mode

`** STRETCH **`                                    Switches to scale mode
`<Stretch to point>/Base point/Copy/`
`Undo/eXit:` *Press button 1 or spacebar*
*three times*

`** SCALE **`
`<Scale factor>/Base point/Copy/Undo/`   Dynamically scales entities in proportion
`Reference/eXit:` *Move the cursor*

`<Scale factor>/Base point/Copy/Undo/`   Scales entities to 3/4 original size
`Reference/eXit:` **.75** ↵

Save the drawing. It should now look like figure 6.29.

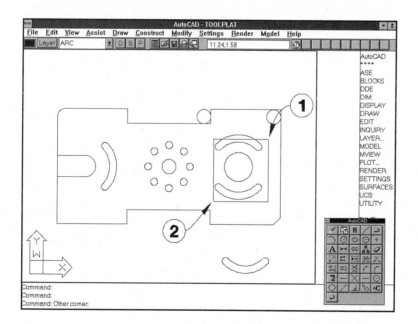

**Figure 6.28:**

Crossing selection of slots.

**Figure 6.29:**

Scaled slots.

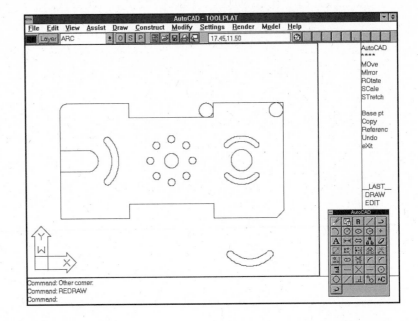

Because the proper scale—usually full—is so important in a CAD data base, be sure to scale entities to their proper size. The scale mode is handy for scaling text, title blocks, borders, and so on to finish off a drawing. The autoediting modes have the same effect on text as on other graphic entities. You can scale, copy, move, and rotate text just like any other entity.

The next section further explains the entity selection options you may want to explore.

# Changing Entities with DDMODIFY

Earlier in this chapter, you used the autoediting modes to modify entities. Chapter 8 shows you how to use many of AutoCAD's other editing commands, as well as other aspects of the autoediting modes. To give you a taste of single-entity editing, the chapter finishes with a look at the DDMODIFY command, which enables you to change many of the characteristics of individual drawing entities by using dialog box controls.

The DDMODIFY command is an editing command that lists information about the selected entity. It also enables you to change the selected entity. DDMODIFY is issued by the E**n**tity item of the **M**odify pull-down menu. The Modify dialog box options differ, depending on the entity selected. In the case of the circle shown in figure 6.30, the radius can be edited by changing the value in the edit box. The center coordinates can be changed this way as well, or the **P**ick Point option can be used to select a new center point. If you choose Cancel instead of on OK, any changes made are disregarded.

Try the DDMODIFY command in the following exercise.

## Using DDMODIFY To Change Entities

Continue with the TOOLPLAT drawing from the previous exercise.

| | |
|---|---|
| Command: *Choose* **M**odify, *then* E**n**tity | Autoloads and starts the DDMODIFY command |
| Select object to list: *Pick the .5"* *radius circle in the middle of the tool plate* | Opens the Modify Circle dialog box |
| *Double-click in the* **R**adius *edit box,* *then enter* **1.5** | Highlights and replaces the radius data |
| *Choose* **P**ick Point | Redraws circle with new radius and prompts for a new center point |
| Center point: *Pick a point near the* *top of the screen* | Returns to the dialog box |
| *Choose* OK | Changes the circle's location |

Quit AutoCAD and discard the last changes to the drawing.

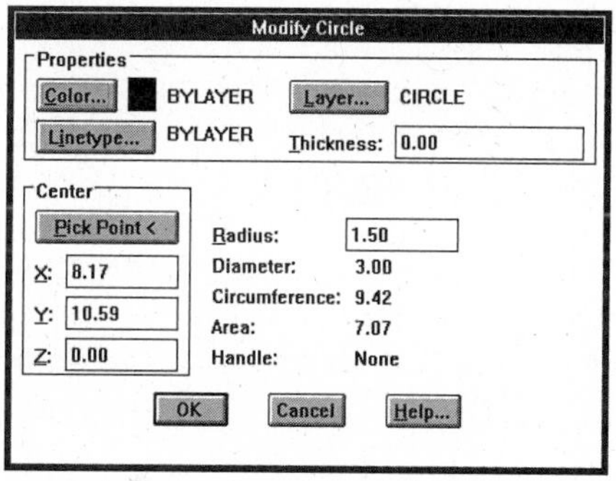

**Figure 6.30:**

Changing a circle with DDMODIFY.

The DDMODIFY dialog box also controls properties such as linetype, layer, and color of the selected entity. When you choose one of these options, a child dialog box displays for the appropriate selections.

# Summary

This chapter showed you how to create a drawing by using just a few of the basic drawing and editing commands. The LINE and CIRCLE commands are often used in CAD drafting. You learned some similarities between the way the drawing commands operate. They can be issued from a pull-down or screen menu. Sometimes, the most efficient method is entering commands from the keyboard, if you can remember how to type the command. Commands that have shortcut keys are easiest to type.

Remember to read the command line to see what type of input AutoCAD is looking for. Points can be specified by coordinates, or by picking them with object snaps or grips. AutoCAD offers several options for the arc and circle commands, so that you can draw them with whatever information you have. The option of absolute, relative, or polar coordinates also gives you powerful drawing capabilities without having to use a calculator to obtain unknown information. Try not to pick points unassisted, or your drawing accuracy can suffer.

Many more drawing and editing techniques are explained in the following chapters. The first challenge is to master the drawing and editing commands themselves, then start to develop a style of CAD drafting that best fits your needs. Each time you complete a drawing, you think of ways to draw it more efficiently the next time. Eventually, you find the techniques that perform best for your line of work.

Chapter 7 explains more of the entity-creation commands that you commonly use for your drawings. A drawing containing more detail and a greater variety of graphic entities is used to illustrate the use of these commands. Turn to Chapter 7 to learn more about graphic entities.

# CHAPTER 7

# Graphic Entities

Just as you find collections of tools around a manual drafting board for making lines, text, and curves, AutoCAD gives you a collection of electronic tools to perform similar functions. This chapter continues to discuss AutoCAD's drawing commands. You use these tools to build the drawing shown in figure 7.1. Each command creates an *entity*, which is the most fundamental piece of a drawing. The LINE command, for example, creates a line entity; the ARC command creates an arc entity. These drawing entities are sometimes called *graphic primitives* (see fig. 7.2). Primitives are the primary entities from which more complex components, symbols, and whole drawings are built. You may, for example, make an annotation bubble symbol from primitive line, circle, and text entities.

On paper, your drawing is static. As you saw in Chapter 6, AutoCAD graphic entities are *dynamic*. An AutoCAD arc, for example, has handles so that you can move it. Text has changeable height, width, and slant. Lines have two endpoints, but when two lines cross, AutoCAD can find the exact intersection.

*In addition to the entities illustrated in figure 7.2, AutoCAD has several 3D primitives, which are covered in the 3D chapters of this book. Other entities include blocks and attributes (covered in Chapters 11 and 16) and dimensions (in Chapter 15). You already learned about viewport entities in Chapter 5.*

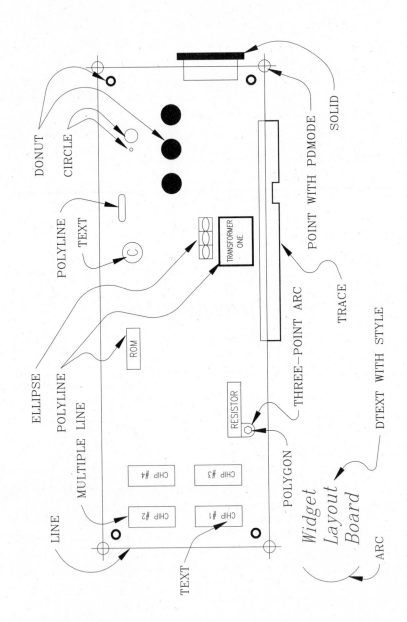

**Figure 7.1:**

Entities used in the
WIDGET drawing.

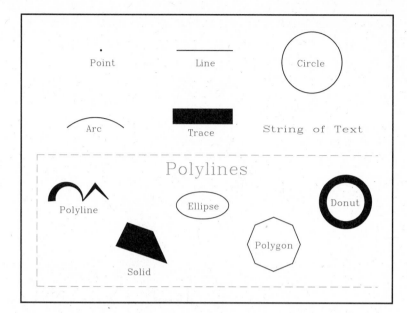

**Figure 7.2:**
Graphic primitives in AutoCAD.

# Establishing Drawing Tools and Drawing Goals

Chapter 6 introduced you to the LINE, ARC, and CIRCLE commands. The POINT and DTEXT commands were used briefly in earlier chapters. These commands and their associated commands—PLINE, DONUT, POLYGON, ELLIPSE, TRACE, TEXT, and SOLID—are used in this chapter.

The principal drawing commands are in the floating toolbox and the Draw pull-down menu (see fig. 7.3); all the drawing commands are also on the screen menu. To access the screen menu commands, select DRAW from the root screen menu. You also can use a tablet menu if you have one configured in AutoCAD (see Appendix A).

*Several of the command items in the floating toolbox menu are modified commands. You can preset parameters for these commands using system variables and the Entity Modes options in the Settings pull-down menu.*

**Figure 7.3:**

The Draw pull-
down menu and
DRAW screen
menu.

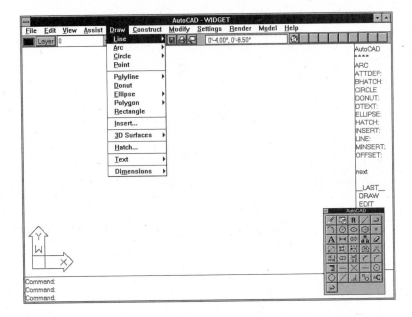

The goals for this chapter are two-fold. The first goal is to learn about different graphic entities and how they are used. The second goal is to work through a drawing that contains more features than the one in Chapter 6. In the exercises, you use graphic entities to build a design by drawing a widget controller circuit board layout. In the next chapter, you manipulate your drawing using AutoCAD's powerful editing commands, which enable you to move, copy, and change entities.

By the end of the next chapter, you should have a complete widget layout on your drawing area and an understanding of AutoCAD's drawing and primary editing commands. The widget may only faintly resemble a real board layout, but it does contain all of the primitive 2D entities of AutoCAD. Figure 7.1 shows the entities that you use to create the widget drawing.

# Setting Up for Drawing Entities

To start, you must create a new drawing with the settings shown in table 7.1. You can set up the WIDGET drawing by using the IAW DISK file named IAWWIDGE as a prototype.

## Table 7.1
## WIDGET Drawing Settings

| COORDS | GRID | SNAP | UCSICON |
|---|---|---|---|
| On | .5 | .1 | ORigin |
| **UNITS** | Engineering, 2 decimal places, 2 fractional places for angles, default all other settings. | | |
| **LIMITS** | 0,0 to 11,8.5 | | |

| Layer Name | State | Color | Linetype |
|---|---|---|---|
| 0 | On/Current | 7 (White) | CONTINUOUS |
| BOARD | On | 2 (Yellow) | CONTINUOUS |
| HIDDEN | On | 1 (Red) | HIDDEN |
| PARTS | On | 4 (Cyan) | CONTINUOUS |
| TEXT | On | 3 (Green) | CONTINUOUS |

The following exercise uses the technique described in Chapter 5 for saving and restoring paper space viewports. The BLOCK and INSERT commands are covered in detail in Chapter 11.

## Setting Up for the WIDGET Drawing

Command: *Choose* **F**ile, *then* **N**ew, *and enter* **WIDGET=IAWWIDGE** — Starts a new drawing called WIDGET

Command: *Choose* **V**iew, *then* **Z**oom, *then* **A**ll

Command: *Choose* **V**iew, *then* **T**ilemode — Switches to paper space

Command: *Choose* **V**iew, *then* Mvie**w**, *then* **3** Viewports — Issues MVIEW with three viewports

```
Command: _mview
ON/OFF/Hideplot/Fit/2/3/4/Restore/
<First Point>: 3
```

```
Horizontal/Vertical/Above/Below/
Left/<Right>: A ↵
```
Specifies a large viewport above the others

*continues*

```
Fit/<First Point>: From the screen
menu, choose Fit
```
Fits the viewports to the drawing area

```
FIT Regenerating drawing.
```

Next, use the BLOCK and INSERT commands to save and restore the viewports.

```
Command: Choose Construct, then BLOCK
```
Issues the BLOCK command

```
_block Block name (or ?): 3VIEW ↵
```

```
Insertion base point: 0,0 ↵
```

```
Select objects: Enter a W, then press
and hold button 1 at ① (see fig. 7.4), drag
to ②, and then release the button
```
Creates a crossing window selection

```
Other corner: 3 found
```

```
Select objects: Press Enter
```

**Figure 7.4:**

Drawing with restored paper space viewports.

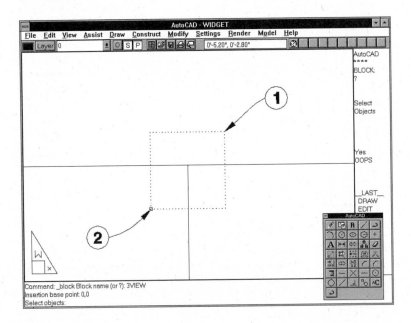

```
Command: Choose Draw, then Insert
```
Opens the Insert dialog box

*Click on Block*
Opens the Blocks Defined in this Drawing dialog box (see fig. 7.5)

*Double-click on 3VIEW*
Specifies the name of the block to insert

*Turn on the Explode check box*
. Explodes the block on insertion

| | |
|---|---|
| *Turn off the* **S***pecify Parameters on Screen check box* | Uses the settings in the dialog box |
| *Choose* OK | Closes the dialog box and completes the INSERT command |

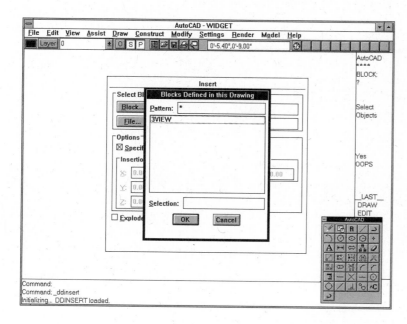

**Figure 7.5:**

The Blocks Defined in this Drawing dialog box.

You cannot see the viewports' contents until you turn the viewports on again.

| | |
|---|---|
| Command: *Choose* **V***iew, then* Mvie**w***, then* Viewport **O**N | Turns on the viewports |
| ON/OFF/Hideplot/Fit/2/3/4/Restore/ <First Point>: _on | |
| Select objects: *Enter a* **C***, then press and drag the same two corner points as earlier* | Selects the viewports with a crossing window |
| Other corner: 3 found | |
| Select objects: *Press Enter* | |
| Command: *Turn off paperspace with the* **P** *toolbar button* | Issues the _MSPACE command and switches to model space |
| Command: *From the toolbar, choose* QSAVE | Saves the drawing |

After you finish, your current layer should be layer 0. The crosshair cursor should be active in the upper viewport because it is current.

## Using a Scratch Layer To Experiment

Each exercise in this chapter shows you how to use one or more drawing command options for each graphic entity. As you work through this chapter's exercises, you use each drawing command. Some commands, such as PLINE and DTEXT, have several options that you can explore on your own. If you want, you can make a layer named SCRATCH on which to experiment (it is not used in the basic widget drawing). If your practice entities get in the way, simply turn off the SCRATCH layer.

## Using Snap and Object Snaps

The drawing-entity exercises show absolute or relative coordinate values for drawing or picking points. Assume that exercise instructions refer to absolute points unless they specifically call out relative points, use the coordinate display to pick relative points, or show the point with the relative @ symbol, like @ 2,3. When the @ symbol is shown for polar coordinates, you can enter it with the coordinates, or pick the relative polar coordinates with help from the coordinate display. Use object snap whenever possible for selecting any of these points, or you can pick the points in the drawing window by using snap and the grid and watching the coordinates. If you are unsure about a coordinate value, you can always pick or enter the value shown in the exercise. If you enter the values from the keyboard, you can omit any trailing zeros or inch marks.

# Establishing the Reference Points

The point is the most fundamental drawing entity. Points are helpful in building a drawing file. Although points are hard to see, you can control their size and use them as drawing reference points. In the following exercise, you lay out the four reference points for the widget board by using the POINT command, and then use the Point Style dialog box to set a point type that is easier to see.

### Setting a Point Type

Make the top viewport active by clicking in it.

Command: *From the toolbox, choose* POINT — Issues the POINT command

point Point: **2.50",3.30"** ↵ — Puts a small blip at the point

Command: *From the toolbox, choose* REDRAW — Redraws, leaving only a dot

Command: *From the screen menu, choose* POINT:, *then* Type — Accesses the Point Style dialog box

Double-click on the icon in the second row, third column, from the upper left corner (a plus in a circle). Then place three more points using the Point item from the **D**raw pull-down menu, which repeats the command.

Command: point Point: **2.5,5.8** ↵

Command: point Point: **9.5,5.8** ↵

Command: point Point: **9.5,3.3** ↵

Command: point Point: *Press Ctrl-C*

Command: **REGENALL** ↵                Regenerates to redisplay the first point

Regenerating drawing.

Command: *From the toolbar,
choose* ZOOM, *then pick window
corner points that enclose the points
you drew in the top viewport*

After you zoom in, your drawing area should look like figure 7.6.

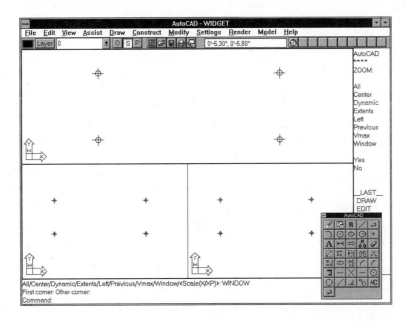

**Figure 7.6:**

Point Styles changed with the Point Style dialog box.

When you drew the first point, a mark appeared in the drawing window. This mark is actually larger than the point that you placed—it was simply the construction marker (blip) for the point. The REDRAW command cleared the construction marker and left a small dot—the default point type—in the drawing.

Resetting your point style mode gave you the circle-with-cross points. You can set about 20 combinations of point types by using the Point Style dialog box, as shown in figure 7.7. You can also enter PDMODE as a system variable and change it directly by entering a new value. The PDMODE settings for the point styles shown in figure 7.7 are shown in table 7.2.

## Table 7.2
### PDMODE Settings for Point Styles

| Row | Settings | | | | |
|---|---|---|---|---|---|
| Top row | 0 | 1 | 2 | 3 | 4 |
| 2nd row | 32 | 33 | 34 | 35 | 36 |
| 3rd row | 64 | 65 | 66 | 67 | 68 |
| 4th row | 96 | 97 | 98 | 99 | 100 |

**Figure 7.7:**

Some of the point styles available in AutoCAD.

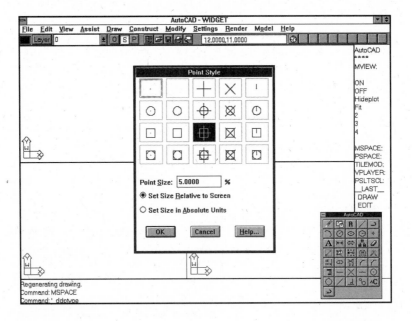

You control the size of the points by using the PDSIZE system variable. Set PDSIZE to a positive number to place its height in current drawing units. Set PDSIZE to a negative number to make its point size a consistent percentage of drawing window area or current viewport height, regardless of the zoom factor. A setting of 8, for example, makes points eight units high; a setting of -8 makes points eight percent of the drawing window area or current viewport height. You can change the point size from the POINT screen menu, the Point Style dialog box, or you can enter PDSIZE to change it.

A reference layer that is set up with points or a few lines helps organize your drawing file when you place other elements. After you finish making your placements, turn off the reference layer. You also can snap to a point using the NODe object snap. Points are useful to include as snap nodes in blocks (blocks are discussed in Chapter 11).

Continue the drawing exercise by using the LINE command. This important drawing command was used in several earlier chapters, and it is fully explained in Chapter 6.

## Drawing the Board Outline

| | |
|---|---|
| `Command:` *From the toolbar layer list box,* *choose* BOARD | Makes BOARD the current layer |
| `Command:` **DDOSNAP** ↵ | Opens the Running Object Snap dialog box |
| *Select the* **N**ode *check box,* *then choose* **OK** | Sets the running object snap mode to NODe |
| `Command:` *From the toolbox, choose* LINE | Issues the LINE command |
| `line From point:` *Pick the point* *entities in the order drawn in* *the previous exercise* | Selection is snapped to each point by the node object snap |
| `To point:` *From the screen menu,* *choose* close | Completes the rectangle |
| `Command:` **OSNAP** ↵ | Issues the direct command to set the object snap |
| `Object snap modes:` **NONE** ↵ | Turns off the current running object snap |

You also can use the DDOSNAP command to deselect NODe and turn off running object snap.

When you have completed the previous exercise, your drawing should resemble figure 7.8.

**Figure 7.8:**

The completed
widget board
layout.

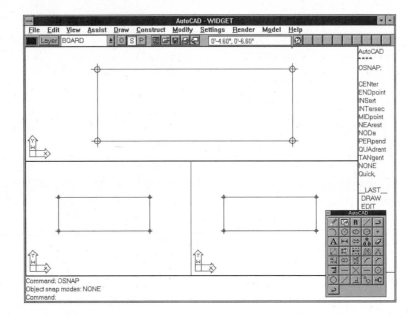

## Drawing Rectangles

In the steps that follow, you add a port to the widget's right side to see how the
RECTANG (rectangle) command functions. If you know the coordinates for two of
the rectangle's corners, the RECTANG command is faster than drawing four separate
lines. RECTANG is an AutoLISP-defined command, defined by the ACAD.MNL
file. The RECTANG command is on the **D**raw menu and actually creates one polyline
instead of four separate line segments.

### Drawing a Port Connector

`Command:` *Choose* **D**raw, *then* **R**ectangle    Issues the RECTANG command

`First corner:` *Pick point 9.30,3.70*

`Other corner:` *Pick point 9.60,4.50*

The rectangle is really a single polyline, which is a special type of entity covered later
in this chapter. Your drawing should look like figure 7.9 after you finish drawing the
port connector.

As you know, you can press Enter to repeat the previous command. You also can make
AutoCAD repeat commands automatically.

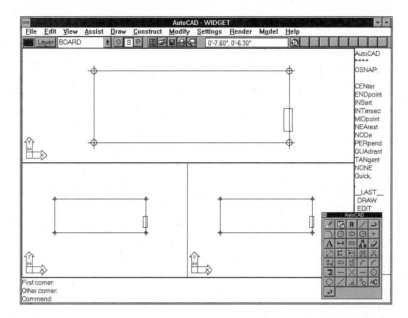

**Figure 7.9:**
The widget board
with the port
added.

# Using MULTIPLE To Repeat Commands

You can repeat commands automatically by preceding them with the MULTIPLE command. Use the MULTIPLE command in the following exercise to fill up the left side of the widget board. In the steps, the MULTIPLE command draws four rectangles by repeating the LINE command. These rectangles are RAM chips, and, as you draw them, you practice various forms of coordinate entry.

---

### Using the MULTIPLE Command To Repeat Commands

Click in the bottom left viewport to make it current.

Command: *From the toolbar layer list,*       Makes PARTS the current layer

Command: *From the toolbar, choose*
ZOOM *and create a window*
*surrounding the left side of the board*
*(see fig. 7.10)*

Command: **MULTIPLE LINE** ⏎

Notice that no Command: prompt appears when you press Enter or the spacebar after typing **MULTIPLE**.

*continues*

`From point:` *Pick point 2.80,3.70*

`To point:` *Pick the relative polar point @0.70<90.00 (press F6 if necessary to display coordinates in polar mode)*

`To point:` *Pick the relative polar point @.3<0*

`To point:` *Pick the relative polar point @0.70<270.00*

`To point: C ⏎`        Closes the line and MULTIPLE starts a new LINE command

`LINE From point:` *Pick point 2.80,4.70*

`To point: @0,.7 ⏎`        Specifies a relative Cartesian point

`To point:` *Pick the relative polar point @0.30<0.00*

`To point: @.7<-90 ⏎`        Specifies a relative polar point

`To point: C ⏎`        Closes and starts LINE again

`LINE From point: 3.4,4.7 ⏎`

`To point:` *Pick or enter the relative polar points @.7<90 to @.3<0 to @.7<270 and enter C to close*

`Line From point:` *Pick points 3.4,3.7 to @.7<90 to @.3<0 to @.7<-90 and enter C to close*

`Line From point:` *Press Ctrl-C*        Cancels the MULTIPLE LINE command

`Command:` *From the toolbar, choose* QSAVE

---

Your drawing should resemble the one shown in figure 7.10.

# Drawing with TRACE

The TRACE command operates much like LINE except for the Width option. You draw traces the same way you draw lines, with a From point and a To point. AutoCAD first asks you how wide you want the trace. As figure 7.11 illustrates, you can create any desired width of traces. When you draw traces, AutoCAD lags one segment behind in displaying the trace because it must calculate the miter angle between the previous trace segment and the next segment.

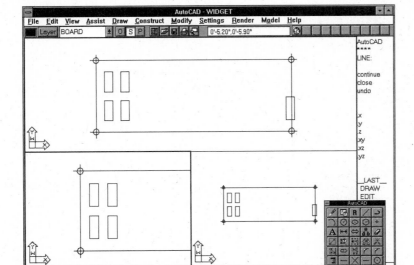

**Figure 7.10:**

The widget board with RAM chips added.

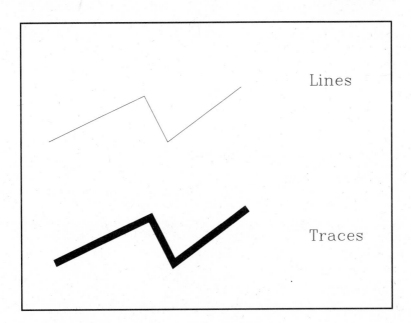

**Figure 7.11:**

Lines and traces.

Try using TRACE to draw a connector on the lower right side of the widget by typing or picking the points.

## Using TRACE To Draw a Wide Line

Click in the top viewport to make it current.

| | |
|---|---|
| Command: *From the toolbar layer list, choose* BOARD | Makes BOARD the current layer |
| Command: **TRACE** ↵ | Starts the TRACE command |
| Trace width <0'-0.05">: **.01** ↵ | |
| From point: **5.5,3.3** ↵ | |
| To point: *Pick the relative polar point* @.2<270 | |
| To point: *Pick the relative polar point* @2.00<0 | |
| To point: *Pick the relative polar point* @.1<90 | |
| To point: *Continue with* @.3<0 *to* @.1<270 *to* @.9<0 *to* @.2<90 | |
| To point: *Press Enter* | Ends the TRACE command |
| Command: *From the toolbox, choose* LINE *to add an interior line from 5.50,3.30 to* @.1<90 *to* @3.2<0 *to* @.1<270 | Draws the remainder of the connector (see fig. 7.12) |
| Command: *From the toolbar, choose* ZOOM *and specify window points surrounding the left end of trace and line* | Zooms in for a closer look at the trace and line |
| Command: **U** ↵ | Undoes the zoom |

Your drawing should look like figure 7.12.

You should see a noticeable thickness to the trace (see fig. 7.13). Numerous wide traces slow down regenerations, redraws, and plots. Read about the FILL command later in this chapter to see how to increase regeneration speed by temporarily turning off the interior filling of traces.

Traces do have limitations. You cannot, for example, perform the following actions:

- Curve a trace
- Close a trace
- Continue a trace
- Undo a trace segment

To create thick lines, use either colors assigned to thick plotter pens or the PLINE command (covered later in this chapter). If you need mitered ends and corners, use TRACE.

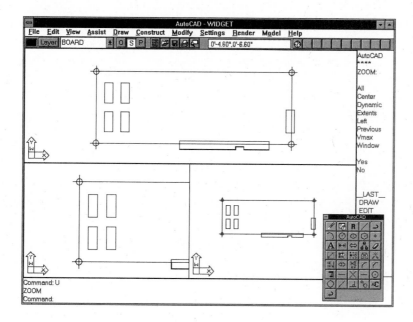

**Figure 7.12:**

The connector drawn with TRACE.

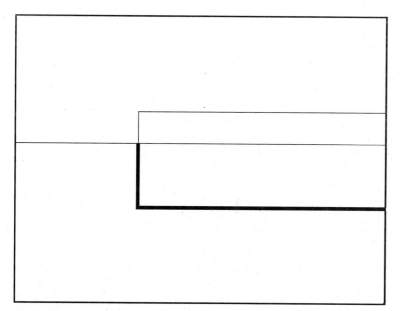

**Figure 7.13:**

A close up view of the line and trace.

*To create a finished end using a miter, draw an extra segment and erase it. The remaining segment will have a mitered end, depending on the direction of the trace that is deleted from the finished end.*

*Because traces are stored the same way as four-sided solids, snapping to them is limited. Object snap INT and ENDP both find the corners. MID finds the middle of any side. Because traces are drawn centered on their endpoints, you use MID, not ENDP, on the end of a trace to find the original From and To points.*

# Exploring More ARC and CIRCLE Options

To continue this drawing, experiment with the ARC and CIRCLE commands. These commands, already covered in Chapter 6, have many options, depending on what information you have available on these entities.

## Drawing the Capacitors

| | |
|---|---|
| Command: *Use the toolbar to make* PARTS *the current layer* | |
| Command: **MULTIPLE CIRCLE** ↵ | Issues a repeating CIRCLE command |
| 3P/2P/TTR/<Center point>: **6.80,5.30** ↵ | Sets the center point |
| Diameter/<Radius>: **0.15** ↵ | Sets the radius |
| CIRCLE 3P/2P/TTR/<Center point>: **2P** ↵ | Specifies the 2P method for the center of the switch |
| First point on diameter: **8.40,5.30** ↵ | |
| Second point on diameter: **8.60,5.30** ↵ | |
| CIRCLE 3P/2P/TTR/<Center point>: **8.30,5.30** ↵ | Specifies the center point for the switch contact |
| Diameter/<Radius> <0'-0.10">: **D** ↵ | |
| Diameter <0'-0.2">: **.05** ↵ | |
| CIRCLE 3P/2P/TTR/<Center point>: *Press Ctrl-C* | Stops the MULTIPLE command |

Three circles, as shown in figure 7.14, have now been added to the drawing.

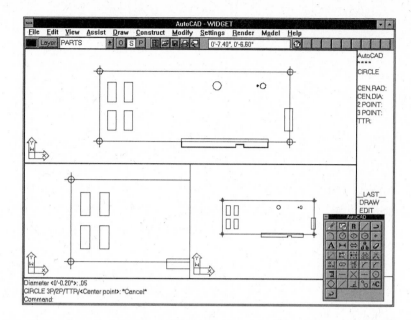

**Figure 7.14:**

Capacitors drawn with circles.

In the following exercise, you use the ARC command to draw part of the logo.

## Using ARC with Start Point, End, and Direction

Make the bottom right viewport current.

Command: *Use the toolbar to make*
TEXT *the current layer*

Command: *From the toolbar, choose* ZOOM
*and window the lower left quarter of the*
*viewport (see fig. 7.15)*

Command: *Choose* **S**ettings, *then*
**D**rawing Aids, *and set the X and*
*Y grid spacing and snap to .05 units*

Command: *From the toolbox, choose ARC*

arc Center/<Start point>:
*Pick point  2.2,2.8. at* ① *(see fig. 7.15)*

Center/End/<Second point>: *Pick the*          Drag comes on automatically
*second point 2.0,2.35 at* ②

Endpoint: *Pick the endpoint 2.2,1.9*
*at* ③

**Figure 7.15:**

A three-point arc
for a future logo.

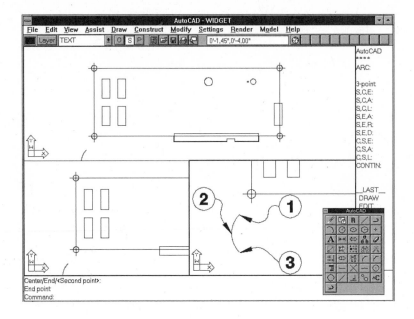

In the next exercise, you zoom in closer in the lower left viewport, and then use the LINE and ARC commands to draw the resistor.

## Drawing a Resistor

Make the bottom left viewport current.

Command: *Make* PARTS *the current layer*

Command: *Use ZOOM and pick window*
*points at 3.90,3.40 and 5.10,4.20*

Command: **DDVIEW** ↵          Opens the View Control dialog box

Click on **N**ew and enter the **N**ew Name: RESISTOR. Then choose **S**ave View, then OK.

Command: *From the toolbox, choose* LINE
*draw from 4.1,3.9 to @.8<0 to @.2<270 to*
*@.8<180, and enter* **C** *to close*

Command: *Press Enter, then draw a line*
*from 4.10,3.60 to @.1<90*

Command: *Press Enter twice, then draw a*
*line from 4.30,3.60 to @.1<90*

Command: *Choose* **D**raw, *then* **A**rc,
*and then* Start,End,**D**irection

| | |
|---|---|
| `Center/<Start point>:` *From the toolbox, choose* ENDPOINT | Specifies the ENDPoint object snap |
| `endp of` *Pick the endpoint of first line at ① (see fig. 7.16)* | |
| `Center/End/<Second point>: _e` | Specifies the End option |
| `Endpoint:` *From the toolbox, choose* ENDPOINT *again* | Specifies ENDpoint object snap |
| `endp of` *Pick the endpoint of the last line at ②* | |
| `Angle/Direction/Radius/<Center point>:_d Direction from start point:` *Enter* **270**, *or drag and pick point at 270 degrees* | Menu enters d (Direction) option, then 270 specifies direction |
| `Command:` *Choose* **V**iew, *then* **Z**oom, *then* **P**revious | |

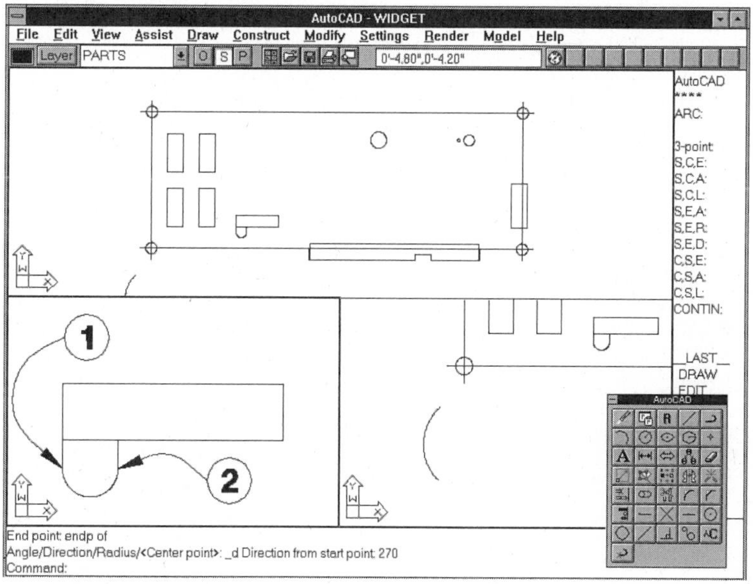

**Figure 7.16:**

A resistor drawn with a Start, End, Direction arc.

You explored the most common entities—the line, arc, and circle—in Chapter 6 and in this chapter. Given what you already know about entities, how would you create thick lines or thick, tapered lines, other than by using the TRACE command? Can you draw a continuous series of lines and arcs? Can you make a closed polygon with three straight sides (lines) and one curved side?

# Creating Polylines

To draw these symbols, consider using the PLINE command to draw polylines. Instead of creating multiple lines to get a thick line, or creating independent arcs and then connecting them to lines, you can create a polyline. Some samples of polylines are shown in figure 7.17.

**Figure 7.17:**

You can create many kinds of polylines.

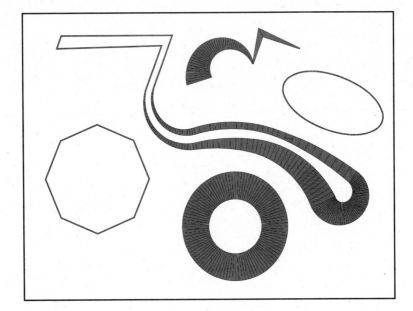

## Polylines versus Lines

Polylines are different from independent line entities created using the LINE command, which visually appear to be joined. AutoCAD treats a multisegment polyline as a single drawing entity. Polylines can include both line and arc segments connected at vertices (endpoints). Information such as tangent direction and line width is stored at each vertex.

Polylines offer two advantages over lines. First, polylines are versatile. They can be straight or curved, thin or wide, one width or tapered. You can, for example, draw a curved leader with an arrowhead as a single polyline.

Second, the fact that a polyline is a single entity makes editing operations easier and reduces errors if you use crosshatching or work in 3D. You can edit a polyline by selecting any segment because all of a polyline's segments are selected. In contrast, if you want to copy one of the RAM chip rectangles made up of four individual line entities in the widget drawing, you must select each individual line segment. If you crosshatch or create 3D objects from 2D lines, you must have edges that connect. Objects drawn with lines and arcs can have tiny gaps that cause hatch or 3D errors. Use polylines to draw any closed or connected object or polygon, particularly if you anticipate hatching it or working with your drawing in 3D.

You already created a polyline by choosing **R**ectangle from the **D**raw menu. Use the PLINE command to create another widget rectangle, the ROM chip, in the center of the board.

---

## Using PLINE To Draw a ROM Chip

Make the bottom right viewport current.

Command: *Choose* **S**ettings, *then*
**D**rawing Aids, *and set snap to .1"*

Command: *Choose* **V**iew, *then* **P**an,
*and center the board in the viewport*
*(see fig. 7.18)*

Command: *From the toolbox,*                    Starts the PLINE command
*choose* POLYLINE

pline From point: **5.1,5.2** ↵          Starts the polyline

Current line-width is 0'-0.00"

Arc/Close/Halfwidth/Length/Undo/
Width/<Endpoint of line>: **@0,0.2** ↵

Arc/Close/Halfwidth/Length/Undo/
Width/<Endpoint of line>: **@.6<0** ↵

Arc/Close/Halfwidth/Length/Undo/
Width/<Endpoint of line>:
*Pick the point @.2<270*

Arc/Close/Halfwidth/Length/Undo/        Ends the polyline
Width/<Endpoint of line>:
*From the screen menu, choose* Close

---

After you choose Close, your drawing should look like figure 7.18.

This new rectangle looks similar to the RAM chips on the left. In the next chapter, you are shown that this single ROM chip entity includes all four segments, whereas the other rectangles actually are four separate entities.

**Figure 7.18:**

A ROM chip
drawn with PLINE.

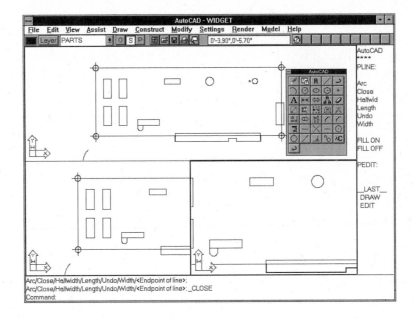

Because PLINE can draw two basic kinds of segments, straight lines and curves, some PLINE prompts are similar to the line prompts, but others are similar to the arc prompts. If you draw straight polyline segments, prompts such as Endpoint, Close, and Undo appear. Check out the possibilities on the PLINE prompt line. The following list describes the PLINE options:

- **Arc.** This option switches from drawing polylines to drawing polyarcs and issues the polyarc options prompt.

- **Close.** This option closes the polyline by drawing a segment from the last end-point to the initial start point, and then exits from the PLINE command.

- **Halfwidth.** This option prompts you for the distance from the center to the polyline's edges (half the actual width).

- **Length.** This option prompts you to enter the length of a new polyline segment. AutoCAD then draws the new segment at the same angle as the last polyline segment or tangent to the last polyarc segment.

- **Undo.** This option reverses the changes made in the last drawn segment.

- **Width.** This option prompts you to enter a width (default 0) for the next segment to create polylines. To taper a segment, define different starting and ending widths. After drawing the tapered segment, AutoCAD draws the next segment with the ending width of the tapered segment.

- **Endpoint of line.** This option prompts you, as the default, to specify the endpoint of the current line segment.

The Arc option presents another set of options, including some familiar arc prompts, such as Angle/CEnter/Radius, Second pt, and Endpoint of arc.

The PLINE Arc options include the following:

- **Angle.** This option prompts you to enter the included angle (a negative angle draws the arc clockwise).

- **CEnter.** This option prompts you to specify the arc's center.

- **Close.** This option closes the polyline by connecting the initial start point to the last endpoint with an arc segment, and then it exits the PLINE command.

- **Direction.** This option prompts you to specify a tangent direction for the segment.

- **Halfwidth.** This option prompts you to specify a halfwidth, the same as for Line options.

- **Line.** This option switches back to Line mode.

- **Radius.** This option prompts you to specify the arc's radius.

- **Second pt.** This option selects the second point of a three-point arc.

- **Undo.** This option undoes the last drawn segment.

- **Width.** This option prompts you to enter a width, the same way as for Line mode.

- **Endpoint of arc.** This option prompts you to specify the endpoint of the current arc segment. This option is the default.

*Although drawing lines and arcs with PLINE is similar to drawing the equivalent elements using LINE and ARC, note several important differences. First, you get all the prompts every time you enter a new polyline vertex. Second, additional prompts, such as for Halfwidth and Width, control the width of the segment. When a polyline has width, you can control the line fill by turning FILL on or off. Third, you can switch back and forth from straight segments to curved segments, and add additional segments to your growing polyline.*

# Using PLINE To Draw Arcs and Wide Lines

You can try using these extra polyline features by putting two more objects on your widget. Create a diode (the little narrow object with arcs on both ends) by combining line and arc segments. Then draw a rectangular transformer using a wide polyline. The diode is located between the circles at the top and the transformer near the bottom center of the board. Continue working in your right viewport. When you start PLINE, the first prompt is for drawing straight segments. Using the Arc option displays the Arc prompts in the polyline command.

## Using PLINE To Draw a Diode and a Transformer

Command: *Choose* **V**iew, *then* **P**an, *and pick points to show the right end of the board in the viewport (see fig. 7.19)*

Command: *Choose* **D**raw, *then* **P**olyline, *then* 2D

`_pline From point:` *Pick point 7.30,5.40*

| | |
|---|---|
| `Current line-width is 0'-0.00"`<br>`Arc/Close/Halfwidth/Length/`<br>`Undo/Width/<Endpoint of line>:`<br>`@0.30,0 ↵` | Draws a line segment |
| `Arc/Close/Halfwidth/Length/Undo/`<br>`Width/<Endpoint of line>: A ↵` | Specifies the Arc option |
| `Angle/CEnter/CLose/Direction/`<br>`Halfwidth/ Line/Radius/Second pt/`<br>`Undo/Width/<Endpoint of arc>: A ↵` | Specifies the Angle option |
| `Included angle: 180 ↵` | |
| `Center/Radius/<Endpoint>:`<br>`@0.10<90 ↵` | Draws an arc segment |
| `Angle/CEnter/CLose/Direction/`<br>`Halfwidth/ Line/Radius/Second pt/`<br>`Undo/Width/ <Endpoint of arc>: L ↵` | Specifies the Line option |
| `Arc/Close/Halfwidth/Length/`<br>`Undo/Width/ <Endpoint of`<br>`line>: @0.30<180 ↵` | Draws a line segment |
| `Arc/Close/Halfwidth/Length/Undo/`<br>`Width/ <Endpoint of line>: A ↵` | Specifies the Arc option |
| `Angle/CEnter/CLose/Direction/`<br>`Halfwidth/ Line/Radius/Second pt/`<br>`Undo/Width/<Endpoint of arc>: CL ↵` | Closes the polyline with an arc segment |

You can zoom in for a better look. Afterward, select UNDO or issue ZOOM with the Previous option.

After you complete the preceding exercise, your drawing should look like figure 7.19 (without the transformer).

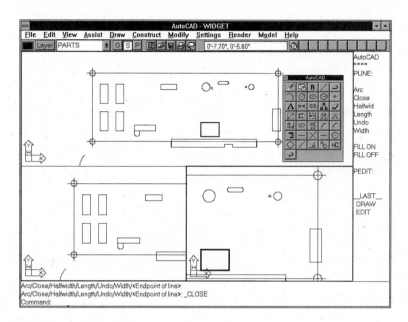

**Figure 7.19:**

A diode and a transformer drawn with polylines.

Next, draw the transformer with a wide polyline by using a preset width. The PLINEWID system variable enables a polyline width to be specified for any subsequent polylines.

---

## Drawing a Polyline with a Preset Width

Command: **PLINEWID** ↵                    Presets the width

New value for PLINEWID
<0'-0.00">:**.02** ↵

Command: **PL** ↵                          Starts the PLINE command

From point: *Pick point 6.60,3.50*

Current line-width is 0'-.02"

Arc/Close/Halfwidth/Length/Undo/
Width/ <Endpoint of line>:
**@0.50<90.00** ↵

Arc/Close/Halfwidth/Length/Undo/
Width/ <Endpoint of line>:
**@0.70<0.00** ↵

*continues*

```
Arc/Close/Halfwidth/Length/Undo/
Width/ <Endpoint of line>:
@0.50<270.00 ↵
```

```
Arc/Close/Halfwidth/Length/Undo/
Width/ <Endpoint of line>:
```
*From the screen menu,*
*choose* Close

*Save the drawing*

*You also can preset PLINEWID for the RECTANG command you used earlier in this chapter.*

*With polylines, you can create complex objects; PEDIT enables you to modify a polyline without redrawing it from scratch. See Chapter 9 for more information on PEDIT.*

The **R**ectangle item on the **D**raw menu is one of several commands in AutoCAD that enable you to create a polyline instead of individual entities.

# Creating Donuts, Polygons, and Ellipses

You can use polylines to create many different objects. AutoCAD has several commands that use the basic polyline entity to draw different symmetrical closed shapes. The DONUT, POLYGON, and ELLIPSE commands take advantage of the power of the simpler PLINE command.

## Creating Donuts

As you can imagine, the DONUT command creates an entity that looks like a donut. Donuts can have any inside and outside diameter. In fact, as figure 7.20 demonstrates, a donut with a 0 inside diameter is a filled-in circle; this shape is a good dot.

In the following exercise, put three filled dots on the right of the board as capacitors. Then put regular donuts at each corner of the widget as ground holes.

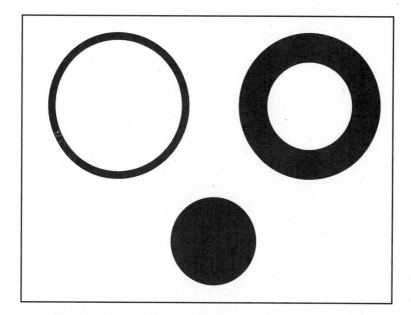

**Figure 7.20:**

Some examples of donuts.

## Using DONUT To Create Donuts

Command: **DONUT** ↵

Inside diameter <0'-0.50">:**0** ↵          Sets the donut's inside diameter
                                            to 0, creating a solid dot

Outside diameter
<0'-1.00">:**.3** ↵

Center of doughnut:
*Pick point 8.80,4.70*

Center of doughnut:
*Pick point 8.30,4.70*

Center of doughnut:
*Pick point 7.80,4.70*

Center of doughnut:
*Press Enter*                               Ends the command

Command: *Press Enter*                      Repeats the command

DONUT Inside diameter                       Specifies a new interior diameter
<0'-0.00">: **0.1** ↵

*continues*

```
Outside diameter <0'-0.30">:
0.15 ⏎
```

```
Center of doughnut:
```
*Pick point 9.30,5.60*

```
Center of doughnut:
```
*Pick point 9.30,3.50*

*Click in the top viewport*                    Makes the top viewport current

```
Center of doughnut:
```
*Pick point 2.70,3.50*

```
Center of doughnut:
```
*Pick point 2.70,5.60*

```
Center of doughnut:
```
*Press Enter*                    Ends the DONUT command

Your drawing should look like figure 7.21.

**Figure 7.21:**

Using DONUT to add parts.

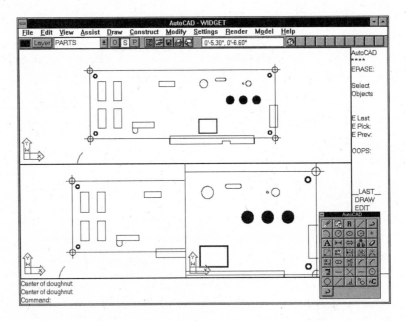

As you can see, DONUT keeps on prompting for the center of the donut until you press Enter to exit the command.

*You can type **DONUT** or **DOUGHNUT**; AutoCAD accepts either spelling.*

The donut that AutoCAD constructs is not a new primitive. The donut is actually a polyline that has the following three polyline properties: it is made of arc segments, it has width (you set the widths by entering the inside and outside diameter), and it is closed.

## Drawing Regular Polygons

If you want multisegmented polygons with irregular segment lengths, use polylines or closed lines. If you want nice, regular polygons, use the POLYGON command. A polygon is actually another polyline in disguise. POLYGON gives you two ways to define the size of your figure (see fig. 7.22). You can show the length of one of the edges or define it relative to a circle. The polygon can then be inscribed in or circumscribed about the circle.

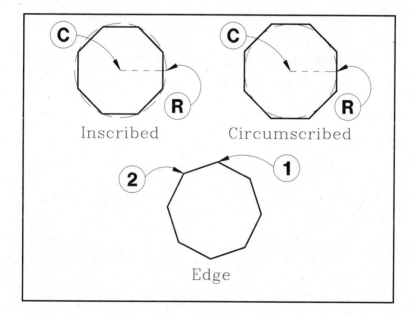

**Figure 7.22:**

Two basic ways to draw polygons.

Six-sided polygons make good hex nuts. In the next exercise, put a six-sided polygon in the mounting tab on the bottom of the resistor.

# Using POLYGON To Draw Regular Polygons

Make the bottom left viewport current and restore the RESISTOR view.

`Command:` *From the toolbox, choose*
POLYGON

`polygon Number of sides <4>: 6` ↵

`Edge/<Center of polygon>:`
*From the toolbox, choose* CENTER

`center of` *Pick anywhere on the arc*

`Inscribed in circle/Circumscribed`
`about circle (I/C) <I>: C` ↵
*(or choose* C-scribe *from the screen menu)*

`Radius of circle: .05` ↵          Draws a hexagon

After you enter the polygon's radius, the hexagon should resemble the one shown in figure 7.23.

**Figure 7.23:**

Drawing a polygon on the resistor tab.

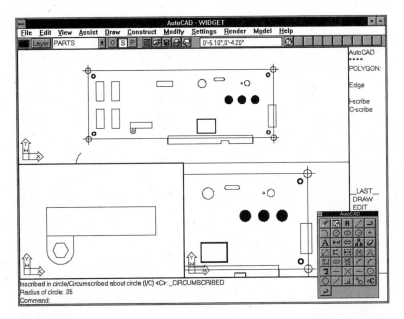

If you know the center point, the inscribed or circumscribed method is probably what you need. The edge method is handy for aligning an edge of the polygon with existing objects. The *edge* method generates a polygon that continues counterclockwise from two edge endpoints that you select. If you want to see a slow circle, draw a polygon with a thousand edges.

# Drawing an Ellipse

The ELLIPSE command creates a polyline in disguise. AutoCAD first prompts you for the major axis, defined by two endpoints or the center and one endpoint. You then can define the minor axis by distance or rotation, or by dragging the ellipse if you pick the point or angle. Figure 7.24 shows the various ellipse-creation methods.

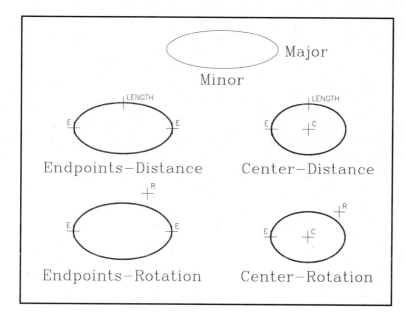

**Figure 7.24:**

Some examples of ellipses.

In the next exercise, you create a rectangle just above the transformer and put three ellipses in it. This part is called a *jumper*.

---

## Using ELLIPSE To Draw a Jumper

Make the bottom right viewport current.

Command: *From the toolbar, choose*
ZOOM *to zoom to the area just*
*above the transformer (see fig. 7.25)*

Command: *From the toolbox, choose*          Issues the PLINE command
POLYLINE

*continues*

```
pline
```
From point: *Choose* **S**ettings, *then*
**D**rawing Aids, *and set snap to .05",*
*then choose* OK

```
'_ddrmodes
Resuming PLINE command.
```

From point: **6.70,4.10** ↵

```
Current line-width is 0'-0.02"
```

```
Arc/Close/Halfwidth/Length/Undo/
Width/<Endpoint of line>:
```
*From the screen menu, choose* Width

*Set the Starting and Ending widths to*
*zero and draw from @0.2<90 to @0.6<0*
*to @0.2<270 and close*

Command: *Start the LINE command*
*and use snap to create two lines*
*that divide the rectangle into thirds*

| | |
|---|---|
| Command: *Choose* **D**raw, *then* **E**llipse, *then* **C**enter, Axis, Axis | Issues the ELLIPSE command with Center and Axis options |

```
ellipse <Axis endpoint
1>/Center:  c
```

| | |
|---|---|
| Center of ellipse: *Pick point 6.80,4.20* | Places the center point |
| Axis endpoint: *Pick the polar point @0.10<0.00* | Specifies the axis' endpoint |
| `<Other axis distance>/Rotation:` *Pick polar point @0.05<270.00* | Specifies the other axis' endpoint |
| Command: *Press Enter* | Repeats the ELLIPSE command |
| `ELLIPSE`<br>`<Axis endpoint 1>/Center:` *Pick point 6.90,4.20* | Specifies the axis' start point |
| Axis endpoint 2: *Pick the polar point @0.20<0.00* | Places the axis' endpoint |
| `<Other axis distance>/Rotation:` *Pick the polar point @0.05<270.00* | Sets the other axis' endpoint and length |

Next, draw an end/rotation ellipse in the right box.

| | |
|---|---|
| Command: *Press Enter* | Repeats the ELLIPSE command |
| ELLIPSE<br><Axis endpoint 1>/Center: *Pick point 7.10,4.20* | Specifies the axis' start point |
| Axis endpoint 2: *Pick the polar point @0.20<0.00* | Specifies the axis' endpoint |
| <Other axis distance>/Rotation: *From the screen menu, choose* Rotation | Specifies the Rotation option |
| _ROTATION<br>Rotation around major axis: **60** ⏎ | |

*Save the drawing*

After you finish, your drawing should look like figure 7.25.

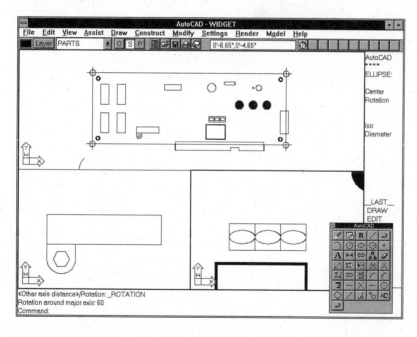

**Figure 7.25:**

A jumper created with the ELLIPSE command.

ELLIPSE is the last type of polyline. If you want to try more polylines, create a layer named SCRATCH and experiment on this layer.

# Creating Solids

The SOLID command creates a filled-in polygon—a two-dimensional boundary (polygon) filled with color. This area is defined by three or four points that form a triangular or quadrilateral shape. You can construct more complex shapes by continuing to add vertices. The order in which you enter vertices and the spatial relationship between these points determines the solid's appearance (see fig. 7.26). If you try to create a quadrilateral shape from four points, you might mistakenly create a bow tie. Users often first create bow ties or butterflies instead of quadrilaterals.

**Figure 7.26:**

Examples of SOLIDS.

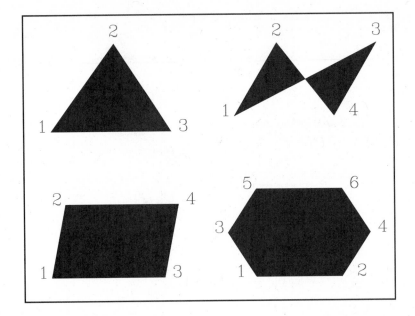

 *Do not confuse the SOLID command, which has been around for many years, with the relatively new concept of AME solid modeling. The advanced modeling extension of AutoCAD is a three-dimensional, solid modeling addition to AutoCAD.*

In the following exercise, use SOLID to create a vertical solid at the outer edge of the port on the right side of the widget.

## Using SOLID To Make a Solid Shape

Command: *Choose* **V***iew, then* **Z***oom, then* **D***ynamic, and magnify the area around the port (see fig. 7.27)*

Command: *Enter* **SNAP**, *and set*
*snap spacing to .1*

Command: **SOLID** ↵

First point: *Pick point 9.60,4.60*

Second point: *Pick point 9.70,4.60*

Third point: *Pick point 9.60,3.60*

Fourth point: *Pick point 9.70,3.60*      Draws the solid and prompts for more

Third point: *Press Enter*      Ends the SOLID command

Your drawing should resemble figure 7.27, showing the solid filled area around the
port.

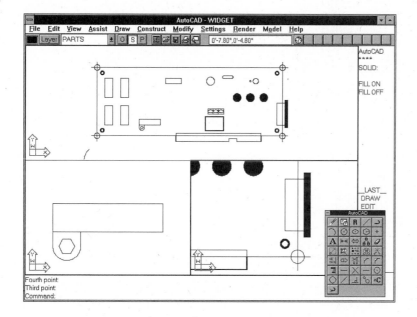

**Figure 7.27:**

Enhancing the
port with a solid.

If you keep entering points, SOLID keeps prompting for new third and fourth points,
drawing new solids from the previous third and fourth points to the new points.

After solids and traces are created, they are identical except in name. Both types of
entities fill and snap with object snaps in the same way.

# Using Fill Control with Solids, Traces, and Polylines

When the FILL command is turned off, it reduces solids, polylines, and traces to single-line outlines of their boundaries. If FILL is on, solids, polylines, and traces are shown and plotted filled-in.

*Turn off FILL to decrease redraw, regeneration, and plotting times.*

The FILL command is either on or off. The steps that follow show you how to turn on and off the widget's filled entities.

## Using the FILL Command

Command: **FILL** ⏎

ON/OFF <ON>: **OFF** ⏎                      Turns off FILL

The FILL command does not affect existing entities until after the next regeneration. To see the effect of FILL, regenerate the drawing now. Regenerating the screen also resizes the point entities.

Command: **REGENALL** ⏎                     Regenerates all viewports

Command: *Choose* Settings, *then* Drawing       Turns FILL back on
Aids, *and put a check in the* Solid **F**ill
*box, then choose* OK

Command: *From the toolbar, choose* QSAVE

---

Figure 7.28 shows the WIDGET drawing with FILL off.

Notice the pie-shaped wedges in the donuts in figure 7.28. When fill is off, each polyline segment shows as an outline. The number of wedges is determined by the VIEWRES setting.

# Using AutoCAD's Text Commands

The rest of this chapter explains the commands associated with placing text in a drawing. AutoCAD text has a set of default parameters that define how text is placed and stored. You must select a beginning point for your text, a height for the characters, and the way the text is to be placed and formatted. Then you enter the characters. You already used text in its default AutoCAD form.

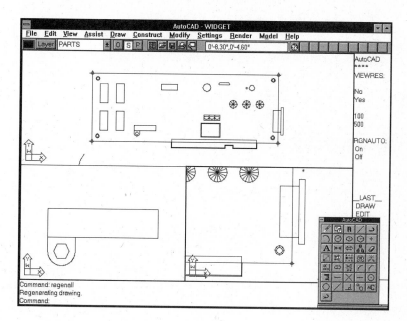

**Figure 7.28:**

Fill off.

# Style Settings

If you draw the letter A, you need 7, 19, or more line strokes, depending on the font. Rather than store each stroke of a character in a string of text, AutoCAD stores characters in special files called shape files. *Shape files* efficiently store each character definition as a series of *vectors* (directions and distances). These shape files are compiled into even more efficient binary SHX files, from which AutoCAD can rapidly extract graphics information. When displaying or plotting text translated from the compiled shape files, AutoCAD passes the text through several filters that incorporate your preferences for the appearance of the text.

*Text style* is the set of parameters AutoCAD uses in translating text from a shape into strokes on the plotter or pixels on the monitor. A text style is a named collection of instructions in the current drawing that does not change the original shape file font definition.

As you have seen, AutoCAD supplies many default settings. The default text style is called STANDARD. This style is defined with the simple TXT font and with default width, rotation angle, and justification (alignment).

# Using STYLE To Create and Maintain Text Styles

Use the STYLE command to create new styles or change the parameters for existing styles. The job of setting your style is really part of the setting-up process. Set your styles early in the drawing before you get into any intensive text input.

Because the default TXT font used in the STANDARD style is a bit awkward, use the following exercise to respecify the font used with your STANDARD style.

## Using STYLE To Modify a Text Style

Continue from the previous exercise, or begin a new drawing named WIDGET=IAWWIDG2 to overwrite the existing WIDGET drawing.

Command: **STYLE** ↵

Text Style name (or ?) <STANDARD>:          Accepts the default name (STANDARD) as
*Press Enter*                                the style to modify

When the Select Font File dialog box appears, change to the subdirectory in which the AutoCAD font files are located (usually \ACADWIN or \ACADWIN\FONTS), select the ROMANS.SHX font file, and click on OK.

Existing style.

Height <0'-0.00">: *Press Enter*          Accepts the 0 default for variable height

Width factor <1.00>: .8 ↵                 Makes the style narrower

Obliquing angle <0.00>: *Press Enter*

Backwards? <N>: *Press Enter*

Upside-down? <N>: *Press Enter*

Vertical ? <N>: *Press Enter*

STANDARD is now the current
text style.

Regenerating drawing.

Now your STANDARD style uses the ROMANS font and is slightly narrower than normal.

To help you select fonts graphically, AutoCAD has a Select Text Font dialog box with pages of icons from which you can select your text styles. Two pages are shown in figures 7.29 and 7.30. All of the standard AutoCAD fonts are included in the icon pages. Select a font from the icons to create a new style, with the same style name as the font.

To get to these icons, choose **T**ext from the **D**raw pull-down menu, then choose **S**et Style.

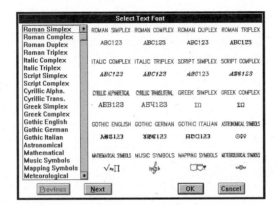

**Figure 7.29:**

The first icon page for creating text styles.

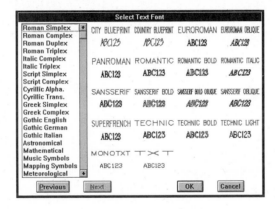

**Figure 7.30:**

The second icon page for creating text styles.

## Style Options

As figure 7.31 shows, AutoCAD offers several text style parameters. The following are the text style options:

- **Style name.** This option prompts you to name a new style to create or an existing style to edit. This style becomes the current default.

- **?.** This option lists named styles defined in the current drawing. You can enter an asterisk (the default) to list all named styles or use wild cards to list a specific set of styles.

- **Font.** This option prompts you to choose a font file name for the style to reference, using the Select Font File dialog box for the style to reference. The default <TXT> references the TXT.SHX file.

- **Height.** This option prompts you to specify text height for a fixed height style, or enter **0** (the default) for a variable height style. Text commands do not prompt for height unless you use a variable height style.

- **Width factor.** This option prompts you for a width factor to expand or condense text (default 1 = normal).

- **Obliquing angle.** This option prompts you to specify a number to slant the text characters, italicizing them (default 0 = vertical). To slant toward the right, use a positive number; to slant toward the left, use a negative number. Use small angles; a little slant looks like a lot.

- **Backwards.** This option mirrors text horizontally.

- **Upside-down.** This option mirrors text vertically.

- **Vertical.** This option orients text vertically, one character below.

# Notes on Style

Here are some notes on using the AutoCAD STYLE command:

- Style definition names for AutoCAD are maintained in a tables section of the drawing database file. You can store many style names in a single drawing file. These style names refer to font files in the default font path and affect only the current drawing.

- If you are using the STYLE command, press **?**, then press Enter in response to the text style name prompt to see a list of the styles currently defined in the drawing file.

- If you give a new name in response to the text style name prompt, AutoCAD creates a new style in the style table.

- If you give an existing style name in response to the text style name prompt, AutoCAD assumes that you want to change or edit the existing style. It prompts you for all the style parameters and offers the old settings as defaults.

- If you change the Font or Vertical option of a style that is currently defined in the drawing file, AutoCAD regenerates the drawing. Any existing text of that style is updated with the new style definition. Changes to all other options are ignored for existing text.

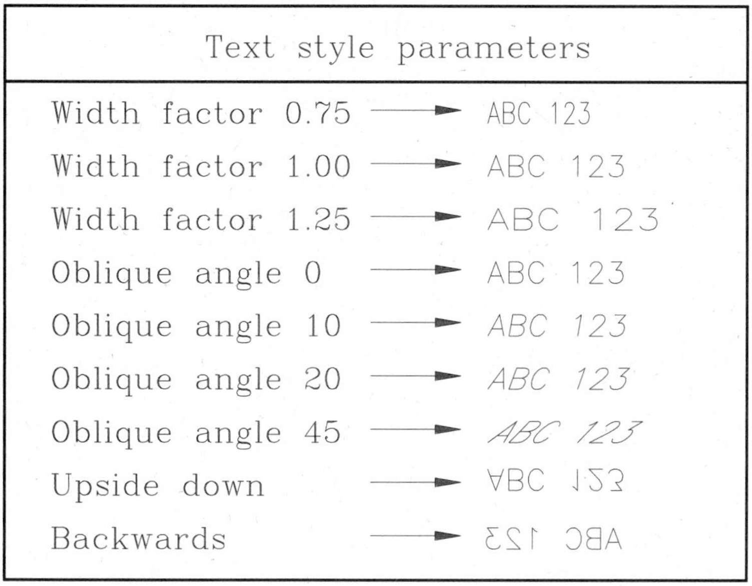

---

| Text style parameters | |
| --- | --- |
| Width factor 0.75 ——► | ABC 123 |
| Width factor 1.00 ——► | ABC 123 |
| Width factor 1.25 ——► | ABC 123 |
| Oblique angle 0 ——► | ABC 123 |
| Oblique angle 10 ——► | ABC 123 |
| Oblique angle 20 ——► | ABC 123 |
| Oblique angle 45 ——► | ABC 123 |
| Upside down ——► | ∀BC 123 |
| Backwards ——► | ƐƧ1 ƆᗺA |

**Figure 7.31:**

Examples of text styles.

*Do not bother to define a standard set of styles each time you start a new drawing. You can add your standard styles to your standard prototype drawing (see Chapter 18 and Appendix C). Or, you can save them as part of another drawing file and insert them as a block (this does not override any existing definitions in an existing drawing). See Chapter 12 for more information.*

# Dynamic Text versus Regular Text

After you create the styles you want for your drawing, AutoCAD offers two commands that you can use to input the text: DTEXT and TEXT. Either command places text. The only difference is that DTEXT does it *dynamically,* enabling you to see each character in the drawing as it is typed.

If you use TEXT, AutoCAD waits for all your text input and then places the text in the drawing when you exit the TEXT command.

To get started with TEXT (and to see the new style definition), label the resistor in the lower left part of the widget in the next exercise.

---

## Using TEXT To Add Labels

Make the bottom left viewport current.

`Command:` *Use the toolbar to make* TEXT
*the current layer*

`Command:` **TEXT** ↵

`Justify/Style/<Start point>:` **J** ↵       Issues the full justification prompt

`Align/Fit/Center/Middle/Right/`       Specifies the Middle option
`TL/TC/TR /ML/MC/MR/BL/MC/BR:` **M** ↵

`Middle point:` *Pick point 4.50,3.80*

`Height <0'-0.20">:` **.1** ↵

`Rotation angle <0.00>:` *Press Enter*

`Text:` **RESISTOR** ↵       Displays the text after you press Enter

*Save the drawing*

---

Your drawing should now look like figure 7.32.

Notice that the prompt options are the same as for the DTEXT command you used earlier, in Chapter 2.

# Formatting Text

The first thing AutoCAD wants to know about the text is how you want to format it. You have several options for formatting your text:

- **Justify.** This option issues the prompt for text justification.

- **Style.** This option enables you to specify a new text style default. The style must have already been created with the STYLE command.

- **Start point.** This default option prompts you to specify a point for the default bottom-left justification.

- **Press Enter.** This option highlights the last text entered and prompts for a new text string when you press Enter at the prompt. AutoCAD places the new text directly below the highlighted text, using the same style, height, and rotation. You also can pick a new point with DTEXT before you enter the text.

- **Height.** This option prompts you to specify the text height (the default is 0.2). You are not prompted for height when using Align justification or any text style with a predefined height.

- **Rotation angle.** This option prompts you to specify the text placement angle (the default is 0).

- **Text.** This option prompts you to enter the text string.

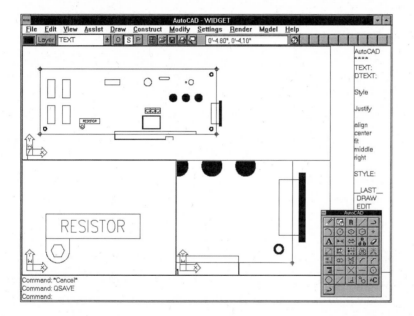

**Figure 7.32:**

The resistor, labeled with TEXT.

# Text Justification

Justification (or alignment) specifies the way in which the text is aligned, relative to the start and optional endpoint(s) you give it. You have used Middle, Center, and the default Left justifications. The justification prompt shows the complete list:

```
Align/Fit/Center/Middle/Right/TL/TC/TR/ML/MC/MR/BL/BC/BR:
```

The following list describes what you must specify for each of these options:

- **Align.** You specify the beginning and ending points of the text baseline. The text height is scaled so that the text between these points is not distorted.

- **Fit.** You specify the beginning and ending points of the text baseline. The text width is distorted to fit the text between these points without changing the height.

- **Center.** You specify a point for the horizontal center and the vertical baseline of the text string.

- **Middle.** You specify a point for the horizontal and vertical midpoint of the text string.

- **Right.** You specify a point for the bottom-right baseline of the text string.

- **TL.** You specify a point for the left of the text string, aligned with the top of the tallest character.

- **TC.** You specify a point for the center of the text string, aligned with the top of an uppercase character.

- **TR.** You specify a point for the right side of the text string, aligned with the top of an uppercase character.

- **ML.** You specify a point for the left side of the text string, aligned halfway between the top of an uppercase character and the text baseline.

- **MC.** You specify a point for the center of the text string, aligned halfway between an uppercase character and the bottom of the text baseline.

- **MR.** You specify a point for the right side, between the top of an uppercase character and the text baseline.

- **BL.** You specify a point for the left side of the text string, aligned at the bottom of a descender.

- **BC.** You specify a point for the center of the text string, aligned at the bottom of a descender.

- **BR.** You specify a point for the right side of the text string, aligned at the bottom of a descender.

Figure 7.33 presents a graphical depiction of each option.

The TL, TC, TR, ML, MC, MR, BL, BC, and BR justifications are the nine possible combinations of the Top, Middle, and Bottom vertical justifications and the Left, Center, and Right horizontal justifications. The default Left and the simple Center and Right justifications are all baseline justifications, which could have fit into this same matrix if B was not already taken by Bottom. Fit, TL, TC, TR, ML, MC, MR, BL, BC, and BR-justified text cannot be used with vertical text styles; the others work vertically or horizontally.

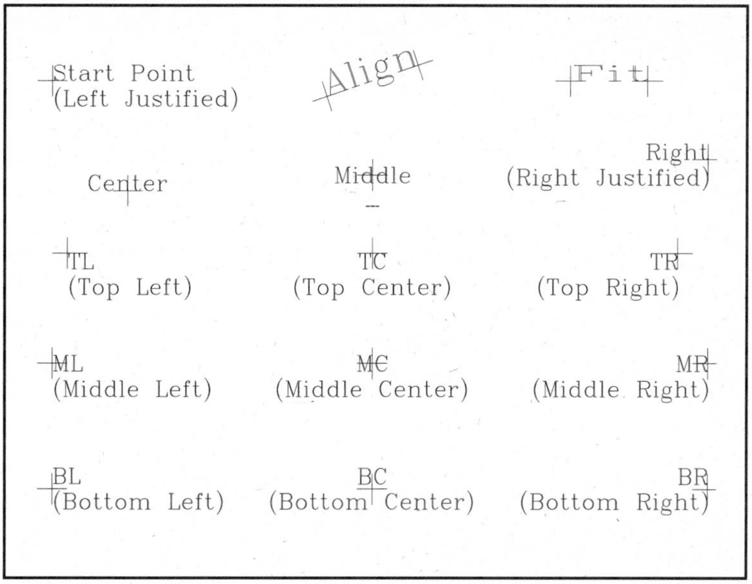

**Figure 7.33:**

Text justification options.

```
Start Point                  Align            Fit
(Left Justified)

                                                    Right
     Center            Middle            (Right Justified)

  TL                    TC                     TR
(Top Left)        (Top Center)           (Top Right)

 ML                     MC                     MR
(Middle Left)    (Middle Center)       (Middle Right)

 BL                     BC                     BR
(Bottom Left)    (Bottom Center)       (Bottom Right)
```

Middle-justified text (unlike ML, MC, and MR) floats vertically, depending on whether the particular text string includes uppercase characters or characters with descenders. The other options have three vertical positions relative to a standard text cell height. The Standard cell height is the height of a capital letter. The options TL, TC, TR, ML, MC, MR, BL, BC, and BR each maintain vertical text positioning, regardless of the string entered. Middle is designed to always be centered in both axes, for use in bubbles and similar applications. The other justifications are designed to give consistent results for most other applications.

 *If you respond to the DTEXT (or TEXT) start point prompt by pressing Enter, the new text starts one line below the last text you entered in the drawing. The new text assumes the height, style, and justification of the previous text, even if you have used intervening AutoCAD commands.*

# Using DTEXT To Place Text

DTEXT can be more flexible to use than TEXT. Input for DTEXT is always shown left-justified, regardless of the chosen format. The justification is corrected after the command is finished. You also can reposition the box cursor on the drawing area at any point during text entry by picking a new point with your crosshairs. This feature enables you to place text throughout your drawing with a single DTEXT command. The trade-off for this flexibility in picking new points is that the menus are disabled.

What happens if you make a mistake entering text? If you are using DTEXT, you can backspace and correct your errors as you type. If you do not realize that you have a mistaken text entry until you see it in the drawing window, do not panic—all is repairable. You learn to edit text in the next chapter. For now, just undo the text and try again.

Input more text with DTEXT by labeling other parts of the widget. Add text by entering the justifications and starting points shown, and either type or drag answers to the height and angle prompts. Start on the left and label the RAM chips with Middle/Left text. Figure 7.34 shows the labeled chips.

## Using DTEXT To Label the Widget Drawing

Command: *Choose* **V**iew, *then* **Z**oom, *then* **D**ynamic, *and zoom to enclose the RAM chips*

Command: *Enter* **SNAP**, *and set Snap to 0.05*

Command: *Choose* **D**raw, *then* **T**ext, *then* **D**ynamic            Issues the DTEXT command

\_dtext Justify/Style/<Start point>: **J** ↵

Align/Fit/Center/Middle/Right/         Specifies the Middle-Left option
TL/TC/ TR/ML/MC/MR/BL/BC/BR: **ML** ↵

Middle/left point: *Pick at 2.95,3.8*

Height <0'-0.10">: **.08** ↵

Rotation angle <0.00>: **90** ↵

Text: **CHIP #1** ↵             Displays the text, but does not yet justify it

*Move the cursor by picking at point 2.95,4.8*

Text: **CHIP #2** ↵

*Move the cursor by picking at point 3.55,3.8*

Text: **CHIP #3** ↵

*Move the cursor by picking at point 3.55,4.8*

Text: **CHIP #4** ↵

Text: *Press Enter*          Ends the DTEXT command and
                            displays the justified text

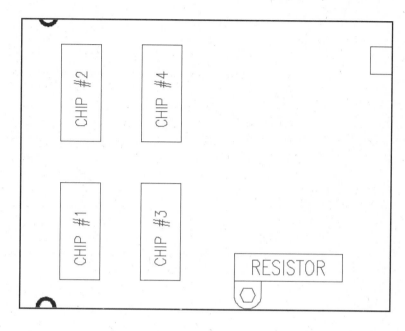

**Figure 7.34:**
Detail of the chip
labels.

Pan or zoom to the center of the board.

Command: **DTEXT** ↵          Starts the DTEXT command

Justify/Style/<Start point>: **M** ↵          Specifies the Middle option

Middle point: *From the toolbox,*          Specifies the CEN object snap mode
*choose* CENTER

center of *Pick any point on the circle
shown in figure 7.35*

Height <0'-0.08">: **.15** ↵

Rotation angle <90.00>: **0** ↵

Text: **C** ↵

Text: *Press Enter*

Command: *Press Enter*          Reissues the DTEXT command

Justify/Style/<Start point>: **F** ↵          Specifies Fit justification

*continues*

| | |
|---|---|
| `First text line point:` *Pick point 6.65,3.80* | Specifies the left end of the text string |
| `Second text line point:` *Pick the polar point @0.60<0.00* | Specifies the right end |
| `Height <0'-0.15">:` **.08** ↵ | |
| `Text:` **TRANSFORMER** ↵ | Displays the text, but not yet justified |
| `Text:` *Press Enter* | Draws the text so that it is squeezed between points; ends the DTEXT command |
| `Command:` *Press Enter* | Repeats the DTEXT command |
| `Justify/Style/<Start point>:` **C** ↵ | Specifies Center justification |
| `Center point:` *Pick point 6.95,3.65* | |
| `Height <0'-0.08">:` *Press Enter* | |
| `Rotation angle <0.00>:` *Press Enter* | |
| `Text:` **ONE** ↵ | |
| `Text:` *Press Enter* | |
| `Command:` *Press Enter* | Repeats the DTEXT command |
| `Justify/Style/<Start point>:` **MC** ↵ | Selects the Middle-Center justification option |
| `Middle point:` *Pick point 5.40,5.30* | |
| `Height <0'-0.08">:` *Pick the polar point @0.10<90.00* | |
| `Rotation angle <0.00>:` *Press Enter* | |
| `Text:` **ROM** ↵ | |
| `Text:` *Press Enter* | |
| `Command:` *Choose* **V***iew, then* Redraw **All** | Erases blips |

Figure 7.35 shows the results of this exercise.

AutoCAD never forgets. The default prompts during the text commands show your previous parameter settings. You can speed parameter entry by pressing Enter to accept the defaults.

Next, try the Middle, Fit, Center, and Middle/Center justifications.

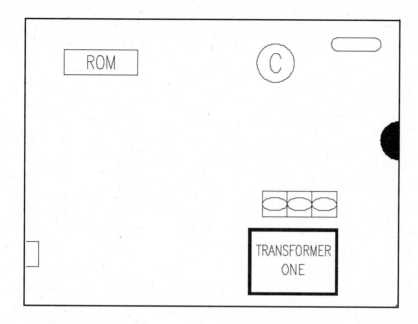

**Figure 7.35:**

Detail of the new labels.

DTEXT automatically lines up successive lines of text, one under the other, if you press Enter after each line. If you press Enter at the first text prompt, the lines of text you enter align with the previous text entered. Before trying this technique in the next exercise, change your text style to one with an oblique slant to give the widget drawing a title with a unique look.

## Defining an Oblique Text Style

Make the bottom right viewport current and zoom to the logo in the lower left corner of the board. Then take the following steps to create a new style for the title.

```
Command: STYLE ↵
```

```
Text Style name (or ?) <STANDARD>:
TITLE ↵
```

After the Select Font File dialog box appears, change to the subdirectory that contains ROMANC.SHX and select ROMANC.SHX.

```
New style. Height <0'-0.00">: .2 ↵     Specifies a fixed height
```

```
Width factor <1.00>: .8 ↵              Makes the font thin
```

```
Obliquing angle <0.00>: 15 ↵           Slants the font 15 degrees
```

*continues*

```
Backwards? <N>: Press Enter

Upside-down? <N>: Press Enter

Vertical ? <N>: Press Enter

TITLE is now the current text style.
```

Next use the TITLE style and have DTEXT automatically line up the words "Widget," "Circuit," and "Board" under one another. After you finish, change your drawing window to a single view and zoom for a good look.

## Creating Successive Lines of Text

`Command:` *Choose* **D**raw, *then* **T**ext, *then*
**D**ynamic, *or enter* **DTEXT**

`Justify/Style/<Start point>:` *Pick*     Left-justifies the text at the picked point
*or enter point 2.50,2.60*

`Rotation angle <0.00>:` *Press Enter*

`Text:` **Widget** ↵

`Text:` **Layout** ↵

`Text:` **Board** ↵

`Text:` *Press Enter*

*Make the top viewport current*

`Command:` *Choose* **V**iew, *then* **T**ilemode     Switches the TILEMODE system variable from 0
                                                        to 1 and returns to a single viewport

`Command:` *Issue ZOOM with the Extents*     Fills the viewport with the drawing
*option*

`Regenerating drawing.`

*Save the drawing*

Your drawing now should resemble figure 7.36.

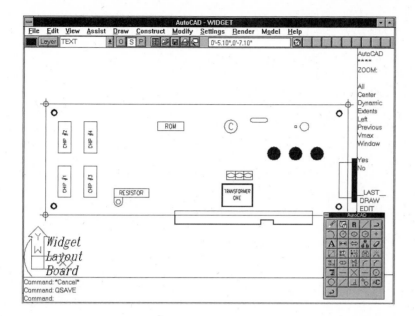

**Figure 7.36:**

A zoomed widget board with text.

Two more special, quick text topics await you. But first, here are some points to remember about text entry.

- Whenever you want to jog your memory, enter **J** at the first text prompt to see the full justification prompt. You do not, however, need the full prompt to use any of its justifications. You can enter any of them at the first prompt. Often, you can set height and angle once (as you set up your drawing file for example) and press Enter to use these defaults for all future text use.

- You also can use object snap modes to help you place your text. To add a line to existing text, use DTEXT with object snap mode INSert, pick the existing text, and enter only a space on the first line. Then press Enter to space down for the next line.

- You can enter text upside down by using an angle definition to the left of the starting point (180 degrees).

*The default height shown in the TEXT command is rounded off to your units setting and may not accurately display its true value.*

# Using Special Text Characters

Occasionally, you may need to use special symbols or angle text on a drawing. This section describes how to create some special effects. If you want to practice some of the special text examples, use your SCRATCH layer.

## Text Underscore and Overscore

You use underscores, superscripts, and special symbols regularly in text strings on drawings. You do not find these symbols on standard keyboards. Figure 7.37 shows some special text. The underscored and overscored text in the illustration was entered into the DTEXT command, as follows:

```
Text: %%u88%%u %%o88%%o
```

You can enter the special character switches, %%u (**u**nderline) and %%o (**o**verscore), any time you are typing a text string in response to the text prompt.

**Figure 7.37:**

Examples of special text.

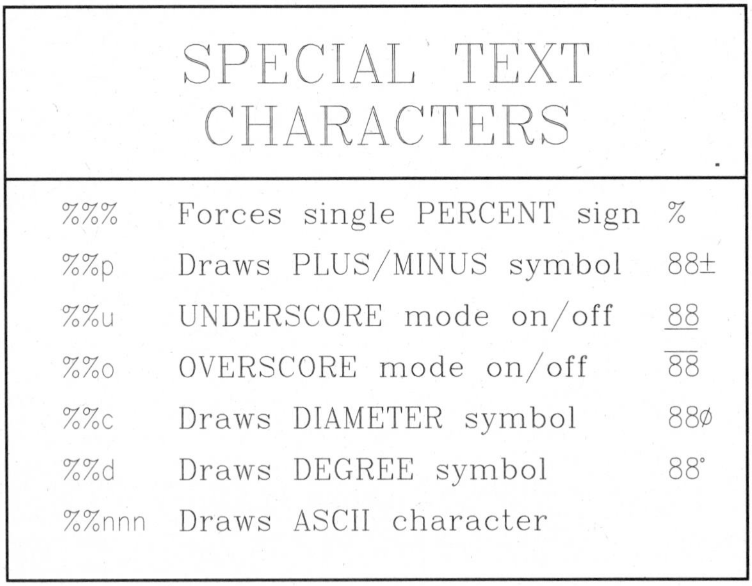

```
            SPECIAL TEXT
            CHARACTERS

   %%%     Forces single PERCENT sign   %
   %%p     Draws PLUS/MINUS symbol      88±
   %%u     UNDERSCORE mode on/off       88
   %%o     OVERSCORE mode on/off        88
   %%c     Draws DIAMETER symbol        88⌀
   %%d     Draws DEGREE symbol          88°
   %%nnn   Draws ASCII character
```

## Angled versus Vertical Text

Most text reads horizontally from left to right. Sometimes, however, you may want text that reads top to bottom.

You can use the normal DTEXT or TEXT command parameters to rotate or align your text at any angle. If you want your text to read vertically, you can create a style and give it a vertical orientation. A vertical orientation aligns characters one below the other. You can give any standard AutoCAD font a vertical orientation.

## Quick versus Fancy Text

As your drawing file fills up with drawing entities, it takes longer and longer to zoom, redraw, or regenerate the drawing window. Sooner or later, you want to cut down the regeneration time. AutoCAD offers two options for speeding up the rate at which text is displayed. First, you can do all your text work in a simple font, such as TXT, while you are creating the drawing or while you are making test plots. When creating the final plot, you can enhance the drawing by replacing the simple font with a more elegant font, such as ROMANC. You save time during initial drawing editor work, but your drawings still look good with the last-minute font change.

*An easy way to substitute simple fonts for complex ones is to create a directory of temporary "fake fonts." Make multiple copies of TXT.SHX, renaming them to represent all the other fonts. Keep the real font files in another directory. AutoCAD will find and use the fake fonts, and all the text will appear as TXT. Then, when you want to use the real fonts, simply copy the REAL.SHX files back into the font directory and reload (or plot) your drawing.*

*Because font-character definitions differ in width, and font respecification does not attempt to compensate, you may find the new fancy text does not fit where you placed the old simple text.*

A second option (to speed regeneration time) is to use the AutoCAD QTEXT command. QTEXT (for Quick TEXT) enables you to temporarily replace lines of text with a rectangle outlining their position.

## The QTEXT Command

QTEXT is available from the keyboard or from the SETTINGS screen menu. It does not replace text until the next regeneration. Try using the QTEXT command on the widget drawing.

CHAPTER 7

---

## Looking at QTEXT

Command: **QTEXT** ↵

ON/OFF <Off>: **ON** ↵

Command: **REGEN** ↵                          Replaces the text with boxes (see fig. 7.38)

Regenerating drawing.

Command: **QTEXT** ↵

*Turn off QTEXT*

*Exit from AutoCAD*

---

Figure 7.38 shows the widget drawing with QTEXT turned on.

**Figure 7.38:**

The widget after
QTEXT is turned
on.

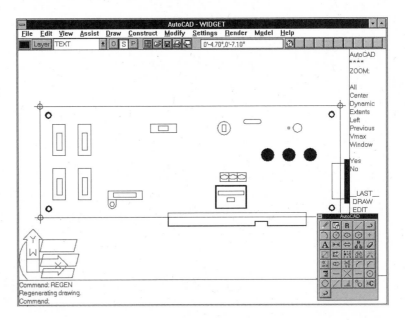

The text regenerates when you reload the drawing in the next chapter. Notice that
QTEXT did not accurately represent the justification and text line lengths. To do so,
AutoCAD must do the full text entity vector calculations, and that would save little
time over the normal display of text.

# Summary

In this chapter, you covered much material. Toolbox, toolbar, pull-down, screen, and tablet menus (if you use one) are becoming familiar, like road signs in a new town. Although the number of side streets for different drawing commands may seem endless, you are beginning to understand how the primary drawing commands get you almost all the way to your destination.

You may put aside learning additional commands and options until you need them or have some extra time to explore AutoCAD. If you like Sunday drives into the country, AutoCAD enables you to "wander" through some of the less frequently used commands without letting you stray too far off the beaten path.

Here are some reminders about the entities you used in this chapter:

- Points are useful reference locators for a later object snap. They can be displayed in various sizes and styles.

- Lines are the pillars of the drawing community. Connected lines are the norm; press Enter to stop a connected line run. Continue starts a line at the last endpoint. Close makes a polygon by returning a connected line series to the first point. Take advantage of TRACE's mitered edge to get angled ends for fat lines. Otherwise, you find PLINE superior to TRACE for every other purpose.

- CIRCLE requires minimal information to generate full circles. Center point/radius is the most common circle-creation method. A three-point arc is the most convenient to create. The start,center series also is useful.

- Polylines enable you to create single graphic elements composed of linear and curved segments. Donuts, polygons, and ellipses are made from polylines.

- Text gets to the drawing window through a filtering process that controls style, justification, height, and rotation. DTEXT dynamically places text as you key characters at the keyboard. Style gives you flexibility in creating type styles that are tailored to your needs. The justification options give control over placement. Keep text on its own layer or use QTEXT to keep redraw and regeneration times to a minimum as drawing files expand.

Think ahead about the sequence for entering solid vertices. It can be difficult to avoid drawing a bow tie.

In this chapter, you began earnest work on a real drawing. Every entity that you used works the same in a 3D drawing, although AutoCAD has a few more graphic entities especially designed for 3D, which you can see later in Part 5.

You have already mastered setting layers, drawing lines and circles, and inserting text. By the end of the next chapter, this drawing will be a complete, four-layer, full-color widget layout drawing.

# 8 CHAPTER

# Introduction to Editing

The one certainty in the drawing business is change. Change this! Change that! Drawing revision numbers keep mounting! If you are to use AutoCAD successfully, you must become familiar with the program's editing functions. In fact, you may find yourself spending more time editing existing drawings than creating new ones.

So far in this book, you have spent most of your tutorial time creating new drawing entities. Chapter 6 used the basic options of several editing commands in the form of grip editing. AutoCAD, however, includes several more powerful and versatile editing commands and options. In this chapter, you expand your drawing knowledge by using more of AutoCAD's editing commands and options.

The benefits of electronic drawing editing are simple. When you master AutoCAD's editing capabilities, you can stay on top of changes to your project without falling behind in your drawings. You can erase, move, copy, and resize individual objects quickly without disturbing other entities in the drawing. You also can create multiple copies of objects—and even arrange those copies in an arrayed pattern—with minimal original entry. Figure 8.1, for example, shows how simple editing techniques can enhance a drawing. You learn how to make these changes to the widget drawing in this chapter.

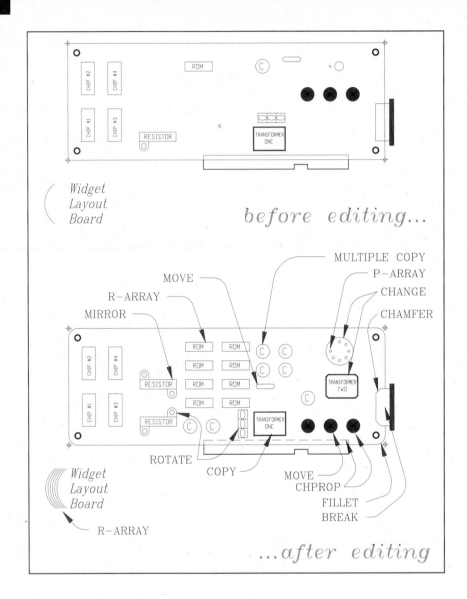

**Figure 8.1:**

The widget drawing before and after editing.

You can perform three basic kinds of activities when you edit a drawing: changing, copying, and erasing entities in your drawing. You can change an existing entity's location, layer, and visual properties, such as color and linetype. You also can *break* entities by deleting portions of line and arc segments. Breaking an entity reduces its length or divides it into multiple entities. You can copy entities, either one at a time or in an arrayed pattern. You also can erase entities to get rid of previous mistakes.

AutoCAD offers more advanced editing functions—such as trimming, extending, stretching, and scaling—as well as some editing construction techniques. The following chapters cover these advanced functions. Part Five includes 3D variations of these editing commands.

# Exploring the Editor's Toolkit

Most of AutoCAD's editing commands are gathered on the **M**odify pull-down menu and the EDIT screen menus (see fig. 8.2). Some of the key editing commands (such as COPY) can be found in the toolbox. The **S**ettings pull-down menu includes settings for some of the editing commands. The **C**onstruct pull-down menu also contains commands that are sometimes thought of as editing commands.

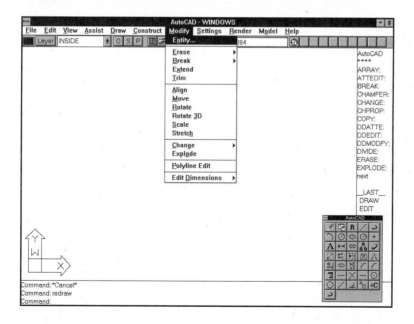

**Figure 8.2:**

The **M**odify pull-down and the EDIT screen menus.

This chapter discusses the basics of editing. In the following exercises, you are shown ways to change both the spatial (location) and appearance (color and linetype) properties of existing entities. To perform these simple editing functions, you need to use only a few basic editing commands.

The basic editing commands form two groups. The first group, which changes the location, quantity, and orientation of objects, includes the following commands:

| Command | Function |
| --- | --- |
| MOVE | Moves selected objects |
| ROTATE | Rotates selected objects about a base point |
| COPY | Creates one or more copies of selected objects |
| MIRROR | Creates a reverse copy of selected objects |
| ARRAY | Creates a rectangular or polar array of selected objects |

You have already used the grip-editing mode of these basic commands, but have not used all of their options. In this chapter, you explore these commands and all their options, as well as these additional commands used for editing objects:

| Command | Function |
| --- | --- |
| BREAK | Removes a portion of the selected object |
| CHAMFER | Inserts a chamfer segment between two continuous lines or polylines |
| FILLET | Inserts a fillet arc between two continuous lines, two polyline segments, or all segments of an entire polyline |

In addition to these two groups of commands, this chapter shows you how to use the ERASE command to delete entities and offers further practice with the various grip editing modes that you examined in Chapter 6.

# How Editing Commands Work

Most editing commands involve a four-step process. Before you actually edit an object, you must think about the kind of edit you want to do, which objects you want to edit, and how you want to edit them. The process includes these steps:

1. Issue the editing command

2. Select the entities

3. Enter the appropriate parameters and pick points

4. Watch the edit as it takes place

Noun/verb selection of entities means that the entities (the nouns) are selected before the verb (the command) is issued. This method of entity selection is different from the verb/noun process, in which entities are not selected until after the command is issued.

When you invoke an editing command, AutoCAD switches to object-selection mode. In object-selection mode, you tell AutoCAD which entity or entities you want to edit. Most commands require you to select one or more objects. You can, however, reverse the order of steps 1 and 2, if the PICKFIRST system variable is on (set to 1). This variable enables you to select the entities before issuing the command. You can turn on PICKFIRST by checking in the **N**oun/Verb Selection box in the Entity Selection Settings dialog box. You can display this dialog box by using the DDSELECT command or by choosing **S**election Settings from the **S**ettings menu. Setting PICKFIRST on adds versatility to editing; you can pick first, or you can still perform editing by first issuing an editing command, and then selecting entities. A pick box is displayed on the cursor at all times when either GRIPS or PICKFIRST is turned on.

*Although most editing commands work well with noun/verb selection, this method of selection is not compatible with some editing commands, such as FILLET or TRIM. Such commands ignore the PICKFIRST selection set.*

The following section describes how to build a selection set, whether you pick first or issue the editing command first.

## Selecting Before Editing

In AutoCAD, you have the option of selecting entities before an editing command is issued (noun/verb), or first issuing the command and then selecting entities. With the PICKFIRST system variable turned off (0, the default), the only method permitted is "verb, then noun." You issue the ERASE command, for example, then pick the entities you want to erase.

With PICKFIRST turned on, the method can be "noun, then verb." You select the entities you want to erase, then issue the ERASE command, which erases the entities without any other input from you. The next exercise demonstrates both of these methods and shows how to select between the two. The exercise uses the IAWCHAP8 drawing from the IAW DISK as a prototype; it is identical to the TOOLPLAT drawing from the end of Chapter 6.

## Selecting Before Editing

Use the NEW command to begin a new drawing named TOOLPLAT=IAWCHAP8, replacing the existing TOOLPLAT drawing.

| | |
|---|---|
| Command: **PICKFIRST** ↵ | Accesses PICKFIRST system variable |
| New value for PICKFIRST <1>: **0** ↵ | Turns off PICKFIRST mode |
| Command: *From the toolbox, choose* ERASE | Starts the ERASE command |

Select two circles ① and ②, and the extra radial slot with a window ③ and ④ (see fig. 8.3). Remember to use Shift to add the second circle and the slot to the selection set.

| | |
|---|---|
| Select objects: *Press Enter* | Erases the entities |
| Command: **U** ↵ | Brings the entities back |
| Command: **PICKFIRST** ↵ | Accesses PICKFIRST system variable |
| New value for PICKFIRST <0>: **1** ↵ | Turns on PICKFIRST mode |
| Command: *Select the circles and the slot again* | Displays grips |
| Command: *From the toolbox, choose* ERASE<br>erase 6 found | Erases the selection set without additional input |

# Building the Selection Set

AutoCAD offers over a dozen ways to collect objects for editing. You can, for example, pick individual objects or enclose a group of objects within a window. As you select objects, AutoCAD sets up a temporary selection set and highlights the objects by temporarily changing their colors, making them blink, or giving them dotted lines. This highlighting enables you to confirm that you have selected the correct entities. If you make an error at the Select objects: prompt, AutoCAD prompts you with all the available modes. When you have selected all the desired objects, press Enter to end object selection and continue the editing command.

The selection process is also controlled by a system variable called PICKADD. When this variable is set to 0 (off), selecting additional entities replaces the ones already selected. Selecting with PICKADD off clears the selection set and starts a new one, unless you hold down Shift. Holding down Shift while choosing additional entities adds them to the existing group. To remove previously selected entities from the selection set, hold down Shift as you select them. If you select a group that contains both unselected and previously selected entities, with Shift down, the unselected ones are added, but the previously selected ones are not removed. If PICKADD is set to 1 (on), entities are automatically added to the selection set as they are chosen, but you can still use Shift to remove entities from the set. A check mark in the <u>U</u>se Shift to Add box of the Entity Selection Settings dialog box indicates that PICKADD is off.

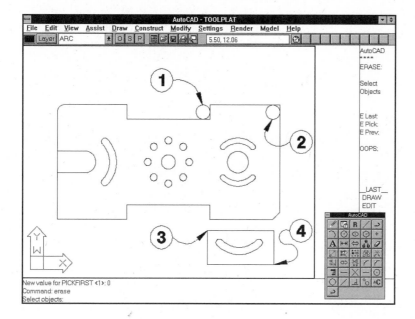

**Figure 8.3:**

Selection points for editing.

AutoCAD provides the following methods for adding objects to a selection set:

- **Object pick.** This method enables you to pick individual objects. This option is the default. When picking, AutoCAD finds the most recently created object that falls within or crosses the pick box. If snap and object snap are used together, AutoCAD snaps first, then performs the object snaps from that snapped point.

- **Window.** This method adds objects within the corners of a window you specify. AutoCAD selects only those objects that are enclosed entirely within the window. Lines that are overlapped by the window edge are considered to be within this window.

- **Last.** This method adds the last object created to the selection set.

- **Crossing.** This method works the same as Window, except that Crossing also includes any object that is partially within (or crossing) the window.

- **ALL.** This method selects all entities in the drawing that are not on a layer which is locked or frozen.

- **Fence.** This method enables you to draw an unclosed polyline fence with which to select objects. All objects touched by the fence line are selected.

- **Wpolygon.** This method is similar to Window selection but enables you to draw an irregular polygon to select objects. All entities completely within the polygon are selected.

- **Cpolygon.** This method is similar to the Crossing selection but enables you to draw an irregular polygon to select objects. All entities inside or crossed by the polygon are selected.

- **Add.** This method switches from Remove mode back to normal, so that you again can add to the selection set. If PICKADD is off, you also can use Shift to add selected objects to the set.

- **Remove.** This method switches to Remove mode, so that you can remove selected objects from the selection set (not from the drawing). You also can use Shift when you select to remove objects from the set.

- **Multiple.** This method enables you to pick multiple objects in close proximity and speeds up selection by enabling multiple selections without highlighting or prompting. An extra Enter is required to complete the multiple selection and return to normal object selection.

- **Previous.** This method selects the entire preceding selection set (from a previous command) as the current selection set.

- **Undo.** This method undoes or reverses the last selection operation. Each U undoes one selection operation.

When do you use which mode? The default option, Object Pick, is fast and simple, even for picking three or four objects, and it requires no mode setting. Last and Undo are obvious. Previous is great for repeated operations on the same set of objects, like a copy and rotate operation.

Sometimes objects are so close to each other that you cannot pick the one you want; AutoCAD just keeps finding the same object over and over again. If this happens, use Multiple and pick repeatedly, and AutoCAD finds multiple objects within the pickbox. Then remove from the set the object(s) you do not want.

 *A number of editing commands, such as FILLET, TRIM, and EXTEND, require individual entity selection, part or all of the time. In these cases, you must select your objects by picking them instead of Crossing, Window, and so on.*

# Windows and Crossing Modes Settings

You can choose between Window and Crossing, depending on which option best extracts the group you want from the crowd, simply by the order in which you pick the two corner points. In grips editing, as you saw in Chapter 6, picking left to right makes a window and right to left makes a crossing window. If the PICKAUTO system variable is on (1), object selection during editing commands behaves in the same way as grips editing selection. If it is off (0), you must use the W and C options. PICKAUTO on is indicated by a check in the **I**mplied Windowing box of the Entity Selection Setting dialog box. PICKAUTO on causes object selection to automatically enter Box mode if the first pick does not find an object to select.

*The Window selection process ignores objects that have portions that fall partly outside of the current drawing window. If all visible portions of an object are in the Window box, it is selected.*

The Wpolygon, Cpolygon, and Fence options are powerful tools for building complex selection sets, particularly when selections must be made in a crowded area of the drawing. These selection methods take longer to implement than the Window and Crossing options, but they are more flexible and can actually save steps.

The PICKDRAG system variable, explained in Chapter 6, controls whether one or two picks are needed to show a window. If PICKDRAG is set to 1 (on), press down on the pick button at the first corner and hold it down while you drag the window. When this variable is set to 0 (off), a window requires a pick at both corners. This setting is shown in the Entity Selection Settings dialog box as **P**ress and Drag.

# Setting Object Selection Behavior

You already set PICKADD off (the **U**se Shift to Add box is checked in the Entity Selection Settings dialog box) and PICKDRAG on (**C**lick and Drag is checked) in Chapter 6. To take advantage of the flexibility of **N**oun/Verb Selection, you need to turn PICKFIRST on by putting a check in the **N**oun/Verb Selection box. You also should turn PICKAUTO on by putting a check in the **I**mplied Windowing box, or you may find the difference between the behavior of grips mode editing selection and selection during editing commands to be confusing.

In the next exercise, set these two selection controls on and leave them on for the rest of the exercise in this book.

# Additional Selection Set Options

AutoCAD has three other selection set options: BOX, AUto, and SIngle. These options are designed primarily for use in menus and offer no real advantages over the options discussed in the preceding list when specifying modes from the keyboard. Note that BOX, AUto, and SIngle are used by some of the pull-down menu items in the following exercises.

- **BOX.** This option combines Window and Crossing into a single selection. To pick the points of your box (window) from left to right is the same as a Window selection; right to left is the same as a Crossing selection.

- **AUto.** This option combines individual selection with the BOX selection. This selection performs the same as BOX, except that if the first pick point finds an entity, that single entity is selected and the BOX mode is aborted. AUto mode is always on if the PICKAUTO system variable is on (1).

- **SIngle.** This option works in conjunction with the other selection options. If you precede a selection with SIngle, object selection automatically ends after the first successful selection without having to use the Enter that is normally required to exit object selection.

When specifying modes from the keyboard, you know how you intend to select the object(s), so you can use Window, Crossing, or just pick the object(s) with PICKAUTO on, rather than use BOX or AUto.

# Setting Up for Editing

This chapter uses the IAWWIDG3.DWG drawing file from the IAW DISK, which is identical to the WIDGET drawing created in Chapter 7. In the following exercise, you use IAWWIDG3 as a prototype to create a new file, WIDGEDIT, in which you try out the editing options.

### Setup for Editing the WIDGEDIT Drawing

Command: *Choose* File, *then* New,          Creates the WIDGEDIT drawing
*and enter* **WIDGEDIT=IAWWIDG3**

## Table 8.1
### Setup for Editing the Widget Drawing

| COORDS | GRID | SNAP | UCSICON |
|--------|------|------|---------|
| On | .5 | .1 | OR |
| **UNITS** | Engineering, 2 decimal places, 2 fractional places for angles, default all other settings | | |
| **LIMITS** | 0,0 to 11,8.5 | | |
| **VIEW** | Saved as RESISTOR | | |

| Layer Name | State | Color | Linetype |
|------------|-------|-------|----------|
| 0 | On | 7 (White) | CONTINUOUS |
| BOARD | On | 2 (Yellow) | CONTINUOUS |
| HIDDEN | On | 1 (Red) | HIDDEN |
| PARTS | On | 4 (Cyan) | CONTINUOUS |
| TEXT | On/Current | 3 (Green) | CONTINUOUS |

You should have a full view of the widget. The following exercises do not make use of the viewports stored with the widget drawing, but you can use viewports in the exercises. You can restore the viewports by using TILEMODE=0. Your current layer is not important to the exercises; editing commands work on any layer. If you want additional practice using individual editing commands, use a layer named SCRATCH, make it the current layer, create some new entities, and practice the editing command on the entities. After you finish practicing, undo, erase, or freeze the SCRATCH layer and continue with the widget drawing.

# Making Some Quick Moves

The process of making a move is quite simple. You grab what you want and move it where you want it. Try moving the solid donuts by using a Window selection. When you are prompted for a base point or displacement, pick a base point. After you pick this point, you can drag the selection set by using your pointer and pick a second displacement point to place the objects. As the following exercise demonstrates, whenever you want to see the full object selection options prompt, you can display it by entering a question mark (or any other irrelevant input).

## Selecting and Windowing Donuts To Move

Choose <u>S</u>election Settings from the <u>S</u>ettings menu. Make sure the check boxes in the <u>N</u>oun/Verb Selection box and the <u>I</u>mplied Windowing box are turned on.

`Command:` *From the toolbox, choose* MOVE    Begins the Move command

`Command: move`
`Select objects: ?` ↵

`*Invalid selection*`    Displays a full selection prompt because ? was
`Expects a point or Window/Last/`    invalid input
`Crossing/BOX/ALL/Fence/Wpolygon/`
`Cpolygon/Add/Remove/Multiple/`
`Previous/Undo/AUto/SIngle`

`Select objects:` *Pick the left donut*
*at* ① *(see fig. 8.4)*

`1 found.`

`Select objects: W` ↵    Specifies window selection mode

`First corner:` *Click and hold button 1 at*
② *(see fig. 8.4)*

`Other corner:` *Drag to second corner at*    Selects the right two donuts with a window
③ *and release button 1*

`2 found.`

`Select objects:` *Press Enter*    Tells AutoCAD that you are through selecting
objects

`Base point or displacement:` *Pick any*    Specifies the "from" point of the move
*point near the donuts*

`Second point of displacement:` *Use the*    Specifies the "to" point and completes the
*coordinates to pick at point 1.00<270*    move (see fig. 8.5)

After you move the donuts, they should appear near the bottom of the widget, as seen in figure 8.5.

---

With <u>I</u>mplied Windowing (PICKAUTO) on, you did not need to use the Window option to select a window. Sometimes, however, using the Window or Crossing option explicitly is essential. <u>I</u>mplied Windowing and AUtomode can find an object within the pickbox (if any), instead of entering Window/Crossing selection. If there is such an object at the corner of the desired window selection area, you must use the W or C options to make your selection.

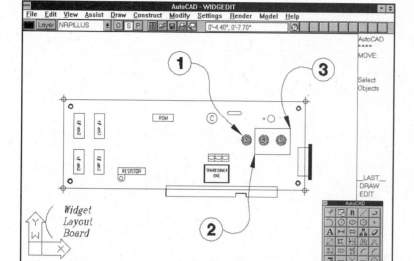

**Figure 8.4:**

Selecting donuts for a Move.

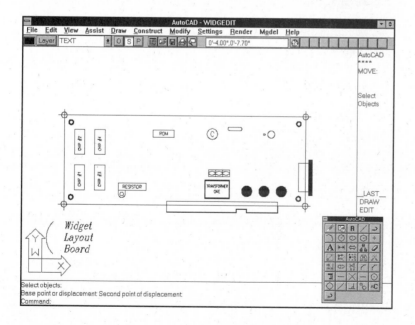

**Figure 8.5:**

The donuts after being moved.

As you see, object selection and moving is easy. After you select the donuts with a window, they are highlighted. You tell AutoCAD you are through collecting by pressing Enter in response to the Select objects: prompt. After you finish selecting, pick your displacement points, and your donuts are moved.

> *Another way to control which entities are selected by a pick is to change the pick-box size by changing the PICKBOX system variable. Enter **PICKBOX**, and then enter a new value. You also can change the pick box size transparently in the middle of a command by using 'SETVAR or 'PICKBOX. The DDSELECT dialog box also controls the pick-box size.*

## Moving with Noun/Verb Selection

The previous exercise using the MOVE command can also be done using the Noun/Verb selection process. Try selecting the three donuts with a window and then issuing the MOVE command. You are not prompted to select entities because AutoCAD recognizes that it has already been done. The next exercise demonstrates that method of moving the donuts.

### Using Move with the Noun/Verb Selection

| | |
|---|---|
| Command: **U** ↵ | Undoes the previous MOVE command |
| Command: *Select the three donuts using a window* | Selects the entities |
| Command: *From the toolbox, choose* MOVE | Issues the MOVE command |
| move 3 found<br>Base point or displacement: **0,-1** ↵ | Specifies a displacement |
| Second point of displacement:<br>*Press Enter* | Moves the donuts |

You also can use Move grip mode to move objects, just as you did in Chapter 6. Next, undo the previous MOVE command, and then perform the same edit by using Move grip mode.

## Using Move Grip Mode

`Command:` **U** ↵                    Undoes the previous MOVE command

`Command:` *Select the three donuts using*    Displays grips
*a window*

`Command:` *Pick one of the grips*          Enters stretch mode

`** STRETCH **`                      Switches to move mode
`<Stretch to point>/Base point/Copy/`
`Undo/eXit:` **MO** ↵

`** MOVE **`                        Moves the donuts
`<Move to point>/Base point/Copy/`
`Undo/eXit:` **@1<270**

The Grip editing feature combines several of the most common editing commands into one command with different mode options. Grip editing always begins in the stretch mode. You can switch between the various modes by pressing Enter or the spacebar. The shortcut keys may be a quicker method of accessing the proper mode. The modes and the shortcut keys are as follows:

- **ST.** Stretch
- **MO.** Move
- **RO.** Rotate
- **SC.** Scale
- **MI.** Mirror

One of the most difficult parts of learning AutoCAD is that the software offers so many ways of doing things. Editing is no exception. Although moving an entity seems simple, there are many ways of defining the distance, or *displacement*, to move it.

# Displacement and Drag

When you change the location of objects in a selection set, you use a displacement. If you know the absolute X,Y, or polar displacement, you can enter it at the `Base point or displacement:` prompt. Entering **0,-1** or **1<270** (do not preface the displacement with an @), for example, duplicates the move you just did. Then press Enter, instead of a value, at the `Second point:` prompt to tell AutoCAD to use the first value as an absolute offset.

Often, you want to show a displacement by entering two points. Think of the first point (base point) as a handle on the selection set. The second point is where you want to put the handle of the set down. The *displacement* is an imaginary line from the base point to the second point. AutoCAD calculates the X and Y differences between the base and second points. The new location of the object(s) is determined by adding this X,Y displacement to its current location.

AutoCAD does not actually draw a displacement line; it gets the information it needs from the displacement points. When you pick displacement points, AutoCAD shows a temporary rubber-band line trailing behind the crosshairs from the first point to the second.

As you move the donuts, an image of the selection set also follows the crosshairs. AutoCAD provides a visual aid to help you pick your second displacement point. This action is called *dragging*. Without dragging, it can be difficult to see if the selection set fits where you want it.

When you set a base point, try to pick a base point that is easy to visualize (and remember). If the base point is not in, on, or near the contents of the selection set, you appear to be carrying the selection set around magically without touching it. Sometimes you use object snap mode to move the points to a different but related object. Otherwise, it is a good idea to make this drag anchor (base-displacement point) a reference point, such as an object snap point on one of the objects.

## Using DRAGMODE

When you edit large selection sets, you may want to control dragging. You can turn dragging on or off by using the DRAGMODE system variable. The default for DRAGMODE is Auto, which causes AutoCAD to drag everything that makes sense. Turn DRAGMODE on to be more selective about what you drag. If DRAGMODE is on, and you want to drag while using a command, type **Drag** and press Enter before picking the point that you want to drag. The option Off turns DRAGMODE off entirely and ignores a previously typed Drag.

## Add and Remove Modes for the Selection Set

You often need to remove objects from a selection set when too many objects are in the set. Although, with **U**se Shift to Add turned on (PICKADD off), you rarely need to use them, AutoCAD has two modes for handling selection set contents: an Add mode and a Remove mode. In Add mode, the default Select objects: prompt appears. If you pick individual objects or use any other object-selection mode, such as Window or Last, the objects are placed in the selection set. If **S**hift to Add is on, Remove mode overrides it, but Add mode has no effect other than ending Remove mode.

You also can press **R** (for Remove) in response to the normal Add mode prompt. When the Remove objects: prompt appears, remove objects from the selection set by using any type of object selection in the Remove mode. Press **A** to return to Add mode.

# Using a Crossing Window

A second type of window-object selection is a *crossing window*, which selects everything that falls within your selection window or crosses the boundary of the window. A crossing window is handy when you want to select objects in a crowded drawing. The number of picks (one or two) that are required to show a window depends on whether the PICKDRAG system variable is 1 or 0. This setting is also known as <u>P</u>ress and Drag in the Entity Selection Setting dialog box. AutoCAD also differentiates between objects in the window and objects crossing the window. Some advanced editing commands, such as the Stretch command, treat selected objects in the window differently from those crossing the window boundary.

The next exercise uses a polar displacement to combine a crossing window and the Remove mode to move the ROM chip. Select the capacitor and the ROM chip together by using Crossing, and then remove the capacitor from the selection set. (The *capacitor* is the circle containing a C.)

## Using Crossing, Add, and Remove Selection Set Modes

| | |
|---|---|
| Command: *Pick in an empty area of the drawing* | Clears the selection set |
| Command: *From the toolbox, choose* MOVE | Issues the MOVE command |
| Command: move<br>Select objects: *Press and hold at* ①<br>*(see fig. 8.6)* | |
| Other corner: *Drag to* ② *and release* | Selects the objects with a crossing window |
| 4 found. | Highlights four objects |
| Select objects: **R** ↵ | Begins Remove mode |
| Remove objects: *Pick the circle* | |
| 1 found, 1 removed | Removes the circle from the selection set |
| Remove objects: *Pick the text character* C | |
| 1 found, 1 removed | Removes the C from set |
| Remove objects: *Press Enter* | Ends selection |
| Base point or displacement:<br>**1.1<270** ↵ | Specifies a polar displacement |
| Second point of displacement:<br>*Press Enter* | Uses the previous input as the displacement |

**Figure 8.6:**

Using a crossing window to move objects.

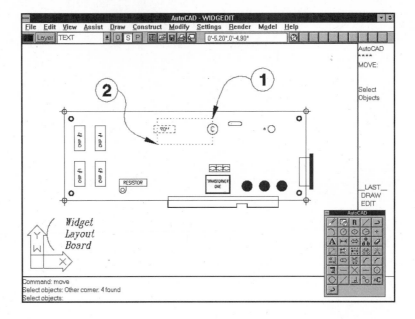

As figure 8.7 shows, this operation moves the chip and leaves the capacitor in its original location.

**Figure 8.7:**

The ROM chip in its new location.

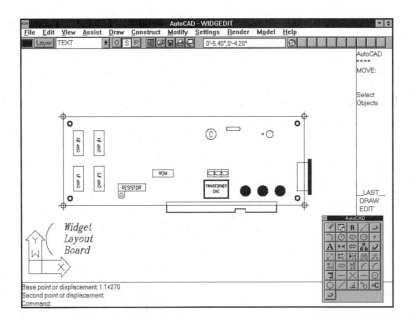

Next, use automatic selection and the Move Grip mode to perform the same edit again.

### Removing Entities with Shift to Add

| | |
|---|---|
| Command: **U** ↵ | Undoes the previous MOVE command |
| Command: *Press and hold at* ① *(see fig. 8.6), drag to* ② *and release* | Selects the capacitor and ROM with a crossing window and displays grips |
| Command: *Hold down Shift and select a window around the capacitor* | Removes the capacitor from the selection set |
| Command: *Pick any of the ROM's grips* | Enters stretch mode |
| ** STRETCH **<br><Stretch to point>/Base point/Copy/<br>Undo/eXit: *Press Enter* | Enters Move mode |
| ** MOVE **<br><Move to point>/Base point/Copy/<br>Undo/eXit: **@1.1<270** | Moves the ROM chip |
| Command: *Pick in an empty area of the drawing* | Clears the selection set |

This exercise used a relative point to define the move distance because the Grip modes do not support the displacement option. You also can enter a displacement with the Base point option and a second point.

## Understanding the Selection Set

In a complex drawing, you may notice the time it takes AutoCAD to search through the drawing file for entities that qualify for the selection set. Every time you select more objects for the selection set, AutoCAD shows the number you selected and the number it actually found. These numbers are not always the same, for two reasons. First, you can select objects that do not qualify for editing. Second, you may have already selected an entity. In the latter case, AutoCAD informs you that it found a duplicate. In all cases (except Multiple mode selections), AutoCAD uses the highlighting feature to show you what is currently in the selection set.

*To speed up the selection of large selection sets, turn the HIGH-LIGHT system variable off. To do so, enter **HIGHLIGHT** and set it to 0 (off). If you do so, select carefully because you cannot tell which objects are selected. Highlight off is useful for selecting large, easily defined portions of the drawing. Also, consider using the DDSELECT dialog box to*

set <u>E</u>ntity Sort Method to fit your selection situation. (Entity Sort is discussed later in this chapter.)

# Using the SIngle Option for Object Selection

Menu items—such as <u>E</u>rase, then <u>Si</u>ngle on the <u>M</u>odify pull-down menu—expect you to select exactly one object, so they use the SIngle mode of object selection. As soon as an object (or group of objects) is selected, object selection ends without having to press Enter. Try SIngle and an absolute displacement to move the diode from the top of the widget down to the left. Remember that the diode was made with a polyline, so it selects and moves as a single entity.

---

## Using the SIngle Option for Object Selection

`Command:` *Choose* <u>M</u>odify, *then* <u>M</u>ove

`Command: _move`

`Select objects:` **SI** ↵           Specifies single object selection mode

`Select objects:` *Pick any point on the diode*

`1 found.`           Highlights the diode and completes the selection set

`Base point or displacement:`    Specifies a negative absolute displacement
**-.6,-.9** ↵

`Second point of displacement:`    Uses the preceding input as the displacement
*Press Enter*

*Save the drawing*

Figure 8.8 shows the diode in its new location.

---

You can precede any of the object selection modes with SI (for SIngle), but SIngle was intended primarily for use in menu macros.

# Using the Previous Selection Set Option

The Previous selection option is helpful when you cancel an editing command or use several commands on the same selection set. Previous object selection reselects the object(s) that you selected in your previous editing command.

Previous enables you to edit the preceding set without having to select its objects individually again. Previous is different from the Last option, which selects the last created object visible in the drawing area. Previous includes objects from the preceding set even if they are now outside the visible drawing area. Previous does not work with some editing commands, such as STRETCH, in which a window, crossing, or point selection is required.

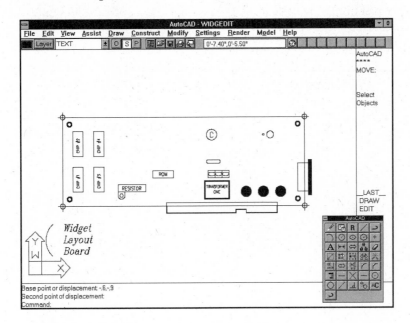

**Figure 8.8:**

The diode's new location.

# Controlling Entity Sorting

Unlike earlier versions of AutoCAD, which always sorted entities in their order of creation, Release 12 normally uses an oct-tree (octal tree) method of sorting the entity data base. Entity sorting affects the order in which entities are found by object selection and object snapping; it also affects the order in which they are displayed or output by redraws, regenerations, MSLIDE, plotting, and PostScript output. The old method of sorting favored the most recently created entities during selection and object snapping, and displayed or output entities in their order of creation. The oct-tree method sorts, selects, displays, and outputs entities in a grid arrangement. The oct-tree method divides the drawing up into rectangular areas, making object selection and object snapping much faster because they need only consider the local area instead of the whole drawing. These areas are visually evident during a redraw or regeneration of a complex drawing because AutoCAD redraws or regenerates each area in turn.

*If you want to see the effect of an oct-tree sort, create a 50-row-by-60-column array of circles and perform a ZOOM All.*

In most cases, the order of the entities is of little consequence. For cases in which the order matters, you can use the Entity Sort Method dialog box (see fig. 8.9) to override oct-tree sorting and consider the order of creation for specific operations.

**Figure 8.9:**

The Entity Sort Method dialog box.

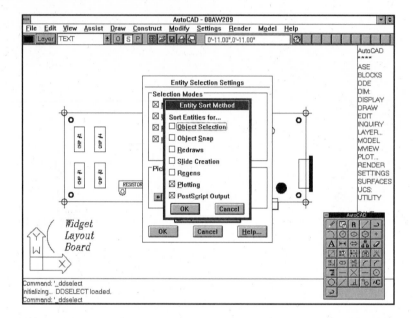

To display the Entity Sort Method dialog box, first enter DDSELECT or choose **S**ettings, then **S**election Settings, and then choose **E**ntity Sort Method. With this dialog box, you choose between the default oct-tree sorting method and an entity creation sorting method (by checking a box) while performing selected operations. The operation options in the Entity Sort Method dialog box are as follows:

- **Object Selection**. When picking an entity with oct-tree sorting, if several entities fall within the pickbox, it is hard to predict which entity will be found. With entity creation sorting selected (placing a checkmark in the box), the most recent entities will be found. When you are editing recent entities, as is often the case, setting oct-tree off will help select them. When making a window or crossing selection with oct-tree on, entities will be selected in an unpredictable order. With oct-tree off, they will be selected in the reverse of the creation order. This sometimes makes a difference when creating a block; for example, if the block contains attributes which need to prompt in a specific order, you need to control their order of selection (see Chapter 16).

- **Object <u>S</u>nap**. As with <u>O</u>bject Selection, oct-tree affects the finding of entities when using object snap. Turn it off when using the QUIck object snap option if you want the most recent entities to be found predictably.

- **<u>R</u>edraws**. If the order in which entities appear during a redraw really matters to you, turn oct-tree off to make them appear in their order of creation. Because many zooms merely redraw instead of regenerating, this might be important to you. If, for example, you first draw a basic part outline, framework, or building grid in your drawings, you can use it to locate your zooms. With oct-tree off, that first-drawn outline, framework, or grid appears first. You can do a rough zoom, cut the zoom short with a Ctrl-C, and then zoom more precisely, using the outline, framework, or grid. With oct-tree on, the order of appearance is less predictable.

- **S<u>l</u>ide Creation**. As with redraws, oct-tree controls the order of appearance of objects in slides created by MSLIDE. This order is often important in a complex slide; a presentation might look odd if all the windows of a building appeared before the wall outlines.

- **<u>R</u>egens**. As with redraws, oct-tree controls the order of appearance of objects during regenerations. See the preceding discussion of redraws.

- **<u>P</u>lotting**. Because AutoCAD's plot routine and many plotters perform their own vector sorting, oct-tree is generally not important to plotting. If, however, you are plotting to an image file format, you may want to control the order of appearance, as discussed in the preceding <u>S</u>lide Creation option.

- **PostS<u>c</u>ript Output**. As with slides and plotting to image files, if you need to control the order of appearance in the PostScript file, set oct-tree off.

Setting oct-tree off for any option causes only that option's operations to use the old-style sorting; other operations still use an oct-tree sort. When an option box in the Entity Sort Method dialog box is checked, it sets oct-tree off for that option. The SORTENTS system variable stores the current oct-tree sort setting; see Appendix C for more information.

# Using the COPY Command

The basic COPY command is similar to the MOVE command. The only difference between a copy and a move is that COPY leaves the original objects in place.

In the steps that follow, use a Wpoly (Window Polygon) selection to copy the widget's transformer and capacitor. Wpoly provides a multisided window for selection. Try canceling the command and using Previous to reselect the selection set that is to be copied.

## Using the COPY Command, Wpoly, and Previous

| | |
|---|---|
| Command: *From the toolbox, choose* COPY | Begins the COPY command |
| Command: copy | |
| Select objects: **WP** ↵ | Specifies WPolygon mode |
| First polygon point: *Pick at* ① *(see fig. 8.10)* | Starts polygon selection |
| Undo/<Endpoint of line>: *Pick at* ② | Continues selection |
| Undo/<Endpoint of line>: *Pick points* ③ *through* ⑦ | Creates the polygon |
| Undo/<Endpoint of line>: *Pick at* ⑧, *and press Enter* | Closes the polygon |
| 5 found | Highlights and selects the transformer and ROM |
| Select objects: *Press Enter* | Ends selection |
| <Base point or displacement>/ Multiple: *Press Ctrl-C* | Cancels the COPY command |
| Command: *Press Enter* | Repeats the COPY command |
| Command: COPY | |
| Select objects: **P** ↵ | Uses the previous selection set |
| 5 found | Highlights the transformer and ROM |
| Select objects: *Hold down Shift and select a window around the capacitor* | Removes ROM from the selection set |
| 2 found, 2 removed | |
| Select objects: *Press Enter* | |
| <Base point or displacement>/ Multiple: *From the toolbox menu, choose* INTERSECTION | |
| int of *Pick the transformer's lower left corner* | Specifies the "from" point |
| Second point of displacement: **8.20,4.30** ↵ | Copies the transformer |

Figure 8.11 shows the board with the newly copied transformer.

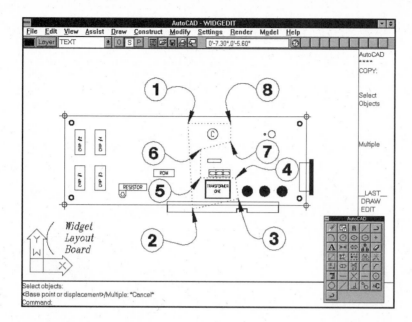

**Figure 8.10:**

Selecting the transformer and capacitor.

Remember, you can always use object snap and snap modes to help you get an exact displacement location or to help select objects for the selection set.

*Now that you have practiced using object selection, most exercises in the rest of the book omit the nnn found and Select objects: prompts and their responses. Most exercises simply tell you what to select, leaving you to complete the selection set on your own.*

# Using the COPY Command Options

The COPY command options are similar to the MOVE options. COPY options include displacement points identification, object-selection options, and a new option: Multiple, which stands for multiple copies. (Do not confuse the new Multiple option with Multiple object selection.)

## Working with the COPY Multiple Option

The Multiple option of the COPY command enables you to copy the contents of your selection set several times, without having to respecify the selection set and base point. If you respond to the Base point or displacement: prompt by entering **M**, AutoCAD reprompts for base point, then repeatedly prompts you for multiple second point of displacement points. Press Enter or Ctrl-C to get out of the Multiple loop.

**Figure 8.11:**

The copied
transformer.

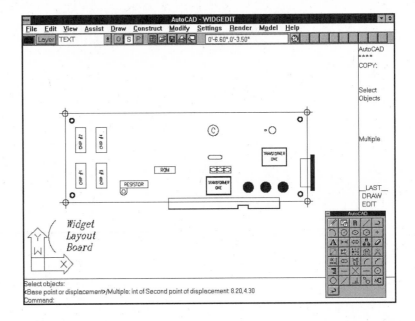

Follow the steps in the next exercise to make multiple copies of the capacitor. Put three copies next to the original capacitor and put one copy between the transformers. Finally, put two more copies next to the resistor on the bottom of the board. The polar coordinates shown are for your reference. To maintain accuracy, the coordinates are all snap points. As you begin the next exercise, your drawing should look like figure 8.12.

## Using COPY Multiple To Make Copies of the Capacitor

Command: *Select the capacitor with a window*

Command: *From the toolbox, choose* COPY

copy 2 found         Selects the preselected set

<Base point or displacement>         Invokes the Multiple Copy option
/Multiple:*Enter* M *or choose* Multiple
*from the screen menu*

Base point: *From the toolbox,*
*choose* CENTER, *then select the circle*

Second point of displacement: *Pick at*     Makes the first copy
*polar point 0.40<270.00*

Second point of displacement: *Pick at*     Makes another copy
*polar point 0.50<0.00*

`Second point of displacement:` *Pick at polar point 0.64<321.34*

`Second point of displacement:` *Pick at polar point 2.26<225.00*

`Second point of displacement:` *Pick at polar point 1.94<235.49*

`Second point of displacement:` *Pick at polar point at 1.41<315.00*

`Second point of displacement:` *Press Enter*         Exits from the Copy option

Figure 8.13 shows the copies.

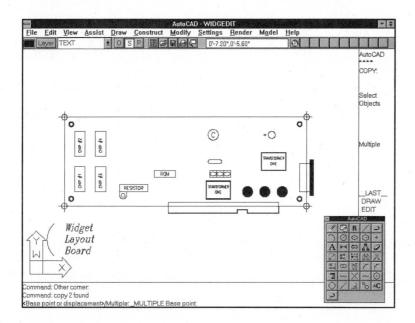

**Figure 8.12:**

Before the multiple copy.

# Using ARRAY To Make Multiple Copies in a Pattern

Making arrays is another type of multiple copying. Often, you want to make multiple copies of an object or group of objects in a regular pattern. Suppose, for example, you have a rectangle that represents a table in a cafeteria. AutoCAD can place a table every nine feet in the X direction and every 14 feet in the Y direction to make five rows and eight columns of tables. Another example of the usefulness of arrays is to draw evenly spaced bolt holes around the circumference of a tank top.

**Figure 8.13:**

Detail of the completed multiple copy.

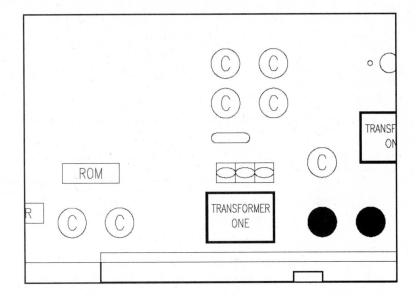

The ARRAY command functions similarly to the COPY command. Unlike COPY, however, ARRAY makes a regular pattern of entities instead of making individually placed copies of the selection set. You determine the number of copies and the repetition pattern. The two basic array patterns are rectangular and polar.

# Using Rectangular Arrays

You make a *rectangular array* by specifying the number of rows and columns you want and an X,Y offset distance. You can have a single row with multiple columns, a single column with multiple rows, or multiple rows and columns.

You can show the displacement between rows or columns by picking two points (as you would a window) at the Distance between rows (—): and Distance between columns ( | | | ): prompts. You also can specify the offsets by entering positive or negative offset values (see figs. 8.14 and 8.15). The *offset distance* is the X and Y direction from the original selection set. Negative values produce an array in the negative X or Y (or both) directions. A positive X value generates columns to the right; a negative X value generates columns to the left. A positive Y value generates rows up; a negative Y value generates rows down.

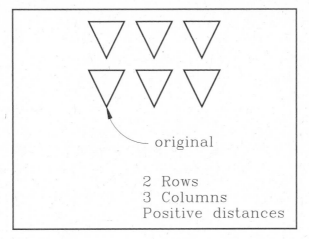

**Figure 8.14:**

Positive array offsets.

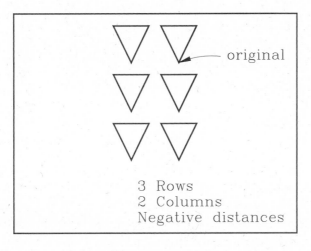

**Figure 8.15:**

Negative array offsets.

Try making a rectangular array by using the ROM chip.

---

## Using ARRAY To Make a Rectangular Array

Command: *Select the ROM chip and its text*

Command: *Choose* **C**onstruct, *then* **A**rray      Begins the ARRAY command

Command: `_array 2 found`      Selects the preselected set

`Rectangular or Polar array (R/P)`      Specifies a rectangular array
`<R>:` *Press Enter or choose* Rectang
*from the screen menu*

*continues*

```
Number of rows (--) <1>: 4 ↵

Number of columns (¦¦¦) <1>: 2 ↵

Distance between rows (--): 0.40 ↵

Distance between columns (¦¦¦):
0.80 ↵                              Draws the array (see fig. 8.16)
```

**Figure 8.16:**

The completed rectangular array.

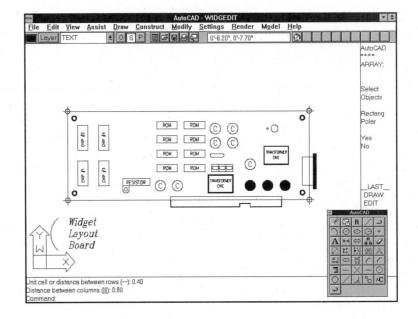

If you set up a big array (with many rows and columns), AutoCAD asks if you really want to repeat the selection set that many times. If an array gets too big, you can stop it by pressing Ctrl-C, and then reverse the array by using UNDO.

*ARRAY is useful, even if you want to make only one row or column of entities. This command is quicker than COPY Multiple.*

In the following exercise, make a set of logo arcs next to the widget layout text at the bottom left area of your drawing. This is the single-row array of arcs shown in the next example.

## Making a Single-Column Array

```
Command: ARRAY ↵

Select objects: Pick the logo arc

Rectangular or Polar array (R/P)
<R>: Press Enter

Number of rows (--) <1>: Press Enter    Accepts the default value of one row

Number of columns (¦¦¦) <1>: 6 ↵       Specifies six columns

Distance between columns (¦¦¦):        Draws the array (see fig. 8.17)
0.05 ↵
```

**Figure 8.17:**
Detail of the logo after the array.

# Using Polar Arrays

In *polar arrays,* you place copies of the entities in the selection set around the circumference of an imaginary circle or arc. Polar arrays are useful for creating mechanical parts, such as gear teeth or bolt patterns. Figures 8.18 and 8.19 show examples of regular and rotated circular arrays.

When you form a polar array, you specify the number of items you want in the array, the angle you want to fill, and whether or not you want the items rotated. One *item* is one copy of the selection set to be arrayed. When you count your items, remember to include the original. You can array around a full circle or part of a circle. If you array around part of a circle, you need one more item than the total arc angle, divided by the incremental angle. If, for example, you are arraying 90 degrees, and you want the items at 30-degree increments, you need $90/30 + 1 = 4$ items.

**Figure 8.18:**

A rotated polar array.

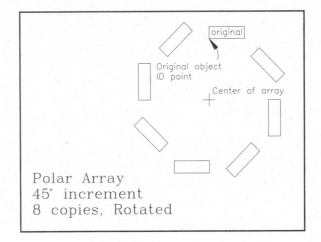

**Figure 8.19:**

A nonrotated polar array.

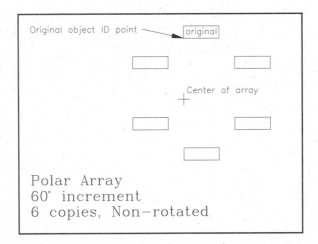

The following exercise shows how to array the contact around 270 degrees of a circle. You need seven items (270/45 + 1 = 7). The contact is the small circle to the left of the switch (large circle) on the right side of the widget. It does not matter whether you rotate the contact as it is copied because you are arraying circles.

## Using Polar Array on Switch Contacts

Command: *Select the small circle to the left of the switch as shown by ①*

Command: *Choose* **C**onstruct, *then* **A**rray

```
_array 1 found
```

Rectangular or Polar array (R/P):          Specifies a polar array
*Enter* **P** *or choose* Polar *from the*
*screen menu*

Center point of array: *From the*
*toolbox, choose* CENTER

center of *Pick any point on the*          Specifies the center of the array
*large circle*

Number of items: **7** ↵

Angle to fill (+=ccw, -=cw)
<360>: **270** ↵

Rotate objects as they are
copied? <Y> *Press Enter*

Figure 8.20 shows a zoomed view of this array.

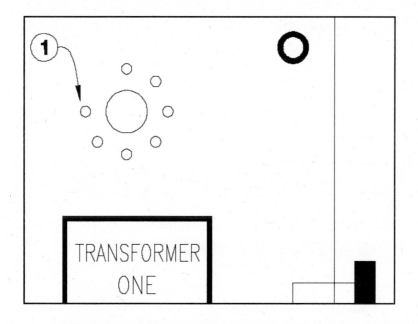

**Figure 8.20:**

Detail view of the switch after the array.

*If you array a line (using a polar array) twice around its midpoint or four times around its endpoint, you create a cross. A large number of lines creates a sunburst.*

If an array can rotate entities, AutoCAD also must be able to rotate individual entities.

# Turning Entities by Using the ROTATE Command

The ROTATE command enables you to turn existing entities at precise angles. RO-TATE, like MOVE, requires you to specify a first point as a base point. This rotation base point does not need to be on the object that you are rotating—you can put it anywhere and AutoCAD turns your selected entities relative to the base point. Never-theless, be careful when you use ROTATE; it is easy to become confused with rotation base points (such as bad drag handles) that are not on the entities you intend to rotate. After you specify the base point, give a rotation angle. Negative angles produce clock-wise rotation; positive angles produce counterclockwise rotation (with the default direction setting in units).

An alternate way to specify an angle is to use a reference angle. You can change the angle of an entity by giving AutoCAD a reference angle that should be set equal to the new angle. You can say, for example, "Put a handle on 237 degrees and turn it to 165." This is often easier than calculating the difference (72 degrees clockwise) and entering that number at the prompt. You need not even know the actual angles; you can pick points to indicate angles. To align with existing objects, use object snaps when picking the points of the angle(s).

Try two rotations in the next two exercises. First, use ROTATE to reposition the jumper. The *jumper* is the rectangular object with three ellipses in it, located just above the transformer. Rotate the jumper into position vertically at the left of the transformer.

*In the following exercise, and throughout much of the rest of the book, exercises simply tell you what to select and omit the full set of prompts and responses.*

## Using the ROTATE Command

Command: *From the toolbox, choose*     Begins the ROTATE command
ROTATE

Command: rotate

Select objects: *Select the jumper with a window from* ① *(see fig. 8.21) to* ②

Base point: **6.45,4.3** ↵

<Rotation angle>/Reference: **-90** ↵     Specifies the rotation angle

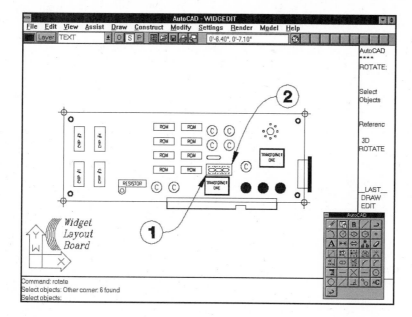

**Figure 8.21:**

Selecting the jumper with a window.

Figure 8.22 shows the base point and the rotation the jumper has been put through.

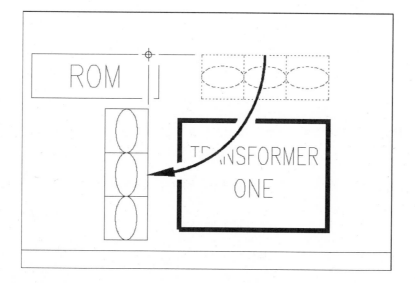

**Figure 8.22:**

Detail of the jumper's rotation.

Next, you combine a Copy operation and a Rotate operation to place another mounting tab and nut above the resistor. This Copy and Rotate technique is an efficient trick. You can accomplish the task by first using the COPY command, then the ROTATE command, but it is easier to use the Copy option of Rotate Grip mode—you then only have to perform one operation, instead of two.

## Using the Copy and Rotate Technique

| | |
|---|---|
| Command: *Choose* **V**iew, S**e**t View, *and* **N**amed View | Opens the View Control dialog box |
| *Choose* RESISTOR, *then* **R**estore, *then* OK | Restores the RESISTOR view |
| First, select the entities. | |
| Command: *Select the tab and nut with a window from* ① *(see fig. 8.23) to* ② | |
| Command: *Pick any one of the grips* | Enters stretch mode |
| \*\* STRETCH \*\*<br><Stretch to point>/Base point/Copy/<br>Undo/eXit: **RO** ↵ | Switches to rotate mode |
| \*\* ROTATE \*\*<br><Rotation angle>/Base point/Copy/<br>Undo/Reference/eXit: **C** ↵ | Specifies the Copy option |
| \*\* ROTATE (multiple) \*\*<br><Rotation angle>/Base point/Copy/<br>Undo/Reference/eXit: **B** ↵ | Specifies the Base point option |
| Base point: *Pick point 4.50,3.80* | |
| <Rotation angle>/Base point/Copy/<br>Undo/Reference/eXit: *Pick at polar point 0.50<180* | Copies the entities |
| <Rotation angle>/Base point/Copy/<br>Undo/Reference/eXit: *Press Ctrl-C* | Cancels rotate Grip mode |

After you complete this exercise, your drawing should look like figure 8.24.

*The preceding exercise shows how handy Copy and Rotate can be for avoiding redrawing entities in new positions. Also, you could have chosen any of the options from the screen menu instead of typing them.*

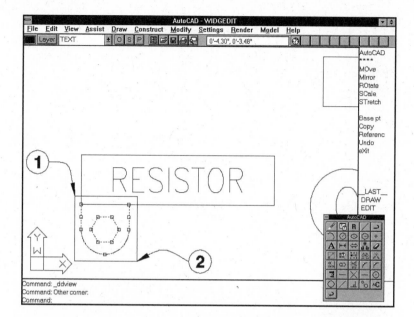

**Figure 8.23:**

Selecting a resistor tab and nut with window.

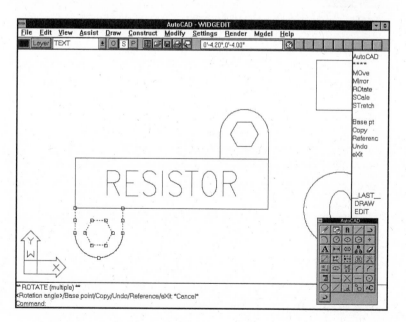

**Figure 8.24:**

A nut after you use the Copy and Rotate options.

# Copying through the Looking Glass

The MIRROR command creates a mirrored copy of objects. You can mirror the contents of a selection set at any angle. MIRROR prompts you to identify a selection set; it then initiates a mirror operation. AutoCAD prompts you for the beginning and endpoint of a mirror line. The line can be in any direction. If you want a perfect 180-degree flip, use Ortho to help you create an orthogonal mirror line. If you want mirroring at a precise angle, use relative polar coordinates (@8<60, for example) or use a rotated snap or UCS.

Finally, AutoCAD asks if you want to keep the original entities in place or to delete them. Think of this as copying or moving the contents of the selection set through the mirror.

If you have text in your selection set (as the example does), you need to consider whether you want to pass the text through the mirror unchanged or mirrored. If you do not want text mirrored, set the MIRRTEXT system variable to 0, enabling graphics, but not text, to be inverted.

Mirror the resistor you have been working on, keeping the original. Set the MIRRTEXT system variable to 0 so that text is not mirrored.

---

## Using MIRROR To Mirror the Resistor

Command: **MIRRTEXT** ↵

New value for MIRRTEXT <1>: **0** ↵      Turns off MIRRTEXT

Zoom Previous.

Command: *From the toolbox,*      Starts the MIRROR command
*choose* MIRROR

Command: mirror

Select objects: *Select the resistor with
a window from 4.00,3.40 to 5.00,4.20*

First point of mirror line: *Pick
5.00,4.20*

Second point: *Turn on ortho,*      Specifies the mirror line
*then pick any point to the left*

Delete old objects? <N> *Press Enter*      Mirrors the resistor and retains the original

Save and continue or end and take a break.

---

Figure 8.25 shows a zoomed view of the mirrored resistor and the location of the mirror line.

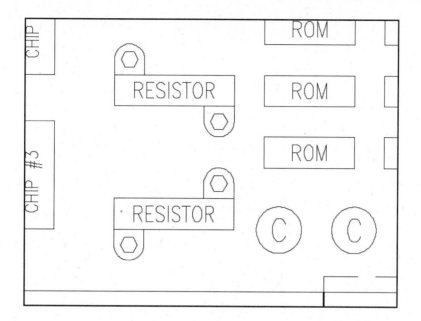

**Figure 8.25:**
Detail of the
resistor after
being mirrored.

So far, the editing commands that you have worked with are variations on a theme—moving or copying single entities, or making multiple copies of entities. The next group of editing commands involves deleting portions of entities, or—in the case of ERASE—deleting entire entities.

# Deleting and Restoring by Using ERASE and OOPS

Like a hammer, the ERASE command can be a constructive tool. But, like a hammer, you must watch how you use it. The ERASE command has been the scourge of many drawing files.

The following exercise uses ERASE and its complement, the OOPS command. OOPS is prominently displayed on the ERASE screen menu. OOPS uses no prompts; it just restores whatever was last obliterated with ERASE.

In the steps that follow, get rid of the original resistor by using ERASE. You can reload your WIDGEDIT drawing or continue from the preceding exercise. In either case, your drawing now should resemble figure 8.26.

**Figure 8.26:**

The layout board before erasing.

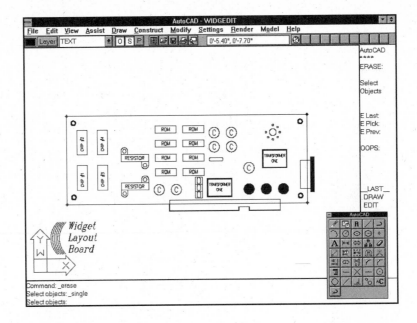

## Using ERASE

Command: *Press and drag a window to select the top resistor* — Selects the resistor

Command: *From the toolbox, choose* ERASE — Issues the ERASE command

Command: `_erase 3 found` — Deletes the resistor immediately (see fig. 8.27), without repeating the `Select objects:` prompt

Use REDRAW to clear any debris from the screen.

When you use the **E**rase option on the **M**odify pull-down menu, the ERASE command uses the Auto and SIngle object selection modes to act immediately on the selection. If you enter **ERASE** at the Command: prompt or use the toolbox or screen menu, ERASE uses normal object selection.

Every time you execute an erase, AutoCAD keeps a copy of what you erased, in case you want to bring it back into the file by using OOPS. Only the most recent erasure is kept ready. Try OOPS now to restore your resistor.

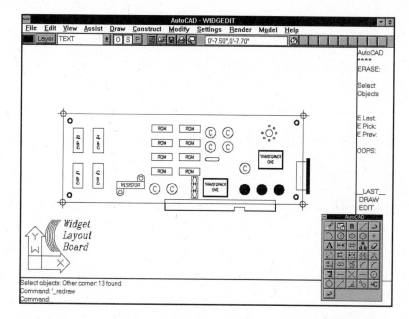

---

## Using OOPS To Restore an Erased Object

Command: *From the screen menu,*          Restores the mirrored resistor
*choose* OOPS

---

OOPS enables you to recover from the unthinkable. After you have mistakenly deleted an entity from your drawing, you can recover the last deletion (under most circumstances) by using OOPS, even if you have used other commands since then. However, the OOPS command does not recover an entity after you plot or end and then resume a drawing.

# Using BREAK To Cut Objects

BREAK cuts existing objects in two or erases portions of objects. Use any of the standard selection-set techniques to let AutoCAD know which entity you want to break. The safest way to select the object you want is by picking it. By default, AutoCAD uses the pick point as the start of the break and prompts you for the second point. If you use Crossing, Window, or Previous, the first entity in the oct-tree is selected and you are prompted for the first point (the start of the break) and second point (the end of the break). If you pick the same first point again or choose **M**odify, **B**reak and use the At Selected **P**oint option, AutoCAD cuts your object in two at the selected point, but does not delete any of it.

The process of picking does not work as well when breaking between intersections because AutoCAD may select the wrong entity. You can pick the object to be broken at another point, and then respecify the first break point. To do this, enter an **F** at the Enter second point (or F for first point): prompt, and AutoCAD reprompts you for the first point.

The following exercise breaks out the line at the port on the right side of the widget.

## Using BREAK To Break a Line

| | |
|---|---|
| `Command:` *Choose* **M**odify, *then* **B**reak, *then* Select Object, **T**wo Points | Begins the BREAK command |
| `Command: _break Select object:` *Pick at ① (see fig. 8.28)* | Specifies what to break and the default first break point |
| `Enter second point (or F for first point): F` | Issues the First option |
| `Enter first point:` *From the toolbox, choose* INTERSECTION, *then pick at ②* | Specifies the first break point |
| `Enter second point:` *From the toolbox, choose* INTERSECTION, *then pick at ③* | Locates the break's endpoint and completes the break (see fig. 8.29) |

**Figure 8.28:**

The board end before breaking.

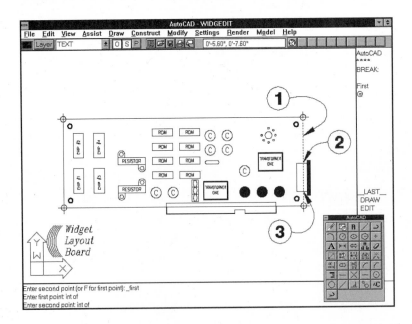

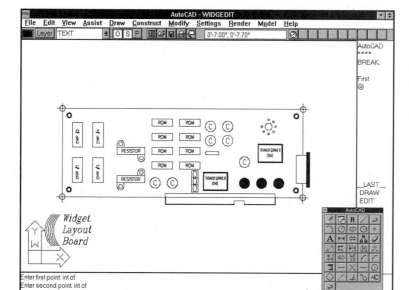

**Figure 8.29:**
The board after
breaking the end.

BREAK works on lines, arcs, circles, traces, and polylines (including polygons and donuts). Take care to select the first and second points in counterclockwise order when breaking circles and arcs. Closed polylines need a little experimentation. BREAK's effects depend on the location of the polyline's first vertex. The break cannot extend across this vertex. If a point is off the entity, it acts as if you used object snap NEArest. If one point is off the end of an arc, line, trace, or open polyline, that end is cut off instead of breaking the entity in two.

# Rounding Edges Using the FILLET Command

A *fillet* is a tangent arc swung between two lines to create a round corner. The FILLET command is simple; AutoCAD asks you to identify the two lines that you want joined. You identify the lines by picking them. AutoCAD then shortens or extends the lines and creates a new arc for the fillet corner.

You can specify the radius of the arc to create the fillet corner. The default radius is 0. The fillet radius you set becomes the new default. The most common use for FILLET is to round corners, but a fillet with a zero radius (the original default) is good for cleaning up underlapping or overlapping lines at corners. FILLET with a zero radius creates a corner but does not create a new entity (see fig. 8.30). You pick the portions of the line that you want retained, and AutoCAD trims the other ends.

FILLET works on any combination of two arcs, circles, and non-parallel lines; or on a single polyline. You can select lines or a polyline by using Window, Last, or Crossing, but the results may be unpredictable. Selection by picking is safer and is required for arcs or circles. Arcs and circles have more than one possible fillet and are filleted closest to the pick points.

Try filleting the four corners of the layout board. First, set a default fillet radius with the Radius option, and then fillet the board.

---

### Using FILLET To Round Corners

`Command:` *From the toolbox, choose* Fillet          Begins the FILLET command

`fillet Polyline/Radius/<Select`
`first object>:` *From the screen menu,*
*choose* radius

`Enter Fillet radius <0'-0.00>:.25` ↵          Sets the radius and repeats the FILLET command

`_FILLET Polyline/Radius/`
`<Select first object>:` *Pick one line at*
*a corner of the widget board*

`Select second object:` *Pick the other*          Builds a fillet arc between the selected lines
*line at the same corner*

`Command:` *Press Enter*          Repeats the FILLET command

Fillet each of the three remaining corners.

`Command:` *From the toolbox, choose*
REDRAW

Your board's corner should resemble the example shown in figure 8.31.

---

**Figure 8.30:**

Examples of
fillets.

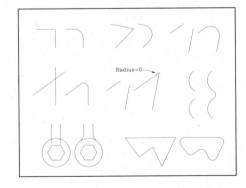

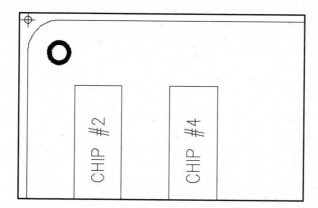

**Figure 8.31:**

Detail of a filleted corner.

*When fillets have the same radius arc (as in the preceding exercise), you can speed up the edit by preceding FILLET with the Multiple command to make multiple fillets.*

AutoCAD offers two ways to fillet polylines: one vertex or all vertices. If you select the polyline by Window, Crossing, or Last, the most recent vertex within the selection set is filleted. If you pick two points on adjacent segments, the vertex between those segments is filleted. If you enter a **P** at the first fillet prompt, you are prompted to select a polyline and all of its vertices are filleted. Try this technique in the following exercise by using the CHAMFER command, which works much like the FILLET command.

# Applying the CHAMFER Command

A *chamfer* is a beveled edge. CHAMFER works only on two lines or a single polyline. To get the chamfer, you supply a chamfer distance along each line that you want to join, rather than an arc radius. The distance that you supply is the cut-back distance from the intersection of the lines (see fig. 8.32).

Try two sets of chamfers. First, chamfer all four corners of the second transformer polyline with 45-degree chamfers (equal distances). Then, chamfer two corners on the right side port.

---

## Using CHAMFER on the Layout Board

| | |
|---|---|
| Command: *From the toolbox,* *choose* CHAMFER | Begins the CHAMFER command |
| chamfer Polyline/Distances/ <Select first line>: **D** ↵ | Specifies the Distances option |

*continues*

| | |
|---|---|
| `Enter first chamfer distance`<br>`<0'-0.0">:` *.05 ↵* | Resets the first distance |
| `Enter second chamfer distance`<br>`<0'-0.05">:` *Press Enter* | Accepts the new first distance as the default second distance |
| `Command:` *Press Enter* | Repeats CHAMFER |
| `Polyline/Distances/<Select first`<br>`line>:` *Enter* **P** *or from the screen menu,*<br>*choose* polyline | |
| `Select 2D polyline:` *Select the*<br>*transformer polyline on the right* | Chamfers all four vertices in one pick |
| `4 lines were chamfered` | |
| `Command:` *Press Enter* | Repeats CHAMFER |
| `Chamfer Polyline/Distances/`<br>`<Select first line>:` *From the screen*<br>*menu, choose* distance | Enters the Distance option and makes the chamfer command repeat later |
| `Enter first chamfer distance`<br>`<0'-0.05">:` *.1 ↵* | Resets the first distance distance |
| `Enter second chamfer distance`<br>`<0'-0.10">:` *Press Enter* | Accepts the new first distance as the default second distance |
| `_CHAMFER Polyline/Distances/`<br>`<Select first line>:` *Select the top*<br>*horizontal port line* | CHAMFER repeats |
| `Select second line:` *Select the vertical*<br>*port line* | |
| `Command:` *Press Enter* | Repeats CHAMFER |
| `Chamfer Polyline/Distances/ <Select`<br>`first line>:` *Select the bottom horizontal*<br>*port line* | |
| `Select second line:` *Select the vertical*<br>*port line* | |

As you can see from the exercise, it is easy to chamfer polylines. All four corners of the transformer were modified at the same time (see fig. 8.33).

The following sections discuss the CHANGE and CHPROP commands, which modify existing entities.

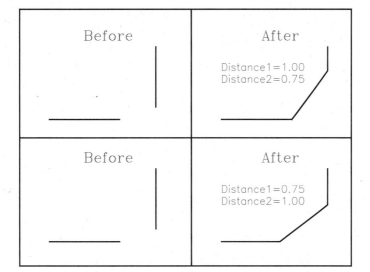

**Figure 8.32:**
Examples of chamfered line intersections.

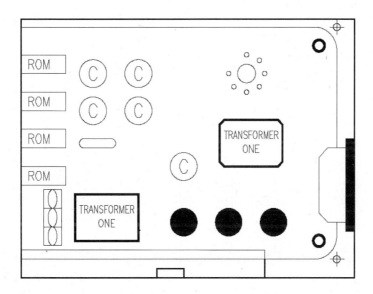

**Figure 8.33:**
Detail of a transformer and the port after chamfering.

# Modifying Entities by Using the CHANGE Command

The CHANGE command can selectively edit one or more parameters that give a drawing entity its identity, location, and appearance in the drawing file. Use CHANGE in 2D drawings to modify entity points, text, or attribute definitions (see Chapter 16); and use a second command, CHPROP (discussed in the next section), to modify appearances. CHPROP works in both 2D and 3D.

When you select objects to change, AutoCAD prompts you for the points and parameters that are changeable for the entities that you select. These points and parameters vary with the type of entity.

The CHANGE command affects different entities in the following ways:

- **Lines.** Change point, which is the default for the change command, changes the endpoint of a line. If several lines are selected, their nearest endpoints converge at the picked change point. If Ortho is on, lines are forced orthogonal to the relevant coordinate of the picked change point, instead of converging on it.

- **Circles.** Change point alters the circumference of an existing circle, forcing it to pass through the change point, while keeping the same center point.

- **Text (and attribute definitions).** Change point alters the location, rotation angle, height, style, and text string. CHANGE acts as a second chance to reset your text parameters.

- **Blocks.** CHANGE enables you to alter the insertion point or rotation angle. (See Chapter 11.)

If you select several different entities, even different types, CHANGE ignores any change point you pick; it instead cycles through the entities in the order selected, prompting for the appropriate changes.

*Entities on a locked layer are not altered by the editing commands. Locked layers are a good way to protect certain entities and maintain a well-organized drawing.*

First, use CHANGE to change the text of the second transformer from "ONE" to "TWO." Then, change the diameter of the switch circle on the right side of the board. Figure 8.34 shows the board before these changes are made.

## Using CHANGE To Modify the Layout Board

`Command:` *From the toolbox, choose*
CHANGE

`Command: change`

`Select objects:` *Select the text string*
ONE *in the transformer on the right*

```
Properties/<Change point>: Press
Enter
```

```
Enter text insertion point: Press        Keeps the same point
Enter
```

```
Text style: STANDARD                      Displays current and prompts for new style
New style or RETURN for no change:
Press Enter
```

```
New height <0'-0.08">: Press Enter        Keeps the same height
```

```
New rotation angle <0.00>: Press Enter    Keeps the same angle
```

```
New text <ONE>: TWO ⏎                      Changes ONE to TWO
```

Now, change the diameter of the switch.

```
Command: Press Enter                      Repeats the command
```

```
Select objects: Select the center
switch circle inside the array
```

```
Properties/<Change point>: Pick           Specifies a new circumference point and changes
point 8.20,5.30                            the circle
```

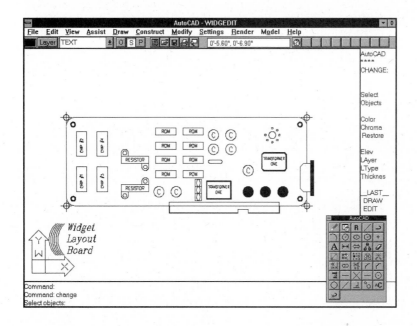

**Figure 8.34:**

The right transformer text and switch circle before changes.

Figure 8.35 shows a zoomed view of the changed switch and transformer.

**Figure 8.35:**

Detail of the switch and transformer after changes.

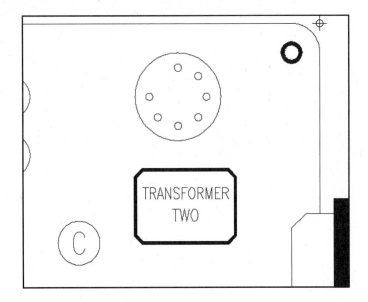

You also can use CHANGE to modify the properties of entities. Using CHANGE to modify properties in 2D drawings works fine, but it may not always work in 3D drawings. For 3D, use the CHPROP command, which always works.

*When you redefine an existing text style by using STYLE, only changes to the font and vertical orientation affect existing text. You can use the CHANGE command to force existing text to reflect modifications to width, height, obliquing angle, and so on. If you enter a style name at the new style prompt, AutoCAD updates all text parameters, even if the style name entered is the same as the currently defined style. Press Enter to leave all parameters unchanged.*

# Using CHPROP To Change Properties

CHPROP changes properties in a 2D or 3D drawing. So far, you have changed the location, size, or shape of entities already in place. In the next section, you learn how to change their properties.

As discussed in Chapter 3, all entities have properties that you can edit. These properties are the following:

- Color
- Layer
- Linetype
- Thickness

When you created the lines in your widget drawing, you gave them a color and linetype. You created the individual widget parts on the layer PARTS with both entity color and linetype BYLAYER. (PARTS has a cyan [4] color default and a continuous linetype default.) When you created the parts, these entities picked up their characteristics from the layer defaults. While you were editing these lines, they retained their BYLAYER color and linetype. At this point, the widget's entities have 0 elevation and thickness. These properties apply to 3D drawings. (You learn about them in Part Five, which covers 3D drawing and editing.)

The CHPROP command is the best way to change the properties of entities that you have already drawn. In the first exercise, you use CHPROP to change the interior connector line's layer property to the HIDDEN layer. The object-selection prompts are abbreviated in this exercise and in most of the remaining exercises. After you select the objects, you see a prompt for the property that you want to change.

## Using CHPROP To Change Layers

Command: *Select the connector lines using a window*

Command: *From the screen menu, choose* EDIT, *then* CHPROP:

Command: _CHPROP 10 found

Change what property (Color/LAyer/    Specifies the Layer property
LType/Thickness) ? **LA** ↵

New layer <BOARD>: **HIDDEN** ↵    Specifies HIDDEN, and then reprompts for
    other properties

Change what property (Color/LAyer/    Completes the changes (see fig. 8.36)
LType/Thickness) ? *Press Enter*

Your drawing should show red, hidden connector lines (see fig. 8.36). The linetype and color properties are still BYLAYER.

Entity color and linetype properties can be independent of layer. In fact, an entity can have any color or linetype. However, setting a color or linetype different from those of an objects layer can cause serious editing difficulties when things start changing.

**Figure 8.36:**

The connector
after the change.

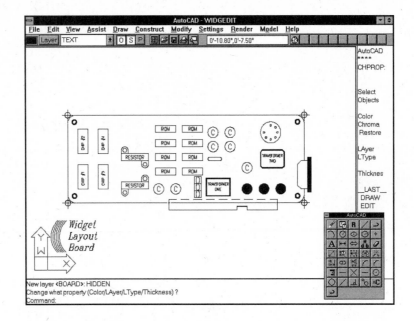

## Using the Change Properties Dialog Box

The Change Properties dialog box is a convenient alternative to the CHPROP command (see fig. 8.37). You can display it by entering **DDCHPROP** or by choosing Change, and then Properties from the Modify pull-down menu. The four existing properties are displayed with child dialog boxes for selecting new properties instead of typing them. Remember that typing the first letter of a name takes you to that alphabetic point in a list, which is useful in a drawing with a large number of layers.

Change the entity color of the three donuts (the solid dots) by using the DDCHPROP dialog box. Then, take one last look at your widget layout drawing with all its edits.

### Using DDCHPROP To Change the Color of Donuts

Continue from the preceding exercise.

| | |
|---|---|
| `Command:` *Choose* **M**odify, *then* **C**hange, *then* **P**roperties | Starts the DDCHPROP command |
| `Select objects:` *Select the three solid dots* | Displays the Change Properties dialog box |
| *Choose* **C**olor | Displays the Select Color dialog box |
| `New color <BYLAYER>:` *Click on the magenta box, then choose* OK | Selects magenta and returns to the Change Properties dialog box |

*Choose* OK                              Closes dialog box and executes change

Zoom All, then save the drawing.

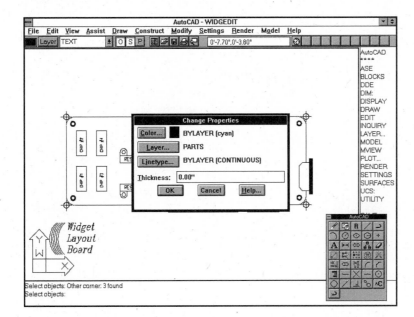

**Figure 8.37:**

The Change
Properties
dialog box.

Now the donuts are magenta, overriding the cyan PARTS layer default.

CHPROP provides an easy method for changing entity properties. For organized
controlled drawings, it is usually best to work with color and linetype by layer settings.
Instead of changing color and linetype properties, try expanding and redefining the
layers you set up in your drawings.

Another dialog box is available, which enables changing of properties and entity
geometry, such as points and radii. The DDMODIFY command first prompts for an
entity to be selected, shows all of its properties and coordinate data, and enables the
entity to be changed. This dialog box, almost a combination of the CHANGE and
CHPROP commands, can be displayed by choosing **E**ntity from the **M**odify pull-down
menu. Unlike CHANGE, CHPROP, and DDCHPROP, which can modify several
entities at one time, DDMODIFY only modifies a single entity.

As promised, you now have a full color widget layout board (see fig. 8.38). Save this
drawing; you can use it later when you experiment with plotting in Part Three.

**Figure 8.38:**

The completed WIDGEDIT drawing.

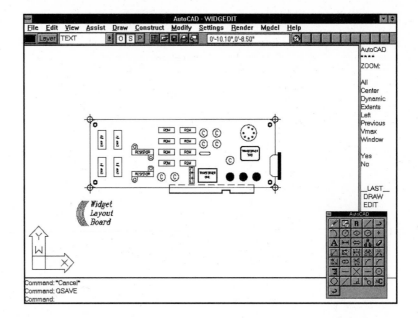

*You can now delete the WIDGET, PSPLOT, MVPLOT, and VPLAYER drawings; you no longer need them.*

# Summary

You can see how important editing is in constructing a drawing. In the beginning of the chapter on graphic entities, you learned that drawings are dynamic. With a first course in editing under your belt, you can see just how dynamic a drawing can be.

Are you ready for the next engineering change order? Use the following Editor's Guide to Editing to be prepared:

- Plan ahead for editing. When you first set up a drawing, think about how you are going to use your multiple layers. If you have everything on one layer, editing can be complicated. Think about repetitive features and building blocks. Draw it once, copy it forever. Start by defining your basic components and building your drawing up from there.

- Use all of the editing commands. Try to use grips when possible to simplify editing. Use snap, ortho, and object snaps to set up your MOVE and COPY displacements. MIRROR and ARRAY can help you complete a repetitive drawing in a hurry. Be careful with ERASE. To avoid disasters, you can always use OOPS and UNDO.

- Learn to use all of the object-selection options, including using the Remove option and using the Shift key with object selection. All selection-set options have their roles. Last and Previous can be used when you realize that AutoCAD did what you said, not what you meant. The object-picking method is best for detail work, especially with object snap. If you want to edit most of the entities at once, use the All option, then remove the entities you did not want to include.

- Window is powerful, but it does not do it all. Remember, what you see in the window is what goes into the selection set. You can use Crossing as a knife to slice out a selection set. BOX and SIngle are best for menu macros, as you can see when you get to customization. The use of AUto is a good habit. You can use it as a window, a crossing, or just to select an object. The WPOLY window is nice when a rectangular window cannot enclose the entities. Previous saves time in repetitive editing. Do not forget, a U undoes the last object selection operation.

- Think ahead about individual edits. Keep your field of view small and your concentration level high. Do not get caught setting up the base point of a displacement, only to find that the second point is not in the viewport. (If that happens, use a transparent pan or dynamic zoom, and try again.) Do not underestimate the power of the CHANGE command—it is an effective tool. Changing an endpoint is often easier than erasing and then adding a new line segment. You can almost always change text style, height, or rotation more easily than you can erase and replace it. Use CHPROP when you need to change the layer, color, linetype, and thickness properties of existing entities. When you are unsure of the change options, try DDCHPROP or DDMODIFY for a more graphic interface.

- Watch the current layer name on the status line. Note the edit prompts on the prompt line; it is easy to start creating a selection-set window while the prompt line is waiting for you to enter **W** to initiate the window selection. Change from the text screen to the graphics screen and back again, to see AutoCAD's status.

So far, you have looked at some of AutoCAD's basic editing commands. The next chapter moves on to more advanced editing commands that you use with electronic drafting techniques to get more productivity from editing your drawings.

# Advanced 2D AutoCAD Drafting

*Introduction*

*Advanced Editing*

*Drawing Construction Techniques*

*Grouping Entities into Blocks and Xrefs*

*Construction Techniques with Blocks and Xrefs*

*Sheet Composition, Scaling, and Plotting*

*Drawing Enhancements and Inquiry*

*Dimensioning*

# PART 3

# Introduction

In previous chapters, you learned to use AutoCAD's many basic drawing features to create and edit various types of drawings. You also learned how to control the graphics display and how to use the coordinate system and electronic drawing aids to draw entities accurately.

Part Three of *Inside AutoCAD Release 12 for Windows* introduces you to the program's new and more advanced features. The following seven chapters show you how to use these features in the most productive ways. The chapters cover Release 12's new advanced commands and show you how to use the AutoCAD dimensioning and plotting tools to finish your drawings.

## How Part Three Is Organized

Part Three contains seven chapters, which cover the following four topics:

- Advanced drawing and editing commands
- Grouping entities together to create symbols and insertable drawing files (such as overlays, backgrounds, and title blocks)
- Preparing and printing your drawing
- Basic dimensioning of drawings

When you finish Part Three, you will be able to produce and plot nearly any type of 2D drawing.

# Advanced Drawing and Editing

Chapter 9 covers AutoCAD's more advanced editing commands, which enable you to extend, stretch, trim, scale, and offset objects. The chapter also shows you how to edit polylines to create continuous drawing lines. These advanced editing techniques are extremely productive in 2D drafting, and they are essential in the 3D environment.

All of this book's drawing and editing chapters offer tips and tricks, but Chapter 10 is a "pure techniques" chapter. It shows you how to combine construction lines, electronic point filters, and editing commands to build accurate drawings quickly. Chapter 10 also teaches you how to place editing marks and controls in your editing sequences, so that you can try different edits without wasting time. Chapter 10 also teaches you how to take maximum advantage of AutoCAD's undo functions.

As you apply AutoCAD's drawing and editing commands to your drawings, you may begin to recognize patterns in your own command usage. The trick for improving productivity is to learn the drawing and editing commands that enable you to build fast, accurate drawings, and then to incorporate these editing sequences and techniques into your daily AutoCAD work. If you are looking for advanced editing techniques, you can learn them by working through chapters 9 and 10.

# Blocks (Symbols) and Reference Files

AutoCAD enables you to save groupings of entities as symbols, which AutoCAD calls *blocks*. You can save drawing time and file space by learning how to use blocks to insert repetitive objects in your drawings. Chapter 11 shows you how to use blocks and how to update your drawings quickly and easily by redefining the blocks. This chapter also introduces you to the basics of external reference files (xrefs). A drawing that contains an *xref* refers to another drawing file for information contained in the other file. Reference files coordinate the cooperative editing of a master drawing by enabling several people to work on component parts of it simultaneously.

Chapter 12 continues with block usage by teaching you construction techniques with blocks and xrefs. The exercises in this chapter involve developing a site plan—called "Autotown"—with houses, trees, and cars. The chapter shows how fast you can develop a drawing by using existing geometry, and how to use Windows' drag-and-drop feature to insert one drawing into another.

# Plotting, Presentation, and Dimensioning

Chapter 13 teaches you a variety of methods for successfully plotting output. You learn how and when to use paper space to compose drawings and to make multiple-view plotting a cinch. You also discover dozens of plotting tips and take advantage of Windows' multitasking capabilities to plot one drawing while you work on another.

Chapter 14 contains techniques for hatching, linetypes, and free-hand sketching for dressing up finished drawings. This chapter concludes with a discussion of AutoCAD's inquiry commands and Region Modeler, which give you information about what you are drawing, including information such as center-of-gravity.

Chapter 15 guides you through the basics of AutoCAD's dimensioning commands and settings. (Advanced dimensioning is discussed in Chapter 17.)

# CHAPTER 9

# Advanced Editing

To take advantage of AutoCAD's power, you need to combine AutoCAD's editing commands with CAD drafting techniques. Although the editing commands you learned in the last chapter help speed up your drafting, the editing commands and techniques discussed in this chapter enable you to change the way you create your drawings. You can use advanced editing commands, such as EXTEND, STRETCH, TRIM, and OFFSET for more than copying and moving entities. These commands build on AutoCAD's geometrical recognition of the entities in your drawing. By combining these commands with construction techniques, such as setting up construction lines, parallel rules, and construction layers, you can make a rough draft of a drawing quickly, and then finish it perfectly.

Besides construction techniques, this chapter shows you how to use polylines and PEDIT to create continuous two-dimensional lines. Continuous polylines are important for AutoCAD's hatch patterns and 3D, and they provide continuity when you form three-dimensional faces and meshes. If your two-dimensional drawing has breaks in its line profile, you cannot form a complete three-dimensional surface. Figure 9.1 shows a 3D mesh formed from a continuous polyline profile.

Before you work with 3D drawings, you must master basic 2D skills, such as drawing polylines and using PEDIT to modify polylines and convert or join existing entities into polylines. The exercises in this chapter show you how to use PEDIT and other advanced editing commands to combine entity creation and CAD construction techniques into a single drawing process.

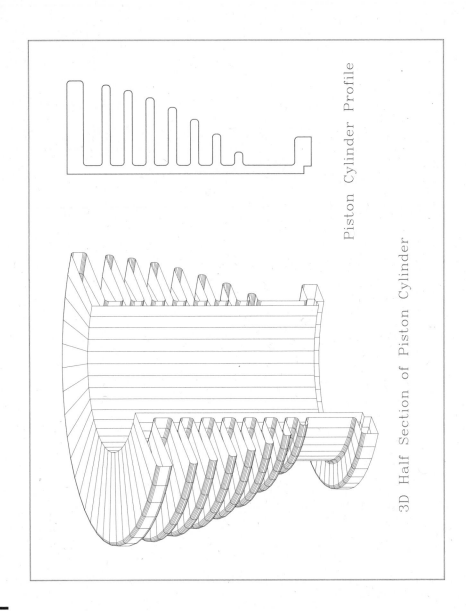

Piston Cylinder Profile

3D Half Section of Piston Cylinder

**Figure 9.1:**

3D piston
cylinder and
profile.

The editing commands covered in this chapter's exercises include EXTEND, OFFSET, SCALE, STRETCH, TRIM, and PEDIT. The trick to using these advanced editing commands is to plan ahead. The operations of commands such as EXTEND, STRETCH, and TRIM can involve a number of entities. These commands require some setup so you must think ahead to the way you are going to use them. PEDIT, for example, requires continuity to join lines and arcs.

# Setting Up the Cylinder Drawing

The drawing that you create in this chapter's exercises is the piston cylinder profile (see fig. 9.2). The full cylinder is approximately 10 by 14.60 inches.

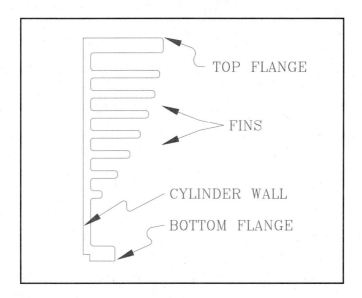

**Figure 9.2:**

The cylinder profile target drawing.

The following sample calculations estimate a drawing scale factor and set a sheet size:

```
Finned Piston Cylinder Wall 14.60" x 10.00"
Plot sheet size      11" x 8 1/2"
Test 1/2" = 1" scale is a scale factor of 2.
11" x 2 = 22" and 8 1/2" x 2 = 17" 22" x 17" limits
```

In the steps that follow, create a new drawing called CYLINDER. Use the default decimal units (each unit represents one inch). If you dimension this drawing, you can use the AutoCAD dimensioning feature to add inch marks automatically. Set your limits at 22x17. In the first exercise, you begin your CYLINDER drawing by setting it equal to the IAWCYLIN.DWG file from the IAW DISK. Table 9.1 shows the drawing's initial settings.

## Table 9.1
### Cylinder Drawing Settings

| COORDS | GRID | SNAP | ORTHO |
|--------|------|------|-------|
| On | 1 | 0.1 | ON |
| **UNITS** | Default decimal units, 2 digits to right of decimal point, default all other settings. | | |
| **LIMITS** | 0,0 to 22,17 | | |
| **ZOOM** | Zoom All | | |

| Layer Name | State | Color | Linetype |
|------------|-------|-------|----------|
| 0 | On | 7 (White) | CONTINUOUS |
| 2D | On/Current | 1 (Red) | CONTINUOUS |
| 3D | On | 3 (Green) | CONTINUOUS |

If you want to practice individual editing commands as you work through the chapter, create a layer named SCRATCH. Create some entities on this layer, try out some editing variations, then freeze your SCRATCH layer and pick up again with the exercise sequences.

# Using Lines and Polylines To Rough-In a Drawing

Start to create the cylinder by roughing-in the section profile of the cylinder in the following exercise. First, use a polyline to draw the top, side, and bottom of the cylinder. Then draw one line and array it to form the construction lines for what later becomes the cylinder fins. Finally, draw an arc on the right side as a construction line to help form the ends of the fins. Your current layer is 2D.

## Using PLINE, LINE, and ARC To Rough-In the Cylinder Wall

Command: *Choose* **F**ile, *then* **N**ew, *enter* **CYLINDER=IAWCYLIN** *and choose* OK — Begins drawing with settings shown in table 9.1

Command: *From the toolbox, choose* POLYLINE — Issues the PLINE command

Command: pline

From point: *Pick point 17,12*

Current line-width is **0.00**

Arc/Close/Halfwidth/Length/Undo/
Width/<Endpoint of line>: **@3<180** ↵

Arc/Close/Halfwidth/Length/Undo/
Width/<Endpoint of line>: **@8<270** ↵

Arc/Close/Halfwidth/Length/Undo/
Width/<Endpoint of line>: **@1<0** ↵

Arc/Close/Halfwidth/Length/Undo/
Width/<Endpoint of line>: *Press Enter*

| | |
|---|---|
| Command: *From the toolbox, choose* LINE *and draw a line from 14.00,11.00 to @1<0* | Issues the LINE command and draws the line |
| Command: *Select the line you just drew, then choose* **C**onstruct, *and* **A**rray | Selects the line and starts the ARRAY command |
| Command: _array 1 found | Finds the preselected line |
| Rectangular or Polar array (R/P) <R>: *Press Enter* | |
| Number of rows (--) <1>: **7** ↵ | |
| Number of columns (¦¦¦) <1>: *Press Enter* | |
| Unit cell or distance between rows (--): **-.8** ↵ | Makes six copies of the line at .8 spacing |
| Command: *From the toolbox, choose* ARC, *then draw an arc from 17,12 to 16.1,8.7 to 14,5.7* | Issues the ARC command and draws the arc |

Your drawing should resemble the one shown in figure 9.3.

Your arc should extend down from the polyline endpoint on the top right, intersect the last line of the array, and intersect the polyline on the left just below the intersected line. This arc is a construction line boundary that you use to form the cylinder fins. The fin lines are formed by extending the lines to the arc.

**Figure 9.3:**

The rough
construction lines
of a cylinder wall.

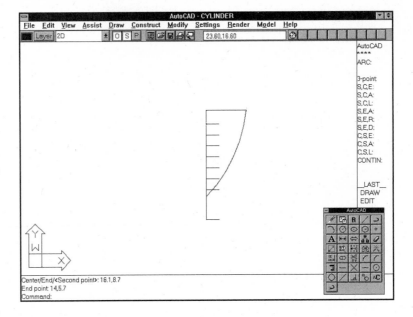

# Extending Entities

To extend the lines to the arc, use the EXTEND command, which extends lines, polylines, and arcs. The boundary edge(s) can be lines, polylines, arcs, circles, and viewport entities (when in paper space). Use normal object selection to select the boundary edge(s) to which you want to extend, then pick the objects that you want to extend. You must pick individually each object to extend. You cannot use other modes to fill a selection set full of objects that you want to extend, and then extend them all at once. Objects to extend are ignored unless EXTEND can project them to intersect a boundary object.

Use EXTEND if you do not know the drawing intersection points or if you do not want to calculate them. In these cases (and in the current exercise), it is easier to use a construction line and then extend the entities. EXTEND has a few constraints: you cannot extend closed polylines or shorten objects (use the TRIM command to shorten lines).

In the following exercise, use EXTEND to lengthen the fin lines until they meet the construction arc.

## Using EXTEND To Extend Lines to an Arc

Use ZOOM Window and zoom to view shown in figure 9.4.

| | |
|---|---|
| Command: *From the toolbox, choose* EXTEND | Issues the EXTEND command |
| Command: extend<br>Select boundary edges(s)... | |
| Select objects: *Pick the arc and press Enter* | |
| <Select object to extend>/Undo:<br>*Starting from the top, pick each of the seven short lines at or near the endpoint closest to the arc* | Extends all the lines except the bottom one |
| Entity does not intersect an edge | Fails to extend |
| <Select object to extend>/Undo:<br>*Press Enter* | Exits from the EXTEND command |

The zoomed view and extended lines should look like figure 9.4.

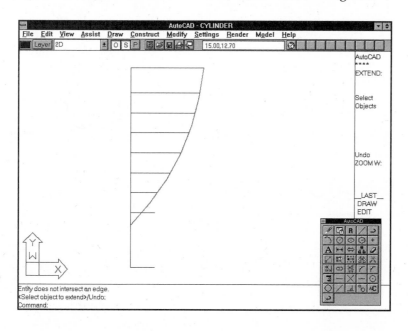

**Figure 9.4:**

Extending lines to the arc.

The EXTEND command cannot adjust the bottom line because it crosses the arc. You can use TRIM on this line, but in a later exercise, you attach the line and the arc using STRETCH instead. In another exercise, you use TRIM for something more complicated.

# Using the OFFSET Command

The cylinder wall and each cylinder fin is made up of parallel lines. The OFFSET command enables you to create parallel drawing lines. You pick each entity individually that you want to offset and AutoCAD creates a parallel copy.

You cannot offset some types of entities. Entities that you can offset include lines, arcs, circles, and 2D polylines. Polylines include donuts, ellipses, and polygons. Each offset creates a new entity with the same linetype, color, and layer settings as the original entity. Polylines also have the same width and curves.

You can use two techniques to offset entities. You can provide an offset distance and then indicate the side (direction) of the offset. You can input values or pick a point to show the offset distances, but you must use a pick to show the side for placement. Offset distances cannot be negative values.

The second way to offset entities (the default) is to pick the entity you want to offset and then pick a point through which the entity is to be offset. If the through point falls beyond the end of the new entity, the offset is calculated as if the new entity extended to the through point, but it is drawn without that imaginary extension.

In the following exercise, use OFFSET with a through point to create a double cylinder wall and to double the lines that form the fins. After you offset these lines, close the ends of the wall and fins.

## Using OFFSET To Create Wall and Fin Lines

| | |
|---|---|
| Command: *Choose* Construct, *then* Offset | Issues OFFSET with the default distance |
| Command: _offset<br>Offset distance or Through<br><Through>:.3 ↵ | Sets a default for the distance |
| Select object to offset: *Pick polyline on the left* | |
| Side to offset? *Pick any point to the left of the polyline* | Draws a new parallel polyline |
| Select object to offset: *Pick the bottom fin line* | |
| Side to offset? *Pick any point above the line* | Draws a new parallel line |

`Select object to offset:` *Continue to offset the fin lines, picking each offset above the selected line, then press Enter (see fig. 9.5)*

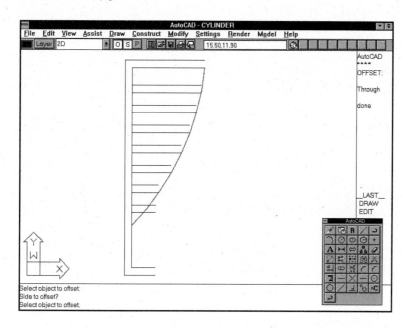

**Figure 9.5:**

The cylinder after offset.

| Command: *Choose* **S**ettings, *then* **O**bject Snap, *put a check in the* **E**ndpoint *box, and choose OK* | Sets the running object snap to ENDPoint |
| --- | --- |
| Command: *From the toolbox, choose* LINE, *and draw vertical lines closing the ends of each pair of fin lines, including the top and bottom polylines* | Issues the LINE command and draws lines |
| Command: *Choose* **S**ettings, *then* **O**bject Snap, *clear the* **E**ndpoint *check box, and choose OK* | Sets the running object snap to NONe |

Figure 9.6 shows the cylinder with its closed fins.

You can use OFFSET to offset lines and polylines (as you saw in the preceding exercise), and you also can use OFFSET to form concentric circles.

**Figure 9.6:**

The cylinder with
connecting lines.

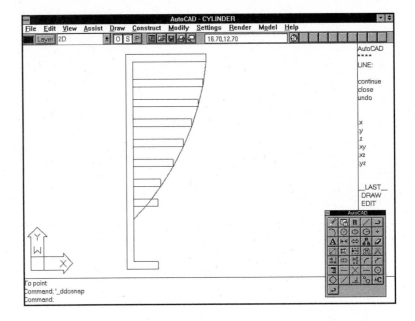

*OFFSET forms a new entity by drawing the entity parallel to the
original entity. OFFSET cannot form a new entity inside an arc or
circle if the offset distance exceeds the original radius. (You cannot
create a negative radius.) Donuts, polygons, and arc or short
segments in other polylines are treated similarly. OFFSET attempts to duplicate
small zig-zag segments and loops with polylines, but you may get confused results.
Use PEDIT to clean up offset polylines if you do not like the results.*

In the exercise that follows, you learn how to thicken the flanges and shorten the
bottom fin by using the STRETCH command.

# Using STRETCH for Power Drawing

The STRETCH command enables you to move and stretch entities. You can lengthen
entities, shorten them, and alter their shapes.

The STRETCH command is normally used with a crossing window. After you select
your objects with a crossing window (see fig. 9.7), you show AutoCAD where to stretch
your objects with a displacement from a base point, to a new point. Everything that
you selected inside the crossing window moves, and entities crossing the window are
stretched. The expression *inside the window* means that all of an object's endpoints or
vertex points are within the window. The expression *crossing the window* means that the
endpoints or other elements of an object are both inside and outside the window.

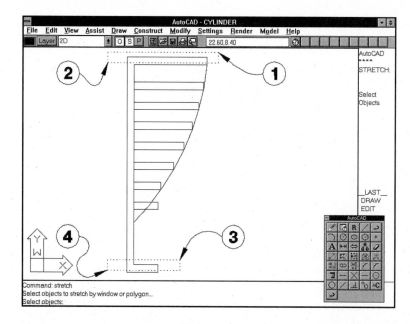

**Figure 9.7:**
Select crossing windows to stretch the flanges.

The STRETCH command uses the crossing window selection set. (A standard window moves the selected entities, but it does not stretch them.) If you want any objects that fall within the crossing window left unchanged, you can use the Remove mode to remove them from the selection set. With a window, you can add only objects you want moved to the new destination. If you use Crossing or Window to add or remove entities, the results may not be what you want because STRETCH uses only the most recent Crossing or Window selection.

STRETCH interacts differently with different entities. In the following exercise, use STRETCH on lines and polylines by widening the top and bottom of the cylinder.

## Using STRETCH To Widen the Flanges

| | |
|---|---|
| Command: *From the toolbox, choose* STRETCH | Issues STRETCH with a Crossing selection |
| Command: stretch<br>Select objects to stretch by window<br>or polygon... | |
| Select objects: *Press at point* ①<br>*(see fig. 9.7), drag to* ②, *release,*<br>*and press Enter* | Sets the crossing window |
| other corner: 2 found | |
| Base point: *Pick any point* | |

*continues*

| | |
|---|---|
| `New point:` *Pick or enter point* `@.3<90` | Stretches the flange |
| `Command:` *Press Enter* | Repeats the command |
| `STRETCH` `Select objects to stretch by window or polygon ...` | |
| `Select objects:` *Press at the upper right corner at ③, drag to ④, release, and press Enter* | Selects the bottom flange |
| `Base point:` *Pick any point* | |
| `New point:` *Pick or enter point at* `@.3<90` ↵ | |

Use dynamic ZOOM and PAN to obtain the view extents shown in figure 9.8 and save the drawing.

**Figure 9.8:**

The top and bottom flanges after being stretched.

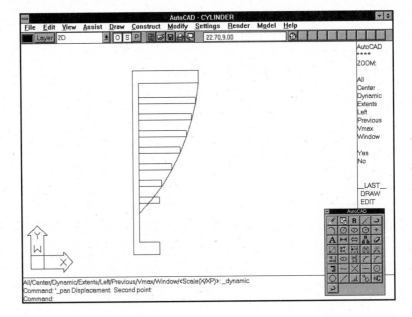

*Unlike the MOVE and COPY commands, STRETCH does not accept absolute X,Y or polar displacements. When you use MOVE or COPY, and enter an X,Y or dist<angle value at the first prompt, it becomes an absolute displacement if you press Enter at the second point prompt. The STRETCH equivalent to an absolute displacement is picking any point for the base point and then typing relative coordinates, such as @0,-7.5.*

Use STRETCH again in the following exercise to shorten the bottom fin so that it is in line with the arc.

## Using STRETCH To Shorten the Fin

`Command:` *From the toolbox, choose* STRETCH

`Command: stretch`
`Select objects to stretch by window...`

`Select objects:` *Pick corners at* ①
*and* ② *(see fig. 9.9) and press Enter*

`Base point:` *From the toolbox,*
*choose* ENDPOINT, *then pick at* ③

`New point:` *From the toolbox, choose*          Shortens the fin
INTERSECTION, *then pick the*
*intersection of the arc and line at* ④

When you are finished, the bottom fin should look like the one in figure 9.10.

As you work through the steps in the preceding exercise, you notice that the construction arc is highlighted by the crossing window, but it does not change with the stretch. The arc is not moved or stretched because its endpoints are not enclosed in the window. STRETCH operates differently with different entities.

Some significant points to remember when you use STRETCH with entities follow:

- The endpoints or vertex points of lines, arcs, polyline segments, viewports, traces, and solids determine what is stretched or moved.

- The center points of arcs or polyline arcs are adjusted to keep the sagitta constant. The *sagitta* is the altitude or distance from the chord midpoint to the nearest point on the arc.

- Viewport contents remain constant in scale.

- The location of a point, the center of a circle, or the insertion point of a block, shape, or text entity determine whether these entities are moved. These points are never stretched.

**Figure 9.9:**

A crossing window for stretching the fin.

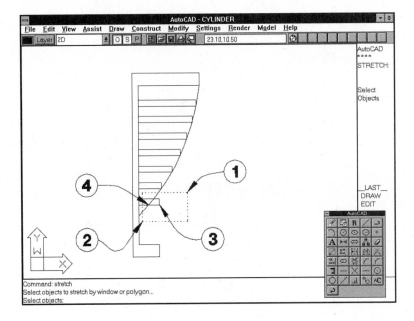

**Figure 9.10:**

A detail of the stretched fin.

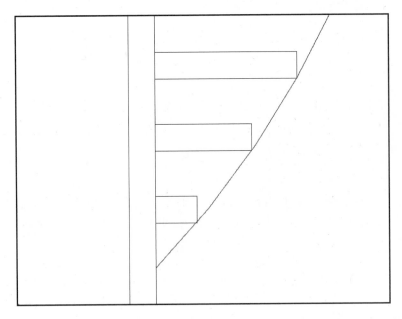

# Using TRIM in Quick Construction

Frequently, you need to trim existing lines in a drawing. If you are working with a large number of entities, breaking individual entities is tiresome and cumbersome. You can get the same results faster by using TRIM. Like EXTEND, TRIM makes use of boundary entities that include lines, arcs, circles, polylines, and, in paper space, viewports. The entities that you select as your boundary edge become your cutting edge(s). After you select your cutting edge, you pick the individual entities that you want to trim. You can trim lines, arcs, circles, and polylines. Other entity types are ignored by the TRIM command; therefore, you can select extra objects that are in the area.

Figure 9.11 shows the trimmed interior lines of the top three cylinder fins. Compare those fins with the untrimmed ones, and then use TRIM in the following steps to cut the interior lines of all cylinder fins. You may have to turn off snap (F9) to pick the lines you want to trim.

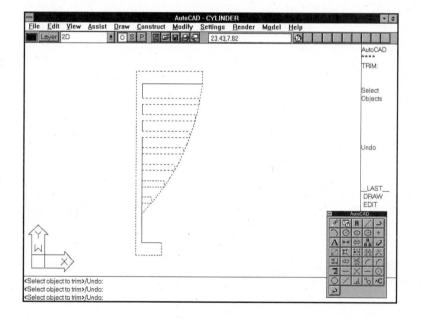

**Figure 9.11:**

The cylinder with top three fins trimmed.

---

## Using TRIM To Cut Fin Lines

`Command:` *From the toolbox, choose* TRIM          Issues the TRIM command

`Select cutting edge(s)...`

`Select objects:` **ALL** ↵          Selects all the entities in the drawing

*continues*

```
26 found
Select objects: Press Enter
```

<Select object to trim>/Undo:
*Turn snap off, then pick a point on the
cylinder wall between fin lines*                    Trims the cylinder wall line

<Select object to trim>/Undo:
*Continue picking until all the cylinder
wall fin lines are trimmed*

*If you make an error, enter **U** to undo it*

<Select object to trim>/Undo:
*Turn snap on, then press Enter*                    Resets snap and ends the command

The results of trimming the interior walls of the cylinder are shown in figure 9.12.

**Figure 9.12:**

The cylinder after trim.

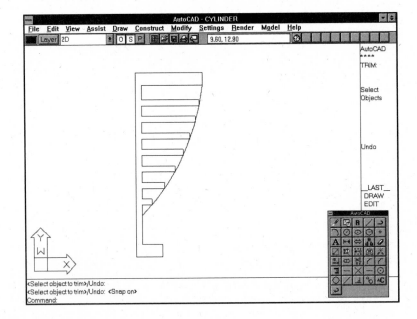

 *The same entity can be a cutting edge and be cut as an object to trim. After it has been trimmed, it is no longer highlighted, but it still functions as a cutting edge.*

# Using the SCALE Command

Occasionally, you may use the wrong drawing symbol and text scale or you may have to change an object's size in mid-drawing. The SCALE command enables you to shrink or enlarge objects that you already placed in your drawing. When you rescale drawing objects, you use a scale factor to change the size of entities around a given base point. The base point you choose remains constant in space; everything around it grows or shrinks by your scale factor. Also, the distance from the base point to the entities that you scale changes by the scale factor. You can enter an explicit scale factor, pick two points to show a distance as a factor, or specify a reference length. To use a reference length, define a length (generally on an entity), and then specify the length you want it to become.

The piston cylinder is supposed to be 10 inches high. In the following exercise, use SCALE with the Reference option to change the cylinder profile to make it exactly 10 inches. After you finish, save your drawing.

---

## Using SCALE To Enlarge the Cylinder

Command: *Choose* **M**odify, *then* **S**cale       Issues SCALE

Command: _scale

Select objects: **ALL** ↵

Use the ENDPOINT object snap from the toolbox with each of the following picks.

Base point: *Pick at* ①
*(see fig. 9.13)*

<Scale factor>/Reference: **R** ↵       Specifies the Reference option

Reference length <1>: *Pick at* ①       Sets the first point of the original
*again (see fig. 9.13)*       reference length

Second point: *Pick at* ②       Defines the original reference length

New length: **10** ↵       Resizes to exactly 10" (see fig. 9.14)

Zoom All, then save the drawing and continue, or end and take a break.

---

*The scale base point is also the base point of the new length in the Reference option. If you want to show the length by picking points on another object, place the base point there, scale the selection, then use the MOVE command to adjust its location. Use Previous to select the object scale and object snaps to specify the move.*

**Figure 9.13:**

A cylinder profile with pick points before scaling.

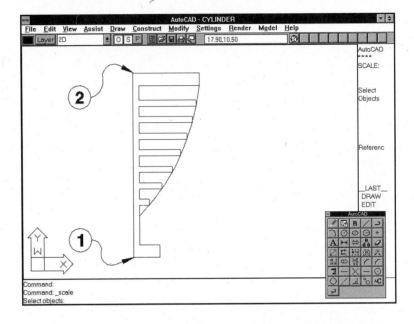

**Figure 9.14:**

The cylinder profile after scale and zooming.

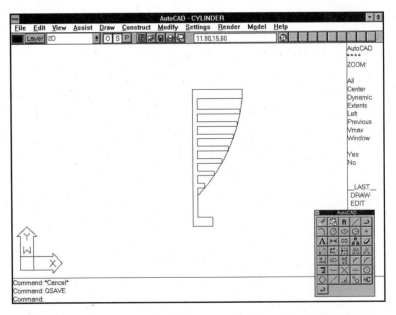

Your CYLINDER drawing should now be the same as the IAWCYLI2 drawing from the IAW DISK. In the next section, you use your CYLINDER drawing to experiment with selection filters, and then you continue drawing by using the IAWCYLI2 file.

Now is a good time to introduce a new method of entity selection—filters. *Filters* enable you to include and exclude specific types of entities from your object selection sets. The next section explains the method you use.

# Controlling the Selection Set

Even with all of the selection set options available for entity selection, it is still sometimes difficult and time-consuming to select the right entities in a complex drawing. Entity-selection filters enable you to select only those entities that have been specified in the filter description. Common filters can include entity type, color, layer, or coordinate data. Although the concept of specifying filters is simple, the process may seem confusing because AutoCAD provides so many filter specifications and options for using them. You can display the Entity Selection Filter dialog box, which contains all of these options, by choosing Object Filters from the **A**ssist pull-down menu (see fig. 9.15). Entering the FILTER command also displays the dialog box, and you can enter '**FIL-TER** to use it transparently in another command when prompted for entity selection.

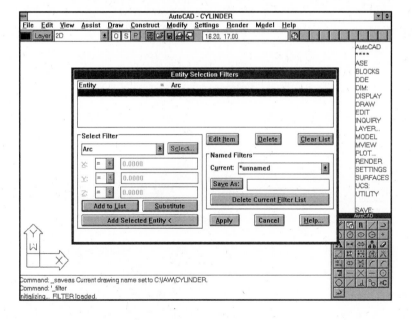

**Figure 9.15:**

Entity Selection Filters dialog box.

# Using Entity Selection Filters

You can specify entity-selection filters by choosing an item from the drop-down list under Select Filter, then clicking on the Add to **L**ist button. That filter then appears in the current filter list at the top of the dialog box. You can repeat this process to add more filters. If you want to save the filter list to use at a later time, enter a name (up to

18 characters) in the edit box next to Save As and then click on the Save As button. You can find and retrieve all of the defined filter names in the list box next to the **C**urrent button. Choosing **A**pply closes the dialog box and prompts for object selection, using the current filter. Choosing Cancel leaves the dialog box without applying the filter.

Try using entity filters in the following exercise.

## Selecting Objects by Using FILTERS

Continue with the CYLINDER drawing from the previous exercise.

| | |
|---|---|
| Command: *Choose* **A***ssist, then* **O***bject Filters* | Opens the Entity Selection Filters dialog box |
| *With* Arc *displayed in the* Select Filter *drop-down list box, choose* Add to List | Adds the arcs to the filter list at the top of the dialog box |
| *Choose* **A**pply | Closes dialog box and prompts to select objects |
| Applying filter to selection. Select objects: *Select a window enclosing all of the entities in the drawing* | Creates a selection set, but filters out everything except the arc (see fig. 9.16) |
| 33 found 32 were filtered out. | |
| Select objects: *Press Enter* | Ends object selection |
| Exiting filtered selection. | |
| Command: *From the toolbox, choose* ERASE | Starts the ERASE command |
| Select objects: **P** ↵ | Selects the previous set |
| 1 found | |
| Select objects: *Press Ctrl-C* | Cancels the ERASE command |

Remember that when a filter is active, only the selected entities that conform to that filter are selected; all other entities are disregarded. In the previous exercise, the prompt displayed the number selected and the number filtered out by the active filter. Only the arc entity was selected. The Previous select set option can be used to recall those entities during a subsequent editing command, or you can use 'FILTER transparently.

In the Filters dialog box, you can create a list of filters to apply. After a filter has been added to the list, you can highlight it by clicking on it. You may need to follow this procedure before you use the **D**elete, Edit **I**tem, or **S**ubstitute buttons. The next exercise continues to define and use entity filters.

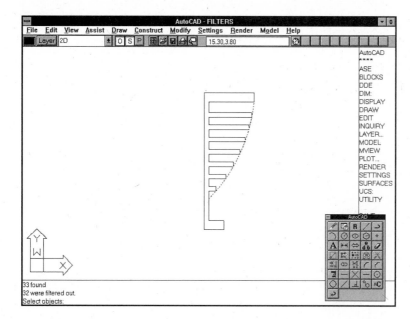

**Figure 9.16:**
The arc is selected by filtering out the lines.

# Filtering Specific Entity Characteristics

In addition to the entity filters, you can specify coordinate information to further filter the entities. Click on the X, Y, and Z coordinate boxes to specify entity data, such as start and endpoints of lines or arc radius and center points. These coordinate descriptions are found in the select filter list box, as are properties such as layer, color, and linetype. To give additional clarification to these filters, relational operators can be specified with the coordinate data. The more commonly used ones include equal (=), not equal (!=), less than (<), and greater than (>). By placing these operators in the small edit box next to the coordinates, you specify how the coordinates are to be used. Try these in the following exercise, which selects lines whose X,Y endpoints are greater than 16.5,16.1.

## Filtering Specific Entity Characteristics

Command: *Choose* **A**ssist, *then* **O**bject Filters

*Choose* **C**lear List

| | |
|---|---|
| *Scroll through the* Select Filter *drop-down list box to find and select* Line End | Displays Line End in in the Select Filter box |
| *Click on* = *in the box beside* X: *in the* Select Filter *area* | Opens a drop-down list box of logical operators |

*continues*

| | |
|---|---|
| *Select greater than (>)* | Closes the drop-down list |
| *Double-click on 0.0000 in the* X: *row, then type* **16.5** | Highlights and replaces 0.0000 |
| *Click on = beside* Y: *in the* Select Filter *area, then choose* less than (<) | Selects a logical operator |
| *Double-click on 0.0000 in the* Y: *row, then type* **16.1** | |
| *Choose* Add to **L**ist | Adds Line End selection to filter list |
| *Choose* **A**pply | Closes the dialog box and prompts for object selection |

```
Applying filter to selection.
```

| | |
|---|---|
| `Select objects: ` **ALL** ↵<br>`33 found`<br>`23 were filtered out.` | Selects lines that fit the search criteria (see fig. 9.17) |
| `Select objects: ` *Press Enter* | |

```
Exiting filtered selection.
```

**Figure 9.17:**

Lines selected using logical operators.

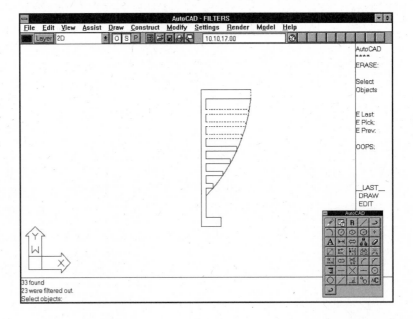

# Using Conditional Testing

The entity filters can be extremely flexible when conditional testing is applied between the filters. This logic is the same logic that AutoLISP or other programming languages use. The four grouping operators—AND, OR, XOR, NOT—each have a Begin and End option. It is important that they are balanced and are used in pairs. These operators are also selected from the Select Filter drop-down list and can be applied to the other properties or coordinates. Try it in the next exercise.

## Using Conditional Tests

Use the CIRCLE command to draw two circles with a 0.50" radius, a third circle with a 1.00" radius, and a fourth circle with a 2.00" radius (see fig. 9.18).

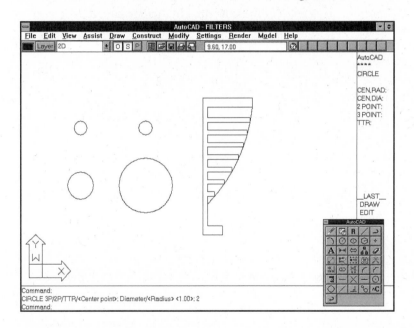

**Figure 9.18:**

Four circles are added for conditional testing.

| | |
|---|---|
| Command: *Select the 2" radius circle* | Creates the selection set and displays grips |
| Command: **CHPROP** ⏎ | Starts the CHPROP command with the 2" radius circle selected |

```
1 found
Change what property (Color/LAyer/
LType/Thickness) ? C ⏎

New color <BYLAYER>: Y ⏎
```

*continues*

| | |
|---|---|
| `Change what property (Color/LAyer/`<br>`LType/Thickness) ?` *Press Enter* | Ends the command and changes the circle<br>to yellow |
| `Command:` *Choose **A**ssist, then **O**bject*<br>*Filters* | |
| *Choose **C**lear List* | |
| *From the Select Filter list, select*<br>Circle, *then choose* Add to **L**ist | Adds Circle to the filter list |
| *From the bottom portion of the*<br>*Select Filter list, select*<br>** Begin NOT, *then choose*<br>Add to **L**ist | Adds ** Begin NOT to the filter list, above<br>Circle |
| *From the Select Filter list, select*<br>Circle Radius, *then double-click on*<br>0.0000 *in the X: row, type* **1**, *and*<br>*choose* Add to **L**ist | Sets the filter to exclude any circle with a<br>radius of 1" |
| *From the Select Filter list, select*<br>** End NOT, *then choose* Add to **L**ist | Ends the NOT operation |
| *From the Select Filter list, select*<br>** Begin NOT, *then choose* Add to **L**ist | Adds ** Begin NOT to the filter list |
| *From the Select Filter list,*<br>*select* Color, *then choose* S**e**lect,<br>*click on the standard yellow box,*<br>*choose* OK, *then* Add to **L**ist | Sets the filter to exclude any circle<br>with color 2 (yellow) |
| *From the Select Filter list, select*<br>** End NOT, *then choose* Add to **L**ist | Ends the NOT operation |

Use the scroll button beside the filter list to view the entire filter list, then enter **1 AND YELLOW** in the Save As edit box and choose the Sa**v**e As button to save the filter list for future use.

| | |
|---|---|
| *Choose **A**pply* | Prompts for object selection |
| `Select objects:` *Window select all of*<br>*the circles, then press Enter* | |
| `4 found`<br>`2 were filtered out.` | Selects only the .5" circles |

The named 1 AND YELLOW filter set will be the default the next time FILTER is used in this drawing. In later drawing sessions, you can select this filter set from the Named Filters drop-down list.

> *To create a filter set for selecting multiple entity types, use OR. Do not use AND. To select lines and arcs, for example, use \*\* Begin OR, Entity = Line, Entity = Arc, and \*\* End OR. AND attempts to find entities that were simultaneously lines and arcs—a geometric impossibility. OR finds all entities that are lines or arcs.*

You can apply filters from within another command. In fact, the true power of using filters comes from using them within another command. This process is similar to accessing the toolbar for point filters or the toolbox for object snaps when a command is prompting to select objects. Enter '**FILTER** as a transparent command when you are asked to select objects. The last exercise in entity filters demonstrates this procedure.

---

### Using Transparent, Named Filters within a Command

| | |
|---|---|
| `Command:` *From the toolbox, choose* ERASE | Begins the ERASE command |
| `Select objects:` `'FILTER ↵` | Opens the Entity Selection Filters dialog box, with 1 AND YELLOW shown as current in the Named Filters area |
| *Click on* **A**pply | Resumes the ERASE command with entity filter selection |
| `Applying filter to selection.`<br>`Select objects:` `ALL ↵` | |
| `37 found`<br>`35 were filtered out.` | |
| `Select objects:` *Press Enter* | |
| `Exiting filtered selection. 2 found` | |
| `Select objects:` *Press Enter* | Erases the two small circles |

---

You can define and then save filters with a name that you specify, so that you can later recall and use them again. Although setting up filters may seem to take much effort, filters increase your productivity as you become more familiar with them. If your drawings are really not that complicated, using locked layers might be a little easier to master, but remember what the filters can do for you.

## Limiting Selections with Locked Layers

Another new feature of AutoCAD Release 12 is its capability to lock a layer. In Chapter 3 you learned that turning a layer off hides the entities that are on it, and freezing it removes the entities from the active entity group, which must be recalculated during drawing regenerations. What if you want to see the entities on a certain layer but do not want to select and modify them? Lock the layer. You can still see the entities, list them, and use object snaps with them. Changing the color and linetype is all that you can do to modify entities on locked layers, however. Layers can be locked and unlocked the same way you turn them on and off. An L appears under the State column of a locked layer. The following exercise illustrates this concept.

## Controlling Selection with Locked Layers

| | |
|---|---|
| Command: *Select the 2" radius circle* | Creates the selection set and displays grips |
| Command: **CHPROP** ↵ | Starts the CHPROP command with the 2" radius circle selected |
| Change what property (Color/LAyer/ LType/Thickness) ? **LA** ↵ | |
| New layer <2D>: **3D** ↵ | |
| Change what property (Color/LAyer/ LType/Thickness) ? *Press Enter* | Ends the command and changes circle to layer 3D |
| Command: **DDLMODES** ↵ | Opens the Modify Layer dialog box |
| *Select layer 3D, choose* Lock, *then choose* OK | Locks layer 3D |
| Command: *From the toolbox, choose* ERASE | Begins the ERASE command |
| Select objects: *Use a window to select both of the circles* | |
| 2 found 1 was on a locked layer. | |
| Select objects: *Press Enter* | Erases the 1" radius circle, but ignores the 2" radius circle on the locked layer |

If your drawings have the entities well organized by layer, the concept of locking layers should be easy to apply. If you have trouble isolating groups of entities by layer, better drawing organization helps you. Now that you have explored some of the additional entity-selection options, continue with the cylinder drawing.

The cylinder drawing you are constructing in this chapter is a mixture of polylines and lines. In the next section, you practice editing by changing polyline width. The next section also shows you how to form a new polyline by joining the individual entities that make up the cylinder profile.

# Controlling Polylines by Using PEDIT

Polylines can contain a complex continuous series of line and arc segments. Because of this complexity, AutoCAD provides the PEDIT command, which you use only to edit polylines. PEDIT also contains a large list of subcommands for polyline properties. To manage this list, AutoCAD divides PEDIT into two groups of editing functions. The primary group of functions works on the whole polyline you are editing and the second group works on vertices connecting segments within the polyline.

The PEDIT command has more restrictions when you edit three-dimensional polylines, as you can see in Part Five on 3D Drawing. Although you are now concentrating on editing two-dimensional polylines, you learn how to form a three-dimensional polyline mesh from two-dimensional polylines at the end of this chapter.

The primary PEDIT options are as follows:

- **Close/Open.** This option adds a segment (if needed) and joins the first and last vertices to create a continuous polyline. When the polyline is open, the prompt shows Close; when closed, the prompt shows Open. A polyline can be open, even if the first and last points coincide and it appears closed. A polyline is open unless you use the Close option when you draw it, or later use the PEDIT Close option.

- **Join.** This option enables you to add selected arcs, lines, and other polylines to an existing polyline. Their endpoints must coincide exactly to be joined.

- **Width.** This option prompts you to specify a single width for all segments of a polyline. The new width overrides any individual segment widths that are already stored.

- **Edit vertex.** This option presents a separate set of options for editing vertices and their adjoining segments.

- **Fit.** This option creates a smooth curve through the polyline vertices.

- **Spline.** This option creates a curve controlled by, but not usually passing through, a framework of polyline vertices. The type of spline and its resolution are controlled by system variables.

- **Decurve.** This option undoes a Fit or Spline curve back to its original definition.

- **Ltype gen.** This option regenerates the polyline by using current system variable settings.

- **Undo.** This option undoes the most recent editing function.

- **eXit.** This option is the default <X> and exits PEDIT to return you to the Command: prompt.

# Using PEDIT Join To Create a Polyline

In the following exercise, use PEDIT to join the cylinder lines into a single closed polyline. Use a window to select all entities that you want to join. After you create the polyline, increase its width to .02 inch. In the final steps of the exercise, after you exit the PEDIT command, you use FILLET to fillet all the corners in the polyline profile. Use the IAWCYLI2 drawing from the IAW DISK to replace your existing CYLINDER drawing. IAWCYLI2 has been zoomed in, the construction arc and the entities you used for filtering have been erased, and ortho is off; otherwise, the drawing is the same as CYLINDER.

The exercise uses the AutoLISP-defined AI_PEDITM command, which is issued by the pull-down, screen, and tablet menu PEDIT and Polyline Edit selections. The AI_PEDITM command behaves like PEDIT, except that it filters its initial selection set and controls the screen menus to display appropriate selections of PEDIT's numerous options. When you enter the ordinary PEDIT command from the keyboard or toolbox, you have to enter the options as needed.

## Using PEDIT To Join and Change a Polyline

Open a new drawing named CYLINDER=IAWCYLI2, replacing the current CYLINDER drawing.

| | |
|---|---|
| Command: *Choose* **M**odify, *then* **P**olyline Edit | Issues the AutoLISP-defined AI_PEDITM command |
| ai_peditm | |
| Select objects: *Pick the bottom line of one of the middle fins* | Issues the PEDIT command with that selection |
| _.PEDIT Select polyline: Entity selected is not a polyline | |
| Do you want to turn it into one? <Y> *Press Enter* | Converts the line to a polyline |
| Close/Join/Width/Edit vertex/Fit/ Spline/Decurve/Ltype gen/Undo/eXit <X>: *From the screen menu, choose* Join | |
| _JOIN Select objects: **ALL** ↵ | |
| 32 found | |
| Select objects: *Press Enter* | |
| 35 segments added to polyline | Creates a closed polyline |

```
Open/Join/Width/Edit vertex/Fit/
Spline/Decurve/Ltype gen/Undo/eXit
<X>: From the screen menu, choose Width
```

WIDTH

```
Enter new width for all
segments: .02 ↵
```
Increases the lineweight (see fig. 9.19)

```
Open/Join/Width/Edit vertex/
Fit/Spline/Decurve/Ltype gen/
Undo/eXit <X>: Press Enter
```

Command: *From the toolbox,*
*choose* FILLET

```
Command: _fillet Polyline/Radius/
<Select first object>: From the
```
*screen menu, choose* radius

```
Enter fillet radius <0.00>:
0.125 ↵
```
Sets default radius and reissues
FILLET command

```
FILLET Polyline/Radius/
<Select firstobject>: From the
```
*screen menu, choose* polyline
Specifies all vertices of a single polyline

```
POLYLINE Select 2D polyline:
```
*Pick the polyline*
Fillets all corners (see fig. 9.20)

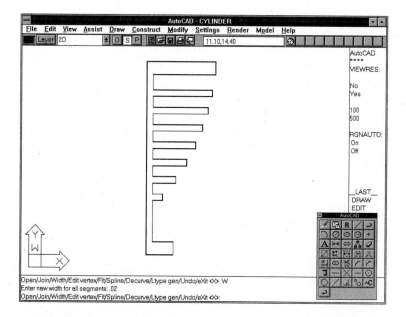

**Figure 9.19:**

The joined
polyline with
changed width.

*As with linetype scale, you set polyline width so that it is readable and accurate when it plots. Polyline width may look irregular in the graphics window, or it may not show its width at some zoom levels or video resolutions.*

**Figure 9.20:**

Detail of the filleted polyline.

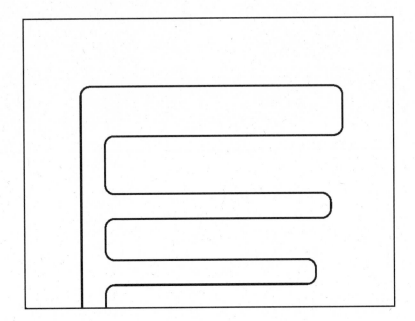

Two common edits involve joining polylines and changing their width properties. Later in this chapter, you learn how to use other PEDIT options, including the curve fit options.

*The process of joining polylines is tricky—it can fail if the endpoints of the entities do not coincide exactly. Problems can be caused by not using snap and object snaps when drawing, and by occasional round-off discrepancies. Edit or replace stubborn entities by using object snap mode to select the adjacent endpoints, and then use PEDIT again. A good way to make endpoints coincide is to use the FILLET command with a zero radius.*

Each polyline segment belongs to, and is controlled by, the preceding vertex. The Edit vertex option makes available a separate set of Edit vertex subcommands. When you use these commands, the current vertex of the polyline is marked with an X. This X shows you the vertex you are editing. Move the X until you mark the vertex you want to edit.

Options for the Pedit Edit vertex command are as follows:

- **Next/Previous.** This option moves the X marker to a new current vertex. Next is the initial default.

- **Break.** This option splits the polyline into two, or removes segments of a polyline at existing vertices. The first break point is the vertex on which you invoke the Break option. Use Next/Previous to access another vertex for the second break point. The Go option performs the break.

  The BREAK command usually is more efficient than invoking PEDIT with the Break option, unless curve or spline fitting is involved.

- **Insert.** This option adds a vertex at a point you specify following the vertex currently marked with an X. This option can be combined with Break to create a break between existing vertices.

- **Move.** This option changes the location of the current (X-marked) vertex to a point you specify.

- **Regen.** This option forces a regeneration of the polyline so that you can see the effects, such as width changes, of your vertex editing.

- **Straighten.** This option removes all intervening vertices from between the two you select, replacing them with one straight segment. It also uses the Next/Previous and Go options.

- **Tangent.** This option sets a tangent to the direction you specify at the currently marked vertex to control curve fitting. The tangent is shown at the vertex with an arrow, and can be dragged or entered from the keyboard.

- **Width.** This option sets the starting and ending width of an individual polyline segment to the values you specify.

- **eXit.** This option exits vertex editing and returns to the main PEDIT command menu.

# Using PEDIT Edit Vertex Options

After you form a polyline, you often need to move a vertex or straighten a line segment. Try these two edits in the steps that follow by removing two of the fillets. Remove one fillet at the top left of the cylinder profile and another on the bottom flange. After you enter the PEDIT Edit Vertex option, move the X to mark the desired segment. Use the Move option to move the top left vertex to the corner. This move creates a small bump at the corner from the existing fillet arc segment. You can use a transparent 'ZOOM to better view the bump. Use the Straighten option to make a 90-degree corner and eliminate the bump.

## Using PEDIT Vertex Editing To Remove Fillets

Command: *Choose* **M**odify, *then* **P**olyline Edit

Select objects: *Pick the polyline and press Enter*

_.PEDIT Select polyline:

Close/Join/Width/Edit vertex/ Fit/Spline/Decurve/Ltype gen/ Undo/eXit <X>: *From the screen menu, choose* Ed Vrtx | Changes the screen menu to the edit vertex selections and displays an X on the current vertex

Next/Previous/Break/Insert/Move/ Regen/Straighten/Tangent/Width/ eXit <N>: *From the screen menu, choose* Next *or press Enter, and repeat until the X is located as in figure 9.21* | Moves the current vertex along the polyline

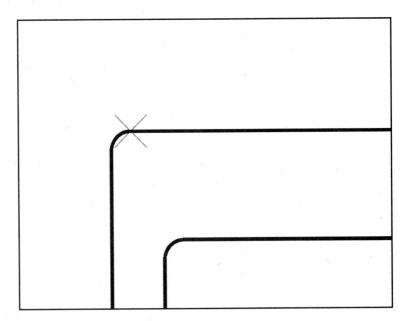

**Figure 9.21:**

Detail of the location of the edit X before the move.

Next/Previous/Break/Insert/Move/ Regen/Straighten/Tangent/Width/ eXit <N>: *From the screen menu, choose* Move | Specifies the Move option and the vertex location

Enter new location: *Enter or pick polar point @0.12<180* | Creates a bump, as shown in figure 9.22

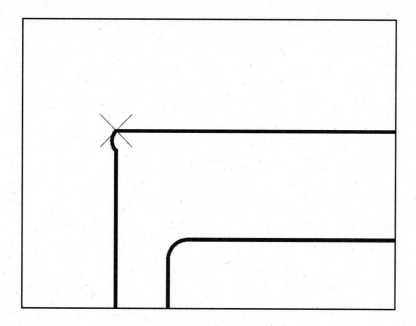

**Figure 9.22:**
Detail after the move, before straightening.

In the next steps, you straighten the bump. Use 'ZOOM if you want to see the bump better, then zoom back out.

```
Next/Previous/Break/Insert/Move/
Regen/Straighten/Tangent/Width/eXit
<N>: From the screen menu, choose Straight
```

```
Next/Previous/Go/eXit <N>:          Moves the X below the bump
Press Enter
```

```
Next/Previous/Go/eXit <N>:          Moves X to match figure 9.23
Press Enter
```

```
Next/Previous/Go/eXit <N>:          Straightens the line (see fig. 9.24)
From the screen menu, choose Go
```

```
Next/Previous/Break/Insert/Move/
Regen/Straighten/Tangent/Width/
eXit <N>: Stay in the command for
the next exercise
```

**Figure 9.23:**

The location of the X before straightening.

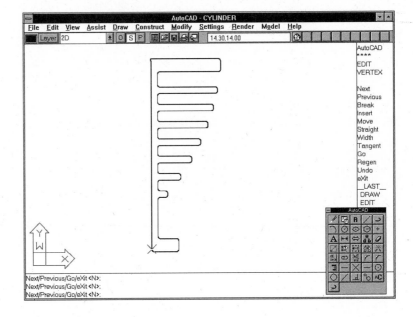

**Figure 9.24:**

Detail of the location of the X after straightening.

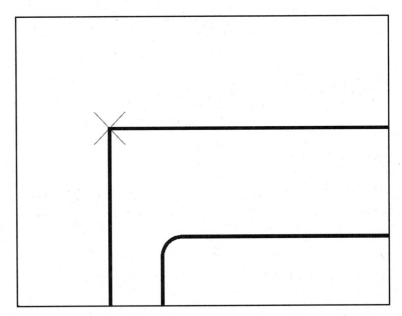

*If you make a mistake, exit the Edit vertex mode to the primary PEDIT mode and use the Undo option. Then re-enter Edit vertex mode and continue your work. The UNDO command undoes all operations of the Edit vertex session. As you edit a long polyline with a number of steps, exit and re-enter Edit Vertex mode occasionally to protect your work.*

You can repeat the preceding Move and Straighten options to clean up the lower right corner. For the rest of this polyline editing session, try entering the options from the keyboard.

## Straightening the Lower Right Corner

Continue in the PEDIT command from the previous exercise.

`Next/Previous/Break/Insert/Move/`     Moves the X to match figures  9.25 and 9.26
`Regen/Straighten/Tangent/Width/`
`eXit <N>:` *Press Enter three times*

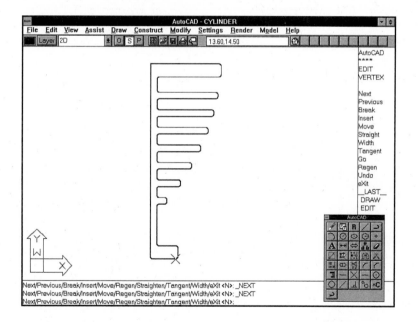

**Figure 9.25:**

The location of the edit X before the second move.

*continues*

**Figure 9.26:**

Detail of the lower right corner of the cylinder before the move.

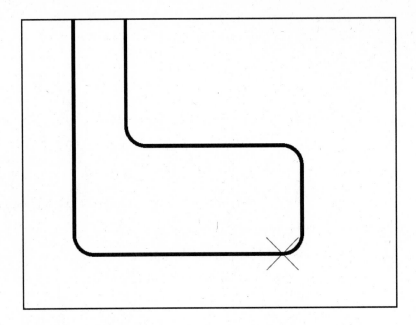

```
Next/Previous/Break/Insert/Move/
Regen/Straighten/Tangent/Width/
eXit <N>: M ↵
```

```
Enter new location: @0.125<0 ↵
```
Creates a bump (see fig. 9.27)

**Figure 9.27:**

Detail of the cylinder corner after the move, and before straightening.

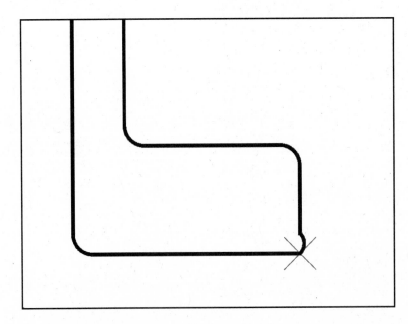

```
Next/Previous/Break/Insert/Move/
Regen/Straighten/Tangent/Width/
eXit <N>: S ↵
```

Next/Previous/Go/eXit <N>: *Press*     Moves the X to match figure 9.28
*Enter twice*

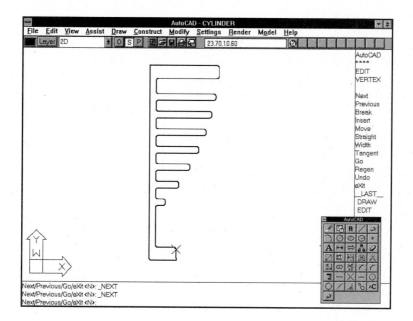

**Figure 9.28:**

The location of the X before the second straightening.

Next/Previous/Go/eXit <N>: **G** ↵     Straightens the line (see fig. 9.29)

```
Next/Previous/Break/Insert/Move/
Regen/Straighten/Tangent/Width/
eXit <N>:
```
*Stay in the command for the next exercise*

You can add a vertex to an existing polyline. In the following exercise, add a notch to the lower left corner of the cylinder profile. The following editing sequence uses the Insert and Move vertex options to perform two moves and one insertion.

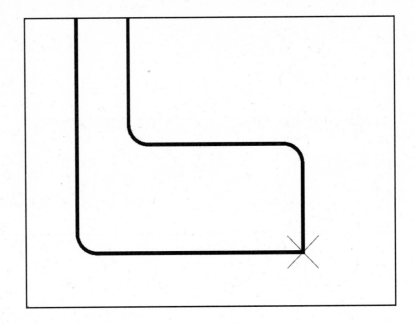

**Figure 9.29:**

Detail of the lower right corner of the cylinder after straightening.

---

## Using PEDIT To Add a Notch

Continue in the PEDIT command from the previous exercise.

| | |
|---|---|
| `Next/Previous/Break/Insert/Move/`<br>`Regen/Straighten/Tangent/Width/`<br>`eXit <N>:` *Type* **P** *and press Enter twice* | Moves the X to match figure 9.30; notice the default change from N to P |
| `Next/Previous/Break/Insert/Move/`<br>`Regen/Straighten/Tangent/Width/`<br>`eXit <P>:` **M** ↵ | |
| `Enter new location:` `@0.175<90` ↵ | Makes a bump, as shown in figure 9.31 |
| `Next/Previous/Break/Insert/Move/`<br>`Regen/Straighten/Tangent/Width/`<br>`eXit <P>:` **I** ↵ | Prompts for a new vertex point |
| `Enter location of new vertex:`<br>*Pick polar point at 0.30<0* | Makes a V-notch (see fig. 9.32 and 9.33, 0.175 + 0.125 = 0.3" notch) |
| `Next/Previous/Break/Insert/Move/`<br>`Regen/Straighten/Tangent/Width/`<br>`eXit <P>:` *Type* **N** *and press Enter twice* | Moves the X to the vertex shown in figure 9.33 |

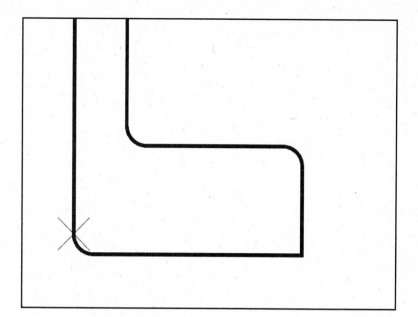

**Figure 9.30:**
Before the move.

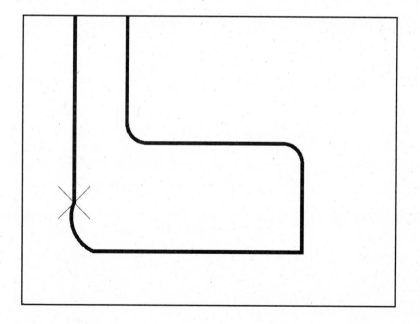

**Figure 9.31:**
The lower left corner after the move and before the insert.

*continues*

**Figure 9.32:**

The cylinder corner after the insert.

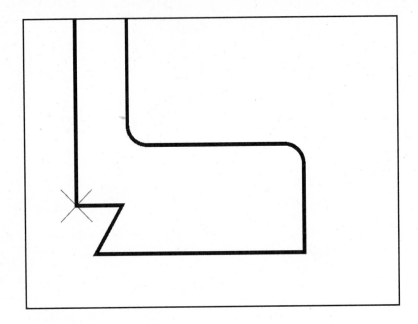

**Figure 9.33:**

The location of the edit X before the second move.

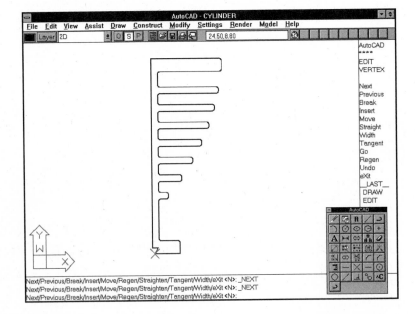

```
Next/Previous/Break/Insert/Move/
Regen/Straighten/Tangent/Width/
eXit <N>: M ↵
```

```
Enter new location: @0.175<0 ↵
```
Squares off the notch (see fig. 9.34)

```
Next/Previous/Break/Insert/Move/
Regen/Straighten/Tangent/Width/
eXit <N>: X ↵
```
Exits from Edit vertex mode

```
Open/Join/Width/Edit vertex/Fit/
Spline/Decurve/Ltype gen/Undo/
eXit <X>: Press Enter
```
Exits from PEDIT

Command: *From the toolbar, choose* QSAVE

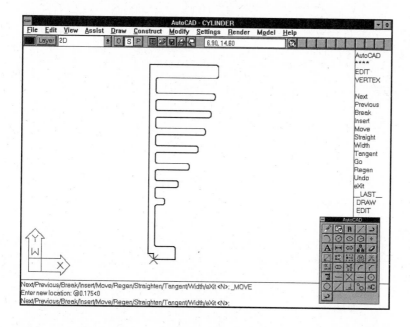

**Figure 9.34:**

The completed cylinder, with the notch.

# Using EXPLODE on Polylines

If you must edit a polyline extensively, it may be easier to edit the vertices or to explode the polyline into individual segments, and then rejoin the segments after you perform your edits. The EXPLODE command breaks a polyline into its individual segments. One disadvantage of using EXPLODE is that polylines lose their width and tangent information after they are exploded. EXPLODE locks in curves and splines by converting the polyline to many arcs or small straight lines. If wide polylines are exploded, only their center lines show (see fig. 9.35). If you explode the cylinder's polyline, 72 entities emerge.

**Figure 9.35:**

A polyline before and after explosion.

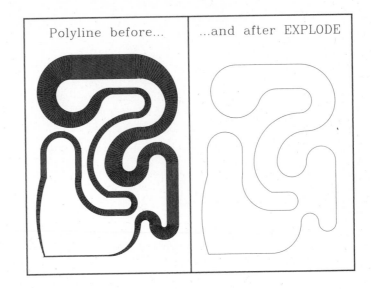

Polyline before...    ...and after EXPLODE

# Using PEDIT Fit and Spline Curves

The PEDIT command provides two options for making polyline curves that pass through control points: a fit curve and a spline curve. As you see in the next exercise, the cylinder profile dramatically shows the different results between fit curves and spline curves. A *fit curve* passes through vertex control points and consists of two arc segments between each pair of vertices (see fig. 9.36). A *spline curve* interpolates between control points but does not usually pass through the vertices (see fig. 9.37). The framework of vertices is called the *spline frame*.

PEDIT spline curves create arcs or short-line segments approximating the curve of the arc. To help you visualize a spline curve, AutoCAD provides a system variable called SPLFRAME. You can set SPLFRAME to 1 to show you the reference frame and vertex points for a spline curve. The fineness of the approximation and type of segment is controlled by the SPLINESEGS system variable. The numeric value controls the number of segments. A positive value generates line segments; a negative value creates arc segments. Arcs are more precise, but slower. The default is 8 (line segments).

You can generate two kinds of spline curves: a quadratic b-spline (type 5) or a cubic b-spline (the default, type 6). Both spline curves are controlled by the SPLINETYPE system variable.

In the next exercise, try both fit and spline curves by using the cylinder fins as your control points. After you generate the spline curve, turn SPLFRAME on to see the reference frame for the curve. The exercise shows you how to regenerate the drawing in the PEDIT command, to make the frame visible. After you finish, use the Undo option to restore the original cylinder profile. Be careful using the Decurve option; it removes the fillets in the drawing. If you try it, undo to recover the fillets.

## Using PEDIT To Make a Fit and a Spline Curve

Command: *Choose* **M**odify, *then*
**P**olyline Edit

Select objects: **L** ↵       Selects the polyline

Select objects: *Press Enter*

_.PEDIT Select polyline:

Open/Join/Width/Edit vertex/Fit/    Creates a fit curve, as shown in figure 9.36
Spline/Decurve/Ltype gen/Undo/
eXit <X>: *From the screen menu,*
*choose* Fit Curv

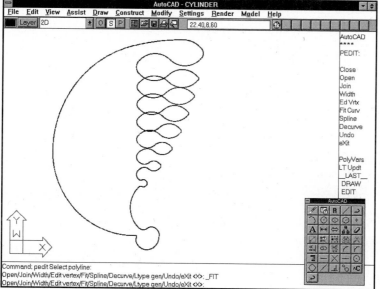

**Figure 9.36:**

The piston cylinder after fit curve.

Open/Join/Width/Edit vertex/Fit/    Creates a spline curve, as shown in figure 9.37
Spline/Decurve/Ltype gen/Undo/
eXit <X>: *From the screen menu,*
*choose* Spline

*continues*

**Figure 9.37:**

The piston
cylinder after
spline curve.

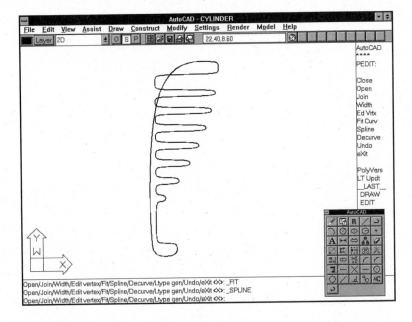

```
Open/Join/Width/Edit vertex/Fit/
Spline/Decurve/Ltype gen/Undo/
eXit <X>: 'SPLFRAME ↵

>>New value for SPLFRAME <0>: 1 ↵        Turns on frame

Resuming PEDIT command.
```

The frame does not appear until you use Edit vertex to regenerate the polyline.

```
Open/Join/Width/Edit vertex/Fit/
Spline/Decurve/Ltype gen/Undo/eXit
<X>: From the screen menu, choose Ed Vrtx

Next/Previous/Break/Insert/Move/        Regenerates the image to display the frame
Regen/Straighten/Tangent/Width/eXit     (see fig. 9.38)
<N>: From the screen menu, choose Regen

Next/Previous/Break/Insert/Move/        Exits from Edit vertex mode
Regen/Straighten/Tangent/Width/eXit
<N>: From the screen menu, choose eXit


Open/Join/Width/Edit vertex/Fit/        Undoes the change to the SPLFRAME setting
Spline/Decurve/Ltype gen/Undo/
eXit <X>: From the screen menu,
choose Undo
```

```
Open/Join/Width/Edit vertex/Fit/          Exits from PEDIT
Spline/Decurve/Ltype gen/Undo/eXit
<X>: From the screen menu, choose eXit

Command: U ↵                              Undoes the PEDIT, restoring the original
                                          cylinder profile
```

Figure 9.38 shows a spline curve with its associated frame.

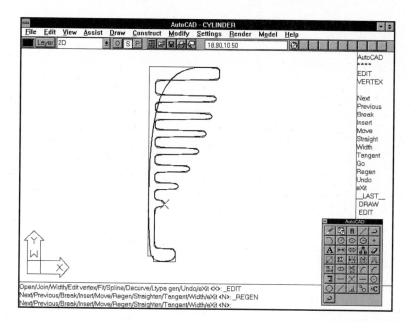

**Figure 9.38:**

A spline curve with frame.

When you displayed the reference frame for spline curves, the original cylinder profile and points appeared. If you are editing a spline curve and you need to know the location of the control points, use the SPLFRAME system variable to view your frame of reference.

After you undo your curve fitting, your drawing should look like the original in figure 9.34. Although you have moved, stretched, and curved the polyline, it still is a continuous polyline.

**NOTE**

*The BREAK and TRIM commands make curve- and spline-fitting permanent. The PEDIT Break option and EXTEND command enable subsequent polyline edits to decurve and refit curves or splines. Curve-fit and spline-fit polylines can become complex. See the Autodesk manual,* Using AutoCAD for Windows, *for their quirks and interactions with other editing commands.*

# Controlling Polyline Linetype Generation

When broken linetypes (such as Hidden) are used with polylines, short and spline or curve fit segments may appear continuous because there is not enough space between vertices to display the broken line pattern. In such cases, you can use the PLINEGEN system variable to control how the linetype is generated. When the variable is set to 0 (off is the default) each vertex of the polyline starts the linetype pattern over again. When PLINEGEN is set to 1 (on), the linetype pattern is generated uniformly over the whole polyline. This displays a uniform linetype pattern across vertices, but sometimes corners fall in a gap in the pattern. The PLINEGEN variable controls linetype generation of new polylines. To change existing polylines, use the Ltype gen option of PEDIT to change the linetype generation. Both of these methods are used in the following exercise and illustrated in figures 9.39 and 9.40. Notice the differences in the corners and fillets.

## Controlling Polyline Linetype with PLINEGEN

Continue with the CYLINDER drawing from the previous exercise.

Command: *Select the polyline*                Displays grips

Command: **CHPROP** ↵

1 found
Change what property (Color/LAyer/
LType/Thickness) ? **LT** ↵

New linetype <BYLAYER>: **HIDDEN** ↵

Change what property (Color/LAyer/        Changes the polyline to a hidden linetype
LType/Thickness) ? *Press Enter*          (see fig. 9.39)

Command: **PLINEGEN** ↵

New value for PLINEGEN <0>: **1** ↵

Command: **PEDIT** ↵

Select polyline: **L** ↵                  Selects Last

Open/Join/Width/Edit vertex/Fit/          Specifies the Ltype generation option
Spline/Decurve/Ltype gen/Undo/
<X>: **L** ↵

Full PLINE linetype ON/OFF <OFF>:         Regenerates the polyline with a uniform
**ON** ↵                                   linetype (see fig. 9.40)

Open/Join/Width/Edit vertex/Fit/          Exits from PEDIT
Spline/Decurve/Ltype gen/Undo/
eXit <X>: *Press Enter*

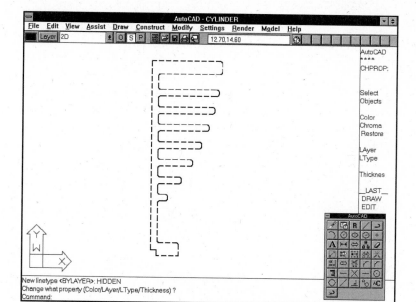

**Figure 9.39:**

The polyline with a per-segment hidden linetype.

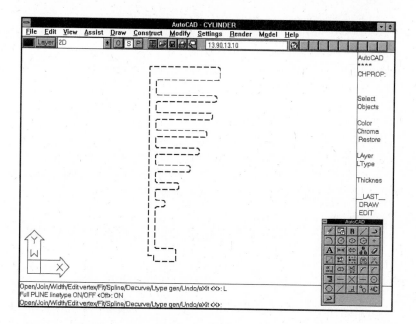

**Figure 9.40:**

The polyline with a smooth, continuous hidden linetype.

# Using PLUD

An AutoLISP-defined command called PLUD (short for PolyLine UpDate) can be used to control linetype generation. PLUD asks you whether you want to use the Full or Segment approach to generate linetypes in a polyline. You then are prompted to select a polyline. This routine is a combination of PLINEGEN and the Ltype gen option of PEDIT. This feature is used in the following exercise.

---

## Controlling Polyline Linetypes with PLUD

Command: **PLUD** ↵                          Loads and issues the PLUD command

Initializing...Full/Segment
<Full>: **S** ↵

Select objects: *Pick the polyline,*         Changes the linetype, as seen previously in
*then press Enter*                           figure 9.39

1 Polyline(s) updated.

Command: *Press Enter*                       Repeats PLUD command

PLUD Full/Segment <Full>: *Press Enter*      Accepts default

Select objects: *Pick the polyline,*         Changes the linetype, as seen previously in
*then press Enter*                           figure 9.39

1 PoLyline(s) updated

---

The system variable PLINEGEN should be set in your prototype drawing for the setting that works out best in your drawings. If you need to change a polyline you already created, use the PLUD command.

Another command that should be discussed with creating and editing polylines is XPLODE, which breaks apart polylines. You can, of course, use BREAK or TRIM, or you can use the XPLODE command, which is explained next.

# Using the XPLODE Command

The XPLODE command is an AutoLISP-defined command that you can use to break up complex entities, such as polylines, blocks, and dimensions, into simpler entities like lines, arcs, and text. Although complex entities are usually preferred, they must sometimes be broken apart to change or regroup them. The XPLODE command, which must be loaded before it can be used, is similar to the EXPLODE command except that it gives you more control over what happens to the color, layer, and linetype of the entities created after they are broken up. The following options are available with this command:

- **All.** This option enables all of the properties to be changed for the entities created from the XPLODE command.

- **Color.** This option enables you to set the color of the component entities or use the BYlayer choice.

- **LAyer.** This option enables a layer to be specified. The default is the current layer.

- **LType.** Similar to the LAyer option, any loaded linetype can be named or the default is the current linetype.

- **Explode.** The default option Explode works like the regular XPLODE command.

Try the XPLODE command in the following exercise. The XPLODE.LSP file is normally located in the SAMPLE subdirectory of AutoCAD. You must load it before use, using the **Applications** item in the **File** menu.

## Using the XPLODE Command

Command: *Choose* **F**ile, *then* App**l**ications,    Loads XPLODE
*then* **F**ile, *and select* xplode.lsp *from
the C:\ACADWIN\SAMPLE directory,
then choose OK, then* **L**oad

Loading C:\ACADWIN\SAMPLE\
XPLODE.LSP

C:XPlode loaded. Start command
with XP or XPLODE.

Command: **XP** ↵      Begins XPLODE

XPlode, Version 2.00, (c) 1991
by Autodesk, Inc. Select entities
to XPlode. *Select the polyline and
press Enter*

1 entities found.

All/Color/LAyer/LType/Inherit from
parent block/<Explode>: **ALL** ↵

New color for exploded entities.    Chooses White for the exploded entity
Red/Yellow/Green/Cyan/Blue/    color
Magenta/White/BYLayer/BYBlock/
<BYLAYER>: **W** ↵

Choose from the following list    Chooses the continuous linetype
of linetypes. Enter new linetype    for exploded entities
name. BYBlock/BYLayer/CONTinuous/
HIDDEN/<BYLAYER>: **CONT** ↵

XPlode onto what layer? <2D>:    Leaves entities on their current layer
*Press Enter*

Entity exploded with color of 7,
linetype of CONTINUOUS, and layer 2D.

The polyline exploded into individual lines and arcs on layer 2D, and the entity's color and linetype changed to white, continuous. Next, verify that the profile is no longer a polyline.

---

### Checking the Results of EXPLODE

`Select objects:` *Select one of the fin line segments*

`Command:` *From the toolbox, choose* ERASE      Erases the line

`Command:` **U** ↵      Undoes ERASE

`Command:` **U** ↵      Undoes XPLODE and restores the hidden linetype

`Command:` **CHPROP** ↵

`Select objects:` *Select the polyline and press Enter*

`Change what property (Color/LAyer/ LType/Thickness) ?` *From the screen menu, choose* LType

`New linetype <HIDDEN>:` *From the screen menu, choose* bylayer

`Change what property (Color/LAyer/ LType/Thickness) ?` *Press Enter*      Changes the polyline linetype

---

Use caution with the XPLODE command. Unless you are changing visible properties, it is hard to see if the command really worked. You may need to use XPLODE repeatedly to explode through nested levels of complex entities. Careless use of XPLODE may disable the database updating in some drawings. Exploded dimensions cannot be updated, exploded polylines lose special properties (such as segment widths), and exploded blocks have no associated attributes.

# Using REVSURF To Create a 3D Surface Mesh

You can use your cylinder profile to create a 3D surface mesh. The following exercise guides you through a quick 3D setup. The steps use a 3D viewpoint that looks down at the cylinder, so that you can see the surface mesh as it is formed. You use a 3D entity command called REVSURF (REVolve SURFace) to form the surface mesh, which forms a polyline surface mesh from the two-dimensional polyline that makes up the cylinder profile.

Do not worry about fully understanding the commands or the sequence used to create the 3D cylinder. Try the exercise to see how easily a complex 3D part is created. After you finish, save your drawing as 3DCYLIND.

## Using REVSURF To Make a Quick 3D Mesh

Reopen drawing CYLINDER (discarding changes), or continue from the "Using PEDIT To Add a Notch" exercise.

Command: *Turn off grid with F7, then*
*ZOOM All*

Command: *From the toolbox, choose* LINE          Defines axis of rotation line
*and draw from the point 10,15*
*to the polar point @13<270*

Command: *Use the toolbar layer drop-down*
*list to set layer* 3D *current*

Command: **SURFTAB1** ↵

New value for SURFTAB1 <6>: **24** ↵          Sets the vertical mesh density

Command: **SURFTAB2** ↵

New value for SURFTAB2 <6>: **4** ↵          Set the horizontal mesh density

Command: **WORLDVIEW** ↵

New value for WORLDVIEW <1>: **0** ↵          Sets for viewpoints relative to UCS

Command: *Choose* **D**raw, *then* **3**D Surfaces,     Issues REVSURF
*and choose* **S**urface of Revolution

Command: _revsurf

Select path curve: *Pick the polyline*
*cylinder profile*

Select axis of revolution: *Pick near*
*the bottom of the rotation axis line*

Start angle <0>: *Press Enter*

Included angle (+=ccw, -=cw)          Draws a half-cylinder surface
<Full circle>: **180** ↵

Command: *From the toolbar, choose* Layer
*and freeze layer* 2D

Command: *Choose* **S**ettings, *then*          Issues the UCS command with prompt
U**C**S, *then* **A**xis, *then* **X**          for rotation

*continues*

```
Rotation angle about X axis <0>:
-90 ↵
```

Note that the UCS Icon changes to a broken pencil to warn you that the current view does not match the current drawing plane.

Command: *Choose* **V**iew, *then* **S**e**t** View,          Displays the Viewpoint Presets dialog box
*then* **V**iewpoint, *then* **P**resets

*Double-click in the X* **A**xis *edit box and*
*enter* **225**, *then double-click in* XY **P**lane
*edit box and enter* **17**, *then choose OK*

The viewpoint is rotated –45 degrees horizontally, and 17 degrees in the vertical from the XY axis (see fig. 9.41).

Command: *Choose* **F**ile, *then* Save **A**s,          Saves under new name
*then enter* **3DCYLIND** *and choose* OK

---

If you like the results shown in figure 9.41, see the 3D exercise in Part Five.

**Figure 9.41:**

A rotated half-section of a 3D cylinder.

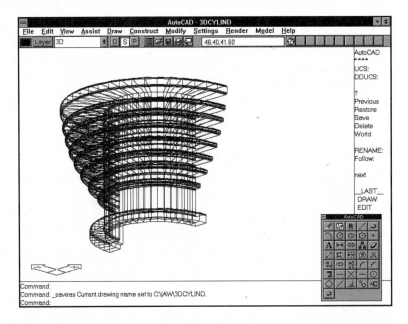

To cut down on computing time, the exercise only created a half-section of the cylinder. You can revolve the polyline 360 degrees to draw the full cylinder. If you have some time to kill or a fast 486-based computer, invoke the HIDE command to get rid of the hidden lines (see fig. 9.42).

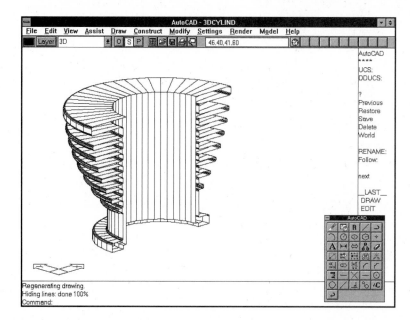

**Figure 9.42:**

A 3D piston half-cylinder after Hide.

---

## Using Hide To View Cylinder

Command: *Choose* **R**ender, *then* **H**ide          Issues HIDE

Command: Hide Regenerating drawing.     Redisplays the drawing with
Hiding lines: done nn%                  hidden lines removed

Quit AutoCAD and discard the changes to the drawing.

---

You see how powerful 3D editing commands are; it is easy to create the complex cylinder surface mesh from your cylinder's two-dimensional polyline. Continuity becomes important in 3D. To show the effect of discontinuity, the cylinder polyline was nicked in two places. The nicked cylinder was then revolved with REVSURF to form a 3D surface mesh.

The nicked profile is shown in figure 9.43. The two Xs mark the places at which the polyline was broken. The resulting 3D image is shown in figure 9.44. As you can see, the 3D mesh formation halts at the break points. The nicked 2D profile looks almost the same as your original profile, but it gives vastly different results when you form a 3D surface image.

**Figure 9.43:**

A cylinder profile
with breaks
creating two open
polylines instead
of one closed one.

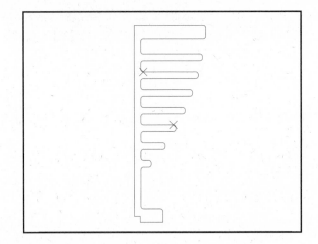

**Figure 9.44:**

A 3D half-cylinder
created with a
nicked polyline.

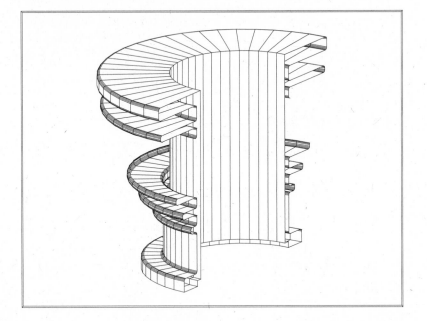

 *You can erase the CYLINDER drawing; you will not need it again.*

# Summary

After you start editing, your drawings become dynamic. You now have an advanced editing course under your belt and you see that the editing process itself can give you added power and control. The editing commands—EXTEND, OFFSET, STRETCH, TRIM, SCALE, and PEDIT—are new tools that do not have exact counterparts in the manual world. These editing commands operate on multiple entities. When you combine these advanced editing tools with the electronic equivalent of construction lines, you can create fast, accurate drawings.

One trick to using these commands is to plan ahead. Do not get trapped into traditional thinking. It would have been a laborious process to draw the cylinder profile line-by-line and point-by-point. Plan on using EXTEND, OFFSET, STRETCH, and TRIM to refine a rough drawing, and use PEDIT to obtain the detailing features you want.

A second trick to using these new editing commands is to think about how the drawing is constructed. As you work with the more complex commands, the behind-the-scenes construction is almost as important as the appearance of the final drawing. You saw how two little nicks in a 2D polyline drastically affect a 3D object.

# Drawing Construction Techniques

The process of learning individual AutoCAD commands is an important step for becoming proficient in CAD drafting. The real challenge, however, is to use the drawing and editing tools in a productive manner to create CAD drawings. Typically, there are many ways to approach a drawing project. The methods you have used in the past with manual drafting or other CAD software can determine the AutoCAD methods that work well for you.

## Using Advanced Construction Methods

This chapter is about methodology—it shows you ways to combine many of the drawing and editing commands that you learned in previous chapters with construction lines, point filters, and undo marks. You learn to use these powerful tools rapidly and efficiently in constructing your drawings.

# Point Filters and Construction Lines

*Point filters* are construction tools. The best way to visualize point filters is to consider them as invisible construction lines. Figure 10.1 compares construction lines and point filters. Construction lines are as important in CAD as they are in manual drafting. When you use a construction line to help draw an entity, you are really looking for an X- or Y-coordinate value to use as a guideline.

**Figure 10.1:**

Construction lines and point filter techniques compared.

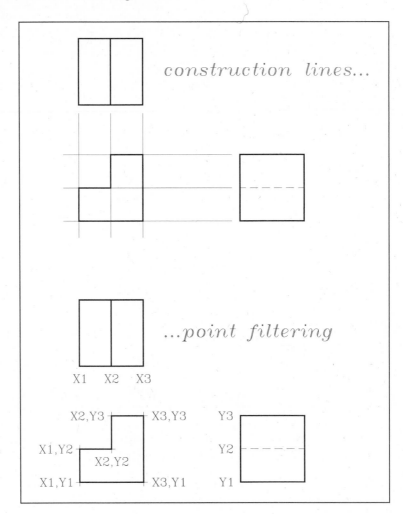

Point filters give you the advantages of construction lines without requiring extra work ahead of time. Point filters enable you to indicate the coordinate values of the existing geometry and eliminate the need for drawing a construction line. After you become accustomed to using point filters, they can increase your drawing productivity.

The following drawing exercise, called MOCKUP, demonstrates the use of these construction techniques. The MOCKUP drawing setup is stored on the IAW DISK as the IAWMOCK drawing. A second drawing on the disk, IAWMOCK2, has the completed left view of the flange. Point filters are used to help construct the section view on the right. If you want to jump directly to the section on point filters, turn to "Using XYZ Point Filters for Section Construction," in this chapter and use the IAWMOCK2 drawing as your starting drawing.

# UNDO Marks

You have seen the U or UNDO commands reverse the effects of a previous command. The U command is issued by the Undo option of the **E**dit menu, and the UNDO command is found on the toolbox and on the EDIT screen menu. As you design and draft, you often try alternatives that may or may not work well. These alternatives often involve a long series of commands. Although you can undo repeatedly to back up and try again, it is often easier to place a mark in your drawing session at the beginning of the alternative branch, so that you can backtrack to that editing point in a single step. *Undo marks* are like editing bookmarks in your drawing. After placing a mark, you can try a command sequence, go back to your mark if it does not work, and then try an alternate sequence.

You place a mark by choosing Mark from the UNDO command on the EDIT menu. When Back is chosen from the UNDO command options, AutoCAD backs up through the previous commands until the mark is found. Each time you start a drawing session, AutoCAD keeps track of every command you execute by writing it to a temporary file on disk. This temporary file records all of your moves whenever you are in the drawing editor. You do not find this file on disk when you in an editing session because it is a hidden file. At the end of an editing session, AutoCAD wipes out its temporary files and cleans up the disk. While you are in an editing session, however, you can play your drawing sequence in reverse, undoing each command, or you can redo parts of your past command sequence if you undo too much.

*If you have a printer hooked up to your system, you can get a hard copy of all command prompts and your responses by echoing your command line output to the printer. With your printer on and ready to print, press Ctrl-Q to turn printer echo on or off.*

The Mark and Back options, as well as several other options, are seen when the UNDO command is typed or chosen from the toolbox or EDIT screen menu.

## Editing Tools

In addition to point filters and UNDO, this chapter's exercises also use the OFFSET, ARRAY, TRIM, FILLET, CHAMFER, CHANGE, CHPROP, and PEDIT editing commands, as well as the various grip modes. If you need to review these commands, refer to the two previous editing chapters and to Chapter 6.

# Setting Up for the Mockup Drawing

The mockup drawing is actually a plan and section view of a flange. As in the widget drawing, you do not have to know anything about flanges to learn the basic concepts of undo marks, construction lines, and point filters. The dimensions needed to create the drawing are shown in figure 10.2.

**Figure 10.2:**

The dimensioned mockup drawing.

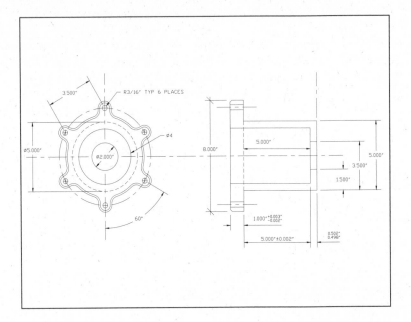

The first exercise creates a new drawing with the settings shown in table 10.1 by using the IAWMOCK drawing from the IAW DISK as a prototype. Although most drawings like this probably would be drawn in decimal units, the book uses this example to demonstrate fractional units, as shown in table 10.1. The drawing limits are set to 34"×22". The plotting scale factor is 1:2 for a 17"×11" final drawing.

**Table 10.1**
**Mockup Drawing Settings**

| COORDS | GRID | LTSCALE | ORTHO | SNAP |
|--------|------|---------|-------|------|
| On | 1 | 1 | ON | 1 |
| **UNITS** | Set UNITS to 5. Fractional, 64ths denominator. Default the other Units settings. | | | |
| **LIMITS** | Set LIMITS from 0,0 to 34,22. | | | |
| **ZOOM** | Zoom All. | | | |
| **VIEW** | Save view as A. | | | |

| Layer Name | State | Color | Linetype |
|------------|-------|-------|----------|
| 0 | On | 7 (White) | CONTINUOUS |
| CENTER | On/Current | 1 (Red) | CENTER |
| DIMS | On | 2 (Yellow) | CONTINUOUS |
| HIDDEN | On | 4 (Cyan) | HIDDEN |
| PARTS | On | 3 (Green) | CONTINUOUS |

# Using Construction Lines

The first step in making the mockup is to rough-in the construction lines. Create these lines by using your CENTER layer as a background layer. This step defines the two major sections of the drawing. You then can use the PARTS layer to draw the flange and its section view.

## Using OFFSET To Create Construction Lines

Choose File, then New, and enter **MOCKUP=IAWMOCK**. Use the LINE command to draw a line from 4,13 to @24<0, then another line from 10,7 to @12<90.

Command: *From the toolbox, choose CIRCLE,*
*and draw a 3" radius circle at 10,13*
*(see fig. 10.3)*

Command: *Choose* **C**onstruct, *then* **O**ffset

*continues*

| | |
|---|---|
| Offset distance or Through <Through>: 16 | Specifies the offset distance |
| Select object to offset: *Pick the vertical line* | |
| Side to offset? *Pick any point to the right of the line* | Shows which direction to offset |
| Select object to offset? *Press Enter* | Ends the command |
| Command: *Press Enter* | Repeats the OFFSET command |
| _OFFSET Offset distance or Through <16>: *Offset circle to outside with distance 1 to create a 4" radius circle (see fig. 10.4)* | |

**Figure 10.3:**

The construction lines and circle.

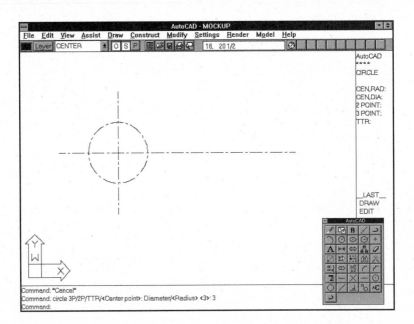

The two circles in your drawing are temporary construction lines that help you form the complex entity that makes up the perimeter of the flange.

Look at figure 10.2 again. The perimeter of the top flange is a polyline with six lugs sticking out, so it is difficult to draw this entire perimeter as a single polyline. The next three exercises show you how to create one-sixth of the perimeter, array this to get the basic perimeter, and then form a polyline by joining all of the adjoining entities.

Because you are creating several entities to represent the top flange and because you are also using several different editing commands, this is a good place in the drawing sequence to put an undo mark in your drawing file. If the next three sequences produce undesirable results, you can easily come back to this point.

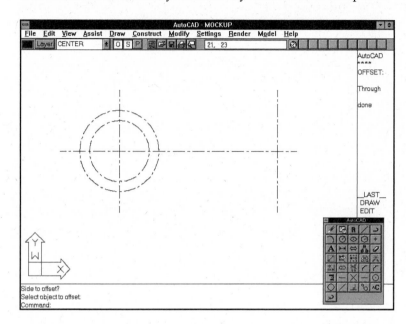

**Figure 10.4:**

An offset of the circle and line.

Use UNDO to place a mark in your drawing, and then resume construction of the lug that sticks out from the top of the flange perimeter. The lug is constructed on the PARTS layer.

## Using Construction Entities To Draw a Lug

Command: *From the toolbox, choose* UNDO

Command: undo Auto/Back/Control/End    Places a mark
/Group/Mark/<number>: **M** ↵

Command: *From the toolbar, choose* Zoom
*and select the view shown in figure 10.5*

Command: *Use the toolbar drop-down layer
list to set the* PARTS *layer current*

Command: *From the toolbox, choose* Circle

circle 3P/2P/TTR/<Center point>:
*From the screen menu, select* 2-Point:

*continues*

```
_2p First point on diameter:
```
*Pick at ① in figure 10.5*

```
Second point on diameter:
```
*Pick at ②*

```
Command:
```
*From the screen menu, choose CEN,DIA:*

```
Command: circle 3P/2P/TTR/
<Center point>:
```
*Pick at ③*

```
_D Diameter <1>: 3/8 ↵
```

```
Command:
```
*From the toolbox, choose LINE*    Starts the LINE command

Make sure SNAP is on, so the start and end points of the next two lines can be picked easily. Draw the two lines shown in figure 10.6, starting at ④ and ⑤.

```
Command:
```
*From the toolbar, choose QSave*    Saves the drawing

---

**Figure 10.5:**

Starting a lug construction with circles.

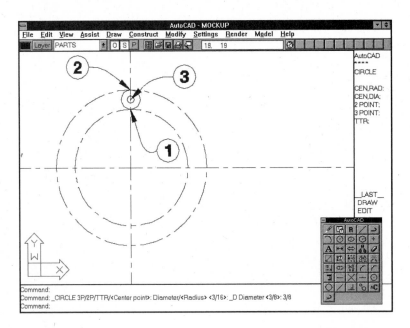

This is a good place in the drawing to experiment with undoing and redoing commands.

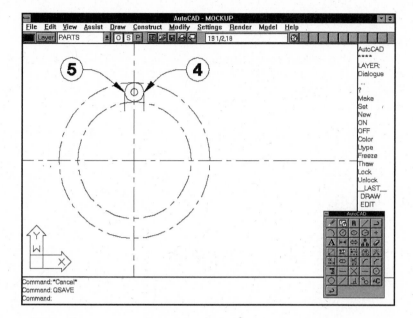

**Figure 10.6:**
The lug construction after adding lines.

# Controlling AutoCAD's UNDO

AutoCAD provides several commands to make changes or to correct mistakes made during the drawing process. Many of these commands have already been mentioned, and they are now demonstrated in this exercise. The most-used editing command, ERASE, is easy to use; and the OOPS command quickly brings back entities that are accidentally erased.

Erasing the last item you drew, however, is only part of the process of going back through your drawing file. When you do decide to go back, it is often to undo a whole sequence of draw and edit commands.

## The U Command

The U command is a "mini-undo," which backs up by one step or command. Whatever you did immediately before issuing the U command is undone when you type **U**. Unlike the OOPS command, however, U works many times, stepping back through each previous last command, one by one. In this sense, U is similar to the Undo option in LINE or PLINE, which deletes line or polyline segments by going back one segment at a time. You can even undo an OOPS or an ERASE by using the U command.

# The UNDO Command

The UNDO command, when entered or selected from the toolbox or EDIT screen menu, offers more control than does the U command. By using UNDO, you can specify the number of steps you want to return. You also can set marks or group a series of commands together, so that if the process does not work, you can undo the whole series at once.

# The REDO Command

If you issue REDO immediately after the UNDO command, REDO reverses, or cancels, the UNDO. Thus, you can experiment if you are not sure how far back you want to go. You can do something drastic—undo 20 commands for example—and then recover with a REDO. You can even play back your drawing sequences with UNDO (see fig. 10.7), and then use REDO to show or teach someone else what you have done.

**Figure 10.7:**

The Mockup drawing after UNDO 4.

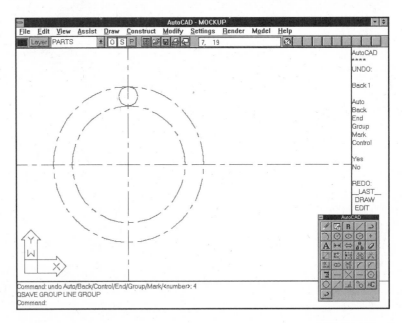

Use the following illustrations and exercise sequence to test the U, UNDO, and REDO commands. When the test is complete, your drawing should look the same as it does now.

## Using U, UNDO, and REDO on an Editing Sequence

Command: *Choose* Edit, *then* Undo        Undoes the last command

_U QSAVE                                    Shows the last command it undid

Although UNDO showed QSAVE as an undone command, commands that write to the disk are never actually undone.

Command: *Choose* **E**dit, *then* **R**edo    Reverses the U command

_redo

Command: *From the toolbox, choose* UNDO

Auto/Back/Control/End/Group/Mark    Undoes the last four commands
/<number>: **4** ↵

QSAVE GROUP LINE GROUP

Command: *Choose* **E**dit, *then* **R**edo    Reverses the UNDO command

_redo

Command: *From the toolbox, choose* UNDO

Auto/Back/Control/End/Group/Mark/    Backs up to the previously set
<number>: **B** ↵    mark (see fig. 10.8)

QSAVE GROUP LINE GROUP GROUP
CIRCLE LAYER ZOOM
Mark encountered

Command: *Choose* **E**dit, *then* **R**edo    Reverses the UNDO command (see fig. 10.6)

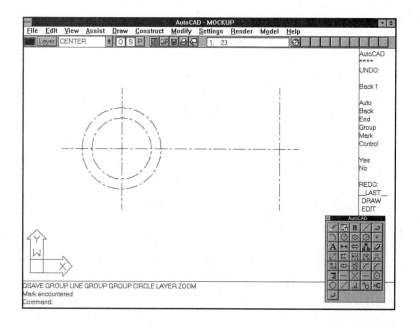

**Figure 10.8:**

The Mockup drawing after an UNDO Back.

If you accidentally undo too much and you cannot recover the data, reload your saved drawing. Remember, commands that write to the disk are never actually undone. The UNDO Back option used in the exercise is only one of six options that control UNDO. The following section lists the UNDO options.

# UNDO Options

- **<number>.** This option is the UNDO default. It enables you to enter a number, and AutoCAD steps back by that many steps.

- **Auto.** An ON/OFF setting, the Auto option affects menu items only. Sometimes, a single menu item creates or edits many entities. Normally, everything done by one command is one step back in Undo. If Auto is set to ON (the default), it causes an entire menu item to be treated as a single step by making it an undo *group*.

- **Back** and **Mark.** The UNDO Back option undoes until it returns to the beginning of the editing session, an undo mark, or a PLOT command (because AutoCAD re-initializes the undo file as if the editing session started after the plot). If no mark has been placed, you get a warning: This will undo everything. OK <Y>. Respond with a **Yes** or **No.** You set an undo mark by executing the UNDO command with the Mark option. This option is available from the UNDO screen menu by choosing Mark. You can mark as many times as you like, each time setting a stop for the next UNDO Back. UNDO Marks are not saved with the drawing file. UNDO Back removes the mark it encounters, so you must set another Mark if you want to undo back to the same point.

- **Control.** The creation of the temporary undo file can take a large amount of disk space. The Control option enables you to specify how active the temporary file is with the following three options: All/None/One. All is the default. None turns UNDO off. One limits UNDO to just one step back. When set to One, none of the other UNDO options are available. All restores UNDO to its full function.

- **Group** and **End.** Like Back and Mark, the Group and End options put boundaries on the series of commands in the temporary file, so that you can undo the series in one step. You begin a group with the Group option, end the group with the End option, and then continue working. Later, you step back using U or UNDO <number>. When the backstep gets to an End, the next UNDO step wipes out everything between the End and Group markers as a single step.

Be careful not to undo too much. Any settings during a command, including toggles or transparent commands, are undone with the main command. Although UNDO can wipe out your entire drawing, you can save it if you catch it immediately with REDO.

*In the exercises in the rest of the book (and in your own work), place undo marks to give yourself additional checkpoints in the editing session. If you then need to retry a sequence, you can easily step back and do it.*

# Using Array Techniques To Construct the Flange Perimeter

Continue drawing the flange. First, finish the lug by using the TRIM command, which is easier than trying to calculate the exact arc and line lengths that make up the lug. It also ensures that all the endpoints match.

### Using TRIM To Draw First Lug of Flange

`Command:` *Use the toolbar, F9, or Ctrl-B to turn off snap*

`Command:` *From the toolbox, choose* TRIM

`trim`
`Select cutting edge(s)...`

`Select objects:` *Select the 3" circle at ①, shown in figure 10.9, and use the shift key to add the lines at ② and ③*

`Select objects:` *Press Enter*  Completes the cutting edge selection

`<Select object to trim>/Undo:`  Trims the line
*Pick the line at ②*

`<Select object to trim>/Undo:`
*Pick the line at ③*

`<Select object to trim>/Undo:`
*Pick the circle at ④*

`<Select object to trim>/Undo:`
*Pick the circle at ⑤*

`<Select object to trim>/Undo:`  Finishes the TRIM command (see fig. 10.10)
*Press Enter*

`Command:` *Use the toolbar to turn snap back on*

**Figure 10.9:**

Picks for the circle
and line trim.

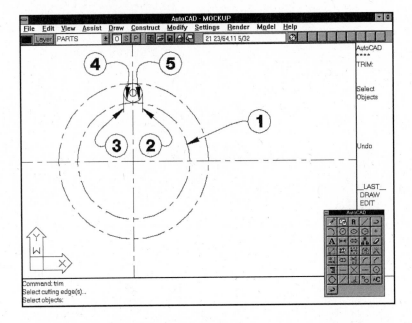

**Figure 10.10:**

A completed lug
after trimming.

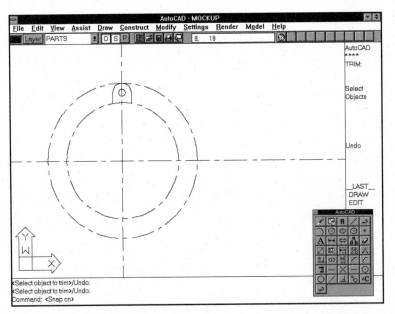

The first lug is now complete, as shown in figure 10.10. The perimeter in the target
drawing showed the lug in six places. You can array the lug now and draw the remaining entities between the arrayed lugs, but it is more efficient to complete one-sixth of
the perimeter and then perform the array.

# Completing a One-Sixth Portion To Array

AutoCAD's editing commands are used here to do the calculation and construction. Use the rotate autoedit mode to set up a one-sixth segment of the circle. Then use the ARC and FILLET commands and object snaps to complete the segment.

## Using Autoedit Rotate and ARC To Construct a Perimeter Segment

Command: *Select the short lug line on the right side (see fig. 10.11)*　　Displays grips

Command: *Pick any grip*

```
** STRETCH **
<Stretch to point>/Base point/Copy/
Undo/eXit: RO ↵
```
Enters rotate mode

```
** ROTATE **
<Rotation angle>/Base point/Copy/
Undo/Reference/eXit: B ↵
```
Issues the base option

```
Base point: 10,13 ↵
```
Sets the base point at the center of the flange

```
** ROTATE **
<Rotation angle>/Base point/Copy/
Undo/Reference/eXit: 60 ↵
```
Rotates the lug line 60 degrees counterclockwise

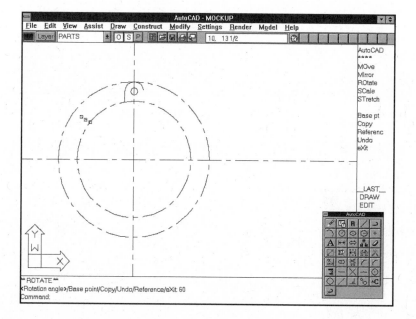

**Figure 10.11:**

The rotated lug line, with grips.

*continues*

Command: *From the toolbox, choose* ARC
*then from the screen menu choose* S,C,E

_ARC Center/<Start point>: *From the
toolbox, choose* ENDPOINT

endp of *Pick at* ① *(see fig. 10.12)*

Center/End/<Second point>:_c Center:
*From the toolbox, choose* INTERSECTION

int of *Pick at* ②                        Picks the arc's center

Angle/Length of chord/<End point>:      Picks the arc's endpoint
DRAG *From the toolbox, choose* ENDPOINT

endp of *Pick at* ③                       Draws arc from ① to ③

**Figure 10.12:**

The arc is added
to the one-sixth
segment.

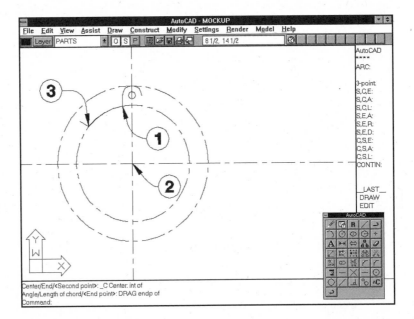

# Using FILLET To Complete the Perimeter Segment

Command: *Use the toolbar to turn off snap*

Command: *From the toolbox, choose* Fillet

Command: fillet Polyline/Radius/
<Select first object>: *From the
screen menu, choose* radius

| | |
|---|---|
| `Enter fillet radius <0>: 1/2 ↵` | Sets radius and reissues FILLET |
| `Command: _FILLET Polyline/Radius/`<br>`<Select first object>:` *Pick the arc*<br>*at ① and the line at ② (see fig. 10.13)* | Fillets the arc and line |

If you have difficulty selecting the small arc instead of the large arc, zoom in or use DDLMODES to temporarily lock the CENTER layer.

| | |
|---|---|
| `Command:` *Press Enter and pick the line*<br>*at ③ and the arc at ④ (see fig. 10.14)* | Repeats FILLET and fillets line and arc |

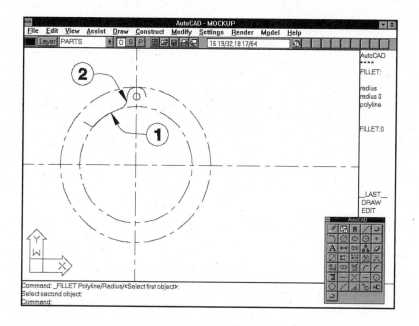

**Figure 10.13:**

Pick points and the first fillet.

You now are ready to create the perimeter by arraying the one-sixth segment. If you followed the construction sequence, all the entity points should line up. Notice that you have made only one trivial calculation: dividing the circle into sixths (60 degrees). By using object snaps and editing commands, you let AutoCAD do all the hard calculations and locations.

# Using ARRAY and PEDIT To Create the Perimeter

Use a polar array to replicate the one-sixth segment to complete the perimeter of the flange (see fig. 10.15). Then, use PEDIT with the Join option to group the entity segments into a single polyline. After you have joined the segments, create two circles in the interior of the flange.

**Figure 10.14:**

Pick points and the second fillet.

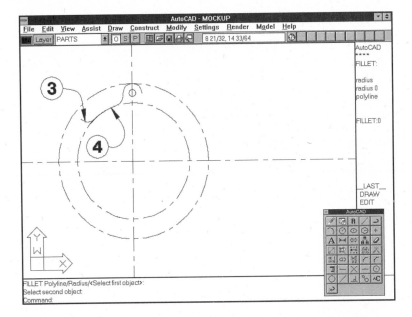

**Figure 10.15:**

The top flange after the array.

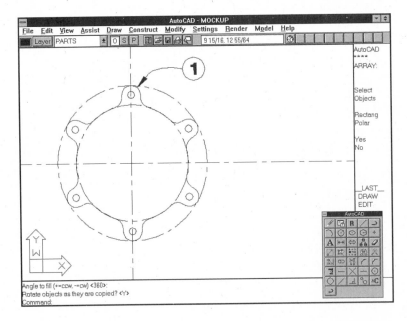

# Using ARRAY and PEDIT To Complete the Flange

Command: *Use FILTER or a window to*     Displays grips
*select all the green entities*

Command: *Choose* **C**onstruct, *then* **A**rray

`_array 7 found`

`Rectangular or Polar array (R/P)`
`<R>:` **P** ↵

Center point of array: *From the*     Specifies the center of the flange
*toolbox, choose* INTERSECTION, *then*
*pick at 10,13*

`Number of items:` **6** ↵

`Angle to fill (+=ccw, -=cw) <360>:`     Specifies a full circle
*Press Enter*

`Rotate objects as they are copied?`     Creates the array (see fig. 10.15)
` <Y>` *Press Enter*

Next, you join the flanges.

Command: *From the toolbox, choose* PEDIT

`Select objects:` *Pick first arc created*
*on top flange at* ① *in figure 10.15*

`Select objects:` *Press Enter*

`Entity selected is not a polyline`
`Do you want to turn it into one? <Y>`
*Press Enter*

`Close/Join/Width/Edit vertex/`
`Fit/Spline/Decurve/Ltype gen/`
`Undo/eXit <X>:` **J** ↵

`Select objects:` **ALL** ↵

`47 found`

`Select objects:` *Press Enter*

`35 segments added to polyline`     Join ignored the extra entities

`Open/Join/Width/Edit vertex/Fit/`     Creates a single polyline
`Spline/Decurve/Ltype gen/Undo/`
`eXit <X>:` *Press Enter*

Next, create the inside wall of the flange and the center hole in the bottom. Draw a 4"
diameter circle and a 2-1/2" diameter circle, both at 10,13.

Your drawing now should resemble figure 10.16.

*The PEDIT Join option requires that each entity endpoint match the adjacent endpoint exactly. For this reason, the command rejected the construction lines. If you do not get a complete join (if the Close option did not change to Open), undo it and try again.*

**Figure 10.16:**

Inner circles added to the top view of the flange.

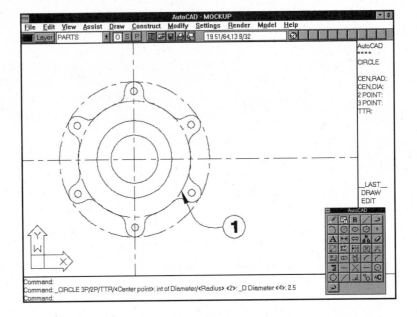

*You can use a far-off drawing corner, viewport, or a scratch UCS for background construction, putting together pieces of a drawing that you can later move, copy, or array into place.*

# Editing by Recycling Entities

You can save drawing time by recycling surplus construction circles, rather than by creating new ones. Change the inner construction circle's layer (linetype) and radius to make a hidden line for the outer wall. Then change the outer circle's radius to make a bolt ring center line (see fig. 10.17). You could use both the CHPROP (or DDCHPROP) and CHANGE commands, but a single DDMODIFY command can do it all.

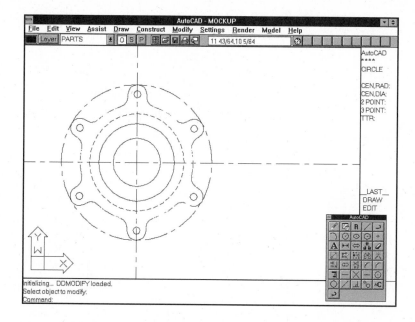

The first construction circle with changed layer and radius.

## Using DDMODIFY and CHANGE To Complete Top View

Command: *Choose **M**odify, then **E**ntity*

Select objects: *Select center line* | Selects circle and opens Modify
*construction circle at ① (see fig. 10.16)* | Circle dialog box
*and press Enter* |

*Click on **L**ayer..., select HIDDEN,* | Changes the circle layer to HIDDEN
*then click on OK* |

*Double-click in the **R**adius: edit box,* | Resets radius, closes dialog box, and
*type **2.5**, and choose OK* | modifies circle

Command: *Press Enter to repeat*
*DDMODIFY and change the **R**adius of*
*the outside circle to **3-1/2**" (see fig. 10.18)*

Command: *From the toolbox, choose*
REDRAW

Command: **QSAVE** ↵

**Figure 10.18:**

The second
construction circle
with changed
radius.

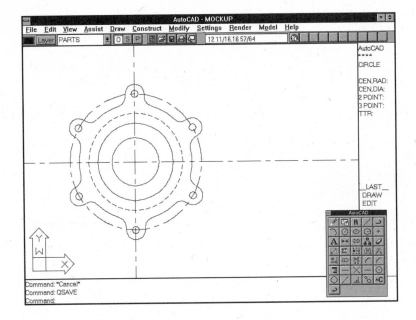

As the exercise demonstrates, you can still type a decimal entry when using fractional units.

The plan view of the flange is finished. This is a good point to take a break before using XYZ point filters to construct the section view of the flange.

# Using XYZ Point Filters for Section Construction

Figure 10.19 reveals that most of the geometry you need to draw the section view on the right already exists in the plan view. You can draw an accurate section quickly by aligning the new section lines with intersections of the lines and entities making up the plan view. You cannot draw the lines by simply aligning your crosshair cursor, however, because most of the intersection points are not on snap increments.

Using XYZ point filters makes this alignment an easy procedure. Point filters enable you to pick X, Y, and Z coordinates independently. Although Z filtering is extremely useful in 3D drawings, you can ignore it for now.

To use point filters, precede a point that you pick (or enter) with a .X or .Y (pronounced dot-X or dot-Y). The dot (period) distinguishes the point filter from command options that begin with an X or Y. AutoCAD then takes only the specified coordinate from the following point, and prompts you for the other coordinate values.

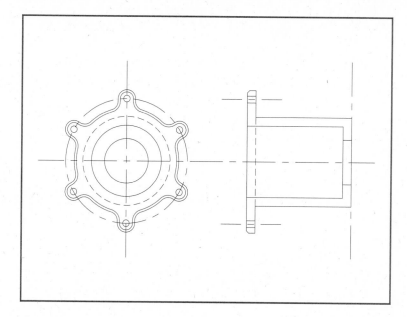

**Figure 10.19:**

A mockup target drawing.

When you specify a .X value, for example, you pick a point, or snap with object snap to an entity with the X value you want. AutoCAD then tells you that you need a Y value. You can pick, type, or use an object snap to get the Y value, which gives you the X,Y intersection point.

Because the flange is symmetrical, you only need to draw half of the section view, and then mirror the other half. Use the next exercise sequence with X and Y filters to create the lower half of the section, as shown in figures 10.20 through 10.23.

You can resume drawing by using the IAWMOCK2 drawing from the IAW DISK. It contains the completed plan view of the flange. Your current layer should be PARTS.

## Using XYZ Point Filters To Draw a Section View

Continue from the previous exercise, or choose File, New, and enter MOCKSECT=IAWMOCK2.

Command: *Zoom into area shown in figure 10.20*

Command: *Choose Settings, then Object Snap, put checks in the Intersection and Endpoint check boxes, then choose OK*  Sets running INT, ENDP object snap

Command: *Turn off snap*

Command: **APERTURE ↵**

*continues*

```
Object snap target height         Adjusts the size of the aperture box
(1-50 pixels)<10>: 6 ↵

Command: From the toolbox, choose LINE

From point: From the screen menu,
choose .X

.X of Pick anywhere on vertical base line
at ① (see fig. 10.20)

(need YZ): Pick intersection of hole and
vertical center line at ②

To point: @-.5,0 ↵               Draws the first line

To point: .X ↵

of Pick left side of last line drawn
at ③

  (need YZ): Pick inside of flange circle  Draws the second line
and vertical center line at ④
```

**Figure 10.20:**

The first and second lines of the section.

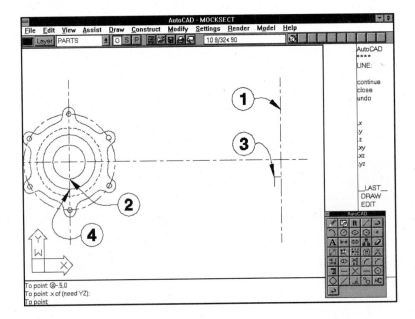

```
To point: @-5.5,0 ↵              Draws the third line (see fig. 10.21)

To point: From the screen menu,
choose .X
```

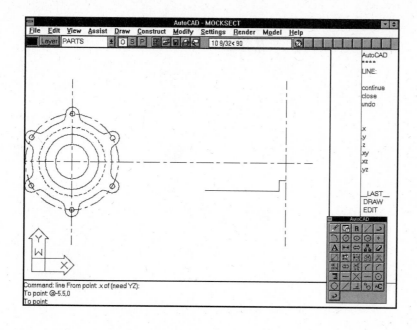

**Figure 10.21:**
The third line of
the section.

.X of  *Pick left side of last line drawn at*
⑤ *in figure 10.22*

(need YZ): *Pick intersection of arc and*
*vertical center line at* ⑥

Draws the fourth line (see fig. 10.22)

To point: @1/2,0 ↵

Draws the fifth line

To point: *From the screen menu,*
*choose .X*

of *Pick right side of last line drawn*
*at* ⑦ *(see fig. 10.23)*

(need YZ): *Pick intersection of hidden*
*circle and vertical line at* ⑧
*(see fig. 10.23)*

Draws the sixth line

To point: *From the toolbox,*
*choose* PERPENDICULAR

Uses PER to override running object snap

per to *Pick anywhere on vertical base*
*line at* ⑨

To point: C ↵

Closes to the beginning point

**Figure 10.22:**

The fourth and fifth lines of the section.

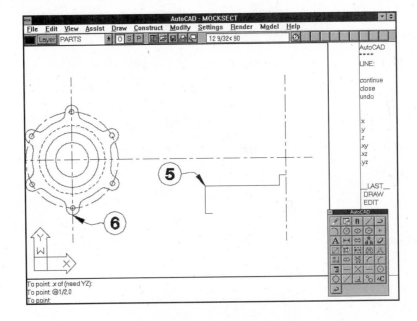

**Figure 10.23:**

A completed section outline.

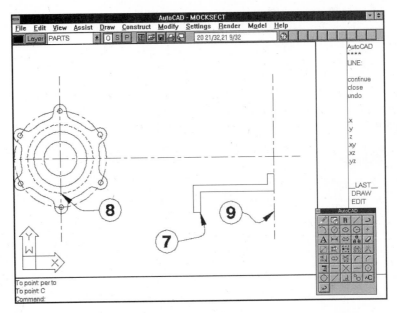

You used both command-line entry and the screen menu to select the .X filter. As you work on your own drawings, try different methods to see which is most efficient for you.

Your drawing should now show half a section view of the mockup part. Next, you complete the section half by using XYZ filters to add the lines for the hole in the top flange.

## Using XYZ Filter To Draw a Hole in the Section View

Command: *From the toolbox, choose* LINE    Issues the LINE command and displays filters on the screen menu

From point: *From the screen menu, choose* .x

.x of *Pick line of top flange in the section view at* ① *(see fig. 10.24)*

(need YZ): *Pick where the drilled hole and center line intersect at* ②

To point: *From the toolbox, choose* PERPENDICULAR

per to *Pick line in the section view at* ③

To point: *Press Enter*

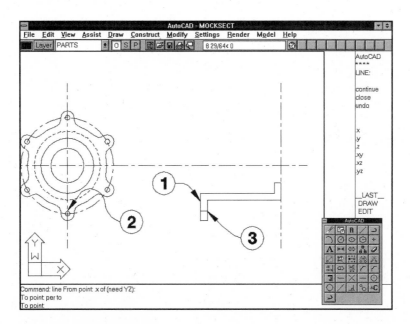

**Figure 10.24:**

A section view with hole lines.

`Command:` *From the toolbox, choose* LINE, *and repeat the process for the line at the bottom of the hole*

`Command:` *Use the toolbar layer list to set the* CENTER *layer current*

`Command:` *From the toolbox, choose* LINE

`From point:` `.X` ⏎          Begins center line for hole

`of` *Turn on snap momentarily to assist you in picking a point about 1" to the right of the bottom flange at* ④ *(see fig. 10.25)*

`(need YZ):` *Without snap, pick the center of the lug hole at* ⑤

`To point:` *Use snap again to pick a point 1" to the left of the top flange at* ⑥

`To point:` *Turn off snap and press Enter*

`Command:` *Use the toolbar layer list to set the* PARTS *layer current*

**Figure 10.25:**

A center line through the hole.

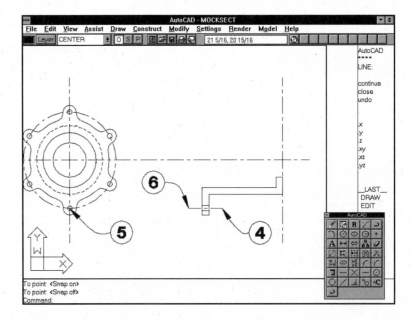

In the following exercise, to get the rest of the section view, mirror the lower half and add four more lines.

## Completing the Section View

| | |
|---|---|
| `Command:` *Select the section and center line, then pick a grip* | Enters stretch grip mode |
| `** STRETCH **`<br>`<Stretch to point>/Base point/`<br>`Copy/Undo/eXit:` *From the screen menu, choose* Mirror | Switches to mirror grip mode |
| `MIrror`<br>`** MIRROR **`<br>`<Second point>/Base point/Copy/`<br>`Undo/eXit:`*From the screen menu, choose* Base pt | |
| `B`<br>`Base point:` *From the toolbox, choose* INTERSECTION *and pick at* ① *(see fig. 10.26)* | Sets the base point |
| `** MIRROR **`<br>`<Second point>/Base point/Copy/`<br>`Undo/eXit:`*From the screen menu, choose* Copy | Enters Copy mode |
| `Copy`<br>`** MIRROR (multiple) **`<br>`<Second point>/Base point/Copy/`<br>`Undo/eXit:`*Pick a point to the left of the base point (the mirror image appears above the centerline)* | |
| `** MIRROR (multiple) **`<br>`<Second point>/Base point/Copy/`<br>`Undo/eXit:`*Press Enter* | Completes the mirror copy |
| `Command:` *Use the toolbar layer list to set the* HIDDEN *layer current* | |
| `Command:` *Choose* **D**raw, *then* **L**ine, *then* **1** Segment, *and draw a hidden line from* ② *to* ③ *(see fig. 10.27)* | |
| `Command:` *Use the toolbar layer list to set the* PARTS *layer current* | |

*continues*

Command: *Draw the three lines at* ④      Completes the section

Command: *Choose* **S**ettings, *then* **O**bject      Resets object snap to NONE
Snap, *clear the* Endpoint *and* **I**ntersection
*check boxes, then choose* **OK**

Command: **QSAVE** ↵      Saves to the default drawing

---

**Figure 10.26:**

The section after
mirroring.

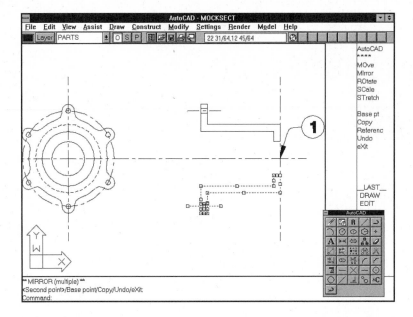

---

The target flange has a chamfer. Take a moment to chamfer the section view, and then
add the chamfer to the plan view by offsetting the perimeter. The following illustrations and exercise can help you do this procedure.

---

## Chamfer Edge of Flange

Zoom to the view shown in figure 10.28.

Command: *From the toolbox, choose*
CHAMFER

```
_chamfer Polyline/Distances
/<Select first line>: From the screen
menu, choose distance

_D Enter first chamfer distance
<0>: 1/8 ↵
```

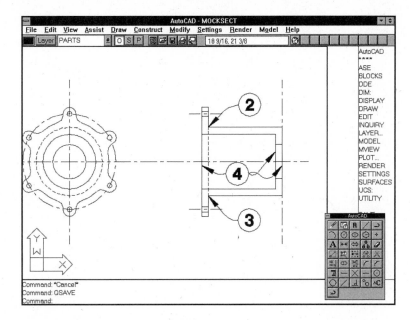

**Figure 10.27:**

The completed section.

| | |
|---|---|
| Enter second chamfer distance <1/8>: *Press Enter* | Sets distance and reissues CHAMFER command |
| _CHAMFER Polyline/Distances/ <Select first line>: *Pick the top flange line at ① (see figs. 10.28 and 10.29)* | |
| Select second line: *Pick the flange end line at ②* | Chamfers the lines |
| Command: *Press Enter* | Repeats the command |
| CHAMFER Polyline/Distances/<Select first line>: *Pick top flange line at ③* | |
| Select second line: *Pick the flange end line at ④* | |
| Command: *Choose **V**iew, then **Z**oom, then **P**revious* | |
| Command: *Choose **C**onstruct, then **O**ffset* | |
| _offset | |
| Offset distance or Through <16>: 1/8 ↵ | Changes the offset distance |

*continues*

**Figure 10.28:**

The section after chamfering.

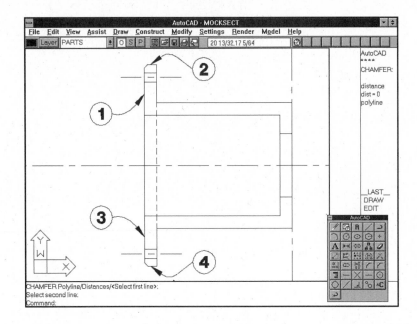

**Figure 10.29:**

Detail of the chamfer.

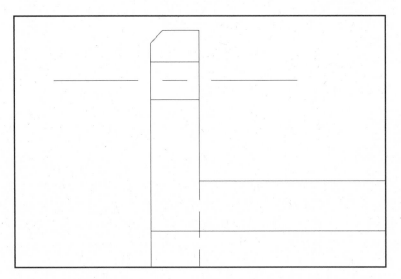

`Select object to offset:` *Pick any perimeter point on the top flange in the plan view*

Selects the entity to offset

`Side to offset?` *Pick a point inside the perimeter*

Draws offset polyline

`Select object to offset:` *Press Enter*    Exits command

*Save the drawing*

Figures 10.30 and 10.31 show the plan view of the flange with the new offset.

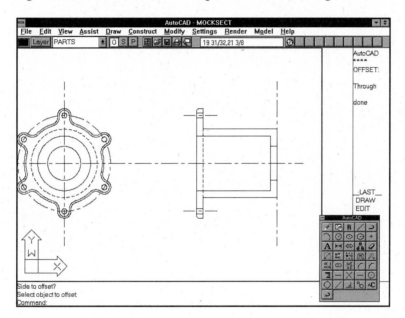

**Figure 10.30:**
The top view after offsetting.

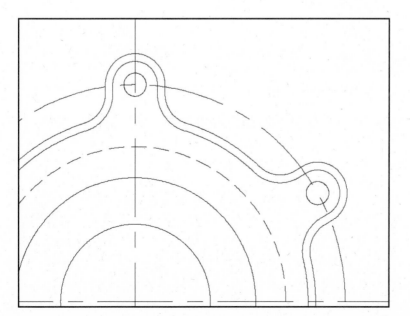

**Figure 10.31:**
Detail of the offset.

You use this MOCKSECT drawing later when you practice dimensioning.

*You can delete the MOCKUP drawing, which is no longer needed.*

# Defining Boundaries with BPOLY

A fast and easy way of defining a boundary around the inside of a group of entities is with the BPOLY (Boundary POLYline) command. This command brings up the Polyline Creation border dialog box (see fig. 10.32). The easiest way to use the command is to choose the **P**ick Points button, which accepts the default values in the dialog box and prompts you to choose an internal point. AutoCAD then draws a polyline around the area you selected, assuming that it is closed off with entities. To speed up the process and to give you more control over it, you may choose the Make **N**ew Boundary Set< button, which enables you to select the entities that AutoCAD uses in determining a boundary. **R**ay Casting gives additional control by enabling you to specify which direction to search from the selected point for entities to form the boundary. BPOLY also is used as part of the BHATCH command; see Chapter 14 for details on BHATCH.

**Figure 10.32:**

The BPOLY Polyline Creation dialog box.

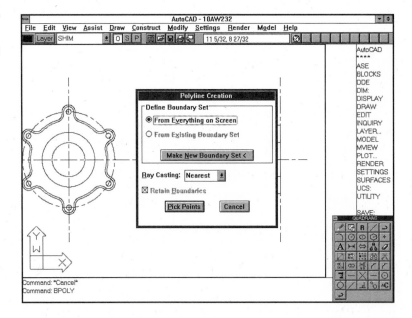

Next, use the BPOLY command to create an outline of a partial shim for the flange. After you create the shim outline, move it above the two existing views of the flange. To stop MOVE from finding the original entities, lock layers PARTS and CENTER.

## Defining Boundaries with BPOLY

Continue with the MOCKSECT drawing from the previous exercise.

Command: *Select the circle at ①*  Selects and shows grips
*(see fig. 10.33)*

Command: *From the toolbox, choose* ERASE  Erases hidden circle

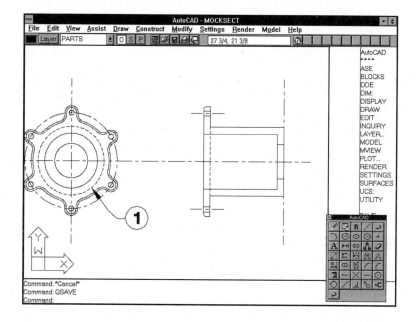

**Figure 10.33:**
The flange before BPOLY.

Use DDLMODES to create a new layer named SHIM with color yellow, and set it current. Lock layers PARTS and CENTER.

Command: **BPOLY** ↵  Opens the Polyline Creation dialog box

*Choose* **P**ick Points  Prompts for point

Select internal point *Pick at ②*  
*(see fig. 10.34)*

Selecting everything...  Searches for and highlights boundary  
Selecting everything visible...  
Analyzing the selected data...

*continues*

```
Select internal point Pick at ③,
```
④, *and* ⑤ *(see fig. 10.34)*

```
Select internal point Press Enter
```
Creates four boundary polylines

```
Command: From the toolbox, choose MOVE
```
Begins MOVE command

```
move
```

```
Select objects: Select a window
```
*enclosing the entire flange front view*
Selects entities on unlocked SHIM layer

```
15 found
11 were on a locked layer.
```

```
Select objects: Press Enter
```

*Turn ortho off and snap on*

```
Base point or displacement: From
```
*the toolbox, choose* INTERSECTION,
*then pick the intersection of the center
lines at the center of flange*

```
Second point of displacement:
```
*Pick a point near 17,20*

Pan to the view shown in figure 10.34 and redraw to clean up the image. Quit the drawing, discarding the changes.

**Figure 10.34:**

The shims added to the flange drawing.

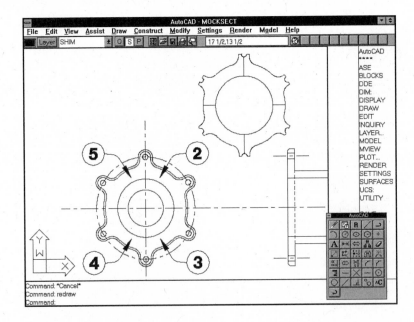

The BPOLY command saved considerable time and effort, and created a polyline that could be moved and modified in another part of the drawing. The task of generating Computer Numerical Control (CNC) tool paths from a mechanical part drawing is something for which this command is well suited. Boundary polylines are used later to automatically define hatch boundaries.

# Summary

AutoCAD's drawing construction tools are as much a frame of mind as they are a framework of commands and options. In the course of constructing the mockup, you learned ways to drop construction lines, use a construction underlayer, and trace over construction lines. You also learned ways to use point filters—combining them with object snaps to create a section view.

There is never only one way to build an AutoCAD drawing. In fact, the opposite is true—you can always find other ways to build the same drawing. The trick is to find the methods that work most intuitively and efficiently for you.

You can plan ahead and save many unnecessary steps, and you can recycle entities to save erasing and drawing again. Try to envision well in advance the commands you are going to use. If you can visualize the construction technique ahead of time, your drawing productivity increases dramatically.

You can use point filters and construction lines to line up entities, and you can use construction lines for center lines, base lines, and lines to align large numbers of points. You can use point filters for entity alignments, and you can use object snaps to help pick filtered points. Set up one or more layers for your construction lines. Construction lines do not have to be linear—use arcs and circles for angular or curved tracing. A few extra construction lines can make your life easier.

You can use the UNDO command to protect your work sequences. REDO can rescue from an UNDO error—but only immediately after the UNDO. Marks and Groups help control undos and make going back easier. Watch out for PLOT when you plan to undo. Going back to a mark is no substitute for saving regularly. Frequent saves are still the best way to protect your drawing file.

Would it be useful if you could save the contents of the selection set and use it as a rubber stamp whenever you need it? You can—with blocks, which is the topic of the next chapter.

# CHAPTER 11

# Grouping Entities into Blocks and Xrefs

In this chapter, you learn how to create, store, and use blocks. The process of grouping entities into blocks enables you to repeat them easily and efficiently in one or more drawing files and to make them into permanent symbols in a symbol library.

You also learn to work with *external reference files (xrefs)*, which are similar to blocks. Xrefs make work-group drafting (in which several people work on different parts of the same drawing) simple and less error-prone—xrefs are the key to effective distributed design. Externally referenced drawing files, when attached to a master drawing as an xref entity, become visible in that drawing without adding their data to the master drawing file. Xrefs are more efficient than blocks, and they automatically update drawings when changes are made. (Xrefs are examined as a separate topic following the section on blocks.)

## Using Block Parts, Symbols, and Features

Figure 11.1 illustrates an entire town that was created from different types of drawing blocks. *Blocks* group individual entities together and treat them as one object. Drawing symbols and parts are typical candidates for such groups (see fig. 11.2). Drawing *parts*, such as a car or desk, represent real objects, drawn full-size or at one-unit scale. *Symbols*, such as section bubbles, electrical receptacles, or welding symbols, are symbolic objects, which you can scale appropriately for plot size.

The Autotown
drawing with
simple and
complex blocks.

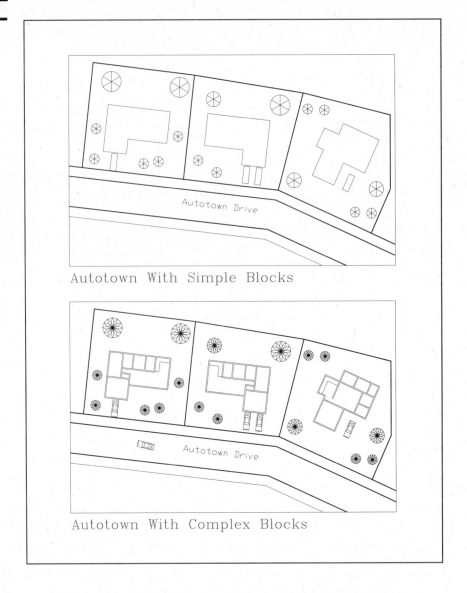

Autotown With Simple Blocks

Autotown With Complex Blocks

To move or copy symbol objects as individual drawing entities, you collect the individual entities into a selection set. As drawings become crowded, however, it becomes more difficult to select the entities you want. Selection is much easier if the entities are grouped together as a block. A block is saved with a name and can be reused in the same drawing later or reused in other drawings.

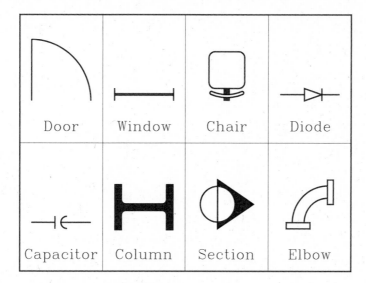

**Figure 11.2:**
Some common symbols and parts.

AutoCAD blocks enable you to operate on the group as a whole. Entities in blocks stick together; move one part of the block and the whole block moves. You can, of course, break up a block by exploding it if you need to edit it.

## Block Speed and Versatility

Libraries of frequently used blocks speed the process of creating AutoCAD drawings. A *library* can consist of many individual drawing files, each used as a single block; a few files, each containing many blocks; or a combination of both. To build such a library takes time, but it dramatically reduces design time for future projects.

Besides their convenience, blocks provide additional drawing and editing benefits. A block insertion is faster than redrawing the same objects 20 times in 20 different drawings or copying those objects 20 times in the same drawing. When you insert blocks into your drawing file, you can change their scale and rotation. You can use one block, such as a window or bolt head, to represent many different sizes of the same object instead of using multiple instances of the block. This method enables you to build your drawing quickly by modifying simple blocks. You also can globally replace one block with another, revising an entire drawing with a single command.

## Block Efficiency and Storage

One of the biggest advantages in using blocks is that they help minimize a drawing's file size. A smaller file takes less disk space and uses less memory when it loads. When you draw 100 lines, for example, you add 100 entities to your drawing. When you make a block containing 100 lines, AutoCAD creates a block definition containing 100 entities. This block of 100 lines is then stored as one entity in the drawing file. When you insert a block in your drawing, you add only one new entity—a reference to the block definition.

If you insert a block containing 100 lines into your drawing in 12 places, AutoCAD must store only 112 entities. These 112 entities include 100 lines in the block definition and 12 block references for the visible references. Without blocks, if you draw and copy 12 groups of 100 lines, you add 1200 entities to your drawing file. Blocks can save huge amounts of disk and memory space. Reducing the size of the drawing file with blocks lowers the time required to load it and leaves more memory free for AutoCAD program modules.

## Following the Block Exercises

You can use this chapter's exercises in two ways. First, the exercises in the early part of the chapter guide you through the basic block commands, including writing blocks to disk files and redefining blocks in a drawing. These blocks are also used for the Autotown exercise in Chapter 12.

Second, the section on xrefs guides you through creating, attaching, detaching, controlling, and converting xrefs. The exercises in this section are independent from the rest of the chapter.

# Examining Block Editing Tools

The process of grouping entities into blocks is quite simple. You use the BLOCK command to create a block definition, INSERT to place a block reference in a drawing, and WBLOCK to store a block's entities as a separate drawing file on disk. You find INSERT, BLOCK, and WBLOCK with two other block commands, BASE and MINSERT, on the BLOCKS screen menu. In addition, INSERT can be found under the **D**raw pull-down menu.

*This chapter uses commands from the screen menu; the next chapter explains using INSERT from the pull-down menu.*

In addition to these block commands, you learn in this chapter about three additional commands that you use with blocks: EXPLODE, DIVIDE, and MEASURE. These three commands are located on the EDIT screen menus.

*AutoCAD has another type of symbol entity, called a* shape. *Text is a special form of the shape feature. To learn more about shapes, see* Maximizing AutoCAD Release 12 *(New Riders Publishing).*

# Setting Up for Blocks

The next exercise helps you set up a drawing to create some simple blocks that you need·for developing Autotown in the next chapter. "Autotown" is a simple site plan that encompasses three building lots along an elegant street known as "Autotown Drive." The drawing uses feet and decimal inches. Be sure that the drawing limits are set at 360'×240'—a 36"×24" D-size sheet plotted at 1" = 10'.

## Setting Up for the Blocks Exercise

Choose <u>F</u>ile, then <u>N</u>ew. Make sure <u>N</u>o Prototype is checked and enter **IABLOCKS**.

*Choose* <u>S</u>ettings, *then* <u>U</u>nits Control *and set the* Units *and* Angles *as shown in table 11.1*

*Choose* <u>S</u>ettings, *then* <u>D</u>rawing Aids *and set up* <u>S</u>nap *and* <u>G</u>rid *as shown in table 11.1*

*Choose* <u>S</u>ettings, *then* U<u>C</u>S, *then* <u>I</u>con *and make sure that* Origin *is selected*

*Choose* <u>S</u>ettings, *then* Dra<u>w</u>ing Limits *and set the limits as shown in table 11.1*

*Choose* <u>V</u>iew, *then* <u>Z</u>oom, *then* <u>A</u>ll

## Table 11.1
### Blocks Drawing Settings

| *COORDS* | *GRID* | *SNAP* | *UCSICON* |
|---|---|---|---|
| ON | 10' | 6" | OR |
| **UNITS** | Engineering, 2 decimal places, decimal degrees, default all other settings. | | |
| **LIMITS** | 0,0 to 360', 240' | | |

Your current layer should be layer 0. Before you can do anything, you need to draw some objects (on layer 0) that will be made into blocks.

## Making Objects for Blocks

The first objects you make for Autotown are a part representing a car, and a symbol representing a tree. The car is drawn and inserted full-size, but the tree is drawn small (one unit in diameter), so that it can be scaled easily to make different sizes of trees when you insert it.

---

### Creating Objects for the Blocks Exercise

Issue the ZOOM command, and then use the Center option to zoom to the center of the drawing with a height of 15'.

Draw a car by using the dimensions shown in figure 11.3.

Zoom by using the Center option, picking a point below the car and entering a height of 2." Set snap to .25.

Draw a 1"-diameter tree, as shown in figure 11.4.

---

**Figure 11.3:**

A car for the block exercise.

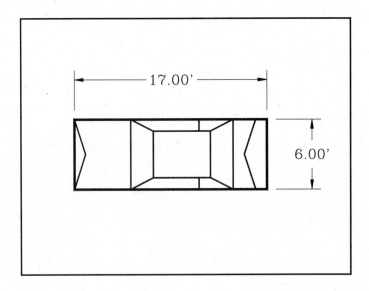

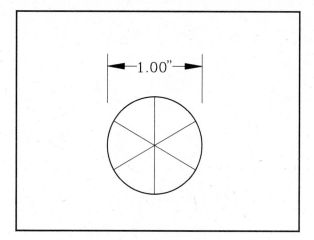

**Figure 11.4:**

A tree for the block exercise.

# The BLOCK Command

Turn the car and tree into blocks by following the steps in the next exercise. When you execute BLOCK, AutoCAD first prompts you for a block name. Name the blocks TREE1 and CAR2. AutoCAD then prompts you for an insertion *base point*, which is the reference point that you later use to put the block in a new location. After you identify a base point, AutoCAD prompts you to select the entities that form the blocks.

## Using Block To Create Your First Blocks

Command: *From the screen menu, choose* BLOCKS, *then* BLOCK:                 Issues the BLOCK command

_BLOCK Block name (or ?): **TREE1** ↵                 Specifies the block name TREE1

Insertion base point: *Pick the center of the tree symbol*

Select objects: *Select all the tree's entities (see fig. 11.5)*

4 found

Select objects: *Press Enter*                 Stores the block definition and removes the tree entities

Command: *Choose* <u>V</u>iew, *then* <u>Z</u>oom, *and then* <u>P</u>revious

*continues*

Command: *Choose* Settings, *then* Drawing
Aids, *and set* Snap *back to 6"*

Command: **BLOCK** ↵

Block name (or ?): **CAR2** ↵          Specifies the block name CAR2

Insertion base point: *Use the MID*
*object snap to pick the front of the car at*
① *(see fig. 11.6)*

Select objects: *Use a crossing window to*
*select all the car's entities*

17 found

Select objects: *Press Enter*          Ends object selection

*Save the drawing*

---

**Figure 11.5:**

The TREE1 block.

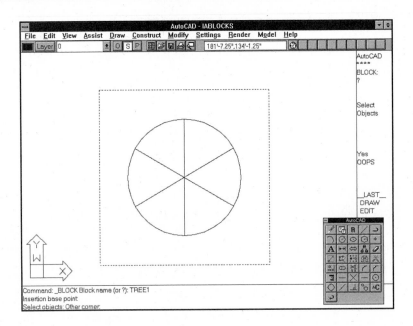

You now should have a blank drawing. After you selected each drawing's entities, they disappeared. The entities are not lost; they are stored safely in memory as two blocks named CAR2 and TREE1.

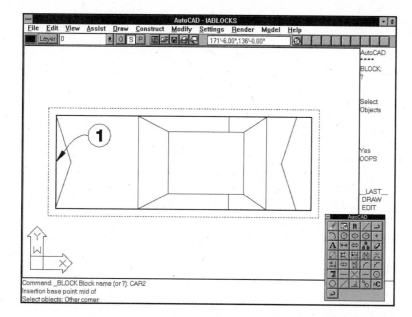

**Figure 11.6:**
The CAR2 block.

AutoCAD keeps track of all blocks in an invisible part of the drawing file called the *block table*. When you used the BLOCK command, it created a definition of the car and the tree and stored the definitions in the block table (see fig. 11.7). Each block definition defines the entities associated with the block name. When you save the drawing, the block definitions are stored as part of the drawing file.

*When you purge an unreferenced block from a drawing, you remove the block's definition from the block table.*

# Using the INSERT Command

Leave the tree in storage for now (in memory). To get the car back, use the INSERT command to insert CAR2 from the block table into the active part of the drawing file. First, AutoCAD wants to know which block you want to insert. If you respond with a question mark, AutoCAD lists the names of all the blocks currently defined in the table area of your drawing. The following steps look at these names.

**Figure 11.7:**
BLOCK and
INSERT use the
block table area.

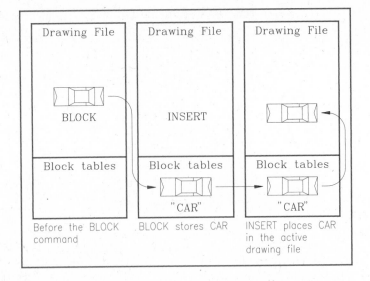

---

## Using INSERT ? To List Block Names

`Command:` *From the screen menu,*          Issues the INSERT command
*choose* DRAW, *then* INSERT:

`Block name (or ?):` *From the screen*       Specifies the List option and all
*menu, choose* ?, *then* *                    (*) block names

*Press F2 to display the AutoCAD*
*Text window*

`Block(s) to list <*>: * Defined`            Displays the defined blocks
`blocks.`
`CAR2`
`TREE1`

`User      Unnamed`
`Blocks    Blocks`

`    2         0`

*Press F2 to return to the AutoCAD graphics window*

Instead of selecting the INSERT: item from the screen menu, you can enter **INSERT** at the Command: prompt, or you can use Window's drag-and-drop feature to insert a drawing file as a block. See Chapter 12 for a drag-and-drop example.

## Using INSERT To Insert the Car Block

*Use ZOOM with the Left option, picking the left corner at 168',110' and entering a height of 40'*

Command: **INSERT** ↵

Block name (or?): **CAR2** ↵

Insertion point: *Drag the car and pick at 174',118'*

X scale factor <1>/Corner/XYZ: *Press Enter*                   Defaults the X scale factor to 1:1

Y scale factor <default=X>: *Press Enter*                   Defaults the Y scale factor to 1:1

Rotation angle <0.00>: *Press Enter*      Inserts the car with 0 rotation (see fig. 11.8)

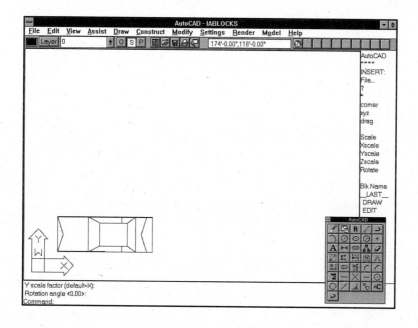

**Figure 11.8:**

The inserted car.

*continues*

Next, you copy the car.

Command: *From the toolbox, choose* COPY

Select objects: *Select any line on the car and press Enter*

<Base point or displacement>/          Specifies the last point
Multiple: @ ↵

Second point of displacement:          Copies the car with a polar displacement
@30'<0 ↵                                (see fig. 11.9)

**Figure 11.9:**

The copied CAR2 block.

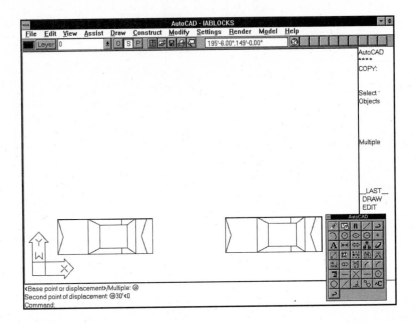

Your car reappeared in the drawing after you inserted CAR2, but the car you see is not the same collection of individual entities as your original car. When you copied the car, you selected it with a single object pick. After you insert a block in your drawing, you can move and copy all of its information as a single entity.

What happened when the block was inserted? INSERT created a block reference to the block definition. Then INSERT drew an image representing the entities that make up the block definition at the point of insertion. The original block definition is still in place in the block table area.

*You can insert not only blocks that you created in the current drawing but also any drawing file saved on disk. A previously saved drawing inserts as a block in the current drawing. The saved drawing's origin becomes the insertion base point, unless you set another base point by using the BASE command (discussed later in this chapter).*

The process of inserting a drawing creates a new block definition containing all the entities of that drawing. If AutoCAD cannot find a block that you know you have on disk, check its location against the list of directories that AutoCAD searches for files (see Appendix A).

# Scaling and Rotating Block Insertions

When you insert a block reference, you can enter different values for the block's scale and rotation. You can scale by entering X and Y scale factors. The default scale prompt for the Y factor uses the X factor you enter. This simplifies the process of scaling your drawing symbol at a 1:1 ratio. You can use different X and Y scales by entering different responses (the XYZ option is for 3D control). You also can give an angle of rotation by entering an angle or by dragging the rotation and picking a point.

Try two modified car block insertions. First, insert your car using different X and Y scale factors. Use the values given in the following exercise to elongate the car to make it look like a stretch limousine. Second, insert another car at an angle. If you make a mistake, use UNDO or ERASE LAST to remove the block insertion.

---

### Using INSERT with Scale and Rotation Changes

Command: **INSERT** ↵

Block name (or?) <CAR2>: *Press Enter*     Accepts the default of CAR2

Insertion point: *Pick at 174',128'*

X Scale factor <1>/Corner/XYZ: **1.5** ↵     Applies an X scale of 1.5 to the block

Y Scale factor (default=X): **1** ↵     Keeps the Y scale at 1

Rotation angle <0.00>: *Press Enter*     Accepts the default rotation of 0.00 (see fig. 11.10)

Next, you use INSERT and leave the scale factor at 1, but rotate the car 45 degrees.

Command: *Press Enter*     Repeats the previous INSERT command

*continues*

```
INSERT Block name (or ?) <CAR2>:        Accepts the default of CAR2
Press Enter

Insertion point: Pick at 205',128'

X Scale factor <1>/Corner: Press Enter

Y Scale factor <default=X>: Press Enter

Rotation angle <0.00>: 45 ↵            Applies a rotation angle of 45 degrees
                                       (see fig. 11.10)
```

**Figure 11.10:**

A stretched
limousine and
an angled car.

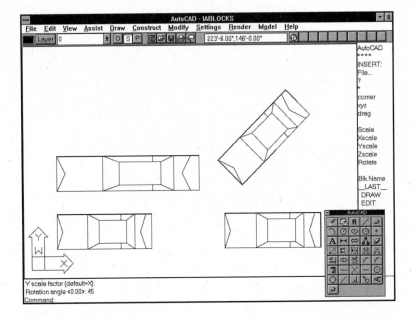

What happened when you inserted blocks this time? The INSERT command again
made reference to the block table, but the values retrieved were modified by the scale
and rotation values. These modifications are stored with each inserted entity's data,
and visible in the image of the car in the active drawing (see fig. 11.11).

*A handy trick for inserting objects that normally are horizontal or
vertical is to use your pointer to pick a rotation angle with ortho
(Ctrl-O) turned on. This method limits the rotation angle to 0, 90,
180, or 270 degrees.*

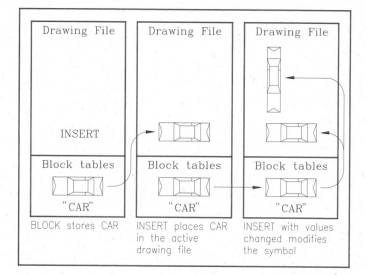

**Figure 11.11:**

A standard and a modified block insertion from the block table.

While you were entering the scale values in the preceding exercise, you may have noticed a second option, called Corner. When you use the Corner option to enter your scale values, you can scale the block by indicating the X and Y size of a rectangle. The insertion point is the first corner of the rectangle. Drag and pick the other corner to determine scale. AutoCAD uses the width as the X scale and the height as the Y scale. The width and height are measured in current drawing units.

You do not need to enter a C to use corner point scaling—if you move the mouse at the X scale prompt, you see the block being dynamically scaled. The Corner option is used in menus because it limits scale input to corner point-picking and issues an Other corner: prompt.

*Whether you use keyboard scale entry or the Corner option, you can specify negative scale factors to mirror the block's insertion, turn it upside-down, or both.*

Be careful with corner point scaling. The dragged scale is relative to one unit (1") square, and it works well if your block definition is about one unit in size. If your block definition is many drawing units in size (like CAR2), however, even a small rectangle gives a large scale factor.

When you use a corner scale input, use snap or object snap to control accuracy. Corner scale input is most useful when inserting unit scale blocks, such as parts (see fig. 11.12).

CHAPTER 11

**Figure 11.12:**

The TREE1 block
inserted with corner
scaling.

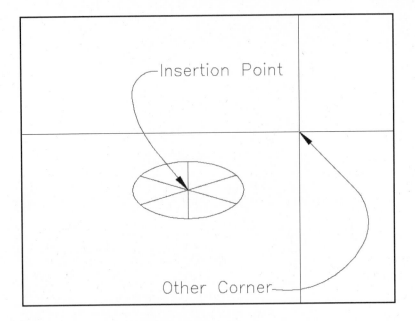

## Using Unit Scale To Make Flexible Blocks

At first, you may think the capability to scale and rotate blocks during insertion is an
option used only occasionally. However, under many circumstances, they are valuable
features of the INSERT command.

The trick of effective block scaling is to create your parts in a 1×1-unit cell. When you
insert a block, you can then stretch or shrink it. The block is good at any scale with any
insertion-scale factor. You can, for example, store a door or window part so that the
endpoints are on the left and right edges of the unit cell. You can then insert the symbol
with appropriate scale factors to fill the area you need. If you draw a unit block at 1"
and you want to insert it scaled to 3', remember that you use a scale factor of 36, not 3
(see fig. 11.13).

To illustrate the versatility of one-unit blocks, insert the tree in the following steps and
scale it down to a bush.

### Using Corner Point Scaling To Insert a One-Unit Block

Command: *From the screen menu, choose*
INSERT:

INSERT Block name (or ?)<CAR2>: **TREE1** ↵

Insertion point: *Pick any clear point*

X scale factor <1> / Corner/XYZ: **C** ↵  Specifies the Corner option

Other corner: *Drag it to a good bush shape and size (use the car as a size reference), then pick the other corner*

Rotation angle <0>: *Press Enter*

Next you create a block called BUSH, which you can use again later.

Command: **BLOCK** ↵

BLOCK Block name (or ?): **BUSH** ↵

Insertion base point: *Pick the center of the bush*

Select objects: *Pick the bush*

Select objects: *Press Enter*

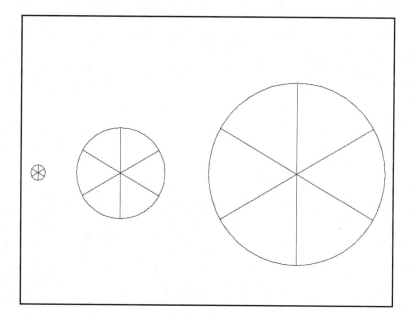

**Figure 11.13:**

The one-unit TREE1 block inserted at scales of 12 (1'), 72 (6'), and 144 (12').

One-unit blocks are extremely useful. You can create libraries full of one-unit parts and then insert them at different sizes, depending on the situation. Do not create whole libraries full of different sizes of windows or bolts—create a single one-unit part, and then insert it at whatever scale you need.

# Using Preset Scales

You have inserted blocks by specifying an insertion point, a scale, and an angle. You can preset the scale factor and rotation angle before selecting the insertion point. When you preset the block's scale and angle, insertion point dragging is suspended until you finish setting those options. You then see the block's scale and angle as you drag it to pick the insertion point.

Try making one more stretch limousine by using preset values.

---

### Using INSERT with Preset Scales

Command: **INSERT** ↵

Block name (or ?) <TREE1>: **CAR2** ↵

Insertion point: **X** ↵ — Specifies the X scale preset option

X scale factor: **1.3** ↵ — Presets the X scale value

Insertion point: **Y** ↵ — Specifies the Y scale preset option

Y scale factor: **1** ↵ — Presets the Y scale value

Insertion point: **R** ↵ — Specifies the rotation preset option

Rotation angle: **180** ↵ — Presets the rotation angle value

Insertion point: *Drag the car around, then pick at 196',138'*

---

The newly inserted car appears in figure 11.14.

# Preset Scale and Rotation Options

Several options for presetting values are available, but they are not shown as prompts during the INSERT command. The following list displays every option.

- **Scale** and **PScale.** These options prompt for scale factor—preset to X, Y, and Z axes.

- **Xscale** and **PXscale.** These options preset only the X-scale factor.

- **Yscale** and **PYscale.** These options preset only the Y-scale factor.

- **Zscale** and **PZscale.** These options preset only the Z-scale factor.

- **Rotate** and **PRotate.** These options preset the rotation angle. Enter this value from the keyboard or by picking two points.

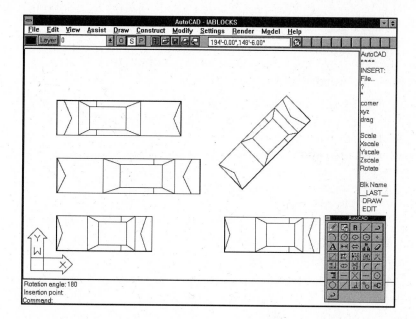

**Figure 11.14:**
A stretch limousine inserted with a preset scale and rotation.

Type the first one or two characters of the preset option to tell AutoCAD what you want to preset.

The letter P stands for preliminary, not preset. Options prefixed with a P establish a preliminary scale and rotation value to visually aid in insertion. After the insertion point is selected, the normal insert prompts and defaults are displayed.

Preset scale factors have limitations. You cannot mix fixed presets (such as Xscale) with preliminary presets (such as PYscale). If you try to mix them, the preliminary presets become fixed, and AutoCAD does not prompt you again for their values.

*Preset options are most valuable when you use them in custom menu macros. Macros can apply preset options transparently, which simplifies the task of placing the Block by enabling dragging during an insertion.*

# Inserting Blocks as Individual Entries

You use the BLOCK command to collect entities into a single group. When you insert the block in a drawing file, the insertion is a single entity. When you erase a block, the block reference (but not its stored definition) is erased. The same holds true for moving and copying blocks.

When is a block not a block? A block is not a block when it is *inserted or exploded.

After you insert a block, you may want to individually edit the different entities that make up the block. As you learned earlier, however, individual entities lose their identities when they are stored as a block.

What if you want to edit a block after you insert it? To edit individual pieces of a block after insertion, AutoCAD provides an option for the INSERT command. Place an asterisk (*) in front of a block name when you insert it to tell AutoCAD to break the block back into its individual entities. This is commonly called an *insert-star* or *star-insertion*. A star-insertion (denoted as *\*insertion*) does not insert a block reference; it duplicates the original entities of the block definition. Unlike using COPY to duplicate entities, a *insertion enables you to modify the scale and rotation of the copy.

The insertion of a separate drawing file into the current drawing creates a block in the current drawing unless the *insertion option is used. The *insertion option inserts only individual entities without creating a block definition.

Zoom in to your drawing in the next exercise and insert the car in the clear area of the drawing. To prove that the new car is really a collection of separate entities, change it into a sports car. Use some editing commands on the *inserted car and create a car as complex as you like, making sure it differs from the original. The sports car is used in a later exercise.

## Using *INSERT To Break Blocks into Components

Command: *Choose **V**iew, then **S**et View,*
*then **N**amed View, then **N**ew*

*Enter **CARS** in the **N**ew Name: box, then*      Saves the view CARS
*choose **S**ave view, then OK*

Now zoom in to a height of 15' in a clear area and revise the CAR2 block.

Command: **INSERT** ↵

Block name: **\*CAR2** ↵

Remember that CAR2 inserts on the midpoint of the front end.

Insertion point: *Pick a point at the*      Inserts the block as individual entities
*left, then accept the default scale and*
*rotation (see figure 11.15)*

Command: *From the toolbox, choose ERASE,*
*then select the windshield line and two*
*lines on the trunk and hood and press Enter*

`Command:` *From the toolbox, choose*
STRETCH *and stretch the rear glass*
*toward the back to make the roof smaller*
*(see fig. 11.16)*

`Command:` *From the toolbox, choose* ARC
*and draw a new windshield*

`Command:` *From the toolbox, choose* FILLET
*and use the FILLET command to round the*
*corners of the car with a 6" radius*

Use the same method you used at the start of the exercise to save the current view
as SPORTS_CAR.

`Command:` *Choose* **V**iew, *then* **S**et View,    Restores the view of the CAR2 blocks
*then* **N**amed View. *Select* CARS, *then*
*choose* **R**estore, *then* OK

`Command:` *From the toolbar, choose* QSAVE    Saves the file

---

When you use the star option to insert a block, AutoCAD restricts your flexibility in
rescaling the objects as they are placed. You can only specify a single, positive scale
factor in the * mode. Negative and unequal X and Y scales are not allowed. You can,
however, reshape your *inserted blocks with MIRROR, SCALE, STRETCH, and the
other editing commands after insertion to achieve the same effect.

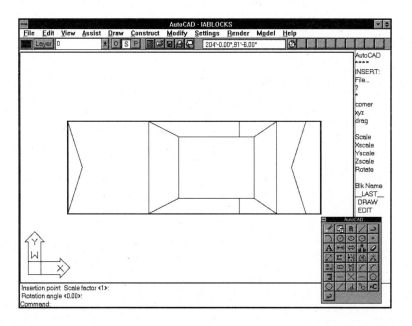

**Figure 11.15:**

The *inserted CAR2
block before editing.

**Figure 11.16:**

A sports car.

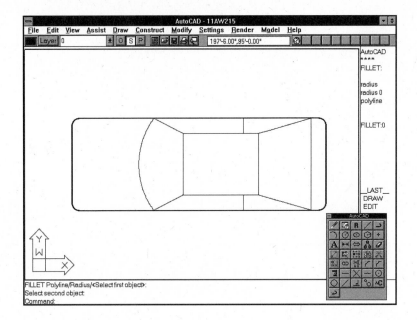

*If you place a complex *inserted block in the wrong place, use UNDO to get rid of all the pieces.*

What if you want to modify a block after it has already been inserted? You explode it.

# Using the EXPLODE Command

You can use another command similar to INSERT to modify blocks that have already been inserted. The EXPLODE command separates a block back into its original entities. To test this command, try exploding the first car you inserted on the bottom left of your drawing.

### Using EXPLODE To Explode a Block

*Zoom Previous*

`Command:` *From the screen menu, choose EDIT, then EXPLODE:*

`_EXPLODE`

`Select objects:` *Pick the first car in the lower left corner and press Enter*     Redraws the block as it is exploded

The exploded car pieces look identical to the image before the explosion. Some components of the drawing, such as byblock, color, linetype, and layer assignments, may change because they can come undone when you explode a block. If an exploded block contained nested blocks, the nested blocks are not exploded. (Nesting and byblock properties are examined a little later in this section's discussion of block properties.)

Some entities cannot be exploded. You cannot explode an *inserted block, for example, because it already is exploded. You cannot explode a block with different X-, Y-, and Z-scale factors including mirrored blocks (which have a negative scale factor). And, you cannot explode a block that has been inserted by the MINSERT command.

# Using the MINSERT Command

A block is more than a block when the MINSERT command is used to insert it. Suppose you want to put many cars (or desks, printed circuit board drill locations, or other symbols you may have stored as blocks) in your drawing. You can insert one copy of the block and then use ARRAY to make several columns and rows of copies. Each of these copies contains its own inserted entity information.

The MINSERT command provides another option. Think of MINSERT (Multiple INSERTion) as a single command that combines inserts and rectangular arrays. (You cannot use polar arrays with MINSERT.) Each entity generated by ARRAY is an individual entity in the drawing file—it can be edited, deleted, copied, or even arrayed individually. MINSERT differs from ARRAY in that each block component in the array that MINSERT generates is part of a single inserted entity. You cannot edit the individual component blocks, but you are saving memory by not storing all that repetitive information.

Use MINSERT in the following steps to fill your drawing with cars. Continue the steps by panning to the right side of your drawing to access a clear space. After you insert the cars by using MINSERT, use ERASE with the Last option to get rid of them.

---

### Using MINSERT To Insert a Block

Command: *Choose* **V**iew, *then* **P**an, *pick a point and specify a displacement of* @60'<180

Command: *From the main screen menu, choose* BLOCKS, *then* MINSERT:     Issues the MINSERT command

_MINSERT Block name (or ?) <*CAR2>:
**CAR2** ↵

Insertion point: *Pick a point in the lower left corner (see fig. 11.17)*

*continues*

X Scale factor <1>/Corner/XYZ: *Press Enter*

Y Scale factor <default=X>: *Press Enter*

Rotation angle <0>: *Press Enter*

Number of rows (---) <1>: **4** ↵

Number of columns (¦¦¦) <1>: **2** ↵

Unit cell or distance
between rows (---): **8'** ↵

Distance between columns (¦¦¦):     Displays eight cars, arranged in two columns
**19'** ↵                            (see fig. 11.17)

Command: *Choose* **M**odify, *then* **E**rase,
*then* **L**ast *and note that all the cars are
tied to one another*

**Figure 11.17:**

Some cars drawn
with MINSERT.

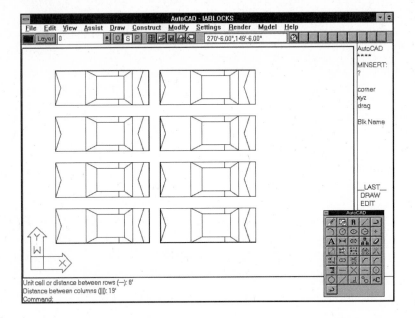

*When you specify a rotation in MINSERT, the array is rotated and
the individual blocks maintain their position in the array.*

MINSERT is an efficient way to place multiple copies of a block in a drawing file. In an array, every entity occurrence takes up disk space. If you insert by using MINSERT, the block reference occurs once and only includes information about the number of rows, columns, and spacing of elements.

Two additional commands, DIVIDE and MEASURE, can be used to insert multiple copies of a block.

# Using the DIVIDE Command

Blocks often need to be placed in a drawing at set intervals. You can use the DIVIDE command to divide an entity, such as a polyline, into parts of equal length, and to then insert a block at the division points. DIVIDE does not actually break the polyline (or other entity); it only marks the division points. You can divide lines, arcs, circles, and polylines.

In the steps that follow, you learn the use of the DIVIDE command by creating a new car block from CAR2 in the same space in which you erased the cars that were inserted with the MINSERT command. Call this new car block **CAR3**, and change its insertion point so that the cars are set back from the polyline when they are inserted. Next, create a polyline. The direction in which you draw the polyline determines the side in which the cars are inserted. Finally, use DIVIDE to divide the polyline into five segments and then insert the new car blocks.

---

### Using DIVIDE To Insert a Car Block

Command: **INSERT** ↵

Block name (or ?) <CAR2>: *Press Enter*

Insertion point: *Pick a point in the center of the drawing and accept the default X and Y scales*

Rotation angle <0>: **-90** ↵                     Inserts the car rotated –90 degrees

Command: **BLOCK** ↵

Block name (or ?): **CAR3** ↵

Insertion base point: **@0,3'** ↵                 Places the insert point 3' in front of the car

Select objects: **L** ↵

1 found.

*continues*

`Select objects:` *Press Enter*

`Command:` *From the toolbox, choose* POLYLINE *and draw a polyline from* 275',129' *to* @22'<180 *to* @ 17'<–90

`Command:` *From the toolbox, choose* FILLET *and fillet the corner with a radius of 12'*

Creates CAR3 as a nested block containing CAR2

Draws the polyline (see fig. 11.18)

**Figure 11.18:**

A polyline for the
DIVIDE command.

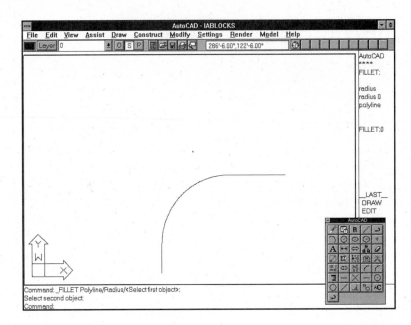

Next, you insert the block at divisions along the polyline.

`Command:` *Choose* **C***onstruct, then* **D***ivide*

`Select object to divide:` *Pick the polyline*

Specifies the object to be divided

`<Number of segments>/Block:` **B** ↵

Allows a block to be named to insert during the divide

`Block name to insert:` **CAR3** ↵

Specifies the block to be inserted

`Align block with object?`
`<Y>` *Press Enter*

Aligns the block insertions to the orientation of the polyline

`Number of segments:` **5** ↵

Specifies the number of blocks to be inserted

After you finish, your drawing should have four cars, one between each of the five segments (see fig. 11.19). Each inserted block is a separate entity.

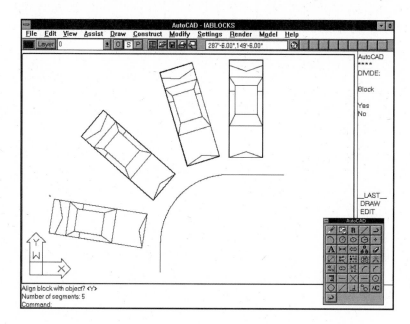

**Figure 11.19:**

Some cars inserted with DIVIDE.

You can divide a line or polyline even if you do not use blocks. As a default, the DIVIDE command inserts point entities that you can snap to by using NODe. You can make them display more visibly by using Pdmode and Pdsize.

When you use DIVIDE to insert blocks (or points), AutoCAD saves the inserted entities as a Previous selection set. You can select the group again for editing by using the Previous selection set option. If, for example, you want to change the layer of the cars, you can select all of them by using the Previous option when prompted to select objects in the CHPROP command.

*You can use a construction entity for your block inserts, and then erase it after you perform your DIVIDE (or MEASURE) insert.*

DIVIDE (and MEASURE) do not enable you to scale a block. If you wanted to insert the original one-unit size trees at a different scale, for example, you would need to create a larger block and insert it, or rescale each block after it is inserted.

# Using the MEASURE Command

The MEASURE command works like DIVIDE, but, instead of dividing an entity into equal parts, MEASURE enables you to specify the segment length. After you specify a block name to insert and a segment length (either by entering a value or by picking two points), AutoCAD inserts the block at the segment-length intervals.

Are you getting tired of placing cars in your drawing? Try adding some bushes to the parking area by following the next exercise.

## Using MEASURE To Insert BUSH Blocks

Command: *Choose* **C**onstruct, *then* **M**easure

Select object to measure:
*Pick the polyline*

<Segment length>/Block: **B** ↵          Prompts for the block's name

Block name to insert: **BUSH** ↵          Specifies the block to be inserted

Align block with object? <Y>:
*Press Enter*

Segment length: 60 ↵          Places a bush every five feet

As figure 11.20 shows, your enhanced parking area is beginning to look more realistic.

**Figure 11.20:**

Some bushes inserted with the MEASURE command.

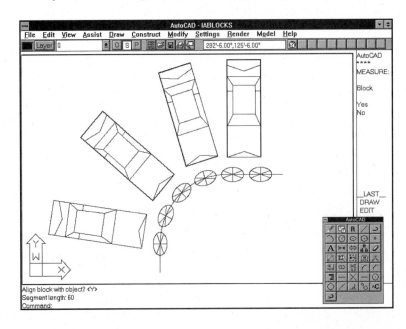

Like DIVIDE, MEASURE works with blocks or points; it forms a Previous selection set that you can use for subsequent editing.

# Using the WBLOCK Command

So far, the blocks you have created and stored in the block table have been self-contained in the current drawing file. The blocks are stored in this drawing when you save it or end it. Whenever you work in this drawing file, these block definitions are available. Sooner or later, however, you need to copy blocks from one drawing file to another drawing.

## Sending Blocks to Disk as Drawing Files

WBLOCK enables you to save any block in your current drawing as a separate drawing file on disk. You also can use WBLOCK to select a set of entities and write them to a separate drawing file without making them into a block in the current drawing. Any block or selection set can be stored as a separate drawing file, and any drawing file can be inserted as a block.

The drawing file created by WBLOCK is a normal drawing that contains the current drawing settings and the entities that make up the block definition. The entities are normal drawing entities and are not defined as a block in the new file unless they were nested blocks within the original block.

Store CAR2 as a separate file called CAR2.DWG and store TREE1 as the file TREE1.DWG.

---

### Using WBLOCK To Write a Block to Disk

Command: *From the root screen menu,*
*choose* BLOCKS, *then* WBLOCK:

| | |
|---|---|
| *Enter* **CAR2** *in the* File **N**ame: *edit box* | Names the new file |
| `Block name: = ↵` | Specifies a block name equal to the file name |
| Command: *Press Enter* | Repeats the WBLOCK command |
| *Enter* **TREE1** *in the* File **N**ame: *edit box* | |
| `Block name: = ↵` | Specifies that the block name equals the file name |

---

*If you have a block that you use often, use WBLOCK to save it to a disk file. Group these new symbols into library subdirectories to organize them.*

To insert (or *INSERT) CAR2.DWG into another drawing file, use the INSERT command and specify the block by using its disk file name, CAR2. Figure 11.21 shows how this process works.

**Figure 11.21:**

WBLOCK and
INSERT.

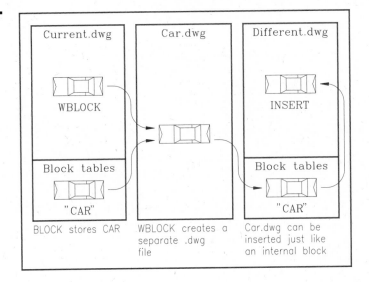

## Using WBLOCK with Entity Selection To Create a File

You can make a block file without first creating a block. When the block name prompt appears, press Enter instead of giving an existing block name. You are prompted for an insertion-base point and object selection. You can use any of the standard object-selection techniques with WBLOCK to select items for storing to disk. If you plan ahead, you can use SELECT to create a Previous selection set to use with WBLOCK. When you finish with your selections, press Enter and the entities are copied to the disk file you specified.

The entities are not defined as a block in the current drawing unless you also insert them. The drawing file created by WBLOCK is a normal drawing, containing the selected entities and current drawing settings. The entities are not defined as a block in the new file.

In the following exercise, use WBLOCK to store the sports car to the file called MY-CAR. When you use BLOCK or WBLOCK, the selected entities are erased. You can use OOPS to restore them, just as you can use it to restore entities deleted by the ERASE command. After you create the drawing file, use UNDO or OOPS to bring the entities back.

## Using Entity Selection To Create a Block Drawing File

Command: *Choose* **V**iew, *then* S**e**t View,      Restores the view of the Sports car
*then* **N**amed View. *Select* SPORTS_CAR
*and then choose* **R**estore, *then* OK

Command: **WBLOCK** ⏎

*Enter* **MY-CAR** *in the* File **N**ame: *edit box*

Block name: *Press Enter*      Prompts you to select the objects
     for the new file

Insertion base point: *Pick the car's
front midpoint*

Select objects: *Select all the sports
car's entities*

Select objects: *Press Enter*

Command: **OOPS** ⏎      Returns the car to the drawing

---

Just as you can insert an entire drawing file as a block, you can use WBLOCK to store an entire current drawing to disk as a new file.

> *Remember that the drawing file created by WBLOCK is like any other drawing file. WBLOCK does not create any blocks—it creates a drawing file that contains the entities that you select or that make up an existing block.*

# Using WBLOCK* To Write Most of a Drawing

If you respond to the WBLOCK block name prompt with an asterisk, it writes most of the entire current drawing to a disk file. AutoCAD does not write any unreferenced table definitions, such as unused blocks, text styles, layers, or linetypes. Drawing-environment settings for UCSs, views, and viewport configurations, however, are written.

---

### Using WBLOCK* To Write All of a Drawing

Command: **WBLOCK** ↵

*Enter* AUTOCITY *in the* File **N**ame: *edit box*

Block name: **\*** ↵                                    Writes the entire drawing to a new file on disk

---

*Like the PURGE command, WBLOCK\* often is used to remove unused blocks, layers, linetypes, and text styles. If you use WBLOCK\* with the same file name as the current drawing, AutoCAD prompts if you want to replace it. If you answer Yes, the current drawing is saved without any unused blocks, layers, and so on. Then simply quit the current drawing. This trick is commonly called a* wblock star.

# Using the PURGE Command

As you work with blocks, you can build up extraneous blocks in the block table by inserting them and then later deleting them. Use the PURGE command to remove unused block definitions from the block table of the current drawing file.

PURGE only works in an editing session before you modify your drawing database, either by creating a new entity or by editing an existing entity. PURGE is selective and prompts you extensively. When you invoke this command, it provides information on the blocks stored in the block table area and asks you explicitly if you want to delete any of the listed blocks. You also can use PURGE to clean out unused layers, views, or styles—anything that you named during a drawing editor session. A good drawing habit is to use PURGE before you back up a drawing. To use PURGE, load your drawing and issue PURGE as the first command. Some circumstances, such as nested blocks, may make it necessary to use PURGE more than once. When archiving a drawing, use PURGE repeatedly until it reports that no unreferenced items were found. PURGE does not remove layer 0, the CONTINUOUS line type, or the STAN-DARD text style, even if they are not referenced.

# Using the BASE Command

When you create drawing files that you later might use as blocks, you need an easy way to control their insertion-base points. The BASE command sets the INSBASE system variable, which establishes the insertion-base point for a drawing file. (Setting INSBASE directly has the same effect as using BASE). The *base point* is an insertion handle like the insertion-base point on a regular block. (It is not an entity or visible point.) If you make a drawing, store it on disk, and later insert it in another drawing, the insertion-base point defaults to 0,0 unless you specify a base point. If you use WBLOCK to create a drawing, the insertion-base point you specify becomes the INSBASE value for the resulting drawing file. Figure 11.22 shows how the BASE command works. The INSBASE in the TABLE.DWG, set at point Ⓐ, is the insertion-base point (Ⓑ) you use to place the TABLE.DWG in the ROOM.DWG.

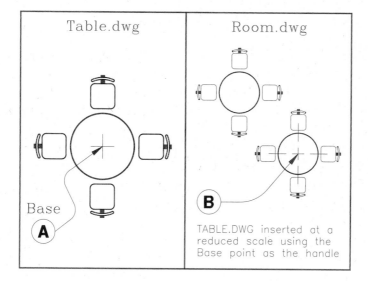

**Figure 11.22:**

Inserting a drawing as a block into another drawing.

# Naming Conventions for Blocks

As your list of blocks and drawing files grows, the need for some convention for naming the blocks also grows. Give your blocks useful names. For example, CAR1 and CAR2 are better than C1 and C, but not as descriptive as VWBUG and PORSCHE.

Although AutoCAD enables you to choose block names up to 31 characters long, make your block names the same number of characters (or fewer) than what your operating system allows for file names. You later may want to store them by using WBLOCK. A block name that is an allowable file name enables you to specify = for the file name instead of typing it. You also can use common prefixes for similar classes of blocks (and drawings), so that you can use wild cards during file management operations.

*Keep an alphabetical log of block names in a disk text file and print it out as it changes so that you do not accidentally insert the wrong block or duplicate block names.*

# Defining Block Structure

Blocks are powerful tools and they can make drawing easier. You should be aware of two additional block properties when you use blocks: blocks can include other blocks and blocks can include entities on different layers.

## Nesting Blocks

A block can be made up of other blocks; this is called *nesting*. You can place a block inside a block inside a block. AutoCAD does not place a limit on the number of block-nesting levels, although editing nested blocks can get confusing if you go more than a few levels deep. (When you created the BUSH block, it contained a TREE1 block as a nested block.)

To include one block in another block, select the first block when you create the second. You can use standard editing commands with nested blocks, such as ARRAY, COPY, and MOVE, just as you use them with normal blocks.

Nested blocks further increase the efficiency and control of blocks. The BUSH block contains only one entity (the TREE1 block), instead of one circle and three lines. In figure 11.23, the chair is a nested block; the outer TABLE block only needs to contain four block references, instead of all the entities that make up each chair. Another advantage to nesting the TABLE block is that the CHAIR block can be redefined (changed) easily and independently of the TABLE block definition.

**Figure 11.23:**

An example of a nested block.

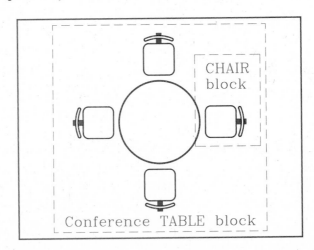

# Blocks and Layers

When you work with blocks and layers, you need to know on which layers the entities are located in the block definition. In the blocks you have used so far, all the entities have been drawn on layer 0. You can, however, create a block with entities on different drawing layers (see fig. 11.24). You can, for example, create a block with graphic entities on layer ABC and text on layer XYZ. When you create the block, AutoCAD stores the entities inside the block on their appropriate layers.

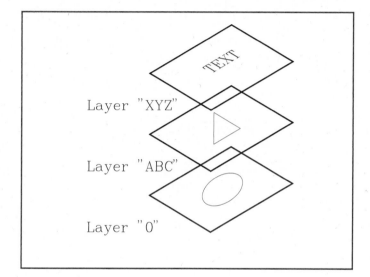

**Figure 11.24:**

A block can have entities on many layers.

When you insert multiple-layer blocks, each entity in the block displays, according to the color and linetype of the layer on which the entities were created. Entities included in a block can have color or linetype specification set to Bylayer (the default), Byblock, or by explicit color or linetype settings. If the current drawing file does not contain all the layers or linetypes in the block, they are created in the new drawing when the block is inserted as they are defined in the block. If the layers or linetypes do exist, the drawing's definition for them supersedes the blocks definitions. Figure 11.25 shows a block insertion with an entity that retains its original explicit color when inserted on a different active layer.

## Using Layer 0's Special Block-Insertion Properties

Blocks made from layer 0 Bylayer entities act as chameleons—they adopt the colors of their drawing environment. When a layer 0 block entity's color or linetype (or both) is set to Bylayer it adopts the layer settings of the layer on which it is inserted. If any entities in the block have explicit color or linetype (including Byblock), they retain those definitions (see fig. 11.26). Block entities assigned to any other layer reflect the settings of that layer regardless of the layer they are inserted on.

**Figure 11.25:**

An example of a block retaining its original layer's color.

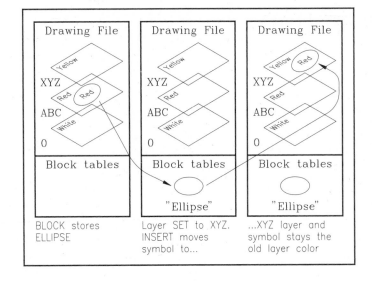

**Figure 11.26:**

An example of a block adopting a new layer's color.

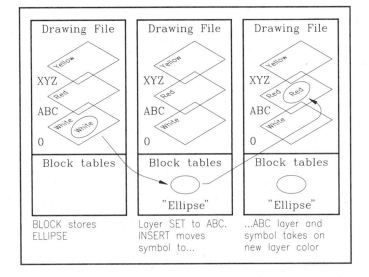

*When you use a \*insertion, or when you explode a block containing any entities that were assigned to layer 0 at the time the block was created, the entities return to layer 0 and resume their original color and linetype.*

## Using Byblock Colors and Linetypes

Entities assigned the Byblock property (or existing entities changed to Byblock by using CHPROP) can take advantage of the special features of layer 0. Byblock entities take on any current entity color and linetype settings when the block is inserted, whether explicit (like red), Bylayer, or even Byblock (for nesting). Byblock entities are completely flexible, unlike blocked layer 0 Bylayer entities, which are predestined to assume only the default color/linetype of the layer on which the block is inserted.

## Working with Blocks and Frozen Layers

If you insert a block with entities on multiple layers, and then freeze only the layer it was inserted on, all the block's entities disappear from view. How does this happen?

When you give a block an insertion-base point, that invisible reference point is defined in the block at the time it is created. The reference point anchors the block into the drawing file by its insertion point coordinates. When you insert a block, AutoCAD does not insert all the information that makes up the block—only a block reference back to the invisibly-stored block table definitions. Thus, whatever layer you use to insert the block contains the block reference at the insertion point. When you freeze the layer, you suppress the block reference, even though the block has entities on other layers that you have not frozen.

# Substituting and Redefining Blocks

The properties discussed in previous sections sound good in theory, but what about some practical techniques? This first section on blocks ends with two useful block techniques: using substitute blocks and redefining blocks. The Autotown block exercises show you how to substitute working blocks and perform block redefinitions.

## Substituting Block Names

As you insert a block, you can assign a different block name by using an equal sign. You can use an assignment, such as IAW-TREE=TREE1, to tell AutoCAD to use the block name IAW-TREE with the graphic information stored in the TREE1.DWG file on disk. The TREE1 symbol is then inserted in your drawing with the name IAW-TREE.

## Redefining Blocks

If a block name already exists in your drawing, reinserting it with an equal sign redefines all existing insertions of the block.

To see how block redefinition works, replace all CAR2 blocks with MY-CAR blocks (the sports car you saved to disk). You can use the INSERT command to replace blocks and to insert them. You do not have to complete the INSERT command to redefine existing blocks. Cut the command short by pressing Ctrl-C, and the redefinition still occurs.

# Using INSERT To Redefine Blocks

Use ZOOM with the dynamic option to create a view of all the cars (see figure 11.27).

```
Command: INSERT ↵

Block name: CAR2=MY-CAR ↵          Replaces CAR2 with MY-CAR from the disk

Insertion point: Press Ctrl-C        Cancels the command

*Cancel*

Command: From the toolbar, choose QSAVE
```

Figure 11.27 shows the redefined blocks.

**Figure 11.27:**

The CAR2 blocks redefined to equal the MY-CAR block.

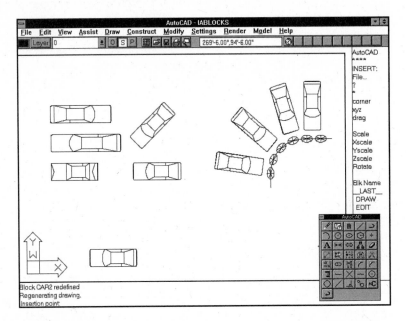

You should see sports cars all over the place. To replace cars with a few different cars may seem trivial. On the other hand, if you have a minor revision to make on a block that occurs several hundred times in a drawing, replacing blocks becomes no trivial matter. You can replace all your blocks globally by using a revised block in a single insertion redefinition.

*If you are satisfied with a certain portion of a drawing, and you are not expecting to work on that portion again for a while, make a WBLOCK of it and replace it with a simple block to improve redraw speed and reduce drawing clutter. When you are ready, put the drawing back together by inserting the block with an equal sign.*

# Using External References (Xrefs) for Design Distribution

Assume that your building project's design team consists of four people—one is working on the building's structure and floor plan, one on the electrical system, one on the plumbing and other facilities, and the other on the interior design.

These people need to know the basic outline of the building and the location of walls, doors, windows, and other features. They cannot wait for the floor plan to be finalized and completely drawn—they must get to work right away to stay on schedule with the project. If any change is made to the floor plan, the rest of the team must know it as soon as possible.

The best way to solve this problem is for each person on the team to insert the floor plan into their drawings as an xref. Every time a designer loads his drawing to work on it, the latest revision of the floor plan automatically loads. If a wall has moved, the designer has the change right away and can respond to it.

Even if you do not design buildings, this example should give you ideas for ways to incorporate xrefs into your own applications.

*Xrefs (external references)* are collective entities similar to blocks. They can contain multiple entities, such as lines and arcs. You can insert xrefs in your drawing as you do blocks, and you can select them as a single entity, whether the xref contains one entity or a hundred.

Unlike blocks, which condense multiple drawing entities to a single insert entity in a drawing file by moving them to a hidden block table, xrefs are represented solely by an insert entity. An xref has no block table entry in a drawing.

When you create a block that contains 100 lines, you add a block table entry to your drawing database that includes the definition for each of those lines, including each line's layer setting, color setting, and linetype. You cannot list this data, even if you list the drawing database's contents. Although buried in the block-definition table, the data for all 100 lines is still in memory. When you insert more copies of your block onto your drawing, you duplicate only the insert block reference, not the original data. The original lines always have to be in the block definition table for the block to exist.

# Using Xrefs for Efficiency

Xrefs remove the need to store block table data in a drawing. Xrefs do exactly what their name implies—they reference external drawings. When you insert an xref, you are inserting only its name. A few other bits of information also are inserted that AutoCAD needs in order to display an image of the xref in the drawing. The entities that make up the image are still located on disk in the drawing file referenced by the xref. Your drawing file saves only a reference to the external reference file.

Xrefs are like ghost images of other files. You can use them to insert images of parts and symbols into your drawing without actually inserting the data that make up the part or symbol. Like blocks, you can snap to objects in the xref. If a block (such as a title block) contains hundreds of drawing entities and you insert an xref in its place, those entities can be removed (purged) from the drawing file, which makes the file size much smaller. Repeat the process over a number of drawings, and the space savings become substantial.

# Using Xrefs To Control Drawings

Another reason to use xrefs is the control they offer. When several people work on parts of the same drawing, these parts can be incorporated into one master drawing as xrefs. By inserting the separate files as xrefs, the drafters ensure that every time the master drawing is loaded or plotted, the latest revisions to the referenced drawings automatically are used. The TABLET.DWG file on the Release 12 sample disk is one example that uses three referenced drawings (TABLET-A, B, and S).

Xrefs ensure that parts are automatically updated throughout an entire library of drawings. If you have parts that change from time to time and they need to be updated to the latest revision in a number of existing drawings, you can use block redefinition, for each block, one drawing at a time. If you insert them as xrefs instead, they automatically update whenever a drawing is loaded or plotted.

Xrefs are best when used to save common parts that may be revised during your project. The use of xrefs can significantly reduce the errors normally associated with copying data from one drawing to another. As you now know, xrefs always reflect the most current revision of the data they reference—if you make a change to the xref's source file, that xref is updated in every drawing in which it is referenced.

*The impact of using xrefs is realized best in a network environment where there is only one common xref source file to all the work stations. On independent systems the xref's source file would have to be updated on each machine that used it, including any plotter support machines.*

# Using Xrefs with Options

The following command options can be used with XREF:

- **Attach.** This option enables you to enter a drawing file name to attach it to the current drawing as an xref.

- **?.** The ? option lists the xrefs in the current drawing and their associated drawing files. Press Enter to accept the default asterisk for a complete list, or use wild-card characters to specify a specific set of names.

- **Bind.** This option enables you to enter a single xref name or several xref names, separated by commas. You can also use wild cards in the selection. Each of the xrefs specified become permanent by converting them to blocks, and the xref's dependent symbols (layers, linetypes, and so on) are renamed to replace the vertical bar ( | ).

- **Detach.** Detach has the same selection options as Bind. Detach is used to specify xrefs to be removed from the drawing.

- **Path.** Path has the same selection options as Bind. Path is used to change the directory path of attached xrefs.

- **Reload.** Reload has the same selection options as Bind. Reload is used to update xrefs to the latest versions of their referenced files without exiting the current drawing.

The commands for using xrefs are issued from a submenu of Xref under the File pull-down menu and by the XREF: and XBIND: items on the BLOCKS screen menu.

In the following exercise, attach an xref to a drawing. Begin a new drawing named XSYMBOL. Then draw a new symbol on a layer called SYMLAYER (see fig. 11.28). After you save the drawing, attach the drawing as an xref in a new drawing.

## Attaching an Xref to a Drawing

Command: *Choose* File, *then* New, *and*
*enter* **XSYMBOL**

Make a red layer named SYMLAYER and set it current. Turn on snap and draw the symbol shown in figure 11.28, with 1" radius.

Command: *From the screen menu, choose*          Sets the insertion point
BLOCKS, *then* BASE:, *and pick the center*
*of the object*

Command: *From the toolbar, choose* QSAVE

*continues*

**Figure 11.28:**

A symbol on layer
SYMLAYER in the
XSYMBOL
drawing.

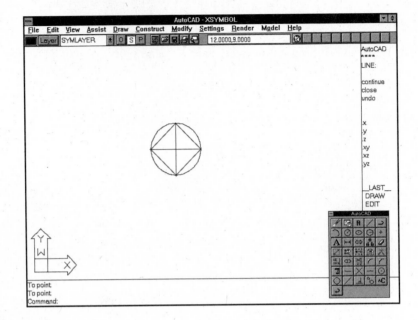

Command: *Choose* File, *then* New,
*and enter* **XTEST**

Command: *Turn on snap*

Command: *Choose* File, *then* Xref, *then*                 Issues XREF with the Attach option
Attach

Xref to Attach: *Choose* XSYMBOL                 Specifies the xref's name
*and* OK

Attach Xref XSYMBOL: XSYMBOL
XSYMBOL loaded.

The rest of the prompts are identical to the prompts for the INSERT command.

Insertion point: **5,5** ↵

X scale factor <1> / Corner / XYZ:
*Press Enter*

Y scale factor (default=X): *Press Enter*

Rotation angle <0>: *Press Enter*                 Attaches and displays the xref

Command: *From the toolbar, choose* QSAVE

You can see that attaching an xref is similar to inserting a block—xrefs function like blocks. If you select any part of the xref by using the ERASE command, the entire xref is deleted, as if it were a block. You cannot explode an xref to edit its entities, but, unlike blocks, you can edit the external file. When you update an xref file, you affect every drawing in which that file is referenced.

## Using Xrefs for Workgroup Design Distribution

One reason xrefs were designed was to facilitate workgroup design. You can allocate different parts of a large project to members of your design team and combine all the pieces at the end to make the final project. Use the XSYMBOL drawing in the next exercise as an example of xref's capability to provide automatic updates. Load it, then add two more circles to it, and save the drawing. Finally, load XTEST again to see XSYMBOL as it automatically updates.

---

### Updating an Xref

Command: *From the toolbar, choose* OPEN
*and enter* **XSYMBOL**

Command: *From the toolbox, choose* CIRCLE
*and add two concentric circles around
the symbol*

Command: *From the toolbar, choose* QSAVE

Command: *From the toolbar, choose* OPEN
*and enter* **XTEST**

Resolve Xref XSYMBOL: xsymbol                Loads and displays the current revision when
you load the drawing

---

When you load a drawing that contains xrefs, AutoCAD automatically reloads any external references. You loaded XSYMBOL, changed it, then ended it. When you loaded the drawing that contained XSYMBOL as an xref, the updated version of XSYMBOL appeared in the file automatically.

If you are part of a design team, you probably are on a network with other designers. What happens to your xrefs if someone edits a file you have referenced in your drawing while you are still working on the drawing? Nothing happens, unless you reload the xref.

## Reloading Xrefs

You can reload xrefs in two ways. The first way, which you just used, is to load the drawing again. The other way is to use the XREF Reload option. When AutoCAD asks you which xrefs you want to reload, you can specify one or more xrefs by name or type * to reload them all.

In the following steps, change the original XSYMBOL external file by drawing a new square symbol (see fig. 11.29), and use WBLOCK to overwrite its file. Then reload XSYMBOL in your XTEST drawing to update it (see fig. 11.30). XTEST still should be loaded.

**Figure 11.29:**

The new square symbol before using the WBLOCK command.

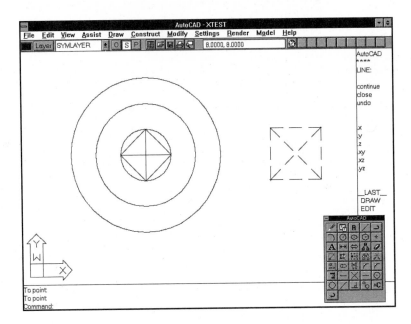

## Reloading an Xref after its File Changes

Create a layer named SYMLAYER and set it current. Set the new layer's color to yellow and the linetype to DASHED. Draw a 2"-square symbol with an X through it.

| | |
|---|---|
| Command: *From the screen menu, choose* BLOCKS, *then* WBLOCK: | Displays the Create Drawing File dialog box |
| *Choose the file name* **XSYMBOL**, *pick the center of the square as the insertion point, and select the six lines in the square as the entities to define the block* | Saves the square and overwrites the existing file |
| Command: *Choose* **F**ile, *then* Xre**f**, *then* **R**eload | Issues XREF with the Reload option |

```
Xref(s) to reload: *              Updates all xrefs
    Scanning...
Reload Xref XSYMBOL: XSYMBOL.dwg
XSYMBOL loaded. Regenerating drawing.
```

The updated xref appears in figure 11.30.

When you reload xrefs with the * wild card, AutoCAD scans your drawing for any xref(s) and rereads the drawing file(s) from disk. AutoCAD then updates the symbol(s) in the current drawing.

In an earlier exercise, you created a new SYMLAYER layer. This layer was created before storing the symbol to make its layer name match the original xrefs.

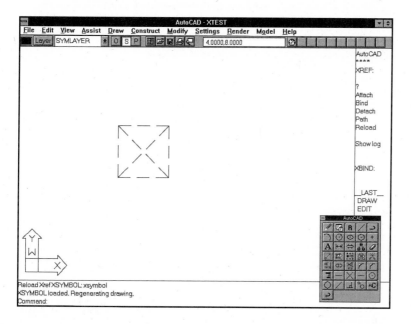

**Figure 11.30:**

The xref symbol after reloading XSYMBOL.

## Understanding Xref Layers

When you insert a block into a drawing, any layers in the block's definition are added to the drawing. If a layer in a block already exists in the drawing, and the entities are set by using the BYLAYER command, the block's entities take on the characteristics of the existing drawing layer.

Xrefs work a little differently than blocks. When you attach an xref that contains layers other than layer 0, AutoCAD modifies the xref layer names to avoid duplication. A vertical bar (|) prefixes the xref layer names to separate the prefix from the layer name.

You created the XSYMBOL data on layer SYMLAYER. When you attach XSYMBOL as an xref, AutoCAD renames the XSYMBOL's SYMLAYER as XSYMBOL | SYMLAYER in the drawing in which the xref is attached. The renaming of the layers prevents the xref's entities from taking on the characteristics of existing layers in the drawing.

In the steps that follow, check the layers in XTEST to see that the layer has been renamed.

---

### Listing Xref Layers

Command: *From the toolbar, click on the* Layer *button*     Displays the Layer Control dialog box, listing the following:

| Layer name | State | Color | Linetype |
|---|---|---|---|
| 0 | On. | WHITE | CONTINUOUS |
| SYMLAYER | On. | Yellow | CONTINUOUS |
| XSYMBOL | SYMLAYER | On | Yellow | XSYMBOL | DASH |

*Choose* OK     Exits from the Layer Control dialog box

Command: *From the toolbar, choose* QSAVE

---

Layer 0 is again the exception to xref layer renaming. As with block insertions, any data in xref files that reside on layer 0 loads on layer 0 in the current drawing; it assumes any settings you have assigned to layer 0.

# Removing Xrefs from Drawings

A block's definition remains in memory, even after all visible insertions are erased. If you erase an xref, the reference to the external file still is in your drawing. When the drawing is reloaded, AutoCAD looks for the external file, even though visibly it does not appear.

Use XREF's Detach option to remove the xref from your drawing. The following steps use Detach to remove XSYMBOL from your XTEST drawing.

---

### Detaching an Xref from a Drawing

Command: **XREF** ↵

?/Bind/Detach/Path/Reload/<Attach>:
**D** ↵

Xref(s) to Detach: **XSYMBOL** ↵

    Scanning...     Detaches the xref; it is no longer part of your drawing

---

# Using Bind with Xrefs

Sometimes you want to make your xref data a permanent part of your drawing, instead of a reference to an external file. When you finish a project and want to archive it, for example, separate xref files force you to archive all the drawings referenced in the main drawings. If the xref drawings are not available when you try to load your drawing, AutoCAD displays an error message that says it cannot find the xrefs. Without xrefs, AutoCAD cannot load and display them as part of the drawing. If you bind the xrefs, they are converted into permanent blocks in the drawing file.

Whenever you remove a drawing from its original environment (when you copy it onto a floppy disk for distribution to a client or contractor, for example), you either must bind the xrefs or include the xref drawings. Binding xrefs is usually the safest method unless you send drawings to a consultant as a work in progress.

Return to the XTEST drawing and use the Bind option to make the xref XSYMBOL a permanent part of the drawing.

---

## Using Bind To Make an Xref Permanent

`Command:` *Choose* **F**ile, *then* Xre**f**, *then* **A**ttach

`Xref to Attach:` *Choose* XSYMBOL

`Attach Xref XSYMBOL: XSYMBOL`
`XSYMBOL loaded.`

`Insertion point:` **5,5** ↵

`X scale factor <1> / Corner`
`/ XYZ:` *Press Enter*

`Y scale factor (default=X):` *Press Enter*

`Rotation angle <0>:` *Press Enter*

`Command:` *Press Enter*                    Repeats XREF

`/?/Bind/Detach/Path/Reload/<Attach>:`
**B** ↵

`Xref(s) to bind:` **XSYMBOL** ↵

`    Scanning...`

---

The Bind option merges xrefs into the drawing file in which they are contained. The xref becomes a standard block in the drawing. After it is bound, you can explode it and manipulate it just as you can any other block created or inserted directly in the drawing. To prove the XSYMBOL is now an ordinary block, you can explode and edit it, or list it with the BLOCK or INSERT command ? option.

Bind also changes the layers that belong to xrefs. It replaces the vertical bar ( | ) in the layer name with $n$ ($n$ is a number). If you list the drawing layers again, layer XSYMBOL|SYMLAYER has been renamed XSYMBOL$0$SYMLAYER. When AutoCAD renames binded layers, it first uses 0 for the number. If a layer by that name already exists, AutoCAD substitutes a 1. AutoCAD continues trying higher numbers until it reaches a unique layer name. You can use the RENAME command to change these strange layer names to whatever layer name you like.

*If you want to insert a drawing as a block into your current drawing (and there are conflicting layer names), attach the drawing as an xref first, then bind it as a block. This step preserves the incoming block's unique layers.*

In addition to ensuring unique layer names, AutoCAD prevents xrefs and blocks from having the same names.

## Controlling Xref Name/Block Conflicts

If you try to attach XSYMBOL again, the following error message appears:

```
** Error: XSYMBOL is already a standard block in the current drawing.
*Invalid*
```

If you need to attach the XSYMBOL xref again, you can substitute a different name in the current drawing as you do for blocks. Another option is to use RENAME to rename the XSYMBOL block to remove the conflict. To see which file name is referenced by an xref already loaded with a substitute name, use the ? option. You also can use the BLOCK command's ? option to view information on blocks and xrefs.

In the next exercise, attach XSYMBOL by using the name XSYM2=XSYMBOL. Then use the XREF ? option, the BLOCK ? option, and the LAYER ? option to list the new name.

---

### Attaching an Xref with a Substitute Name

Command: **XREF** ↵

?/Bind/Detach/Path/Reload/<Attach>:
*Press Enter*

Xref to Attach <XSYMBOL>:                          Makes XSYM2 the xref name and XSYMBOL
**XSYM2=XSYMBOL** ↵                                the external file name

```
Attach Xref XSYM2: XSYMBOL
XSYM2 loaded.
```

`Insertion point:` *Pick 9,5 and accept*
*the default scale and rotation*

`Command:` *Press Enter*　　　　　　　　　　Repeats XREF

`?/Bind/Detach/Path/Reload/<Attach>:`　　Prompts for names to list
`? ↵`

`Xref(s) to list<*>:` *Press Enter*　　　Lists all xrefs

*Press F2 to display the AutoCAD Text window*

```
   Xref Name                  Path

- - - - - - - - - - - - - - - - - - - -    - - - - - - - - - - - - -

   XSYM2                      XSYMBOL

Total Xref(s): 1
```

*Press F2 to return to the AutoCAD graphics window*

`Command:` *From the root screen menu, choose*
**BLOCKS**, *then* **BLOCK:**, *and then* ?

`Blocks(s) to list<*>:` *Press Enter*　　Lists all blocks

*Press F2 to display the AutoCAD*
*Text window*

```
Defined blocks.
   XSYM2                           Xref: resolved
   XSYMBOL


User       External     Dependent    Unnamed
Blocks     References    Blocks       Blocks
  1            1            0            0
```

*Press F2 to return to the AutoCAD graphics window*

`Command:` *From the toolbar, click on the*　　Displays the Layer Control dialog
Layer *button*　　　　　　　　　　　　　　box, with the following listing:

| Layer name | State | Color | Linetype |
| --- | --- | --- | --- |
| 0 | On... | White | CONTINUOUS |
| SYMLAYER | On... | Yellow | DASHED |
| XSYM2 \| SYMLAYER | On... | Yellow | XSYM2 \| DASHE |
| XSYMBOL$0$SYMLAYER | On... | Yellow | XSYMBOL$0$D |

*Choose* OK　　　　　　　　　　　　Exits from the Layer Control dialog box

When you listed the xrefs by using XREF and BLOCK, XSYM2 appeared as the xref name in the current drawing. XSYMBOL appeared as its path which is the externally referenced file name.

Although you can attach an xref with an equal sign, you cannot redefine an existing xref as you can for blocks. You can rename an xref, however, by using the Block option of the RENAME command. If you do so, the following RENAME warning appears:

```
Caution! XSYM2 is an externally referenced block.
Renaming it also renames its dependent symbols.
```

What are dependent symbols, and what do XSYM2 | DASHED linetype and Xdep: XSYM2 mean in the list from the preceding exercise?

## Understanding Xref's Dependent Symbols

Layers, linetypes, text styles, blocks, and dimension styles are symbols (not to be confused with graphic symbols such as TREE1); that is, they are arbitrary names that represent definitions in reference tables such as layers or styles. The symbols that are carried into a drawing by an xref are called *dependent symbols* because they depend on the external file, rather than on the current drawing, for their characteristics.

To avoid conflicts, dependent symbols are prefixed in the same manner as XSYM2 | SYMLAYER and XSYM2 | DASHED. The only exceptions are unambiguous defaults like layer 0 and linetype CONTINUOUS. You can vary text style STANDARD, however, which means it is prefixed.

Prefixed dependent symbols also apply to nested xrefs. If the external file XSYMBOL includes an xref named TITLEBLK, for example, the external file has the symbol name XSYMBOL | TITLEBLK. If TITLEBLK includes the layer LEGEND, XSYMBOL gets the symbol XSYMBOL | TITLEBLK | LEGEND. Xrefs may be nested deeply (xrefs within xrefs), or a drawing may contain many xrefs.

*AutoCAD maintains a log file of all xref activity in ASCII-text format. The log file is stored in the same directory as your drawing, and it uses your drawing's name with an XLG extension. The log file continues to grow as the drawing is edited over many sessions. Occasionally, you may want to delete all or part of the log file to save disk space.*

To protect the integrity of an xref, AutoCAD limits the capability to change dependent symbols in your current drawing. You cannot make an xref the current layer and draw on it, for example, as you can with a standard drawing layer. You can modify an xref's appearance, however, by changing the color, linetype, and visibility of an xref's layer. Any changes you make are only temporary. The xref reverts to its original state when it is reloaded, even if you save the drawing after making changes to an xref's layer settings. This occurs because, as you have seen, the xref is updated at the start of each drawing session.

You can selectively import the dependent symbols into your current drawing.

# Using XBIND To Bind Dependent Xref Symbols

In an earlier exercise, you used the Bind option of XREF to convert XSYMBOL from an xref to a block. AutoCAD converted all the layers and data in the xref's file to become part of the new block.

You also can use the XBIND command to bind only portions of an xref to the current drawing. Use XBIND if you only want to bring in a text style, block, or layer defined in the xref without binding the entire xref.

To see how XBIND works, bind only the SYMLAYER layer in XSYMBOL, not the entire xref. Only the layer definition is bound, not the data drawn on that layer.

---

## Binding Only Parts of an Xref by Using XBIND

Command: *From the screen menu,*
*choose* BLOCKS, *then* XBIND:

```
Block/Dimstyle/LAyer/LType/Style:
```
*From the screen menu, choose* Layer

```
Dependent Layer name(s): XSYM2¦SYMLAYER ⏎
```

```
    Scanning...
Also bound linetype XSYM2$0$DASHED:
it is referenced by layer
XSYM2$0$SYMLAYER.
```

```
1 Layer(s) bound.
```

Use DDLMODES or LAYER to see that the layer and linetype have been bound and renamed with ($0$) rather than ( ¦ ).

Command: *From the toolbar, choose* QSAVE

---

In addition to any symbols you explicitly bind by using XBIND, linetypes and other symbols that are bound to those symbols are automatically bound to the current drawing. A linetype bound to a layer is one example of symbols bound together. The entities (lines and so on) contained in the xref are not bound to the drawing. If you bind a block, however, its definition is added to the block table and you can then use INSERT to insert it in the current drawing.

*You can transfer blocks and other symbols from one drawing to your current drawing. To do this, attach the drawing on disk as an xref, bind what you need, detach the xref, and rename the items you wanted.*

Use BIND if you want to bind the entire xref to make it a block. Use XBIND if you only want to bind layer, linetype, dimension styles, nested blocks, or text styles without binding any actual entities in the xref.

# Summary

Without blocks, you cannot keep track of all the individual components that make up even a simple drawing. Blocks help you organize your drawing by grouping useful collections of entities.

Xrefs give the same benefits as blocks, but they work with multiple drawings. Xrefs are most useful for keeping file size to a minimum and for ensuring that a drawing has the most up-to-date revision of the parts it contains. Xrefs act like blocks, and you can consider them special types of blocks. If controlling the proliferation of common data, keeping drawing size down, and decreasing disk usage are critical problems, use xrefs.

A well-planned system usually includes a well-organized library of blocks. Do not be afraid to create blocks when you need them. If you find that you are copying the same group of unblocked objects all the time, make them blocks. If you need a new block similar to an existing block, explode the old block, edit it, and make it a new block with a new name.

After you create a new library part with WBLOCK, take time to edit the part's drawing file. Move the part to the vicinity of the origin, reset the limits to just encompass it, and reset the INSBASE to the desired insertion point. Consider the generic advantages gained by placing all the entities on layer 0 with properties set to Bylayer or Byblock. Remember, a polluted block contaminates every drawing it is placed in.

Use drag to see how a block is going to fit as you insert it. Use preset scale and rotation to see the block accurately as you drag it. Plan ahead to make groups of insertions so that you can use AutoCAD's insertion default prompts instead of typing block names and options over and over.

Use MINSERT, MEASURE, and DIVIDE to place many blocks with one command. Use an INSERT* or EXPLODE command to reconvert your blocks into their individual entities.

Block redefinitions can be a big time saver. If you are doing a project that requires a schematic or simple layout to precede a more accurate and detailed drawing, a global replacement can automate an entire drawing-revision cycle. You also can update a drawing by redefining obsolete blocks or by using xrefs instead of blocks.

Be careful when you insert from a disk file. Existing named symbols and objects and their parameters take precedence over incoming ones. When you insert from a disk file, all named objects and symbols in the outside file get copied into the receiving file. If a layer (or style) already exists in the receiving drawing, it takes precedence. This may change text styles in the newly inserted parts or add to the current drawing file. To avoid that possibility, insert your parts as xrefs. Any duplicate layer names or other dependent symbols in the incoming drawing are thus renamed, avoiding duplication. Then, if you need the data to become a permanent part of your drawing, use XREF BIND or XBIND to make it permanent.

Use PURGE or a `Wblock *, Quit` sequence to keep your drawing file clean. PURGE is selective, but `Wblock *, Quit` wipes out all unused blocks. To remove unused xref definitions, use XREF DETACH.

You now have a basic understanding of blocks and xrefs. In the next chapter you apply these commands in the development of a housing site plan.

As the next chapter demonstrates, there is no single tool in AutoCAD that enables you to develop a large, complex drawing more easily than blocks and external references. Once you have drawn an object, you never need to develop it again. The capability to redefine blocks is the single most powerful tool for most users of AutoCAD.

# Construction Techniques with Blocks and Xrefs

In this chapter, you use blocks and xrefs to develop a site plan that contains houses, trees, and cars. This site plan is called Autotown. The Autotown exercises will show you how quickly you can develop a drawing through the application of existing geometry.

In addition to leading you through a further exploration of blocks and xrefs, the Autotown exercises teach you several techniques. One of these techniques involves the use of an AutoLISP-defined command—DLINE—which draws double lines.

The "Laying Out Autotown Drive and Lots" exercise lays out the ATLAYOUT site plan and demonstrates drawing-input techniques in surveyor's units. This site plan is also available on the IAW DISK. If you do not want to try surveyor's units, you can skip the exercise.

In the "Attaching the Site Layout as an Xref" exercise, you open a drawing file and attach the ATLAYOUT site plan drawing file as an xref.

The "Creating Blocks for Autotown" demonstrates the development of a set of simple and complex blocks, which are used for subsequent exercises.

In the "Aligning Working Blocks with a UCS" exercise, you practice inserting and redefining blocks, substituting block names, and setting temporary UCSs to align the blocks when they insert.

In the "Inserting Blocks with Windows' Drag-and-Drop Feature" exercise, you use the AutoLISP-defined ALIGN command in lieu of a temporary UCS to align a block after insertion. In the same exercise, you use the Windows drag-and-drop feature to insert a drawing file as a block in the current drawing.

In the exercises called "Using DDINSERT to Insert Car Blocks" and "Grouping Blocks with BMAKE," you use dialog boxes to create and insert blocks.

In the "Using Grips with Blocks" exercise, you change the ATLAYOUT xref that defines the site plan, which redefines it in the AUTOTOWN drawing as well. After you make this change, some of the trees do not fit on the property. By using grips, you reposition the trees so that they are again within the property lines.

The first step in the Autotown exercises is to set up and save the AUTOTOWN.DWG and ATLAYOUT drawing files.

# Setting Up Autotown

To prepare for the Autotown exercises, you must first start a site plan layout drawing named ATLAYOUT. The drawing uses feet, decimal inches, and surveyor's angles. You set your drawing limits at 360'×240', sizing the drawing to fit a 36"×24" (D-size) sheet plotted at one inch equal to ten feet.

Set up the Autotown drawing according to the settings shown in table 12.1.

### Table 12.1
### ATLAYOUT Drawing Settings

| COORDS | GRID | SNAP | UCSICON |
|--------|------|------|---------|
| **ON** | 10' | 6" | OR |
| **UNITS** | Engineering, 2 decimal places, angles in surveyor's units, default all other settings. | | |
| **LIMITS** | Set LIMITS from 0,0 to 360',240'. | | |
| **ZOOM** | Zoom ALL. | | |
| **VIEW** | Save as A (for All). | | |

| Layer Name | State | Color | Linetype |
|------------|-------|-------|----------|
| 0 | On | 7 (White) | CONTINUOUS |
| PLAN | On | 4 (Cyan) | CONTINUOUS |
| SITE | On/Current | 3 (Green) | CONTINUOUS |

## Setting Up ATLAYOUT and Saving AUTOTOWN.DWG

*Choose* **F**ile, *then* **N**ew, *make sure there is a check in the* **N**o Prototype *box, then enter* **AUTOTOWN** *in the* File **N**ame *input box*
Begins the drawing with the defaults

Set up the drawing to match the settings listed in table 12.1. Set the units before snap, grid, and the limits. Make sure that SITE is the current layer.

*From the toolbar, choose* QSAVE
Saves AUTOTOWN for use in later exercises

Command: *Choose* **F**ile, *then* Save **A**s, *and enter* ATLAYOUT *in the* File **N**ame *input box*
Sets current drawing name to ATLAYOUT and saves it

You continue working in this ATLAYOUT drawing, giving the drawing a border and adding the street by using the PLINE and DLINE commands.

# Using DLINE To Draw Double Lines

The AutoLISP-defined DLINE command draws a continuous double line by using straight or arc line segments. You can assign the width of the lines at any time. You can leave the end of the lines *capped* (closed) or open. The key element of this command is that it automatically cleans up intersecting lines as they are drawn. Like the LINE and PLINE commands, DLINE uses a rubber-band line (called the *dragline*) to show where the current segment is being drawn.

You can use the following command options with DLINE:

- **Break.** This option enables you to specify (by entering either the On or Off suboption) whether you want DLINE to create a gap between intersecting lines.

- **Caps.** This option controls caps at the end of double lines. You can specify Both to place a cap on both ends; End places one on the last end; None draws no caps; Start places a cap at the beginning points; and Auto places caps on any open ends.

- **Dragline.** This option enables you to specify where the original line is placed, in relation to the offset line. You can choose from Left, Center, or Right.

- **Offset.** This option starts a new double line a relative distance from a base point, which usually is at an existing double line.

- **Snap.** This option gives you the choice of three suboptions: On, Off, and Size. On and Off specify whether the DLINE command enables you to snap to existing objects. The Size suboption determines the area (in pixels) to search for an object to snap to when you select a point.

- **Undo.** This option reverses the last operation.

- **Width.** This option enables you to specify the perpendicular distance between the two double lines.

- **Start point.** This option enables you to specify the double line's first point.

To issue the DLINE command, choose the <u>D</u>raw pull-down menu, then choose <u>L</u>ine, then <u>D</u>ouble Lines. Otherwise, you can enter **DLINE** at the Command: prompt.

## Laying Out Autotown Drive and Lots

Begin by adding the border with polylines, then use DLINE for the streets.

Command: *Choose <u>D</u>raw, then <u>P</u>olyline, then <u>2</u>D, and draw the border from 12'6,15' (set the width to 1') to 347'6,15' to 347'6,225' to 12'6,225' and close it*

| | |
|---|---|
| Command: *Choose <u>D</u>raw, then <u>L</u>ine, then <u>D</u>ouble Lines* | Issues the DLINE command |
| Dline, Version 1.11, 1990-1992 by Autodesk, Inc. | |
| Break/Caps/Dragline/Offset/Snap/ Undo/Width/<start point>: **C** ↵ | Specifies the Caps option |
| Draw which endcaps? Both/End/None/Start/<Auto>: **N** ↵ | Specifies no caps |
| Break/Caps/Dragline/Offset/Snap/ Undo/Width/<start point>: **D** ↵ | Specifies the Dragline option |
| Set dragline position to Left/Center/Right/ <Offset from center = 0.00">: **C** ↵ | Specifies the dragline in the center of the double lines |

```
Break/Caps/Dragline/Offset/Snap/        Specifies the Width option
Undo/Width/<start point>: W ↵

New DLINE width <0.05">: 600 ↵         Sets the width to 600 inches

Break/Caps/Dragline/Offset/Snap/        Specifies the drag line's starting point
Undo/Width/<start point>: 6',91' ↵

Arc/Break/CAps/CLose/Dragline/Snap/     Specifies the next point
Undo/Width/<next point>: 221',65'9 ↵

Arc/Break/CAps/CLose/Dragline/Snap/     Specifies the next point
Undo/Width/<next point>: 335'8,4'6 ↵

Arc/Break/CAps/CLose/Dragline/Snap/     Ends the DLINE command
Undo/Width/<next point>: Press Enter
```

To finish the road in the following steps, use DLINE again with an offset of 360 to create the road with a curb line. Then use TRIM to remove the ends that protrude past the border.

```
Command: Press Enter                    Repeats the DLINE command

Break/Caps/Dragline/Offset/Snap/
Undo/Width/<start point>: W ↵

New DLINE width <50'>: 360 ↵           Sets the offset width to 360 inches

Break/Caps/Dragline/Offset/Snap/        Specifies the start point for the center drag line
Undo/Width/<start point>: 6',91' ↵

Arc/Break/CAps/CLose/Dragline/Snap/
Undo/Width/<next point>: 221',65'9 ↵

Arc/Break/CAps/CLose/Dragline/Snap/
Undo/Width/<next point>: 340'3,1'7 ↵

Arc/Break/CAps/CLose/Dragline/Snap/     Ends the DLINE command
Undo/Width/<next point>: Press Enter

Command: From the toolbox, choose TRIM
and trim all lines that extend beyond
the border

Command: From the toolbar, choose QSAVE
```

Your drawing should resemble the one shown in figure 12.1.

**Figure 12.1:**

The ATLAYOUT drawing with the Autotown border and drive.

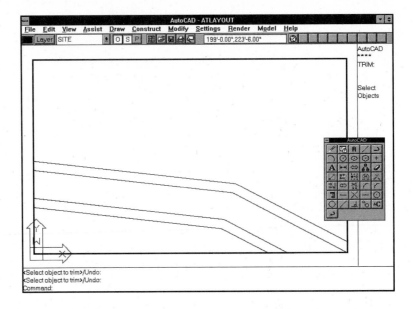

In manual drafting, converting and using surveyor's units is always a nuisance. As you will see in the following section, AutoCAD can convert these figures for you.

# Using Surveyor's Angles

Autotown's setup contains surveyor's angles. AutoCAD still accepts normal decimal angle input for surveyor's angles and enables you to enter a simple **N**, **S**, **E**, or **W** for 90-, 270-, 0-, and 180-degree angles. You can specify angles in survey nomenclature, such as N14d52'00"E for north 14 degrees, 52 minutes and 00 seconds east. In the next exercise, you use surveyor's angles to draw the lot lines for the three lots. You also use object snap modes as you pick drawing points. The easiest way to specify the object snap modes is to pick them from the toolbox; see the annotated illustration of the toolbox inside the book's front cover.

---

### Using Surveyor's Angles To Draw Autotown's Lot Lines

`Command:` *From the toolbox, choose* LINE     Starts the LINE command

`From point:` *From the toolbox, choose* INTERSECTION *and pick the bend in the road at* ① *(see fig. 12.2)*     Specifies the starting point

| | |
|---|---|
| `To point: @100'2.5<N14d52'E ↵` | Draws a line 100' long at a direction of 14 degrees north and 52 minutes east |
| `To point: @112'5.5<N80d47'W ↵` | Draws a line 112' long at a direction of 80 degrees north and 47 minutes west |
| `To point:` *From the toolbox, choose* PERPENDICULAR *and pick the north side of the road at* ② | |
| `To point:` *Press Enter* | Ends the LINE command |
| `Command:` *Press Enter* | Repeats the LINE command |
| `LINE From point:` *From the toolbox, choose* ENDPOINT *and pick the northwest corner of the center lot at* ③ | |
| `To point: @105'<N82d57'W ↵` | Draws a line 150' long at a direction of 82 degrees north and 57 minutes west |
| `To point:` *From the toolbox, choose* PERPENDICULAR *and pick the north side of the road at* ② | |
| `To point:` *Press Enter* | Ends the LINE command |
| `Command:` *Press Enter* | Repeats the LINE command |
| `From point:` *From the toolbox, choose* ENDPOINT *and pick the northeast corner of the center lot at* ④ | |
| `To point: @91'8<S76d7'E ↵` | Draws a line 91' long at a direction of 76 degrees south and 7 minutes east |
| `To point: @74'<S ↵` | Draws a line 74' long to the south |
| `To point:` *From the toolbox, choose* PERPENDICULAR *and pick the north side of the road at* ⑤ | |
| `To point:` *Press Enter* | Ends the LINE command |

Your lot should now look like the lot in figure 12.2.

**Figure 12.2:**

The ATLAYOUT
drawing depicting
Autotown with
surveyed lot lines.

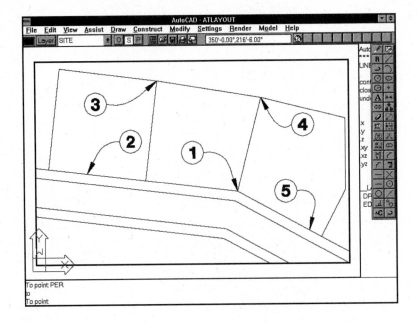

In the following steps, you finish the site layout by using DTEXT to finish the road.

*To align text with an existing object, use an object snap to set the*
*text angle, then pick the real location to place the text.*

## Using DTEXT To Label the Road

Command: *Choose* **S**ettings, *then*
**D**rawing Aids, *and set snap to 1'*

Command: *From the toolbox, choose* DTEXT

Justify/Style/<Start point>:                    Sets one point to specify the angle
*Use the INT object snap to pick the*
*southwest corner of the center lot*

Height <0.2000>: **6'** ↵

Rotation angle <E>:

*Use INT to pick the southeast corner*          Completes the angle specification
*of the center lot*

Text: *Pick at absolute point 133',75'*     Specifies the real location
*with the crosshairs*

Text: **Autotown Drive** ↵

Text: *Press Enter*     Ends the DTEXT command

Command: *Choose* **S**ettings, *then* **D**rawing
Aids, *and set snap back to 6"*

Command: *From the toolbar, choose* QSAVE

Figure 12.3 shows Autotown's new road and lots.

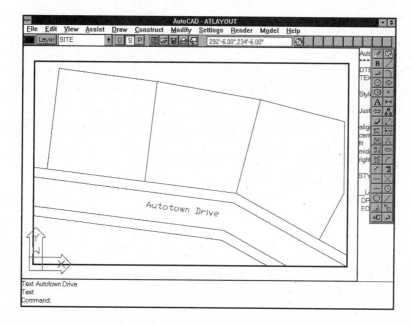

**Figure 12.3:**
The ATLAYOUT
drawing of the
completed
Autotown Drive,
with text.

# Using the Site Layout as an Xref

In the following exercise, you open the AUTOTOWN.DWG setup drawing and attach
the site layout drawing to it as an xref. If you modify the site layout drawing, the
changes automatically update in the finished Autotown drawing.

## Attaching the Site Layout as an Xref

*From the toolbar, choose* OPEN, *then choose*
AUTOTOWN *from the* File **N**ame *list box,*
*then* OK

*continues*

*From the toolbar, use the layer list to*
*set layer 0 current*

`Command:` *Choose* **F**ile, *then* Xre**f**, *then* **A**ttach,
*then from the* File **N**ame *list box, choose*
ATLAYOUT, *then* OK

`Attach Xref ATLAYOUT: ATLAYOUT`

`ATLAYOUT loaded.`

`Insertion point: 0,0` ↵          Specifies the origin as the xref's insertion point

`X scale factor <1> / Corner / XYZ:`   Accepts the default scale
*Press Enter*

`Y scale factor (default=X):` *Press Enter*

`Rotation angle <E>:` *Press Enter*          Accepts the default rotation angle

`Command:` *From the toolbar, choose* QSAVE

# Using DLINE and WBLOCK To Prepare Autotown's Blocks

To study siting options, you can insert and arrange houses and site improvements as blocks. Throw in a car or two to dress up your presentations. You will not see much difference in regenerations and redraws of the Autotown drawing because it only contains three lots. If Autotown had three dozen lots, however, the complexity of the blocks used would make a big difference in regeneration and redraw speeds. The solution is to use matching pairs of simple and complex blocks, then use redefinition to swap them. Use the simple blocks during site design, then substitute the complex blocks for presentation plots.

You already have two blocks—CAR2 and TREE1—that you created in Chapter 11. Six other blocks are required to continue with the Autotown exercises.

The six other blocks are stored on the IAW DISK, but you may want to perform these exercises to get some practice with the DLINE and WBLOCK commands. If you choose to follow these exercises, you can use WBLOCK to overwrite the blocks in your IAW directory when you store your creations.

Start with a floor plan and use figure 12.4 as a guide. The DLINE command breaks (or cleans up) all intersecting lines. If you make a mistake, issue the UNDO command.

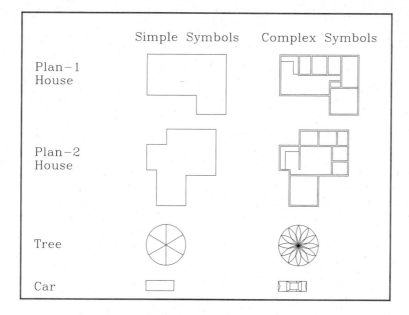

**Figure 12.4:**

Examples of simple and complex blocks.

## Creating Blocks for Autotown

Zoom in on one of the lots as a construction area and turn on ortho. Draw the SIMPLE1 floor plan with the dimensions shown in figure 12.5.

Next, you save the SIMPLE1 floor plan as a block, by using the WBLOCK command.

Command: *From the screen menu,*          Creates SIMPLE1.DWG file
*choose* BLOCKS, *then* WBLOCK:

*Use* WBLOCK *to store the floor plan*
*as* SIMPLE1

In the following steps, you draw the COMPLEX1 floor plan, as shown in figure 12.6. Use the DLINE command to create the object, using the same dimensions you used in the SIMPLE1 floor plan.

Command: *Choose* **D**raw, *then* **L**ine,
*then* **D**ouble lines

*continues*

**Figure 12.5:**

The SIMPLE1 floor plan.

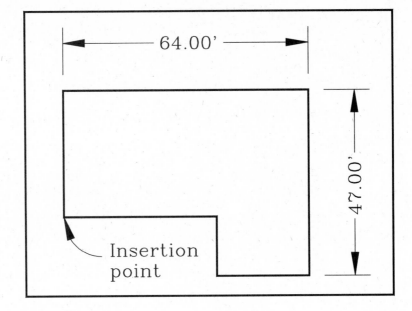

64.00'

47.00'

Insertion point

**Figure 12.6:**

Interior walls in the COMPLEX1 floor plan.

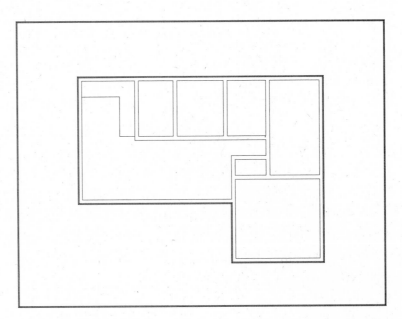

```
Break/Caps/Dragline/Offset/Snap/
Undo/Width/<start point>: D ↵
```

```
Set dragline position to              Places dragline to the left of the
Left/Center/Right/                    original line
<Offset from center = 0.00">: L ↵
```

```
Break/Caps/Dragline/Offset/Snap/
Undo/Width/<start point>: W ↵
```

```
New DLINE width <5'>: 6 ↵            Specifies the width
```

```
Break/Caps/Dragline/Offset/Snap/
Undo/Width/<start point>: Pick a point to
be the upper left corner of the floor plan
```

```
Arc/Break/CAps/CLose/Dragline/Snap/
Undo/Width/<next point>: @64'<0 ↵
```

```
Arc/Break/CAps/CLose/Dragline/Snap/
Undo/Width/<next point>: @47'< – 90 ↵
```

```
Arc/Break/CAps/CLose/Dragline/Snap/
Undo/Width/<next point>: @20'<180 ↵
```

```
Arc/Break/CAps/CLose/Dragline/Snap/
Undo/Width/<next point>: @10'<90 ↵
```

```
Arc/Break/CAps/CLose/Dragline/Snap/
Undo/Width/<next point>: @44'<180 ↵
```

```
Arc/Break/CAps/CLose/Dragline/Snap/      Closes the outside wall
Undo/Width/<next point>: CL ↵
```

In the following steps, you use DLINE with the Offset option to draw the interior wall section shown in figure 12.7.

```
Command: DLINE ↵
```

```
Break/Caps/Dragline/Offset/Snap/      Specifies the Offset option
Undo/Width/<start point>: O ↵
```

```
Offset from: Use the ENDP object snap to   Specifies the base from which to offset
pick the inside corner of the plan at ①    the second line
```

```
Offset toward: Use the ENDP object snap   Sets the offset direction
to pick the corner to the right of the
intersection at ②
```

*continues*

```
Enter the offset distance          Sets starting point for the double line,
<13'—7.00">: 15' ↵                 defining the room's size
```

```
Arc/Break/CAps/CLose/Dragline/Snap/
Undo/Width/<next point>: @15'<—90 ↵
```

```
Arc/Break/CAps/CLose/Dragline/Snap/
Undo/Width/<next point>: @35'<0 ↵
```

```
Arc/Break/CAps/CLose/Dragline/Snap/
Undo/Width/<next point>: Use the PER
object snap to pick the top inside wall line
```

**Figure 12.7:**

Interior walls in
the COMPLEX1
floor plan.

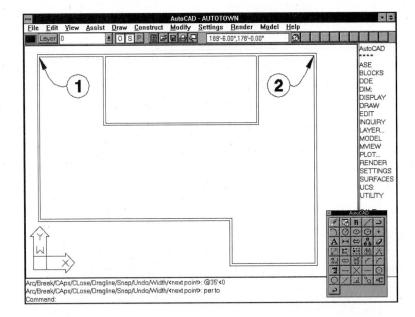

Finish COMPLEX1 by using DLINE to draw additional interior walls. Because SNAP is set to 6, you can pick points for the starting and ending points of the double lines. Next, use WBLOCK to store the floor plan as COMPLEX1.

Use LINE and WBLOCK to create and save the SIMPLE2 floor plan with the dimensions shown in figure 12.8.

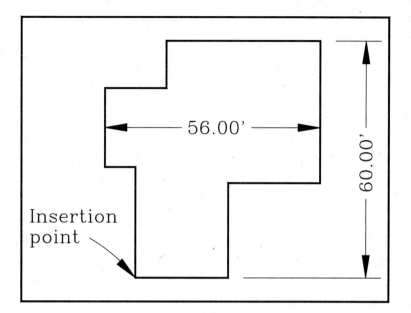

**Figure 12.8:**
The SIMPLE2 floor plan.

Use DLINE and WBLOCK to create and save the COMPLEX2 floor plan shown in figure 12.9. Make the floor plan as complex as you like.

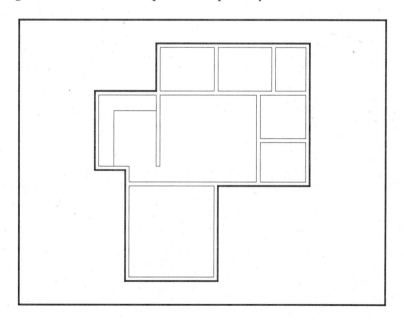

**Figure 12.9:**
The COMPLEX2 floor plan.

*continues*

In the following steps, you continue by making a simple car and a complex tree. You already have CAR2 and TREE1 from Chapter 11.

Draw the CAR1 symbol with the dimensions shown in figure 12.10.

Use WBLOCK to store the car symbol as CAR1.

Zoom in and set snap to .125 to draw the TREE2 tree symbol one unit (1") in diameter (see fig. 12.11).

Use WBLOCK to store the tree symbol as TREE2.

Command: *Choose* **V**iew, *then* S**e**t *View,*          Restores the view named A
*then* **N**amed *View, then choose* A, *then*
**R**estore, *then* OK

**Figure 12.10:**

The CAR1 simple block.

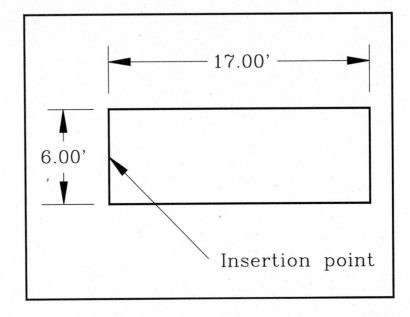

**Figure 12.11:**

The TREE2 complex block.

Now that you have finished the blocks, you can build the rest of the subdivision.

# Using a UCS To Insert Blocks

To insert the houses, set a UCS at the corner of each lot. This setting helps align the house plan in relationship to the lot. As you insert each block, substitute a working name (such as PLAN-1=SIMPLE1). This substitution tells AutoCAD to use the SIMPLE1.DWG file on disk, but to name the block PLAN-1 in the drawing. The preliminary subdivision is shown in figure 12.12.

## Aligning Working Blocks with a UCS

Command: *From the toolbar, use the* layer
*list to set layer* PLAN *current and*
*turn off ortho*

Command: *From the main screen menu,*
*choose* UCS:, *then* next, *then* 3point

*continues*

**Figure 12.12:**

Autotown with
the first two floor
plans.

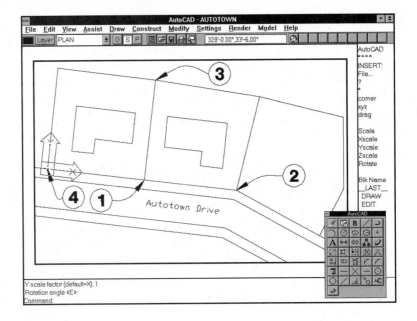

Origin point <0,0,0>: *Use ENDP to*
*pick the lower left corner of the lot at* ①
*(see fig. 12.12)*

Point on positive portion of the
X-axis <131'−3.02", 101'−5.66",
0'−0.00">: *Use ENDP to pick the*
*lower right corner of the lot at* ②

Point on positive-Y portion of the
UCS X-Y plane <131'−2.13",
101'−6.66", 0'−0.00">:*Use ENDP to*
*pick the upper left corner of the lot at* ③

Next you insert the SIMPLE1 plan on the center lot as PLAN-1.

Command: **INSERT** ↵

Block name (or ?): **PLAN-1=SIMPLE1** ↵     Inserts the SIMPLE1 block and renames it
                                            PLAN-1 upon insertion

Insertion point: **17',36'** ↵      Positions the block with respect to the corner of the lot

*Accept the scale and rotation defaults*

Command: *From the main screen menu, choose* UCS:, *then* next, *then* Origin

*Use the ENDP object snap to pick the left lot at lower left corner at* ④

Next, you use a –1 X scale to insert a flipped PLAN-1 on the west lot. You do not need an = sign because the previous insertion defined PLAN-1 in your drawing's block table.

Command: **INSERT** ↵

Block name (or ?) <PLAN-1>: *Press Enter*

Insertion point: **88',36'** ↵

X scale factor <1> / Corner /      Flips the block with the negative scale
XYZ: **–1** ↵

Y scale factor (default=X): **1** ↵

Rotation angle <E>: *Press Enter*

Command: *From the screen menu, choose* UCS:, *then* next, *then* Origin, *and set the origin for the east lot at the lower left corner (⑤ in fig. 12.13)*

Next, you use the Z option with the INT object snap to rotate about the Z axis, making the X axis parallel to the front lot line.

Command: *From the screen menu, choose* UCS:, *then* next, *then* Z

Rotation angle about Z axis <E>: *Use the ENDP object snap to pick the lower left corner of the lot at* ⑤

Second point: *Use ENDP to pick the lower right corner of the lot at* ⑥ *(see fig. 12.13)*

AutoCAD and Windows have an interface capability involving the insertion of drawing files.

**Figure 12.13:**

Establishing a UCS at the third lot.

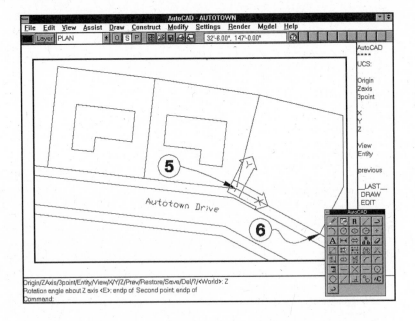

# Using Windows To Insert a Drawing File

The practice of maintaining parts in a separate directory referred to as a library is common (and wise). There are times, however, when you cannot remember where the part you want to insert is stored. You can use the Windows File Manager to get parts from another directory, to insert them into your drawing, and even to help find a lost file. To accomplish these tasks, you use the drag-and-drop feature introduced in Chapter 2.

If File Manager is open, you can hold the Alt key and press Tab until the name of the drawing you want displays, then release both keys to switch to it. If it is not open, locate and double-click on its icon, which is in the Main group of Program Manager. You can use the Alt and Tab keys to switch to Program Manager.

With AutoCAD at the Command: prompt, you activate the Windows File Manager and size it so that AutoCAD is still partially visible. Use the File Manager to select the drive and directory that holds the drawing file you desire. You can use the By File **T**ype feature in the **V**iew menu to limit the file display to *.DWG files. Press the mouse button with the pointer on the file name you want to insert, and then drag the file icon out of the File Manager window into AutoCAD, and release it. You are automatically taken from the Windows File Manager to AutoCAD. AutoCAD issues the INSERT command, using the file name you have selected, and prompts for an insertion point.

Use the Windows File Manager to insert the SIMPLE2 block into the third lot, as shown in figure 12.15. In the previous exercise, the file SIMPLE1 was renamed as PLAN-1 as it was inserted. This time, you insert SIMPLE2 and then use the RENAME command to change the block name.

## Inserting Blocks with Windows' Drag-and-Drop Feature

*Locate and double-click on the Windows File Manager icon*     Opens File Manager

Size and locate the window so that AutoCAD is partially visible (see fig. 12.14).

Choose <u>V</u>iew, make sure there are check marks beside the T<u>r</u>ee and Directory and the <u>N</u>ame items. Choose the C drive icon, find and select the IAW directory folder icon in the directory window, then choose <u>V</u>iew, then By File <u>T</u>ype, enter **\*.DWG** in the <u>N</u>ame box, and choose OK.

*Press and hold on the file name* simple2.dwg, *drag it anywhere over the AutoCAD window, and release it (see fig. 12.14)*     Leaves the File Manager window and issues the INSERT command in AutoCAD

```
Command: INSERT Block name (or ?)
<PLAN-1>: C:\IAW\SIMPLE2.DWG
Insertion point: 25'6,28' ↵
```

```
X scale factor <1> / Corner /
```
XYZ: *Press Enter*

```
Y scale factor (default=X):
```
*Press Enter*

Rotation angle <E>: *Press Enter*     Inserts PLAN-2 on the east lot with a relative east rotation

Command: **RENAME** ↵

```
Block/Dimstyle/LAyer/LType/Style/
Ucs/VIew/VPort: B ↵
```

Old block name: **SIMPLE2** ↵

New block name: **PLAN2** ↵     Renames block

File Manager is still in the background; you can leave it open or switch back to it and choose <u>F</u>ile, then <u>E</u>xit to close it.

No subdivision is complete without a few cars scattered around. In the next section, you insert several cars by using the DDINSERT command.

**Figure 12.14:**

Dragging
SIMPLE2 from
File Manager
to AutoCAD.

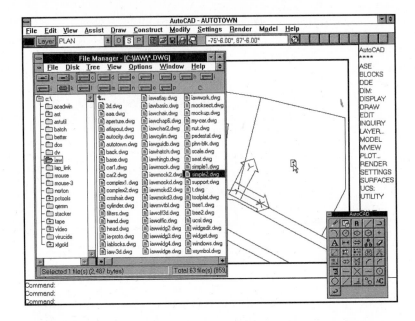

**Figure 12.15:**

Autotown with
the last floor plan.

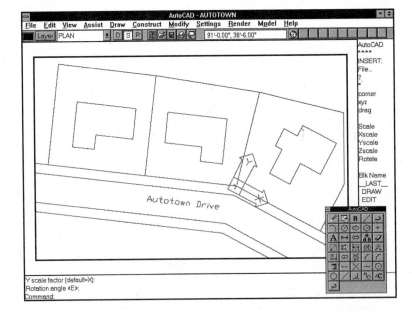

# Using the Insert Dialog Box

The DDINSERT command displays the Insert dialog box for inserting blocks. To issue the command, choose Insert from the Draw pull-down menu.

This dialog box has the same options as the INSERT command. You can choose the buttons for Block and File to display a second dialog box with the available blocks or drawing files. You can also type the name in the input box. Activating the Explode option performs the same function as *INSERT. The Specify Parameters on Screen box, when checked (the default), generates all the normal prompts during the insertion.

You can also specify the insert parameters by turning off the Specify Parameters on Screen box and setting the Insert Point, Scale, and Rotation values (or accept the defaults) in the boxes provided. This action turns off all the normal prompts and performs the insertion as soon as you click on OK.

During the following insertion, you make the file CAR1 equal to the block CAR.

## Using DDINSERT To Insert Car Blocks

| | |
|---|---|
| Command: *From the screen menu, choose* UCS:, *then* World | Restores the World UCS |
| Command: *Choose* Draw, *then* Insert | Displays the Insert dialog box |
| *Click on the* File *button and select* CAR1, *then* OK | Specifies the file to insert |
| *Enter* **CAR** *in the* Block *input box* | Performs the same function as block_name=file_name |
| *Choose* OK | Prompts for all the normal INSERT options |

Pick your own insertion points, stretch the scales or use the defaults, and drag the angles. Figure 12.16 shows one possible arrangement for the cars. Use INSERT or DDINSERT to insert CAR for the remaining cars.

# Using Preset Scale Insertions

After you finish inserting the cars, spruce up the subdivision with some trees. Remember that you drew the tree block with a one-unit (1") diameter. In the following exercise, you use different scale values to create trees with different diameters. Enter the desired diameter in inches, because scale does not accept feet—only a factor by which it scales. Preset the scale factors, as it is hard to place 1" trees accurately with drag before they are scaled. The trees then display at the desired scale as you drag them.

**Figure 12.16:**

Autotown with
inserted cars.

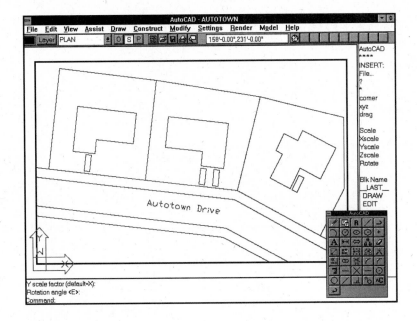

## Using Preset Scale To Insert Trees

Command: *Choose* **D**raw, *then* **I**nsert          Displays the Insert dialog box

*Click on the* **F**ile *button and select*
TREE1, *then* OK

*Enter* **TREE** *in the* **B**lock *input box*          Renames TREE1 as TREE upon insertion

*Choose* OK

Insertion point: **S** ↵          Specifies the preset scale options

Scale factor: **240** ↵          Creates a tree 20' in diameter

Insertion point: *Pick a point (see fig. 12.17)*

Rotation angle <E>: *Press Enter*

Continue inserting more 20' diameter trees, using TREE as the inserted block name.

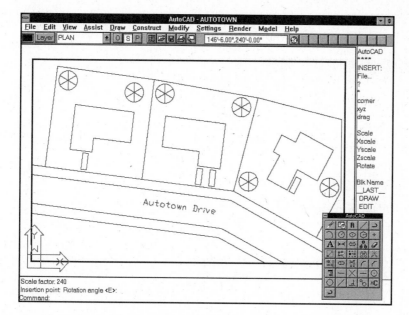

**Figure 12.17:**

Autotown with inserted trees.

# Using BMAKE To Group Blocks

In developing a drawing, it can be productive to group several existing blocks as nested blocks in a single block. You can then insert this new block throughout the drawing.

Figure 12.18 shows three similarly arranged trees in the corner of each lot. In the following exercise, you insert one group of trees, make them into a block named 3-TREES, and then insert the new block into each of the lots. You use the AutoLISP-defined command BMAKE to define the 3-TREES block. The BMAKE command enables you to define blocks through a dialog box. This command is not built into the menus; you must load it before use. You load BMAKE by issuing the APPLOAD command, or by choosing the Application item from the **F**ile pull-down menu. You can also use the windows drag-and-drop method in the same way you used it to insert the PLAN-2 block.

The BMAKE.LSP file and its BMAKE.DCL supporting file are located in the ACADWIN\SAMPLE directory. BMAKE.DCL must be copied or moved to the ACADWIN\SUPPORT directory before BMAKE can be used. As an alternative, you could choose **F**ile, then P**r**eferences, then **E**nvironment, and add ;C:\ACADWIN\SAMPLE to the Environment dialog box **S**upport Dirs: list. (See Chapter 18 for more on the Environment dialog box.)

## Making and Inserting Nested Blocks with BMAKE

Command: **INSERT** ↵

Block name (or ?) <TREE>: *Press Enter*

| | |
|---|---|
| Insertion point: **S** ↵ | Preset the scale factor |
| Scale factor: **60** ↵ | |
| Insertion point: *Pick a point in the left lot* | Inserts one of the three trees |
| Rotation angle <E>: *Press Enter* | |

*Use* INSERT *or* COPY *and add two more trees to develop the pattern as seen in figure 12.18*

Now that you have created one set of trees, group them into a block and insert them in the drawing. First, make sure that you have BMAKE.DCL in the ACADWIN\SUPPORT directory or that ACADWIN\SAMPLE is on AutoCAD's search path as discussed in the text prior to this exercise.

| | |
|---|---|
| Command: *Choose* **F**ile, *then* App**l**ications, *then* **F**ile | Displays the Select LISP/ADS dialog box |
| *Double-click on the* \, *then select* ACADWIN, *then* SAMPLE *in the* \ACADWIN\SAMPLE Directories *list* | Displays files in the subdirectory |
| *Double-click on* BMAKE, *then choose* **L**oad | Specifies BMAKE and loads it |

The AutoLISP command BMAKE is now available in the drawing; you can issue the command by entering **BMAKE** at the Command: prompt. The BMAKE (BlockMAKE) command defines a block in the same way as the BLOCK command, but BMAKE enables you to use a dialog box to specify the block's parameters.

Command: **BMAKE** ↵

| | |
|---|---|
| *Pick the* Select **P**oint *button* | Prompts for insertion point |
| Insertion base point: *Pick a point in the middle of the three trees* | Defines an insertion point |
| *Pick the* **S**elect Objects *button* | Prompts for specification of the object to be included in the block |
| Select objects: *Select the three trees and press Enter* | Number found: 3 appears under Select Objects < |

| | |
|---|---|
| *Enter* **3-TREES** *in the* Block Name *input box as the name of the block* | Defines the block's name |
| *Turn off the* **R**etain Entities *option* | Removes the 3 trees from the drawing |
| *Click on the* OK *button to close the dialog box and complete the command* | |

Use INSERT to place the block 3-TREES in each of the lots. Use the Rotate option to place the block in the lot on the right, as shown in figure 12.18.

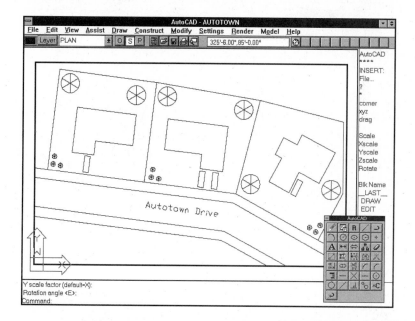

**Figure 12.18:**

Autotown with all simple blocks inserted.

You are finished with Autotown's simple symbols. If you try different arrangements, drawing regeneration is quick because you inserted simple blocks. Before you redefine them with the complex blocks for presentation, review the blocks in your drawing and on your hard drive.

# Displaying Blocks and Drawing Files

As you use AutoCAD, there are times when you need a list of the blocks and files that are available. Although it is important to give your blocks meaningful names, you may forget a block's name from time to time. Or you may make a typing error during the

BLOCK command. When this happens, you may need to find out what you actually named the block. For these and many other reasons, you may need to display a list of block names or drawing files.

Use **U**tility and **L**ist Files from the **F**ile pull-down menu to look at your current drawing directory files. Use the ? option of the BLOCK command to list blocks in a drawing. The files listed in your File List dialog box may differ from those shown in figure 12.19.

**Figure 12.19:**

The File List dialog box.

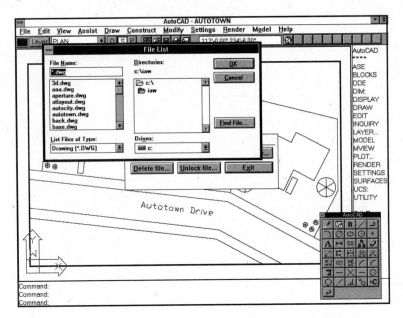

## Displaying Blocks and Drawing Files

| | |
|---|---|
| Command: *Choose* **F**ile, *then* **U**tilities, *then* **L**ist Files | The FILES command displays the File List dialog box (see fig. 12.19) |
| *Choose* **C**ancel, *then* E**x**it | Returns to the drawing editor |
| Command: **BLOCK** ↵ | |
| Block name (or ?): **?** ↵ | |
| Block(s) to list <*>: *Press Enter* | Displays listing in the text window |
| *Press F2 to open the* AutoCAD *Text window and review the listing* | |

```
Defined blocks.
ATLAYOUT            Xref: resolved
CAR
PLAN-1
PLAN-2
TREE
3-TREES

User      External    Dependent   Unnamed
Blocks    References   Blocks      Blocks
5         1            0           0
```

*Press F2 to return to the*
AutoCAD - AUTOTOWN *graphics window*

Each working block has two corresponding drawing files you created by using WBLOCK. The working blocks in the current drawing have simple PLAN-1, PLAN-2, TREE, and CAR names because you used an equal sign when you inserted them (as in PLAN-1=SIMPLE1). Maintain the files (created with WBLOCK) separately to keep track of the simple and complex symbols. The BLOCK command also lists the xref site layout ATLAYOUT.

# Redefining Blocks

You can use block redefinition to swap final blocks for the currently inserted simple blocks. To redefine blocks, use the equal-sign option of the INSERT command. You do not have to complete the INSERT command; cut it short by pressing Ctrl-C, and the redefinition occurs.

## Using Insert = To Redefine Blocks

Command: **INSERT** ↵

Block name (or?) <3-TREES>: **PLAN-1=COMPLEX1** ↵

Block PLAN-1 redefined

Regenerating drawing.

Insertion point: *Press Ctrl-C to cancel*

Your drawing should now look like figure 12.20.

**Figure 12.20:**

Autotown with
PLAN-1 updated.

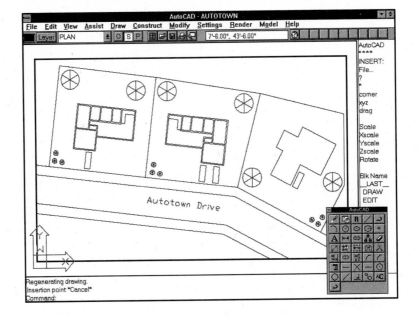

*If you must redefine several blocks, enduring the regeneration each time can be a nuisance. To avoid this, turn REGENAUTO off until you finish. When you turn REGENAUTO back on, a single regeneration is performed.*

In the following steps, you redefine the rest of the drawing's working blocks.

## Completing the Block Redefinitions with REGENAUTO Off

Command: **REGENAUTO** ↵

ON/OFF <On>: **OFF** ↵                    Turns off automatic regenerations

*Use INSERT to insert* PLAN-2=COMPLEX2

Regen queued.
Insertion point: *Cancel the INSERT command*

*Use INSERT to insert* TREE=TREE2
*and cancel the INSERT command*

*Use INSERT to insert* CAR=CAR2
*and cancel the INSERT command*

Command: **REGENAUTO** ↵

ON/OFF <Off>: **ON** ⏎                    Turns automatic regeneration back on and
                                            regenerates the redefined blocks

In the following steps, you insert one final car along the road (see fig. 12.21).

Command: **INSERT** ⏎

Block Name (or ?) <3-TREES>: **CAR** ⏎

Insertion point: **90'6,81'** ⏎

X scale factor <1>/Corner/XYZ: *Press Enter*

Y scale factor (default = x): *Press Enter*

Rotation angle <E>: **172** ⏎

Command: *Choose* <u>F</u>ile, *then* <u>S</u>ave

All the blocks are now redefined in the drawing. The last insertion used the new
CAR=CAR2 block definition.

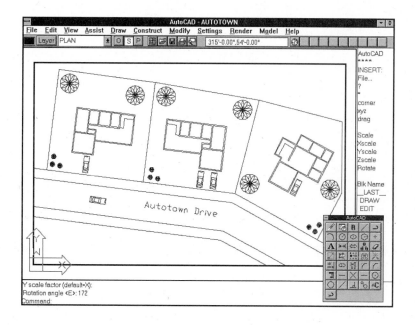

**Figure 12.21:**

Autotown with
complex blocks.

# Updating the Externally Referenced Site Plan

In the following drawing, the site plan is from the drawing ATLAYOUT, which is attached with XREF. As explained in Chapter 11, the primary advantage of using an xref over a block is that you can modify the xref source drawing independently from the drawing in which it is attached. After an xref source drawing has been modified, when you reload the xref (or the next time the drawing is opened), the xref is scanned and updated. Try updating the site plan file, and then reload AUTOTOWN to see the changes.

## Updating an Xref

Command: *From the toolbar, choose* OPEN, *then double-click on* ATLAYOUT     Loads the externally referenced file

Next, you use the STRETCH command to change the plan.

Command: **STRETCH** ↵

Select objects: *Pick and drag to develop a crossing window across the top of the lots (see fig. 12.22)*

Select objects: *Press Enter*

Base point or displacement: *Press Enter*

Second point of displacement:     Stretches the lot lines
**@15'<S12dW** ↵

Command: *From the toolbar, choose* QSAVE     Saves changes

Command: *From the toolbar, choose* OPEN, *then double-click on* AUTOTOWN     Reloads AUTOTOWN

When you reopened AUTOTOWN, the changes to ATLAYOUT placed your trees over the property line. You can use grip-editing techniques to move the trees.

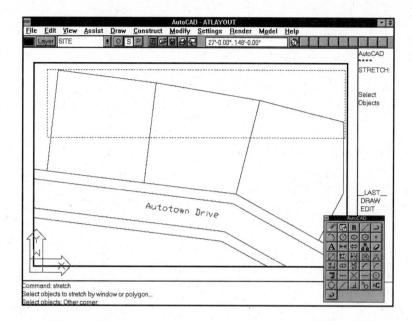

**Figure 12.22:**
Specifying the crossing window for STRETCH.

**NOTE**

*Grips are available in blocks just as in any entity. To access grips within a block, use the Grip dialog box and turn on both Enable Grips or Enable Grips Within Blocks. Enable Grips places one grip at the insertion point of the block. Enable Grips Within Blocks displays grips attached to all the entities in the BLOCK and is less desirable because of the confusion created in a complex block.*

---

## Grip-Editing Blocks

| | |
|---|---|
| Command: *Choose* **S**ettings, *then* **G**rips | Displays Grips dialog box |
| *Click as needed to put checks in both the* **E**nable Grips, *and the* **E**nable Grips within **B**locks *boxes, then choose* OK | Displays all grips within the entities of a block |
| Command: *Pick one of the trees* | Displays the tree's grips |
| *Pick one of the tree's grips* | Makes the grip hot |
| *Drag inside the property line and click* | Moves the tree |

*continues*

Use grips to move the remaining trees. When you are finished, use cancel to clear the displayed grips, then use the Grips dialog box to turn off Enable Grips within **B**locks.

Command: *From the toolbar, choose* QSAVE

Take one last look at Autotown (see fig. 12.23). Your finished AUTOTOWN drawing file has about 200 entities. If you had created the drawing without blocks and xrefs, you would have created about 1000 entities. As you can see, blocks and xrefs are efficient tools for both drawing in AutoCAD, and conserving storage space.

**Figure 12.23:**

The finished Autotown drawing.

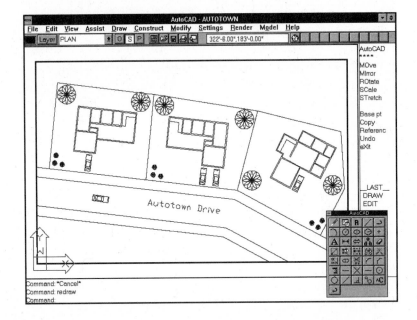

*Now you can delete all the files created in this chapter (for use in Chapter 14, the IAW DISK includes the IAWHATCH and IAWATLAY files; they are identical to the finished AUTOTOWN and ATLAYOUT).*

# Summary

AutoCAD's blocks feature enables you to develop a large detailed drawing quickly and reduces the number of entities in the drawing.

Use the technique of first adding simple block representations to the drawing. After the drawing is complete, you can use = to update to a more detailed symbol, which keeps the computer from slowing down during the design process. You end up with a sophisticated-looking drawing quickly.

When you group blocks within blocks and create nested blocks, you reduce drawing time. After a grouping pattern is recognized and stored, you can use INSERT to develop the geometry.

Dialog boxes for the BLOCK and INSERT commands help you develop a drawing. These features can be particularly helpful for specifying BLOCK names. As with all dialog boxes, however, it is sometimes much faster if you type the command and options.

Use the XREF command any time a drawing (or symbol) is to be shared by many drawings, and you plan to change the shared drawing during the development of any new drawing. An xref drawing enables all drawings to have immediate access to the most current version of the referenced drawing or symbol. Xref drawings are also extremely efficient when used to replace complex blocks that appear once in a multiple number of drawings (such as a title block or common drawing notes). With blocks that you insert often in a drawing (such as an electrical symbol), or a reference drawing you do not use often and do not plan to make changes to, use the BLOCK command.

Grips are available with blocks, just as they are within singular entities. Use grips to quickly manipulate blocks within a drawing. Remember that because blocks are single objects, some modifications are not possible.

You have created a lot of drawing data—it is now time to plot it. Although CAD replaces manual drafting in many ways, you generally need to have a paper copy of your drawing. As in manual drafting, the drawing must be scaled to fit on a piece of paper and may require different view and linetype characteristics. The next chapter explores plotting and composition of finished drawings.

# CHAPTER 13

# Sheet Composition, Scaling, and Plotting

A CAD drawing is fundamentally different from a drawing created with paper and pencil. The final product of a manual drawing is the sheet of paper on which it is drawn. The final product of a CAD drawing is a database that represents all of the graphic entities and text associated with the drawing. AutoCAD's drawing editor builds a collection of data in memory. When you save your drawing, that data—lists and tables full of coordinates, numbers, and other information—is stored in a file on disk. Visually, this database has no resemblance to a drawing. When you edit the drawing, AutoCAD represents the data in the drawing editor by reading the database and issuing instructions that convert the data into the image you see. Figure 13.1 shows a sample printed drawing.

The process of generating a plot is similar to that of representing a drawing on-screen. Instead of converting the data into pixels on your monitor, however, AutoCAD translates the information into a raster or vector image that a plotter can understand. After you initially set up the plotter, these commands for a vector plotter usually amount to little more than moving a pen up and down and from one coordinate to another on the paper. If the pen is down when the command is issued, a line is drawn. Many little line segments combine to plot arcs and text.

**Figure 13.1:**

A detail viewport
and layout
plotted from a
paper space
sheet.

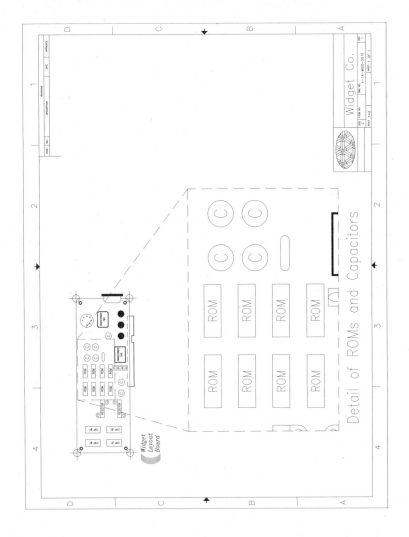

Fortunately, AutoCAD takes care of translating the data in your file into plotter commands. All you have to do is set up the plotter, select the drawing, tell AutoCAD what to plot, and watch it plot. So many plotters and printers are available that it would be impractical to explain the configuration and setup of each one, especially because most output devices control many of the plotting parameters and functions from the plotter, rather than through AutoCAD. This chapter focuses on composing your drawing for plotting, and on actually creating plots.

AutoCAD Release 12 for Windows enables you to run multiple instances of AutoCAD. This means that you can edit one drawing while another is plotting or rendering.

AutoCAD Release 12 for Windows allows up to three instances of AutoCAD to be running under Windows at the same time.

# Getting Ready To Plot

The task of plotting involves more than just issuing the PLOT command. When you install AutoCAD, you have to tell AutoCAD the type of plotter you have, how the plotter is connected, and what default settings to use. When you draw, you have to compose your finished drawing for plotting. When you plot, you have to load paper into the plotter, put in the right type of pens for the plotting media you are using, and make sure the plotter is ready to start receiving information. When you finally issue the PLOT command, you have to check each of its parameters to make sure it is correct for that particular plot. With the drawing file ready to plot, you issue the PLOT command, which passes the data through with parameters that control the size and appearance of the finished plot, convert the data into plotter commands, and send them to the plotter.

## Configuring AutoCAD for Your Output Device

AutoCAD must be properly configured for your output device. This can be accomplished by choosing **C**onfigure from the **F**ile pull-down menu, or by entering the CONFIG command, and then using Option 5, Configure plotter. Device configuration is covered in more detail in Appendix A. Before you try to configure an output device, you may have to know certain information about the device, such as model number, emulation capabilities, and communications parameters. Consult your output device manufacturer's instructions and your *Installation and Performance Guide*.

The plotter configuration option of AutoCAD offers the following options:

- **Add** a plotter to the configuration
- **Delete** a plotter from the active configuration list
- **Change** a plotter configuration
- **Rename** a plotter configuration

All raster output devices, such as dot matrix printers and laser printers, use the Windows system printer driver. If an AutoCAD ADI driver exists for your plotter, use the ADI driver rather than the Windows system printer. The AutoCAD ADI drivers are faster and more reliable.

## Multiple Plotter and Printer Configurations

The CONFIG command can configure AutoCAD for one or more output devices and file formats. During configuration, you can assign your own special device names to any plotter, output device, or file format configuration. The PLOT command conveniently enables you to select, from a list, what configuration you want to use for a given plot.

*If you have both a printer and plotter connected to your system, install drivers for both devices using the Plotter option in AutoCAD configuration. You can then select the desired output device from the Plot Configuration dialog box when you plot.*

 *If you reconfigure AutoCAD, write or print out the current configuration in case the settings are accidentally lost or overwritten. You can use the AutoCAD log file to save text window output to a file that can be edited and printed.*

The plotting examples in this chapter are based on a generic D-size (34×22) plotter and a generic printer. Your default pen speed, sheet size, and linetypes may vary from the examples in this book, but these settings do not affect the exercises. If you want to change some of the configuration settings for your output device, you can set different values during the PLOT command.

# First-Time Checklist

The following checklist outlines items you should check when you configure your plotter initially:

- Is the plotter plugged in?

- Is the plotter connected to the correct port on the computer?

- Does the interface cable between the plotter and computer match the connections shown in the *Installation and Performance Guide*?

- Has the plotter been configured in AutoCAD?

- Are the software configuration settings correct?

- Does the plotter self-test run properly and does the drawing output look OK?

- Is the paper alignment correct and do the pens operate properly?

If you are using a printer instead of a plotter, or a smaller plotter, most of the discussion in this chapter still applies. If you do not have a printer or plotter but can carry a floppy disk to a system with one, you can plot to a disk file and then copy it to the plotter. This process is covered later in this chapter.

If your plotter or printer requires an ADI driver for AutoCAD that was not supplied by Autodesk, see the manufacturer's instructions and be sure to add any required commands to your CONFIG.SYS or AUTOEXEC.BAT files.

## Every-Time Checklist

The plotting process involves two steps: setting up the plotter to run, and readying your drawing file with the proper scale and other plotter assignments in AutoCAD. After you have configured the plotter in AutoCAD, you only need to check and adjust parameters such as paper size and pen selection when you plot. Use the following checklist.

- Is the paper or other media loaded and properly aligned in the plotter? Does it move freely without striking the wall, cables, or other obstructions?

- Is the plotter adjusted for that size of paper?

- Are the pens in the holder? Are they primed and flowing freely? If the plotter uses removable carousels, is the correct carousel in the plotter? Does the carousel type match the pen type? Are the correct pens for the media being used, and is the speed set so the pens work without skipping?

- If the plotter shares a single COM port with another device such as a digitizer, has the selection switch been switched to the plotter, or has the cable been connected to the plotter?

- Does the plotter need to be in Remote mode to sense incoming commands?

Try performing a plot based on the following procedures.

# Accessing the PLOT Command

AutoCAD offers a number of ways to access the PLOT command. You can plot by choosing Print/Plot from the File pull-down menu, specifying the plotting options in the Plot Configuration dialog box, and then clicking on OK. The Plot Configuration dialog box is shown in figure 13.2. You can also issue the PLOT command from the screen menu, the toolbar, or enter it at the Command: prompt. The toolbox can be modified to include the PLOT command as well. All these methods bring up the Plot Configuration dialog box, shown in figure 13.2, if the system variable CMDDIA is on (set to 1—the default). If CMDDIA is set to 0, you are prompted for the plot options at the command line. Later in the chapter, you learn how to plot without first bringing up the drawing. This is done if you start AutoCAD by using the -P switch in the command line of the AutoCAD for Windows startup icon's properties.

*The PRPLOT command, found in previous releases of AutoCAD, is no longer valid. Printers are supported along with plotters through the standard Plot Configuration dialog box. In AutoCAD for Windows, Printers are supported through the system printer driver.*

The Plot Configuration dialog box sets parameters and plots a drawing. Many of these parameters are the same as in the CONFIG command's plotter option, and you can use the Plot Configuration dialog box to select from any configured devices. However, if you need to add a new device, or delete or rename an existing one, use the CONFIG command, not PLOT.

You can also use scripts to run plots automatically. The SCRIPT command is on the UTILITY screen menu. The task of plotting from a script file is covered later in this chapter.

If you want to run another copy of AutoCAD to plot your drawings while editing another drawing, simply double-click on the startup icon again. You will need a minimum of 8M of RAM for the first instance of AutoCAD and 4.5M of ram for each additional instance of AutoCAD for acceptable performance. Each instance of AutoCAD started will use the same configuration files.

# Creating a Checkplot To Fit the Paper

When you plot a drawing to fit, AutoCAD calculates a ratio between the width of the drawing area you specify and the width of the plotting area. AutoCAD performs the same calculation for the height of the drawing area and the height of the plotting area. The larger of the two dimensions determines the actual size of the plot. Because the drawing is plotted in proportion to its true size, some blank space may be left on the plot either for the width or height, depending on which proportion is smaller. The following exercise shows the prompts for a printer configured as a PostScript printer in AutoCAD. If you are configured for a plotter or a system printer, this exercise should work fine. You can plot to the default device or choose another device from the dialog box, if one is available.

Begin by plotting the drawing extents in the following exercise. You are fitting them to the sheet, rather than scaling the drawing to a specific size. If you plot by using the Extents and Fit options, everything in the drawing is plotted as large as possible on the paper. Throughout this chapter, you can use either the WIDGEDIT drawing from Chapter 9 or the IAWWIDG4 drawing from the IAW DISK. In this exercise you can use any drawing, however, because it is plotted to fit the paper. Your plotting area dimensions probably differ from the numbers shown in the exercise, but your plot should appear similar to that shown in figure 13.3.

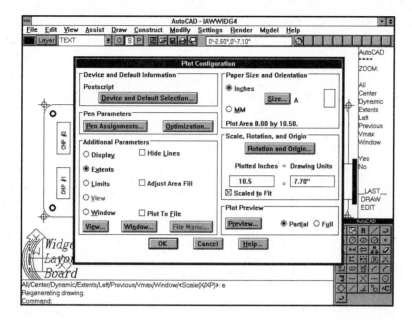

**Figure 13.2:**

The Plot Configuration dialog box.

## Plotting the Extents To Fit the Paper

Start AutoCAD using the IAW startup icon.

Start a new drawing named FRSTPLOT=IAWWIDG4, then zoom with the Extents option.

| | |
|---|---|
| Command: *Choose* **F**ile, *then* **P**rint/Plot *or choose the* PLOT *toolbar button* | Displays the Plot Configuration dialog box (see fig. 13.2) |
| *Choose the* **Ex**tents *radio button in the* Additional Parameters *area* | Specifies the area of the drawing to plot |
| *Put a check mark in the* Scaled **t**o Fit *check box in the* Scale, Rotation, and Origin *area* | Scales the plot to fit the paper |

Make sure Device and Default Information is set up for the correct plotter, and make sure your printer or plotter and paper are ready.

*Choose* OK        Starts the PLOT command

```
Effective plot area: 10.50 wide
by 5.51 high
```

*continues*

```
Position paper in plotter.              Starts the plot
Press RETURN to continue or S to
Stop for Hardware setup: Press Enter

Regeneration done: nn
```

AutoCAD cycles through the drawing, displaying the percent finished in place of nn at left, and displays "Plot Complete" on the command line.

**Figure 13.3:**

The WIDGET draw-
ing, plotted with
extents, and scaled
to fit.

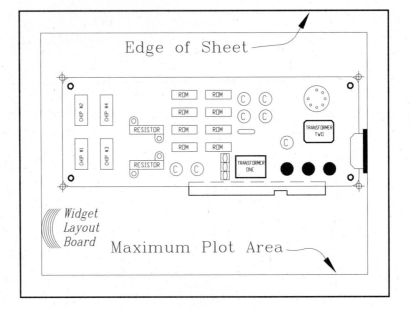

If you used the WIDGEDIT or IAWWIDG4 drawing, your plot should resemble the one shown in figure 13.3. If the drawing plotted extremely small, perform a ZOOM Extents on the drawing, then replot. The drawing may need to be rotated to best fill the sheet on your printer or plotter; you learn how to rotate plots later in this chapter.

*If you plot a drawing using the system printer and you do not have a color printer, check your advanced printer setup to make sure the All Colors to Black option is on. Otherwise, colored lines will be converted to grey scale and will not appear solid or may not appear to be plotted at all.*

*Take advantage of plotting to a printer to make quick, easy, and inexpensive checkplots. If your printer has high enough resolution, it also is useful for 11" × 8 1/2" detail prints.*

The steps described in the preceding exercise are basically what it takes to get a plot. But you should compose your plot before you even turn on the plotter.

# Composing and Finishing a Drawing for Plotting

The IAWWIDG4 drawing makes a nice plot, but it is not a finished drawing. A finished drawing is composed with a title block and usually includes more than one view of the object it represents. Often, detailed views are included—views that may be at different scales than the original drawing. A finished drawing often includes annotations and dimensions. Some layers, like construction layers, for example, may be turned off. Finished drawings usually include more than one line weight—usually controlled by plotting with different pens.

In the plot you just did, AutoCAD's defaults were used for all of the plotting-control parameters. Most finished drawings require changing one or more of those parameters for each plot. These parameters include:

- **Select the Part of the Drawing to Plot.** This parameter selects how much of the drawing to plot by choosing the Display, Extents, Limits, View, or Window radio buttons.

- **Select the Plotting Area.** This parameter specifies a sheet size, such as C, D, and so on, for plotting area, or specifies a custom plot size by plot length and width if you are using an odd-sized sheet or need the plot to be a certain finished size. Select either option by clicking on the Size button.

- **Select the Plot Scale.** This parameter checks the Scaled to Fit check box to scale the drawing to fill the plotting area, proportional to the model, but not to any certain scale. To plot to a specific scale, enter values in the Plotted Inches and Drawing Units edit boxes.

Paper space makes it easy to finish and compose a drawing for plotting. You simply treat paper space as an electronic sheet of paper, sized to match your plotter media, and compose your drawing. When you plot, what you see in the graphics window is what you get in the plot—at the full precision and resolution of your plotter.

The task of finishing and composing a drawing without paper space is more complicated. Model space is the environment in which you model your design, whether 2D or 3D. In model space, you can plot only the current viewport. You need to do some manual cut-and-paste operations by using commands such as COPY, SCALE, and TRIM to plot several views of a drawing on one sheet of paper from model space.

*Think ahead about leaving room for a border and a title block. Set the drawing limits equal to the paper size and plot Limits. Size and position your title block and border margins to compensate for the area the plotter needs to grasp the paper.*

# Controlling What To Plot

When you compose a drawing, your first consideration should be to decide what to plot. Many times, whether from model space or paper space, you want to plot only a portion of your drawing. You may, for example, need a checkplot of only one viewport or of part of a viewport. If you use layers and colors to segregate your data, you may want to plot only certain layers, areas, or colors. The LAYER command controls which layers are plotted. The PLOT command enables you to specify how much of the drawing to include in the plot and to control how colors plot. The PLOT command also enables you to move the location of the plot on the paper, scale the plot, and fit it to the paper, giving you fine control over the finished plot, even without paper space.

The PLOT command has five options that control how much of the drawing will plot. The Plot Configuration dialog box gives you the choice of Display, Extents, Limits, View, or Window. Anything that falls outside the selected area is clipped and not plotted. The following list describes what each choice does:

- **Display.** This option uses the image currently displayed in your graphics window to determine what to plot. Everything inside the area of the current viewport is plotted. (Remember, paper space itself or a single full-drawing area view in paper space is considered a viewport.)

- **Extents.** This option specifies the extents of your drawing. When used in coordination with Fit, this option plots everything visible in the drawing to fit the paper.

- **Limits.** This option specifies everything in the drawing limits.

- **View.** This option specifies a named view you previously saved. You can save several different views with different names, then use View to plot each one by name. You can save an appropriate view named PLOT in every drawing, which makes plotting easy to standardize.

- **Window.** This option enables you to define a rectangular window around the area of the drawing you want to plot. Normally, you use the Window option only when you are plotting or printing with the drawing loaded into the drawing editor. If, however, you select Window when plotting or printing from a *freeplot* session (a session started with ACAD -P), you can use the Window button to specify the coordinates of the opposing corners of the window to determine what to plot.

# Setting the Plotting Scale

In the first exercise, you plotted the IAWWIDG4 drawing to fit the paper in the plotter. Although this gave you a plotted image proportional to the original model, it was not set to any specific scale. Most of the time your drawings do need to be plotted to scale.

In paper space, you compose your drawing in paper space limits that equal your sheet size and plot the drawing at full scale.

In model space, sizing your plot to a particular scale is more involved, but fairly straightforward. You size your plot by finding a ratio between the actual size of the model and the scale at which you want it to plot. Suppose, for example, that you have a house plan drawn to actual size, and you want to plot it at a scale of 1/4"=1'-0". When you specify a plot scale in the PLOT command, you enter the corresponding scale in units that AutoCAD can interpret, instead of typing Fit. In this case, you can enter either **1/4"=1'0** or **1=48**, and the drawing plots to that scale. Optionally, you can enter the same value in decimal form, such as **.25=12**, or **.020833=1**. This scales the model correctly, but what about scaling the annotations?

## Scaling Annotations, Symbols, and Dimensions

How can you determine what size your text, bubbles, and dimensions will plot? The key is to understand that everything in your model is related to model space or real-world dimensions. You almost always draw objects actual size, and scale them when it is time to plot. In the preceding example, the house plan would have been drawn actual size. Suppose, for example, that you want your text to plot 1/8" high. If you create your text and other annotations at 1/8", the dimensions and notes would be so small relative to the house plan itself that you could not read them. It would be like standing 200 feet above the house while trying to read a newspaper resting on the ground.

When you create your dimensions and text, you need to know at what size you will eventually plot the drawing. In this example, you want to determine the relationship between 1/8" on the paper and the size of the text in the model. If 1/4" on paper equals 12" in the model, then 1/8" equals 6", so text and dimensions should be drawn 6" high in this drawing to plot 1/8" on paper at this scale. Dimension text and symbols are scaled similarly.

Consider one more example. If you find that your house plan is too big to fit on the paper at 1/4" = 1'-0", you might decide to scale the drawing to 3/16" = 1'-0" instead. But you still want all text to plot 1/8" high. 1/8" is two-thirds of 3/16" (2/16 compared to 3/16), and 8" is two-thirds of 12", so you need 8" text to get 1/8"-high characters on paper.

These same scales apply to text and annotations you put on your model in model-space viewports—even if you compose the final drawing in paper space. Later, some paper space alternatives are explored.

Table 13.1 shows the model space text size needed to achieve a specific plotted text size at some common scales.

# Composing a Title Block in Model Space

Drawing in full scale brings up the problem of how to place a D-size sheet border and title block around a model that may be a hundred feet wide. The answer is simple: create the title block full size (34×22 or 36×24 for a D-size sheet). Then insert it as a block in your drawing by using the inverse of the scale that you would use to plot the drawing.

## Table 13.1
## Common Text Sizes at Various Scales

| Scale | Plotted Text Size | Text Size (Model Space) |
|-------|-------------------|-------------------------|
| 1/8"=1'-0" | 1/8" | 12" |
|  | 3/16" | 18" |
|  | 1/4" | 24" |
| 3/16"=1'-0" | 1/8" | 8" |
|  | 3/16" | 12" |
|  | 1/4" | 16" |
| 1/4"=1'-0" | 1/8" | 6" |
|  | 3/16" | 8" |
|  | 1/4" | 12" |
| 1/2"=1'-0" | 1/8" | 3" |
|  | 3/16" | 4.5" |
|  | 1/4" | 6" |
| 1"=1'-0" | 1/8" | 1.5" |
|  | 3/16" | 2.25" |
|  | 1/4" | 3" |
| 1 1/2"=1'-0" | 1/8" | 1" |
|  | 3/16" | 1.5" |
|  | 1/4" | 2" |
| 1:2 | .125" | .25" |
|  | .1875" | .3875" |
|  | .25" | .5" |

| Scale | Plotted Text Size | Text Size (Model Space) |
|-------|-------------------|-------------------------|
| 1:10  | .125"             | 12.5"                   |
|       | .1875"            | 18.75"                  |
|       | .25"              | 25"                     |
| 2:1   | .125"             | .0625"                  |
|       | .1875"            | .09375"                 |
|       | .25"              | .125"                   |

Consider the same example shown earlier—a house plan drawn actual size that needs to go on a D-size sheet at a scale of 1/4" = 1'-0". You enter a scale of 1/4"=1'0 (equal to 1:48) when prompted for a scale in Plot. Your title block is also drawn actual size, only 34" or 36" wide. When you insert the title block by using the INSERT command, it has to be scaled up proportionally to the model. So if you insert the title block drawing into the model and scale it 48 times larger to fit around the plan of the house, it scales back to its original size when the drawing is plotted.

## Model Space Alternative: Faking Paper Space

Another approach would be to scale the model drawing down and insert it into the title block before you plot. This approach has the advantage of always plotting at a standard 1=1 scale, and it enables you to preview the "what you see is what you will plot" image in the graphics window. It also makes it much easier to combine multiple scales of details in a single drawing. You can do this in two ways.

One solution is to do it in a single drawing file. First, create a block of your entire drawing; do not use the OOPS command to bring back the erased entities. Next, insert your title block at 1=1 scale on its own layer and zoom to the title block. Then, insert your entire drawing into the title block on the title block layer at the scale you would have used to plot it in the previously discussed method. In this example, you would insert it at 1/48. If you later need to make changes to the drawing model, freeze the title block layer, *Insert the drawing block at 1=1 scale, zoom out and make changes, and reblock it to the same name. When you thaw and zoom back to the title block layer, you find the changes because of the block redefinition.

A second solution is to create a separate 1=1 scale title block drawing and insert the model drawing file into it at the appropriate scale. If you make changes to the model drawing file, reinsert it with an equal sign to redefine it in the title block drawing.

In either case, you plot the results at full scale. If you need to add annotations or title text, you do it at the real-world scale you want it to be in the plot. This method makes multiple model views or detail with varying scales in one drawing easier, but it is not as easy as using paper space.

## Plotting Multiple Model Views or Details

Multiple model views or details with varying scales in one drawing are easy to compose in paper space. Set up each desired view or detail in its own viewport, scale it, and plot everything at once from paper space. That full process is covered later in this chapter.

You can fake the paper space technique by inserting a block for each desired view or detail into your 1=1 title block. Scale each insertion as if you were plotting it to scale by itself. As you see in the 3D chapters, you can use UCSs when you write your blocks to disk to create varying viewpoints of the same model. Then you can insert these into a single title block.

A third alternative is to scale and plot each view or detail separately, but all on the same sheet of paper. This alternative requires the capability to position each plot where you want it on the plotter sheet.

# Positioning the Plot on Paper

Whichever way you compose and scale your plot, whether you plan to plot it all at once or plot separate views or details on the same sheet of paper, your next decision is how to place the plot on the paper.

*All plotters have a limit to how wide a drawing they can plot, and cut sheet plotters are also limited in how long a plot they can produce. Roll feed plotters (plotters that use a roll of plotting media instead of cut sheets) are limited as to width, but can often plot a drawing as long as the length of the media on the roll. Because cut sheet plotters are much more common than roll feed plotters, cut sheet plotters are used in the following discussion.*

## Plot Origin versus Area-to-Plot Origin

A plotter's starting pen position is the *plotter origin*. The plot places the lower left corner of the area to plot (display, extents, limits, view, or window) at the plotter origin. On a pen plotter, the plotter origin usually is at or near the lower left corner of the paper. For a printer plotter, it is the upper left corner. If you tell AutoCAD to rotate the plot, the origin changes. The rectangular boundary that defines the maximum plotting area for a plotter is called its *hard clip limits*. If you place a point in each of the opposite corners of the hard clip limits, one of the points becomes the plotter origin.

You can determine your plotter's origin and hard clip limits by separately plotting a vertical line and a horizontal line (length is not important). Plot them on the same sheet by using Extents and Fit. Both options start at the plotter origin and extend to the X or Y limits.

As already mentioned, AutoCAD normally places the lower left corner of the part of the drawing you specify to plot at the plotter origin. To plot the drawing at a particular point on the sheet, as you would to plot multiple views separately, tell AutoCAD to move the plotter origin. Do this by specifying an X,Y displacement in plotter units at the plot origin prompt or in the Plot Rotation and Origin dialog box. By specifying a different displacement for each view or detail, you can plot multiple images on a sheet, one at a time.

# Plot Standardization

Even normal plots (one per sheet) are easier if you standardize the relationship of the plotter origin to the lower left corner of the area you specify to plot. You standardized the book's drawings by setting limits to the sheet size (in drawing units). If your plotter can plot the full sheet from edge to edge, you can plot limits at the default plot origin (home position at the lower left corner of the sheet). Most plotters, however, grip a portion of the paper during the plot. This means that the lower left corner of the paper is not at the plotter origin, so you cannot plot limits to scale. You still can get an accurately scaled plot by doing a window plot or by plotting a named view. Set the lower left corner of the window or view in the drawing at an offset from the lower left corner of the limits. This offset should be equal to the distance from the lower left corner of the sheet to the plotter origin for your plotter. Unless you are plotting at full scale, you need to convert this offset to drawing units (offset times scale factor). Set the upper right corner to encompass the area you want to plot; anything outside the window or view (or outside your plotter's hard clip limits) will be clipped. Make sure any title block you use fits in the window or view and is within your plotter's hard clip limits.

By using a view named PLOT, you can standardize plotting at the appropriate scale at the default plotter origin. You can further standardize your plotting by combining this technique with using paper space or the fake paper space method. That way, you always plot a view named PLOT at full scale at the default plotter origin.

# Plotting a Standard View Named PLOT to Scale

To see how this works and to practice plotting a drawing to scale, plot the IAWWIDG4 again. IAWWIDG4 was created with 11"×8.5" limits, matching an A-size sheet at 1=1 scale or a C-size (22×17) sheet at 2=1 scale (twice real size). You will plot it at 2=1 scale.

Assume that the generic plotter's origin is offset 1/2" in the X axis and 3/4" in the Y axis from the lower left corner of the sheet. This makes your offset .25,.375 (.5,.75 divided by a 2:1 plot-to-drawing scale). You can place the lower left of your PLOT view at .25,.375 to place the 0,0 point of your limits precisely at the corner of the plot sheet. If your plotter origin offset is different, substitute your X,Y offset divided by 2. If you are using a printer or if your maximum sheet size is smaller than C-size, plot to an A-size sheet at 1:1 scale and adjust your offset to match.

As in the earlier plot, your plot area may differ from that shown in the following PLOT command.

## Plotting to Scale and Moving the Origin

Start a NEW drawing named SCALPLOT=IAWWIDG4, then zoom All.

```
Command: VIEW ↵

?/Delete/Restore/Save/Window: W ↵
```

| | |
|---|---|
| `View name to save: PLOT ↵` | Names the view |
| `First corner: .25,.375 ↵` | Sets the first window corner (substitute your calculated offset) |
| `Other corner: 11,8.5 ↵` | Sets the other corner and saves the view |

Draw a border, using a 2D polyline, no larger than half your hard clip limits, centered on the image.

Set the PDMODE system variable to 0, and by using POINT, draw a point at your calculated offset point.

| | |
|---|---|
| Command: *Choose* **F**ile, *then* **P**rint/Plot *or, from the toolbar, choose* PLOT | Opens the Plot Configuration dialog box |
| *Choose the* **Vi**ew *button* | Opens the View Name dialog box |
| *Double-click on* PLOT *in the View Name list* | Selects the view, closes the dialog box, and turns on the **V**iew radio button |
| *Choose* **S**ize, *then select* A *if you are plotting to a printer, or* C *if you are plotting to a plotter, then choose* OK | Sets the paper size |
| *If you are using a printer, choose* Rotation and Origin, *click on the* 90 *radio button, then choose* OK | Sets the plot orientation on the paper |
| *Clear the* Scaled **t**o Fit *check box* | Allows the scale to be set |
| *Double-click in the* Plotted Inches *edit box and enter* **1** *and press Enter for A-size, or enter* **2** *and press Enter for C-size* | Sets the appropriate scale |

Make sure Drawing Units are set to 1.

| | |
|---|---|
| *Choose* OK | Closes the dialog box |

```
Effective plotting area: 21.00 wide
by 16.00 high
Position paper in plotter.
```

Make sure your printer or plotter and paper are ready.

```
Press RETURN to continue or S to        Starts the plot
Stop for Hardware setup: Press Enter
```

```
Regeneration done: nn
```

When the plot finishes, close the drawing and discard your changes.

---

The widget should have plotted at twice its real-world size for C-size, or at its exact size for A-size, with the lower left corner of the border exactly at your plotter origin and the lower left limits at the sheet corner, as shown in figure 13.4.

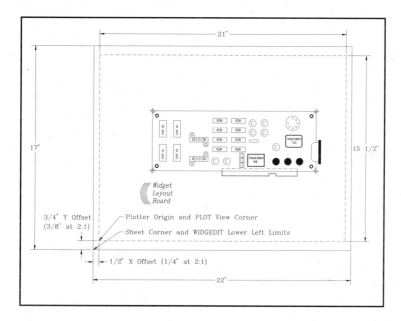

**Figure 13.4:**

Plot offset for WIDGEDIT at 2=1 scale.

*If your plotter offset is too large and your hard clip limits are too small to accommodate your standard title sheet, perhaps you can expand them.*

*You cannot choose the **V**iew radio button unless a named view has previously been specified by choosing Vi**e**w and selecting a named view.*

## Expanding the Plotting Area

Sometimes your drawing does not fit in the hard clip limits, perhaps by a fraction of an inch. In some cases, the hard clip limits of the plotter can be expanded by increasing the plot area half an inch or more. Check your plotter documentation to see if your plotter offers an expanded mode. Usually, expanded mode is controlled by a small switch on the plotter. Expanded mode moves the location of the 0,0 plotter origin to the corner of the expanded area.

Sometimes, the expanded plotter origin comes too close to the pinch wheels that hold the paper against the plotter drum, at times even moving past the wheels. If this happens with an ink plot, the wheels smear anything drawn inside their area. To eliminate this problem, you can adjust the plotter origin away from the pinch wheel by entering a small origin offset.

You may find that composing a plot in paper space is even easier than using the technique just described.

## Composing a Plot in Paper Space

One of paper space's primary functions is to make plotting easier, particularly in 3D work. The process you go through each time you take your drawing from the design stage to a finished plot is much the same. The following checklist gives you an idea of what steps to take after your design is drawn.

- Enter **PSPACE** and use MVIEW to create as many viewports as you need for the various views and details you want to plot. If your viewports exceed 15, turn them on, 15 at a time, and plot twice on a single sheet, or put details in separate drawing files and insert them or attach them as externally referenced files in paper space before plotting. You can also create and draw in viewports that you do not intend to plot, to work on the main or master model from which the other views are derived. You can do the bulk of your design work now or after you plan the arrangement of views in the title sheet.

- Insert your title sheet into paper space at full scale or attach it as an externally referenced file. Put it on its own layer so you can freeze it as you work on your drawing. Plan how the viewports to be plotted are to be arranged and scaled in the title sheet. You can draw construction lines on a layer that will not be plotted to keep track of your arrangement. Freeze the title sheet layer.

- Enter model space and create or finish drawing your views and details. Compose each view to be plotted as if it were a separate drawing in its own viewport. You do not need to have the viewports in their final arrangement as you work—arrange and size them for drawing convenience. But keep the planned scale and size of each in mind, particularly as you add annotations. You can control layers independently in each viewport, so annotations for one do not show up in others. Finish the model, complete with most dimensions, notes, and other details.

- Enter paper space and thaw your blank title sheet. Erase or freeze the layers of viewports that will not be plotted.

- Resize, stretch, and move the viewports to be plotted to match your planned arrangement in the sheet.

- Enter model space and use the ZOOM command's *n*XP option (*n* is your scale value) to scale each view or detail to the correct plotted scale. This technique is covered in the next section.

- Re-enter paper space. Add any annotations or dimensions you want to do in paper space (dimensions can be automatically scaled to the viewport's contents). Insert any details or attach any externally referenced files stored as separate drawing files. (These could be ordinary blocks or blocked viewports. If they are viewports, you have to turn them on.) Fill in your title block information.

- Create a view named PLOT with its lower left corner offset to match your plotter's offset. Restore the view. What you see is what you will get. Make any final layer on/off or freeze/thaw adjustments.

- Use the PLOT command to plot the PLOT view at full scale.

 *If you plot by using the Display option and have multiple viewports set, you get a plot of whatever is displayed in the current viewport.*

The procedure outlined earlier introduced something new: zooming relative to paper space.

## Scaling Viewports Relative to Paper Space

In the ZOOM command, entering a scale factor, followed by XP causes the image to display relative to paper space units. (The XP stands for *times paper space*.) If you enter a factor of 1XP, the viewport displays the image at full scale (1=1) relative to paper space (and your paper plot). When you plot the drawing at full scale from paper space, the viewport plots at the scale factor specified by ZOOM with the XP option. A zoom factor of .5XP causes the image in the viewport to display at half size.

You determine the ZOOM XP scale as a decimal scale factor in the same manner that you figure scale if you were plotting that viewport by itself. If, for example, you want a view of your model at 1/4" = 1'-0", which is 1:48, divide 1 by 48 to get 0.020833 and enter **0.020833XP** at the ZOOM command as your scale factor.

After you use the ZOOM XP option, be careful not to zoom in or out in model space. PAN is safe and good for fine-tuning the view. If you use ZOOM with the Dynamic option for panning, be sure you do not change the size of the zoom box.

*Scaling a viewport like this only makes sense if you are working in model space (MSPACE). ZOOM with the XP option still works in paper space or tiled viewports, but its effect is identical to the ZOOM X option in those cases.*

# Setting Up Paper Space Views for Plotting

Whether you use tiled or untiled viewports, you model your design in one or more model space viewports, and then compose your title block sheet in paper space for plotting as outlined earlier.

If all your views and details require more than one title sheet, you can insert more than one copy of your title block and then open viewports accordingly on each sheet. You can define plot views by using names like PLOT1, PLOT2, and so on. If you have more than 15 total viewports, you have to use MVIEW to turn them on and off as you plot the different plot views. This keeps you from having to duplicate the model in separate files for each sheet.

The composition of a sheet involves more than haphazardly opening viewports on the page and scaling the views inside them. You can overlap viewports if you want. You can turn viewport frames off by layer control if you do not want them to plot. Their contents still plot unless their appropriate layers are frozen.

Try to compose a new plot and arrange the viewports. Compose two viewports on a 22"×17" sheet and plot it at full scale. One viewport contains a full view of the widget board, and the other shows a 4X detail view. If you do not have a C-size or larger plotter, compose it on an 11"×8.5" sheet. A simple polyline border can be drawn to represent the title block sheet that normally would be inserted or attached. Before you pan and zoom the viewports, your drawing should look like the one shown in figure 13.5.

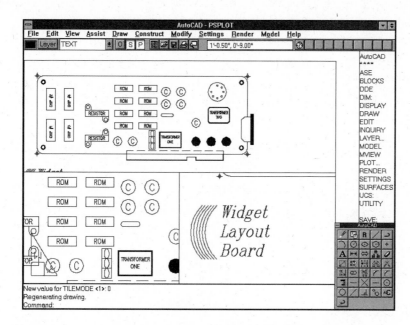

**Figure 13.5:**

The widget in paper space, before rearranging the viewports.

---

## Composing a Plot in Mview Viewports

Begin a new drawing named PSPLOT=IAWWIDG4.

Command: **TILEMODE** ↵

| | |
|---|---|
| New value for TILEMODE <1>: **0** ↵ | Turns off TILEMODE |
| Regenerating drawing. | Displays Viewports from Chapter 7 |
| Command: *Select all three viewports, then issue the* ERASE *command* | Leaves blank paper space sheet |
| Command: *Choose* **S**ettings, *then* Dra**w**ing Limits, *and set limits from 0,0 to 11,8.5 for A-size, or from 0,0 to 22,17 for C-size* | Sets paper space limits, independent from model space |

Zoom with the All option.

If you are using an A-size sheet, set snap to .125 and use RECTANG (choose **D**raw, then **R**ectangle) to draw a border from .5,.375 to 10.5,8.125.

If you are using a C-size sheet, set snap to .25 and use RECTANG to draw a border from 1,.75 to 21,16.25.

*continues*

| | |
|---|---|
| `Command:` *Choose* **V**iew, *then* Mvie**w**, *then* **C**reate Viewport | Issues MVIEW command |
| `ON/OFF/Hideplot/Fit/2/3/4/Restore/` `<First Point>:` *From the toolbox, choose* INTERSECTION | |
| `_int of` *Pick the upper left hand corner of the border at* ① *(see fig. 13.6)* | |
| `Other corner:` *Enter* **9,4.5** *for A-size or* **18,9** *for C-size* | Displays widget in a viewport |
| `Command:` *Press Enter* | Repeats MVIEW |
| `ON/OFF/Hideplot/Fit/2/3/4/Restore/` `<First Point>:` *Enter* **3.5,1** *for A-size or* **7,2** *for C-size* | |
| `Other corner:` *From the toolbox, choose* INTERSECTION | |
| `_int of` *Pick lower right corner of upper viewport at* ② | Displays widget in another viewport |
| `Command:` **MS** ↵ | Enters model space and allows the contents of the viewports to be zoomed and panned |
| `Command:` *Click on upper viewport* | Makes it active |
| `Command:` **Z** ↵ | |
| `All/Center/Dynamic/Extents/Left/` `Previous/Vmax/Window/<Scale(X/XP)>:` *Enter* **.5XP** *for A-size or* **1XP** *for C-size* | Scales the image to .5=1 or 1=1 relative to paper space |
| `Command:` *Use ZOOM Center and pick the center point on the image, then press Enter at the height prompt* | Centers the image without changing the default height (see fig. 13.6) |
| `Command:` *Click on lower right viewport and use ZOOM 2XP for A-size or 4XP for C-size* | Makes it active and scales its image to 2=1 or 4=1 |
| `Command:` *Use ZOOM Center and pick the middle of the eight ROMs, and then press Enter at the height prompt* | Pans the image without changing the default height (see fig. 13.6) |

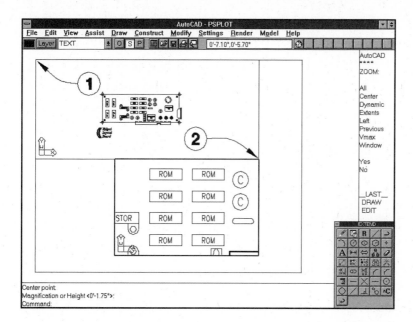

**Figure 13.6:**
Widget viewports arranged and scaled.

Layer visibility can be turned on or off on a viewport-by-viewport basis. Normally, you add annotations and other finishing touches by using unique layers to prevent visibility in other viewports. If you have done that, you may also want to add annotations in paper space. You can use object snaps when in paper space to snap to objects in viewports. This helps align and position your paper space objects and annotations.

*Use the MVIEW Hideplot option in 3D work to specify which viewport(s) should have hidden lines removed when plotted.*

In the following exercise, turn the viewport frames off and tie the 4X scale viewport to the full image with two dashed rectangles and dashed zoom lines, as shown in figure 13.7. This shows where the 4X image comes from.

## Annotating in Paper Space

Continue from the previous exercise.

Command: **PS** ⏎                    Re-enters paper space

Command: **LINETYPE** ⏎

?/Create/Load/Set: **L** ⏎

Linetype(s) to load: **DASHED** ⏎

*continues*

| | |
|---|---|
| *Select* ACAD *from the* \ACADWIN \SUPPORT *directory* | Loads DASHED from the ACAD.LIN file in your AutoCAD support directory |

```
Linetype DASHED loaded
```

```
?/Create/Load/Set: Press Enter
```

| | |
|---|---|
| `Command:` *Enter* **DDLMODES**, *then create layer DONTPLOT and turn it off, then create layer DASHED and set it current, with linetype DASHED* | Uses Layer Control dialog box to create and set layers |
| `Command:` *Using RECTANG with INT object snap, trace over frame of bottom viewport* | Draws dashed box |
| `Command:` *Type* **DDCHPROP** *and press Enter, select both viewports (remove the polyline rectangle from the set), then use the* **L**ayer *button to place them on the DONTPLOT layer* | Uses Change Properties dialog box to make viewport borders invisible |
| `Command:` *Enter* **LTSCALE**, *and set linetype scale to .5* | Regenerates with new linetype scale |

Next, create a 1/4-scale duplicate of the polyline box and move it over the widget board in the upper viewport.

| | |
|---|---|
| `Command:` *Select the dashed viewport* | Starts a selection set |
| `Command:` *Pick the lower left grip* | Enters stretch mode |

```
** STRETCH **
<Stretch to point>/Base point/Copy/
Undo/eXit: SC ↵
```
Switches to scale

```
** SCALE **
<Scale factor>/Base point/Copy/Undo/
Reference/eXit: C ↵
```
Specifies Copy option

```
** SCALE (multiple) **
<Scale factor>/Base point/Copy/Undo/
Reference/eXit: .25 ↵
```
Creates 1/4-scaled copy

```
** SCALE (multiple) **
<Scale factor>/Base point/Copy/Undo/
Reference/eXit: Press Enter
```
Exits grip mode

| | |
|---|---|
| `Command:` *Select the 1/4-scale dashed box, then pick its lower left grip* | Selects box and enters stretch mode |

```
** STRETCH **
Stretch to point>/Base point/Copy/
Undo/eXit: MO ↵
```
Switches to move mode

```
** MOVE **
<Move to point>/Base point/Copy/
Undo/eXit:
```
*Move 1/4-scale box over the part of upper image that matches the 4X view (see fig. 13.7)*

**Command:** *Enter* **L**, *then draw two lines connecting the two boxes*     Shows 4X detail zooming from full widget image

You can add any annotations and title text you want while in paper space by using the DTEXT command with text height set to the actual desired text height in the plot.

Finally, you create a plot view and plot the drawing.

Use the VIEW command's Window option to create a view named PLOT, set the lower left corner of the window at your calculated plotter offset, and set the upper right corner to encompass the border.

*Save the drawing*

**Command:** **PLOT** ↵     Opens Plot Configuration dialog box

*Click on* Vi**e**w, select PLOT, *then choose* OK     Selects view PLOT

Make sure plot scale is 1=1.

*Click on* OK     Plots the drawing

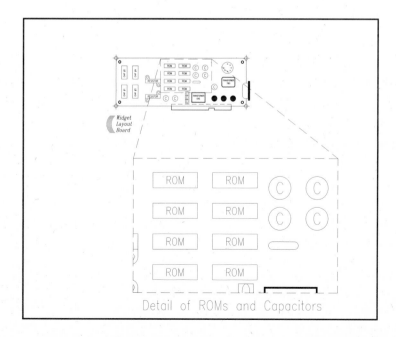

**Figure 13.7:**

The plotted widget with two viewports.

The advantage of annotating in paper space is that you do not have to scale at plot time. You draw your model at real size, compose your plot sheet at full size, and plot it at 1=1. The only scaling is setting the viewport zoom scale relative to paper space for the plot. The disadvantage of annotating in paper space is that the annotation is not tied to the viewport contents.

Now that you know how to set up your title block and viewports manually, you may appreciate the fact that AutoCAD can automate this creation and insertion of title blocks and viewport configurations.

# Automating Your Plot Setup Using MVSETUP.LSP

The MVSETUP.LSP routine is an AutoLISP-defined command accessed from the Layout option of the View pull-down menu. If you chose not to install all files when you installed AutoCAD, you may not have MVSETUP.LSP on your system. If not, copy the file MVSETUP.LSP from your original AutoCAD disks into your AutoCAD support directory, your IAW directory, or any directory on AutoCAD's support path.

To use MVSETUP.LSP, choose View, then Layout, then MV Setup from the pull-down menu. The first time you use MVSETUP, it takes longer than subsequent uses because MVSETUP sets itself up on your system. The first time each title block size is used also takes longer because MVSETUP builds the title block from scratch. The routine offers you the option of saving the title blocks to disk, so it can speed up sheet layout in subsequent uses. After you initially load MVSETUP, you can execute it in the current drawing as a command with the name MVS.

MVSETUP has options for aligning, creating, and scaling viewports, and for inserting a title block. Not all of these apply to your initial setup, so you may use MVSETUP more than once on each drawing.

Use MVSETUP in the following exercise to insert a title block and viewports in the IAWWIDG4 drawing. If you are using a C-size or larger plotter, insert a C-size title block (see fig. 13.8); otherwise insert an A-size title block. Save the title block it creates for use later in the book.

---

## Setting Up a Widget Plot with MVSETUP

Enter **NEW**, then enter the file name **MVPLOT=IAWWIDG4**.

| | |
|---|---|
| `Command:` *Choose* View, *then* Layout, *then* MV Setup | Loads and issues MVSETUP command |
| `Initializing... MVSETUP loaded.` | Executes MVSETUP automatically |
| `Paperspace/Modelspace is disabled.`<br>`The pre-R11 setup will be invoked`<br>`unless it is enabled. Enable Paper/`<br>`Modelspace?` `<Y>:` ↵ | |

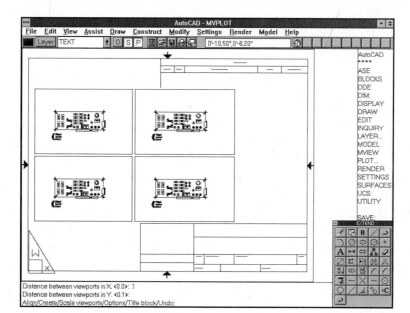

**Figure 13.8:**

A title block and viewpoints inserted by MVSETUP.

| | |
|---|---|
| Regenerating drawing. | Displays three existing viewports |

First, you need to delete the existing viewports, then you need to insert a title block.

| | |
|---|---|
| `Align/Create/Scale viewports /Options/Title block/Undo:` **T** ↵ | Specifies title block option |
| `Delete objects/Origin/Undo/<Insert title block>:` **D** ↵ | Specifies the delete option |
| `Select the objects to delete:` *Select all existing viewports* | Deletes viewpoint |
| `Delete objects/Origin/Undo/<Insert title block>:` *Press Enter* | Displays title block insertion choice |

*Press* F2 *to switch to the text window*

```
Available title block options:

0:      None
1:      ISO A4 Size(mm)
2:      ISO A3 Size(mm)
3:      ISO A2 Size(mm)
4:      ISO A1 Size(mm)
5:      ISO A0 Size(mm)
6:      ANSI-V Size(in)
7:      ANSI-A Size(in)
```

*continues*

```
8:      ANSI-B Size(in)
9:      ANSI-C Size(in)
10:     ANSI-D Size(in)
11:     ANSI-E Size(in)
12:     Arch/Engineering (24 x 36in)
13:     Generic D size Sheet (24 x 36in)
```

Add/Delete/Redisplay/<Number of    Inserts A-size or C-size title block
entry to load>: *Enter* **7** *for A-size or* **9**
*for C-size*

Create a drawing named ansi-c.dwg?    Saves title block for later
<Y>: *Press Enter*

Next, you need to insert new viewports.

Align/Create/Scale viewports/    Specifies the Create option
Options/Title block/Undo: **C** ↵

Delete objects/Undo/    Displays viewport layout choices
<Create viewports>: *Press Enter*

Available Mview viewport layout options:

```
0:      None
1:      Single
2:      Std. Engineering
3:      Array of Viewports
```

Redisplay/<Number of entry to    Specifies Array option
load>: **3** ↵

Bounding area for viewports.    Specifies upper left corner
Default/<First point >: *Enter* **.5,7**
*for A-size or* **1,16** *for C-size*

Other point: *Enter* **8,2.2** *for A-size*    Specifies lower right corner
*or* **16,2.5** *for C-size*

Number of viewports in X. <1>: **2** ↵

Number of viewports in Y. <1>: **2** ↵

Distance between viewports in X.    Specifies viewport spacing
<0.0>: *Enter* **.1** *for A-size or* **.5** *for C-size*

Distance between viewports in Y.    Creates 2×2 array of viewports with
<0.5>: *Press Enter (defaults to X spacing)*    .1 or .5" spacing

Finally, scale the upper right viewport relative to paper space.

Align/Create/Scale viewports/    Specifies Scale option
Options/Title block/Undo: **S** ↵

Select objects: *Select the upper right viewport, then press Enter*

Enters model space to zoom view

Enter the ratio of paper space units to model space units...

Number of paper space units. <1.0>: *Press Enter for A-size or enter* **2** *for C-size*

Number of model space units. <1.0>: *Press Enter*

Scales A-size view 1:1 or C -size 2:1 (see fig. 13.9)

Align/Create/Scale viewports/ Options/Title block/Undo: *Press Enter*

Exits MVSETUP

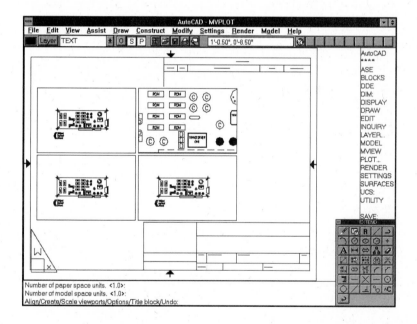

**Figure 13.9:**

Viewports scaled by MVSETUP.

You now have a title block that shows four viewports of IAWWIDG4. If it is C-size, the upper right viewport has a plot scale of 2:1, as shown in figure 13.9. But that is not all MVSETUP can do. You can use MVSETUP automatically to align images in two different viewports.

*The Std. Engineering MVIEW viewport layout option sets up standard top, front, right, and 3D isometric viewports and viewpoints of a 3D model.*

# Aligning Viewport Images

Often, you want common elements in adjacent views of your drawing to line up with each other. This alignment is particularly important in multiview 3D plots. Although you can do this manually, MVSETUP makes it much easier. To use MVSETUP to align your images, start in paper space and zoom in on the two bottom viewports. Enter model space and misalign the bottom left viewport with PAN so that the viewports approximate figure 13.10. Then use MVSETUP to realign the image between the two viewports. When you finish the following command sequence, your drawing window should look like the one shown in figure 13.11.

**Figure 13.10:**

Misaligned images.

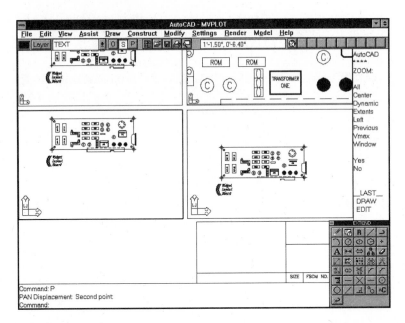

---

## Realigning Views with MVSETUP

Continue from the preceding exercise.

Command: *Use* ZOOM Window *to zoom in on two bottom viewports (see fig 13.10)*

Command: *Enter* **MS***, then click on the bottom left viewport*

Enters model space and makes viewport current

Command: *Enter* **P***, then pan the viewport contents up a little*

Issues PAN command and misaligns images (see fig. 13.10)

Next, use MVSETUP to realign the two views.

Command: **MVS** ↵                                     Executes MVSETUP

Align/Create/Scale viewports                          Specifies the Align option
/Options/Title block/Undo: **A** ↵

Angled/Horizontal/Vertical                            Specifies Horizontal
alignment/Rotate view/Undo? **H** ↵

Basepoint: *Pick the endpoint of a line*
*in the left viewport*

Other point: *Click in right viewport,*              Pans right viewport up to match left
*and then pick the endpoint of a*                    (see fig. 13.11)
*corresponding line*

Angled/Horizontal/Vertical
alignment/Rotate view/Undo?
*Press Enter*

Align/Create/Scale viewports                          Exits MVSETUP
/Options/Title block/Undo:
*Press Enter*

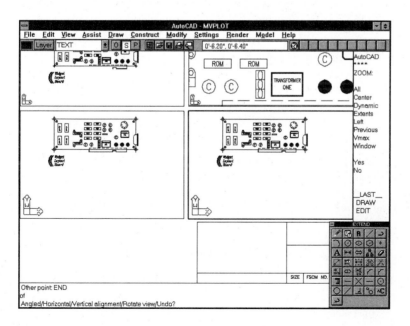

**Figure 13.11:**

Images realigned
by MVSETUP.

Now, your viewport images should be lined up again. When PAN, ZOOM, and other operations misalign views and change the scale of a drawing you have already composed for plotting, you should realign and rescale all your views just before plotting.

## Customizing MVSETUP

You can customize the MVSETUP setup routine to use your own title blocks, custom viewport layouts, and more. Its defaults are contained in an ASCII file named MVSETUP.DFV, which contains instructions on how to customize it. The easiest form of customization is to simply edit the standard title block drawings it creates, making them conform to your standards and adding your standard title text.

# Controlling Layer Visibility in Plots

Several references have been made to controlling layer visibility when plotting. You have seen how you can place mview viewports on layers that you turn off to prevent their plotting. AutoCAD works like overlay drafting, turning on and off combinations of layers to view the drawing data you need to see. This layer control gives you great flexibility in getting a number of finished plots out of a single drawing file. The layers that are on and thawed get plotted, and the layers that are off or frozen do not get plotted. Because layer control is more sophisticated in mview viewports in paper space than it is in tiled viewports or model space, that concept is examined first.

## Layer Control in Paper Space

The capability to control your plot by layer is one of the most important aspects of plotting. Used properly, this technique can save you from duplicating work and filling up your disk with duplicate drawings. The following discussion uses a facilities plan as an example, but the same concept applies to nearly any type of drawing you create in AutoCAD.

Suppose, for example, that a site plan and a floor plan exist, as well as electrical, piping, and equipment layouts. This master facilities plan is used to create five separate plots—one for each of the areas listed. Five copies of the drawing could be made, erasing everything except what is needed in each, but that presents some major problems. If a change is made to the facility, all five drawings must be revised. Plus, if you make a change to one of the drawings, it is difficult to see how it affects the other areas if they are detailed on separate drawings. That does not have to be a problem.

The five different systems on the master drawing are all separated onto different layers. When you work on the drawing, you can leave all the layers turned on so that all of the pertinent information is displayed. Any change to the electrical system, for example, shows conflicts with the other systems.

To plot the finished drawings, you can create five different title sheets in paper space and named plot views, one for each finished plot. Then, opening model space viewports on each sheet, position and scale the model images for each, adding any additional notation or details needed. Use the LAYER command to freeze the unnecessary layers for each sheet when you plot it. If you freeze a layer in one viewport, AutoCAD freezes it in all. Of course, the work of all that freezing and thawing as you go from view to view to work or plot becomes a nuisance. To get around that problem, you can use the VPLAYER (View Port LAYER) command or the Layer Control dialog box to freeze layers selectively in one viewport without affecting other viewports.

The same principles apply to any multiview drawing in which you have annotations and dimensions specific to the views in each viewport. You just freeze those annotation layers in all other viewports.

In Chapter 5, both methods were discussed and you used the VPLAYER command. Try the Layer Control dialog box in the following exercise (see fig. 13.12). The Cur VP buttons control the freeze/thaw status of layers in the current viewport, and the New VP buttons control whether layers are frozen or thawed in the subsequently created viewports.

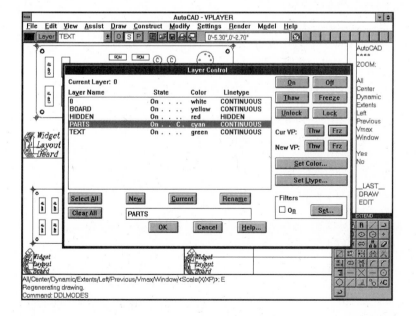

**Figure 13.12:**

The Layer Control dialog box.

The IAWWIDG4 drawing shown in figure 13.13 is used again in the next exercise to see how the Layer Control dialog box selectively freezes layers, as shown in figure 13.14.

**Figure 13.13:**

VPLAYER before
freezing layers.

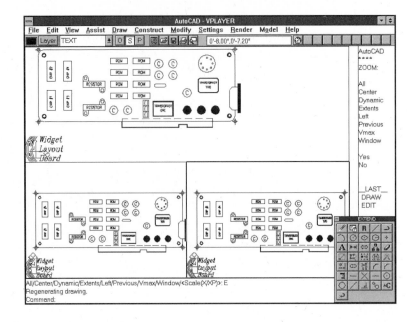

## Freezing Layers Selectively with VPLAYER

Enter **NEW**, discard changes, then enter **VPLAYER=IAWWIDG4**.

| | |
|---|---|
| Command: *Set TILEMODE to 0, then enter* **MS** | Enters paper space, and then model space |
| Command: *Use* ZOOM Extents *in each viewport, then click in lower right viewport* | Leaves right viewport current |
| Command: **DDLMODES** ↵ | Opens Layer Control dialog box |

*Set layer 0 current, and review layer list
(see fig. 13.12)*

| | |
|---|---|
| *Choose* **Clear** All, *select the PARTS layer in the list box, and click on Cur VP*: Frz | Freezes PARTS in current viewport |

The dialog box now displays a C on the PARTS line in the fourth column in the State
column in the layer list box.

| | |
|---|---|
| *Choose* OK | Redisplays without cyan parts in lower right viewport |
| Command: *Click in lower left viewport* | Sets it current |

| | |
|---|---|
| **Command:** *Press Enter, then select the BOARD layer in the list box, and click on Cur VP:* Frz | Repeats DDLMODES command and freezes BOARD in current viewport |

The dialog box now displays a C on the BOARD line (but not on the PARTS line) in the State column in the layer list box.

| | |
|---|---|
| *Choose* OK | Redisplays without yellow board in lower left viewport |
| **Command:** *Click in upper viewport* | Sets it current |
| **Command:** *Press Enter, then select the TEXT layer in the list box, and click on Cur VP:* Frz, *then choose* OK | Repeats DDLMODES, freezes TEXT in current viewport and redisplays without green text in upper viewport |

Quit AutoCAD and discard changes to the drawing.

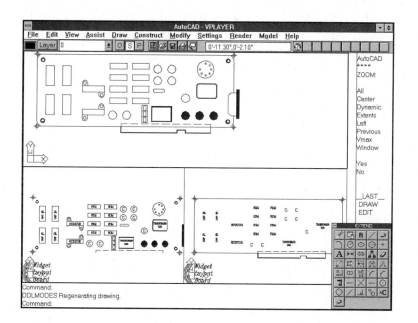

**Figure 13.14:**

VPLAYER after freezing layers.

Although you have frozen each of the main layers in one of the viewports, those layers still are visible in the other two viewports.

Even without mview viewports, you can achieve control over layers almost as well, but it requires more effort.

## Controlling Layers in Model Space or Tiled Viewports

In model space, you can only control your layers globally—a change to a layer's visibility affects all views. To compose your drawing for plotting, make sure the data you want to plot is on a different layer from the data you do not want. By using the facilities plan example, you would start with the same model (each of the different systems for the facility would be on separate layers). You can use the LAYER command to turn on and off or freeze and thaw the correct layers for each desired combination of layers when you plot it. The key to doing this successfully is in knowing what to separate from what. Too many layers usually are better than too few layers.

To create a title block for each sheet, for example, put the blank title block and common text on a layer by itself. Create unique layers for title block text that differs from sheet to sheet. Place common data, such as the building outline, on a layer by itself and turn it on for all plots. Make sure that any data unique to a certain sheet is either on the layer for its system or on a layer by itself. That enables you to turn it on or off when you need it to plot. You can ease the nuisance of turning layers on and off, or freezing and thawing, by naming layers to enable you to use wild-card character filters to specify groups of names.

# Using Other Methods To Plot

Although the Plot Configuration dialog box is a nice addition to AutoCAD Release 12, it is sometimes advantageous to plot from the command line. Scripts use command-line plotting, so, if you want to write a script for unattended plotting, you should be familiar with the prompts. The defaults are listed on-screen, and you have several options to go into some of the detailed areas, if you want them. The system variable called CMDDIA controls whether the PLOT command brings up the dialog box or shows the prompts at the Command: line. The default value is 1 (on) to display the dialog box, although plotting from a script file by-passes the dialog box no matter what CMDDIA is set to. This variable is demonstrated in the next exercise.

Another method of plotting which is new to AutoCAD is the *freeplotting* feature. This is a mode *module* started from Windows, similar to starting AutoCAD, but is dedicated to plotting. Freeplotting is started by using a -p modifier on the startup icon's command line when starting AutoCAD. On some systems you would enter **C:\ACADWIN\ ACAD -p** in the command-line text box. The screen looks like AutoCAD, but most commands do not function. In a networking situation, starting this mode is not counted by the server authorization as an active copy of AutoCAD. You can view slides in this mode as well as preview plots and run script files for plotting.

Freeplot commands include the following:

| | | |
|---|---|---|
| ABOUT | HELP | SCRIPT |
| COMPILE | PLOT | STATUS |
| CONFIG | QUIT | TEXTSCR |
| DELAY | REINIT | TIME |
| FILE | RESUME | VSLIDE |
| GRAPHSCR | RSCRIPT | |

If you use the Plot Configuration dialog box in freeplot mode, you can use the Full Preview option to see and pan or zoom a drawing.

Try the next exercise by using the CMDDIA system variable and the Freeplotting module.

---

### Using Freeplot Mode

Command: **CMDDIA** ↵

New value for CMDDIA <1>: **0** ↵        Turns off command dialog boxes

COMMAND: **QUIT** ↵        Exits AutoCAD

From Program Manager, create a program item named IAW Freeplot similar to the one you created in Chapter 1. Enter **C:\ACADWIN\ACAD -P** in the Command Line text box.

If AutoCAD is installed in a directory other than \ACADWIN, or is installed on a drive other than C, substitute the appropriate path in the previous step.

Start AutoCAD using the new IAW Freeplot startup icon.

Command: **LINE** ↵        Issues LINE command

** Command not allowed. AutoCAD
was invoked only to plot. **

You can issue only a limited set of commands in freeplot mode.

---

If you later want to turn on AutoCAD's dialog box input, just set CMDDIA=1. First, however, read through the next section to learn about pen assignment, and then plot a drawing in freeplot mode without the Plot Configuration dialog box.

# Controlling Pens, Line Weights, and Linetypes

Another dimension of plotting, which often is carried over from manual drafting, is to use a variety of line weights and colors. Many drawings require different line weights or colors to communicate the content of the drawing. New CAD users often settle for a single line weight, not realizing they can use different pens on one plot even with a single-pen plotter. If you use a single-pen plotter, AutoCAD prompts you to change pens.

You can control three factors with drawing colors. You can plot with different pens (for different colors or sizes of pens), with different plotter linetypes, and with different pen speeds. (A *plotter linetype* is defined internally in the plotter, independently of AutoCAD's *software linetypes*.) You can control any of these three factors easily because AutoCAD separates the plot data by color. Everything that is the same color on your drawing plots by using the same pen number, plotter linetype, and pen speed. If you have not organized specific parts of the drawing by entity or layer color, use the CHPROP command to regroup them.

# Pen Color

If you use the PLOT command to assign pen number 1 to the drawing color red, everything that is red in your drawing plots with pen number 1. Then you place a red pen in pen slot number 1 (or place a red pen in the pen holder when prompted to do so for single-pen plotters). If you want pen number 1 to plot with thick black lines, put a thick black pen in slot number 1. Drawing colors do not necessarily have to match plot colors. The task of plotting with different sizes of pens is exactly the same as that of plotting with different colors of pens. Just use drawing color as a logical alias for line weight and assign the same pen number to each color that needs to be plotted at the same line weight. You can assign more than one drawing color to a particular pen number. You could, for example, assign blue and red to pen number 1. Then, anything in the drawing that is either blue or red would plot with pen number 1. To avoid frequent swapping of pens, AutoCAD's plot optimization sorts by pen number as it generates the plot data.

# Plotter Linetype

The second plot factor you can control with drawing color is plotter linetype. Many plotters can generate internal plotter linetypes. They do not have anything in common with AutoCAD's linetypes, so do not confuse the two. You can assign a linetype for each drawing color in the PLOT command. The linetype is specified by a number. Plotter linetype 0 is continuous, which is the default. If you enter a linetype number for a certain drawing color, AutoCAD plots all entities with that drawing color by using that plotter linetype. Be careful to avoid plotting entities that have a software linetype other than continuous with a plotter linetype other than continuous; the result is an inconsistent combination of the two. The pros and cons of software versus plotter linetypes are covered after the exercise. Plotter linetypes are assigned to drawing color independently of pen numbers, so more than one pen can use the same linetype, and one pen can use more than one plotter linetype. Some plotters have internally programmable linetypes/pen assignments that override AutoCAD's plot settings.

# Pen Speed

The final plot factor you can control with drawing color is pen speed. The best speed varies with the pen type, size, type of ink, and plotting media. Use trial and error to set the fastest speeds that plot consistently. Pen speed is assigned to drawing color independently of pen numbers and plotter linetypes. The pen speed numbers are in cm/second. Some plotters have internally programmable speed/pen assignments that override AutoCAD's settings.

Try plotting from the command line in the next exercise and note the many settings that can be viewed and adjusted if necessary.

---

## Plotting with Different Colors, Line Weights, and Linetypes

Continue from the previous exercise in freeplot mode. For a multipen plotter, place different colored pens or different size pens in slots 1, 2, and 3. For a single-pen plotter, place a pen in the plotter, and you are prompted to change pens at the appropriate time. After you prepare the plotter for plotting, just plot the Limits to Fit.

Command: **PLOT** ↵                          Issues PLOT command and opens the Open
                                             Drawing File dialog box

*Scroll through the file list to select*       Selects file to plot but does not load the drawing
IAWWIDG4, *or type* **IAWWIDG4** *in the*      file
*File edit box, then choose* OK

AutoCAD switches to text screen, and logo information appears.

```
What to plot — Display, Extents, Limits,
View or Window <D>: L ↵

Number of copies = 1
Plot device is Hewlett-Packard (HP-GL/2) ADI 4.2 - by Autodesk
Description: HP DraftMaster
Plot optimization level = 4
Plot will NOT be written to a selected file
Sizes are in Inches and the style is landscape
Plot origin is at (0.00,0.00)
Plotting area is 44.72 wide by 35.31 high (MAX size)
Plot is NOT rotated
Area fill will NOT be adjusted for pen width
Hidden lines will NOT be removed
Scale is 1=1.00"

Do you want to change anything?
(No/Yes/File/Save) <N>: Y ↵
```

*continues*

```
Do you want to change plotters?
<N> Press Enter

How many copies of this plot would
you like? , 1 to 99 <1>: Press Enter

Pen widths are in Inches.
```

| Entity Color | Pen No. | Line Type | Pen Speed | Pen Width | Entity Color | Pen No. | Line Type | Pen Speed | Pen Width |
|---|---|---|---|---|---|---|---|---|---|
| 1 (red) | 1 | 0 | 36 | 0.010 | 9 | 1 | 0 | 36 | 0.010 |
| 2 (yellow) | 2 | 0 | 36 | 0.010 | 10 | 2 | 0 | 36 | 0.010 |
| 3 (green) | 3 | 0 | 36 | 0.010 | 11 | 3 | 0 | 36 | 0.010 |
| 4 (cyan) | 4 | 0 | 36 | 0.010 | 12 | 4 | 0 | 36 | 0.010 |
| 5 (blue) | 5 | 0 | 36 | 0.010 | 13 | 5 | 0 | 36 | 0.010 |
| 6 (magenta) | 6 | 0 | 36 | 0.010 | 14 | 6 | 0 | 36 | 0.010 |
| 7 (white) | 7 | 0 | 36 | 0.010 | 15 | 7 | 0 | 36 | 0.010 |
| 8 | 8 | 0 | 36 | 0.010 | 16 | 8 | 0 | 36 | 0.010 |

```
Linetypes:  0 = continuous line
            1 = ..............................
            2 = ──    ──    ──    ──
            3 = ──   ──   ──   ──
            4 = ──── . ──── . ──── . ──── .
            5 = ── .  ── .  ── .  ── .
            6 = ─ . . ─ . . ─ . . ─ . .
            7 = ── ..  ── ..  ── ..  ── ..
            8 = ─ . .. ─ . .. ─ . .. ─ . ..

Do you want to change any of the above
parameters? <N> Y ↵

Enter values, blank=Next, Cn=Color n, Sn=Show n, X=Exit
```

| Layer Color | Pen No. | Line Type | Pen Speed | Line Width | |
|---|---|---|---|---|---|
| 1 (red) | 1 | 0 | 36 | 0.010 | Pen number <1>: *Press Enter* |
| 1 (red) | 1 | 0 | 36 | 0.010 | Line type <0>: *Press Enter* |
| 1 (red) | 1 | 0 | 36 | 0.010 | Pen speed <36>: *Press Enter* |
| 1 (red) | 1 | 0 | 36 | 0.010 | Pen width < 0.01>: *Press Enter* |
| 2 (yellow) | 2 | 0 | 36 | 0.010 | Pen number <2>: *Press Enter* |
| 2 (yellow) | 2 | 0 | 36 | 0.010 | Line type <0>: 2 *Press Enter* |
| 2 (yellow) | 2 | 2 | 36 | 0.010 | Pen speed <36>: *Press Enter* |
| 2 (yellow) | 2 | 2 | 36 | 0.010 | Pen width < 0.01>: *Press Enter* |
| 3 (green) | 3 | 0 | 36 | 0.010 | Pen number <3>: *Press Enter* |
| 3 (green) | 3 | 0 | 36 | 0.010 | Line type <0>: 4 *Press Enter* |
| 3 (green) | 3 | 4 | 36 | 0.010 | Pen speed <36>: *Press Enter* |
| 3 (green) | 3 | 4 | 36 | 0.010 | Pen width < 0.01>: *Press Enter* |
| 4 (cyan) | 4 | 0 | 36 | 0.010 | Pen number <4>: X *Press Enter* |

```
Write the plot to a file? <N>
```
*Press Enter*

```
Size units (Inches or Millimeters)
<I>: Press Enter

Plot origin in Inches <0.00,0.00>:
Press Enter

Standard values for plotting size
Size      Width    Height
ANSI paper sizes
A         10.50     8.00
B         16.00    10.00
C         21.00    16.00
D         33.00    21.00
E         43.00    33.00
F         40.00    28.00

DIN/ISO paper sizes
A4        11.20     7.80
A3        15.60    10.70
A2        22.40    15.60
A1        32.20    22.40

Max and User paper sizes
MAX       44.72    35.31

Enter the Size or Width,Height
(in Inches) <MAX>: Press Enter

Rotate plot clockwise 0/90/180/270
degrees <0>: Press Enter

Adjust area fill boundaries for pen
width? <N> Press Enter

Remove hidden lines? <N> Press Enter

Specify scale by entering:
Plotted Inches=Drawing Units or Fit
or ? <1=1.00">: F ↵

Effective plotting area:  44.72 wide
by 34.56 high
Position paper in plotter.
Press RETURN to continue or S to Stop
for hardware setup Press Enter
```

Regeneration done *nn*                Counts *nn* vectors

```
Plot complete.
```

Command: **QUIT** ↵                   Exits freeplot and AutoCAD

Your plotted drawing should look like the one shown in figure 13.15.

**Figure 13.15:**

The widget
plotted with
plotter linetypes
and line weights.

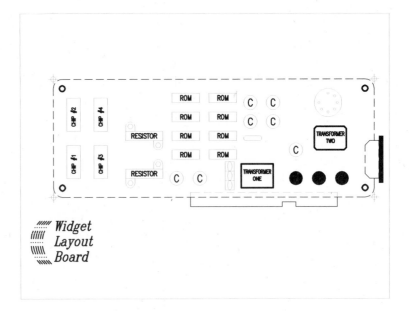

The color, pen, linetype, and speed parameters have three more options, which were not used in the preceding exercise. If you enter an **S**, it redisplays the settings made up to that point. If you enter **C** in which *n* is a color number, the dialog jumps to that color number. Enter **C** with no number to jump to the next color. If you enter an asterisk in front of a pen number, linetype number, or pen speed, such as **\*3** for pen 3, PLOT assigns that setting to the current color and all higher numbered colors.

# Plotter Linetypes, Software Linetypes, and Pen Widths

Plotter linetypes have advantages and disadvantages over software linetypes. Plotter linetypes are independent of scale, although you have to calculate and set an appropriate linetype scale for software linetypes. Wherever possible, you should use AutoCAD's software linetypes, but only lines, circles, arcs, and two-dimensional polylines accept software linetypes. Short polyline segments or spline and curve fit polylines generally plot continuous because the distance between vertex endpoints usually is too short to break the line. AutoCAD linetypes intelligently adjust to balance between endpoints, so corners always are closed. Plotter linetypes often fail to close at corners but do work well for polylines with short segments or curves. Consider using plotter linetypes when you need curved polyline linetypes or a special effect like applying a linetype to 3D meshes or even text. If you use a plotter linetype, make sure your entities are drawn in a unique color for that linetype only.

The pen width setting (default 0.010) in the PLOT command does not directly affect the pen selections. This setting controls the spacing of the closely spaced lines that AutoCAD plots to fill wide polylines, solid entities, and traces. Set it to match the smallest pen used to plot these entities to avoid gaps. The pen width setting also affects text. If plotted text shows partial skips in characters, or if characters run together, check your pen width plot setting. Too large a value causes these symptoms.

*The* line weight *of PostScript printers (which are configured as plotters) is controlled by the pen width setting; 0.005 works well for 300 dpi printers. The thinnest line a 300 dpi printer can produce is 0.003 inches wide; a 1200 dpi printer can produce lines 0.00083 inches wide.*

# Pen Motion Optimization

To minimize pen changes and time spent in pen-up moves (between the end of one line and the start of the next), AutoCAD includes configurable plot optimization. The settings are as follows:

0. No optimization

1. Adds endpoint swap

2. Adds pen sorting

3. Adds limited motion optimization

4. Adds full motion optimization

5. Adds elimination of overlapping horizontal or vertical vectors

6. Adds elimination of overlapping diagonal vectors

Each successive level of optimization includes the features of the preceding levels. The default is 4: endpoint swap, pen sorting, and full motion optimization. Some plotters do their own internal optimization, which may be more efficient. Items 5 and 6 are primarily for 3D work because then you may have many overlapping lines in a plot. You can adjust the level of optimization by reconfiguring your plotter, after first selecting item 2. Allow detailed configuration from the configuration menu. See your AutoCAD *Installation and Performance Guide* for details.

Plot settings can really take time and effort to set up correctly. To change them each time you plot can be time-consuming; it would be nice if you could save settings and reuse them.

# Controlling Pen Assignments from a Dialog Box

The Pen Assignments dialog box, which you access by clicking on the Pen Assignments button in the Plot Configuration dialog box, enables you to control pen number, linetype, speed, and width. You turn the CMDDIA system variable back on (1) to access the Plot Configuration dialog box in the next exercise. Figure 13.16 shows the Pen Assignments dialog box.

**Figure 13.16:**

The Pen Assignments dialog box.

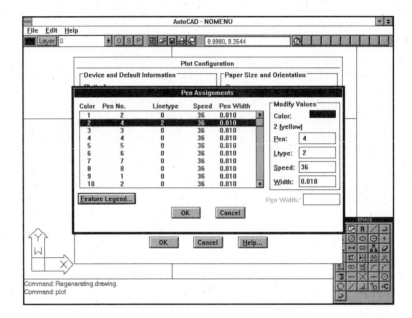

Try using the Pen Assignments dialog box in the next exercise to change some pen number and linetype assignments for your next plot.

## Using the Pen Assignments Dialog Box

Exit AutoCAD and click on the IAW icon to restart AutoCAD without Freeplot mode.

Enter **NEW**, discard changes, then enter **PENBOX=IAWWIDG4**.

Command: **CMDDIA** ↵

New value for CMDDIA <0>: **1** ↵                 Turns on command dialog boxes

Command: **PLOT** ↵                              Displays the Plot Configuration dialog box

*Put a check mark in the* Plot To File
*check box*

| | |
|---|---|
| *Click on the* File N**a**me *button and enter* **PENBOX**, *then choose* OK | Displays Plot Configuration dialog box and specifies drawing drawing to plot |
| *Click on* **P**en Assignments | Opens the Pen Assignments dialog box |
| *Click on color 1 in the list box* | Displays values for pen assignment in Modify Values area |
| *Double-click in the* **P**en *edit box, then enter* **2** | Assigns pen 2 to color 1 |
| *Click on color 1, then click on color 2* | Deselects color 1 and selects color 2 |
| *Double-click in the* **P**en *edit box, then enter* **4** | Assigns pen 4 to color 2 |
| *Double-click in the* Ltype *edit box, then enter* **2** | Assigns linetype 2 to color 2 |
| *Choose* OK | Closes dialog box and returns to Plot Configuration dialog box |

At this point, you could change other settings or choose OK to plot. Instead, choose **C**ancel to cancel the plot.

Quit AutoCAD, discarding changes.

The previous exercise demonstrated using the Plot Configuration dialog box to change pen color and linetype settings when CMDDIA is set to 1.

# Saving Default Plot Settings

AutoCAD maintains your most recent plot parameters from plot to plot and from one AutoCAD session to the next in the ACAD.CFG file. This is convenient; you do not have to reset all of the settings if it takes several attempts to get a plot correct, or if you use the same settings day in and day out. You may need several different sets of standard settings, or you may need to use more than one type of plotter. AutoCAD provides three ways to save and restore settings and plotter configurations.

You can configure several different output devices in AutoCAD, or you can simply configure one device several times with different settings. Each configuration can be saved under a different name, and each time that configuration is used to plot, the same settings used the last time are remembered.

You can use configuration subdirectories to save and use several sets of defaults. At the beginning of the book, the IAW directory was set as the configuration directory. You can create as many configuration directories as you like, in exactly the same manner as you created IAW. You can change the configuration for each plotter or set of standards with the SET ACADCFG= line in the different batch files, and AutoCAD remembers the settings from plot to plot.

You can also use scripts to store and execute standard plot setups. *Scripts* give you a way to make AutoCAD push its own buttons. Scripts are like the macros you find in many other programs—they are really nothing more than automated input that simulates strings of keystrokes. AutoCAD users often overlook the fact that scripts can start and run plots. Scripts are unique in being started outside the drawing editor. You can use a script, for example, to load a drawing, create some entities, and then end the drawing. You can use any input for scripts that you can use in your drawings or in AutoCAD's configuration menus. You can reconfigure plotters with scripts. You can end one drawing and start another, edit it, plot it, end it, and so on. If you have a specific set of operations to run on a group of drawings, you can use a script file to batch process the drawings.

You can also run a script from inside the drawing editor. If you have four standard plotting sequences, each requiring resetting parameters in the PLOT command, you can create four standard scripts, one for each setup. If you set up a standard view to plot named PLOT, your script might look like the example shown in table 13.2. This script is provided on the IAW DISK as DPLOT.SCR. It plots to a D-size sheet at a 1=1 scale. (The right-hand comments are not part of the script file.) The script file to run your plotter may be slightly different; this script file was designed to plot directly to an HP 7585 plotter. You can try entering the responses (listed in table 13.2) to a plot at the command line with CMDDIA turned off to see if they run your plotter.

## Table 13.2
## A Standard Plot Script

| | |
|---|---|
| PLOT | The Plot command |
| V | View |
| PLOT | Plot view name |
| Y | Yes, change some parameters |
| N | No, do not change plotters |
| 30 | Wait 30 seconds for plotter time-out |
| Y | Yes, request hard clip limits |
| N | No, do not change pen/color/linetypes |
| N | No, do not plot to file |
| I | Inches |

| | |
|---|---|
| 0,0 | Origin |
| D | Size |
| 0 | Do not rotate the plot |
| N | No, do not adjust for pen width |
| N | No, do not hide |
| 1=1 | Scale |
| Add a blank line | Starts the plotter |

*The comments shown on the right in table 13.2 are not part of the script file. Do not put comments in your script file.*

If you named the preceding script DPLOT.SCR, you could run the script from the Command: prompt by using the following commands:

```
Command: SCRIPT ⏎
Script file <SCRTEST>: DPLOT ⏎
```

AutoCAD runs through the PLOT command, plots the drawing, and returns to the drawing editor after the plot is complete. Examine (and modify) the script from the IAW DISK to adapt it to your own use. You can edit or create scripts using a text editor.

# Plotting to a File and Spooling

What if you do not have a plotter? Or you are at home and the plotter is at work? Or you need to create a plot file to import into a desktop publishing program?

Sometimes you may want to plot your drawing to a file, rather than to a plotter or printer. When you plot to a file, AutoCAD issues the same plot commands that it would if you were plotting to a plotter. The only difference is that AutoCAD redirects those commands to a file on disk, instead of to the plotter.

You may, for example, have a plot spooling program that enables you to plot multiple drawings one after the other without user intervention. (Plot spooling programs are discussed later in this chapter.) In that case, you plot your drawing to a file, instead of sending it to the plotter. Then, the plot spooler can pick up the file and send it to the plotter.

You may also want to plot to a file when you are transferring your drawings to other programs, such as desktop publishing programs or presentation graphics programs. Many programs import HPGL or PostScript plot files. HPGL files contain plot commands for Hewlett-Packard plotters. Even if your plotter is not a Hewlett-Packard plotter, you can configure AutoCAD for an HP plotter and plot an HPGL file to disk. Then, you can import your plots into CorelDRAW!, PageMaker, Ventura Publisher, and other graphics and desktop publishing programs.

The task of plotting to a file is simple. If CMDDIA is set to 1, use the Plot To File option in the Plot configuration dialog box, then click on File Name and enter a file name in the File Name text box. If you need a special type of file, such as an HPGL file, remember to first select the correct plotter by choosing it from Device and Default Selection dialog box.

If CMDDIA is off and you issue the PLOT command, one of the questions AutoCAD asks you is whether you want to plot to a file or not. If you answer yes, AutoCAD redirects the plot commands to the file name you specify. If you need a special type of file, remember to first select the correct plotter by using the Configure option from the pull-down menu.

A plot spooler is a program that can control access to a plotter by one or more workstations and queue multiple plot requests through a single plotter. Because there are as many different possibilities for spooling as there are spoolers, this book cannot go into much depth about each one. Most spoolers, however, share some common features.

SPOOL is an acronym for Simultaneous Peripheral Output On-Line. On a single-user system, the spooler receives your plot as fast as AutoCAD can send it and trickles it out to the plotter, so you can go on working instead of waiting for the plotter to finish. Plot and print spoolers also enable several people to access a single device. The spooler logs their requests and schedules their plot or print into a queue to be printed when the device is available. Spooling is an integral part of UNIX and most other multi-user/ multiprocessing operating systems and networks. Third-party programs are available for DOS systems that can handle spooling.

Depending on the spooler you are using, you may need to plot your drawing to a file first, then direct the file to the spooler as a job request. See the documentation that comes with your spooler for specifics on installing and using it.

Print Manager is a spooler you can use in Windows. To use Print Manager as a plot spooler for AutoCAD for Windows, you must configure AutoCAD to use the system printer plotter driver and configure your Windows printer driver to use Print Manager. However, using the system printer driver may cause your plot job to take several times longer to print than the AutoCAD ADI drivers.

# Plotting Tips

The following sections offer some general advice on plotting. The visible quality of finished plots is as dependent upon the media and pens you use as it is upon properly controlling AutoCAD. Also, by knowing your plotting device well, you are capable of producing the fastest and highest quality plots possible.

## Plotting Media

The type of media you use depends on the plotter, the project, and whether you need a checkplot or finished drawing. For checkplots, you usually can use the least expensive type of paper you can put through the plotter. Large cut sheets are relatively inexpensive if you purchase them in 1000-sheet quantities. To really save money, buy a roll of butcher paper from your local paper supplier. Roller-ball pens or fiber-tip pens usually are best for checkplots. Because butcher paper is not smooth, roller-ball pens work better than fiber-tips, which tend to bleed through this type of paper.

The choice of vellum and mylar depend mainly on personal preference and the nature of the project. Some types of vellum and mylar do not work well with the inks used in plotter pens. Major drawing media suppliers have special vellum and mylar for use in plotters.

## Pen Type, Speed, and Force

Three types of pens are common for plotting: roller-ball, fiber-tip, and ink pens. Roller-ball and fiber-tip pens are disposable, and ink pens are available in both disposable and refillable types. Four factors affect the efficiency of your pens—speed, acceleration, force, and point quality. You can change the speed of most plotters, as well as the force applied to the pen against the media. Many plotters use a default speed and force settings for the type of pen it thinks is installed. But you can override those settings to fine-tune your plot.

Pen speed typically is expressed in inches per second (ips) or centimeters per second (cps or cm/sec). Acceleration is stated in G-force. Acceleration is important because with short segments, text, and curves, the pen has little room to get up to full speed. Roller-ball pens offer the fastest acceleration, which is why they are ideal for checkplots. Roller-ball pens can go as high as 60 cps with good results. Fiber-tip pens often work best around 40 to 50 cps, and slowing their speed does not affect the quality much, either. With ink pens though, fine-tuning the speed and acceleration often makes a difference. Normally, ink pens plot well anywhere from 10 cps to 30 cps. Jewel tips outwear tungsten or ceramic, which outwear stainless, but all pens wear out eventually. Mylar wears tips much faster than vellum. Cross-grooved tips (not single grooved) can plot at higher speeds than plain tips.

## Keeping Your Plotter and Pens Working

Most plotters are fairly maintenance-free (see your manufacturer's instructions for specifics). You can, however, do a few things every month or so for preventive maintenance. The first is to keep the roller and pinch wheels clean. The pinch wheels press the paper against the roller, and the roller moves the paper in and out of the plotter. Keep the pinch wheels clean of paper particles with a stiff toothbrush. The other item to check is the paper sensors (if your plotter uses photo-diodes to measure the ends of the paper when you load it). If so, two holes are in the plate over which the paper moves, one in back and one in front. These holes have glass covers to keep dust and paper fibers out. When the covers get dirty, you may have problems loading the paper. Use a cotton-tipped swab with a little alcohol on it to clean the covers.

The secret to pen maintenance is to keep them capped, even if your pens normally sit in a pen carousel. Ink pens sometimes need a little extra care. The disposable pens usually come with caps that have a small rubber cushion inside, which keeps the tip from drying out and clogging. Even so, you may want to place capped pens in a carousel or sealed container with a damp sponge. Then a quick tap of the top end of the pen (not the tip) should get it running again. Finally, do not try to refill disposable pens; the nibs wear out too soon to make reusing them worthwhile.

# Solving Plotter Problems

Even after you set everything up correctly, plots fail. The reasons are often simple, but it is the nature of plotting for things to go wrong. The following sections describe a few frequent plotter problems and some possible solutions.

## No Communication between Computer and Plotter

Sometimes after you issue the PLOT command, AutoCAD gives you an error message saying the plotter is not responding. This usually means that the computer cannot make contact with the plotter. If this happens, check for the obvious first and use the checklist from the beginning of this chapter. If AutoCAD still fails to plot, you may have a bad cable. Although it does not happen often, cables sometimes just go bad. Or someone might have accidentally pulled the cable and disconnected one of the contacts in the connector at one end of the cable. With a spare pretested cable available, you can confirm or rule out cabling problems with a simple swap.

## Paper Jams

Paper jams usually are caused by misaligning the paper or by having one of the pinch wheels half-on, half-off the sheet. If one pinch wheel is completely off the paper, the paper jams. Make sure the edges of the sheet are square with each other, or the plotter cannot measure it properly and may try to run it out past the pinch wheels, causing a jam. Check and adjust or replace worn rollers.

## No More Ink or a Pen Skips

The most irritating occurrence when you plot is to run out of ink or have the pen skip in the middle of the plot. If this happens, do not remove the sheet from the plotter. You can replot over the original. The next step is to get the pens working again. You might as well check them all while you are at it. If the plot is a relatively short one, just issue the PLOT command again, and AutoCAD plots over the entities. If you are plotting a drawing that takes a long time to plot, resave the drawing, then erase the entities that plotted the first time. Then, reissue the PLOT command to finish the plot.

## Wrong Linetypes

If lines plot with a different linetype than you expected, or if the scale of dashed linetypes seems wrong, check to see if plotter linetypes are specified in the PLOT command's default settings. If the linetype for a color is anything other than 0, those entities plot by using the plotter's internal linetypes instead of AutoCAD's linetypes. If the scale of your lines is off, check the drawing's LTSCALE setting and adjust it for correct plotting.

# Summary

Now you have followed the CAD drafting process from start to finish: setting up a new drawing, creating and editing entities, and finally, plotting. Continue to explore AutoCAD for Windows Release 12 by mastering the commands in Chapter 14, which add many enhancements to your drawings. Hatching with AutoCAD is powerful and can be used in many creative ways to dress up your drawings. Many examples of this are shown in the next chapter. Creative use of linetypes is also explained, including how to define your own new linetypes. Freehand sketching is also available in AutoCAD, if you like to give drawings a personal touch.

Finally, a major portion of Chapter 14 explains all of the inquiry commands. Once you have a CAD drawing properly drawn to scale, you will be pleasantly surprised at how easy it is to obtain information such as area, perimeters, distances, and entity properties. Turn to Chapter 14 now and see for yourself.

# Drawing Enhancements and Inquiry

Up to this point, your drawings have been simple. If you want to make your drawings look more professional, you can enhance them with patterns, shading, annotation, dimensioning, and linetypes. Figure 14.1 shows some of AutoCAD's hatch patterns and styles you might use. You also may need to sketch in freehand or trace lines, such as contours in the Autotown site plan. You have already learned text annotation, and dimensioning is the topic of the next chapter. The rest you learn in this chapter.

You also learn how to use AutoCAD's inquiry commands to get information about your drawings and their entities. You have already used the ID, HELP, and STATUS commands. This chapter discusses the AREA, DBLIST, DIST, ID, LIST, and TIME commands. You are also introduced to the Region Modeler and how it applies to retrieving drawing database information.

The discussion of hatching was deferred until after the blocks chapter, because AutoCAD's hatch patterns are really a type of blocks. When you use the HATCH command to place a pattern, such as a brick pattern in a walkway area, you are really inserting a block with the brick pattern.

**Figure 14.1:**

Some AutoCAD hatch patterns.

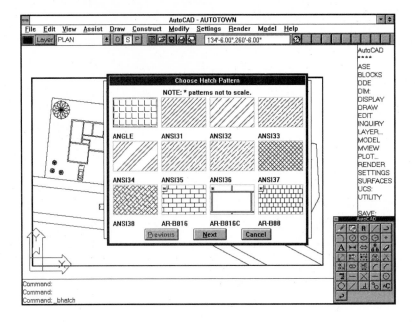

*Hatches* are specialized blocks. They do not share the efficiency or easy insertion-point control of normal AutoCAD blocks, and they require some care in setting up boundaries. Good results may require a little practice.

Otherwise, the basic scaling and rotating techniques you have learned about inserting blocks also apply to placing hatch patterns. AutoCAD's standard hatch patterns are sized as unit blocks. When you insert these patterns in your drawing, you scale and rotate the pattern. If you are composing your drawing in paper space, you can have AutoCAD automate hatch scaling.

Because you normally want to fit these patterns in predefined areas in your drawing, the focus of this chapter is to give you a set of techniques to help you define the boundaries that control the insertion of the hatch block. These boundaries can be defined by using POLYLINE to develop a boundary, BREAK to segment the area into a contiguous boundary, or by using BHATCH. The BHATCH command stands for *boundary hatch* and uses the same dialog box and methods as BPOLY to create a boundary by "tracing" the entities surrounding a selected point in the drawing.

# Setting Up for Drawing Enhancements

The hatching and sketching exercises in this chapter represent a suburban renewal project for Autotown. You are going to pave the road, brick the sidewalk, add detail to some yards with hatching, and improve the drainage by sketching some contour lines.

To select a hatch pattern, you can type the name within the HATCH command, or use the dialog box with the BHATCH command. To know what hatch patterns are available within the HATCH command, you can enter a **?** within the command. Doing this displays a listing of all the hatch pattern names and a description. The BHATCH command displays the hatch patterns with an icon menu. You can select the hatch pattern by pointing and picking the icon of the desired pattern.

You use the IAWHATCH drawing from the IAW DISK, which is identical to the AUTOTOWN drawing you saved at the end of Chapter 12. Add two more layers called SCRATCH and HATCH, and check the other settings in table 14.1. You also bind the IAWATLAY drawing (the same as the ATLAYOUT drawing from the IAW DISK) to the current drawing, and explode it so you can select its component entities when you hatch.

Your drawing should appear similar to figure 14.2 as you begin.

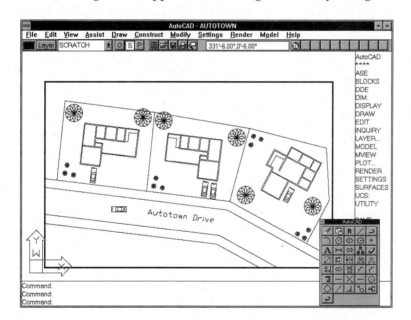

**Figure 14.2:**
The Autotown drawing.

## Table 14.1
## Autotown Drawing Settings

| APERTURE | COORDS | GRID | SNAP | ORTHO | UCSICON |
|---|---|---|---|---|---|
| 6 | On | 10' | 6" | OFF | OR |

*continues*

## Table 14.1
## Continued

| | |
|---|---|
| **UNITS** | Engineering units, 2 decimal places, surveyor's angles with 8 places of precision, default angle 0. |
| **LIMITS** | 0,0 to 360',240' |
| **ZOOM** | Zoom All. |
| **VIEW** | View saved as A. |

| Layer Name | State | Color | Linetype |
|---|---|---|---|
| 0 | On | White | CONTINUOUS |
| IAWATLAY$0$PLAN | On | Green | CONTINUOUS |
| IAWATLAY$0$SITE | On | Cyan | CONTINUOUS |
| HATCH | On | Magenta | CONTINUOUS |
| PLAN | On | Green | CONTINUOUS |
| SCRATCH | On/Current | White | CONTINUOUS |
| SITE | On | Cyan | CONTINUOUS |

## Setting Up for Enhancing Autotown

Choose <u>F</u>ile, then <u>N</u>ew, and enter `AUTOTOWN=IAWHATCH`, replacing your previous Autotown drawing.

`Command:` *From the screen menu, choose*
BLOCKS, *then* XREF:

`?/Bind/Detach/Path/Reload/<Attach>:`
`B ↵`

`Xref(s) to bind:` **`IAWATLAY`** ↵           Binds IAWATLAY as a BLOCK
  `Scanning...`

Create the HATCH and SCRATCH layers and check the other settings shown in table 14.1. Set layer SCRATCH current.

`Command:` *From the screen menu, choose*           Explodes bound block into individual entities
EDIT, *then* EXPLODE, *then select the*
*border and press Enter*

`Command:` *From the toolbar, choose* QSAVE

The process of hatching often requires building boundaries to control your hatch inserts. You are starting with the SCRATCH layer current, and you build your hatch boundaries there. You can also use it as a pure scratch layer to experiment with any of the predefined hatch patterns that seem interesting to you.

Autotown would look better if the road had some character. The next exercise shows you how to view by name available hatch patterns to locate a brick pattern for the road.

# Examining the Patterns Stored in ACAD.PAT

To view the patterns in ACAD.PAT by name with the HATCH command, use a ?, as shown in the following exercise.

---

## Viewing Hatch Patterns

| | |
|---|---|
| `Command:` *From the screen menu,* *choose* DRAW, *then* HATCH: | Starts the HATCH command |
| `Pattern (? or name/U, style): ?` ↵ | Displays the name and description of available hatch patterns |
| `Pattern(s) to List <*>` *Press Enter* | Displays all hatch patterns |

Press Enter twice more to complete the list; press F2 to see the list in the text window. You should see a listing of hatch pattern names and their descriptions similar to figure 14.3.

---

When you are in the HATCH command, entering the name of a HATCH pattern places this pattern in the drawing. A sample image of each of these patterns can be found in the Appendix of the Autodesk manual, *Using AutoCAD for Windows*. Later in the chapter, you are introduced to the BHATCH command, which enables you to view and select pattern images.

# Using the HATCH Command

You use the brick pattern to add detail to the Autotown street. The most important part of creating a hatch is defining the boundary for the pattern. The HATCH command requires a boundary consisting of a closed polygon or contiguous entities. To use the HATCH command to fill an area, you must completely define a closed boundary. When you define a boundary, avoid overlapping and open-ended intersections, or your pattern can spill out of bounds.

**Figure 14.3:**

Hatch pattern
names and
descriptions.

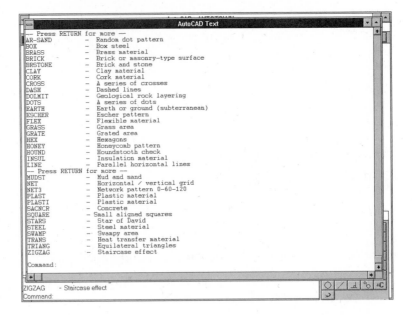

One method is to use a polyline to trace over the perimeter of the area you want to hatch. This method eliminates the uncertainty of whether your drawing has any questionable endpoints (like the endpoints where Autotown Drive meets the border line) or your fill area is open or closed. Create such boundaries on a scratch layer so they do not affect the rest of the drawing.

Create a boundary for Autotown Drive by tracing over the road perimeter with a polyline. Use object snaps to help pick the endpoints.

## Using HATCH To Insert a Brick Pattern

Set a running INT object snap, and then use the PLINE command to trace the road area's perimeter. Use the PLINE Close option to create an accurate closed boundary. Set the running object snap back to NONE after you are done.

| | |
|---|---|
| Command: *From the toolbar, open the Layer pop-up list and select* HATCH | Sets HATCH current |
| Command: *From the screen menu, choose* DRAW, *then* HATCH: | Starts the HATCH command |
| Pattern (? or name/U, style): **BRICK** ↵ | Specifies a BRICK pattern |
| Scale for pattern <1.0000>: **120** ↵ | Scales the pattern by a factor of 120 |
| Angle for pattern <0.0000>: **45** ↵ | Specifies an angle of 45 degrees for the pattern |

| | |
|---|---|
| `Select objects:` *Select polyline boundary, text, and car in road* | Specifies the boundary for the HATCH |
| `Select objects:` *Press Enter* | Draws the hatch |
| `Command:` *Press F7* | Turns off grid (see fig. 14.4) |
| *Zoom in on the car in the road* | |

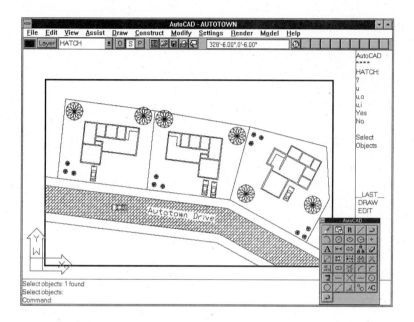

**Figure 14.4:**

Autotown with a bricked drive.

Look closely at your bricked drive. What is wrong with the car? (Look at fig. 14.5.)

# Solving the Hatch Donut-and-Hole Problem

The brick hatch pattern drew directly over the car in the road. This classic hatching problem is called the *donut-and-hole* problem. If you select something as simple as a circle or rectangle, the HATCH command fills it in, stopping the pattern at the edges. If you want to fill in a more complex boundary that also contains other objects, you must tell the HATCH command not to draw the hatch pattern across those objects. A boundary inside another boundary, such as a circle (hole-and-donut), is called a *nested boundary*.

**Figure 14.5:**

Detail of the car.

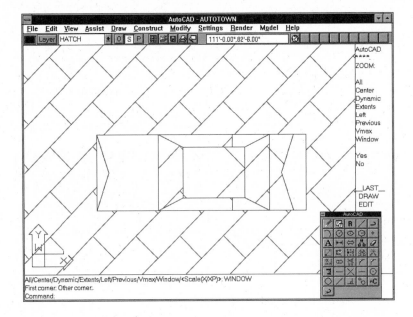

The HATCH command tries to decide what is the donut and what is the hole when it figures out where to hatch. In the Autotown Drive case, the text is a hole, but the car is a number of holes. (Text is treated as if surrounded by an invisible boundary.) AutoCAD normally hatches by starting the pattern at the perimeter boundary and stopping at the next boundary, and then starting again at the next boundary. The car is made up of many lines, creating many interior boundaries, so the pattern fills over parts of the car. The HATCH command offers three hatch style options to help solve this problem.

## Using HATCH Prompts and Options

As you work with hatches, you also need to set the scale and angle to get the effects you want. The following lists the HATCH command prompts and options you have to work with:

- **Pattern...name...** This option enables you to enter a predefined hatch pattern name. Precede the name with an asterisk to insert the hatch as individual line entities instead of as a block reference. You can also append a comma and style code to the name.

- **?.** This option displays a list of all defined hatch pattern names and their descriptions. You can use wild cards for a specific list.

- **U.** This option creates a user-defined array or double-hatched grid of straight lines. You answer the following prompts to define the pattern:

```
Angle for crosshatch lines <0>:

Spacing between lines <1.0000>:

Double hatch area? <N>
```

- **,style.** This option enables you to append a comma and style code to the hatch pattern name, unless you want the default Normal style. The style code determines the way nested boundaries are hatched. The three style choices are the following:

    **N.** Normal (the default) hatches every other boundary.

    **O.** Outermost hatches only the area between the outermost boundary and the next inner boundary.

    **I.** Ignore hatches everything inside the outermost boundary, ignoring inner boundaries.

- **Scale for pattern <1.0000>.** This option establishes scale. Most predefined patterns are designed to look correct at a scale of 1 when plotted at 1:1 scale. In paper space, use a scale of 1. In model space, scale the pattern to the inverse of the plot scale. Enter a factor as scaleXP to scale the hatch to match what you get by using scale in paper space. In an mview viewport scaled to paper space with ZOOM XP, you can enter the hatch scale as 1XP.

- **Angle for pattern <0>.** This option enables you to enter the rotation angle; pick two points to show the angle.

- **Select objects.** This option specifies objects to define the hatch boundaries. Each boundary should consist of a contiguous series of entities. If you select a block, all entities in it are considered hatch boundaries. Mview viewport borders can be selected as hatch boundaries. If you select text, attributes, shape, trace, or solid entities, the hatch stops at their perimeters unless you use the Ignore style. The perimeters for text, attributes, and shapes include a small margin space to ensure readability. For hatching complex areas or areas without clearly defined boundaries, trace the perimeter with a polyline on a reference layer and select the polyline as the boundary. If you select entities that are not parallel to the current UCS, the boundaries are projected to and hatched in the current construction plane of the current UCS.

# Using HATCH Outermost

Try the Outermost option to repave the road, so the car appears as shown in figure 14.6. The HATCH command considers only the entities you select when it calculates the interior boundaries, so be sure to select all interior objects you do not want hatched.

## Using HATCH Outermost To Hatch Around Objects

Command: *Choose* **V**iew, *and then* **Z**oom, *then* **P**revious
Zooms to the previous display

Command: *Choose* **M**odify, *then* **E**rase, *then* **L**ast
Erases the last hatching

Command: *From the screen menu, choose* DRAW, *then* HATCH:
Starts the HATCH command

Pattern (? or name/U, style) <BRICK>: **BRICK,O** ↵
Specifies a BRICK pattern with the Outermost style

Scale for pattern <120.00>: *Press Enter*
Scales the pattern by a factor of 120

Angle for pattern <N45d0'0"E>: *Press Enter*
Specifies an angle of 45 degrees for the pattern

Select objects: *Select polyline boundary, text, and car in road*
Specifies the boundary for the HATCH

Select objects: *Press Enter*
Draws the hatch

Figure 14.6 shows the results of this exercise.

**Figure 14.6:**

Detail of the car.

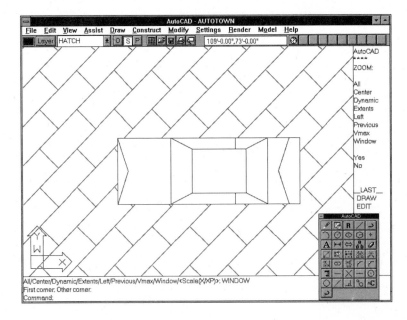

# Breaking Existing Entities for a Hatch Boundary

In the Autotown drawing, you place a grass pattern between the three lot lines and the drawing border. In this case, it is easier to break the four intersections where the border and the outer lot lines meet Autotown Drive than it is to trace the entire lot and border perimeters.

In this exercise, use BHATCH and pick the segments as the hatch boundary and fill the area with a grass pattern. Figure 14.7 and the following exercise show the break points on Autotown Drive's polyline.

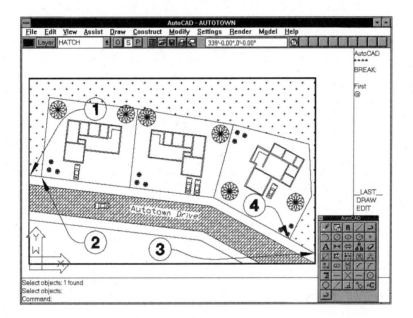

**Figure 14.7:**

Inserted grass pattern in Autotown.

The BHATCH command works in the same way as the HATCH command, except it uses a dialog box and has additional options for defining hatch boundaries in the same way as BPOLY. You issue the BHATCH command by selecting **H**atch under the **D**raw pull-down menu.

---

## Using BREAK and BHATCH To Insert a Hatch Pattern

`Command:` *Choose* **M**odify, *then* **B**reak,
*then* Select Object, **T**wo Points

`Select object:` *Pick the border near*          Selects the object to break
*(not at) point* ① *(see fig. 14.7)*

*continues*

| | |
|---|---|
| `Enter second point (or F for first point):_first` | The menu enters the First option, enabling you to respecify the first point |
| `Enter first point:` *Use the* ENDP *object snap to pick point* ① | Specifies the first point to break the object |
| `Enter second point:` *Choose @ from the screen menu* | Repicks at the first point and breaks line |
| *Repeat the BREAK command for sidewalk at point* ②, *border at point* ③, *and sidewalk at point* ④, *using First for first point and the* ENDPoint *object snap and* @ | |
| `Command:` *Choose* **D**raw, *then* **H**atch | Starts the BHATCH command |
| *Choose the* Hatch **O**ptions *button, then* **N**ormal | Resets the style option to Normal |
| *Choose the* **P**attern *button* | Displays first page of available patterns |
| *Choose* **N**ext *twice, then click on the* Grass *image* | Displays and selects the pattern |
| *Enter* 120 *in the* Sca**l**e *input box* | Specifies the pattern scale |
| *Enter* 0 *in the* **A**ngle *input box* | Specifies the pattern angle |
| *Choose the* OK *button* | Returns to the Boundary Hatch dialog box |
| *Choose the* **S**elect Objects *button* | Redisplays the drawing area |
| `Select Objects:` *Select the border polyline, two broken ends of sidewalk, and all six lot lines adjoining hatched area shown in figure 14.7* | Specifies the HATCH boundary |
| `Select Object:` *Press Enter* | |
| *Choose the* Apply *button* | Draws the pattern in the drawing |

You may notice that the grass slightly overlaps the wide border polyline. Hatch draws its pattern to the center line of wide polylines.

# Using BHATCH To Define a Boundary

When using the BHATCH command, notice that there are several options in addition to the normal HATCH command options. You may also use the **P**ick Points option to pick a point inside the grass boundary area. The BHATCH command develops a polyline around the selected area. This polyline is temporary for use during the BHATCH command unless you choose **A**dvanced Options and set Retain **B**oundaries to keep the border polyline after the HATCH pattern is added to the drawing.

After using Hatch **O**ptions in BHATCH, to set the type of pattern, angle, scale, and hatching style, you can use **P**ick Points to create a border. To use the **P**ick Points option with the BHATCH command, the area to hatch must be a closed area. The entities need not connect at endpoints, but they must intersect. If they do not, you see an error message telling you that the boundary is not closed. To be sure of finding the correct boundary, pick the point near one line of the boundary. **V**iew Selections shows the selected entities (or boundaries) before hatching. The Previe**w** Hatch option displays the hatch pattern in the drawing, enabling you to change any hatch option (or cancel the command) before the hatch pattern is applied. The Apply button draws the final pattern and exits.

Use BHATCH and the **P**ick Points option to place a brick stone sidewalk along the road. To use the **P**ick Points option with the BHATCH command, the area to hatch must be a closed area. The entities need not connect at endpoints, but they must intersect. If they do not, you get an error message telling you the boundary is not closed.

The BHATCH command works the same way as the HATCH command except that it uses a dialog box and can define hatch boundaries in the same way as BPOLY. You issue the BHATCH command by selecting **H**atch under the **D**raw pull-down menu.

## Hatching the Sidewalk

Command: *Choose* **D**raw, *then* **H**atch

*Choose the* Hatch **O**ptions *button*

*Choose the* **P**attern *button*                          Displays the available patterns

You can use the **S**elect Objects option in BHATCH to add boundary-defining entities to the selection set created by **P**ick Points. **S**elect Objects can also be used to select a set of contiguous objects to hatch in exactly the same way as at the HATCH command's Select objects: prompt.

*Choose* **N**ext, *then* Brstone                          Displays and selects the pattern

*Enter* 60 *in the* Sca**l**e *input box*                  Specifies the pattern scale

*Enter* 45 *in the* **A**ngle *input box*                  Specifies the pattern angle

*Choose the* OK *button*                          Returns to the Boundary Hatch dialog box

*Choose the* **P**ick Points *button*                          Displays drawing to pick a point inside the area to hatch

*continues*

| | |
|---|---|
| `Select internal point` *Pick a point inside the sidewalk area (see fig. 14.8)* | Calculates and highlights hatch boundary |
| `Select internal points` *Pick a point inside the sidewalk area on the opposite side of the road* | Specifies another boundary |
| `Select internal points` *Press Enter* | Returns to the dialog box |
| *Choose the* Previe**w** Hatch *button* | Displays the potential HATCH pattern on-screen |
| `Press RETURN to continue` *Press Enter* | Returns to the BHATCH dialog box |
| *Choose the* Apply *button* | Draws the hatch pattern |

**Figure 14.8:**

Inserted brick stone pattern in sidewalk.

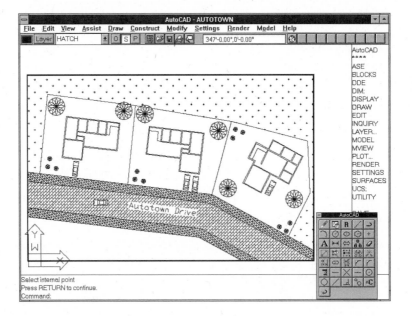

When using the BHATCH command, you must be able to see on-screen all the entities used to define the boundary by using the pick points option to define a boundary. If you need to hatch a very narrow area, or are working on a large drawing, the **A**dvanced Options dialog box enables you to create a selection set from which the hatch boundary is made. When you create a selection set for **P**ick Points to consider, you speed up the process in a complex drawing; otherwise, **P**ick Points considers all entities on the screen.

> When picking internal points to create a BHATCH border, select
> the point inside the area near an entity that defines the area. By
> default, BHATCH selects the nearest object. The Advanced Options
> dialog box enables you to control how the Pick Point option locates
> the first entity for the boundary (by default, the nearest entity). Use the Ray
> Casting dialog box to change this so that a ray is projected in an +X, −X, +Y, −Y
> direction from the selected point.

# Hatching Complex Areas

Next, show some mud on the east lot. This situation presents a more difficult hatch problem because you want to fill around the house, tree, and car blocks. This lot can only be hatched by tracing boundaries around the objects in the lot. The Outermost hatch style does not work; the result of using Outermost (note the missing hatch in some areas) is illustrated in figure 14.9.

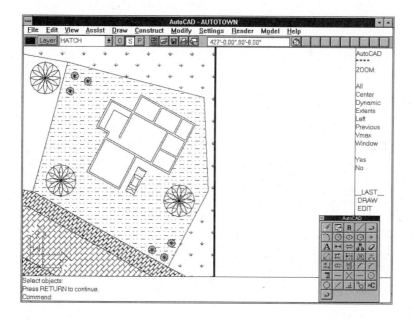

**Figure 14.9:**

Imperfect HATCH Outermost.

To insert the mud hatching properly, first trace the interior features with a polyline, then hatch it using the BHATCH command with the MUDST hatch pattern.

# Hatching Complex Boundaries

Command: *From the toolbar, open the*
*layer pop-up list and set* SCRATCH *current*

Command: *Choose* **V**iew, *then* **Z**oom, *then*
**W**indow, *then zoom in on the east*
*(right) lot*

*Use OSNAP to set running object snap to*
*INT, use PLINE to trace the perimeters*
*of the house and car, and then use OSNAP*
*to set object snap to QUA*

Command: *Choose* **D**raw, *then* **C**ircle,
*then* **2**-point *to draw circles around*
*each tree*

*Turn off layer PLAN, and set layer*
*HATCH current*

Use OSNAP to set running object snap back to NONE.

Command: *Choose* **S**ettings, *then* **E**ntity
Modes, *set color to YELLOW, then*
*choose* OK *twice*

Command: *Choose* **D**raw, *then* **H**ATCH

| | |
|---|---|
| *Choose* Hatch **O**ptions, *then* **N**ormal | Defines the hatch style |
| *Choose the* **P**attern *button* | Displays the available patterns |
| *Choose* **N**ext *three times, then select*<br>Mudst | Displays and selects the pattern |
| *Enter* **120** *in the* Sca**l**e *input box* | Specifies the pattern scale |
| *Enter* **0** *in the* **A**ngle *input box* | Specifies the angle |
| *Choose the* OK *button* | Returns to the Boundary Hatch dialog box |
| *Choose the* **P**ick Points *button* | |
| Select internal points: *Pick a point*<br>*inside the lot, not inside a tree,*<br>*house, or car* | |
| Select internal points: *Press Enter* | Returns to the dialog box |
| *Choose the* **S**elect Objects *button* | Specifies the option to select the boundary<br>objects on-screen |
| Select Objects: *Select the outline*<br>*of the trees, car, and house* | Specifies additional hatch boundaries |

Select Object: *Press Enter*

*Choose the* Apply *button*                          Draws the hatch pattern

*Turn layer PLAN on*

Command:  *Choose* **S**ettings, *then*
**E**ntity Modes, *then the* **C**olor *button,*
*and set color back to BYLAYER*

Command:  **QSAVE** ↵

The result appears in figure 14.10.

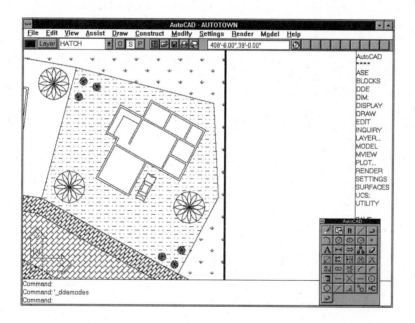

**Figure 14.10:**

A better hatch with traced boundaries.

You can see that hatching complex areas can be a lot of work.

*When creating blocks you are likely to hatch around, draw a boundary on a scratch layer around the entities to be blocked before you create the block. When you insert the blocks, they already have boundaries included with them. Turn layers on and off as needed to get just the boundary visible, and then hatch.*

*When creating simple and complex block pairs for redefinition, make sure you have clean hatch boundaries in the simple blocks. Then you can hatch before you redefine simple blocks with complex blocks.*

So far, you have used both the Normal and Outermost hatch styles. The third style option ignores any interior boundary. If you want to test the Ignore hatch style, make the SCRATCH layer current and experiment with it.

If you place a pattern with the wrong scale or angle, you can always use Erase Last or U to get rid of the pattern and try again. Press Ctrl-C to stop a pattern fill in progress. Any other editing of hatches, however, is more complicated.

# Editing Hatch Patterns

You probably noticed that a single Erase Last command erases an entire hatch pattern. Hatch patterns are *unnamed blocks* with insertion points at 0,0. Normal editing commands like MOVE, COPY, and ARRAY operate on the entire pattern, just like on a named block. If you hatch multiple areas in a single HATCH command and then try to move them individually, the hatches move as a group.

If you want to edit individual lines in a pattern, explode the pattern by prefacing the pattern name with an asterisk. *BRICK, for example, works just like an *insertion of a block. Because this process creates lots of little lines, an Undo is the best way to get rid of an erroneous hatch inserted in this manner.

*The 0,0 insertion point of hatches causes a problem with STRETCH. STRETCH ignores hatch patterns, blocks, and text unless the insertion point is included in the selection window. For hatches, this means that you must include 0,0 in your window to get STRETCH to move it.*

Several items are worth noting when deciding whether to explode hatches or insert them with an asterisk. If you explode hatches, the bits and pieces migrate to layer 0, making it easy to select and modify the entities if you keep layer 0 clean. The use of an asterisk before the pattern name places hatch entities on the current layer. A normal hatch creates an unnamed block definition, containing all the hatch's lines and a block reference. When you explode the hatch, the drawing temporarily contains twice as much data. You get a new set of individual lines, but the block definition remains until the drawing is ended and reloaded. HATCH creates a set of individual lines, but no block definition, so it uses less data.

Because HATCH uses blocks to group the lines as one entity, every use of the HATCH command creates a unique block definition. Normally, blocks save data storage space through multiple insertions of the same object. But the simultaneous hatching of identical multiple areas with the same pattern does not save data space. If you copy a hatch, however, the copy uses the same block definition and saves space.

*When you are hatching several identical areas, hatch one and copy it several times to save data storage space.*

# Customizing Hatch Patterns

One more technique is useful when using the HATCH command. Assume that you want to use some simple parallel lines as a shading pattern to fill a boundary. Immediately after you invoke the HATCH command, pick the U option from the screen menu or tablet, or press U. U stands for *User-specified* hatch pattern. This hatch option enables you to create parallel or perpendicular crossed-line patterns.

The U option with zero- or 90-degree rotation is good for ruling or gridding areas such as pavement, ceiling plans, or section cuts. Use the U option in the next exercise, in which you also explore controlling hatch alignment.

# Controlling Hatch Alignment

So far, you have used hatches to fill an area and to indicate a type of material. The precise alignment of the pattern relative to objects in the drawing is not important in these uses. When hatches are used to lay out patterns such as for pavement, floor tile, or ceiling grids, however, the alignment is critical.

The base point of a hatch pattern's alignment is at 0,0 of the current UCS. You can relocate your UCS or use the SNAP command's Rotate option to relocate your hatch insertion point, rather than letting it default to 0,0. The best option is to relocate the UCS.

Assume you live in the house on the muddy east lot, and you want to turn your garage into a family room. You want to tile it with a user-defined hatch of 36×36 carpet tiles. If you set a hatch angle to match the family room angle, its alignment with the walls is made purely by chance. A better method is to set the UCS to the lower left corner of the family room, and then hatch it. You may have to adjust the UCS and perform the hatch again to center the tile pattern and balance the cut-edge pieces.

---

## Aligning a Hatch U Pattern with a UCS

*Zoom in to the garage/family room
(see fig. 14.11)*

| | |
|---|---|
| Command:  *From the screen menu,* *choose* AutoCAD, *then* UCS:, *then* next, *then* 3point, *and pick points* ①, ②, *and* ③ *with INT object snap (see* *fig. 14.11)* | Sets UCS to corner of room |
| Command: *Choose* **D**raw, *then* **H**atch | |
| *Choose* Hatch **O**ptions | |
| *Choose* **U**ser Defined Pattern (U) | Specifies a user defined hatch pattern |
| *Enter* **0** *in the* **A**ngle *input box* | Aligns the HATCH with the UCS and the walls |
| *Enter* **36** *in the* **S**pacing *input box* | Sets spacing for 36×36 carpet tiles |
| *Choose* **D**ouble Hatch | Places a cross hatch in the drawing |
| *Choose* OK | Returns to the Boundary Hatch dialog box |
| *Choose* **P**ick points | |
| Select internal points *Pick a* *point inside the room and press Enter* | Returns to the dialog box |
| *Choose the* Apply *button* | |

Now that you have added the hatch pattern, save the drawing.

Command: **QSAVE** ↵

---

 *User-defined hatches are not restricted to simple patterns. Try hatching in different linetypes and at different linetype scales to generate some interesting patterns.*

You can create your own hatch patterns like the linetype you create in the next section. The process of creating hatch patterns is much more complex than creating linetypes. You can learn how to create hatch patterns in *Maximizing AutoCAD Release 12* (New Riders Publishing).

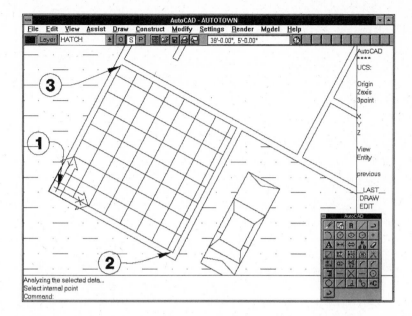

**Figure 14.11:**

Hatching tiles in the family room.

# Using Linetypes and Linetype Scales

Do not overlook the opportunity of enhancing drawings by using AutoCAD's standard linetypes or by creating and using your own custom linetype patterns. Every linetype is a pattern of spaces, short-line segments, or dots. You create your own patterns using the LINETYPE command. LINETYPE affects only lines, arcs, circles, and polylines, and entities in blocks.

The LINETYPE or LAYER commands set different linetypes. You control the overall scale of these patterns with LTSCALE. The easiest way to select linetypes is to use the **S**ettings pull-down menu and then **E**ntity Modes. Then click on the L**i**netype button. The Select Linetype dialog box appears (see fig. 14.12), which graphically displays all currently loaded linetypes. You must use the LINETYPE command or the Ltype option of the LAYER command, however, to load linetypes before they show up in the dialog box. The LINETYPE command has a ? option to list any or all linetypes in any linetype file.

## Controlling Line Pattern Spacing

You have used the LTSCALE command to adjust linetype scales. If you do not remember how LTSCALE works, review the following examples.

**Figure 14.12:**

The Select
Linetype dialog
box with standard
linetypes.

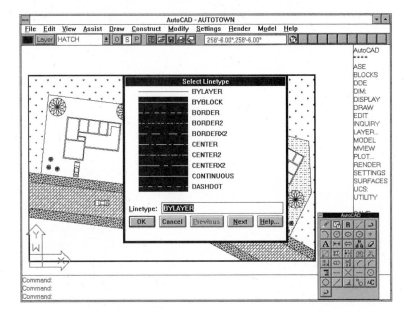

Each standard line pattern is defined to look good when plotted at full scale when LTSCALE is set to 1, the default. By setting LTSCALE to the desired scale factor, you can condense or stretch the pattern. Use your drawing scale factor as a starting scale, although you may need to adjust it slightly to personal preference or standards. Set LTSCALE for the plot appearance, not the screen appearance. Whatever setting meets your standards, remember to adjust it for your drawing scale for other than 1=1 plots. For example, a 1/4" = 1'-0" plot with a 0.375 standard linetype scale yields 48×.375 = 18 as the actual setting.

You can have only one linetype scale, which is applied to all linetypes. However, each of the standard linetypes comes in three variants—a standard scale pattern with a name such as PHANTOM, a half-scale pattern with a name such as PHANTOM2, and a twice-scale pattern with a name such as PHANTOMX2. Many users find the half-scale variants best for most purposes. Figure 14.13 shows how several of the standard, half-scale, and twice-scale linetypes look at different linetype scales.

*If your lines generate slowly or appear continuous instead of broken, try resetting LTSCALE higher.*

| | LTSCALE = 1 | LTSCALE = 4 | **Figure 14.13:** |
|---|---|---|---|
| Dashed | – – – – – – – – – | ―― ―― ―― | Ltscale and linetype examples. |
| 2 | ------------------------------ | ― – ― – ― – ― | |
| X2 | – ― – ― – ― – ― – ― | ―――――  ―― | |
| | | | |
| Dot | ......................................... | . . . . . . . . . . | |
| 2 | ......................................... | . . . . . . | |
| X2 | ......................................... | ......................... | |
| | | | |
| Hidden | ------------------------------ | – ― – ― – ― – ― | |
| 2 | ......................................... | - - - - - - - - - | |
| X2 | - ― - ― - ― - ― - ― | ―――  ――  ―― | |
| | | | |
| Phantom | – – ―― - - ―― - - ―― - - - | ―  ―――  ―― | |
| 2 | --------------------------------- | ― – ― – ― – ― | |
| X2 | ―――  - - ―  ―― | ――――  ―――― | |

**TIP**

*In complex drawings with a lot of patterned linetypes, your regenerations may slow down. To speed things up, you can temporarily use continuous linetypes while drawing, and then change them to the correct linetypes before plotting.*

# Creating Your Own Linetypes

Autotown is getting a new gas line. Rather than use a standard linetype to draw it, the next set of exercises show you how to make your own linetype (named GASLINE), scale it, and then use it to draw the proposed gas line.

The LINETYPE command enables you to define your own dot-and-dash pattern and store that pattern in a linetype file. AutoCAD's standard linetypes are stored in a disk file named ACAD.LIN. You can add linetypes to ACAD.LIN or create your own file, like the MYLINES.LIN file in this exercise.

First, you create a new linetype, GASLINE, and store it. GASLINE consists of a dash, then five dots, and so on, all entered on one line. The process is explained further after the exercise.

---

## Using LINETYPE To Create a Linetype

Continue from the preceding exercise, or from the "Setting Up" exercise at the beginning of the chapter.

| | |
|---|---|
| `Command:` *From the screen menu,* choose AutoCAD, *then* SETTINGS, *then* LINETYP: | Starts the LINETYPE command |
| `?/Create/Load/Set:` *From the screen menu, choose* Create | Creates a new linetype |
| `Name of linetype to create:` **GASLINE** ↵ | Specifies the name of the new linetype |
| *Enter* **MYLINES** *in the* File **N**ame *text box, and then choose the* **O**K *button* | Specifies the DOS file where the linetype is stored |
| `Creating new file` | |
| `Descriptive text:` **GASLINE** _____ ......_____ ......↵ | Simulates the linetype with five underscores and periods |
| `Enter pattern (on next line):` **A,.4,-.1,0,-.1,0,-.1,0,** **-.1,0,-.1,0,-.1** ↵ | Specifies a .4 unit dash, then five zeroes for five dots, with .1 unit gaps between ends |
| `New definition written to file.` | |
| `?/Create/Load/Set:` *Press Enter* | Exits the LINETYPE command |

The linetype has been created and stored but is not yet loaded.

---

What went on in the linetype definition sequence? Here is an explanation of the prompts and responses.

- **Name of linetype to create.** Name of the linetype you want to create. Use a good descriptive name for the linetype to make it easy to identify later.

- **File for storage of linetype.** Name of the disk file where the linetype definition is to be stored. It is safer to store linetype definitions in your own file, rather than to use the ACAD.LIN file where AutoCAD stores the standard linetypes. If you want them all in one file, copy the ACAD.LIN file to your name, and then add your linetypes to it.

- **Descriptive text.** What you see when you issue a ? query to list the named linetypes. The pattern is a dot-and-dash representation of the linetype that shows on a text screen. Just type underscores (___) and periods (. . .) as descriptive text.

- **Enter pattern (on next line).** AutoCAD is asking for the actual definition of the linetype pattern to repeat when it draws the line. You separate values with commas. The pattern codes include:

    **The A,** is entered for you. A is the alignment code to balance the pattern between endpoints. No other alignments are currently supported.

    **A positive number** like .4. The positive number gives the unit length of a pen downstroke. The first stroke must be pen down; it is the maximum line length that appears as the first segment.

    **A negative number** like –.1. The negative number gives the unit length of a pen upstroke. In other words, it is the length of the blank space.

    **A zero** represents a dot.

After you have stored one or more linetypes in a linetype file, you can load the linetypes for use. Load these linetypes with the Load option of the LINETYPE command. You can list several names with commas between names. Use wild cards, such as * and ?, to load several or all linetypes at once. The process of loading a linetype does not set it current. You use the LAYER command to set it for layers or the LINETYPE Set option to set the linetype as an explicit entity linetype.

Try loading and setting GASLINE.

## Using LINETYPE To Load a Linetype

`Command:` *From the screen menu, choose*
*AutoCAD, then* SETTINGS,
*then* LINETYP:

| | |
|---|---|
| `?/Create/Load/Set: L` ↵ | Loads linetypes from a file |
| `Linetype(s) to load: *` ↵<br>Linetype File dialog box | Specifies all linetypes and opens the Select |
| *Press Enter* | Accepts the default file name of MYLINES |
| Linetype GASLINE loaded. | |
| `?/Create/Load/Set: S` ↵ | Sets the linetype |
| `New entity linetype (or ?)`<br>`<BYLAYER>:` **GASLINE** ↵ | Specifies the new default linetype |
| `?/Create/Load/Set:` *Press Enter* | Sets GASLINE current |

After it is loaded, a linetype is stored in the drawing, and, unlike text font and xref files, the drawing file does not need to reference the linetype file in order to use it. You also can use the Entity Creation Modes Select Linetype dialog box to set the current entity linetype.

Any entities you create now show the new GASLINE linetype. Try drawing the gas line between the curb and setback property line on the north side of Autotown Drive.

---

## Testing and Scaling a Linetype

Command: *From the screen menu, choose*     Sets UCS to World
AutoCAD, *then* UCS, *then* World

*Issue the ZOOM command with the All option, then issue the LAYER command and set layer* SCRATCH *current and freeze* HATCH

Command: *Choose* **D**raw, *then*
**P**olyline, *then* **2**D, *and draw a line between the curb and property lines, border to border*

The line looks as if it is continuous.

Command: *From the screen menu, choose*
AutoCAD, SETTINGS, *then* next,
*then* LTSCALE:

New scale factor <1.0000>: **120** ⏎

Regenerating drawing.

The linetype is still too small to be sure it is right (see fig. 14.14).

Zoom in close enough to see the dots. Now it looks correct (see fig. 14.15). It should plot fine at 1"=10'.

Command: *Choose* **V**iew, *then* **Z**oom,
*then* **P**revious

*Erase the gas line*

Command: *Choose* **F**ile, *then* **S**ave

---

Just like text, properly scaled linetypes are not always legible when you are working on your drawing. When you are zoomed way out or in, they may appear continuous or invisible.

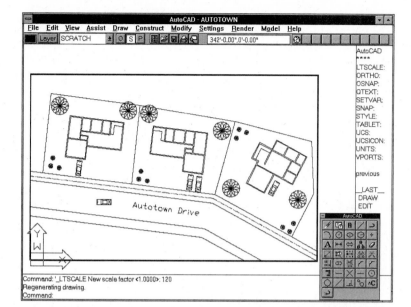

**Figure 14.14:**
GASLINE at
LTSCALE 120.

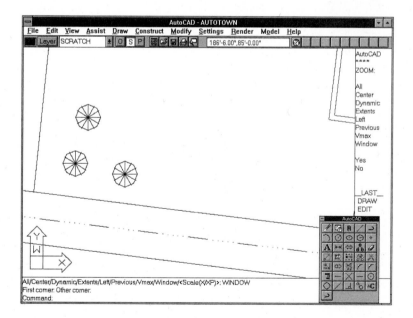

**Figure 14.15:**
GASLINE zoomed.

*If you cannot discern linetypes on-screen in large-scale drawings, you may want to set a temporary linetype scale for screen appearance. Just remember to set it back to the correct scale before plotting.*

*Like replacing blocks and styles, loading a new definition of a linetype causes a regeneration and replaces old linetypes with new unless you suppress regeneration using REGENAUTO. Adjustments to LTSCALE do not affect existing entities until after a regeneration.*

Complete the Autotown drawing by sketching some contour lines between the road and the lower border, to redirect the drainage away from the east lot and its new family room.

# Drawing Freehand Using SKETCH

The SKETCH command enables you to draw lines freehand, without being bothered by point specification and other alignment or input parameters. You sketch just as you would doodle or draw on a piece of paper. SKETCH is also useful for tracing curves such as contour lines.

## How SKETCH Works

AutoCAD stores sketch entities in the drawing file as successive short-line segments. It draws wherever you move your cursor, as you move it. Because AutoCAD does not know where your sketching may lead, both you and the program have to take precautions to keep the amount of sketch information from getting out of hand. Just a few quick motions of the cursor in sketch mode can create a huge number of short segments in the drawing file.

To help AutoCAD keep sketch information under control, you tell it how short a line segment to use for storing your sketch data. This measurement is known as the *record increment*. AutoCAD stores a new segment every time your pointer moves more than the record increment away from the last stored segment endpoint. Try to keep the record increment as large as possible to minimize the number of lines.

The record increment is in current drawing units, but the effect on your input coordination also depends on the area your mouse or digitizer cursor has to move in your currently zoomed view. For example, if the width of your screen represents 300 feet (3600 inches), and the screen pointing area on your digitizer is six inches wide, a 60-inch increment means your sketch segments are five feet and that AutoCAD records a new segment every time you move your pointing device about one-tenth of an inch (six inches times 60 inches, divided by 3600 inches).

*Variable speed mice vary in their mouse-to-screen scaling—move them at a steady speed for best results.*

You also have to let AutoCAD know when to consider the sketching pointer up (off the paper) or down (sketching). AutoCAD keeps all sketch input in a temporary buffer until you press R to record it into the drawing file database. You can press E to erase sketched lines before you record them. If you record sketched lines, AutoCAD turns them into regular line (or polyline) entities.

## Contour Polylines

Try making some contour lines using the SKETCH command. This example was chosen because it is a common and extremely useful application of SKETCH. To get smooth contour curves, you need to sketch with polylines rather than with lines (the default). Use the SKPOLY system variable to switch SKETCH from lines to polylines. If SKPOLY is 0, SKETCH draws lines. If it is 1, SKETCH draws polylines.

*Polylines can be easily stretched and edited, but their biggest advantage is that you can curve fit polylines and get a smooth curve. When you set SKPOLY to sketch polylines, set your record increment larger than you would when you sketch with lines. Use an increment half of the smallest radius or turn that you sketch. This increment may seem too large until you apply a curve fit to it.*

Try sketching the contour lines. It takes a little time to become familiar with sketching, so do not be shy about undoing or erasing and trying again. Do not worry if your sketch ends extend over the drive and border lines. You can trim the loose ends later. Set the linetype back to continuous because broken linetypes do not work well for short-line segments, like those that SKETCH creates. Set up SKETCH in the following exercise, and then sketch and edit the contour polylines.

## Using SKETCH and SKPOLY To Draw Contour Lines

Continue from the preceding exercise, or from the "Setting Up..." exercise at the beginning of the chapter.

`Command:` *Choose* <u>V</u>*iew, then* <u>Z</u>*oom, then* <u>W</u>*indow, then zoom to the area shown in figure 14.16*

`Command:` *Choose* <u>S</u>*ettings, then* <u>E</u>*ntity Modes, then the* <u>L</u>*inetype button*

*Choose* CONTINUOUS, *then choose* OK,          Selects continuous linetype
*then choose* OK *again*

`Command:` **SKPOLY** ⏎          Accesses the SKPOLY system variable

`New value for SKPOLY <0>:` **1** ⏎          Sets SKETCH to draw polylines

`Command:` *From the screen menu, choose* DRAW, *then* next, *and then* SKETCH:

`Record increment <0'-0.10">:` **60** ⏎          Specifies the length of a sketch line segment

`Sketch.  Pen eXit Quit Record Erase Connect.`

*Press* P *and move cursor*          Puts pen down and begins sketching a line

`<pen down>`

*Press* P          Picks pen up and stops sketching

`<pen up>` *Press* R          Records the line

`1 polyline with 14 edges recorded.`

*Press* X          Exits SKETCH

Next, smooth the sketch polyline.

`Command:` *Choose* <u>M</u>*odify, then* <u>P</u>*olyline Edit*

`Select objects:` **L** ⏎          Selects the last entity

`Select objects:` *Press Enter*

`Close/Join/Width/Edit vertex/`          Performs a fit curve on the sketch line
`Fit curve/Spline curve/Decurve/`
`Undo/eXit <X>:` *From the screen menu,*
*choose* Fit Curve

`Close/Join/Width/Edit vertex/`
`Fit curve/Spline curve/Decurve/`
`Undo/eXit <X>:` *Press Enter*

Draw the remaining contours shown and fit curves to them.

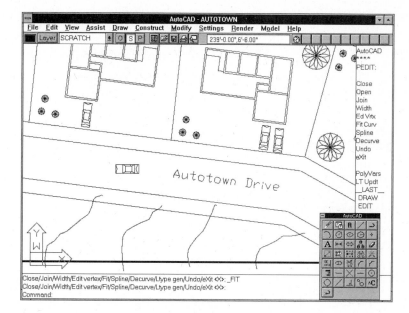

**Figure 14.16:**

Autotown with sketched contours.

# SKETCH Options

When you are in the SKETCH command, all other input is ignored, except for the sketch mode controls (and toggles like F8 for ortho and F9 for snap). To control SKETCH using the following options, press the first character of the option without pressing Enter.

- **Pen.** This option tells AutoCAD the pointer is up or down. Just type **P**, without pressing Enter, to change the toggle. You can also click to move the pen up or down.

- **eXit.** This option records the sketch segments you have been creating in the drawing file and gets you back to the Command: prompt. You can also exit by pressing the spacebar or Enter, which does the same thing as eXit.

- **Quit.** This option leaves SKETCH without storing the segments you have been creating. Pressing Ctrl-C does the same thing.

- **Record.** This option keeps you in SKETCH, but stores the segments you have been creating so far in the drawing file. This function is just like a save, but after you record, segments that get stored are not available for Erase from SKETCH.

- **Erase.** This option erases any unrecorded segment from a point you pick to the last segment drawn.

- **Connect.** This option connects the pen to the end of the last endpoint of an active sketch chain. You can also use normal AutoCAD editing techniques to connect finished sketch lines to other elements after you finish the sketch.

Now, trim any loose sketch ends, so the finished lines resemble those shown in figure 14.17.

**Figure 14.17:**

The sketched lines after trimming.

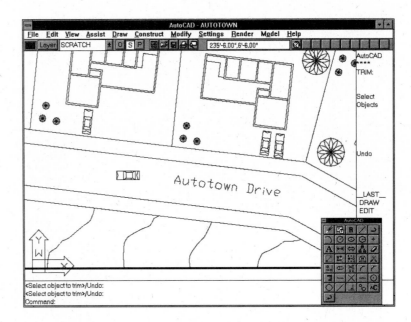

## Using TRIM To Trim Sketch Polylines

Command: *Choose* **M***odify, then* **T***rim*

Select cutting edge(s)...
Select objects: *Select the road and border lines*

Select objects: *Press Enter*

<Select object to trim>/Undo: *Pick each of the overlapping ends of the sketch lines, then press Enter*

Command: *Choose* **V***iew, then* **Z***oom, then* **A***ll*

ZOOM All and thaw layer HATCH if you want to view the complete drawing.

Command: **QSAVE** ↵

The added contour lines were the last step in Autotown's suburban renewal. Your drawing should now resemble figure 14.18.

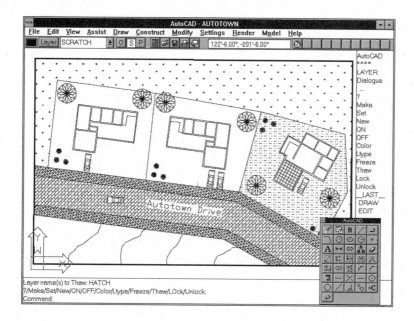

**Figure 14.18:**

The enhanced Autotown drawing.

Not everyone feels confident about freehand drawing skills. If you would rather trace, AutoCAD provides a way to trace contours (or any kind of data) from an existing paper drawing.

# Tracing and Sketching Using the Tablet

If you have a digitizer, you can use it to trace and digitize drawings into AutoCAD. AutoCAD has two modes for using digitizers: the screen pointing mode you usually use and a calibrated digitizing mode. You use the calibrated digitizing mode to establish a relationship between points on a drawing taped to the tablet and points in your AutoCAD drawing. After that relationship has been calibrated, you can pick points in the AutoCAD drawing fairly accurately by digitizing the corresponding points on the paper drawing. Although this is not as accurate as creating a new drawing entirely from accurate coordinate and measurement data, it is often the only efficient way to import existing drawing data.

Digitizing is well-suited to tracing contours, which do not demand absolute precision, with sketched lines. Digitizing is not limited to sketching, however. You can use the full range of drawing commands and controls, even inserting blocks at datum points picked on the tablet.

To digitize, first use the CAL (calibrate) option of the TABLET command. It prompts you for two known points on the paper drawing and for the drawing coordinates to assign to them. After calibration, the relationship between the drawing and tablet is maintained even if you pan and zoom. The X and Y axes are calibrated with equal scales. If the tablet drawing is distorted (as are many paper drawings), you can compensate after tracing by blocking the results and inserting them with differing X and Y scales. If your paper drawing does not fit on the tablet menu's screen pointing area, you can reconfigure the tablet to use its full area for digitizing. To exit the calibrated tablet mode, use the TABLET command's OFF option; to re-enter tablet mode, use ON. You can also switch between tablet mode and screen pointing mode with F10 or Ctrl-T.

You are not going to change the Autotown drawing any more, but you are now going to use AutoCAD's inquiry commands to take another look at it. Autotown has defined distances and areas that make it a good practice drawing for retrieving information.

# Using Inquiry Commands

AutoCAD's inquiry commands are useful for providing information about drawings. When lines are placed into a drawing file, they often represent distances and locations with real-world relationships. Part of creating a good drawing is to help the person reading the drawing understand these spatial implications.

You have used the ID, HELP, and STATUS commands in earlier chapters. With these and other inquiry commands, you can measure, identify, and generally find out what is in a drawing file. AutoCAD already has much of the spatial information you may need built into the drawing. The DISTANCE and AREA commands, for example, return line distances and polygon area values from the data base. Start an inquiry session with a look at AutoCAD's timing features, and set the clock to see how long this last section of the chapter takes to examine.

# Using TIME To Track Your Drawing Time

Unlike the other inquiry commands, TIME is really a management tool. TIME gives you a list of times and dates about your drawing and editing sessions. This information includes the current system time, the date and time a drawing was created, the date and time of the last update, time in the editor, and elapsed time.

Choose the TIME command, and set time ON. This acts as an elapsed timer that you can check at the end of these inquiry exercises to measure your time spent in the drawing editor.

These inquiry exercises can use any version of the Autotown drawing, as long as it has the lot lines in it. If you are starting after a break, reload your AUTOTOWN drawing.

If you are jumping into the chapter at this point, do the quick "Setting Up for Enhancing Autotown" exercise at the beginning of the chapter, then do the following exercise. Start by turning on an elapsed timer built into the TIME command.

---

## Using TIME To Track Your Drawing Time

Choose <u>F</u>ile, then <u>O</u>pen, then enter **AUTOTOWN**.

`Command:` *From the screen menu, choose*
INQUIRY, *then TIME:, then press F2*

Your dates and times vary from those shown.

```
Current time:          05 Jan 1993 at 10:29:27.000
Drawing created:       02 Jan 1993 at 12:17:08.000
Drawing last updated:  04 Jan 1993 at 14:10:23.000
Time in drawing editor: 0 days 1:49:15.000
Elapsed timer:         0 days 1:49:15.000
Timer on.
```

`Display/ON/OFF/Reset:` **R** ↵          Resets the elapsed timer

`Timer reset.`

`Display/ON/OFF/Reset:` *Press Enter*

---

You can also access the time data with AutoLISP, which enables you to create drawing time management and billing programs.

Check the elapsed time after you look at the other inquiry commands. The simplest inquiry, ID, deserves a second look.

# Using the ID Command

You have used ID before to locate points. ID returns the X,Y,Z location of a point.

*The ID command is useful for resetting the last point without drawing anything, so you can use relative coordinates from the reset point. The last point is stored as the system variable LASTPOINT.*

Use ID to reset the last point.

# Using ID To Reset LASTPOINT

*Set layer 0 current and freeze the* SCRATCH
*and* HATCH *layers*

| | |
|---|---|
| `Command: `**`LASTPOINT`**` ↵` | Accesses the system variable LASTPOINT |
| `New value for LASTPOINT <168'-6.00",`<br>`46'-6.00",0'-0.00">: ` *Press Enter* | Displays LASTPOINT value; yours may be different |
| `Command: `**`ID`**` ↵` | |
| `Point: ` *Use the ENDP object snap*<br>*and pick point at ① (see fig. 14.19)* | Identifies the point |
| `ENDP of X: 140'-2.34" Y: 190'-2.66"`<br>`Z: 0'-0.00"` | Returns the exact location |
| `Command: `**`LASTPOINT`**` ↵` | |
| `New value for LASTPOINT <140'-2.34",`<br>`190'-2.66",0'-0.00">: ` *Press Enter* | Displays new values set by ID |

**Figure 14.19:**

ID corner point
between lots.

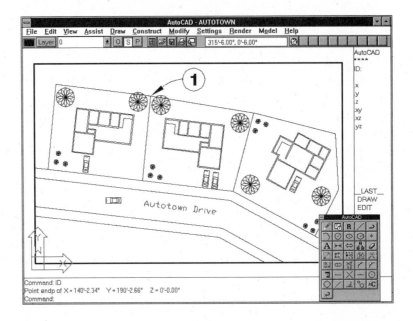

# Using DIST To Get Line Lengths—and More

DIST gives the 3D distance between two points, its angles in and from the X,Y plane, and the X, Y, and Z offset distances. The measured distance is stored as the system variable DISTANCE.

Assume that you need to check the length of the lot line between the east lot and the middle lot. Use object snaps for accuracy, and DIST gets you this information.

---

### Using DIST To Get a Lot Line Length and Angle

**Command:** *Choose* **A**ssist, *then* **I**nquiry, *then* **D**istance      Issues DIST command transparently

`'_dist First point:` *Use the ENDP object snap to pick corner of lot at* ①
*(see fig. 14.20)*

`Second point:` *Use the ENDP object snap to pick corner of lot at* ②      Displays distances and angles

```
Distance = 85'-2.76", Angle in X-Y Plane =
S15d 22'16"W, Angle from X-Y Plane = E
Delta X = -22'-7.10", Delta Y = -82'-2.18",
Delta Z = 0'-0.00"
```

---

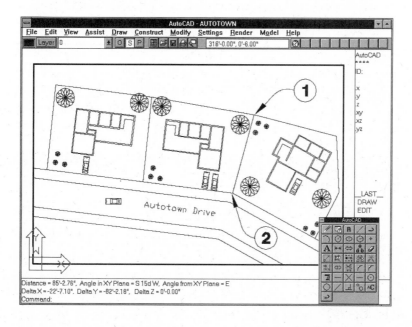

**Figure 14.20:**

Distance and angle of lot line.

You can also issue DIST from the screen menu by choosing AutoCAD, then INQUIRY, then DIST.

If units are set to decimal degrees, DIST displays the angle in decimals, such as 255.1333.

Next, survey the perimeter and areas.

# Using AREA To Get Area and Perimeter Values

AREA gives you the area surrounded by a straight-sided polygon, defined by temporary points you pick. Or, you can select an entity such as a polyline or circle, and AREA automatically calculates its area, including curves. AREA keeps a running total you can add to or subtract from to calculate complex areas or groups of areas. In the Add or Subtract mode, the AREA command stays active until you exit it by pressing Enter. Add and Subtract only accumulate in the current command; each use of the AREA command restarts from 0. The area is stored as the system variable AREA, and the calculated perimeter is stored as the system variable PERIMETER.

Try surveying the area and perimeter of the east lot, using object snaps for your pick points.

---

### Using AREA To Calculate a Lot and Perimeter Area

Command: *Set a running object snap of INT,END*

Command: *Choose* **A**ssist, *then* **I**nquiry, *then* **A**rea
\<First point>/Entity/Add/Subtract:

*Pick corner of the lot at* ① *(see fig. 14.21)*

Next point: *Pick corner of the lot at* ②

Next point: *Pick corner of the lot at* ③

Next point: *Pick corner of the lot at* ④

Next point: *Pick corner of the lot at* ⑤

Next point: *Press Enter*                          Closes the boundary

Area = 1450045.00 square in.
(10069.7570 square ft.),
Perimeter = 391'-10.46"

---

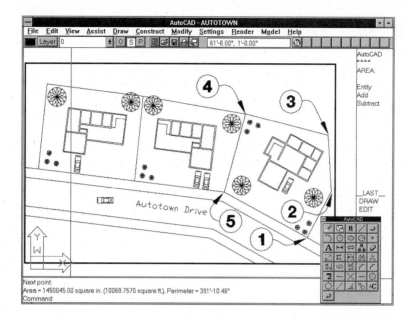

**Figure 14.21:**

Getting the area of the east lot.

You can also issue AREA from the screen menu (choose INQUIRY, then AREA:). Another way to get an area is to pick an entity. AREA recognizes polylines and circles. Use the Entity option when you need the area of an existing boundary. Use BPOLY or PLINE to trace a temporary polyline over your drawing if you need to define the boundary.

If you hatched the muddy east lot, try getting the area of the east house by picking the hatch boundary you drew around it earlier.

## Using AREA To Find the Area of the East House

Use OSNAP to set the running object snap to NONE, then use LAYER to thaw layer SCRATCH.

Command: *From the screen menu, choose* INQUIRY,
*then* AREA:

<First point>/Entity/Add/Subtract:
*From the screen menu, choose* Entity

Select circle or polyline: *Select
polyline boundary around house*

Area = 340992.00 square in. (2368.0000
square ft.), Perimeter = 232'-0.00"

*An area is always a closed calculation. AutoCAD assumes a closure line between the first and last pick points of your area boundaries. Likewise, when you select an open polyline, AREA treats it as if it were closed.*

You can access the last-calculated area, distance, and perimeter values using the SETVAR command.

---

## Using the AREA and PERIMETER System Variables

Command: **SETVAR** ↵

'setvar Variable name or
?<LASTPOINT>: **AREA** ↵

AREA = 340992.00 (read only)          Shows the area in square inches

Command: **SETVAR** ↵

'setvar Variable name or ?<AREA>:
**DISTANCE** ↵

DISTANCE = 100'-2.50" (read only)

Command: **SETVAR** ↵

'setvar Variable name or
?<DISTANCE>: **PERIMETER** ↵

PERIMETER = 232'-0.00" (read only)

---

# Using the Region Modeler as a Drawing and Inquiry Tool

Another powerful set of drawing and inquiry tools is available in the Region Modeler of AutoCAD. The Region Modeler is included with AutoCAD and enables you to create closed 2D areas or regions. The Region Modeler is a 2D subset of the 3D features of the Advanced Modeling Extension (AME), AutoCAD's optional solid modeler, which enables you to create 3D solid models.

Both tools add real-world properties to the model, enabling you to analyze the model according to its physical properties.

By using a region model, you can calculate mass properties such as area, weight, center of gravity, and moments of inertia. This information can be useful for making engineering decisions. Although modeling generally has been the province of mechanical designers, AutoCAD's region modeling features are also useful to spatially oriented designers such as architects and to drafters of many disciplines. By using regions, you can easily define closed areas that contain voids. You can also easily calculate a region's area or other properties.

You build a region or solid model in much the same way you would actually manufacture the item being modeled. You can, for example, start with a simple shape, punch holes in it (subtract an opening), and perform other modeling operations that mimic the actual manufacturing operation.

The object in figure 14.22 was originally drawn with polylines, fillets and circles, which were then combined into a single *region*. A region is a single entity with properties such as those shown in table 14.2.

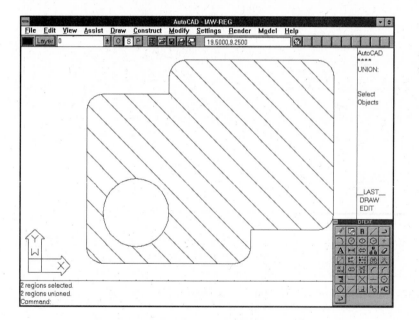

**Figure 14.22:**

Region created from a polyline and circles.

## Table 14.2
## Mass Properties Data for a Region

| | |
|---|---|
| Area: | 146.146 sq cm |
| Perimeter: | 63.99115 cm |
| Bounding box: | X: 4  --  19 cm |
| | Y: 1  --  13 cm |

*continues*

## Table 14.2
## Continued

| | |
|---|---|
| Centroid: | X: 11.88693  cm |
| | Y: 7.257955  cm |
| Moments of inertia: | X: 9181.801  sq cm sq cm |
| | Y: 23147.01  sq cm sq cm |
| Product of inertia: XY: | 12924.38  sq cm sq cm |
| Radii of gyration: | X: 7.926299  cm |
| | Y: 12.58502  cm |

Principal moments(sq cm sq cm) and X-Y directions about centroid:

```
                         I: 1392.867 about [0.9614603 0.274944 ]
                         J: 2586.962 about [0.274944 -0.9614603 ]
```

The following exercise demonstrates some region modeling basics as you learn to create, edit, and analyze a region.

# Creating a Region Model

Defining regions is a simple process. You can combine lines, arcs, circles, polylines, or any AutoCAD entities that enclose an area, and join them to define a region. The command to join them is SOLIDIFY. When you solidify entities, they become a new entity—a region. In this exercise, you define several simple 2D entities that form a closed area. You use the SOLDELENT variable to tell AutoCAD whether to retain the defining entities or discard them. Finally, you solidify the entities to create a single region entity.

## Creating a Region

Begin a new drawing named IAW-REG. Set snap to 0.25, grid to 1, and turn on coordinate display. Set the limits from 0,0 to 20,14 and then zoom All.

Command: *From the toolbox, choose*          Draws closed polyline square
POLYLINE, *draw from point 4,1 to 14,1*
*to 14,11 to 4,11 and enter* **C**

Next, give the polyline rounded corners using the FILLET command.

Command: *From the toolbox, choose* FILLET

```
Polyline/Radius/<Select first
object>: From the screen menu,
choose radius
```

```
Enter fillet radius <0.0000>: 1 ↵
```
Defines radius and repeats FILLET

```
Command: _fillet Polyline/Radius/
<Select first object>: P ↵
```

```
Select 2D polyline: L ↵
```
Fillets last object, the polyline (see fig. 14.23)

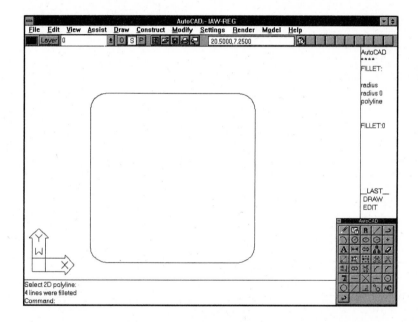

**Figure 14.23:**

The 2D polyline with rounded corners.

Next, set the SOLDELENT variable to prompt before deleting entities, and then use the SOLIDIFY command to create the initial region.

```
Command: SOLDELENT ↵
```

```
Initializing...
No modeler is loaded yet. Both AME
and Region Modeler are available.
```

```
Autoload Region/<AME>: R ↵
```

```
Initializing Region Modeler.
```
Loads the Region Modeler

```
Delete the entity after
solidification?
(1=never, 2=ask, 3=always)<3>: 2 ↵
```

*Choose M**o**del, then **S**olidify*

*continues*

```
Command: _solidify Delete the entities
that are solidified? <N> Y ⏎
```

Select objects: *Select the polyline*          Creates region
*and press Enter*                                (see fig. 14.24)

**Figure 14.24:**

The newly defined
region, evident by
its hatch pattern.

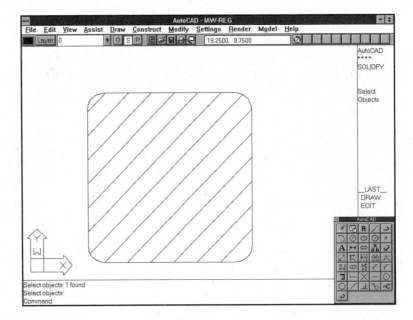

The SOLIDIFY command uses the closed polyline to define a new entity: a region. The region is, by default, automatically crosshatched. This crosshatching helps you visually discern a region from any other collection of 2D entities. You can control the region's hatching with the SOLHANGLE, SOLHPAT, and SOLHSIZE variables.

The SOLHANGLE variable sets the angle of region hatching. For this exercise, you use the default 45-degree angle, but SOLHANGLE accepts any real number, just like the Angle option of AutoCAD's HATCH command. A change to this value does not affect existing regions unless that region is modified.

SOLHPAT enables you to instruct AutoCAD to use a particular hatch pattern on regions. SOLHPAT uses that same pattern file used by the AutoCAD HATCH command. Like SOLHANGLE, SOLHPAT does not affect existing regions until they are modified.

The SOLHSIZE variable defines the current region hatch scale, similar to the HATCH command's Scale option. The advantage to using variables for these values, rather than simply duplicating the HATCH command's prompts, becomes apparent when creating multiple regions. You can simply set the values once, and then go about the process of creating your regions, without unnecessary prompts.

In the first exercise, you used the default region hatching values. In the next exercise, you adjust those settings and review the results after editing the region. To modify the region, you define a new region, subtracting it from the first region with the SOLSUB command to create a "hole." Then you use a basic AutoCAD command, COPY, to create an overlapped copy of the new region. Finally, you use the SOLUNION command to define the final region.

## Subtracting and Joining Regions

*Draw a circle with center point at 7,4
and a radius of 2 units*

Command: **SOLHANGLE** ↵

Hatch angle <45.000000>: **135** ↵

Command: **SOLIDIFY** ↵

Delete the entities that are
solidified <N> **Y** ↵

Select objects: *Select the circle and
press Enter*

Solidification and hatching occur. Note how the hatch angle differs (see fig. 14.25).

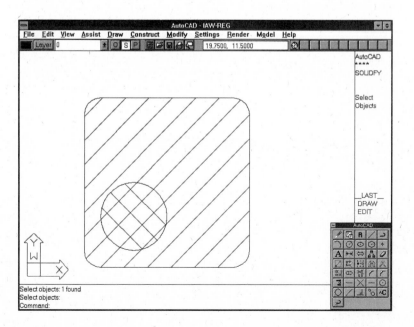

**Figure 14.25:**

A second region is defined.

*continues*

Next, you copy the circular region and subtract it from the first region.

Command: *Choose M<u>o</u>del, then Su<u>b</u>tract*     Issues SOLSUB command

Command: _solsub

Source objects...
Select objects: *Select the original*
*rectangular region and press Enter*

Objects to subtract from them...     Creates a single region with a hole
Select objects: *Select the*     (see fig. 14.26)
*circular region and press Enter*

**Figure 14.26:**

A region with a
"hole."

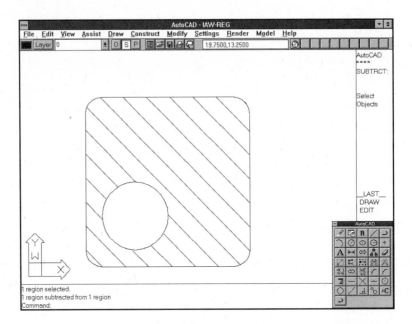

Notice how the hatching of the original region took on the new angle specified by the
SOLHANGLE variable. Finally, use the basic AutoCAD COPY command to duplicate the
region, and then unify the two regions with SOLUNION.

Command: *From the toolbox, choose* COPY

_copy
Select objects: *Select the region and*
*Press Enter*

<Base point or displacement>/
Multiple: **5,2** ↵

| | |
|---|---|
| Second point of displacement: *Press Enter* | Copies the region |
| Command: *Choose* M**o**del, *then* **U**NION | Issues SOLUNION command |
| _solunion Select objects: *Select the two regions, then press Enter* | Creates single region (see fig. 14.27) |

You have seen a few of the basic region modeling commands. Now take a look at the data you can extract from regions.

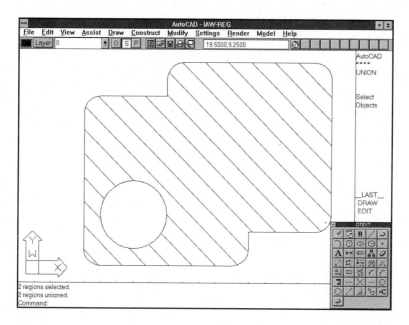

**Figure 14.27:**

The region.

# Analyzing a Region Model

Region models can be analyzed much like solid models. You can, for instance, calculate the region's area, or its material properties. In the following exercise, you calculate the area of the region you generated in the first two exercises.

## Extracting Data from a Region

Continue from the previous exercise.

| | |
|---|---|
| Command: *Choose* M**o**del, *then* In**q**uiry, *then* **A**rea Calculation | Issues SOLAREA command |

*continues*

| | |
|---|---|
| ```_solarea```<br>```Select objects:``` *Select the region and*<br>*press Enter* | |
| ```One region selected.```<br>```Surface area of regions is```<br>```146.146 sq cm``` | Calculates area of region |
| ```Command:``` *Choose* **M**o**del***, then* **In**q**uiry***,*<br>*then* **M**ass Property | Issues DDSOLMASSP command |
| ```_ddsolmassp```<br>```Select objects:``` *Select the region and*<br>*press Enter* | |
| ```One region selected.```<br>*(see fig. 14.28)* | Displays Mass Properties dialog box |
| *Choose* **F**ile *and press Enter* | Writes data to IAW-REG.MPR<br>(see table 14.2) |
| *Choose* OK | Exits dialog |

You can discard drawing \IAW\IAW-REG; it is no longer needed.

**Figure 14.28:**

The Mass Proper-
ties dialog box.

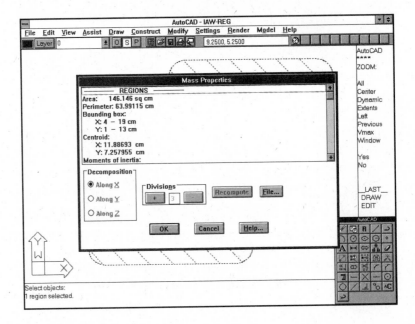

# The Region Modeler Command List

You can create, edit, and analyze region models with several other commands. The following list describes the subset of AME commands that work with region models:

 *Most of these commands create or modify either regions or solids, depending on whether you have loaded the Region Modeler or the full AME.*

- **SOLAREA.** This command, as exemplified by the preceding exercise, calculates the combined area of all selected regions.

- **SOLCHP.** This command enables you to change the properties of a solid or region primitive. With this one command, you can change the color, copy, move, replace, delete, or resize any primitive. This command is described in further detail later in this chapter.

- **SOLFEAT.** This command enables you to create standard AutoCAD entities from any region or solid model.

- **SOLINT.** This is the Boolean intersection operator, which creates a new region by calculating the common area of two intersecting regions.

- **SOLLIST.** This command displays the information that defines a region.

- **SOLMASSP.** This command calculates and displays the mass properties of the selected regions and solids. Mass properties calculated for regions include moments of inertia, product of inertia, radii of gyration, principal moments, and principal directions.

- **SOLMAT.** This command enables you to assign the current material, edit an existing material, or create a new material. AutoCAD uses the material assignments to perform the mass property calculations.

- **SOLMESH.** This command displays regions as a 3D mesh. Use SOLMESH where the model must be processed with the SHADE or HIDE commands.

- **SOLMOVE.** This command enables you to move and rotate regions in one command.

- **SOLPURGE.** This command erases the entities from which a composite region is built, reducing file size and improving performance.

- **SOLSEP.** This command separates composite regions created using the SOLUNION, SOLINT, and SOLSUB commands. SOLSEP enables you to separate the specific primitives you select.

- **SOLSUB.** This Boolean function subtracts one region from another.

- **SOLUCS.** This command aligns the current UCS with the face or edge of an existing region.

- **SOLUNION.** This is the Boolean union function, which creates composite regions by combining the area of two or more existing regions.

- **SOLWIRE.** This command displays selected regions as wireframes.

These commands are a subset of the AME command, but they work in much the same way. Even if you do not have AME, you can use the region modeler to familiarize yourself with most of the same commands and techniques used in AME. Of course, you can also use most of the standard AutoCAD drawing and editing commands as well.

# Using LIST and DBLIST Inquiry Commands

AutoCAD has two other inquiry commands you should know about: LIST and DBLIST. LIST gives a complete list of entities you select, including where the entities are located. The LIST command gives the closed area of a closed polyline, including curves. LIST also lists the length of selected polylines. The length equals the perimeter reported by AREA if it is closed.

LIST is often used to check the block name, dimension style, color, layer, or pertinent coordinate points of existing entities, so you can use this information for drawing new entities. The following exercise lists information about a block and a polyline.

## List Entity Data

`Command:` *Choose* **A**ssist, *then* **I**nquiry, *then* **L**ist

`Select objects:` *Select car and the polyline border around it in east lot*

| | | |
|---|---|---|
| `POLYLINE` `Layer: SCRATCH` | | The polyline data begins |
| `Space: Model space` | | |
| `Closed` | | |
| `starting width` `0'-0.00"` | | |
| `ending width` `0'-0.00"` | | |
| `VERTEX` `Layer: SCRATCH` | | Polyline continues with four vertices |
| `Space: Model space` | | |
| `at point, X=297'-3.17"` `Y=108'-8.77"` `Z= 0'-0.00"` | | |
| `starting width` `0'-0.00"` | | |
| `ending width` `0'-0.00"` | | |

Three more vertices are listed, then:

```
      END SEQUENCE  Layer: SCRATCH              The polyline ends
                    Space: Model space
    area  15120.00 sq in (105.0000 sq ft)      Saved in AREA system variable
    perimeter 46'-0.00"                         Saved in PERIMETER system
                                                variable
      BLOCK REFERENCE Layer: PLAN              Displays the block data
                   Space: Model space
        CAR                                    Displays the block name
    at point, X=300'-0.00"  Y=107'-6.00"   Z= 0'-0.00"
      X scale factor    1.0000
      Y scale factor    1.0000
    rotation angle 245d19'23"
      Z scale factor    1.0000
```

You can also access LIST from the screen menu (choose INQUIRY, then LIST:). The color and linetypes also are listed when they are anything other than the default BYLAYER.

DBLIST gives a complete data list of every entity in the drawing file. After you issue a DBLIST command, you might never do it again. Issuing this command causes the entire database to scroll by the screen. Cancel with Ctrl-C to stop this display.

# Using TIME To Get Elapsed Editing Time

Finish this chapter by looking at TIME again to see how long you spent in this editor session.

---

### Using TIME To Get Elapsed Drawing Time

Command: *From the screen menu, choose*     Displays time in the AutoCAD Text window
INQUIRY, *then* TIME:, *then press F2*

```
Current time:            05 Jan 1992 at 10:29:27.000
Drawing last updated:    04 Jan 1992 at 14:10:23.000
Time in drawing editor:  0 days 1:49:15.000
Elapsed timer (on):      0 days 0:13:00.000
```

The elapsed time is about 13 minutes; your time varies.

Display/ON/OFF/Reset: *Press Enter*

Command: *Choose* **F**ile, *then* E**x**it AutoCAD

---

# Summary

AutoCAD provides nearly limitless possibilities for enhancing drawings. In this chapter, you have covered the essentials to get you started. Here are some other reminders about hatching and sketching.

AutoCAD needs fully closed boundaries for hatching; use BHATCH or PLINE to create closed continuous boundaries. Standard AutoCAD patterns are designed to be scaled by your drawing scale factor. Use HATCH U when you just want a quick hatch. You can press Ctrl-C to terminate hatching in progress. Use ERASE with the Last option to get rid of hatch patterns as a block. When hatching, take time to find the patterns that work best for your drawings. Do not overlook the possibility of creating your own hatch patterns and linetypes to give your drawings a unique look.

Be careful with SKETCH. Use it with a relatively large increment, and set SKPOLY to 1 and curve fit with PEDIT for smooth, efficient curves. Use the calibrated digitizer mode when you need to sketch or trace data from existing paper drawings.

Use AutoCAD's inquiry commands to measure, identify, and generally find out the status of entities and what is in a drawing. Consider using the TIME command as a management tool. Use ID to identify coordinates and reset the last point. Use DIST for distances and angles. Use AREA for areas and perimeters. Use LIST to check coordinates and properties of existing entities. Do not forget the system variables that store these data.

The Region Modeler is an excellent engineering tool for obtaining useful information about the drawing entities. Try to apply this feature to some of your own applications to see how it can easily provide you with engineering data that may be helpful in determining material or manufacturing requirements.

# Dimensioning

To communicate designs, drawings must convey more than just graphic entities and annotations. Many drawings require dimensions, tolerances, and other key information to define the design well enough so that it can be built or manufactured. This information is often just as important as the drawing. An object that is not drawn to scale might not affect the project, as long as the dimensions are correct. If you put down a wrong dimension, however, the chances of an error in production increase dramatically.

This chapter shows you how to dimension your drawings in AutoCAD by defining spatial relationships between objects. You learn about many basic dimensioning techniques and commands. In Chapter 17, "Advanced Dimensioning," you learn more about dimensioning with AutoCAD, including how to use dimension styles and associative dimensions. This chapter, therefore, lays the groundwork for Chapter 17.

## Understanding Dimensioning

AutoCAD takes as much work out of dimensioning as possible: distances are calculated automatically; dimension arrows are consistently sized; standards for settings, such as extension line offsets, are maintained and applied to the drawing; and the entities that make up a dimension are created automatically.

After specifying the type of dimensions to draw, identify what to measure (usually endpoints, arcs, or other points of existing entities). For greater accuracy, use object snaps. Then pick a location for the dimension line and text. Finally, accept AutoCAD's measurements as dimension text or enter your own text.

*The key to accurate dimensioning relies more on drawing technique than on dimensioning. The accuracy of your drawing controls the accuracy of the drawing's dimensions because AutoCAD calculates dimensions based on the points you specify. When you draw an object out of scale or to an incorrect size, the drawing's dimensions reflect that error unless you override them. If you override these dimensions, you defeat the advantage AutoCAD provides by calculating dimensions for you. Accuracy in drawing makes dimensioning much easier.*

AutoCAD can create dimensions in many different styles and to nearly any standard. The default style of dimensioning works, but it may not suit your standards. To dimension in AutoCAD, you usually create a group of standard settings that control the appearance and placement of your dimensions. Then, you select the type of dimension and the points or entities to dimension, and AutoCAD does the rest. System variables called *dimension variables* (or *dimvars*) provide almost complete control over size, placement, and appearance of dimensions. The easiest way to adjust the dimension variables is by using the Dimension Style option of the Settings pull-down menu. This dialog box contains a list of dimension variable groupings that brings up child dialog boxes that enable those variables to be viewed and adjusted. If you know them quite well, you also can set dimension variables using the SETVAR command by entering the variable names as commands, or by choosing them from the list provided on the screen menu. Table 15.1 lists all of AutoCAD's dimension variables.

You usually have several standard sets of dimension variables that you use. You can save these as *dimension styles* (*dimstyles*). Dimstyles are groups of settings that you can save and recall by name, to easily set up different styles for different applications. Dimension styles are explained in detail in Chapter 17. The following list describes a few of the characteristics you can control by using dimension variables (and dimension styles):

- The appearance and size of your dimension arrows (or what you use instead of arrows)

- The size and style of the dimension text

- What tolerance ranges, if any, are included with the text

- Where the dimension text goes relative to the dimension line

- The layer on which arrows, text, and extension lines are placed (to control plotted line weight by color)

**Table 15.1**

**AutoCAD Dimension Variables**

| Variable Name | Default Setting | Default Meaning | Description |
|---|---|---|---|
| DIMALT | 0 | OFF | Controls the drawing of additional dimension text in an alternative-units system: 1 = On, 0 = Off |
| DIMALTD | 2 | 0.00 | The decimal precision of dimension text in alternative units |
| DIMALTF | 25.4000 | | The scale factor for dimension text alternative units |
| DIMAPOST | " " | NONE | The user-defined suffix for alternative dimension text (RO) |
| DIMASO | 1 | ON | Controls the creation of associative dimensions: 1 = On, 0 = Off |
| DIMASZ | 0.1800 | | Controls the size of dimension arrows and affects the fit of dimension text inside dimension lines when DIMTSZ is set to 0 |
| DIMBLK | " " | NONE | The name of the block to draw, rather than an arrow or tick (RO) |
| DIMBLK1 | " " | NONE | The name of the block for the first end of dimension lines. *See DIMSAH* (RO) |
| DIMBLK2 | " " | NONE | The name of the block for the second end of dimension lines. *See DIMSAH* (RO) |

*continues*

## Table 15.1
## Continued

| Variable Name | Default Setting | Default Meaning | Description |
|---|---|---|---|
| DIMCEN | 0.0900 | MARK | Controls center marks or center lines drawn by radial DIM commands: Mark size = value Draw center lines = negative (mark size = absolute value) |
| DIMCLRD | 0 | COLOR | The dimension line, arrow, and leader color number: 0 = BYBLOCK 256 = BYLAYER |
| DIMCLRE | 0 | COLOR | The dimension extension line's color |
| DIMCLRT | 0 | COLOR | The dimension text's color |
| DIMDLE | 0.0000 | NONE | The dimension line's extension distance beyond ticks when ticks are drawn (when DIMTSZ is nonzero) |
| DIMDLI | 0.3800 | | The offset distance between successive continuing or baseline dimensions |
| DIMEXE | 0.1800 | | The length of extension lines beyond dimension lines |
| DIMEXO | 0.0625 | | The distance by which extension lines originate from dimensioned entity |
| DIMGAP | 0.0900 | | The space between text and a dimension line; determines when text is placed outside a dimension **(Creates reference dimension outlines if negative)** |

| Variable Name | Default Setting | Default Meaning | Description |
|---|---|---|---|
| DIMLFAC | 1.0000 | NORMAL | The overall linear dimensioning scale factor; if negative, acts as the absolute value applied to paper space viewports |
| DIMLIM | 0 | OFF | Presents dimension limits as default text: 1 = On, 0 = Off *See DIMTP and DIMTM* |
| DIMPOST | " " | NONE | The user-defined suffix for dimension text, such as "mm" (RO) |
| DIMRND | 0.0000 | EXACT | The rounding interval for linear dimension text |
| DIMSAH | 0 | OFF | Enables the use of DIMBLK1 and DIMBLK2, rather than DIMBLK or a default terminator: 1 = On, 0 = Off |
| DIMSCALE | 1.0000 | | The overall scale factor applied to other dimension variables except tolerances, angles, measured lengths, or coordinates 0 = Paper space scale |
| DIMSE1 | 0 | OFF | Suppresses the first extension line: 1 = On, 0 = Off |
| DIMSE2 | 0 | OFF | Suppresses the second extension line: 1 = On, 0 = Off |
| DIMSHO | 0 | OFF | Determines whether associative dimension text is updated during dragging: 1 = On, 0 = Off |

*continues*

## Table 15.1
### Continued

| Variable Name | Default Setting | Default Meaning | Description |
|---|---|---|---|
| DIMSOXD | 0 | OFF | Suppresses the placement of dimension lines outside extension lines: 1 = On, 0 = Off |
| DIMSTYLE | *UNNAMED | | Holds the name of the current dimension style (RO) |
| DIMTAD | 0 | OFF | Places dimension text above the dimension line, rather than within: 1 = On, 0 = Off |
| DIMTFAC | 1.0000 | | The scale factor, relative to DIMTXT, for the size of tolerance text |
| DIMTIH | 1 | ON | Forces dimension text inside the extension lines to be positioned horizontally, rather than aligned: 1 = On, 0 = Off |
| DIMTIX | 0 | OFF | Force dimension text inside extension lines: 1 = On, 0 = Off |
| DIMTM | 0.0000 | NONE | The negative tolerance value used when DIMTOL or DIMLIM is on |
| DIMTOFL | 0 | OFF | Draws dimension lines between extension lines, even if text is placed outside the extension lines: 1 = On, 0 = Off |

| Variable Name | Default Setting | Default Meaning | Description |
|---|---|---|---|
| DIMTOH | 1 | ON | Forces dimension text to be positioned horizontally, rather than aligned, when it falls outside the extension lines: 1 = On, 0 = Off |
| DIMTOL | 0 | OFF | Appends tolerance values (DIMTP and DIMTM) to the default dimension text: 1 = On, 0 = Off |
| DIMTP | 0.0000 | NONE | The positive tolerance value used when DIMTOL or DIMLIM is on |
| DIMTSZ | 0.0000 | ARROWS | When assigned a nonzero value, forces tick marks to be drawn (rather than arrowheads) at the size specified by the value; affects the placement of the dimension line and text between extension lines |
| DIMTVP | 0.0000 | | Percentage of text height for vertical dimension text offset |
| DIMTXT | 0.1800 | | The dimension text height for nonfixed text styles |
| DIMZIN | 0 | | Suppress the display of zero inches or zero feet in dimension text 0 = Feet & Inches = 0 1 = Neither 2 = Inches only 3 = Feet only |

(RO) indicates read-only.

## Overview of the Exercises

The exercises in this chapter are organized into two major groups:

- The first group explains how to use the dimensioning commands, including center, radius, diameter, angular, and linear dimensions. In this group of exercises, you also learn how to set some dimensioning variables.

- The second group of exercises, beginning with "Understanding Dimension Variables," goes deeper into the discussion of AutoCAD's dimension variables by explaining the process of working with and setting these variables.

*If you already are familiar with AutoCAD's basic dimensioning features, you might want to begin with the second group of exercises. Before you begin, however, make the settings shown in table 15.2 and complete the "Setting DIMTXT, DIMASZ, and DIMSCALE" exercise in the first section.*

# Using Dimensioning Tools

AutoCAD provides many dimensioning commands and settings, and makes them available on various pull-down, screen, icon, and tablet menus that are used throughout this chapter. Because dimensioning has so many options, it has its own command mode and prompt, accessed through the DIM and DIM1 commands.

*You can abbreviate any dimensioning command to the fewest characters that are unique to that command, such as HOR for Horizontal. Six commands require three characters: HORizontal, HOMetext, REStore, REDraw, STAtus, and STYle. Six dimensioning commands can be abbreviated to one character: Baseline, Diameter, Newtext, Exit, Leader, and Undo. All others can be abbreviated to their first two characters.*

## Working with Dim Mode, the Dim Prompt, and Dim Commands

When you enter the dimensioning mode, you see a new prompt, Dim:, instead of the usual AutoCAD command prompt. The DIM command places you in dimensioning mode and leaves you there. The DIM1 command automatically exits dimensioning mode after one dimensioning command. All dimensioning is done in dimensioning mode. When you are in dimensioning mode, you cannot execute the regular AutoCAD commands, but function keys, control-key combinations, object snap overrides, menus, dialog boxes, and most transparent commands still function normally. After you are finished dimensioning, exit the dimensioning mode and return to the regular Command: prompt.

Dimensioning has a unique vocabulary, and AutoCAD has its own dialect within that vocabulary. The following list describes AutoCAD's dimensioning terms:

- **Alternate Units.** This term stands for dimensions in which two separate measurement systems are used, such as inch and metric units.

- **Angular.** This term stands for a set of dimension lines, extension lines, arrows, and text that shows the measurement of an angle.

- **Arrow.** Also called *terminator*, this term stands for the block attached to the end of a dimension line. Other entities, such as ticks, dots, and user-defined blocks, also may be used as terminators.

- **Associative Dimension.** This term stands for a dimension created as a single entity instead of individual lines, arrows (solids), arcs, and text. Associative dimensions can be moved, scaled, and stretched along with the entities being dimensioned, and the dimension text adjusts automatically. This option is the default dimensioning mode.

- **Baseline Dimensions.** This term stands for a series of successive linear dimensions, starting at the same extension line.

- **Center Mark/Center Line.** This term stands for a line that identifies the center point of a circle. AutoCAD's dimensioning commands draw these automatically.

- **Continuing Dimensions.** This term stands for a series of successive linear dimensions that follow one another. Also referred to as *chained dimensions*.

- **Datum or Ordinate Dimension.** This term stands for a dimension consisting only of a leader and dimension text indicating the feature's horizontal or vertical distance from a 0,0 base point. Datum dimensions are generally used as a series of dimensions referencing a common base point.

- **Dimension Line.** This term stands for a line that shows which angle or distance is being dimensioned. It usually has arrows at both ends.

- **Dimension Styles.** This term stands for a named group of dimension variable settings that can be stored to disk with the drawing. After you fine-tune your dimension variable settings, you can save that setup by name for future use.

- **Dimension Text.** This term stands for the text string that displays the dimension value. You can use AutoCAD's default value or enter your own value to override the default.

- **Dimension Variables.** This term stands for a set of variables (also called *dimvars*), some user-controlled, which controls size, style, location, and appearance of dimensions.

- **Extension Line.** This term stands for a short line segment that shows each end or extent of the element being dimensioned (also called *witness line*).

- **Leader.** This term stands for a line that extends from the dimension text to the element being dimensioned or annotated.

- **Limits.** This term stands for a type of tolerance dimensioning that shows the minimum and maximum dimensions, rather than a single value.

- **Linear Dimensions.** This term stands for a set of dimension lines, extension lines, arrows, and text that shows the distance between two (or more) points in a straight line.

- **Tolerances.** This term stands for plus and minus amounts that can be attached to a dimension text. To use tolerance dimensions, you must set their values with dimension variables.

# Setting Up for Dimensioning

The first exercise in this chapter begins with the MOCKSECT drawing that you created in Chapter 10. You can use the identical IAWMOCKD.DWG file from the IAW DISK. It contains the settings shown in table 15.2. Because you use this drawing to explore a wide variety of dimensioning features, many of the dimensions deviate from what is considered the usual dimensioning for this type of drawing. When you are finished, your completed drawing should resemble figure 15.1.

**Figure 15.1:**

The MOCKDIM drawing with a variety of dimensions.

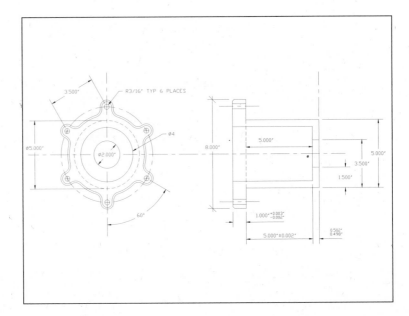

## Table 15.2
## MOCKDIM Drawing Settings

| COORDS | GRID | LTSCALE | OSNAP | ORTHO | SNAP |
|---|---|---|---|---|---|
| On | 1 | 1 | NONe | On | On |

| Layer Name | State | | Color | Linetype |
|---|---|---|---|---|
| 0 | On | | 7 (White) | CONTINUOUS |
| CENTER | On | | 1 (Red) | CENTER |
| DIMS | On/Current | | 2 (Yellow) | CONTINUOUS |
| HIDDEN | On | | 4 (Cyan) | HIDDEN |
| PARTS | On | | 3 (Green) | CONTINUOUS |

The initial MOCKDIM drawing looks like figure 15.2.

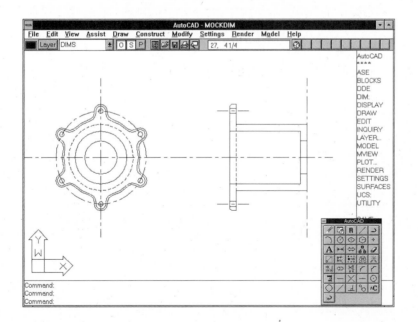

**Figure 15.2:**

The starting MOCKDIM drawing.

Before you start dimensioning, consider the topic of scaling dimensions. Assume that MOCKDIM is scaled 1=2 (a half-scale factor) when plotted or composed in a paper space sheet.

# Scaling Dimensions

AutoCAD's defaults make assumptions about dimension setup parameters, including the scale of your dimension text and arrows. The defaults may be acceptable for a drawing that is plotted at full scale, but if your drawing is to be scaled, the default settings may make your dimensions huge or nearly invisible. On a 60'×100' facilities planning drawing, for example, the default arrow of 0.18 inches is invisible at almost any drawing scale and sheet size. Setting a scale factor for sizing dimensions is similar to setting a scale for annotating your basic drawing.

You could reset all the dimension variables to get the right size, but AutoCAD has a better answer: DIMSCALE. Every scalar dimension variable is multiplied by DIMSCALE before it is applied to the drawing. DIMSCALE does not affect the measured value of the dimension, only its physical size relative to the drawing. You can use DIMSCALE to change all the dimensioning variables with a single scale factor. The default for DIMSCALE is 1.0000. Set DIMSCALE to the drawing-scale factor (drawing units divided by plot or paper space sheet units). If you scale the drawing down, you need to scale the dimensions back up to their intended size. If you scale a drawing up when you plot, you need to scale the dimensions down. MOCKDIM will be plotted at half scale (1 plotted inch = 2 drawing units), which means the drawing scale is 2. You can set the DIMSCALE variable at the Feature Scaling setting in the Features dialog box.

Set the scalar dimension variables, such as dimension text and arrow size, to the actual sizes you want in the plotted output. DIMTXT is for text, and DIMASZ is for arrows. These settings are multiplied by DIMSCALE. A .125 DIMTXT setting will be .25" in the drawing (.125×2), but it will plot half that size (.125).

Set these values in the following exercise. Set DIMTXT for the text, set DIMASZ for arrows, and then set DIMSCALE to 2, making your dimension scale offset your drawing scale. Use the screen menus to set various dimension variables. The dialog boxes are used more extensively later in the chapter.

---

### Setting DIMTXT, DIMASZ, and DIMSCALE
### To Scale Dimensions

Begin a new drawing called MOCKDIM=IAWMOCKD.

| | |
|---|---|
| `Command:` *From the screen menu, choose* DIM:, *then* Dim Vars | Enters dimensioning mode and displays dimension variable screen menu |
| `_DIM Dim:` *From the screen menu, choose* dimasz | Issues the DIMASZ variable prompt |

| | |
|---|---|
| `Dim: _DIMASZ Current value <3/16>`<br>`New value: 0.14 ↲` | Sets the arrowhead size |
| `Dim:` *From the screen menu, choose* next,<br>*then* dimscale | Displays the next page of the Dim Vars<br>screen menu |
| `Dim: _DIMSCALE Current value`<br>`<1.000000> New value: 2 ↲` | Sets DIMSCALE to 2 |
| `Dim: DIMTXT ↲` | Prompts for DIMTXT setting |
| `Dim: _DIMTXT Current value <3/16>`<br>`New value: .125 ↲` | Makes text 1/4" high in the drawing<br>(.125 DIMTXT ×2 DIMSCALE) |
| `Dim:` *Press Ctrl-C or, from the screen*<br>*menu, choose* AutoCAD | Exits to the `Command:` prompt |

*Save the drawing*

By choosing the Dimension Style option of the **S**ettings menu, you adjust these variables from dialog boxes. DIMSCALE is found under the **F**eature Scaling option of **F**eatures, and DIMASZ is listed as Arrow Si**z**e. The DIMTEXT can be set from the Text **H**eight setting in the Text Position area of that same dialog box.

*Be careful when you use UNDO after you exit the dimensioning mode. If you set any variables, a command-prompt level UNDO or U cancels everything from the preceding dimensioning mode session in a single UNDO step. You can easily undo dimension variable settings accidentally. Always exit the dimensioning mode immediately after you set dimension variables, then re-enter dimensioning mode to dimension objects. This step protects settings from an accidental undo.*

*You can exit dimensioning mode by using the EXIT command; abbreviate it with just an E, or press Ctrl-C.*

# Using Undo in Dimensioning Mode

The DIM command's Undo option is similar to Undo in the LINE command. DIM's Undo removes the results (extension lines, arrows, text, and so on) of the last dimensioning command. Enter **U** to undo at the `Dim:` prompt. As discussed in the preceding

Caution, you also can undo dimensions with the normal UNDO command from the Command: prompt, but one Undo then wipes out an entire dimensioning session.

## Dimensioning the MOCKDIM Plan View

To start dimensioning, use the plan view (the left side) of the MOCKDIM drawing to test some of the basic dimensioning commands. Figure 15.3 shows the dimension types covered in this first section.

**Figure 15.3:**

Some dimension examples.

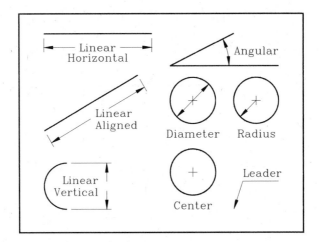

# Dimensioning with Center Marks

The plan view has a series of small circles in the lugs on the flange's edge. Begin your dimensioning sequence in the following exercise by using the CENTER command to place center marks in these circles. The CENTER command puts a cross at the center of an arc or circle.

Put the first mark in the circle at the upper right, and then work your way around the flange.

### Using CENTER To Place a Center Mark

Use ZOOM with the Window option to zoom in on the flange top view.

Command: *Choose* **D**raw, *then*       Enters dimensioning mode and issues
Di**m**ensions, *then* **R**adial, *then*    CEN command
**C**enter Mark

Command: _dim1

```
Dim: _center Select arc or circle:
```
*Turn off snap and pick the hole's*
*circumference near ① (see fig. 15.4)*                Draws a center mark

Next, use the screen menu to access the CENTER command.

```
Command: From the screen menu, choose          Enters dimensioning mode and issues
DIM:, then next, then CENTER                     CEN command
```

```
_CENTER Select arc or circle: Pick              Adds center marks to another hole
another hole
```

```
Dim: Press Enter                                Repeats CENTER command
```

```
_CENTER Select arc or circle:
```
*Repeat the process to add center marks to*      Adds center marks to remaining holes
*the remaining holes*

---

The center mark should appear as shown in figure 15.4.

 *The DIMCEN dimension variable sets the size of the center marker.
If you give DIMCEN a negative value, center lines extending
beyond the circumference are added to the center mark. In either
case, the value of DIMCEN is half the width of the cross it creates.*
*To set DIMCEN using the dialog boxes, change the Center Mark Size value in the
Features dimensioning dialog box.*

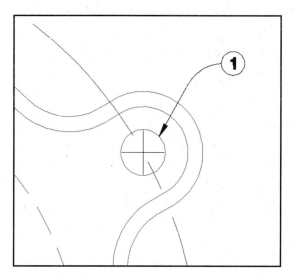

**Figure 15.4:**

Detail of a center mark.

# Dimensioning a Radius

Place a radius dimension in the inner flange circle. The RADIUS command measures from an arc or circle center point to a circumference point. In the following example, the dimension text does not fit inside the circle. Drag the dimension outside the circle and place it by picking a point. The point determines the leader's length, not its endpoint. The dimensioning screen menu is already displayed; use it instead of the dialog box.

## Using RADIUS To Place a Radius Dimension

Continue in the DIM command from the previous exercise.

| | |
|---|---|
| Command: *From the screen menu, choose* previous, *then* RADIUS | Issues RADIUS command |
| Dim: _RADIUS Select arc or circle: *Select the inner circle at point* ① *(see fig. 15.5)* | Specifies dimension line location |
| Dimension text <1 1/4>: *Press Enter* | Accepts default |
| Enter leader length for text: *Pick point outside circle* | Sets leader length and draws dimension |

Your drawing should appear as shown in figure 15.5.

**Figure 15.5:**

A radius
dimension.

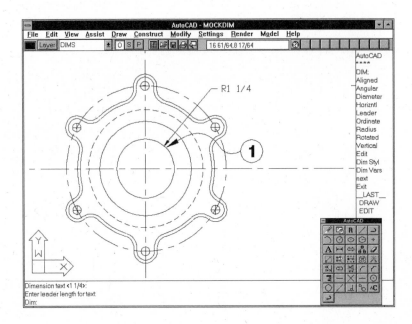

AutoCAD measured the radius for you and drew the correct dimension with default text. (You can input your own text instead of using the default dimension text, if necessary.)

Because the dimension lines, arrow, and text would not fit inside the circle, AutoCAD asked you for a leader length. (You are not limited to picking a point; you also can enter a distance for the length.) The angle of the leader is determined by the center of the circle and the point picked to select the circle.

# Forcing the Text inside the Circle or Arc

Text size and pick point determine whether the dimension text fits in the circle. What do you do if you want the radius dimension inside the circle in all circumstances? AutoCAD provides a variable for this control. With radial dimensions, the variable DIMTIX On forces the value inside the circle or arc, even if AutoCAD would normally prompt you to place it outside. DIMTIX Off forces it outside.

To see how this variable works, undo this first radius in the following exercise. Then, set DIMTIX On and execute the radius command again. This time, select the circle by picking at about the 85-degree point on the circumference.

## Forcing a Radius Dimension inside a Circle

| | |
|---|---|
| `Dim:` *Choose* **E**dit, *then* **U**ndo | Undoes the first radius dimension |
| `Dim:` *Choose* **S**ettings, *then* Di**m**ension Style | Cancels the DIM command, and displays Dimension Styles and Variables dialog box |
| `*Cancel*`<br>`Command: ddim` | |
| *Choose* **T**ext Location | Displays Text Location dialog box |
| *Click on* Default *to open the* **H**orizontal *drop-down list, then select* Force Text Inside, *then choose* OK, *then* OK *again* | Sets DIMTIX on and exits dialog boxes |
| `Command:` *Choose* **D**raw, *then* Di**m**ensions, *then* **R**adial, *then* **R**adius | Enters dimensioning mode and issues the RADIUS command |
| `Dim: _radius Select arc or circle:`<br>*Pick  circle at point* ① *(see fig. 15.6)* | |
| `Dimension text <1 1/4>:` *Press Enter* | Draws dimension with text inside |
| `Command:` **QSAVE** ↵ | Saves the file |

The dimension should appear as shown in figure 15.6.

**Figure 15.6**

Detail of a radius dimension.

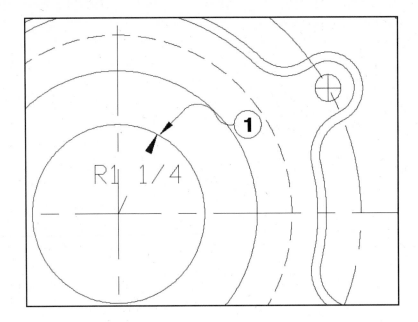

The dimension text was placed in the circle, and you were not prompted for leader length.

*Use a text style with a width factor of 0.75 to condense the dimension text.*

AutoCAD always writes dimension text horizontally, even for angular dimensions, unless you change the dimension variables.

*You get vertical dimension text if your current text style is vertical when you enter dimensioning mode. Reset your text to a horizontal style before executing the dimension commands.*

# Dimensioning a Diameter

Now that the text fits in the circle, replace the radius with a diameter dimension. *Diameter* measures between two diametrically opposed points on the circumference of a circle or arc. Placing a diameter is similar to placing a radius. When you select the circle that you want to dimension, Diameter uses the point you pick as a diameter endpoint. AutoCAD automatically determines where the second endpoint goes. (If the text does not fit, a leader also stems from this first picked point.) Diameter dimension text placement is controlled by DIMTIX, just as radius dimensions are.

Undo the radius and put in a diameter dimension in the following exercise. Because DIMTIX is still on, the dimension is automatically placed inside the circle.

## Using DIAMETER To Place a Diameter Dimension

Select the previous radius dimension, and then issue the ERASE command to erase it.

Command: *Choose* **D**raw, *then*　　　　Enters dimensioning mode and issues
Di**m**ensions, *then* **R**adial, *then* **D**iameter　DIA command

Dim: _diameter Select arc or
circle: *Pick the circle at* ① *(see fig. 15.7)*

Dimension text <2 1/2>: *Press Enter*　　Draws the dimension

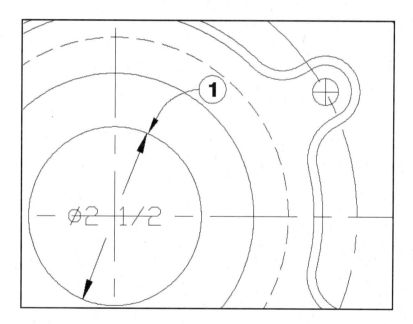

**Figure 15.7:**

Detail of a diameter dimension.

The diameter dimension should appear as shown in figure 15.7.

# Forcing an Inside Dimension Leader

If DIMTIX is on, it forces the text and leader inside the arc or circle; if DIMTIX is off, it forces them outside. When the leader and text are outside, no leader or arrows are drawn inside. Your dimensioning standards may require a radius or diameter leader drawn from or through the center to the pick point, even if the text is outside. The DIMTOFL dimension variable controls the inside leader. To force AutoCAD to draw outside text with both an outside and inside leader, set DIMTOFL on and DIMTIX off. DIMTOFL off (the default) suppresses the inside leader. If the inside leader is drawn, the arrows are drawn inside.

# Adding Text to a Default Dimension

You may have noticed that AutoCAD precedes the radius and diameter text with an R or a diameter symbol, but it does not put a space between the symbol and the measured text. How can you place a space between them? This section discusses working with dimension text, including forcing spaces, adding text, and overriding the measured dimension.

When you create a dimension, AutoCAD measures the value and displays it for you as a default. If you press Enter at the default, AutoCAD uses that value. Sometimes you may want to add text to the dimension, or change it altogether. To do this, enter the desired text at the default dimension text prompt. If you want the text to appear with your added text, represent the dimension in your typed text by a pair of angle brackets. For example, if the default is <2 1/2">, then enter **<> NOT TO SCALE** to create the text as 2 1/2" NOT TO SCALE.

Add text to a measured dimension in the following exercise. Return to the lug circle at the top of the flange and place a radius dimension with some added text. Use the exercise's prompt sequence to get your text input, including the angle brackets, and a leader offset value. Because AutoCAD recognizes the angle brackets as the default text value, the text includes the calculated value, plus any text added after the <>.

---

## Adding Text to a Dimension

| | |
|---|---|
| Command: *Choose* **S**ettings, *then* Di**m**ension Style | Opens dialog box |
| *Choose* **T**ext Location | Displays Text Location dialog box |
| *Click on* Force Text Inside *to open the* **H**orizontal *drop-down list, then select* Default, *then choose* OK, *then* OK *again* | Sets DIMTIX off and exits dialog box |
| Command: *Choose* **D**raw, *then* Di**m**ensions, *then* **R**adial, *then* **R**adius | Enters dimensioning mode and issues RAD command |

```
Dim: _radius Select arc or circle:
```
*Pick the top small hole at point ①*
*(see fig. 15.8)*

Figure 15.8 shows the pick point for the dimension that is to receive text.

```
Dimension text <3/16>:                  Adds to the dimension text
<> TYP 6 PLACES ↵
```

```
Enter leader length for text:           Draws dimension (see fig. 15.9)
```
*Pick a point at upper right of circle*

The inserted text should appear, as shown in figure 15.9.

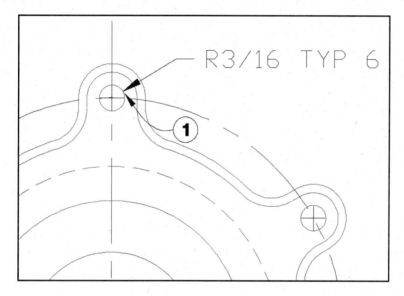

**Figure 15.8:**

Detail of a radius dimension.

Table 15.3 shows some other text examples.

### Table 15.3
### Alternative Text Examples

| When AutoCAD offers: | Enter this: | To get this: |
|---|---|---|
| `Dimension text <2.5000>:` | *Press spacebar* | |
| `Dimension text <2.5000>:` | **Not important** | Not important |

*continues*

### Table 15.3
### Continued

| When AutoCAD offers: | Enter this: | To get this: |
| --- | --- | --- |
| Dimension text <2.5000>: | **about <>** | about 2.5000 |
| Dimension text <2.5000>: | **roughly <>"** | roughly 2.5000" |

**Figure 15.9:**

A radius dimension with added text.

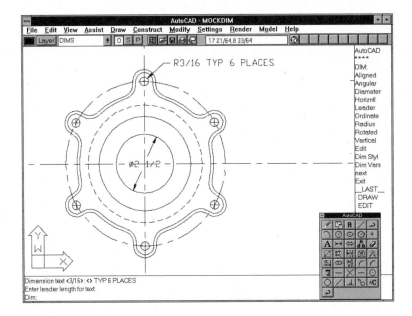

# Dimensioning with Leader Dimensions

In both the radius and diameter dimensions, a leader was used to place text outside the circle (or arc). A leader is like a combination of an arrow block insert, the LINE command, and the TEXT command. It enables you to create a *callout* to point text to a specific location. Use the Leader command to create an arrow, with one or more continuous line segments, to place text away from the entities you are dimensioning (see fig. 15.10).

Use a leader to dimension the hole in the flange in the following exercise. AutoCAD prompts for a starting point for the leader line. You do not need to pick a point for the leader's short horizontal extension line—AutoCAD automatically places a horizontal extension onto the end of the leader for the text.

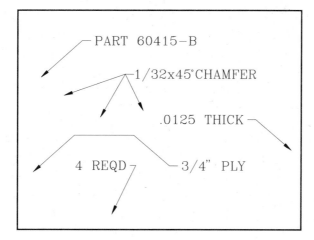

**Figure 15.10:**

Some leader examples.

---

## Using LEADER To Place a Leader Dimension

| | |
|---|---|
| `Command:` *Choose* **D**raw, *then* Di**m**ensions, *then* Lea**d**er | Issues the LEADER dimensioning command |
| `Dim: _leader Leader start:` *From the toolbox, choose* NEAREST | Issues NEA object snap |
| `nea to` *Pick right side of the large circle at point* ① *(see fig. 15.11)* | |
| `To point:` *Turn ortho off and pick point* ② | Defines leader line |
| `To point:` *Press Enter* | Creates a short line at end of leader |
| `Dimension text <3/16>:` `%%C4` ↵ | Adds diameter symbol to text 4 |

Your drawing should appear as shown in figure 15.11.

---

If you enter **%%C4** as the dimension text, you get the same effect as if you had dimensioned the hole by using the DIAMETER dimensioning command. You can use leaders to annotate any feature with a note—not just circles and arcs—and you can use multisegmented leaders in dense drawings.

New text is usually entered each time a leader is created. After locating the points for the leader and pressing Enter, you are prompted for the text. After you enter the text, the LEADER command places the text at the end of the leader (near the last point indicated). If the last segment of the leader line is pointed toward the right, the text is left-justified. If the last leader segment points left, the text is right-justified. This prevents the text from overwriting its leader.

**Figure 15.11:**

Creating a leader
dimension.

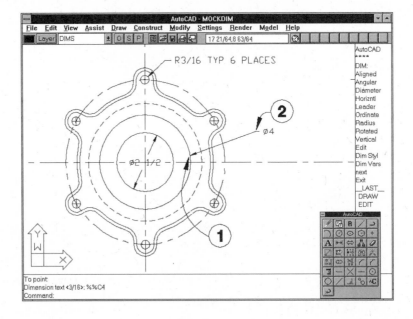

AutoCAD offers the default text value of the previous radius dimension as the default
leader text. This procedure enables you to use the previous dimension value as all or
part of the leader text.

*To use a previous dimension value, execute any dimension, such as
a DIAMETER dimension, then cancel it at the text prompt. Execute
the LEADER dimension command and accept the default dimension, or use angle brackets with added text.*

# Dimensioning an Angle

The measure of the angle between two of the outer flange holes is an *angular dimension*.
The ANGULAR command measures the inner or outer (acute or obtuse) angle between
two specified nonparallel lines, the angle of an arc, or the angle between three points
(see fig. 15.12). You can select an arc, circle, line, or polyline entity to dimension; or pick
three points for the vertex, start, and endpoints of the angle—virtually any situation
you can imagine.

In the following exercise, dimension the angle between the two outer holes at the lower
right of the flange. Use object snaps to pick the points and zoom in if necessary. Notice
that using the dimensioning commands from the pull-down menu are like the DIM1
command, which brings you back to the Command: prompt instead of the DIM: prompt.

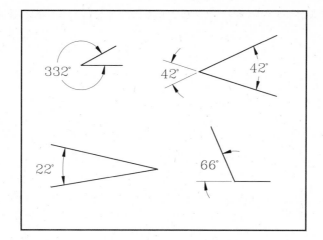

**Figure 15.12:**
Angular dimension examples.

---

## Using ANGULAR To Place an Angular Dimension

| | |
|---|---|
| Command: *Choose* **D**raw, *then* Di**m**ensions, *then* **A**ngular | Enters dimensioning mode and issues the ANGULAR command |
| Dim: _angular Select arc, circle, line, or RETURN: *Press Enter* | Specifies three-point method |
| Angle vertex: *From the toolbox, choose* INTERSECTION, *then pick point at* ① *(see fig. 15.13)* | Sets vertex point |
| First angle endpoint: *From the toolbox, choose* CENTER | |
| center of *Pick hole in tab at* ② | Sets one angle point |
| Second angle endpoint: *From the toolbox, choose* ENDPOINT | |
| endp of *Pick bottom center line at* ③ | Sets other angle point |
| Enter dimension line arc location: *Pick* ④ | |
| Dimension text <60>: *Press Enter* | Accepts text |
| Enter text location (or RETURN): *Press Enter* | Defaults to arc location |

Your new dimension should appear as shown in figure 15.13.

Creating
an angular
dimension.

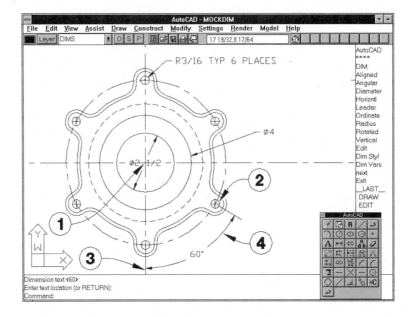

# Drawing Angular Dimensions

The ANGULAR command gives you a number of options. The following list explains the Angular options and the action that occurs:

- **Arc.** This option measures the arc from endpoint to endpoint and prompts you to place the dimension text. The ANGULAR command calculates the angle of the arc automatically, using the arc's center and its two endpoints.

- **Circle.** When this option is used, AutoCAD assumes you want to measure from the pick point to the next point you pick on the circle. The angle is then measured from the center of the circle.

- **Line.** When this option is used, AutoCAD assumes you want to dimension the angle between two lines and prompts for a second line.

- **Press Enter and pick three points.** This option is used to measure and dimension any angle, instead of selecting an entity. Usually, you use object snap to locate the points on existing entities.

No matter what kind of entity you dimension, the result is an arc angle between two points about a center point. Two angles exist for every set of points: one obtuse angle and one acute angle. The angle that is dimensioned depends on the location you pick for your dimension line arc. If you pick it between the two points, you get an acute angle with a small-dimension arc; if you pick it outside the two points, you get an obtuse angle.

# Dimensioning with Linear Dimensions

*Linear dimensions* refer to a group of dimensioning commands that measure between two points. The points can be endpoints, intersections, arc chord endpoints, or any two points you can identify (usually by selecting an entity or using object snap). Linear dimensions include the following measurements:

- **HORIZONTAL.** This linear dimension creates horizontal dimension lines.

- **VERTICAL.** This linear dimension creates vertical dimension lines.

- **ALIGNED.** This linear dimension creates dimension lines that are aligned (parallel) to an object or two specified points.

- **ROTATED.** This linear dimension creates dimension lines rotated to a specified angle, not necessarily aligned with the points.

- **CONTINUE.** This linear dimension creates a series of dimensions, with each dimension using the previous dimension's second extension line as the new dimension's first extension.

- **BASELINE.** This linear dimension creates a series of dimensions, all from the same first extension line.

## Making Horizontal and Vertical Linear Dimensions

The Horizontal and Vertical commands work exactly the same, except that one dimensions horizontally and the other vertically. When using either command, pick two points as the origins of two extension lines, or select an object (like a line, arc, or circle) and automatically dimension the full length or breadth of that object. If space allows (or if you set the variables to force it), the dimension line and text are drawn between the extension lines.

Dimension the dashed (hidden line) circle in the following exercise. Use Vertical and select the circle. The Vertical command selects the circle's top and bottom quadrant points as starting points for your extension lines, then prompts you for the location of the dimension line. Place the dimension line to the left of the circle.

### Using Linear VERTICAL To Place a Vertical Dimension

| | |
|---|---|
| Command: *Choose* **D**raw, *then* **Di**mensions, *then* **L**inear, *then* **V**ertical | Enters dimensioning mode and issues VERTICAL command |
| Dim: _vertical | |
| First extension line origin or RETURN to select: *Press Enter* | Specifies the entity selection method |

*continues*

```
Select line, arc, or circle: Pick
```
*any point on the hidden circle*

```
Dimension line location:
```
*Pick point at about 5,15*

```
Dimension text <5>: %%C<>          Adds the diameter symbol to the text and draws
                                    dimension
```

The vertical dimension should appear as shown in figure 15.14.

**Figure 15.14:**

A linear vertical
dimension on a
circle.

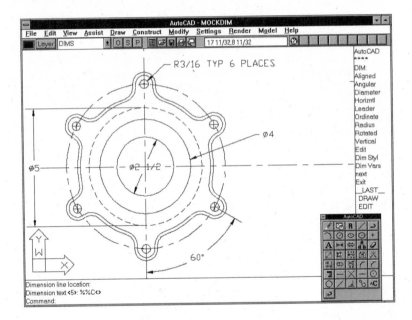

The text conflicts with the center line. The dimension text location is set automatically, but you can control it with dimension variables or change it after placement, as you can see in the associative dimensioning section of Chapter 17.

# Aligning Dimensions

The next exercise demonstrates the process of dimensioning a distance that is neither horizontal nor vertical, such as the distance from the center of one outer flange hole to the center of another. A vertical dimension measures only the Y-axis distance from the first hole to the second hole. Aligned, however, measures the actual distance between the two holes. Aligned works the same way as any linear dimensioning command: select an object or pick points to locate your dimension lines. The dimension is drawn parallel to the two points or object. Try this command on the two holes at the upper left of the flange.

## Using Linear Aligned To Place an Aligned Dimension

Command: *Choose* **D**raw, *then*
Di**m**ensions, *then* **L**inear, *then* **A**ligned

Enters dimensioning mode and issues
ALIGNED command

Dim: _aligned

First extension line origin or
RETURN to select: *From the toolbox,*
*choose* CENTER

center of *Pick hole at* ①
*(see fig. 15.15)*

Sets first alignment point

Second extension line origin:
*From the toolbox, choose* CENTER

center of *Pick the center of hole at* ②

Sets second alignment point

Dimension line location :
*Pick point 8,17*

Dimension text <3 1/2>: *Press Enter*

Accepts AutoCAD's default text

Zoom out a little if necessary to view the dimensions.

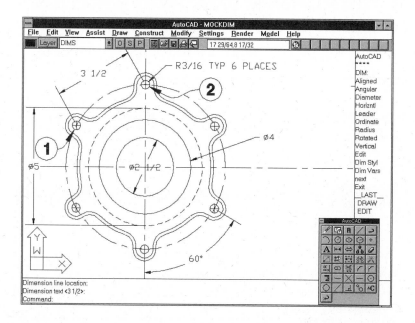

**Figure 15.15:**

An aligned
dimension.

The result is an aligned dimension, as shown in figure 15.15. Of course, if the origin points align vertically or horizontally, an aligned dimension produces identical results to vertical or horizontal.

# Creating Rotated Dimensions

If you do not want the dimension line to align with the two points you are dimensioning, AutoCAD provides a type of linear dimension called a *rotated dimension*. The rotated linear dimension is similar to the other linear dimensions except that you must specify the angle of the dimension line. Although it is not as practical as the other methods, you can use Rotated for vertical and horizontal dimensioning by specifying an angle of 90 or 0 degrees, respectively.

Use a rotated dimension to mark the distance between the lower right flange hole perpendicular to a line from the center of the 2 1/2" circle through the upper right flange hole. The dimension line should be at 120 degrees.

---

### Using Linear ROTATED To Place a Rotated Dimension

Command: *From the screen menu, choose* DIM:, *then* ROTATED

Enters dimensioning mode and issues ROTATED command

Dim: _ROTATED
Dimension line angle <0>: **120** ↵

First extension line origin or RETURN to select: *From the toolbox, choose* CENTER

center of *Pick point on 2 1/2" circle*

Second extension line origin: *From the toolbox, choose* CENTER

center of *Pick point on lower right flange hole*

Dimension line location:
**16.5,15.5** ↵

Dimension text <3 1/32>: *Press Enter*    Draws the dimension

Dim: **E** ↵    Exits dimensioning mode

*Save the drawing*

The rotated dimension should appear as shown in figure 15.16.

---

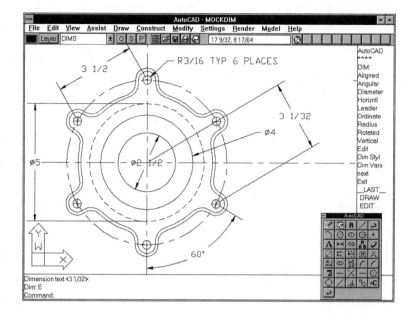

**Figure 15.16:**

A rotated dimension.

Your quick tour through the basics of dimensioning is now complete. To dimension, graphically define what you want to dimension, and then define where the dimension entities are to be located. You may have to practice to get the effects you want. Use the MOCKDIM drawing to try some variations, and then undo or discard those practice variations before you proceed.

The next section explores controlling dimension appearance using additional dimension variables and explains more of AutoCAD's dimensioning dialog boxes.

# Understanding Dimension Variables

From the dimension variables you have changed already, you can see the effect on the appearance of certain dimensions. AutoCAD has over 40 dimension variables. These variables can be set in different combinations to create dimensions that match nearly any standard. You will probably use several different combinations in your own work. Chapter 17 explains how to save and restore these sets as customized dimstyles.

The dimension variable names are cryptic acronyms for what the variables do. You should be able to decode them from the list in table 15.1 or the list that the Status dimensioning command provides. The acronyms are easier to remember if you think of them in terms of their functions.

# Examining the Default Dimension Variables

The following exercises look at the dimension variables with two different commands and in two different systems of units. Begin a new drawing to ensure that all variables show their default values. Use the SETVAR command with the default decimal units and the Status dimensioning command with fractional units, like the units in the MOCKDIM drawing. The complete lists are not shown in the following exercise—only dimension variables that already have been discussed or that are discussed in this section.

*To print a list of dimension variables, choose **F**ile, then **P**references. Put a check in the Log File **O**pen check box, and choose OK. Issue the SETVAR command, and list variables using the pattern DIM\*. Then use the Preferences dialog box to close the log file. Open the resulting log file with Windows Notepad, Write, or any ASCII text editor, and print it. The default log file is ACAD.LOG in the ACADWIN directory. If the file already contains data when you use **P**references to open it, the dimension variables listing will be added to the end of the file. See Chapter 18 for more information on the ACAD.LOG file.*

## Looking at Dimension Variables

Choose **F**ile, then **N**ew, and enter the drawing name **DIMVARS**.

| | |
|---|---|
| Command: **SETVAR** ↵ | Issues SETVAR command |
| Command: Variable name or ?: **?** ↵ | Prompts for names |
| Variable(s) to list <\*>: **DIM\*** ↵↵ | Lists all dimension variables (they all begin with DIM), including the following: |

```
DIMASZ      0.1800
DIMCEN      0.0900
DIMDLI      0.3800
DIMEXE      0.1800
DIMEXO      0.0625
DIMGAP      0.0900
DIMSCALE    1.0000
DIMSTYLE    "*UNNAMED" (read only)
DIMTIX      0
DIMTOFL     0
DIMTXT      0.1800
```

Press F2 to view text window, then press Enter once or twice to return to the Command: prompt.

| | |
|---|---|
| Command: *Press F2 to return to the graphics window, then choose* **S**ettings, *then* **U**nits Control | Opens the Units Control dialog box |

Set Units to Fractional, precision to 1/64, leave the rest at their defaults, and choose OK.

| | |
|---|---|
| Command: **DIM** ↵ | Enters dimensioning mode |
| Dim: **STATUS** ↵ | Lists the current settings, including the following: |

```
DIMASZ      3/16      Arrow size
DIMCEN      3/32      Center mark size
DIMDLI      3/8       Dimension line increment for continuation
DIMEXE      3/16      Extension above dimension line
DIMEXO      1/16      Extension line origin offset
DIMGAP      3/32      Gap from dimension line to text
DIMSCALE    1.000000  Overall scale factor
DIMSTYLE    *UNNAMED  Current dimension style (read-only)
DIMTIX      Off       Place text inside extensions
DIMTOFL     Off       Force line inside extension lines
DIMTXT      3/16      Text height
```

Again, switching to the text window shows all of these variables.

You can discard the drawing at this point.

---

As you can see, the dimensioning Status list is more than just a list of the variables. Both methods display in current units; the units were changed in the previous exercise to illustrate the following warning:

*The current units mislead you when the list rounds off the default settings. For the DIMTXT variable, for example, STATUS with fractional units shows it as 3/16, but .1800 is still its actual value. The values displayed as defaults are rounded to the drawing units settings. This difference becomes important when you mix annotations generated by the dimension commands with ones created with TEXT, DTEXT, and other drawing commands. Text heights will not match, and you will have trouble aligning items. Therefore, you should change all scalar dimension variables to exact fractional values when using any system of units that does not display true values. If, for example, you enter 3/16 as a new value for DIMTXT, it becomes .1875; however, if you press Enter at the default <3/16> prompt, it is unchanged and remains .1800.*

In the rest of this chapter, all scalar dimension variables are reset to precise decimal equivalents of these fractions. Several ways to set dimension variables are examined.

# Using the Dimensioning Dialog Boxes

You can set dimension variables by using the SETVAR command or by entering the name of the dimension variable at the Command: prompt or the Dim prompt. You also can set the dimension variables by selecting Dim Vars from the dimensioning screen menu. You get a list of dimension variables menu items covering three full-screen menu pages.

Because the dimension variable names are cryptic and sometimes hard to remember, AutoCAD has devoted a group of dialog boxes for setting dimension variables and creating dimension styles. These dialog boxes use check boxes, edit boxes, radio buttons, and list boxes to control dimension features. The DDIM command or Dimension Style item on the **S**ettings pull-down menu displays the main Dimension Styles and Variables dialog box (see fig. 15.17). From this dialog box, you can select an item from the list to access the other dialog boxes.

**Figure 15.17:**

The Dimension
Styles and
Variables
dialog box.

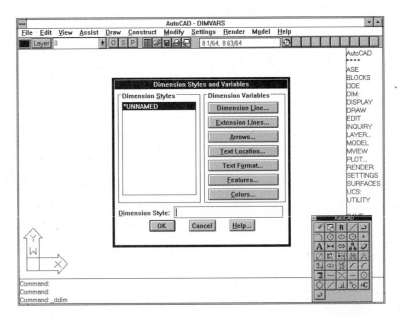

The Features dialog box controls the more popular display characteristics of dimensions (see fig. 15.18). Radio buttons enable selection of the type of arrows to be used and list boxes, such as the one for extension-line visibility, offer several options when the box is chosen. The check boxes can be chosen to turn features off or on. Change the values in the edit boxes by choosing the box and editing the value, or by double-clicking on the box and entering a new value. Another convenience of the dialog boxes is the capability to see the whole group of variables that affect a certain feature. For this reason, some dimension variables appear in more than one dialog box.

*The dimensioning dialog boxes are most effective when you do not know the name of the dimension variable you need to set or do not know which variables must be set to work together. If you know which ones to set, however, it may be faster to change the dimension variables directly.*

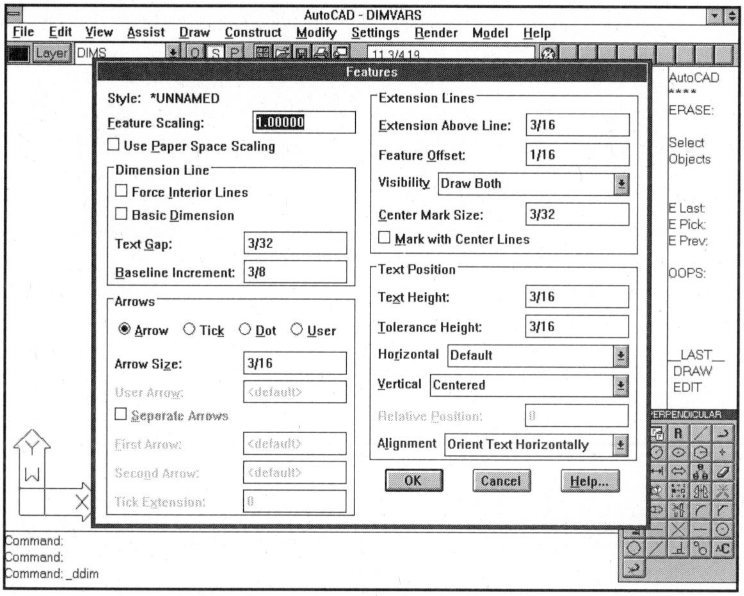

**Figure 15.18:**

The Features dialog box.

The following exercises show both the dimension variable names and values and the dialog box instructions for setting them. As you make dialog box selections, try to keep track of the dimension variables that are affected. With some practice, you learn the dimension variables well enough to set them manually.

Return to the MOCKDIM drawing in the following exercise and practice controlling the dimension variables from the dialog boxes.

## Setting Dimension Variables with Dialog Boxes

Open the drawing file MOCKDIM, or begin a new file called MOCKDIM, using the file IAWMOKD2.DWG from the IAW DISK as a prototype.

| | |
|---|---|
| Command: *Choose* **S**ettings, *then* Di**m**ension Style | Opens Dimension Styles and Variables dialog box |
| *Choose* **T**ext Location | Opens Text Location dialog box |
| *Click on* Default *to open the* Ho**r**izontal *drop-down list, then select* Force Text Inside, *and choose* OK | Sets DIMTIX on and returns to previous dialog box |
| *Choose* **E**xtension Lines, *then verify that* Feature **O**ffset *is set to* 1/16 | Sets DIMEXO variable to 1/16" |
| *Verify that* **E**xtension Above Line *is set to* 3/16, *then choose* OK | Sets DIMEXE variable to 3/16" and returns to previous dialog box |
| *Choose* **F**eatures, *double-click in the* **B**aseline Increment *edit box, and enter* **5/8** | Sets DIMDLI variable to 5/8" |
| *Verify that* **F**eature Scaling *is set to* 2 | Sets DIMSCALE variable to 2" (verifies setting made earlier in chapter) |
| *Verify that* Text **G**ap *is set to* 3/32 | Sets DIMGAP variable to 3/32 |
| *Choose* OK | Returns to main dialog box |
| *Choose* **T**ext Location, *and verify that* Te**x**t Height *is set to* 1/8, *then choose* OK | Sets DIMTXT to 1/8" and returns to previous dialog box |
| *Choose* OK | Returns to Command: prompt |

Save the drawing, to be used in Chapter 17, then quit AutoCAD.

# Summary

You now have some experience with most of AutoCAD's basic dimensioning commands, and you can place linear, radius, and diameter dimensions, as well as leaders. Chapter 17 explains the rest of AutoCAD's many dimensioning commands and features.

The most important point to remember about dimensioning with AutoCAD has nothing to do with dimensioning: be as precise as possible when you draw. Always use object snaps or exact coordinates whenever possible to ensure that AutoCAD calculates the correct values when the drawing is dimensioned.

Control the appearance of your dimensions with dimension variables. As you learned in the last exercise, you can set dimension variables most easily by using AutoCAD's dialog boxes. After you have used the variables for some time, you can remember them by name. Then you can speed up the process of setting dimension variables by entering their variable names at the Command: prompt.

The last several chapters have shown that when a drawing has been properly created, it becomes a valuable database. Chapter 16 begins Part Four: "Advanced AutoCAD Features," and provides a rest from dimensioning while you learn about AutoCAD's attributes and data extraction. Chapter 16 shows several examples of how to use attributes—AutoCAD's way of storing nongraphical (ASCII text) information in a drawing. AutoCAD gives you limitless possibilities for storing this kind of data with your drawing geometry.

In the next chapter, you learn how to create attribute definitions, edit them, and combine attribute definitions with graphical entities into blocks. When blocks with attributes are inserted, the data for attributes is requested. Chapter 16 also shows you how to modify attribute data after insertion and how to extract the data for use in other programs for tabulation or reporting. You can perform all of these operations by using standard commands or dialog box alternates. Chapter 17, "Advanced Dimensioning," takes you further into dimensioning.

# Advanced AutoCAD Features

# PART 4

# Introduction

This book's first three parts taught you how to create an accurate drawing, dimension it, and print it out as hard copy. These tasks are all that many users really expect of AutoCAD. If you are a more sophisticated user, however, you probably want to take advantage of AutoCAD's additional built-in capabilities, which can help you enhance your drafting productivity. Part Four of *Inside AutoCAD Release 12 for Windows* introduces you to AutoCAD's new and more advanced features.

## How Part Four Is Organized

Part Four consists of four chapters, which cover:

- Storing and retrieving information in drawings by using attributes

- Using dimension styles and other advanced dimensioning features

- Customizing AutoCAD Release 12 for Windows to maximize its capabilities and adapt it to your preferences

- Exchanging data and images between AutoCAD and other programs

# Using Attributes To Store and Retrieve Information

As a drafter, designer, or artist, you understand that drawings are much more than just collections of graphic entities and annotations. Drawings convey ideas. For example, drawings are often used to keep track of equipment in a commercial facility, to define items to be purchased for a project, and to generate bills of materials for items to be manufactured. Electronic drawings, such as those maintained by AutoCAD, have the capability to store many different types of nongraphic information.

In Chapter 16, you learn about AutoCAD's attribute entities. *Attributes* are like informational tags you can attach to various items in your drawing. These tags maintain information about the items to which they are attached. If you are creating a drawing that shows the equipment in a factory, for example, you can assign attributes to each piece of equipment to keep track of cost, function, manufacturer, purchase date, maintenance data, and other types of information.

Stored information is not useful, however, unless you have a method of retrieving it from the drawing in some meaningful way. Chapter 16 also shows you how to extract data from attributes in a drawing, so that you can export the data to a database program for analysis, create bills of materials, or otherwise collect and analyze the data contained in your drawings.

# Additional Dimensioning Capability

Chapter 17 increases your dimensioning capability by showing you how to create and use AutoCAD's dimension styles. As you learned in Chapter 15, AutoCAD's dimensions are controlled by a wide range of dimension variables. AutoCAD has so many dimension variables, and their names are so cryptic, that they can be difficult to keep track of—even for experienced AutoCAD users. Dimension styles overcome this problem by enabling you to define a style of dimensioning, save it by name, and then specify the dimension style's name whenever you want to use it again. Chapter 17 also explains several advanced dimensioning features, including commands for ordinate, chain, and datum dimensioning.

Chapter 18 introduces you to techniques and commands for customizing AutoCAD's environment and interface. You learn to create a custom prototype drawing, which you can load automatically with each new drawing, if you want to. You learn to customize the ACAD.PGP file to execute commands with one or two (or more) character abbreviations. AutoCAD Release 12 for Windows also enables you to add often-used commands and macros to the AutoCAD toolbar and menus. *Macros* enable you to program command sequences, including preset options and input, so that you can save time and avoid entering repetitive steps manually. You can easily add commands and macros to the AutoCAD for Windows interface to make them immediately accessible. Chapter 18 also examines how to set preferences you may have, such as setting default directories and changing the fonts and colors used for the AutoCAD interface.

# Exchanging CAD Data with Other Software

The final chapter in this part shows you how to exchange AutoCAD data and images with other software packages. Chapter 19 explains the two file formats that have been used for data conversion with AutoCAD for many years (the IGES and DXF formats). Chapter 19 also discusses a new and exciting feature of Release 12: the capability to import and export graphics file formats, such as GIF, TIFF, PCX, and PostScript files. The capability to copy a drawing—or part of a drawing—to another document can save considerable time in developing training materials, manuals, reports, and other documents.

In addition to these formats, Chapter 19 explores features unique to the Windows version of AutoCAD. In Chapter 19, you learn how to use the Windows Clipboard and OLE features to copy or link data from AutoCAD to other applications in order to create reports or manuals that contain AutoCAD-created data or graphics. The capability to copy or link a drawing or part of a drawing to another document can also save time.

# Attributes and Data Extraction

So far, the drawings in this book have been based on graphic entities or on spatial relationships between graphic entities. AutoCAD also can produce drawings from other types of data. In the Autotown subdivision you created in Chapter 12, for example, you can add "House Model Name," "House Size (Sq. Ft.)," and "House Exterior Finish" data to each house block to provide even more information about the real-world objects that are represented by the graphic blocks. This kind of extra information can be helpful to the person who is reading your drawing.

In AutoCAD, you can assign attributes to any item in your drawing to provide extra information about that item. *Attributes* are like paper tags attached to merchandise with a string. They can contain all kinds of information about the item to which they are tied: the item's manufacturer, model number, materials, price, stock number, and so on. The information stored in the attribute is the attribute's *value*.

In this chapter, you learn how to make your drawings more informative by adding text attributes to the drawing's blocks. You also learn how to extract this data in report form. By tagging entities with attributes, you can extract automatic bills of materials, schedules, and other tabular lists of data, or you can view the information in graphic form. You do not need to clutter your drawing with attribute data that you do not want to display. You can store data invisibly in the drawing file until you are ready to turn it into a report.

# Understanding How Attributes Work

You store an attribute (such as a name) in a block the same way you store graphic entities in a block. Just as you create and carefully lay out graphic entities before you include them in a block, you define attributes before you create an *attribute-laden* block.

AutoCAD provides an attribute-definition command called ATTDEF and a dialog box (called DDATTDEF) for attribute definition. You use ATTDEF or DDATTDEF to create attribute definitions, which determine how and what kind of attribute values are stored. Then you use the BLOCK command to group graphic entities and attribute definitions to form a block. This action places the attribute definitions into the same block definition as the graphic entities.

## Tagging Blocks with Attributes

You often may want to tag a group of graphic entities that already are in a block. If you design printed circuit boards, for example, you can assign text to an integrated circuit (IC) chip by labeling the chip with the manufacturer's name and pin assignments. If you are the facilities manager of an office building, you can tag each desk with an employee's name, title, department, phone number, and workstation description, as shown in figure 16.1. The desk (or IC chip for the PC board) probably already is stored as a block. In these cases, you can explode and reblock or form a new nested block (a block within a block) by including the attribute definition tags and the original block in the new block definition.

After you form an attribute-laden block, you use the INSERT command to insert the block into your drawing. You use the following commands to control attribute display and attribute editing:

- **ATTDISP.** This command controls the visibility of attributes in the drawing.

- **ATTEDIT.** This command changes attribute values after you insert them in your drawing.

- **ATTEXT.** This command extracts attribute values and block information, which you can place in a report.

- **ATTREDEF.** This command redefines a block and its associated attributes through the Attribute Redefinition dialog box.

- **DDATTEXT.** This command performs attribute extraction through a dialog box.

- **DDEDIT.** This command displays the Edit Attribute Definition dialog box (see fig. 16.2) when you select an attribute definition that has not been blocked. (DDEDIT displays the Text Editing dialog box when you select a text entity.)

- **DDATTE.** This command displays the Edit Attributes dialog box (see fig. 16.3), which enables you to edit attribute values in blocks after they have been inserted into the drawing. When you insert a block and the ATTDIA system variable is set to 1 (the default is 0), this dialog box prompts you for initial attribute data.

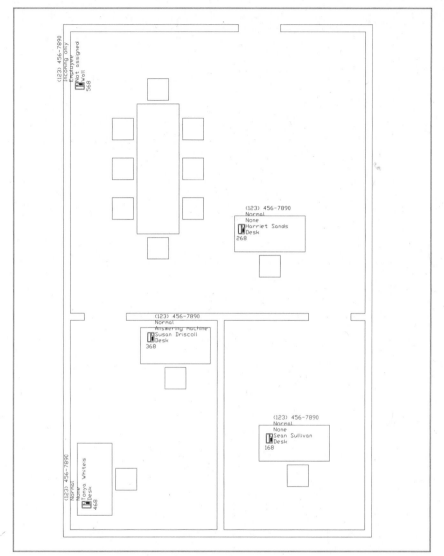

**Figure 16.1:**

A facility drawing with phone attributes.

**Figure 16.2:**

The DDEDIT Edit Attribute Definition dialog box.

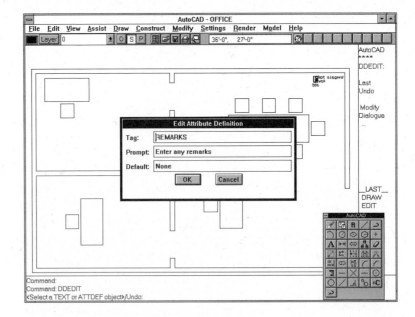

**Figure 16.3:**

The DDATTE Edit Attributes dialog box.

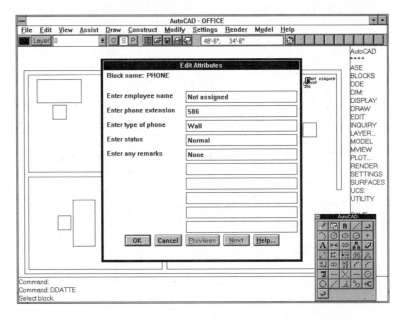

An *attribute definition* is the attribute entity before it is blocked; an *attribute entity* exists only as a subentity in a block insert.

Menu items for the attribute commands are scattered throughout different screen menus. From the screen menu, choose BLOCKS, then choose ATTDEF: to issue the ATTDEF command. Then you can choose DISPLAY, and then ATTDISP: to issue ATTDISP. Choose EDIT, then DDEDIT:, DDATTE:, or ATTEDIT: to issue those commands. You can choose DDEDIT: and then choose Modify Dialogue to issue the DDMODIFY dialog box. Choose UTILITY, then ATTEXT: to issue the ATTEXT command, or choose Att Ext Dialogue to issue the DDATTEXT command.

From the pull-down menu, choose **D**raw, **T**ext, then **A**ttributes, and then **D**efine to issue the DDATTDEF command, or **E**dit to issue the DDATTE command, or E**x**tract to issue the DDATTEXT command. To use ATTREDEF, choose **F**ile, then App**l**ications, and load ATTREDEF.LSP from the \ACADWIN\SAMPLE directory; you can then enter AT or ATTREDEF to issue the command.

## Following the Attribute Exercises

This chapter's attribute exercises are straightforward. First, you set up a facility drawing in which to work. Then you learn how to define attribute definitions, how to insert a block with attributes, and how to display and edit the attributes after they are in the drawing. Finally, you learn how to extract the data in a text report. Once this is done, you redefine the block with different attributes and extract the data to a second text report.

# Setting Up for Attributes

Facility management drawings commonly employ attributes. In this chapter, imagine that you are working in the offices of the Acme Tool Co. One of your responsibilities is to maintain drawings and produce reports on the equipment in the office. This equipment includes telephones, copiers, fax machines, and computers. Each piece of equipment in the office has information—such as an identification number and name assignment—that is stored in a drawing in the form of attributes. In the following exercises, you develop a drawing that shows the telephone equipment for a small section of the office complex, and you extract a telephone report. Table 16.1 lists the information you need to store and extract in your drawing.

### Table 16.1
### Telephone Report for Acme Tool Co.

| Name | Number | Ext | Type | Status | Remarks |
|------|--------|-----|------|--------|---------|
| Not Assigned | (123) 456-7890 | 586 | Wall | In only | Employee |
| Tonya Whiteis | (123) 456-7890 | 486 | Desk | Normal | None |

*continues*

## Table 16.1
## Continued

| Name | Number | Ext | Type | Status | Remarks |
|------|--------|-----|------|--------|---------|
| Susan Driscoll | (123) 456-7890 | 386 | Desk | Normal | Ans.Mach. |
| Harriet Sands | (123) 456-7890 | 286 | Desk | Normal | None |
| Shawn Sullivan | (123) 456-7890 | 186 | Desk | Normal | None |

In this chapter, you are more concerned with manipulating the attributes associated with the graphics than with manipulating the graphic entities. Nevertheless, you still need a drawing. Create a new drawing, named OFFICE, that uses architectural units. The drawing scale factor is 24 for a scale of 1/2" = 1'-0", sized to plot on a 36"×24" sheet.

In the first exercise, you start your OFFICE drawing using the IAWOFFIC.DWG file from the IAW DISK as a prototype. It contains the office plan shown in figure 16.4 and the settings shown in table 16.2. The desks, tables and chairs are drawn with the SOLID command, for later use in the 3D chapters.

## Table 16.2
## Office Drawing Settings

| COORDS | GRID | ORTHO | SNAP | FILL | UCSICON |
|--------|------|-------|------|------|---------|
| ON | 24 | OFF | 3 | OFF | OR |

| | |
|------|-----|
| **UNITS** | Set UNITS to 4 Architectural, default the rest |
| **LIMITS** | Set LIMITS from 0,0 to 72',48' |
| **ZOOM** | Zoom All |
| **VIEW** | Save view as A |

| Layer Name | State | Color | Linetype |
|------------|-------|-------|----------|
| 0 | On | 7 (White) | CONTINUOUS |
| DATA | On | 7 (White) | CONTINUOUS |
| PLAN | On/Current | 3 (Green) | CONTINUOUS |

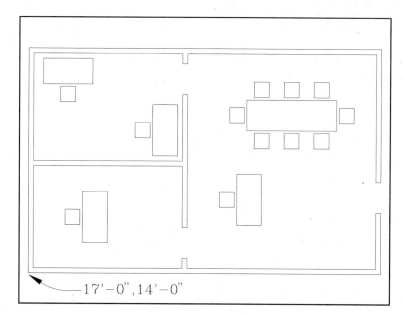

**Figure 16.4:**

The floor plan before attribute blocks are added.

17' – 0", 14' – 0"

Also on the IAW DISK is a telephone symbol in a drawing called PHN-BLK.DWG (PHoNe-BLocK). To create the attribute-laden phone block, you first insert the PHN-BLK drawing with its insertion point (the lower left corner of the phone symbol) at 0,0.

## Setting Up the Office and Telephone Symbol

*Choose* **F**ile, *then* **N**ew, *and enter*
`OFFICE=IAWOFFIC`

Makes OFFICE drawing with IAWOFFIC as its prototype

`Command:` *From the toolbar, click on the Layer button, set layer 0 current, and turn off the* PLAN *layer*

`Command:` *From the screen menu, choose* DISPLAY, *then* ZOOM:, *then* Center, *pick a point near 0,0 and specify a height of 36"*

Zooms in to work on the symbol

`Command:` *Choose* **S**ettings, *then* **D**rawing Aids, *and set snap to .25 and grid to 2"*

*continues*

Next, insert the phone using the following step:

**Command:** *Choose* **D**raw, *then* **I**nsert, *put a check in the* **E**xplode *box, clear the check from* **S**pecify Parameters On Screen, *enter* **PHN-BLK** *in the* **F**ile *input box, then choose OK twice*

Uses DDINSERT to insert exploded phone symbol at default 0,0 as shown in figure 16.5

**Figure 16.5:**

The telephone symbol.

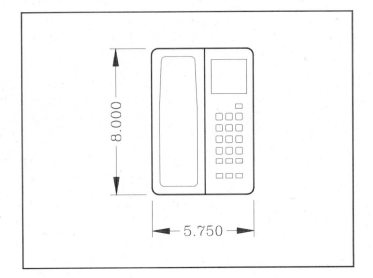

You now are ready to add attribute definitions.

# Using the ATTDEF Command To Define Attributes

To create an attribute, first use the ATTDEF command. Start by defining the EXTEN-SION attribute for the phone. Attributes have several definition modes, including normal (the initial default), Invisible, Preset, Constant, and Verify. In this drawing, define the EXTENSION attribute for the phone as normal.

## Understanding Variable Attributes

A *variable* attribute is an attribute that is not constant. You usually enter a variable attribute's value when its block is inserted, but you can change it later. You can define a value as a default that appears on the prompt line when you insert the block into the drawing. In addition, you set attribute definition modes and set text parameters to define the way the attribute appears on-screen (and in the drawing).

The process for defining variable attributes sounds more complicated than it really is. The following exercise shows you how to use the ATTDEF command to define a variable attribute.

---

## Using ATTDEF To Define a Variable Attribute

| | |
|---|---|
| Command: *From the screen menu, choose* BLOCKS, *then* ATTDEF: | Issues the ATTDEF command |
| Attribute modes - Invisible:N Constant:N Verify:N Preset:N | Displays current attribute modes |
| Enter (ICVP) to change, RETURN when done: **V** ↵ | Turns on Verify |
| Attribute modes - Invisible:N Constant:N Verify:Y Preset:N | Displays new attribute modes |
| Enter (ICVP) to change, RETURN when done: *Press Enter* | Accepts the attribute modes' settings |
| Attribute tag: **EXTENSION** ↵ | Specifies the attribute tag |
| Attribute prompt: **Enter phone extension** ↵ | Specifies the new attribute prompt |
| Default attribute value: *Press Enter* | Specifies that no default attribute value will be used |
| Justify/Style/<Start point>: **C** ↵ | Specifies the Center text option |
| Center point: **2.875,-5** ↵ | Centers the attribute under the telephone |
| Height <0'-0 3/16">: **3** ↵ | Specifies 1/8"-high text at 1/2"=1'-0" |
| Rotation angle <0>: *Press Enter* | Creates the attribute definition |

---

Your screen should show the extension attribute tag centered under the telephone, as shown in figure 16.6.

**Figure 16.6:**

The telephone
with EXTENSION
attribute
definition.

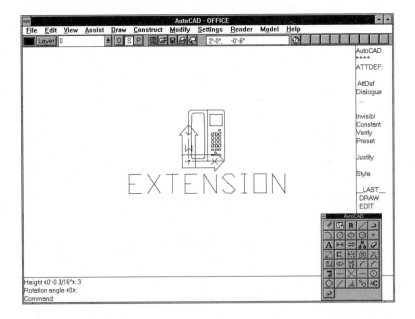

## Using Attribute Modes

Before AutoCAD prompts you to control the appearance of the attribute text, it
prompts you for several attribute modes. These modes control the attribute's visibility
and the treatment of block insertions. You can choose from the following modes:

- **Invisible.** The Invisible mode makes the attribute data invisible. Invisible mode is
  useful when you want to store data in the drawing, but you do not want to
  display or plot the data, or wait for it to regenerate.

- **Constant.** The Constant mode creates attributes with a fixed text value. Constant
  mode is helpful when you want to write boilerplate notes with attribute text. You
  cannot edit a constant attribute after it is inserted as a block without redefining
  the block. The default is Constant:N, which means the attribute is variable. You
  can edit variable attributes after you insert them by using the ATTEDIT command
  or the DDATTE dialog box.

- **Verify.** The Verify mode enables you to check variable attribute values before you
  insert them into the drawing file. If an attribute has the Verify mode, AutoCAD
  displays the attribute value on the prompt line after you type it. AutoCAD waits
  for you to press Enter before inserting the text. You can see what you have typed,
  check for errors, and correct them before the attribute is inserted.

- **Preset.** The Preset mode enables you to create attributes that automatically accept their default value. When the block is inserted, attribute values are not requested. Preset is the most flexible mode. Preset attributes function the same as Constant attributes, except that you can edit Preset attributes after you insert them by using the ATTEDIT command or the DDATTE dialog box.

Attributes can be Constant, Invisible, Preset, and Verified at the same time, or in any combination. The initial default setting is N (no) for all modes. To turn one of the ATTDEF modes on or off, type **I, C, V,** or **P,** then press Enter. AutoCAD redisplays the mode's prompt with a Y (yes) or N (no) next to the item. The last settings are saved as new default modes for the next use of ATTDEF.

# Defining Attributes

You define attributes by giving them a tag name, an optional prompt, and an optional default or constant text value. The default value is entered in the drawing, unless you provide a new value when you insert the attribute block. After you define the default value, you set its location, style, alignment, height, and angle, exactly as you do with the TEXT and DTEXT commands.

## Using Attribute Tags

Each attribute has a *tag*, such as "Name," "Employee-No.," "Extension," and "Part-Number." You can think of a tag as the name of the attribute value you insert (such as block names). The only restriction on tag names is that they cannot include blanks. Use a hyphen in place of a blank (as in "Employee-No.") to separate the tag name's elements. AutoCAD translates all tags into uppercase letters, even if you type them in lowercase letters.

## Using Attribute Prompts

In addition to naming the attribute, you can assign an instructional prompt to use at insertion time. You can assign, for example, the prompt Enter the Part Number of this widget here to the tag name "Part-Numbers." Prompts are most useful when you do not use the Enter Attributes dialog box (you use this dialog box in later exercises).

*A prompt longer than 24 characters is truncated in the Enter Attributes dialog box.*

You can use any text you want for your prompts. Gimme the number now, Dummy is as valid as Would you please enter the number here.... If you think the attribute tag name says it all, you do not need to add a prompt. The attribute tag name is used as the default prompt if you do not enter a prompt when you define the attribute. Press Enter to use the attribute tag as the attribute prompt.

## Using Default Attribute Values

When you define attributes, AutoCAD asks you for the default values. Practical defaults for variable attributes are "Not Yet Entered" or "XXX.NN". These defaults show up in the drawing if you accept the default by pressing Enter instead of entering an attribute value at the time of insertion. Constant and Preset attributes insert automatically, without showing you their default values.

## Displaying Attributes

After assigning the attribute value, AutoCAD prompts you for information about how to display attribute-value text. This series of AutoCAD prompts is identical to the standard TEXT prompts. After you set all the text parameters, AutoCAD draws the attribute on-screen just as it draws text. You can edit attribute definitions before they are blocked by using the CHANGE command or the DDEDIT dialog box.

# Creating a Block with Many Attributes

Earlier in this chapter, you defined the extension attribute as a variable attribute. Before you build the complete phone block, you need to analyze the other attribute data types you include in your phone report. Use table 16.1 as a guide to the following attribute definitions.

All the telephones have the same number in table 16.1, which makes the telephone number an obvious candidate for a Constant attribute with the value "(123) 456-7890". The rest of the attribute tags have different values; make them Variable or Preset. Define the status and remarks attributes as Preset to accept their defaults and avoid the prompt on insertion. The status and remarks attributes are not likely to change often.

The extension, telephone type, and employee name are important to this project, so keep them visible. The telephone number, status, and remarks, however, are not pertinent to your report. Define them as Invisible, so that the data is available for other reports.

## Creating the Rest of the Attribute Definitions

You create the rest of the attribute definitions in the following exercise. To start, make DATA the current layer. This change gives you the option of displaying or plotting the drawings with only the extension visible (on the layer of insertion), or of including the type and name on the DATA layer.

Look for the different attribute modes, tags, and defaults in the exercise. Notice that you can repeat the ATTDEF command to place the next line of text just below the first, just as you do for the TEXT command. Answer all the attribute-specific prompts first. Then, when the `Justify/Style/<Start point>:` prompt appears, AutoCAD highlights the last attribute-defined line on the screen. If you press Enter, the current attribute definition is placed immediately below the old one.

## Using ATTDEF To Define Attributes

First, set the DATA layer current. Next, make the NUMBER attribute Constant and Invisible, as follows.

| | |
|---|---|
| `Command:` *From the screen menu, choose* BLOCKS, *then* ATTDEF: | Issues ATTDEF command |
| `Attribute modes - Invisible:N Constant:N Verify:Y Preset:N` | Displays the current attribute modes |
| `Enter (ICVP) to change, RETURN when done:` **V** ↵ | Turns off Verify |
| `Attribute modes - Invisible:N Constant:N Verify:N Preset:N` | Displays the new attribute modes |
| `Enter (ICVP) to change, RETURN when done:` **I** ↵ | Turns on Invisible |
| `Attribute modes - Invisible:Y Constant:N Verify:N Preset:N` | |
| `Enter (ICVP) to change, RETURN when done:` **C** ↵ | Turns on Constant |
| `Attribute modes - Invisible:Y Constant:Y Verify:N Preset:N` | |
| `Enter (ICVP) to change, RETURN when done:` *Press Enter* | Accepts the attribute modes' settings |
| `Attribute tag:` **NUMBER** ↵ | Specifies the attribute tag |
| `Attribute value:` **(123) 456-7890** ↵ | Specifies the attribute value |
| `Justify/Style/<Start point>:` **6.75,20** ↵ | Specifies the starting point |
| `Height <0'-3">:` *Press Enter* | Accepts the height |
| `Rotation angle <0>:` *Press Enter* | Accepts the rotation angle |

Next, make the STATUS attribute Invisible and Preset.

| | |
|---|---|
| `Command:` *Press Enter* | Repeats the ATTDEF command |

*continues*

```
ATTDEF Attribute modes - Invisible:Y
Constant:Y Verify:N Preset:N

Enter (ICVP) to change, RETURN          Turns off Constant
when done: C ↵

Attribute modes - Invisible:Y
Constant:N Verify:N Preset:N

Enter (ICVP) to change, RETURN          Turns on Preset
when done: P ↵

Attribute modes - Invisible:Y
Constant:N Verify:N Preset:Y

Enter (ICVP) to change, RETURN
when done: Press Enter

Attribute tag: STATUS ↵

Attribute prompt: Enter status ↵

Default attribute value: Normal ↵

Justify/Style/<Start point>: Press Enter
```

Next, make the REMARKS attribute Invisible and Preset.

```
Command: Press Enter                     Repeats the ATTDEF command

ATTDEF Attribute modes - Invisible:Y
Constant:N Verify:N Preset:Y

Enter (ICVP) to change, RETURN
when done: Press Enter

Attribute tag: REMARKS ↵

Attribute prompt: Enter any remarks ↵

Default attribute value: None ↵

Justify/Style/<Start point>: Press Enter
```

Next, use the DDATTDEF command to make the NAME attribute. The DDATTDEF command displays a dialog box that defines an attribute using the same information as ATTDEF.

## Using a Dialog Box To Define Attributes

| | |
|---|---|
| Command: *From the screen menu, choose* DRAW*, then* ATTDEF:*, and then* AttDef Dialog | Issues the DDATTDEF command and displays Attribute Definition dialog box |
| *Remove the checkmarks from the* **I**nvisible *and the* **P**reset *boxes* | Turns off Invisible and Preset |
| *Enter* NAME *in the* **T**ag: *input box* | Specifies the Tag name |
| *Enter* Enter employee name *in the* **P**rompt: *input box* | Specifies the attribute prompt |
| *Enter* Not assigned *in the* **V**alue: *input box* | Specifies the default value |
| *Put a check in the* **A**lign below previous attributes *box* | Sets the new attribute location below the last one |
| *Choose* OK | Defines the attribute |

Finally, make the TYPE attribute by using DDATTDEF.

| | |
|---|---|
| Command: *Press Enter* | Repeats the DDATTDEF command |
| *Enter* TYPE *in the* **T**ag *input box* | Specifies the Tag name |
| *Enter* Enter type of phone *in the* **P**rompt *input box* | Specifies the attribute prompt |
| *Enter* Desk *in the* **V**alue *input box* | Specifies the default value |
| *Choose the* **A**lign below previous attributes *box* | Sets the new attribute below the last one |
| *Choose* OK | Defines the attribute |
| Command: *Choose* **V**iew*, then* **P**an*, if needed, and pan to see everything* | |
| Command: *From the toolbar, choose* QSAVE | |

Your screen should show all six attribute definitions, even though some of the attributes become invisible when you block the phone (see fig. 16.7).

The telephone
with the attribute
definitions.

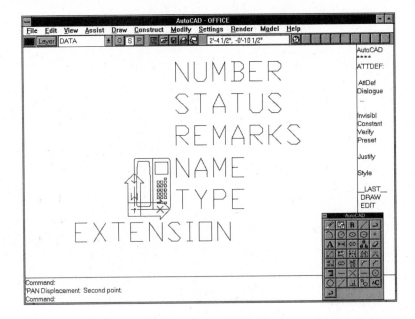

An attribute definition displays the attribute tag, but when blocked and inserted, the
attribute value is shown instead.

# Using BLOCK To Group Graphics and Attribute Definitions

The next step is to group all the graphic entities (lines, polylines, and so on) and
nongraphic entities (attribute definitions) together by using the BLOCK command.
After you block the attribute definitions, you cannot edit the definitions without a
block redefinition. Now, you can edit the attribute definitions by using the CHANGE
command or the DDEDIT or DDMODIFY dialog boxes, just as you edit strings of text.
You can also erase the attribute definitions and replace them by using the ATTDEF
command if you need to make major changes.

Block your telephone symbol and use the lower left corner as an insertion base point.
The order in which you select attribute definitions is important because the selection
order controls the prompting order when you insert the block. Name the block
PHONE.

## Using BLOCK To Group Graphics and Attribute Definitions into a Block

`Command:` *From the screen menu, choose* BLOCKS, *then* BLOCK:

`Block name (or ?):` **PHONE** ⏎

| | |
|---|---|
| `Insertion base point:` **0,0** ⏎ | Specifies the UCS point of origin |
| `Select objects:` *Pick the* NAME *attribute first* | Starts selection with the attribute definition |
| `Select objects:` *Shift-pick the* EXTENSION *attribute* | Adds to the set |
| `Select objects:` *Shift-pick the* TYPE *attribute* | Adds the attribute definition to the block |
| `Select objects:` *Shift-pick the* NUMBER *attribute* | Adds to the set |
| `Select objects:` *Shift-pick the* STATUS *attribute* | Adds to the set |
| `Select objects:` *Shift-pick the* REMARKS *attribute* | Adds to the set |
| `Select objects:` *Shift-pick entities for the* PHONE *block* | Adds entities to the set |
| `Select objects:` *Press Enter* | Defines the block from the selection set |

All graphic elements and attribute definitions disappear, just as in normal block creation.

You have just formatted your first attribute-laden block. Attribute block creation does not involve anything special, other than remembering to select the attribute definitions in the order you want them. You can block, insert, redefine an attribute block, and write to disk using WBLOCK the same way you do a normal block.

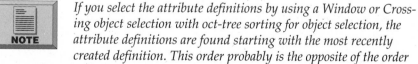

*If you select the attribute definitions by using a Window or Crossing object selection with oct-tree sorting for object selection, the attribute definitions are found starting with the most recently created definition. This order probably is the opposite of the order you want, unless you plan ahead and create them in reverse order. With oct-tree on, the selection order is unpredictable (see Chapter 8 for details).*

## Using INSERT To Insert Attribute Blocks

When the ATTDIA system variable is on 1 (the default is off or 0), you can use the Enter Attributes dialog box to enter attribute values during block insertions (see fig. 16.8). Fortunately, the dialog box enables you to edit or change the defaults in any order you want. The dialog box displays all attribute prompts and defaults (including preset attributes), except those defined as Constant. Except for the title, this dialog box is identical to the DDATTE command's Edit Attributes dialog box.

**Figure 16.8:**

The Enter Attributes dialog box.

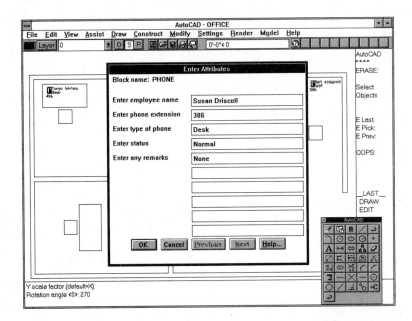

Locate the telephones in the offices by inserting them at the appropriate places in the floor plan. Turn ATTDIA on, then start by inserting the employee telephone on the wall in the conference room on the right.

### Using INSERT To Insert Attribute Blocks

Set layer 0 current and turn on the PLAN layer, then zoom to the view shown in figure 16.9.

Command: *From the screen menu, choose*     Sets the UCS to World
AutoCAD, *then* UCS:, *then* World

*Choose* **S**ettings, *then* **D**rawing
Aids, *and set snap to 6" and grid to 2'*

Command: **UCSICON** ↵

| | |
|---|---|
| `UCSicon ON/OFF/All/Noorigin/ORigin`<br>`<ON>:` **`OFF`** `↵` | Turns off the UCS icon |
| `Command:` **`ATTDIA`** `↵`<br>`New value for ATTDIA <0>:` **`1`** `↵` | Turns on Enter Attributes dialog<br>box for INSERT |
| `Command:` *Choose* **D***raw, then* **I***nsert* | Issues the INSERT command |
| *Enter* **PHONE** *in the* **B***lock input box, then*<br>*choose* OK *twice* | Specifies the PHONE |
| `Insertion point:` *Pick a point in the*<br>*upper right corner of conference room*<br>*(see fig. 16.9)* | Positions the block |
| `X scale factor <1> / Corner:`<br>*Press Enter* | Accepts the X scale |
| `Y scale factor <default=X>:`<br>*Press Enter* | Accepts the Y scale |
| `Rotation angle <0>:` *Press Enter* | Accepts the rotation angle |

The Enter Attributes dialog box automatically displays input boxes for entering the attribute values.

| | |
|---|---|
| *Enter* **586** *in the* Enter phone extension<br>*input box* | Specifies the extension |
| *Enter* **Wall** *in the* Enter type of phone<br>*input box* | Specifies the phone type |
| *Leave the employee name unchanged and*<br>*choose* OK | Inserts the block and the attributes |

Zoom in for a look (see fig. 16.10), then zoom back to the previous view.

---

The PHONE block should appear on-screen with all the attributes in their correct positions. The NUMBER, STATUS, and REMARKS attributes are invisible. They are stored in the correct position, but not displayed. If you turn off the DATA layer, only the phone symbol and extension attribute, which were created on layer 0, are visible.

Next, insert three more telephones in the following steps. Use the following list for the attributes:

| *Rotation* | *Name* | *Ext* | *Type* |
|---|---|---|---|
| 0 | Tonya Whiteis | 486 | Desk |
| 270 | Susan Driscoll | 386 | Desk |
| 270 | Harriet Sands | 286 | Desk |

**Figure 16.9:**

An inserted wall
telephone.

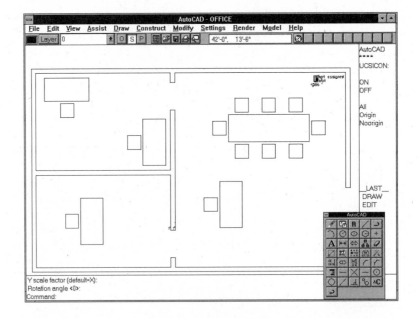

**Figure 16.10:**

A detail of the
telephone.

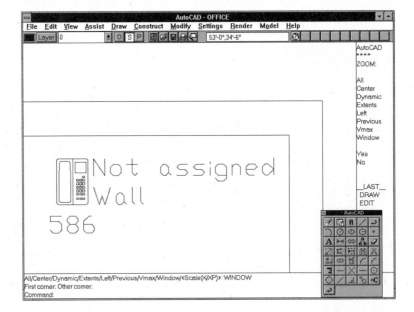

## Inserting Three More Attribute Phones

Command: *Choose* **D**raw, *then* **I**nsert,
*and insert the phone for Tonya Whiteis*
*at* ① *(see fig. 16.11)*

*Insert phone for Susan Driscoll at* ②

*Insert phone for Harriet Sands at* ③

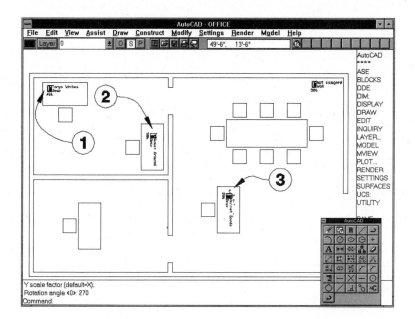

**Figure 16.11:**

Three more telephones inserted in the office.

# Using the Attribute Prompts

In the steps that follow, insert the last telephone by using the attribute prompts you entered when you first made the attribute definitions. The next steps also give you an opportunity to test the verify mode you applied to the EXTENSION attribute. The final telephone goes on the desk in the lower left office. Use the INSERT command, with the ATTDIA system variable set to 0 so that the attribute prompts display to accept attribute values in place of the Enter Attributes dialog box.

## Using Attribute Prompts To Insert an Attribute Block

```
Command: ATTDIA ↵

New value for ATTDIA <1>: 0 ↵

Command: INSERT ↵
```

Block name (or ?): *Insert the PHONE
block at ① at 270 (see fig. 16.12)*

```
Enter employee name <Not assigned>:     Specifies the value for employee name
Shawn Sullivan ↵

Enter phone extension: 186 ↵            Specifies the value for the phone extension

Enter type of phone <Desk>:             Accepts the default value
```
*Press Enter*

```
Verify attribute values

Enter phone extension <186>:            Double-checks the value of the EXTENSION
```
*Press Enter*                          attribute

Command: *Choose* **F**ile, *then* **S**ave

Shawn Sullivan's telephone should be placed on the desk shown in figure 16.12. Your screen should now show the floor plan with all five PHONE blocks.

The dialog box is easier to use than the standard insertion prompts, and sometimes faster. It enables you to accept defaults and verify entries without any overt action on your part. Later, you learn how to use the same dialog box to change values of an inserted attribute.

*You can suppress attribute prompting by setting the ATTREQ system variable to 0. This suppression forces block insertion to accept all the attribute defaults, but you still can edit attributes at a later time. If ATTREQ is set to 0, variable attribute block insertions act as if they were preset.*

*AutoCAD may truncate your attribute prompts depending on the text size set for the interface and the length of the prompt you entered in the Enter Attributes dialog box (it should be less than 24 characters).*

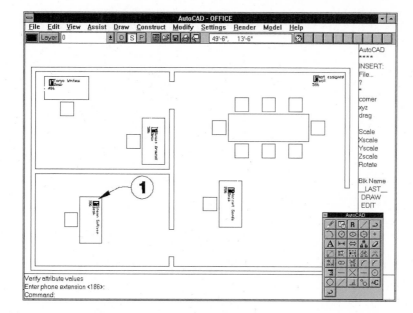

**Figure 16.12:**

The floor plan, showing five PHONE blocks.

**TIP**

*You can form an attribute block with no graphic entities in it. Simply create a block with attributes and insert it in the drawing. You can use these nongraphic blocks to automate drawing text entry, and to associate invisible or nongraphic information in a drawing. Be sure at least one attribute has a visible value when inserted, or you will insert an invisible block of attributes.*

# Using ATTDISP To Control Attribute Display Visibility

You can control an attribute's visibility by using the ATTDISP (ATTribute DISPlay) command. ATTDISP temporarily reverses visibility, turning on invisible attributes, or turning off visible attributes. To return to the default condition set by the ATTDEF command, set ATTDISP to N (for Normal).

Use ATTDISP first to turn off all attributes, then change them back to normal, then on. On forces all attributes to display. When you regenerate the screen, you can see how you have stored the STATUS, REMARKS, and other DATA layer attributes.

---

## Using ATTDISP To Control Attribute Visibility

*Zoom in on the upper left office*
*(see fig. 16.13)*

| | |
|---|---|
| Command: *From the screen menu, choose* DISPLAY, *then choose* ATTDISP: | Issues the ATTDISP command |
| Command: ATTDISP Normal/ON/OFF <Normal>: *From the screen menu, choose* OFF | Turns all attributes off |
| Regenerating drawing. | Regenerates the drawing, turning off all attributes (see fig. 16.13) |

Next, you set ATTDISP back to Normal.

| | |
|---|---|
| Command: *Press Enter* | Repeats the ATTDISP command |
| ATTDISP Normal/ON/OFF <Off>: *Choose* Normal *from the screen menu* | Displays attributes as they were defined |
| Regenerating drawing. | Returns the display to normal |
| Command: *Press Enter* | Repeats ATTDISP |
| ATTDISP Normal/ON/OFF <Normal>: *Choose* ON *from the screen menu* | Turns all attributes on |
| Regenerating drawing. | Regenerates the drawing, showing all invisible attributes (see fig. 16.14) |

---

## Using Layers To Control Attribute Display

You can extend your control of attribute visibility by putting your attribute data on different layers. Insert or define the attributes on the layer you normally keep attributes on, then use layer visibility controls to turn data on and off. Do not forget that in paper space, viewports can have independent layer visibility settings.

# Editing Attributes Using ATTEDIT

If attributes could not be edited in AutoCAD, they would not be as useful as they are. If you suddenly realized, for example, that Shawn spells his name Sean, you need some way to change the contents of the attribute. Fortunately, AutoCAD enables you to edit attributes by using the ATTEDIT command.

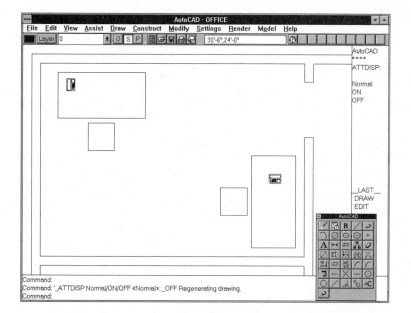

**Figure 16.13:**

The corner office, with no attributes showing.

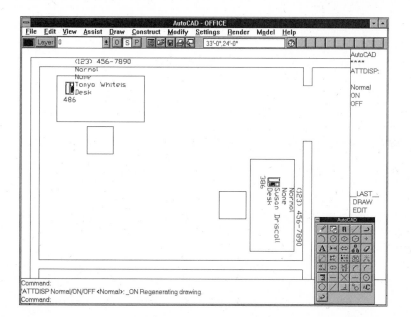

**Figure 16.14:**

The corner office, with all attributes showing.

An attribute must be displayed to be edited. It can be hidden again as soon as all editing has been completed.

The ATTEDIT (ATTribute EDIT) command enables you to change attributes. When you use ATTEDIT, you first form a selection set for editing attributes. ATTEDIT provides additional filters to help you select attributes and a graphic X cursor to identify the attribute being edited. You explore these filters and other attribute features in more detail later. For now, try a simple pick selection to change Shawn's name to Sean.

---

## Using ATTEDIT To Edit Individual Attributes

`Command:` *Choose* <u>V</u>*iew, then* <u>P</u>*an,*
*and pan down to Shawn's office*

`Command:` *From the screen menu,*            Starts the ATTEDIT command
*choose* EDIT, *then* ATTEDIT:

`Edit attributes one at a time? <Y>:`        Specifies editing attributes one at a time
*Press Enter*

`Block name specification <*>:`              Specifies all editing attribute tags
*Press Enter*

`Attribute tag specification <*>:`           Specifies editing all attributes' values
*Press Enter*

`Attribute value specification <*>:`         Specifies all attributes' values are
*Press Enter*                                available to edit

`Select Attributes:` *Choose the text*       Highlights and displays an X after
*string* Shawn Sullivan *and press*          selection (see fig. 16.15)
*Enter*

`1 attributes selected.`

`Value/Position/Height/Angle/Style/`         Specifies an editing value
`Layer/Color/Next <N>:` **V** ↵

`Change or Replace? <R>:` **C** ↵            Tells AutoCAD that you want to change the
                                             value

`String to change:` **Shawn** ↵             Specifies the old value (you cannot use wild
                                             cards here)

`New string:` **Sean** ↵                     Specifies new value

`Value/Position/Height/Angle/Style/`         Completes the name change
`Layer/Color/Next <N>:` *Press Enter*

`Command:` *Choose* <u>F</u>*ile, then* <u>S</u>*ave*

Zoom in to view the change (see fig. 16.16), then zoom back to the previous view.

---

You should notice two nice features on-screen. First, an X appears adjacent to the attribute you want to edit (see fig. 16.15). Second, AutoCAD asks if you want to change part of the attribute value text string or replace it. In this exercise, you changed part of it (see fig. 16.16).

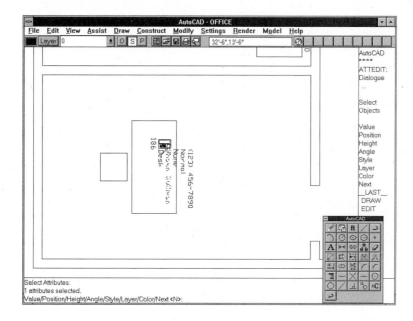

**Figure 16.15:**

A selected attribute, indicated by an X.

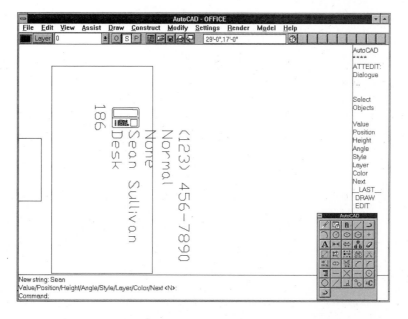

**Figure 16.16:**

A detail of the corrected attribute.

You can change much more than the text value when you edit attributes individually. Frequently, attributes overlap graphic objects. For the invisible attributes, this may not be a concern. The appearance of visible attributes, however, is an important part of your final drawing. Fortunately, you can use ATTEDIT to fine-tune their appearance by changing the text position and angle, the text style, height, layer, and color.

In the preceding exercise, you changed Sean's name fairly easily. What if you want to make global changes, such as change the 86 in all the extensions to 68, or selectively change 86 to 68 only on employee phones throughout the building?

# Making Global Attribute Edits with ATTEDIT

Your facility drawing has only five telephones; individually picking each attribute for editing is not a problem. An entire office complex might have 500 telephones. A considerable amount of time would be needed to edit five hundred attributes individually. You could gather all the tags named EXTENSION and do the replacement in one window—or could you? You could if you were able to tell AutoCAD exactly which characters in the EXTENSION attribute you want to edit. In other words, you need to set up a selection set filled with just the precise group. Regular selection set techniques do not work for this type of task.

## Using Wild Cards To Edit Attributes Selectively

Instead of individually picking attributes from the screen, you can use a combination of wild-card filters and standard selection set options to select your attributes. The following common scenarios can be used:

- Select all attributes in blocks with a name you specify (wild cards are acceptable). Use * to select all blocks.

- Select all attributes that match a tag name you specify (wild cards are acceptable). Use * to select all tag names.

- Select all attributes that match a specified value (wild cards are acceptable). Use * to select all values.

- Narrow the selection process further by picking an individual attribute object, or by using the Window, Last, Crossing, or BOX options.

- Use any combination of the selection options described previously.

You can narrow the field of attributes you want to edit by using wild cards to filter the selection. The following wild cards are available:

| Wild card | Meaning |
|-----------|---------|
| @ | Matches any alphanumeric character. |
| # | Matches any number. |
| * | Matches any string, even an empty (null) string. You can use an asterisk at the beginning, middle, or end of a string. |
| . | Matches any nonalphanumeric character. |
| ? | Matches any single character. |
| ~ | Matches any character but the one that follows the tilde. The string ~?86, for example, matches any telephone extension except those ending in 86. |
| [ ] | Matches any single instance of any characters you enclose between the brackets, such as [xyz] to match either an x, y, or z. |
| [~ ] | Matches anything except any enclosed characters. |
| - | Matches a range of characters when used in brackets, such as [1-5] to match 1, 2, 3, 4, or 5. |
| ' | Matches the special character that follows, such as '? matches a ? instead of using the ? as a wild card. |

You can use individual wild cards or combine them. Do not be overwhelmed by the possibilities; you usually use the question mark and asterisk. The other wild cards are available if you need them.

## Using Tag Selection To Edit Attributes

After you select and filter your attributes, AutoCAD prompts you to edit them. If you ask for individual editing (the default), AutoCAD prompts for your changes one at a time. As you saw in the preceding exercise, you can tell which attribute you are editing by looking for the highlighting or X on-screen.

Use AutoCAD's attribute-editing capabilities to change the wall phone status from "Normal" to "Incoming only" by following the next exercise. Narrow your attribute selection by specifying the STATUS attribute to edit, then select all five workstations with a window. Watch the X cursor to know which attribute AutoCAD wants you to edit. Use the <N>, which is the Next default, to skip to the wall phone status. Change the text value of the wall phone status. Then, use the <N> to skip past the rest, or terminate ATTEDIT by pressing Ctrl-C.

## Using an Attribute Tag To Specify an Attribute Edit

Command: *Choose* <u>V</u>iew, *then*                     Displays the entire office
<u>Z</u>oom, *then* <u>E</u>xtents

Command: **ATTEDIT:** ↵

Edit attributes one at a time? <Y>:
*Press Enter*

Block name specification <*>:
*Press Enter*

Attribute tag specification <*>:          Specifies editing only the attribute tag
**STATUS** ↵                               STATUS

Attribute value specification <*>:
*Press Enter*

Select Attributes: *Enter* W *and select*    Specifies attributes to edit
*all phones by using a window*

5 attributes selected.

Value/Position/Height/Angle/Style    Moves the X to the next attribute
/Layer/Color/Next <N>: *Press Enter*
*until an* X *is on the wall phone*
*(see fig. 16.17)*

Value/Position/Height/Angle/Style    Specifies Value
/Layer/Color/Next <N>: **V** ↵

Change or Replace? <R> *Press Enter*      Specifies Replace

New attribute value:                 Specifies a new value
**Incoming only** ↵

Value/Position/Height/Angle/Style    Ends the ATTEDIT command
/Layer/Color/Next <N>: *Press Enter*

Zoom in to view the wall phone (see fig. 16.18), then zoom back to the previous view.

The preceding editing sequence is convenient if you are making selective changes to many attributes. If you have a change that applies to all or a filterable subset of a large group of attributes, however, you can use a global selection.

The following exercise shows you how to make a division-wide reorganization by changing the last two digits in all the telephone extensions from "86" to "68". Use the default * wild card and a window to include all your telephone extensions.

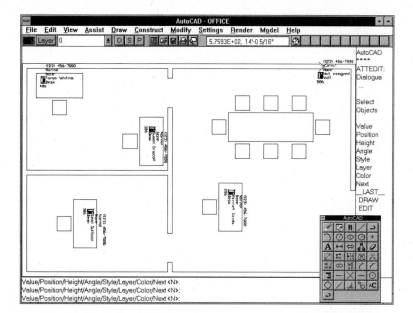

**Figure 16.17:**

Editing the wall phone by its tag.

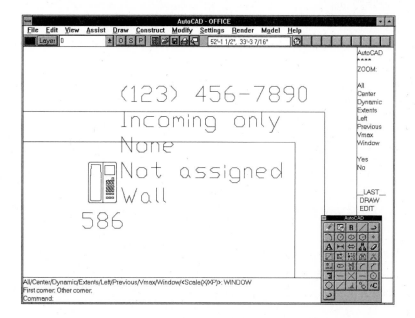

**Figure 16.18:**

A detail of the wall phone.

---

# Using ATTEDIT for a Global Edit

Command: **ATTEDIT** ⏎

Edit attributes one at a time?          Edits all attributes globally
<Y>: N

Global edit of Attribute values.

Edit only Attributes visible on          Specifies editing only attributes on-screen
screen? <Y>:  *Press Enter*

Even though all the attributes are on-screen, you have the option to include those off-screen.

Block name specification <*>:
*Press Enter*

Attribute tag specification <*>:          Limits the selection to the specified tag
**EXTENSION** ⏎

Attribute value specification <*>:
*Press Enter*

Select Attribute: *Enter* W *and select
all the telephones by using a window*

5 attributes selected.

String to change: **86** ⏎          Specifies old text string

New string: **68** ⏎          Specifies new text string

Zoom in to examine the wall phone (see fig. 16.19), then use the ZOOM Previous option to resume the previous view.

---

All your extensions now should end in 68. If you want to change all but the wall phone (extension 586), enter **~586** at the Attribute value specification prompt.

# Using the Attribute Dialog Box To Edit Attributes

You can use the DDATTE dialog box to edit attributes. DDATTE presents the Edit Attributes dialog box, which is the same as the Enter Attributes dialog box you used when you inserted the first PHONE blocks earlier in this chapter. You can edit the text string values of any number of attributes, but you can edit only the text string values of one block at a time. If you use a window selection, AutoCAD edits only the first block it finds.

In the following exercise, use the dialog box to edit two preset REMARKS attributes.

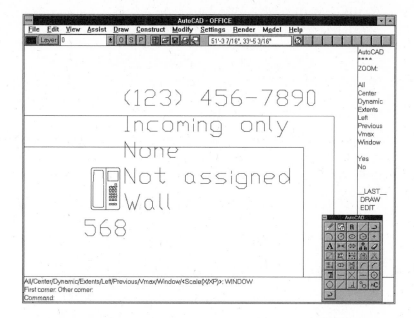

**Figure 16.19:**
A detail of the wall phone.

## Using the DDATTE Dialog Box To Edit Attributes

`Command:` *From the screen menu, choose* EDIT, *then* DDATTE:

Issues the DDATTE command

`DDATTE Select block:` *Select the wall phone*

The Edit Attributes dialog box appears (see fig. 16.20)

*Enter* Employee *in the* Enter any remarks *input box*

Changes the attribute value

*Choose* OK

Closes the dialog box

`Command:` *Press Enter*

Repeats DDATTE

When the DDATTE `Select block:` prompt appears, select Susan's phone, and enter **Answering machine** in the Enter any remarks input box. When you are finished, choose OK.

`Command:` *From the screen menu, choose* DISPLAY, *then* ATTDISP:, *then* Normal

Sets ATTDISP back to normal

`Command:` **QSAVE**

**Figure 16.20:**

Editing attributes by using the Edit Attributes dialog box.

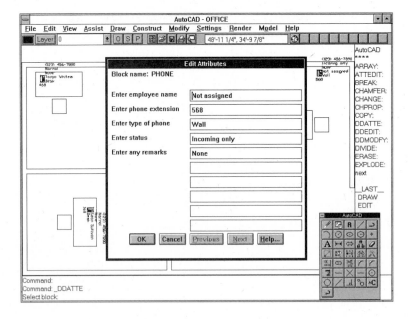

## Plotting the Office Drawing

If you want to see how AutoCAD plots attributes, make a quick plot of your office plan. AutoCAD offers four ways to plot the drawing attribute data:

- Turn off all the attributes

- Plot the extension number, employee name and phone type (Normal)

- Plot the extension number only (layer 0)

- Turn on all the attributes

The next step is to extract the data to format a telephone report, similar to a simple telephone directory or part of an equipment report. You also use this office drawing in Part Five of the book, when you extrude it into a 3D drawing.

# Using the ATTEXT Command To Extract Attributes

Although the ATTEXT command sounds like a text operation, it stands for ATTribute EXTraction. ATTEXT provides a way to extract attribute information from the drawing file and print that information in a text report. In addition to ATTEXT, another command, DDATTEXT, performs the same function with the Attribute Extraction dialog box. DDATTEXT is used later in the chapter.

# Setting Up an Attribute Report

When you set up the facility drawing earlier in the chapter, you listed in a simple table the data for the employee names, status, remarks, type, and extension for each of the five telephones. Similar kinds of tables form the basis for bills of materials (BOM), lists, schedules, and specifications that regularly accompany professional drawings. These tables organize the data scattered around drawing files.

# Examining ATTEXT Formats

AutoCAD provides three ways to extract attribute values from a drawing file and format them in a disk file. You can print these lists or use the data in other programs, such as dBASE III or IV, Lotus 1-2-3, or a word processor. You can also put the list into a table and bring it back into your drawing. The following attribute extraction formats are templates that define the way the data is formatted in the extracted text file:

- **CDF (Comma Delimited Format).** CDF is easy to use with BASIC programs or with dBASE's "APPEND FROM . . . DELIMITED" operation. (See the following example.)

- **SDF (Standard Data Format).** SDF is for FORTRAN and other programs that read a dBASE "COPY . . . SDF" file, or a dBASE "APPEND FROM . . . SDF" operation. (See the following example.)

- **DXF (Drawing Interchange Format).** DXF is a subset of AutoCAD's full DXF file format that is used by many third-party programs.

You can extract data in any format suitable for your application. Many users (and vendors of third-party software) now have applications built around AutoCAD by using one or more of these data extraction interfaces.

# Extracting Attribute Data Using CDF or SDF

CDF creates a file that has commas separating the data fields in the attribute extraction. The following is a simple example of a CDF format:

## CDF Format

```
'Name1','Type1','Extension1'

'Name2','Type2','Extension2'

 ...

 ...

 ...

'Name9','Type9','Extension9'

'Name10','Type10','Extension10'
```

To format extract files, you need to place alphanumeric characters, commas, and spaces. In the CDF format, each data field is separated by a comma. The spacing of the data field is dependent on the data width in the field. Name10 in the preceding example takes up more room than Name9.

The SDF format creates a file similar to CDF, but without commas and with a standard field length and spacing, as shown in the following list.

### SDF Format

```
Name1    Type1    Extension1

Name2    Type2    Extension2

...      ...      ...

...      ...      ...

Name9    Type9    Extension9

Name10   Type10   Extension10
```

In SDF format, the data field length is standardized and preformatted to a standard value, regardless of the data value length. If the data exceeds the length, the data is truncated.

## Creating an Attribute Report Template File

Before you can extract attributes, AutoCAD needs a template file to create the SDF or CDF file. The template file is a format instruction list that tells AutoCAD what to put where in the extract data file. The IAW DISK contains a template file called PHONE.TXT. This file provides an SDF template for the telephone data, which you can use to create the report.

This file was created as an ASCII text file. You can create similar files by using EDLIN, EDIT (in DOS 5), Notepad, Write, or your word processor. Use spaces, not tabs. Make sure you end the last line of your file with a return character (↵). Also, make sure you do not have any extra spaces at the end of lines, or extra returns after the last line of text.

Table 16.3 shows the PHONE.TXT template file for your sample telephone data. The template assumes that NAME comes first, TYPE second, and EXTENSION third. The NUMBER, STATUS, and REMARKS are not included in the report.

## Table 16.3
## Viewing an SDF Template File

| | |
|---|---|
| BL:NAME | C011000 |
| BL:X | N006002 |
| DUMMY1 | C002000 |
| BL:Y | N006002 |
| DUMMY2 | C002000 |
| NAME | C015000 |
| TYPE | C008000 |
| EXTENSION | N005000 |

If you look at the right column, you can easily decipher the formatting information. The first C or N says this is a character or a number. The next three digits (011 in the BL:NAME line) tell the number of spaces to leave for the data. The final three digits specify the number of decimal places for floating point (decimal) numeric data. Integer data have 000 in the last three columns.

The BL:X and BL:Y are not blocks or attributes. They extract the X,Y coordinate values for the block.

DUMMY1 and DUMMY2 only appear in the template file. They are not blocks or attributes; they are used to provide space in the report. These dummy lines force a two-space blank between the X,Y coordinates (BL:X,BL:Y) and a two-space blank between the Y coordinate and the NAME, making the output easier to read.

Table 16.4 shows the complete list of the kinds of data that ATTEXT or DDATTEXT can extract.

## Table 16.4
## ATTEXT Template Fields

| Field | Data Type | Description | Field | Data Type |
|---|---|---|---|---|
| BL:LEVEL | integer | Block nesting level | BL:XSCALE | decimal |
| BL:NAME | character | Block name | BL:YSCALE | decimal |
| BL:X | decimal | X insert coord | BL:ZSCALE | decimal |

*continues*

**Table 16.4**
**Continued**

| Field | Data Type | Description | Field | Data Type |
|-------|-----------|-------------|-------|-----------|
| BL:Y | decimal | Y insert coord | BL:XEXTRUDE | decimal · |
| BL:Z | decimal | Z insert coord | BL:YEXTRUDE | decimal |
| BL:NUMBER | integer | Block counter | BL:ZEXTRUDE | decimal |
| BL:HANDLE | character | Entity handle | *attribute* | integer |
| BL:LAYER | character | Insertion layer | *attribute* | character |
| BL:ORIENT | decimal | Rotation angle | | |

Integer fields are formatted Nwww000, floating point (decimal) fields are Nwwwddd, and character fields are Cwww000, in which www is overall width (such as 012 for 12 characters wide and 000 is 000) and ddd is the width to the right of the decimal point.

# Extracting the Data File

After you have the template file, you can extract data for all or some of the attributes. If you have the PHONE.TXT file, switch to AutoCAD. Extract the attribute data into a file called PHN-DATA.

## Using ATTEXT To Create an SDF Data File

`Command:` *From the screen menu, choose*
UTILITY, *then* ATTEXT:

`ATTEXT CDF, SDF, or DXF Attribute`          Specifies a space-delimited file and displays
`extract (or Entities) <C>:` **S** ↵          the Select Template File dialog box

*Select the file* PHONE.TXT *in your*          Selects the template and displays the
\IAW *directory and choose* OK          Create Extract File dialog box

*Enter* PHN-DATA *in the* File **N**ame          Specifies the *input* extract file name
*box and choose* **O**K          and saves the file to disk

`5 records in extract file.`

`Command:` **SAVE** ↵

In the preceding exercise, if you enter an E for entities, AutoCAD prompts for object selection to extract data from specific blocks, and then prompts for CDF, SDF, or DXF.

*Do not use the same name for your template file as that of your extract file, or the extract file overwrites the template.*

The extracted SDF report file is shown in the following list. You can examine the file by using a text editor or your word processor. Take a look at your data text file.

### SDF Report Example

| | | | | | |
|-------|--------|--------|--------------|------|-----|
| PHONE | 408.33 | 435.79 | Not assigned | Wall | 568 |
| PHONE | 60.00  | 441.00 | Tonya Whiteis | Desk | 468 |
| PHONE | 198.00 | 396.00 | Harriet Sands | Desk | 268 |
| PHONE | 303.00 | 318.00 | Susan Driscoll | Desk | 368 |
| PHONE | 123.00 | 294.00 | Sean Sullivan | Desk | 168 |

Notice that the extracted data gives useful spatial information about this drawing as well as the attribute data. The X and Y data fields give the X and Y insertion points of each PHONE block. Your X,Y fields can vary from the ones shown here, depending on where you insert the blocks. The PHONE column is set up to print the name of the block that acts as the attribute data source. The PHONE column has character data (see the C in the template) and an 11-character print width.

The next two columns give the X and Y locations of the block insertion point in numeric form (see N in the template). (Your data can vary from the example.) The X and Y data have two decimal places and the decimal point in a six-character print width. The X and Y fields and the employee name would all run together if the two-character dummy fields were not included. The other extracted attribute fields (a character field and a numeric field) are in the last two columns. If an employee's name is unusually long, you can see that the name would be truncated by the print width.

## Redefining a Block with Attributes

Redefining a block without attributes is as simple as creating the geometry and using the BLOCK command. To redefine the attributes in a block, you can insert the block exploded, edit its attribute definitions, and then use BLOCK or the AutoLISP-defined ATTREDEF command to redefine it.

In this exercise, use DDEDIT to redefine the attribute REMARKS to BUILDING. Once this is done, use ATTREDEF to redefine the block and update the drawing.

## Using DDEDIT To Edit an Attribute

Command: *Issue the ZOOM command
and zoom to a center point of 46',18'
and a height of 6'*

Command: **INSERT** ↵

Block name (or ?): **\*PHONE** ↵               The * specifies an exploded block insertion

Insertion point: **46',18'** ↵

Scale factor: *Press Enter*

Rotation angle <0>: *Press Enter*          Displays the block and attribute definitions

Use DDEDIT to change the values of the attribute definition.

Command: *From the screen menu,*          Starts the DDEDIT command
*choose EDIT, then DDEDIT:*

<Select a TEXT or ATTDEF object>      Specifies the attribute definition to modify
/Undo: *Select the attribute definition*
REMARKS

*Enter* BUILDING *in the* Tag *input box*       Replaces REMARKS

*Enter* Enter building name *in the*       Specifies the new prompt
Prompt *dialog box*

*Enter* Green Tree *in the* Default         Specifies the default value
*dialog box*

*Choose* OK                                 Closes the dialog box and makes the  changes
                                            (see fig. 16.21)

---

The ATTREDEF command is an AutoLISP program that must be loaded before use. You can load it from the File menu's Applications selection. Once you load the ATTREDEF command, you can modify the attributes associated with a block, redefine the block, and AutoCAD updates the entire drawing.

Load the ATTREDEF command and redefine the phone block and associated attributes.

## Using ATTREDEF To Redefine Attributes in a Block

Command: *Choose* File, *then* Applications,      Clears file list and displays Select LISP/ADS
*then* File                                       Routine dialog box

Clear the Save list box, then select any existing file names and choose Remove.

*In the directories list, double-click on*          Displays the files in the SAMPLE subdirectory
*the* C:\, *then* ACADWIN, *then*
SAMPLE C:

| | |
|---|---|
| *In the* **F**iles *list, double-click on* ATTREDEF.LSP, *then choose* **L**oad | Loads the ATTREDEF command |
| Command: **AT** ↵ | Starts the ATTREDEF command |
| Name of Block you want to redefine: **PHONE** ↵ | |
| Select entities for new Block... | |
| Select objects: *Select all the attribute definitions and the phone geometry* | Specifies the new block definition |
| Select objects: *Press Enter* | |
| Insertion base point of new Block: *Pick the lower left corner of the phone* | |

*Zoom to the previous view*

The finished drawing, with ATTDISP set to ON, should now look like figure 16.22. The attributes now display "Green Tree" instead of "None".

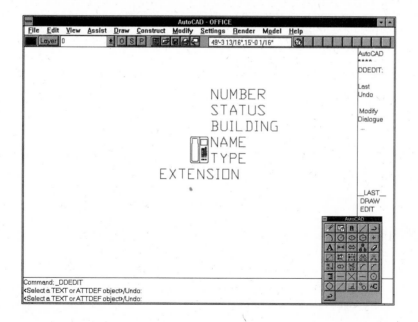

**Figure 16.21:**

The redefined attribute definition.

**Figure 16.22:**

The redefined
blocks and
attributes.

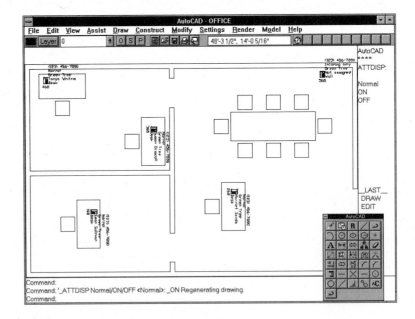

# Attributes versus DXF, DXB, and IGES Drawing Data Exchange

AutoCAD provides additional methods for extracting spatial and graphic data from the drawing file. Block layers and block levels (levels of nesting for nested blocks, block rotation, and scale) are extractable. These spatial attributes are useful for handing off data to engineering programs in which the block orientation or relationship among drawing entities is as critical as the text or numeric data associated with the block.

DXF, AutoCAD's Drawing Interchange Format, is used in many add-on programs and for drawing file exchange. You use the DXFOUT command to extract the DXF file from a drawing. An ATTEXT DXF file includes only block reference and attribute information, but the DXFOUT command exports either the full drawing file or selected entities. A full DXFOUT creates a complete ASCII text description of the drawing. DXFOUT also utilizes a binary option to create a more compact binary file for faster processing by sophisticated third-party programs.

The DXFIN command imports a DXF file. You can use DXFIN to import an entire drawing, but this requires a new drawing file, created by starting a new drawing with no prototype, such as *NAME* = ↵. You can use DXFIN to import into an existing drawing, but you get the following message:

```
Not a new drawing - only ENTITIES section will be input
```

In such a partial DXF import, data such as block definitions and layer information are not imported. A partial import functions the same as an insert, in which the current drawing definitions override the imported definitions.

The IGES format is another drawing exchange format. You get data in and out by using the IGESIN and IGESOUT commands. IGES is not perfect, and you usually need to edit the resulting drawing. IGESOUT loses attribute definitions and solid fills, and 3D data may be represented differently. When you register your AutoCAD program, you receive a detailed IGES Interface Specifications document.

DXB, another file format used by AutoCAD, is a binary drawing file format. DXBIN imports binary drawing files. You can output a limited DXB format file (everything converted to straight line segments) by configuring the AutoCAD file output for an ADI driver and selecting AutoCAD DXB file as the output format.

To learn more about DXF and other types of file exchange with AutoCAD, see Chapter 19 and *Maximizing AutoLISP*, from New Riders Publishing.

# The AutoCAD SQL Extension (ASE)

In addition to attributes, AutoCAD has a Structured Query Language (SQL) extension. Through the use of SQL, AutoCAD can directly pass information back and forth with a traditional relational database. SQL enables a direct linkage between the graphical information in AutoCAD and the nongraphical information in the relational database. This information need not be associated only with a block.

The advantage of this system is a smaller drawing, because the nongraphical information can be stored in the relational database. Information is shared directly between AutoCAD and the relational database, which increases speed, accuracy, and flexibility. Finally, an expansion in the type of data is enabled because the SQL extension can share any type of graphical data—not just that type stored in a block.

# Summary

Attributes provide power and flexibility for annotating your drawings and producing reports. When you use attributes, you make AutoCAD manage both graphic and nongraphic information.

To better use and organize attributes, design your report formats before you define attributes. Develop a rough table to plan ahead for field name, size, and prompting. Good layout and design of attribute fields is critical to creating a useful attribute file. Test your extraction before you fill up your drawing with information in a format you cannot use.

Place your attribute definitions on different layers or create them with different colors to distinguish them from regular text. The names you use for tags are important; try to make them explanatory but also brief. The tag name is the default prompt when no other prompt is given, and it is used in attribute edits and extracts. Break your attribute data into useful fields. Use enough fields to capture all the variable information you need. Avoid fields filled with extra long strings of output.

ATTEDIT is an extremely flexible and powerful command. When you work with this command, make sure you check your results often. You can easily introduce an ATTEDIT error that creates global havoc. You can have AutoCAD prompt you for all changes if you take advantage of grouping attributes by layer, tag name, and value.

Use attributes in place of normal text for standardized boilerplate entries and title blocks. Attributes offer more input control, automation, and sophisticated editing than regular text does.

This chapter has shown you how to do more with AutoCAD than just create and plot drawings. In the next chapter, you learn how to make the most of AutoCAD's dimensioning commands, as well as the important role that associative dimensions play in your design process.

# Advanced Dimensioning

In Chapter 15, you learned to use AutoCAD's basic dimensioning commands to create linear and radial dimensions. Chapter 15 also introduced you to the use of dimension variables to control the appearance and other characteristics of dimensions. The complexity of working with so many dimension variables, however, can be hard to control. This chapter teaches you how to control dimension variables by introducing you to AutoCAD's dimension styles.

You also learn how to use several advanced dimensioning commands that were not examined in Chapter 15. AutoCAD's commands for creating ordinate, baseline, and chain dimensions, among others, are covered in this chapter's exercises. Perhaps the most important topic in this chapter is the topic of associative dimensions. As you soon learn, *associative dimensions* enable you to update an object or feature while its associated dimensions automatically update to reflect the change as well.

AutoCAD gives you a variety of choices for accessing dimensioning commands and variables. Pull-down menus and dialog boxes with easy-to-follow controls are available, but they require several steps to issue the commands and variables (see fig. 17.1). You also can use screen menus. If you know the command and variable names, you can enter them directly from the keyboard, abbreviating the commands if you like. The exercises in this chapter demonstrate all three methods; therefore, you can decide which method you prefer.

**Figure 17.1:**

One of AutoCAD's many dimensioning dialog boxes.

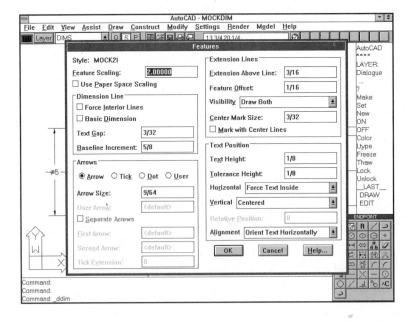

Before you begin using the advanced dimensioning commands, however, you should have a good understanding of dimension styles. The following discussion introduces you to this convenient AutoCAD feature.

# Saving Sets of Dimension Variables as Dimension Styles

Even with the help of dialog boxes, dimension variables can be a nuisance to set. Many effects you want to achieve do not depend on a single setting, but rather on many dimension variable settings working together. Remembering all of the combinations necessary for the variety of dimensioning in a typical drawing is difficult at best. Fortunately, the dimension settings in most drawings can be grouped into a few types. AutoCAD's dimension style feature enables you to save named sets of dimension variable settings. (All settings except DIMASO and DIMSHO are saved with the dimension style.) Dimension styles enable you to easily save as many different groups of settings for as many types of dimensions as you need. You also can restore any style at will.

Furthermore, associative dimensioning saves dimension styles along with the dimension entities. This feature protects the style of the associative dimension from accidental changes while you edit the drawing. It also enables you to update a style simply by selecting a dimension entity that uses it. Associative dimensions are described in detail later in this chapter.

When you save a style, you must assign it a name. The default style name is *UN-NAMED, which is not saved in associative dimension entities. Any time you change a dimension variable, it creates a new *UNNAMED style. If you want the dimensions to be protected from change, always have a named style current when you create new dimensions. The easiest way to manage dimension styles is to use the Dimension Styles Variables dialog box. Use the DDIM command or choose **S**ettings, then Di**m**ension Style to display this dialog box.

In the following exercise, load the MOCKDIM drawing you created at the end of Chapter 15, then save the current settings as a style named MOCK2I (2 for half scale, I for Inside text because DIMSCALE and DIMTIX were the only significant deviations from the defaults). If you have not yet created MOCKDIM, you only need to perform the last exercise in Chapter 15 to create it.

## Saving the Current Dimension Variables
## as Dimension Style MOCK2I

| | |
|---|---|
| Command: *Choose* **F**ile, *then* **O**pen, *then select the file* MOCKDIM | Loads the drawing MOCKDIM |
| Command: *Choose* **S**ettings, *then* Di**m**ension Style | Issues DDIM, which displays the Dimension Styles and Variables dialog box |
| *In the* **D**imension Style *edit box, enter* **MOCK2I** | Assigns a name to the current settings and creates a style |

The message New style MOCK2I created from *UNNAMED appears at the bottom of the dialog box when you press Enter, and the new style name appears in the list box in place of *UNNAMED.

| | |
|---|---|
| *Choose* OK | Closes the dialog box |
| Command: **QSAVE** ↵ | Saves the drawing |

Dimension styles are that easy to save. When a new style is named, its settings are the same as the current one until some changes are made in the dimension variables. Do not, however, confuse the dimension mode SAVE style command with the drawing file SAVE command.

You can restore dimension styles by using the Restore dimensioning command or the Dimension Styles and Variables dialog box. You define and save styles within the drawing, not as separate files on disk such as you do with text fonts or linetypes. Later in this chapter, however, you learn how to save dimension styles within drawing files that you can use as dimension style storage files.

# Creating a Dimension Style for Paper Space Dimensioning

Sometimes you may want to dimension objects in a model space viewport while you are preparing to plot in paper space. Most of the preparation is the same as in the plotting chapter in which you composed a paper space plot sheet. You learned to set up the viewport and scale its contents relative to the paper space sheet with Zoom XP.

*One disadvantage of dimensioning in paper space versus an mview viewport or tilemode is that associative dimensions are not tied to the model space objects and not automatically updated when the drawing is edited.*

Two features make dimensioning model space objects from paper space possible. First, you can snap to model space from paper space by using object snap. Second, a special feature of the DIMLFAC dimension variable also adjusts the dimensions measured in model space to the scale factor of the viewport. DIMLFAC is a factor by which all measurements are multiplied before dimension text is generated. This global scale factor enables dimensioning at scales other than the current units. Usually this factor is set to 1. If DIMLFAC is set to a negative value, it multiplies all paper space dimensions by the absolute value of that value. (Model space dimensioning ignores a negative setting and uses 1, so you do not have to create a separate dimension style for this purpose.) To simplify setting for paper space, the DIMLFAC dimension variable enables you to select a viewport, and then it calculates the value for you.

The following exercise sets up an mview viewport and new layer for dimensioning the section view of MOCKDIM from paper space. The existing dimensions on the DIMS layer are then frozen in the new viewport.

## Setting Up for Paper Space Dimensioning

| | |
|---|---|
| Command: *Choose* **V**iew, *then* **T**ilemode | Turns TILEMODE off and enters paper space |
| Command: *From the screen menu, choose* MVIEW: | |
| ON/OFF/Hideplot/Fit/2/3/4/Restore/ <First Point>: *Pick points 3,2 and 10,8* | Defines a viewport and displays the drawing |
| Command: **MS** ↵ | Enters model space |
| Command: *Select the 3 1/32 rotated dimension, then issue the ERASE command* | Erases the dimension |

| | |
|---|---|
| Command: *Use ZOOM and enter a zoom scale factor of* .5XP | Zooms the image to half-scale relative to paper space |
| Command: *Choose* **V**iew, *then* **P**an, *and pan from right to left to match figure 17.2* | |
| Command: *From the toolbar, click on* Layer, *create a new layer named* PSDIMS *with color magenta, and set it current* | Opens Modify Layer dialog box and creates layer |
| *Deselect* PSDIMS *and select* DIMS *in the list box, and click on* Cur VP **F**rz, *then choose* OK | Freezes DIMS in the current viewport |
| Command: **DDIM** ↵ | Displays the Dimension Styles and Variables dialog box |
| *Click on* MOCK2I *in the list box* | Selects the MOCK2I style |
| *Choose* Text F**o**rmat, *double-click in the* Length **S**caling *edit box, and enter* **2** | Displays the Text Format dialog box and sets the inverse of .5 ZOOM XP factor |
| *Choose* OK *twice* | Closes the dialog box and saves changes as MOCK2I |
| Command: **PS** ↵ | Enters paper space |

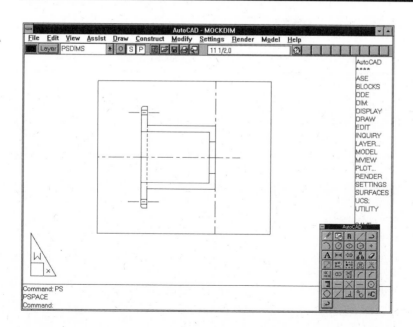

**Figure 17.2:**

An mview viewport set up for paper space dimensioning.

# Changing Styles with Dimension Variables

If you change any dimension variable at the Command: or Dim: prompts, a new *UN-NAMED style is created. Any change made in the Dimension Styles and Variables dialog box (the DDIM command), however, changes the settings of the currently selected style. Unfortunately, this makes it difficult to use the dialog box when you want to make only a couple of variable changes to apply to only one or two dimensions. When you create a new style with the dialog box, it inherits the settings of the previously current style, and you can then make changes to that new style. However, you may not want to create a new style each time you encounter such a situation. The solution is to apply the current settings to a new *UNNAMED style.

*In the DDIM dialog box, to create a new *UNNAMED style, select the style on which you want to base the new style, make the settings changes you want, and exit the dialog box by choosing OK. The selected style's dimensions are updated, but you then use the U (Undo) command to reverse that update. Fortunately, the settings changes you made in the dialog box are not undone in the resulting *UNNAMED style, which is now current. See the "Overriding a Dimension Style" exercise for an example.*

# Placing Ordinate Dimensions

Now you are ready to create some ordinate dimensions of the section. *Ordinate dimensions* (sometimes called *datum dimensions*) are a series of dimensions that are offset from a common base point, without dimension lines. They have only one extension line—a leader on which the dimension text is placed. The dimension text is always aligned with the leader, regardless of the values of the dimension variables DIMTIH and DIMTOH. Ordinate dimensions measure the X datum or Y datum of the point you specify from the current 0,0 origin. Use UCS to place the current origin at the desired base point and object snap to ensure accurate datum points. Use ortho to ensure straight leader lines. Otherwise, if you pick a point for the end of the leader that is not in line with the dimension point, AutoCAD draws an offset line or "dogleg" as the leader. Doglegs can be useful, however, for avoiding overlapping dimension text in closely spaced dimensions.

In the following exercise, enter paper space and add a few ordinate dimensions to the section view. Set the UCS, using XYZ point filters to get the bottom left corner at the chamfer. Pick all the dimension leader endpoints so that they line up. Turn ortho off for the last dimension, however, to keep it clear of the top one.

## Placing Ordinate Dimensions

*Issue ZOOM with the Extents option to fill paper space with the viewport, and turn snap off*

| | |
|---|---|
| `Command:` *Choose* **S**ettings, *then* U**C**S, *then* **I**con, *and then* Ori**g**in | Sets UCSICON to Origin |
| `Command:` *Choose* **S**ettings, *then* U**C**S, *then* **O**rigin | Issues the UCS Origin prompt |
| `Origin point <0,0,0>:` **.X** ↵ of *Use the INT object snap to pick at* ① *(see fig.17.3)* | Specifies an X filter |
| `(need YZ):` *Use the INT object snap to pick at point* ② | Moves the UCS to the corner (see fig. 17.3) |
| `Command:` *Choose* **S**ettings, *then* **D**rawing Aids, *set* **S**nap *to 1/8 and turn it on, then turn on* **O**rtho, *and choose* OK | |
| `Command:` *Choose* **D**raw, *then* Di**m**ensions, *then* **O**rdinate, *then* **Y**-Datum | Enters dimensioning mode and issues the ORDINATE command with the Y-datum option |
| `Dim: _ordinate` | |
| `Select Feature:` **0,0** ↵ | Dimensions the UCS origin |
| `Leader endpoint (Xdatum/Ydatum):` Y | The menu issues the Y option |
| `Leader endpoint:` *Pick at @1<180* | Locates the end of the dimension leader |
| `Dimension text <0>:` *Press Enter* | Places the dimension |
| `Command:` *Choose* **D**raw, *then* Di**m**ensions, *then* **O**rdinate, *then* **Y**-Datum | |
| `Select Feature:` *From the toolbox, choose* INTERSECTION, *then pick at* ① | |
| `Leader endpoint:` *Pick at @1<180* | Locates the end of the dimension leader |
| `Dimension text <2>:` *Press Enter* | |
| `Command:` **DIM** ↵ | |
| `Dim:` **ORD** ↵ | |
| `Select Feature:` **.X** ↵ | |

*continues*

`.X of` *From the toolbox, choose*
`INTERSECTION,` *then pick at point* ①

`(need YZ):` *From the toolbox, choose*
`ENDPOINT,` *and pick a point on the top*
*edge of the flange*

| | |
|---|---|
| `Leader endpoint (Xdatum/Ydatum):` **Y** ↵ | Specifies the Y datum option |
| `Leader endpoint:` *Pick at @1<180* | Locates the leader's endpoint |
| `Dimension text <8>:` *Press Enter* | Places the dimension |

*Turn ortho off*

| | |
|---|---|
| `Dim:` *Press Enter* | Repeats the ORDINATE command |

`Select Feature:` *From the toolbox,*
*choose* `ENDPOINT,` *then pick at* ③

`Leader endpoint (Xdatum/Ydatum):` **Y** ↵

| | |
|---|---|
| `Leader endpoint` *Pick at point* ④ | Specifies the offset point |

`Dimension text <7 1/2>:` *Press Enter*

*Turn ortho back on*

`Dim:` **E** ↵

---

**Figure 17.3:**

Ordinate dimen-
sions in paper
space.

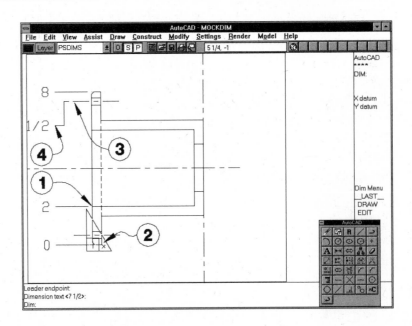

AutoCAD rounds off the angle between the first and second points in 90-degree increments to determine whether to calculate the X datum or Y datum in the Automatic mode. The Xdatum and Ydatum options of ORDINATE enable you to override AutoCAD and specify whether you want an X coordinate or a Y coordinate.

Although the preceding exercises required you to dimension in paper space, you dimension more often in model space.

# Dimensioning the Section View in Model Space

The rest of this chapter demonstrates a wide variety of dimensioning commands, settings, and styles, in both fractional and decimal units. Figure 17.4 shows the final results after switching to decimal units.

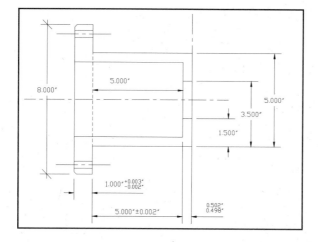

**Figure 17.4:**

The MOCKDIM section view target drawing.

When dimensioning in model space, you must be sure that DIMSCALE is appropriately set for the final plotting scale. The point of composing a drawing in a paper space sheet is to plot the sheet at full scale. The process of composing the sheet before dimensioning can set DIMSCALE relative to paper space scale. When you set DIMSCALE to 0, it calculates an appropriate scale value relative to the scale of the current viewport in paper space. This value is the inverse of the Zoom XP scale value used for that viewport. When you are in paper space, or using TILEMODE viewports, the 0 setting is ignored and treated as if set to 1.

The following exercise sets up a viewport and uses DIMSCALE to scale the dimensions. Create and zoom the viewport for half scale. Set two other dimension variables to get the dimension appearance you want. Figure 17.6 shows that the 1/2" dimension at the bottom of the view has no text or dimension lines between the extension lines. You need to turn off DIMTIX and DIMTOFL to allow the text outside and to suppress the inside dimension line. Save the changes as a new dimension style named MOCK2O (2 for 1/2 scale and the letter O for Outside text and dimension lines). Use the dialog boxes or enter the dimension variables at the dimension mode prompt.

## Setting Up for Dimensioning the Section View in Model Space

Command: *Select the viewport border and dimensions, then issue the ERASE command*  — Clears the drawing area

Command: *Choose **S**ettings, then U**C**S, then **N**amed UCS, click on \*WORLD\*, then **C**urrent, and then OK*  — Sets the UCS to World

*Set layer DIMS current*

Command: *Choose **V**iew, then Mvie**w**, and then **C**reate Viewport*

ON/OFF/Hideplot/Fit/2/3/4/Restore/ <First Point>: *Pick or enter* **.5,.5** *and* **12,8**  — Creates a new viewport

*Issue ZOOM with the Extents option*

Command: *From the toolbar, choose* P  — Enters model space

Command: *Enter* **Z**, *then enter* **.5XP**  — Zooms image half scale relative to paper space

*Pan to the view shown in figure 17.5*

Command: **PS** ⏎  — Switches to paper space

Command: *Choose **S**ettings, then* Di**m**ension Style  — Opens the Dimension Styles and Variables dialog box

*In the* **D**imension Style *edit box, enter* **MOCK2O** *(enter the letter O, not zero)*  — Creates a new style MOCK2O from MOCK2I

*Choose **T**ext Location, then open the* **H**orizontal *drop-down list box, and select* Default  — Turns on DIMTOH

| | |
|---|---|
| *Verify that* **A**lignment *is set to* Orient Text Horizontally | Turns off DIMTIX |
| *Clear the* Use **P**aper Space Scaling *check box, double-click in the* **F**eature Scaling *edit box, and enter* **2**, *then choose* OK | Sets DIMSCALE to 2 |
| *Choose* Text **F**ormat, *double-click in the* Length **S**caling *edit box, enter* **1**, *then choose* OK | Sets linear scaling for model space (DIMLFAC=1) |
| *Choose* OK | Saves the new style as MOCK2O |
| Command: **MS** ↵ | Enters model space |
| *Save the drawing* | |

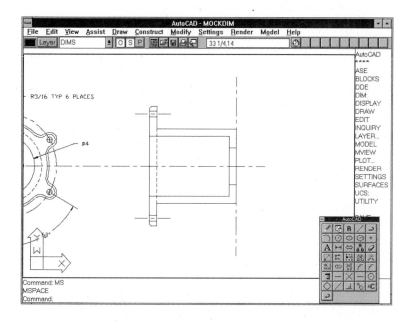

**Figure 17.5:**

The viewport, ready to dimension.

Figure 17.5 shows the completed setup.

Even though you only changed three dimension variables, including DIMSCALE, the last exercise is a typical example of modifying a dimension style to create a new one. The DIMSCALE 0 setting for model space dimensioning and the earlier DIMLFAC 2 setting for paper space dimensioning are compatible—this style can now be used for either.

*If you need to zoom an image, do not zoom in model space. This action throws off the DIMSCALE sizing of the dimension relative to paper space. Instead, use PAN, or enter paper space and zoom, then re-enter model space.*

Take another look at figure 17.4. The linear dimensions along the bottom form a set of continuing dimensions; the dimensions on the right are baseline dimensions.

# Dimensioning with Continued Dimensions

Begin with a normal linear dimension. Then use the Continue command to string subsequent dimensions together in a series. Continue begins each new dimension line where the last dimension line left off. Continue uses the previous extension line as the first extension line for the new dimension. If the dimension line needs room to clear the last text, Continue offsets the new dimension line by the DIMDLI value. You previously set DIMDLI to 5/8.

In the following exercise, you draw a horizontal dimension (see fig. 17.6) along the bottom of the section view and continue by adding new extension lines (to the right). Remember to use object snaps to ensure accuracy.

**Figure 17.6:**

The first horizontal dimension.

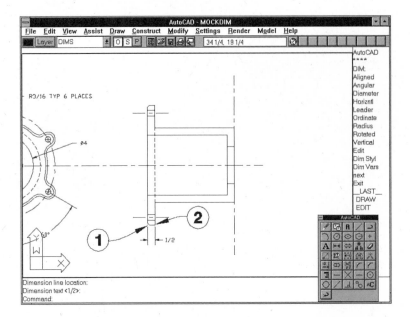

## Using HORIZONTAL CONTINUE Dimensions

Make sure that you are in model space.

| | |
|---|---|
| **Command:** *Choose* **D***raw, then* **Di***m***ensions, *then* **L***inear, then* **H***orizontal* | Enters dimensioning mode and issues the Horizontal command |
| `Command: _DIM1` | |
| `Dim: _horizontal` | |
| `First extension line origin or RETURN to select:` *With snap on, pick at* ① *(see fig. 17.6)* | |
| `Second extension line origin:` *Pick at* ② | |
| `Dimension line location:` *Pick point 21,8* | |
| `Dimension text <1/2>:` *Press Enter* | Accepts the default dimension text |
| **Command:** *From the screen menu, choose* DIM:, *then* next, *then* CONTINUE | Re-enters dimension mode and issues CONTINUE |
| `Dim: _CONTINUE` | |
| `Second extension line origin or RETURN to select:` *Pick point at* ③ *(see fig. 17.7)* | |
| `Dimension text <5>:` *Press Enter* | Accepts the text |
| `Dim:` *Press Enter* | Repeats CONTINUE |
| `_CONTINUE` | |
| `Second extension line origin or RETURN to select:` *Pick point at* ④ *and press Enter* | Draws the dimension with default text |

AutoCAD put the text "1/2" from the first dimension outside the extension line because it could not fit into the dimensioned space. To place the text on the left side, just reverse the pick order of the two points.

**Figure 17.7:**

The continued
horizontal
dimensions.

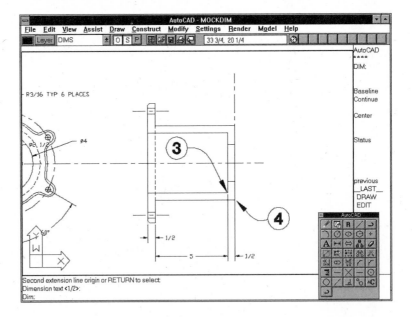

AutoCAD automatically placed the continued dimension line below the first one. The distance between the two dimension lines is controlled by DIMDLI. If the first horizontal dimension, 1/2, had been drawn right to left, its text would have been on the left and all three dimension lines would have been drawn aligned with each other.

By default, Continue strings dimensions from the last linear dimension drawn in the current drawing session. The RETURN to select option enables you to select an existing linear dimension from which to continue.

A series of vertical baseline dimensions is next. Like continued dimensions, baseline dimensions begin from an existing linear dimension. You need a normal vertical dimension to begin with, but if you use the current dimension style as it is, it puts the text outside the extension lines (see fig. 17.8). Therefore, restore and redefine the MOCK2I dimension style in the following exercise, change DIMSCALE to 0 for model space, and save it. Use the MOCK2I dimension style because it turns on DIMTIX, forcing AutoCAD to place the dimension text within the dimension lines. Then, turn DIMTOFL off to avoid drawing a dimension line through the text. Update MOCK2I's DIMSCALE to 0 for model space scaling to paper space.

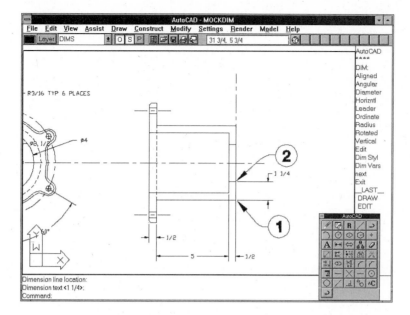

**Figure 17.8:**

The vertical dimension with DIMTIX off.

# Restoring, Redefining, and Examining Existing Dimension Styles

The primary dimension commands for working with existing dimension styles are Save, Restore, and Variables. (The Update and Override commands are examined in the associative dimensioning section of this chapter.) The Save command saves changes you make to a style, redefining it.

*Use caution when using the DDIM dialog box or the Save (dimension style) option of the DIM command to redefine an existing dimension style; this process changes every existing dimension entity in the drawing using that style.*

The Restore command changes the current dimension style to a previously saved style. Enter a dimension style name to restore or press Enter to adopt the dimension style of an existing dimension entity that you choose.

*An excellent way to prevent errors is to restore dimension styles by selecting existing dimensions—what you see is what you get. You can enter the DIMSTYLE system variable as a command to see what the current style name is, but you cannot change it that way. You can, however, rename an existing dimension style by using the RENAME command. (RENAME is not a dimension mode command.)*

The Variables command lists the dimension variable settings of any saved dimension style. It lists them in the same format that STATUS lists the settings of the current dimension style.

The Save, Restore, and Variables commands each have an inquiry option. If you enter a question mark, these commands list existing style names. Use wild cards to list all styles.

In the following exercise, you use Restore to reload the MOCK2I dimension style and adjust its DIMSCALE and DIMTIX settings. Remember, a change to any dimension variable changes the current dimension style to *UNNAMED, so use the Save option under DIM to redefine MOCK2I and make it the current style before you use it.

## Restoring and Redefining a Dimension style

| | |
|---|---|
| `Dim:` *Choose* **S**ettings, *then* Di**m**ension Style | Opens the Dimension Styles and Variables dialog box |
| *Click on* MOCK2I *in the list box* | Selects MOCK2I |
| *Choose* **F**eatures, *then put a check mark in the* Use **P**aper Space Scaling *check box, then clear the* Force **I**nterior Lines *check box, and choose* OK | Effectively sets DIMSCALE to 0 and turns DIMTOFL off |
| *Choose* Text F**o**rmat, *then double-click in the* Length **S**caling *edit box, enter* **1**, *then choose* OK | |
| *Choose* OK | Saves the changes to the style MOCK2I |

Now the vertical dimension fits within the extension lines when you create it in the next exercise.

Just as you create a library of blocks, you can create a library of dimension styles. AutoCAD provides two ways to save dimension styles and reload them from separate disk files. One way is to define all of the dimension styles you need in a prototype drawing. Then, when you begin new drawings by specifying a prototype, new drawings already contain those dimension styles.

The other method is to create a drawing file containing one or more dimension styles and insert them as blocks into any drawing where you need to use those styles. You can accomplish this in several ways. Use the WBLOCK command to save the dimension entities with those styles to a new file. Then insert it as a block, but cancel the insertion before the entities themselves become part of the drawing. Or, define the styles in an empty drawing and insert it without needing to cancel it. You also can create a style-laden empty drawing by erasing dimension entities from a drawing created with WBLOCK. In any case, the insertion makes any dimension styles in the inserted file a part of the current drawing.

# Dimensioning with Baseline Dimensions

Now you can draw the first vertical dimension line (see fig. 17.9), and use the BASELINE command to continue it. BASELINE is a cross between continuous and ordinate dimensioning. It works like CONTINUE, except that it uses the first extension line (base extension line) as the origin for all successive dimension calculations and line placements. Each successive dimension line is offset by the DIMDLI setting.

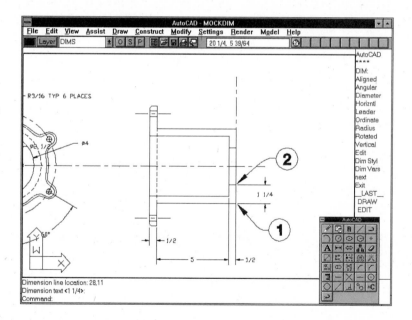

**Figure 17.9:**

The first vertical dimension for BASELINE.

In previous exercises, you used snap to locate your dimension points. Although this method works, it is a good habit to use object snaps instead to ensure that you select the exact points for the dimensions. In the remainder of the exercises, you turn snap off and use object snaps to locate your points.

## Using BASELINE for a Series of Vertical Dimensions

Command: *Turn off snap and ortho*

| | |
|---|---|
| Command: *Choose* **D**raw, *then* Di**m**ensions, *then* **L**inear, *then* **V**ertical | Enters dimensioning mode and issues the VERTICAL command |
| Dim: _vertical | |
| First extension line origin or RETURN to select: *From the toolbox, choose* INTERSECTION, *then pick corner at* ① *(see fig. 17.9)* | |
| Second extension line origin: *From the toolbox, choose* INTERSECTION, *then pick corner at* ② | |
| Dimension line location: **28,11** ↵ | |
| Dimension text <1 1/4>: *Press Enter* | Places the text inside the dimension line |
| Command: *From the screen menu, choose* DIM:, *then* next, *then* Baseline | Issues the BASELINE command |
| Dim: _BASELINE | |
| Second extension line origin or RETURN to select: *With object snap INT, pick corner at* ③ *(see fig. 17.10)* | Sets the origin point |
| Dimension text <3 3/4>: *Press Enter* | Accepts the text and draws the dimension |
| Dim: Press Enter | Repeats BASELINE |
| _BASELINE | |
| Second extension line origin or RETURN to select: *With object snap INT, pick at* ④ *and press Enter* | Sets point, accepts text, and draws dimension |
| Dim: **E** ↵ | Exits dimensioning |

*Save the drawing*

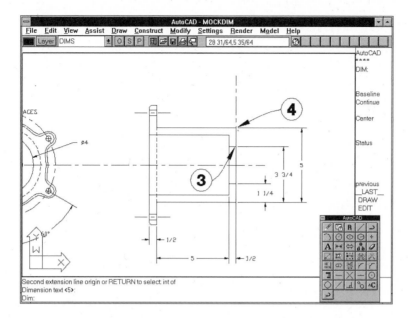

**Figure 17.10:**
Vertical dimensions after baseline.

In the next set of exercises, you stretch, scale, and update the drawing. You also use two more dimension variables to add inch tick marks to the dimension text and to increase the extension line offset.

## Appending a Units Suffix to Dimension Text

If you look closely at the current drawing, you see that the dimension text does not show any units. You are using the multipurpose fractional style of units. You can set an automatic dimension suffix with DIMPOST to append any text character or string to dimensions. You set it to a period to clear the suffix. Commonly used suffixes or prefixes include ', ", cm, fathoms, R (radius), or the diameter symbol. The next exercise shows you how to add inch marks to the dimension text.

Add a suffix, prefix, or both by typing custom characters before or after < > at the dimension text prompt. AutoCAD inserts the characters and replaces < > with its calculated text. See Chapter 15 for details on using this feature.

## Controlling Extension Line Offset from Objects

When you are setting dimension variables in the next exercise, reset DIMEXO to increase the offset for extension lines. The default 1/16 is too small to clearly separate extension lines from objects.

## The Efficiency of Dimension Styles

You might think that dimension styles add more work to dimensioning. Why not just set the dimension variables and be done with it? That might be easier for a few dimensions. But when you create several types of dimensions over and over, you are constantly resetting dimension variables as you switch between types. With dimension styles, you can just restore the style to switch between types instead of resetting several dimension variables. Overall, dimension styles are faster and easier—well worth the time it takes to set them up.

You have already created associative dimensions whether you knew it or not. In the next section, you use the MOCKDIM drawing to take a closer look. You also learn how to tailor them further by including tolerances, changing the terminator (arrow) type, and editing the characteristics of existing dimensions.

# Understanding Associative Dimensions

An associative dimension is a single entity that is linked to the dimensioned entity. As you move, scale, and stretch the dimensioned entity, the associative dimension moves, scales, or stretches as well. The associated dimension's text also adjusts automatically. Associative dimensioning is the default dimensioning mode. If the DIMASO dimension variable is on, AutoCAD creates associative dimensions (except for leader dimensions, which are always individual entities). If DIMASO is off, AutoCAD draws dimensions with individual lines, arrows (solids), arcs, and text entities. DIMASO is on by default.

An associative dimension is a special kind of unnamed block. Exploding an associative dimension creates individual lines, arrows (solids), arcs, and text entities that look the same as the associative dimension block. Individual components of associative dimensions can only be edited with special associative dimensioning commands or by STRETCH. Of course, exploded associative dimensions or dimensions created with DIMASO off can be edited as ordinary entities.

The dimension style name that is current when an associative dimension entity is created is stored with it. If it is a named dimension style, the associative dimension is protected from any subsequent changes to dimension variables (unless the dimension style is redefined). If the current dimension style is *UNNAMED, any associative dimensions change to assume the current dimension style, text style, and units settings, which is usually not wanted. Accidental updates to associative dimensions occur easily with the STRETCH or SCALE commands as well as several dimensioning commands. To protect the integrity of the dimensions, be sure a named dimension style is current whenever you create a new dimension.

AutoCAD has no dimension variables to control associative dimensions. Use the normal AutoCAD UNITS command to set units and the dimension mode STYLE command or the normal AutoCAD STYLE command to set text style. The dimension mode STYLE command is limited to setting styles; it cannot define a style.

*A named dimension style does not protect the text style or units from accidental updating. The safest method is to limit the dimensions to a single text style. If you need more than one type of unit, keep one type set with the UNITS command and create the other(s) with the dimension variables DIMALT, DIMALTD, DIMALTF, DIMPOST, and DIMLFAC.*

Associative dimensioning creates *definition points*. Associative dimensions use these points to control their rescaling and updating. Definition points are kept on a special layer called DEFPOINTS. They do not plot but are always visible when the dimension is visible. Exploding an associative dimension converts definition points to point entities on layer DEFPOINTS. The point locations vary with the type of dimension. For linear dimensions, there is one at each extension line origin and one at the dimension line intersection with the second extension line. You can snap to definition points with object snap NODe, even though layer DEFPOINTS is frozen. You also can use object snap NODe to snap to the midpoint of the associative dimension text, although it is not a true definition point.

Subentities of associative dimensions respond to the object snap modes just like subentities of ordinary blocks. You can snap, for example, to the end of a dimension arrow by using the ENDPoint object snap.

# Using Associative Dimensions

Associative dimensions make it easy to update and rescale a fully dimensioned drawing. In the following exercises, you learn three ways to use associative dimensions: to update dimension variables, including redefining and reassigning dimension styles; to stretch dimensions to relocate dimension text; and to stretch and rescale drawing entities and their associated dimensions to automatically update measurements.

## Associative Dimensioning Commands

AutoCAD offers the following seven dimensioning commands for editing existing associative dimensions:

- **HOMETEXT.** This command restores text of selected associative dimensions to its default (home) position.

- **UPDATE.** This command reformats selected associative dimensions to the current dimension style.

- **NEWTEXT.** This command enables editing of associative dimension text or restoration of the default measurement as text.

- **OBLIQUE.** This command changes extension lines of selected associative dimensions to an oblique angle.

- **OVERRIDE.** This command changes one or more dimension variable settings of the current dimension style and applies them to one or more selected associative dimensions as dimension style *UNNAMED.

- **TEDIT.** This command changes the position or rotation of selected dimension text.

- **TROTATE.** This command changes the rotation of selected dimension text.

## Updating Associative Dimensions

The UPDATE command changes selected associative dimensions by applying the current dimension style, text style, and units settings to them. Be sure a current named dimension style exists before using UPDATE, or the associative dimension adopts an *UNNAMED dimension style. All nonassociative dimension entities are ignored even if they are part of the selection set, so window and crossing selections are easy and convenient.

Update all the associative dimensions in the following exercise with new DIMPOST and DIMEXO settings. For simplicity, return to a single TILEMODE viewport and reset DIMSCALE to 2. Update the current MOCK2I dimension style, and then repeat the process for MOCK2O.

---

### Updating Dimensions with Suffix Text and Increased Extension Line Origin Offsets

Continue with your present MOCKDIM drawing, or begin a new drawing called MOCKDIM using the file IAWMOKD3 from the IAW DISK as a prototype.

Command: **TILEMODE** ↵

New value for TILEMODE <0>: **1** ↵     Returns to a single tiled viewport (see fig. 17.11)

*Issue ZOOM with the Extents option*

Command: *Choose* **S**ettings, *then*     Opens the Dimension Styles and Variables
Di**m**ension Style     dialog box

| | |
|---|---|
| *Select MOCK2I in the list box* | Makes MOCK2I the current style |
| *Choose* **E**xtension Lines, *double-click in the* Feature **O**ffset *edit box, enter* **1/8,** *then choose* OK | Sets DIMEXO to 1/8" |
| *Choose* Text F**o**rmat, *double-click in the* Te**x**t Suffix *edit box, and enter* **"**, *then choose* OK | Sets DIMPOST to " |
| *Choose* **F**eatures, *clear the* Use **P**aper Space Scaling *check box, double-click in the* **F**eature Scaling *edit box, enter* **2,** *then choose* OK | Sets DIMSCALE to 2 |
| *Choose* OK | Saves the changes as MOCK2I |

The vertical baseline associative dimensions with the MOCK2I style are immediately redefined with added " and larger offsets.

| | |
|---|---|
| Command: *Choose* **M**odify, *then* Edit **D**imensions, *then* **U**pdate Dimension | Enters dimension mode and issues the UPDATE command |
| Dim: _update | |
| Select objects: *Select all dimensions in the flange top view, but not those in section, then press Enter* | Updates the dimensions in the top view (see fig. 17.11) |

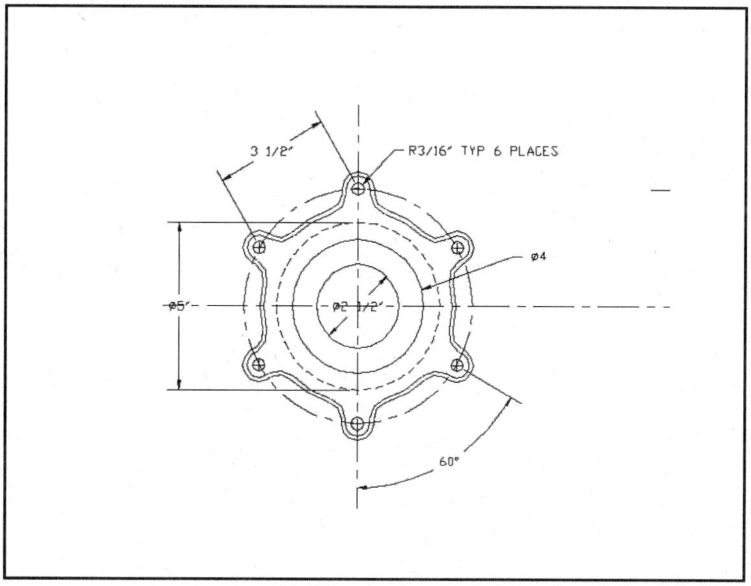

**Figure 17.11:**

The top view after updating dimensions.

The dimension entities are redefined to the MOCK2I style, adding " and increasing offsets. Any other entities are ignored. The drawing's continued dimensions still need to be updated; MOCK2I style, however, is unsuitable for the "R3/16" TYP 6 PLACES" dimension. The following exercise restores the MOCK2O style from the continued dimensions, makes the same changes to it as to MOCK2I, and updates this dimension. Enter the commands and variables from the keyboard. You can abbreviate them as shown.

## Restoring and Updating Dimensions

```
Command: DIM ↵

Dim: RES ↵                                      Issues RESTORE

Current dimension style: MOCK2I

?/Enter dimension style name or
RETURN to select dimension:
Press Enter

Select dimension: Pick one of the             Extracts the style from the dimension
horizontal continue associative dimensions

Current dimension style: MOCK2O             Resets the current style

Dim: DIMEXO ↵

Current value <1/16> New value:             Increases the offset
1/8 ↵

Dim: DIMPOST ↵

Current value <> New value: " ↵             Sets the suffix to "

Dim: DIMSCALE ↵

Current value <2.000000> New value:
2 ↵

Dim: SA ↵                                      Issues SAVE

?/Name for new dimension style:
MOCK2O ↵

That name is already in use,
redefine it? <N> Y ↵
```

The continue dimensions with the MOCK2O style are immediately redefined with added " and larger offsets.

| | |
|---|---|
| Dim: **UP** ↵ | Issues UPDATE |
| Select objects: *Select the* R3/16" TYP 6 PLACES *and press Enter* | Updates it (see fig. 17.11) |
| Dim: **E** ↵ | Ends dimensioning |

*Save the drawing*

Now, as figure 17.11 demonstrates, all the dimension text (except the 60-degree radius and ø4 leader dimensions) has inch marks. Angular dimensions ignore DIMPOST and leader dimensions are not associative. With DIMEXO at 1/8, the dimensions are separated more clearly from the objects they dimension. The extension lines on the 5" diameter vertical dimension at the left, however, still look too close because of the circle's large radius. This problem is solved in the next exercise. Before you proceed, however, take a quick look at other controls for dimension line and extension line appearance.

# Controlling Dimension and Extension Lines

Do not confuse DIMEXO with the similar-sounding DIMEXE, which controls how far extension lines extend beyond the dimension line. You can also use the following dimension variables for controlling dimension and extension lines:

- **DIMDLE.** This variable extends the dimension line through tick marks by its value when DIMTSZ is on (nonzero).

- **DIMGAP.** This variable controls the gap between text and the break in the dimension line, or optionally draws a box around the text if you set a negative value.

- **DIMTAD.** This variable puts text above the dimension line, with no break, when on. The variable DIMTVP controls how far above the line the text goes.

- **DIMSE1.** When turned on, this variable suppresses the first extension line. Suppression off means draw the line.

- **DIMSE2.** This variable suppresses drawing of the second extension line.

*Setting DIMGAP to a negative number causes AutoCAD to draw a rectangular box around the extents of dimension text. This box is offset from the text by the absolute value of DIMGAP, precisely intersecting the dimension line break. The negative setting is controlled by the Basic **D**imension check box of the Dimension Line group of the Features dialog box. Note that, according to ANSI Y14.5M standards, this dimension type is known as a Basic dimension.*

DIMSE1 and DIMSE2 are commonly used as exceptions to various dimension styles. You might, for example, need a dimension whose extension line would overlap the object itself or another line if an extension line were not suppressed. Suppress DIMSE1 or DIMSE2, especially if the extraneous extension line overlaps a dashed or hidden line. If you do not suppress these extra entities, drawing regenerations are slowed down and drawings may not plot neatly. You also can suppress overlapping lines with plot optimization.

Occasionally, it is more expedient to override one or two dimension variables for a single dimension rather than to create another special dimension style. Try a DIMSE1 and DIMEXO override in the next exercise.

Dimension styles can be overridden in two ways. Change one or more dimension variables before drawing the odd dimension, and then restore the previous style and continue working. Or, use the Override command to change the settings of the current style. Override then prompts you to select one or more associative dimensions to update according to the modified dimension variables. If the associative dimension has a named dimension style, you can update the style (redefining it for all entities assigned to it). The current dimension style is not changed, unless it also is the associative dimension's style.

Alter the 5" diameter vertical dimension at the left of the plan view in the following exercise. Give it an even larger DIMEXO, and then draw a horizontal dimension inside the flange hole on the section with DIMSE1 on. The setting of DIMSE1 demonstrates the earlier tip on using DDIM to create an *UNNAMED style.

## Overriding a Dimension Style for Odd Cases

`Command:` *From the screen menu, choose*
DIM:, *then* Dim Styl, *and then* Restore

Issues RESTORE

`Dim: _RESTORE`

`Current dimension style: MOCK2O`

`?/Enter dimension style name or`
`RETURN to select dimension:` *Press*
*Enter*

`Select dimension:` *Select the vertical*
*5" at the right side*

`Current dimension style: MOCK2I`

Restores MOCK2I

`Dim:` *From the screen menu, choose*
Override

Issues OVERRIDE

`Dim: Override`

| | |
|---|---|
| `Dimension variable to override:` `DIMEXO` ↵ | Specifies the DIMEXO variable |
| `Current value <1/8> New value:` `1/2` ↵ | Sets a new override value |
| `Dimension variable to override:` *Press Enter* | Ends variable specification |
| `Select objects:` *Select the 5" diameter dimension at the left side of the circle* | Increases the offsets |
| `Select objects:` *Press Enter* | |
| `Modify dimension style "MOCK21"?` `<N>` *Press Enter* | Leaves the style unchanged |

Next, you create an *UNNAMED style with the first extension line suppressed.

| | |
|---|---|
| Dim: *Choose* **S**ettings, *then* **Di**mension Style | Opens the Styles and Variables dialog box and cancels DIM mode |
| *With no style name displayed in the* **D**imension Style *edit box, choose* **E**xtension Lines, *open the* **Visibility** *drop-down list box, and select* Suppress First | Turns DIMSE1 on to suppress the first extension line |
| *Choose* OK, *then* OK *again* | |

The MOCK2I dimensions update to suppress the first extension line, but a new style called *UNNAMED has been created and made active, as you see in the next step.

| | |
|---|---|
| Command: `U` ↵ | Undoes the update on the MOCK2I dimensions but leaves *UNNAMED intact |
| Command: *Choose* **S**ettings, *then* **Di**mension Style | Opens the Dimension Styles and Variables dialog box |
| *Notice the current *UNNAMED style, then choose* Cancel | Closes the dialog box without any changes |
| Command: *Choose* **D**raw, *then* **Di**mensions, *then* **L**inear, *then* **H**orizontal, *and use object snap* NEA *to draw dimension from* ① *to* ②, *picking dimension line location at* ② *(see fig. 17.12)* | Draws a 5" dimension inside the hole in the section with no extension line at the left side |
| Command: *From the screen menu, choose* DIM:, *then* Dim Styl, *then* Restore | |

Dim: `_RESTORE`

*continues*

```
Current dimension style: *UNNAMED

?/Enter dimension style name or
RETURN to select dimension:
MOCK2I ↵

Dim: E ↵                              Exits from dimensioning mode
```

*Save the drawing*

---

**Figure 17.12:**

5" diameter after OVERRIDE, and 5" horizontal dimension with DIMSEI on.

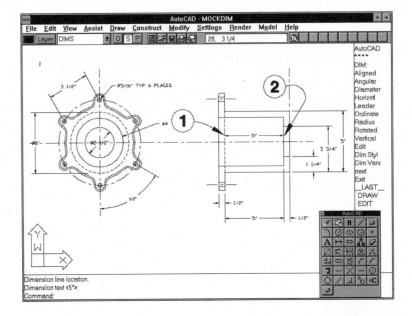

The offset, as illustrated at the far left in figure 17.12, should now be quite distinct. You can see no first extension line from the new horizontal dimension over the hidden line. You might be able to see the second extension line in yellow, overlapping the green bottom line of the hole. Notice that changing DIMSE1 changed the current style from MOCK2I to *UNNAMED.

*Beware of the difference between OVERRIDE and UPDATE. OVERRIDE assigns dimension style *UNNAMED to the associative dimension(s) unless you ask it to update the dimension style. The dimensions are not protected from accidental updating. UPDATE assigns the current dimension style, named or unnamed.*

*If the associative dimensions have the current dimension style, answer yes to update the dimension style with OVERRIDE. The result is equivalent to changing dimension variables and redefining the current dimension style.*

Until now, you have been using fractional units. Drawings like this one are usually dimensioned in decimal units. Update the current units to decimal.

# Controlling Units

Controlling units is simple and automatic—the current drawing units are used in the dimensioning text. Almost as simple is applying a round-off factor with the DIMRND dimension variable. If DIMRND is nonzero, all measurements (except angular dimensions) are rounded to the nearest increment of its value. For example, if DIMRND is set to .5, the dimension text is rounded to the nearest half unit. DIMRND does not truncate trailing zeros; the number of decimal places and display of zeros are controlled by the UNITS command and the DIMZIN dimension variable.

*Units are not saved or controlled by dimension styles.*

If you use DIMZIN, controlling units can be tricky. Measurements can be formatted in several possible ways. For example, in feet and inches, 1/4", 8", and 3' also can be formatted 0'0 1/4", 0'8", and 3'0". You can control this confusion by setting DIMZIN to 1, 2, or 3, 4.

- 0 suppresses both zero feet and zero inches (the default).

- 1 includes both zero feet and zero inches.

- 2 includes zero feet but suppresses zero inches.

- 3 suppresses zero feet but includes zero inches.

If a measurement includes fractional inches, zero inches are not suppressed, regardless of the setting. This automatic override helps avoid hard-to-read values like 6'1/2".

DIMZIN also controls decimal zeros, using settings of 4 and 8. These settings are additive; you can use them both for a sum of 12 and you can add them to the 0, 1, 2, or 3 settings for feet and inches control. A value of 4, 5, 6, or 7 suppresses all leading zeros

(0.7500 becomes .7500). A value of 8, 9, 10, or 11 suppresses (truncates) trailing zeros (0.7500 becomes 0.75). A value of 12, 13, 14, or 15 suppresses both leading and trailing zeros (0.7500 becomes .75). Update the drawing's dimensions with decimal units and suppress zeros in the horizontal dimensions.

Figure 17.13 shows the section before DIMZIN.

**Figure 17.13:**

Decimal dimensions before DIMZIN.

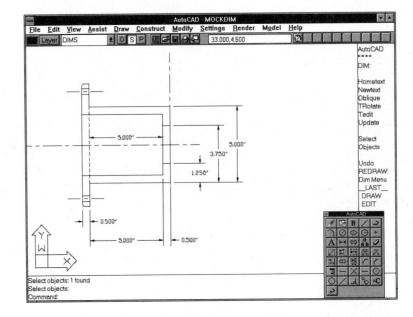

## Updating to Decimal Units and Controlling Zeros

Zoom to the view shown in figure 17.13.

Command: *Choose* **S**ettings, *then* **U**nits Control, *and set* De**c**imal *units, with 0.000 Precision*

| | |
|---|---|
| Command: *Choose* **M**odify, *then* Edit **D**imensions, *then* **U**pdate Dimension | Issues the UPDATE command |
| Dim: _update | |
| Select objects: *Select all vertical dimensions and press Enter* | Updates to decimal, but the DIMPOST " suffix remains |

| | |
|---|---|
| Command: Choose **S**ettings, *then* **Di**mension Style, *select MOCK2O in the list box, then choose* **F**eatures, *clear the* Use **P**aper Space Scaling *check box, and set* **F**eature Scaling to 2.0, *then choose* OK *twice* | Sets the style MOCK2O and updates three horizontal dimensions |
| Command: *Choose* **M**odify, *then* Edit **D**imensions, *then* **U**pdate Dimension | Issues the UPDATE command |
| Dim: _update | |
| Select objects: *Select the inside 5" horizontal dimension and press Enter* | Updates to decimal (see fig. 17.13) |
| Command: **DIM** ↵ | |
| Dim: **OV** ↵ | |
| Dimension variable to override: **DIMZIN** ↵ | |
| Current value <0> New value: **12** ↵ | |
| Dimension variable to override: *Press Enter* | |
| Select objects: *Select all the horizontal dimensions and press Enter* | |
| Modify dimension style "MOCK2O"? <N> *Press Enter four times* | Answers no for each selected MOCK2O dimension |

Examine the dimensions before undoing the DIMZIN override (see fig. 17.14).

| | |
|---|---|
| Dim: *Choose* **E**dit, *then* **U**ndo | Undoes the override |
| Dim: *Enter* **OV**, *then override the 5" horizontal dimension inside the hole, setting DIMSE1 back on, without modifying the existing style* | Suppresses the first extension line |
| Dim: **E** ↵ | Exits from dimensioning mode |
| *Save the drawing* | |

Figure 17.14 shows the horizontal dimensions after DIMZIN.

**Figure 17.14:**

Horizontal
dimensions
after DIMZIN.

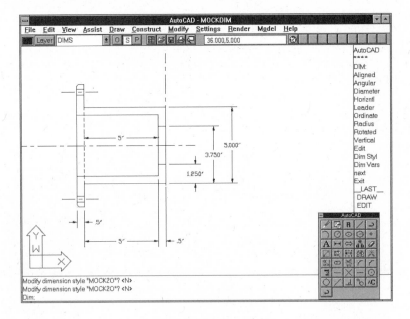

Experiment with different units and DIMZIN settings for other combinations you might use in your work.

You also can alter the linear scale of units and combine two alternate forms of units into one dimension.

## Dimensioning with Alternative Units

AutoCAD uses the units settings and actual distances you set up when you draw entities to calculate dimensions. If these units are not the lengths you want to show, apply a standard multiplier to alter the default calculations. You might, for example, use this feature to dimension an inserted scaled-down or metric detail.

To multiply all linear default dimensioning measurements by a standard factor, set the DIMLFAC dimension variable. When DIMLFAC is nonzero, AutoCAD uses the factor as a multiplier to calculate the dimension text. For example, if the measured dimension is 7.05", set DIMLFAC to 2.54 to generate the metric equivalent (17.907). Then to show the dimension as 17.907cm, set DIMPOST to cm. DIMLFAC has no effect on angular dimensioning.

## Using Two Measurement Systems at the Same Time

To display alternative dimension text strings on a dimension line, set DIMALT on. When you do, AutoCAD formats the dimension to match the *number* [*alternative number*] setting on the dimension line.

The first number is the standard dimension measurement (multiplied by DIMLFAC). The alternative number, shown in brackets, is that number multiplied by DIMALTF (dimension alternative factor). The alternative number of decimal places is set by DIMALTD (dimension alternative decimals). The default for DIMALTF is 25.4, the number of millimeters in an inch. The default for DIMALTD is two decimal places. The optional alternative suffix is set by DIMAPOST. For example, if the measured dimension is 7.05 and you want the text line to read 7.05" [17.907cm], set these dimension variables: DIMAPOST to cm; DIMALT on; DIMALTF to 2.54; and DIMALTD to 3.

Another popular dimensioning task is to include tolerances in dimensions. AutoCAD makes it easy.

# Adding Tolerances and Limits to Dimension Text

The dimension variables that control tolerances and limits are DIMTOL, DIMLIM, DIMTM, DIMTP, and DIMTFAC. The DIMRND round-off dimension variable also is useful. DIMTOL On turns tolerances on and DIMLIM On turns limits on. These dimension variables are mutually exclusive; turning one on turns the other off. DIMTP is the plus tolerance/limit value, and DIMTM is the minus value. DIMTFAC controls the size of the plus and minus tolerance and limits text strings (relative to DIMTXT size).

If you have only a few tolerance or limit dimensions in a drawing, use Override. If you use them frequently, create dimension styles for them. A convenient compromise is to create tolerance and limits dimension styles that you can override for specific DIMTP and DIMTM values. This method, however, sacrifices the dimension style protection against accidental changes.

Tolerances and limits work the same whether you update existing dimensions or create new ones with their settings. In the following exercise, update the existing horizontal associative dimensions below the section to try tolerances and limits. Also, turn DIMTAD on to place dimension text above unbroken dimension lines. To create tolerances (see fig. 17.15), set DIMTOL on, DIMTP to .003, DIMTM to .002, and DIMTFAC to .8 (.8×.125 DIMTXT = .1 text), and save a new dimension style. Then, override those settings to update the lower 5" dimension with equal DIMTP and DIMTM tolerance values. To create limits (see fig. 17.16), update the lower right dimension with DIMLIM on.

**Figure 17.15:**

Horizontal
dimensions above
a line with
tolerances.

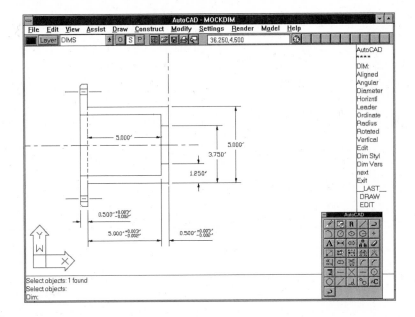

---

## Creating and Using Tolerance and Limits Dimensions

| | |
|---|---|
| Command: *Choose* **S**ettings, *then* **Di**mension Style, *click in the* **D**imension Style *edit box, and enter* MOCK2OTP3M2 | Starts a new style |

The message New Style MOCK2OTP3M2 created from MOCK2O appears at the bottom of the dialog box.

| | |
|---|---|
| *Choose* **T**ext Location, *open the the* **V**ertical *drop-down list box, select* Above, *then choose* OK | Turns on DIMTAD |
| *Choose* Text F**o**rmat, *then click on the* **V**ariance *radio button* | Turns on DIMTOL |
| *Double-click in the* U**p**per Value *edit box, then enter* .003 | Sets DIMTP |
| *Double-click in the* Lo**w**er Value *edit box, then enter* .002 | Sets DIMTM |
| *Choose* OK | Returns to the main dialog box |

| | |
|---|---|
| *Choose* **T**ext Location, *then double-click in the* **T**olerance Height *edit box and enter* `0.1` | Sets DIMTFAC to .8 (ratio of text height to tolerance text height) |
| *Choose* OK, *and then* OK *again* | Saves new settings for MOCK2OTP3M2 and returns to `Command:` prompt |

The style name was derived from: DIMSCALE 2 Outside Tolerance Plus .003 Minus .002.

| | |
|---|---|
| `Command:` *Choose* **M**odify, *then* Edit **D**imensions, *then* **U**pdate Dimension, *and select the bottom three horizontal dimensions* | Updates dimensions with tolerances (see fig. 17.15) |
| `Command:` **DIM** ↵ | |
| `Dim:` **DIMTP** ↵ | |
| `Current value <0.003> New Value:` `.002` ↵ | Sets plus tolerance same as minus |
| `Dim:` *Choose* **M**odify, *then* Edit **D**imensions, *then* **U**pdate Dimension, *and update the toleranced 5.000" dimension* | Overrides its style |
| `Command:` **DIM** ↵ | |
| `Dim:` **DIMLIM** ↵ | |
| `Current value <off> New Value:` **ON** ↵ | Turns limits on and tolerances off |
| `Dim:` *Choose* **M**odify, *then* Edit **D**imensions, *then* **U**pdate Dimension *and update right-most 0.500" toleranced dimension* | Overrides its style |
| *Save the drawing* | |

The left-most horizontal dimension now reads 0.500" +0.003"/-0.002", the middle dimension is 5.000" -0.002", and the right-most one reads 0.502"/0.498".

*For more complete coverage of geometric dimensioning and tolerancing to ANSI Y14.5M-1982 (R1988) standards, consult* AutoCAD Drafting and 3D Design *(New Riders Publishing).*

**Figure 17.16:**

Horizontal
dimensions with
tolerances and
limits.

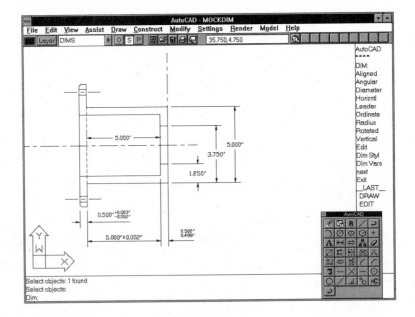

# Controlling Dimension Text

In addition to the settings you have already used, AutoCAD offers other ways to control dimension text, as described in the following list of dimension commands and dimension variables:

- **HOMETEXT.** This command restores text of selected associative dimensions to their default (home) position.

- **NEWTEXT.** This command enables you to edit the contents of selected associative dimension text, or restore the default measurement as text if you enter <>. Embedded <> measurements and text are accepted.

- **TROTATE.** This command changes the rotation angle of dimension text.

- **TEDIT.** This command changes the location of selected dimension text without affecting its contents. You can justify it left or right, pick a new location, restore it to its home position, or change its angle. TEDIT includes the features of Hometext, Newtext, Trotate, and STRETCH, but you can only edit one associative dimension at a time with TEDIT.

- **DIMTIH.** This variable keeps text that is inside extension lines horizontal when on (the default). When DIMTIH is off, the angle of the text takes on the angle of the dimension line.

- **DIMTOH.** Similar to DIMTIH, this variable places text outside the extension lines.

- **DIMCLRT.** This variable assigns a color to associative dimension text for plotting pen line weight control.

*You might want to use the STRETCH command instead of TEDIT. The regular STRETCH command is useful for relocating dimension text to locations not allowed by the TEDIT command.*

Use STRETCH in the following exercise to relocate the 0.500" +0.003"/-0.002" horizontal section view dimension. Figure 17.17 shows its appearance before editing.

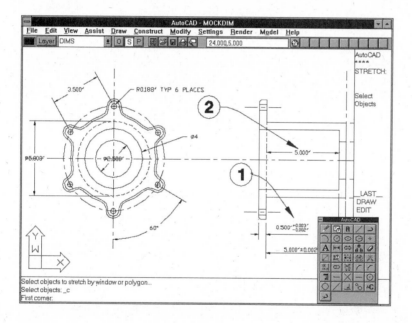

**Figure 17.17:**

MOCKDIM before editing.

When you are selecting dimension text with STRETCH, the crossing window only needs to catch the node point in the center of the dimension text. Then use TEDIT to relocate the dimensions shown. The 5" vertical dimension text is located on top of the flange center line, so move it up a little. While you are editing the dimensions, break the center lines going through the inner circle's dimension. Also set DIMCLRT to red, both to try it out and to use it as a visible flag to see which dimension text values are changed by the TEDIT and STRETCH commands.

## Relocating Text and Controlling Color with TEDIT, STRETCH, and DIMCLRT

Zoom and pan to the view illustrated in figure 17.17.

Command: *Choose* **S**ettings, *then*
**Di**mension Style, *and click on* MOCK2I
*in the list box, then choose* OK

Restores the MOCK21 style

Command: *Choose* **M**odify, *then* Edit
**D**imensions, *then* **U**pdate Dimensions,
*select all dimensions in top view
(except R3/16"...), and press Enter*

Command: *Choose* **S**ettings, *then*
**Di**mension Style

Opens the Dimension Styles and Variables
dialog box

*Click on* MOCK2I, *choose* **C**olors, *click in
the color box to the right of BYBLOCK in
the* **D**imension Text Color *drop-down list
line, click on red, then choose* OK *three
times*

Changes text color of MOCK2I dimensions
(changes *DIMCLRT* variable for MOCK21)

Command: *Choose* **M**odify, *then* Stretc**h**,
*and select the dimension text at* ①
*(see fig. 17.17), and press Enter*

Selects 0.500" toleranced dimension

Base point or displacement: *With object
snap NODe, pick text at* ①

Second point of displacement: *Turn
on ortho, drag text to left and pick point
to place it where shown in figure 17.18*

Relocates text

Command: *Turn off ortho*

Command: *Choose* **M**odify, *then* Stretc**h**
*and stretch the 5.000" dimension
at* ② *to the left and up (see figs.
17.17 and 17.18)*

Makes text red and moves it above the
dimension line, which "heals" itself

Command: **DIMSHO** ⏎

New value for DIMSHO <1>: **0** ⏎

Turns off dynamic updating of dimension
during edit

Command: *Choose* **M**odify, *then* Edit
**D**imensions, *then* **D**imension Text, *then*
**M**ove Text

Issues TEDIT

```
Dim: _tedit
```

**Select dimension:** *Pick the 5" diameter dimension at the far left of plan view and press Enter*

**Enter text location (Left/Right /Home/Angle):** *Pick new location shown in figure 17.18*

Moves it above center line

**Command:** *Choose* **M***odify, then* **B***reak, then* Select Object, **T***wo Points, and break the center lines to clear the 2.500" diameter dimension*

*Save the drawing*

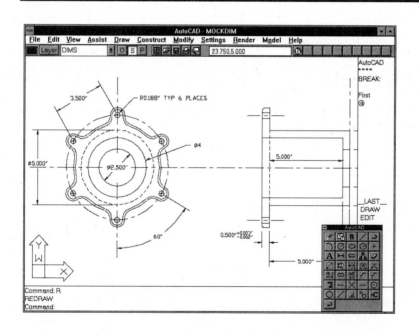

**Figure 17.18:**

MOCKDIM after STRETCH, TEDIT, and BREAK.

Setting DIMCLRT made the current dimension style *UNNAMED. However, the first STRETCH and the TEDIT did not change their dimension's text values because they had named dimension styles stored with them. Stretching the 5" horizontal dimension updated it to the current dimension variable settings and changed its color because it began as an *UNNAMED associative dimension. When you stretch an associative dimension's text out of the dimension line, the line "heals" itself. The Hometext command makes the associative dimension text snap back to its default home.

Did you notice a difference in dragging with DIMSHO off? If DIMSHO is on, AutoCAD recalculates the dimension value and updates the dimension while dragging; if DIMSHO is off, no recalculation occurs. DIMSHO on might produce jerky and slow results on some computers; if so, turn it off. DIMSHO is not stored in the dimension style, so changing it does not change the current dimension style to *UNNAMED.

Editing other objects, such as center lines, might be the easiest way to clear up conflicts. When you have a choice in modifying an associative dimension, it is usually better to use dimensioning utility commands rather than normal AutoCAD commands. Instead of using STRETCH to move text, use TEDIT. Instead of exploding a dimension so you can edit its text or change its color, use Newtext or DIMCLRT.

# Controlling Dimension Color and Line Weight

In addition to using the DIMCLRT dimension variable to set color for dimension text, you can use DIMCLRD to set color for dimension lines, arrows, and leaders. DIMCLRE similarly controls the color of extension lines. You can set them to any color, or to BYLAYER or BYBLOCK. They are set to BYBLOCK by default, so the entities within the dimension take on current color settings when created or changed with CHPROP. This also is the reason why the leader dimension is white. Leaders and center marks are not associative dimensions; they act like associative dimensions that have been exploded.

Try using EXPLODE on an associative dimension. Because they are really special forms of blocks, EXPLODE changes associative dimensions to individual entities with linetype BYLAYER and the color set by the DIMCLRx dimension variables. With default DIMCLRx settings, leaders are drawn with color BYBLOCK, which appears white. Change them by setting colors or using CHPROP. Undo is the only way to restore associativity.

The STRETCH and SCALE commands are the links to maintaining associativity of dimensions as you edit drawing objects.

# Stretching and Scaling Entities and Associative Dimensions

Remember that associative dimensions contain invisible definition points at their extension line origins. If you select a dimension when using SCALE or catch a definition point in the crossing window when stretching, the dimension text automatically is recalculated.

To examine this effect, use STRETCH in the following exercise to double the flange thickness from .5" to 1" on the left side of the section view. Then use SCALE and STRETCH to resize the inner circle's hole diameter from 2.5" to 2" in both the plan view and the section view. Figure 17.19 shows the selection points for the STRETCH crossing windows.

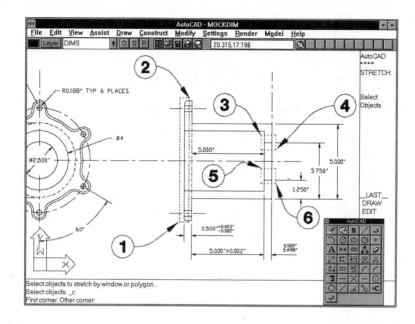

**Figure 17.19:**
Crossing window for changing the flange.

## Using STRETCH and SCALE To Edit Objects and Associative Dimensions

Zoom to the view shown in figure 17.19.

| | |
|---|---|
| Command: *Choose* **S**ettings, *then* Di**m**ension Style, *click on* MOCK2OTP3M2, *then choose* OK | Restores MOCK2OTP3M2 dimension style |
| Command: *Choose* **M**odify, *then* Edit **D**imensions, *then* **D**imension Text, *then* **H**ome Position | Enters DIM mode and issues HOMETEXT |
| Dim: _hometext | Returns text to default position |
| Select objects: *Select the left-most tolerance 0.500" dimension and press Enter* | Returns text to default position |

*continues*

Command: *Choose* **M**odify, *then* Stret**ch**

Command: Stretch

Select objects to stretch by window
or polygon...
Select objects: _c

First corner: *Pick point at* ①
*(see fig. 17.19)*

Other corner: *Pick point at* ②                    Thickens by .5" and increases dimension
Select objects: *Press Enter*                     (see fig. 17.20)
Base point: *Pick any point*
New point: **@-.5,0** ↵

Command: *Select the 2.500" dimension*           Creates selection set and enters Stretch mode
*and circle, then pick the center grip*

** STRETCH **                                      Switches to Scale mode
<Stretch to point>/Base point/Copy/
Undo/eXit: **SC** ↵

** SCALE **                                        Specifies the Reference option
<Scale factor>/Base point/Copy/Undo/
Reference/eXit: **R** ↵

Reference length <1.000>: **2.5** ↵              Specifies the reference length

<New length>/Base point/Copy/Undo/               Scales the circle and the dimension
Reference/eXit: **2** ↵

Command: *Double-click in an empty space*        Clears the selection set and grips

Command: **R** ↵                                 Redraws the screen

Command: *Choose* **M**odify, *then* Stret**ch**, *and*
*select crossing* ③ *and* ④
*(see fig. 17.19) to stretch edge of*
*hole and vertical 3.750" dimension to 3.500"*
*(if the 5.000" dimension gets selected,*
*Shift-pick it to deselect it)*

Command: *Choose* **M**odify, Stret**ch**, *and*
*select crossing* ⑤ *and* ⑥ *to*
*stretch other edge of hole and vertical*
*1.250" dimension to 1.500"*

*Save the drawing*

All of the associated dimensions are selected and updated to match the stretched and scaled entities. As illustrated in figure 17.20, the drawing remains accurate after editing.

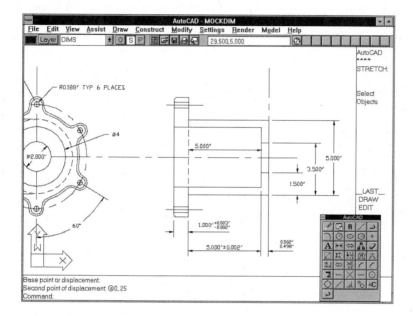

**Figure 17.20:**

The stretched flange and rescaled holes.

# Changing the Dimension Terminator (Arrow)

A terminator is the symbol placed at the intersection of a dimension line and an extension line. The default terminator is an arrow, but ticks or dots can be substituted simply by setting dimension variables. Whenever DIMTSZ (dimension tick size) has a value greater than 0 (the default), ticks of that size are drawn instead of arrows.

In the following exercise, set DIMTSZ to a value of .125 for the tick size. Also set DIMDLE to .125 to extend the dimension line through tick marks. Then place a vertical dimension using tick marks instead of the normal dimension line arrows (see fig. 17.21). Draw the overall vertical dimension of the flange section 1 inch to the left of the face.

**Figure 17.21:**

A vertical dimen-
sion with tick
marks.

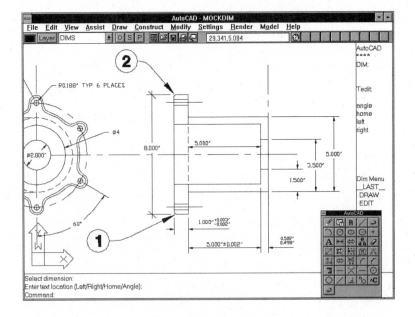

## Dimensioning with Tick Marks

| | |
|---|---|
| Command: *Choose* **S**ettings, *then* **Dim**ension Style, *and select* MOCK2I | Selects MOCK2I style |
| *Choose* **A**rrows, *click on the* Tick *radio button, double-click in the* Tick E**x**tension *edit box, and enter* **.125** | Selects ticks instead of arrows and sets DIMDLE to .125 |
| *Double-click in the* Arrow Si**z**e *edit box, then enter* **.125**, *and choose* OK, *then* OK *again* | Sets DIMTSZ, closes dialog boxes, and updates MOCK2I dimensions |
| Command: **U** ↵ | Undoes dimension change, but retains dimension style changes as \*UNNAMED |
| Command: *Turn on snap* | |
| Command: *Choose* **D**raw, *then* **Dim**ensions, *then* **L**inear, *then* **V**ertical, *and pick extension line origins* ① *and* ② *(see fig. 17.21), dimension line location at 18,12 and accept the default text* | Enters dimension mode and draws 8" Vertical dimension |

`Command:` *Turn off snap*

`Command:` *Choose* **M**odify, *then* Edit **D**imension, *then* **D**imension Text, *then* **M**ove Text, *and move the text up above center line (see fig. 17.21)*

Save the drawing and quit AutoCAD.

---

You also can use dots or any drawing or block as a customized dimension terminator.

You can easily set the size of dimension arrows with the DIMASZ dimension variable. You also can substitute dots, custom arrows, or any symbol you want. If the DIMBLK (dimension block) dimension variable contains the name DOT, AutoCAD creates a block named DOT and uses it as a terminator. If DIMBLK contains the name of any other block, AutoCAD uses that block in place of the default arrow (unless overridden by a nonzero DIMTSZ).

If you create a custom symbol oriented for the right end of the dimension line, AutoCAD can flip it 180 degrees for the left side and rotate it for angular dimensions. Dimension blocks can be any shape you want. A few examples are shown in figure 17.22.

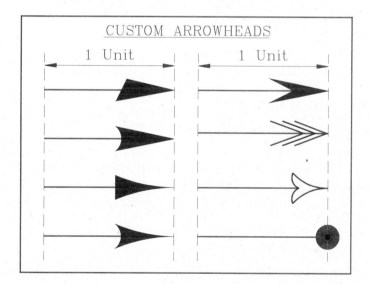

**Figure 17.22:**

Some DIMBLKS examples.

*Make your symbol one drawing unit wide. AutoCAD draws the dimension line or leader up to one unit away from the extension line. If the symbol is not one unit wide, there is a gap between the symbol and the dimension line. Point the symbol or arrow to the right and make the symbol or arrow's tip the block insertion base point.*

You can create different dimblocks for the right and left sides. To use them, set the DIMBLK1 dimension variable to the name of the left side dimension block and DIMBLK2 to the name of the right side dimension block. Then, turn the DIMSAH dimension variable on to tell AutoCAD to use the separate blocks.

You can now erase the MOCKSECT and DIMVARS drawing. You do not need them again.

# Summary

Associative dimensions are one of the most useful features of any CAD system when used properly. Associative dimensions ensure that the dimension values always reflect the current size of the objects in the drawing. If you change the objects, you do not need to change the dimensions—they are updated automatically. Associative dimensions also make it easier to make global changes to the dimensions. Remember the following points to use associative dimensioning most effectively:

- Draw precisely, so the dimensions are accurate. Do not draw out of scale unless you absolutely have to.

- When modifying the drawing by stretching or scaling, make sure you include the dimensions in the selection set so they are updated as well.

- Let AutoCAD do the work of making changes by using the associative dimension utility commands such as NEWTEXT, TEDIT, and TROTATE.

- Use named dimension styles to protect associative dimensions from accidental updating. Standardize your dimensioning into as few dimension styles as possible. Save those dimension styles in a prototype drawing or in a drawing you can insert as a block. Use the Restore option to set the current dimension style by selecting existing dimensions. You can reduce the chance of error by seeing what you are setting the dimension style to.

- Use overrides to named dimension styles sparingly and check instances of their use before plotting to be sure they have not accidentally changed.

- Put the dimensions on a separate layer with a different color than the one used for the main body of the drawing. Use the DIMCLRX set of dimension variables to assign colors to parts of dimensions so you can plot different line weights. This way, extension lines and dimensions stand out and are not mistaken for actual drawing elements.

- Adjust dimension text to the same height as the annotation text for consistency and to make text changes and additions easier.

# Maximizing AutoCAD for Windows

In previous chapters, you learned to use AutoCAD's functions and commands to create and annotate drawings. This chapter examines a completely new topic—customization.

You can do so much to customize AutoCAD that New Riders Publishing offers two other books on the subject, *Maximizing AutoCAD Release 12* and *Maximizing AutoLISP*. These two books cover almost every aspect of AutoCAD customization in detail. To give you a head start on customizing AutoCAD, this chapter examines a few of the simpler methods of customizing AutoCAD itself, and explains techniques specific to maximizing your use of AutoCAD for Windows.

You start by learning how to use prototype drawings to quickly customize your AutoCAD drawings. Next you look at the ACAD.PGP file and command aliases. Then you explore ways to customize the appearance and functionality of AutoCAD for Windows. Finally, you learn how to add new features to its toolbar and toolbox.

Some of the changes you can make to AutoCAD, such as creating and using a custom prototype drawing, or adding new functions to the toolbox, affect your productivity directly by providing a tailored working environment and quick access to often-used commands and features. Other changes, such as changing the font used for the screen menu or text window, also can increase your productivity with AutoCAD but in a more subtle way. Minor changes to the interface can make AutoCAD a more useful tool for your application. A smaller font for the graphics window, for example, gives you a larger drawing area, more items on the screen menu, and more buttons on the toolbar.

The simplest way to begin maximizing your AutoCAD setup is to use custom prototype drawings.

# Using Custom Prototype Drawings

Many users overlook the fact that they can customize their drawing setup by starting a drawing session with a prototype drawing that they can modify. This simple task can save time-wasting setups.

Chapter 3 discussed how a default working environment is established for the units, grid, and snap settings by setting no prototype or loading a prototype drawing called ACAD.DWG. The ACAD.DWG file comes with the AutoCAD program. (All the ACAD.DWG variables and their default values are listed in the table of system variables, which appears in Appendix C.) Specifying **N**o Prototype is equivalent to using the original ACAD.DWG file.

Instead of always using the ACAD.DWG prototype drawing, however, you can create your own prototype drawing and use it to initialize your drawings. After you create this drawing with the defaults (and any standard graphics, such as a title block) that you want, you can save it on disk with a name that you prefer. Then you can load the drawing as an option, or set up AutoCAD to load it automatically.

Use the following exercise as a guide to creating a prototype drawing file. Although you can modify the ACAD.DWG file, it is better to create your own prototype drawing with your own default settings and standard graphics. In this example, the new prototype drawing is named IAW-PROT.

 *This exercise is just an example. Do not set up for this book's exercises by using the following exercises. If you perform the following exercises, set your default prototype drawing back to none when you are finished.*

For simplicity, IAW-PROT uses an 8 1/2 by 11-inch setup at full scale with engineering units. If you use a different scale factor and sheet size, adjust your text and dimension scales accordingly. You can make sure the drawing is started with the standard defaults by putting a check in the **N**o Prototype box from the Create Drawing File dialog box, and entering **IAW-PROT** in the New **D**rawing Name text box.

## Table 18.1
## IAW-PROT Drawing Settings

| APERTURE | COORDS | GRID | LTSCALE | SNAP | ORTHO |
|----------|--------|------|---------|------|-------|
| 10 | ON | .5 | .375 | .0625 | ON |

**UNITS**  Engineering units, default all other settings

**LIMITS**  0,0 to 11,8.5

**ZOOM**  Scale of .75X

**VIEW**  Save view ALL

| Layer Name | State | Color | Linetype |
|------------|-------|-------|----------|
| 0 | On | White | CONTINUOUS |
| CENTER | On | Green | CENTER |
| DASHED | On | Yellow | DASHED |
| DIM | On | Yellow | CONTINUOUS |
| HATCH | On | Red | CONTINUOUS |
| HIDDEN | On | Blue | HIDDEN |
| NO-PLOT | On | Magenta | CONTINUOUS |
| OBJECTS | Current | Green | CONTINUOUS |
| TEXT | On | Cyan | CONTINUOUS |
| TITLE | On | Yellow | CONTINUOUS |

## Customizing a Prototype Drawing

Choose File, then New. Make sure there is a check in the No Prototype check box, and enter the drawing name **IAW-PROT**.

Create the layers and make the settings shown in table 18.1.

*Set the TEXTSIZE system variable to .125*

*Set the following dimension variables:*

*continues*

*DIMDLI to 0.375*
*DIMTXT to 0.125*
*DIMASZ to 0.1875*
*DIMEXE to 0.1875*
*DIMCEN to 0.0625*
*DIMEXO to 0.9375*

| | |
|---|---|
| *From the toolbar, choose* QSAVE | Saves IAW-PROT for future use |

## Loading a Prototype Drawing As An Option

Now that you have saved IAW-PROT, you can load it as an option by setting any new drawing so that the new drawing is equal to IAW-PROT. This technique is used throughout the book. You can use it now to check IAW-PROT in the following exercise.

### Testing a Prototype Drawing

| | |
|---|---|
| *Choose* File, *then* New, *and enter drawing name* **TEST=IAW-PROT** | Starts new drawing; if it is identical to IAW-PROT, it is okay |

## Loading a Prototype Drawing Automatically

You can set up AutoCAD to use IAW-PROT automatically for your new drawing in two ways. One way is to copy IAW-PROT.DWG to the name ACAD.DWG in the AutoCAD program directory, replacing the original default ACAD.DWG. If you do this and later you want to restore the standard ACAD.DWG prototype drawing, just begin a new drawing in your AutoCAD program directory named ACAD= and then save it.

This method has an advantage when you routinely create several different types of drawings. By default AutoCAD always looks for a drawing named ACAD.DWG in the current directory; therefore, different prototype drawings can be created, saved as ACAD.DWG in different working directories, and automatically selected by starting a new drawing in the appropriate directory. You specify the working directory in Windows, when you create an icon to start AutoCAD, as you did in Chapter 1.

The other way to automate IAW-PROT is to set it as the default prototype drawing in AutoCAD's Create New Drawing dialog box. The following exercise shows you the steps for changing the name of the default prototype drawing this way.

*The following exercise is an example showing how to change the default prototype drawing. DO NOT perform this exercise if you plan to perform other exercises in this book because other exercises depend on the default ACAD.DWG or No Prototype. If you do change the default prototype, change it back to No Prototype for the rest of the book.*

## Configuring a Prototype Drawing

*Choose* **F**ile, *then* **N**ew      Displays the Create New Drawing dialog box (see fig. 18.1)

If the No Prototype check box has an X in it, click on it to turn it off.

*In the text box beside* **P**rototype, *enter* **IAW-PROT**

*Choose* **R**etain as Default, *then* OK

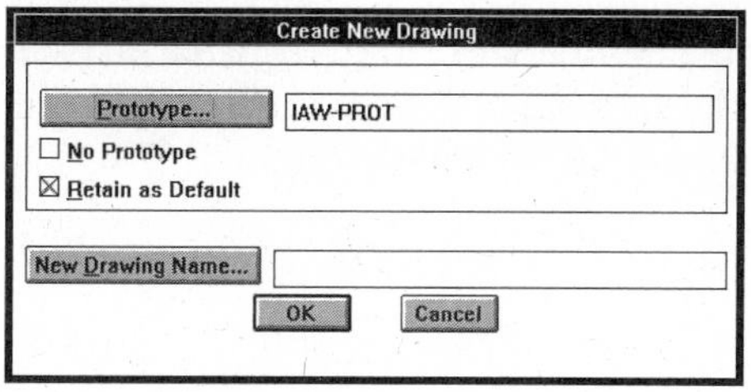

---

**Create New Drawing**

Prototype...    IAW-PROT

☐ **N**o Prototype
☒ **R**etain as Default

New **D**rawing Name...

OK    Cancel

**Figure 18.1:**

The Create New Drawing dialog box.

This procedure has the same effect as changing the default prototype drawing name in AutoCAD's configuration menu, but is much quicker. Now, when you create a new drawing with the current configuration, the drawing starts up with IAW-PROT's defaults.

Later in the chapter, you learn to set up multiple configurations of AutoCAD. Because the default prototype drawing name is saved in the ACAD.CFG file, by creating separate configurations with different default prototype drawings you can achieve the same result as described earlier.

Prototype drawings are a powerful tool for standardizing drawings, reducing repetitive setup effort, and tailoring AutoCAD to the way you work. Another useful tool for setting up a productive custom working environment is the ACAD.PGP file.

# Customizing the PGP File

You can run other programs, utilities, or DOS commands without ending your AutoCAD drawing session. The Windows environment enables you to have any number of other applications running simultaneously with AutoCAD, including additional sessions of AutoCAD itself. This capability is one of the great features available to users of AutoCAD for Windows.

When you run most applications under DOS, you must leave the application if you want to run another program or use operating-system commands. With the DOS version of AutoCAD, you can enter these names directly at the Command: prompt. To enable AutoCAD to do this, a few *external commands*, such as SHELL, are defined in a file named ACAD.PGP. An *external command* is any program that is external to AutoCAD. You can use the external commands to run a text editor, for example, or to design third-party AutoCAD applications.

To provide compatibility with the DOS version, AutoCAD for Windows includes the capability of defining external commands in the ACAD.PGP file, which resides in the AutoCAD support directory. The PGP extension stands for ProGram Parameters. ACAD.PGP contains the information that AutoCAD needs to execute the external program, and return when the external program finishes. This file can be easily modified to add external programs of your own choosing.

You can use the SHELL command to run any DOS programs or commands you want. The SHELL command is a generic external command that gives you temporary access to the operating-system prompt. Enter **EXIT** to return to AutoCAD.

You will probably find that using the Windows interface, which enables external programs to be loaded concurrently with AutoCAD and accessed with a single short-cut key, is a quicker and more efficient way to accomplish tasks outside AutoCAD. But the ACAD.PGP file also has another purpose: defining command aliases.

## Using AutoCAD Command Aliases

Although its ability to run external commands is less important in AutoCAD for Windows, the ACAD.PGP file still performs an important function; it defines abbreviated aliases for AutoCAD commands. For example, instead of entering **REDRAW**, you can simply enter **R**, because R has been defined as an alias for REDRAW.

You can use your preferred ASCII editor to display the contents of the standard ACAD.PGP file, which should be in the SUPPORT directory. The following listing shows the external commands and some of the aliases that are stored in the standard ACAD.PGP file.

# The PGP File

```
; acad.pgp - External Command and Command Alias definitions

; External Command format:
;    <Command name>,[<DOS request>],<Memory
;      reserve>,[*]<Prompt>,<Return code>

; Examples of External Commands for DOS

CATALOG,DIR /W,33000,File specification: ,0
DEL,DEL,      33000,File to delete: ,0
DIR,DIR,      33000,File specification: ,0
EDIT,EDLIN,   42000,File to edit: ,0
SH,,          33000,*OS Command: ,0
SHELL,,       127000,*OS Command: ,0
TYPE,TYPE,    33000,File to list: ,0

; Command alias format:
;    <Alias>,*<Full command name>

; Sample aliases for AutoCAD Commands
; These examples reflect the most frequently used commands.
; Each alias uses a small amount of memory, so don't go
; overboard on systems with tight memory.

A,      *ARC
C,      *CIRCLE
CP,     *COPY
DV,     *DVIEW
E,      *ERASE
L,      *LINE
LA,     *LAYER
M,      *MOVE
MS,     *MSPACE
P,      *PAN
PS,     *PSPACE
PL,     *PLINE
R,      *REDRAW
Z,      *ZOOM


3DLINE, *LINE

; easy access to _PKSER (serial number) system variable
SERIAL, *_PKSER

; These are the local aliases for AutoCAD AME commands.
; Comment out any you don't want or add your own.
; Note that aliases must be typed completely.
```

(Aliases for AME commands follow.)

The ACAD.PGP file contains aliases for a number of AutoCAD commands, but not for all of them. You can add alias names for any AutoCAD command. Typically, the alias is a one- or two-letter mnemonic that you can type in place of the command's full name. Unless your system has lots of available memory, you should define aliases only for those commands you use frequently, because each alias uses a small amount of memory.

To add command aliases, make a backup of ACAD.PGP in the AutoCAD program directory. Then use your text editor to edit the file. Enter the alias, followed by a comma and the command to be referenced by that alias. The AutoCAD command must be prefixed with an asterisk, as shown in the preceding listing. The IAW DISK includes an IAW-ACAD.PGP file with aliases for every command; you can append it to your existing ACAD.PGP file. You can edit it to remove any aliases you do not need.

*After editing the ACAD.PGP file, you can either exit and reload AutoCAD to load the new definitions, or you can use the REINIT command.*

Prototype drawings and the ACAD.PGP file are basic tools for customizing AutoCAD, common to the DOS version as well. With AutoCAD for Windows, however, the easiest changes you can make are changes to its operating environment, such as the colors and fonts used by the AutoCAD interface. The next section looks at the way AutoCAD maintains its environment configuration and the ways you can change that configuration.

# Customizing the AutoCAD Interface

In Chapter 2, you learned how you could tell AutoCAD to display either icons or text labels in several of the pull-down menus. You can also make a number of other changes to AutoCAD that quickly change the appearance of its interface. The setting for icons versus text labels is set by the Menu **B**itmaps selection on the **S**ettings pull-down menu. You can control most of the other interface configuration options by using the AutoCAD Preferences dialog box, which is shown in figure 18.2. To access the AutoCAD Preferences dialog box, choose **F**ile and then P**r**eferences, or enter **PREFERENCES** at the command prompt.

As with other Windows dialog boxes, the controls in the AutoCAD Preferences dialog box are separated into different groups. There are four boxed groups; AutoCAD Graphics Window, AutoCAD Settings, AutoCAD Text Window, and Digitizer Input. Then there are three buttons that open additional dialog boxes, which affect AutoCAD settings; Co**l**or..., **F**onts..., and **E**nvironment. The AutoCAD Settings group is covered last, after you look at the various ways to fine-tune the AutoCAD for Windows interface.

**Figure 18.2:**

The AutoCAD Preferences dialog box.

# Controlling the Screen Menu and Command Prompt

The AutoCAD Graphics Window group controls the Screen **M**enu, Scroll **B**ars, **T**oolbar, Toolbo**x**, Command **P**rompt, and Window **R**epair options. The following list explains the controls in the AutoCAD Graphics Window group:

- **Screen M**enu check box. This option turns on or off the screen menu.

- **Scroll B**ars check box. This option turns on or off the scroll bars. It is only available if you have configured AutoCAD to use the non-display list Windows video driver. See Chapter 5 for specific information on using the scroll bars.

- **T**oolbar check box. This option turns on or off the toolbar.

- **Toolbox** check box. This option turns on or off the floating toolbox.

- **Command P**rompt drop-down list box. This option specifies the number of lines AutoCAD uses for the command prompt area, from zero to three lines. (0 turns off the Command: prompt.)

- **Window R**epair drop-down list. This option specifies the type of screen update method AutoCAD uses when a portion of the AutoCAD window must be repaired (such as when a dialog box is closed). If Window Repair is set to Bitmap (the default), AutoCAD replaces its display with a bit-map image after each redraw. This setting is fastest for VGA (640×480) and Super VGA (800×600) displays. For high-resolution displays that require more pixels and time to display, such as 1024×768 and 1280×1024, the Fastdraw option is better.

You can change these and other options any time AutoCAD is active and waiting for your input. To change an item, choose the control you want to change, choose the option you want, and then choose OK. The change takes effect immediately.

Try changing a few of AutoCAD's features in the following exercise by using the options in the AutoCAD Graphics Window group.

## Changing the AutoCAD Command Interface

| | |
|---|---|
| *Choose* **F**ile, *then* **P**references | Opens the AutoCAD Preferences dialog box |
| *Make sure the* Screen **M**enu *check box is cleared* | Suppresses the screen menu |
| *Click on the* Command **P**rompt *list box drop-down arrow and select* 1 line | Sets command prompt to a single line |
| *Choose* OK, *then* **C**ontinue | Puts change into effect and closes the dialog box |
| *Choose* **F**ile, *then* **N**ew, *and enter* **TEST** | Starts a new drawing named TEST |

When the drawing displays (see fig. 18.3), notice that the Command: prompt is reduced to a single line, and the screen menu no longer appears.

**Figure 18.3:**

Single command line and no screen menu.

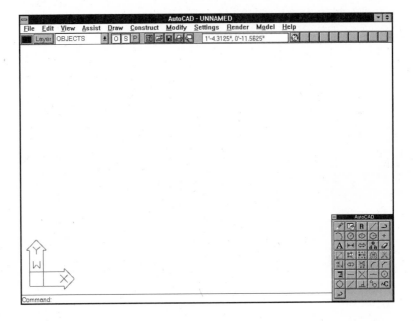

You can just as easily return the AutoCAD display options to normal. Turn on the screen menu again and reset the command prompt to three lines, as shown in the following exercise.

## Restoring Interface Settings

| | |
|---|---|
| *Choose* **F**ile, *then* **P**references, *and put a check in the* Screen **M**enu *check box* | Turns on screen menu |
| *Click on the* Command **P**rompt *list box drop-down arrow, then choose* 3 lines | Sets command prompt to three lines |
| *Choose* OK, *then* **C**ontinue | Puts the change into effect and closes the dialog box |

*The Alert box that pops up when you close the Preferences dialog box is warning you that the changes you have made will not be saved permanently. Later in the chapter you learn how to make the changes to your AutoCAD environment permanent.*

# Controlling the Text Window and Log File

The AutoCAD Text Window group has two settings that enable you to control aspects of AutoCAD's text window. The following sections describe these controls and how they work. Figure 18.4 shows the controls that affect the text window.

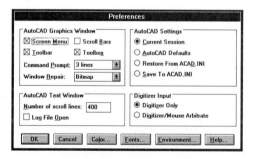

**Figure 18.4:**

The AutoCAD Text Window group in the Preferences dialog box.

## Controlling Text Window Scrolling

The first option in the AutoCAD Text Window group, **N**umber of scroll lines, defines the total number of lines AutoCAD maintains in the text window. The default is 400 lines, meaning that AutoCAD saves the last 400 lines of command-line dialog in memory. The text window includes a vertical scroll bar you can use to view text that already has scrolled outside the window (see fig. 18.5). If you want to view a command you entered earlier, a value that AutoCAD has calculated for you, or AutoCAD's response to one of your previous commands, use the scroll bar to locate the command or value in question.

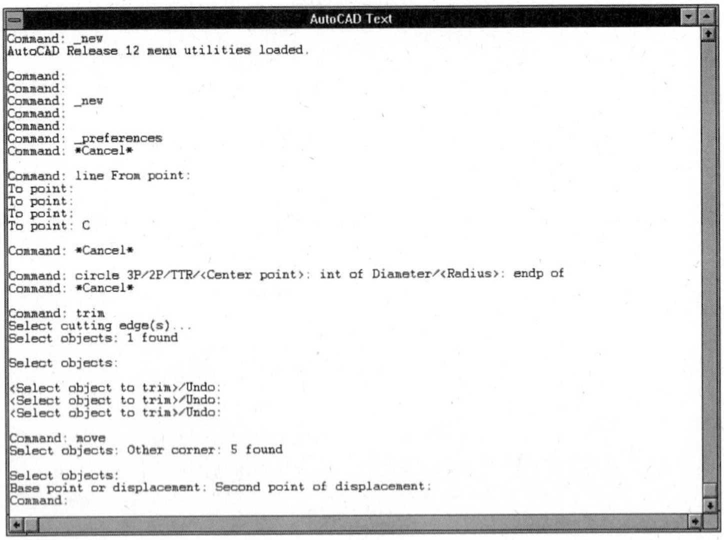

**Figure 18.5:**

AutoCAD's text
window includes
scroll bars.

The Number of scroll lines option sets the size of AutoCAD's text window buffer,
which controls the number of text lines that you can view in the text window by using
the scroll bars. You may prefer to maintain more lines in memory, making them
available for viewing with the scroll bars, or you may want to reduce the number of
lines to conserve memory. To change the number of lines, enter the new value in the
Number of scroll lines text box and choose the OK button. Valid entries are from 200 to
1500.

## Using a Log File

The AutoCAD Text Window group also contains a control for the AutoCAD log file,
ACAD.LOG. All commands that you enter and all of AutoCAD's command responses
(everything that appears in the text window) can be echoed to this file, giving you a log
of your editing session in AutoCAD.

By default, echoing of the text window to a file is turned off. To turn on echoing, click
on the Log File Open check box.

If you then need a hard copy of your AutoCAD session, you can print the file, using
any ASCII text editor, such as Notepad or Write. If you log your editing session to disk,
you can capture AutoCAD command input and output for use in tracking down
problems with your drawing, verifying calculations, or preparing text for AutoCAD
tutorials.

The following exercise illustrates the use of the log file.

# Echoing Commands to a Log File

| | |
|---|---|
| *Choose* **F**ile, *then* **N**ew, *and enter* **TEXTWIN** | Starts a new drawing |
| **Command:** *Choose* **F**ile, *then* **P**references, *and put a check in the* Log File **O**pen *check box* | Turns on text window logging |
| *Choose* OK | Closes dialog box |
| **Command:** *From the toolbox, choose* LINE, *and draw a line* | |
| **Command:** *From the toolbox, choose* CIRCLE, *and draw a circle* | |
| **Command:** *Choose* **A**ssist, *then* **I**nquiry, *then* **L**ist | |
| **Select objects:** *Select the circle and the line* | |
| **Select objects: 2 selected, 2 found** | |
| **Select objects:** *Press Enter, then F2* | Displays text window, listing the entity data (see fig. 18.6) |

Next, you will close and view the log file that AutoCAD has been maintaining for you.

| | |
|---|---|
| **Command:** *Choose* **F**ile, *then* **P**references, *make sure the* Log File **O**pen *check box is not checked, and then choose* OK | Turns off text window logging and closes the log file |
| *Click in the AutoCAD graphics window, and then choose the minimize button (the down-arrow button at the upper right)* | Minimizes AutoCAD to the IAW icon |

Use the text editor of your choice to view the ACAD.LOG file or to use Windows Write, open the Accessories group in the Windows Program Manager, double-click on the Write icon, and perform the following steps:

| | |
|---|---|
| *Choose* **F**ile, *then* **O**pen, *and enter* **\ACADWIN\ACAD.LOG**, *and then choose* OK | Selects the AutoCAD log file for opening |
| *Choose the* **N**o Conversion *button* | Loads file in ASCII format, not in Write's format (see fig 18.6) |

Use the vertical scroll bar to scroll through the ACAD.LOG file and locate the Line, Circle, and List commands you entered previously (see fig. 18.6).

*continues*

*Choose* **File**, *and then* **Ex**it *to exit*
*Write*

*Double-click on the IAW icon at* Restores AutoCAD to a window
*the bottom of the screen*

**Figure 18.6:**

Result of List
command in text
window, and
loaded into Write.

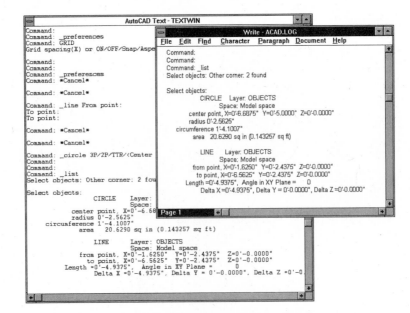

The last boxed group in the Preferences dialog box affects the way AutoCAD works
with your digitizer and/or mouse.

# Controlling Digitizer and Mouse Options

The two radio buttons in the Digitizer Input group, in the Preferences dialog box,
control the way AutoCAD interacts with the mouse and digitizer (if one is installed).
The Digitizer Input group contains the **D**igitizer Only and Di**g**itizer/Mouse Arbitrate
radio buttons. These two options work as described in the following list:

- **Digitizer Only.** This option specifies that AutoCAD accepts input only from the
  digitizer. If no digitizer is configured, AutoCAD accepts input from the mouse. If
  both a digitizer and mouse are connected to the system, AutoCAD ignores input
  from the mouse. You still can use the mouse with the Windows environment and
  other Windows applications.

- **Digitizer/Mouse Arbitrate.** This option specifies that AutoCAD arbitrates input
  from both the mouse and digitizer. AutoCAD accepts input from whichever

device last updated the cursor position or last sent a coordinate sample to AutoCAD.

Now that you have seen the effects of the controls in the Preferences dialog box itself, look at the options available from the buttons at the bottom.

# Controlling Colors and Fonts

The AutoCAD Preferences dialog box provides buttons that enable you to control the fonts and colors used for the AutoCAD interface. Choose the Color button to open the AutoCAD Window Colors dialog box (see fig. 18.7). This dialog box enables you to specify colors for some of the AutoCAD interface components.

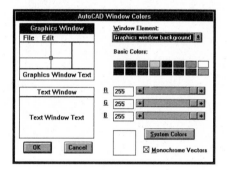

**Figure 18.7:**

The AutoCAD Window Colors dialog box.

The AutoCAD Window Colors dialog box enables you to change the color of the graphics window background, the background color of the command prompt area and screen menu, and the color of the text used for the command prompt and screen menu. You also can change the color of the text window's background and text. The Basic Colors section of the dialog box contains the 16 basic VGA colors, each of which can be selected by clicking on the color.

In addition to the basic colors, you can create custom colors by mixing varying amounts of red, green, and blue by using the RGB color slider controls. These slider controls (scroll bars) specify color values for each of the three primary light colors from a minimum of zero to a maximum of 255. Custom colors, however, are approximated by dithering on most displays. *Dithering* displays a pattern of pixels of various basic colors that average out to the custom color you specify. This results in a coarse display and generally is not useful.

To change a color by using the controls in the AutoCAD Window Colors dialog box, select the element to change by using the Windows Element drop-down list box. You also can click on the element in the Graphics Window or Text Window sample display. Next, specify the new color by clicking on one of the Basic Colors boxes or by using the custom color slider controls. To use the default colors that are assigned to your Windows environment, click on the System Colors button.

The following exercise changes the colors that are used by both the graphics and text windows.

---

## Changing Interface Colors

*Choose* <u>F</u>ile, *then* <u>P</u>references

| | |
|---|---|
| *Choose the* Co<u>l</u>or button | Opens the AutoCAD Window Colors dialog box |
| *Choose* Graphics Text Background *from the Window Element drop-down list box* | |
| *Click on the fifth box in the first row of the* Basic Colors *color boxes* | Selects blue |
| *Click on* Graphics Window Text *in the Graphics Window sample display* | Selects graphics text color in Window Element list |
| *Click on the last box in the first row of the* Basic Colors *color boxes* | Selects white |
| *Click on the words* Text Window Text *in the Text Window sample display* | Selects Text Window Text as the element as to change |
| *Choose the white box in the* Basic Colors *color boxes* | Sets text to white |
| *Choose* Text Window Background *from the Window Element drop-down list box* | Selects Text Window Background as the element to change |
| *Click on the first box in the first row of the* Basic Colors *color boxes* | Selects dark gray |
| *Choose* OK, *then* OK *again, and then* <u>C</u>ontinue | Makes the change take effect |
| *Press F2* | Displays the text window |

---

You can see from the preceding exercise that you can select an interface element to change color in two ways. You can select the element by using the Window Element drop-down list box, or by clicking on the element in the sample display.

Now, change the colors back to the Windows default system colors in the following exercise.

## Resetting Colors

| | |
|---|---|
| *Press F2* | Hides the text window |
| *Choose* **F**ile, *then* **P**references, *and then the* Co**l**or button | Opens the AutoCAD Window Colors dialog box |
| *Choose the* **S**ystem Colors *button, then* OK, *then* OK *again, and then* **C**ontinue | Restores your default system colors |

*Although AutoCAD provides its own Color and Fonts dialog boxes, as a Windows application it inherits some elements of its interface from the settings you choose in the Colors and Fonts utilities in Windows' Control Panel.*

*The title bars and borders of AutoCAD's graphic and text windows always have the colors you choose in the Control Panel Colors utility, whether you choose them individually or select a predefined color scheme. Choosing the System Colors option in AutoCAD's Colors dialog box applies the other colors in the current Windows color scheme to the "user-selectable" AutoCAD window elements.*

*The Control Panel Fonts utility lists the text fonts that are installed on your system and available to your applications. If you purchase additional fonts, you use this utility to install them. Your font choices in AutoCAD's Fonts dialog box are limited to the fonts in this list.*

The last of the options on the AutoCAD Window Colors dialog box, the **M**onochrome Vectors check box, controls the way AutoCAD displays colors in the graphics window. If you put a check mark in the **M**onochrome Vectors check box, AutoCAD displays all drawing entities in a single color (either black or white, depending on the background color). This arrangement is useful if you want to transfer an image to the Windows Clipboard but want to remap all entities to either black or white.

The **F**onts button in the AutoCAD Environment Settings dialog box opens the Font dialog box (see fig. 18.8). The Font dialog box enables you to control the font face name and size used for text in both the graphics and text windows. This size affects the text used for the AutoCAD interface, not the text that appears in your drawing as text entities.

To see how the Font dialog box works, perform the following exercise and change the font that is used for the graphics window to Times Roman. Then change the font that is used for the text window to Courier.

**Figure 18.8:**

The Font dialog
box.

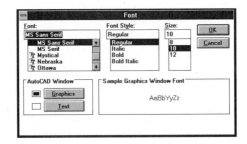

---

## Changing Interface Fonts

| | |
|---|---|
| *Choose* File, *then* Preferences, *and then the* Fonts button | Opens the Font dialog box |

The Graphics option in the AutoCAD Window group already is selected.

| | |
|---|---|
| *Select* Times New Roman *from the* Font *combo box* | Sets Times New Roman as font for graphics window |
| *Choose* Bold *in the* Font Style *combo box* | Selects bold for font |
| *Choose* 12 *in the* Size *combo box* | Selects font size of 12 |
| *Choose the* Text *button in the* AutoCAD Window *group, then* MS Sans Serif *in the* Font *combo box* | Selects MS Sans Serif as font for text window |
| *Choose* OK, *then* OK *again, and then* Continue | Makes change take effect (see fig. 18.9) |
| *Press F2 to view the AutoCAD Text Window* | |
| *Choose* File, *then* Exit AutoCAD, *and then* Discard *changes* | Quits the drawing |

---

Although changing colors and fonts may make the AutoCAD for Windows interface easier to use, several less obvious but more powerful tools for tailoring AutoCAD to work for you are available in the Environment dialog box.

# Controlling AutoCAD's Environment

Choose the Environment button at the bottom of the Preferences dialog box to open the Environment dialog box, which enables you to set AutoCAD's DOS environment variables.

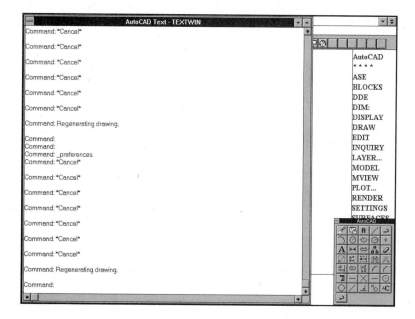

**Figure 18.9:**

Times New Roman and MS Sans Serif used for the AutoCAD interface.

AutoCAD for Windows provides as many as three different means of setting its environment variables. First, as with the DOS version, you can use the DOS SET command. Second, you can use command-line switches in the Windows Program Manager New Program Item or Properties dialog boxes, which override any variables set in the DOS environment or set by the third method. See Chapter 1 or the "Cloning ACAD.INI..." exercise in this chapter for examples.

The third, and most accessible, method of assigning values to AutoCAD's environment variables is to enter them in the text boxes in the Environment dialog box (see fig. 18.10). Settings made here override any DOS environment variable settings, but not those made on the Windows command line. Whether or not they are permanently applied depends on the setting of the **S**ave to ACAD.INI check box (described later in this chapter), in the Preferences dialog box.

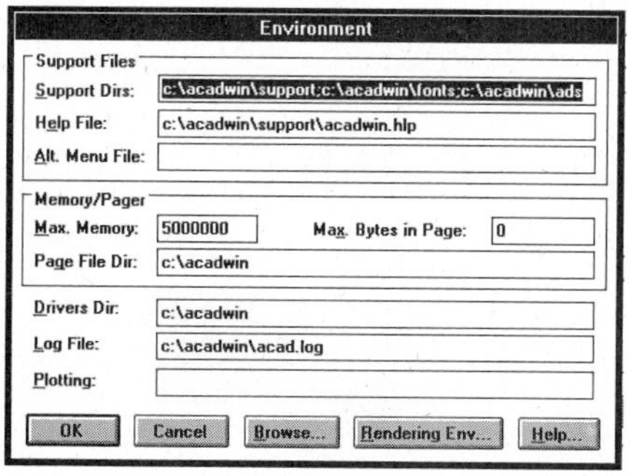

**Figure 18.10:**

The Environment dialog box.

The functions of the text boxes in the Support Directories group are described in the following list:

- **Support Dirs:** This box is a list of directories; the search path AutoCAD uses to find its support files. It corresponds to the ACAD environment variable, and the /s command-line switch.

- **Help File:** This box shows the name of the AutoCAD for Windows help file, which corresponds to the ACADHELP variable.

- **Alt. Menu:** If you use a digitizer, you can name an alternate menu here, which is loaded when you pick Change Template on the AutoCAD template menu. This corresponds to the ACADALTMENU variable.

The Autodesk manual, *Using AutoCAD for Windows*, recommends against changing the values in the text boxes in the Memory/Pager group, unless you have a clearly defined and understood need. These values function as follows:

Three more text boxes are included in the Environment dialog box:

- **Drivers Dir:** This value is a directory or list of directories that limits the paths AutoCAD searches for its driver files. It corresponds to the ACADDRV environment variable, and the /d switch.

- **Log File:** This value is the name of the file to which AutoCAD writes the data sent to its text window, when the Log File **O**pen box is checked in the Preferences dialog box. This corresponds to the ACADLOGFILE variable.

- **Plotting:** This specifies a command that is sent to a plot spooler, and corresponds to the ACADPLCMD variable.

In addition, the Environment dialog box provides two buttons which access dialog boxes of their own. The **B**rowse... button provides a Windows-standard file selection interface, from which you can select directory and file names to place in a selected text box. The **R**endering Env... button pops up a dialog box in which you can specify locations for files used in generating rendered images.

If you exit AutoCAD and restart the program, the default colors, fonts and environment settings are again used by AutoCAD. The next section explains the reason the changes you made to the interface in previous exercises were not permanent.

# Understanding ACAD.INI

Like many Windows programs, AutoCAD maintains many of its settings in an *initialization* file. AutoCAD's initialization file is called ACAD.INI. A typical INI file is separated into sections, with each section labeled by a header in square brackets. Figure 18.11 shows part of the ACAD.INI file loaded into Notepad.

**Figure 18.11:**

ACAD.INI loaded into Notepad.

The [AutoCAD General] section of ACAD.INI contains settings that define the size of AutoCAD's toolbar, the functions assigned to toolbar buttons, and other global AutoCAD parameters. The [AutoCAD Graphics Screen] section contains settings that control the size and appearance of the AutoCAD graphics window. The [AutoCAD Text Screen] section contains settings that control the size and appearance of AutoCAD's text window. Finally, the [AutoCAD Toolbox] section contains settings that define the form-factor and position of AutoCAD's floating toolbox, and the functions assigned to toolbox buttons.

The four sections described above do not appear in figure 18.11—only the Graphics Screen and Text Screen headings.

You can change ACAD.INI settings in two ways. You can edit the file manually, or you can let AutoCAD do it for you automatically. Later in this chapter, you learn how to modify ACAD.INI manually. First, you are shown the way AutoCAD makes changes to ACAD.INI for you.

## Saving Changes in ACAD.INI

Examine the AutoCAD Preferences dialog box again and notice the AutoCAD Settings group, which contains four radio buttons (see fig. 18.12).

The four radio buttons in the AutoCAD Settings group perform the following functions:

The AutoCAD
Settings group in
the AutoCAD
Preferences dialog
box.

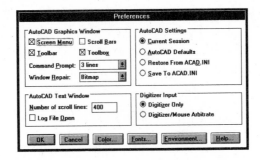

- **Current Session.** Changes that you make to the environment, such as color or font changes, are applied only to the current AutoCAD session. They are not stored in ACAD.INI for future sessions. This option is the default.

- **AutoCAD Defaults.** This setting restores all environment settings to AutoCAD's built-in defaults.

- **Restore From ACAD.INI.** With this setting, AutoCAD reads the settings currently stored in ACAD.INI and applies those settings to the current AutoCAD environment.

- **Save To ACAD.INI.** With this setting, AutoCAD stores the current AutoCAD environment parameters in the appropriate settings in the ACAD.INI file.

As the preceding list indicates, the Current Session option is the default and its radio button automatically is selected when you enter the AutoCAD Environment Settings dialog box. Any changes you make to the AutoCAD environment affect only the current AutoCAD session, not future sessions of AutoCAD.

If you want your changes to become permanent, choose the Save To ACAD.INI radio button before choosing OK to exit the dialog box. Any changes you have made to fonts, colors, or other AutoCAD environment parameters are then stored in ACAD.INI. The next time AutoCAD starts, it looks in ACAD.INI and retrieves the settings.

You can use different ACAD.INI files for different projects, configurations, or users. The default location of ACAD.INI is the AutoCAD for Windows program directory. If, however, you use the /c switch on the AutoCAD for Windows command line to specify an alternate configuration directory (see Chapter 1), ACAD.INI is read from and saved to that directory.

## Restoring ACAD.INI Settings

If you make changes to AutoCAD's environment settings and discover you prefer AutoCAD's defaults, you can easily restore the default settings. Choose the AutoCAD Defaults radio button in the AutoCAD Settings group, then choose OK. AutoCAD restores its built-in default settings. If you also want to save the defaults in ACAD.INI, choose the **S**ave To ACAD.INI radio button before choosing OK to close the dialog box.

If, on the other hand, you make changes to the environment in the current session and you want to restore the settings currently in ACAD.INI, choose the **R**estore From ACAD.INI radio button. AutoCAD reads ACAD.INI and resets its operating parameters accordingly.

The following are the key points to remember about modifying settings in ACAD.INI:

- AutoCAD can automatically change settings in ACAD.INI, which affects future AutoCAD sessions.

- Environment changes you make in AutoCAD are not stored in ACAD.INI (made permanent) unless you select the **S**ave To ACAD.INI radio button before closing the dialog box.

- You can restore AutoCAD's built-in default settings at any time by using the **A**utoCAD Defaults radio button.

- Some changes require that you edit ACAD.INI manually.

 *Although you can directly open and edit the ACAD.INI file with any ASCII text editor while AutoCAD is running, doing so may yield unpredictable results. AutoCAD maintains some INI settings in memory and writes them to the INI file when AutoCAD exits, possibly overwriting changes made directly to the ACAD.INI file.*

## Maintaining Multiple ACAD.INI Files

Clearly, the ACAD.INI file is central to creating and maintaining your custom AutoCAD for Windows environment. If you need to maintain several different working environments, consider creating multiple copies of this critical file, each assigned to a different program-item by Windows' Program Manager.

The idea is simple, and depends on understanding only two key elements of the way AutoCAD works in Windows. First, any application (AutoCAD included), once it has been installed into one of Windows' program groups, can have its icon copied any number of times into the same, or other program groups. Any of these icons can launch the application. Second, AutoCAD can be started with the **/c** command-line switch specifying a certain directory for its configuration files, which consist of ACAD.CFG and ACAD.INI. Because each copy of the AutoCAD icon can be set to point to a different directory, you can create multiple copies of ACAD.INI in multiple directories, with a corresponding AutoCAD icon for each.

*If you make multiple configuration directories and specify a configuration directory with a /c switch on the Windows Program Item or Properties command line, AutoCAD may be unable to find support files. To solve this problem, you should do one of the following.*

*The easiest alternative is to copy currently working ACAD.CFG and ACAD.INI files into the configuration directory and then make changes. The other alternative, if you must create a new configuration, is to edit the Preferences' Environment dialog box settings. When AutoCAD fails to find the support files, choose OK or Cancel to all of the error messages and file dialogs you receive, and then enter the PREFERENCES command. Choose* **E**nvironment *and enter a new* **S**upport Dirs *path, such as:*
**C:\ACADWIN;C:\ACADWIN\SUPPORT;C:\ACADWIN\FONTS**.

Although AutoCAD currently supports up to three concurrent sessions of itself, all concurrent sessions share the same configuration, with the exception of changes made in the Preferences dialog box. The technique described here has nothing to do with running multiple sessions of AutoCAD. This technique is intended as a way of maintaining multiple configurations which can be selected when you start up AutoCAD, each designed for a specific type of work.

The following exercise illustrates the technique.

## Cloning ACAD.INI and the AutoCAD Program-item

Open the Main program group in Program Manager, and then double-click on the File Manager icon.

Use the scrollbars to find the \IAW directory in the File Manager's directory window and double-click on it to display its files.

| | |
|---|---|
| *Choose* **F**ile, *then* C**r**eate Directory, *and enter* **OPTION** | Creates \IAW\OPTION subdirectory |
| *Find and click on the ACAD.INI file, then hold down Ctrl and click on the ACAD.CFG file* | Selects the files |
| *Choose* **F**ile, *then* **C**opy, *click on the* **T**o *text box, and enter* **OPTION** | Specifies the new subdirectory |
| *Choose* OK | Copies the files |
| *Double-click on the File Manager control menu button (at upper left) and choose* OK | Closes the File Manager |

| | |
|---|---|
| *Double-click on the Main program group control menu button and choose* OK | Closes the Main program group |
| *Double-click on the group that contains the IAW icon* | Opens the program group |
| *Hold down Ctrl while you click on and drag the IAW icon to a new location* | Creates a new copy of the program-item |
| *Click on the new icon to highlight it, then choose* <u>F</u>ile, *then* <u>P</u>roperties | Opens the Program Item Properties dialog box |

Click in the <u>C</u>ommand Line: text box and use the left and right cursor keys to examine it. Edit the string that follows the /c switch to `C:\IAW\OPTION`. Also, either change the string in the <u>D</u>escription: text box, or use the Change <u>I</u>con... button to select another icon, so that the new program item can be distinguished from the old.

| | |
|---|---|
| *Choose* OK | Saves changes and closes the dialog box |

You have just created a new and potentially distinct AutoCAD environment. To use it, start the new version from Program Manager. Then any customizing you do in the new environment is saved in the new ACAD.INI (if you choose <u>S</u>ave to ACAD.INI, in the Preferences dialog box).

Now that you have practiced some of the simpler ways to customize AutoCAD's interface, learned how to save the changes you make, and are familiar with AutoCAD's initialization file, you are ready to learn how to customize the command tools unique to AutoCAD for Windows: the toolbar, the floating toolbox, and pull-down menu icons.

# Customizing AutoCAD for Windows' Command Tools

AutoCAD for Windows takes advantage of its environment to provide three unique tools for issuing commands, macros, and even AutoLISP routines. These tools are: the toolbar, the floating toolbox, and icon items in pull-down menus. Each of these areas enables you to create a custom working environment by associating commands with icons and arranging their locations to suit the way you work.

Two means of customization apply to the use of icons instead of text labels in AutoCAD's pull-down menus. You can choose <u>S</u>ettings, then Menu <u>B</u>itmaps to turn icon display on or off, and you can create new icon bit maps and include them in the ACAD.DLL file, as described in the final section of this chapter.

Customizing the toolbar and floating toolbox offers a variety of opportunities to make your working environment more efficient. Start by exploring the AutoCAD for Windows equivalent of the status line: the toolbar.

# Customizing the Toolbar

AutoCAD's toolbar, even without customizing, provides access to many of the most-used AutoCAD commands. The toolbar is also another aspect of the AutoCAD interface that you can customize. The default toolbar, shown in figure 18.13, contains the following items:

- **Current color box.** This choice displays the current color with which entities are drawn. Clicking on this box pops up the Entity Creation Modes dialog box.

- **Layer button.** You can click on this button to pop up the Layer Control dialog box.

- **Layer name drop-down list box.** This option displays the name of the current layer; clicking on it displays a list of layers from which you can choose a new current layer.

- **Preset buttons.** These buttons turn ortho mode and snap mode on and off, and select between paper space and model space (if TILEMODE is set to 0).

- **Coordinate window.** This setting shows the last digitized point (when coordinate display is off). When coordinate display is on, it shows the absolute or relative coordinate of the current cursor position.

- **Programmable buttons.** Depending on the configuration of AutoCAD's graphic window, up to 26 programmable toolbar buttons are available.

Although most of the items in the AutoCAD toolbar are fixed, you can customize the programmable buttons by assigning any AutoCAD command macro to them.

The number of buttons that appear on the toolbar varies according to the value of ToolbarSize in the ACAD.INI file, the size of the font selected for the graphics window interface, and the size of the AutoCAD graphics window. When the AutoCAD window is reduced in size, buttons disappear from the toolbar to accommodate the new window size. When the graphics window is enlarged, additional buttons appear. Figure 18.14 shows the toolbar that results on an 800×600 display when ToolbarSize is set to 12. Figure 18.15 shows a toolbar sized to 24.

Each of the possible 26 toolbar buttons can display a different bit map or character on the button face. AutoCAD includes two DLLs (Dynamic Link Libraries), which contain standard bit maps you can use for button faces. These two DLLs—TBAR16.DLL, and TBAR24.DLL—contain identical bit-mapped images and character sets. The only difference is in the size of the bit maps. TBAR16.DLL contains bit maps that are 16×16 pixels, and TBAR24.DLL's bit maps are 24×24 pixels.

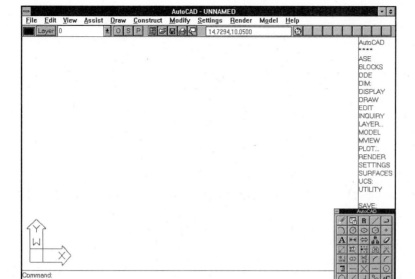

**Figure 18.13:**

The default
AutoCAD toolbar.

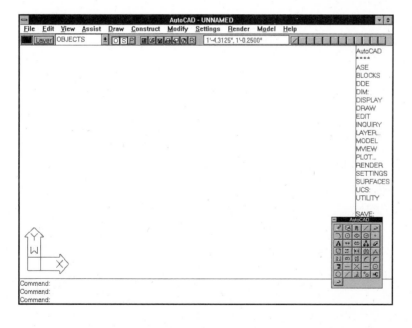

**Figure 18.14:**

The effect of
ToolBarSize=12.

The size of the toolbar and its buttons is controlled by the text font you set for the graphics window. AutoCAD automatically chooses a specified bit map from one of these two DLLs based on the size of the toolbar buttons by using a "best-fit" algorithm.

If the ToolBarSize variable in ACAD.INI is set to 16, for example, AutoCAD uses the bit maps contained in TBAR16.DLL. If ToolBarSize is set to 18, the 16×16 bit maps still are closer to the required size than the bit maps contained in TBAR24.DLL (which are 24×24), so AutoCAD still uses TBAR16.DLL. AutoCAD scales the bit maps as necessary to fit the buttons when the toolbar size is not one of the two standard sizes (16 or 24 pixels).

**Figure 18.15:**

The effect of ToolBarSize=24.

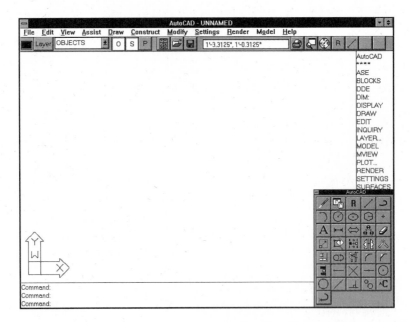

## Customizing Toolbar Buttons

Because toolbar button definitions are stored in the ACAD.INI file, you should make a backup copy of your ACAD.INI file before you begin to customize the AutoCAD toolbar. If you make a change that you do not like and cannot get the toolbar back to normal, you can copy the backup of ACAD.INI to replace the modified file. The following exercise creates a backup copy of ACAD.INI called ACADINI.OLD.

### Backing Up ACAD.INI

Open the Main program group in Program Manager, and then double-click on the File Manager icon.

Use the scrollbars to find the \IAW directory in the File Manager's directory window and double-click on it to display its files.

*Find and click on the ACAD.INI file*        Selects the file

| | |
|---|---|
| *Choose* **F**ile, *then* **C**opy, *click on the* **T**o *text box, and enter* `ACADINI.OLD` | Specifies the new file name |
| *Choose* OK | Copies the file |
| *Double-click on the File Manager control menu button (at upper left) and choose* OK | Closes the File Manager |

Now that ACAD.INI is backed up, you are ready to begin making some changes to ACAD.INI through AutoCAD.

Although you can edit ACAD.INI directly to add new button definitions and change existing ones, you might find that making the changes from AutoCAD's graphics window is easier. To define a button, simply click on the button with the right mouse button. This opens the AutoCAD Toolbar Button *n* dialog box, as shown in figure 18.16 (*n* is the number of the button you have selected to modify).

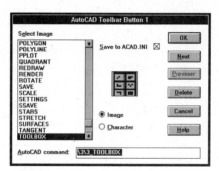

**Figure 18.16:**

The AutoCAD Toolbar Button dialog box.

Try changing one of the toolbar buttons. The following exercise assigns the 'REDRAW command to toolbar button 1.

## Modifying a Toolbar Button

| | |
|---|---|
| *Choose* **F**ile, *then* **N**ew, *and enter* **BUTTON** | Begins a new drawing named BUTTON |
| *Right-click on the first toolbar button to the right of the paper space button* | Chooses the Toolbox button and displays AutoCAD Toolbar Button 1 dialog box |
| *Make sure the* **C**haracter *radio button is turned on* | Uses letters rather than icons for the face of the button |
| *Select R in the* Select Character: *list box* | |

*continues*

| | |
|---|---|
| *Double-click on the* **A**utoCAD Command *text box, and enter* **'REDRAW** | Assigns transparent REDRAW command |
| *Choose* **M**odify | Applies the change (see fig. 18.17) |
| *Click on the new* R *toolbar button* | Issues REDRAW command |

**Figure 18.17:**

The 'REDRAW command as-signed to button 1.

Your new toolbar button definition continues to work as you have programmed it until you exit AutoCAD. You can begin a new drawing and the 'REDRAW button will still be available. The change, however, is not stored in ACAD.INI for the next AutoCAD session unless you access the P**r**eferences dialog box and choose **S**ave to ACAD.INI.

Because the first five programmable toolbar buttons are already assigned useful general-purpose functions, do not save the modified button 1. In the next exercise, however, you can assign the 'REDRAW command to button 6 and make the change permanent.

The first step is to change button 1 back to its original state, so that the Toolbox bit map displays. The following exercise accomplishes three tasks: it changes the size of AutoCAD's toolbar (if necessary), assigns the 'REDRAW command to toolbar button 6, and assigns the LINE command to button 7. If your configuration already displays at least seven programmable buttons, you can skip the file editing steps.

## Changing Toolbar Size and Customizing Buttons

If you need to increase the number of toolbar buttons on your display, perform the follow-ing steps. Use the ASCII text editor of your choice, or open Program Manager's Accessories group and double-click on the Notepad icon to use the Windows Notepad.

| | |
|---|---|
| *In Notepad, choose* **F**ile, *then* **O**pen, *enter* **\IAW\ACAD.INI** *and choose* OK | Opens ACAD.INI for editing |

Notice that the ToolBar1 line still contains the Toolbox command.

| | |
|---|---|
| *Find and edit the ToolBarSize entry to read* **ToolBarSize=12** | Reduces the size of the toolbar |
| *Choose* **F**ile, *then* E**x**it, *and then choose* **Y**es | Closes Notepad and saves ACAD.INI |

| | |
|---|---|
| *In AutoCAD, choose* **F**ile, *then* **P**references, *click on the* **R**estore *from ACAD.INI radio button, and choose* OK | Reads the setting from the modified ACAD.INI file |

If you changed the ToolBarSize value, note that the toolbar is now smaller than in the preceding exercise and more buttons are displayed (see fig. 18.14).

| | |
|---|---|
| *Right-click on button 7 (the first blank button)* | Opens the AutoCAD Toolbar Button 7 dialog box |
| *Make sure* **S**ave to ACAD.INI *is off* | |
| *Make sure the* **C**haracter *radio button is turned on* | |
| *Choose* **R** *in the* Select Character: *list box* | |
| *Click on the* **A**utoCAD Command *text box, and enter* `'REDRAW` | |
| *Choose* **N**ext | Applies the changes and moves to edit the next button (7) |
| *Make sure the* **I**mage *radio button is turned on* | Uses icons for the face of the button |
| *Choose* **LINE** *in the* Select Image: *list box* | Selects the LINE icon |
| *Click on the* **A**utoCAD Command *text box, and enter* `\3\3LINE` | Assigns the actual AutoCAD command (explanation of the \3 codes follows the exercise) |
| *Choose* OK | Applies the changes and stores new settings in ACAD.INI |
| *Click on the LINE toolbar button* | Starts the LINE command |
| *Click on the 'REDRAW toolbar button* | Issues transparent REDRAW command |
| *Enter several more points* | Draws lines |

If you changed the size of your toolbar, edit your ACAD.INI file to return the toolbar size back to 16 and then restore the ACAD.INI file from the Preferences dialog box.

*Before you continue, you may want to edit your ACAD.INI file and change the toolbar size to the height you prefer. Making it larger reduces the number of buttons displayed. Similarly, selecting a different font, adjusting the size of the graphics screen text, or*

*resizing the AutoCAD graphic window can cause AutoCAD to display more or fewer toolbar buttons.*

When you choose the Save All button in the AutoCAD Toolbar Button dialog box, AutoCAD saves in ACAD.INI the currently assigned values of all toolbar buttons. If you want to verify that the new toolbar button 6 and 7 settings are updated in the file, load ACAD.INI into Notepad and view it. The ToolBar6 and ToolBar7 settings in ACAD.INI now should read like the following settings:

```
ToolBar6='REDRAW #R
ToolBar7=\3\3LINE ^LINE^
```

Note that the setting for ToolBar6 includes the characters **#R** after the 'REDRAW macro command. The pound character (#) indicates that the button face uses a character on its face, rather than a bit map. The ToolBar7 setting, however, includes the directive **^LINE^** after the LINE macro command. The carets (^) surround a bit-map resource ID, which in this case is LINE. The bit-map resource LINE is contained, along with bit maps for forty other common commands and object snaps, in two sizes in the DLL files TBAR16.DLL and TBAR24.DLL.

## Using Special Characters in Toolbar Macros

Notice also that the default ToolBar1 setting begins with two combinations of **\3**. The (\3) is AutoCAD's way of issuing the Ctrl-C key combination in toolbar macros. This cancels any command pending when the toolbar button is used. You can also use \n for the newline character, \t for Tab, or \nnn for any ASCII character (*nnn* is a variable that represents the decimal number of the character). Another special character you can use in toolbar macros is the semicolon. When you create a toolbar macro, AutoCAD appends a space to it, which is interpreted as a return when the macro is used. To suppress this space/return, end the macro with a trailing semicolon. Note that this trailing semicolon is interpreted differently in menu macros, in which a semicolon also is interpreted as a return.

*If you are familiar with AutoLISP, you can include AutoLISP expressions in toolbar macros. When you create toolbar macros, however, you are limited to 256 characters.*

## Customizing the Floating Toolbox

One of the handiest features of AutoCAD for Windows, and one that has no equivalent in the DOS version, is its floating toolbox. This tool provides constantly available access to as many as 128 commands, macros, and AutoLISP routines with a single pick. And one of the toolbox's most powerful features is the ease with which you can tailor it to your particular needs, and the job at hand.

If the toolbox is not currently visible, click on the toolbox icon on the toolbar. Choosing this icon repeatedly cycles the toolbox through three configurations: 1) fixed vertically along the right side of the graphic window, 2) floating, 3) fixed vertically on the left, and 4) not visible. Click on the toolbox icon until the toolbox is in its floating configuration, with its AutoCAD title bar visible (see fig. 18.18).

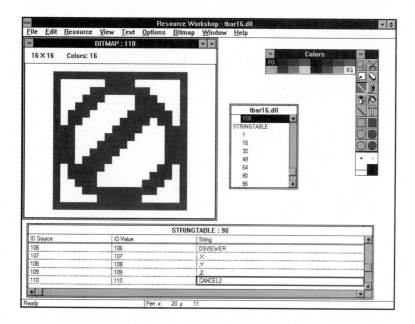

**Figure 18.18:**

The floating toolbox.

*Because the button definitions for the toolbox are stored in the ACAD.INI file, it is a good idea to create a backup of this critical file before making changes to it. See the exercise titled "Backing Up ACAD.INI," in the section on customizing the toolbar.*

To make a change to any button in the toolbox, just right-click on it. The Toolbox Customization dialog box opens (see fig. 18.19), which is quite similar to the Toolbar Button *n* dialog box described earlier in the chapter. The following exercise redefines a toolbox button to issue the EXPLODE command, and changes the default number of buttons in each row.

## Changing Toolbox Size and Customizing Buttons

If you have not already done so, click on the toolbox icon (the first one to the right of the paper space button, P) until the toolbox appears, similar to figure 18.18.

| | |
|---|---|
| *Right-click on one of the toolbox buttons* | Pops up the Toolbox Customization dialog box |
| *Make sure* **S***ave to* ACAD.INI *is off* | |
| *Use the scroll bars to choose* **EXPLODE** *in the* **I***mage Name list box* | Selects the EXPLODE bit map |
| *Double-click in the* **A***utoCAD Command: text box, and enter* **\3\3EXPLODE** | Assigns the actual command to the button |

See the section on using special characters in toolbar macros, earlier in this chapter, for a description of the \3 codes.

| | |
|---|---|
| *Double-click on the* **F***loating: text box of the* Toolbox Width *group, and enter* **5** | Changes the width of the toolbox |
| *Choose* OK | Applies the changes |

**Figure 18.19:**

The Toolbox Customization dialog box.

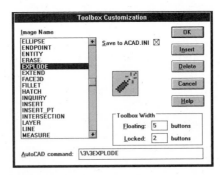

The other buttons in the Toolbar Customization dialog box function as follows:

- **Insert**. This button enables you to insert a new button at the current location.

- **Delete**. This button removes the selected button from the toolbox.

- **Save All**. This button stores the new definition and configuration information for the entire toolbox to ACAD.INI.

Most of the information provided in the preceding section on customizing toolbar buttons applies to toolbox buttons as well. You can assign AutoCAD commands, macros, and even short AutoLISP routines to any button, and have them always handy.

Clearly, AutoCAD for Windows provides far greater flexibility in the manner of issuing commands than does the DOS version. The ability to associate almost any command with an icon in the toolbar, the floating toolbox, or the pull-down menus, offers an incredible opportunity for customization.

However, the variety of bit maps available to use for these icons is somewhat limited. The next section describes a fairly simple means of overcoming this limitation.

# Creating Custom Bit Maps

You can create your own custom DLLs and add your own bit maps to the toolbar and toolbox buttons. To create new Windows DLLs, you generally need a resource editor to create the bit maps, as well as the Windows Resource Compiler (RC), the Microsoft Segmented Executable Linker, and MASM (macro-assembler) to compile the DLLs. To modify existing DLLs, you need only a resource editor.

The easiest way to create custom bit maps for the AutoCAD toolbar and toolbox is to add them to the existing TBAR??.DLL files. Resource editors, such as the Borland Resource Workshop (see fig. 18.20) and Whitewater Resource Toolkit, enable you to edit resources in existing files (including EXE, DLL, and other file types), and to add new resources to existing files. You do not need to understand programming at any level to add these new resources to AutoCAD. The Borland Resource Workshop is included with Borland programming languages for Windows and Object Vision Pro. The Whitewater Resource Toolkit is available through many software dealers and from Symantec.

To add custom bit maps to your existing toolbar/toolbox DLLs, use the following procedure. Because the process requires a third-party resource editor, the procedure is not included as an exercise; see your chosen resource editor's documentation for details on its use.

1. Create backup copies of the existing AutoCAD toolbar DLLs.

2. Load the appropriate toolbar/toolbox (such as TBAR16.DLL) DLL into a resource editor capable of adding new resources to existing and DLL files.

3. Create a new bit-map resource by using the bit-map editing tools in the resource editor.

4. Assign a name to the bit-map resource. The name of the bitmap must be the next whole number above the current highest bit map number. If you add a new bit map to the default TBAR16.DLL, for example, you would name it 110.

**Figure 18.20:**

Using the Borland Resource Work-shop to edit TBAR16.DLL.

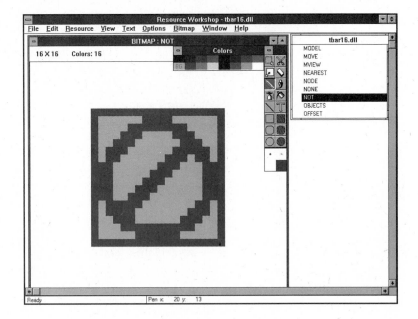

5.  If you are editing the TBAR16 or TBAR24 DLL's, edit the DLL's STRINGTABLE by using the resource editor's String editor and add an entry with an ID Source that matches the name of the bit-map resource (such as 110, if you use the ex-ample from step 4). Next, give the new entry a string value. The string value must not match any existing string values or AutoCAD will crash. This is not required for ACAD.DLL.

6.  Save the file to add the resources to the DLL without requiring compiling or linking.

*Do not give an AutoCAD toolbar DLL's stringtable ID sources identical string values or AutoCAD will crash. For example, you can not have 2 string values of CANCEL. Name one CANCEL and name the other CANCEL2.*

Although the process may seem confusing to you if you have never used a resource editor such as the two just described, it is really quite simple. All you have to do is create a bit map by using the editor's built-in paint program, create the resource IDs by using a few menu commands, and then save the file. In minutes and without any programming knowledge at all, you can add new bit-map resources to your toolbar DLLs, making them available in AutoCAD.

To assign a custom bit-map resource to a toolbar button, use the same procedure as for one of the standard bit-map resources—click on the toolbar button with the right mouse button, then select the custom bit-map resource ID from the Enter Resource ID drop-down list box. Remember to add the custom bit-map and resource ID string to each of the standard toolbar DLLs to ensure that your custom bit maps are available for any button size. Figure 18.21 shows a new bit-map resource added to the toolbar.

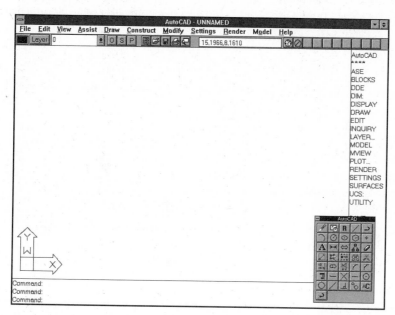

**Figure 18.21:**

Custom CANCEL2 bit map added to toolbar button 7.

# Creating Custom Menu Bit Maps

You can also use the Borland Resource Workshop or Whitewater Resource Toolkit to add custom bit maps to your AutoCAD pull-down menu. Each AutoCAD menu consists of a source menu file with an MNU extension, a compiled menu file with an MNX extension, and a DLL file that has the same name as the menu file but that has a DLL file extension.

For a complete treatment of menus, see *Maximizing AutoCAD Release 12* from New Riders Publishing. A brief explanation of the process, however, can help you understand how to add new bit maps to the existing AutoCAD menu and replace some of the existing text items with bit maps.

# Examining Menus

Each AutoCAD menu begins as an ASCII text source file containing sections that define the screen menu, pull-down menus, tablet menus, dialog boxes, and other features of the AutoCAD menu interface. The menu source file uses an MNU file extension. When the menu source file is complete, you can load the menu into AutoCAD by using the MENU command, which instructs AutoCAD to automatically compile the menu file into a format that AutoCAD can use more efficiently. The compiled menu file receives the same name as the MNU file but uses a file extension of MNX. AutoCAD then uses the MNX file to index the menu file.

In addition to the MNU and MNX files, a DLL file is used to supply bit maps that appear in the AutoCAD for Windows pull-down menus. The standard AutoCAD for Windows menu, ACAD.MNX, uses a corresponding ACAD.DLL file.

# Creating and Using New Menu Bit Maps

Although creating a new menu takes time, adding new bit maps to the existing ACAD.DLL file and to the ACAD.MNU source menu file does not. You add a bit map to a menu DLL in exactly the same way you add new button bit maps to a toolbar DLL. Use a resource editor that enables you to add bit maps to an existing DLL.

The existing bit maps in ACAD.DLL are 32×32 pixels. This is a suitable size for pull-downs containing only bit maps, but if you want to mix bit maps and text labels in the same pull-down, you may find that 16×16 bit maps look better. The following procedure adds a bit map called REDRAW to ACAD.DLL:

1. Create a backup copy of ACAD.DLL.

2. Load ACAD.DLL into the Whitewater Resource Toolkit (or other resource editor).

3. Use the resource editor to create a new bit map, and assign to it the Resource ID REDRAW.

4. Save the new bit map in the DLL by using the resource editor's file commands. This step adds the new bit map to the DLL.

 *The existing bit maps in ACAD.DLL use cryptic names, such as X19, but you can use more informative names.*

After you add the bit map to the menu DLL, you can use it in your menu. The following exercise adds a bit map with the resource ID REDRAW to the **R**edraw command option in the **V**iew pull-down menu. You enclose the REDRAW bit-map resource ID in carets to inform AutoCAD that it is a bit-map reference.

*The following exercise is for example only.* **Do not** *perform the exercise unless you have used the preceding steps to add a new REDRAW bit map to ACAD.DLL.*

## Adding Custom Bit Maps to a Menu

Create a backup copy of ACAD.MNU by using the Windows File Manager.

Open the Accessories group in the Program Manager and double-click on the Write icon.

| | |
|---|---|
| *In Write, choose* **F**ile, *then* **O**pen, *enter* `\ACADWIN\SUPPORT\ACAD.MNU`, *and choose* OK | Begins to load the AutoCAD menu source file |
| *Choose* **N**o Conversion | Loads file in ASCII format |
| *Choose* Fi**nd**, *then* **F**ind, *then enter* `***POP3`, *and choose* **F**ind Next | Locates character String ***POP3, which is the header for the **V**iew menu |
| *Click on the Find dialog box* Cancel *button* | Cancels the Find dialog box |
| *The second line under the ***POP3 header reads:* `[/RRedraw]'_redraw` | |
| *Change the second line to read as follows:* `[^REDRAW^/RRedraw    ]'_redraw` | |
| *Choose* **F**ile, *then* E**x**it, *and then* Yes | Exits Write and saves the changes |
| *Make the AutoCAD window active* | |
| Command: **MENU** | Displays the Select Menu File dialog box |
| *Choose* ACAD.MNU *from the* File **N**ame *list box, and then choose* **O**K | Selects and reloads the menu file, causing AutoCAD to recompile the file |
| *Choose* **V**iew *to see the new REDRAW bit map (see fig. 18.22)* | |

You can see from the preceding exercise that assigning a bit map to a menu item is a relatively simple task—you locate the menu item to which you want to add the bit map and then add the bit map resource ID enclosed in carets (^REDRAW^, for example) inside the square brackets that define the menu label.

The Menu **B**itmaps item on the **S**ettings pull-down menu will not
turn on and off the display of the new Redraw bit map. The turning
on and off of bit maps is down by swapping alternate pages in the
ACAD.MNU file. The swapped pages are identical except for the bit
maps in the labels of alternate pages. See the book Maximizing AutoCAD Release
12, from New Riders Publishing, to learn how to swap menu pages.

**Figure 18.22:**

Custom menu bit
map added to the
Redraw menu
item.

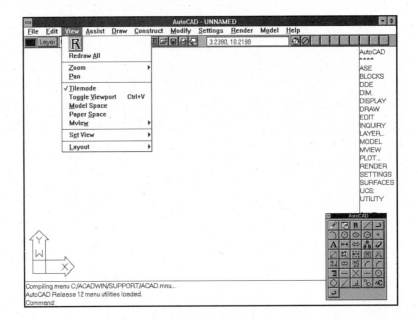

# Summary

You have learned in this chapter that you can customize AutoCAD in numerous ways.
You can use the AutoCAD Preferences dialog box to customize AutoCAD's graphic
and text windows, set up and control a text log file, control digitizer input, change the
fonts and colors used for the AutoCAD interface, and save and restore settings in
ACAD.INI.

You can redefine toolbar and toolbox buttons as simply as clicking on a button with the
right mouse button, then using the dialog boxes to assign to the button a macro command string and resource ID. Use the Save All button in the dialog box to save all of
your custom button definitions in ACAD.INI.

Although the creation of new toolbar and toolbox DLLs requires programming experience and various programming tools, the addition of new bit maps to an existing DLL

for use on custom buttons is a simple task with resource editors such as the Borland Resource Workshop or Whitewater Resource Toolkit. These resource editors enable you to add bit maps and other resources to existing DLL and EXE files without any programming tools or experience. The process of adding new bit maps to menu DLLs is equally easy by using these types of resource editors.

This chapter showed you how to to start making the most of AutoCAD for Windows' advanced features to change the way you work with AutoCAD. Chapter 19 introduces you to the wide variety of methods available for exchanging data between AutoCAD and other applications. These methods include two capabilities that only the Windows version of AutoCAD offers—Object Linking and Embedding (OLE), and Dynamic Data Exchange (DDE). As you will learn, these techniques enable you to apply the power of AutoCAD to tasks ranging from illustrating a word-processed document to performing parametric modeling with a spreadsheet program.

# CHAPTER 19

# Data Exchange with Other Applications

The popularity of AutoCAD, in part, is based on the strength of its "open architecture"—features that enable you to tailor it to work the way you need it to, including integrating it with other software. The previous chapter examined some of the customization options. In this chapter, you look at the variety of methods AutoCAD provides for exchanging data with other applications.

Several of these methods have been available since the earliest versions of AutoCAD, and some are new to Release 12. AutoCAD for Windows extends these data exchange capabilities by capitalizing on one of the primary benefits of the Windows environment—its built-in tools for integrating applications and sharing data. The capability to exchange data easily with other applications is one of AutoCAD for Windows' most important new features.

In this chapter, you learn how to move data in and out of AutoCAD and to share drawing data with other applications. Whether you want to copy a selection from a drawing to use in a report, or perform more extensive data sharing for parametric design, this chapter shows you techniques for exchanging AutoCAD and other application data.

Some types of data exchange are easier to accomplish than others. You can, for example, export a drawing easily from AutoCAD to a document processor, such as PageMaker, or another graphics program, such as Paintbrush or InterGraph MicroStation. Extensive exchanges of more complex data may require programming with AutoLISP, ADS (the AutoCAD Development System), or a Windows programming environment, such as Visual Basic.

This chapter begins by describing the data exchange tools unique to AutoCAD for Windows. You learn to use the Clipboard to paste images from AutoCAD into documents, and how to use Object Linking and Embedding (OLE) techniques to automate the process of revising these images. Then you look at the tools available for creating custom data exchange systems within Windows. Finally, you explore the file formats used for AutoCAD data exchange, which work in the DOS environment as well.

# Understanding Windows Data Exchange Methods

Windows provides three methods for direct exchange of data between applications. The first two methods use the Windows Clipboard. The Clipboard is an area in memory that all Windows applications share. You can use this area of memory to perform static data exchanges of information between applications. This type of data exchange is referred to as static because a change to the original source data does not affect the copied data (the copy is unchanging, or static). Figure 19.1 shows a drawing copied through the Windows Clipboard from AutoCAD to the Windows Paintbrush application.

The second method, called *Object Linking and Embedding*, or OLE, differs from a simple static data exchange in that the resulting image retains its association with the program that created it. This linking and embedding enables you to revise the object by a simple direct means, described later in the chapter.

The third method for data sharing in Windows is called *Dynamic Data Exchange*, or DDE. As its name implies, DDE enables you to share data dynamically among applications. When such a link is established between AutoCAD and another application, changes made to the data in one are automatically reflected in the other. DDE also enables you to create *parametric designs*, which use programs such as Microsoft Excel or Lotus 1-2-3 for Windows as design programs, and AutoCAD as the drawing generator. After you create a parametric DDE link, changes you make to the values of the design program's data (the design parameters) automatically alter the appearance of the drawing in AutoCAD.

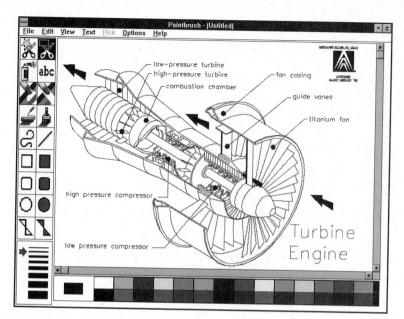

**Figure 19.1:**

An AutoCAD drawing copied to Paintbrush.

Although AutoCAD includes some commands and features for direct use of DDE, the effective use of DDE in AutoCAD requires some programming. Your exploration of data exchange with AutoCAD, therefore, starts with a simpler approach—the Windows Clipboard.

## Understanding the Windows Clipboard

Windows sets up a common area in memory that all applications running under Windows can share. This memory structure is called the *Clipboard*. An application can place data in the Clipboard and retrieve data from it. This capability enables applications to share data; the source application places the data in the Clipboard, and the destination application retrieves it from the Clipboard.

The Main program group in Windows includes an application called the *Clipboard Viewer*. Although the Clipboard Viewer is titled and generally referred to as "Clipboard," it is different from the Clipboard. The Clipboard Viewer is a Windows application that enables you to view the contents of the Clipboard in various formats, save the contents to disk, and retrieve data from disk to place in the Clipboard.

In most cases, you do not need to use the Clipboard Viewer to move data from one application to another. You can copy data easily from AutoCAD to another application by using just the application's menus and commands. The Clipboard Viewer is most useful for verifying the current contents of the Clipboard, determining which types of data are available, and saving Clipboard contents to disk.

# Choosing Clipboard Data Formats

The Clipboard can contain many types of data or the same data in many different formats. A single image, for example, can be stored in the Clipboard as a bit map (Bitmap format, BMP extension), metafile (Picture format, WMF extension), Device-Independent-Bitmap (DIB format and extension), or in a proprietary format controlled by the source application (owner format and extension). Additional data types, such as text and spreadsheet data, also have special formats in the Clipboard.

A Windows application that places data in the Clipboard controls the types and formats that appear in the Clipboard. The application provides the data in as many different formats as possible. An application that is retrieving data from the Clipboard uses the most appropriate available format. Some Windows applications enable you to select the format you want to use to import from the Clipboard.

AutoCAD provides four methods for copying drawing data to the Clipboard, each of which places different types of data in the Clipboard. The following selections are available in AutoCAD's <u>E</u>dit menu:

- **Copy <u>I</u>mage**. This option places an image of selected entities in the Clipboard, in bit-map format.

- **Copy <u>V</u>ectors**. This option places the selected entities in both Picture (Windows Metafile) format and native AutoCAD format in the Clipboard.

- **Copy <u>E</u>mbed**. This option places the selected entities in Picture and native AutoCAD format, as well as OwnerLink data (information about the server application) in the clipboard.

- **Copy <u>L</u>ink**. This option places the entire drawing's entities in Picture format and OwnerLink and ObjectLink data (information about the data file for the server application) in the clipboard.

*AutoCAD for Windows also provides two options for writing the entire current drawing to files that other Windows applications can use. In the <u>F</u>ile menu, the Save DI<u>B</u> selection writes the drawing to a Device-Independent-Bitmap file, with a DIB extension. One of the options under the <u>I</u>mport/Export selection is W<u>M</u>F Out, which writes the drawing to a Picture (Windows metafile) format file, with a WMF extension.*

What is the difference between bit maps and Picture files? A *bit map* is a graphic representation of an image that is composed of dots. A monochrome bit map uses alternating dots of black and white to create an image. A color bit map is similar, but uses colored dots to create the image. These dots are the only entities that make up the image—lines, circles, and other graphic shapes are converted to patterns of dots. After a drawing is converted to a bit map, the lines and other entities are no longer recognized as objects. The entire image is simply a collection of dots. Bit-map images are used by many paint programs.

A *metafile*, which is represented by the *Picture* format name in the Clipboard Viewer, is more like an AutoCAD drawing. Lines, circles, and other graphic entities in a metafile are recognized as objects, not just as patterns of dots. Programs that edit metafile images enable you to delete objects selectively from the image, move them, and resize the image without losing its proportional scale or image quality. These capabilities are similar in concept to the editing tools available in AutoCAD.

The method you use to copy AutoCAD data to the Clipboard depends on the receiving application and the format you want to use to import the file. The process for accomplishing the transfer, however, is similar. The next exercise illustrates the method for copying drawing data to the Clipboard as a bit map using the EXCHANGE.DWG file from the IAW DISK.

---

## Copying Data to the Clipboard in Bitmap Format

Command: In AutoCAD, *choose* **F**ile, *then* **O**pen, *and enter* **EXCHANGE**   Opens an existing drawing named EXCHANGE

Command: *Choose* **E**dit, *then* Copy **I**mage   Begins a Windows bit-map copy

The large AutoCAD crosshair is replaced by a smaller crosshair.

*Pick a point to the left and above the circle*   Defines the upper left corner of a boundary box

*Pick a point to the right and below the circle*   Defines the second corner of the box and copies the image

---

Figure 19.2 shows the Copy Image process.

You can see from the preceding exercise that copying a bit-mapped image to the Clipboard is simple. You place a boundary box around the portion of the image you want to copy, and Windows automatically places the image in the Clipboard in Bitmap format.

*The boundary box specification is controlled by Windows, not AutoCAD, so it does not behave exactly like an AutoCAD Window selection.*

**Figure 19.2:**

Copying a bit-
map image from
AutoCAD to the
Clipboard.

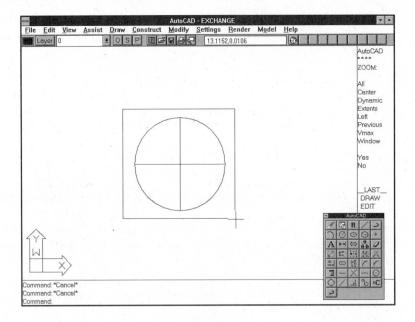

How can you verify that the data is really in the Clipboard, and that it is in the right format? Open the Clipboard Viewer application to view the contents of the Clipboard and the available formats. The next exercise shows you how to start the Clipboard Viewer and view the data in the Clipboard.

## Starting the Clipboard Viewer

Continue from the previous exercise.

*In Program Manager, double-click on the Clipboard Viewer icon in the Main program group*          Starts the Clipboard Viewer

*In Clipboard, choose Display, then Bitmap*          Produces no change in the image

Notice that the viewer defaulted to Auto mode, and that Bitmap is the only other choice.

*Click in the AutoCAD window*          Returns to AutoCAD and leaves the Viewer open

Figure 19.3 shows the Clipboard Viewer displaying a bit-map image copied from AutoCAD.

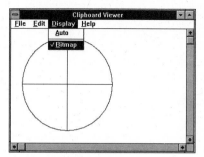

**Figure 19.3:**

The Clipboard
Viewer.

In the preceding exercise, the Clipboard Viewer **D**isplay menu included two options: **A**uto (the default) and **B**itmap. Data sent to the Clipboard can exist in more than one format. The **A**uto option directs the Clipboard Viewer to display the data in the format that shows the data in the greatest detail. Some data formats provide additional detail that other formats cannot display (such as formatted text versus unformatted text).

The **B**itmap option that you selected in the preceding exercise had no effect because the AutoCAD Clipboard data was only in the Bitmap data format. When you copy data to the Clipboard in multiple formats, however, you can change the view of the data in the Clipboard Viewer by selecting the desired data format from the **D**isplay menu.

The next exercise completes the exchange process by copying the contents of the Clipboard to a Paintbrush document.

## Copying AutoCAD Graphics to Other Programs

Continue from the previous exercise.

| | |
|---|---|
| *In Program Manager, double-click on the Paintbrush icon in the Accessories group* | Starts Paintbrush |
| *Choose* **O**ptions, *then* **I**mage Attributes | Opens the Image Attributes dialog box |
| *Choose the* pels *radio button in the* **U**nits *group box* | Specifies pixel units |
| *Enter* **640** *in the* **W**idth *box and* **480** *in the* **H**eight *box, then choose* OK | Sets size to 640×480 pixels |
| *Choose* **E**dit, *then* **P**aste | Displays the Clipboard image in Paintbrush |
| *Click outside the boundary box* | Pastes the image |
| *Choose* **F**ile, *then* E**x**it, *then* **N**o | Exits and discards the Paintbrush document |

The process you used in the preceding exercise to move data from the Clipboard to Paintbrush is the same for any Windows application that supports static data exchange. You can use AutoCAD's Copy **I**mage selection to place the image in the Clipboard, then use **P**aste in the receiving application's **E**dit menu to paste the image from the Clipboard.

The process for copying an image from AutoCAD to the Clipboard either in vector (Picture) format, or as an *object* (OLE format) is similar to that for copying in Bitmap (image) format. In the following exercise, you copy the same image to the Clipboard as before, but this time as vectors.

## Copying Data to the Clipboard in Picture Format

Continue from the previous exercise, with AutoCAD and the Clipboard Viewer open, *or* start the Clipboard Viewer and AutoCAD, and, in AutoCAD, open the existing drawing named EXCHANGE.

| | |
|---|---|
| *In AutoCAD, choose* **E**dit, *then* Copy **V**ectors | Issues COPYCLIP command |
| `Command: _COPYCLIP` | |
| `Select objects:` *Select the circle and the lines* | Builds a selection set |
| `Select objects:` *Press Enter* | Ends selection and copies the data to the Clipboard |
| *In the Clipboard Viewer, choose* **D**isplay | Displays the available formats |
| *Choose* **F**ile, *then* E**x**it | Closes the Clipboard Viewer and returns to AutoCAD |

Figure 19.4 shows the data in the Clipboard in Picture format.

**Figure 19.4:**

An image in the Clipboard in Picture format.

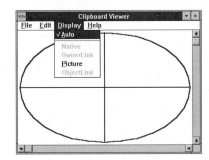

You can see from the exercise that the only difference between copying data to the Clipboard in Picture format rather than Bitmap format is the method you use to select the data. Notice that the Display options are different. The Clipboard now contains the data in two forms—Picture, and native AutoCAD. The AutoCAD option is grayed-out because the Clipboard Viewer does not have the capability of displaying this format.

*The image presented in the Clipboard Viewer seems coarser than the bit-map image was, and may be somewhat distorted. This effect is the result of the way the viewer displays it, not the quality of the image itself. Picture format stores the graphic data as entities, much like AutoCAD's. Therefore, when you copy Picture format data to another application, it can still be manipulated as entities (not just dots), and displays and prints at the resolution(s) supported by that application and the output devices you have available.*

*Try changing the size and shape of the Clipboard Viewer window, first with a bit map and then a Picture format loaded, to see how the display affects each format.*

If you have an application that can import metafiles (Picture format), you can use the application's **E**dit menu and **P**aste command to import the data, just as you did with the Bitmap format in Paintbrush. Also, if the data was copied from an AutoCAD drawing, you can also use this technique to copy the contents of the Clipboard into AutoCAD, as a block.

By copying data to the Clipboard, you can use your AutoCAD drawings to create illustrations and graphic data for other applications. Nevertheless, this process has a few disadvantages. If the source drawing changes in AutoCAD, the change does not appear in any other documents into which you have pasted the drawing or portions of the drawing. In addition, the drawing data is duplicated in the destination document, which means that additional disk space is required to hold the copy of the data.

The greatest disadvantage, however, is that if you want to modify the image in the final document, you have a lot of work to do. First, you need to know what application created it, and, if it was saved to a file from that application, what the file name is. Then you need to launch the other program, and either edit or re-create the drawing, then copy it to the Clipboard. Finally, you need to delete the existing image from the document, and replace it with the revised one, along with any sizing or placement editing that may require.

AutoCAD for Windows has an easier way. Recall that AutoCAD provides three options for copying data to the Clipboard. The two previous exercises have used Copy Image and Copy Vector. The third option—Copy Object—is the key to Object Linking and Embedding, which can overcome the limitations of the other two.

# Using Windows Object Linking and Embedding (OLE)

Windows' *Object Linking and Embedding* techniques provide an easy, direct method of integrating AutoCAD drawing data into documents and materials prepared using other software applications. When you link or embed an object from one application into a file created in another, you set up a mechanism that makes it simple to maintain and update the resulting document.

You begin the process by copying entities from AutoCAD to the Clipboard in Object format. Again, use the EXCHANGE drawing from the IAW DISK. This step creates a collection of AutoCAD drawing data with a special set of properties, as you see in the next exercise.

---

### Copying Data to the Clipboard for Embedding

Continue from the previous exercise, with AutoCAD and the Clipboard Viewer open, *or* start the Clipboard Viewer and AutoCAD, and open the existing drawing named EXCHANGE.

*In AutoCAD, choose **E**dit, then*
Copy **E**mbed

```
Command: _COPYEMBED
```

| | |
|---|---|
| `Select objects:` *Select the circle and the lines* | Builds a selection set |
| `Select objects:` *Press Enter* | Ends selection and copies the data to the Clipboard |
| *In the Clipboard Viewer, choose **D**isplay* | Displays the available formats |
| *Choose **F**ile, then E**x**it* | Closes the Clipboard Viewer and returns to AutoCAD |

---

Notice that the Clipboard Viewer now shows three types of data in the **D**isplay menu, with all but the Picture option grayed out. All of these data types are applicable to the current object in the clipboard, but those that are grayed out are not displayable. The following is a list of the possible data types from AutoCAD OLE objects.

- **Picture:** This data is the vector representation of the entities from AutoCAD. If the object is being embedded, the selected entities of the current drawing are represented. If the object is being linked, the entire drawing is represented.

- **Native:** This is the actual data from the server application. This data is used when you edit an embedded image.

- **OwnerLink:** This information is used to associate the object in the clipboard with the application that created it. This format is used when an object is embedded or linked.

- **ObjectLink:** This information is used to specify the name and location of the original file in which the data resides. This data is present when you link an object.

Embedded objects will have Picture, Native, and OwnerLink data. Objects that are linked will have Picture, OwnerLink, and Object Link data.

Depending on the way you intend to use the final document, and how you want to control the effect of changes made to the original drawing, you can choose to either *embed* or *link* the drawing data into the document. The following sections describe each option, with an exercise that shows you how to achieve either result.

*Windows refers to the application in which an object is created as the* Server, *and the application with which the final document is generated as the* Client. *AutoCAD can be used only as a Server application.*

## Embedding Objects with OLE

An embedded object contains all the data that would be required by its server application if it were a stand-alone file, along with information Windows needs to launch that application. In the case of AutoCAD, this means that an embedded drawing object is the equivalent of an AutoCAD DWG file, with information attached that tells Windows how to start up AutoCAD.

You can edit an embedded AutoCAD illustration by simply double-clicking on the figure itself. If everything is properly set up, Windows starts AutoCAD, loads the illustration, and waits for you to make any changes you need. The OLE interface adds an item to the <u>F</u>ile menu—<u>U</u>pdate docfile—which writes the changes back to the document, and switches Windows back to the client application.

*In order for Windows to recognize AutoCAD objects, and to know how to launch the program itself, AutoCAD must be registered in the Windows Registration Database. The install program should take care of this, but check it if you have problems using the OLE functions described. Consult your Windows documentation or the Windows Resource Kit documentation for more information on the Registration Database.*

Windows Write, a simple word processor which is located in the Accessories group, can import Picture format images, and can be used as an OLE client application. You use it in the next exercise to see how OLE works, using the EXCHANGE drawing from the IAW DISK.

## Embedding an AutoCAD Object in Windows Write

*In AutoCAD, choose* **F**ile, *then* **O**pen, *then enter* **EXCHANGE**      Opens the existing drawing EXCHANGE

Command: *Choose* **E**dit, *then* Copy **E**mbed      Starts the object creation process

Select objects: **ALL** ↵

Select objects: *Press Enter*      Copies everything to the Clipboard

The Clipboard should now contain the AutoCAD image, as an object. You can use the Clipboard Viewer to verify this.

*From Program Manager, double-click on the Write icon in the Accessories group*      Starts Windows Write

*In Write, choose* **E**dit, *then* **P**aste      Copies the AutoCAD object into Write

The **P**aste option causes the object to be embedded. If you choose Paste **L**ink at this point, you create a linked object (see the section following this one).

*Click on the picture*      Selects the object for editing

*Choose* **E**dit, *then* **S**ize Picture      Enables you to resize the image (see tip following exercise)

*Click outside the picture*      Deselects the object

The picture in Write should look approximately like the AutoCAD drawing, depending on how you sized the picture's boundary box.

*Double-click on the picture*      Loads the new object back into AutoCAD

In AutoCAD, use the OFFSET command to create a smaller circle, concentric with the original.

Command: *Choose* <u>F</u>ile, *then*          Sends the updated drawing data back to Write
<u>U</u>pdate [untitled]

Switch back to Write, and click outside the picture to deselect it. Notice that the change to the AutoCAD object has been transferred. If you like, you can click on the end-of-file mark at the lower left, press Enter once or twice, and enter a text caption for your embedded image. It should look something like figure 19.5.

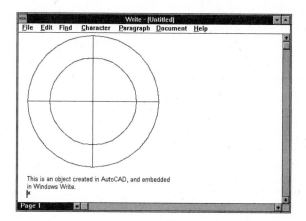

**Figure 19.5:**

An AutoCAD object embedded in a Write document.

*Windows Write's picture-editing tools are not very sophisticated, and it may take some practice to control the size of the image. Moving the cursor to the edge of the window scrolls the image the opposite way (revealing more of the image in the direction you move the cursor). If you start with the cursor within the figure's boundary box and move it toward an edge, the first boundary line encountered attaches to the cursor. Moving to a corner attaches both adjacent boundary lines. Click to fix the new edge or corner.*

If everything worked the way it is supposed to, the process you just witnessed probably seems deceptively simple. Review what actually happens when you double-click on an embedded object. First, Windows switches its focus to AutoCAD. If you did not have a session of AutoCAD open at the time, Windows would launch one. Then Windows opens a temporary drawing, with the data from the embedded object. If you had a drawing open in AutoCAD, with changes you had not saved, you would be prompted to save it, just as if you had initiated the OPEN command yourself. Finally, Windows moves the AutoCAD window to the foreground, with the object loaded for you to edit. Notice that the Title Bar displays the message AutoCAD - Drawing in [Untitled].

A document with an embedded object, such as the one you just created, has properties and advantages similar to those of an AutoCAD drawing with a block inserted in it (see Chapter 11). The data that defines the object is self-contained, which means you can give the file to someone else to edit or print. If their system also has AutoCAD for Windows, they can even modify the illustration, since the object contains the additional "hook" that enables it to start AutoCAD. Also, either the illustration or the drawing from which it was copied can later be modified, without the one affecting the other.

This method of sharing AutoCAD drawing data has several drawbacks. First, because the equivalent of an AutoCAD drawing has been embedded into the document, it has grown significantly in size. For example, the WRI file shown in figure 19.5 is 5,376 bytes, although the caption alone, saved to a file, is only 640 bytes. Second, if you later modify the original drawing and *do* want the illustration to reflect the changes, it requires a good memory and a number of steps.

The other option in OLE, linking an object, is performed in almost exactly the same manner, but effectively swaps the advantages and disadvantages of embedding.

## Linking Objects with OLE

Like embedding, linking an object into a document gives you the power to initiate the process of editing the object with a simple double-click. Unlike embedding, the data you then edit is contained in the original source file.

If you want to try linking an object, you can follow nearly the same steps as in the previous exercise for embedding, with three exceptions. In AutoCAD, choose the Copy **L**ink option from the **F**ile menu. You do not need to select entities because the entire drawing is used. In Write, choose the Paste **L**ink option in the **E**dit menu, instead of just **P**aste, to insert the object.

*If you do try the exercise to practice linking, you should switch back to AutoCAD after you insert the picture, and close the file you linked, before you double-click on the new illustration to modify it. Otherwise, Windows may try to launch a second session of AutoCAD to open the linked drawing.*

A linked object has many properties in common with an External Reference file in an AutoCAD drawing (see Chapter 11). Embedding an object copies all the data into the document, but linking creates a "link" with the data. The data itself continues to reside only in the original file in which it was created.

The linking technique has two real advantages. First, the client file does not increase in size nearly as much as with embedding. The example file created for figure 19.5 with embedding was 5,367 bytes; with the object linked, it is only 2,304 bytes. Second, because the data is stored in only one place, any changes made to it can be automatically applied to every document into which it has been linked. These links are maintained as long as the files remain in the same directory locations on the same system. If you move the server file, you can use the Lin**k**s option in the client's **E**dit menu to change the path and re-establish the link.

The downside to linking objects into your documents is that you set up a dependent relationship. If you give someone the document file without the linked file, they cannot use the object. Similarly, you must be careful to maintain all the files on your own system that are linked to documents you want to preserve.

In this section, you have seen how you can use Windows' ready-made OLE tools to share data between AutoCAD and other applications. More powerful and dynamic methods are available for exchanging AutoCAD data, but they require more work, as you see in the next section.

# Understanding Dynamic Data Exchange (DDE)

Although Object Linking and Embedding techniques enable you to easily place AutoCAD drawing data into documents created by other applications, the potential for data exchange is limited to a single direction. Windows provides a set of tools that applications can use to establish true dynamic exchange of data, in which changes in one file are immediately and automatically reflected in the other—Dynamic Data Exchange, or DDE.

Like Object Linking, DDE can be used to maintain a link between a drawing file and data in another format, so that changes you make to the drawing are always reflected in the other document. The real power of using DDE with AutoCAD, however, is that the exchange of data can flow in either direction, from an AutoCAD drawing to another application's data file, or vice versa.

By using this kind of link, you can create a parametric drawing environment. As a typical example, you could use a spreadsheet application such as Microsoft Excel or Lotus 1-2-3 for Windows as a design and calculation program, linked to AutoCAD to generate a graphic representation of your design. Entering or changing values in the cells of the spreadsheet (the *parameters* of the design) produces corresponding changes in the AutoCAD drawing. The proper structuring of the link can enable the reverse; the application of AutoCAD's editing commands to the drawing elements would cause the values in the spreadsheet to change.

Such an environment could enable a designer to quickly evaluate the results of modifying some aspect of a complex design, while maintaining previously developed design constraints and interdependencies. The key to effective use of this technique is to identify and exploit the strengths of each individual application, and integrate the results.

If you have Excel or 1-2-3 on your system, you can experiment with the sample DDE functions that are included with AutoCAD. The commands in the **D**DE option of the **E**dit menu enable you to create and explore a variety of exchanges between AutoCAD and a spreadsheet. AutoCAD also includes a fully developed sample parametric link, also using Excel, in which a drawing of a machined shaft is modified by values placed in the spreadsheet, and edits made to the drawing are reflected in the numeric data. These sample functions are described in the Autodesk manual, *Using AutoCAD for Windows*.

## Creating DDE Functions with AutoLISP and ADS

Developing a truly useful DDE link, or parametric drawing, of your own can involve a substantial amount of work. AutoCAD provides programming tools designed to provide access to DDE functions from AutoLISP and the AutoCAD Development System (ADS).

Most Windows programs that are capable of DDE need to handle only one or two data types, typically text strings and possibly graphic data (in Windows metafile format). As you have seen, with OLE, linking objects into such a program is a matter of first copying the object to the Clipboard, and then using the built-in Paste Link function.

AutoCAD supports such a variety of data types that the process of creating data exchange "hooks" in AutoCAD, aside from the export of simple graphic images, requires a more sophisticated toolkit. If you are an experienced AutoLISP or ADS programmer, you can use the function libraries provided with AutoCAD to accomplish this.

Once again, however, the Windows environment provides a more accessible option. Microsoft Visual Basic is a graphically oriented programming environment, which can be used to set up DDE links. Although Visual Basic requires an understanding of basic programming concepts, it is much easier to understand and use than a language such as C. The speed and ease with which you can create stand-alone programs using Visual Basic make it an excellent choice for developing AutoCAD add-on programs.

So far you have looked at methods of exchanging data between AutoCAD and other programs, which are unique to the Windows environment. In the next section you look at the variety of methods AutoCAD provides for exchanging data between applications in the DOS environment.

# Exchanging Data in the DOS Environment

Although Windows provides a new set of tools for exchanging data between AutoCAD and other applications, several reliable, if less elegant, methods of doing so have been around for a while. These other methods do not depend on Windows' resources. In the DOS environment, data exchange involves the use of specific intermediary file types. Data is written from one program to a file, then the data is read into another program from that file. The file type is selected on the basis of the type of data to be exchanged and the formats used by the applications involved.

One advantage of using these simpler file-exchange methods to integrate AutoCAD with other programs is that they are portable. If you work alternately in DOS and Windows, or if others in your office need tools that work on either platform, and you need to transfer data from AutoCAD to some other applications' files, consider using one of the following file formats:

- **DXF.** This ASCII-format file (see below) describes an AutoCAD drawing. Autodesk provides the specification of the codes used in DXF files, primarily as a means of enabling other CAD programs to create files that can be read into AutoCAD.

- **DXB.** DXB is a special compact binary file format.

- **IGES.** IGES is a public domain specification for CAD drawing data exchange. IGES stands for Initial Graphics Exchange Specification, and is defined by the U.S. National Computer Graphics Association.

- **ASCII.** This is the standard text file format. ASCII stands for American Standard Code for Information Interchange.

- **Raster Image.** This includes a large number of file formats which encode graphic information as a pattern of dots or pixels. Some examples are: PCX, TIFF, GIF, and BMP.

- **PostScript.** This format uses a page composition language (PCL) that is proprietary to Adobe Systems. PostScript is primarily used to create documents for printing to raster devices, such as laser printers.

Each of the previous formats is discussed, in turn, in the rest of this chapter.

## Using DXF for Data Exchange

The *Drawing Interchange File* (DXF) was developed by Autodesk to accurately describe an AutoCAD drawing file in an ASCII text-file format. Although AutoCAD's proprietary binary (or compiled) DWG drawing file is efficient for a computer to use, it is difficult to manipulate outside of AutoCAD. An ASCII text file, on the other hand, is a more cumbersome file, but it is one that most software applications can read and write to. Because of AutoCAD's market dominance, the DXF format has become an industry standard.

You can find **D**XF In and D**X**F Out in the **I**mport/Export option of the **F**iles pull-down menu. The DXFOUT command prompts for a file name, so that you can give the DXF file a different name than the drawing name. The DXF extension is automatically added. You can also specify a number of decimal places of accuracy for the file. Six is the default and works well in most cases. Some high-precision applications may require more decimal places of precision. The DXFOUT command can output to an ASCII file, unless you specify the Binary option. The Binary option outputs to a more efficient binary DXF file. Try creating a DXF file in the next exercise, using the EX-CHANGE drawing from the IAW DISK as a prototype.

---

### Using DXFOUT To Export Data

| | |
|---|---|
| Command: *Choose* **F**ile, *then* **N**ew, *and enter* **DXFTEST=EXCHANGE** | Starts a new drawing identical to EXCHANGE |
| Command: *Choose* **F**ile, *then* **I**mport/Export, *then* D**X**F Out | Issues the DXFOUT command and displays the Create DXF File dialog box |

AutoCAD supplies the drawing name as the default (in this case, DXFTEST) in the File **N**ame: text box. Check the Dri**v**es: and **D**irectories: list boxes, and use the scroll bars if necessary, to make C:\IAW the current directory.

| | |
|---|---|
| *Choose* OK | Accepts the default DXFTEST.DXF |
| `Enter decimal places of accuracy (0 to16)/Entities/Binary <6>:` *Press Enter* | Accepts the default accuracy and creates DXF file |

---

This simple exercise created a text file that accurately describes the drawing database. At first glance, the text file may look a little confusing, but it is not difficult to learn to read this type of file. Because there were so few entities in this drawing, most of the file is filled with the first two sections, called the header and tables, which define all of the drawing's variables, settings, and feature definitions. The last part of the file, which lists the entities and their coordinates, is simple. The next exercise shows how to change a coordinate in the DXF file.

## Inside a DXF File

You can view a DXF file with any editor or word processor that can read an ASCII text file. Most word processors use a special file format, and asks you if you want your file converted to it when you load an ASCII file. The word processor may require a special save command so that the file is saved in ASCII format. Be sure to retain the DXF extension, or AutoCAD cannot read the file.

Windows provides both the Notepad and Write programs, either of which can edit DXF files. Notepad is best suited to small files, although the size of file you can open in Write is limited only by available memory. Because DXF files can be quite large, Write is the better choice for the following exercise.

---

## Viewing and Editing a DXF File

| | |
|---|---|
| *From Program Manager, double-click on the Write icon in the Accessories group* | Starts Windows Write |
| *In Write, choose* **F**ile, *then* **O**pen | Opens the Open dialog box |
| *Use the* **Dri**ve: *and* **D**irectories: *list boxes, if necessary, to go to* C:\IAW, *then select* DXFTEST.DXF, *then* OK, *then enter* DXFTEST.DXF *in the* File **N**ame: *box* | Selects DXFTEST.DXF for editing |
| *Choose* **N**o Conversion *in the alert box* | Leaves file in ASCII format |
| *Choose* Fi**nd**, *then* **F**ind..., *enter* **CIRCLE**, *then choose* **F**ind Next | Goes to the first occurrence of CIRCLE in the file (see fig. 19.6) |
| *In the* CIRCLE *section, locate the line that reads* 2.0, *and change it to* 4.0 | Changes the radius of the circle |
| *Choose* **F**ile, *then* **S**ave | Saves the changes |

Switch back to AutoCAD, and use the NEW command to start a new drawing. It does not need to be named.

| | |
|---|---|
| Command: *Choose* **F**ile, *then* Import/Export, *then* **D**XF In | Issues the DXFIN command and displays the Select DXF File dialog box |
| *Double-click on* DXFTEST *or enter* **DXFTEST** | Issues the DXFIN command and reads the file (see fig. 19.7) |

---

By finding the entity-coordinate information in the DXF file, you were able to modify the circle radius and then see that change after you read the file back into AutoCAD graphics. This technique is the way many third-party applications manipulate a drawing file. You may have noticed how much other data was in that file. In many cases, the drawing setup information is not required in the DXF file. By using the Entities option of the DXFOUT command, only the entities themselves are exported to the file. This option is used in the following exercise.

**Figure 19.6:**

Editing a DXF file
in Write.

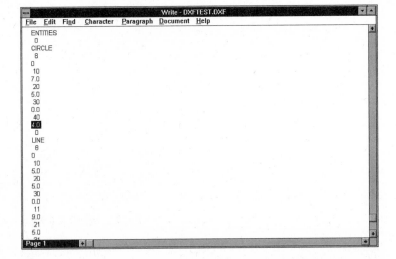

**Figure 19.7:**

The modified DXF
file imported into
AutoCAD.

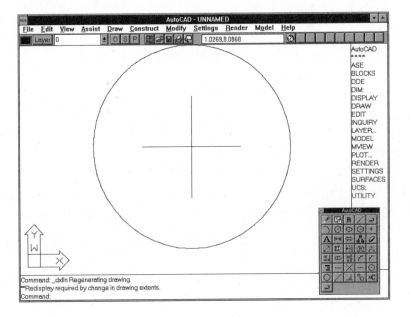

## Exporting Selected Entities with DXFOUT

| | |
|---|---|
| Command: *Choose* **F**ile, *then* **I**mport/Export, *then* D**X**F Out | Opens the Create DXF File dialog box |
| *Enter* **LINES** *in the* File **N**ame *text box* | Specifies the file name LINES.DXF |
| `Enter decimal places of accuracy (0 to 16)/Entities/Binary <6>:` **E** ↵ | Specifies the Entities option |
| `Select objects:` *Select the two lines and press Enter* | |
| `Enter decimal places of accuracy (0 to 16)/Binary <6>:` **3** ↵ | Specifies three decimal places of accuracy and creates the DXF file |
| Command: *Choose* **F**ile, *then* **N**ew, *click on* **D**iscard Changes, *then choose* OK | Begins a new drawing with no name |
| Command: *Choose* **F**ile, *then* **I**mport/Export, *then* **D**XF In | Issues the DXFIN command and displays the Select DXF File dialog box |
| *Double-click on* LINES *or enter* **LINES** | Issues the DXFIN command and reads the file |

To import block insertions into a drawing, however, the block definitions must exist in the receiving drawing, or you must import a full (not Entities-only) DXF file into a new drawing. If you look at this DXF file, it appears much shorter than the previous one because only those entities that you chose were included. This method is often preferred to creating a file because the drawing parameter section does not have a potential conflict with the file you want to import. You should use this option if you want to import data into an existing drawing file, rather than into a new one.

 *A full DXF file can only be imported into a new, empty drawing file. To create an empty drawing, you must use the default original ACAD.DWG prototype file, specify no prototype, or specify the new drawing name equal to nothing (blank), such as NAME= in the New Drawing Name: box.*

The DXFOUT command also features the Binary option. This option creates a binary DXF file, which is about 25 percent smaller than a text file and can be read much faster by AutoCAD. A binary DXF file can be read and written by sophisticated third-party programs, but you cannot read or edit the file with a text editor.

## Using Binary Drawing Interchange (DXB) Files

Another file format that is more compact than a binary DXF file is the DXB format. This file format is not as complete as DXF, but it can handle large amounts of entity data very efficiently, and it maintains greater accuracy. A special command called DXBIN is used to read in a DXB file. Although AutoCAD has no direct command for creating one of these files, it can be done indirectly by configuring an ADI plotter driver to plot in a DXB format.

## Exchanging Data with IGES

The Initial Graphics Exchange Specification (IGES) has been an industry standard file-translation format for many years. IGES is especially popular for transferring the large three-dimensional product design files used in manufacturing. Because the IGES specification was developed for no specific CAD program, each CAD program conforms differently to the standards. Many different entity types are supported, but not all CAD systems use identical entity definitions. For this reason, you can lose data or have it altered in the exchange process. The success of this translator varies, depending on which CAD software packages are sending and receiving the information. AutoCAD has the IGESIN and IGESOUT commands built into the software, and they are easy to use because they have no options. The following exercise creates an IGES file in model space (because IGES does not support paper space).

---

### Using IGESOUT To Export Data

Open the MOCKDIM drawing, which you created in Chapter 17, or start a new drawing MOCKDIM=IAWMOKD3. Discard changes to the current drawing. Set TILEMODE to 1.

Command: *Choose* **V**iew, *then* **Z**oom, *and then* **E**xtents

Command: *Choose* **F**ile, *then*           Issues the IGESOUT command and displays
**I**mport/Export, *then* IGES **O**ut      the Create IGES File dialog box

*Choose* OK                             Accepts the default file name (MOCKDIM.IGS)
                                      and exports to file

```
Writing Start section
Writing Global section
Writing line type 1 (HIDDEN)
Writing line type 2 (CENTER)
Writing view 1 (A)
Translating AutoCAD entity 1 (LINE)
Translating AutoCAD entity 13 (CIRCLE)
Translating AutoCAD entity 44 (LINE)
Translating AutoCAD entity 64 (DIMENSION)
Translating AutoCAD entity 70 (DIMENSION)
```

```
Copying DE data record 416 of 416
Copying Parameter data record 311 of 311
Writing Terminate section
```

As you can see from the command prompt activity, the IGES file is a rather substantial file that contains several sections that define its file type, the parameters, and the entity data. Because it is an ASCII text file, you can attempt the same type of coordinate modification as you did with the DXF file. Some of the more advanced features of AutoCAD are not supported in the IGES file; therefore, they may be lost or modified. When you are importing IGES files into AutoCAD, you must start with a new drawing file that contains no defined entities, as previously was noted for a full DXF import. You see an error if you do not follow this procedure.

In the following exercise, you import the IGES file MOCKDIM.IGS that you created in the previous exercise. After you complete the exercise, you see that, although IGES offers a standard by which most CAD applications can exchange data, it loses something in the translation.

## Using IGESIN To Import Data

Start a new drawing, saving the changes to MOCKDIM for later exercises. The new drawing does not need a name. Set VIEWRES for fast zooms, and a circle zoom percent of 2000.

Command: *Choose* **F**ile, *then* **I**mport/Export, *then choose* **I**GES In          Opens the Select IGES File dialog box

*Double-click on* MOCKDIM.IGS          Imports MOCKDIM.IGS

```
Read 416 directory and 311 parameter records.
Found 2 status, 3 global, 416 directory, and 311 parameter records.
Checking T record. Bypassing START section. Reading GLOBAL section.
Product id: MOCKDIM
IGES file created by: AutoCAD-Q.W.06
Version: IGESOUT-3.04
Processing independent, non-annotation entities.
Read 414 directory and 205 parameter records.
Processing annotation or logically dependent entities.
Read 28 directory and 11 parameter records.
Warning: Inconsistent parameter data for entity in section P, record 220
Read 185 directory and 95 parameter
Read 22 directory and 15 parameter records.
Regenerating drawing.
Drawing extents undefined.  Zooming to limits.
Regenerating drawing.
```

Set TILEMODE to 1, then issue ZOOM with the EXTENTS option. The drawing should look like figure 19.8.

**Figure 19.8:**

The result of
importing
MOCKDIM.IGS.

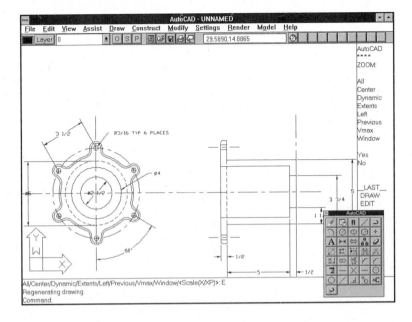

The visual result of the previous exercise may not show it, but some exploration of the resulting drawing reveals that the translation process is not perfect. Look at the list of layers, for instance. This drawing is a simple one; the more complex the drawing, the more likely that information may change or be lost in translation. The *AutoCAD/IGES Interface Specification* document details which AutoCAD entities are supported in IGES, and contains tips on how to obtain the best results in file translations. If you need to exchange IGES files with other sources, it may be beneficial for you to document some drawing-setup procedures to minimize the effects of the IGES translation.

# Importing and Exporting to Raster Files

DXF and IGES files can be very large and complex, but they try to maintain the accuracy and flexibility of the entities in a CAD database. If you are interested in the picture itself, a raster image may be much more practical. Similar to the difference between a pen plotter output versus a dot-matrix hard copy, a raster image defines shapes as a series of closely grouped dots on a screen or on paper. AutoCAD Release 12 includes capabilities to create raster files for use in other applications and to import common raster files. Although a raster image does not contain the inherent accuracy of a vector file, this image is much easier to edit and transport between software-application packages.

Some of the more common raster image file formats include FAX, Tagged Image File Format (TIFF), and Graphics Interchange Format (GIF). Bit-map (BMP) files are common to paint programs, and the PCX format also is widely used. These types of files have become the industry standard for exchanging raster image files. You can find many applications for using this type of CAD output, in which absolute drawing accuracy is not required. Desktop publishing, rendering and animation, electronic FAX, and logos are commonly transferred in these file formats. One parameter that is important is the resolution of these raster files. The advantage of viewing and printing sharp-looking, high-resolution files must be weighed against the large file sizes that are generated.

AutoCAD can output to various types of raster files by configuring the plotter to the proper specifications, then plotting to a file. The following exercise illustrates this technique.

## Configuring a Raster Plot Device

Command: *Choose* **F**ile, *then* **C**onfigure        Starts AutoCAD Configuration

*Select option 5 to configure a plotter*

```
Plotter Configuration Menu
    0. Exit to configuration menu
    1. Add a plotter configuration
    2. Delete a plotter configuration
    3. Change a plotter configuration
    4. Rename a plotter configuration

Enter selection, 0 to 4 <0>: 1 ↵

Searching for files. Please wait.

Available plotters:

    1.   None
    2.   AutoCAD file output formats (pre 4.1) - by Autodesk, Inc
    3.   Calcomp ColorMaster Plotters ADI 4.2 - by Autodesk, Inc
    4.   Calcomp DrawingMaster Plotters ADI 4.2 - by Autodesk, Inc
    5.   Calcomp Electrostatic Plotters ADI 4.2 - by Autodesk, Inc
    6.   Calcomp Pen Plotters ADI 4.2 - by Autodesk, Inc
    7.   Canon plotter ADI 4.2 - by Autodesk, Inc
    8.   Hewlett-Packard (HP-GL) ADI 4.2 - by Autodesk, Inc
    9.   Hewlett-Packard (HP-GL/2) ADI 4.2 - by Autodesk, Inc.
   10.   Houston Instrument ADI 4.2 - by Autodesk, Inc
   11.   IBM 7300 Series ADI 4.2 - by Autodesk, Inc
   12.   PostScript device ADI 4.2 - by Autodesk, Inc
   13.   Raster file export ADI 4.2 - by Autodesk, Inc
   14.   System Printer ADI 4.2 - by Autodesk, Inc
   15.   UNIX Plot device ADI 4.2 - by Autodesk, Inc

Select device number or ? to repeat list <1>: 13 ↵
```

*continues*

Supported models:

```
 1.  320 x 200    (CGA/MCGA Colour)
 2.  640 x 200    (CGA Monochrome)
 3.  640 x 350    (EGA)
 4.  640 x 400
 5.  640 x 480    (VGA)
 6.  720 x 540
 7.  800 x 600
 8.  1024 x 768
 9.  1152 x 900   (Sun standard)
10.  1600 x 1280  (Sun hi-res)
11.  User-defined
```

Enter selection, 1 to 11 <1>: **5** ↵

You can export the drawing in any of the following raster file formats. Please select the format you prefer.

```
 1.  GIF (CompuServe Graphics Interchange Format)
 2.  X Window dump (xwd compatible)
 3.  Jef Poskanzer's Portable Bitmap Toolkit Formats
 4.  Microsoft Windows Device-independent Bitmap (.BMP)
 5.  TrueVision TGA Format
 6.  Z-Soft PCX Format
 7.  Sun Rasterfile
 8.  Flexible Image Transfer System (FITS)
 9.  PostScript image
10.  TIFF (Tag Image File Format)
11.  FAX Image (Group 3 Encoding)
12.  Amiga IFF / ILBM Format
```

In which format would you like to export
the file, 1 to 12 <1>:**4** ↵

You can write the file using any of the following colour gamuts. The more colours you use, the larger the file is, usually.

```
 1. Monochrome
 2. 16 colours
 3. All 256 standard AutoCAD colours
```

How many colours do you want to use, 1 to 3 <3>: *Press Enter*

You can specify the background colour to be any of AutoCAD's 256 standard colours. The default of 0 selects a black screen background.

Background colour (0 = black), 0 to 255 <0>: **7** ↵

Sizes are in Inches and the style is landscape
Plot origin is at (0.00,0.00)
Plotting area is 640.00 wide by 480.00 high (MAX size)
Plot is NOT rotated

```
Hidden lines will NOT be removed
Plot will be scaled to fit available area
Do you want to change anything? (No/Yes/File) <N>:
```
*Press Enter*

```
Enter a description for this plotter:
```
**Windows DIB (BMP) file** ↵

Your current plotter is: Hewlett-Packard (HP-GL) ADI 4.2 - by Autodesk, Inc
(your current plotter may differ).

```
Description: Windows DIB (BMP) file
```

Repeat the process to install any other raster plot drivers you require, then exit from the
Configure program and save your changes.

*If your system shows only a few plotter options and omits* Raster
file export ADI ..., *make sure that you have specified a directory
for driver files in the Environment dialog box, from the Preferences
dialog box (see Chapter 18).*

Now, try out the raster plot on your MOCKDIM drawing. In the following exercise,
you export the drawing to a Windows BMP file. If you have added a different raster
plot device to your configuration, simply select it instead.

First, reload MOCKDIM. Then use the PLOT command to create a BMP file.

## Plotting to a Raster Plot Device

Command: *Choose* **F**ile, *then* **O**pen, *then*
**D**iscard Changes, *then enter* **MOCKDIM**    Reloads MOCKDIM

Command: *Choose* **F**ile, *then* **P**rint/Plot    Displays the Plot Configuration dialog box

*Choose* **D**evice and Default Selection    Opens the Device and Default Selection dialog
box (see fig. 19.9)

*Select* Windows DIB (BMP) file *in the*
Select device *list box, then choose* OK

*Choose* File Na**m**e, *then enter*    Specifies a name for the BMP file
**MOCKDIM.BMP** *(include the BMP file
extension) then choose* OK

*Choose* OK    Begins plot

```
Command: _plot Effective plotting
area: 640.00 wide by 431.11 high
Regeneration done 100%
Plot complete.
```
Creates the raster file (see fig. 19.10)

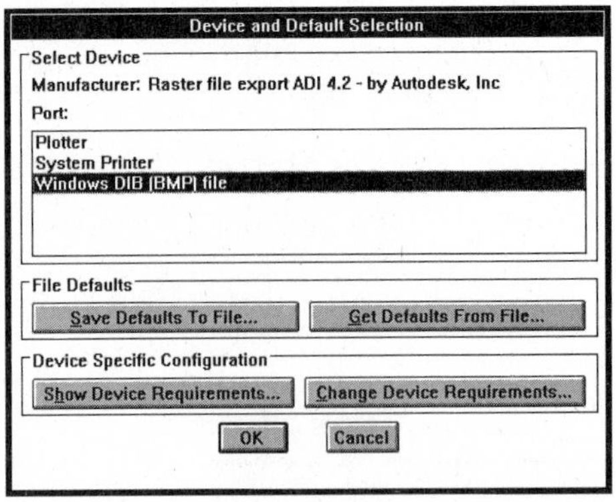

**Figure 19.9:**

The Device and
Default Selection
dialog box.

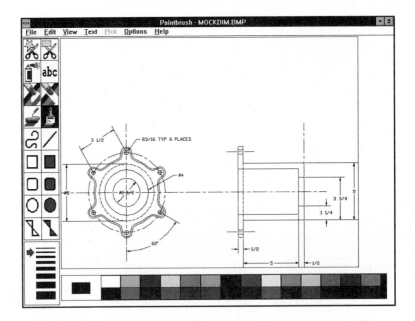

**Figure 19.10:**

MOCKDIM.BMP
displayed in
Windows Paint-
brush.

You may want to try configuring AutoCAD to plot to another type of raster file,
especially if you have software that can use that type of file. If AutoCAD does not
output to the type of raster file you need, there is a good chance that if you use a
standard format, such as PCX, GIF, or BMP, you can later translate the file. Many
common programs, such as Graphics Workshop, Paintshop, or WinGIF, are readily
available, often as shareware. They can read or write to several of the popular formats
(see fig. 19.9).

# Importing Raster Images

One of the new ADS applications available in AutoCAD is the capability to read raster files into the drawing editor. Raster files can be useful for graphics, such as logos or images, which are often available in popular formats such as GIF, PCX, or TIF. Some images are easier to create using other graphics software and can be imported into AutoCAD to enhance a drawing created in a CAD environment. Unless a scanned image has been converted into a vector file, it is often a raster image and must be brought into CAD accordingly.

Three separate commands, depending on the type of file to be read, can be issued: GIFIN, PCXIN, and TIFFIN. These commands, named for the type of file to be read, are very similar in the way they operate. Entering the command produces prompts very similar to the BLOCK command. The file name must be entered, along with the appropriate path. The extension is not needed if it is the standard GIF, TIF, or PCX extension. An insertion point and scale factor must also be given. When you drag the image in, it appears as a rectangle with the file name shown inside. This helps you visualize the location and scale factor for fast and efficient dragging.

A raster file is brought in as a block containing many solid entities that define the shape of the image. The colors may be a little unpredictable due to the process of assigning AutoCAD color numbers to all the dithered entities. As you might have guessed, best results occur with small files of well-defined images. Once you import the image you can leave it as is, explode and modify it, or simply trace over and discard it.

Six ADS functions, which operate just like system variables, can be altered to change the way the raster image is imported. Each of them begins with the RI (Raster In) designation.

- **RIASPECT.** The image ASPECT ratio controls the roundness of circles, or the X to Y ratio, to compensate for different graphics resolutions.

- **RIBACKG.** The BACKGround color is adjustable, depending on the predominant background color of the image and what your screen background is set to. This variable controls which predominant color will not be converted to solid images. The most common settings are 0 for a black screen background and 7 for a white screen background.

- **RIEDGE.** This integer controls the EDGE detection capabilities for importing an image in which you want highly defined edges. The higher the number (up to 255), the more contrast is required on an image to show the edges.

- **RIGAMUT.** The number of colors used (GAMUT) is defined by this variable. Popular settings are 256, 16, or 8.

- **RIGREY.** A GREYscale image can be obtained by setting this variable to 1, which turns on the greyscale option. This option can reduce the file size by effectively reducing the number of colors available.

- **RITHRESH.** This TRESHhold feature enables filtering out some of the background "noise" by enabling only the brighter entities to be captured. The higher the number, the more filtering takes place.

As you can see, importing raster images involves some complexity and is difficult to define with hard and fast rules. You will have to experiment on your hardware.

## Exchanging Data through PostScript

PostScript is a type of graphics file that is popular for illustrations and desktop publishing. The advantage that PostScript has over regular raster images is that it contains special shapes and fonts that are stored more efficiently and generated with better resolution than most raster images. You can use PostScript fonts in AutoCAD drawings, rather than the AutoCAD fonts. PostScript makes the file much more compatible with other devices or applications that recognize PostScript entities. The standard file extension for PostScript is EPS (Encapsulated PostScript). This file is a text file and can be read by many different graphics software packages, as well as by hard-copy output devices (see fig. 19.11).

**Figure 19.11:**

A portion of
MOCKDIM.EPS in
Windows Write.

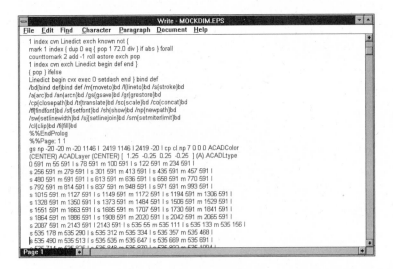

You can access the PostScript commands, PSOUT and PSIN, from the Import/Export option of the Files pull-down menu. The process of creating an EPS file is very similar to plotting. If you have used a PostScript text font (by using a style defined with a font file that has a PFB extension) or a PostScript fill pattern (by using the PSFILL command), these fonts and fills will be exported along with the rest of the image. If FILEDIA is set to 1, a file dialog box appears to name the file. The next prompt offers the same five choices as plotting for the area to output: Display, Extents, Limits, View, or Window. A screen preview may be added to the EPS file in either an EPSI or TIFF format, and several choices are offered for the resolution of that image. Then the scale and output size is specified. The next exercise shows how to plot to a PostScript file.

## Plotting to a PostScript File

Continue with the MOCKDIM drawing from the previous exercise.

| | |
|---|---|
| Command: *Choose* **F**ile, *then* **I**mport/Export, *then* Post**S**cript Out | Starts PSOUT command and displays the Create PostScript File dialog box |
| Command: _psout | |
| *Choose* OK | Accepts the default file name MOCKDIM.EPS |
| Command: _psout | |
| What to plot -- Display, Extents, Limits, View, or Window <D>: **E** ↵ | Specifies the Extents option |
| Include a screen preview image in the file? (None/EPSI/TIFF) <None>: *Press Enter* | Includes the TIFF screen preview image in the file |
| Screen preview image size (128 x 128 is standard)? (128/256/512) <128>: *Press Enter* | Accepts the default resolution for the preview |
| Size units (Inches or Millimeters) <Inches>: *Press Enter* | |
| Specify scale by entering: Output Inches=Drawing Units or Fit or ? <Fit>: *Press Enter* | |

Standard values for output size

| Size | Width | Height |
|---|---|---|
| A | 8.00 | 10.50 |
| B | 10.00 | 16.00 |
| C | 16.00 | 21.00 |
| D | 21.00 | 33.00 |
| E | 33.00 | 43.00 |
| F | 28.00 | 40.00 |
| G | 11.00 | 90.00 |
| H | 28.00 | 143.00 |
| J | 34.00 | 176.00 |
| K | 40.00 | 143.00 |

*continues*

```
A4           7.80        11.20
A3          10.70        15.60
A2          15.60        22.40
A1          22.40        32.20
A0          32.20        45.90
USER         7.50        10.50
```

```
Enter the Size or Width,Height
(in Inches) <USER>: A ↵
```

Effective plotting area:  8.00          Exports image to file
wide by 5.22 high

200 entities

*If you want to be able to import Encapsulated PostScript files into AutoCAD, the EPS files must not have a screen preview image (sometimes called a preview header).*

## Using PostScript To Import Data

The PSIN command inserts an EPS file similarly to inserting a block. If FILEDIA is set to 1, a file dialog box assists in selecting the EPS file. The PSQUALITY system variable is used to define the resolution of the image. A higher number provides higher resolution. A negative number outlines the polygons instead of filling them.

Because you have the MOCKDIM.EPS file, use it in the following exercises to experiment with the PSIN command. First, import the file with the default PSQUALITY setting of 75. Then decrease the setting to see what effect it has on the imported drawing quality.

### Using PSIN To Import an EPS File

Start a new drawing, discarding changes to the current one.

| | |
|---|---|
| Command: *Choose* **F**ile, *then* **I**mport/Export, *then* **P**ostscript In | Starts PSIN command and displays Select PostScript File dialog box |
| Command: psin .................. | The command line displays dots as the file imports |
| *Double-click on* MOCKDIM.EPS | Starts the import process, then displays drawing |
| Insertion point<0,0,0>: *Press Enter* | Accepts the default insertion point |
| Scale factor: 1 ↵ | Specifies scale factor of 1 |

Issue ZOOM with the Extents option to view the results (see fig. 19.12).

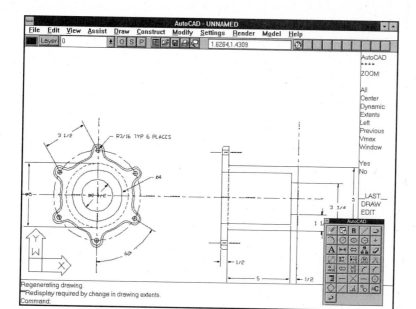

**Figure 19.12:**

The MOCKDIM.EPS file imported into AutoCAD with PSQUALITY=75.

You may need to experiment with the PSQUALITY variable to see which resolutions work the best for graphics display and hard-copy output. A balance between a good image and a reasonable file size must be maintained. Figure 19.13 shows the MOCKDIM drawing with a PSQUALITY setting of 10.

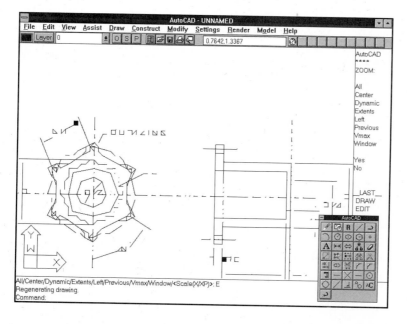

**Figure 19.13:**

MOCKDIM.EPS imported with PSQUALITY=10.

PostScript capability enables you to use AutoCAD to exchange information with other software packages without converting the image to a raster image. PostScript also gives AutoCAD a better interface with output devices that directly support this type of file.

# Using ASCTEXT To Import Text

Standard text files, conforming to the ASCII format, are commonly used in software programs because most application packages can read and write to that format. On a DOS computer, the CONFIG.SYS and AUTOEXEC.BAT files are ASCII files. UNIX configuration files, such as .profile, also are ASCII files. Some of the AutoCAD files, such as the ACAD.PGP file, are ASCII. AutoCAD has an AutoLISP-defined command called ASCTEXT, which can read an ASCII text file into the drawing editor. This command, which is actually an AutoLISP routine that uses the TEXT command, works much like a block insertion.

Because AutoCAD is not a good text editor, you may find it more practical to create your notes and product descriptions in a text editor, then insert them into your drawings as needed. The DOS commands EDLIN or EDIT (for DOS 5.0) create an ASCII text file. Keeping your text in ASCII files is preferable to having blocks that contain nothing but text, because you can use them in documents other than AutoCAD drawings. You can create a library of common text strings, much like a block library, that you can use in your drawings. Of course, you can edit the text after it is imported by using the regular AutoCAD text-editing options.

If the ASCTEXT command is executed, you must specify the path and file name, including the extension. The rest of the prompts look similar to the prompts you see when you use the TEXT command. You must specify the placement and justification, along with the text height and rotation angle. If you choose the change text options, you can specify several other parameters that affect the appearance and placement of the text. You see these options in the next exercise, in which you import a text file by using the ASCTEXT command.

In the next exercise, you begin a new drawing, then import your CONFIG.SYS file. If you want to use a different ASCII file (or are working on a different operating system), substitute the appropriate file name.

## Using ASCTEXT To Import Text

Start a new drawing named TEXTIN.

Command: **ASCTEXT** ↵                    Starts the ASCTEXT command, and opens the
                                          File to Read dialog box

*Choose* **T**ype It, *and enter* **\CONFIG.SYS**

| | |
|---|---|
| `Start point or`<br>`Center/Middle/Right/?:`<br>*Pick a point near .5,8.5 (the upper*<br>*left corner of drawing area)* | Specifies the text's starting location, left-justified |
| `Height <0.2000>:` *Press Enter* | Accepts the default text height |
| `Rotation angle <0>:` *Press Enter* | Accepts the default text rotation |
| `Change text options? <N>:` *Press Enter* | Places text |
| `Command:` *Press Enter* | Repeats the ASCTEXT command |
| *Choose* T*ype* It, *and press Enter* | Specifies same file |
| `Start point or Center/Middle/Right`<br>`/?:` **C** ↲ | Specifies the Center option |
| `Center point:` *Pick a point near 6,3* | Sets the text's location, center-justified |
| `Height <0.2000>:` *Press Enter* | Accepts the default text height |
| `Rotation angle <0>:` *Press Enter* | Accepts the default text rotation |
| `Change text options? <N>:` **Y** ↲ | |
| `Distance between lines/<Auto>:` **.5** ↲ | Sets line spacing |
| `First line to read/<1>:` **2** ↲ | Starts at line 2 |
| `Number of lines to read/<All>:` **3** ↲ | Tells AutoCAD to read from line 2 to line 4 |
| `Underscore each line? <N>:` *Press Enter* | |
| `Overscore each line? <N>:` **Y** ↲ | |
| `Change text case? Upper/Lower/`<br>`<N>:` **U** ↲ | |
| `Set up columns? <N>:` *Press Enter* | ASCTEXT imports the text in uppercase<br>(see fig. 19.14) |

The first time you used the ASCTEXT command in this exercise was similar to the way you used the TEXT command, except that you did not type the text. Using it the second time with the change text options showed the additional capabilities of the command.

# Understanding the AutoCAD SQL Extension

Another feature that is new to AutoCAD in Release 12 is the module called the AutoCAD SQL Extension (ASE). This interface uses Structured Query Language (SQL) to manipulate information in a standard relational database-management system (DBMS). The capability to form strong links between graphic entities and nongraphic data helps develop a small drawing file with a great deal of external data connected to it. This feature provides many advantages over the attribute definition and extraction that is presently being done.

**Figure 19.14:**

Text imported with ASCTEXT.

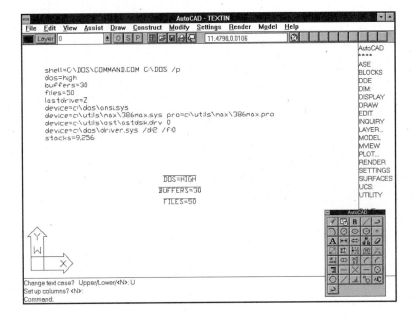

To use the ASE, you must have a database program that uses SQL and is supported by database drivers supplied with AutoCAD or your database vendor. Using the ASE is not difficult, but a strong knowledge of database operation is recommended. See the *AutoCAD SQL Extension Reference Manual* for more information.

# Summary

AutoCAD for Windows offers a wide range of options for sharing data and integrating your work with other applications, adding the new functionality of the Windows environment to the already strong stable of methods available under DOS.

For simple copy operations from AutoCAD to other programs, consider using the Clipboard to transfer AutoCAD drawing data in either Bitmap or Picture format to other programs. This technique is useful for using AutoCAD drawings in reports or presentations you create with other Windows applications, such as Windows Write, PageMaker, or CorelDraw. You can use the OLE option to make this a more flexible process, and maintain the ability to edit the images after you have placed them.

More complex data transfers with AutoCAD may require DDE. The trade-off for this power is that, due to AutoCAD's unique and complex data structure, using DDE with

AutoCAD generally requires some programming knowledge. Once again, however, the Windows environment has a new and powerful tool to help in this area. Visual Basic is an excellent development tool for creating DDE applications to interact with AutoCAD, offering a full range of standard functions as well as strong support for Dynamic Data Exchange.

Though somewhat lackluster compared to many Windows methods, there are many options for data exchange in the DOS environment. Because many of your suppliers or clients may use other CAD packages, you will probably be faced eventually with the need for data translation. IGES is an attempt at an industry standard, but DXF usually provides better results when AutoCAD files are used. Developing drawing standards can help to obtain the best results when you translate files.

Most people would not purchase and implement a CAD package as extensive as AutoCAD just to create and export graphic files. But because you have already learned to use the software and created graphic files for engineering and design purposes, you can do many things with these files in other software packages.

As computers and software applications continue to mature, it is becoming easier to transport data successfully between application packages. AutoCAD for Windows provides many new features for doing this. Try using some of the examples shown in this chapter for your own applications.

# AutoCAD and 3D Drawing

*Introduction*

*Getting Started with 3D*

*Using 3D Entities*

*Dynamic 3D Displays*

# PART 5

# Introduction

At this point, you should realize how easily you can increase your design and drafting productivity by using AutoCAD rather than a drafting machine or drawing board. When you know AutoCAD's commands, you can create, edit, and plot drawings in much less time than is required to draw them manually. You can store more information in an AutoCAD drawing file than you can on a typical paper drawing, and the information is portable.

The techniques you have learned so far, however, are similar to those used in manual drafting, in that you have concentrated on flat 2D drawings. In this final part of *Inside AutoCAD Release 12 for Windows*, you learn how to take advantage of AutoCAD's third dimension. Instead of showing you how to create more 2D drawings, the following chapters show you how to build 3D models. You also learn how to define a 2D drawing as one or more views of a 3D model.

You can use AutoCAD's 3D capabilities to increase your drafting productivity, but this is not the only consideration. When you develop a design, you generally must describe one or more 3D objects. You must convey the design to others, including those who must create the real objects from your information. You may think that your 2D drawings accurately convey your 3D design, but others may miss points you think are obvious. Indeed, your 2D drawings may actually convey something other than the message you originally intended, because of conflicts between views, missing elements, or other errors. When you create a 3D model to document your design, however, you can rest assured that all views are consistent. In many—but not all—applications, 3D modeling is essential.

# Understanding the Benefits of 3D Modeling

So far, you have worked with 2D images on your screen, much as you would on paper. But paper drawings are hopelessly inadequate when you need to manipulate a 3D object. In AutoCAD, you can draw, edit, rotate, scale, and stretch 3D objects in much the same manner as you work with 2D objects. You can move your viewpoint around the 3D model, using different views of it to help visualize, create, and present the design. If you need a side view, you just move your viewpoint around to that side. If you need to see the underside of the model, you simply move your viewpoint again. This visualization can solve many difficult design problems.

You can use 3D models to create complex shapes or to find intersections and other design relationships that would be difficult or impossible to draw manually.

# Learning the Building Blocks of 3D

The task of building a 3D model is not difficult if you take it one step at a time. You can use simple shapes such as cubes, spheres, surfaces, and cones to build more complex objects. You can use 2D entities such as lines, polylines, and circles to build part of your model, and then switch to 3D entities and objects, such as faces, surfaces, spheres, cubes, and cylinders. But no matter how you put your model together, you are simply making smaller parts and assembling them into larger parts.

# How Part Five Is Organized

Part Five leads you step by step through the entire process of building 3D models. The explanations and exercises in Part Five take you from building simple 3D shapes with planar and extruded 2D entities to full 3D surface modeling. The three chapters comprising Part Five cover the following topics:

- The basics of 3D drawing
- Entities in 3D
- Viewing and presenting your 3D drawings

By the time you complete Part Five, you may find yourself envisioning uses for 3D you never considered before.

## 3D Basics

Chapter 20 teaches you how to manipulate the user coordinate system (UCS) for positioning construction planes anywhere in 3D space. In Chapter 20, you draw on these construction planes by using standard 2D AutoCAD drawing commands. You learn how to use UCSs to move, rotate, and tilt your X,Y,Z axes so that you can create a 3D model from extruded 2D entities. Viewports take on additional importance for visualizing your model in 3D. The exercises show you how to see a more realistic view of your model with hidden lines removed. At the end of the chapter, you have a 3D model of the drafting board that AutoCAD replaces.

## 3D Entities

Chapter 21 introduces you to new entities such as 3D polylines, 3D faces, and 3D surface meshes. You model an office chair by creating 3D parts and inserting them as blocks for assembling the chair. In addition to the basic surface commands, Chapter 21 shows you how to use AutoLISP-defined commands that create 3D objects such as boxes, wedges, cones, and spheres. Surface shading is used for hidden-line removal and for viewing your model quickly and clearly.

## Viewing in 3D

Chapter 22 shows you how to adjust your 3D viewpoint dynamically and create perspective views, by using the DVIEW command as a single 3D substitute for the VPOINT and ZOOM commands. You learn advanced 3D viewing techniques that make 3D drawing easier and help you plan and preview 3D presentations. The chapter shows you how to put together dynamic views, slides, and scripts to create a walk-through of successive views in a simple 3D office model.

# Learning When To Use 3D

One of your goals in this 3D section is to learn how to determine when 3D modeling is useful and when it is not. Many projects do not require 3D modeling. Good examples are simple plans, diagrams, and flowcharts.

On the other hand, much of what you design and build is three-dimensional, and 3D modeling can be the most natural way to create and document your design. Three-dimensional modeling may add time and complexity to the design process, so you should know how to determine when the added complexity is worthwhile. Only you can make this determination, but you must be proficient in 3D to do so.

In any case, once you see how easy 3D can be, you can probably find some indispensable use for it in your everyday work.

# CHAPTER 20

# Getting Started with 3D

In a 3D view, what you see is one of many possible views of the 3D model you are creating in AutoCAD. You need to remember this distinction between the model itself and the view of the model. AutoCAD provides one set of tools that you use to build 3D models, and provides another set of tools for viewing your models.

This chapter teaches you the basics of working in 3D. First, you learn how to create a 2D drawing—called an *isometric drawing*—that emulates 3D. Next, you create a *wireframe drawing*, consisting of familiar AutoCAD entities, but built in 3D dimensional space. This chapter shows you how to use the VPOINT command to control the angle from which you view your 3D model, and then shows you how to use viewports in 3D. You learn about moving and rotating your UCS and about drawing and editing in 3D with extruded 2D entities.

This chapter also shows you how to use the HIDE command to remove hidden lines for more realistic 3D images, how to create and insert 3D blocks into your drawings, and how to compose multiple 3D views.

In the following lessons, you focus on using the UCS and 2D entities to build 3D models. AutoCAD provides two methods for using 2D entities to represent 3D objects. First, you can draw isometrically, just as you do in manual drafting. Second, you can create a true 3D drawing with 2D entities by controlling the entities' positions in 3D space and by extruding them along their Z axes.

Before you begin working with a true 3D drawing, consider the ways in which you can create 3D views by working entirely in 2D with an isometric drawing.

# Understanding Isometric Drawing

*Isometric drawings* are 2D representations of a 3D object. Why should this chapter include a section on 2D drawing? Mechanical and piping designers frequently use isometric drawings to help the fabricator visualize the product, as shown in figure 20.1.

**Figure 20.1:**

An isometric drawing of a pulley bracket.

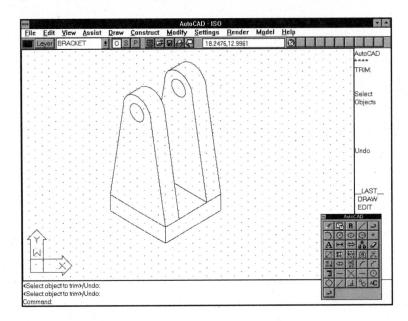

Isometric drawing offers several advantages, which make it a viable alternative to true 3D drawing. Here are several of the advantages of isometric drawing:

- In AutoCAD, isometric drawing uses familiar 2D commands. You do not need to master new commands or concepts.

- In some cases, you can create an isometric drawing more quickly than you can generate a 3D model.

- You can draw isometrics alongside other standard 2D drawings without using multiple viewports or paper space.

Isometric drawing also has a few disadvantages, including the following:

- You cannot view isometrics from different angles, as you can a 3D model.

- You cannot view isometrics in perspective mode.

- You cannot automatically remove hidden lines from an isometric drawing.

- When you make changes to one isometric view, all views do not automatically update, as 3D models do.

In this section, you learn how to create an isometric drawing by using some of AutoCAD's basic 2D tools. As you develop your isometric drawing and continue to learn about 3D construction, you begin to understand how each technique can be applied for specific needs.

## Setting Up for an Isometric Drawing

You can create an isometric drawing using lines and ellipses, but you can get correct angles much more easily using AutoCAD's built-in isometric drawing tools. The isometric SNAP style option enables you to rotate your drawing's snap and grid settings to create an isometric drawing. With the SNAP style set to isometric, the ISOPLANE command enables you to set the current drawing plane to the top, right side, or left side.

 *Isometric drawing planes are entirely different from AutoCAD's true 3D construction planes. You learn more about these drawing planes later, but remember that isometric drawings are really only 2D.*

AutoCAD provides two snap styles: standard and isometric. *Standard* is the default style, in which the crosshair cursor's X and Y axes are perpendicular. *Isometric* skews the crosshairs and the snap angle to an isometric angle.

Figure 20.2 illustrates the three isometric planes you can work in: Right, Left, and Top. The ISOPLANE command enables you to set the isometric plane you want to use.

**Figure 20.2:**

The Right, Left, and Top ISOPLANE options.

The following exercise changes the SNAP command's Style option and the ISOPLANE command as you prepare to draw the baseplate for the pulley bracket. You begin by creating a new drawing, named ISO, using IAW-ISO from the IAW DISK. The ISO drawing uses the settings shown in table 20.1.

**Table 20.1**
**Isometric Drawing Settings**

| COORDS | TILEMODE | GRID | ORTHO | SNAP | UCSICON |
|--------|----------|------|-------|------|---------|
| ON | OFF (0) | ON | OFF | .5 | OR |
| **UNITS** | Defaults for all UNITS settings | | | | |
| **LIMITS** | From 0,0 to 21,14 | | | | |
| **ZOOM** | Zoom All | | | | |
| **SPACE** | In model space with one mview viewport sized to fit | | | | |

| Layer Name | State | Color | Linetype |
|------------|-------|-------|----------|
| 0 | On | White | CONTINUOUS |
| BRACKET | On/Current | White | CONTINUOUS |

## Starting an Isometric Drawing

Use the NEW command to begin a new drawing named ISO=IAW-ISO. The drawing settings should match those shown in table 20.1. The mview viewport is sized to fit a maximized 800×600 pixel window. If the viewport does not fill your window, you can erase it and make a new one in paper space, then return to model space.

```
Command: SNAP ↵

Snap spacing or ON/OFF/Aspect/        Specifies the snap Style option
Rotate/Style <0.5000>: S ↵

Standard/Isometric <S>: I ↵           Specifies the Isometric style

Vertical spacing <0.5000>: Press Enter   Accepts the snap spacing

Command: ISOPLANE ↵                   Prompts for a new isometric plane

Left/Top/Right/<Toggle>: R ↵          Specifies the Right isometric plane
```

Notice how the grid dots and the crosshairs change orientation, as shown in figure 20.3. ORTHOMODE also changes to correspond with this new grid, and the current ISOPLANE setting. You may find it helpful to turn ORTHO on for some of the operations in the following exercises.

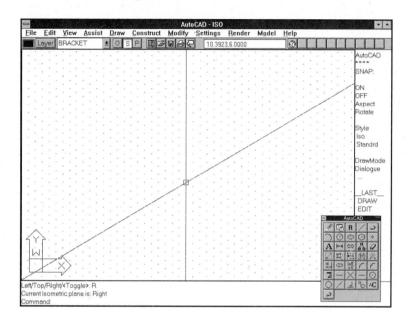

**Figure 20.3:**

The effect of choosing the Isometric SNAP Style.

Now you are ready to begin drawing your isometric pulley bracket. Begin by using the LINE command to create isometric rectangles to outline the baseplate. When the snap and grid settings are properly defined, you should be able to use the coordinate display to pick the coordinates directly from the drawing area, without typing them. Click in the coordinates box on the toolbar when you need to switch between X,Y and distance<angle input.

## Creating an Isometric Baseplate

Continue drawing in the ISO drawing.

Command: *From the toolbox, choose* LINE

Command: line From point: *Pick the first corner at 9.0933,2.25*

To point: *Pick the second corner at 1.0<90*

*continues*

```
To point: Pick the third corner at
4.0<30
```

```
To point: Pick the final corner at
1.0<270
```

| | |
|---|---|
| `To point:` **C** ⏎ | Closes the rectangle |

`Command:` *From the toolbox, choose*
**MIRROR**

`Command: mirror`

| | |
|---|---|
| `Select objects:` *Use a crossing window to select the lines shown in figure 20.4* | Selects three lines for mirroring |

`Select objects:` *Press Enter*

`First point of mirror line:` *From the toolbox, choose* ENDPOINT *and pick at* ①

`Second point:` *From the toolbox, choose* ENDPOINT *and pick at* ②

| | |
|---|---|
| `Delete old objects? <N>` *Press Enter* | Copies the lines in a mirror image |

You have now begun your first isometric drawing. Next, you learn a fast way to switch between isometric planes and a way to easily create isometric circles.

**Figure 20.4:**

The first half of the baseplate, before MIRROR.

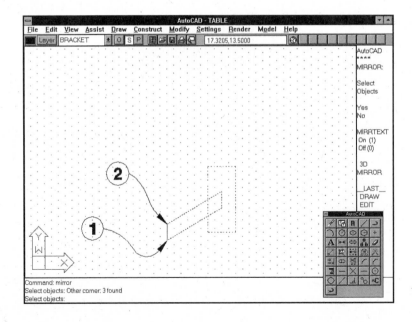

# Drawing the Support Arms

Now you create the bracket's support arms. You can create one arm, using the LINE and ELLIPSE commands, then copy and modify the other arm.

## Creating the Bracket Arms

Command: **ISOPLANE** ↵

Left/Top/Right/<Toggle>: **L** ↵       Specifies the left isometric drawing plane

Current Isometric plane is: Left

Command: *From the toolbox, choose* LINE

Command: line From point:
*Pick at 9.0933,3.25*

To point: *Pick at 8.2272,9.75*

To point: *Pick at 6.4952,10.75*

To point: *Pick at 5.6292,5.25*

To point: *Press Enter*

Command: *From the toolbox, choose* ELLIPSE

Command: ellipse

<Axis endpoint 1>/Center/Isocircle:
**I** ↵       Chooses the Isocircle option

Center of circle: *From the toolbox,*
*choose* MIDPOINT *and pick the short*
*line at* ① *(see fig. 20.5)*

<Circle radius>/Diameter: *From the*       Draws an isometric circle
*toolbox, choose* ENDPOINT *and pick*
*the short line at* ②

You have now drawn the support arm's basic outline, as shown in figure 20.5. The short line at the top of the arm is a temporary construction line. Next, you clean up and complete the arm.

*You have learned how to use the ISOPLANE command to change the current isometric plane, but there is an easier way. You can press Ctrl-E or F5 to switch modes, even during another command, in Left-Top-Right order.*

*You can also change the current isometric plane by using the Drawing Modes dialog box. To reach that dialog box, choose Settings, then Drawing Modes. In this dialog box, you can change the current isometric plane and turn the isometric snap style on or off.*

**Figure 20.5:**

The support arm begins to take form.

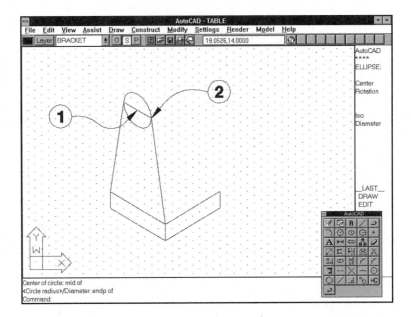

In the next exercise, you complete the support arm. First use the ELLIPSE command to create a "hole," then copy the first support arm to create the second arm.

## Completing the Support Arm

`Command:` *From the toolbox, choose* ELLIPSE

`Command: ellipse`

`<Axis endpoint 1>/Center/`
`Isocircle: I ↵`

| | |
|---|---|
| `Center of circle:` *From the toolbox, choose* MIDPOINT *and pick the short line at the top of the arm* | Uses the same center as the last circle |
| `<Circle radius>/Diameter: 0.5 ↵` | Specifies the radius |

Turn off snap in the following steps, then trim the large ellipse.

```
Command: From the toolbox, choose TRIM

Command: trim

Select cutting edge(s)

Select objects: Select only the short       Selects the cutting edge
construction line

<Select object to trim>/Undo:               Removes the lower half of the ellipse
Pick the lower half of the large ellipse
```

Use the ERASE command to remove the construction line. Then change back to the Right isometric drawing plane, using any of the four methods available.

```
Command: From the toolbox, choose COPY

Command: copy

Select objects: Select the trimmed
ellipse and the right-hand support
line

<Base point of displacement>/Multiple:
Pick any point in the drawing area

Second point of displacement:
Turn on snap and pick at 1.000<30
```

Issue ZOOM, and window an area around the top of the arm.

```
Command: From the toolbox, choose LINE

line From point: From the toolbox, choose
TANGENT and pick at ① (see figure 20.6)
```

```
To point: From the toolbox, choose
TANGENT and pick at ②
```

```
To point: Press Enter
```

Use the TRIM command to remove the portion of the second large ellipse below the short tangent line you just drew. Then issue ZOOM with the Previous option, so your drawing matches figure 20.7.

To complete the bracket, you copy the first support arm, trim the hidden lines, and add a line where the second support arm meets the baseplate. To simplify the process of picking points from the drawing area, work in the TOP isometric plane.

Finishing the
details of the
support arm.

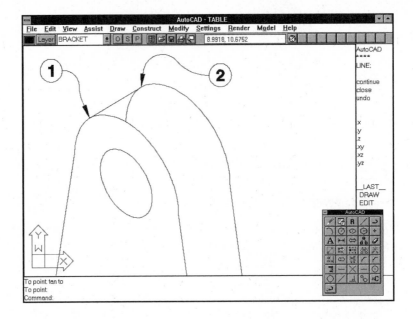

The first support
arm completed.

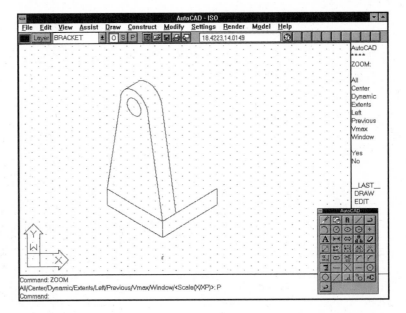

## Completing the Pulley Bracket

`Command:` *From the toolbox, choose COPY*

`Command: copy`

`Select objects:` *Pick the entities that make up the first bracket*

`<Base point or displacement>`
`/Multiple:` *Pick a point near the baseplate corner*

`Second point of displacement:`          Copies the support arm
*Drag the selected entities 3 units at 30 degrees*

Finally, draw a line where the arm meets the base and use the TRIM command to clean up the second arm, which is obscured by the first arm. Your finished bracket should look like the one shown in figure 20.8.

This is a good time to save your drawing and take a break.

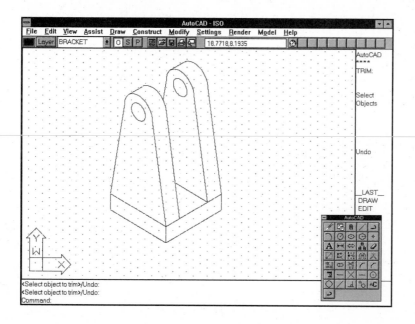

**Figure 20.8:**

The completed isometric pulley bracket drawing.

You can reset the Snap Style to Standard and annotate your isometric drawing, or you can combine isometric and orthographic drawings in the same drawing without using paper space. You also save the processing time normally required for AutoCAD to perform the HIDE command on a true 3D model. If you need to see another view of the pulley, however, you have to draw it. Your isometric drawing is not truly 3D and cannot be properly viewed from different angles.

As you see, AutoCAD's isometric tools are quick and easy, but not well-suited for multiple views. If your drawing requires a single, simple 3D view for illustrative purposes, isometric drawing works well.

But what if you need to generate multiple views of a model? You can do this by using AutoCAD's powerful 3D tools. AutoCAD has many 3D commands; many of the 2D commands work in 3D space, too. One of the key concepts behind 3D in AutoCAD is the *User Coordinate System*, or *UCS*. Before you begin working with 3D tools, you must learn how to use the UCS to your advantage.

# Using the User Coordinate System (UCS)

Up to this point, you have been working in AutoCAD's basic coordinate system—the *World Coordinate System*, or *WCS*. In fact, you have been working in the X,Y plane of the WCS. The WCS is the coordinate system of AutoCAD's model space. All drawing entities are defined in terms of their coordinate values in this coordinate system.

The principal difficulty of 3D modeling lies in the 2D nature of your workstation. Your workstation's input and output devices are two-dimensional devices. You can use the mouse or digitizer to interactively specify X and Y coordinates, but not Z coordinates. To construct 3D models, however, you must specify X, Y, and Z coordinate values for points and displacements.

To solve this problem, AutoCAD enables you to define your own coordinate systems, or UCSs. You have only one WCS, but you can create as many UCSs as you want. You can define your UCSs at any angle and location in the 3D space defined by the WCS. The X,Y plane of a UCS is its default construction plane, as is the X,Y plane of the WCS. A *construction plane* is like a transparent sheet of plastic on which you can draw by using standard 2D or 3D AutoCAD commands. You can rotate and align that transparent sheet to any orientation in 3D space by using the UCS command.

The Z elevation of points defaults to the construction plane, unless you explicitly specify a different elevation above or below the construction plane. You can give the construction plane a nonzero Z elevation, or you can relocate the UCS to control the Z coordinate. In both cases, the end result is the same, because entities are defined in terms of WCS coordinate values, regardless of how they are specified.

Look at the table drawings in figure 20.9. The four views are of a single table drawn in 3D. Each view has an associated UCS that enables you to work on a different plane, as if it were a 2D X,Y plane. In the following exercises, you learn how to create and edit this table by using 2D drawing entities and editing commands. The key to using 3D efficiently is learning how to locate your UCS in your drawing.

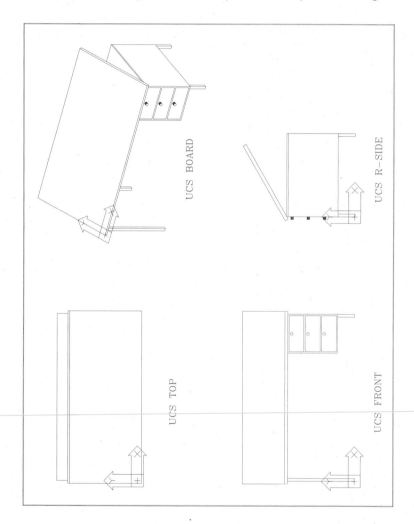

**Figure 20.9:**

The table drawings, with UCS icons.

You can draw 2D entities in any UCS construction plane and then extrude them in the Z direction. The drawing board, for example, is drawn at a 30-degree angle to the table top. It was drawn by first placing the UCS on the table top, then rotating the X-axis angle of the UCS 30 degrees to the top of the table. To give the board thickness, the artist extruded it in the Z direction. All 2D drawing and editing commands work for drawing and editing in any construction plane, set by the UCS anywhere in 3D space. If you know how to locate and use your UCS, you have an immediate advantage because you can use everything you already know about 2D drawing and editing to create work in 3D.

# Getting around in Simple 3D Drawings

Every entity you have drawn so far has been in the same plane as the WCS construction plane. All the entities' X and Y values have been in a flat plane, and the Z value for all these entities has been 0. Just as you have control over X and Y locations for entities, AutoCAD gives you Z-axis control for creating 3D objects.

You can draw some entities directly in 3D. A point or line does not have to lie flat on the X,Y construction plane. The simplest way to give 3D life to your drawing is to add a Z coordinate when you pick point coordinates. The LINE command, the full 3D-entity commands (3DPOLY, 3DFACE, and 3DMESH), and several surfacing commands accept Z input for any point. Other 2D-entity commands accept a Z coordinate for their first point only, and that coordinate is applied to the rest of their points so that they are created parallel to the current construction plane.

*If you encounter problems in any exercise, check your current UCS, thickness, and object snap settings.*

Although many 3D objects look complex, they are easy to draw. The following simple exercise shows you how to use all three coordinates (X,Y,Z) to create lines in 3D space. Later you draw a drafting table in 3D, but first, draw a few simple 3D entities and then view them from several different angles to become familiar with viewpoints in 3D space. To begin, set up a new drawing called UCS.

---

## Using LINE To Make 3D Lines

Use the NEW command to begin a new drawing named UCS. Turn on the coordinate display and grid, and set snap to .5. Zoom Center with a center point of 0,0 and a height of 3.

Command: **UCSICON** ↵

ON/OFF/ALL/Noorigin/ORigin<ON>: **OR** ↵    Displays the UCS icon at the drawing's origin

Command: *From the toolbox, choose* LINE *and draw a line along the X axis from 0,0,0 to 1,0,0*    Draws a white horizontal line

Command: *Choose* **S**ettings, *then* **E**ntity, *and set the color to red*    Changes the default Modes, entity color from BYLAYER to red

| Command: *From the toolbox, choose* LINE *and draw a line along the Y axis from 0,0,0 to 0,1,0* | Draws a red vertical line |
|---|---|
| Command: *Choose* **S**ettings, *then* **E**ntity Modes, *and set the color to green* | |
| Command: *From the toolbox, choose* LINE *and draw a line along the Z axis; pick point 0,0,0 and enter point* **0,0,1** ↵ | Draws a green line toward you, which appears as a dot |

Notice that you used three values for each coordinate. The third value is for the Z axis. Although the first two lines did not actually require a Z value, the Z coordinates are included to clarify the exercise. Your drawing should resemble the one shown in figure 20.10, with the lines in different colors.

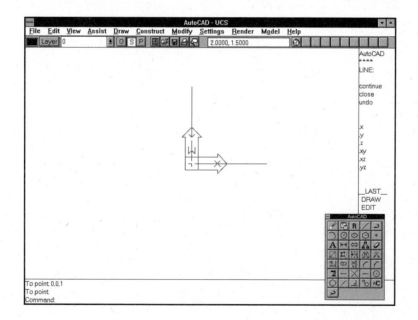

**Figure 20.10:**

Three lines in 3D space (the Z-axis appears as a green dot).

Take a look at your drawing. You see two lines and the UCS icon. Although you drew three lines, only the two lines in the X,Y plane are clearly visible (see fig. 20.10). From your current viewing direction, you cannot see the third line because you are looking directly down at its endpoint. It looks as if the line is coming directly out of the screen at you, so you see it as a single point. You need a way to view the drawing from a better angle. Fortunately, you can use AutoCAD's VPOINT command to change your viewing angle.

# Using VPOINT To Get Around

Until now, your graphics window has represented the X,Y plane only. Your vantage point, in front of the screen, is actually some distance above the X,Y plane, looking down along the Z axis. If the plane of the screen represents flat ground, you look at that flat ground from a perch on top of a flagpole. Figure 20.11 shows you how the real-world X, Y, and Z axes are oriented on your screen in a normal plan view.

**Figure 20.11:**

The orientation of the X, Y, and Z axes, relative to the screen.

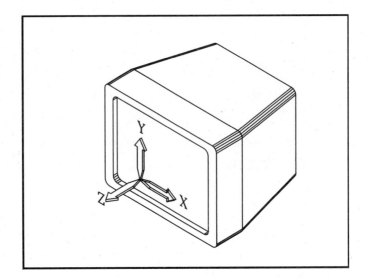

In AutoCAD, the direction from which you view your drawing or model is called the *viewpoint*. AutoCAD's VPOINT command controls this direction in relation to the drawing. The default viewpoint is 0,0,1, which indicates that your viewpoint is directly over the X,Y origin. Your line of sight is along a line from 0,0,1 to 0,0,0 (the origin). This view of a drawing is called the *plan view*. As long as you are directly above your drawing and looking down the Z axis, everything you create with 2D entities looks flat.

To see 3D, you have to move to a point that is not looking straight down at your model. Your viewpoint must have a nonzero X or Y, or both. For example, a 1,1,1 setting gives you a 45-degree angle in the X,Y plane and a 45-degree angle above the X,Y plane. This perspective enables you to look back at 0,0,0, where your lines are located. You can use VPOINT to set the viewpoint to any X,Y,Z location.

Although you can enter values to locate your viewpoint, the easiest way to use VPOINT is by using its predefined icon selections or by using the VPOINT command's globe and axes. Figure 20.12 shows the Viewpoint child pull-down menu, including Axes, which issues the VPOINT command with the globe and axes option. The child menu also offers the Presets option for the Viewpoint Presets dialog box (the

DDVPOINT command), which enables you to preset views and coordinate-defined viewpoints. The menu also offers the Set Vpoint option, which issues the VPOINT command.

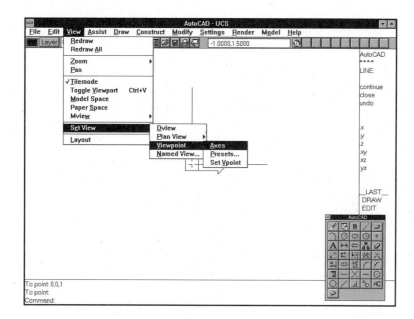

**Figure 20.12:**

The Viewpoint child pull-down menu.

## Using the VPOINT Globe and Axes

The viewpoint globe (see fig. 20.13) looks like a bull's-eye with crosshairs. You can display the viewpoint globe by pressing Enter at the VPOINT command's Rotate/<0.0000,0.0000,1.0000>: prompt. You also can choose S**e**t View, **V**iewpoint, **A**xes from the **V**iew pull-down menu.

To understand VPOINT, think of your drawing as being located at the center of a transparent globe, so that the X,Y plane is in the same plane as the globe's equator. The default viewpoint is sitting at the North Pole, looking down to the center of the globe, at your drawing. The globe's concentric circles represent the world's globe; the center point represents the North Pole, the inner circle represents the equator, and the outer circle represents the South Pole.

When you move the cursor around the viewpoint globe, you move around the outside of the world globe's sphere. If the cursor is in the inner circle, as shown in figure 20.13, you are above the equator, looking down on your model (that is, you are in the northern hemisphere, looking down toward the equator). If the cursor is in the outer circle, you are looking up at the drawing from *underneath* it (that is, you are in the southern hemisphere, looking up toward the equator).

**Figure 20.13:**

The VPOINT globe and axes.

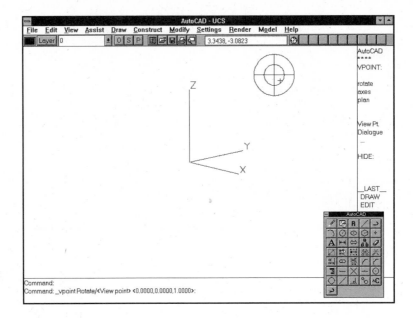

If you move the cursor to a point directly on the inner circle, you are looking directly at the drawing's edge. From this view, a 2D drawing appears as a single line. The horizontal and vertical lines represent the X and Y axes, dividing the globe into four quadrants, just as the AutoCAD X and Y axes divide your drawing.

The dynamically moving X,Y,Z axes shown in your graphics window (see fig. 20.13) reflect the position of your viewpoint as you move the cursor. For some users, this process is an intuitive way to select a viewpoint, although it does take some getting used to.

In the following exercise, you display the VPOINT globe, use the illustrations to position your cursor in the concentric circles, and then pick your viewpoint. Your drawing regenerates to reflect your VPOINT position.

## Using the VPOINT Globe and Axes

Continue working in the drawing \IAW\UCS.

| | |
|---|---|
| `Command:` *Choose* **V***iew, then* **S***e***t** *View, then* **V***iewpoint, and finally* **A***xes* | Displays the globe and axes and prompts for a viewpoint |
| `Rotate/<0.0000,0.0000,1.0000>:` *Move your pointing device until it matches figure 20.13, then press the pick button* | Displays the lines in 3D, in the lower left of the drawing area |

Use the ZOOM and PAN commands to size and position your three drawn lines in the center of the graphics window (see fig. 20.14).

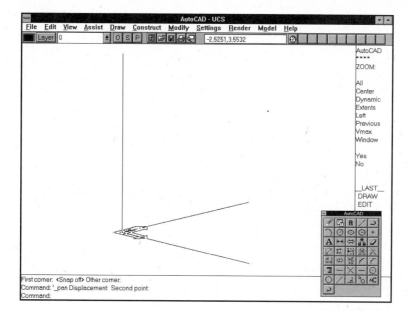

**Figure 20.14:**

The view of the lines, after VPOINT and PAN.

The VPOINT command always causes a regeneration and displays the image zoomed to the drawing extents. You can cancel the regeneration as soon as you see how the drawing will be displayed, and then you can zoom in to the desired view. For frequently used viewpoints, you can save and restore named views by using the VIEW command, described in Chapter 5.

## Selecting Predefined Viewpoints

You can also select any of nine predefined viewpoint directions from the Viewpoint Presets dialog box (the DDVPOINT command), shown in figure 20.15. You can select the viewpoint by choosing one of the eight preset angles (0 degrees through 315 degrees), then selecting the angle from the X,Y plane. If none of the preset angles suits you, you can enter specific angles in the X **A**xis and XY **P**lane boxes. To return to a plan view, select Set to Plan **V**iew, which sets your viewpoint to 0,0,0. You also can control which coordinate system the viewpoint is set to by selecting either the Absolute to **W**CS or Relative to **U**CS button. Normally, you set the viewpoint absolute to the WCS, as is the case in the following exercises. After you specify both angles, AutoCAD calculates the viewpoint and regenerates the drawing.

*The Viewpoint Presets dialog box is quick and foolproof. To get a precise view at other than the preset angles, use the X **A**xis and XY **P**lane angle entry boxes to type in the angle.*

**Figure 20.15:**

The Viewpoint
Presets dialog box.

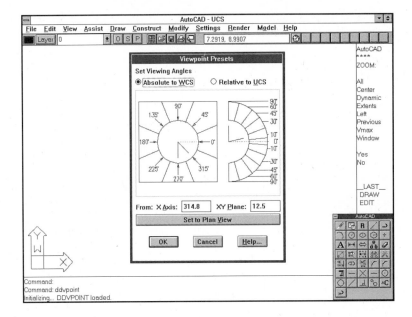

## Using Polar Angles To Select a Viewpoint

If you look at the VPOINT prompt on the command line, you see the Rotate option. The VPOINT icon menu uses Rotate to set its two angles. You also can set the viewpoint by entering two angles at the Command: prompt. The first angle determines the rotation in the X,Y plane from the X axis (X axis equals 0 angle) and the second angle determines the Z angle (inclination) from the X,Y plane. The Rotate option seems more natural to many users than specifying an X,Y,Z coordinate point in space. Use the following exercise to experiment with the VPOINT options to see which you like. First, use the dialog box again.

### Using VPOINT Options

| | |
|---|---|
| Command: *Choose **V**iew, then S**e**t View,* **V**iewpoint, *then* **P**resets | Displays the Viewport Presets dialog box |
| *Click in the area labeled 225 degrees (arrow pointing to upper right), then enter **30** in the* X,Y **P**lane *edit box, then* OK | Applies the angles and regenerates the view shown in figure 20.16 |

Next, you use the VPOINT command and supply coordinate values.

| | |
|---|---|
| Command: *Select **V**iew, then S**e**t View, then **V**iewpoint, then Set **V**point* | Starts the VPOINT command |

```
_vpoint Rotate/<View point>
<-2.8756,-2.8756,2.3479>: 1,1,.5 ↵
```

Regenerates the view shown in figure 20.17

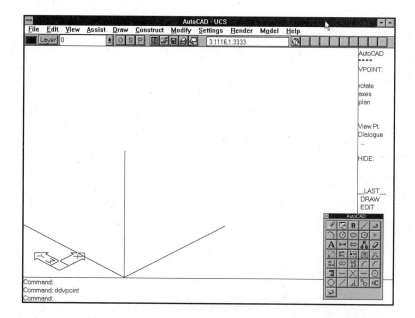

**Figure 20.16:**

A viewpoint
established with
the dialog box.

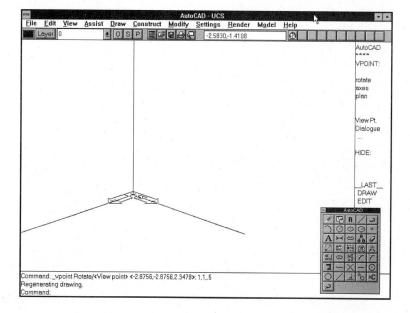

**Figure 20.17:**

A viewpoint
established with
coordinate values.

*continues*

Now use the VPOINT command and Rotate option.

```
Command: VPOINT ↵

Rotate/<View point>
<1.0000,1.0000,0.5000>: R ↵

Enter angle in X-Y plane from
X axis <45>: 200 ↵

Enter angle from X-Y plane <19>:          Regenerates the view shown in figure 20.18
50 ↵
```

Finally, use the Rotate option to view lines from below the X,Y plane:

```
Command: Press Enter                      Repeats command

VPOINT Rotate/<View point>
<-0.9060,-0.3298,1.1491>: R ↵

Enter angle in X-Y plane from
X axis <200>: Press Enter

Enter angle from X-Y plane <50>:          Regenerates the view shown in figure 20.19
-50 ↵
```

**Figure 20.18:**

A viewpoint
established with
the Rotate option.

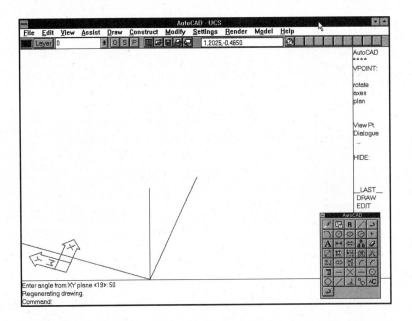

Notice that the box is now gone from the UCS icon (see 20.19). It appears only when your viewpoint is above the X,Y plane, as shown in figure 20.18.

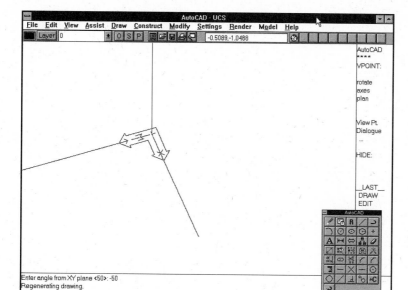

**Figure 20.19:**

A bottom view, using the Rotate option.

Practice with VPOINT for a few minutes to get a feel for the way it works. VPOINT makes sense if you remember that you are always looking through the specified viewpoint toward 0,0,0 (and beyond). Remember, too, that you are moving around the drawing; it does not move around. The entire drawing is always displayed. As you try different options, you find that the X,Y,Z axes icon matches your three lines. The lines' three colors and their intersection at 0,0,0 help you identify your vantage point.

If you select a viewpoint parallel to the current X,Y construction plane, the UCS icon turns into a *broken pencil* icon. Because AutoCAD projects distances from the screen to the X,Y plane, a small distance on the screen projects to a large one on the X,Y plane, resulting in a loss of precision. If the broken pencil appears, AutoCAD cannot project the points with acceptable precision.

*If you have trouble picking a viewpoint, try to set the angle in the X,Y plane first, and then adjust the inclination.*

## The WORLDVIEW System Variable

By default, VPOINT always bases your views on the World Coordinate System, not on the current UCS. The WORLDVIEW system variable's setting determines whether VPOINT bases the view on the WCS or UCS. The default WORLDVIEW of 1 enables you to specify your viewpoint relative to the WCS. If you set WORLDVIEW to 0, your coordinates and viewpoint-rotation angles are interpreted by VPOINT in the current UCS rather than the WCS. If you want to specify a viewpoint relative to the WCS while a UCS is current and WORLDVIEW is set to 0, prefix the coordinates with an asterisk and the UCS is ignored.

Generally, you should set WORLDVIEW to 1 (the default). It then provides a constant viewpoint reference to the World Coordinate System and makes it easier not to get "lost in space." As you become more comfortable in AutoCAD's 3D world, you can use the WORLDVIEW system variable for greater flexibility in positioning your models in the graphics window. Regardless of the WORLDVIEW setting or current UCS, the VPOINT command always regenerates the drawing looking through your viewpoint at the WCS origin.

## Using the PLAN Command

What do you do if you lose your bearings? The PLAN command quickly returns your view to the default orientation. It automatically resets the viewpoint to 0,0,1 in the current UCS (default), the WCS, or a named UCS you have saved.

Try using a quick PLAN command in the following exercise.

---

### Using PLAN To Return to a Plan View

Command: *Choose* **V**iew, *then* **S**et View,      Displays the lines at the lower left corner
**P**lan View, **W**orld      in plan view in the WCS

*Zoom Center at 0,0,0 with a height of 2*      Centers the lines

Save the drawing and continue, or end the drawing session and take a break.

---

You could have chosen Plan View, Current UCS because the WCS is the current UCS in this exercise.

The preceding drawing exercise showed how you can use AutoCAD's basic LINE command in 3D space. The next section shows you how to use other 2D commands in the 3D drawing world.

## Drawing 2D Entities in 3D Space

You can draw most of AutoCAD's basic 2D entities with a Z-coordinate value. 2D entities, such as polylines, circles, arcs, and solids, are constrained to the X,Y plane of the UCS. For these entities, the Z value is accepted only for the first coordinate to set the elevation of the 2D entity above or below the current plane.

When you pick entity coordinates, AutoCAD assumes a Z value of 0 (unless you use object snap). Until you began the 3D section of this book, you allowed AutoCAD to operate this way. Picking coordinates above or below the X,Y plane (when a Z value is allowed) is as easy as adding a Z value when AutoCAD asks for a point. When you pick a point by using an object snap mode, AutoCAD uses the X,Y, and Z values of the matching point.

The following tips can assist you in creating 3D objects from familiar 2D entities:

- Circles are best for making closed cylinders. Donuts make good open-ended cylinders with thick walls.

- Solids quickly make rectilinear closed objects. Keep Fill turned off to speed up regenerations.

- Lines and polylines make good open rectilinear objects. Polylines show their width.

- Lines can approximate any object in wireframe but cannot hide anything unless extruded.

- Solids, wide polylines, and traces fill only in plan view and do not plot filled in other views.

# Three-Dimensional Thickness

You can create a 3D model by positioning flat 2D entities at various angles in 3D space. You can create 3D models more efficiently, however, by extruding 2D entities (lines, polylines, arcs, circles, and solids) to give them a *thickness* in their Z direction. When you assign a thickness to a 2D entity, you give the entity *height* in its Z direction. If you draw a line on the X,Y plane, for example, its thickness appears as a wall, stretching from the line itself to the height of the thickness given it. Figure 20.20 shows how a 3D object "grows" from flat 2D entities.

You can create new entities with thickness by first setting a value for the THICKNESS system variable. All entities are created with a thickness equal to the value of the THICKNESS variable. The default value is 0, which produces planar entities—that is, entities with no thickness. You also can use the CHPROP command to edit the thickness of an existing entity.

*Thickness can be positive (up in the Z direction) or negative (down in the Z direction). Thickness is relative to the Z axis of 2D entities, even if applied by CHPROP with the current UCS in a different orientation. For 3D entities that can accept thickness, such as points and lines, thickness is always relative to the current UCS. These entities appear oblique if they do not lie in or parallel to the current UCS. If thickness is added to a line drawn directly in the Z direction, it appears that the line extends beyond its endpoint in the positive or negative thickness direction.*

**Figure 20.20:**

Growing a 3D
drawing from 2D
entities.

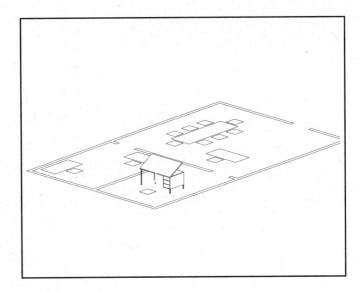

## Using THICKNESS To Draw Table Legs

Your table drawing begins with its legs. Make TABLE the current layer and then set a thickness for the extruded height of the legs. Draw one table leg with lines and a second with a polygon, and then copy both to create the table's other two legs. You may find this process easier if you first turn on ortho. Create the table by using the settings shown in table 20.2.

### Table 20.2
### Table Drawing Settings

| COORDS | FILL | GRID | ORTHO | SNAP | UCSICON |
|--------|------|------|-------|------|---------|
| ON | OFF | 2 | ON | .25 | OR |
| **UNITS** | Use defaults for all UNITS settings. | | | | |
| **LIMITS** | Set LIMITS from 0,0 to 68,44. | | | | |
| **ZOOM** | Zoom All. | | | | |

| Layer Name | State | Color | Linetype |
|------------|-------|-------|----------|
| 0 | On | White | CONTINUOUS |
| SCRATCH | Off | White | CONTINUOUS |
| TABLE | On/Current | White | CONTINUOUS |

## Using the THICKNESS Variable To Extrude a 2D Entity

Use the NEW command to begin a new drawing named TABLE, and then make the settings shown in table 20.2. Be sure TABLE is the current layer and the SCRATCH layer is off.

Command: *Choose* **V**iew, *then* **Z**oom, *then* **A**ll

Zooms to show grid

Command: *Choose* **S**ettings, *then* Entity Modes..., *double-click in the* **T**hickness *box, enter* **25**, *and then choose* OK

Sets the entity thickness to 25

Command: *From the toolbox, choose* LINE, *and draw a 1" square with its lower left corner at 4,7.5*

Command: *Choose* **D**raw, *then* **P**olygon, *then* **C**ircumscribed, *and draw a polygon with four sides at center point 51.5,8 circumscribed around a .5 radius circle*

Command: *From the toolbox, choose* COPY, *and copy the two legs 29 inches up in the Y direction*

As figure 20.21 shows, you now have four squares for table legs, but you need to view the legs from a different viewpoint to see the thickness. A common problem of drawing in 3D is that you cannot see what you have done unless you first change your viewpoint. Multiple views of your drawing help you work most effectively in 3D.

# Using Multiple Viewports To Control Drawing Display and 3D Viewing

You can view your 3D model in several viewports, which can have different snap, grid, zoom, and viewpoint settings. MVIEW and VPORTS are the commands that create multiple viewports.

Chapters 5 and 13 taught you how MVIEW and VPORTS set up and control 2D drawing viewports. As you may recall, the VPORTS command divides the AutoCAD graphics window into as many as 16 tiled viewports, and the MVIEW command creates up to 15 MVIEW viewports. (One viewport number is reserved by the system for the main paper space viewport in paper space.)

You can work in only one viewport at a time—that is, the *current* viewport. Make the viewport current by clicking on it with your pointer. When you work in a viewport, you can use all your normal display controls, as if you were working with a single viewport. As you draw or edit in one viewport, however, the drawing is updated in all viewports.

When you work in 3D, you should set up three viewports as a starting configuration. Set up one viewport for your UCS plan view, use a second viewport as a 3D viewport for visualizing and building your 3D model, and use the third viewport to hold a WCS view or a second 3D view of your drawing.

**Figure 20.21:**

Table legs drawn with THICKNESS, as seen from plan view.

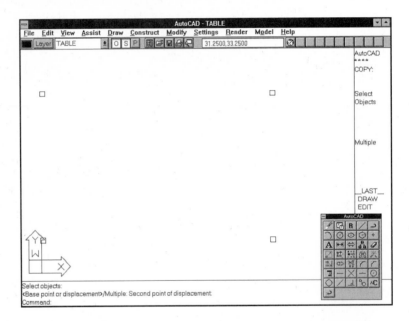

# Using Viewports To View the 3D Table's Construction

In the next exercise, you set up three viewports so you can see the 3D table construction as you draw it (see fig. 20.22). Split the graphics window into a large top view for construction and two smaller views below. The lower left viewport gives you a left-front 3D view of the table from above. The lower right viewport gives you a right-front 3D view of the table from below. The top view is your plan view. The table you are building appears in each viewport. When your views are set up, save the viewport configuration with the name TABLE.

## Using MVIEW To Set Three Viewports

Command: *Choose* View, *then* Tilemode      Enters paper space

Command: *Choose* View, *then* Mview, *then*      Issues Mview with the 3 option
**3** Viewports

```
Command: _mview
ON/OFF/Hideplot/Fit/2/3/4/Restore/
<First Point>: 3
```

| | |
|---|---|
| `Horizontal/Vertical/Above/Below`<br>`/Left/<Right>:` **A** ↵ | Specifies Above |
| `Fit/<First Point>:` **F** ↵ | Fits three viewports to the drawing area |

Click on the P (Paperspace) toolbar button to return to model space.

| | |
|---|---|
| `Command:` *Click in the bottom left viewport* | Makes the viewport current |

*Use VPOINT to set the viewpoint to -.6,-1,.8*

`Command:` *Select the lower right viewport*

*Set the viewpoint to -1,-1,-.4*

`Command:` *Select the lower left viewport*

| | |
|---|---|
| *Use* VIEW *with the* Save *option to save*<br>*the view as* TABLE | Saves the model-space view |

Click on the P (Paperspace) toolbar button again to enter paper space.

| | |
|---|---|
| *Use* VIEW *with the* Save *option to save*<br>*the view as* TABLEP | Saves the three-viewport paper-space view |

The table legs should be visible in all three viewports (see fig. 20.22). Their thickness makes them 25 inches high. Notice that the lower right viewport's viewpoint is looking up from below the table. It may sometimes appear backwards as the wireframe image plays tricks on your eyes.

*When you use multiple viewports and you want to redraw or regenerate all viewports, use the REDRAWALL or REGENALL command.*

# Using the SOLID Command To Make a 3D Object

Now you are ready to put a top on the table. You want the table top to show as a solid surface, so you make it a solid entity. The top is 1/2" thick; you can extrude the top by assigning a thickness to it. The only constraint on using solids in 3D is that all the extruded Z points must lie in a plane parallel to the X,Y plane.

**Figure 20.22:**

The table legs
shown in three
viewports.

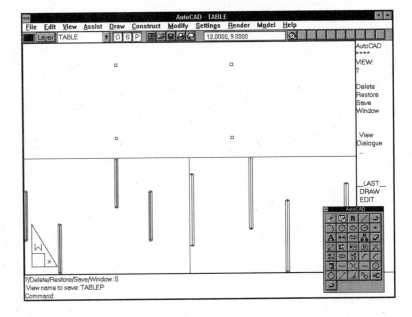

## Using XYZ Filters in 3D

How do you get the table top on top of the legs? You have two choices. You can assign
a thickness of 0.5 inches for your table top, and then begin your solid at the Z height of
25 inches above the current UCS construction plane. The second option is to set a new
UCS 25 inches above the current one—so that the X,Y plane is at the top of the legs—
and to begin drawing the solid from that spot.

You use the first method in the following exercise, which shows how to start the solid
at the correct Z height by using XYZ filters. First, set THICKNESS to 0.5 inches. Then
use the SOLID command to create the table top by picking the X,Y coordinates and
entering the Z value at the keyboard.

### Using SOLID and XYZ Filters To Make a 3D Table Top

Click on the P (Paperspace) toolbar button again to enter model space.

Command: *Click in the top viewport*          Makes the viewport current

Command: *Choose* Settings, *then* Entity
Modes..., *double-click in the*
Thickness *box, enter* **.5** *and choose* OK

Command: *Choose* Settings, *then*          Opens the Running Object Snap dialog box
Object Snap

| | |
|---|---|
| *Select the* **E**ndpoint *snap mode, then choose* OK | Selects the running object snap mode |
| `Command:` *From the screen menu, choose* DRAW, *then* next, *then* SOLID: | |
| `Command: SOLID First point:` **.XY** ↵ | Specifies the XY filter |
| `of` *Pick near corner of leg at* $bub1 *(see fig. 20.23)* | Sets the X and Y values |
| `(need Z):` **25** ↵ | Specifies the elevation |
| `Second point:` *Pick the second, third, and fourth corners in the sequence shown by the bubbles in fig. 20.23, then press Enter* | Draws solid top (see fig. 20.24) and ends the command |
| `Command:` *Choose* **S**ettings, *then* **O**bject Snap | Opens the Running Object Snap dialog box |
| *Click to clear the* **E**ndpoint *snap mode, then choose* OK | Turns off the running object snap mode |
| *Save the drawing* | |

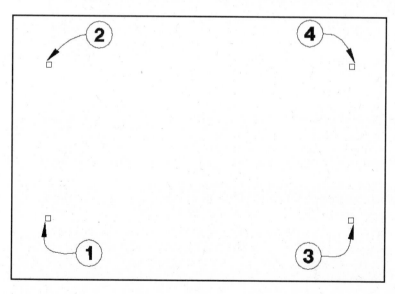

**Figure 20.23:**

Detail of the pick points.

Note that you had to enter the Z value only for the first coordinate point; AutoCAD assumed the same Z value for the three remaining points. This technique works for all extrudable 2D entities. For 3D entities, such as lines that accept different Z coordinates for their different points, you must specify X, Y, and Z values for each point.

**Figure 20.24:**

The table top, added with SOLID.

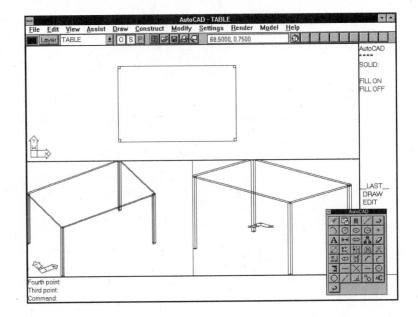

*XYZ point filters are efficient for creating entities at various Z elevations without changing your UCS. You can use object snap to snap the X,Y point to an existing object, and then enter a Z value. You also can use object snap to pick the Z elevation from an entity in a different viewport.*

## Z Values and Thickness

You made a simple 3D table by extruding the legs and top, assigning thickness values, and drawing the entities at the Z height you wanted. When you draw in 3D, remember that the draw commands do not prompt for thickness. You can check the current thickness setting by using the THICKNESS system variable or by displaying the Entity Creation dialog box. You can find the Z value and thickness of an existing entity by using the LIST command. If you want to change the thickness of an existing entity, use the CHPROP or DDMODIFY command. You select the entity, respond with thickness as the property you want to edit, and then input a new value. You can check the X,Y,Z coordinates of points on existing entities with the ID command by snapping to them with object snap in a suitable view.

*The ELEV command can assign a thickness value, but it is better to control thickness by using the THICKNESS system variable. ELEV can also set an ELEVATION variable, but it is better to enter elevations directly by using object snaps when appropriate. The*

ELEV command may eventually be eliminated from AutoCAD, and it can be confusing to use with varying UCSs.

AutoCAD ignores the thickness setting when you create text. If you want text with a 3D thickness, use CHPROP or DDLIST to set a thickness after you create the text.

You now have a good 3D drawing of a simple table. Before moving on to more 3D drawing and editing, take a minute to see how the table drawing looks with its hidden lines removed.

# Using HIDE To Remove Hidden Lines

In the bottom viewports, the different views of the table are *wireframe* representations. These wire edges help you visualize the table's appearance in 3D space. When AutoCAD generates a wireframe image, it does not consider whether a line would be visible from your viewpoint if the objects on the screen were solid. Instead, AutoCAD shows it as if it were transparent or constructed of wires. This method is the quickest way for the program to display the view.

Once you get a view you like, you can make it look more realistic by using the HIDE command to remove lines that should be hidden. The HIDE command is simple to use and takes only a little longer than a screen regeneration. While HIDE works, AutoCAD keeps you informed by displaying the percentage of hiding that has been completed.

Try hiding the table in the following exercise; it uses a simple drawing, so the process is rapid.

---

### Using HIDE To Remove Hidden Lines in the Table

Command: *Click in the bottom left viewport*   Makes the viewport current

Command: *Choose **R**ender, then **H**ide*

Command: _hide Regenerating drawing   Regenerates and displays the HIDE
Hiding lines: done 100%   operation's progress

The results are shown in figure 20.25.

---

AutoCAD clears the viewport, regenerates the drawing, processes the drawing, and finally displays the drawing with the hidden lines removed. Now, the table top obscures the back leg.

**Figure 20.25:**

The table after
HIDE in the lower
left viewport.

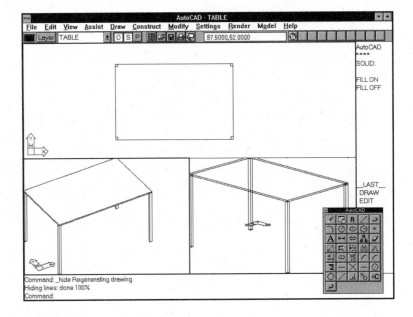

*The HIDE command performs hidden-line removal only on the
current viewport. Be sure you are in model space and the correct
viewport is active before issuing the HIDE command.*

# What Gets Hidden with HIDE?

To help you understand hidden lines, imagine that your 3D wireframe model is
constructed of clear, non-reflective plastic; you can see all the edges in the model,
regardless of their positions. If you then paint the model so the surfaces are opaque,
you can see only the edges not hidden by surfaces. AutoCAD simulates the painting
process in software and displays the result.

It helps to know the ways AutoCAD treats various entity surfaces when it calculates
hidden-line removal. AutoCAD puts an opaque cap on the bottom and top of most
graphic entities that surround an area. Circles and solids, for example, have top and
bottom surfaces that hide lines enclosed within or behind them. (You saw the effect of
the solid table top in your table view.) A polyline (or trace) hides only what is behind
its thickness extrusion or what is concealed by its width. Areas enclosed by closed
polylines are not hidden because they have no top or bottom. Remember that polygons, ellipses, and donuts are really polylines. Other 2D extruded entities hide only
what is behind their extrusions. Text entities are ignored by HIDE, and are never
hidden.

*When the HIDE command determines what to display, it includes entities on layers that are turned off. This can result in invisible objects hiding visible ones. Use frozen layers if you want to suppress unwanted objects when hiding.*

*All normal editing commands work on 3D-generated displays, but a regeneration or any zoom unhides the drawing. When you edit a hidden-line display, turn REGENAUTO off to avoid accidentally regenerating the drawing.*

*You should freeze layers that contain extraneous information before you use the HIDE command. AutoCAD should not spend time removing hidden lines unnecessarily.*

*If you have created top and bottom objects from entities that do not hide lines behind them, fill in the surface boundaries with circles, solids, or wide polylines.*

The HIDE command hides one entity when it is behind another. If two entities intersect or coincide in the same plane, small rounding errors make it impossible to predict which one hides the other. When two entities intersect, cut a tiny slice out of one at the intersection. If they coincide, move one a short distance in front of the other.

Remember that all the editing tools you have learned so far also can be applied to 3D.

# Using Familiar Editing Commands as 3D Tools

The editing commands that reposition entities are valuable in 3D drawing. Often you can more easily draw an entity in the current UCS and then move, copy, or rotate it than you can by using more advanced 3D techniques. The COPY and MOVE commands accept 3D points or displacements. COPY Multiple is useful for positioning several identical entities at different points in 3D space. The ROTATE command rotates only objects that are parallel to the current UCS, but, by setting different UCSs, you can rotate objects to any orientation in space.

## Using MOVE as a 3D Construction Tool

In the following exercise, you construct a cabinet on the table's right side. The new cabinet overlaps the legs. Later, you shorten the legs and add drawers. You draw the cabinet at the UCS origin and then move it into place, instead of picking the corner points in space. You can set a new color to distinguish the cabinet from the table. Use SOLID to draw the cabinet and extrude it in the Z direction with a thickness of 18 1/2 inches.

## Drawing and Moving the Cabinet in 3D

Use the **O** Orthomode toolbar button to make sure ORTHO is on.

Command: *Choose* **S**ettings, *then* **E**ntity Modes, *double-click in the* **T**hickness *box, enter* **18.5**, *and choose* OK

Command: *From the screen menu, choose* DRAW, *then* next, *then* SOLID:

Command: _SOLID First point: **0,0,0** ↲      Specifies the UCS origin

Second point: *Enter* **14,0**, **0,30**, *and* **14,30** *for the second, third, and fourth corners and press Enter*      Draws a 3D cabinet (see fig. 20.26)

*Zoom in close on the table top's right corner (see fig. 20.27)*

Next, you move the cabinet to below the top at the right front corner.

Command: *From the toolbox, choose* MOVE

Command: _move
Select objects: *Click in the lower right viewport and select the cabinet*

Base point or displacement: *From the toolbox, choose* ENDPOINT

endp of *Pick corner at* ① *(see fig. 20.26)*

Second point of displacement: *From the toolbox, choose* ENDPOINT

endp of *Click in the lower left viewport and pick the outside corner of the right leg at* ② *(see fig 20.27)*

Command: *Choose* **V**iew, *then* **Z**oom, *then* **P**revious

Use QSAVE and continue, or take a break.

If all went well, you should have a good solid cabinet mounted under the right side of the table, as shown in figure 20.27. The cabinet overlaps the legs, but that is fixed later.

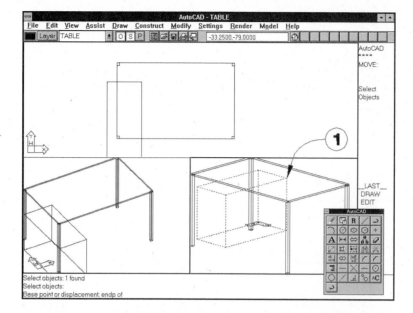

**Figure 20.26:**

The table with the cabinet at UCS origin and the MOVE command's base point.

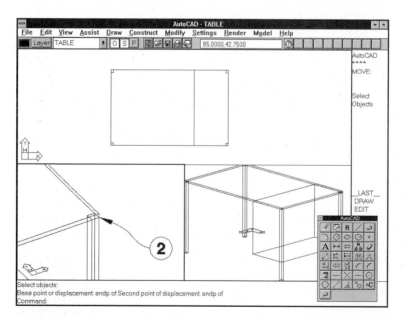

**Figure 20.27:**

The table with the cabinet moved up beneath the top.

Although THICKNESS settings, Z coordinate values, object snap, and the editing commands are useful for constructing 3D drawings, they cannot handle all 3D construction tasks you encounter. In the next set of exercises, you add drawers and a drawing board at a 30-degree slant on top of the table. Think about ways to draw these entities by using the tools you have learned about so far. The drawers are pretty simple, but the slanted drawing board is easier to do with a reoriented UCS.

# Establishing a UCS in 3D

Start this section by taking a closer look at the UCS command and the UCS icon. So far, you have been using AutoCAD's WCS, the default coordinate system, and UCSs that share its X,Y plane. You can create your own coordinate system, however, by using the UCS and UCSICON commands. These commands were developed for 3D to enable you to work with 2D entities and editing commands by locating your coordinate system anywhere in 3D space.

You can establish or modify a UCS by using the UCS command, the UCS screen menu, the UCS item on the SETTINGS screen menu, or the UCS item in the Settings pull-down menu, which displays a child menu of five UCS menu items. The Named UCS pull-down item uses the DDUCS command to display the UCS Control dialog box (see fig. 20.28). The UCS Presets selection displays the UCS Orientation dialog box with a group of predefined UCSs (see fig. 20.29). The UCS Icon selection enables you to change the origin and visibility of the UCS icon. The Axis option enables you to rotate the current UCS about the X, Y, or Z axis. Finally, the Origin option enables you to change the origin of the current UCS.

**Figure 20.28:**

The UCS Control dialog box.

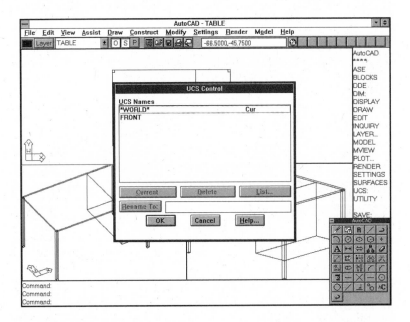

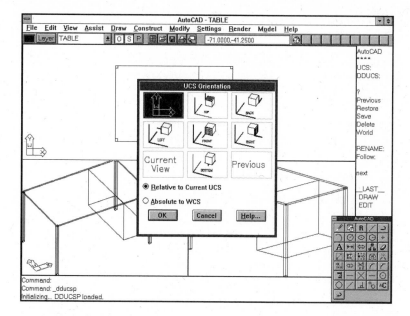

**Figure 20.29:**
The UCS Orientation dialog box.

You can establish a new UCS in 3D in the following ways:

- Specify a new origin, a new X,Y plane, or a new Z axis
- Copy the orientation of an existing entity
- Align the new UCS to your current view
- Rotate the current UCS around any one or all X, Y, or Z axes

You can set a UCS by using these methods, or you can combine them by executing the UCS command several times in succession. A complex UCS move is easier to visualize in several steps. You can define any number of UCSs by naming and saving them. Only one UCS can be current at any one time, however, and the current UCS defines all coordinate input. If you are using multiple viewports, they all share the current UCS.

## Understanding the UCS Command's Options

As you construct the rest of the table, you learn how to use most of the command options to define, name, and save UCSs. The following list describes all of the UCS command's options (more details appear in the exercises):

- **Origin.** This option specifies a new UCS origin point, without changing the orientation.

- **ZAxis.** This option specifies a new UCS origin point and defines a new UCS by specifying a positive point on the Z axis.

- **3point.** Use this option to define a new UCS by specifying three points: an origin, a positive point on the X axis, and a positive point on the Y axis.

- **Entity.** This option aligns the current UCS with the coordinate system of a selected entity.

- **View.** You can use the view option to align the UCS to your current viewpoint.

- **X.** Use this option to rotate the UCS about the X axis.

- **Y.** Use this option to rotate the UCS about the Y axis.

- **Z.** Use this option to rotate the UCS about the Z axis.

- **Prev.** This option restores the previous UCS. You can repeat this option to step back up to ten previous coordinate systems in paper space or ten in model space.

- **Restore.** This option restores a previously named and saved UCS. Enter a question mark for a list of named UCSs.

- **Save.** This option saves the current UCS. You specify a name (up to 31 characters). Enter a question mark for a list of named UCSs.

- **Del.** This option deletes a saved UCS by name. Enter a question mark for a list of named UCSs.

- **?.** This option lists named UCSs. You can use wild cards to create a specific list. A current unnamed UCS is listed as *NO NAME*, unless it is the WCS, which is listed as *WORLD*.

- **World.** This option restores the WCS, and is the default.

*The X,Y plane of the current UCS also is the current construction plane, unless you have used the ELEV command to set a nonzero elevation. A* nonzero elevation *creates a current construction plane above or below the UCS X,Y plane and can make drawing in 3D confusing. Thus, you should not use ELEV to set elevations. For brevity and simplicity, the term UCS is often used rather than the term* construction plane.

In the following section, you return to the table drawing, in which you define and save two UCSs.

# Defining and Saving a 3Point UCS

In the following exercises, you establish two more UCSs: at the front of the table and on the right side. You use the 3point option for the front UCS. (You can use 3point to establish any UCS.) If you do not pick up all the options immediately, learn this option first.

You define the UCS by entering three coordinate points: the first point defines the origin, the second point defines the positive X axis from the new origin point, and the third point defines the X,Y plane (and, consequently, the Z axis). The third point need not be on the Y axis (because the Y axis must be perpendicular to the X axis), but it defines the direction of the positive Y axis. The only constraint for the 3point option is that all three points cannot lie in a straight line. The prompts for each of the points present defaults that set a point or axis equal to the current UCS.

In the following exercise, you define the UCS so that it lies at the base of the table's left front leg. You pick the first origin point on the front lower left corner of the leg, the second on the right leg, and the third on the front edge of the top. After picking the points, you save the UCS with the name **FRONT**. The exercise also shows you how to return to a single viewport and set a larger grid, so that you can more easily see the object snap points and UCS icon as you work.

---

## Using 3Point To Create a UCS

Continue from the preceding exercise in the TABLE drawing or begin a new drawing named TABLE=IAW-TBL1. Select the bottom left viewport. Turn on the P toolbar button to switch to paper space.

Command: *Choose* **V**iew, *then* **Z**oom, *then* **W**indow, *and fill the graphics window with the lower left viewport*

Turn off the P toolbar button to return to model space.

Command:  *Choose* **V**iew, *then* **Z**oom, *then* **A**ll, *then press Enter, and enter* **0.9X**       Enables some working room around the figure in the graphics window

Command: *Choose* **S**ettings, *then* **D**rawing Aids, *and set the grid to 6*

Command: *From the screen menu, choose* UCS:, *then* next, *then* 3point       Issues UCS 3point option

Origin point <0,0,0>: **INT** ↵

of *Pick at* ① *(see fig. 20.30)*

Point on positive portion of the X-axis
<5.0000,7.5000,0.0000>: **INT** ↵

of *Pick at* ②

Point on positive-Y portion of the
UCSX-Y plane <4.0000,8.5000,0.0000>:
**MID** ↵

*continues*

| | |
|---|---|
| of *Pick at* ③ | Creates the UCS |
| Command: *Press Enter, and from the screen menu choose* SAVE | Repeats UCS command, with Save option |
| ?/Desired UCS name: **FRONT** ↵ | Saves UCS |

**Figure 20.30:**

The table with a UCS at the front, defined with the 3point option.

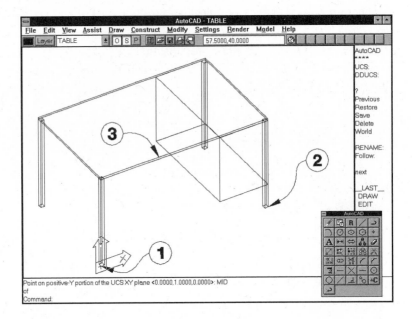

Your UCS icon's origin should be on the base of the front left leg, with the X axis pointing toward the right leg and the Y axis pointing up the left leg. Notice that you did not change your view of the drawing by setting the UCS. When you save the UCS, the FRONT UCS is listed as an option the next time you display the UCS Control dialog box.

Now you can define a second UCS on the right side.

## Using the ZAxis Option To Define a UCS

In the following exercise, you use the ZAxis option to define a UCS at the right leg, with the X,Y plane on the table's right side. The ZAxis option enables you to specify a new positive Z axis by picking an origin and a point on the Z axis. This option rotates the X,Y plane, based on your new Z axis. Again, this is an easy option to use.

In this case, the new Z direction must face out from the table's right side, as shown in figure 20.31. After you pick your origin point at the corner of the right front leg, you specify the second point with relative polar coordinates at 0 degrees. The new UCS is saved with the name R-SIDE.

## Using ZAxis To Create R-Side UCS

Command: **UCS** ↵

Origin/ZAxis/3point/Entity/View/
XYZ/Prev/Restore/Save/Del/?/
<World>: **ZA** ↵

Origin point <0,0,0>: **INT** ↵

of *Pick at ② from previous
exercise (see fig. 20.30)*

Point on positive portion of Z-axis    Positions UCS, as in figure 20.31
<48.0000,0.0000,1.0000>: **@1<0** ↵

*From the screen menu, choose* UCS:,
*then* Save

?/Desired UCS name: **R-SIDE** ↵

*Save the drawing*

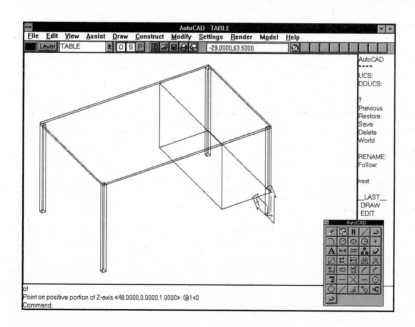

**Figure 20.31:**

The table with the new UCS at the right side.

Your new UCS icon origin should be at the base of the right front leg with the X axis pointing toward the back of the table, the Y axis pointing toward the table top, and the Z axis pointing to the right.

# Using the UCS Icon To Keep Track of UCS Orientation

You may come to rely heavily on the UCS icon as a reminder of your construction plane's orientation and to confirm that you have defined your UCS the way you want it.

Looking closely at your drawing, you see that the icon's X and Y axes point along the axes of the table. The + on the icon means that it is located at the origin of the current UCS. The W on the Y axis is missing, which indicates that your current coordinate system is not the WCS. A box at the icon's base means you are viewing the UCS from above (a positive Z direction). No box means you are looking at the icon from below (a negative Z direction). Figure 20.32 shows a collection of icon views you encounter. When you see a *broken pencil* icon, your view is within one degree of parallel (edge-on) to the current UCS, making point picking unreliable. When you see the paper-space icon, you know to switch to model space in order to draw.

To control the visibility and location of the UCS icon, use the UCSICON command. You can find this command by choosing Settings, then UCS, then Icon. The UCSICON settings can be controlled separately in each viewport, enabling the user to selectively turn the icon on or off.

*The UCSICON settings do not have any effect on the UCS. It is recommended that you keep the UCS icon on, which serves as a reminder of the current UCS.*

## UCSICON Options

The following list reviews the UCSICON options for controlling the UCS icon's display.

- **ON.** This option turns on the UCS icon so it appears in the drawing area.

- **OFF.** This option turns off the UCS icon.

- **All.** This option displays the UCS icon in each viewport when you use multiple viewports.

- **Noorigin.** This option always displays the UCS icon at the lower left corner of each viewport.

- **ORigin.** This option displays the UCS icon at the 0,0 origin of the current UCS, unless the origin is outside the drawing area or too close to the edge for the icon to fit. The icon is then visible at the lower left corner of the viewport.

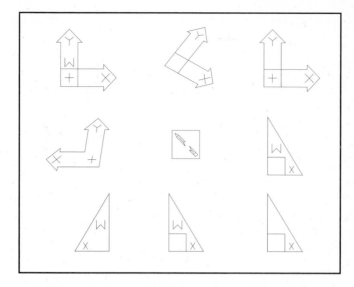

**Figure 20.32:**
Different views of
the UCS icon.

When you are working with three viewports, AutoCAD displays the UCS icon in each viewport. You can set different display settings for the icon in each viewport.

# Setting the UCS Origin and a Plan View

Depending on what you are doing, it may be clearer to draw in a 3D viewpoint or in a plan view of the current UCS. Use the PLAN command to set a plan view if it is easier to find your pick points that way.

In the following exercise, you restore the FRONT UCS and use the UCS origin options to set the UCS at the lower left corner of the cabinet. Then you use the PLAN command to set a plan view for constructing the drawers. When the view is set, you can draw the first (lower) drawer on the cabinet face with a 2D polyline, and then use the COPY command's Multiple option to add the next two drawers. When you are done, you restore your 3D view named TABLE.

## Using UCS in Plan View To Add Drawers to the Table

Command: *Choose* **S***ettings, then* U**C**S, *then* **N***amed UCS, highlight* **FRONT**, *click on the* **C***urrent button, then* OK

Makes FRONT the current UCS

*Choose* **S***ettings, then* U**C**S, *then* **O***rigin*

Prompts for a new UCS origin

Origin point <0,0,0>: **INT** ↵

of *Pick the cabinet's lower left corner*

*continues*

Save the current UCS as CABINET. Next, use the Entity Modes dialog box to set a thickness of .01, because when entities are in the same plane, you cannot always predict when one entity hides another. The .01 thickness makes the drawer polylines protrude slightly beyond the face of the cabinet, ensuring that they are not hidden accidentally.

| | |
|---|---|
| Command: *Choose* **V**iew, *then* S**e**t View, *then* **P**lan View, *then* **C**urrent UCS | Displays PLAN viewpoint |
| *Zoom in on the cabinet, as shown in figure 20.33* | |
| Command: *From the toolbox, choose* POLYLINE, *then draw from .5,.5 to @13<0 to @5.5<90 to @13<180 and enter* **C** | Creates the first drawer |
| Command: *From the toolbox, choose* COPY, *and select the drawer, then enter* **M**, *and add two drawers above the original at a 6" spacing* | Creates a total of three drawers as shown in figure 20.34 |

Use VIEW to restore the view named TABLE (see fig. 20.34), and save the drawing.

**Figure 20.33:**

The cabinet front— the plan view from the CABINET UCS.

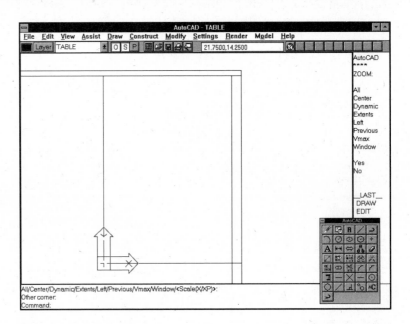

Aside from the Origin, 3point, and ZAxis options you have used so far, there are several other ways to set a UCS.

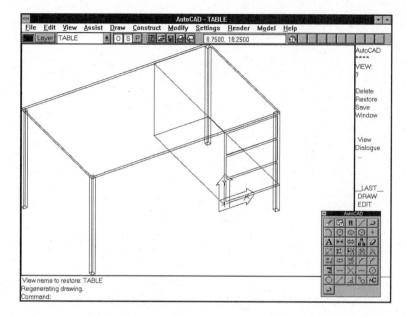

**Figure 20.34:**

The table with drawers added.

# Setting a UCS with the X/Y/Z, View, and Entity Options

The X/Y/Z options enable you to rotate the current UCS around either the X, Y, or Z axis. The angle of rotation is relative to the specified axis of the current UCS through the right-hand rule of rotation. The *right-hand rule of rotation* means that if you close your right fist and extend your thumb to point in the positive direction of the specified axis, your curled fingers point in the direction of positive rotation. Figure 20.35 shows the direction of the rotations. If you want to rotate more than one axis, re-execute the UCS command to rotate the second (or third) axis. (You use the X/Y/Z options in some of the remaining exercises.)

The View option is simple; it sets the X,Y plane of the UCS so it is parallel to the screen's orientation. The origin does not change. The Entity option is a bit more complex.

## Using Entity Selection To Establish a UCS

You can define a new UCS by selecting an existing entity. This action aligns the UCS with the entity. You use entity selection in the next set of exercises when you create and insert a block to form the drawing board. If you select an entity, the entity type and your pick point determine the new UCS. You cannot, however, base a UCS on either 3D polyline entities or 3D meshes. (You learn about these two entities in the next chapter.) The following list describes the ways in which entities can determine a new UCS:

- **Arc.** The arc's center becomes the new origin point, and the X axis goes through the endpoint nearest your pick point.

- **Circle.** The circle's center becomes the new origin point, and the X axis passes through your pick point.

- **Line.** The endpoint nearest your pick point becomes the new origin, and the second endpoint is on the positive X axis. (The second point's Y coordinate is 0.)

- **Point.** The point becomes the new origin point.

- **2D Polyline.** The polyline's start point becomes the new origin point; the X axis lies along the line to the first vertex point. (The first vertex Y coordinate is 0.)

- **Solid.** The first point becomes the new origin point, and the X axis lies along the line between the first two points.

- **Trace.** The first point of the trace becomes the new origin point, and the X axis lies along the trace's center line.

- **3DFace.** The first point determines the new origin point, the X axis lies along the first and second points, and the positive Y axis is determined by the first and fourth points.

- **Dimension.** The new origin is the middle of the dimension text, and the X axis is parallel to the X axis in effect when the dimension text was drawn.

## Figure 20.35:

Rotation angles from viewpoint 1,1,1.

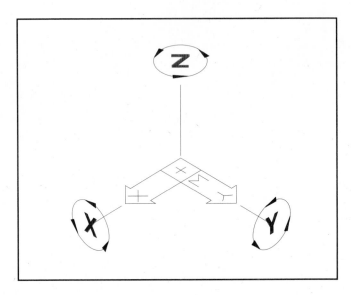

- **Text, Attribute, Attdef, Shape, Insert.** The new origin is the entity's insertion point. The X axis is defined by the entity's rotation about the extrusion direction (Z axis). In effect, the entity you select has a zero rotation angle in the new UCS.

For all these entities, the positive Z axis of the resulting UCS is parallel to the Z extrusion direction of the selected entity. Because each entity type behaves differently, you should play with each to see how it behaves when you establish a new UCS. Set an undo mark and use your SCRATCH layer to draw and test any entity type, then use it to define a new UCS. When you are done, undo back, and resume with the next exercise on blocks.

You now have a table with a decent set of drawers. The last item to add to the drafting table is the drawing board.

# Using BLOCK and INSERT To Insert Blocks in 3D

The drawing board is 1 1/4 inches thick and overlaps the table top on all sides by 1 inch. The next two exercises show you how to create the drawing board and insert it as a block, slanted at a 30-degree angle.

You can insert 3D blocks into a drawing the same way you insert 2D blocks. The standard INSERT command accepts a 3D insertion point and gives you the options of X-scaling, Y-scaling, and Z-scaling the block's entities. The current UCS defines the X,Y plane for the block when it is created.

## Using BLOCK To Create a Unit 3D Block

As in 2D, unit-scaled blocks are versatile in 3D. To make the drawing board, you use SOLID to build a 1×1×1 block, name it CUBE, and extrude the solid in the Z direction by setting its thickness to 1. The resulting block can be inserted with various scales to represent any rectilinear 3D box.

In the following exercises, you use the UCS Entity and Z options to set the construction plane on the table top to build the block. Save the UCS with the name TOP, and then make the block. If you like, you can replace your TABLE drawing with IAW-TBL2 from the IAW DISK.

---

### Using the SOLID Command To Make a Building Block

Continue from the previous exercise, in the TABLE drawing, or begin a new drawing named TABLE=IAW-TBL2.

```
Command: UCS ⏎
```

*continues*

```
Origin/ZAxis/3point/Entity/View/XYZ/
Prev/Restore/Save/Del/?/<World>: E ↵
```

| | |
|---|---|
| `Select object to align UCS:` *Pick the table top* | Sets the UCS on top |
| `Command:` *Press Enter and enter* **Z** | Repeats the UCS command with Zaxis option |
| `Rotation angle about Z axis <0>:` **-90** ↵ | Aligns X and Y axes with edges of top |
| `Command:` *Press Enter and enter* **S** | Repeats the UCS command with Save option |
| `?/Desired UCS name:` **TOP** ↵ | Names the UCS TOP |

Use the Entity Creation Modes dialog box to set the following: Color and Linetype BYLAYER, and Thickness 1.0. Use the Layer... option to set layer 0 Current. This setting enables the CUBE block you are about to create to assume the properties of the layer it is inserted on.

*Zoom Center to a height of 3 in a clear area of the drawing*

| | |
|---|---|
| `Command:` *Choose* Settings, *then* Drawing Aids *and set Grid to 1* | |
| `Command:` *From the screen menu, choose* DRAW, *then* next, *then* SOLID: *and draw a 1" square* | Creates a 1×1×1 cube |
| `Command:` *From the screen menu, choose* BLOCKS, *then* BLOCK: | |
| `Command: _BLOCK Block name (or ?):` **CUBE** ↵ | |
| `Insertion base point:` *Pick ① at lower left corner of solid (see fig. 20.36)* | |
| `Select objects:` *Select the solid* | Defines the CUBE block and erases the solid |

*Set THICKNESS to 0, set GRID back to 6, and zoom Previous*

The cube is now defined and stored in your drawing.

# Using INSERT To Insert a 3D Block

You can use the INSERT command to insert the cube into the drawing, stretching its scale into a drawing board. When you insert a 3D block, the block's X,Y plane is aligned so it is parallel to the current UCS.

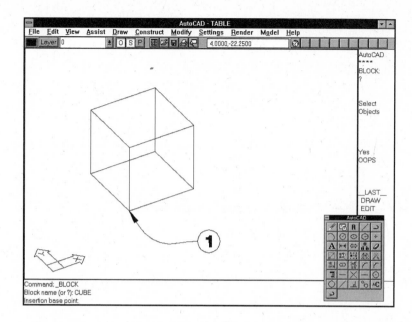

**Figure 20.36:**
A 1x1x1 building block, showing its insertion point.

The TOP UCS is the current UCS. To slant the drafting board 30 degrees, use the UCS X option and rotate the UCS 30 degrees about the X axis. Offset the insertion by one inch to provide an overlap at the front of the table. The INSERT command's Corner option tells INSERT to prompt first for the opposite X,Y corner, then the Z scale. The following exercise uses an X that extends the board 12 inches beyond the right side of the table. You can later edit the drawing to make it fit.

---

## Inserting a 3D Block as a Drawing Board

Command: *Make TABLE the current layer*

Command: **UCS** ↵

Origin/ZAxis/3point/Entity/View/XYZ/
Prev/Restore/Save/Del/?/<World>: **X** ↵

Rotation angle about X axis <0>:     Tilts UCS 30 degrees
**30** ↵

Command: *Press Enter and enter* **S**     Repeats the UCS command with Save option

?/Desired UCS name: **BOARD** ↵

Command: *Choose* **D***raw, then* **I***nsert...*     Opens the Insert dialog box

*continues*

*Click in the **B**lock... edit box, and enter* **CUBE***, then clear the* Specify **P**arameters on **S**creen *check box, then set the* Insertion Point *to -1,-1,0, and the* Scale *to 62, 31, 1.25, and choose* OK

*Zoom Extents and save the drawing*

Predefines the insertion parameters and inserts the block

**Figure 20.37:**

The Insert dialog box (DDINSERT command).

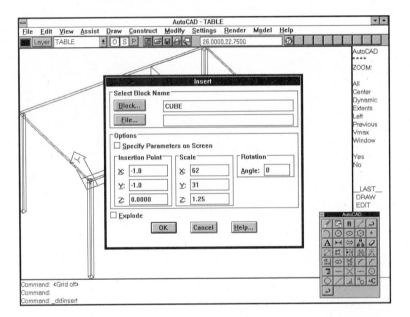

When you finish, the drawing board lies in the same X,Y plane as your X-rotated UCS. The UCS icon should appear to lie just under the drawing board at the table's left corner (see fig. 20.38). The Z-scale value of 1.25 scaled the board's thickness in the positive Z direction from the rotated UCS icon. You could also have rotated the block. When you provide a rotation angle, it rotates the block in the current X,Y plane around the insertion point.

## Building a Library of 3D Blocks

As you work in 3D, you can build a library of blocks like the CUBE—a wedge, a pyramid, a cone, various roof shapes, and a pipe elbow are examples of useful shapes you can easily insert and scale in different drawings. By using the same blocks repeatedly, you can create drawings quickly and reduce the size of your drawing files.

AutoCAD also provides AutoLISP routines that create primitive shapes made of 3D meshes. These routines are accessed from the 3D Surfaces pull-down menu (see fig. 20.39) and the 3D Objects icon menu under the **D**raw pull-down menu (see fig. 20.40).

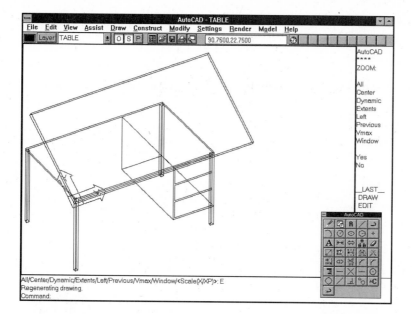

**Figure 20.38:**

The table, with the drawing board added.

These mesh commands are documented in the *AutoLISP Programmer's Reference*, but you do not have to be a programmer to use them. The routines form custom shapes from 3D meshes. Although they are not blocks, 3D mesh objects behave somewhat like blocks. You can select an entire object with a single pick, just like a block. You can also explode these objects into individual 3DFace entities. Unlike multiple occurrences of scaled blocks that all reference the same block definition, each occurrence of these mesh objects is composed of separate data. If you use the same primitives frequently, you can block and insert them for greater efficiency. You make and use 3D meshes in the next chapter.

# Editing in 3D

Meanwhile, back at the table, the drawing looks a bit funny. The board overhangs on the right, and the two right legs extend up through the cabinet. Now it is time for you to start editing your 3D drawing.

Wireframes can quickly become confusing. As you edit, you can do several things to avoid picking the wrong entities or getting lost in 3D space. First, use color extensively to help identify entities. Second, keep track of the UCS you used when you created an entity. Many users encounter problems during wireframe editing because they pick objects that are at an oblique angle to the UCS. Several 2D editing commands work only with entities parallel to the current construction plane. In these cases, you must adjust your UCS to match the entity's UCS. The easiest way to do this is to use the UCS Entity option. If you have any doubts about the outcome of your edits, work in multiple viewports.

**Figure 20.39:**

The 3D (mesh) Surfaces pull-down menu.

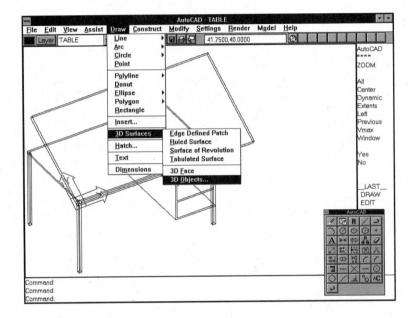

**Figure 20.40:**

The 3D (mesh) Objects icon menu.

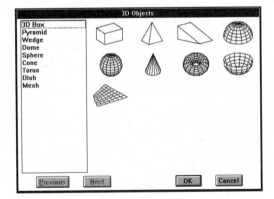

You have already used MOVE and COPY in 3D. In the following section, you use CHPROP, STRETCH, TRIM, EXTEND, BREAK, FILLET, CHAMFER, and OFFSET. You also try HATCH, another drawing command.

# Using CHPROP and DDMODIFY
# To Edit an Entity's Thickness

The CHPROP, DDCHPROP (CHange PROPerties dialog box), and DDMODIFY commands work on any entity with any current UCS setting. Often it is easier to create or copy entities with the current settings and then use CHPROP, DDCHPROP, or DDMODIFY to alter them, than it is to change settings, create an entity, and change the settings back. CHPROP and DDMODIFY are the only commands that can assign a thickness to text, shape, and attribute-definition entities.

In the following exercise, you fix the right two legs of the table by using DDCHPROP to change their thickness.

---

### Using DDCHPROP To Edit Entity Thickness

`Command:` *Choose* **M**odify, *then* **C**hange, *then* **P**roperties...

`Command:` `_ddchprop`

`Select objects:` *Select the two right legs*

`Select objects:` *Press Enter*  — Displays the Change Properties dialog box

*Double-click in the* **T**hickness *text box and enter 6.5, then choose* OK  — Changes the length of the legs

`Command:` *From the toolbox, choose* REDRAW

---

Figures 20.41 and 20.42 show the table before and after the change to the right legs.

*The CHANGE command is "pickier" than CHPROP and DDLIST. Several of its options require that selected entities be parallel to the current UCS, so it does not select nonparallel entities. Use CHPROP or DDLIST instead, whenever possible.*

**Figure 20.41:**

The original table legs.

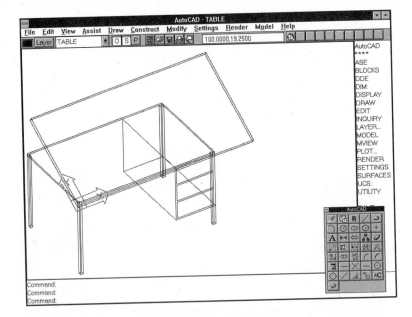

**Figure 20.42:**

The table legs after being edited.

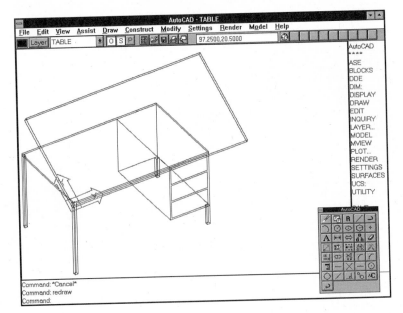

# Using STRETCH To Edit in 3D

The results of STRETCH depend on the entity and current UCS. 3D entities, such as lines (and 3D meshes), can be stretched to and from any point in 3D space, regardless of the current UCS. For 2D and extruded 2D entities, the entities being stretched should be aligned with the STRETCH displacement. Otherwise, entities' construction planes may be changed by STRETCH, and the results are difficult to predict.

In the next exercise, you stretch the table to fit the length of the drawing board. All entities align with the X axis of the current BOARD UCS. You stretch the cabinet, drawers, top, and right legs 12 inches along this X axis.

---

## Stretching the Table

Command: *From the toolbox, choose* STRETCH

stretch
Select objects to stretch by window
or polygon...
Select objects: c

First corner: *Pick at* ① *(see fig. 20.43)*      Starts a crossing window

Other corner: *Pick at* ②

Select objects: *Press Enter*

Base point or displacement: *Pick any point*

Second point of displacement: from the base **@12<0** ↵      Stretches the table 12 inches along the X axis point (see fig. 20.44)

Command: *From the toolbox, choose* REDRAW

---

Like CHANGE and STRETCH, several other editing commands require more care and attention in 3D.

The following editing commands work correctly only for entities in which the current UCS is in or parallel to the construction plane of their entity coordinate system(s). The easiest way to use these commands is to use the UCS Entity option to make your UCS parallel to the entities you want to edit. Use special care when you use the following editing commands in 3D:

- **BREAK.** This command projects the entity and break points to the current UCS.

- **TRIM.** This command projects the trim edge and entities to the current UCS.

- **EXTEND.** This command projects the extend edge and entities to the current UCS.

- **FILLET and CHAMFER.** All objects being filleted or chamfered must lie in a plane parallel to the current UCS (the extrusion thickness is parallel to the current Z axis).

- **OFFSET.** This command performs relative to the current UCS.

You may find it easiest to work with these commands in plan view while observing the results in multiple 3D viewports.

**Figure 20.43:**

The crossing window for STRETCH.

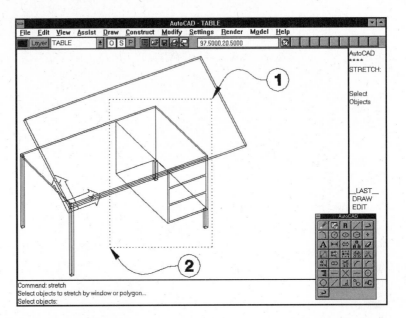

## Using FILLET To Edit in 3D

To demonstrate the FILLET command's behavior in 3D, the following exercise shows you how to fillet the polylines of the cabinet drawers by using a 0.5 radius in the next exercise. First, you try it in the current UCS to see the type of error messages that appear.

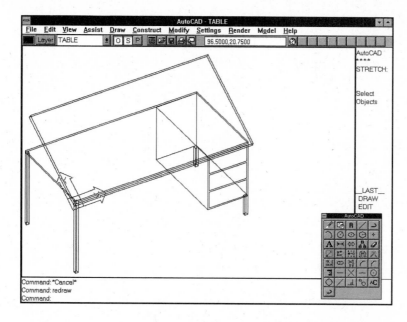

**Figure 20.44:**

The stretched table.

## Using FILLET To Fillet Drawers in 3D

Zoom in to the front of the cabinet so all drawer fronts are visible.

Command: *From the toolbox, choose* FILLET

```
Command: fillet
View is not plan to UCS. Command
results may not be obvious.

Polyline/Radius/<Select first
object>: R ↵
```

Enter fillet radius <0.000>: **.5** ↵          Specifies the radius

Command: *Press Enter*                        Repeats the command

```
Command: FILLET
View is not plan to UCS. Command
results may not be obvious.

Polyline/Radius/<Select first
object>:P ↵
```
Specifies the polyline option

Select 2D polyline: *Pick any drawer*

```
The entity is not parallel to
the UCS.
```
Rejects selection

*continues*

Select 2D polyline: *Press Enter* — Ends the FILLET command

Command: *Choose* **S**ettings, *then* U**C**S, *then* **N**amed UCS, *then highlight* CABINET, *choose* **C**urrent, *and click on* OK — Restores the CABINET UCS, used to create the drawers

Command: *From the toolbox, choose* FILLET

Command: fillet
View is not plan to UCS. Command results may not be obvious — Warns you that results may not be clear, but try it anyway

Polyline/Radius/<Select first object>: **P** ⏎

Select 2D polyline: *Pick any drawer* — Fillets the drawer

4 lines were filleted

*Repeat to fillet the second and third drawers* — Fillets all the drawers, as shown in figure 20.45

Command: *Choose* **V**iew, *then* **Z**oom, *then* **P**revious

**Figure 20.45:**

The filleted drawers.

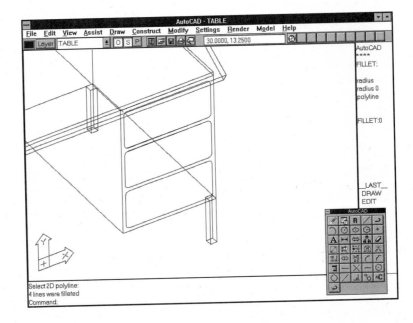

If you are wondering why your CABINET UCS icon seems to be floating in space, remember that you stretched the table 12 inches to the right, away from the UCS origin. The FRONT UCS also works for these fillets.

*When you edit in 3D, you find that it pays to name and save your UCSs so you can later restore them. If you forget their names, you can get a list by using the UCS command or the UCS Control dialog box.*

## Supplemental 3D Editing Commands

If you have installed AutoCAD's sample and supplemental programs, you have access to additional editing commands designed specifically for editing 3D models. If you have the ACAD.MNU loaded, the ALIGN, MIRROR3D, and ROTATE3D commands (in the GEOM3D.LSP file) and the 3DARRAY command (in the 3DARRAY.LSP file) are auto-loaded from the ACADWIN\SUPPORT directory when you use them. You can load the PROJECT.LSP command from the ACADWIN\SAMPLE directory, using the Applications dialog box from the **F**iles pull-down menu. This ADS application defines the following new commands:

- **ALIGN.** This command works like an efficient combination of the MOVE and ROTATE commands. Uses three pairs of source and destination points.

- **MIRROR3D.** This command enables you to mirror a selection set about a 3D plane. The plane can be defined by an existing entity, the last-used plane, a viewpoint, or by user-definition.

- **ROTATE3D.** This command enables rotation in the X, Y, or Z direction.

- **PROJECT.** This command creates a 2D copy of a 3D view.

- **3DARRAY.** This command enables you to create rectangular and polar arrays that, unlike the standard ARRAY command, can be nonparallel to the current UCS. 3DARRAY does not, however, enable you to create an array in three directions at once.

# Hatching in 3D

You can spruce up your 3D images by filling their surfaces with hatch patterns. You usually have to set the UCS on the surface to be hatched and then draw new boundary edges to hatch in. The HATCH command projects the hatch boundaries onto the X,Y plane of the current UCS. In the following exercise, you create a boundary with lines on layer 0 and try to hatch the board.

## Trying To Hatch the Drawing Board

Make layer 0 current, use OSNAP to set INT as the running object snap mode, then draw a line around the top of the drawing board. You may have to turn snap off and transparently zoom in on the front left corner to pick it.

Command: *Choose* **D**raw, *then* **H**atch

Command: _bhatch

| | |
|---|---|
| *Choose* Hatch **O**ptions, *then* **P**attern, *then* next *three times, and select the* LINE *pattern, set the scale to 6, choose* OK, *then* **S**elect objects | Defines the hatch parameters and prompts for object selection |
| Select objects: *Select the boundary polyline, and press Enter* | |
| *Choose* Previe**w** hatch | Displays the hatch pattern (see fig. 20.46) |
| *Press Enter to return to the* Boundary Hatch *dialog box, then choose* Cancel | Cancels the HATCH command |

**Figure 20.46:**

The table with an incorrect hatch.

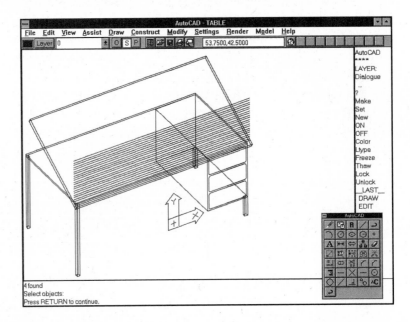

The hatch was projected to the current UCS, which is not the effect you want. To get the hatch right, locate the UCS on the plane of the drawing board's surface.

Restore the UCS named BOARD, and try again to correct the hatch. The BOARD UCS is on the underside of the board, so use the UCS Origin option to move the origin 1.25 inches up to the board top.

## Hatching the Drawing Board

Command: *Choose* **S**ettings, *then* **O**bject     Turns off running object snaps
Snap, *clear all check boxes, and*
*choose* OK

Command: **UCS** ↵

Origin/ZAxis/3point/Entity/View/
XYZ/Prev/Restore/Save/Del/?/
<World>: **0** ↵

Origin point <0,0,0>: **0,0,1.25** ↵     Moves the UCS to the top of the board

Repeat the BHATCH command from the previous exercise, this time finishing by clicking on Apply rather than Cancel. Save the drawing.

Your table should now have a hatch on the plane of the drawing board (see fig. 20.47).

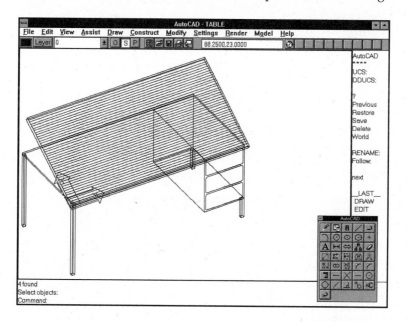

**Figure 20.47:**

The correctly hatched table.

Both the TRIM and EXTEND commands behave like HATCH, projecting their boundary edges and entities onto the construction plane of the current UCS to calculate the trim or extension. The trimmed or extended entities, however, remain in their own planes after modification.

# Viewing the Table

Before you put the table drawing to rest, clean up the drawing by erasing the hatch and boundary lines, then review its construction by looking at the plan views of the TOP, FRONT, and R-SIDE UCSs you saved.

## Using UCSFOLLOW To Automate Plan Views

Viewing the TOP, FRONT, and R-SIDE UCSs in their plan views shows the top, front, and right sides of the model. When the UCSFOLLOW system variable is set to 1, AutoCAD automatically generates a plan view whenever you change UCSs. Set UCSFOLLOW to 1 in the next exercise, and look at your drawing's UCSs in plan view. Try this with both the UCS command and the dialog box.

### Using UCSFOLLOW To View Saved UCS Planes in Plan

*Erase the hatch and boundary lines from layer 0*

```
Command: UCSFOLLOW ↵

New value for UCSFOLLOW <0>: 1 ↵

Command: UCS ↵

Origin/ZAxis/3point/Entity/View/X/Y
/Z/Prev /Restore/Save/Del/?/<World>:
R ↵
```

`?/Name of UCS to restore: TOP`          Restores the TOP UCS

`Regenerating drawing.`

Issue ZOOM with the All option, to display the entire plan view of the TOP UCS, as shown in figure 20.48.

`Command:` *Choose* **S**ettings, *then* U**C**S, *then*          Restores FRONT UCS and displays the
**N**amed UCS, *highlight* FRONT, *choose*          plan view (see fig. 20.49)
**C**urrent, *and then* OK, *and zoom 0.9X*

*Use either method to restore the R-SIDE*          Restores R-SIDE UCS
*UCS, and zoom 0.9X*          (see fig. 20.50)

*Set UCSFOLLOW back to 0 (off)*

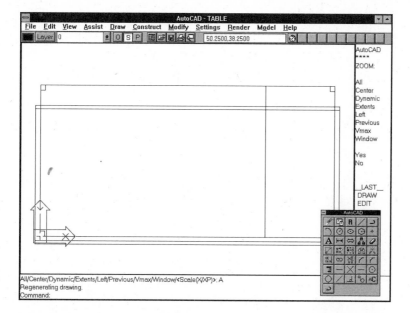

**Figure 20.48:**
Plan view of the top.

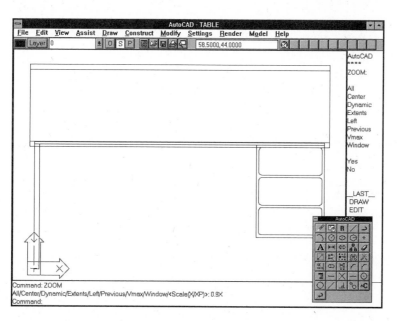

**Figure 20.49:**
Plan view of the front.

**Figure 20.50:**

Plan view of the right side.

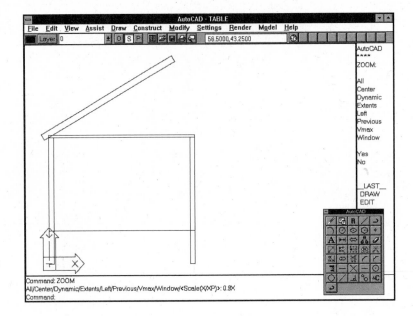

Now that you have reviewed your drawing, you can restore your 3D view and hide the table's hidden lines in the next exercise. The following exercise also shows you how to change some settings for later use. Finally, you end the drawing session.

## Hiding the Table's Hidden Lines

Turn on the P toolbar button to enter paper space.

Command: *Choose* **V**iew, *then* **Z**oom, *then* **A**ll

*Erase all three viewports*

Command: *Choose* **V**iew, *then* **T**ilemode          Returns to a single tiled viewport

*Use VIEW to restore the 3D view TABLE, then ZOOM Extents*

Command: *Choose* **S**ettings, *then* U**C**S, *then* **P**resets, *and double-click on the WCS icon*          Sets the UCS to the WCS

Command: *Choose* **R**ender, *then* **H**ide

```
Regenerating drawing.
Hiding lines: 100% done
```
Regenerates the drawing as in figure 20.51

*Save the drawing; the table model is complete.*

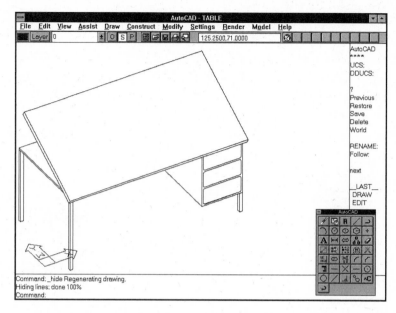

**Figure 20.51:**

The finished table, after HIDE.

When you edit 3D views with hidden lines removed, the hidden lines may reappear. If so, execute HIDE again when you finish editing.

Congratulations! You have created (and edited) a 3D table from start to finish. You should have gained a feel for the power and ease built into 3D drafting. Once you get the hang of it, using a UCS is like 2D drafting. The only difference is that, like a fly, you can climb all over your drawing.

To document the results of your 3D designs, you can create assembly drawings. The next section shows you how to assemble a multiple-view drawing.

# Creating 3D Multiple-View Drawings

Once you have a basic 3D drawing, you can easily create a multiple-view drawing. The next exercise shows you how to have a plan, top, right side, and 3D view in the same drawing. You use MVIEW viewports in paper space to view the same 3D model from several viewpoints.

Setting up a multiple-view drawing is easy. All you have to do is enter paper space, insert your title block (if you have one), and open up as many viewports as you need to contain the different views of your model (see fig. 20.52). Then you orient the views by simply setting the desired UCS in each viewport and using the PLAN command. The ZOOM command, when used with the XP options, scales the viewport contents relative to the paper-space sheet for plotting.

**Figure 20.52:**

MVIEW viewports before reorienting views.

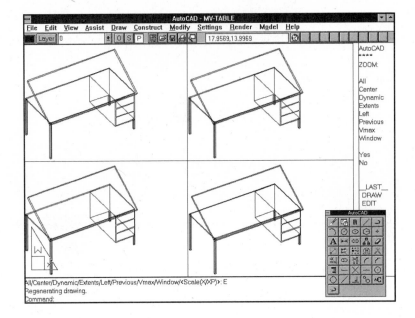

## Assembling a Multiple-View Drawing in Paper Space

Use the NEW command to begin a new drawing named MV-TABLE=IAW-TBL3. Turn off the grid, and set TILEMODE to 0 (off).

Command: *Choose* **V***iew, then* Mvie**w***, then* **4** Viewports    Issues MVIEW with the 4 option

```
Command: _mview
ON/OFF/Hideplot/Fit/2/3/4/Restore/
<First Point>: 4
```

Fit/<First Point>: **1,2** ↵    Sets the lower left corner

Second point: **20,15** ↵    Opens four viewports

Command: *Choose* **S***ettings, then* Dra**w***ing* Limits

```
Command: '_limits
Reset Paper space limits:
ON/OFF/<Lower left corner>
<0.0000,0.0000>: Press Enter
```

```
Upper right corner <12.0000,    Sets the limits for a 22"×17" sheet
  9.0000>:22,17 ↵
```

*Use ZOOM Extents*                                    Displays the views shown in figure 20.52

Turn off the P toolbar button to re-enter model space.

Command: *Select the upper left viewport*

Command: *Choose* **V***iew, then* **Se***t View,*      Reorients viewpoint for top view
*then* **P***lan View, then* **W***orld*

Command: **ZOOM** ⏎

All/Center/Dynamic/Extents/Left/        Scales the viewport relative to paper space
Previous/Vmax/Window/<Scale(X/XP)>:     sheet for 1=8 scale
**.125XP** ⏎

The following steps reorient the viewpoint for the front view.

Command: *Select the lower left*
*viewport, then restore* UCS FRONT

Command: *Choose* **V***iew, then* **Se***t View,*
*then* **P***lan View, then* **C***urrent UCS*

*Zoom .125XP (1=8 scale)*

The following steps reorient the viewpoint for the side view.

Command: *Select the lower right*
*viewport, then restore* UCS R-SIDE

Command: *Choose* **V***iew, then* **Se***t View,*
*then* **P***lan View, then* **C***urrent UCS*

*Zoom .125XP (1=8 scale)*

*Select the upper right viewport and*
*ZOOM .6 (not .6XP)*

Turn on the P toolbar button again, to return to paper space.

*Make TABLE the current layer and*       Makes the viewport borders disappear
*freeze layer 0*                         (see fig. 20.53)

*Save the drawing and exit*

You now have four different views of your table, and you did not have to copy or
insert anything to do it. To align the viewports and get the drawing ready for plotting,
see Chapter 13.

**Figure 20.53:**

The completed multiple-view table drawing in paper space.

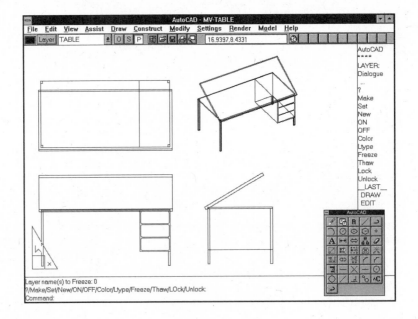

*You can also create 2D copies of your 3D model from any viewpoint, projected onto any UCS. The PROJECT command is a supplemental program which "projects" a view of your model onto the desired 2D plane. This command is particularly useful when you need to include a two-dimensional 3D view within a 3D model. If you like, experiment with this concept by creating a block of a projected 3D view, and then inserting that block on your drafting table. The result is a 2D "drawing" (of a 3D view) lying on the desktop of your 3D model. Load PROJECT.LSP from the ACADWIN\SAMPLE using the Applications dialog box, and run the program by entering **PROJECT**.*

# Summary

Two-dimensional isometric drawings provide a quick and simple method of emulating 3D views. They work well for simple drawings in which multiple views are not required.

Good layer and color management can greatly ease and speed 3D work. Colors help clarify a mass of overlaid wireframe images. Layers enable you to turn objects off to help with picking points in complex drawings and to freeze unneeded layers to speed up regenerations and hidden-line removal. Paper space gives you individual layer visibility control in each viewport.

Use multiple viewports when drawing in 3D. Sometimes it can be hard to select objects and pick points in a single viewport, particularly when using object snap to select an existing object. Remember that you can use XYZ point filters, and even switch viewports in the middle. You can, for example, select your objects in one or more viewports, pick your X,Y point in another viewport, and then switch to a third viewport to pick the Z value by using object snap.

A standard set of named UCSs, views (viewpoints), and viewports makes moving around in 3D a breeze. Remember that each viewport can have its own set of snap and grid settings. Save your settings in a 3D prototype drawing. Use the UCS Entity option for quick edits to existing entities or to add new entities parallel to existing ones. The X,Y orientation may look unusual, but it seldom matters.

For 2D entities constrained to be parallel to the current UCS, you need not change the UCS just to place them above or below the current UCS. A Z value entered for their first coordinate point establishes their position in 3D space. Do not confuse things by setting elevation or by using the ELEV command.

Remember that you can use editing commands in 3D. COPY and MOVE, for example, can place any entity up and down in the current Z axis.

The next chapter shows you how to work with 3D entities. Now that you have created a drafting table, you need a chair—a 3D chair.

**CHAPTER**

# Using 3D Entities

In the last chapter, you used 2D entities and extrusions to build a table in 3D space. In this chapter, you learn how to draw and edit objects by using true 3D entities, including 3D polygon meshes. You can use these 3D entities to construct complex shapes bounded by flat and curved surfaces. You can also combine these 3D objects into complex assemblies by making and inserting blocks of 3D entities to build a drawing.

Now that you have drawn a table, you need a comfortable chair to go with it. As you draw the chair, shown in figure 21.1, you use all of AutoCAD's 3D entities.

## Selecting 3D Entities and Meshes

AutoCAD has only four true 3D entities: points, lines, 3Dfaces, and a family of special polylines. The simplest of the polylines is the 3D polyline, which is a polyline without width or curvature whose vertices can be at any X, Y, or Z coordinate in space. The 3Dface entity is much like a 2D solid entity except that each of its three or four corners can be at any X, Y, and Z coordinate in space, whereas a solid is planar. The sides of the chair's legs are constructed of 3Dfaces. Although you can create multiple 3Dfaces in a single 3DFACE command, these 3Dfaces exist as individual entities. The polyline mesh entities are more efficient and versatile.

**Figure 21.1:**

The completed 3D chair.

Most 3D commands you work with in this chapter construct faceted surface meshes. The chair's seat, back, and pedestal have multiple faces. Although you can build these surfaces by using individual 3Dfaces, AutoCAD's 3D mesh commands automatically generate 3D polygon meshes that can approximate any possible surface in 3D space. They can be either planar, like the square center of the seat; or curved, like the pedestal, back, edges, corners, and casters.

AutoCAD has various types of polyline meshes. Polyface meshes are the most general and versatile because they can be arbitrarily irregular. You can create polyface meshes with the PFACE command, and they can contain any number of edges, vertices, and visible or invisible interior divisions. Other polygon meshes are less general. You use the 3DMESH command, for example, to create topologically rectangular meshes; although the meshes can be warped and distorted, they must be bounded by four lines or curves. Opposite sides must have the same number of subdivisions, although a side can converge to a single point (that is, it can have a zero length).

# Applying 3D Drawing Tools

AutoCAD provides numerous commands, menu items, and AutoLISP- and ADS-defined commands for constructing regular polyline meshes. On the **D**raw pull-down menu is the 3D Surfaces option, which provides access to the 3D surface commands, as well as to the 3D Objects icon menu. The 3D Objects icon menu, which includes selections that use AutoLISP to create 3D geometric objects like spheres, cones, and tori from the surface meshes, is shown in figure 21.2. The 3D Surfaces pull-down menu of surfacing-command selections is shown in figure 21.3.

The 3D commands are also found on the screen menu. Choose SURFACES or DRAW, and then choose 3D Surfs to find items for the following 3D drawing commands: 3DFACE, 3DPOLY, PFACE, 3DMESH, EDGESURF, REVSURF, RULESURF, and TABSURF. The choices for 3D and objects at the bottom of the menu open a menu of the same AutoLISP-defined commands as the 3D Objects icon menu.

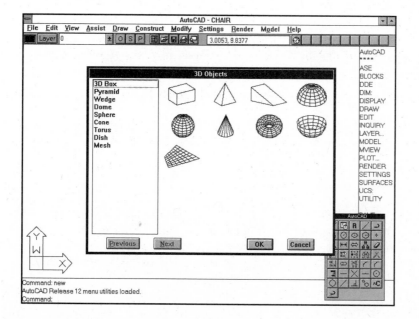

**Figure 21.2:**

The 3D Objects icon menu.

**Figure 21.3:**

The 3D Surfaces child
pull-down menu.

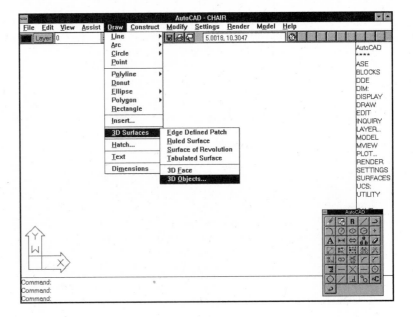

## Understanding Mesh Generation

Think of a mesh as a piece of net or chicken wire that you can mold or stretch into various shapes. The wires or cords that make up the net enable you to visualize the shape of a surface, even though your model is essentially transparent. You can model simple shapes with a coarse net, but you need a finer net to model complex shapes or shapes with small features. AutoCAD creates meshes with a preset number of four-sided areas, which you can control through the use of system variables.

You can use the PFACE and 3DMESH commands to create irregularly shaped surfaces. In most cases, you want to use commands that take advantage of symmetry or regularity to generate a mesh. The RULESURF command generates a surface defined by ruling lines between two existing edges, which may be lines or curves—two of the ruling lines form the other two edges. The EDGESURF command generates a mesh that fills the area bounded by four existing lines or curves.

The process of generating a mesh often involves specifying the profile of the mesh and line it is to be rotated about or translated (moved) along. The REVSURF command makes a circular mesh when you specify a path profile and an axis of rotation (the *path profile* is a cross section of the surface you want). If you rotate the profile 360 degrees, you get a cylindrical or globular surface, similar to the chair's pedestal or casters.

You can also generate a mesh by using the TABSURF command, translating a direction vector along a path curve (profile). The results of using TABSURF look like the results of extruding a 2D entity into 3D, except that the TABSURF command can create oblique or skewed surfaces. Figure 21.4 shows how these commands are used to create your chair.

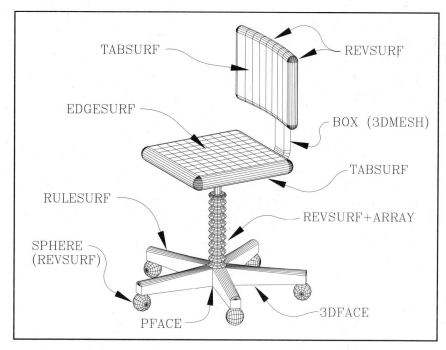

**Figure 21.4:**

The 3D commands used to construct the chair parts.

That is all there is to meshes: defining edges, path profiles, direction vectors, or rotation axes, and a few system variable settings.

# Following the Chair Exercises

As you use each 3D drawing command to build the parts of the chair, you get some practice and tips on using UCSs to draw and edit entities in 3D space. You also edit some of the chair's meshes by using the PEDIT command. As you create the parts, you make them into 3D blocks. Then you assemble the chair by inserting the casters on the legs, the legs on the pedestal, the pedestal on the seat, and so on, just as you might assemble a real chair. You use 3D blocks by applying the standard BLOCK and INSERT commands.

Because the chair is built in parts, you can do it all or pick and choose the commands you want to learn by working on particular components. The IAW DISK contains the component blocks for assembling the chair, even if you do not want to draw all the parts.

Set up the drawing by using the upper right viewport as a scratch viewport. Use the SCRATCH layer for practicing the 3D commands. When you are through practicing, restore the previously current layer and freeze the SCRATCH layer.

# Setting Up for Using 3D Entities

The CHAIR drawing uses two layers, CHAIR and BUILD, with default drawing units and limits large enough to contain the chair at full scale. The chair is 35 inches high and about 25 inches wide at the base, with varied entity colors to help your viewing in 3D.

The IAW DISK contains the IAW-CHR1.DWG file, which has the settings shown in table 21.1, and also includes three viewports: a full-height viewport on the left (in which you spend most of your time building the chair); a lower right viewport with a plan view of the chair; and an upper right viewport to use as a scratch viewport. If you want to practice setting up a drawing for 3D work, you can perform the steps in the following exercise. Otherwise, just start a new drawing CHAIR, equal to IAW-CHR1, and examine the settings.

## Table 21.1
### 3D Chair Drawing Settings

| COORDS | FILL | GRID | SNAP | UCSICON |
|--------|------|------|------|---------|
| ON | OFF | Off | .25 | OR |
| **UNITS** | Use defaults for all settings. | | | |
| **MODEL** | | | | |
| **SPACE** | | | | |
| **LIMITS** | 0,0 to 68,44 | | | |

| Layer Name | State | Color | Linetype |
|------------|-------|-------|----------|
| 0 | On | 7 White | CONTINUOUS |
| BUILD | On | 1 Red | CONTINUOUS |
| CHAIR | On/Current | 7 White | CONTINUOUS |
| SCRATCH | On | 4 Cyan | CONTINUOUS |

## Setting Up for 3D Entities

If you want to practice the 3D drawing setup, begin a new drawing named CHAIR, make the settings shown in table 21.1, and perform the following steps. Otherwise, begin a new drawing named CHAIR=IAW-CHR1, check the settings, and simply read through the following.

*Choose* **V**iew, *then* S**e**t View, *then*
**V**iewpoint, *and then set* **V**point

```
_vpoint Rotate/<View Point><0.0000,0.0000,
1.0000>: − 1, − 1,0.5 ⏎
```

*Choose* **V**iew, *then* **T**ilemode            Sets TILEMODE to 0 and enters paper space

*Choose* **V**iew, *then* Mvie**w**, *then*        Issues MVIEW command
**3** Viewports

```
Command: _mview
ON/OFF/Hideplot/Fit/2/3/4/Restore
/<First Point>: 3
Horizontal/Vertical/Above/Below/Left
/<Right>: L ⏎
```

```
Fit/<First Point>: F ⏎
```
Fits three viewports to the screen

*Turn off the* P *(paper space) toolbar*        Enters model space
*button*

*Click in the upper right viewport to*
*make it current*

*Use ZOOM with the Center option at 0,0*
*with a height of 10*

*Turn the UCS icon off*

*Use VIEW to save the current view as*
*CHAIR*

*Make the left viewport current*

*Choose* **S**ettings, *then* U**C**S, *then* **O**rigin

```
Origin point <0,0,0>: 0,88,0 ⏎
```
Creates new UCS named HUB

*Save the current UCS as HUB*

*Use ZOOM with the Center option at 0,0*
*and a height of 20*

*Save view as BUILD*

*continues*

*Select lower right viewport*

*Choose* **V**iew, *then* **Se**t View, *then*
**P**lan View, *then* **C**urrent UCS

*Use ZOOM with the Center option at 0,0
and a height of 5*

*Save your drawing*

---

When you finish this first exercise, your screen should look like figure 21.5, with layer CHAIR current and the UCS icon located in the center of the left viewport and in the center of the lower right viewport. The lower right viewport should be current.

**Figure 21.5:**

Viewports for the
CHAIR drawing.

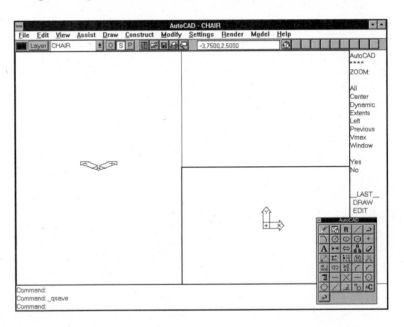

The job of creating 3D entities requires preparation. Drawings can become complex and difficult to visualize. Your ability to visualize and select entities depends on your display resolution—a high-resolution, large-screen display makes matters easier, especially for tired eyes. The following exercises specify the required ZOOM, SNAP, ORTHO, and object snap settings, but you may want to zoom in further, and more often. If this is the case, follow each additional "zoom in" with a ZOOM Previous, so that you can track the exercises and illustrations.

# Using the 3D Objects Mesh Commands

You can extrude a 2D polyline to create the chair's hub, but you should create it as a true 3D surface. The *hub* is a pentagon-shaped cylinder. AutoCAD does not have a specific command to draw five-sided cylinders, but it does include some AutoLISP-defined commands that you can use to draw many different types of 3D objects. These routines are included in the AutoLISP file, 3D.LSP, and can be used just like built-in commands—by selecting them from the 3D Objects icon menu. The routines are Cone, Wedge, Torus, Sphere, Pyramid, Mesh, Dome, Dish, and Box.

This 3D AutoLISP file also defines the general command, 3D, which you can use to access any of these routines. The 3D command issues the following prompt so that you can select the surface shape you want:

```
Box/Cone/DIsh/DOme/Mesh/Pyramid/Sphere/Torus/Wedge:
```

These options are documented in the AutoCAD *Extras* manual, but they are so easy to use that you probably do not need to look them up.

*Although the 3D object routines are AutoLISP programs, they are easily accessed through the 3D Objects icon menu. Choose **D**raw, then **3**D Surfaces, then 3D **O**bjects to display the icon menu. Selecting an icon or a routine name from this menu automatically loads and executes the requested routine in much the same way as AutoCAD's built-in commands are loaded and executed.*

The 3D objects mesh routines do not include a pentagon, but you can use the CONE command to create one because of the way that AutoCAD draws surface entities.

## Using CONE To Construct the Chair's Five-Sided Hub

The AutoLISP-defined Cone routine is versatile. It enables you to specify a top as well as a bottom diameter for drawing a truncated cone. If the diameters are equal, the result is a cylinder. You can also specify the resolution (number of segments) it uses to represent the cone or cylinder. The Cone routine normally uses 16 segments to approximate a circular cone; five segments generates a pentagon.

Use Cone in the following exercise to create the hub of the chair.

## Drawing a Five-Sided CONE

Continue from the previous exercise, or begin a new drawing named CHAIR=IAW-CHR1.

| | |
|---|---|
| *Choose* **D**raw, *then* **3**D Surfaces, *then* 3D **O**bjects, *and double-click on* CONE *or the cone icon* | Loads 3D.LSP and issues the CONE routine |

```
Command: ai_cone
Initializing...  3D Objects loaded.
Base center point: 0,0,-2.5 ↵

Diameter/<radius> of base: 1.55 ↵

Diameter/<radius> of top <0>: 1.55 ↵

Height: 2.5 ↵
```

Number of segments <16>: 5 ↵      Specifies five "sides"

The hub created in this exercise looks like figure 21.6. You should have a plan view of the hub polygon in the right viewport and a 3D view of it in your left viewport.

**Figure 21.6:**

The hub of the chair.

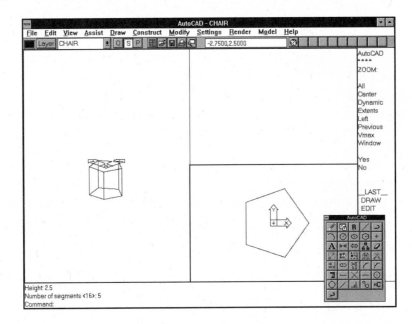

# Using 3DFACES To Create the Chair Leg

Next, create the chair's leg with 3Dface entities. 3Dfaces are defined by three or four edges (they always have four corner points, but the third and fourth may coincide). The 3DFACE command prompts are similar to those for a 2D solid entity (not an AME solid), but the pick-point order is more natural.

You can pick clockwise or counterclockwise, rather than in a crisscross bow tie (if you pick the points in the same sequence as for the SOLID command, the result is a bow-tie shape). A 3D solid is confined to a single plane (in any UCS); edges and points of a 3Dface can be anywhere in space. A non-extruded 2D solid and a 3Dface may look the same if they both lie in the same plane, but they have different edge and transparency properties. If all points and edges of a 3Dface lie in a single plane, the HIDE command treats the 3Dface as opaque. If the 3Dface is not planar, it is transparent and does not hide. Unlike a 2D solid, you cannot extrude a 3Dface; it always has zero thickness.

Use 3Dfaces when you want to draw simple three-point or four-point planar faces. For the chair leg, you want an end cap, an underside, and two simple planar sides.

Create a four-sided 3Dface as the leg's end cap in the following steps, working in the left viewport. The easiest method is to create the 3Dface at the origin, then move it where you want it. After you create and move the end cap, use 3DFACE again to create the bottom and the two sides, snapping to endpoints on the cap and hub. You can leave the top open for now.

---

## Using 3DFACE To Make the First Leg

Continue from the previous exercise. Make the left viewport current.

*Choose* **D**raw, *then* **3**D Surfaces, *then*
3D **F**ace

```
Command: _3dface
```

```
First point: 0,0 ↵
```
Specifies first corner

```
Second point: 0,0,1.25 ↵
```

```
Third point: 0,1.5,1.25 ↵
```

```
Fourth point: 0,1.5,0 ↵
```

```
Third point: Press Enter
```
Ends the 3DFACE command and creates end cap of leg at the UCS origin (see fig. 21.7)

*continues*

**Figure 21.7:**

The end cap of
the leg at UCS
origin.

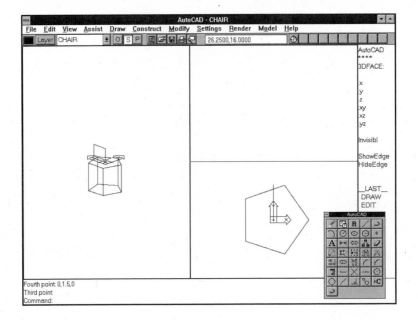

From the toolbox, choose MOVE, and move
the 3Dface with a displacement of
–12.5,–.75,–2

Use PAN to move to the view shown in
figure 21.8 to see the end cap

| | |
|---|---|
| Choose **S**ettings, then **O**bject Snap | Displays OSNAP dialog box |
| Click on the **E**ndpoint box, then OK | Sets running ENDP object snap to draw the leg faces |
| Choose **D**raw, then **3**D Surfaces, then 3D **F**ace, and draw the leg's left face first, then remaining faces, selecting points ① (see fig. 21.9) through ⑧ in sequence, then press Enter | |
| Set the running object snap mode back to NONE | |
| Choose **R**ender, then **H**ide | Removes hidden lines to confirm drawing (see fig. 21.10) |
| Save the drawing | |

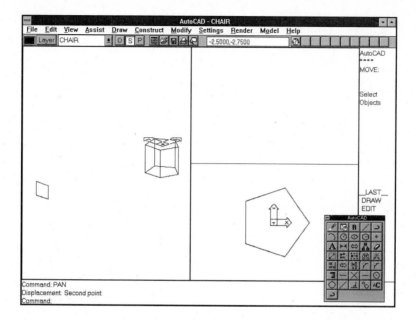

**Figure 21.8:**

The end cap of the leg moved into place.

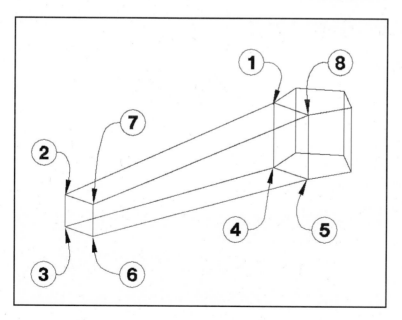

**Figure 21.9:**

Detail of pick points.

**Figure 21.10:**

The chair leg
constructed with
3Dfaces, after
HIDE.

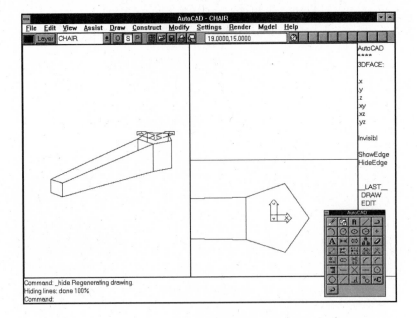

# Utilizing 3Dfaces with Invisible Edges

By using multiple adjoining 3Dfaces with invisible edges, you can create what appears to be a single surface. The SPLFRAME system variable controls whether the invisible edges display. SPLFRAME is the same variable that you use to control the frame points for a curve fit polyline in 2D.

When SPLFRAME is 0, invisible edges are invisible; when SPLFRAME is 1, all edges are visible. To draw an invisible edge during a 3DFACE command, enter an **I** before the first pick for that edge.

You can use invisible edges to make the top of the chair hub look like one piece, even though you create it with five separate 3Dfaces. Use 3DFACE to create a triangular surface that you can later array with the leg to complete the chair base. Use SPLFRAME to make invisible edges visible to confirm the results.

## Using 3DFACE with Invisible Edges To Cap the Chair Hub

Continue from the previous exercise. Make the lower right viewport current.

*Choose* **D**raw, *then* **3**D Surfaces, *then*
3D **F**ace

```
Command: _3dface
```

| | |
|---|---|
| `First point:` *Enter* **I** *and use the ENDP object snap to pick the first corner at* ① *(see fig. 21.11)* | Begins invisible edge |
| `Second point:` *Enter* **I** *and use the ENDP object snap to pick the polygon's second corner at* ② | Completes first invisible edge |
| `Third point:` *Enter* **I***, then enter* **0,0** | Specifies center of cap at ③ |
| `Fourth point:` *Press Enter* | Makes it three-sided, but invisible |
| `Third point:` *Press Enter* | Ends 3DFACE command |
| *Set SPLFRAME system variable to 1* | Turns on edge visibility |
| *Regenerate the drawing* | Displays the 3Dface |
| *Save the drawing* | |

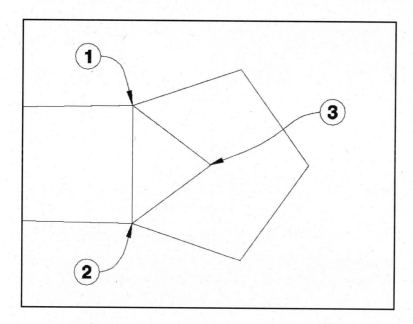

**Figure 21.11:**

Detail of edges and pick points.

*Leave SPLFRAME on until you use HIDE or end the drawing. If you create a 3Dface with all edges invisible and SPLFRAME off, AutoCAD does not select it, even with Window or Last. You may even forget the 3Dface is there.*

*Invisible edges can be hard to set up correctly when drawing 3D faces. The AutoCAD Sample disk includes the EDGE.LSP AutoLISP program, which is probably installed in your ACADWIN\SAMPLE directory. This program edits the visibility of existing 3Dface edges after they are drawn, making 3D face constructions much easier. Enter (load "\\ACADWIN\\SAMPLE\\EDGE") to load it and EDGE to use it as a command. You can also load EDGE.LSP through the Applications dialog box, found on the File pull-down menu.*

So far, you have used simple, flat 3D entities. The rest of the chair construction involves curves and contours. The following section discusses the mesh tools for such 3D surface constructions. You then come back to the chair leg and put a ruled surface on top of it.

# Introducing 3D Polyline Meshes

AutoCAD has only two 3D mesh entities, both of which are polyline variants: polyface meshes, created by the PFACE command, and polygon meshes, for which there are five drawing commands. All mesh commands, except PFACE, create meshes of *n* rows by *m* columns. The basic polygon mesh command is 3DMESH. Although the 3DMESH command generates a mesh directly, point-by-point, the other four commands rely on existing entities to establish the edges, directions, paths, and profiles of the resulting surface.

## Working with Polyface and Polygon Meshes

The following is a list of the commands that create polyface and polygon meshes:

- **3DMESH.** This command creates a rectilinear wireframe blanket, composed of *m* column lines by *n* row lines, passing through a matrix of *m*×*n* 3D points in space. You have complete control over *m*, *n*, and the coordinate location of each of the 3D points.

- **RULESURF.** This command creates a ruled surface. RULESURF is like stretching and bending a ladder in 3D space. You select any two lines, polylines, or curves that make up the rails, and AutoCAD fills in the ladder with straight rungs. If you select a point, the rungs converge to that point.

- **TABSURF.** This command creates a tabulated surface. AutoCAD sweeps or translates a line you select (called a direction vector or *generatrix*) along any curve you select (called the *directrix*) to define the surface. If, for example, you translate a straight line along a circle, you create a cylinder.

- **REVSURF.** This command creates a surface of revolution. AutoCAD sweeps any curve you select about an axis of revolution. If, for example, you sweep a 90-degree arc about a line through one of its endpoints, you create a bowl shape.

- **EDGESURF.** This command creates a four-sided surface defined by four boundary lines or curves you select. AutoCAD fills in $m{\times}n$ column and row lines to define the surface, as in a 3D meshed flying carpet.

- **PFACE.** This command constructs a mesh of any topology you want. You specify arbitrary locations of vertices and then specify which vertices are part of which face. You can have any number of edges and any number of faces, each with any number of sides or vertices. Any side can be any color, be located on any layer, or be invisible.

Figure 21.12 shows examples of these entities.

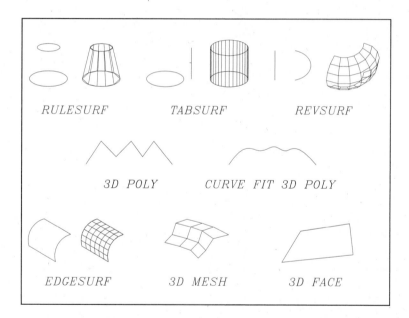

**Figure 21.12:**

Mesh entity primitives.

RULESURF    TABSURF    REVSURF

3D POLY    CURVE FIT 3D POLY

EDGESURF    3D MESH    3D FACE

*The 3DMESH command is provided primarily as a tool for AutoCAD application developers to build 3D meshes without using other entities as paths. The following section shows how the 3DMESH command works—keep in mind, however, that the other mesh commands usually provide simpler solutions.*

## Using the 3DMESH Command

You rarely use the 3DMESH command unless you are using AutoLISP to generate mesh points automatically. A 3D mesh is made up of rows and columns. The directions *m* and *n* are indices that specify the number of rows and columns that make up the mesh, up to 256×256. These indices determine the number of vertices required in the mesh. After you set *m* and *n*, you input each vertex as X,Y,Z coordinates. Meshes can be open or closed, depending on whether the mesh joins in either the *m* or *n* direction, or both.

Figure 21.13 shows an example of a 3D mesh, showing the *m* and *n* directions. This is an open mesh. A donut mesh is an example of a mesh closed in both directions. An example of a mesh closed in *m* and open in *n* is a tube; an auto tire (without a rim) is open in *m* and closed in *n*. Later, when you edit a mesh, you identify the vertices to see how the mesh vertex information is displayed.

**Figure 21.13:**

A 3D mesh example.

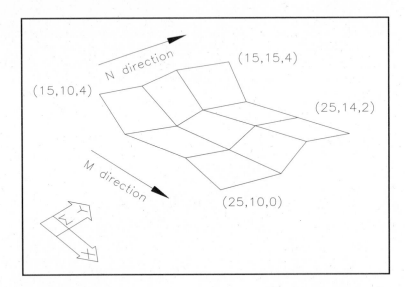

The 3DMESH command is difficult to use because the points must be entered in rigid row-by-row, column-by-column order. The PFACE command is more flexible.

## Using the PFACE Command

Like the 3DFACE command, PFACE can create surfaces with invisible interior divisions. Unlike the other meshes, you can specify any number of vertices and create any number of faces by using PFACE. First, pick all vertex points, remembering their numerical order, and then create faces by entering the vertex numbers that define their edges. To make an edge invisible, you respond to the first vertex prompt of that edge with a negative, instead of a positive, vertex number. Like 3Dfaces, invisible polyfaces are visible when SPLFRAME is set to 1 and invisible when it is set to 0.

You can also assign a color or layer by responding to any `Face n, vertex n:` prompt using C for color or L for layer. It then re-prompts for the vertex number. If you do so, the current face and all subsequent faces get that color or layer until you specify otherwise.

Although the PFACE command is capable of making more complex surfaces, you can use it in place of 3DFACE to cap the hub. You use it to put a bottom on the hub, for comparison. Use the ENDP running snap mode to pick all except the center vertex point. SPLFRAME is set to 1 so that all edges are visible until you set it to 0 and regenerate.

## Putting a Bottom Surface on the Hub with PFACE

Continue from the previous exercise. Make the left viewport current, zoom in on the hub, and set a running object snap to ENDPoint.

`Command:` *From the screen menu,*
*choose SURFACES, then PFACE:*

`Command: _PFACE`                      Specifies the center vertex ① (see fig. 21.14)
`Vertex 1: 0,0,-2.5` ↵

`Vertex 2:` *Pick* ②

`Vertex 3:` *Pick* ③

`Vertex 4:` *Pick* ④

`Vertex 5:` *Pick* ⑤

`Vertex 6:` *Pick* ⑥

`Vertex 7:` *Press Enter*            Ends vertex specification

*continues*

**Figure 21.14:**

PFACE vertex
numbers and pick
points.

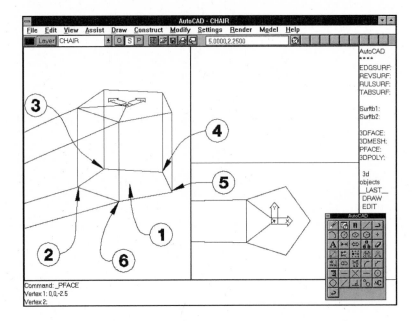

Next, you specify which vertex numbers define each face.

Face 1, vertex 1: **−1** ↵          Negative makes following inside edge invisible

Face 1, vertex 2: **2** ↵           Positive makes following outside edge visible

Face 1, vertex 3: **−3** ↵

Face 1, vertex 4: *Press Enter*          Completes face 1

Face 2, vertex 1: **−1** ↵

Face 2, vertex 2: **3** ↵

Face 2, vertex 3: **−4** ↵

Face 2, vertex 4: *Press Enter*

Face 3, vertex 1: **−1** ↵

Face 3, vertex 2: **4** ↵

Face 3, vertex 3: **−5** ↵

Face 3, vertex 4: *Press Enter*

Face 4, vertex 1: **−1** ↵

Face 4, vertex 2: **5** ↵

Face 4, vertex 3: **−6** ↵

Face 4, vertex 4: *Press Enter*

Face 5, vertex 1: **− 1** ↵

Face 5, vertex 2: **6** ↵

Face 5, vertex 3: **− 2** ↵

Face 5, vertex 4: *Press Enter*

Face 6, vertex 1: *Press Enter*            Completes all faces (see fig. 21.15)

*Set SPLFRAME to 0, and regenerate*            Makes edges invisible

*Set object snap back to* NONE, *set*
*SPLFRAME back to 1, and zoom Previous*

*Save your drawing*

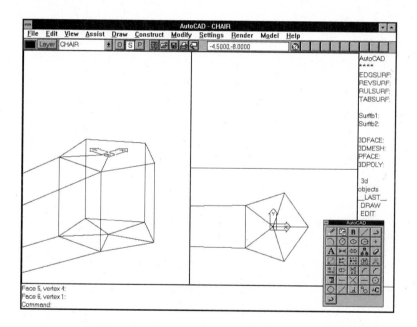

**Figure 21.15:**

A completed PFACE closes the bottom of the hub.

You generally do not know all the surface points required to create a surface entity; calculating these points may be too difficult. You can use the four "surf" commands, however, to generate 3D surfaces based on boundaries, curves, and direction vectors that are relatively easy to specify or determine. AutoCAD then handles the tedious calculations.

*The IAW DISK includes an AutoLISP-defined command named PFACE2. You load it by entering (load "pface2") and use it in place of the PFACE command. PFACE2 displays numbered markers at the vertices during the command to make it easier to keep track of the vertices. The AutoCAD Sample disk includes the MFACE.LSP AutoLISP program, which is probably installed in your ACADWIN\SAMPLE directory. This program enables you to generate a polyface with invisible interior edges by entering only the perimeter vertices. Enter (load "\\ACADWIN\\SAMPLE\\MFACE") to load it and MFACE to use it as a command. You can also use the APPLOAD command (choose File, then Applications) to load MFACE.LSP, or PFACE2.LSP from the IAW directory.*

Although you may not use the 3DMESH command often, you still need to set the system variables that control the *m* and *n* indices to control mesh density in the other commands. The SURFTAB1 system variable sets the *m* index, and SURFTAB2 sets the *n* index. Although you can use values up to 256 for either, you should use the lowest values that generate acceptably smooth surfaces. Values of 8 to 16 are suitable for most purposes. Dense meshes significantly increase your drawing processing time. If you do not like the mesh that appears, you cannot re-specify these variables for an existing mesh. You have to erase the mesh, reset the SURFTAB values, and then create a new mesh.

# Using RULESURF To Create the Leg Top

The RULESURF command creates a ruled surface between two boundaries of nearly any type. RULESURF creates a 2×*m* polygon mesh between the two boundaries; that is, it defines a one-way mesh of straight ruled lines between the boundaries. The entities that define the boundaries can be points, lines, arcs, circles, 2D polylines, or 3D polylines. (If you use a point, only one edge can be a point.) You only need to set the SURFTAB1 system variable, which controls the spacing of the rules.

You use RULESURF to finish the leg's top surface and to add a little arched cap to the end. The top surface runs as a ruled surface from an arc drawn above the end cap to the top edge of the hub. To create the arc, use the UCS Entity option to set the UCS in the plane of the end cap.

## Preparing for RULESURFs

Continue from the previous exercise. Make the left viewport current, and set the current layer to BUILD.

```
Command: UCS ↵

Origin/ZAxis/3point/Entity/View/X/Y/Z
Prev/Restore/Save/Del/?/<World: E ↵
```

| | |
|---|---|
| Select object to align UCS: *Pick the end cap at ① (avoid selecting the 3Dface sides (see fig. 21.16)* | Aligns the UCS with the leg's end cap |
| *Set PDMODE system variable to 66* | Makes points visible |
| *Use the POINT command and MID object snap to put a point at ①* | |
| *Use the ENDP object snap to draw a line from ② to ③* | |
| *Use the ARC command's Start, End, Angle options with the ENDP object snap to pick start and endpoints at ④ and ⑤, then enter angle 135* | |
| *Use UCS to restore the HUB UCS.* | |

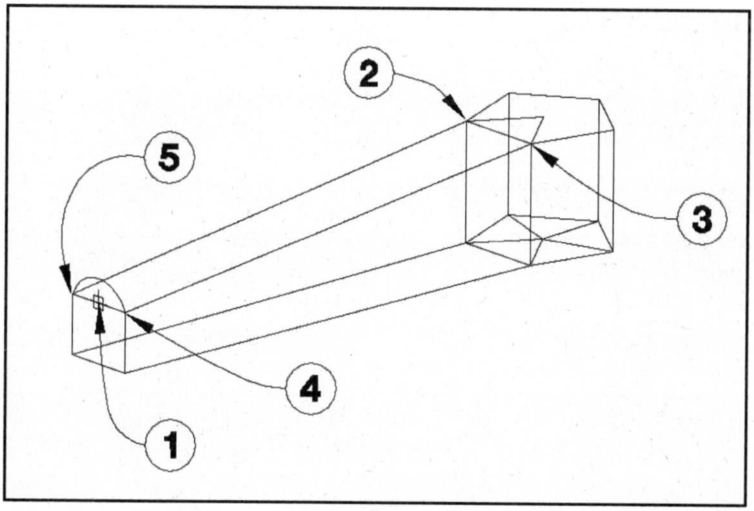

**Figure 21.16:**

Detail of creating profiles for the ruled surfaces.

After you have defined the curves for RULESURF, you can begin the surfacing. In the previous exercise, you created a point, a line, and an arc that defines a curve for the top of the leg and the space at the end cap.

**TIP**

*Picking the line to draw the top mesh surface can be difficult, because AutoCAD may find the hub or the 3Dface on its top instead. Even if you manage to draw the top mesh surface, it may be impossible to pick the arc for the arched end cap surface because the top surface gets in the way. To avoid these problems, you use the LAYER command to display only the defining entities (or profiles), and cause the meshes to be drawn on an invisible layer.*

Use the preceding tip to make the two meshes, then use LAYER again to see the results.

## Using RULESURF To Complete the Leg

Continue from the previous exercise. Set SURFTAB1 to 8. Make CHAIR the current layer, then turn it off (answer Yes to `really want to turn off current layer...`). This setting leaves visible only the point, line, and arc you just drew, but draws the new surfaces on the correct layer, where they will not interfere with your picks.

| | |
|---|---|
| *Choose* **D**raw, *then* **3**D Surfaces, *then* **R**uled Surface | Begins RULESURF command |
| `Command: _rulesurf`<br>`Select first defining curve:` *Pick* ①<br>*(see fig. 21.17)* | |
| `Select second defining curve:` *Pick* ② | Draws the surface |
| `Command:` *Press Enter* | Reissues the RULESURF command |
| `Select first defining curve:` *Use NODe object snap and pick* ③ | |
| `Select second defining curve:`<br>*Pick arc at* ② | |

Turn the CHAIR layer back on and issue the HIDE command, then save the drawing. Your drawing should look like figure 21.18.

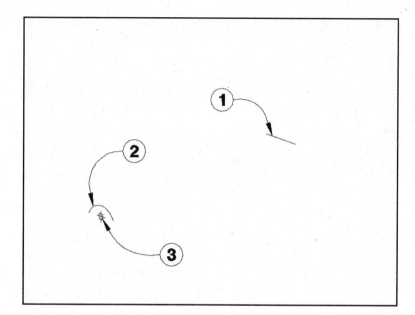

**Figure 21.17:**

Detail of pick points used to create the ruled surfaces.

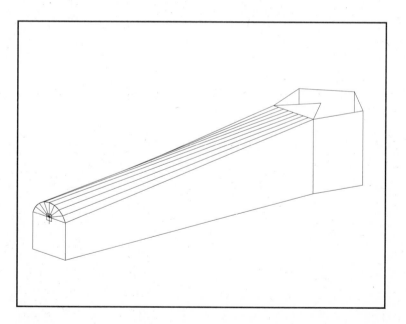

**Figure 21.18:**

The completed leg surfaces.

When you work with RULESURF, your pick points can be critical. If your edge curves are open, the rule is built from the endpoint nearest your pick point on each entity. The ruled surface can twist if you do not pick the nearest endpoints on the edge entities.

You can also get a twist with closed entities. The generated mesh starts from the 0-degree point of circles and from the starting vector of closed polylines. If you are generating a mesh between two circles or between a circle and closed polyline, make sure that your zero points and first points are aligned in order to avoid a twist in the mesh.

*You may want to use RULESURF between a circle and a polyline ellipse. Aligning the zero point on the circle with the starting vector of the ellipse is almost impossible. It is easier to achieve the correct alignment if both entities are created by using the ELLIPSE command.*

The mesh commands require that you pick the entities for creating the ruled surface. When creating meshes with a common boundary entity, you need to get the first mesh out of the way to pick the boundary entity for the second mesh. Otherwise, it is almost impossible to pick it. You can put the defining curves on a different layer, make the layer for the meshes current, and turn it off, as you did in the previous exercise. Another strategy is to create new meshes on a temporary layer, and use CHPROP to move them to their destination layer (which is turned off) as soon as you create them.

*Besides using layer control, other methods for temporarily removing an interfering entity include: temporarily erasing and then restoring the entity with OOPS; using BLOCK to store it to a temporary block name and performing an \*INSERT later; or moving it to another location and back again.*

# Completing the Base Assembly

To complete the base, draw a caster, and then duplicate the leg and caster to make the other four legs. You can take advantage of one of the AutoLISP-defined 3D mesh drawing commands from the 3D Objects icon menu to draw the caster. Select the Sphere icon from the 3D Objects menu. This command is an AutoLISP routine that uses the REVSURF command to revolve an arc about an axis line.

## Using a 3D SPHERE To Construct the Chair's Casters

You select the Sphere icon from the 3D Objects icon menu. You are prompted for the sphere's center point and radius. The routine draws the arc and axis line, generates the sphere, and then automatically cleans up by erasing the arc and axis lines.

## Using the AutoLISP SPHERE Command To Make a Caster

Continue from the previous exercise.

*Choose* **D**raw, *then* **3**D Surfaces,
3D **O**bjects, *then double-click on the*
*Sphere icon*

```
Command: ai_sphere
Initializing...  3D Objects loaded.
Center of sphere: 0,0 ↵

Diameter/<radius>: 1.25 ↵

Number of longitudinal segments <16>:
12 ↵

Number of latitudinal segments <16>:  Draws the sphere (see fig. 21.19)
12 ↵
```

*Zoom in for a closer look*

*Move the caster with displacement*          Completes one leg
*–12,0,–3.25 (see fig. 21.20)*

```
Command: REDRAWALL ↵                Redraws all viewports
```

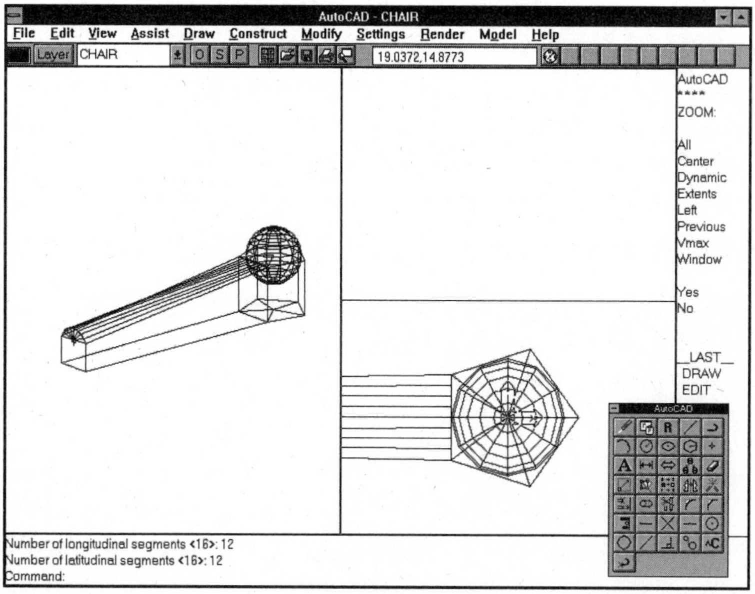

**Figure 21.19:**

The chair caster before MOVE.

**Figure 21.20:**

The chair caster in place.

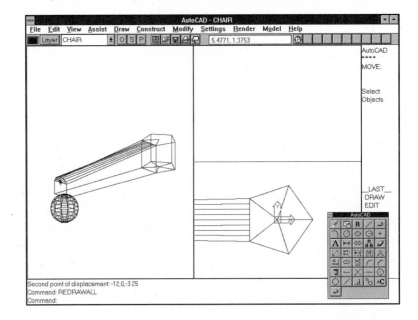

## Using ARRAY To Complete the Chair Base

Now you can array the first leg and caster to complete the chair's base, and then block the base as a finished component. Use the standard ARRAY command to array the leg and BLOCK to create the BASE block.

### Using ARRAY To Complete the Base

Continue from the previous exercise. Make the lower right viewport current, and use ZOOM with the Center option at 0,0, and a height of 28. Turn off the BUILD layer.

*Use ARRAY to polar array all entities except the hub and bottom cap, about center point 0,0; 5 items to fill 360 degrees and rotate as copied (see fig. 21.21)*

Command: **HIDE** ↵

*Use BLOCK to block everything to name BASE with insert base point 0,0*

Save your drawing and continue, or end and take a break.

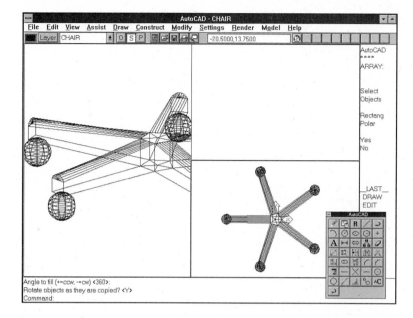

**Figure 21.21:**

The completed base, after ARRAY.

The BASE block is stored in your current CHAIR drawing. You also have the base stored on the IAW DISK, as IAW-BASE.DWG.

# Using the REVSURF Command

You saw REVSURF in action, generating the sphere, although you did not actually enter the command by name. REVSURF creates a surface by revolving a path curve around an axis of revolution. In the case of the sphere, the SPHERE routine created the path curve, an arc, and the axis of revolution for you. You can select a line, arc, circle, or 2D or 3D polyline as the path curve. You can select a line or open polyline to specify the axis of rotation. If you select a polyline as the axis of revolution, AutoCAD uses an imaginary line between the first and last vertices as the axis, ignoring the intermediate vertices.

You then enter the angle at which the rotation starts, and the included angle of rotation: 360 degrees for a full cylinder or sphere. You can offset the start angle if you do not want to start from a 0-degree angle.

## Creating a Shaft Profile of the Pedestal

You use REVSURF to create a complex surface (the chair's accordion-shaped pedestal cover), which covers the shaft. The pedestal mesh is made up of two different revolved shapes. Create a single pleat at the bottom and the top closure as two polyline profiles, and then revolve them into 3D surfaces by using REVSURF. You array the bottom piece vertically to complete the pedestal.

In the following exercise, you set up a UCS, create a vertical line for the axis of revolution, and create a polyline path profile for the bottom pleat. You use PEDIT to add tangent information to the first and last vertices, and then curve fit the polyline so that it smoothly meets adjoining sections. You can continue from the previous exercise, or use the IAW-CHR2 drawing from the IAW DISK.

## Preparing Axis and Bottom Path Curve for REVSURF

Continue in the CHAIR drawing you created in the first section of the chapter, or begin a new drawing named CHAIR=IAW-CHR2.

If you are continuing with your own drawing, make the left viewport current, and set BUILD as the current layer. Then erase the arc, line, and point left from the base construction.

Use UCS with the X option and rotate the UCS 90 degrees about the X axis.

Command: *From the toolbox, choose* LINE          Designates axis of revolution
*and draw a line from 0,0 to 0,13*

*Choose* **V**iew, *then* **S**e**t** View, **P**lan View,          Displays plan view
*then* **C**urrent UCS

*Zoom in on bottom half of the line*

Command: *From the toolbox, choose*
POLYLINE *and draw a polyline from*
*1.25,0 to 0.75,0.5 to 1.25,1*

Next, you set tangents and curve fit the profile.

Command: *From the toolbox, choose* PEDIT

pedit Select polyline: **L** ↵

Close/Join/Width/Edit vertex/Fit/Spline/
Decurve/Ltype gen/Undo/eXit <X>: **E** ↵

Next/Previous/Break/Insert/Move/Regen
/Straighten/Tangent/Width/eXit <N>: **T** ↵

Direction of tangent: **90** ↵

Next/Previous/Break/Insert/Move/Regen
/Straighten/Tangent/Width/eXit <N>:
*Press Enter twice*

```
Next/Previous/Break/Insert/Move/Regen
/Straighten/Tangent/Width/eXit <N>: T ↵

Direction of tangent: 90 ↵

Next/Previous/Break/Insert/Move/Regen
/Straighten/Tangent/Width/eXit <N>: X ↵

Close/Join/Width/Edit vertex/Fit curve
/Spline curve/Decurve/Undo/eXit <X>: F ↵

Close/Join/Width/Edit vertex/Fit/Spline/
Decurve/Ltype gen/Undo/eXit <X>:
```
*Press Enter*

The results appear in figure 21.22.

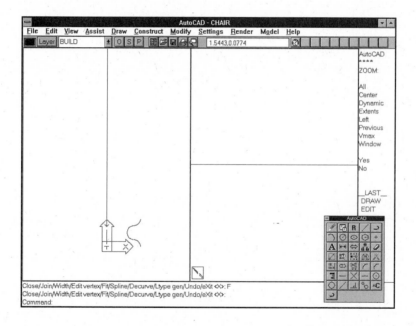

**Figure 21.22:**

The bottom path curve and axis for REVSURF.

The top of the pedestal terminates with a shaft. Draw the second path curve to establish the top shaft profile and a closure where it meets the arrayed bottom piece. This shaft profile combines polyline arc and line segments.

## Creating Top Path Curve for the Shaft Top

Continue from the previous exercise. Use PAN to display the top half of the line.

Command: *From the toolbox, choose*
POLYLINE

```
pline
From point: .5,13 ↵

Current line-width is 0.0000
Arc/Close/Halfwidth/Length/Undo/Width/
<Endpoint of line>: @0,-2.75 ↵

Arc/Close/Halfwidth/Length/Undo/Width/
<Endpoint of line>: @.5,0 ↵

Arc/Close/Halfwidth/Length/Undo/Width/
<Endpoint of line>: A ↵

Angle/CEnter/CLose/Direction/Halfwidth/
Line/Radius/Second pt/Undo/Width/
<Endpoint of arc>: @.25, − .25 ↵

Angle/CEnter/CLose/Direction/Halfwidth
/Line/Radius/Second pt/Undo/Width/
<Endpoint of arc>: Press Enter
```

The results appear in figure 21.23.

**Figure 21.23:**

The top path
curve for the
pedestal shaft
REVSURF.

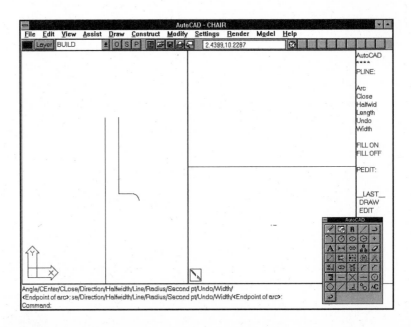

# Using REVSURF To Complete the Shaft

Now you can complete the shaft by using REVSURF. Adjust the SURFTAB1 and SURFTAB2 settings to achieve acceptably smooth surfaces. When you execute REVSURF, pick your profile entity first, then pick the axis line. Accept the default start angle of 0 degrees and the default included angle of 360 degrees for a full circle. After you have revolved the bottom, repeat REVSURF for the top. Finish the pedestal by using a rectangular array to create nine copies (ten rows, one column) of the bottom piece. When done, reset your UCS and define the block, PEDESTAL, which includes the top shaft and all pleats in the cover.

## Using REVSURF To Make the Pedestal Surface

Restore the view named BUILD and use PAN to display both path profiles, then set the current layer to CHAIR.

*Set SURFTAB1 to 12 and SURFTAB2 to 4*

| | |
|---|---|
| *Choose* **D***raw, then* **3**D Surfaces, *then* **S**urface of Revolution | Issues REVSURF command |
| `Command: _revsurf`<br>`Select path curve:` *Pick top profile at* ① *(see fig. 21.24)* | |
| `Select axis of revolution:` *Pick the axis at* ② | |
| `Start angle <0>:` *Press Enter* | |
| `Included angle (+=ccw, -=cw)`<br>`<Full circle>:` *Press Enter* | Creates top of pedestal |

*Set SURFTAB2 to 6*

| | |
|---|---|
| *Repeat REVSURF on the bottom profile, picking path curve at* ③ *and axis of revolution on line at* ② *with included angle a full circle* | Creates bottom of pedestal |
| *Use ARRAY to create a rectangular array of the bottom piece, 10 rows and one column, at one-unit spacing (see fig. 21.25)* | Completes pedestal |

*Restore HUB UCS and turn layer BUILD off*

*Create a block named PEDESTAL selecting everything and using insertion base point 0,0*

*Save your drawing*

**Figure 21.24:**

Detail of REVSURF
pick points.

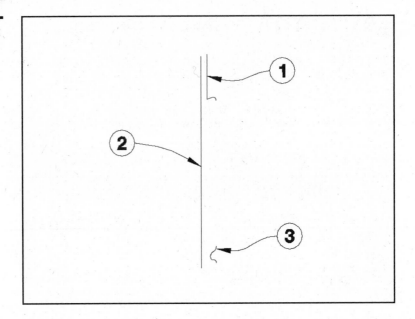

**Figure 21.25:**

The completed
pedestal.

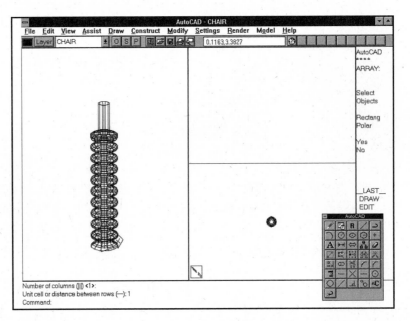

The pedestal used the default (full-circle) rotation. The next exercise uses a partial, 90-degree REVSURF to connect rectangular frames made with BOX, one of the AutoLISP 3D mesh drawing commands. You make the frames first, and then connect them with a partial REVSURF.

# Using the BOX Command

BOX is another one of the AutoLISP-defined 3D mesh drawing commands on the 3D Objects icon menu. This command prompts for the starting corner, length, width, height, and rotation angle. You can enter the values or pick points. The cube option requires only one dimension. Remember that length is measured along the X axis of the current UCS, width along the Y axis, and height along the Z axis.

Use BOX to draw the three frame pieces. After the menu has loaded the BOX command, you can also enter it at the Command: prompt to create the seat support base (see fig. 21.26). You can continue from the previous exercise, or use the IAW-CHR3 drawing from the IAW DISK.

## Using BOX To Create Seat and Back Support Frames

Continue in the CHAIR drawing you have already created, or begin a new drawing named CHAIR=IAW-CHR3. Make sure that the left viewport and CHAIR layer are still current.

*Choose **D**raw, then **3**D Surfaces, then 3D **O**bjects, and then double-click on the Box icon*

Command: ai_box

Corner of box: **− 1.5, − 1.25** ↵

Length: **10.5** ↵

Cube/<Width>: **2.5** ↵

Height: **1** ↵

Rotation angle about Z axis: **0** ↵     Draws seat support base (see fig. 21.26)

*Zoom all viewports to views shown in figure 21.26*

Command: **AI_BOX** ↵

Corner of box: **10, − 1.25,2** ↵

Length: **1** ↵

Cube/<Width>: **2.5** ↵

Height: **13** ↵

Rotation angle about Z axis: **0**     Creates back support (see fig. 21.26)

Command: *Press Enter*     Repeats AI_BOX command

*continues*

Corner of box: **9.25, – 1.25,11.5** ↵

Length: **.75** ↵

Cube/<Width>: **2.5** ↵

Height: **1.5** ↵

Rotation angle about Z axis: **0** ↵        Creates back support spacer (see fig. 21.26)

**Figure 21.26:**

The seat and back supports, created with BOX.

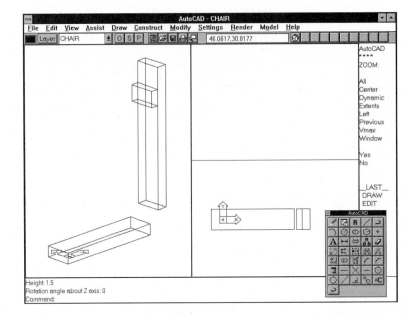

# Using 3D Polylines

Now, connect the frames by using REVSURF to revolve a 3D polyline. Use 3D polylines when you need to draw a polyline with vertices that do not lie in a single plane. 3DPOLY draws polylines with independent X,Y, and Z axis coordinates for each vertex. A 2D polyline can exist in any 3D construction plane, but all of its vertices must lie in a single plane. A 3D polyline is not subject to this limitation. A 3D polyline, however, consists of straight-line segments only, with no thickness. You can spline fit 3D polylines by using PEDIT; the resulting "curve" consists of short, straight segments (this is also true of spline fit 2D polylines).

The process of editing a 3D polyline with PEDIT is similar to editing a 2D polyline, but with fewer options. You cannot join 3D polylines, curve fit them with arc segments, or give them a width or tangent. The PEDIT prompt for 3D polylines looks like this:

```
Close/Edit vertex/Spline/Decurve/Ltype gen/Undo/eXit <X>
```

You use the LINE command to draw the axis of rotation for REVSURF, and you use a 3D polyline to create a rectangular path curve. You do not need to adjust the UCS to draw with 3DPOLY.

## Creating the Axis and Path Curve for REVSURF

Continue from the previous exercise. Make BUILD the current layer and erase the leftover pedestal construction entities.

| | |
|---|---|
| *Draw a line from 9,1.25,2 to @0,–2.5 (see fig. 21.27)* | Designates the axis of revolution |

*Choose **D**raw, then **P**olyline, then **3**D (use ENDP object snap to pick points shown)*

```
Command: _3dpoly
From point: Pick at ① (see fig. 21.28)
```

```
Close/Undo/<Endpoint of line>: Pick at ②
```

```
Close/Undo/<Endpoint of line>: Pick at ③
```

```
Close/Undo/<Endpoint of line>: Pick at ④
```

| | |
|---|---|
| `Close/Undo/<Endpoint of line>: C ↵` | Completes the rectangle |

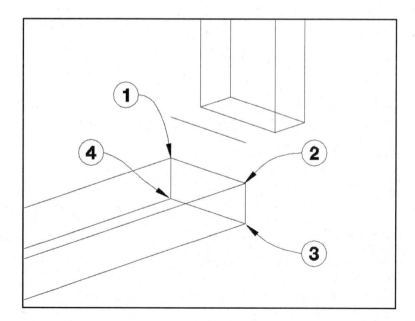

**Figure 21.27:**

Detail of the axis for the 90-degree REVSURF and the 3DPOLY pick points.

Now that you have the axis and polyline path profile, you can connect the two frames by using a partial REVSURF.

# Understanding Partial REVSURFS and the Direction of Rotation

The direction of surface rotation for REVSURF is determined by your pick point on the axis of rotation and the right-hand rule. When you pick an axis of rotation, the end nearest your pick point is considered the origin of that axis. Recall the *right-hand rule of rotation* from Chapter 19: if you curl the fingers of your right hand around an axis, with your thumb pointing away from the origin, your fingers naturally curl in the direction of positive rotation. Assigning a nonzero start angle offsets the mesh in this direction, and a partial rotation sweeps in this direction from the starting angle.

In the next exercise, you revolve the 3Dpoly profile through a 90-degree arc to create a mesh section that connects the two frames. After you get the supports connected, define a block named SUPPORT, consisting of the frames and the mesh. As you do the REVSURF, visualize the right-hand rule.

---

### Using a 90-Degree Revsurf To Connect Back and Seat Frames

Continue from the previous exercise. Turn off the CHAIR layer, and set SURFTAB1 to 6.

*Choose* **D**raw, *then* **3**D Surfaces, *then* **S**urface of Revolution

```
Command: _revsurf
Select path curve: Select rectangle on
near side edge at ① (see fig. 21.28)

Select axis of revolution: Select line
at ② (see fig. 21.28)

Start angle <0>: Press Enter

Included angle (+=ccw, -=cw)
<Full circle>: -90 ↵
```

| | |
|---|---|
| `Command:` *Choose* **M**odify, *then* **C**hange, *then* **P**roperties | Starts CHPROP command |
| `Select objects: L` ↵ | Selects the mesh and starts the Modify Entities dialog box |

| | |
|---|---|
| *Choose* **L***ayer, select* CHAIR, *then choose* OK, *and* OK *again* | Changes the mesh to layer CHAIR |

*Set layer CHAIR current, and turn off layer BUILD*

*Create a block named SUPPORT, selecting everything and using base point 0,0*

Save your drawing

Figure 21.29 shows the connected supports.

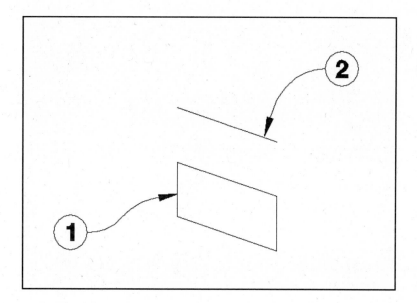

**Figure 21.28:**

Detail of REVSURF pick points.

The seat and back support construction involves simple surfaces. In the next section, you encounter curved surfaces and corners that require more complex meshes.

**Figure 21.29:**

The supports after REVSURF and LAYER.

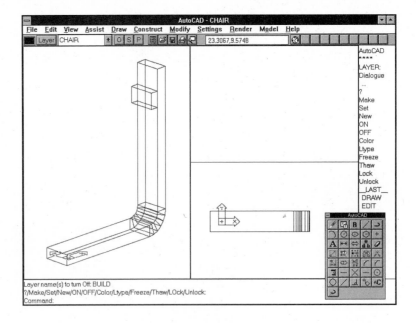

# Combining 3D Surfaces for Complex Mesh Construction

Many 3D objects are made by combining different 3D meshes. You need to make a curved back cushion with curved corners and edges. You can create the backrest with seven mesh entities. When you work with multiple mesh entities, you frequently encounter edges that coincide. When the arched ruled surface mesh was added to the end cap of the chair leg, you used layer control to get the preceding mesh out of the way. As you work with several meshes at once in the following exercises, you use one of the alternate techniques mentioned earlier—temporarily moving meshes out of your way.

In plan view, the main body of the chair back is slightly curved and is 1.5 inches thick with semicircular ends. You create its profile as a polyline by drawing a large arc, offsetting it 1.5 inches, and closing the ends with two small arcs. You create a major axis line at the center of the large arc to use with surfacing commands (discussed later). The top, bottom, and corners of the back are also curved. You create another small arc and minor axis at one corner to use with the surfacing commands as you define the curved parts of the back. You build these profiles and axes in plan view in the lower right viewport. You can continue from the previous exercise, or use the IAW-CHR4 drawing from the IAW DISK.

## Creating a Polyline Path Curve for the Back Cushion

Continue in the CHAIR drawing you have already created, or begin a new drawing named CHAIR=IAW-CHR4. Make the lower right viewport current, and zoom Center at 0,0 with height 21. Make BUILD the current layer and erase leftover entities.

First, you draw an arc for the inside profile of the back.

*Choose* **D***raw, then* **A***rc, then*
Start, **E**nd, Angle

```
Command: _arc
Center/<Start point>: 0, - 7 ↵

Center/End/<Second point>: _e
End point: 0,7 ↵

Angle/Direction/Radius/<Center
point>: _a Included angle: 20 ↵
```

*Draw a line from the center of the arc*     Designates direction vector and rotation axis line
*to @0,0,–9*

Make the left viewport current and use ZOOM with the Extents option to see the line, then make the lower right viewport current again.

*Use OFFSET with distance 1.5 to offset*     Creates outside profile of back
*the arc to the right*

*Draw another* Start, **E**nd, Angle *arc,*     Connects end of large arcs with a short arc
*using ENDP object snaps to pick start*
*point at* ① *and endpoint at* ②,
*and enter* **180** *degree included angle*
*(see fig. 21.30)*

*Use PEDIT to join all three arcs into*     Creates fourth arc segment at other end
*single polyline and close it*     of large arcs (see fig. 21.31)

*continues*

**Figure 21.30:**

Detail of the first
arc pick points.

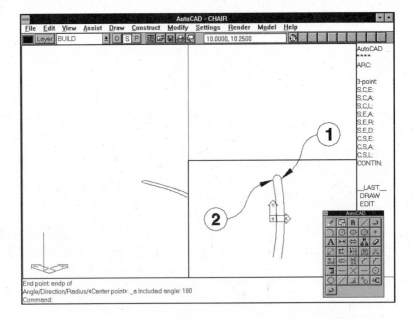

**Figure 21.31:**

The backrest
profile and axis
line.

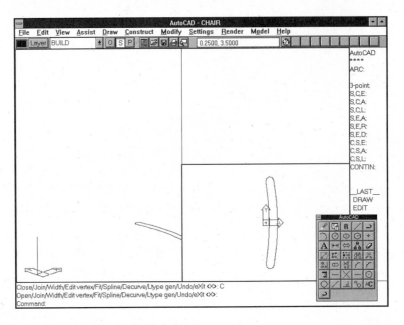

Make the left viewport current (to draw small arc and axis for path curve of both rounded
corner and top surfaces), and zoom to the left end of the polyline.

| | |
|---|---|
| *Use ENDP object snap to draw a line between ① and ② (see fig. 21.32)* | Connects the ends of the small arc segment |
| *Use* UCS Entity *option to align the UCS with the line just drawn, and then rotate the UCS 90 degrees about the X axis* | |
| *Draw another* Start, <u>E</u>nd, Angle *arc, using object snaps to pick start point at ①, endpoint at ②, and then enter* **180** *as angle* | |
| *Use Zoom with Extents option to see the major axis line and profile paths (see fig. 21.33)* | |
| *Save the drawing* | |

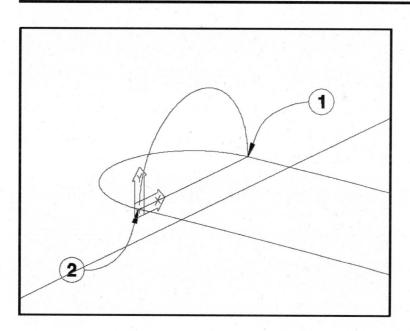

**Figure 21.32:**

Detail of axis line and arc pick points, with rotated UCS.

**Figure 21.33:**

An axis and profile curve for rounded edges and corners.

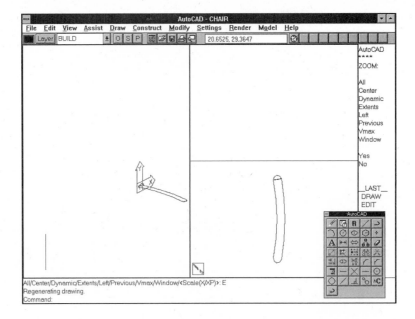

Now you are ready to create the mesh entities, starting with TABSURF for the main body of the backrest.

# Using the TABSURF Command

TABSURF creates a *tabular* surface by using a path curve (directrix) and a direction vector (generatrix). As with the RULESURF command, you only need to set SURFTAB1. TABSURF uses the usual set of entities for the path curve: line, arc, circle, or 2D or 3D polyline. After you select the entity to use for the path curve, select the direction vector. The surface lines it creates are parallel to the direction vector. The direction vector does not need to be on the path curve; it defines the direction and distance in which TABSURF extrudes your path profile. The direction of extrusion is away from the end of the direction vector nearer the pick point.

As noted earlier, you must move surfaces out of the way as you create them. You can move them to the WCS origin, using a special form of coordinate input, so that they appear in the upper right viewport.

Prefixing any coordinate value with an asterisk makes AutoCAD interpret the coordinate value in the WCS. Using the MOVE command with a first point of 0,0 (in the current UCS) and a second point of *0,0 moves the mesh surfaces to the WCS coordinate point that corresponds to their current UCS locations.

Now use TABSURF to create the main part of the chair's back, and then move it to *0,0 so that you can create the top and corner meshes.

## Using TABSURF and *0,0 To Create and Move the Back

Make CHAIR the current layer, and set SURFTAB1 to 8.

| | |
|---|---|
| *Choose **D**raw, then **3**D Surfaces, then* **T**abulated Surface | Issues TABSURF command |
| Command: _tabsurf<br>Select path curve: *Pick the joined polyline profile* | |
| Select direction vector: *Pick top of major axis line at* ① *(see fig. 21.34)* | Specifies direction and draws back |
| *Move the mesh from 0,0 to *0,0 (see fig. 21.35)* | Moves mesh to 0,0 of WCS |
| Command: REDRAWALL ↵ | Redraws all viewports |

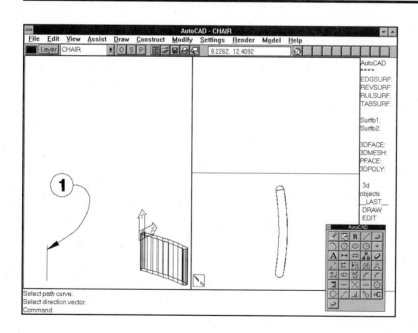

**Figure 21.34:**

The body of the back created with TABSURF.

**Figure 21.35:**

The body of the
back moved to the
WCS.

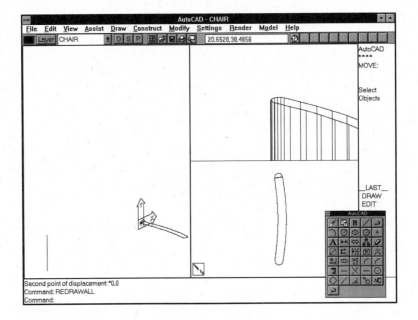

# Using REVSURF To Create Revolved Surfaces

Use REVSURF to surface the top edge and a corner of the backrest. First, create a 20-degree partial revolved surface by revolving the small arc at the corner about the major axis. This surface becomes the top edge of the back. Move the revolved surface to 0,0 in the WCS. Finally, use REVSURF with a 90-degree included angle to create the first rounded corner with the same arc, but revolve it 20 degrees (matching profile angle) about the short axis between its endpoints.

## Using REVSURF To Surface Top Edge and Corner of Backrest

Continue from the previous exercise. Set SURFTAB2 to 8.

*Choose **D**raw, then **3**D Surfaces,*
*and then **S**urface of Revolution*

```
Command: _revsurf
Select path curve: Pick arc at ①
```
*(see fig. 21.36)*

```
Select axis of revolution: Pick line
```
*at ③ (see fig. 21.37)*

Start angle <0>: *Press Enter*

Included angle (+=ccw, -=cw) <Full      Creates top edge of chair back
circle>: 20 ⏎

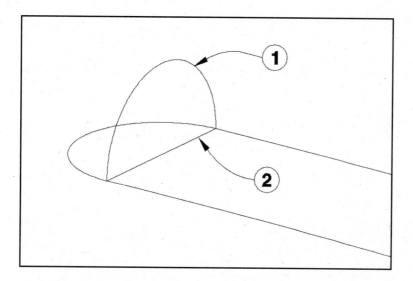

**Figure 21.36:**

Detail of REVSURF
path curve pick
point.

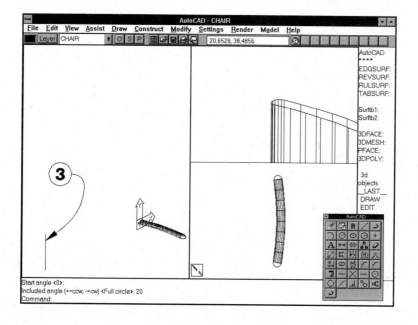

**Figure 21.37:**

Surface for the
top edge of the
backrest.

*continues*

*Move the mesh from 0,0 to \*0,0*

*Use ZOOM to display the left end of polyline, as shown in fig. 21.38*

Next, you use REVSURF to make the first corner of the backrest.

```
Command: REVSURF
Select path curve: Pick the arc at ①

Select axis of revolution: Pick the
short line at ②

Start angle <0>: Press Enter

Included angle (+=ccw, -=cw) <Full      Draws first corner
circle>: 90 ↵
```

*Move the meshes in upper right viewport from \*0,0 back to 0,0*

*Use ZOOM with the Dynamic option to fill left viewport with back surfaces (see fig. 21.39)*

*Save your drawing*

**Figure 21.38:**

The first backrest corner, created with REVSURF.

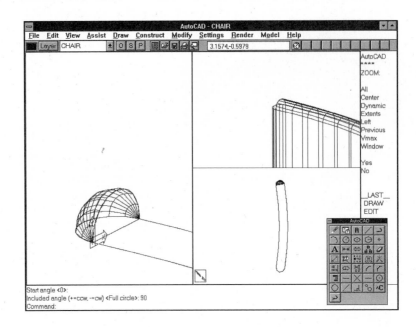

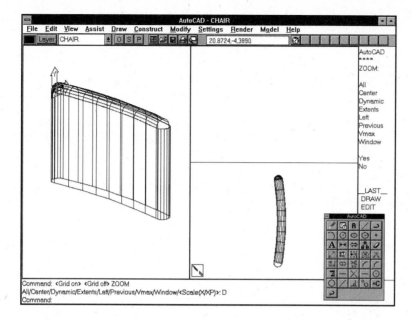

**Figure 21.39:**

The three backrest components assembled.

You now have all the entities you need to complete the backrest. You can create the remaining edges and corners of the backrest in the same way, but it is much easier to mirror the existing entities. Before you mirror the entities, make the mirroring easier by changing the UCS to HUB and moving the back to center its back surface on the UCS origin. After completing the backrest with two MIRROR commands, select everything to create a block named BACK.

---

## Using MIRROR To Complete the Backrest

Continue from the previous exercise. Make the lower right viewport current, and restore UCS HUB.

Command: *From the toolbox, choose* MOVE

Command: _move
Select objects: *Select everything*

Base point or displacement: *Use ENDP
object snap to pick middle of back side
at* ① *in lower right viewport
(see fig. 21.40)*

*continues*

| | |
|---|---|
| `Second point of displacement:` | Moves the back |
| **`0,0,4.5`** ↵ | |

*Use UCS with the Y option to rotate the UCS –90 degrees around the Y axis (see fig. 21.41)*

**Figure 21.40:**

Picking the midpoint of the back.

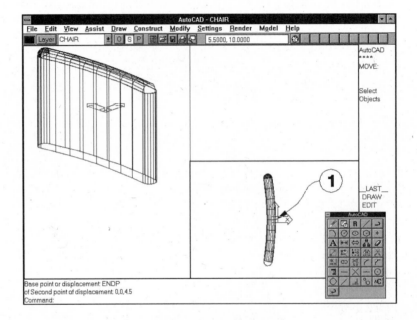

**Figure 21.41:**

The UCS oriented for mirroring.

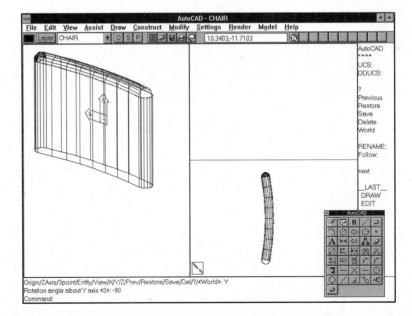

Next, you mirror the corner mesh to the other side.

`Command:` *From the toolbox, choose* **MIRROR**

`Command: _mirror`
`Select objects:` *Select corner mesh*

`First point of mirror line:` **0,0** ↵

`Second point:` **1,0** ↵

`Delete old objects? <N>` *Press Enter*    Draws opposite corner (see fig. 21.42)

Make the left viewport current, repeat the MIRROR command, and mirror top edge and both corner meshes to bottom of back, specifying mirror line from 0,0 to 0,1 and not deleting old objects (see fig. 21.43).

*Restore UCS HUB and turn layer BUILD off*

*Create a block named BACK, selecting everything and using base point 0,0*

Save and continue or end and take a break.

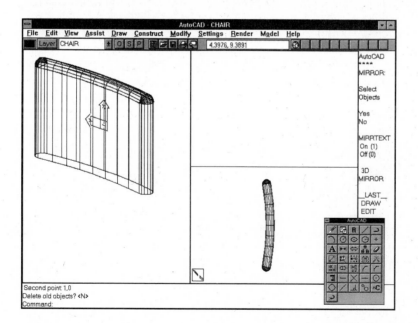

**Figure 21.42:**

The first corner mirrored.

**Figure 21.43:**

The completed
backrest before
restoring UCS
HUB.

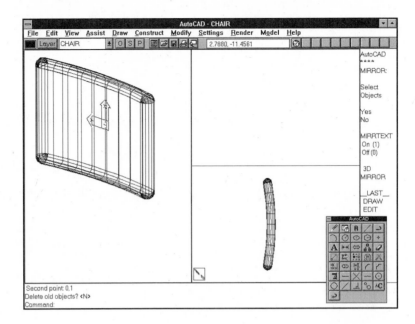

You now have all chair components except the seat itself. In the next section, you create the chair's seat and use PEDIT to change the surface contours of the seat. You can use PEDIT to move mesh vertices and to smooth meshes by spline fitting. First, use EDGESURF to create the seat body. Later, finish the seat construction by using a 3Dface for the seat bottom and by using REVSURF and TABSURF to create rounded edges and corners. Finally, assemble the chair by inserting the blocks that store its component parts.

# Creating a Surface Using the EDGESURF Command

EDGESURF creates a polygon mesh from four adjoining edges. The edges can be lines, arcs, or open 2D or 3D polylines, but the four edges must touch at their endpoints. A polyline is a single edge, no matter how many vertices it has. You need to set SURFTAB1 and SURFTAB2 to specify your *m* and *n* mesh density. The EDGESURF command is easy; simply select the four edge entities. The first pick sets the SURFTAB1 *m* mesh direction along the edge picked.

In the following exercise, you create four lines to define the planar edges of the top surface of the seat cushion, and then use EDGESURF to fill it in with a 10×10 mesh. Pick the edges so that the *m* and *n* directions match the illustrations in figure 21.46.

Temporarily go back to a single viewport, so that you can better see the results when you experiment with PEDIT mesh smoothing. Because the cushion is two inches thick, begin by drawing the line edges with a Z value of 2. You can continue from the previous exercise, or use the IAW-CHR5 drawing from the IAW DISK.

## Using EDGESURF To Create the Top Surface of the Seat Cushion

Continue in the CHAIR drawing you have already created, or begin a new drawing named CHAIR=IAW-CHR5.

If you are continuing in your own drawing, first make sure the left viewport is current. Then perform the next three steps.

*Set TILEMODE to 1*                    Exits from the mview viewports and returns to single viewport

*Zoom Center at 0,0,3 with height 15*

*Set layer BUILD current, and erase leftover entities*

If you started with a copy of IAW-CHR5.DWG, begin here.

*Set SURFTAB1 to 10 and SURFTAB2 to 10*

*Draw a line from 7,7,2 to 7,–7,2 to –7,–7,2 to –7,7,2, and close it*

*Make CHAIR the current layer*

Next, you use EDGESURF to create a 10×10 mesh 2" above seat bottom.

Command: *Choose* **D**raw, *then* **3**D Surfaces,    Issues EDGESURF
*and then* **E**dge Defined Patch              command

```
Command: _edgesurf
Select edge 1: Pick line at ①
```
*(see fig. 21.44)*

```
Select edge 2: Pick line at ②
```

```
Select edge 3: Pick line at ③
```

```
Select edge 4: Pick line at ④
```                    Draws seat bottom (see fig. 21.45)

*Save your drawing*

**Figure 21.44:**

Picking the edges to create the mesh.

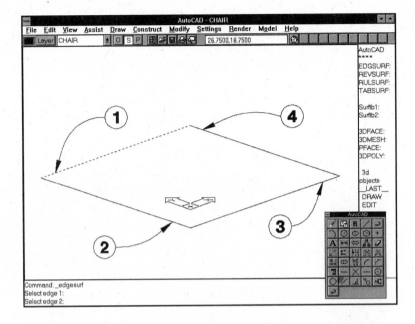

**Figure 21.45:**

The EDGESURF mesh.

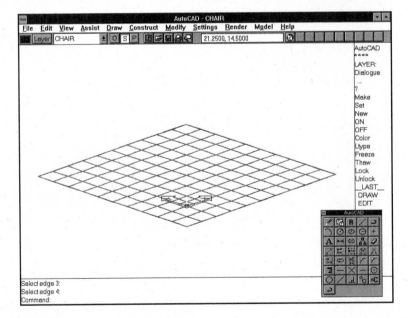

You can change the surface contours of a 3D polyline polygon mesh by editing the 3D vertex points with PEDIT.

# Using PEDIT To Edit 3D Meshes

PEDIT is an intelligent command. When you select a mesh, PEDIT prompts with the only options available for editing meshes. (The options also change with 2D or 3D polylines, but polyface meshes cannot be edited.) You can use PEDIT to move a mesh vertex point by identifying the vertex point and entering a new 3D coordinate. You can also smooth and unsmooth the mesh by spline fitting the vertex mesh points.

When editing meshes, PEDIT has several options for moving the vertex editing X marker from vertex to vertex, in addition to the familiar Next and Previous options. Look at the prompt line in the following exercise. The X starts at the corner nearest the first pick point used in EDGESURF. The Vertex (*m,n*) prompt indicates your current vertex (the location of the X). You move the X up (away from the starting corner) and down the *m* direction or right (away from the starting corner) and left in the *n* direction. The Next option initially moves in the right direction.

To get a feel for editing vertices and spline fitting meshes, try the following exercise. It exaggerates the movement of the vertex points so that you can see the effects of different curve fits. Watch the (*m,n*) prompt and X mark as you work. Set an undo mark so you can easily undo the experiment. First, move vertex (3,3).

## Using PEDIT To Edit Mesh Vertex Points

Command: **UNDO** ↵

Auto/Back/Control/End/Group/           Sets a mark
Mark/<number>: **M** ↵

*Choose* **M***odify, then* **P***olyline Edit*

Command: ai_peditm
Select objects: *Pick mesh and
press Enter*

PEDIT Select polyline:
Edit vertex/Smooth surface/Desmooth/
Mclose/Nclose/Undo/eXit <X>: **E** ↵

Vertex (0,0). Next/Previous/Left/Right/
Up/Down/Move/REgen/eXit <N>: *Press Enter*

Vertex (0,1). Next/Previous/Left/Right/
Up/Down/Move/REgen/eXit <N>: **R** ↵

Vertex (0,2). Next/Previous/Left/Right
/Up/Down/Move/REgen/eXit <R>: **U** ↵

*continues*

```
Vertex (1,2). Next/Previous/Left/Right
/Up/Down/Move/REgen/eXit <U>: Press
```
*Enter twice*

```
Vertex (3,2). Next/Previous/Left/Right
/Up/Down/Move/REgen/eXit <U>: R ↵
```

```
Vertex (3,3). Next/Previous/Left/Right
/Up/Down/Move/REgen/eXit <R>: M ↵
```

```
Enter new location: @0,0,3 ↵
```
       Moves vertex (3,3) 3" in Z direction

```
Vertex (3,3). Next/Previous/Left/Right
/Up/Down/Move/REgen/eXit <R>:
```
*Press Enter*

```
Vertex (3,4). Next/Previous/Left/Right
/Up/Down/Move/REgen/eXit <R>: M ↵
```

```
Enter new location: @0,0,2 ↵
```
       Moves vertex (3,4) 2" in Z direction

*Go to vertex (4,4) with Up option
and move the vertex 2" in Z by
entering @0,0,2*

*Go to vertex (4,3) with Left option
and move the vertex 2" in Z by
entering @0,0,2*

*Go to vertex (7,4) with Up Up Up
Right and move the vertex 1" in Y
and 9" in Z by entering @0,1,9*

*Go to vertex (8,5) with Up Right and
move the vertex -5" in Z by entering
@0,0,-5 (see fig. 21.46)*

```
Vertex (8,5). Next/Previous/Left/Right   Exits vertex editing
/Up/Down/Move/REgen/eXit <R>: X
```

```
Edit vertex/Smooth surface/Desmooth
/Mclose/Nclose/Undo/eXit <X>:
```
*Press Enter*

The smooth surface option enables you to perform three types of spline fitting. Each type produces a different smooth surface, based on formulas that produce a surface passing near the vertex points. You control the type of spline fit by setting the SURFTYPE system variable. Two other system variables, SURFU and SURFV, control the fineness of the fit in the *m* and *n* mesh directions. You use the SPLFRAME system variable to control whether the spline fit or original mesh displays. A value of 0 (off—the default) displays the spline fitting, if any, and a value of 1 (on) displays the original mesh and vertices regardless of spline fitting.

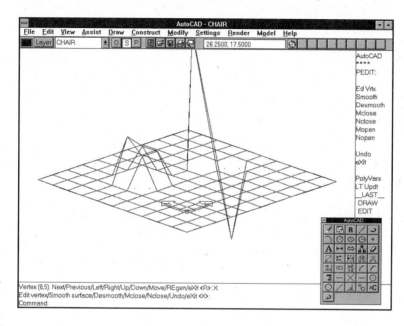

**Figure 21.46:**

The seat after mesh editing.

# Choosing Smooth Surface Options

The three smooth surface options and their variables are as follows:

- **Cubic B-spline curve.** SURFTYPE 6 (AutoCAD's default).
- **Quadratic B-spline curve.** SURFTYPE 5.
- **Bezier curve.** SURFTYPE 8.

Try all the smoothing options on the mesh to see the effect each has. Use the exercise that follows to configure the SURFU, SURFV, and SURFTYPE settings. Use PEDIT to smooth the mesh to a cubic B-spline surface, with default SURFTYPE 6.

## Using PEDIT To Smooth Mesh Surface Fitting

Continue from the previous exercise. Set SURFU system variable to 24 and SURFV to 24.

*Choose* **M**odify, *then* **P**olyline Edit

*continues*

```
Command: ai_peditm
Select objects: Pick mesh and
press Enter

PEDIT Select polyline:
Edit vertex/Smooth surface/Desmooth
/Mclose/Nclose/Undo/eXit <X>: S ↵

Edit vertex/Smooth surface/Desmooth
/Mclose/Nclose/Undo/eXit <X>:
Press Enter
```

Nothing happened because SPLFRAME was set to 1 for polyface and 3Dmesh visibility in an earlier exercise.

| | |
|---|---|
| *Set SPLFRAME to 0 and regenerate drawing* | Makes spline fitting visible (see fig. 21.47) |
| *Set SURFTYPE to 5* | Specifies quadratic B-spline surface |
| *Use PEDIT Smooth again (see fig. 21.48)* | |
| *Set SURFTYPE to 8* | Specifies Bezier surface |
| *Use PEDIT Smooth again (see fig. 21.49)* | |

```
Command: UNDO ↵

Auto/Back/Control/End/Group/
Mark/<number>: B ↵
```

Restores flat mesh

**Figure 21.47:**

SURFTYPE 6 smoothing.

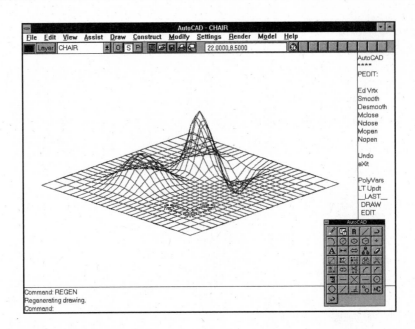

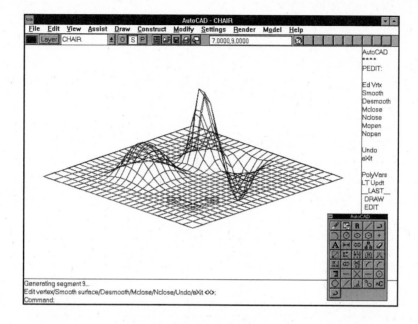

**Figure 21.48:**
SURFTYPE 5 smoothing.

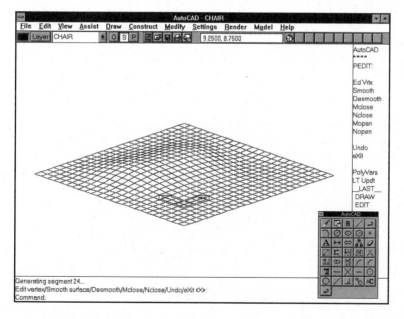

**Figure 21.49:**
SURFTYPE 8 smoothing.

You have to look closely to see the difference between SURFTYPEs 5 and 6, but 8 is dramatically smoother. You can regenerate to see the effects of a SPLFRAME change, but you have to use PEDIT to resmooth the mesh to see the effects of changing

SURFTYPE, SURFU, or SURFV. When you finish, you should have the flat starting mesh restored. If you like, try to edit the mesh into a comfortable seat contour.

## Other PEDIT Mesh Options

The Mclose and Nclose options control whether a mesh connects the first vertex to the last vertex of the mesh. A mesh in the shape of a dish (half a sphere) is closed in the M direction and open in the N direction. If you open the dish in the M direction by selecting Mclose, the dish is redrawn with a wedge segment missing. Likewise, if you close the dish in the N direction, the dish is redrawn with a mesh going from the edge to the center of the dish, creating a cone inside the dish. The M and N options display either close or open prompts, depending on the current status of the mesh being edited.

# Finishing the Seat by Using 3DFACE, TABSURF, and REVSURF

Now you can finish the seat. Make a simple seat bottom with the 3DFACE command, and then use REVSURF to make curved corners and TABSURF to close the curved edges.

After drawing the seat bottom by using 3DFACE, you create the arc and axis for REVSURF. You also move the existing mesh out of the way so that you can select one of its edge lines when you use TABSURF to create the arc. You utilize the same techniques here that you used to build the backrest.

---

### Using 3DFACE and Creating Arc Path and Axis for REVSURF and TABSURF

Continue from the previous exercise.

| | |
|---|---|
| *Set TILEMODE to 0* | Returns to mview viewports |
| *Make left viewport current, then use ZOOM with the Center option at 0,0 and height 36* | |
| Command: *Choose* **D**raw, *then* **3**D Surfaces, *then* 3D **F**ace, *and draw seat bottom from 7,7 to 7,–7 to –7,–7 to –7,7, and press Enter* | Draws seat bottom (see fig. 21.50) |
| *Make BUILD the current layer* | |
| *Draw a line from –7,7 to @0,0,2* | Designates axis for corner REVSURF |
| *Move seat top mesh from 0,0 to \*0,0* | Moves mesh out of the way |

| | |
|---|---|
| *Make top right viewport current, then use ZOOM with the Center option at \*0,0 and height 16* | |
| *Use UCS Entity option and pick bottom of axis line in left viewport* | Aligns UCS with line |
| *Use UCS with the Y option to rotate the UCS –90 degrees about Y axis (see fig. 21.51)* | |
| *Use ARC with* Start, **E**nd, Angle *option, entering start point* **2,0**, *endpoint* **0,0**, *and angle* **180** *degrees* | Creates profile curve for seat corner REVSURF and edge TABSURF (see fig. 21.51) |

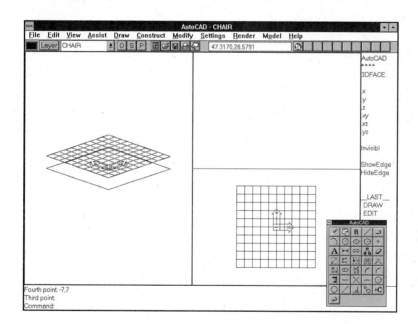

**Figure 21.50:**

The seat with a 3DFACE bottom.

Now you can use REVSURF and TABSURF to create the first corner and edge. Afterward, use a polar array to complete the seat cushion. The use of ARRAY takes advantage of the fact that the seat is symmetrical and saves mirroring (or individually creating) the edges and corners.

**Figure 21.51:**

Arc and construc-
tion lines ready
for surfacing.

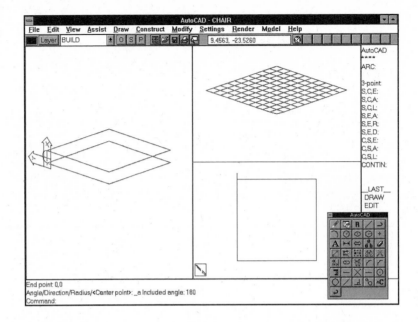

## Using REVSURF, TABSURF, and ARRAY To Complete the Seat

Continue from the previous exercise.

*Make CHAIR the current layer*

*Choose* **D**raw, *then* **3**D Surfaces,
*then* **S**urface of Revolution

```
Command: _revsurf
Select path curve: Pick arc at ①
(see fig. 21.52)

Select axis of revolution: Pick
line at ②

Start angle <0>: Press Enter

Included angle (+=ccw, -=cw)        Forms the corner
<Full circle>: 90 ↵
```

*When picking points with the REFSURF command, use care to pick
the point shown in figure 21.52.*

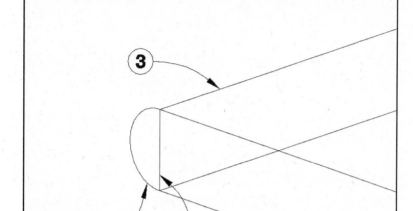

**Figure 21.52:**

Detail of seat corner and edge mesh creation pick points.

| | |
|---|---|
| *Restore UCS HUB* | Centers UCS on seat |
| *Move seat corner from 0,0 to \*0,0 and issue REDRAW* | |
| *Choose **D**raw, then **3**D Surfaces, then **T**abulated Surface* | |
| `Command: _tabsurf`<br>`Select path curve:` *Pick arc at* ① | |
| `Select direction vector:` *Pick line at* ③ | Creates seat edge |
| *Move meshes from upper right viewport, back from \*0,0 to 0,0* | |
| *Turn BUILD layer off* | |

Next, create a polar array of the edge and corner mesh to create the three remaining sides.

`Command:` *Choose **C**onstruct, then **A**rray*

`Command: _array`
`Select objects:` *Select TABSURF edge mesh and REVSURF corner mesh*

`Rectangular or Polar array (R/P):` **P** ↵

*continues*

Center point of array: **0,0** ↵

Number of items: **4** ↵

Angle to fill (+=ccw, -=cw) <360>:
*Press Enter*

Rotate objects as they are copied? <Y>    Creates rest of corners and edges
*Press Enter*                             (see fig. 21.53)

*Create a block named SEAT, selecting*
*everything and using base point 0,0*

*Save your drawing*

**Figure 21.53:**

The completed
seat cushion.

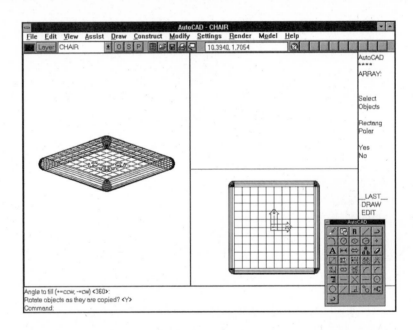

Congratulations! You now have all your chair components stored in your drawing as
blocks.

# Inserting 3D Blocks

In 3D, building complex parts as a series of smaller blocked parts offers several productivity benefits. First, you only have to work with a limited number of entities on the
screen for a particular part, which makes construction and editing less confusing (other
parts do not get in your way). This technique also makes redraws, regenerations, and

interim hidden-line removals faster. Another benefit is that you can easily change the components. For example, with a variety of seat, back, pedestal, and base blocks, you can use block redefinition to build a different chair from other parts.

Use the INSERT command to construct the chair from the components you have blocked. Even if you did not create all the blocks, you can insert them from files on the IAW DISK (the file names are given in the exercise). When all the parts are inserted, use the BASE command to set an insertion base point at floor level so that you can easily insert this drawing into other drawings. You can continue from the previous exercise, or use the IAW-CHR6 drawing from the IAW DISK.

## Using INSERT To Assemble the 3D Chair

Continue in the CHAIR drawing you have created in this chapter, or begin a new drawing named CHAIR=IAW-CHR6. This file already has the settings made by the first four steps of the exercise, but you will need to insert the parts from the IAW-???? files on the IAW DISK.

If you are continuing in your own drawing, do the following:

*Set TILEMODE to 1*                          Returns to single viewport

*Set UCS Origin to 30,22,0*

*Turn on all layers, zoom extents, and erase any leftover entities*

*Use ZOOM with the Center option at 0,0,18 and height 42*

If you are using the IAW-CHR6 file, begin here:

*Insert BASE block (or BASE=IAW-BASE) at 0,0,4.5 with default scale and rotation*

*Insert PEDESTAL (or PEDESTAL=IAW-PDST) at 0,0,4.5 with default scale and rotation*

*Insert SUPPORT (or SUPPORT=IAW-SPPT) at 0,0,17.5 with default scale and rotation*

*Insert SEAT (or SEAT=IAW-SEAT) at 0,0,18.5 with default scale and rotation*

*Insert BACK (or BACK=IAW-BACK) at 9.25,0,30 with default scale and rotation*

Command: **BASE** ↵

Base point <-30.0000,-110.0000,0.0000>:
**0,0,0** ↵

*Choose* **R***ender, then* **H***ide*

*Save your drawing*

Now the chair is complete (see fig. 21.54).

**Figure 21.54:**

The assembled chair, with hidden lines removed.

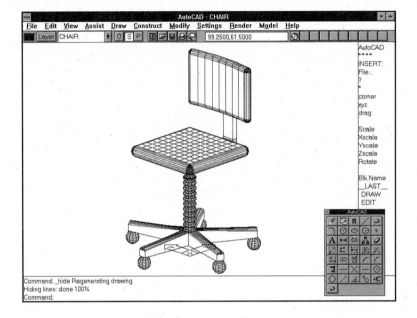

## Summary

When you construct a 3D drawing, use the entities and commands you need for your specific drawing. Meshes may not always be the most efficient drawing entities. Extruded 2D entities require less memory and hard disk space, so use them if they adequately represent what you need to show.

You will most often use a mix of 2D extruded entities and 3D mesh entities. If you are building a complex drawing, consider using the approach taken in this chapter: build your drawing in components and assemble it by using the BLOCK and INSERT commands.

When you use meshes, set reasonable surface mesh density by using SURFTAB1 and SURFTAB2. Keep track of these settings; if you forget to set the desired values, you have to erase the mesh and create a new one. Keep mesh profile entities on a separate layer to avoid conflicts with 3D model entities. If you have meshes with common edges, use temporary layers or blocks, moves, or erasures to remove one mesh so that you can pick the edge entity for the second mesh. If you really want to control your meshes, create some AutoLISP routines. For details, consult *Maximizing AutoLISP* (available from New Riders Publishing).

In Chapter 22, you are shown how to walk through a 3D drawing. You generate perspectives and partial hides and view an office drawing dynamically.

With these techniques, you will be able to present your 3D drawings to others with the greatest possible impact. Even simple schematic drawings and mass models are impressive when displayed using tools like perspective projection, shading, hidden-line removal, and clipping planes.

# Dynamic 3D Displays

In the preceding two chapters, you used extruded 2D entities and 3D surface entities to draw 3D models. This chapter presents advanced 3D viewing techniques that make drawing in 3D easier and help you plan and preview your 3D presentations. When you create a presentation, you use a variety of views in 3D space. This chapter teaches you how to use the DVIEW command to dynamically adjust your viewpoint and other parameters that control the appearance of the display, so that you can create the individual views that comprise a 3D presentation.

Often, the correct 3D view can save you time and money. Systematically revolving a drawing in 3D space might reveal an unanticipated design condition, such as interference between machinery and a wall. You can create winning presentations by learning to use tools such as DVIEW.

This chapter shows you how to use DVIEW as an interactive 3D substitute for the VPOINT and ZOOM commands, as well as how to display perspectives in AutoCAD. You also learn how to create slides of these views and construct a slide show using a script file.

## Viewing Drawings Dynamically

By combining DVIEW with paper space viewports, you can draw and annotate a single drawing with any combination of views, including perspectives. By combining

DVIEW, the RENDER and SHADE commands, slides, and scripts, you can quickly create preliminary or simple presentations. Then you can go on to create impressive full-motion video presentations by using Autodesk RenderMan, 3D Studio, AutoFlix, and Autodesk Animator (all Autodesk products).

DVIEW includes all the facilities of the VPOINT and ZOOM command, plus a few additional features. Rather than using the VPOINT globe and axes, DVIEW enables you to display all or part of your drawing as you adjust your viewpoint directly. Using DVIEW, you can zoom, pan, and adjust your viewpoint in a single command. Unlike VPOINT, DVIEW provides parallel (orthographic) or perspective views. Figure 22.1 shows both parallel and perspective views of an office. In the perspective view, parallel lines recede from your view toward a vanishing point. In the parallel view, parallel lines always remain parallel. Note that VPOINT is limited to defining parallel views. Parallel views often seem unnatural because your eyes are accustomed to viewing the real world. Parallel lines appear to converge as they recede from your viewpoint.

The VPOINT command zooms the new view to the drawing extents, but DVIEW gives you full control over the display of your view. VPOINT forces you to look through the entire drawing toward 0,0,0. DVIEW enables you to look from any point to any other point and control the zoom factor. You can clip the foreground or background to temporarily remove objects that obscure the object you want to see.

DVIEW uses an interactive camera and target metaphor to control your drawing view. To select a view, you point an imaginary camera at a target in your drawing. The line from the camera to the target is your line of sight. You can move the camera and target to get different views. The camera metaphor is carried further in perspective views to enable you to change your field of view by changing the lens length. You can also cut away sections of your drawing by clipping the front or back plane of your view. This useful feature enables you to look at an office interior in a building plan or create a section view of a part.

Although each of these features gives you more control over your drawing views, DVIEW's most powerful advantage is its *interactive interface*. The VPOINT command displays the globe and axes to preview the line-of-sight orientation, which requires trial and error to find the correct view. DVIEW, however, displays a selection set of drawing objects or a 3D icon (see fig. 22.2) if no objects are selected so that you can visualize the orientation of the line of sight in complex drawings. You can easily adjust the viewpoint using only a few selected entities and then regenerate the view of the entire drawing from this new perspective.

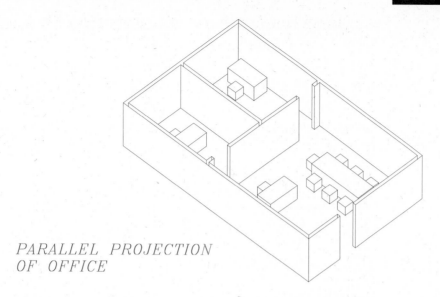

PARALLEL PROJECTION
OF OFFICE

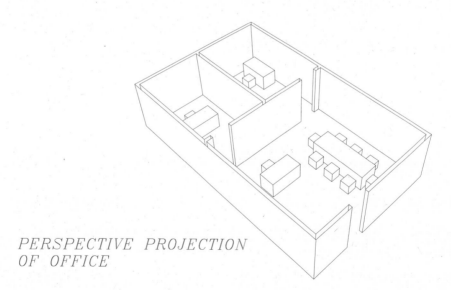

PERSPECTIVE PROJECTION
OF OFFICE

**Figure 22.1:**

Parallel and
perspective views
of an office
interior.

**Figure 22.2:**

The default DVIEW
icon.

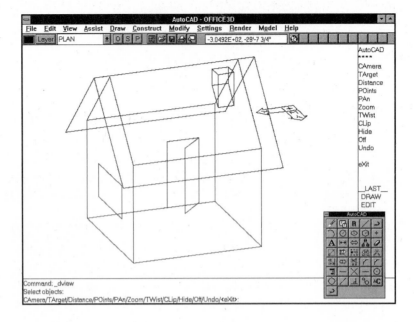

# Setting Up for DVIEW

For the exercises in this chapter, you use an office plan based on the drawing you did in Chapter 16 (see fig. 22.3). This drawing provides a variety of perspective views from the different rooms, and it regenerates quickly.

*Although the OFFICE3D drawing is simple, it illustrates a time-saving technique. You can work with simple shapes that regenerate quickly, such as those in this drawing, to develop a presentation, then replace them with complex blocks before plotting or presenting your work.*

The IAW DISK has the IAW-OFF1.DWG file, with extruded walls and furniture blocks (see fig. 22.4), ready for the first DVIEW exercise. Use the NEW command to begin a drawing named OFFICE3D=IAW-OFF1, and examine it to see that the settings match those in table 22.1. You use this drawing in the rest of this chapter.

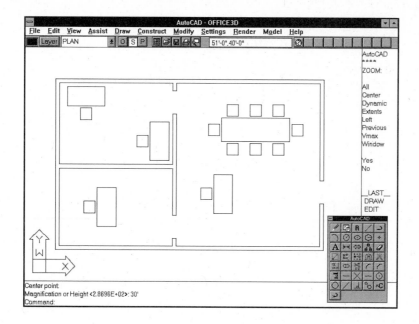

**Figure 22.3:**

The office plan with primitive table, desks, and chairs.

## Table 22.1:
## Dynamic View Office Drawing Settings

| COORDS | GRID | ORTHO | FILL | SNAP | UCSICON |
|--------|------|-------|------|------|---------|
| ON | 2' | OFF | OFF | 3" | ON and OR |
| **UNITS** | 4 (Architectural), defaults for the rest. | | | | |
| **LIMITS** | From 0,0 to 72',48'. | | | | |
| **VIEW** | Saved views named OFFICE1, and VIEW-1 thru VIEW-4. | | | | |

| Layer Name | State | Color | Linetype |
|------------|-------|-------|----------|
| 0 | On | 7 White | CONTINUOUS |
| PLAN | On/Current | 3 Green | CONTINUOUS |

You see the lower left room of the floor plan, which contains a simple chair and desk in the center of the room. You should be in the WCS with the UCS icon showing in the lower left corner of the drawing area. The thickness of the extrusions does not appear until the first dynamic view because your viewpoint is at 0,0,1—directly above the WCS origin.

**Figure 22.4**

The initial view of the OFFICE3D drawing.

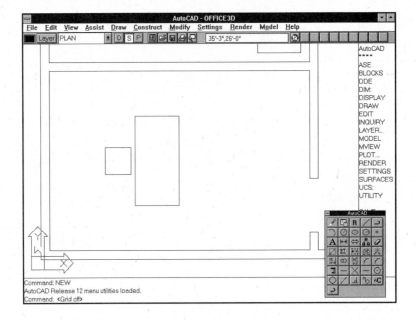

# Understanding the DVIEW Command

DVIEW is complex because it has 12 options; however, the command is easy to use after you learn these options and their effects. First, DVIEW asks for a selection set to use as the dynamic display. After you select objects or accept AutoCAD's default house icon, set your *viewpoint* (camera location) and the *focus* (target) by picking or setting points. These two points establish a line of sight or viewing direction. Then refine the view by zooming, panning, clipping, or hiding. After you have the view you want, exit DVIEW. AutoCAD regenerates the drawing according to the parameters you set. DVIEW's default view is parallel projection, but you can specify a perspective view.

You can access DVIEW from the S**e**t View option of the **V**iew pull-down menu. You can also choose DVIEW from the Display screen menu.

## Understanding DVIEW Options

Use the following options to control DVIEW:

- **CAmera.** This option rotates the viewpoint. CAmera is similar to the VPOINT Rotate option, but rotates the viewpoint around the target point rather than around 0,0.

*The target point default is 0,0,0 until you change it by using the
TArget option.*

- **TArget.** This option rotates the target point around the camera viewpoint. The
  TArget option is the opposite of the CAmera option. CAmera rotates the viewpoint around the target point.

- **Distance.** This option changes the distance from the camera to the target along
  the current line of sight. It switches the view from parallel to perspective.

- **POints.** This option sets the camera position (viewpoint) and target point. These
  points define the viewing direction.

- **PAn.** This option moves the camera and target points parallel to the current view
  plane. Because both points move by the same displacement, the angles between
  the viewing direction vector and the axes do not change.

- **Zoom.** This option enlarges or shrinks the image on the screen without changing
  the camera and target locations in the WCS—perspective angles are not affected.

- **TWist.** This option rotates the image around the line of sight.

- **CLip.** This option removes foreground or background objects from the image by
  setting clipping planes perpendicular to the line of sight.

- **Hide.** This option performs a temporary hidden-line removal in the DVIEW
  command. The image regenerates after you exit DVIEW.

- **Off.** This option turns off perspective mode and returns the image to parallel
  projection.

- **Undo.** This option undoes the other options.

- **eXit.** This option ends the DVIEW command. AutoCAD displays the `Command:`
  prompt and regenerates all drawing entities except portions that are clipped or
  outside of the current view as specified with the DVIEW command. If perspective
  mode is set, the drawing regenerates in perspective.

*You cannot use transparent commands in DVIEW; however, you
can turn on and off toggles such as SNAP, ORTHO, and the
coordinate display. You cannot use ZOOM, PAN, SKETCH, or
pick points from a perspective view generated by DVIEW.*

# Setting a Line-of-Sight View with POints

In the following exercise, you select the room and its contents to dynamically view your drawing. Then you use the POints option to set the camera position in the upper left corner of the room at approximately eye level and set a target point on the center of the desk top. You locate the target point, and then the camera point with XYZ point filters. After you pick the target point, a rubber-band line appears from the target point to the camera point to help you visualize the line of sight.

---

## Using POints To Set the DVIEW Camera Line of Sight

Continue in the OFFICE3D drawing you started at the beginning of the chapter.

Command: *Choose* **V***iew, then* **Se***t View,*
*then* **D***view*

Command: _dview

Select objects: *Use a window to select*    Specifies objects to view dynamically
*the room and its contents, then press*
*Enter*

CAmera/TArget/Distance/POints/
PAn/Zoom/TWist/CLip/Hide/Off/
Undo/<eXit>: *Enter* **PO***, or from the*
*screen menu, select* Options, *then* POints

Enter target point <25'-0 7/16",    Applies XY filter to next point
19'-6", 4'-0">: **.XY** ↵

*Pick a point in the middle of the desk*    Specifies XY coordinates of the "look at" point

(need Z): **3'6** ↵    Supplies Z coordinate

Enter camera point <26'-5 1/8",    
19'-6", 4'-1">: **.XY** ↵

of *Pick upper left corner of room*    Specifies XY coordinates of the "look from"
point

(need Z): **5'6** ↵    Sets camera point at eye level

CAmera/TArget/Distance/POints/    Regenerates the entire view using
PAn/Zoom/TWist/CLip/Hide/Off/Undo/    DVIEW parameters
<eXit>: *Press Enter*

---

Figure 22.5 shows your drawing after you input the points. Figure 22.6 shows what you see after you exit DVIEW.

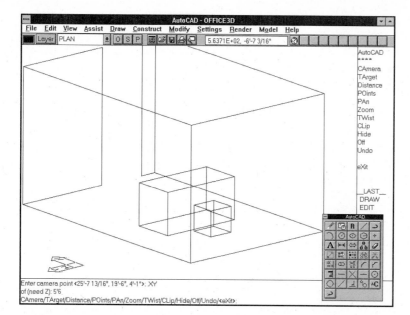

**Figure 22.5:**

The DVIEW display after point selection.

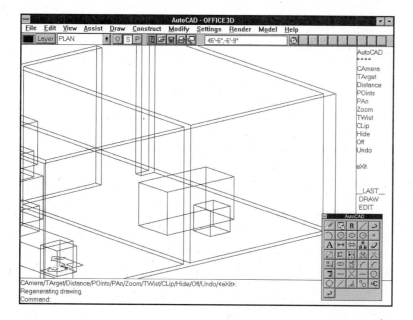

**Figure 22.6:**

An office viewed from the corner of the room.

Your drawing regenerates after you exit DVIEW. The drawing should show a view of the desk with the office doorway in the left background. If you study the location of the camera and target points in relation to the plan view and the new view, you discover that the display includes objects in back of the camera as well as in front of it. These objects appear because you did not set clipping planes to remove from the display objects that a real camera cannot see.

> *DVIEW automatically turns off snap, but you can turn it back on for snapping to points by pressing F9 or Ctrl-B. You can also use object snap overrides to pick points.*

> *The DVIEW default target and camera point prompts, as well as other default values and pick points, vary from those shown in this book. The exact defaults and points depend on your display and on the locations of your desks and chairs.*

## Using DVIEW's Undo Option

Like other complex commands, DVIEW has an Undo option to step back through the settings, angles, and point changes made while using the current DVIEW command. If you have exited DVIEW, you can use the UNDO command to undo an entire DVIEW operation.

## Understanding the DVIEW House Icon

If you press Enter in response to the DVIEW object selection prompt instead of selecting objects, AutoCAD displays a 3D house icon to orient you in space during a DVIEW operation. As you adjust your DVIEW settings, the house icon moves dynamically. After you exit DVIEW, your drawing regenerates in the view you established by manipulating the house icon.

You can replace the house icon with your own icon by defining a block named DVIEWBLOCK. You might prefer an icon that relates better to the subject of your drawings—a car, airplane, tool, video camera, or just a set of arrows. DVIEW scales the icon to fit your drawing and aligns it to the axes of your current UCS; therefore, create your block as a 1×1×1 unit block. Align the X,Y,Z axes with an origin point at the front lower left corner. Use a custom icon block instead of selecting complex objects to make DVIEW use quick and efficient. The house icon can be seen in figure 22.2.

*Create an easily recognizable DVIEW block with a unique top, bottom, left, right, front, and back side so that its orientation is easy to determine at a glance. Keep the block simple so that it drags smoothly in DVIEW.*

## Changing the Camera Location

The CAmera option rotates the point of view around the target point. The CAmera option is like the VPOINT Rotate option except that the order of the angle prompts is reversed. The first CAmera prompt asks for the angle from the X,Y plane. You can adjust this angle to move the camera up and down. The second prompt asks for the angle from the X axis (in the X,Y plane). This angle moves the camera from side to side. You can input the angles from the keyboard, or you can dynamically rotate your view by moving your crosshairs up, down, left, and right. When you move the crosshairs up, you increase the camera angle from the X,Y plane, while moving them to the right increases the angle from the X axis (in the X,Y plane). This dynamic rotation enables you to effectively select both angles with a single pick. As figure 22.7 shows, sometimes certain lines disappear while you are dynamically rotating the camera angle.

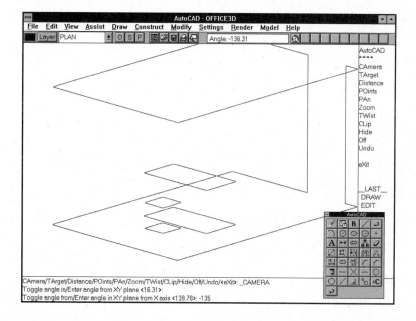

**Figure 22.7:**

The DVIEW display during camera angle selection.

# Using Dynamic Rotation

If you know the angles that produce the desired line of sight in advance, you can produce the view best by entering the angles from the keyboard. If not, you can use the cursor to find the right image interactively. As you move the cursor, AutoCAD dynamically redraws the selected objects to represent the new view. AutoCAD updates the angle display and the image as you move the cursor. AutoCAD provides similar dynamic editing features, such as slider bars to change distance settings.

*The angles in DVIEW are always in the WCS unless you set the WORLDVIEW system variable to 0. If you have a UCS current, and WORLDVIEW is 1 (the default), AutoCAD switches to the WCS during DVIEW, and then switches back to the UCS. A camera angle of 0 from the X,Y plane looks edge-on to the UCS or WCS construction plane.*

Next, you try the CAmera option by changing the angle in the X,Y plane to a view from the lower left corner of the room (with respect to the original plan view), looking back at the desk. The office doorway appears on the right (see fig. 22.7). Leave the angle above the X,Y plane unchanged.

## Using CAmera Option To Locate DVIEW Camera

Continue from the previous exercise.

```
Command: Choose View,
```
*then* **Se**t View, *then* **D**view

```
Select objects: P ↵
```
Selects walls of room, desk, and chair

```
Select objects: Press Enter
```
Completes the selection

```
CAmera/TArget/Distance/POints/
Zoom/TWist/CLip/Hide/Off/Undo/
<eXit>: From the screen menu,
choose Options, then CAmera
```

```
Toggle angle in/Enter angle from
XY plane <16.31>: Press Enter
```
Retains the current angle

```
Toggle angle from/Enter angle
in X-Y plane from X axis
<139.78>: -135 ↵
```

```
CAmera/TArget/Distance/POints/Zoom/
TWist/CLip/Hide/Off/Undo/<eXit>:
Press Enter
```
Exits DVIEW command and regenerates the screen

```
Regenerating drawing.
```

The resulting view appears in figure 22.8.

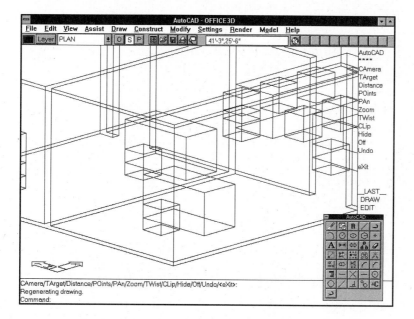

**Figure 22.8:**

The view with the camera moved to the lower left corner.

 *If you select an option that uses slider bars, the initial image depends on your cursor location and usually is different than the view displayed when you selected the option. To restore the view you just lost, move the diamond on the slider back to the end of the slider control. The illustrations with slider bars show the cursor and slider at their current default positions.*

The disadvantage of dynamically picking the camera's viewpoint is that precise values are hard to pick. Use the CAmera option's dynamic rotation ability to pick approximate views, but for precise views, enter the specific angles required.

If you want to experiment with the dynamic rotation, move the "camera" around. After you are done, use the Undo option to return the camera to -135 degrees.

## Setting a Distance for Perspective Views

You switch from parallel to perspective view by using the Distance option. AutoCAD prompts you for a new distance from the camera to the target, with your current distance as the default. The line of sight remains unchanged. You can enter a distance or use the top slider bar. The slider values range from 0X (on the left) to 16X (on the right). Your current distance factor is 1X. Move to the right, and you are farther away from the target; 2X is twice the distance. A continuous update of your distance displays in the coordinate display box of the toolbar.

> *Remember that the default prompt and coordinate display show the distance, but the slider is a multiplication factor, not a distance.*

If you select the Distance option, you also see your UCS icon replaced with a perspective icon (a small cube) in the lower left corner of the graphics window. This icon reminds you that you are in perspective mode. To turn off perspective, use the DVIEW Off option.

In the next exercise, you set a new camera/target distance to get a perspective view. The current distance is about seven or eight feet. Press Enter to accept the default distance so that you can see the desk in perspective at the current distance (see fig. 22.9). Then increase the distance to about 19 feet (about 2.7X). Use the VIEW command to save this view as a named view so you can return to it later.

## Using Distance Option To Create a Perspective View

Continue from the previous exercise.

`Command:` *Choose* **V**iew, *then*
**Se**t View, *then* **D**view

`Command: _dview`

`Select objects: P↵`                        Selects the same entities again

`Select objects:` *Press Enter*

`CAmera/TArget/Distance/`                    Starts the Distance option
`POints/PAn/Zoom/TWist/CLip/`
`Hide/Off/Undo/<eXit>: D↵`

`New camera/target distance`                 Displays view shown in figure 22.9
`<7'-1 7/16">: 8'↵`

`CAmera/TArget/Distance/POints/`
`PAn/Zoom/TWist/CLip/Hide/Off/`
`Undo/<eXit>: D↵`

`New camera/target distance <8'-0">:`
*Enter* **19'** *or select approximate distance*

`CAmera/TArget/Distance/POints/`            Displays view shown in figure 22.10
`PAn/Zoom/TWist/CLip/Hide/Off/`
`Undo/<eXit>:` *Press Enter*

Use VIEW to save the view with the name OFFICE1.

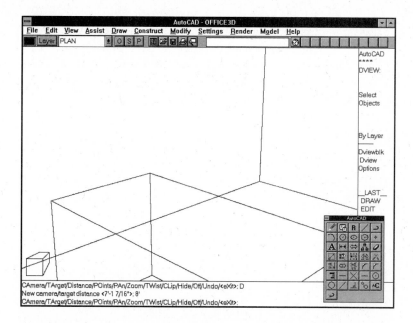

**Figure 22.9:**

The desk at a distance of 8'-0".

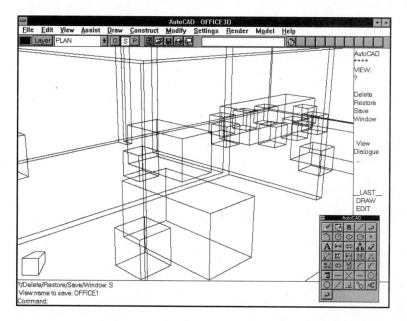

**Figure 22.10:**

The desk at a distance of 19'-0".

When you change the distance, you change the perspective. You can magnify an image by using the Zoom option without changing distance. Zoom acts like switching camera lenses, or using a zoom lens. After you set the perspective, you can use the POints, CAmera, and TArget options to change the perspective by changing points.

In the next section, you leave perspective on and change the target point.

# Rotating the View Using the TArget Option

One frustration of the VPOINT command is that it always looks at the WCS origin point. DVIEW's POints and TArget options, however, enable you to move the target point as well as the viewpoint. The TArget option prompts are similar to the CAmera prompts. The first prompt is for a new angle from the X,Y plane, and the second prompt is for a new angle in the X,Y plane from the X axis. The effect is the opposite of the CAmera option's effect; you are changing the target's location relative to your vantage point (the camera point). If you adjust only the angle in the X,Y plane, the effect at the camera is like turning your head to look around the room (or rotating the room around your head).

In the following exercise, you use the TArget option to aim the point of view at the office door on the right (see fig. 22.11). Change the target angle in the X,Y plane to get a view with the doorway near the center, leaving the angle from the X,Y plane unchanged.

---

### Using the TArget Option To Get a Viewpoint of Door

Continue from the previous exercise.

Command: *Choose **V**iew, then*
S**e**t View, *then* **D**view

Command: _dview

Select objects: **P** ↵

Select objects: *Press Enter*

CAmera/TArget/Distance/POints/
PAn/Zoom/TWist/CLip/Hide/Off/
Undo/<eXit>: **TA** ↵

Toggle angle in enter angle
from XY plane <-16.31>: **-16** ↵

Enter angle in X-Y plane          Displays view shown in figure 22.11
from X axis <45.00>: *Enter* **25**
*or pick approximate point*

CAmera/TArget/Distance/POints/
PAn/Zoom/TWist/CLip/Hide/Off/
Undo/<eXit>: *Press Enter*

---

You should see the corner of the building in the upper right of the drawing area (see fig. 22.12).

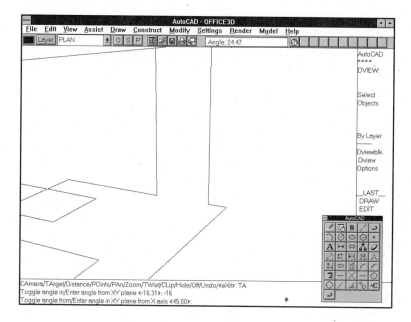

**Figure 22.11:**

The DVIEW TArget option.

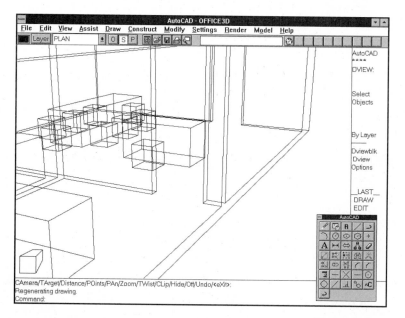

**Figure 22.12:**

The room with a new target setting.

# Selection Sets and Dragging in DVIEW

As you adjust these perspective images, you get a feel for your system's performance in updating DVIEW's preview image. Complex images slow the responsiveness. If your entities are extremely complex (with 3D meshes), you might not get a fully formed preview. The solution is to select only enough entities to orient you in the drawing while you are in DVIEW. Remember that the whole drawing regenerates with the view after you exit DVIEW.

# Using the PAn Option To Center the Room View

The PAn option enables you to change your view by moving the camera and target point side to side and up and down relative to the plane of your current view. The target and camera points move by the same displacement, so that the angle of the viewing direction and distance between the target and camera points remains unchanged. You pan by picking a base point and second point to show the displacement. AutoCAD dynamically drags the image as you drag the second point. In parallel projection, this effect is just like the effect of the PAN command. The entire image shifts, but the relative visual positions of objects remain unchanged. In perspective projection, the relative visual positions shift in the perspective as the image pans.

Try centering the desk in your current view of the room with the next exercise until it looks like figure 22.13.

---

## Centering the Room with PAn

Continue from the previous exercise.

```
Command: Choose View,
then Set View, then Dview

Command: _dview

Select objects: P ↵

Select objects: Press Enter

CAmera/TArget/Distance/POints/      Starts the PAn option
PAn/Zoom/TWist/CLip/Hide/Off/
Undo/<eXit>: PA ↵

Displacement base point: Pick
any point near the desk

Second point: Drag desk to center
of viewport and pick, then press Enter
```

---

You should have a perspective view with the desk centered in the room (see fig. 22.13).

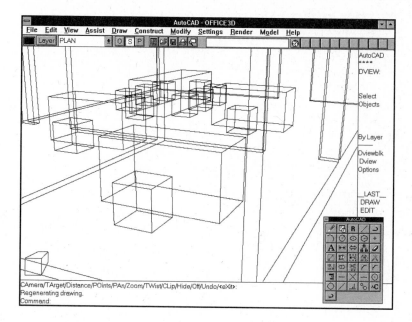

**Figure 22.13:**

The view after using DVIEW's PAn option.

*Sometimes it can be difficult to make the perspective view pan to fill the drawing area. But you should be able to achieve the effect you want by using a combination of PAn and Distance. Use, for example, PAn to center your view, and then use the Distance slider bar or try entering different distances to get the view you want.*

## Organizing Your Views

After you set up perfect perspectives, you can save and later restore them by using the VIEW command or its dialog-equivalent: DDVIEW. In the Distance option exercise, you saved the original perspective view as a view named OFFICE1. You use the DDVIEW command to restore it in the next exercise. DDVIEW, like VIEW, can name and save perspective views just like normal views. By saving a view, you store all of the current DVIEW settings so that you can go about your work and later use DDVIEW to return your saved perspective view to the current viewport.

You can also save a collection of views including perspectives in multiple viewports. See Chapter 5 for details.

# Previewing Hidden-Line Removal Using the Hide Option

DVIEW's Hide option has two purposes. The first is to check your clipping settings while you are in DVIEW. (You do clipping in the next section.) The second is to preview a selection of objects and get the view you want before doing a more time-consuming hidden-line removal with HIDE. DVIEW Hide works like the HIDE command, except you see the hide in perspective. DVIEW Hide, however, is temporary and affects only the entities selected. When you exit DVIEW, AutoCAD regenerates the drawing without the hide. To hide the full drawing, use the HIDE command.

You already have a perspective view saved as the OFFICE1 view, so use DDVIEW to restore it (see fig. 22.14). Then try the Hide option.

---

### Using DVIEW's Hide Option

Continue from the previous exercise.

*Choose* **V**iew, *then* **S**e**t** View,
*then* **N**amed view, *select view*
*OFFICE1 (see fig. 22.14), then*
*choose* **R**estore, *and then* OK

Command: *Choose* **V**iew, *then*
**S**e**t** View, *then* **D**view

Command: _dview

Select objects: **P** ↵

Select objects: *Press Enter*

CAmera/TArget/Distance/                    Starts the Hide option
POints/PAn/Zoom/TWist/
CLip/Hide/Off/Undo/
<eXit>: **H** ↵

Hiding lines: done 100%                     Hides everything (see fig. 22.15)

CAmera/TArget/Distance/                     Regenerates the drawing and undoes
POints/PAn/Zoom/TWist/CLip/                 the Hide
Hide/Off/Undo/<eXit>: *Press Enter*

---

Figure 22.15 shows that everything is hidden. You cannot see anything but the nearest corner of the wall. You must set up a front clipping plane to see what is inside.

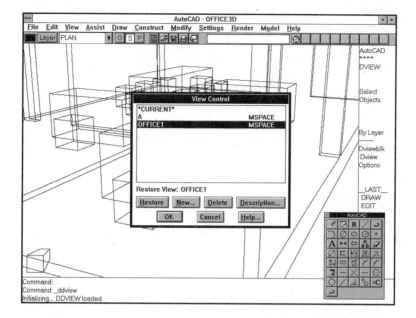

**Figure 22.14:**

Using DDVIEW to restore view OFFICE1.

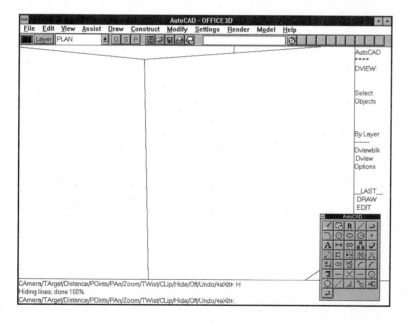

**Figure 22.15:**

Results of DVIEW Hide.

# Using DVIEW Clip To Remove Obstructions

When you used the DVIEW Hide option on the office, the two walls forming the nearest corner obstructed your view. To present the objects of interest in your drawing, you often want to remove objects in the foreground from the view. When you work in complex 3D wireframes, you often need to suppress the display of objects in the foreground or background that cannot be off with the LAYER command. The DVIEW CLip option enables you to place a front and a back clipping plane (or both) to get these effects. A *back clipping plane* obscures all objects behind it; a *front clipping plane* removes all objects in front of it. Clipping works in both parallel and perspective projection.

Clipping planes are perpendicular to the line of sight between the camera and the target. You place clipping planes by specifying their distances from the target. A positive distance puts the plane between the target and the camera (or behind the camera), whereas a negative distance puts it beyond the target. You can also set the front clipping plane to be at the camera with the CLip Front Eye option sequence. The CLip option gives you a Back/Front/<Off> prompt, which you use to set the back or front clipping distances or turn clipping off. Off turns both planes off, but the Back option also has an independent on/off option to control it.

When working with the first perspective drawing, before setting the camera-to-target distance to 19 feet, you might have noticed the front plane clipping effect. After you switch perspective mode on, it turns the front clip on and defaults its location to the current camera position (like the Eye option).

Next you try clipping the nearest corner and background (see fig. 22.16). Put your front clipping plane about two-and-a-half feet from the target. Then issue the Hide option again for an unobstructed view of the desk and chair (see fig. 22.17). Before you exit Dview to see the full drawing, set the back clipping plane to about minus 10 feet (just beyond the room) to clip out the background clutter. Then issue a SHADE or HIDE command.

---

## Using CLip To See into the Room and Remove Background Clutter

Continue from the previous exercise.

Command: **DVIEW** ↵

Select objects: **P** ↵

Select objects: *Press Enter*

CAmera/TArget/Distance/POints/
PAn/Zoom/TWist/CLip/Hide/Off/
Undo/<eXit>: *From the screen menu,
choose* Options, *then* CLip

| | |
|---|---|
| Back/Front/<Off>: **F** ↵ | Specifies the front clipping plane |
| Eye/<Distance from target><br><19'-0">:**2'8** ↵ | Sets clipping plane |

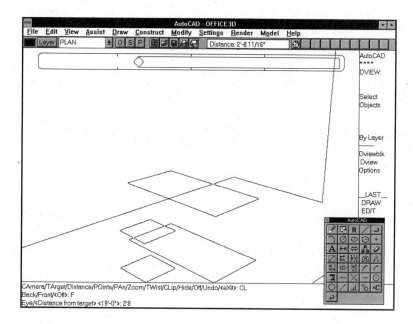

**Figure 22.16:**

Setting the front clipping plane interactively with DVIEW.

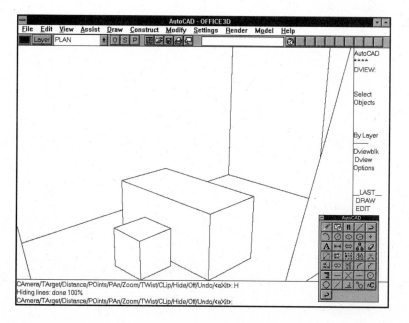

**Figure 22.17:**

Result of DVIEW Hide with a front clipping plane set.

*continues*

Next, you use the Hide option to see into the room.

```
CAmera/TArget/Distance/
POints/PAn/Zoom/TWist/CLip/
Hide/Off/Undo/<eXit>: H ↵

Hiding lines: done 100%

CAmera/TArget/Distance/POints/
PAn/Zoom/TWist/CLip/Hide/Off/
Undo/<eXit>: CL ↵
```

| | |
|---|---|
| `Back/Front/<Off>: B ↵` | Sets the back clipping plane |
| `ON/OFF/<Distance from`<br>`target> <4'-0">:` *Move slider*<br>*bar back and forth, and then position*<br>*the clipping plane just beyond the*<br>*back corner at about -10'-6" and pick* | Moves clipping plane forward and back,<br>and then sets it |
| `CAmera/TArget/Distance/POints/`<br>`PAn/Zoom/TWist/CLip/Hide/Off/`<br>`Undo/<eXit>:` *Press Enter* | Exits DVIEW and regenerates the<br>drawing (see fig. 22.18) |

Now you can see the objects you want to present. It becomes easier to work in the
drawing because most of the background clutter is gone. A little clutter remains in
front of the back clipping plane.

**Figure 22.18:**

View of the room
with both clipping
planes set.

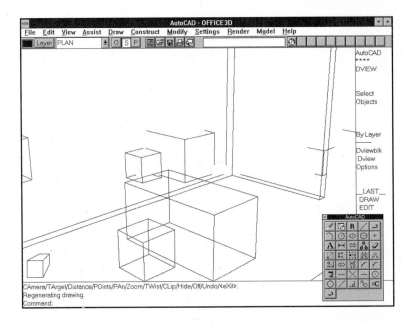

*The HIDE command is faster than the SHADE command in simple drawings, but in complex drawings using the SHADE option is much quicker (see fig. 22.19).*

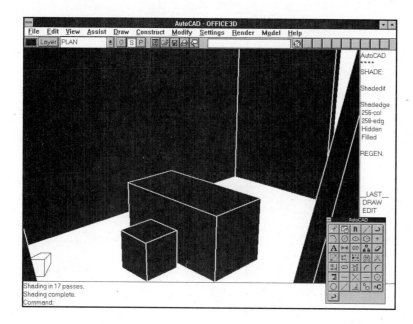

**Figure 22.19:**

The clipped view with SHADE.

 *Watch your clipping values. These values remain in effect after you exit the DVIEW command. If you think you have suddenly lost portions of your drawing, you probably left clipping on. If so, turn DVIEW CLip off.*

## Zooming To Change Camera Lenses

You cannot use the ZOOM command in a perspective view, but you can use the DVIEW command to change your field of view. The Dview Zoom option enables you to "change lenses" to include more (or less) of the image in your view, without changing the location of camera and target points. The default lens length is 50mm, which provides a field of view that looks natural, just as a normal lens (50mm to 55mm lens for a 35mm camera) does for a real camera. An increased lens length (105mm in the next exercise) has a telephoto effect (see fig. 22.20). A decreased lens length (35mm) gives a wide-angle effect (see fig. 22.21). The ZOOM command used on parallel projection acts just like AutoCAD's standard ZOOM Center. The zoom slider and the coordinate readout show the zoom ratio, instead of a lens length.

Use your current view in the following exercise to try switching lenses.

## Using ZOOM To View Room with Different Lenses

Continue from the previous exercise.

```
Command: DVIEW ↵
```

```
Select objects: P ↵
```

```
Select objects: Press Enter
```

| | |
|---|---|
| `CAmera/TArget/Distance/POints/`<br>`PAn/Zoom/TWist/CLip/Hide/Off/`<br>`Undo/<eXit>: Z ↵` | Starts the Zoom option |
| *Drag the slider back and forth* | Changes only the image scale, not the perspective |
| `Adjust lens length`<br>`<50.000mm>: 105 ↵` | Creates a telephoto effect (see fig. 22.20) |
| `CAmera/TArget/Distance/POints/`<br>`PAn/Zoom/TWist/CLip/Hide/Off/`<br>`Undo/<eXit>: Z ↵` | |
| `Adjust lens length`<br>`<105.000mm>: 35 ↵` | Creates a wide-angle effect (see fig. 22.21) |
| `CAmera/TArget/Distance/POints/`<br>`PAn/Zoom/TWist/CLip/Hide/Off/`<br>`Undo/<eXit>: X ↵` | |

Save the drawing and continue.

*The 35mm lens is a good choice for interior room views because its wider angle encompasses more of the room.*

Contrary to popular belief, the lens length does not affect perspective. Only the distance and angle from camera to target determine perspective. The lens length determines only the width of the view. Many people think lens length affects perspective because wide-angle (short) lenses coincidentally tend to be used for close distances and telephoto (long) lenses are used for distant subjects. Unlike real lenses (especially short fish-eyes), AutoCAD's lenses are perfect, with no distortion. They always yield a geometrically true perspective.

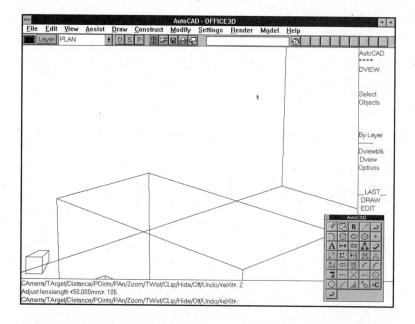

**Figure 22.20:**
View with a
105mm lens.

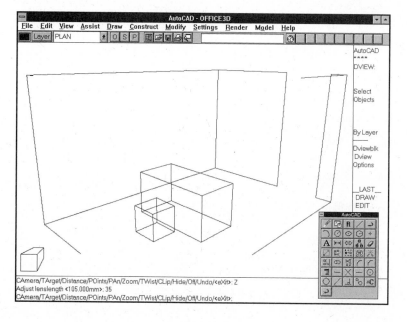

**Figure 22.21:**
View with a
35mm lens.

# Using the TWist Option

DVIEW's TWist option enables you to rotate your view around your line of sight by specifying an angle. Because TWist uses the right-hand rule of rotation, a positive angle is counterclockwise. If you try using the TWist option, you can see how easy it is to turn the room upside down. After you try this option, you can undo the operation to restore the current view.

As you develop a set of views, you might want to capture them as slides for later reference or presentation.

# Making a 3D Slide Presentation

Slides have been the mainstay of AutoCAD presentations since their early use in computer shows. Slides are easy to create and easy to display. When you make a slide, you save a screen image that AutoCAD can quickly recreate on-screen.

## Using the MSLIDE Command To Make a Slide

The MSLIDE (Make SLIDE) command creates a disk file with the extension SLD. AutoCAD does not store all the drawing file information in the SLD file. It only stores the display vector list and colors needed to paint the screen quickly. AutoCAD cannot edit slides. If you want to change a slide, you must edit the drawing file that was used to create the slide and then create a new file.

You make a slide of your current office view in the next exercise (see fig. 22.22). You must exit the DVIEW command and use the HIDE or SHADE commands to get a hidden or shaded view. Then you can use MSLIDE to make a slide named VIEW-1.

---

### Using MSLIDE To Create a Slide of the Office

Continue in the OFFICE3D drawing from the previous exercise.

| | |
|---|---|
| Command: **HIDE** ⏎ | Removes hidden lines |
| Command: **MSLIDE** ⏎ | Opens the Create Slide File dialog box |
| Enter **VIEW-1** *in the* File **N**ame *text box* | Stores image on disk as VIEW-1.SLD |

---

## Using VSLIDE To Display a Slide

The VSLIDE (View SLIDE) command recalls the SLD file from the disk and displays the slide image. When you display a slide, it temporarily paints over the graphics window and leaves whatever you were working on intact and active, but invisible.

To see how this feature works, follow the next instructions to return to a plan view (WCS) of the office, then display the VIEW-1 slide.

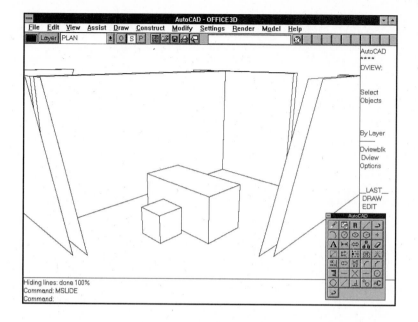

**Figure 22.22:**
View of the office
for slide VIEW-1.

---

## Using VSLIDE To View the Slide

Continue from the previous exercise.

*Choose* **V***iew, then* **S***et View,
then* **P***lan View, then* **W***orld*

| | |
|---|---|
| `Command:` **VSLIDE** ↵ | Opens the Select Slide File dialog box |
| *Enter* **VIEW-1** *in the* File **N**ame *text box or double-click on* VIEW-1 *in the file list* | Displays the slide (see fig. 22.22) |
| `Command:` *From the toolbox, choose* REDRAW | Removes the slide |

---

After you redraw the window, you should be back in plan view.

*Slides appear over your actual drawing. Any attempt at drawing on or editing the slide actually appears on your drawing, which is obscured by the slide.*

*Use a viewport to display a slide for reference while you work in another viewport.*

# Making Slides for a Slide Show

Next you produce a brief slide show, but first you need to create at least three more slides. You create three more perspective views and make a slide of each. These next three views take you around the office plan. VIEW-2 and VIEW-3 provide two views of the large room on the right (see figs. 22.23 and 22.24). VIEW-4 gives a view of the office with two desks in the upper left (see fig. 22.25). Remember these view names because you need them to prepare corresponding AutoCAD Render images in the next chapter. After you create the slides, you use Windows' Notepad to a script file.

## Using MSLIDE To Create Three More Slides

Continue from the previous exercise. (You can cheat and use VIEW with the Restore option and restore the predefined views VIEW-2, VIEW-3 and VIEW-4, if you do not want to go through the whole process with DVIEW.)

Command: **DVIEW** ↵

*Select a representative sampling of walls, desks, and chairs from the large room on the right*

| | |
|---|---|
| *Use POints to set target to 33',33', 2' and camera to 51'6,21'6,5'6* | Sets viewpoint for VIEW-2 slide |
| *Use Distance and accept default* | Turns on perspective |
| *Use Clip to set clipping off* | |
| *Use ZOOM to set lens to 35mm, then exit* | |
| *Use HIDE or SHADE on the drawing* | |
| *Use MSLIDE to make a slide named VIEW-2 (see fig. 22.23)* | |

Command: **DVIEW** ↵

| | |
|---|---|
| *Select Previous objects and use POints to set the target point to 52',35'6,0' and camera to 33',14'6,6', and then exit* | Adjusts viewpoint, but not lens perspective |

*Use SHADE or HIDE and make a slide named VIEW-3 (see fig. 22.24)*

Command: **DVIEW** ↵

*Select Previous objects and use POints to set target to 38',33'6,0' and camera to 18'6, 26',6', and then exit*

*Use SHADE or HIDE and make a slide
named VIEW-4 (see fig. 22.25)*

*Return to WCS plan view of office*

*Use ZOOM with the All option*

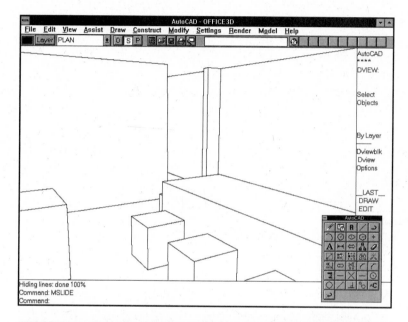

**Figure 22.23:**
Slide VIEW-2.

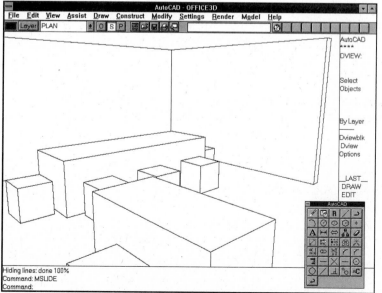

**Figure 22.24:**
Slide VIEW-3.

**Figure 22.25:**

Slide VIEW-4.

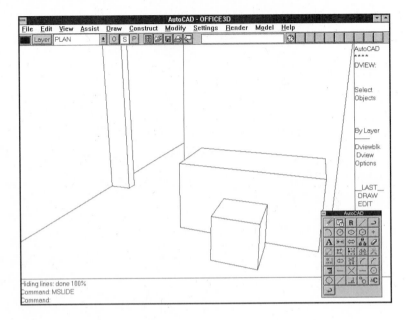

# Automating Slide Shows Using Script Files

You have the slides. Now how do you make a script? SCRIPT is a utility command for hands-free operation. A *script file* is a list of commands, input, and responses stored in a text file and played character for character exactly as if it were typed directly at the keyboard. Like slides, scripts are designed for self-running demonstrations of AutoCAD at presentations and shows.

## Making a Script File for Slide Presentations

Scripts are ideally suited for controlling AutoCAD shows. Script files are ASCII text files and have an SCR extension. To create or modify a script, you need a text editor or word processor that creates ASCII text files. Windows' Notepad accessory works fine.

The IAW DISK has the IAW-SHOW.SCR script file to run the four-slide show. You can examine the script, or create it yourself with Notepad. Enter it exactly as shown in the next exercise.

The SCRIPT command loads and starts a script. Scripts use a DELAY command to control each slide's display time. Delays are in milliseconds (2000 is 2 seconds). The RSCRIPT command repeats a script.

The IAW-SHOW.SCR script (shown following) controls the display of the slides, VIEW-1 through VIEW-4, by stringing together a series of VSLIDE and DELAY commands. The final RSCRIPT command loops the script to start over. After you create the file, move on to the next exercise to run the script.

---

### Creating a Script for a Slide Show

From Program Manager, double-click on the Accessories group, then on the Notepad icon, to start Notepad. Choose **F**ile, **O**pen and double-click on IAW-SHOW.SCR in the list box. If you choose **N**ew and create your own script file, be sure not to use tabs or any trailing spaces, and press Enter to end the last line.

*You see (or enter) the following:*

```
vslide view-1
delay 2000
vslide view-2
delay 2000
vslide view-3
delay 2000
vslide view-4
delay 2000
rscript
```

Save the IAW-SHOW.SCR if you created a new one, close Notepad, and return to AutoCAD.

---

## Using Scripts for Other Purposes

Scripts can do other things besides run slide shows. Scripts offer three unique advantages. First, you can start them outside the drawing editor from the operating system prompt. Second, they can end a drawing, run through the configuration menu, the plot dialogues, and into another drawing. The third advantage is that scripts can loop indefinitely. Scripts are sometimes used to modify or plot a batch of drawing files. For details, see Chapter 13 on plotting.

## Using Script To Run a Slide Show

You now have a script for AutoCAD's SCRIPT command to run. Run the script, sit back, and enjoy the slide show. The slides show in the drawing area, cycling through in sequence and repeating until you cancel the script by pressing Backspace or Ctrl-C.

---

## Using SCRIPT To Run the Slide Show

Continue in the OFFICE3D drawing.

| | |
|---|---|
| Command: **SCRIPT** ⏎ | Opens the Select Script File dialog box |

*Double-click on* IAW-SHOW.SCR *in the list box*

The script commands scroll by on the command line, and the slides display.

Command: vslide

Slide file <OFFICE3D>: view-1

Other script commands and slides appear.

| | |
|---|---|
| Command: delay Delay time in milliseconds: 2000 | Issues a two-second delay |
| Command: rscript | Repeats the script sequence |

Command: vslide

Slide file <OFFICE3D>: view-1

| | |
|---|---|
| Command: *Press Backspace* | Halts the script |

---

If a script has an error, it stops and returns to the Command: prompt. You can correct it with your text editor. Look for the error following the last command that executed correctly.

After you run the slide show, you can adjust the delay or slide name sequence to alter the show. If you want to show slides of your own, substitute your own names and extend the script by repeating the VSLIDE *name*, DELAY *number* pattern.

# Stopping and Resuming Scripts

You can stop a script by pressing Backspace or Ctrl-C. The script finishes its current command and returns to the Command: prompt. You can do some work, and then pick up where you stopped the script by using the RESUME command.

# Slide Library Files

Although slides were invented for presentations, they now have an important use as images for icon menus. To avoid cluttering your disk with dozens of slide files, you can group and store slides in slide library (SLB) files.

To display a slide from a library, use the format *libraryname(slidename)* as the slide name in your script or with VSLIDE at the Command: prompt. When you display an icon menu, you are displaying slides from the standard ACAD.SLB slide library file.

## Making a Slide Library File

You can create your own slide library files by using AutoCAD's SLIDELIB.EXE program. The process of creating a slide library requires the following three steps:

• Make all the needed slides.

• Create an ASCII text file (as an example, call it SLDLIST.TXT), listing each slide name (without the SLD extension) on a separate line. Do not include any extra carriage returns or spaces. Make sure you press Enter after the last name.

• Run the SLIDELIB.EXE program from the DOS prompt to create a SLB library file from your *slidelist*.TXT file and the listed slide files.

Assuming that the slides and a slide list file named SLDLIST.TXT are in your current IAW directory and that the SLIDELIB.EXE program is in the ACADWIN\SUPPORT directory, do the following: From Windows' Program Manager, choose File, then Run, and enter:

```
C:\ACADWIN\SUPPORT\SLIDELIB IAW-LIB <SLDLIST.TXT
```

to create a slide library named IAW-LIB.SLB.

# Using AutoFlix, the Low-Cost Animator

If you like slide shows, you should look into AutoFlix, another Autodesk program. AutoFlix can combine AutoCAD and AutoShade slides with text files and even simple musical notes to create a movie. AutoFlix includes AutoLISP programs to automate the production of slides and shaded images. It can even follow animation sequences. You can make the movies self-running or interactive. Interactive movies prompt the user for a choice and then branch to various movie subsections or even run external programs. AutoFlix requires an EGA (or VGA) standard video card. The AutoFlix program is *shareware*, meaning that you can copy and distribute it freely. If you find AutoFlix useful, you are required to pay Autodesk $35 for it.

If you are a member of CompuServe, you can download AutoFlix from the ACAD Forum. AutoFlix is available in a file called AFEGA.ZIP for EGA card owners, or AFVGA.ZIP for VGA card owners. Before you download either file, though, you might want to read the file AFLIX.TXT, which describes what AutoFlix can do in more detail. Many ready-made AutoFlix movies are also available in the ACAD forum. All of the files mentioned here are located in the Shade/Flix/Rman files library. AutoFlix is also included with the AutoShade program.

# Using Autodesk Animator, Animator Pro, and 3D Studio for Creating Presentations

Sometimes putting together a group of slide files using AutoFlix or a script file is not an impressive enough presentation. Maybe you need to add a splash of color, add text and titles, use special effects such as dissolves and wipes, or even add real character animation. For those cases, Autodesk has other answers: Autodesk Animator (320 x 200 pixels), Animator Professional (resolution-independent), and 3D Studio.

Animator offers all the features just mentioned and more. Animator can add color, special effects, and titles to your animation to achieve professional-quality animated sequences.

In addition to AutoCAD slides, AutoCAD Render and AutoShade RenderMan rendering files, Animator can import GIF images. GIF is the popular graphic format standardized by CompuServe. With additional hardware, you can even incorporate videotaped sequences and photographs in your presentation and export presentations to videotape. For an in-depth look at Animator, see *Inside Autodesk Animator* (New Riders Publishing).

Autodesk 3D Studio is a combined modeling, rendering, and animation package designed for presentation graphics. It features a low price and an easy-to-use interface. You can load AutoCAD models into 3D Studio by using DXF or filmroll files, and then manipulate the models in 3D Studio. Or you can create 3D models in 3D Studio with its integrated modeling tools. The modeler in 3D Studio is not as precise as AutoCAD, however, and cannot take advantage of the AutoCAD third-party products available. Nor can you plot out your 3D designs from 3D Studio; you can only print them or output to video tape. You can, however, render and animate your models in 3D Studio in many ways. The quality of renderings made in 3D Studio approaches those of real photographs because you can assign life-like materials and textures to surfaces. You can also simulate realistic shadows and atmospheric effects. When animated to produce motion effects, your 3D models come alive with presentation power. *AutoCAD 3D Design and Presentation* (New Riders Publishing) details the integrated use of Animator Pro, 3D Studio, and AutoShade RenderMan with your 3D AutoCAD models to create professional presentations.

Drawing and editing commands work normally in parallel projection views created by VPOINT or DVIEW, with or without clipping. But drawing and editing are restricted in perspectives.

# Editing, Annotating, and Plotting Perspectives

How do you edit perspective drawings? The big limitation in perspective is not being able to pick points. Several commands do not enable entity selection in perspective because they *require* picking by point. These commands include BREAK, FILLET, CHAMFER, TRIM, EXTEND, the UCS Entity option, and dimensioning by entity picking, but you can still use these commands by typing coordinates or picking in other viewports. Normal object selection, including entity picking, still works with some exceptions.

The PAN, ZOOM, and SKETCH commands are not enabled in perspective. These commands cancel themselves, and AutoCAD prompts: `This command may not be invoked in a perspective view`. Rather than use PAN and ZOOM, use DVIEW's PAn and Zoom options. These limitations are not severe, largely because you can easily use DVIEW in multiple viewports.

## Using Viewports To Work with Perspective Views

Rather than trying to work directly in a perspective view, you can use multiple viewports. Enter points in one viewport while you observe your perspective in another. Any command you execute in a normal viewport is reflected in the perspective viewport. As you modify your drawing, the perspective view updates to match the changes.

This last exercise has three mview viewports set up: use one for a perspective view, another for editing in parallel projection, and a third for plan view editing (see fig. 22.26). Use the HIDE option in the perspective viewport because you cannot select objects after invoking the SHADE command.

---

### Editing a Perspective in Viewports

Begin a drawing named OFFICE3D=IAW-OFF2.

Make the right viewport active and issue the HIDE command.

`Command:` *From the toolbox, choose* MOVE

`Command: move`

`Select objects:` *Select desk and chair and press Enter*　　　Object selection work fine

*continues*

Base point or displacement: *Try to pick a point in perspective*

Pointing in perspective view not allowed here

*Make upper left viewport current*

Base point or displacement: *Use INT object snap to pick rightmost bottom corner of desk*

*Make lower left viewport current*

Second point of displacement: *Drag and pick in lower left viewport to place desk in upper right corner (see fig. 22.27)*

---

As you dragged the desk and chair in the lower left viewport, the images dragged along in all viewports (see fig. 22.27). When you issue REDRAWALL, you clean up the upper left viewport, but the right viewport requires re-hiding. If the right viewport were not hidden, a REDRAWALL would clean it up too.

**Figure 22.26:**

The three viewports before editing.

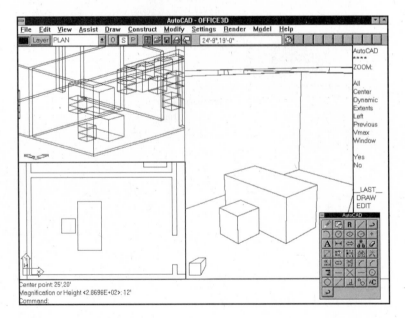

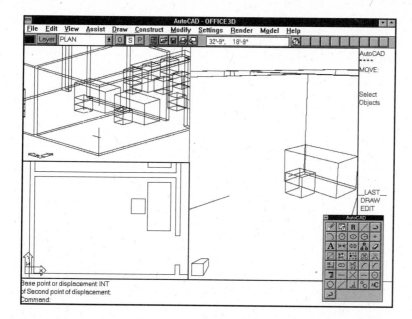

**Figure 22.27:**

The three viewports after MOVE.

# Annotating and Plotting Perspective Drawings

Sooner or later, you will want to enhance or annotate a 3D perspective image. You can plot a single perspective image by plotting the current viewport. What you see is what you get, except for any hides or shades. You can use the PLOT command's hidden-line removal option if you want to.

But you might want to plot the perspective on a sheet with a title or other images, or with annotations, or do a bit of rendering to it before plotting. It is practically impossible to add title text, annotations, or draw a border around a perspective view in 3D. Placing 3D trees and shrubs around a building perspective is impractical and makes the drawing slow to regenerate.

The best way to compose and annotate a perspective is to use paper space. Then you can use all of AutoCAD's commands to annotate and add rendering details to the drawing. Treat a perspective view in a paper space viewport just like any other viewport. You can add 2D annotation and other details to the view in paper space and plot the results. If you plot in paper space, the view(s) that are current at plot time, parallel or perspective, clipped or not, are the views that get plotted. To have the plot remove hidden lines in a particular viewport, select it by using the MVIEW Hideplot option. See Chapter 13 for details on composing and plotting in paper space.

# Summary

Do not get carried away with 3D and perspectives. Use them when you need to, but 2D is simpler and quicker if 3D is not really required.

Here are some techniques for speed and efficiency when you use DVIEW:

- Use the DVIEW house icon (or your own custom icon) instead of selecting complex entities.

- Select a representative subset of entities to use in DVIEW.

- Use block redefinition, substituting simple blocks for complex ones until you get it right, and then swap them back for the final presentation images.

- Use object snaps and point filters to set points in DVIEW instead of using trial and error (unless in perspective). If you know where you want to look from (camera point) and what you want to look at (target point), then you can use object snaps and XYZ point filters to align them with known geometry. When setting perspectives, get the points ahead of time using the ID command.

- Use sliders for dynamic image adjustment, and then enter exact values if you need precision in your views.

- Use named views to save and restore your perspectives and other DVIEW settings after you get them right.

Your introduction to 3D drawing in AutoCAD is now complete. In Chapter 20, you saw how to simulate 3D with isometric drawing techniques, explored the use of User Coordinate Systems, and applied the 2D tools you already knew to manipulating objects in 3D. In Chapter 21, you looked at AutoCAD's special 3D objects, used AutoCAD's 3D mesh creation tools to model complex surfaces, and practiced using 3D blocks as components to assemble a sophisticated model. Finally, in this chapter you learned to create any view of your 3D model you need, and got some ideas about using your 3D skills to prepare persuasive and informative presentations.

# APPENDIX A

# Installing, Configuring, and Troubleshooting

This appendix explains the AutoCAD workstation and installation setup you need to be able to work through the exercises in this book. In addition, the appendix discusses the following topics:

- Installing and configuring AutoCAD on your system

- Managing your hard drive

- Resolving common AutoCAD errors

- Using AutoCAD's tablet menu

This appendix discusses many of the configuration settings and setup techniques that control AutoCAD and improve its performance. It is not practical for this book to discuss all possible configurations and their variables in detail. The aim, instead, is to acquaint you with the possibilities available. For more information, refer to the *Installation and Performance Guide*, or the README.DOC file that comes with AutoCAD for Windows.

# Preparing for Installation

As with any program, the way you use AutoCAD determines the type of hardware best suited to your application. If you use AutoCAD in an educational environment, for example, your hardware requirements are naturally not as critical as those of a production environment. AutoCAD for Windows requires the following minimum hardware and software configuration:

- **An 80386-based computer.** In an educational environment, an 80386SX-based system is adequate for 2D work. For maximum efficiency, production drafters need a 33 MHz 80386DX-based system or better. AutoCAD for Windows uses special features of the 80386 to operate faster. You may encounter difficulties if you try to run AutoCAD on computers that have incompatible ROM BIOS, older 16 MHz 386 computers, or computers using add-in SX or 386 cards.

- **A math coprocessor for 80386- or 80486SX-based systems.** An 80486DX chip contains an integrated coprocessor.

- **A hard disk with at least 40M of free disk space.** This free disk space must be large enough to contain your AutoCAD files and drawing files.

- **At least 8M of RAM.** AutoCAD operates faster if you add more than the 8M minimum, especially when working with large drawings.

- **A graphics card and monitor.** Your system must display at VGA or better resolution, and it must be able to display Windows. A coprocessed or an accelerated graphics card is recommended on production AutoCAD systems.

- **A pointing device.** This device can be a mouse or a digitizing tablet with a stylus or puck.

- **Floppy disk drives.** At least one floppy disk drive with 1.2M or 1.44M capacity is required.

- **PC or MS-DOS version 3.3 or later.** MS-DOS version 5.0 or later is strongly recommended.

- **Microsoft Windows 3.1.** Your computer must be able to run Windows in 386-enhanced mode. AutoCAD does not run in standard mode.

*For best results, update your DOS operating system to version 5.0 or later. You can easily remember to keep AutoCAD software up to date, but you might forget to update your operating system. DOS version 5.0 offers valuable features for a customized environment and for optimizing Windows' performance. It also handles memory limitations better.*

# Installing AutoCAD

The following sections list the important processes for installing AutoCAD.

## Backing Up Your Original Software Disks

*Before beginning any software installation, make a backup copy of your original software disks. Always install the software from the backup set of disks, not the originals. Before making backup copies, place a write-protect tab on each original disk to prevent accidental erasure or damage to it. You must have the same number and type of backup disks as your distribution set.*

---

### Using File Manager To Back Up Your Disks

| | |
|---|---|
| *In Windows, double-click on the Main icon, then on the File Manager icon* | Opens File Manager from the Main group in Program Manager |
| *Place source diskette to be copied from in drive and click on that drive's icon* | |
| *Choose **D**isk, then **C**opy Disk, enter the drive letter in the **S**ource In: and **D**estination In: boxes, choose OK, and follow the prompts* | Copies the diskette |
| Repeat this process for each diskette to be copied. | |
| *Double-click on the control button (left side of the File Manager title bar)* | Closes File Manager |

---

The *source* disk is the disk you are copying (your original distribution disk), and the *destination* disk is your duplicate (backup) disk. The destination disk does not need to be formatted. File Manager automatically formats it if necessary.

## Preparing Your Hard Drive for AutoCAD Installation

The speed with which files are accessed on your hard disk drive significantly affects AutoCAD's performance, because Windows must swap program and drawing data in and out to disk when the drawing becomes too big to fit entirely into available RAM. Disk-access time is also important when loading and storing drawing files, inserting blocks, and loading other files.

## Disk Defragmenting and Reformatting

When DOS stores files on your hard disk drive or floppy disk, it must sometimes break the files up and scatter them around, rather than store the file in *contiguous* (side-by-side) sectors. The more you use the disk, and the more files you store on it, the more likely this *fragmentation* will occur. If your drive has been in use for a long time, you might want to defragment or pack the disk. The process of *packing* reorders the files, moving the data around so that your files are once again stored in contiguous sectors. Any small groups of unused sectors that were previously between files are reallocated in larger groups.

To maximize space, you can reformat the disk, rather than just pack it. Because the entire disk is freed by reformatting, you achieve the same effect as packing by copying your files back onto the disk—they are copied into contiguous sectors because there is plenty of free space on the disk. Beware—packing is done without losing data, but reformatting destroys any existing data on the disk.

*Before you consider reformatting any disk or drive, make sure you have a complete backup of all files on it, that you know how to restore them after you reformat it, and that you have a bootable diskette containing your CONFIG.SYS and AUTOEXEC.BAT files, as well as any files referenced by your CONFIG.SYS and AUTOEXEC.BAT files.*

*Use a disk optimizer or defragmentation program frequently to speed up file access on your hard disk. Some commercial disk-management programs not only pack the disk, but repair errors and/ or check and adjust performance and operating parameters of your hard drive, such as the disk's* interleave *factor (the ordering of the sectors on the disk). See any software dealer for recommendations.*

*It helps to keep each application, such as AutoCAD, in its own subdirectory. File access is faster, you are not as likely to get files mixed up, and future program upgrades are easier to install. In addition, it is much easier to back up your file system when programs are separated into individual directories.*

# Using the AutoCAD Installation Program

AutoCAD for Windows includes an installation program that automatically creates the necessary directories, copies files, and personalizes AutoCAD for you. It also enables you to install only those groups of files you want, which can save you disk space if you do not want source, bonus, and sample files installed on your hard disk.

You need at least 15M of free space on your disk for executable and support files to install a minimum AutoCAD configuration. If you install the sample ADS programs, you need an additional 6M of free space. If you do not have enough space to install the files you have selected, INSTALL alerts you to that fact. INSTALL is fully menu-driven, so you should have no difficulty installing AutoCAD. Because the installation program creates the necessary directories, you do not need to create them beforehand.

To install AutoCAD, start Windows, insert your AutoCAD for Windows Disk #1 in drive A:. Next, in Program Manager, choose **F**ile, then **R**un, and then type **A:INSTALL** in the Command Line text box and choose OK. Then follow the instructions and prompts. If you use a drive other than A, substitute its drive letter for A when you type **A:INSTALL**.

If any of your hardware requires an ADI driver not supplied with AutoCAD, install it according to the manufacturer's instructions and reconfigure AutoCAD.

# Configuring Your System

The first time AutoCAD is started you must configure AutoCAD for your system's hardware, network use, and other configuration parameters. You will need to know what type of graphics controller, plotter, and pointing device you have. If your version of AutoCAD for Windows is licensed for multiple users, you will need to know the maximum number of users supported, and have the server authorization code ready for input.

If you want to create more than one configuration of AutoCAD, create a separate startup icon for each configuration. Each different configuration can specify different ACAD.CFG and ACAD.INI files to support a different set of devices—such as digitizers or plotters, different setups for the same devices, and/or a different set of support directories for different types of projects.

If you need to reconfigure AutoCAD for a different hardware device, the AutoCAD configuration menu enables you to identify and change selected parameters for the graphics display, digitizer, and plotter that make up your workstation configuration.

# Reconfiguring AutoCAD

After AutoCAD for Windows is installed and configured, you can examine or change your configuration setup.

---

## Reconfiguring AutoCAD for Windows

*Choose* **F**ile, *then* **C**onfigure
        Displays release information, serial number, and the following current configuration in the text window

```
Configure AutoCAD.
Current AutoCAD configuration

Video display:....Your current display

Digitizer:        Your current input device

Plotter (#):      Your current plotters

Press RETURN to continue: Press Enter    Displays the configuration menu

Configuration menu

   0.  Exit to Main Menu
   1.  Show current configuration
   2.  Allow detailed configuration

   3.  Configure video display
   4.  Configure digitizer
   5.  Configure plotter
   6.  Configure system console
   7.  Configure operating parameters

Enter selection <0>:
```

---

To configure or change a device driver, select the item you want to change from the configuration menu. AutoCAD asks you questions about your hardware setup, and you respond with answers or a number selection from a list of choices AutoCAD provides. Configuration is dependent on your specific hardware. AutoCAD prompts you to supply values for each device. If you need more information, consult your *Installation and Performance Guide* or the device manufacturer's documentation.

When you choose to configure a particular device in AutoCAD's configuration menu, AutoCAD looks in the ACADWIN program subdirectory and the subdirectory specified in the Environment dialog box for the appropriate driver files.

*If you move the driver files from their installed location, edit the ACAD.INI file to indicate the new driver directory before starting AutoCAD. Change the path after the ACADDRV= setting to the new driver directory. This enables you to reconfigure AutoCAD when you start it the next time.*

*If you need to reconfigure a device that AutoCAD for Windows is already configured for, and you want to start out with or restore that device's default settings, select that device type from the configuration menu and answer* **Yes** *at the* Do you want to select a different one <N> *prompt, and then select the same device from the available device list.*

## ADI Drivers

*Autodesk Device Interface* (ADI) drivers are device driver programs for display adapters, plotters, and digitizers. All AutoCAD for Windows drivers, other than null drivers, are ADI drivers. AutoCAD for Windows ADI drivers only work with AutoCAD for Windows; real mode and protected mode ADI drivers used with DOS AutoCAD 386 and 286 do not work with AutoCAD for Windows. If your printer or plotter requires an ADI driver for AutoCAD that was not supplied by Autodesk, see the manufacturer's instructions. Also, be sure to add any required commands to your CONFIG.SYS or AUTOEXEC.BAT files.

## Configuring Your DOS Boot Files

When your system boots, the CPU runs through a self-test, then reads two hidden files from the root directory of your boot drive. With MS-DOS, these files are called IO.SYS and MSDOS.SYS. The system then looks for two startup files in your root directory: CONFIG.SYS and AUTOEXEC.BAT.

The CONFIG.SYS file contains entries that load system-level device drivers, such as memory managers, RAM drives, and disk caches. You can also load device drivers for peripherals (a mouse, for example) in CONFIG.SYS. In addition, this file contains entries that set the number of files that a program can have open at one time, and that specify the number of disk buffers to be created by the system.

The AUTOEXEC.BAT file contains entries to set your system prompt, set your path and other DOS environment variables, and call batch files or other programs to execute automatically during startup.

You can view and edit these files with Windows' ASCII text editor, Notepad. The icon to launch Notepad is located in Windows' Accessories group. Although Notepad cannot process extremely large files (it is limited to files of fewer than approximately 50,000 characters), it should be adequate for creating or editing most of the text files discussed in this book. For instructions on using Notepad, see your Windows reference manual, or launch Notepad and press F1 or choose **H**elp.

> *Keep your AUTOEXEC.BAT and CONFIG.SYS files as unclut-*
> *tered as possible. Keep your path down to the absolute minimum to*
> *avoid possible conflicts, and only install device drivers that are*
> *necessary in CONFIG.SYS.*

If you edit your CONFIG.SYS and AUTOEXEC.BAT files, your changes do not take effect until you reboot your computer. To perform a warm reboot of your system, press Ctrl-Alt-Del.

## Tailoring Your CONFIG.SYS File

The CONFIG.SYS file is read automatically by the system at boot, and it must be located in the root directory of the boot disk. To examine or edit your CONFIG.SYS file, open it in Notepad, as shown in the following exercise, or use the ASCII text editor of your choice.

### Examining CONFIG.SYS

*From the Windows Program Manager, double-click*
*on the Accessories icon, then on the Notepad icon*

*Choose* **F**ile, *then* **O**pen *and enter* \**CONFIG.SYS**
*in the* File name *box, and choose* OK

Your CONFIG.SYS displays. A typical CONFIG.SYS file includes:

```
DEVICE=HIMEM.SYS
DEVICE=EMM386.SYS
BUFFERS=24
FILES=48
SHELL=C:\COMMAND.COM /P /E:256
DEVICE=SMARTDRV.SYS
```

HIMEM.SYS and EMM386.SYS are memory managers used by Windows and DOS 5.0. Your system may use other memory managers, such as QEMM386.SYS, instead of

HIMEM.SYS and/or EMM386.SYS. QEMM386.SYS (and associated utilities from Quarterdeck Office Systems) can often provide better memory management and more available memory than HIMEM.SYS and EMM386.SYS can.

BUFFERS allocate RAM to hold your recently used data. Use BUFFERS=20 or more for AutoCAD for Windows. If a program frequently accesses recently used data, buffers reduce disk accesses and increase speed. Each two-buffer increment uses 1K of base (conventional) DOS memory. You may have to use a smaller number if AutoCAD runs short of memory.

NOTE

*If you use a disk cache program, such as PC-CACHE, NCACHE, or SMARTDRIVE, set BUFFERS to one. The cache program provides better performance than the use of BUFFERS. One is the smallest value BUFFERS accepts.*

FILES tells DOS the maximum number of files your applications expect to have open at one time. Use FILES=40 or more for AutoCAD for Windows. FILES does not use much memory; a large value helps with AutoCAD and AutoLISP.

SHELL defines the command processor to be used by DOS. By default, the system command interpreter is COMMAND.COM. The setting of SHELL in CONFIG.SYS enables you to specify the amount of RAM to store environment variable settings and other information. Use /E:256 or more for DOS 3.2 or later. If you receive the error message Out of environment space, you may need to try a higher number. Increase the number, reboot, and try the operation that caused the error again. Repeat the process, if needed, until the error message disappears.

SMARTDRV.SYS is a disk-caching utility that speeds up hard-disk access. You may instead have another disk-caching utility installed, such as PC-CACHE from Central Point Software, Inc. Some disk-caching utilities may be installed in your CONFIG.SYS and others may be in your AUTOEXEC.BAT file.

## Tailoring Your AUTOEXEC.BAT File

The AUTOEXEC.BAT file is a batch file like any other, with one important exception: it is automatically executed every time the system is booted. Like CONFIG.SYS, it must be in the root directory.

The AUTOEXEC.BAT file is the place to install your TSR (Terminate-and-Stay-Resident) programs and to declare DOS environment settings you need to complete an application environment (such as the ACAD support variable or the ACADCFG variable). Examine your AUTOEXEC.BAT file—it should include at least the lines shown in the following exercise.

To examine or edit your AUTOEXEC.BAT file, open it in Notepad, as shown in the following exercise, or use the ASCII text editor of your choice.

## Examining the AUTOEXEC.BAT file

*From the Windows Program Manager, double-click*
*on the Accessories icon, then on the Notepad icon*

*Choose* <u>F</u>ile, *then* <u>O</u>pen *and enter* \\**AUTOEXEC.BAT**
*in the* File name *box, and choose* OK

Your AUTOEXEC.BAT displays. A typical AUTOEXEC.BAT file includes:

```
C:\BOOT\MOUSE
PROMPT=$P$G
PATH C:\;C:\DOS;C:\BAT;C:\WINDOWS
SET TEMP=C:\WINDOWS\TEMP
```

C:\BOOT\MOUSE loads a mouse driver. Mouse drivers are sometimes loaded in CONFIG.SYS instead of in AUTOEXEC.BAT.

PROMPT=$P$G tells DOS to display the current directory as part of the DOS command prompt, which helps you keep track of the current directory.

PATH C:\;C:\DOS;C:\BAT;C:\WINDOWS specifies the order of directories that DOS searches when you enter an executable program or batch file name. Your path may include other directories, and it probably contains additional directories. In fact, when you install Windows, your Windows directory is automatically added to your path by the Windows installation program if you choose. You do not have to place your AutoCAD for Windows directory on your path; you specified the location of the AutoCAD executable file when you added the AutoCAD icon to Windows' Program Manager.

PATH is essential for automatic directory access to programs and DOS commands. The C:\ (root) and C:\DOS paths are essential to the recommended setup. If your DOS files are in a different directory, substitute the directory name for DOS in your path line.

*Keep your path short; a long path takes DOS longer to search (the path line cannot exceed 144 characters). Many programs use an installation process that adds the program's directory to your path. In most cases, you can shorten the path by including a batch file directory, such as C:\BAT, on your path and by creating batch files in that directory to change directories and launch programs, instead of having each program's*

*directory on the path. For example, a batch file named WIN.BAT that contains the following lines starts Windows and enables you to delete C:\WINDOWS from your path:*

```
C:
CD \WINDOWS
WIN
CD \
```

The SET line tells Windows where to place temporary files. Your batch file may include lines other than those listed here. Use whatever is relevant to your setup in your AUTOEXEC.BAT file.

## Launching AutoCAD with Specific Drawing Files

You may want AutoCAD to automatically enter the Drawing Editor and load a particular drawing when it launches. You can run the application and load an associated data file by double-clicking on the file name in File Manager.

# Troubleshooting Common Problems

The following sections list some common problems you can encounter in setting up and running AutoCAD.

## Common Problems with CONFIG.SYS

If your CONFIG.SYS settings do not run smoothly, your only indication may be that some AutoCAD features do not work. If you receive the following error message, DOS cannot find the file as it is specified:

```
Bad or missing FILENAME
```

Check your spelling, and provide a full path. The following message means that you made a syntax error, or your version of DOS does not support the configuration command:

```
Unrecognized command in CONFIG.SYS
```

Check your spelling.

Watch closely when you boot your system. These error messages flash by quickly. If you suspect an error, temporarily rename your AUTOEXEC.BAT file so that the system stops after loading CONFIG.SYS. You can also try to send the screen messages to the printer by pressing Ctrl-PrtSc as soon as DOS starts reading the CONFIG.SYS file. Press Ctrl-PrtSc again to turn the printer echo off.

# Common Problems with AUTOEXEC.BAT

Errors in the AUTOEXEC.BAT file can have many causes and are harder to trouble-shoot. Often, the system just does not behave as you think it should. The following lists some troubleshooting tips:

- Isolate errors by temporarily editing your AUTOEXEC.BAT file. You can disable a line with a leading colon, as in the following:

  ```
  : NOW DOS WILL IGNORE THIS LINE!
  ```

- Many AUTOEXEC.BAT files have echo to the screen turned off by the command ECHO OFF or @ECHO OFF. Disable echo off to see what they are doing and put a leading colon on the line.

- To record or study what is happening more closely, echo to the printer by pressing Ctrl-PrtSc while booting.

- Make sure the prompt, path, and other environment settings precede any TSR (memory-resident) programs in the file.

- Check your path for completeness and syntax. Unsophisticated programs that require support or overlay files, in addition to their EXE or COM files, may not work, even if they are in the path. Directories do not need to be in the path unless you want to execute files in them from other directories.

- The APPEND command (DOS 3.3 or later) works like PATH to enable programs to find their support and overlay files in other directories. It uses about 5K of RAM. All files in an appended directory are recognized by programs as if they were in the current directory.

*If you use APPEND, use it* cautiously. *If you modify a file in an appended directory, the modified file is written to the current directory,* not *to the appended directory. When you load an AutoCAD MNU file from an appended directory, you create an MNX file in the current directory. AutoCAD searches an appended directory before completing its normal directory search pattern, so appended support files are loaded instead of those in the current directory.*

- SET environment errors are often obscure. Enter **SET** to see your current environment settings. If a setting is truncated or missing, you probably are out of environment space. Fix it in your CONFIG.SYS file (refer to the discussion of the DOS shell command, earlier in this chapter). Do not use extraneous spaces in a SET statement.

- If your AUTOEXEC.BAT file does not seem to complete its execution, you may have tried to execute another BAT file from your AUTOEXEC.BAT file. If you nest execution of BAT files, the second one takes over and the first is not completed. To solve this problem with DOS 3.3 or later, use the following:

```
CALL NAME
```

- If you are fighting for memory, insert temporary lines in the AUTOEXEC.BAT file to check your available memory. After you determine the amount of memory allocated to each, you can decide what to sacrifice. Use the following at appropriate points to display the remaining memory:

```
CHKDSK
PAUSE
```

In DOS 5.0 or later, replace CHKDSK with MEM. Reboot to see the effect. Remove the lines after you are done.

- Run CHKDSK /F at the DOS prompt on a regular basis. It verifies your hard disk file structure and frees up any lost clusters found. *Lost clusters* are sometimes created when programs crash. Answer **N** when it asks if you want to convert the clusters to files. You cannot run CHKDSK /F from the Shell command in AutoCAD or from a Windows DOS prompt.

- If you have unusual occurrences or lockups, and you use TSRs, the TSRs may be the source of the problems, although cause and effect can be hard to pin down. Disable TSRs one at a time in your AUTOEXEC file, then reboot and test.

## Memory Problems

If you exit AutoCAD for Windows, and then try to reopen it, you may see an `insufficient memory to run application` error message in an alert box. If so, choose OK and try again. It usually works the second time. If this does not work, you have to completely exit Windows, and then start Windows again.

## Problems with ADI Drivers

If you have a problem with a device that uses an ADI driver, contact your dealer or the manufacturer for help.

## Finding Support Files

When you ask AutoCAD to find a support file (such as a menu file), it searches in a particular order. AutoCAD typically searches the current directory, then the current drawing's directory, then the designated support directory(ies), and finally the program directory, home of ACAD.EXE. If you keep AutoCAD's search order in mind, you can prevent AutoCAD from finding the wrong support files. If AutoCAD loads the wrong support files, you may find that the designated support directory(ies) are set incorrectly.

In AutoCAD for Windows, you have three ways to specify configuration and support directories. You can set DOS environment variables before starting Windows, set parameters in the Environment dialog box, and use command line parameters in the startup icon. The order of supersession is: command line parameter > environment dialog > DOS environment variable.

Be sure to clear DOS environment variables when you are not using them. Doing so frees environment space and so lessens the likelihood of configuration problems.

## Tracing and Curing Errors

You are your own best source for error diagnosis. Log any problems as they occur so that you can begin to recognize any patterns. Here are some tips and techniques:

- Scroll back through the text window to see what happened.

- If you can repeat the problem, turn on the log file to capture it, then print the file after you close it. (Refer to Chapter 18 for a discussion of the log file.)

- Write down what you did in as much detail as possible, as far back as you can remember.

- Use the AutoCAD STATUS command to check settings.

- Check related system variable settings.

- Check the AutoCAD for Windows environment settings.

- Check AutoCAD startup command line parameters.

- Use the DOS command SET to check settings.

## Clearing Up File Problems After a System Crash

When your system goes down unexpectedly in the middle of an AutoCAD session, you can end up with extraneous files on disk or with files locked and inaccessible.

Run CHKDSK /F at the DOS prompt after exiting Windows to restore any disk space occupied by abandoned sessions. Do not run CHKDSK /F from the AutoCAD Shell or from Windows.

## Removing Extraneous Files After a Crash

When AutoCAD terminates abnormally, you may find files on your hard drive with the extension ac$. Normally, AutoCAD erases these files whenever you exit the program. If the system is turned off, crashes, or locks up for some reason, however, the files remain on your disk until you erase them. The $ is the convention for designating a temporary file. As long as no application programs are currently running, you can delete any file names that begin with a $ or that have a $ in their extension.

Look for these files in the drawing directory, the ACAD directory, and in the root directory of the drive from which you started AutoCAD. Use the DOS DEL or ERASE commands or choose **D**elete under the **F**ile pull-down menu in Windows' File Manager to erase these files. From DOS, you can erase all files having an extension of AC$ by entering the following in each directory where they are found:

```
DEL *.AC$
```

## Unlocking Locked Files

If file locking is enabled and your AutoCAD session terminates abnormally, the drawing file you were editing remains locked. If you try to edit it again, AutoCAD refuses access to the file. Locked files are designated by a small lock file with the same name as the file it locks, but with a K as the last letter of its extension. For example, the ACADWIN.MNX file is locked if an ACADWIN.MNK file exists in the same directory.

To unlock a locked file, first verify that the file is not actually in use by someone else, such as on a network. If it is not, choose **F**ile, then **U**tilities to access the File Utilities dialog box. Click on **U**nlock file. A standard AutoCAD file dialog box appears. Select all the files you want to unlock and click on OK. AutoCAD then unlocks the files. The File Utilities dialog box reappears and tells you how many files were unlocked.

## Recovering Corrupted Drawings

If you receive an error message beginning with words like EREAD or SCANDR when trying to load a drawing, the file may be corrupted. AutoCAD itself might be able to salvage some or all of it, and third-party drawing recovery utilities also work well. As a last resort, you may have to draw the work again.

The Reco**v**er damaged drawing option under the **F**ile pull-down menu recovers as much of your drawing as possible. You can process multiple drawings by using the same wild-card conventions available in AutoCAD and by entering several names separated by commas. The option performs an automatic audit of the files and presents you with the results in the drawing editor. Any warning messages AutoCAD displays are also written to a log file with the same name as the recovered drawing except the extension, which is ADT.

# Using AutoCAD's Standard Tablet Menu

AutoCAD comes with a standard tablet menu, shown in figure A.1, and includes a plastic template for an 11×11-inch digitizer tablet. To use the standard AutoCAD tablet menu, affix the AutoCAD standard plastic template to your digitizer and use the AutoCAD TABLET command to let the program know where the tablet "boxes" are located.

## Figure A.1:

The standard
AutoCAD tablet
menu.

## The TABLET.DWG Drawing

AutoCAD also comes with a drawing file, TABLET.DWG, which reproduces the plastic template menu. You can use this drawing to create a custom template drawing for your digitizer.

If you know how to edit drawings and customize the tablet menu, you can make your own tablet drawing, supporting the menu with your own tablet menu programs. If you customize your tablet menu, make a backup copy of TABLET.DWG, call it MYTABLET.DWG, and make your changes to the copy, not to the original. See the book *Maximizing AutoCAD Release 12* from New Riders Publishing for more information on customizing AutoCAD's menus.

# Configuring Your Tablet Menu

This section assumes that you are using an 11×11-inch or larger digitizer configured according to the *Installation and Performance Guide*.

If you are using the AutoCAD template, place it on your digitizer. If you are using the plotted TABLET drawing, trim the drawing, leaving about a 1/2-inch border, and tape it to your digitizer. Because every tablet is different, and because every user trims and tapes differently, you must configure the tablet to let AutoCAD know exactly where the tablet commands are located on the surface of the tablet.

Use the TABLET command from inside the drawing editor to configure the tablet. You see a series of donuts—tablet pick points on the drawing (or template)—that you can use as a guide when picking each of the four menu areas prompted for by the TABLET command.

The standard menu is divided into four menu areas by columns and rows. In figure A.1, for example, the columns are numbered 1 to 25 across the top and the rows are lettered A to Y on the left. Menu area 1 is the top rectangular area. The first donut pick point is near A and 1 in the top left corner. Menu area 1 has 25 columns and 9 rows of menu "boxes."

To configure the tablet, pick three points for each menu area and enter the number of columns and rows. Use figure A.2 as a guide for picking points.

## Configuring the AutoCAD Tablet Menu

Begin a NEW drawing named TEST.

```
Command: TABLET ↵
```

```
Option (ON/OFF/CAL/CFG): CFG ↵
```

```
Enter the number of tablet menus
desired (0-4) <0>: 4 ↵
```

```
Digitize the upper left corner of
menu area 1: Pick point T1-UL
```

```
Digitize the lower left corner of
menu area 1: Pick point T1-LL
```

```
Digitize the lower right corner of
menu area 1: Pick point T1-LR
```

```
Enter the number of columns for
menu area 1: 25 ↵
```

```
Enter the number of rows for
menu area 1: 9 ↵
```

*continues*

Digitize the upper left corner of
menu area 2: *Pick point T2-UL*

Digitize the lower left corner of
menu area 2: *Pick point T2-LL*

Digitize the lower right corner of
menu area 2: *Pick point T2-LR*

Enter the number of columns for
menu area 2: **11** ↵

Enter the number of rows for
menu area 2: **9** ↵

Digitize the upper left corner of
menu area 3: *Pick point T3-UL*

Digitize the lower left corner of
menu area 3: *Pick point T3-LL*

Digitize the lower right corner of
menu area 3: *Pick point T3-LR*

Enter the number of columns for
menu area 3: **9** ↵

Enter the number of rows for
menu area 3: **13** ↵

Digitize the upper left corner of
menu area 4: *Pick point T4-UL*

Digitize the lower left corner of
menu area 4: *Pick point T4-LL*

Digitize the lower right corner of
menu area 4: *Pick point T4-LR*

Enter the number of columns for
menu area 4: **25** ↵

Enter the number of rows for
menu area 4: **7** ↵

Do you want to respecify the screen
pointing area (Y) *Press Enter*

Digitize lower left corner of screen
pointing area: *Pick point S-LL*

Digitize upper right corner of screen
pointing area: *Pick point S-UR*

Try picking a few commands from the tablet and drawing in the screen-pointing area to test the configuration.

Command: **QUIT** ↵                              Quits the TEST drawing

The standard AutoCAD tablet menu is configured for your digitizer and the configuration parameters are stored on your disk in a file.

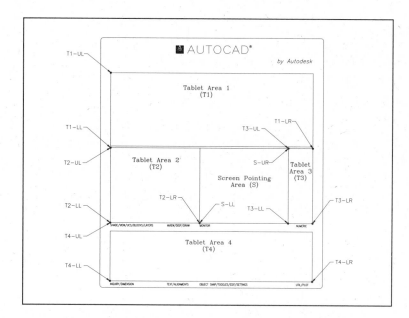

**Figure A.2:**

Configuring the AutoCAD standard tablet menu.

## Swapping Tablet Menu Areas

The process of swapping a menu area changes its function from the default to a different, predefined menu. To swap a particular menu area, select one of the four corresponding tablet swap icons located on the digitizer overlay below the monitor area. The following list describes the default and alternate menus for each swap icon.

- **Menu Area 1**. Top menu area.

    **Default**. AME, Region Modeler, Render and AutoShade menus.

    **Swap**. Replaces AME and AutoShade menus with a blank menu area that can be used for personal applications and menu items.

- **Menu Area 2**. Left menu area.

  **Default**. Display commands are transparent, and VPOINT and DVIEW refer to the WCS.

  **Swap**. Display commands cancel a command in progress, and VPOINT and DVIEW refer to the current UCS.

- **Menu Area 3**. Right menu area.

  **Default**. American units.

  **Swap**. Metric units.

- **Menu Area 4**. Lower menu area.

  **Default**. Object snap picks are temporary.

  **Swap**. Changes object snap picks to running object snap picks.

When you swap a menu area, the corresponding asterisk in the screen menu below [AutoCAD] changes to a number to indicate which menu has been switched. The selecting of [AutoCAD] resets all menu areas to their defaults.

# Windows Basics and Performance

The vast majority of AutoCAD users run AutoCAD under MS-DOS, a command line-oriented, single-tasking operating system. If you are used to DOS, you may at first find Windows bewildering. To help ease the task of learning to use Windows, this appendix provides explanations for the basic operations you use to navigate through Windows.

## Navigating in Windows

You perform tasks in Windows by choosing items from menus, entering text and choosing settings in dialog boxes, clicking on push buttons, and clicking on pictures—called icons—using your mouse. Practically speaking, you cannot use Windows effectively without a mouse or some other pointing device like a digitizing tablet. (To use a digitizer as a mouse in Windows, you must install a driver for the tablet that Windows recognizes as a mouse driver.)

You operate a mouse differently in Windows than you do in AutoCAD, so even though you may have used a mouse for years with AutoCAD, you should read the following section to familiarize yourself with mouse operations under Windows and AutoCAD for Windows.

# Mouse and Keyboard Basics

When you are using a mouse with Windows, you can choose objects or trigger processes with one of several mouse actions or keyboard shortcuts.

## Clicking, Clicking On, and Choosing

The term *click* means to press and release the number one mouse button one time. The number one button is generally the left button, unless you have used the Windows Control Panel to configure your mouse for left-hand use. *Click on* means to place the Windows *cursor* (the small arrow pointing to the upper left) on an object on-screen and click the mouse button once. You may have used this method to select or switch on items in AutoCAD's dialog boxes in DOS versions in the past.

*Choose* is often used in the book in place of "click on" because you can also select most items in Windows by using shortcut keys. For example, "*Choose* File, *then* New" means either to click on the File menu title, and then click on the New item, or it can mean to press Alt-F, and then N on the keyboard. Choose is used instead of *select* in this book for menu items and Windows objects because select is used to refer to AutoCAD's object selection process or to selecting specific text characters in a Windows text entry input box.

## Double-Clicking

*Double-click* means to momentarily press and release the number one mouse button twice in rapid succession. *Double-click on* means to place the Windows cursor on an object and double-click. Double-clicking is new to AutoCAD in its AutoCAD for Windows version.

## Right-Clicking

The term right-click means to press and release the number two mouse button one time. The number two button in Windows is generally the right-hand button unless you have configured your mouse for left-hand use.

*Windows and AutoCAD for Windows ignore the middle button on three-button mice. In AutoCAD for Windows, clicking the right mouse button generally produces the same effect as pressing Enter.*

## Dragging

Dragging in the Windows interface differs from dragging in the AutoCAD drawing. Windows itself enables dragging of Windows objects much like many AutoCAD commands. In Windows, *drag* means to place the cursor on a Windows object, and then press and hold down the number one mouse button while moving the mouse so that the selected object moves on the screen. You release the mouse button to place the object. In AutoCAD, drag means to move the cursor and then click, to specify a window, or to place an object, point, or entity.

## Typing, Entering, and Pressing Keys

The term *type* means to press and release each specified character without any preparatory or further action. For example, *type* **ABC** means only to press and release A, then B, then C.

The term *press* means to press and release a single key, or combination of keys, without any preparatory or further action. *Press Enter*, for example, means only to press and release the Enter key, and *press Ctrl-C* means to press and hold the Control key while pressing and releasing the C key.

The term *enter* means to do whatever is necessary to send the specified characters to a program. This action may include clearing or deleting existing characters from an input box or command line before inputting the specified characters and clicking on an OK button or pressing Enter to send the characters. The characters may be input by typing them or by choosing them from a list, if available.

## Using Shortcut Keys

Many actions in Windows can be accomplished by using shortcut keys. Windows provides two methods of using shortcut keys. The first method uses key combinations indicated in menu titles, menu items, and dialog boxes with underscored characters— indicated in this book with bold underscored characters. To pull down a menu, you hold down the Alt key and type the key indicated in the menu title. To select an item in a menu, you type the indicated key alone. For example, to choose **F**ile, then **N**ew, you press Alt-F, and then N. In dialog boxes, you can generally press the indicated key to select an item in the currently selected group, but selecting an item outside the current group generally requires holding down Alt and pressing the indicated key.

The second method of using shortcut keys is direct access through specially designated keys. The Windows Program Manager **F**ile menu, for example, designates Del as a shortcut for the **D**elete menu item. If you press Del, you select the **D**elete menu item from the **F**ile menu without needing to open the menu. These direct keys are defined in specific applications; AutoCAD for Windows defines Ctrl-V as Toggle VP, Ctrl-B as Snap On/Off, Ctrl-G as Grid On/Off, and Ctrl-O as Ortho On/Off.

## Window Basics

Windows' background screen, on top of which everything happens in Windows, is called the desktop. Applications run, logically enough, inside frames called *windows* on the *desktop* (the screen background). This section discusses how you work with windows. Figure B.1 shows a typical window and the elements it contains.

**Figure B.1:**

Common
application
window elements.

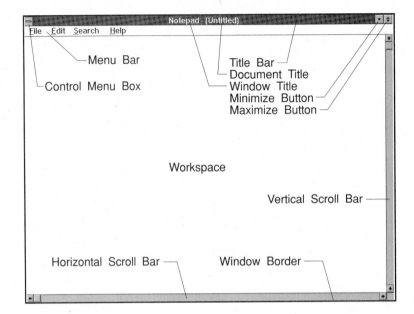

## Scrolling

Down the right side and across the bottom of the window are *scroll bars* (also called slider bars) with scroll arrows at each end. A scroll box is at the left end of the horizontal bar and the top end of the vertical bar. You use scroll bars, arrows, and boxes to bring into view parts of the document that are not in the window. You can click on one of the scroll arrows at the top or bottom of the vertical scroll bar to scroll up or down one line. You can click above or below or to the right or left of the scroll box to move the window's contents forward or backward or to the right or left one window's width or height. If you put the cursor on one of the scroll arrows and hold down the left mouse button, the document scrolls continuously. If you put the cursor on one of the scroll bars but not on the scroll box and hold down the left mouse button, the document scrolls until the scroll box reaches the cursor. Finally, you can drag the scroll box to move to any particular point in the document.

## Closing Windows

Windows offers four ways to close a window (exit from an application). You can exit applications by choosing File, then Exit; you can click on the *control menu box* in the upper left corner of the window to open the *control menu,* and then select Close; you can double-click on the control menu box; or you can press Alt-F4.

# Using the Control Menu

As just mentioned, you can close a window from the control menu. You can also use the control menu to move and resize a window. The next two sections discuss how you can move and size a window directly using a mouse. You can always duplicate these procedures with commands from the Control menu. Refer to your Windows reference manual for specific instructions about using the Control menu.

# Moving and Sizing

You can move a window by positioning the cursor on the window's title bar (where the text `SomeApp - (untitled)` appears in figure B.2) and dragging the window to a new position. To change a window's size, place the cursor on one of the window's borders, and the cursor changes to a double arrow to indicate that you can resize the window. To resize, you simply drag the border. If you place the cursor on one of the border's corners, you can drag diagonally to change both height and width at the same time.

# Minimizing and Maximizing

In the upper right corner of the window shown in figure B.1, notice the button with an arrow pointing down and the button with an arrow pointing up. If you click on the down arrow, the window collapses to an icon at the bottom of the Windows desktop. This action cleans up a cluttered desktop, while the program still runs in the background. If you click on the icon, you open the window's control menu. Double-clicking on the icon restores the window to its previous size. If you click on the up arrow, the window grows to fill the full screen, and the up arrow changes to an up and a down arrow. Clicking on the up-and-down arrow button restores the window to its previous size.

# Using Menus

Below most of Windows' title bars is a *menu bar*. Clicking on one of the headings in the menu bar or pressing Alt-*key* (*key* is the menu name's underscored key letter) pulls down a menu. Figure B.2 shows the File menu pulled down.

You can use the keyboard's up and down arrow keys to highlight a particular item, then press Enter to choose a highlighted item. As discussed earlier, you can also choose a menu item by pressing the key of its key letter.

Some menu items are displayed in gray text, indicating that they are not currently available. To the right of some menu items, a small, right arrow appears, which means that choosing the item causes a submenu, called a *cascading* (or child) menu, to flow from the original menu. Some menu items end with ellipses (...). When you select one of these items, a *dialog box* appears rather than an action being executed immediately.

**Figure B.2:**

A typical
Windows
pull-down menu.

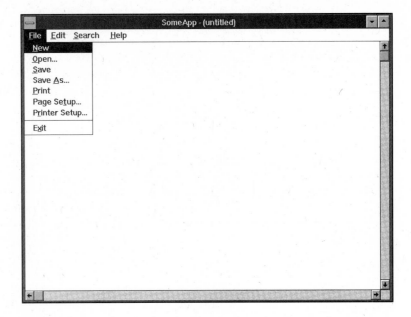

## Dialog Boxes

Windows and AutoCAD for Windows use dialog boxes to request additional information needed to continue a command or to make settings. Small dialog boxes, called message or alert boxes, are used to issue informational, warning, and error messages. Dialog boxes can contain several kinds of buttons and boxes through which you enter information or commands. Figure B.3 shows a typical Windows dialog box, the Record Macro dialog box from Windows' macro recording program, Recorder.

In figure B.3, you can see most of the different kinds of controls used in Windows dialog boxes. The use of AutoCAD for Windows dialog boxes is covered in more detail in Chapter 2.

The following discussion is mostly in terms of using a mouse to activate a dialog box's various controls. As discussed earlier, you can also operate dialog boxes using your keyboard. By pressing Tab, you can move forward through the dialog box's fields and buttons. Press Shift-Tab to move backwards through the box. Usually an outline box indicates the currently selected dialog box feature. You can choose items directly using the underscored *key* characters by pressing Alt-*key* or the underscored key alone.

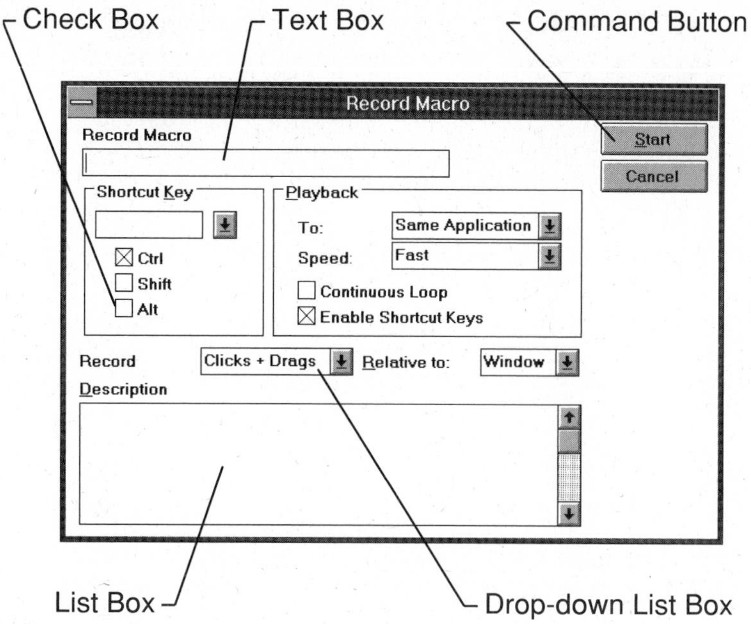

**Figure B.3:**

Typical Windows dialog box controls.

## Command Buttons

In the upper right corner of the dialog box in figure B.3 are two *command buttons*, labeled **S**tart and Cancel. Clicking on a command button initiates an immediate action. When you click on the **S**tart button, for example, Windows begins recording a macro. Clicking on Cancel or pressing Esc immediately closes the dialog box without saving changes. Different dialog boxes have a variety of command buttons, but most have OK and Cancel buttons.

## Text Boxes

Opposite the **S**tart button you see a *text box*, labeled Record Macro. When you click on a text box, a blinking, vertical line cursor appears inside the box. When a text box displays a blinking cursor, you can type text in the box at the cursor position. In this example, you would type a name for the macro to record. You position the cursor in an existing text string by clicking with the mouse or moving it with the arrow keys. You can insert new text in an existing string by positioning at the desired point and typing. The Insert key switches between insert and overstrike mode. In insert mode, the new text is inserted into the old. In overstrike mode, new text overwrites the old.

In many cases, as in the Record Macro text box, after you fill the text box, you can either press Enter or choose a command button such as **S**tart or OK to close the dialog box and execute its action.

You can use the Delete or Backspace keys in text boxes to erase text. Delete erases the character to the right of the cursor; Backspace erases the character to the left of the cursor. To erase more than one character at a time, highlight the text string you want to delete, and then press the Delete key. To highlight text, press the cursor at the beginning or end of the string and drag the cursor with the mouse, or hold down the Shift key while moving the cursor with the right or left arrow keys. To highlight the entire text box, double-click on it.

## Check Boxes

In figure B.3, above the drop-down list box, you see three squares labeled Ctrl, Shift, and Alt. The squares are called *check boxes*. Clicking on a check box either places an X in it or removes an existing X from it. An X in a check box means that the option has been selected; an empty square means that the option has not been selected. You can select none, any number, or all of the options offered in a series of check boxes.

## Radio Buttons

*Radio buttons* resemble check boxes, except that they are presented as circles rather than squares; they are filled when selected rather than checked; and you can select only one of the offered options at a time, whereas you can select as many check box options as you want.

## List Boxes

Figure B.4 shows a dialog box with two list boxes. List boxes may contain more information than can be shown in one box, in which case they include a scroll bar that enables you to display the rest of the choices contained in the box.

To choose a list box, click on it or use the Tab key. To choose and highlight an item in a list box, you can click on it, move up and down the list with the arrow keys, or press the key corresponding to the first character of the desired item. If more than one item has the same first character, pressing that character's key selects each in order.

Some list boxes, called combo boxes, appear directly under associated text boxes. The action of choosing an item from the list enters it in the text box. Double-clicking on an item in such a list is the same as typing text in the text box, then pressing Enter or choosing OK.

In some list boxes, you can choose and highlight more than one item at a time. This type of box can be identified by clicking on an already selected item; if it unhighlights, then multiple selections are enabled. You can choose and highlight items by either clicking on as many as you want or by moving up and down the list with the arrow keys and pressing the spacebar. You can deselect and unhighlight items by clicking on them or pressing the spacebar. Double-clicking on an item in such a list sometimes selects it and completes the command, just as choosing OK does.

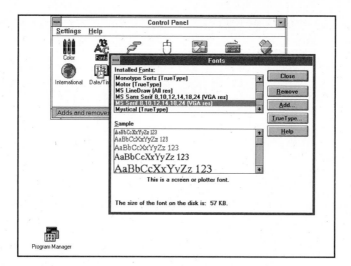

**Figure B.4:**

Typical Windows list boxes.

## Drop-Down List Boxes

In the middle of the dialog box shown in figure B.3, note a box displaying the text `Clicks + Drags` with a downward pointing arrow to the right. This box is a *drop-down list box*. If you click on the drop-down button, the box expands to show a list of choices. Drop-down list boxes work like regular list boxes, except that the list is visible only when you drop it down. You can press a key letter to choose an item without dropping down the box.

# Program Manager

Windows' Program Manager acts as the central control center for Windows activities. In Program Manager, you organize applications into groups, and from Program Manager, you run those applications. You see Program Manager when you first enter Windows. Program Manager runs continuously while you are in Windows. Figure B.5 shows Program Manager.

The *Main* group window is open, showing icons for utility programs you use to set up, configure, and maintain Windows, and program icons for viewing the contents of the Clipboard and for invoking the DOS prompt.

Across the bottom of the Program Manager Window, note the three group icons for Accessories, Games, and Applications. Double-clicking on one of these icons opens a group window that displays icons for programs in these groups. In Program Manager, you can drag the icons in group windows to other groups and to other positions to arrange your desktop. After you exit from Windows, Program Manager remembers your current arrangement in each window (if **S**ave Settings on Exit is checked).

**Figure B.5:**

The Windows
Program Manager.

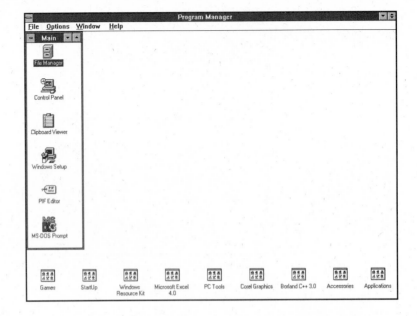

Program Manager can also rearrange icons for you. If you select **A**rrange Icons from the Program Manager's **W**indow pull-down menu, Program Manager neatly arranges all icons in the current window at the bottom of the window. Program Manager can cascade or tile opened windows. Figures B.6 and B.7 show cascaded and tiled windows, respectively. The commands to cascade or tile windows are found in Program Manager's **W**indow menu.

**Figure B.6:**

Group windows
cascaded in the
Program Manager
window.

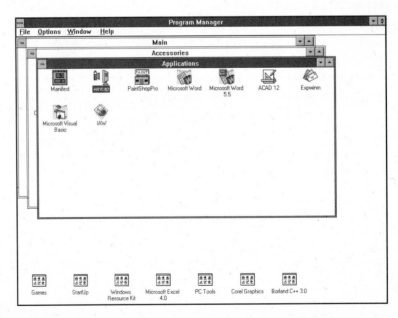

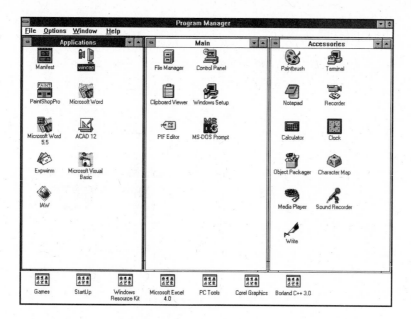

**Figure B.7:**
Group windows tiled in the Program Manager window.

Under the Program Manager's **F**ile menu, you find commands for creating and deleting groups and adding and running applications. The following exercise shows how to create a new program group.

---

## Creating a New Group and Program Icon

| | |
|---|---|
| *In Program Manager, choose* **File,** *then* **New** | Opens the New Program Object dialog box |
| *Choose* Program **G**roup *and click on* OK | Opens the Program Group Properties dialog box |
| *Click on the* **Description** *box and enter* **Inside AutoCAD for Windows,** *then choose* OK | Creates the new group icon |

---

The process for adding an application program icon to the group is similar. Chapter 1 shows how to add a new Inside AutoCAD Release 12 for Windows program icon to a group.

See your Windows reference manual for more detailed information about using Program Manager.

# File Manager

Windows' File Manager enables you to organize your files in directories; to search for, copy, move, rename, and delete files; and to format diskettes. You can find the File Manager icon in the Main group in Program Manager. As shown in figure B.8, when you first run File Manager, you see a directory window displaying the directories on the currently active drive and the files of the currently selected directory. Across the top of the window are drive icons for all disk and logical drives to which you have access. To select a different drive, click on its icon.

**Figure B.8:**

The File Manager directory window.

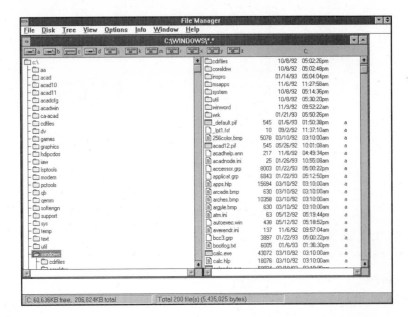

Each entry on the directory tree is designated by a folder icon and a name. Folders with a + symbol contain subdirectories. To see a list of subdirectories, click on the directory icon or name. To see a list of files in a directory, click a directory icon or name. The file list is updated to reflect the file in the newly selected directory. Double-clicking on a directory expands it to show its subdirectories. The + symbols are visible only if the **I**ndicate Expandable Branches option of the **T**ree menu is on.

You can move and copy files from one directory to another with your mouse by holding down Alt or Ctrl, respectively, and dragging the file to the destination directory. You can run applications from File Manager by double-clicking on the executable file name.

You can link applications and the files it creates so that you can double-click on an associated file name to run an application and immediately load the associated file. For specific instructions about creating these associations, see your Windows reference manual or the section in Appendix A on associating AutoCAD drawing files with AutoCAD.

This section about using Windows provides only the most basic information about the program, so that you can get started using the program. Please see your Windows reference manual for a more comprehensive treatment.

# Enhancing Performance

When you run AutoCAD 386 or 286, AutoCAD can use most of your computer's resources for its own needs. When you run AutoCAD for Windows, AutoCAD must share your computer's resources with Windows. This sharing, along with the overhead of the graphical user interface (GUI), affects the performance of AutoCAD for Windows. If all other factors are equal, AutoCAD for Windows runs only slightly slower than AutoCAD 386. However, many of the same strategies you use to increase the performance of AutoCAD 386 or 286 can be implemented to increase the performance of both AutoCAD for Windows and Windows itself.

## Decreasing Initial Load Time

You can decrease the amount of time it takes AutoCAD to load by using a prototype drawing without a menu loaded. When AutoCAD for Windows is started, it loads the ACAD.MNL file associated with the menu defined in the prototype drawing. The default ACAD.MNL file loads AutoLISP and ADS commands and utilities. These files are reloaded when an existing drawing is loaded. The first loading of the support files is unnecessary and wastes time.

To decrease the initial load time, create a drawing without a menu file loaded. You can do this by starting a new drawing, entering the MENU command, choosing **T**ype it, entering a period for the menu file name, and then saving the drawing. Name the drawing NOMENU.

Next, edit the startup icon's properties to have AutoCAD automatically load the drawing without a defined menu. Change the command line that starts AutoCAD to include the name of the drawing you created without a menu. The line should look like this:

```
C:\ACADWIN\ACAD.EXE NOMENU
```

If you use command line switches when starting up AutoCAD, put them after the NOMENU drawing name.

# Creating or Increasing a Permanent Windows Swap File

Windows must be configured with a permanent swap file to permit acceptable AutoCAD performance. The size of the swap file should be as large as Windows allows. The optimum swap file size is 32M or larger. The amount of RAM you have affects the size of the swap file Windows allows.

Windows swaps information to disk when it has used all the available RAM. Normally, Windows creates these files dynamically on your hard drive as it needs space. You can instruct Windows to create a permanent swap file on your hard drive. Performance is enhanced because the permanent swap file occupies contiguous, rather than scattered, disk space. You should defragment your hard drive beforehand if needed to provide a large enough contiguous area of disk space for the swap file. Swap file performance can be further enhanced by enabling 32-bit disk access. The following exercise shows how to set up a permanent swap file.

## Creating a Permanent Swap File

*Double-click on the* 386 Enhanced
*icon in* Control Panel

*Choose* Virtual Memory *in the*
386 Enhanced *dialog box*

The Virtual Memory dialog box appears showing the current swapfile settings.

*Choose* Change

The dialog box expands to show New Settings and displays the largest possible and the recommended swap file size. If you want to create a larger swap file on another drive, change the Drive setting to see if another drive has more space. When a number displays that you are satisfied with, proceed.

*Change* Type *to* Permanent

If the Use 32-bit Disk Access option is available, choose it. See your Windows reference manual for details on 32-bit disk access.

*Choose* OK

You need to restart Windows before your swap file changes take effect.

# Installing Additional Memory

You can enhance your computer's performance inexpensively by installing more RAM. When your drawings grow in size so that they no longer fit in RAM while you work on them in AutoCAD, Windows begins paging drawing and program data to disk. You begin to lose time as Windows reads to and from your disk. The more RAM you can install in your computer, the longer you can put off paging. To determine how much RAM you might need, use this rule of thumb:

3x drawing size + 6M AutoCAD + 2M Windows

A 1M drawing would require 11M RAM to forestall paging. If you typically create 1M drawings, you should have 11M RAM (or more) to accommodate AutoCAD and maximize performance.

## Setting Files and Buffers

DOS limits the number of files that can be open at one time. Because AutoCAD can exceed the default value, you should set FILES=40 or more and BUFFERS=20 or more in your CONFIG.SYS file.

## Maximizing Available Memory

Free as much RAM as you possibly can before running Windows, so that Windows and AutoCAD have as much RAM as possible for their use when you run them. Load only those memory-resident TSR programs you absolutely need. Windows itself reduces the need for TSRs. For example, you may load a TSR program like Sidekick so that you have a text editor available when you are in AutoCAD 386. You can forgo loading this program if you use AutoCAD for Windows, because you can easily run a text editor in Windows' multitasking environment while you are running AutoCAD.

Your disk cache size should also be adjusted smaller for Windows. Many disk cache programs have separate size settings for DOS and Windows. SMARTDRV and PC-CACHE from Central Point Software are such programs. SMARTDRV has a default size of 2048K on machines with 8M of RAM. A cache size of 512K is adequate for Windows.

Use a memory manager such MS-DOS 5's HIMEM.SYS or QEMM386.SYS from QuarterDesq Office Systems, along with DOS=HIGH or DOS's LOADHIGH or QEMM's LOADHI, to maximize your available DOS memory. See an MS-DOS 5 or QEMM 386 manual, or *Maximizing DOS 5* (New Riders Publishing) for details.

## Running Fewer Applications

You can improve performance by running only essential applications in Windows when using AutoCAD for Windows. Avoid running applications that do processing simultaneously when you are working in AutoCAD. The fewer applications you have running, the more system resources are available for AutoCAD's use. In particular, if you have a screen saver utility installed to blank the screen, you should be aware that it may slow down AutoCAD for Windows. (The built-in screen saver in Windows 3.1 does not slow AutoCAD for Windows; you can install it with the Desktop in the Control Panel group.)

# Use Faster Video

A number of manufacturers offer video adapter boards optimized for Windows; they improve screen scrolling and redraw speed in AutoCAD for Windows. Several of these manufacturers as well as other third-party ADI driver developers offer software video drivers that optimize AutoCAD for Windows video performance. See your AutoCAD dealer for details.

# Keep Up to Date

If you are not using them already, install Windows 3.1 and DOS 5.0. They improve performance somewhat.

# Use a Disk Cache

Disk caching programs buffer disk reads to minimize disk access time. SmartDrive, included with Windows and MS-DOS 5, is adequate. The Norton Utilities NCACHE program from Symantec, or PC-Cache from Central Point Software, is better. A hardware caching hard-drive controller is best. (Note: write-caching is not recommended with AutoCAD for Windows.)

# Other Tips

For other performance tips, see the AutoCAD for Windows *Installation and Performance Guide* and README.DOC file. You can also find more detailed information on Windows in *Maximizing Windows 3.1*, *Inside Windows 3.1*, and *Windows 3.1 on Command* (New Riders Publishing).

# System Variables

This appendix contains a table of AutoCAD system variables. Use this table to find AutoCAD's environment settings and their values. Table C.1 presents all the variables available through AutoCAD, AutoLISP, or the AutoCAD Development System (ADS). The system variable name and the default AutoCAD prototype drawing (ACAD.DWG) settings are shown. A brief description is given for each variable, and the meaning is given for each code. Variable names shown italicized must be set by the SETVAR command, because AutoCAD has a command with the same name as the variable. All others can be set directly by entering their name at the Command: prompt (or at the Dim: prompt in the case of dimension variables) or indirectly by using AutoLISP, ADS, or the command(s) shown. All values are saved with the drawing unless noted with (CFG) for ConFiGuration file, or (NS) for Not Saved. Variables marked (RO) are read-only, which means that you cannot change them.

*Variable names and features shown in bold are new in Release 12.*

## Table C.1
## AutoCAD System Variables

| Variable Name | Default Setting | Command Name | Variable Description |
|---|---|---|---|
| ACADPREFIX | C:\ACAD;C:ACAD\SAMPLE;... | | Directory search path set by DOS environment variable ACAD (NS),(RO) |
| ACADVER | 12 | | The release number of your copy of AutoCAD (RO)(NS) |
| AFLAGS | 0 | DDATTDEF, ATTDEF | Current state of ATTDEF modes. The value is the sum of the following:<br>1 = Invisible<br>2 = Constant<br>4 = Verify<br>8 = Preset<br>(NS) |
| ANGBASE | 0 | DDUNITS, UNITS | The direction of angle 0 in the current UCS |
| ANGDIR | 0 | DDUNITS, UNITS | The direction of angle measure:<br>1 = Clockwise<br>0 = Counterclockwise |
| APERTURE | 10 | DDOSNAP, APERTURE | Half the OSNAP target size in pixels (CFG) |
| AREA | 0.0000 | AREA, LIST | The last computed area in square drawing units (RO)(NS) |
| ATTDIA | 0 | | Controls the attribute-entry method:<br>1 = DDATTE dialogue box<br>0 = Attribute prompts |

| Variable Name | Default Setting | Command Name | Variable Description |
|---|---|---|---|
| ATTMODE | 1 | ATTDISP | Attribute display: <br> 1 = Normal <br> 2 = ON <br> 0 = OFF |
| ATTREQ | 1 | | Attribute values used by Insert: <br> 1 = Prompts for values <br> 0 = Uses defaults |
| **AUDITCTL** | 0 | | **Controls the creation of an ADT log file containing AUDIT results:** <br> 0 = No file <br> 1 = ADT file <br> (CFG) |
| AUNITS | 0 | **DDUNITS**, UNITS | The angular unit display code: <br> 0 = Decimal deg. <br> 1 = Degrees/min/sec <br> 2 = Grads <br> 3 = Radians <br> 4 = Surveyors units |
| AUPREC | 0 | **DDUNITS**, UNITS | The number of angular units decimal places |
| BACKZ | 0.0000 | DVIEW | The DVIEW back clipping plane offset in drawing units. *See VIEWMODE* (RO) |
| BLIPMODE | 1 | BLIPMODE | Controls blip display: <br> 1 = Blips <br> 0 = No Blips |

## Table C.1
## Continued

| Variable Name | Default Setting | Command Name | Variable Description |
|---|---|---|---|
| CDATE | 19920702.144648898 | TIME | Current date and time in YYYYMMDD.HHMMSSmsec format (NS),(RO) |
| CECOLOR | BYLAYER | DDEMODES, COLOR | The current entity color |
| CELTYPE | BYLAYER | DDEMODES, LINETYPE | The current entity linetype |
| CHAMFERA | 0.0000 | CHAMFER | The first chamfer distance |
| CHAMFERB | 0.0000 | CHAMFER | The second chamfer distance |
| CIRCLERAD | 0.0000 | | The default radius value for new circle entities:<br>0 = None (NS) |
| CLAYER | 0 | DDLMODES, LAYER | The current layer |
| CMDACTIVE | 0 | CMDACTIVE | Indicates that an AutoCAD command is active (used primarily by ADS):<br>0 = None<br>1 = Ordinary Command<br>2 = Ordinary and Transparent<br>4 = Script<br>8 = Dialog box<br>(NS),(RO) |
| CMDDIA | 1 | | Controls whether the PLOT command issues dialog boxes or prompts; a nonzero setting issues dialog boxes, and 0 issues prompts (CFG) |

| Variable Name | Default Setting | Command Name | Variable Description |
|---|---|---|---|
| CMDECHO | 1 | | Controls AutoCAD Command: prompt echoing by AutoLISP:<br>1 = Echo<br>0 = No Echo<br>(NS) |
| **CMDNAMES** | *""* | | **Names of any active commands (RO)(NS)** |
| COORDS | 1 | [^D] [F6] | Controls the updating of the coordinate display:<br>0 = Absolute upon picks<br>1 = Absolute continuously<br>2 = Relative only during prompts |
| CVPORT | 2 | VPORTS | The current viewport's number |
| DATE | 2448806.36807836 | TIME | The current date and time in Julian format (NS),(RO) |
| **DBMOD** | 0 | Most | **Describes modifications to the current drawing database (sum of the following):**<br>0 = None<br>1 = Entities<br>2 = Symbol table<br>4 = Database variable<br>8 = Window<br>16 = View<br>(RO) (NS) |

**Table C.1**
**Continued**

| Variable Name | Default Setting | Command Name | Variable Description |
|---|---|---|---|
| DIASTAT | 1 | DD????? | The last dialog box exit code:<br>0 = Canceled<br>1 = OK button<br>(RO)(NS) |
| DIMALT | 0 | | Controls the drawing of additional dimension text in an alternative-units system:<br>1 = On<br>0 = Off |
| DIMALTD | 2 | | The decimal precision of dimension text when alternative units are used |
| DIMALTF | 25.4000 | | The scale factor for dimension text when alternate units are used |
| DIMAPOST | " " | | The user-defined suffix for alternative dimension text |
| DIMASO | 1 | | Controls the creation of associative dimensions:<br>1 = On<br>0 = Off |
| DIMASZ | 0.1800 | | Controls the size of dimension arrows and affects the fit of dimension text inside dimension lines when DIMTSZ is set to 0 |

| Variable Name | Default Setting | Command Name | Variable Description |
|---|---|---|---|
| DIMBLK | "" | | The name of the block to draw rather than an arrow or tick |
| DIMBLK1 | "" | | The name of the block for the first end of dimension lines. *See DIMSAH* |
| DIMBLK2 | "" | | The name of the block for the second end of dimension lines. *See DIMSAH* |
| DIMCEN | 0.0900 | | Controls center marks or center lines drawn by radical DIM commands: 0 = no center marks positive value = draw center marks (value = length) negative value = draw center lines (absolute value = mark portion) |
| DIMCLRD | 0 | | The dimension line, arrow, and leader color number, any valid color number, or: 0 = BYBLOCK 256 = BYLAYER |
| DIMCLRE | 0 | | The dimension extension line's color (see DIMCLRD) |

## Table C.1
### Continued

| Variable Name | Default Setting | Command Name | Variable Description |
|---|---|---|---|
| DIMCLRT | 0 | | The dimension text's color (see DIMCLRD) |
| DIMDLE | 0.0000 | | The dimension line's extension distance beyond ticks when ticks are drawn (when DIMTSZ is nonzero) |
| DIMDLI | 0.3800 | | The offset distance between successive continuing or baseline dimensions |
| DIMEXE | 0.1800 | | The length of extension lines beyond dimension lines |
| DIMEXO | 0.0625 | | The distance by which extension line origin is offset from dimensioned entity |
| DIMGAP | 0.0900 | | The space between text and a dimension line; determines when text is placed outside a dimension (creates Basic dimension text boxes if negative) |
| DIMLFAC | 1.0000 | | The overall linear dimensioning scale factor; if negative, acts as the absolute value applied to paper space viewports |

| Variable Name | Default Setting | Command Name | Variable Description |
|---|---|---|---|
| DIMLIM | 0 | | Presents dimension limits as default text:<br>1 = ON<br>0 = OFF<br>*See DIMTP and DIMTM* |
| DIMPOST | " " | | The user-defined suffix for dimension text, such as "mm" |
| DIMRND | 0.0000 | | The rounding interval for linear dimension text |
| DIMSAH | 0 | | Enables the use of DIMBLK1 and DIMBLK2 rather than DIMBLK or a default terminator:<br>1 = ON<br>0 = OFF |
| DIMSCALE | 1.0000 | | The overall scale factor applied to other dimension variables except tolerances, angles, measured lengths, or coordinates<br>0 = Paper space scale |
| DIMSE1 | 0 | | Suppresses the first extension line:<br>1 = On<br>0 = Off |
| DIMSE2 | 0 | | Suppresses the second extension line:<br>1 = On<br>0 = Off |

## Table C.1
## Continued

| Variable Name | Default Setting | Command Name | Variable Description |
| --- | --- | --- | --- |
| DIMSHO | 0 | | Determines whether associative dimension text is updated during dragging:<br>1 = On<br>0 = Off |
| DIMSOXD | 0 | | Suppresses the placement of dimension lines outside extension lines:<br>1 = On<br>0 = Off |
| DIMSTYLE | *UNNAMED | | Holds the name of the current dimension style (RO) |
| DIMTAD | 0 | | Places dimension text above the dimension line rather than within:<br>1 = On<br>0 = Off |
| DIMTFAC | 1.0 | | Scale factor for dimension tolerance text height |
| DIMTIH | 1 | | Forces dimension text inside the extension lines to be positioned horizontally rather than aligned:<br>1 = On<br>0 = Off |

| Variable Name | Default Setting | Command Name | Variable Description |
|---|---|---|---|
| DIMTIX | 0 | | Forces dimension text inside extension lines: <br> 1 = On <br> 0 = Off |
| DIMTM | 0.0000 | | The negative tolerance value used when DIMTOL or DIMLIM is on |
| DIMTP | 0.0000 | | The positive tolerance value used when DIMTOL or DIMLIM is on |
| DIMTOFL | 0 | | Draws dimension lines between extension lines even if text is placed outside the extension lines: <br> 1 = On <br> 0 = Off |
| DIMTOH | 1 | | Forces dimension text to be positioned horizontally rather than aligned when it falls outside the extension lines: <br> 1 = On <br> 0 = Off |
| DIMTOL | 0 | | Appends tolerance values (DIMTP and DIMTM) to the default dimension text: <br> 1 = On <br> 0 = Off |

**Table C.1**
**Continued**

| Variable Name | Default Setting | Command Name | Variable Description |
|---|---|---|---|
| DIMTSZ | 0.0000 | | When assigned a nonzero value, forces tick marks to be drawn (rather than arrowheads) at the size specified by the value; affects the placement of the dimension line and text between extension lines |
| DIMTVP | 0.0000 | | Percentage of text height to offset dimension vertically |
| DIMTXT | 0.1800 | | The dimension text height for nonfixed text styles |
| DIMZIN | 0 | | Suppresses the display of zero inches or zero feet in dimension text, and leading and/or trailing zeros in decimal dimension text: <br> 0 = Feet & Inches=0 <br> 1 = Neither <br> 2 = Inches Only <br> 3 = Feet only <br> 4 = Leading zeros <br> 8 = Trailing zeros <br> 12 = Both leading zeros and trailing zeros |

| Variable Name | Default Setting | Command Name | Variable Description |
|---|---|---|---|
| DISTANCE | 0.0000 | DIST | The last distance computed by the DISTANCE command (NS)(RO) |
| **DONUTID** | 0.5000 | | **The default inner diameter for new DONUT entities; may be 0 (NS)** |
| **DONUTOD** | 1.0000 | | **The default outer diameter for new DONUT entities; must be nonzero (NS)** |
| DRAGMODE | 2 | DRAGMODE | Controls object dragging on screen:<br>0 = Off<br>1 = If requested<br>2 = Auto |
| DRAGP1 | 10 | | The regen-drag sampling rate (CFG) |
| DRAGP2 | 25 | | The fast-drag sampling rate (CFG) |
| **DWGCODEPAGE** | **ASCII** | | **The code page used for the drawing (RO)** |
| DWGNAME | UNNAMED | | The current drawing name supplied by the user when the drawing was begun (RO) |
| DWGPREFIX | C:\ACAD\ | | The current drawing's drive and directory path (RO)(NS) |

**Table C.1**
**Continued**

| Variable Name | Default Setting | Command Name | Variable Description |
| --- | --- | --- | --- |
| DWGTITLED | 0 | NEW | Indicates whether the current drawing has been named or not. 1 = Yes 0 = No (RO)(NS) |
| DWGWRITE | 1 | OPEN | Indicates that the current drawing is opened as read-only: 0 = Read-only 1 = Read/write (NS) |
| ELEVATION | 0.0000 | ELEV | The current elevation in the current UCS for the current space |
| ERRNO | 0 | | An error number generated by AutoLISP and ADS applications. (See the *AutoLISP Release 12 Programmer's Reference* or the *AutoCAD Development System Programmer's Reference Manual*.) Not listed by SETVAR. |
| EXPERT | 0 | | Suppresses successive levels of Are you sure? warnings: 0 = None 1 = REGEN/LAYER 2 = BLOCK/WBLOCK/SAVE 3 = LINETYPE 4 = UCS/VPORT 5 = DIM (NS) |

| Variable Name | Default Setting | Command Name | Variable Description |
|---|---|---|---|
| EXTMAX | -1.0000E+20,-1.0000E+20 | | The X,Y coordinates of the drawing's upper right extents in the WCS (RO) |
| EXTMIN | 1.0000E+20,1.0000E+20 | | The X,Y coordinates of the drawing's lower left extents in the WCS (RO) |
| FILEDIA | 1 | | Controls the display of the dialogue box for file name requests:<br>0 = Only when a tilde (~) is entered<br>1 = On<br>(CFG) |
| FILLETRAD | 0.0000 | FILLET | The current fillet radius |
| FILLMODE | 1 | FILL | Turns on the display of fill traces, solids, and wide polylines:<br>1 = On<br>0 = Off |
| FRONTZ | 0.0000 | DVIEW | The DVIEW front clipping plane's offset, in drawing units; *see VIEWMODE* (RO) |
| GRIDMODE | 0 | DDRMODES, GRID | Controls grid display in the current viewport:<br>1 = On<br>0 = Off |
| GRIDUNIT | 0.0000,0.0000 | DDRMODES, GRID | The X,Y grid increment for the current viewport |

## Table C.1
## Continued

| Variable Name | Default Setting | Command Name | Variable Description |
|---|---|---|---|
| GRIPBLOCK | 0 | DDGRIPS | Controls the display of grips for entities in blocks:<br>1 = On<br>0 = Off<br>(CFG) |
| GRIPCOLOR | 5 | DDGRIPS | The current color code of unselected (outlined) grips; can be a value of 0 to 255 (CFG) |
| GRIPHOT | 1 | DDGRIPS | The current color code of selected (filled) grips; can be a value of 0 to 255 (CFG) |
| GRIPS | 1 | DDSELECT | Controls the display of entity grips and grip editing<br>1 = ON<br>0 = OFF<br>(CFG) |
| GRIPSIZE | 5 | DDGRIPS | The size of grip box in pixels; equals 0 = PICKBOX (CFG) |
| *HANDLES* | 0 | HANDLES | Controls the creation of entity handles for the current drawing:<br>1 = On<br>0 = Off<br>(RO) |

| Variable Name | Default Setting | Command Name | Variable Description |
|---|---|---|---|
| HIGHLIGHT | 1 | | Determines whether current object selection set is highlighted: 1 = On 0 = Off (NS) |
| HPANG | 0 | BHATCH, HATCH | The default angle for new hatch patterns (NS) |
| HPDOUBLE | 0 | BHATCH, HATCH | Controls user-defined hatch-pattern doubling: 1 = On 0 = Off (NS) |
| HPNAME | "" | BHATCH, HATCH | The default name and style for new hatches (NS) |
| HPSCALE | 1.0000 | BHATCH, HATCH | The default scale factor for new hatches; must be nonzero (NS) |
| HPSPACE | 1.0000 | BHATCH, HATCH | The default spacing for user-defined hatch patterns; must be nonzero (NS) |
| INSBASE | 0.0000,0.0000,0.0000 | BASE | Insertion base point X,Y coordinate of current drawing in current space and current UCS |
| INSNAME | "" | DDINSERT, INSERT | The default block name for new insertions. (NS) |

## Table C.1
## Continued

| Variable Name | Default Setting | Command Name | Variable Description |
| --- | --- | --- | --- |
| LASTANGLE | 0 | ARC | The end angle of the last arc in the current-space UCS (NS)(RO) |
| LASTPOINT | 0.0000,0.0000,0.0000 | | The current space and UCS coordinate of the last point entered (recall with "@") (NS) |
| LENSLENGTH | 50.0000 | DVIEW | The current viewport perspective view lens length, in millimeters (RO) |
| LIMCHECK | 0 | LIMITS | Controls limits checking for current space: 1 = On 0 = Off |
| LIMMAX | 12.0000,9.0000 | LIMITS | The upper right X,Y limit of current space, relative to the WCS |
| LIMMIN | 0.0000,0.0000 | LIMITS | The lower left X,Y limit of current space, relative to WCS |
| **LOGINNAME** | "" | **CONFIG** | **The name entered by the user or configuration file during login to AutoCAD (CFG)(RO)** |
| LTSCALE | 1.0000 | LTSCALE | The global scale factor applied to linetypes |

| Variable Name | Default Setting | Command Name | Variable Description |
|---|---|---|---|
| LUNITS | 2 | **DDUNITS**, UNITS | The linear units format:<br>1 = Scientific<br>2 = Decimal<br>3 = Engineering<br>4 = Architectural<br>5 = Fractional |
| LUPREC | 4 | **DDUNITS**, UNITS | Units precision decimal places or fraction denominator |
| **MACROTRACE** | 0 | | **Controls the DIESEL macro-debugging display. Not listed by SETVAR**<br>1 = On<br>0 = Off<br>(NS) |
| MAXACTVP | 16 | | The maximum number of viewports to regenerate (NS)(RO) |
| MAXSORT | 200 | | The maximum number of symbols and file names sorted in lists, up to 200 (CFG) |
| **MENUCTL** | 1 | | **Command-line input-sensitive screen menu-page switching;**<br>1 = On<br>0 = Off<br>(CFG) |

## Table C.1
### Continued

| Variable Name | Default Setting | Command Name | Variable Description |
|---|---|---|---|
| MENUECHO | 0 | | Controls the display of menu actions on the command line; the value is the sum of the following:<br><br>1 = Suppresses menu input<br>2 = Suppresses command prompts<br>4 = Suppresses disable ^P toggling<br>8 = Displays DIESEL input/output strings<br>(NS) |
| MENUNAME | ACAD | MENU | The current menu name, plus the drive/path if entered (RO) |
| MIRRTEXT | 1 | | Controls reflection of text by the MIRROR command:<br><br>0 = Retain text direction<br>1 = Reflect text |
| MODEMACRO | "" | | A DIESEL language expression to control status-line display (NS) |
| OFFSETDIST | -1.0000 | OFFSET | The default distance for the OFFSET command; negative values enable the Through option |

| Variable Name | Default Setting | Command Name | Variable Description |
|---|---|---|---|
| ORTHOMODE | 0 | [^O] [F8] | Sets the current Ortho mode state: 1 = On 0 = Off |
| OSMODE | 0 | **DDOSNAP**, OSNAP | The current object snap mode; the value is the sum of the following: 1 = Endp 2 = Mid 4 = Cen 8 = Node 16 = Quad 32 = Int 64 = Ins 128 = Perp 256 = Tan 512 = Near 1024 = Quick |
| PDMODE | 0 | | Controls the graphic display of point entities |
| PDSIZE | 0.0000 | | Controls the size of point graphic display positive = absolute negative = relative to view |
| PERIMETER | 0.0000 | AREA, DBLIST, LIST | The last computed perimeter (NS)(RO) |
| PFACEVMAX | 4 | | The maximum number of vertexes per face in a PFACE mesh (NS)(RO) |

## Table C.1
### Continued

| Variable Name | Default Setting | Command Name | Variable Description |
|---|---|---|---|
| PICKADD | 1 | DDSELECT | Controls whether selected entities are added to, or replaced (added with Shift+select), the current selection set: 1 = Added (Shift to remove only) 0 = Replace (Shift to add or remove) (CFG) |
| PICKAUTO | 0 | DDSELECT | Controls the implied (AUTO) windowing for object selection: 1 = On 0 = Off (CFG) |
| PICKBOX | 3 | | Half the object-selection pick box size, in pixels (CFG) |
| PICKDRAG | 0 | DDSELECT | Determines whether the pick button must be depressed during window corner picking in set selection (MS Windows style): 1 = On 0 = OFF (CFG) |

| Variable Name | Default Setting | Command Name | Variable Description |
|---|---|---|---|
| **PICKFIRST** | 0 | **DDSELECT** | **Enables entity selection before command selection (noun/verb paradigm):** 1 = On 0 = Off (CFG) |
| PLATFORM | Varies | | Indicates the version of AutoCAD in use: a string such as "386 DOS Extender," "Sun 4/SPARCstation," "Apple Macintosh," etc. (RO)(NS) |
| **PLINEGEN** | 0 | | **The control points for polyline generation of noncontinuous linetypes:** 0 = Vertices 1 = End points |
| **PLINEWID** | 0.0000 | **PLINE** | **The default width for new polyline entities** |
| **PLOTID** | "" | **PLOT** | **The current plotter configuration description (CFG)** |
| **PLOTTER** | 0 | **PLOT** | **The current plotter configuration number (CFG)** |
| **POLYSIDES** | 4 | **POLYGON** | **The default number of sides (3 to 1024) for new polygon entities (NS)** |

## Table C.1
## Continued

| Variable Name | Default Setting | Command Name | Variable Description |
|---|---|---|---|
| POPUPS | 1 | | Determines whether the Advanced User Interface (dialog boxes, menu bar, pull-down menus, icon menus) is supported:<br>1 = Yes<br>0 = No<br>(NS)(RO) |
| PSLTSCALE | 1 | | Paper-space scaling of model space linetypes:<br>1 = On<br>0 = Off |
| PSPROLOG | "" | | The name of the PostScript post-processing section of ACAD.PSF to be appended to the PSOUT command's output (CFG) |
| PSQUALITY | 75 | PSQUALITY | The default quality setting for rendering of images by the PSIN command (CFG) |
| QTEXTMODE | 0 | QTEXT | Sets the current state of Quick text mode:<br>1 = On<br>0 = Off |
| REGENMODE | 1 | REGENAUTO | Indicates the current state of Regenauto:<br>1 = On<br>0 = Off |

| Variable Name | Default Setting | Command Name | Variable Description |
|---|---|---|---|
| RE-INIT | 0 | REINIT | A code that specifies the type(s) of reinitializations to perform. Not listed by SETVAR. The sum of: 1 = Digitizer port 2 = Plotter port 4 = Digitizer device 8 = Display device 16 = Reload ACAD.PGP (NS) |
| SAVEFILE | AUTO.SV$ | CONFIG | The default directory and file name for automatic file saves (CFG)(RO) |
| SAVENAME | "" | SAVEAS | The drawing name specified by the user to the last invocation of the SAVEAS command in the current session (RO) |
| SAVETIME | 120 | CONFIG | The default interval between automatic file saves, in minutes: 0 = Disable automatic saves (CFG) |
| SCREENBOXES | 26 | CONFIG | The number of available screen menu boxes in the current graphics screen area (RO)(CFG) |

**Table C.1
Continued**

| Variable Name | Default Setting | Command Name | Variable Description |
|---|---|---|---|
| **SCREENMODE** | 0 | [F1] | **Indicates the active AutoCAD screen mode or window:**<br>**0 = Text**<br>**1 = Graphics**<br>**2 = Dual screen**<br>**(RO)(CFG)** |
| SCREENSIZE | 574.0000,414.0000 | | The size of current viewport, in pixels, X and Y (RO) |
| SHADEDGE | 3 | | Controls the display of edges and faces by the SHADE command:<br>0 = Faces shaded, edges unhighlighted<br>1 = Faces shaded, edges in background color<br>2 = Faces unfilled, edges in entity color<br>3 = Faces in entity color, edges in background |
| SHADEDIF | 70 | | Specifies the ratio of diffuse-to-ambient light used by the SHADE command; expressed as a percentage of diffuse reflective light |
| **SHPNAME** | "" | **SHAPE** | **The default shape name (NS)** |
| SKETCHINC | 0.1000 | SKETCH | The recording increment for SKETCH sements |

| Variable Name | Default Setting | Command Name | Variable Description |
|---|---|---|---|
| SKPOLY | 0 | | Controls the type of entities generated by SKETCH:<br>1 = Polylines<br>0 = Lines |
| SNAPANG | 0 | **DDRMODES**, SNAP | The angle of SNAP/GRID rotation in the current viewport, for the current UCS |
| SNAPBASE | 0.0000,0.0000 | **DDRMODES**, SNAP | The X,Y base point of SNAP/GRID rotation in the current viewport, for the current UCS. |
| SNAPISOPAIR | 0 | **DDRMODES**, SNAP [^E] | The current isoplane for the current viewport:<br>0 = Left<br>1 = Top<br>2 = Right |
| SNAPMODE | 0 | **DDRMODES**, SNAP [^B] [F9] | Indicates the state of Snap for the current viewport:<br>1 = On<br>0 = Off |
| SNAPSTYL | 0 | **DDRMODES**, SNAP | The snap style for the current viewport:<br>1 = Isometric<br>0 = Standard |
| SNAPUNIT | 1.0000,1.0000 | **DDRMODES**, SNAP | The snap X,Y increment for the current viewport |

## Table C.1
## Continued

| Variable Name | Default Setting | Command Name | Variable Description |
| --- | --- | --- | --- |
| SOLAMEVER | R2.1 | | The Region Modeler software's version number (RO) |
| SOLAREAU | sq cm | | The unit system for area calculations |
| SOLAXCOL | 3 | | The color number of the SOLMOVE MCS icon |
| SOLDELENT | 3 | SOLIDIFY | Controls prompting for original entity deletion by SOLIDIFY command. 1 = Don't delete 2 = Ask 3 = Delete |
| SOLDISPLAY | WIRE | SOLMESH, SOLWIRE | Controls the default display mode for new solids |
| SOLHANGLE | 45.000000 | SOLIDIFY | The default angle of new solid entity hatch patterns |
| SOLHPAT | U | SOLIDIFY | The default pattern name for new solid entity hatching |
| SOLHSIZE | 1.000000 | SOLIDIFY | The default scale for new solid entity hatch patterns |
| SOLLENGTH | cm | SOLLIST, SOLMASSP | The unit system for perimeter calculations |
| SSOLMASS | gm | SOLMASSP | The unit system for mass calculations |

| Variable Name | Default Setting | Command Name | Variable Description |
|---|---|---|---|
| SOLMATCURR | MILD_STEEL | SOLMAT | The default material assigned to new solid entities |
| SOLPAGELEN | 25 | SOLLIST, SOLMASSP SOLMAT | The length of message pages, in lines |
| SOLSECTYPE | 1 | SOLSECT | Controls the type of entities generated by SOLSECT 1 = A block composed of arcs, circles, and lines 2 = A block composed of polylines 3 = Region |
| SOLSUBDIV | 3 | SOLMASSP | The level of subdivisions used by the SOLMASSP command |
| SOLUPGRADE | 0 | | Controls the upgrading of solids from single-precision to double-precision: 0 = Do not upgrade 1 = Upgrade |
| SOLVOLUME | cu cm | SOLMASSP | The unit of measure for volume used by the SOLMASSP command |
| SOLRENDER | CSG | SHADE, SOLMESH, SOLWIRE | The display type for solids CSG = By primitive UNIFORM = As composite |

## Table C.1
### Continued

| Variable Name | Default Setting | Command Name | Variable Description |
|---|---|---|---|
| SOLSERVMSG | 3 | MANY | The level of details displayed by Region Modeler messages:<br>0 = None<br>1 = Errors<br>2 = Errors+progress<br>3 = All |
| SOLSOLIDIFY | 3 | MANY | Controls prompting for entity conversion to solid regions<br>1 = Don't convert<br>2 = Ask<br>3 = Convert |
| SOLWDENS | 4 | MANY | Controls the number of edges used to represent curved solid surfaces displayed as wireframes (Edges=SOLWDENS*4) |
| SORTENTS | 0 | DDSELECT | A bit code corresponding to the type(s) of operations for which AutoCAD should not use spatial database organization and instead sort entities in the order created; |

| Variable Name | Command Name | Default Setting | Variable Description |
|---|---|---|---|
| | | | the value is the sum of the following:<br>**0 = OFF**<br>**1 = Object selection**<br>**2 = OSNAP**<br>**4 = REDRAW**<br>**8 = MSLIDE**<br>**16 = REGEN**<br>**32 = PLOT**<br>**64 = PSOUT**<br>**(CFG)** |
| SPLFRAME | | 0 | Controls the display of control polygons for spline-fit polylines, defining meshes of surface-fit polygon meshes, invisible 3D face edges:<br>1 = On<br>0 = Off |
| SPLINESEGS | | 8 | The number of line segments in each spline curve |
| SPLINETYPE | | 6 | Controls the spline type generated by the PEDIT command's Spline option:<br>5 = Quadratic B-Spline<br>6 = Cubic B-Spline |
| SURFTAB1 | | 6 | The number of RULESURF and Tabsurf tabulations, also the REVSURF and EDGESURF M-direction density |

**Table C.1**
**Continued**

| Variable Name | Default Setting | Command Name | Variable Description |
|---|---|---|---|
| SURFTAB2 | 6 | | The REVSURF and EDGESURF N-direction density |
| SURFTYPE | 6 | | Controls type of surface generated by Pedit smooth option: Quadratic B-Spline=5 Cubic B-Spline=6 Bezier=8 |
| SURFU | 6 | | The M-direction surface density of 3D polygon meshes |
| SURFV | 6 | | The N-direction surface density 3D polygon meshes |
| **SYSCODEPAGE** | **ASCII** | | **The code page used by the system (RO)** |
| **TABMODE** | **0** | **TABLET, [F10]** | **Controls tablet mode:** **1 = On** **0 = Off** **(NS)** |
| TARGET | 0.0000,0.0000,0.0000 | DVIEW | The UCS coordinates of the current viewport's target point (RO) |
| TDCREATE | 2448806.36779607 | TIME | The date and time of the current drawing's creation, in Julian format (RO) |

| Variable Name | Default Setting | Command Name | Variable Description |
|---|---|---|---|
| TDINDWG | 0.00000000 | TIME | The total amount of editing time elapsed in the current drawing, in Julian days (RO) |
| TDUPDATE | 2448806.36779607 | TIME | The date and time when the file was last saved, in Julian format (RO) |
| TDUSRTIMER | 0.00000000 | TIME | User-controlled elapsed time in Julian days (RO) |
| TEMPPREFIX | "" | | The directory configured for placement of AutoCAD's temporary files; defaults to the drawing directory (RO)(NS) |
| TEXTEVAL | 0 | | Controls the checking of text input (except by DTEXT) for AutoLISP expressions: 0 = Yes 1 = NO (NS) |
| TEXTSIZE | 0.2000 | TEXT | The height applied to new text entities created with nonfixed-height text styles |
| TEXTSTYLE | STANDARD | TEXT, STYLE | The current text style's name |
| THICKNESS | 0.0000 | | The current 3D extrusion thickness |
| TILEMODE | 1 | TILEMODE | Release 10 VPORT compatibility setting; enables/disables paper space and viewport entities: 1 = On 0 = Off |

## Table C.1
### Continued

| Variable Name | Default Setting | Command Name | Variable Description |
|---|---|---|---|
| TRACEWID | 0.0500 | TRACE | The current width of traces |
| **TREEDEPTH** | 3020 | **DDSELECT** | A code number (4 digits) representing the maximum number of divisions for spatial database index for model space (first two digits) and paper space (last two digits) |
| **TREEMAX** | 10000000 | **TREEMAX** | The maximum number of nodes for spatial database organization for the current memory configuration (CFG) |
| UCSFOLLOW | 0 | | Controls automatic display of the plan view in the current viewport when switching to a new UCS: <br> 1 = On <br> 0 = Off |
| *UCSICON* | 1 | UCSICON | Controls the UCS icon's display; the value is the sum of the following: <br> 0 = Off <br> 1 = On <br> 2 = At origin |
| UCSNAME | "" | **DDUCS**, UCS | The name of the current UCS for the current space: <br> "" = Unnamed <br> (RO) |

| Variable Name | Default Setting | Command Name | Variable Description |
|---|---|---|---|
| UCSORG | 0.0000,0.0000,0.0000 | DDUCS, UCS | The WCS origin of the current UCS for the current space (RO) |
| UCSXDIR | 1.0000,0.0000,0.0000 | DDUCS, UCS | The X direction of the current UCS (RO) |
| UCSYDIR | 0.0000,1.0000,0.0000 | DDUCS, UCS | The Y direction of the current UCS (RO) |
| **UNDOCTL** | **5** | **UNDO** | **The current state of UNDO; the value is the sum of the following:**<br>**1 = Enabled**<br>**2 = Single command**<br>**4 = Auto mode**<br>**8 = Group active**<br>**(RO)(NS)** |
| **UNDOMARKS** | **0** | **UNDO** | **The current number of marks in the UNDO command's history (RO) (NS)** |
| UNITMODE | 0 | | Controls the display of user input of fractions, feet and inches, and surveyor's angles:<br>0 = Per LUNITS<br>1 = As input |
| USERI1 - 5 | 0 | | User integer variables USERI1 to USERI5. Not listed by SETVAR |
| USERR1 - 5 | 0.0000 | | User real-number variables USERR1 to USERR5. Not listed by SETVAR |

## Table C.1
## Continued

| Variable Name | Default Setting | Command Name | Variable Description |
|---|---|---|---|
| USERS1 - 5 | "" | | User string variables (up to 460 characters long) USERS1 to USERS5. Not listed by SETVAR. (NS) |
| VIEWCTR | 6.2433,4.5000 | ZOOM, PAN, VIEW | The X,Y center point coordinate of the current view in the current viewport (RO) |
| VIEWDIR | 0.0000,0.0000,1.0000 | DVIEW | The camera point offset from target in the WCS (RO) |
| VIEWMODE | 0 | DVIEW, UCS | The current viewport's viewing mode; the value is the sum of the following:<br>1 = Perspective<br>2 = Front clipping on<br>4 = Back clipping on<br>8 = UCSFOLLOW On<br>16 = FRONTZ offset in use (RO) |
| VIEWSIZE | 9.0000 | ZOOM, VIEW | The current view's height, in drawing units (RO) |
| VIEWTWIST | 0 | DVIEW | The current viewport's view-twist angle (RO) |
| VISRETAIN | 0 | VISRETAIN | Controls retention of Xref file layer settings in the current drawing. Off=0 On=1 |

| Variable Name | Default Setting | Command Name | Variable Description |
|---|---|---|---|
| VSMAX | 37.4600,27.0000,0.0000 | ZOOM,PAN,VIEW | The upper right X,Y coordinate of the current viewport's virtual screen for the current UCS (NS)(RO) |
| VSMIN | -24.9734,-18.0000,0.0000 | ZOOM,PAN,VIEW | The lower left X,Y coordinate of the current viewport's virtual screen for the current UCS (NS)(RO) |
| WORLDUCS | 1 | UCS | The current UCS, equivalent to WCS:<br>1 = True<br>0 = False<br>(RO)(NS) |
| WORLDVIEW | 1 | DVIEW,UCS | Controls the automatic changing of a UCS to the WCS during the DVIEW and VPOINT commands:<br>1 = On<br>0 = Off |
| XREFCTL | 0 | | **Controls the creation of an XLG log file that contains XREF results:**<br>**0 = No file**<br>**1 = XLG file**<br>**(CFG)** |

# INDEX

# E

output devices, configuring, 619
OVERRIDE dimensioning command, 830
override modes (OSNAP), 198
overrides, 188-194
overriding
    dimension styles, 834-836
    running OSNAP, 196
overscore (text), 368
OwnerLink data, 909

# P

packing files, 1126
PAN command, 203, 222-224
Pan command
    Aerial View, 228-229
    View menu, 340
PAn option (DVIEW command), 1089, 1100-1101
panning, 222, 232-233
paper
    jams, 666
    space, 244-246
        dimensioning, 812-814
        entering, 247-250
        exiting, 261
        layer control, 648-651
        plotting in, 634-648
        viewports, 1121
parallel
    lines, 440-442
    views, 1084
parametric
    designs, 900
    drawings, 913-914
PATH (DOS) command, 1132
path curve (directrix), 1058
Path option (XREF command), 567

path profiles, 1018
Pattern...name... option (HATCH command), 676
patterns
    brick, inserting, 674
    hatch
        creating, 688
        customizing, 687
        editing, 686-687
        inserting, 679-680
        MUDST, 683
        User-specified, 687
    viewing, 673
PAUSE (DOS) command, 1135
PC DOS, *see* DOS
PC-CACHE program, 1131
PCX file format, 922
PCXIN command, 927
PDMODE system variable, 324
PDSIZE system variable, 324
PEDIT command, 459-473, 1069-1074
    3D meshes, 1069-1074
    fit curves, 474-477
    options
        Close/Open, 459
        Decurve, 459
        Edit vertex, 459-473
        eXit, 459
        Fit, 459
        Join, 459-463, 505-508
        Ltype gen, 459
        Mclose, 1074
        Nclose, 1074
        Spline, 459
        Undo, 459
        Width, 459
    spline curves, 474-477
Pen Assignments dialog box, 660-661

# V

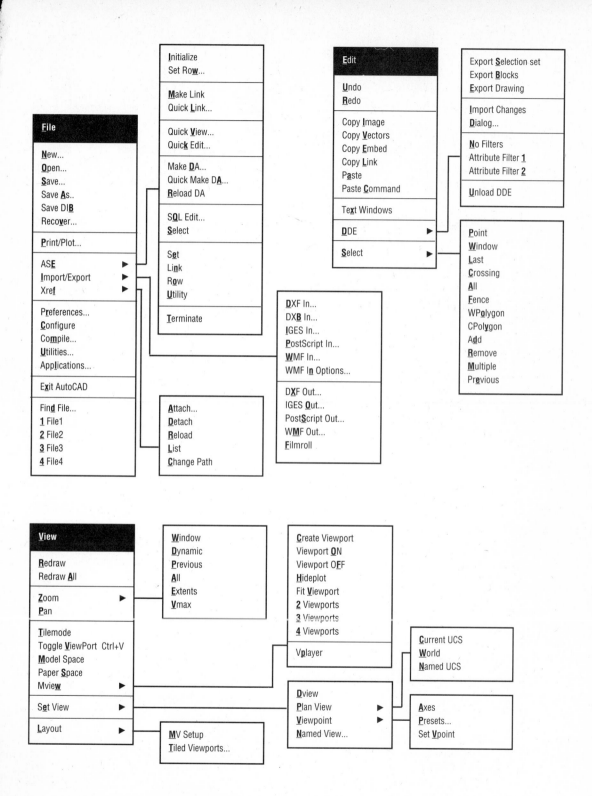

**File**

New...
Open...
Save...
Save As..
Save DIB
Recover...

Print/Plot...

ASE ▶
Import/Export ▶
Xref ▶

Preferences...
Configure
Compile...
Utilities...
Applications...

Exit AutoCAD

Find File...
1 File1
2 File2
3 File3
4 File4

Initialize
Set Row...

Make Link
Quick Link...

Quick View...
Quick Edit...

Make DA...
Quick Make DA...
Reload DA

SQL Edit...
Select

Set
Link
Row
Utility

Terminate

Attach...
Detach
Reload
List
Change Path

DXF In...
DXB In...
IGES In...
PostScript In...
WMF In...
WMF In Options...

DXF Out...
IGES Out...
PostScript Out...
WMF Out...
Filmroll

**Edit**

Undo
Redo

Copy Image
Copy Vectors
Copy Embed
Copy Link
Paste
Paste Command

Text Windows

DDE ▶

Select ▶

Export Selection set
Export Blocks
Export Drawing

Import Changes
Dialog...

No Filters
Attribute Filter 1
Attribute Filter 2

Unload DDE

Point
Window
Last
Crossing
All
Fence
WPolygon
CPolygon
Add
Remove
Multiple
Previous

**View**

Redraw
Redraw All

Zoom ▶
Pan

Tilemode
Toggle ViewPort  Ctrl+V
Model Space
Paper Space
Mview ▶

Set View ▶

Layout ▶

Window
Dynamic
Previous
All
Extents
Vmax

Create Viewport
Viewport ON
Viewport OFF
Hideplot
Fit Viewport
2 Viewports
3 Viewports
4 Viewports

Vplayer

Dview
Plan View ▶
Viewpoint ▶
Named View...

MV Setup
Tiled Viewports...

Current UCS
World
Named UCS

Axes
Presets...
Set Vpoint

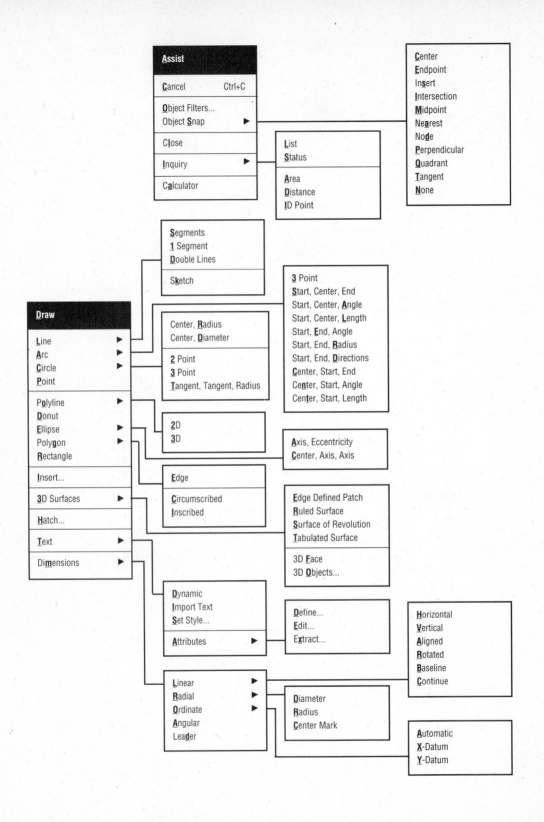

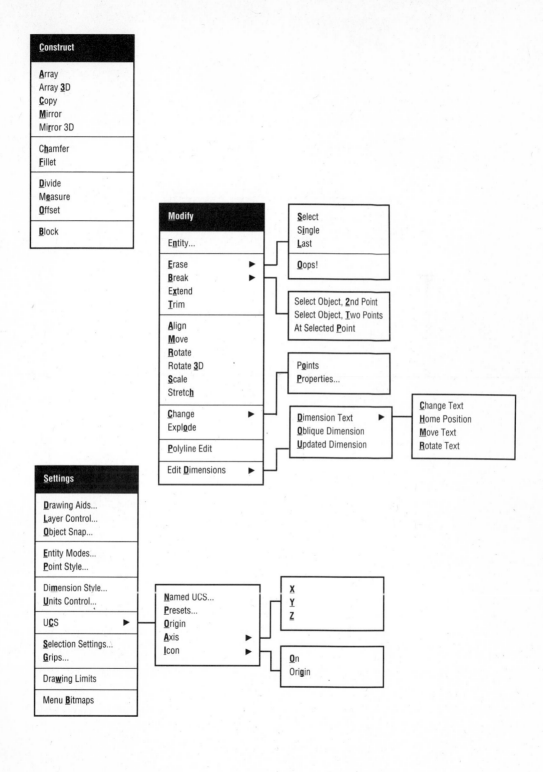

**Construct**

Array
Array 3D
Copy
Mirror
Mirror 3D

Chamfer
Fillet

Divide
Measure
Offset

Block

**Modify**

Entity...

Erase ▶
Break ▶
Extend
Trim

Align
Move
Rotate
Rotate 3D
Scale
Stretch

Change ▶
Explode

Polyline Edit

Edit Dimensions ▶

Select
Single
Last

Oops!

Select Object, 2nd Point
Select Object, Two Points
At Selected Point

Points
Properties...

Dimension Text ▶
Oblique Dimension
Updated Dimension

Change Text
Home Position
Move Text
Rotate Text

**Settings**

Drawing Aids...
Layer Control...
Object Snap...

Entity Modes...
Point Style...

Dimension Style...
Units Control...

UCS ▶

Selection Settings...
Grips...

Drawing Limits

Menu Bitmaps

Named UCS...
Presets...
Origin
Axis ▶
Icon ▶

X
Y
Z

On
Origin

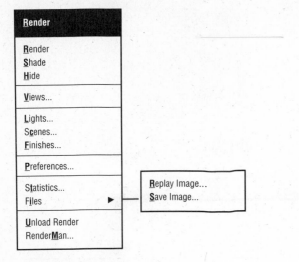

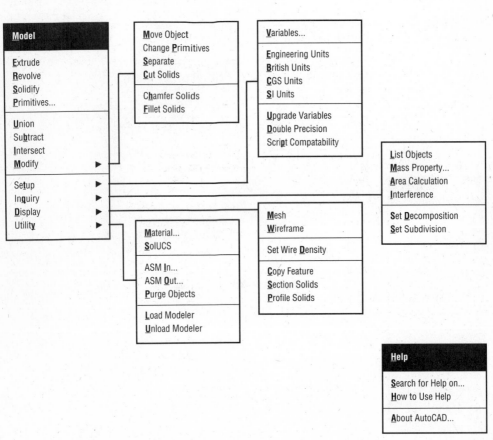